DAD'S ARMY

THE COMPLETE SCRIPTS OF SERIES 5–9

DAD'S

ARMY

THE HOME FRONT

THE COMPLETE SCRIPTS OF SERIES 5–9

Jimmy Perry
& David Croft
Edited by
Richard Webber

As far as possible we have tried to reproduce the original scripts of the television programmes. As you read the scripts you may, therefore, notice that changes did occur during the process of recording each episode.

First published in 2002
by Orion Books Ltd.
Orion House, 5 Upper St. Martin's Lane
London WC2H 9EA

Pictures supplied by: Radio Times, Peter Fitton
Design sketches by Peter Day

A CIP catalogue record for this book
is available from the British Library.

ISBN 0 75284 743 0

Printed and bound in Italy

Contents

ACKNOWLEDGEMENTS

Jimmy Perry, David Croft and Richard Webber would like to thank everyone who helped make this book possible, especially those people who have shared their memories of working on *Dad's Army,* or written about the fine actors who brought the show to life; we're also grateful to Paul Joel, for writing a section about his years spent designing the sets – he was certainly a valuable and hard-working member of the team. Once again, we pass on our thanks to those who supplied photos, including Don Smith.

RICHARD WEBBER
Somerset – March 2002

WHY HAS DAD'S ARMY BECOME SO SUCCESSFUL?

'I'm frequently asked this question and it's never easy to find an answer. Firstly, one does not set out to write a flop, so it would be a falsehood to say that you're surprised by success. You aim all the time for success, although you don't always achieve it.

'I think part of the success of *Dad's* is due to the fact that we were depicting a time when the people of this country behaved exceedingly well. Life was uncomfortable to say the least and for long periods, for a lot of us, it was damned dangerous. It would be wrong to say that people didn't whinge quite a lot, but they faced up to the conditions that were thrust upon them and, by and large, were remarkably brave. They helped and supported each other and that made them a bit proud of themselves. I think this was reflected in the programme. The situation was desperate and even hopeless, but nobody admitted it. We were united and determined. Don't let any historic revisionists persuade you otherwise. I was there.

'It was one of the ground rules of the programme that, either by accident or design, they would succeed. Failure is seldom a good subject for comedy. Financial failure, which did not concern us, is usually a disaster.

'Deep down, the characters all looked after each other. Godfrey had great difficulty mounting the back of the truck, so they all gave him a shove or lent a hand. He in turn always had a good word to say about Mainwaring when things were not going well for him. This sort of thing gives a reassuring atmosphere to the show. The characters rib each other but are not gratuitously unpleasant. The result is a show which sends people to bed in a happy frame of mind. We need this.'

DAVID CROFT

Who Do You Think You Are Kidding, Mr Hitler?

'When I volunteered to write the signature tune for *Dad's Army* I must have been mad; I was so carried away with my own importance. Looking back, 34 years later, it's a wonder I had the gall. In the first place, to quote my old singing teacher when I was a young boy, I was "musically illiterate"; being far too lazy to learn to read music properly, I could only just about manage to do a top line. In my early years, when I earned my living as a singer in various London musicals, I always faked it. During rehearsals for one show called *The Water Gypsies*, the composer, the great Vivian Ellis, would creep up behind me and listen carefully. "Nice tone," he said, "but you are just a teeny-weeny bit off the baritone line, dear boy. Never mind, you look so nice on stage."

'It didn't take me too long to write "Mr Hitler". I often tell people that I just put together a lot of wartime songs. This isn't quite true, but once I had decided on my theme – the brave defiance of the British People against one of the most evil forces the world has known – the words seemed to come quite easily. I sorted out the melody and then I contacted Derek Taverner to put the whole thing together for me.

'I first met Derek just six months after the war in the Far East had ended. He was the pianist for an army concert party I was in that was run by Combined Services Entertainment. Incidentally, he was the original prototype for "Mr La-di-dah" Gunner Graham in the series *It Ain't Half Hot, Mum*. When I contacted Derek to help me, he was musical director for *The Desert Song*, starring John Hanson, which was a surprise success and ran for quite a few months at the Palace Theatre in London. And so it was there, in the orchestra pit, that Derek and I hammered out the finished version of "Mr Hitler", our only audience being the cleaners.

'Come the day of recording, at the old BBC Riverside Studios in Hammersmith, I found myself with the Band of the Coldstream Guards, Bud Flanagan – a music hall legend – and Captain Trevor Sharpe, the Director of Music, who looked like a man who was not to be trifled with. Amongst all this serious talent, my first reaction was to run away and lock myself in the lavatory; fortunately, Derek Taverner was a fine musician and took everything out of my hands, and so I quietly slid away and sat in the sound gallery. After about an hour, while Bud was getting things right, I went to get a cup of tea; when I returned, I pushed open the gallery door and heard, for the very first time, dear old Bud singing: "Who do you think you are kidding, Mr Hitler, if you think we're on the run..."

'It was the greatest moment in my career; I felt goose pimples all over my body: the great Bud Flanagan, whom I had worshipped ever since I was a boy, was singing a song that I had written! Even today, 34 years later, whenever I hear Bud's voice at the start of the show I get those same goose pimples. When we had finished the recording, Bud said goodbye to us all and the last I saw of him was walking up the long corridor towards the exit. Three months later he died and a great music hall legend passed into the halls of fame.'

JIMMY PERRY

LIEUTENANT COLONEL TREVOR L. SHARPE, LVO, OBE, LRAM, ARCM, PSM

'I never really thanked Trevor for all the work he did to make "Mr Hitler", the signature tune, a success. I spoke to him on the phone recently, and he confessed that, at the time, he thought the song rather corny. Well, I must admit, I thought so too, but somehow it just hit the spot.

'What an amazing career Trevor has had; starting out as a young band-boy, distinguishing himself as a clarinettist, he was selected to study for bandmanship at the Royal Military School of Music, Kneller Hall. On graduation he was awarded the Cousins Medal for Musicianship by the Worshipful Company of Musicians. After further service in the Infantry and the Royal Armoured Corps, he was appointed to the prestigious post of Director of Music to the Coldstream Guards.

'Now the closing sequence of *Dad's Army* required a reprise of the opening in a strong military marching style, followed by a credit to the Coldstream Guards, the Regiment and, of course, Trevor. At the start of the series it was *Captain* Sharpe, then *Major* and finally, towards the end, *Lieutenant Colonel*, and so we see the progression of his career through the credits. Unfortunately, however, as the episodes are repeated quite often, and not always shown in chronological order, Trevor is promoted and demoted with amazing rapidity.

'Serving actively with his regiment for some twelve years, Colonel Trevor was then promoted to Senior Director (Army) at the Royal Military School of Music, where his duties involved the training and examination of musicians, at all grades, for the Army. This position he held for five years, before taking the Chair of Professor of Orchestration at Kneller Hall.

'Throughout his career he has been much involved in the music of many State and ceremonial occasions, together with the various mediums of television, radio and films. His compositions and orchestrations are played by musicians in many aspects of the profession. He's now retired, living in Herefordshire, still writing, playing, producing concerts and following his great interest as a watercolourist and, of course, never missing an episode of *Dad's Army*.

'Thank you, Trevor, for helping to create a legend.'

JIMMY PERRY

THE PLATOON

'Right from the start of the planning of *Dad's Army*, David and I worked out that we would need 15 men in the platoon – we had the front row, of course, but needed another ten men behind to make up the three ranks. We decided not to use "extras", as they were called in those days, but individual artistes. The important thing was they had to know how to handle weapons and be able to drill. Now, in 1967, most people had served in the war, so this did not present any problem. The strange thing is, you can teach someone to handle a rifle but, unless they've actually been in the forces, it never looks quite right. And so we cast wide our net.

'One of the first was Colin Bean, who had worked for me in the theatre for many years before *Dad's Army*. Roger Bourne had served with me in the Far East during the war, and was one of the original members of the Royal Artillery Concert Party. He was an excellent dancer and could tackle anything from tap to tango. Hugh Hastings, the playwright (*Seagulls Over Sorrento*) and songwriter, who left us in 1972 to join the Young Vic Company, and George Hancock, a retired opera singer, who had worked at Covent Garden. In his youth he was the youngest baritone to sing at Glyndebourne.

'There was Jimmy Mac, the famous pantomime Dame, Hugh Cecil, the children's entertainer and Punch and Judy man, as well as Frank Godfrey, ex-chorus boy and in his later years, Front of House Manager at the Palace Theatre, Watford. Others included Desmond Cullum-Jones, entrepreneur extraordinaire and Richard Jacques, theatre director, actor, writer – one of the original members of the platoon, who directed the stage version of *It Ain't Half Hot, Mum* for David and me. He emigrated to Canada where he worked continuously until his early death in 2000.

'Michael Moore, a big radio star during the 1950s, was an impressionist and starred in a show called *Ignorance is Bliss* with Harold Berens and Gladys Hay. And then there was Vernon Drake who, because of his immaculate appearance, was known in the profession as "The Duke". He was the straight man, or "feed", in a well known double act, Connor and Drake, and played the London Palladium many times. I shall never forget the wonderful opening of their act: Vernon would enter dressed immaculately in white tie and tails, and chat to the audience for a bit; then Connor would make his entrance looking like something the cat had dragged in. Vernon would look at him with disgust and utter the immortal line: "That's the last time I take you to the Lord Mayor's Banquet!"

'There were, of course, a few others in the platoon over the 80 episodes that I did not know personally, but each man played his part and marched into history.'

JIMMY PERRY

Regular Faces

COLIN BEAN

'Private Sponge was a sort of gofer for Captain Mainwaring. At first he was just a plain member of the platoon but, after a few series, was promoted to a speaking part – the indomitable Sponge. Always at Captain Mainwaring's side, always ready to carry out orders. "I'm leaving you in charge, Sponge." "Take over, Sponge." "I rely on you, Sponge." And so on and so forth.

'Sponge was a farmer and favoured by Mainwaring on the whole, for his loyalty and steadfastness. He was also the spokesman for the rest of the platoon, a sort of trade union leader which Mainwaring did *not* favour. Sometimes he would convey any grumbles from the platoon to the noble Captain, who would regard him as a bit of a troublemaker.

'How did he get the name of Sponge? Well, it first came to us when we were out filming and Colin was sweating quite a lot; in fact, he looked exactly like a sponge. Before we gave him the name, I had to check if it was real or not. I looked it up in the telephone directory and, sure enough, there were two Sponges in it. So that's how the character was born.

'I've always been obsessed by names. I love ones with numbers in them: Twelvetrees, Forboys, Sixsmith, Sevenoaks, Twentyman, etc., all ready for characters to step into them. With the exception of Twelvetrees, which David and I used for the character of the footman played by Jeffrey Holland in *You Rang, M'Lord?*, and the character played by Natalie Kent in the *Dad's Army* episode "High Finance", the others will have to remain tucked away in the drawer, alas, never to see the light of day.'

JIMMY PERRY

HAROLD BENNETT

'My first sight of Harold Bennett was when he was playing an incredibly old Archbishop in a sort of pantomime called *The Rose and the Ring* at, I believe, Stratford East. I had gone along to see Gerry Campion who was well known for playing Billy Bunter in the children's television series. He was a good chum and ran a drinking club called Gerry's in Shaftesbury Avenue. I found Harold very funny indeed and over a pint after the show I asked Gerry about him. "How old is he really, and can he learn his lines?"

'"Terribly old," said Gerry, "but he's absolutely solid on the dialogue."

'I made a note for future reference. Thereafter whenever an ancient character was called for I sent for Harold. He had a remarkable ability to get and time a laugh, and at the same time was always true to his character.

'I never found out the true age of Harold. He was a cabin boy in the First World War and got sunk in the Irish Sea. He then joined the Royal Artillery and was shot down whilst in an observation balloon. Moreover, he didn't have a parachute.

'When I was in the Royal Free Hospital after my first heart attack, Harold was in a ward two storeys below with some sort of bladder complaint. He gallantly came up to see me, but it took him a long time because he had to get out of the lift at each floor to spend a penny.'

DAVID CROFT

JOAN COOPER

'One of Arthur's outstanding traits was his loyalty to his wife, Joan. She was really responsible for him becoming an actor in the first place when she got him a job with her in the repertory company where she was working. When we went away filming with *Dad's Army*, Joan always accompanied Arthur.

'Before we started on a new series, Arthur would always call and say: "Anything for Joan in the coming episodes?" She played many supporting parts in *Dad's Army* including, of course, Godfrey's dotty sister, Dolly. Although people might say it was Arthur's influence that got her the jobs, she always gave very credible performances. She was also in the radio series and the stage show at the Shaftesbury Theatre, London.'

JIMMY PERRY

PAMELA CUNDELL

'Wearing a fox fur and bathed in not too expensive perfume, Mrs Fox was always trying to ingratiate herself with Corporal Jones. It wasn't his uniform that attracted her but rather the fact he was a wartime butcher and she always suspected that he had a little bit of something desirable under the counter.

'Pamela Cundell took the part to her ample bosom. Whether in the meat queue, on a handy sofa or round the table at a parish conference, she always managed to be gushing and rampantly sexy. In the very last episode of *Dad's Army,* after many misunderstandings, she got her man and became Mrs Jones.

'Of late, she has been one of the most loyal supporters of the show. Pamela always appears at any anniversary of the show, and can be relied upon to turn up for all the functions staged by the Dad's Army Appreciation Society. She actually appeared in 13 episodes of the show and played various parts for me in *Up Pompeii!* with Frankie Howerd, and *Are You Being Served?*'

DAVID CROFT

JANET DAVIES

'Janet was very much in on the ground floor of *Dad's Army* because she was a client of my wife, Ann. She performed in quite a lot of television commercials and, when there wasn't too much work about, doubled up as Ann's secretary. Ann, under the name of Ann Callender, was a theatrical agent.

'One of Ann's principal clients was, of course, Jimmy Perry. He was going through a lean time as an actor when he appeared for me in a television show called *Beggar My Neighbour* starring Peter Jones, June Whitfield and Reg Varney. He played the part of Reg Varney's loud-mouthed brother – and incidentally played it very well.

'Jimmy asked Ann if it would be okay to show me a script he'd written called *The Fighting Tigers.* Ann told him to go ahead and she would make sure that I read it. *The Fighting Tigers* became *Dad's Army.* Later, when we were looking for an actress to play young Pike's doting mum and the "landlady" of Sergeant Wilson, Janet hastened to suggest herself for the part. After all, being in the office where the script first saw the light of day, she knew the requirements well.

'She came along to see me and read for the part. She seemed to be just the right age and type to play the role. I engaged her and she quickly made the worried Mrs Pike her very own part, taking advantage and exploiting every hint of the relationship with Sergeant Wilson.'

DAVID CROFT

CAROLINE DOWDESWELL

'From the earliest days of casting *Dad's Army* I was conscious of the fact that we were completely lacking in pretty female characters. I thought this a great disadvantage. Pretty girls are an essential feature of successful TV comedies. We, therefore, proceeded to introduce a young girl counter clerk into the bank. We started to interview likely artistes for the part of Janet King, and in the fullness of time we saw Caroline Dowdeswell. She was pretty, the right age and clearly a good actress.

'She accordingly appeared in the early episodes, but Jimmy and I were at a loss when trying to find something important for her to do. Young Pike was a very strong character, and a wonderful foil for both Mainwaring and Wilson with many facets to his character which we could exploit. Poor Caroline was pretty and very good in the few lines we wrote for her, but we never found a proper function for her in the plot. After the first few episodes we regretfully dropped the character.'

DAVID CROFT

MICHAEL KNOWLES

'Nearly fifty years ago, when I was working in weekly rep as an actor, some of the plays we performed would have a "Silly Ass (pronounced *arse*)" part in them. This is a very English expression; the American version was called a "Dude". I was fortunate to work with, perhaps, the greatest Silly Ass actor of all time, Ralph Lynn.

'He was in his late sixties and I was in my mid-twenties. The play was the famous farce, *Rookery Nook*, and my part opposite him was originally played by Tom Walls. I was a little concerned as there was over forty years difference in our ages. At the start of rehearsals I asked Ralph Lynn how he wanted me to play the part. "Just put some grey in your hair, old boy, and wear a pair of white flannels – we're a couple of sports in our thirties."

'Michael Knowles had done many different parts when he worked for me in weekly repertory but, as a Silly Ass, he was the best. The wonderful thing was that you really believed in him. What could have been a one dimensional, cardboard character came to life in Michael's hands. In *Dad's Army* he nearly always played army captains of one sort or another, but somehow they always came out as Silly Ass parts; David and I didn't mind because he was so very funny. David thought the world of him, and Michael went on to play Captain Ashwood in *It Ain't Half Hot, Mum* and, of course, the prince of Silly Asses, Teddy in *You Rang, M'Lord?*.

'Michael was also a writer and, with Harold Snoad, adapted 67 episodes of *Dad's Army* television scripts for radio.

'He is, perhaps, one of the nicest actors I've ever worked with – never any trouble. In a profession where you can get some right awkward sods, Michael was always spot on, he'd almost apologise for being so good.'

JIMMY PERRY

ERIC LONGWORTH

'In the episode, "The Godiva Affair", residents of Walmington-on-Sea decide to hold a carnival to raise money to buy a Spitfire and so the committee holds a meeting. David and I so enjoyed writing parish-pump politics. Mainwaring in the chair, of course, and everyone else shoving in their four-penn'orth – suggestions, objections and counter objections.

'Now, the centrepiece of the carnival is to be Lady Godiva on a horse, with long silken tresses to cover her... body. Everyone is horrified until Mr Gordon, the town clerk, explains that the lady in question will not be in the altogether but wearing "fleshings", which will cover her from head to toe. The way Eric, who played the town clerk, pronounced the word gave a whole new meaning to it: prim but, at the same time, lascivious. He would roll back his front teeth from his gums and smack his tongue against the roof of his mouth and out would come the word, with a fine spray of spittle: "FLESH...INGS!"'

JIMMY PERRY

GEOFFREY LUMSDEN

'A big Hollywood film mogul once said: "When I cast a part I want the guy to look like what the audience expect him to look. A doctor should look like a doctor, a cop like a cop, and a villain like a villain." Well, dear Geoffrey, who played Colonel Square, really looked every ounce a British Army colonel of the old school: bristling moustache, pop-eyes, red face, and a tendency to shout: "Eh, what!" He never beat around the bush, always called a spade a spade, and insisted on pronouncing Mainwaring the way it is spelt and not as "Mannering".

'David and I loved to write Colonel Square into our scripts but, sadly, Geoffrey was such a popular actor it was difficult to catch him when he was free. Nothing phoney about him playing an army officer: he served with distinction at the Battle of Monte Casino in the Italian Campaign during the war.'

JIMMY PERRY

ROBERT RAGLAN

'One of Robert's great assets was that he didn't look like an actor. I first came across him when I was in Newcastle, directing television for Tyne Tees. The bosses of the outfit were George and Alfred Black. I had written a lot of material for their summer spectacular shows at Blackpool and they gave me my first chance as a TV producer, a show called *Under New Management*, starring Glenn Melvyn, Danny Ross, Jerry

Verno, Graham Stark and Mollie Sugden. It was about Mollie and Glenn taking over a broken-down pub and trying to make a success of it.

'It was one of the happiest shows I was every associated with because Glenn, Jerry and Graham were wild bridge enthusiasts, so as soon as we stopped rehearsing, out would come the cards, hands would be dealt, bidding would get under way and the usual inquests would follow.

'Robert played a not-very-bright police constable. I remember a typical bit of dialogue from Bob when a burglary had taken place in the pub. "Hullo," said Bob. "I want to report a burglary. I'm speaking from a call box opposite the pub."

'"Can you give a description?" asked the sergeant.

'"Well," replied Bob. "It's about eight feet high and it's red."

'Bob was a regular character on the show and a staunch member of the bridge circle. One week, Graham Stark wasn't in the show, so a fourth member had to be found. Melvyn elected Danny Ross to make up the numbers. Danny was a natural, wonderful comedian but he was far from being the Brain of Britain. They each tried to explain the intricacies of bidding, doubling, vulnerability and the one club convention, and it became very obvious that none of it was sinking into the mind of the bewildered Danny. There was an exasperated pause before Bob suddenly had a terrible thought. "My God," he said. "Which one of us is going to tell him about trumps?"

'Bob played the Colonel in *Dad's Army* on demand, which was quite often. He never looked like an actor. He looked like a Colonel.'

DAVID CROFT

STUART SHERWIN

'I always think of Stuart as the very best of what I call "jobbing actors". If ever I was at a loss for an idea as to who to cast for a particular role, Stuart Sherwin could always play the part. I used him time and again – firstly for various assistant air raid wardens to help Bill Pertwee to be a pain in the side of Arthur Lowe. He also played a lighthouse keeper in a radio episode which was, perhaps, a strange part for someone accustomed to saying, "Put that light out!".

'He played many different customers and workers in *Are You Being Served?* and valiantly played the porter in the first act, and a Spanish hotel owner in the second act of the theatre version of that show for a long season at Blackpool.'

DAVID CROFT

TALFRYN THOMAS

'To my mind, he was a very funny man: a complete grotesque, and his character had a dark side. I loved to write for him, perhaps because I have a sort of strange affinity for the Welsh. Although David Croft thought him funny, I'm not sure he shared my enthusiasm, but one person who certainly did not agree with me was John Laurie; I think he thought that Talfryn was poaching on his territory, that he was the only one in the platoon who was entitled to be potty. One day he came up to me and pulled me into a corner. He rolled his eyes and hissed: "Is yon Welsh feller going to be in the next series?"

'"I've really no idea," I said.

'John hunched his shoulders and his face looked like a bird of prey as he hissed again: "He's too funny. Get rid of him, I'm the only mad one around here!"

'Poor Talfryn, but he managed to keep his end up in spite of a lot of opposition from several quarters, and got some huge laughs. Definitely a very strange, funny man.'

JIMMY PERRY

Designing the Sets
by PAUL JOEL

'I worked as a production designer for nearly 30 years at the BBC and no show gave me greater job satisfaction than *Dad's Army*. Within four years of joining the Corporation I was asked to work on Jimmy Perry and David Croft's sitcom about the Home Guard. Little did I know that I'd go on to design sets for 52 of the 80 episodes made between 1968 and '77.

'As far as my design approach to *Dad's Army* was concerned, I regarded it just like I would a drama on video or film. To me, it was real, not just a situation comedy. This really happened during the early part of World War II, so the sets had to be authentic and believable in every detail – that way the comedy enacted in them would be real and believable, too.

Paul and his wife Judy in the St Ives Society of Artists Gallery where they both work.

'My involvement in the whole process would begin with the arrival of a script and the budget allocation via the design department's management office. I would read the script carefully at home (it was quieter there than the hubbub of the open-plan design offices), and "break it down" into filming and studio requirements.

'Before the series of six or seven episodes were recorded in the studio there would always be certain scenes, usually exteriors, which had to be filmed. Quite often, small sets or special props were required, so these would have to be designed first. The requirements for the studio would be more extensive and demand most of the budget: stock sets (which would be rebuilt at the beginning of a series); new sets; particular requirements, such as water, smoke, sand in one episode, etc.; and special props.

'When I started designing all the episodes in a particular series, David and Jimmy would sometimes ask me to discuss the sets with them at an early stage, as well as estimate the possible costs, enabling them to check that everything was affordable within the overall budget. This was very useful for me because the money for sets could be allocated to each episode more cost effectively than simply splitting the budget into six or seven equal amounts.

'Many of the sets needed some form of research, because I was still a baby during World War II, so having built up a small but useful library of reference books at home, a few of which had belonged to my grandfather, I started there. Beyond that the design department had an excellent reference library and the Imperial War Museum was always very helpful. Sometimes I would get tips from older colleagues in the design offices – such as fixing brown paper to the shade of hanging lamps to prevent the light shining towards the windows (as you will see in the back of the church hall).

'Next I would begin sketching the new sets and roughly plan each studio prior to my first "ideas meeting" with David and Jimmy. Various adjustments took place at this stage, ideas were firmed up and rough plans agreed. Onward then to look through the BBC scenery catalogue to choose useful items kept in stock at warehouses in Acton, or, better still, I'd visit the warehouse to check their condition and see if there were any useful uncatalogued items. Occasionally it was necessary to visit scenery companies, such as the one at Pinewood Studios, to hire unusual pieces of panelling, columns or fireplaces that the BBC couldn't supply.

'Having booked all the stock and hired scenery, it was time to do construction drawings to 1:50 scale, with details at 1:20 or bigger, and take them to the scenic servicing estimators. This was always a difficult period in the design process. Inevitably they would say the sets were too expensive, which was very difficult when, in your opinion, you had designed them within the allocated budget. So compromises were made, even to the extent of losing very important details or parts of sets, before the drawings were approved and sent to the BBC workshops or an outside scenery contractor, such as Ackland Snow.

'Scale models (1:50) of the sets were made, usually by my assistant, from the drawings. These enabled everybody from the director and actors to the scenery builder to visualise the sets in three dimensions. They were used by the AFM (Assistant Floor Manager) to help mark out the sets on the rehearsal room floor (see photos in the introduction to the first book of scripts), and were also taken to planning meetings with the director, lighting director, etc. – invaluable in creating a miniature impression of the entire studio set-up to assist in identifying any technical problems.

'Next, I had to compile the prop list, which was a fully itemised list, in set order, of all the props, from furniture to match boxes, sometimes running to many pages. A copy was given to the property buyer, who then accompanied me to the BBC prop store and then those prop hire companies most likely to have the items I'd listed. As with the set construction it was important not to exceed my allocated prop budget, so the buyer kept a running total of expenditure to ensure this didn't happen.

'I once took my young son to a prop house. He was fascinated by the extraordinary variety of things there: exotic statues of Eastern warriors, elaborate drapes, antique furniture, shining silver, leather-bound books, beautiful glass lamps, glorious paintings in ornate gold frames, but couldn't understand why I didn't hire them. He became quite upset, until the prop house manager sat him on a polished leather Chesterfield and gave him a big glass of lemonade and a warm egg sandwich, whilst I went off to select some army cots and barrack room lockers. In fact, the prop houses were often quite generous to their clients. I remember one Christmas when the Louis Koche hire company invited all the designers and buyers with children to the *Aladdin* pantomime at the Palladium, starring Danny La Rue as Widow Twankey – this was a real treat, to celebrate their 50 years in the prop hire business.

'Prop buying would take several days, interspersed with visits to the set builders to monitor progress and answer questions about details, paint finishes, etc., and also rehearsals, most importantly the final one, or tech run, when the heads of all the various teams attended to see how the script had manifested itself. We would all be there: producer, director, production assistant, producer's assistant, AFM, floor assistant, lighting director, sound supervisor, make-up supervisor, costume supervisor, visual effects (when necessary) and, of course, the designer. Any problems to do with the action, scene changes, lighting changes, etc., were discussed and, hopefully, ironed out during and after this rehearsal, prior to rehearsals in the studio. The tech run usually coincided with the "zero date", when props were delivered to BBC movement control and I approved the finished sets before delivery to the studio for the night set, or day set.

'Sets for each episode would arrive at the studio from two directions (sometimes more): the stock sets from the BBC scenery holding bays, and the new sets from the scenery construction company or BBC scenery workshop. Individual scenery units were loaded on to trailers in the inner ring road behind the studios and towed into studio by a "teddy truck" to be re-assembled overnight (a night set), or during the day (a day set), depending on the studio planner's schedule. Of the two, I preferred a day set because I could monitor the re-assembly process as it happened, anticipating problems and, hopefully, solving them before they became a major headache! With a night set, unless I too stayed overnight, and sometimes there was no choice if the sets were complicated, I would arrive in the morning approximately three hours before rehearsals with the problems still unsolved. A set supervisor with a crew of three or four men was responsible for re-assembling the sets using my studio plan, marked with numbers of each individual scenery unit, my 1:50 scale drawings and ever-useful models.

'I always enjoyed the evening recording. The last-minute, on-set checks; the AFM making sure that the action props were ready; the excitement of the audience arriving and taking their seats; and the "warm up". This was when one of the actors, or a comedian, created a jolly atmosphere by telling jokes and involving the audience in amusing repartee to make them receptive to the comedy about to unfold. However, when Bill Pertwee did it, in addition to the cast, he always introduced me as "Our designer who produced the sets before you. I bet you thought they were real rooms on your telly"! – a bit embarrassing, but flattering nonetheless.

'Once the episode was recorded, the stock sets: church hall, Marigold Tea Rooms, Jones' Butcher's Shop, etc., all marked "Keep for Series", were dismantled and taken back to the scenery store holding bays and the sets needed only for that one episode were dismantled and the individual units (doors, windows, walls, etc.) stored in the BBC stock scenery warehouse or taken back to the scenery hire company. Newly made units would be destroyed, unless thought good enough to re-use or add to the stock scenery catalogue.

'Looking back over all the episodes I worked on, there are five in particular that stick in my mind. "Getting the Bird" is memorable because it was a studio full of sets: Jones' Butcher's Shop; the church hall, including the stage and Mainwaring's office; a sandbagged observation post; and the church complete with pews, pulpit and organ.

These were all crammed into less than half the studio, in front of the audience seating. In order for the action to be seen by the audience, some parts of the sets had to be trucked in and out on castors over the floor, or flown in and out on cables from the studio ceiling – not unlike sets in a West End theatre.

'Having read and enjoyed the script, my concern, apart from how to best lay out the sets, was the big church organ, which had to look authentic, with a proper keyboard, stops, foot pedals and pipes. The truth is, it couldn't have been more simple. Opposite the back gates of the Television Centre, leading to the design offices, lived an organ builder and repairer! In his garage store he had everything I needed – it was just a matter of selecting all the units and making relatively minor adjustments to achieve the desired result. With precious little design time, and "Asleep in the Deep" coming up next week, this was a godsend.

'"Asleep in the Deep" was a particularly interest-

LEFT Jones' butcher's shop was just one of the sets designed by Paul Joel.

RIGHT Visual Effects Designer Peter Day created this detailed drawing of the clock tower for 'Time On My Hands'.

ing episode to design. Never having been inside a pumping station in my life, I researched it by going to my local Thames Water building near the reservoirs beside the river at Molesey, and was surprised to see how immaculately clean it was – polished water pipes and tilework, more like a hospital than a pumping station, and certainly very different from David and Jimmy's script. However, technical details of things such as machinery and pipework were useful, even if the architecture wasn't.

'The real challenge was to create the effect of rising water in front of a studio audience. The set of the room in which the platoon was trapped had to be duplicated in as large a tank of water as possible. Obviously there was a limit to the weight of water permissible on the studio floor for safety reasons, especially as the video editing suites were below – not a good idea to flood them too!

'This severely restricted the size of the set, but after carefully calculating that a water depth of 3 foot 6 inches contained in a robust, rubber-lined tank measuring 12 foot by 8 foot by 4 foot deep did not exceed the studio-floor loading, I felt we could, with limited camera angles, just about do justice to the script.

'It's interesting to note from the audience report of this episode that "It was all extremely convincing. It looked as if the scene was real when the water was rising". In fact, the water, although real enough and cold enough for Ian and Bill to wear wet suits under their uniforms, remained at a constant level of 3 foot 6 inches. It was the set that was lowered into the water in between scenes, making it look as though the water had risen. This deception was perpetrated behind curtains drawn across the front of the tank, so even the studio audience did not see how the water appeared to rise. I remember the curtains being opened to a spontaneous round of applause when they saw Mainwaring, Frazer, Godfrey and Walker, now perilously close to the surface of the water on the bunk, with Pike wading up to his chest through the water (he was actually on his knees), and Hodges precariously floating in a small bath, propelled unseen by visual effects designer Peter Day beneath!

'Probably the most complicated episode I ever designed was "Time On My Hands", with a German parachutist hanging helplessly from the town hall clock; animated figures who came out on tracks; a tolling bell; a ladder crashing to the ground; and lots of jolly slapstick requiring concentrated rehearsal. I requested extra time to build the sets in studio and David requested extra time to rehearse the action more thoroughly before recording in front of an audience, but because of the intense demand for studio space in the run-up to Christmas '72, we were, not surprisingly, refused.

'So, overnight and well into the morning, the town hall clock tower was constructed, supported on a scaffolding structure, raised well above the

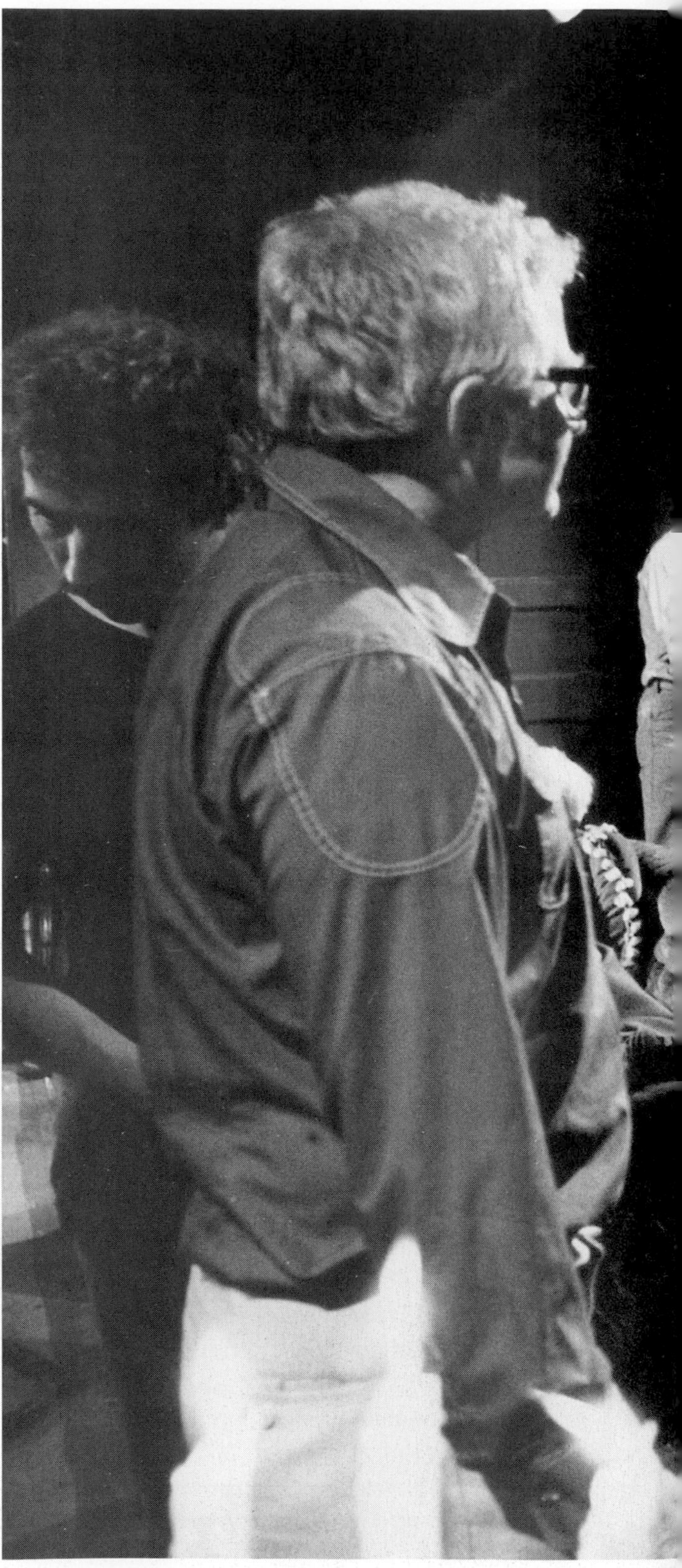

Director David Croft (left) oversees events as the finishing touches are applied to the set in 'Things That Go Bump in the Night'.

studio floor with the clock cantilevered out on an RSJ. Then, dressed with the figures, some beautifully carved in polystyrene, that moved mechanically in and out on a track, a big fibreglass bell, gargoyles and, of course, artificial pigeon droppings were all added. It was a tour de force of organisation and co-operation between the various crews involved in the task. However, finishing everything off had to take place during the day between rehearsals, which were fraught with difficulties as this was the first time the actors had seen the moving figures working. It was especially problematical for Clive who had most of the crazy stunt work to perform on the horse and the clock but, as always, he and the rest were such consummate actors that it all turned out okay in the end. In retrospect, from my point of view, it would have been even better on film – but then we would not have got a live audience's spontaneous reaction to the comedy.

'My penultimate episode was "Things That Go Bump in the Night" – one with no stock sets in the studio, and a chance to design a period drama interior for the spooky "haunted house" without having to match anything to the filming location, which gave me an unusual freedom. So, within the limited confines of the budget I let my imagination wander into creating an old, run-down baronial house full of tapestries, medieval weapons, shields and suits of armour. The most interesting prop,

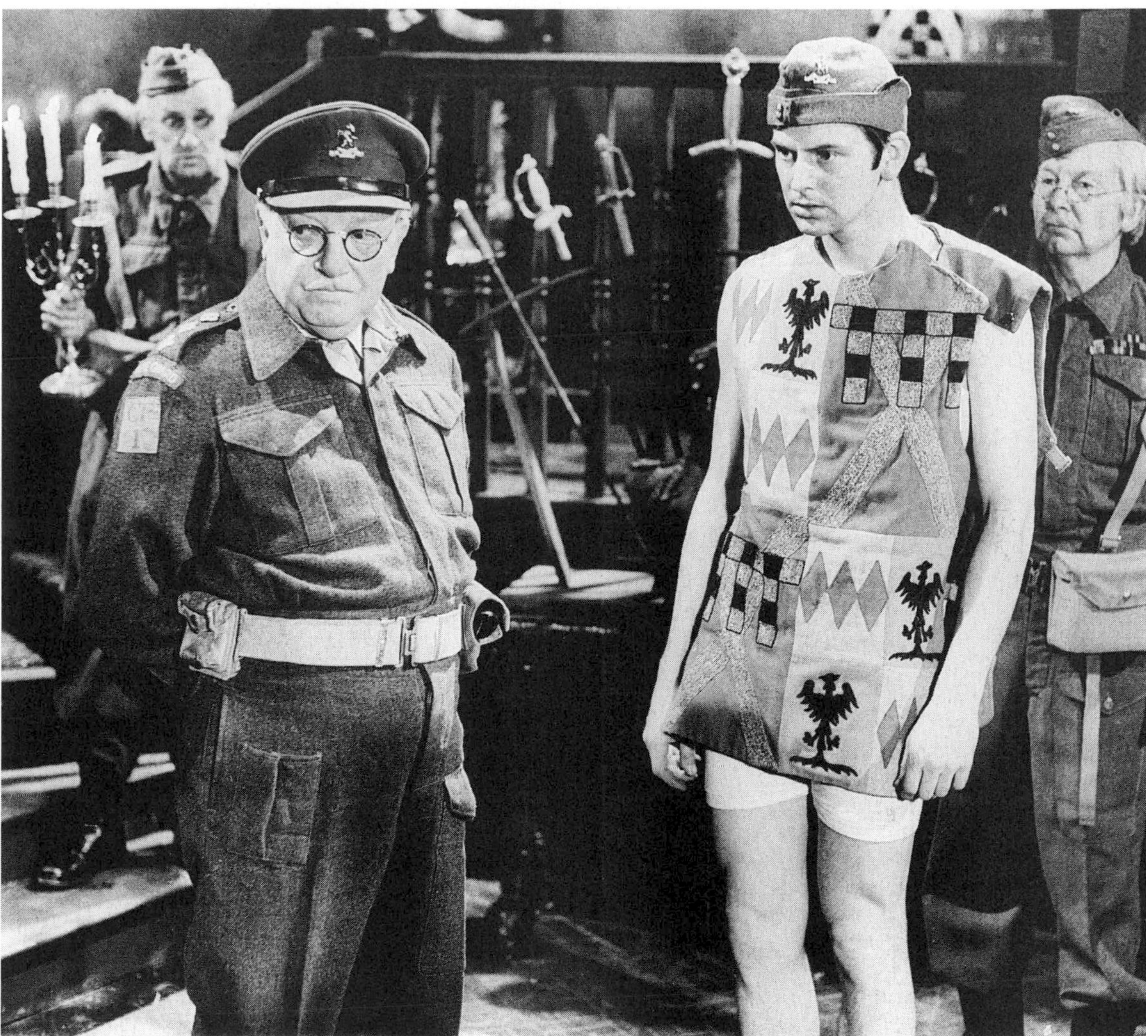

ABOVE 'Things That Go Bump in the Night' afforded Paul the chance to design a period drama interior for the home in which the platoon find themselves fetched up for the night.

LEFT In 'Getting the Bird', one of Paul Joel's tasks involved replicating the interior of a church.

however, was the large, four-poster bed – big enough to sleep six people, three at the head and three at the foot – needless to say, I had to have the base frame strengthened.

'It was also a great script for Ian Lavender, just so long as he didn't mind getting soaking wet, undressing time after time on a cold location in Suffolk, and getting chased up a tree by an angry pack of bloodhounds. In fact, all the hounds were as soppy as puppies and presented no danger at all to the half-naked Pike – it was the water that was more dangerous!

'My last episode of *Dad's Army* was "The Recruit". Alas, nothing special in terms of scenic design, but memorable for me for two reasons: I (above) Creating the effect of rising water in the studio during 'Asleep in the Deep' was particularly challenging for Paul Joel.

was leaving the series to extend my design career by taking the giant leap into the realms of drama plays, and also there was real life drama in *Dad's Army,* too. Sadly, it was obvious that Jimmy Beck would not be able to appear because he was very ill. Indeed he died, at the age of 44, soon after the recording. It was difficult to imagine how the series could carry on without him. I will always remember Jimmy with great affection: his ready wit and the occasional doodles of the cast and crew, in particular. How I wish he'd done one of me! So it was farewell from him and farewell from me.

'I will always regard it as a privilege to have been chosen to design *Dad's Army.*'

Out on Location

'Location was a vital part of the *Dad's Army* operation. Apart from the necessity to stage the outdoor scenes – and, let's face it, *Dad's* was basically an outdoor story – the ability to assemble the actors away from the worries of home and to get them all socialising together was an invaluable dimension in the success of the shows.

'On location there is no escape from the need to concentrate on the show. There is a lot to talk about and a lot of time to do the talking. The crew and I were fiendishly busy all the time, but the actors were forced to spend a lot of time just sitting and waiting. Experiences were exchanged and stories were told and, of course, scenes were rehearsed, dissected and discussed.

'We were lucky with the weather. It was usually spring and I used to say: "It does them good to be waved about in the fresh air once a year." I'm not sure this was the case with Bill Pertwee who would usually get chucked into any nearby river, sea or lake, but at least it gave all the rest of the platoon a good laugh, and Bill always took it in good part.

'I felt very guilty in "Keep Young and Beautiful" when even the older ones were forced to stand while we sprayed hoses on them in order to cause their beautifying and youthful make-up to run down their faces. I did it as quickly as possible but it still took three or four minutes, and the water coming from those nozzles was very cold indeed.

'I avoided filming at night except on a couple of rare occasions. It is a cold and miserable experience and I think it's almost impossible to be funny at half past two in the morning. I tried to arrange that the evenings consisted of a good dinner, a brandy or two in front of a blazing fire and early to bed to be ready for the next day. Nobody objected.'

DAVID CROFT

THE CONTRIBUTORS

JO AUSTIN

Born in Wolverhampton, Jo Austin studied at a business college in London before returning to her home town and working in an estate agents. She eventually moved back to London and, after temping for a while, joined a market research company. Always interested in working within the television industry, Jo applied to the BBC when BBC2 was launched, and was offered a position in 1962. After working as Bill Cotton's secretary for a time, she completed a production course and transferred to the production department at the end of 1963, initially as a production assistant on shows like *It's A Square World, The Beat Room* (an early music show), *The Likely Lads, 'Till Death Us Do Part* and *Top of the Pops*. While working for David Croft, she also helped on *Are You Being Served?* and *It Ain't Half Hot, Mum.*

Jo took early retirement in 1989 after 27 years' service with the Beeb.

COLIN BEAN

Colin wanted to act from childhood and started his career at an early age as a shepherd in a nativity play. After leaving school in 1944 he gained some professional experience before being called up for national service in the army for four years; while serving in Japan he had opportunities for some part-time acting with the BCOF.

He graduated from drama school in 1952, but stayed on to teach for a year before joining Sheffield Rep as ASM. Colin's early career was dominated by the theatre: he spent four years with the Court Players and five with the Victor Graham Players.

His first speaking role on TV was playing a yeoman in 1961's *Richard the Lionheart* with Richard Greene, but he was also seen as an antiques dealer in *Z Cars* and a policeman in *No Hiding Place* before joining *Dad's Army*. Other small-screen credits include being a customer in *Are You Being Served?*, a policeman and a soap box orator in *The Liver Birds,* policemen in *The Goodies* and *The Harry Worth Show,* appearances in 13 episodes of *Michael Bentine Time* in 1973, several roles in *The Gnomes of Dulwich,* a loud supporter in *Fallen Hero* and as the Verger alongside Frank Williams (as the Vicar) at Gladys' wedding in the penultimate episode of *Hi-De-Hi!* in 1988.

Working for Jimmy Perry at Watford's Palace Theatre in 1962 led to the start of almost 20 years playing a pantomime dame, and the role of Sponge in *Dad's Army*. Colin, who gained a master's degree in Speech and Projection during the 1980s via a correspondence course, is now restricted to radio work due to arthritis. He has also turned his hand to writing, completing his autobiography, *Who Do You Think YOU ARE KIDDING!,* in 1998.

GRAHAM BEDWELL

Graham joined the BBC in 1963, just as BBC2 was being launched, as a trainee assistant sound recordist. Early in his career, he worked on productions such as Harold Pinter's play, *Tea Party, The Great War* and the *Tonight* programme.

In 1968, Graham was promoted to sound recordist and added *Nationwide, Wheelbase, The Expert, The Survivors, The Money Programme, Horizon, The Secret War, Z Cars, Poldark, Dixon of Dock Green* and *The Onedin Line* to his list of credits. The last major project he worked on was *Going Live*, which he was involved in for five years before being made redundant in 1995. He now works freelance.

ROBERT BERK

Robert trained as a furniture designer, graduating from the Royal College of Art. After working in the industry for a while, he changed direction and joined the BBC as a design assistant in 1965. Early programmes to which he was assigned included *Sykes, Softly, Softly* and *The Expert* but, other than

Dad's Army, the most famous show he worked on was *Monty Python's Flying Circus*.

In 1968, Robert left the Beeb and spent time out of the profession, renovating an old farmhouse in rural Essex. But he returned to the industry on a freelance basis, working for Channel 4, the Children's Film Foundation and *TV-am*, in 1983. For the last few years, he's been working for Rag Doll Productions.

JONATHAN CECIL

Jonathan, who played loopy Captain Cadbury who talked to his dogs as if they were a platoon, became involved in acting at Oxford. After a university performance at Stratford, he was told he had a future in the profession so, upon graduating, he joined LAMDA.

Rep work followed before he began working in television. Early screen credits include snooty Jeremy Crichton-Jones in two series of *Romany Jones*, *The Ben Travers Farces*, *The Goodies* and *The Dick Emery Show*, but he's probably best known in the medium as Hastings to Peter Ustinov's *Poirot*. As well as a successful television career, Jonathan has had an extensive international film career, appearing in over 20 films, including *Rising Damp*, *The Yellow Rolls Royce*, *Up the Front* and *Alice Through the Looking Glass*.

Jonathan's busy career has graced all areas of the profession, including the theatre. He's recently appeared as Chasuble in *The Importance of Being Earnest* at Chichester and the Haymarket Theatre, and in a season at Shakespeare's Globe.

BRENDA COWLING

As a child, Brenda Cowling wanted to be a film star but, after leaving school, she trained as a shorthand typist. Eventually she changed direction and joined RADA (she was in the same class as Warren Mitchell and Jimmy Perry). She appeared as a drama student in Hitchcock's *Stage Fright* while still at RADA.

Plenty of rep work followed before Brenda made her TV debut. Early appearances include several series of an afternoon keep-fit show and *The Forsyte Saga*. Her career has focused mainly on TV but she has occasionally worked on stage. Brenda was also cast in several films, such as *The Railway Children*, *International Velvet*, *Carry On Girls*, *Carry On Behind* and made brief appearances in two Bond movies.

Post-*Dad's Army*, Brenda worked for David Croft and Jimmy Perry in *It Ain't Half Hot, Mum* as a WVS lady, and a maid in the final instalment of *Hi-De-Hi!* She's played many nurses, including the sister in an episode of *Fawlty Towers* and a matron in *Only When I Laugh*. Brenda was cast as Jane in three series of *Potter*, two of which starred Arthur Lowe.

Other television work includes four series of *You Rang, M'Lord?* playing Mrs Lipton, *The Detectives*, *Casualty* and *The Legacy of Reginald Perrin*, as C.J.'s housekeeper, Mrs Wren.

PAMELA CUNDELL

Both Pamela's parents were in the entertainment business and she never wanted to do anything else. Her training at the Guildhall School of Music and Drama was followed by steady work in rep and summer tours, as a stand-up comic.

She made her TV debut in *Yes, It's the Cathode-Ray Tube Show!* in 1957 with Peter Sellers and Michael Bentine, and worked on *Jim's Inn* during the same period. Other TV credits include: *The Benny Hill Show*, *No Hiding Place*, *The Newcomers*, *Beggar My Neighbour*, *Clochemerle*, *Are You Being Served?*, several episodes of *Bootsie and Snudge*, playing Fat Alice, *On the Buses* and the BAFTA award-winning production, *The Borrowers*.

Pamela's been fortunate enough to work with all the great comics, including Benny Hill, Harry Worth, Bill Fraser and Frankie Howerd. In recent years, she's played Vi Box in three series of BBC's *Big Deal* and Mrs Monk, the housekeeper, in *The Choir*, and remains busy, particularly on stage. She has appeared in three pantos at the Palace Theatre, Watford, all written by Roy Hudd: *Cinderella*, *Jack and the Beanstalk* and *Robinson Crusoe*. In 1977, she played Mrs Orlock in *Plunder* at the Savoy Theatre. She has recently appeared in the film *Paradise Grove*.

PETER DAY

Peter was the visual effects designer on 20 episodes. After training in theatre design, he worked for several companies before joining the BBC in 1958 as a design assistant. Initially he worked on school programmes before concentrating on mainstream TV. Peter retired from the organisation in 1985.

JIM DOWDALL

Jim Dowdall has over 26 years' experience as a stunt co-ordinator/performer, covering a wide range of skills. His first job was in a circus, working with big cats and learning the trapeze, before joining Bapty and Co. as an armourer for three years, during which time he was assigned to films such as *The Dirty Dozen* and *Where Eagles Dare*.

Jim was a member of the Parachute Regiment, as well as an assistant director, before he made the move to stunt work in 1972. Over the last ten years, in addition to normal stunt work, he has been specialising in automotive work, particularly for commericals.

His credits as stunt co-ordinator include such TV shows as *EastEnders, Casualty, Second Sight, Prime Suspect* and *Bergerac*, while in film, he has worked on *Clockwise, Goldeneye, The English Patient, Tomorrow Never Dies* and *The Pianist*.

KEITH ELDRED

Keith moved to Thetford, Norfolk, from Hong Kong in 1965, and a few years later formed the Thetford Music and Drama Society. Whilst chairman of the society, he was approached by David Croft to see if members would be prepared to act as extras in *Dad's Army*. The highlight of Keith's involvement with the sitcom was a party he held at his house attended by members of the cast.

STUART FELL

After serving in the Parachute Regiment, Stuart began a 25-year career as a stunt artist in films and television. Among the productions he's been involved in are *Last of the Summer Wine, Hi-De-Hi!, Blake's 7, Poldark, Doctor Who, A Bridge Too Far,* three *Bond* and three *Superman* movies and a *Star Wars* picture. Nowadays, Stuart works as a freelance entertainer, with a current assignment seeing him work as a jester at stately homes.

PETER FITTON

Peter, who joined the BBC in 1962, worked as an assistant floor manager (AFM) on *Dad's Army*. He worked with David Croft on two further shows: the first series of *It Ain't Half Hot, Mum* and *Are You Being Served?*. He subsequently became a floor manager and held several other positions – including assistant producer/director on children's programmes and outside broadcasts, and consultant to the Singapore Broadcasting Corporation – before leaving the Beeb in 1991, by which time he was an instructor in television training, a job which took him all over the world.

Post-BBC, Peter worked as a freelance producer/director and set up his own company, Television Training International Ltd., before moving to Canada in 2000. Nowadays he still works occasionally as a consultant.

ROBERT GILLESPIE

Gillespie was asked to play actor Charles Boyer in a scene from the 1937 movie, *Marie Walewska*, in which the Frenchman was cast as Napoleon, as a consequence of David Croft not being allowed to use a clip from the actual picture.

Gillespie was cast in his first sitcom by David Croft, playing a Moroccan policeman in *Hugh and I Spy*, a role that led to him playing numerous policemen.

He spent his early years in Nantes, until his parents moved to Manchester. He eventually began performing as a semi-professional at the city's Library Theatre, before joining RADA. After graduating, he worked at the Old Vic until he was offered the role of Matthew in the TV production of *Jesus of Nazareth*.

Although Robert is normally cast in comedy roles, such as the gas man in *Rising Damp*, five series of *Keep It in the Family, The Fall and Rise of Reginald Perrin, Robin's Nest, Butterflies, George and Mildred* and *Whatever Happened To The Likely Lads?*, he's appeared in numerous dramas, including *Maigret, Crane, New Scotland Yard, The Sweeney, Van Der Valk, The Professionals* and *Secret Army*.

Robert, who also writes and directs, has made a

handful of films, and has appeared regularly on stage, including two years with the RSC.

JEAN GILPIN

After graduating from Bristol University, Jean was offered a place at a London drama school. She never completed the course, however, as she was soon offered rep and TV work. She made her debut in *The Duchess of Malfi* in 1972 and made her first film appearance in *To Catch A Spy*. Other credits on the big screen include Miss Field in *The World is Full of Married Men* (1979), the musical *The Bawdy Adventures of Tom Jones* and *The Tip-off*. Her TV work includes playing Margaret Eddington in *Quincy*, Staff Nurse Harper in *Angels* and roles in *Skeletons* and *Survivors*. Jean also worked for David Croft in the sitcom, *Come Back Mrs Noah*, and appeared in an episode of *The Professionals* in 1977.

In 1979 Jean returned to America, where she had lived as a child, and has established a successful career in voice work.

JOHN HART DYKE

John, who'd worked for Jimmy Perry at Watford Rep and Arnold Ridley in a production of *Ghost Train*, began training as a chartered surveyor after his national service. Halfway through his studies he met someone connected with a rep company in Perth, Scotland, and gave up surveying to join the company for three months as an unpaid student, before becoming ASM.

He made his TV debut in an episode of a BBC children's programme, quickly followed by an appearance in *Z Cars* as a furniture removal man. John has never been a regular on TV and most of his work since *Dad's Army* has been in the theatre. However, his TV credits include *The Professionals, Bergerac, Doctor Finlay*, a judge in *EastEnders* and *All Creatures Great and Small*, playing a local squire.

More recently he's played a butler in an episode of *Poirot*, toured the Middle and Far East in the famous *Derek Nimmo Tours*, spent a few weeks in Israel appearing in *Run For Your Wife*, and worked on a cruiser in *Funny Money*, travelling from Bombay to Athens.

MIKE HODGSON

Mike is secretary of the Austin 7 Club (southern branch) and runs a classic car workshop in Sussex. In his own collection of nine classic vehicles he has seven Austin 7s, including a 1931 model, which he bought when he was 15 years old for £5. His cars have appeared in a number of television shows, including *Poirot* and *House of Eliott*. Mike has since sold the vehicle used in *Dad's Army*.

JEFFREY HOLLAND

Jeffrey didn't contemplate acting as a career until joining an amateur company at the age of 15. Unsure what to do with his life, he worked at a wine merchants straight from school, before working in the office of a cardboard box manufacturer. It was then he decided to become an actor.

After more than four years in theatre in Coventry, small TV parts came his way. His first speaking role was a young husband in *Dixon of Dock Green*, but he also played a market stall trader in ten episodes of *Crossroads* in the mid-1970s before *Dad's Army*.

Jeffrey, who classes *Dad's Army* as his favourite programme, was offered the part of the truck-driving soldier after appearing in the stage show. Post *Dad's Army* his career blossomed and the 1980s saw him spend seven years playing Spike Dixon in *Hi-De-Hi!* and appear with Russ Abbot on his *Madhouse* shows. Other TV credits include playing James Twelvetrees in *You Rang, M'Lord?, Are You Being Served?* and Cecil Parkin in *Oh, Doctor Beeching!*

PAUL JOEL

Paul, the designer on 52 episodes of *Dad's Army*, studied architecture in London and worked for several architects before moving into interior design. He joined the BBC in 1965 and was promoted to designer three years later. His career at the Beeb had spanned almost 30 years by the time he left in 1994. Paul, who occasionally works freelance, lives in Cornwall with his artist wife, Judy. Much of his time is now devoted to organising and designing art exhibitions.

VERONICA LAURIE

Veronica is John Laurie's daughter. She now lives on a smallholding in the West Country, but from 1966 to '77 – during the entire making of *Dad's Army* – she was working in New York, before returning to Britain to become administrator of a conservation charity.

ERIC LONGWORTH

When his father died, Eric was only 17 and his ambitions to become an actor were sidetracked while he helped to support the family. He worked as a salesman at a printing company in Shaw, but maintained an interest in acting by joining the Crompton Stage Society, a local amateur company, playing character parts until his call-up in 1939.

In 1943–44, while serving with the army in Bombay, he got involved with the dramatic society and pursued an acting career once demobbed in 1946. His first professional job was at Oldham Rep, where he stayed 11 years. Eric moved behind the scenes and worked as theatre manager there from 1951 to 1957, and then at Guildford until 1963. Christmas Day 1963 saw him return to acting in Granada's 90-minute epic *Mr Pickwick*, with Arthur Lowe playing lead. This was his second TV appearance, the first being in *Shadow Squad* in the late 1950s. Usually cast as businessmen and retired colonels, other early small-screen credits include *Z Cars* and *No Hiding Place*. He also took the leading role in a documentary drama for Yorkshire Television in 1974, *Who Killed Julia Wallace?*, playing William, the husband.

Eric believes his appearance in a 1972 episode of TV's *Lollipop*, written by Jimmy Perry, led to the offer of work in *Dad's Army* later that year. He understudied Arthur Lowe in the *Dad's Army* stage show but didn't tour with the production due to work commitments.

He has made a handful of minor film appearances, including a scene with Ursula Andress in 1970's *Perfect Friday, No Sex Please, We're British* and *Tom Jones*. Other TV parts include two appearances in *Coronation Street*, one playing a policeman alongside Jimmy Beck.

No recent long-running TV roles or theatre parts (his last appearance on TV was in the 1989 BBC production *Oedipus the King*) but Eric, who spent more than five decades in showbiz, is kept busy with commercials. He recently travelled to Amsterdam to film an advert for Dutch Rail, and has also filmed in Stockholm and Oslo. His last commercial for British TV was in 1998, for Macdonald's.

PHILIP MADOC

For someone who only appeared in one episode, it's unbelievable how many people recall vividly Philip's role as the U-boat Captain.

After working as a German interpreter, he entered the industry in the 1960s, studying at RADA. He worked for a while in rep before moving into TV, one of his first TV appearances being in the 1956 production *The Count of Monte Cristo*. Other TV work includes Detective Chief Supt Tate in *Target*, Fison in *A Very British Coup*, *The Avengers* and *Dr Who*. He also appeared in 'Get Me Out Of Here!', an episode of *The Champions*, playing Angel Martes, as Rawlins in a *Randall & Hopkirk (Deceased)* episode, titled 'Never Trust a Ghost' in 1968, and an episode of *Man in a Suitcase*.

Philip also made over 30 films including *The Quiller Memorandum, Daleks: Invasion Earth 2150AD* and *Operation Daybreak*. Recent years have been dominated by theatre. His own TV detective series, *A Mind to Kill*, in which he plays the lead, has been sold all over the world.

ANNIE OGDEN

Annie joined the BBC in 1971, working in the stills library, but within a year she had transferred and was an assistant floor manager on a host of shows, ranging from *Play School* to *It Ain't Half Hot, Mum*. As a floor manager, she worked in news and current affairs, including *Nationwide* and the early breakfast programmes. By the time she left the Beeb in 1992, she was a senior floor manager. Having freelanced ever since, she's currently working at the BBC's political studio at Westminster.

JIMMY PERRY & DAVID CROFT

Between them, Perry and Croft have formed one of Britain's most successful writing partnerships, penning not just *Dad's Army* but other classic sitcoms such as *Hi-De-Hi!, It Ain't Half Hot, Mum* and *You Rang, M'Lord?*. In recognition of their service to television and the enjoyment they've given millions, the writers were awarded the OBE.

BILL PERTWEE

Playing Hodges in 60 TV episodes, the film, stage show and 33 radio instalments, Bill established a character who became the bane of Mainwaring's life. Since the series finished in 1977, he's remained busy, primarily in the theatre. He's also written several books.

DEREK WARE

Between 1960 and 1990, Derek, whose parents were variety artists, worked as a stuntman, fight director and stunt co-ordinator, but his first taste of the entertainment world was as a four year old, touring army bases in the west of England with a children's troupe during the Second World War.

Later, he worked as a child actor in films and television, before attending RADA in 1955. Work in repertory theatres and and the 1959 season at Butlin's followed, but in 1960 he broke into stunting and for the next 30 years worked consistently around the world in all mediums of the profession. He also set up his own stunt agency, HAVOC, which was in business for ten years.

Forced by injury to retire from stunt work in 1990, he has devoted the remainder of his time to his job as fencing coach and staged-combat master at various drama schools and universities in the UK and America. He has also written four books on stunts and swordplay.

FRANK WILLIAMS

For 39 TV episodes, the Vicar was brought to life by Frank Williams, who made his name in *The Army Game*. On the big screen, his debut was in the 1956 film, *The Extra Day*, followed by more than 30 other pictures. Frank, who's a regular in panto, is also a playwright. Over the past few years, there have been successful productions of four of his thrillers.

The Production Team

PRODUCER

David Croft

DIRECTOR

David Croft (all episodes except S9, episodes 1, 2, 4 & 5 which were directed by Bob Spiers)

PRODUCTION ASSISTANT

Gordon Pert (S5; S6)

Bob Spiers (S6, episodes 6 & 7; S7)

Jo Austin (S8; 'My Brother and I'; 'The Love of Three Oranges')

Gordon Elsbury (S9)

PRODUCER'S ASSISTANT

Kay Johnson (S5)

Jo Austin (S6)

Diane Taylor and Jennie Birkett (S7)

Hilary West (S8; S9; 'My Brother and I'; 'The Love of Three Oranges')

ASSISTANT FLOOR MANAGER

Peter Fitton (S5, episodes 1, 3–13; S6)

Steven Morns (S6, episode 1)

Tony Newman (S6, episode 2)

John Cox (S6, episode 7)

Anne Ogden (S7; S8; 'My Brother and I')

Sue Bennett-Urwin (S7, episodes 1, 3–6)

Susan Belbin (S9; 'The Love of Three Oranges')

FLOOR ASSISTANT

Richard Cox (S5, episodes 1–7)

Paul Jackson (S5, episodes 8–13)

Philip Hill (S6)

Richard Boden (S7, episodes 1, 3–6; S8; 'My Brother and I')

Ken Dodds (S7, episode 2)

Judy Littler ('The Love of Three Oranges'; S9)

STUDIO LIGHTING
(also known as TECHNICAL MANAGER 1)

Howard King (S5; S6; S7; S8; S9; 'My Brother and I'; 'The Love of Three Oranges'

TECHNICAL MANAGER 2

Fred Wright (S5, episodes 1–7)

Peter Valentine (S5, episodes 8–10; S6)

Ron Bristow (S5, episode 11; S8, episode 1)

Ray Hider (S5, episodes 12 & 13)

Brendan Carr (S7, episodes 1, 3–6; 'The Love of Three Oranges'; S9, episodes 2–6)

John Barnacle (S7, episode 2; S9, episode 1)

Arthur Relph (S8, episode 2)

Colin Widgery (S8, episodes 3, 4 & 6)

John Carter (S8, episode 5; 'My Brother and I')

STUDIO SOUND SUPERVISOR

Michael McCarthy (S5, episodes 1–7; S6; S7; S8, episode 3; 'The Love of Three Oranges')

John Delany (S5, episodes 8–13)

Alan Machin (S8, episodes 1, 2, 4–6; 'My Brother and I')

Laurie Taylor (S9)

TAPE/GRAM OPERATOR

(Member of team for S5 not listed on production list)

Barry Bonner (S6, episode 1)

Dave Thompson (S6, episodes 2–7; S7; S8, episodes 1, 3 & 6; 'My Brother and I'; 'The Love of Three Oranges')

Ian Tomlin (S8, episode 2 & 5)

Richard David (S8, episode 4)

Keith Bowden (S9, episodes 1, 2, 4 & 5)

Mike Roberts (S9, episodes 3 & 6)

COSTUME SUPERVISOR

Susan Wheal (S5; S6; S7)

Mary Husband (S8; S9; 'Mr Brother and I'; 'The Love of Three Oranges')

MAKE-UP SUPERVISOR

Cynthia Goodwin (S5; episodes 1–7)

Anna Chesterman (S5, episodes 8–13; S6, episode 2)

Ann Ailes (S6, episodes 1, 3–7)

Sylvia Thornton (S7; S8; S9; 'My Brother and I'; 'The Love of Three Oranges')

DESIGNER

Paul Joel (S5; S6)

Bryan Ellis (S7)

Robert Berk (S8; 'My Brother and I')

Tim Gleeson (S9, episode 1, 3 & 4)

Geoff Powell (S9, episode 2, 5 & 6)

Barry Newbery ('The Love of Three Oranges')

VISION MIXER

Dave Hanks (S5; S6; S7, episodes 1, 3–6; S8, episodes 1, 3, 4 & 6)

Ron Isted (S7, episode 2)

Angela Beveridge (S8, episodes 2 & 5; 'My Brother and I'; 'The Love of Three Oranges'; S9)

VISUAL EFFECTS

Peter Day (S5, episodes 1–7 & 12; S6, episode 4)

Tony Harding (S5, episodes 10 & 13)

Jim Ward (S7, episodes 1 & 3)

Martin Gutteridge (S9, episodes 1, 2 & 3)

Peter Pegrum ('The Love of Three Oranges)

FILM CAMERAMAN

Stewart A Farnell (S5, episodes 2, 3, 5 & 7)

James Balfour (S5, episodes 8, 10, 12 & 13; S6, episodes 1, 3–6)

Len Newson (S7, episodes 1, 3, 5 & 6)

Peter Chapman (S8, episodes 1, 3, 4 & 6; S9, episodes 1, 2, 3 & 5)

FILM SOUND

Ron Blight (S5, episodes 2, 3, 5 & 7)

Les Collins (S5, episodes 8, 10, 12 & 13)

John Gatland (S6, episodes 1, 3–6; S7, episodes 1, 3, 5 & 6)

Bill Chesneau (S8, episodes 1, 3, 4 & 6)

Graham Bedwell (S9, episodes 1, 2, 3 & 5)

FILM EDITOR

Bob Rymer (S5, episodes 2, 7 & 8; S6, episodes 1, 3 & 4)

Bill Harris (S5, episodes 3, 5, 10, 12 & 13; S6, episodes 5 & 6; S7, episodes 1, 3, 5 & 6)

John Stothart (S8, episodes 1, 3, 4 & 6)

John Dunstan (S9, episode 1, 2, 3 & 5)

SERIES FIVE **EPISODE ONE**

Recorded: Friday 26/5/72

Original transmission: Friday 6/10/72, 8.30–9pm

Original viewing figures = 17 million

ARTHUR LOWE .... CAPTAIN MAINWARING
JOHN LE MESURIER .... SERGEANT WILSON
CLIVE DUNN.................................. LANCE CORPORAL JONES
JOHN LAURIE .... PRIVATE FRAZER
JAMES BECK .... PRIVATE WALKER
ARNOLD RIDLEY .... PRIVATE GODFREY
IAN LAVENDER .... PRIVATE PIKE
BILL PERTWEE .... ARP WARDEN
COLIN BEAN .... PRIVATE SPONGE
PLATOON..................... VIC TAYLOR, FREDDIE WHITE, HUGH CECIL,
.... GEORGE HANCOCK, LESLIE NOYES, FREDDIE WILES,
.... DESMOND CULLUM-JONES, HUGH HASTINGS, MICHAEL MOORE

ASLEEP IN THE DEEP

• PETER DAY REMEMBERS •

'For the famous scene in which Mainwaring, Hodges and members of the platoon are trapped inside the pumping station with the water rising, the set designer had a tank constructed in the studio, in which the set was built. Fire hoses were then connected to a hydrant outside the building and used to fill up the tank.

'While some of the platoon squeezed on to the top of a double bunk, away from the rising water, Hodges sat in an old water tank and propelled himself across the room, to reach the stop cock and turn off the squirting water (rigged by Visual Effects).

'The water was about three feet deep, and he couldn't keep upright in his tank, so as there were two of us in wet suits in the tank for safety reasons, Brian Marsh, my assistant and a sub-aqua club member, put his air tank and mask on, and swam underwater, controlling the passage of Hodges' "boat", until he fell out and got soaked once again!'

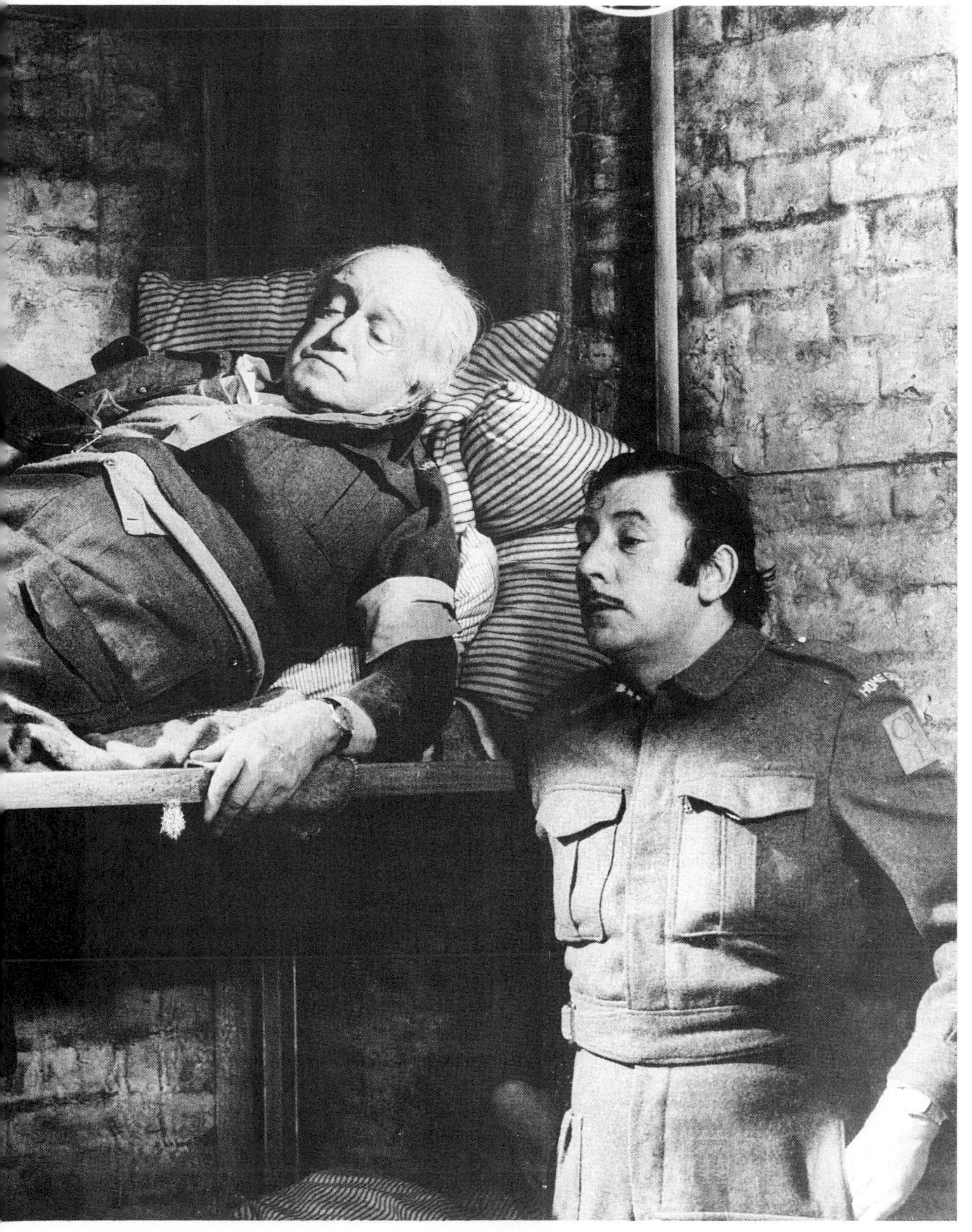

Asleep in the Deep

INTERIOR. COMMAND POST. NIGHT

Small command post made of sandbags. The roof consists of boards about six inches apart with sandbags on top. We can see the sandbags through the gaps.

Mainwaring, Wilson and Pike are looking out through a slit. In the background are the other members of the platoon. They are all wearing steel helmets and equipment. We can hear the drone of planes and ack ack fire. Pike is sucking his thumb.

MAINWARING Do take your thumb out of your mouth, boy. You know, Wilson, I'd give everything I possess to have a go at the enemy. I feel so helpless – our lads are out there bowling Jerry for six – and here we are, stuck in the pavilion.

Jones and Frazer enter, followed by Private Sponge and two other privates. They all have their bayonets fixed. Loud ack ack fire.

JONES Number two patrol reporting, sir.

MAINWARING Yes, Jones.

JONES All quiet, sir.

Several loud bangs.

MAINWARING What?

JONES I said it's all quiet, sir – when I say all quiet – I'm not referring to the noise, if you understand me, sir. The 'all quiet' is official military procedure...

Mainwaring reacts.

FRAZER Ach! What the old fool is trying to tell you, Captain Mainwaring, is that we didn't spot any Nazi parachutists. **(He starts to unfix his bayonet)**

MAINWARING Why have they got their bayonets fixed, Jones?

JONES In case the parachutists come floating down, sir – you've got to be ready for the old upward thrust.

He thrusts his bayonet upwards. It goes into one of the sandbags – a shower of sand falls on Mainwaring.

JONES Sorry, sir – sorry, sir. **(He brushes Mainwaring off)**

MAINWARING Pike, bung up that hole. Go and have a rest in the corner, Jones.

JONES Yes, sir – yes, sir – number two patrol, at the double – go and have a rest in the corner.

WILSON I think it's the best place for him.

MAINWARING **(To Wilson)** You may well scoff – I like that man's spirit, Wilson – you can see the light of battle in his eye – it's exhilarating.

WILSON Yes, sir – awfully good, but rather sandy. **(He has his eyes half closed)**

MAINWARING I wouldn't mind seeing a light of battle in your eyes – that is if you could keep them open long enough. What's the matter? Didn't you get any sleep last night?

WILSON Well, you must admit, sir, we've been going at it pretty hard lately – working at the bank all day – and then being on duty most of the night.

MAINWARING I'm just as tired as you are, Wilson – but I'm not standing here with a dozy look on my face. As an officer, I have to set an example to my men – and you should do the same – now brighten up.

Pike takes a dirty sweet bag out of his pocket.

PIKE **(To Wilson)** Uncle Arthur?

WILSON What?

PIKE Would you like some hundreds and thousands?

WILSON Oh how nice.

Wilson holds out his hand. Pike tips some into his palm.

PIKE Would you like some, Captain Mainwaring?

MAINWARING Not with my cocoa, thank you.

PIKE I always have my sweet ration in hundreds and thousands – they weigh light and you get a lot more for your coupons.

MAINWARING Number three section – get ready for patrol.

Frazer moves down to Mainwaring.

FRAZER If you ask my opinion, Captain Mainwaring, I think it would be sheer folly for them to go out – sheer folly – that shrapnel is coming down like hail.

MAINWARING What do you suggest then – that we crouch in this funk hole for the rest of the night?

FRAZER No, but we can't do very much – we should stay where we are – it's common sense.

MAINWARING War has got nothing to do with common sense, Frazer – I don't want to skulk in here, I want to get out there and get to grips with the enemy.

WILSON Don't you think that they're rather high up for that, sir.

Mainwaring gives him a glare.

JONES Oh, Captain Mainwaring, that's the sort of talk I like to hear. You know, you remind me of a major we had in the trenches in 1916 – he was just like you. Major Willerby D'Arcy, his name was – he wasn't a skulking man – didn't do a lot of skulking at all – just couldn't abide crouching and skulking. You should have seen him, sir – top boots polished like glass – monocle glistening in his eye. Wonderful man – anyhow, one day we was crouching in the bottom of the trench – and he said to us – 'Boys, I've had enough of this. I'm going to get up on that parapet and walk about, just to show those damned Jerries that we're not afraid.' Well, he climbed up to the top of the parapet…

MAINWARING I know what you're going to say, Jones – he walked about and didn't get a scratch.

JONES No, sir – he got shot. In a rather inconvenient place it was – he had to do a lot of crouching after that.

Pause – Pike offers the bag to Jones.

PIKE Would you like a hundred and thousand, Mr Jones?

JONES Thank you, Pikey.

He holds out his hand – there is a loud explosion. He knocks the bag, and the sweets spill on the floor.

PIKE Oh no – that was a whole week's sweet ration.

Hodges the Warden rushes in.

HODGES Blimey that was close. I think it came down in the woods. What are you all hiding in here for? Shouldn't you be out looking for parachutists?

WILSON Just clear off, will you?

MAINWARING Yes, mind your own business.

HODGES Now, don't you start, Napoleon.

JONES Why aren't you out A.R.P.eeing?

HODGES If you must know, I've been A.R.P.eeing all night. I've done my job, mate – all my people are on duty – that's the second bomb we've had tonight, you know.

FRAZER Where did the first one come down?

HODGES Only a small one on the pumping station. It's all right, there's no one in it.

MAINWARING What are you talking about? Godfrey and Walker are on duty there.

HODGES No one told me.

MAINWARING We must get down there at once. Wilson – Jones – Frazer – Pike come with me. Sponge, you take charge here.

SPONGE Right-oh, Mr Mainwaring.

HODGES You can't go interfering – this is an A.R.P. matter.

MAINWARING Mind your own business. (**Pike is bending down**) What are you doing on the floor, Pike?

PIKE I'm trying to pick up my hundreds and thousands.

MAINWARING Come on, you stupid boy.

HODGES You can't go interfering – this is an A.R.P. matter.

MAINWARING Mind your own business.

INTERIOR. FIRST ROOM IN PUMPING STATION. NIGHT

On the far wall of the room are about twenty pipes with stopcocks on. On the other wall is a small grill – next to it is a manhole cover with bolts on the outside. It is big enough for a man to get through. On a rack are several large spanners. There are two doors. One of them opens. Hodges, Mainwaring, Wilson, Jones, Frazer and Pike rush in.

HODGES I told you so – there's nobody here.

MAINWARING They're in the next room.

He runs over to the other door and pulls it open. A pile of bricks and rubble fall into the room. The passage outside is blocked.

MAINWARING The wall's collapsed.

Walker's face appears at the grill.

WALKER Mr Mainwaring! Mr Mainwaring!

Mainwaring climbs on a chair to reach the grill.

JONES Mr Mainwaring – let me give you a bunk up.

MAINWARING Are you all right, Walker?

WALKER Yes – but I can't get out.

MAINWARING What's happened?

WALKER The wall's collapsed against the door. It won't open.

MAINWARING Where's Godfrey?

WALKER He's asleep on the bunk.

FRAZER Did you hear that? Godfrey's asleep! The old fool's asleep on duty, in wartime on active service. That's an offence punishable by death – did you hear what I said, Mr Mainwaring – death! Death!

MAINWARING Oh do be quiet, Frazer. Why are you both in there, Walker? One of you should have been on duty on the roof.

WALKER I did my two hours on duty – then I came down here for Godfrey to relieve me – and I couldn't wake him up. It was then that the bomb came down.

MAINWARING Take Godfrey's name, Wilson. Write it down.

WILSON I know his name

MAINWARING I shall see him in my office tomorrow.

WALKER You don't understand, Mr Mainwaring – I think he's ill.

MAINWARING Why?

WALKER I still can't wake him up – I've tried everything.

MAINWARING Right – we'll soon get you out of there – come on, Wilson!

JONES I'll give you a bunk down. (**He climbs on the rubble out into the passage which is in darkness. Wilson follows**) It doesn't look too bad. I don't think it will take us long to shift this lot.

HODGES Wait a minute – you're not doing any shifting, this is an A.R.P. job. Heavy Rescue – and I'm taking charge. I'm Chief Warden.

MAINWARING Rubbish, you're doing nothing of the sort – I'm taking charge.

HODGES I tell you, I'm taking charge.

Wilson has climbed right out into the passage – he flicks his cigarette lighter.

MAINWARING Those are my men trapped in there – so I'm taking charge and that's that.

WILSON **(Holding up lighter)** Good heavens – look at that, sir.

MAINWARING What? **(He climbs up)**

WILSON Those huge cracks in the wall.

MAINWARING **(Looking right up)** The whole lot could come down any minute.

HODGES **(Looking up)** Blimey! Perhaps you're right, Captain Mainwaring – you should be in charge – as you say, they are your men. **(He moves back)**

MAINWARING Keep perfectly still, Wilson. Now, hold my hand.

WILSON I beg your pardon?

MAINWARING Hold my hand and we'll creep back into the room.

Everything goes quiet – no one speaks. Mainwaring takes Wilson's hand and they gingerly creep back into the room. They all gather in a tight group round Mainwaring.

MAINWARING **(Whispering)** Now, listen to me very carefully, men. Only part of the wall has collapsed. God knows what's holding the rest up. The slightest noise or movement could bring the whole lot down – and we can't wait. Godfrey may be very ill.

FRAZER The question is, how are we going to shift that rubble without bringing the whole wall down on top of us?

MAINWARING There's only one thing for it, men – we must form a chain and pass the rubble back here into this room. I'm afraid it's not going to be too pleasant for whoever's at the head of the chain.

HODGES Pleasant – it's going to be damn dangerous.

JONES Permission to whisper, sir? I should like to volunteer to be the head of the daisy chain. Let me do it, sir – let me lead the daisy chain.

MAINWARING No, Jones – we're going to draw lots. **(He takes a diary out of his pocket and tears out the pages)** Now, I shall mark two of these pieces of paper with a cross – whoever draws them goes to the head of the chain. **(He moves away to mark them)**

PIKE **(Whispering)** Uncle Arthur.

WILSON What is it, Frank?

PIKE I saw them do this in the film – *Each Dawn I Die*.

WILSON Really, who drew the paper with the cross on it?

PIKE The sergeant.

WILSON **(Turning on him)** I do wish you wouldn't keep talking about films all the time, Frank – it's so boring.

PIKE Why have you gone all cross, Uncle Arthur?

WILSON I'm not cross – I'm just er… slightly frightened, that's all.

Mainwaring comes back with the pieces of paper screwed up in his hat.

MAINWARING Now, there are six pieces of paper screwed up in this hat…

HODGES What are you talking about – six pieces? There are only five of you.

MAINWARING I know, but you make six.

HODGES Now, wait a minute – this has got nothing to do with me.

FRAZER Ach! I thought so – you're yellow.

JONES You're right there, Jock – he's got a stripe down his back a foot wide.

MAINWARING Quiet. **(Slowly to Hodges)** Now, are you going to take one or not?

There is a long silence – they all stare at Hodges, who looks round at the group and licks his lips.

HODGES All right, I'll take one – I'm not going to give you lot a chance to have anything on me.

MAINWARING You first, Wilson. **(He offers the hat)**

WILSON **(Takes a paper and unrolls it)** Blank.

MAINWARING Jones.

JONES Nothing on it, sir.

MAINWARING Frazer.

Frazer reaches out – Hodges knocks his hand.

HODGES I'm next. **(He grabs a paper)** Blimey, I've got it.

FRAZER What a pity, I was going to take that one.

Hodges gives him a terrible glare.

MAINWARING Right, I'm next. **(He takes a paper and unrolls it. Cut to close up. We can see that it's blank)** I've got the second one.

JONES Let me go in your place, sir – you're too young to die. Let me go – let me go.

MAINWARING No, Jones – I want you to stay in here at the end of the chain. Right, men, take your equipment off – but keep your steel helmets on. **(To Hodges)** Come on, Chief Warden. **(Climbs through door into the passage)**

INTERIOR. THE PASSAGE. NIGHT

The rubble is about three feet high. It is blocking the door into the second room which opens outwards into the passage. Mainwaring and Hodges reach the door. Mainwaring picks up a piece of rubble and hands it to Hodges.

MAINWARING **(Whispering to Hodges)** The slightest sound could bring this wall down. Tell them not to make any noise. Pass it on.

INTERIOR. FIRST ROOM. NIGHT

Wilson is standing just outside the door. Frazer in doorway. Pike next and then Jones. They are passing pieces of rubble along the chain. Jones puts the pieces on the floor. They are moving like a well oiled machine.

WILSON **(Whispering to Frazer)** Don't make any noise. Pass it on.

FRAZER **(Whispering to Pike)** Don't make any noise whatever you do. Pass it on.

PIKE **(Whispering to Jones)** Don't make any noise.

JONES Don't make…

Pike hands another bit of rubble to Jones who puts it on floor.

WALKER **(Shouting through grill)** Hey, Jonesey – what's going on?

Jones turns to the grill.

JONES Shut up, Joe – you mustn't make any…

Pike passes a brick to Jones whose hands are not there – the brick drops on his foot. Jones goes purple trying to stifle a shout.

INTERIOR. SECOND ROOM. NIGHT

In the corner is a two-tier bunk. Godfrey is asleep on top of it. At the head of the bunk is a manhole cover with bolts – this is covered from view by pillows.

Further along the wall is a rack with spanners on. Next to that is the manhole cover leading to the first room. There are no bolts on it. Next is the grill which is 7 feet from the ground. Underneath is a tin bath which Walker stands on to look through the grill. The top tier of the bunk is 5 feet from the group. Walker is leaning over the bunk trying to wake Godfrey up.

WALKER Oh blimey, what's the matter with him? **(He shakes him)** Wake up, Charlie. **(Godfrey has a lovely smile on his face)** He can't be ill – he wouldn't smile like that if he was. I wonder if his heart's all right? **(He unbuttons Godfrey's blouse and puts his ear to his chest)** I can't hear anything. **(He unbuttons a woollen waistcoat and listens again)** His heart's not beating. **(He unbuttons his shirt and pulls out a large piece of thermogene wool)** No wonder I can't hear anything. **(Listens again)** That's better – sound as a bell. **(He crosses to the grill and stands on the bath)** Hey, Jonesey – what's happening? **(Jones' face appears at the grill)**

JONES Don't worry, Joe – we're nearly through. How's Mr Godfrey?

WALKER I can't make it out – he's sleeping like a baby.

The door opens a few inches and Mainwaring whispers through the crack.

MAINWARING Walker.

Walker rushes over to the door.

WALKER Yes, I'm here, Mr Mainwaring.

MAINWARING Now listen, push the door from your side very slowly.

Walker pushes the door – it slowly opens about two feet. Mainwaring, Hodges and Wilson squeeze through.

MAINWARING A bit more. How's Godfrey?

WALKER I dunno – he looks okay – just won't wake up.

Mainwaring crosses to the bunk.

MAINWARING Godfrey – can you hear me? **(He feels his pulse)** He seems all right. **(Frazer and Pike push through the door)** I thought I told you two to stay in the other room.

FRAZER Well, if the silly old… I mean the poor old man's ill – I want to help.

PIKE Don't forget I've got my scout badge for first aid, Mr Mainwaring.

MAINWARING Frazer.

FRAZER Sir?

MAINWARING Close the door quietly, and, Wilson, tell Jones to stay where he is, and close his door.

INTERIOR. FIRST ROOM. NIGHT

Wilson's face appears at the grill.

WILSON Jonesey – Mr Mainwaring says stay where you are and close the door.

JONES Stay where I am and close the door – right-oh, Mr Wilson.

Jones crosses to the door.

WILSON Quietly.

He slams the door.

JONES What?

There is a creaking sound which gets louder – then a terrific crash as the wall collapses.

INTERIOR. SECOND ROOM. NIGHT

They are all crouched on the floor. Clouds of dust cover them.

WILSON I'm afraid he didn't close it quietly, sir.

HODGES This is a nice mess you've landed us in, Mainwaring.

MAINWARING Shut up!

Mainwaring and Walker rush over to the door. They try to open it.

WALKER It's no use, Mr Mainwaring – there must be a ton of bricks up against that door.

MAINWARING We're trapped!

FRAZER Aye – doomed. Doomed!

Jones' face appears at the grill.

JONES Permission to speak, sir? I'm afraid I closed the door a bit too hard.

MAINWARING **(At grill)** Now listen carefully, Jones – I want you to go to the Command Post and find Private Sponge and tell them to come and rescue us.

JONES Get help – right-oh, sir. Don't panic. Don't panic.

Pike is standing by the bunk.

WALKER Captain Mainwaring, Mr Godfrey's waking up.

MAINWARING What? **(He rushes over to the bunk)**

GODFREY Oh, hello – I'm afraid I must have dozed off for a minute.

WALKER Dozed off – he's been asleep for four hours.

MAINWARING What do you think you're playing at, Godfrey?

GODFREY Well, sir, I haven't been sleeping too well lately – so when I was at the clinic this morning they gave me some tablets – they must have been stronger than I thought.

MAINWARING How dare you take sleeping pills on active service. I've a good mind to…

Jones' face appears at the grill.

JONES Permission to worry you, sir? I can't get out.

MAINWARING What!

JONES I went to open the other door and the handle's come off.

There is a long pause.

FRAZER I knew it – we're doomed – doomed!

MAINWARING Be quiet, Frazer – I'm trying to think.

JONES **(Shouting through grill)** Don't worry, Mr Mainwaring – you'll get an idea in a minute.

Mainwaring draws Wilson away from the others.

MAINWARING Quiet, Jones. Out of the way, Frazer. Keep calm, men. Now listen, Wilson, we've got to keep these men cheerful until help arrives.

WILSON Very well, sir.

MAINWARING Now, whatever I do – you back me up and keep smiling.

WILSON You mean like this. **(He forces a sickly grin)**

MAINWARING I suppose that's better than nothing. Now, pay attention, men, we're in a pretty tight spot, but it's only a matter of time before Private Sponge and the others realise we're missing and come looking for us – meanwhile, to keep our spirits up, we'll have a sing song.

WALKER I'll give you one, Mr Mainwaring. **(Sings)** 'Twas Christmas Day in the workhouse – and the candles had just been lit.

MAINWARING No, Walker, we want something that we can do actions to.

WALKER Well you can do actions to that.

MAINWARING Not those sort of actions – something cheerful.

PIKE I've got an idea, sir – why don't we do one of those camp fire songs we used to have in the boy scouts?

MAINWARING Excellent, Pike – we'll do 'Underneath the Spreading Chestnut Tree'. Wilson will do the cheerful actions, and you follow.

FRAZER If Sergeant Wilson is going to do cheerful actions – I'd rather be miserable.

MAINWARING I don't want any insubordination, Frazer. Now, are you all ready? **(He quickly crosses to Wilson)** I suppose you do know the actions, Wilson?

WILSON Well – I think I saw them once on the Movietone News.

MAINWARING Good – Sergeant Wilson will show you the actions.

WILSON I don't remember them awfully well. Wouldn't it be better if somebody else showed them?

MAINWARING **(Taking him aside)** Now, look here, Wilson. Back me up. Do the actions – that's an order.

WILSON Yes, sir.

MAINWARING Cheerfully.

They all sing – Wilson does the actions.

ALL Underneath the spreading **(Wilson stretches arms overhead)** Chest **(Strikes chest)** Nut **(Taps head)** Tree. **(Spreads arms)** Where I held **(Embraces himself)** you on my knee. **(Strikes knee)** There we raised a family. **(Scowls and emits a growl)** 'Neath the spreading **(Arms outstretched)** Chest **(Strikes chest)** Nut **(Taps head)** Tree.

MAINWARING Now we'll try it all together.

GODFREY Excuse me, sir – do you want me to come down and join in – or stay up here and join in?

MAINWARING Stay where you are, Godfrey – Jones.

JONES Yes, sir.

MAINWARING Don't forget to do the actions.

JONES You've no need to worry, sir. I shall do the actions – even though you cannot see me, sir – I shall do them to the hilt.

MAINWARING Right now – all together, with actions.

They all sing with actions. On the last chestnut tree, Jones' face disappears and there is a loud crash.

MAINWARING Jones – Jones, are you all right?

Jones' face appears.

JONES I fell off the chair, sir – it's difficult to do the actions pressed up against the wall.

MAINWARING Just do the words, Jones. Right, once again.

They all sing. Cut to close up of Pike who is looking uncomfortable. Cut to pipe behind him. Water is pouring out of several large cracks – one jet stronger than all the others is shooting out and hitting Pike in the small of the back – the song finishes.

PIKE Mr Mainwaring, I feel all cold and wet.

WALKER Blimey, look – water's coming out of the pipe.

FRAZER That bomb must have cracked it.

They all clear back from the pipe.

WILSON Perhaps, if we wrapped something round the pipe, that might stop the flow.

MAINWARING Good idea – Pike take your blouse off and wrap it round the pipe.

PIKE Why me?

MAINWARING Because you're already wet. Now, do as you're told.

WALKER If this water keeps on coming in we'll all be drowned.

Pike takes his blouse off.

WALKER What are we going to do if we can't stop it?

MAINWARING There's no such thing as can't, Walker. Get in there, boy, and wrap it round the pipe.

Pike dives in and wraps his blouse round the pipe – the others retreat back to the bunk.

PIKE I don't think it's going to work.

FRAZER Stick at it, laddie – you're doing fine.

MAINWARING Hold your tongue, Frazer – I'll do any encouraging there is to be done.

WILSON I've just remembered, sir – there are a lot of stopcocks in the other room – perhaps Jones could turn the water off.

MAINWARING Good thinking. Walker, tell Jones to try and turn the water off by the stopcocks.

WALKER **(Jumping up on the bath)** Right-oh! **(He shouts through the grill at Jones)** Hey, Jonesey, we're being flooded out. Mr Mainwaring says try and turn the water off.

JONES How can I do that?

WALKER Turn the stopcocks.

JONES What stopcocks?

WALKER **(To Mainwaring)** What stopcocks?

MAINWARING The stopcocks on the pipes.

WALKER **(To Jones)** The stopcocks on the pipes cock.

MAINWARING This is no time for stupid jokes, Walker – tell him to get on with it.

FIRST ROOM. NIGHT

Jones is standing in front of the stopcocks, scratching his head.

JONES I wonder which way is off.

WALKER Hurry up, Jonesey, we're getting wet.

JONES Which way is off, Joe?

WALKER Which way is off?

MAINWARING Anti-clockwise.

WALKER Anti-clockwise.

JONES **(Looking at watch)** Anti-clockwise – that means that way. No it doesn't – it means that way. **(He frantically turns the cocks)** Yes, that's right – that way – it must be that way.

SECOND ROOM. NIGHT

Mainwaring, Wilson, Frazer and Walker are clinging to the bunk. Hodges is standing in the tin bath. Water is coming through cracks in the second pipe as well as the first.

FRAZER The silly old fool – he's making it worse.

Suddenly the first pipe comes apart at the S-bend and water gushes out.

WALKER **(Shouting)** You're turning it the wrong way, Jonesey.

The second pipe comes apart at the S-bend as well. They all shout 'turn it off' etc.

FIRST ROOM. NIGHT

Jones is turning the stopcocks. We can hear shouting from the other room.

JONES Don't panic – don't panic – I'll get it. I'll get it.

SECOND ROOM. NIGHT

Pike is standing in the middle of the room. Mainwaring, Wilson, Frazer, Walker and Godfrey are crouching on the top bunk. Hodges is sitting in the tin bath which is floating. The water is pouring out of the two pipes – the level is just above Pike's knees.

PIKE Mr Mainwaring, can I come up on the bunk please?

MAINWARING I'm sorry, Pike, there's no more room.

PIKE What am I going to do when it reaches my head?

MAINWARING Don't worry, Pike – we'll have thought of something by then.

PIKE Can I get in your bath please, Mr Hodges?

HODGES No you can't get in my bath – there's only room for one – stop mucking about and making waves, the slightest movement will have it over.

WALKER I know – let's have a sing song – how about 'Asleep in the Deep'.

They all give Walker a terrible glare.

SECOND ROOM. NIGHT

The water has now reached Pike's chest. The rest are still on top of the bunk and Hodges is in the bath.

PIKE Uncle Arthur – if you don't let me up on the bunk I shall tell Mum.

WILSON Oh do stop moaning, Frank – you can see there's no room.

PIKE We haven't got much time left, Mr Mainwaring – you said you'd think of something before the water reached my head.

MAINWARING We are thinking, Pike. (**To Wilson**) Have you thought of anything yet, Wilson?

WILSON No, sir, but I'm working on it.

FRAZER The water's getting higher and higher.

GODFREY Perhaps it would be a good idea if we didn't talk very much – then we won't use up the air.

MAINWARING Be quiet, Godfrey – if it hadn't been for you, we wouldn't be in this mess in the first place.

FRAZER We're entombed – entombed. I mind the time when I was a boy on the Isle of Barra – a submarine sunk in the bay – seven brave men were trapped in it and the water rose higher and higher until in the end it came up to their necks – a terrible way to die.

HODGES Oh put a sock in it.

GODFREY Mr Mainwaring, I wonder if I might...

MAINWARING If you want to be excused, it's impossible.

PIKE I agree.

GODFREY What I was going to say was – I think I've found a way out.

MAINWARING Don't be absurd.

GODFREY Here, sir. (**He pulls aside the pillows to reveal the manhole cover**)

MAINWARING And just how do you suggest we undo the bolts?

WALKER (**Pointing to spanners**) Look, Mr Mainwaring, that's what the spanners are for.

MAINWARING By Jove, I believe you're right. Pike, get that large spanner.

WILSON How awfully clever of you, Godfrey.

PIKE I can't reach it, sir.

MAINWARING Hodges – get that spanner.

HODGES Mr Hodges to you, Napoleon.

MAINWARING I presume you want to get out of here?

HODGES Oh, all right. (**He takes his steel helmet off and paddles the bath to below the tool rack**)

HODGES (**Reaching up**) I can't quite reach.

WILSON Well, stand up.

HODGES (**Gingerly standing up and getting the spanner**) If I'm not careful I shall... (**He falls back into the water**)

WALKER Fall in.

Hodges stands up in the water. He has dropped the spanner.

MAINWARING You've dropped it – of all the bungling incompetent...

PIKE I'll get it, Mr Mainwaring.

Pike dives under the water and comes up with the spanner.

WILSON Well done, Frank.

WALKER Give it to me, Pikey.

Walker grabs the spanner and gets to work on the bolts.

MAINWARING Can you manage it?

WALKER A bit stiff but it's coming.

FIRST ROOM. NIGHT

Jones is wrestling with a stopcock.

JONES I've got to close it – no use – it won't budge. I need something to lever it. (**Looks round**) One of those spanners will do.

He rushes over to the tool rack, climbs up on the bench, grabs the spanner. His other hand is on the manhole cover which he notices for the first time.

JONES Blimey, why didn't I think of that before. (**He fixes the spanner on one of the bolts**) It fits! (**He starts to unscrew the bolts and shouts**) Don't worry, my brave lads. I'll get you out of there – I'll rescue you.

SECOND ROOM. NIGHT

Mainwaring and Wilson are the only ones left on the bunk – the rest have gone through the hole. Pike and Hodges are standing in the water holding on to the bunk..

PIKE Give me a hand up, Uncle Sergeant.

WILSON Don't get up here yet, Frank – you'll make us all wet.

HODGES I'd like to make you wet, mate.

WILSON Just clear off will you.

MAINWARING Don't stand there arguing ,Wilson, get through. (**Wilson starts to crawl into the hole**) Then we'll go round and let Jones out.

FIRST ROOM. NIGHT

Jones is unscrewing the last bolt.

JONES I'm coming, boys – I'm coming. (**He pulls the cover off**) Hold on, brave lads – hold on.

SECOND ROOM. NIGHT

Hodges is pushing Pike through the hole.

HODGES Go on, hurry up – hurry up. I'm wet through.

PIKE I'm just as wet as you are.

There is a pause. The manhole cover is pushed into the water and Jones' head and shoulders appear.

JONES It's all right, boys, I've saved you – I've saved... (**He looks round – the room is empty except for seven steel helmets floating on the water**) Oh no – Mr Mainwaring – Mr Mainwaring! Are you there, sir? (**He reaches right through the hole and starts feeling around in the water**)

FIRST ROOM. NIGHT

The door opens, Mainwaring, Wilson, Frazer, Walker, Godfrey, Pike and Hodges dash in – the door closes behind them.

MAINWARING It's all right, Jones – we're here.

WILSON He's gone.

FRAZER No he hasn't. Look! (**He points to Jones' legs poking through the hole. They rush to the hole and pull Jones back into the room**)

JONES Oh thank goodness, Mr Mainwaring – I thought you were all drowned. I'm so pleased to see you.

MAINWARING Come on, I've had enough of this – let's get out of here. (**He crosses to the door – it won't open**) Who shut this door?

GODFREY Well – it was rather draughty, and I didn't want any of you to catch cold.

MAINWARING There's no handle – you've done it again.

ALL Oh no!

JONES How are we going to get out?

MAINWARING (**Slowly**) One of us has got to get through that hole, into the room, and out through the other hole – and then go round and open this door. Whoever it is – is going to get very wet. Right, Wilson, take your trousers off.

SERIES FIVE **EPISODE TWO**

Recorded: Friday 9/6/72

Original transmission: Friday 13/10/72, 8.30–9.00pm

Original viewing figures = 16 million

ARTHUR LOWE .... CAPTAIN MAINWARING
JOHN LE MESURIER .... SERGEANT WILSON
CLIVE DUNN .... LANCE CORPORAL JONES
JOHN LAURIE .... PRIVATE FRAZER
JAMES BECK .... PRIVATE WALKER
ARNOLD RIDLEY .... PRIVATE GODFREY
IAN LAVENDER .... PRIVATE PIKE
BILL PERTWEE .... ARP WARDEN
DEREK BOND .... MINISTER
ROBERT RAGLAN .... COLONEL
JAMES OTTAWAY .... 1ST MEMBER OF PARLIAMENT
CHARLES MORGAN .... 2ND MEMBER OF PARLIAMENT
PLATOON .... COLIN BEAN, DESMOND CULLUM-JONES, EVAN ROSS,
.... GEORGE HANCOCK, HUGH HASTINGS, LESLIE NOYES,
.... HUGH CECIL, FREDDIE WHITE, FREDDIE WILES, MICHAEL MOORE

KEEP YOUNG AND BEAUTIFUL

• BILL PERTWEE REMEMBERS •

'There were certainly a few memorable moments in this episode! The idea of the storyline was a directive requesting that the Home Guard recruit younger men and that some of Mainwaring's older members should join the Wardens, while younger Wardens transfer to the Home Guard.

'Mainwaring thought this was unacceptable, so did Hodges, who got hold of a terrible wig to make himself look older. The ill-fitting wig was also dusted with a white powder which made it worse, making me feel as if I had terrible dandruff. Mainwaring had also bought a wig to make himself look younger. Arthur Lowe's comedy talents again came to the fore when he tried it on in front of the church hall mirror. Sergeant Wilson appears in the middle of this pantomime, walking in a strange way, thanks to an abdominal support, which he was wearing in an attempt to look younger. And then, during the evening parade, the appearance of Jones, Godfrey and Frazer caused much hilarity. Jones and Godfrey had persuaded Frazer to use some of his funeral embalming fluid to tighten the wrinkles on their skin. It had the effect of half closing their eyes as well!

'A later scene finds the platoon on parade, when it suddenly starts to rain (courtesy of the local fire brigade) and all the make-up runs down their faces in black streaks. Actually, this scene nearly started too soon. The fire brigade had a practice first and, luckily, only a few of the technicians got wet. If it had got on to Jones, Frazer and Godfrey prematurely, I'm sure we would have heard a few choice words from them, especially if they'd had to go through the make-up procedure again, which took ages in the first place.'

Keep Young and Beautiful

EXTERIOR SHOT. HOUSES OF PARLIAMENT

INTERIOR. CHAMBER

VOICE OF SPEAKER The Honourable Member for Fifestead East.

Member rises from back bench.

1ST MEMBER Is it not a fact that many of our younger and fitter men joined the A.R.P. at the outset of the War? Is it not further a fact that when the Home Guard was formed only the older and less fit men were left? Would it not be desirable for these younger, fitter men to be drafted into the Home Guard and some of the old war-horses now in the Home Guard drafted into the A.R.P., and given the task of telling us to shut our curtains?

He sits down – another member gets up.

2ND MEMBER Is the Honourable Member for Fifestead aware that in my constituency, hundreds of people can't afford curtains.

Cut to Minister in another part of the House.

MINISTER The Honourable Member has made a very valuable suggestion. I will consult with my colleague – the Home Secretary – and see whether some exchange of personnel could be encouraged at a purely local level. At the same time, let us not forget that the experience and fighting spirit of these older soldiers has been invaluable. The Home Guard is at the ready, ceaselessly on the alert, and make no mistake about it, should the enemy dare set foot on our shores, these men will make most formidable opponents.

FILM: EXTERIOR. A FIELD

Jones' section are running, with a telegraph pole over their shoulders, across a field.

MAINWARING **(Voice)** Come on, men, go to it with a will.

JONES I'm not enjoying this very much.

FRAZER Yon Mainwaring's taken leave of his senses.

GODFREY I'm sure it's not very good for the heart.

WALKER What are you all grumbling about? When the war's over, if anyone wants a telegraph pole delivered in a hurry, we've got ourselves a nice little business.

Cut to Wilson who is standing and watching.

WILSON Don't give up. You really are doing most awfully well.

Cut to Mainwaring.

MAINWARING Right, gather round. Now this is the sort of thing that's being done by our toughest troops, and if they can do it, then so can we.

PIKE Captain Mainwaring, could I have something to pad my shoulder?

MAINWARING No, you can't.

PIKE But it's red raw.

MAINWARING There'll be no mollycoddling in my platoon.

WALKER Trouble is, Captain Mainwaring, Jonesey here spent half the time carrying the pole and the other half dangling.

JONES I was not dangling! Pikey was the one that was dangling.

PIKE I wasn't dangling – you was dangling!

MAINWARING All right, that's enough. Now on the command 'go' – I want to see all three sections charge across the field – under the tarpaulin and then use their poles to cross the stream. I'll stand a pint of beer to every man in the first section across.

JONES Right, my section, we're going to win this, I could just do with a pint.

PIKE Well, don't dangle then.

JONES 'Ere...

MAINWARING Go!

Jones' section moves off before Jones is ready. The three sections charge across the field – Jones' section is left behind.

JONES Come on, lads, charge.

FILM: EXTERIOR. A HEDGE

There is a wide gap – sections two and three come through the gap – Jones' section goes straight through the hedge.

Cut to Wilson.

FILM: EXTERIOR. THE TARPAULINS

Three tarpaulins are pegged down on the meadow. Two and three sections dive under with their poles and scramble to the other side. Jones' section arrive late.

JONES Come on, lads – under the tarpolium.

They scramble under. We see the figures under the tarpaulin as Jones leads them round in a circle.

JONES Mr Mainwaring. Everything's going round and round.

FRAZER You old fool – it's you that's going round and round.

Cut to Mainwaring looking exasperated.

Cut to tarpaulin. Jones' section emerge from the place they first entered.

WILSON Come on, Jones' section, try to catch up.

FILM: EXTERIOR. A STREAM

Two and three sections have up-ended their poles, they let them fall across the stream and then use them to shin across. Cut to Jones' section – they arrive and up-end their pole.

WALKER This should be easy for you, Taffy, like tossing the caber.

FRAZER Belt up or I'll toss you.

WALKER Naughty temper.

JONES Right.

They let go of their pole and it falls across the stream.

FRAZER Come on. You hold it, Pike, and I'll start shinning.

JONES We're not going to shin, we're walking.

• DAVID CROFT REMEMBERS •

'In this episode we used a bloody great hose, courtesy of the local fire brigade, to drench the platoon. We had a problem at first because the make-up and hair colouring wouldn't run, so by the time we sorted that out they were very wet indeed. We set the hose going and there was never any case of stopping, we had to rush round with the camera and take close ups of them all, and it worked well.'

FRAZER What d'you think this is, a circus?

JONES Just hold hands and don't look at your feet. Come on.

He grabs hold of Frazer's hand and leads the section across. Cut to close shots of them inching their way across.

JONES Don't look at your feet, look up – look up – look uuuup...

Cut to a long shot as they all fall into the stream.

INTERIOR. MAIN HALL

Uniform continuity as from the film. The five who fell into the stream are in overcoats. The platoon led by Mainwaring doubles into the hall.

MAINWARING Double mark time.

The platoon forms up – Jones' section enter last.

MAINWARING Halt. Fall out. (**He is all in**) Office, Wilson.

WILSON Yes, sir.

Jones and Frazer stagger towards the office. Jones starts to sink slowly to the ground.

FRAZER (**Grabbing him**) He said fall out– not fall down.

JONES I swallowed so much water my legs won't carry the extra weight.

INTERIOR. SIDE OFFICE. CHURCH HALL

Mainwaring and Wilson enter, they are both very weary. Wilson sits heavily.

WILSON My my, that was tiring.

MAINWARING You're out of condition, that's all. (**He staggers against the bookcase**)

WILSON Are you all right, sir?

MAINWARING Yes, of course. Just all that blood pumping through so fast. Makes you a bit dizzy when you stop.

WILSON I don't think you should have made them double that last two hundred yards.

MAINWARING Didn't want the ones who fell in the stream to catch cold.

INTERIOR. CHURCH HALL

PIKE Mr Godfrey, could I come to your place and dry off. If Mum catches me like this she won't let me come any more.

GODFREY Well, we don't have a fire on Wednesdays. Cissy stays in bed with a hot water bottle – you can't get the coal, you see.

WALKER Don't worry, Pikey, come back to my place, I'll fit you out with a spare uniform – it won't cost you much.

Reaction.

INTERIOR. SIDE OFFICE. CHURCH HALL

WILSON (**Taking off his boots**) Ah, that's better.

MAINWARING You won't leave them in here, will you?

WILSON No, of course not. They did awfully well didn't they?

MAINWARING It was a shambles – Jones' section was a joke.

WILSON They tried very hard though, didn't they?

MAINWARING That won't be good enough when we're up against Hitler and his Prussian Butchers. We shall have to split the platoon into two halves. Those who are young enough and fit enough – and those who aren't up to battle standards.

WILSON I tried that. It looked rather untidy.

MAINWARING What do you mean untidy?

WILSON Well, there were two in one half and twenty one in the other.

MAINWARING I don't mind telling you, Wilson, I sometimes wish I had some younger men under my command.

WILSON (**Picking up a paper**) Others seem to be thinking on the same lines.

MAINWARING What do you mean?

WILSON Well, this note has trickled down from the War Office. It recommends that C.O.s look into the age and fitness of their men with a view to getting together with the A.R.P. and exchanging personnel.

MAINWARING That's an outrageous suggestion – I'll fight that tooth and nail.

WILSON I do agree.

MAINWARING I mean – how can I face – say Godfrey, or Frazer, or Jones – and tell them that I have no more use for them, and they're now in the A.R.P.?

WILSON Well, it seems you won't have to do that. There's going to be a parade and the Area Commander is going to pick out which of us ought to go to the A.R.P. and which Wardens ought to join us.

MAINWARING I don't want any of Hodges' rabble in my unit.

WILSON I quite agree, they should leave well alone. One just doesn't know where a thing like this would end.

MAINWARING Of course not.

WILSON I mean, take Hodges for instance. You say you don't want any of his rabble in your unit. In fact you might find yourself in the A.R.P. and *this* might finish up as *his* unit.

MAINWARING What on earth are you talking about?

WILSON Well, once they start this sort of thing, I mean, anything can happen.

MAINWARING They wouldn't hand my platoon to a man like Hodges – he's a greengrocer. What does he know about the Army?

WILSON Well, he was in the last lot, you know.

MAINWARING (**Rising and going behind Wilson**) That was a different sort of war altogether.

WILSON Still, he did come face to face with the enemy. He looks pretty fit and he's a lot younger than – one or two of us.

MAINWARING Meaning me.

WILSON Well, you're by no means decrepit – I mean – you're not exactly Aubrey Smith.

MAINWARING Thank you very much.

WILSON At the same time, you're not exactly Freddie Bartholomew.

Fade as Mainwaring turns to the mirror.

INTERIOR. CHURCH HALL

The hall is empty – Mainwaring enters carrying a box under a raincoat – he looks around surreptitiously.

MAINWARING Anybody about?

There is silence – he moves to the office door and turns.

MAINWARING (**Louder**) Is anybody about? (**Satisfied, he moves into the office**)

INTERIOR. SIDE OFFICE. CHURCH HALL

Mainwaring goes behind the desk – ensures that nobody is looking and quickly puts the box in a drawer. He hangs up his coat and then goes to the door of the hall again – he opens it – puts his head through and calls.

MAINWARING Is anybody there?

Hearing no reply, he closes the door and locks it – he moves swiftly to the outer door and locks that – he stands the blackout frame against the window and then crosses behind the desk. He removes his hat and puts it on the desk. He opens the drawer and takes out a box and removes something from it. He crosses to the mirror and looks at himself. Rather like a quick change artist, he turns away – makes a swift adjustment and then turns back to the mirror – he is wearing a toupee – it is not a very good one – it is gingerish with a small quiff at the front. He contemplates himself critically and makes an adjustment. He tries it without specs. He is not quite satisfied and he decides what is wrong – he crosses to the coat stand, takes a box of matches from the pocket of the mac – he lights one and lets it burn a little and then blows it out. He crosses to the mirror and etches in his eyebrows a little.

INTERIOR. CHURCH HAL

Enter Wilson – he crosses, walking very stiffly to the office – he tries the door.

INTERIOR. SIDE OFFICE. CHURCH HALL

MAINWARING Just a moment.

He moves swiftly to the desk – he gets the box – he is about to put the toupee back, but hesitates, then changes his mind – he puts the empty box back in the drawer, picks up his hat and crosses to the mirror. He adjusts his hat.

WILSON (**Out of vision**) Are you all right, sir?

MAINWARING Perfectly all right, thank you.

INTERIOR. CHURCH HALL

Wilson moves towards the door to the street.

INTERIOR. SIDE OFFICE. CHURCH HALL

Mainwaring crosses and unlocks the office.

MAINWARING Sorry to keep you waiting, Wilson.

INTERIOR. CHURCH HALL

WILSON (**Stopping halfway across hall**) Oh, I was going round the other way, I thought it was stuck.

MAINWARING No, I was just examining some secret files.

Wilson moves stiffly to the door.

INTERIOR. SIDE OFFICE

Mainwaring notices, but says nothing, he moves behind the desk and sits.

MAINWARING I'm glad you are here early. Sit down.

Wilson doesn't sit.

MAINWARING I've been giving some thought to our conversation yesterday. Sit down, Wilson.

Wilson makes some attempt to sit – finds it difficult and straightens up again.

MAINWARING I said sit down, Wilson.

WILSON I'd rather stand, thank you, sir.

MAINWARING What's the matter with you?

WILSON I'm rather stiff, that's all.

Mainwaring rises and crosses behind him.

MAINWARING Ah, I see, yesterday's little outing left its mark did it? Well, I have to confess I have a slight twinge myself this morning – it hit me about there. (**He puts his hand on the small of Wilson's back – he detects something unfamiliar – Wilson turns quickly. Mainwaring pokes a finger at Wilson's hip**)

WILSON Don't do that, sir, I'm rather ticklish.

MAINWARING Wilson, you're wearing corsets!

Wilson doesn't reply.

MAINWARING Well, am I right?

WILSON Actually, it's a gentleman's abdominal support.

MAINWARING Gentleman's abdominal support my foot, you're wearing corsets!

Wilson sits. After a pause.

MAINWARING You're a rum cove, Wilson. You wear that uniform like a sack of porridge, and yet in other respects you're as vain as a peacock.

WILSON It is nothing whatever to do with vanity. I don't want to risk being put into Hodge's mob, that's all. I'm really quite proud of our platoon. I think you've done a marvellous job putting us all together. I really mean that. So I think it pays, at the moment, not to look any older than one needs.

MAINWARING I'm sorry, Wilson – it was very kind of you to pay that little tribute. I know that sort of thing isn't easy for a person like you.

Wilson reacts.

MAINWARING I was pouring scorn upon you and I had no right to do such a thing. No right at all. I have to tell you that I too have taken steps to appear more, well – more virile.

WILSON My God, not monkey glands.

MAINWARING Certainly not – nothing as drastic as that. What do you think of this?

He removes his hat, revealing the toupee. Wilson corpses but quickly recovers himself.

Mainwaring reacts.

WILSON It's really awfully... (**He giggles again**) It's really awfully good.

Wilson subsides into uncontrollable laughter. Mainwaring is furious.

MAINWARING Watch out, Wilson, you'll snap your girdle.

INTERIOR. CHURCH HALL

Frazer is grouped with Pike, Walker and Godfrey.

FRAZER Well, the result was, I was beneath him, you follow – now as true as I'm standing here, peaking out from under the brim of his hat was a wee kiss curl.

GODFREY It doesn't sound like Captain Mainwaring at all.

FRAZER Precisely, if you're asking me, he's going funny in the head.

WALKER I reckon one of us ought to go into the office and have a butchers.

FRAZER Well I'm not going. I've seen it, I tell you.

WALKER You go, Pike – you're the youngest.

PIKE That's not fair, we ought to dip for it.

WALKER All right, go on then.

PIKE All right then. Eeney, meeney miney moe, catch a nigger by his toe, if he hollers let him go, eeney meeney miney moe.

Walker gets the moe.

PIKE It's you.

WALKER No it isn't. **(He continues the chant)** O-U-T spells out you must go.

Pike is selected.

WALKER It's you.

Pike reacts.

FRAZER Good. Now you'll have to find an excuse to talk to him, and get yourself lower down than he is so you can look under the brim of his cap. You're no paying attention.

PIKE He cheated.

WALKER Never mind about that. Now, when you get in the office, you'll have to make some excuse – tell him you think we ought to go to the local regimental barracks and have more practice at their miniature rifle range.

SIDE OFFICE. INTERIOR. CHURCH HALL

Jones is talking to Mainwaring and Wilson.

MAINWARING Well, at least we can make everyone as fit as possible, so we'll include one extra period of physical training. You can take that, Wilson.

WILSON Yes, sir.

JONES I also think, sir, that as well, and in addition to, also, we should have one hour's instruction in bayonet fighting. We're not doing it as often as we did of yore, and there is no doubt about it, sir, cold steel puts fear into the heart of the Bosche. They do not like it, sir, especially up 'em. I had a very good illustration of this point just outside Wipers.

MAINWARING Yes, thank you, Jones. I'll make a note of that for next week. You can re-join your section now.

There is a knock.

MAINWARING Come in.

JONES Very good, sir.

Jones salutes, turns about and salutes Pike as he enters – Jones goes.

MAINWARING **(Still standing)** Yes, Pike, what is it?

During the next speech, Pike bends his knees to try and get lower to see under Mainwaring's cap.

PIKE **(Saluting)** Excuse me, sir.

MAINWARING Yes.

PIKE Barracks.

MAINWARING I beg your pardon?

PIKE We haven't done it for a long time, sir.

MAINWARING What on earth are you talking about, you stupid boy?

PIKE We ought to shoot at the targets with miniature rifles.

MAINWARING **(Noticing that Pike is behaving strangely in his attempt to see beneath Mainwaring's hat)** Are you all right, Pike?

PIKE Yes, sir.

MAINWARING Are you wearing corsets?

PIKE Am I what?

MAINWARING I asked you a perfectly straightforward question – are you wearing corsets?

PIKE I didn't know we were supposed to.

MAINWARING **(Sitting)** Look, start again.

WILSON I wonder if I could join the platoon? There are one or two things I want to say to them.

MAINWARING Yes, go ahead.

Wilson leaves.

MAINWARING Well, Pike?

PIKE **(Kneeling at the desk)** The men asked me to ask you if we could do more of it.

MAINWARING They surely didn't ask you to pray. Stand up.

PIKE **(Doing so)** Yes, sir. Anyway, we thought, if we could go along to the local one, and borrow theirs, we'd get better at it because we'd have had more practice with the miniature one. **(He belligerently knocks some papers off the desk on to the floor)** Oh dear, how careless of me, I've knocked your papers down, I'll pick 'em up. **(He dives for the floor – grabs some papers then crawls round the desk to look at Mainwaring – he encounters Mainwaring also kneeling behind the desk ready for him)**

MAINWARING Pike, suppose you tell me what you're up to.

INTERIOR. CHURCH HALL

Wilson has the remainder of the platoon gathered round him.

WILSON The point is this, he's done it because none of us want to get split up and drafted into the A.R.P. – and let's face it, we wouldn't want to lose him. At the same time, he's very sensitive about it, so please try not to stare – just treat it as a normal, everyday thing and, for heaven's sake, promise me, chaps – don't laugh.

Mainwaring bursts in.

MAINWARING Right, fall in three ranks.

They fall in quickly.

JONES Fall in three ranks – do as the captain says, fall in.

They settle.

JONES We've falled in three ranks, sir.

MAINWARING Thank you, Jones. It has come to my notice that certain aspects of my appearance have given rise to some speculation and a certain amount of hilarity. Now, I've never been one for beating about the bush, so here it is, straight from the shoulder. I'm wearing a toupee, or a wig if you want to make it plainer still – if any of you fancy a jolly good laugh at my expense, now's your chance because I'm going to give you a good look at it. Here it is.

He takes off his hat with a flourish – in his haste he catches hold of the toupee at the same time and whips that off inside the hat – we still see the normal Mainwaring – the platoon collapse with mirth. Mainwaring reacts. Jones and Godfrey at the far end of the line can't see well enough to understand what all the fuss is about.

JONES **(To Godfrey)** Personally, I think it makes him look older.

INTERIOR. SMALL CORNER OF WALKER'S STORE ROOM

Walker is surrounded by boxes, sacks and general junk. He is on the telephone.

WALKER The point is, Mr Hodges, you might find yourself doing left turn, right turns, under Captain Mainwaring – and you don't get on, do you?

INTERIOR. SMALL CORNER OF WARDEN'S GREENGROCER'S SHOP

Hodges is on the phone.

WARDEN Get on – I'd rather serve under Captain Bligh. **(To an invisible assistant)** Only half a pound of them onions, Beryl, they're like gold. Shove 'em under the counter.

INTERIOR. WALKER'S STORE ROOM

WALKER Now, if your hair was a bit grey like, you wouldn't look quite so young and fit.

INTERIOR. WARDEN'S SHOP

WARDEN What do you mean, young and fit! With my heart and my nerves, I'm a physical wreck.

INTERIOR. WALKER'S STORE ROOM

WALKER Ah, but it's silly to take chances – now, I can let you have something that will whiten your hair instantly. It's pretty expensive, and I can only let you have an ounce – for you it's a quid. Now, are you on?

INTERIOR. WARDEN'S SHOP

WARDEN Well – yes. Silly to take any chances, isn't it.

INTERIOR. WALKER'S STORE ROOM

WALKER Good lad – I'll let you have it right away. **(He puts the phone down – he goes to a tin marked 'Ceiling White' and ladles a spoonful into a small jar)**

EXTERIOR. DOOR OF FRAZER'S FUNERAL PARLOUR. NIGHT

Jones and Godfrey approach and knock – the blind on the door is quickly raised to reveal Frazer holding a candle. He opens the door.

FRAZER What's amiss?

JONES We want to talk to you.

FRAZER Come in.

INTERIOR. FRAZER'S FUNERAL PARLOUR

They move to the counter

FRAZER Sorry about the candles, but my blinds are too thin for gas-light.

GODFREY I – I like candles. I always think they're much more romantic.

FRAZER Now, what would you be wanting?

JONES Well, it's like this, Jock – Mr Godfrey and I was looking in the mirror, and we decided that if that general was going to pick on anybody to go into the A.R.P. it'll be us three 'cause we're the oldest.

FRAZER You're right – I've not slept at night with dwelling on it.

JONES Well, you remember old Mr Armstrong.

FRAZER Him that passed away last month?

JONES That's the one. Well, you made him look not a day over 60, and he was 97.

FRAZER Aye, it's a skill I ha' with my hands. Ah, it's good of you to say so.

JONES Well – couldn't you do the same for us?

FRAZER Ah – I see. It'll be a challenge and no mistakes.

GODFREY We'd be very grateful, Mr Frazer.

JONES And we'd see you weren't out of pocket.

FRAZER Ah – go into the next room and lie on the slab.

INTERIOR: CHURCH HALL. DAY

WILSON Right, fall in everybody.

PIKE Where's Mr Frazer, Mr Jones and Mr Godfrey, Joe?

WALKER I think they're keeping out of the way till the last minute. When he sees 'em, Mr Mainwaring will have kittens right here.

WILSON Come along, Jones – quick as you can.

Jones joins squad.

WILSON Get in the ranks, Jones.

JONES Sorry, Sergeant – without my glasses on I'm a bit hard of seeing.

The platoon are drawn up for inspection in order – reading camera right to left – Pike/Walker/Jones/Frazer/Godfrey.

Jones, Frazer and Godfrey have dark hair, Frazer has filled out his cheeks with cotton wool, Godfrey has applied some preparation that has made his skin tight and shiny – the effect is distinctly Chinese. His hair is also dark.

WILSON Squad. **(Jones comes to attention)** Wait for it, Jones.

JONES Sorry, sir. I'm a bit too alert this afternoon.

WILSON Squad, 'shun.

JONES Was that better? **(He turns and salutes to Mainwaring)**

WILSON Platoon ready for inspection, sir.

MAINWARING Thank you, Sergeant. Now I think you know me well enough to realise that this inspection by the Area Commander is entirely against my wishes, but orders are orders. Rest assured that if any of you are urged to join the A.R.P. against your wishes, I shall protest to the very highest authority. **(He crosses to Pike)**

MAINWARING I think you're safe enough, Pike. **(He moves to Walker)** You too, Walker. **(He moves to Jones) (Reaction)** Who the devil's this?

WILSON Jones, sir.

MAINWARING Good heavens, what on earth have you done to yourself?

JONES I didn't want to leave you, Captain Mainwaring, nor these brave troops that you, captain and I, lance corporal – so Mr Frazer fixed me up.

MAINWARING Frazer, what's the meaning of this?

FRAZER **(He burbles because his cheeks are full of cotton wool)**

WALKER What did Horace say?

JONES He doesn't speak very plainly, sir, on account of his cheeks are puffed out with cotton wool.

MAINWARING Did you know about this, Wilson?

WILSON Well, I turned a blind eye.

MAINWARING Well, you'd no business to. I'm the only one with the authority to turn a blind eye. **(He turns and sees Godfrey)** Godfrey, what in the name of goodness have you done?

GODFREY It's one of Mr Frazer's fluids, sir – it tightens the skin.

Mainwaring crosses to Wilson.

MAINWARING **(To Wilson)** This is ridiculous, he looks like Madame Butterfly. **(To Godfrey)** Get it off at once.

GODFREY I don't think I can, sir.

MAINWARING He can't parade like that – how long does it last, Frazer?

Frazer burbles.

JONES He says he's never dug anyone up to have a look.

The Warden enters in uniform and helmet.

WARDEN Ah, there you are, Napoleon, I just thought I'd let you know that if you've got any idea about getting me in your shower, you can forget it – look. **(He takes off his helmet and shows his white hair)**

MAINWARING Very distinguished.

WARDEN Not bad, eh?

WALKER Wait till he tries to get it off.

MAINWARING All the same, I don't know why you went to all that trouble.

WARDEN Because I'd rather look 107 than serve under you, that's why.

MAINWARING I see. Pity it doesn't show under your helmet.

WARDEN What the matter – I'll stoop. What – I never thought of that. (**He moves away**) You're not getting me in your squad, Mainwaring – the way I'm going on parade they wouldn't have me in the Chelsea Pensioners.

MAINWARING Right, I want you to know that I'm very displeased with this ridiculous charade, but it's too late to do anything about it now, so on your own heads be it.

WILSON I say, that's rather witty.

MAINWARING (**Witheringly**) Carry on, Sergeant.

WILSON Yes, sir. Left turn, by the left wheel, quick march.

Fade as they all march out.

FILM: BARRACKS SQUARE (OR SCHOOL PLAYGROUND)

They are parading – we see the platoon and about the same number of wardens.

The general is inspecting the Home Guard, followed by the colonel and Mainwaring. The general does a slight 'take' on the older ones and then passes on. The colonel salutes and then talks quietly to Mainwaring.

COLONEL He didn't pick any of them – it looks as if you've got away with it.

MAINWARING I sincerely hope so. I really must apologise –

COLONEL (**Interrupting**) Congratulations, Mainwaring, you certainly use your initiative in a crisis.

MAINWARING Ah well – we do our best, sir.

COLONEL I didn't see anything, of course – I hope it comes off all right.

MAINWARING I expect it will.

STOCK SHOT: THREATENING SKY AND LARGE FLASH OF LIGHTNING

FILM: BARRACKS SQUARE

COLONEL Hello, we're just getting through in time. Give the old man three cheers and I'll buy you one in The Fox.

MAINWARING Yes, sir.

COLONEL Blimey, here it comes.

The rain starts very heavily.

MAINWARING Three cheers for the general – Hip, hip hooray.

As they take off their caps and give three cheers we cut to Jones, Frazer and Godfrey – the dye is coursing down their faces.

SERIES FIVE **EPISODE THREE**

Recorded: Friday 2/6/72
Original transmission: Friday 20/10/72, 8.30–9.00pm
Original viewing figures = 17.7 million

ARTHUR LOWE . . . . CAPTAIN MAINWARING
JOHN LE MESURIER . . . . SERGEANT WILSON
CLIVE DUNN . . . . LANCE CORPORAL JONES
JOHN LAURIE . . . . PRIVATE FRAZER
JAMES BECK . . . . PRIVATE WALKER
ARNOLD RIDLEY . . . . PRIVATE GODFREY
IAN LAVENDER . . . . PRIVATE PIKE
BILL PERTWEE . . . . ARP WARDEN
FRANK WILLIAMS . . . . VICAR
ROBERT GILLESPIE . . . . CHARLES BOYER
JOAN SAVAGE . . . . GRETA GARBO
JOY ALLEN . . . . CLIPPIE
COLIN BEAN . . . . PRIVATE SPONGE
PLATOON . . . . DESMOND CULLUM-JONES, MICHAEL MOORE, HUGH HASTINGS, LESLIE NOYES, GEORGE HANCOCK, FREDDIE WHITE, HUGH CECIL, FREDDIE WILES
EXTRAS ON BUS . . . . ELIZABETH CULLUM-JONES, LINDA CARROLL, DORIS KITTS, HUGH ELTON, FRED DAVIES

A Soldier's Farewell

• ROBERT GILLESPIE REMEMBERS •

'David Croft started me off in sitcom. He told me everyone thought it was time Hugh Lloyd and Terry Scott were involved in something more exotic than *Hugh and I* at home, so he'd come up with *Hugh and I Spy*, and the guys were sent off to adventures abroad. I came in to read for a Moroccan police sergeant (French accent, I think). I believe David remarked that he'd tried to get a location in North Africa but, sadly, it was going to be Ealing Studios or wherever, given BBC budgets. However, he went on to say that it was going to be a good year for camels! I remember thinking: "This would be a good bloke to work for."

'I got that job – big laughs in the studio – and can still remember Terry trying to convey some sort of secret code with huge gestures (talking to foreigners, you know) about the moon rising over somewhere or other. Incidentally, that job started me in a line of dead-pan TV policemen, which paid off in *Whatever Happened to the Likely Lads?*, *Robin's Nest*, etc. No way, given my height, could I have got away with playing coppers on stage, especially in those days, but behind a desk, in a television studio, who gave a damn?

'I seemed to get into directors' minds as someone you could call up to do odd things, not quite off the shelf, so after doing quite a bit of work for David, I wasn't entirely surprised when he rang me and said: "Could you do a Charles Boyer?" He said that the owners of the film [*Marie Walewska*] were asking far too much money for a clip from the original, but he wasn't going to be thwarted by them and could I have a go? I just adored the idea of playing Boyer playing Napoleon – it made me giggle just thinking about it. I don't remember too much about the detailed filming, except that we worked at getting my voice down, lower and lower (I've got a deepish voice anyway) to get that kind of vibrant huskiness which was Boyer's stock-in-trade.

'Another thing I remember was David making me be very still, physically, as Boyer – not twitchy – and especially getting me to control my eyebrow gestures. We had a clip to refer to and he'd say: "I think your eyebrows moved, Robert. Better do one more, I think. Watch the eyebrows." Again, David had calculated the effect of the scene brilliantly and it works remarkably well in the episode. I haven't got Boyer's schnozzle, of course, but you can't have everything. Not for two and sixpence, anyway!'

A Soldier's Farewell

INTERIOR. CINEMA. NIGHT

Exterior shot of screen. We see Charles Boyer as Napoleon in the film *Marie Walewska*. It is nearly ending. Audience – composed of the platoon and an assortment of various servicemen and women with a sprinkling of civilians.

Close up of Walker looking at pretty ATS girl who is sitting on his right. We pan along – Jones is sitting at Walker's left and watching intently. Next Frazer is muttering 'Rubbish'. Next Pike leaning forward with his thumb in his mouth. Then Godfrey, asleep. Finally, Mainwaring and Wilson – they are all in uniform.

Cut back to screen – the film finishes..

'The End'.

Audience – lights go up quickly. We hear a roll on the drums – the national anthem starts. The entire audience rushes for the exit. As the audience clears, a dishevelled figure drags himself up from behind a seat. We go into a close up. It is Mainwaring. He stands stiffly to attention. The cinema is empty with a solitary figure standing in the middle.

INTERIOR. A COUNTRY BUS. NIGHT

The windows are painted over. A small round hole is in the centre of each window, just big enough to see out. There is a bell cord running along the roof and the lights are very dim. Mainwaring and Wilson are sitting in the front seat. Behind them, Sponge and Godfrey – across the aisle, Jones and Walker are sitting in the other front seat – behind them, Frazer and Pike. The rest of the platoon are sitting in the other seats.

MAINWARING I've never seen anything so disgraceful in all my life – everybody charging out like that during the national anthem. I thought at least you would have stayed, Wilson – as a sergeant – it was your duty to set an example to the others.

WILSON I couldn't help it, sir – I sort of got carried out in the rush.

MAINWARING Really. (To Godfrey) I'm surprised at you, Godfrey. I'd have thought that you'd have shown more respect.

GODFREY It wasn't that, sir. I had to get out rather quickly for more urgent reasons.

WALKER Did you enjoy the film, Mr Mainwaring?

MAINWARING Not really. I would have thought a film about Napoleon would have been concerned with strategy and tactics. I'd hoped we could learn something from it. Instead of that, he seemed to spend most of his time chasing Greta Garbo round a four-poster bed.

WALKER Well that's strategy and tactics ain't it?

JONES Yeah – I certainly learned something. Mind you, it's a bit late to do anything about it now. (To Frazer) What about you, Jock?

FRAZER Rubbish – sheer rubbish – it was a waste of one and six.

JONES 'Ere, Joe, what about that bit where he took her in his arms in the snow?

WALKER Smashing. (Taking Jones in his arms and doing impressions of Charles Boyer) Oh, my darling – you have such beautiful hair – beautiful eyes – beautiful lips – beautiful moustache.

JONES (Pushing him away) Get off, Joe.

PIKE I liked the part where Napoleon was saying farewell to his troops. I know what – let's take it in turns to do an impersonation of Charles Boyer. Whoever does it the worst has to pay the fares.

WALKER That's a good idea, Pikey – you start.

PIKE (Doing impression) Soldiers of France – our cause is lost – your Emperor must now say goodbye – with this kiss I embrace you all.

FRAZER That was rotten.

JONES How's this? (He does impression using the same words as Pike)

WALKER You're supposed to be doing Charles Boyer, not Harry Champion. My turn. (He does the impression. To Frazer) Right, your turn Taff.

FRAZER I refuse to have anything to do with such childish, moronic nonsense. I'll pay my own fare – and no one else's.

PIKE (To Godfrey) Do you want to do an impersonation of Charles Boyer, Mr Godfrey?

GODFREY I'm not very good at that sort of thing – but my sister Dolly does a very clever impersonation of Greta Garbo.

WALKER Well, why don't you do an impersonation of your sister Dolly doing an impersonation of Greta Garbo?

WILSON (To Sponge) Did you enjoy the movie, Sponge?

SPONGE Not really, Sarge. I couldn't see very much – we should have sat in the ninepennies you know, Mr Mainwaring.

MAINWARING Oh no, I wouldn't sit right down the front in those cheap seats. You never know who's been sitting in them.

JONES Right, let's have a bit of a song, all together now.

They all start to sing 'Roll Me Over in the Clover'.

ALL Now the first is number one, etc…

MAINWARING **(Stopping them)** That will be quite enough of that, thank you very much. Really, Wilson, I don't know what's the matter with everybody – discipline seems to have gone to pot.

A 'clippie' comes down the front of the bus to Mainwaring and Wilson. She is a smart, attractive woman, about forty. Very well spoken. She is carrying a clip containing various bus tickets and is wearing a ticket punch.

CLIPPIE Fares, please – any more fares, please.

MAINWARING **(Holding out money)** Two to Walmington-on-Sea, please. I really must apologise for my men – singing that ribald song.

CLIPPIE That's quite all right. I get far worse than that.

MAINWARING Really – how very distressing for you.

CLIPPIE **(Punching tickets)** I'm used to it – after all, there is a war on.

MAINWARING That's no excuse for slack behaviour.

CLIPPIE How very nice of you to think of me. I don't often get considerate passengers like you on my bus. **(She hands him the tickets)** Thank you. **(She turns away)** Fares, please.

MAINWARING Charming woman, Wilson.

WILSON Awfully nice.

MAINWARING It must be very difficult for her – dealing with men passengers who get over familiar.

WILSON I should think she could take care of herself, sir – she'd probably give them a punch on the nose.

MAINWARING Don't be absurd – one can see at a glance that she's a perfect lady. It must be awfully hard for her working as a clippie.

WILSON Well, she's doing her bit, sir.

MAINWARING I realise that, Wilson – at the same time one can't help wondering if it's right that a lady like her should be exposed to all the riff-raff that use late-night buses.

The bus stops. Hodges, the Warden, gets on. He is wearing civilian clothes and is carrying his gas mask and tin hat.

CLIPPIE Hold tight, please.

The bus starts. Hodges comes down to the front. There are no empty seats, so he stands by Mainwaring.

HODGES Hello, Napoleon – been taking your boy scouts on an outing, have you?

PIKE We've all been to the pictures, Mr Hodges.

HODGES Blimey, that's marvellous that is – Jerry liable to invade any minute and you lot go to the pictures – what did you do – leave a note on the beach saying, 'Dear Hitler, please don't invade tonight, we've all gone to the cinema'.

WILSON If it comes to that, why aren't you on duty?

HODGES If you must know, I've been attending a high-level meeting of Chief Wardens. Top brass only.

WALKER Supposing there's an air raid?

HODGES Don't you worry, mate, I'm fully covered.

JONES Yes, we can all see that.

Hodges reacts.

HODGES **(To the Clippie)** A tuppenny one – a nice big smile and a tickle at the terminus.

MAINWARING A tickle at the terminus? Excuse me, Hodges, how dare you speak to a lady like that?

HODGES What's the matter with you?

MAINWARING Show some respect.

CLIPPIE It's quite all right, sir. Would you please sit down?

HODGES Take no notice of him.

MAINWARING **(Sitting)** Oh, very well.

CLIPPIE **(Leaning over and whispering in Mainwaring's ear)** Thank you all the same – I do appreciate it.

She turns back to Hodges and punches his ticket.

WILSON My – my – we are gallant tonight, sir.

CLIPPIE Walmington-on-Sea next stop.

MAINWARING Listen, Wilson, when the bus stops – I don't want any repetition of what happened in the cinema. I shall get off first – tell the men.

WILSON Right, sir. **(He gets up)** Now, pay attention, everybody – when the bus stops, will you all please sit tight and let Mr Mainwaring off first.

CLIPPIE Walmington-on-Sea, Red Lion.

The bus stops. The platoon all sit tight. Mainwaring gets up, pushes past the Warden and Wilson, and starts to walk slowly down the bus. As he reaches the third seat, the Warden shouts.

HODGES It's closing time in five minutes.

The two men in the third seat jump up and rush out just in front of Mainwaring. Frazer, Pike, Jones and Walker get up next to clear the camera view. Mainwaring is pushed into the empty seat in the rush. There is a general confusion. Mainwaring pulls himself up from behind the seat as in first scene .

INTERIOR. CHURCH HALL. NIGHT

The platoon is drawn up on parade. Mainwaring is addressing them.

MAINWARING …and in conclusion, may I say that I was not only shocked by last night's exhibition in the cinema – but I was also deeply hurt that my platoon should behave in such a disrespectful manner.

FRAZER If I may say a word, Captain Mainwaring?

MAINWARING Yes, Frazer.

FRAZER Well, sir, speaking purely for myself. I did not intend any disrespect – but as an historian and a man of high intellect – I was appalled by the historical inaccuracies in the film. I stuck it as long as I could but in the end I felt I just has to discuss it with the manager – from the intellectual point of view.

MAINWARING What happened?

FRAZER I got one and six back.

Mainwaring reacts.

JONES Permission to speak, sir?

MAINWARING Yes, Jones.

JONES Well, sir, speaking on behalf of the platoon. I think I can say that we're very sorry.

MAINWARING That's all very well, Jones – but fine words butter no parsnips. **(To Wilson)** Get the gramophone, Sergeant.

WILSON Right, sir.

JONES What's he talking about? You can't get butter, and parsnips are out of season.

Wilson crosses to a corner of the hall, picks up a portable gramophone and a chair, and brings it over to Mainwaring.

WALKER I can get you butter.

Wilson puts the gramophone down on a chair and starts to wind it up.

MAINWARING Now be quiet. I don't intend to overlook this. And so I have decided to make the punishment fit the crime – to quote the words of Gilbert and Sullivan.

JONES **(To Pike)** What's Gilbert and Sullivan got to do with it?

Walker sings.

MAINWARING Quiet, Jones. Now, you will all come to attention while Wilson plays the national anthem – and you will stand there and reflect while the notes of this glorious tune float through the hall. Platoon – attention.

Mainwaring nods to Wilson who puts the record on. The German national anthem starts to play. We hear enough of it to establish what it is before Mainwaring realises. He crosses to Wilson, purple with rage.

MAINWARING How dare you? Turn it off at once.

WILSON What?

MAINWARING I said, turn that filth off.

WILSON **(Turning it off)** What's wrong?

MAINWARING What's wrong? That was the German national anthem.

WILSON Oh, sorry – I wasn't really listening.

MAINWARING Now look here, Wilson.

WALKER I've got an idea, sir – why don't we all hum it?

All hum.

MAINWARING That will do. It's all your fault, Wilson.

WILSON I couldn't help it, sir – it just says on the label 'National Anthems of all Nations'.

MAINWARING Well, play the British one.

WILSON The question is, where is the British one on the record?

MAINWARING Where do you expect it to be – first – of course, Wilson. First! Right, Corporal Jones.

JONES Yes, sir.

MAINWARING You will now take charge – and before you dismiss the parade, you will play the national anthem six times. Right, Wilson – office.

Mainwaring crosses to the office door, followed by Wilson. Mainwaring turns at the door.

MAINWARING And see that they stand to attention rigidly, Jones.

JONES Yes, sir – to attention rigidly.

Mainwaring bumps Wilson. Mainwaring opens the office door and goes in, followed by Wilson.

INTERIOR. OFFICE. NIGHT

The Vicar is sitting at the desk, writing. as Mainwaring and Wilson enter.

VICAR **(Looking up)** Good evening.

MAINWARING What are you doing at my desk, Vicar?

VICAR May I remind you, Captain Mainwaring, that this is my office and my desk – and it is only through my good intentions, in this hour of our country's need, that I allow you to share it.

MAINWARING But I've got a lot of work to do.

WILSON The Vicar's got a lot of work to do as well, sir.

MAINWARING You keep out of this, Wilson. Now look here, Vicar, you've got plenty of time to use that desk – while I'm working at the bank all day.

VICAR I'm sorry, Captain Mainwaring – nothing's going to make me get up from this chair – and that's that.

From the hall, the national anthem starts to play. The Vicar gets up and stands to attention. He stands left of the chair. Mainwaring slowly edges round the desk to the chair. They both eye each other. The anthem finishes. They both rush for the chair. The Vicar wins.

INTERIOR. CHURCH HALL. NIGHT

FRAZER We can't stand here all night, Jonesey – the next time, speed it up a bit.

INTERIOR. OFFICE. NIGHT

The Vicar is sitting . The anthem starts again.

VICAR **(Getting up)** Oh really.

After the first few notes, the anthem speeds up and finishes very quickly. It catches the Vicar off his guard. Mainwaring rushes for the chair and sits.

INTERIOR. OFFICE. NIGHT

Mainwaring is sitting at his desk, writing. Wilson is in the corner, fiddling. There is a knock at the door.

WILSON Come in.

Walker enters. He is carrying a parcel and two bottles of beer.

WILSON What is it, Walker?

WALKER I just wanted to have a word with Captain Mainwaring. **(He leans across the desk and whispers)** I've got your cheese.

MAINWARING What?

WALKER **(Raising his voice)** Your cheese! **(He opens it and puts it in front of Mainwaring)** One pound of the finest cheddar.

MAINWARING Oh yes, quite – it's not for me, you understand.

WALKER Of course not.

MAINWARING You know, I don't really approve of this sort of thing.

WALKER Please yourself – I'll take it back.

MAINWARING No – no, leave it there – it's for my wife. **(He picks up the phone)** She's very partial to cheddar cheese. **(Into phone)** Walmington 92 please.

WILSON **(Coming to life and crossing to the desk)** I say, that looks nice, sir. **(He pokes it)**

MAINWARING Don't put your dirty fingers all over it, Wilson – Elizabeth is going to eat that.

WALKER Be hygienic, Mr Wilson – remember, my cheeses are untouched by human hands – they're packed by monkeys. **(He laughs)**

MAINWARING I can't wait to see my wife's face when I show her all this cheese. She's a vegetarian, you know. I planned this as a little surprise. I thought we might have a nice toasted cheese supper together tonight.

WALKER That'll be cosy, won't it?

MAINWARING That will be all, Walker.

WALKER I'll put this on your account – and there's your two bottles of milk stout, Sarge. **(He hands Wilson the two bottles of beer)** Good night, all. **(He goes)**

Mainwaring is still holding the phone.

WILSON **(Sits)** Can't you get any answer from her, sir?

MAINWARING No – it's most strange. Where on earth can she be? **(Looking at cheese)** Doesn't that cheese look delicious, Wilson? **(He breaks of a small piece and eats it. Wilson reacts)** Hmm! Melts in your mouth.

WILSON **(Licks his lips)** Does it really?

MAINWARING Elizabeth will be delighted when I take this home to her tonight. What is she doing? Oh – hello, Elizabeth – you have been a long time answering, dear... Where have you been?... Oh, I see... **(To Wilson)** In the air raid shelter. I thought we might sleep in the house tonight, dear – after all we haven't had any raids for a week... Oh... Yes, dear – yes, dear. Anyhow, I might have a little surprise for you tonight... I've bought – what – yes, dear – oh – but, Elizabeth, I... very well. **(He slowly hangs up)**

WILSON What's the matter, sir?

MAINWARING She's had her supper and she's going to bed.

WILSON Why didn't you tell her about the cheese?

MAINWARING She wouldn't listen – you know it's a funny thing about women, Wilson – every time you plan a surprise, somehow it always goes wrong. I was so looking forward to that toasted cheese supper too. I'll never understand women if I live to be a hundred.

WILSON Look,sir – why don't we have the toasted cheese supper here?

MAINWARING What, just the two of us together?

WILSON Why not, sir? We've got some bread – and I've got these two bottles of milk stout.

MAINWARING That's very thoughtful of you, Wilson.

WILSON Thank you, sir.

MAINWARING You know, someone once wrote somewhere – I forget who it was – 'The love for a woman waxes and wanes like the moon and stars – but the friendship of a man lasts for eternity'. I value your comradeship, Wilson.

WILSON Thank you, sir.

MAINWARING By the way, don't forget to pay me for your half of the cheese.

There is a knock on the door – Pike comes in.

PIKE Excuse me, Mr Mainwaring. **(Whispering to Wilson)** Are you coming, Uncle Arthur?

WILSON Where to?

PIKE Home of course. Mum will have supper ready for us.

WILSON You'll have to go without me – I'm having a toasted cheese supper with Captain Mainwaring.

PIKE Mum will be furious. You're not going to eat all that cheese are you, Mr Mainwaring?

MAINWARING Yes, why not?

PIKE You'll have terrible dreams. Perhaps one of us ought to stay and help you eat it.

MAINWARING I'm sorry, Pike – there's only enough for two.

Pike reacts.

PIKE (**Whispering to Wilson**) What am I going to tell Mum?

WILSON (**Whispering**) Tell her Captain Mainwaring needs my comradeship.

PIKE What's that mean?

WILSON Look – just go, Frank.

PIKE Well, goodnight.

Mainwaring reacts.

PIKE Don't say I didn't warn you about dreaming. (**He goes out of the back door**)

MAINWARING Right, you make the toast, Wilson – I'll cut up the cheese. (**There is a knock at the door**) Oh, really – come in.

Jones enters.

JONES Well, I'm just off – oh – that's a nice bit of cheese. You going to have a snack, are you?

MAINWARING There's only enough for two, Jones.

JONES (**Taking out parcel**) That's a pity – I shall have to eat these kidneys myself.

WILSON What kidneys?

JONES (**Opening parcel**) I was taking these home for my supper.

MAINWARING On second thoughts – I think there's enough to go round, Jones.

JONES And I'll fry these up in my mess tin on the stove. Toasted cheese and kidneys washed down with milk stout – that's what I call a real meal – very tasty – very sweet.

INTERIOR. OFFICE. NIGHT

They are just finishing the meal.

WILSON That was simply delicious . You know, sir, this reminds me of when I was at school – midnight feasts in the 'dorm'.

MAINWARING Really – where I went to school – we didn't have any midnight feasts – we had to make do with a few aniseed balls in the corner of the playground.

JONES Where I went to school – we didn't even have a playground. That was lovely that cheddar cheese – I suppose the fact that it's hard to get makes it more delicious. There's no doubt about it, 'Forbidden fruits are always sweeter'. I shall never forget when I was in the Sudan, there was this native girl – she was beautiful – well, I think she was beautiful. It was a bit difficult to tell really on account of the fact that she was covered up from head to foot, with just her eyes sticking out. I don't mean that they were sticking out on stalks, if you understand my meaning, sir. They only looked as if they were sticking out because the rest of her was covered up. Are you with me, sir?

MAINWARING I think so.

JONES It was love at first sight. I went straight to my colonel and told him – he said, 'Jones, sit down. I'm going to talk to you like a Dutch uncle'. He wasn't really my uncle, sir, that's just a saying. The colonel looked at me and he said – 'Listen, Jones, you only desire this girl because she's covered up. Have no truck with her.' Well, I decided to take his advice. I went round to her house to tell her that I was breaking it off. I was just going to knock on the door when I happened to look through the shutter – and there she was, having a bath – and do you know, sir, the colonel was right – when she wasn't covered up, it wasn't her eyes that were sticking out…

MAINWARING (**Getting up**) Well, I'm off home.

JONES But I haven't finished yet, sir.

MAINWARING I think I've heard enough.

WILSON There's no doubt about it, Jonesey – women are very difficult to understand.

JONES But Captain Mainwaring's got a way with the ladies – haven't you, sir?

MAINWARING Not really – no.

JONES What about last night on the bus – with that nice lady clippie – the way you told the Warden off when he was so rude to her? That was very chivalrous of you, sir.

MAINWARING There's no doubt about it – she was a charming woman – charming – you know, somehow I don't think that she'd have refused a toasted cheese supper… oh well. (**He sighs**) Good night. (**He goes**)

INTERIOR ANDERSON SHELTER. NIGHT

Mainwaring is asleep on the bottom bunk. He is very restless – he wakes.

MAINWARING (**Softly**) Are you awake, Elizabeth? (**We hear**

• COLIN BEAN REMEMBERS •

'Many happy memories come to mind when thinking of *Dad's Army*, particularly of times when location shooting was in progress "somewhere in England" (various parts of Norfolk, usually).

'Some of them weren't too pleasant at the time, but never fail to amuse me in recollection. Lying face down in a muddy pond with Arthur using me as a rescue pad to help a slowly sinking young Pike out of the water; not forgetting Wardrobe standing by with warmed bath towels (and a generous tot of whisky) once the sequence was in the can. Getting my uniform trousers caught upon a protrusion whilst attempting to progress along a telegraph pole which was set over a stream in a marvellous Mainwaring military manoeuvre. "Marshal Ney" secretly scared me to death when so far from the ground seated astride that magnificent horse Caesar in *A Soldier's Farewell*.

heavy breathing from the top bunk. We can see her huge outline a few inches above Mainwaring's face. Mainwaring sits up and knocks his face on it. He puts his glasses on and lights a candles which is on a small table by the bed) I shouldn't have eaten all that cheese – it was far too rich. (He picks up the clock and looks at it) Two o'clock. (He gives a little belch) Where are the bismuth tablets? (He feels around for the tin, opens it and pops two tablets in his mouth, takes his glasses off, leans back on the pillow, closes his eyes and sighs. We hear the distant strains of the 1812 overture – it gradulally gets louder – the picture slowly dissolves)

TELECINE: BATTLE OF WATERLOO. DAY

Stock shots of battle.

TELECINE: FRENCH HILL. DAY

Mainwaring is sitting hunched on a white horse dressed as Napoleon. He is still wearing his glasses and moustache. Beside him is Private Sponge as Marshal Ney. Behind them a Polish lancer is holding the imperial standard. They are all on horseback. Ney is looking through a telescope.

MAINWARING How's the battle going, Marshal Ney? I can't see a thing.

SPONGE It's your own fault, sir. I told you that we should have sat down the front, in the ninepennies.

TELECINE: BATTLE. DAY

Stock shots of battle.

TELECINE: BRITISH HILL. DAY

Wilson as Wellington.,Frazer as Gordon and Hodges as a staff officer. Behing them is a sergeant with the battle standard – Union Jack. They are all on horseback. Gordon is looking through a telescope.

WILSON How's it looking, Gordon?

FRAZER Good news, sir – Bluchner (He pronounces it 'Bluthner') has arrived!

WILSON Oh really – I'm in no mood for playing the piano now.

TELECINE: FRENCH HILL. DAY

Walker rides into the picture dressed as a captain in the Hussars. He is out of breath.

WALKER Your Imperial Majesty.

MAINWARING Yes, Captain Gerard.

WALKER Je avez une news terrible.

MAINWARING What is it?

WALKER You've lost the ruddy battle, mate.

TELECINE: BRITISH HILL. DAY

FRAZER (Pointing) Look, Wellington – there go my brave Highlanders. Give 'em hell, lads.

WILSON Aren't they good?

FRAZER Ach! My feet are so cold – these damn boots leak.

HODGES Well, why don't you wear a pair of Wellingtons?

WILSON He doesn't take my size.

TELECINE: FIELD. DAY

Jones, Pike, Godfrey and several other members of the platoon are standing round a cannon. Pike has a bandage round his head.

JONES Fire!

PIKE Balls.

JONES What?

PIKE We've run out of cannon balls.

JONES Then fix bayonets, lads. Remember, Les Anglais do not like it oopla – they do not like it oopla. **(A cannon ball lands at his feet)** Blimey that's handy – pick it up, lad.

PIKE **(Picks it up)** Ow! It ain't half hot, Corporal.

JONES Never mind about that, lad – ram it up.

Pike puts his ball in the cannon and rams it home with a ramrod.

JONES **(To Godfrey)** Right – fire!

GODFREY Er... excuse me – have you a match?

TELECINE: BRITISH HILL. DAY

WARDEN Those French cannon balls are starting fires everywhere. **(Shouting)** Put those lights out! Put those ruddy lights out.

WILSON Oh, do try and keep your voice down – you're giving me a headache.

A cannon ball lands.

WILSON I say, that looks like one of ours.

FRAZER **(Close up. Shouting)** Dinna waste it, men – fire it back.

TELECINE: FRENCH HILL. DAY

Walker rides into the picture.

WALKER Your Imperial Majesty. Je avez une more news terrible.

MAINWARING What?

WALKER Wellington is waiting for you to sign the surrender.

MAINWARING Very well – but first I must say farewell to my troops.

TELECINE: FARMYARD. DAY

The defeated army comes through the entrance to the yard. First, Mainwaring slumped on his horse, then Pike as drummer boy with a bandage round his head. He is beating single beats on the drum – then the standard bearer, which is Godfrey. The rest of the platoon follow in single file. Jones is last. Mainwaring stops with Pike and Godfrey each side of him. The platoon file past.

JONES Platoon, halt! **(They halt in a single line in front of Mainwaring)** Right turn! **(They turn)** Men ready for saying farewell to, sir.

Mainwaring gets off his horse – a private takes it out of the picture. Walker comes into frame.

WALKER The Duke is waiting for you to sign the surrender, your Imperial Majesty. **(He points – in front of the farmhouse, Wilson is sitting at a table covered in a Union Jack. Frazer and Hodges are standing behind him)**

MAINWARING Very well. **(He crosses over to the farm followed by Walker)**

WILSON How do you do? Sit down, please. **(Mainwaring sits opposite Wilson)** Name?

MAINWARING Bonaparte.

WILSON **(Writing)** Initials?

MAINWARING N.

WILSON Address?

MAINWARING Versailles – The Palace.

WILSON What street is that in?

MAINWARING Oh, it's not difficult to find.

WILSON **(Pushing paper in front of him)** Sign here, please.

MAINWARING May I borrow your pen?

WILSON I'm sorry, I never lend my pen to anybody.

WALKER **(Handing him quill)** Here you are, sir – ten francs.

MAINWARING Why is it so expensive?

WALKER Well, it's very special ain't it – La Plume de ma Tante.

MAINWARING I can't sign this.

HODGES Look – just sign here, Napoleon.

FRAZER You've no alternative, man – you're beaten.

MAINWARING Very well – what are you going to do with me?

WILSON We're sending you to the Isle of Elba.

Jones runs into picture.

JONES Permission to speak, sir? The men are waiting for you to say farewell to them.

MAINWARING **(Getting up)** Right.

JONES What are they going to do to you, sir?

MAINWARING They're sending me to Elba.

JONES Hence the expression – giving you the Elba.

Jones and Walker leave the picture.

WILSON Well, goodbye – may I say how sorry I am that you lost.

They shake hands.

Long shot of Mainwaring walking back to his troops – with his hands behind his back and shoulders hunched. He joins Jones, Pike and Godfrey who are standing in a group in front of the men.

MAINWARING Well, goodbye, Corporal.

JONES (**Tears running down his face**) Permission to kiss you, sir?

Mainwaring kisses him.

GODFREY Goodbye, sir – I'll get my sister Dolly to send you some of her upside-down cakes.

Mainwaring kisses him.

PIKE Goodbye, sir.

Mainwaring kisses him.

PIKE My mum won't half be proud of me, sir, when I tell her that I've been kissed by an emperor.

Mainwaring takes up his position. Godfrey is standing beside him, holding the Imperial Standard.

MAINWARING Soldiers of France – our cause is lost – your Emperor must now say goodbye. With this kiss, I embrace you all.

He kisses the Standard. The Marseillaise starts to play.

Cut to Wilson, Frazer and Hodges.

FRAZER (**Looking at watch**) Look at the time – they're open.

WILSON (**To Hodges**) You know, those Frenchies have fought awfully well – ask them to have a drink with me.

HODGES Right-oh, Duke. (**Shouts**) 'Ere, the Duke wants you all to have a drink with him.

Cut to Mainwaring, standing to attention. The troops all break ranks and swarm towards him. He disappears under the mêlée. The picture clears – he drags himself to his feet as in previous scenes.

EXTERIOR. A SHIP. NIGHT

Mainwaring is standing on deck with the 'Clippie'. She is dressed as Marie Walewska. Mists are swirling around them.

MAINWARING Only two more hours together, my dear, before the ship sails.

CLIPPIE I can't bear to see you leave, Napoleon.

MAINWARING Nor I to leave you – but you must be brave – the fortunes of war, you know.

CLIPPIE But we still have two hours together – why can't we have a farewell toasted cheese supper.

MAINWARING Ah, a toasted cheese supper – just you and I.

CLIPPIE Please let me have something to remember you by, Napoleon – a likeness perhaps.

MAINWARING Here, take this. (**Hands her a small picture about the size of a bus ticket**) Think of me sometimes.

CLIPPIE I shall keep it always.

She is wearing a large fur muff. She drops it. Underneath is a bell punch attached to her coat. She puts the picture in and punches it.

MAINWARING I say – you've punched me on the nose.

INTERIOR. ANDERSON SHELTER. DAY

Close up of Mainwaring asleep. We hear the Clippie's voice – 'Just you and I and a toasted cheese supper together'. Mainwaring wakes, puts on his glasses, and looks at the clock.

MAINWARING Good heavens – it's half past eight. I shall be late for the bank. Are you awake, Elizabeth?

Mainwaring gets out of the bunk and stands up – the top bunk is empty. On it a note – pan into close up. It reads, 'Why were you late last night? – I am not speaking to you today'.

SERIES FIVE **EPISODE FOUR**

Recorded: Friday 19/5/72
Original transmission: Friday 27/10/72, 8.30–9.00pm
Original viewing figures = 17.5 million

ARTHUR LOWE	CAPTAIN MAINWARING
JOHN LE MESURIER	SERGEANT WILSON
CLIVE DUNN	LANCE CORPORAL JONES
JOHN LAURIE	PRIVATE FRAZER
JAMES BECK	PRIVATE WALKER
ARNOLD RIDLEY	PRIVATE GODFREY
IAN LAVENDER	PRIVATE PIKE
BILL PERTWEE	ARP WARDEN
FRANK WILLIAMS	VICAR
EDWARD SINCLAIR	VERGER
PAMELA CUNDELL	MRS FOX
ALVAR LIDELL	NEWSREADER
OLIVE MERCER	MRS YEATMAN
SERRETTA WILSON	WREN
PLATOON	COLIN BEAN, DESMOND CULLUM-JONES, VIC TAYLOR, FREDDIE WHITE, HUGH CECIL, GEORGE HANCOCK, LESLIE NOYES, FREDDIE WILES, HUGH HASTINGS, MICHAEL MOORE
DORIS (WORKS IN JONES' SHOP)	LEILA FORDE
CONGREGATION IN CHURCH	ERNEST BLYTHE, ROSE EDWARDS, PHILIP BECKAR, ERNEST JENNINGS, KATHLEEN HURD, MARY MASTERS, BETSY WHITE

GETTING THE BIRD

• VERONICA LAURIE REMEMBERS •

'One of Frazer's acknowledged skills was story-telling – just like my father. When I was young – perhaps five or six – he'd sometimes tell me bedtime stories made up on the spur of the moment. He created a series of short tales in which the heroine was a fair-haired young girl called Susie (me!) who had amazing adventures and often got into dangerous scrapes from which she emerged triumphant through her own ingenuity or the bravery of her ruffian-with-a-heart-of-gold friend, James.

'There are, of course, aspects of Frazer that are pure invention. The deep negativism ("We're doomed!") was the antithesis of my father, although it must be said that after the pilot series he had strong doubts that *Dad's Army* would go anywhere, and when he was asked to play Frazer in a second series, he at first refused. Fortunately he was persuaded to change his mind and later used to say that playing Private Frazer was a fine pension for an old man.

'And as for Frazer's miserly tendencies – that's a comic stereotype, untrue of most Scots, and certainly of my father; he was unstintingly generous, as were his two sisters who continued to live in Dumfries. Far from counting his piles of pennies, he was more likely to lose a £5 note as he whisked his hanky or his specs from his pocket.

'My father wasn't one for socialising, especially with fellow actors. In fact, I think Ian Lavender was the only member of the *Dad's Army* cast to visit our home. My father wasn't a party animal – he was an avid reader and something of a loner – but when he was in company he was huge fun, though with a mischievous sense of humour which might puncture the pompous – if they had wit enough to understand the joke. Remember the story of "The Auld Empty Barn"?'

Getting the Bird

INTERIOR. JONES' BUTCHERS SHOP

A lady customer has just been served. Mrs Fox is in the queue, followed by Frazer.

JONES **(Wrapping a couple of cutlets and some corned beef)** There you are, Mrs Yeatman. Take two and three please, Doris.

The lady customer takes the meat, and goes to the cash desk.

MRS FOX Good afternoon, Mr Jones.

JONES Good afternoon, Mrs Fox. **(He takes her ration books)** Two books as usual.

He cancels the appropriate page with a small wooden stamp, which he moistens on an ink pad.

MRS FOX No, it's three this time – my brother's on leave from the Army – here's his card. Have I enough for a joint?

She hands the supplementary card. Jones snips the stamp-sized meat-coupon section from the card using a pair of right-angled scissors.

JONES Well, hardly, Mrs Fox, unless you take brisket. That's cheap you see, so you get more of it but, of course, it's tougher – whereas if you 'as cutlets there's less of it, but more toothsome.

MRS FOX I'll have cutlets then.

JONES I haven't got any.

FRAZER If you haven't got any, what are you blabbering on about them for?

JONES Now don't be impatient, Mr Frazer – there's a war on, you know. I tell you what – how about some chump ends? You get quite a lot of them, they're not too tough and yet they're fairly toothsome.

MRS FOX They'll do then. I like to feed him up if I can – he was at Dunkirk, you know.

JONES Dunkirk, was he? In that case, I'll let you have two sausages.

MRS YEATMAN **(Who is hovering after getting change)** I didn't get any sausages.

JONES Well, you wasn't at Dunkirk, was you.

MRS YEATMAN I made tea for them and rolled bandages.

JONES Well, you can't have sausages for that. I've got to draw the line somewhere.

He has weighed out Mrs Fox's meat.

JONES Take three and seven please ,Doris. Now, what can I do for you, Mr Frazer?

FRAZER I didn't have any corned beef last week so I've come for it now.

JONES You should have come this morning, Mr Frazer – look, that's all I've got. **(He shows him a mound of corned beef bits)**

FRAZER That's crumbs. I'll not pay the sliced rate for a lot of crumbs.

JONES You can have the lot for sixpence.

FRAZER Done.

Jones starts to wrap – Frazer leans over the counter.

FRAZER Have you heard about Sergeant Wilson?

JONES No, what about him?

FRAZER They say he's not to be found. Now, as you well know – he's not been at the bank all day. Now, I can't stand gossip and tittle-tattle of any kind, but it's my belief that there's been a rift in the loot.

JONES What loot?

FRAZER Mrs Pike's loot, you old fool.

JONES Oh dear, poor Mr Wilson.

Walker enters.

WALKER Hello, Jonesey.

FRAZER Not a word to a soul.

JONES You can rely on me.

WALKER How's tricks, Jonesey?

JONES Now, it's no use you coming round here, Joe, you're not registered with me and anyway it's closing time. Close the shop, Raymond – cash up, Doris.

WALKER How about a nice bit of rabbit, Jonesey?

JONES You'll be lucky – I haven't even seen a rabbit for six weeks.

WALKER You 'ave now. **(He whips out the dead rabbit from under his coat and slaps it on the counter)**

JONES Where d'you get that?

WALKER It's Bugs Bunny – he decided to give up the pictures and help the war effort – it's five bob and I want the skin back.

JONES What for?

FRAZER I wouldn't put it past him to get it re-filled.

WALKER I've got a friend who makes mink coats. Well, you can't get the mink, can you?

JONES One's no good to me, Joe. It would just make my life a misery. If the word got around I'd got rabbit, there'd be a queue right past Timothy Whites. **(He has now wrapped Frazer's parcel)** Six pence please, Doris.

WALKER Things are bad are they, Jonesey?

JONES They're terrible, Joe – I've had no offal since

Friday, less than half a sausage per book, and two tins of corned beef was blown. And they blame me, you know – I can't sleep at night for it. I'm at my wits' end, Joe, and that's a fact.

WALKER You mustn't take it like that, it's not your fault.

JONES The way they go on, you'd think it was. Now, if I had fifty of them, it might restore their faith in me.

WALKER There's no chance of that, Jonesey. You can't get the ammunition.

JONES I've got to get something off the ration from somewhere.

Walker sees calendar on Jones' wall depicting Trafalgar Square and the pigeons.

WALKER Something off the ration, eh?

Zoom in on picture.

WALKER Now, I might just possibly be able to help you.

The voices fade on the following dialogue as we go in on the picture.

FRAZER Have you heard about Sergeant Wilson?

WALKER No – what about him?

FRAZER Don't breathe a word to a soul – but it came to my notice.

INTERIOR. CHURCH HALL

Godfrey is talking to Frazer and a couple of the platoon.

GODFREY Well, anyway, I was coming out of the library with a new Ethel M Dell for my sister, and I saw him in Alexander Gardens with this girl.

FRAZER I knew it – there's a woman at the bottom of it.

GODFREY He had his arm round her, but I'm sure there's nothing in it.

FRAZER Away with you, man! There's depravity in every line of his face. It'll be the ruin of him – he's gone amuck.

INTERIOR. SIDE OFFICE. CHURCH HALL

Mainwaring is at his desk. Pike enters.

MAINWARING Ah, Pike, any sign of Sergeant Wilson?

PIKE He's not at Mum's, Mr Mainwaring.

MAINWARING It's not like Wilson at all. One thing you can say for him – he's dependable. If he doesn't appear by tonight, I'll have to contact the police.

PIKE I don't think you ought to do that, Mr Mainwaring.

MAINWARING Oh, why not?

PIKE Well – I'm sure he'll turn up sooner or later.

MAINWARING Are you hiding something, Pike?

PIKE No, Mr Mainwaring.

MAINWARING Come on – out with it.

PIKE Well – the night before last, Mum and Uncle Sergeant Wilson had words.

MAINWARING Ah – now we're getting somewhere. What happened?

PIKE Well – I was in bed, so I couldn't hear much, leaning over the banisters, but he shouted at Mum so she pushed him out of the door and threw his ration book after him.

MAINWARING Oh, yes. Go on.

PIKE And then, a bit later, when he threw pebbles at her bedroom window, she said, 'Clear off, you beast,' and she chucked something out of the window and it broke.

MAINWARING Now I'm beginning to understand.

PIKE Mum got up early and picked up the pieces.

MAINWARING I see.

PIKE All except the handle.

MAINWARING Keep this to yourself, Pike.

Knock on door. Jones enters and salutes, etc.

JONES Sergeant Wilson is still absent without leave or, at least, not present without leave, sir. Shall I fall the men in?

MAINWARING Yes please, Corporal Jones. Cut along now, Pike.

Jones goes into the hall.

INTERIOR. CHURCH HALL

JONES Right – fall in three ranks and look sharp about it.

Walker enters still in his civilian suit.

JONES Hurry up, Private Walker – you're late.

WALKER Your troubles are over, Jonesey – I've got 'em.

JONES Got what?

WALKER Your off-ration meat – pigeons – about six dozen of them.

JONES Good heavens – where are they?

WALKER In the boiler house next to Mainwaring's office.

JONES We'll have to get them into my cold room. They'll go off in the boiler house.

WALKER No they won't – they're not dead yet.

JONES Not dead – they're no good to me flapping about, you know.

WALKER Don't worry, they're doped – that's how I caught them.

JONES Where did you get them from?

Mainwaring appears.

MAINWARING Come along, now – no talking, Jones.

JONES Yes, sir – Squad, 'shun. (**He salutes**) Platoon ready for inspection, sir.

MAINWARING Right – fall in, Corporal Jones.

Jones falls in.

MAINWARING Why aren't you in uniform, Walker?

WALKER Sorry, sir – I was supplying essential supplies.

MAINWARING That's no excuse – we're all doing essential work, you know.

WALKER Sorry, sir – there was a bit of a flap on. (**He nudges Jones**)

MAINWARING Right – stand at ease. There is a church parade on Sunday, I shall expect to see you all there.

GODFREY I wonder if you could ask the Vicar to shorten his sermon. He went on rather a long time before and it wasn't very convenient.

MAINWARING I think you'd better take that up with the Vicar yourself, Godfrey. Now, your arms drill has been getting very sloppy. Some of you may not think this is very important, but I'd rather go into battle with a smart lot of soldiers than with shoddy, sloppy soldiers. So we are going to brass it up. Since Sergeant Wilson isn't with us tonight, I'll take it myself. Right, properly at ease – Squad.

Wilson's voice off.

WILSON Oh...

MAINWARING Silence in the ranks – Squad –

WILSON (**Out of vision**) Oooh...

MAINWARING Squad –

WILSON Oooooh...

Mainwaring detects that the noise is coming from the stage – he draws his revolver – climbs on to the stage and opens the curtains – Wilson is revealed asleep in a chair, clutching an empty whisky bottle.

MAINWARING Wilson – Wilson.

Wilson wakes.

WILSON Hah, hey – what? Oh, I'm sorry, I must have dropped off.

MAINWARING Go in my office please, Sergeant Wilson.

WILSON What – oh yes, of course.

Wilson climbs down stairs and sees the platoon.

WILSON Good evening, how nice to see you all.

MAINWARING Wilson – the office.

WILSON Yes, sir.

He crosses to the office.

MAINWARING Carry on here, Corporal Jones.

JONES Yes, sir.

Mainwaring crosses.

JONES Captain Mainwaring, sir?

MAINWARING Yes, Jones.

JONES What shall I carry on doing?

MAINWARING The drill, Jones.

JONES Of course, sir – it just slipped my mind for a moment.

FRAZER I'd give a pound to be a fly on the wall in that office.

GODFREY I don't think it's any of our business.

INTERIOR. SIDE OFFICE. CHURCH HALL

Mainwaring is behind the desk .Wilson is standing.

MAINWARING What's the meaning of this?

WILSON Hmmm?

MAINWARING I said, what is the meaning of this?

WILSON I'm sorry – I'm a bit dizzy.

MAINWARING You look all in, you'd better sit down.

WILSON (**Sitting**) This must all seem a bit strange, I suppose.

MAINWARING (**Sniffing the air**) Have you been drinking?

WILSON (**Remembering and seeing the bottle in his hand**) Oh – oh, yes, there was that as well. Dear oh dear, my head.

MAINWARING You must have had quite a skinful.

WILSON Walker got me a bottle of whisky. I rather think I finished it.

MAINWARING You'd better tell me all about it – the last report I had of you was outside Mrs Pike's.

WILSON Oh yes – what a good job she missed. Well, you see, it was all a misunderstanding, she thought I'd been... (**He trails off – a pigeon has appeared in the bookcase behind Mainwaring's head**) She thought I'd been...

MAINWARING What's the matter?

WILSON Well – she thought I'd been...

Mainwaring sees Wilson's gaze is transfixed and he turns round – the pigeon pops down as Mainwaring turns, so there's nothing there to be seen.

MAINWARING Now, pull yourself together, Wilson – you're getting woolly minded.

WILSON I'm most awfully sorry – you see it really all began many years ago, not long after the last… **(He trails off again – the pigeon appears)** Not long after the last…

MAINWARING Wilson.

WILSON I'm sorry – not long after the last…

Mainwaring turns again – the pigeon pops down.

MAINWARING You keep wandering off in a dream.

WILSON I keep seeing birds

MAINWARING If you take my advice you'll sign the pledge. I'm not going to sit and listen to any more of your miranderings – there's a war on, and those troops need training. If you want to remain part of this platoon you'll go out there and give them half an hour's arms drill.

WILSON Yes, sir. **(Stares)**

MAINWARING Now get a grip on yourself and get on with it.

WILSON Yes, sir. **(He crosses to the door)**

MAINWARING And we'll talk about this after parade.

WILSON Yes, sir. **(He goes into the hall)**

CHURCH HALL

WILSON Right, I'll take over now, Corporal Jones. Right, properly at ease, squad. Squad, 'shun.

The squad do so, except for Pike.

WILSON Pay attention like, slope arms.

PIKE I'm not going to.

In a slight daze, Wilson turns to the office.

FRAZER You've done it now, lad. That was mutiny, you'll be shot.

SIDE OFFICE. CHURCH HALL

MAINWARING **(As Wilson enters)** What is it now?

WILSON I'm awfully sorry to trouble you but Pike says he's not going to.

MAINWARING Not going to what?

WILSON Slope arms.

Mainwaring reacts swiftly and crosses to the hall.

CHURCH HALL

Mainwaring crosses to Pike.

MAINWARING What's all this about, Pike?

PIKE May I talk to you in private, sir?

MAINWARING I think you'd better. Come along.

Followed by Pike, Mainwaring goes to the side office. The platoon are spellbound.

SIDE OFFICE. CHURCH HALL

MAINWARING All right, what have you got to say?

PIKE I'm not going to take any notice of Sergeant Wilson at all. Mum said not too.

MAINWARING Am I hearing you right, Pike?

PIKE Yes, Mr Mainwaring. Mum said, if I saw him, I was just to ignore him, so I did.

MAINWARING Now look here, Pike, I'm running this platoon, not your mother.

PIKE Oh, she didn't say I was to ignore you.

MAINWARING That's very generous of her.

PIKE But she said Uncle Sergeant Wilson was a Cassa… **(His voice trails off as he sees pigeon in the same place)** She said he was a Cassa…

MAINWARING Get on with it, boy.

PIKE Mr Mainwaring, there's a pigeon in your pigeonhole.

MAINWARING What!

Mainwaring turns and looks. There is a pigeon. A couple more pigeons pop out.

MAINWARING Wilson! Jones! My office is alive with pigeons.

CHURCH HALL

WALKER **(To Jones)** Blimey, they must have woken up. Hang on, Captain Mainwaring, I'll take care of it.

Walker runs into the office.

SIDE OFFICE. CHURCH HALL

MAINWARING Open the door, Pike. Get them out.

WALKER No, no, don't do that. **(He bungs his hat over the place from which the pigeons are emerging)** That'll stop 'em. Get that on, Jonesy.

Jones pursues the spare pigeon, making cooing noises.

JONES Coo, coo come along, my darling, coo, coo.

MAINWARING Are you at the bottom of all this, Walker?

WALKER Ah well, yes, sir. You see there was this pal of mine who's a pigeon fancier and he didn't fancy them anymore. So I thought you could train them to take messages.

MAINWARING Where are the coming from?

WALKER I put them in the boiler house next door.

MAINWARING This is too much. My sergeant is incapable, the troops won't obey orders and now my office is an aviary.

The Verger is heard off.

VERGER Mr Mainwaring, Mr Mainwaring.

He knocks on the door.

MAINWARING Yes, what d'you want? Come in, damn you.

Enter Verger with a pigeon on his head.

VERGER Mr Mainwaring, I have a very serious complaint to make.

JONES' SHOP. NIGHT

Jones and Walker are putting pigeons into the cold room. They work by hurricane lamp.

WALKER There you are, Jonesy, that's the last lot.

JONES I'll just take these two as a little present for Captain Mainwaring.

WALKER I've never known him in such tizz-wazz. I thought he was going to have me shot.

JONES How much do I owe you, Joe?

WALKER Five pounds to you. (**Jones reacts**) I had to give ten bob to Ted for topping them.

JONES You'll have cash first thing in the morning.

Enter the Warden with a torch.

WARDEN 'Ere, put that ruddy light out, haven't you 'eard them planes going over.

JONES They won't see that little light.

WARDEN How d'you know? Have you been up there to have a look. I'm going to book you for this.

JONES You're showing just as much light with that torch.

WALKER Here, have a couple of pigeons and forget it.

WARDEN Are these for me?

JONES/WALKER Yes.

WARDEN Eh. Ah, ah well, I suppose it's not a very big light, is it. (**He takes pigeons**)

Jones and Walker react.

COMMAND POST. NIGHT

This is a sand-bag structure . We see Mainwaring, Frazer and Godfrey through the slit out of which they are looking – gun fire is heard. There is a door at the back.

FRAZER That's a fine barrage we're sending up tonight.

MAINWARING Yes – three point sevens mostly.

GODFREY Awfully noisy things, aren't they?

Mainwaring looks at watch.

MAINWARING It's gone nine, turn the wireless on, Pike, we're missing the news.

Enter Jones and Walker – as the door opens, we see flashes of gunfire.

WALKER Sorry we were late. We was getting those pigeons into cold storage.

The news bulletin commences in the background.

MAINWARING I don't think I want to hear any more about them, thank you, Walker.

JONES We bought a brace for you and your good lady, sir.

He gives him two pigeons.

MAINWARING Oh, thank you very much.

ANNOUNCER'S VOICE Smaller raids were carried out on the marshalling yards at Ham. From all these operations, three of our aircraft are missing. The mysterious drop in the number of pigeons in Trafalgar Square formed the subject of a question in Parliament today. The Home Secretary said he saw no cause for alarm and promised a full investigation. Answering a supplementary question, he felt it unlikely that there was a link between this event and the fall in the population of apes on the Rock of Gibraltar.

They all look at Walker.

WALKER Not the apes, cross my heart. I have not touched one single ape.

Mainwaring hands back the pigeons to Jones.

MAINWARING I think these are yours, Corporal.

JONES No, sir, no, sir, they're not. (**He hands them to Walker**) They're Joe's.

WALKER Hang on a minute – you bought 'em, all of 'em, remember?

JONES No I didn't, I didn't pay for 'em, so they're still yours.

The Warden enters.

WARDEN I've just heard the news, I've lost the taste.

He hands Joe the pigeons.

WALKER That's nice, isn't it.

MAINWARING You have my permission to fall out, Jones and Walker, if you have anything particular you want to do.

JONES I'm staying on duty, sir, here's the key to the shop, Joe. You'd better get a move on, hadn't you?

PIKE D'you think MI5 will come round, Mr Mainwaring?

FRAZER I can see the headlines now – Home Guard Commander arrested for chasing birds.

MAINWARING Don't hang about, Walker.

INTERIOR. SIDE OFFICE. CHURCH HALL. DAY

Mainwaring is working – Pike enters from outside and salutes.

MAINWARING Yes, Pike?

PIKE Please sir, Mum says, if you see Uncle Arthur, would you ask him to have a word with her?

MAINWARING I don't expect to see him, Pike, I've given him short compassionate leave to sort himself out.

PIKE I see, only she's white-washing the spare bedroom ceiling, I think she wants some help.

MAINWARING Does she? I wouldn't have thought he was much good at that sort of thing.

PIKE Well, he holds the steps for her, you see.

MAINWARING He's promised to be back for church parade.

INTERIOR. CHURCH HALL

Godfrey is talking to Jones.

GODFREY It seems an awful pity with rations so short – people would have been glad of them.

JONES Well, I don't know what he'd done with them, but they were out of my shop when I got there this morning.

Walker enters and crosses to Jones.

WALKER **(Hisses)** It's done, and it wasn't easy, I can tell you.

JONES Did anyone see you?

WALKER Course not – I put three dozen…

JONES No, don't tell me, I don't want to know nothing about it. I'd better tell Captain Mainwaring to put his mind at ease.

Jones crosses to the office.

FRAZER You didn't destroy them, Joe, I couldn't bear the thought.

WALKER D'you think I'm a mug. In a few days time I might be able to let you have a couple, that's provided we don't have a heat wave.

INTERIOR. SIDE OFFICE. CHURCH HALL

Jones enters – Pike has left.

MAINWARING Yes, Jones.

JONES Captain Mainwaring, sir – I thought you would wish to know that the things with feathers that we don't mention, have been put in a place that I don't want to know about – and you don't either, by someone who shall remain anonymous – and we won't be hearing no more about it.

MAINWARING I see.

JONES **(Winking)** I hope you get my meaning, sir.

MAINWARING Very clearly, Jones.

Vicar enters.

VICAR Ah, Captain Mainwaring, I wonder if you'd approve the hymns for Sunday – I thought 'Lead Kindly Light', 'Rock of Ages', 'God Moves in a Mysterious Way' and 'Onward Christian Soldiers'.

MAINWARING They seem all right to me, nothing very controversial.

VICAR The reason I was asking is because we haven't had an organist since poor Mrs West passed away, so we have to sing unaccompanied, which means the congregation must know the hymns. I give them the first note, of course.

He blows a note on his pitch-pipe.

MAINWARING Yes, well, I expect we'll manage.

JONES Permission to interject, sir?

MAINWARING What is it?

JONES There's no need for the Vicar to use his pipe, sir.

VICAR You mean you think I should 'La' it.

MAINWARING Oh no, we can't have him 'La'ing' it, it's much better for him to use his pipe.

VICAR I quite agree with you, Captain Mainwaring. I'd much rather do this. **(Blows pipe)** Than this. **(La's)**

JONES No, no, what I'm trying to say is – the Vicar can use his pipe for the first three hymns, but I can play the organ for 'Onward Christian Soldiers'.

MAINWARING I didn't know that you played the church organ, Jones.

JONES I was driven to it by passion, sir.

MAINWARING Really.

JONES Yes, sir. You see it all happened many years ago in

Leamington-on-Spa. I fell in love with this beautiful lady, well she wasn't really beautiful, sir – bit of an acid face – very acid it was – but what really attracted me to her was her knees.

MAINWARING Her knees?

JONES Yes, they were very flat – I'd never seen such flat knees – then I found out why – very religious she was – did a lot of praying – I was mad with lust – I had to find a way to make her look favourable on me. Driven by desire, I practiced 'Onward Christian Soldiers' on the organ – day and night I practised, with her flat knees imprinted on my mind, until finally I did it in my repertoire. Flushed with triumph, I went round to her house, but it didn't do me any good, she'd moved to Bournemouth. But I never lost the touch.

Mainwaring reacts.

VICAR Thank you, Corporal Jones, it'll make a nice change, won't it, Captain Mainwaring?

MAINWARING Yes, yes, I'm sure it will.

VICAR See you all on Sunday then.

PORCH ENTRANCE TO CHURCH

The platoon are filing in – and just inside the church, behind the lattice screen, Frazer is handing out prayer books – Mainwaring is watching the troops in.

WARDEN I'm helping her with her black-out curtains.

MAINWARING Walker, put that cigarette out.

WALKER Sorry, sir.

They are all through into the church, except Wilson, who is last.

MAINWARING Glad you were able to join us.

WILSON Yes – it's been rather trying.

MAINWARING Could you spare me the time for a talk after the service?

WILSON Yes, of course.

MAINWARING Thank you.

Wilson stays behind – Mainwaring goes into the church. Wilson is clearly waiting for someone. A very pretty Wren of twenty or so enters with a suitcase – she is in uniform. Frazer's face is in the background.

WILSON Oh dear, you have that case to carry. I am so sorry I couldn't see you off.

GIRL That's all right. I was afraid I was going to miss you.

WILSON I'm glad I saw you in uniform – it suits you terribly well.

GIRL So does yours – I must rush or I'll be late. (**She kisses him**) Goodbye, Daddy.

WILSON Goodbye, my darling – thank you for coming to see me.

GIRL I'm very glad I did – goodbye.

She goes – he calls after her.

WILSON Give my love to your mother.

He turns and sees Frazer – they look at each other – Wilson realises that Frazer has overheard.

FRAZER She's a fine lassie.

WILSON Her mother left me when she was a baby – I've seen very little of her really, though I did manage to send her to a good school.

FRAZER She does you credit.

WILSON Yes – it was worth it, I think. Still, it's all in the past. I didn't really want anyone to know.

FRAZER I'm an old blabbermouth, but I really promise you that nobody'll ever learn anything of this from me.

WILSON Thank you, Frazer – that's very kind of you.

INTERIOR. CHURCH

MAINWARING Get in.

Vicar in the pulpit – after establishing him, we pan along the platoon.

VICAR And so this makes it, does it not, even more necessary that we should look into our hearts – gaze closely at ourselves, using the clear light of truth, and ask ourselves, are we any better than that poor woman – if she stood before us today, are we blameless, would we cast the first stone?

MAINWARING I hope you've been paying attention, Wilson.

WILSON I have heard it before, actually.

VICAR (**Out of vision**) And to God the Father, God the Son, etc…

Jones gets up and moves along the row to the aisle.

WALKER Hello, where's Jonesey off to?

PIKE He's playing the last hymn on the organ, 'Onward Christian Soldiers'.

Walker reacts.

PIKE Are you all right, Joe? You've gone very pale.

WALKER He can't play the organ, I've hid 50 pigeons in the pipes.

VICAR Hymn 385 – 'Onward Christian Soldiers'.

WALKER (**About to go**) See you later.

MAINWARING Where are you going, Walker?

WALKER I thought I'd help with the collection.

MAINWARING Stay where you are.

Cut to Jones at the keyboard.

JONES Pump away, Mr Yeatman.

Cut to the Verger – he is pumping, Jones tries to play the intro. The notes are muffled and strange. Mainwaring, Walker and Pike react. Jones can't understand it.

JONES Come on, can't you give me any more air than that – get pumping.

VERGER I'm doing my utmost.

The Verger pumps very hard. Jones plays. The congregation start to sing. There are one or two loud pops. Cut to organ pipes as pigeons are projected. Cut to congregation as dead pigeons and feathers start to rain down. Cut to Vicar, horrified. Cut to Godfrey – he puts on his tin hat. Mainwaring looks at Walker. Walker wishes he were dead.

SERIES FIVE **EPISODE FIVE**

Recorded: Friday 16/6/72

Original transmission: Friday 3/11/72, 8.30–9.00pm

Original viewing figures = 15.8 million

ARTHUR LOWE .... CAPTAIN MAINWARING
JOHN LE MESURIER .... SERGEANT WILSON
CLIVE DUNN .... LANCE CORPORAL JONES
JOHN LAURIE .... PRIVATE FRAZER
JAMES BECK .... PRIVATE WALKER
ARNOLD RIDLEY .... PRIVATE GODFREY
IAN LAVENDER .... PRIVATE PIKE
BILL PERTWEE .... ARP WARDEN
FRANK WILLIAMS .... VICAR
EDWARD SINCLAIR .... VERGER
ROBERT RAGLAN .... COLONEL
LARRY MARTYN .... SIGNALS PRIVATE
JAMES TAYLOR .... ARTILLERY OFFICER
PLATOON .... COLIN BEAN, HUGH HASTINGS, EVAN ROSS,
.... GEORGE HANCOCK, FREDDIE WILES,
.... LESLIE NOYES, MICHAEL MOORE, HUGH CECIL,
.... FREDDIE WHITE, DESMOND CULLUM-JONES
STUNTMEN .... BILLY HUGHES AND LESLIE CONRAD

THE DESPERATE DRIVE OF CORPORAL JONES

• MIKE HODGSON REMEMBERS •

'A phone call from Kingsbury Motors, and I was asked if I would use my 1925 Austin 7 for a week's filming with *Dad's Army*. Sounded fun, so I drove my Austin through the traffic of London to Kingsbury and from there it was trailered to Thetford.

'I followed the next day to find what David Croft really needed was a wreck of a car that would at least run. What he had got was a car that had, a year earlier, won an award for The Best Vintage Car under 1000 c.c. Back at home, I had exactly what he wanted, undergoing restoration. In the TV work I did subsequently, I always made sure I knew what they wanted.

'I stripped the car of its hood, lamps etc, then we covered the shiny paintwork with Fullers earth paste and drove the car through mud and dust. The first shot was Walker driving up late for parade and offering Captain Mainwaring the car for £10. Leaving the car with Godfrey and Jones, the rest of the platoon set off in Jones' van. Godfrey sets about chopping wood for a fire but Jones realises that the lads are going to the wrong place, which is about to be fired on. He gets on the field telephone, only to discover that Godfrey has chopped through the telephone wire. The film had to show the axe chopping through the wire, but after several retakes the wire was reduced to only six inches long. I helped by holding one end of the wire, which was very risky on the fingers. It was then a case of driving a Vauxhall 14/40 and the Austin to warn Captain Mainwaring. Godfrey was given a quick driving lesson but could not do it, so with not much time left, Jones tied a 60-foot rope between the cars and told Godfrey to steer behind him, but the Vauxhall went one side of the tree and the Austin went the other.

'The Austin was supposed to spin round the tree (which was an impossibility without a little help). A stuntman came to do a handbrake turn around the tree, which I hadn't been told about. You can't do that with a 1920s Austin 7 because the handbrake only works the front brakes. After two failed attempts, I drove the car and span it round the tree using just the footbrakes. Arnold Ridley was put in the car and we lifted it a foot at a time round the tree while still shots were taken which, when put together, looked as if the car span round the tree three times. This took most of the day and at one time Arnold dozed off, but what a real gentleman he was!

'A shot taken through the windscreen meant that the front wheels had to be put on a camera trolley and pulled round in a circle. This meant that all the vehicles used by the crew had to be hidden in the wood, which took about half an hour; then all the crew had to run behind the camera. Jones untied the rope and drove both cars to where the rest of the platoon were guarding an old barn, which was, of course, the target for a 25-pounder gun. The whole platoon ran out and jumped into both cars. Eight big soldiers in an Austin 7 must be some record; the car was so overloaded that we had to pull it on rope to make it look as if it had pulled away under its own power. The poor car had taken a proper beating and it took me a week to bring it back to concours condition.

'The stars of *Dad's Army* were a great bunch of lads. It's such a pity that so many are no longer with us.'

The Desperate Drive of Corporal Jones

INTERIOR. CHURCH HALL. DAY

The squad is lined up – Mainwaring is addressing them.

MAINWARING Pay attention. Those of you who read part two orders will know that we are taking part in a Divisional scheme on Saturday. I'm very pleased to be able to tell you that live ammunition will be used.

WILSON That's good news, sir.

MAINWARING We will also be co-operating with a battery of 25-pounders – it will be firing over our heads.

WALKER How far over?

Mainwaring reacts.

JONES Permission to interlope, sir? Private Walker has no need to fret himself, sir. I have many times had artillery guns firing over my head and I have lived to tell the tale.

FRAZER Aye, so far.

MAINWARING Now, during this exercise, we will be doing some house clearing, so we'll spend the rest of this parade revising the drill. Walker, Frazer – you can be the shooters – do you remember what you have to do?

They all nod.

MAINWARING Good, take your places – at the double.

JONES Do as the officer says.

Walker and Frazer stand five yards from the door. Pike stands to the left of it and Jones to the right.

MAINWARING Jones – that'll do. Right, we'll do this by numbers. Walker –

WALKER At the door – bang, bang, bang.

FRAZER At the lock – shoot, shoot, shoot.

MAINWARING Yes. Jones –

JONES **(Coming to attention)** Yes, sir. I'm ready, sir.

MAINWARING Kick the door open.

JONES Yes sir – at the door – kick, kick, kick, aaaah, aaaah. **(With much staggering he kicks open the door which is ajar)** The door is kicked open, sir.

MAINWARING Wilson –

WILSON Yes, sir?

MAINWARING Well, get on with it – chuck your grenade.

WILSON If Jones stands in the way I can't throw the bomb thing.

MAINWARING Jones, get out of the way.

JONES I'm sorry, sir. **(He moves)** I'm not quite myself, I've been having a lot of trouble at the shop.

MAINWARING Well, try to keep alert.

JONES The brawn didn't set, sir, and that threw me out for the whole day. You see, you cannot sell runny brawn – the customers will sneer at me.

Mainwaring reacts.

WALKER Tell 'em it's cold soup.

MAINWARING That'll do, Walker. Get on with it, Wilson.

WILSON I haven't got a grenade, sir.

MAINWARING Oh yes, here you are. **(He takes a large doorknob out of his pocket)**

WILSON I wondered what that was.

MAINWARING On you go.

WILSON Grenade lob.

He lobs the doorknob through the door.

MAINWARING Good – now Pike.

PIKE Yes, sir.

MAINWARING Well, get on with it.

PIKE I'm awaiting the explosion of the bomb, sir, because I don't want to be blown to smithereens.

MAINWARING Don't be impertinent, Pike, just do as you're told.

Pike yells and runs into the side office.

INTERIOR. SIDE OFFICE. CHURCH HALL. DAY

Pike leaps on to the desk and turns towards the door.

PIKE Bang, bang, bang, bang.

He re-enters the hall.

INTERIOR. CHURCH HALL. DAY

Pike enters.

PIKE Was that all right, Mr Mainwaring?

MAINWARING Don't say, 'Was that all right, Mr Mainwaring?' You report, 'House clear, sir'.

PIKE Sorry, sir – house clear, sir.

MAINWARING That's better. We will now do it at operational speed, using blank ammunition.

They prepare.

MAINWARING Now remember, speed is essential. The Nazi is a slow thinker and he's not accustomed to using his initiative. If you don't give him time to think, you've nothing to worry about. Right now, stand by – load your guns. Wilson – you use a thunder flash.

INTERIOR. SIDE OFFICE. CHURCH HALL. DAY

Vicar, Verger and Warden enter.

WARDEN I want you to tell Mainwaring in front of me, it's my 'all just as much as it's 'is.

VICAR In actual fact, it's my hall.

VERGER If you ask me, Mainwaring's getting too big for his trousers.

Walker and Frazer fire three shots each. Jones yells and kicks at the door. Wilson lobs in a thunder flash which explodes. Pike runs in – jumps on desk and fires his blanks – he then moves back to the door to report.

PIKE House clear, sir, except for the Vicar, the Verger and Mr Hodges.

Fade as Mainwaring and Wilson move to aid the Vicar.

INTERIOR. SIDE OFFICE. CHURCH HALL

Mainwaring is admiring himself in the mirror – he is wearing a new officer's greatcoat.

MAINWARING Come in.

Wilson enters.

WILSON The men are ready when you are, sir.

Wilson sees coat.

WILSON Oh, I say, that's awfully smart.

MAINWARING Well, I thought it advisable to get something warm for when the weather gets chilly. I had it specially tailored. It cost me eighteen guineas.

WILSON Yes, I ought to get something like it myself.

MAINWARING They're for officers only.

Wilson reacts. Mainwaring moves into the hall.

INTERIOR. CHURCH HALL

The platoon is formed up, ready for the exercise, wearing tin hats, respirators, haversacks, water bottles, etc. They carry rifles and greatcoats. Frazer sees Mainwaring.

MAINWARING Squad, 'shun.

They come to attention.

FRAZER Look at this – it's the chocolate soldier himself.

WALKER Nelson Eddy.

MAINWARING I heard that, Walker.

Walker reacts.

MAINWARING Stand at ease. Pay attention. Our task on this exercise will be to occupy a disused barn and deny it to the enemy. **(The telephone rings)** Ah – take that call, Jones – it will be HQ giving us the map reference to the farm house.

JONES Yes, sir. Permission to speak, sir?

MAINWARING Yes, Jones.

JONES The coat, sir, it looks very smart. Kitchener had one very similarly identical.

MAINWARING Thank you, Jones.

JONES Except that it was blue, didn't have brass buttons and it was much longer.

FRAZER Answer the phone, you old crawler.

JONES Now look here, Private Frazer –

MAINWARING The phone, Jones.

JONES Yes, sir. **(He moves to the office)**

About turn business.

MAINWARING **(To Wilson)** Since we're using live ammunition, I'm taking no chances, I've put Jones in charge of guarding the company vehicle park.

WILSON That'll be a relief to us all, sir.

INTERIOR. SIDE OFFICE. CHURCH HALL

Jones picks up the telephone.

JONES Jones, the Butcher.

H.Q. BACKGROUND

COLONEL Ah, Jones – I have the map reference for Captain Mainwaring – will you take it down?

SIDE OFFICE. CHURCH HALL

JONES Yes, I'll take your order now, sir.

SH.Q.

COLONEL It's nine, three, seven, six, four, one.

SIDE OFFICE. CHURCH HALL

JONES Just a moment – nine, three, seven… **(He writes**

those three figures and the pencil breaks) D'you mind holding on, sir – I'll attend to you in a moment, only the lead's broke – I've got nine, three, seven down. **(He goes to drawer)**

CHURCH HALL

MAINWARING On the command 'Fall out', you'll put your kit on Jones' van. **(He sees that Godfrey is carrying a rather large basket)** Godfrey, I don't think we need quite as much first aid kit as that.

GODFREY It's not first aid sir, it's my picnic.

MAINWARING Picnic?

GODFREY Well you said we were to bring food.

MAINWARING I said haversack rations – which means sandwiches.

GODFREY I find that sort of thing awfully indigestible, and so my sister has packed me a vegetable flan and some rice pudding.

MAINWARING Rice pudding! This is war, Godfrey. This is no place for rice pudding. Leave it in my office.

WALKER With the spoon.

MAINWARING That's enough, Walker. Right, fall out, the rest of you.

Jones comes up to Walker.

JONES Have you got a pencil, Joe?

WALKER Here you are, packet of six, half a crown – ready sharpened.

JONES Look, I just want one.

SIDE OFFICE. CHURCH HALL

Godfrey puts his basket down.

H.Q.

COLONEL Hello, hello?

SIDE OFFICE. CHURCH HALL

Godfrey picks up the telephone.

GODFREY Can I be of any assistance?

H.Q.

COLONEL Look here, whoever you are, I can't hang on here all day, just take down these figures – six, four, one.

SIDE OFFICE. CHURCH HALL

GODFREY Just a moment – six, four, one.

He writes above Jones' figures.

COLONEL Six, four, one.

H.Q.

COLONEL That's it – he's got the other figures down, hasn't he?

SIDE OFFICE. CHURCH HALL

GODFREY Yes, sir – so it would appear – nine, three, seven.

H.Q.

COLONEL Good. See Captain Mainwaring gets it.

SIDE OFFICE. CHURCH HALL

GODFREY Certainly, sir, with pleasure. Will that be all sir?

He puts down the telephone and Jones enters.

JONES 'Ere, what are you playing at?

GODFREY I've just taken down a message from the colonel.

JONES You're after my job, aren't you?

Godfrey reacts.

CHURCH HALL

Walker goes up to Mainwaring.

WALKER Captain Mainwaring, I've got some essential supplies to collect, so I'll meet you at the vehicle park if it's all the same to you.

MAINWARING It is not all the same to me, I'm just about fed up with your impertinence – and your black market activities, Walker.

WALKER Black market! That's libel that is, Captain Mainwaring. As a matter of fact, if you want to know –

and you're not entitled to – it's three scooters I've had made up for the kids' hospital at Eastgate, and I'm not selling 'em, I'm giving 'em.

MAINWARING **(Covering himself quickly)** I see.

WALKER See you later then, sir, if it's all the same to you.

MAINWARING Yes, I suppose so.

Walker sings.

FILM: VEHICLE PARK

This is a small compound surrounded by a fence, or hedge or barbed wire or wall. There is a small hut or shack in it. Long shot of Jones' van banging ominously from the big end as it arrives and halts, inside the compound. The engine dies.

MAINWARING What's the matter, Jones?

JONES It won't go, sir.

WILSON I think the big end's gone.

JONES Just my luck. The guarantee's run out.

FRAZER **(Through the trap)** That wee farmhouse we're supposed to go to is two miles away.

MAINWARING Oh never mind, we'll march. Fall the men in, Sergeant.

WILSON **(Getting out)** Fall in, you chaps, we're going for a little stroll.

Jones and Mainwaring get out of the van.

MAINWARING Now listen, Jones, you stay here with the vehicles and when we're in position, you report to HQ on the field telephone.

JONES Yes, sir. How will I know when you're in position?

Pike joins them.

MAINWARING Ah – a good point. We need some kind of signal.

PIKE Please, sir, why don't we make smoke signals like the Indians?

JONES You stupid boy.

MAINWARING That's not stupid at all, it's a very good idea. We'll make smoke when we're in position.

JONES Permission to ask a question, sir?

MAINWARING Yes, Jones?

JONES How will I know you're not a bonfire?

PIKE We could do a victory vee, sir – three little puffs and a big puff.

MAINWARING A good idea, we'll send three victory puffs. Off you go and set up your post. **(Moving round to the back of the van)** Hurry up and fall in there – we're late. Carry your greatcoats and equipment.

Godfrey is sitting on the tailboard.

FRAZER He'll not carry himself, let alone his gear.

GODFREY I'm afraid my gout is playing up a bit, I'm awfully sorry.

MAINWARING Right, you stay here with Jones and guard the vehicles.

Walker arrives driving a small car – in the back are the teddy bears and on the luggage rack at the rear are a couple of scooters made from pram wheels.

WALKER Hello, Captain Mainwaring. Have I missed anything? **(He climbs out)**

MAINWARING What on earth have you got there?

WALKER You can have it for ten quid.

MAINWARING Leave that machine there and fall in at once.

WALKER **(Holding up a large coil of rope which is attached to the front)** It's a bargain, it's got its own cold-weather starter.

WILSON **(To Mainwaring)** Won't you be rather hot marching in that overcoat, sir?

MAINWARING No – it's er very good cloth, cool in summer, warm in the winter.

INTERIOR. JONES' COMMAND POST

This is a small shack or lean-to with one window looking out to the side. The colonel is on the field telephone.

COLONEL Well, I'm on my way back to Battalion H.Q. now – goodbye.

Jones enters and salutes.

JONES Sorry, sir, I thought this was my headquarters – now I see it's your headquarters.

COLONEL No, it's yours all right. There's your telephone and my car's out there. Keep guard on it.

JONES Yes, sir, of course, sir. Who am I guarding it from?

COLONEL The Germans actually – I haven't immobilised it.

JONES Ah yes, sir – I won't let those Germans touch it, you can rely on me.

FILM: EXTERIOR. GATEWAY TO THE RANGE

Red flag is flying – the platoon march through. They approach the sign that reads 'Beware of low flying aircraft'.

INTERIOR. JONES' COMMAND POST

Godfrey has now joined him.

JONES Left, right, left, right – fall out. You sit there, Mr Godfrey, and I'll report to head H.Q. quarters. Now let me see, it's 23 minutes past, Mr Mainwaring has to march two miles to the farmhouse – now a column of marching men goes at three and a half miles an hour, so what time will he arrive?

GODFREY I don't think I march at three and a half miles an hour.

JONES Call it three then. Three miles an hour – two miles. That's three tooths of an hour.

GODFREY No, two thirds – that's 40 minutes – he'll be there three minutes past the hour.

JONES Ah yes, that's right – that's what I'll report. (**He goes to the field telephone**) That was very quick, Mr Godfrey.

GODFREY I always imagine I'm measuring cloth – makes it quite easy.

JONES That's a good idea – I'll have to work it out in chops. Jones the butcher here – he'll be there at three minutes past.

SANDBAGGED DUG OUT. STUDIO

Signaller in dug out.

SIGNALLER Who'll be where at three minutes past what?

INTERIOR. JONES' COMMAND POST

JONES Captain Mainwaring, of course – he'll be at the farm barn at three minutes past two.

SANDBAGGED DUG OUT

SIGNALLER Why didn't you say so in the first place?

INTERIOR. JONES' COMMAND POST

JONES Excuse me – could I enquire your rank please?

DUG OUT

SIGNALLER Signalman.

INTERIOR. JONES' COMMAND POST

JONES Well, I'm a lance corporal, so you'd better be a bit more polite.

FILM: EXTERIOR. FARM HOUSE

The platoon arrive.

MAINWARING Platoon, halt. Fall out into the farmhouse. Light the fire, Pike.

INTERIOR. FARMHOUSE

It is derelict – there is a fireplace on one side, a door and a window. Mainwaring enters.

MAINWARING Pile your equipment in the corner there – coats over there.

He takes off his own coat – he is perspiring visibly.

WILSON Deceptively muggy for the time of the year.

MAINWARING Put that on top of the others – don't want it to get soiled.

INTERIOR. JONES' COMMAND POST

JONES I don't see any smoke yet, Mr Godfrey.

GODFREY I don't suppose I'd see that far even if it was there.

JONES You ought to get some glasses, Mr Godfrey.

GODFREY I had a pair once – I didn't get on with them. They made me look rather old.

JONES They don't worry me. I am old.

FILM: EXTERIOR. FARMHOUSE

Walker, Pike and Frazer are round the fire about to use an overcoat to signal. Wilson is in charge.

WILSON Right, centre it – now away. (**Pause**) Over – away. (**Pause**) Over – away. (**Pause**) Over – away – over. (**He turns to Mainwaring**) How long should the break between letters be, sir?

Cut to Mainwaring who is looking through his field glasses.

MAINWARING Oh, about ten seconds I should think.

WILSON Right – one, two, three, four, five.

The coat catches fire.

PIKE Look out, it's burning.

After general confusion they throw the coat on to the bonfire. Cut to Mainwaring.

MAINWARING What on earth are you doing?

WILSON Well, you would insist on a ten-second pause.

Mainwaring joins them.

MAINWARING You stupid fools, you've destroyed that blanket entirely.

WILSON Actually it wasn't a blanket, it was an overcoat.

MAINWARING Whose was it?

FRAZER I don't know, sir, I definitely don't know.

MAINWARING Well, whoever it belongs to will have to pay for it. Everyone inside and pick up your overcoats – I'm going to get to the bottom of this.

INTERIOR. JONES' COMMAND POST

JONES That's it – three little puffs and a big puff. Right, I'll report to Headquarters and you go and find some wood and we'll brew up. There's a chopper on the wall there.

INTERIOR. FARMHOUSE

The squad are holding their overcoats. They are in three ranks.

MAINWARING I've had just about enough of this carelessness. Whoever it is should be on a charge. Now, who hasn't got an overcoat. **(He checks the ranks)** Rear rank – centre rank – front rank. **(Mainwaring turns to Wilson)** Don't tell me it's you, Wilson.

Wilson holds up his coat. Mainwaring realises that he is the only one without a coat.

MAINWARING Where did you put my coat?

WILSON On top of the pile, like you said. **(He reacts on turn)**

FRAZER It wasn't deliberate, sir, it definitely was not deliberate. I would like to say that, sir.

Cut to Mainwaring's reaction.

INTERIOR. JONES' COMMAND POST

JONES Hello, H.Q. quarters, I want to report that Captain Mainwaring and No. 1 Platoon are in position.

SANDBAGGED DUG OUT

SIGNALLER I see – where?

INTERIOR. JONES' COMMAND POST

JONES Ah – hang on. **(He takes a bit of paper out of his pocket)** At map reference six four one nine three seven.

SANDBAGGED DUG OUT

SIGNALLER You mean nine three seven six four one, don't you? Six four one nine three seven is the target for the 25-pounders.

INTERIOR. JONES' COMMAND POST

JONES Ah – well, yes, that'll be right. Anyway, they've taken up their strategic position.

SANDBAGGED DUG OUT

SIGNALLER T.T.F.N.

Jones exits.

FILM: EXTERIOR JONES' COMMAND POST

Godfrey is chopping a stick on a log – the phone wire goes across it.

JONES **(Out of vision)** Mr Godfrey.

GODFREY **(Turning)** Yes. **(He severs this wire, Jones joins him)**

JONES Here – this'll give you a laugh, Mr Godfrey. I've just been on the phone to H.Q. quarters. 'Captain Mainwaring in position six four one nine three seven,' I said. 'That's the target,' he says. I'd given him the wrong number. I'll forget my own name next.

GODFREY Six four one nine three seven is definitely where Captain Mainwaring went.

JONES Are you sure?

GODFREY Absolutely – I never forget a number. They wanted me to go into the accounts department you know – but I didn't fancy it.

JONES But if that's the target for the 25-pounders, they'll all be blown up.

GODFREY Oh dear.

JONES Don't panic, don't panic. I'll get on the blower and stop the firing – but don't panic.

Jones runs towards hut.

INTERIOR. JONES' COMMAND POST

Jones enters.

JONES Don't panic, don't panic. Stop the firing. (**He turns the handle of the phone**) Hello, hello. (**He turns the handle again**) Hello, hello. It's dead.

See Godfrey.

GODFREY Shall I run to H.Q.?

JONES I don't think we've got time for that.

GODFREY I can go quite swiftly if I have to.

JONES I don't know where it is even.

GODFREY We must warn Captain Mainwaring.

JONES That's right, that's what we must do – we must warn him – and we mustn't waste a minute – that's another thing we must do. Now let's see – it took them 40 minutes to march there. How long would it take us if we run?

GODFREY About an hour.

JONES The firing starts in half an hour. Don't panic – the firing starts in half an hour – we'll have to drive – that's it.

GODFREY But your van's broken.

JONES There's two cars outside, we can pack the whole platoon in them and take 'em away in them. You drive one, I'll drive the other.

GODFREY I can't drive.

JONES There's nothing to it, Mr Godfrey – I'll show you – you see, you switch on...

Godfrey follows and mimics the movements with great intensity.

JONES You pull the starter – twiddle the accelerator a little bit – first gear is there, second there, third's there and top's there. So you shove in the clutch, put the gear in first, then slowly, slowly let the clutch out. Not as slow as that. (**Godfrey pulls. They totter as they go through this motion**) That won't happen – you'll be sitting down. (**Godfrey sits**) Don't sit down now.

GODFREY Can we run through it again?

JONES Yes, well, you – look, I'll show you.

INTERIOR. FARMHOUSE

The platoon are sitting around idly.

PIKE Mr Mainwaring, what are we doing here?

MAINWARING We're denying this farmhouse to the enemy.

WALKER Beats me why he should want it, I wouldn't give you a fiver for it.

WILSON It does have a rather lovely view, don't you think?

MAINWARING It's the strategic importance that concerns us. Keep a good look out, Frazer.

FRAZER Aye, aye, sir.

FILM: EXTERIOR. JONES' COMMAND POST

Godfrey is in Walker's car – the engine is running – he jerks it and it stalls.

JONES It's no good – look, I tell you what – I'll tow you.

He runs out of shot.

GODFREY (**Calling after him**) You – you didn't explain about the steering.

FILM: EXTERIOR. RURAL BACKGROUND

ARTILLERY OFFICER Right, No. 6 Troop – load.

STOCK SHOT: 25-POUNDERS BEING LOADED

INTERIOR. FARMHOUSE

MAINWARING Nothing much is going to happen in the next few minutes, Wilson, so the men had better consume their haversack rations.

WILSON Very good, sir.

FRAZER Come on, lads – eat your sandwiches.

FILM: EXTERIOR

Jones and Godfrey. Jones is now in the colonel's car.

JONES Right, hang on, Mr Godfrey.

He moves off. Cut to long coil of rope unwinding.

GODFREY Mr Jones – which way do I turn the wheel?

He is jolted off.

Long shot of Jones towing Godfrey on the end of a long rope, hell for leather.

Mid shot of Jones elated.

Mid shot of Godfrey scared out of his wits – he turns the wheel wildly.

Long shot of the two cars – the rear car goes wildly from side to side off the road.

Mid shot of Jones.

JONES Don't worry, Mr Mainwaring, I'm coming.

Mid shot of Godfrey, desperately trying to drive. Long shot of cars approaching tree.

Jones is heading one side of the tree, Godfrey the other.

Godfrey is swung round and round the tree on the towing rope. Jones comes to a sudden halt and looks back in alarm. He gets out of the car and runs towards Godfrey.

Cut to Godfrey's car. Jones joins him.

GODFREY I think I'm beginning to get the hang of it now.

JONES Move over, I've got an idea.

Godfrey starts to move across. Jones goes to untie the rope.

GODFREY **(Looking at his watch)** We only have seven minutes according to my reckoning.

JONES We'd better hurry then, hadn't we, or Mr Mainwaring will get blown to Kingdom come.

INTERIOR. FARM HOUSE

MAINWARING It seems hard to believe there's a war on doesn't it, Wilson?

WILSON Yes, it's beautiful. Listen to that – isn't that a skylark?

MAINWARING Hmm, I believe it is. Better not fly too high – he'll get his feathers blown off. **(He turns to the troops)** Listen, you chaps, in a few minutes time the 25-pounders will open up and you'll hear the shells whistling overhead. It's quite a frightening noise but it's nothing to be scared about. These artillery boys know what they're doing.

FILM: EXTERIOR. RURAL BACKGROUND

ARTILLERY OFFICER Elevation 22 – right 9 degrees. Seven thousand yards.

STOCK SHOT: GUNS TRAINING ON TARGET

FILM: EXTERIOR

Jones in Walker's car – he passes the colonel's car and stops 100 yards ahead. He climbs out of the car. He grabs a scooter – he scoots back down the road. Godfrey is mystified. Jones arrives at the colonel's car, he throws the scooter into the back and climbs in. Godfrey is baffled. A sheep is baffled. Jones drives up the road. Jones passes Godfrey. Godfrey waves.

FILM: EXTERIOR

Jones gets out of the colonel's car and runs back – forgetting the scoote. He collects the scooter and scoots off. Mid shot of Godfrey looking at his watch.

GODFREY I wish there was something I could do to hasten matters.

FILM: EXTERIOR. RURAL BACKGROUND

Artillery Officer on the phone.

ARTILLERY OFFICER B troop on target and ready to fire, sir.

INTERIOR. FARMHOUSE

MAINWARING My, my, it really is quite warm.

WILSON Yes – you didn't need your overcoat after all.

Mainwaring reacts.

MAINWARING Two minutes to go – it will be interesting to see how our men react under fire.

WILSON Yes – what are they actually shooting at?

MAINWARING The area around a barn house.

WILSON What happens when all the shooting's over?

MAINWARING Well, that's the end of the exercise and we shan't be here to find out.

WILSON Seems rather pointless.

MAINWARING Yes – the brass hats may learn something, but I don't suppose we'll ever know what it was.

Walker enters from outside.

WALKER Here, who gave Jonesey permission to drive my car?

FILM: EXTERIOR. RURAL BACKGROUND

ARTILLERY CAPTAIN Right – stand by – one minute to go.

FILM: EXTERIOR. FARMHOUSE

Jones arrives with Godfrey – he gets out and rushes into the farm.

INTERIOR.FARMHOUSE

Jones enters, very out of breath.

MAINWARING Jones, what on earth's the matter?

JONES Captain Mainwaring – don't panic.

MAINWARING I've no intention of panicking.

JONES **(Between gasps)** Made mistake – map – farm barn – target for 25-pounders is yourselves – and you've got 45 seconds to leave, starting now.

He runs out.

MAINWARING Right, everybody in the cars.

They all rush out.

FILM: EXTERIOR. FARMHOUSE

They scramble into the cars – those that can't get inside, hang on the running board or luggage rack. Mainwaring hangs on beside Jones. Wilson, Pike and Frazer in the back of the same car. Godfrey in the front. Jones is driving. The ones in the back clutch the teddy bears that were on the seat. Long shot of two cars belting along road. Mid shot of Mainwaring.

MAINWARING Stop – make for cover.

Long shot as cars screech to halt.

FILM: RURAL BACKGROUND

Mid shot of artillery captain.

ARTILLERY CAPTAIN Fire!

STOCK SHOT: GUNS FIRING

FILM: EXTERIOR

Long shot of platoon diving for cover. Close up as shells shriek overhead. They put their heads down as the explosions start. Long shot of farmhouse ringed by explosion. Mid long shot of platoon cowering.

FILM: EXTERIOR. RURAL

ARTILLERY CAPTAIN Stop.

FILM: EXTERIOR

Mainwaring's and Wilson's heads come up.

WILSON Well, that seems to be all over.

MAINWARING **(Raising himself. He notices that he has flopped down in a patch of mud)** I'll have somebody's blood for this – look at my battle dress.

WILSON Yes, just as well you weren't wearing your overcoat, wasn't it, sir?

Mainwaring reacts.

SERIES FIVE **EPISODE SIX**

Recorded: Friday 30/6/72

Original transmission: Friday 10/11/72, 8.30–9.00pm

Original viewing figures = 15.5 million

(The working title for this episode was 'Turnabout')

ARTHUR LOWE	CAPTAIN MAINWARING
JOHN LE MESURIER	SERGEANT WILSON
CLIVE DUNN	LANCE CORPORAL JONES
JOHN LAURIE	PRIVATE FRAZER
JAMES BECK	PRIVATE WALKER
ARNOLD RIDLEY	PRIVATE GODFREY
IAN LAVENDER	PRIVATE PIKE
BILL PERTWEE	ARP WARDEN
CAMPBELL SINGER	MAJOR GENERAL MENZIES
ROBERT RAGLAN	COLONEL
EDWARD SINCLAIR	VERGER
ALEX MCAVOY	SERGEANT
DENNIS BLANCH	SECOND LIEUTENANT
PLATOON	COLIN BEAN, DESMOND CULLUM-JONES, EVAN ROSS, MICHAEL MOORE, FREDDIE WHITE, LESLIE NOYES, GEORGE HANCOCK, HUGH HASTINGS, HUGH CECIL, FREDDIE WILES
PIPER	PIPE MAJOR DONALD MACLEOD
EXTRA	(BARMAN) JAMES HASWELL

IF THE CAP FITS...

• PETER FITTON REMEMBERS •

'I have been working in television since 1962 in various capacities on well over 2000 programmes, ranging from *Jackanory* to *Mastermind.* I'm often asked which programme was the best to work on, and I can honestly say *Dad's Army* was the best without any shadow of a doubt; it's certainly the show I'm most proud to have been associated with.

'*Dad's Army* has proved over and over again to be timeless. Originally made some 34 years ago, the programmes are still being repeated and are now being enjoyed by an entirely new generation of viewers. Why this prolonged success? The scripts, the actors and a team of dedicated professionals behind the camera are the short answers.

'The longer answer is that the writers, Jimmy Perry and David Croft, had a different approach to their craft compared to most other writers because they wrote with specific actors in mind, as opposed to writing a script and then casting the actors.

'The sheer quality of the acting throughout the platoon, and the support team of Vicar, Verger and A.R.P. Warden, was terrific. Even the guest appearances of fine actors, such as Talfryn Thomas as the nosey local reporter and Philip Madoc as the U-Boat Captain stand out in my memory. Also, a young Wendy Richard (later to be a star in another Croft production, *Are You Being Served?* and, of course, *EastEnders*) appeared fairly regularly as Private Walker's girlfriend.

'I believe the quality of the acting was enhanced by the fact that most of the actors were performing caricatures of themselves. Arthur Lowe was, in my opinion, Captain Mainwaring in real life: a bumptious and pompous person, and I know he always thought of me as a "stupid boy". It started on the first day of outside rehearsal on my first episode. The process when a cast first comes together is to read through the script and see how much has to be deleted or added to make it run to time. This is followed by blocking the moves in a representation of the set laid out in a rehearsal room by the AFM. Arthur left his script on the table as everyone went home at the end of the day. Trying to create a good impression I ran after him with the script only to be dismissed with: "I have never taken a script home in my life and I'm not starting for you – good night!" I thought this was a very cavalier attitude to take, but I must admit to being impressed when he arrived the next day totally word perfect. He had to be the quickest study (learner of words) I ever worked with in over 30 years of making programmes.'

IF THE CAP FITS...

INTERIOR. SIDE OFFICE. DAY

Wilson is looking through a sheaf of papers – Mainwaring is standing by him. Jones is sorting through a box of lantern slides, the Verger is hovering round the slides.

MAINWARING Now listen, Wilson, I want you to read those notes out in a loud clear voice – do you understand?

WILSON Yes, sir – a loud, clear voice.

MAINWARING I don't want any mumbling.

WILSON Do I ever mumble, sir?

Mainwaring reacts.

MAINWARING Haven't you finished sorting out those slides yet, Jones?

JONES Not quite, sir – shan't be a tick. I'm very excited – we've never had a lecture like this before – that's what I like about you. Captain Mainwaring, you're always trying out new modern scientific methods.

MAINWARING I try to keep abreast with the times, Jones.

JONES There's no doubt about it – the magic lantern is a wonderful invention.

WILSON Yes, it's only been going a hundred years.

JONES Permission to speak, sir? I do not like the Verger creeping round me when I'm trying to sort out my slides.

The Verger is poking at the slides.

MAINWARING Do stop creeping around Jones when he's trying to get his slides sorted out, Verger.

VERGER I beg your pardon, Mr Mainwaring, I am not creeping.

JONES Yes you are, you're the biggest creeper I've ever met – you're a trouble maker and a creeper.

VERGER You're the trouble maker – I am just here on the instructions of the Vicar to keep an eye on his apparatus – and see that you don't abuse it when you use it.

JONES I won't abuse it when I use it.

VERGER And I'm going to see that you don't abuse it when you use it.

INTERIOR. CHURCH HALL. DAY

The platoon are sitting in front of a sheet that has been rigged up between two pairs of steps and a pole. On the left-hand side of the sheet is a table with two candles in holders on it. The lantern is set up behind the platoon, it is a very old-fashioned type. Walker, Frazer, Godfrey and Pike are sitting in the front. The blackouts are up and the lights on.

FRAZER It's a perfect disgrace. Stuck in here on a beautiful summer's evening like this, with the blackouts up.

PIKE They've got to be up, Mr Frazer – otherwise we won't be able to see the pictures.

FRAZER It's so unhealthy – you can cut the air in here with a knife. **(Pointing to Godfrey who is asleep)** Look at him – the silly old fool's in a deep coma.

WALKER Don't wake him up, Taff – he's tired out – he's been up all day.

FRAZER Come on, boys. **(He claps his hands and sings)** 'Why are we waiting?'

The others join in.

INTERIOR. SIDE OFFICE. DAY

MAINWARING What on earth's going on out there?

WILSON Sounds like Frazer's voice, sir.

Mainwaring crosses to the door and opens it.

MAINWARING I thought so – that will be quite enough of that, Frazer – we'll be out when we're ready – and not before. **(He crosses back)** Are the blackouts up, Wilson?

WILSON Yes, sir.

JONES **(Holding a slide up)** This isn't one of ours – it's a lot of Zulus dancing.

VERGER **(Snatching it)** That belongs to the Vicar – it's his lecture – 'Light into Darkest Africa'.

Wilson sniggers.

MAINWARING What are you sniggering at, Wilson?

WILSON I was just thinking, sir – 'Light into Darkest Africa' with the blackouts up.

MAINWARING Yes – well we'll go in shall we? Bring the slides, Jones.

JONES Yes, sir.

VERGER **(To Jones)** I shall be standing right beside you, to see that you don't put any slides in upside down.

JONES I won't put any slides in upside down.

VERGER And I'm going to see that you don't put any slides in upside down.

MAINWARING Oh come on.

INTERIOR. CHURCH HALL. DAY

Mainwaring and Wilson enter followed by Jones and the Verger. Jones is carrying the slides.

MAINWARING Right, settle down – settle down.

He crosses to the front of the screen. Wilson sits at the table with his notes.

MAINWARING Light the candles, Wilson – put the lights out, Pike. Now, the subject of my lecture is 'Know your Enemy'.

Wilson lights the candles. Pike crosses to the lights and turns them out.

MAINWARING Now, we shall show you pictures of Germans in uniform – and Sergeant Wilson will read out the notes on each one.

The lights are out and Wilson is sitting with the two candles alight – each side of him. He has his elbows on the table, the palms of his hands together and his eyes closed.

MAINWARING You're not in church, Wilson.

Wilson comes to.

MAINWARING Right, are you ready with the first slide, Jones?

JONES Yes, sir – all ready.

MAINWARING Ready to read out the notes, Sergeant?

WILSON **(He turns his face to Mainwaring – he has a monocle in his right eye)** Ready, sir.

Mainwaring looks again. Mainwaring turns and sees the monocle. He is unable to believe his eyes. He stares – Wilson stares back with an expressionless look. No one reacts to Wilson at all. Mainwaring stares, then pulls himself together.

MAINWARING First slide, please.

JONES Permission to speak, sir? Where's your clicker?

MAINWARING What are you talking about?

JONES Your clicker, sir – the little metal frog that you click when you want me to change the slide.

MAINWARING I haven't got one.

JONES Go and get the Vicar's clicker.

VERGER You're not having the Vicar's clicker.

JONES Would you mind saying click then?

MAINWARING That'll do. Just put the first slide in. Read on, Wilson.

A picture of a German infantry rifleman is thrown on screen.

WILSON Private. Infantry Rifleman. Front. Field grey uniform. National colours on right side of steel helmet.

MAINWARING **(Pointing with stick)** Now, here are some interesting points – you'll notice the eyes – mean – shifty – set too close together – typical Nazi – next slide.

JONES Click.

Picture of Private. Infantry Rifleman. Rear.

WILSON Private. Infantry Rifleman .Rear. German Eagle on left side of steel helmet.

MAINWARING Here's another very good point – you'll notice the nasty, fat, red, bull neck, bulging over the collar – a typical feature this – watch out for it. Next.

JONES Click.

A picture of Panzer Grenadier.

WILSON Panzer Grenadier. Light Machine Gunner.

MAINWARING I'd like to draw your attention to the ears – no lobes – this is a well known criminal trait.

They all feel their ears. Walker reacts.

PIKE Excuse me, sir – aren't there any nice looking Germans?

MAINWARING That will do, Pike –

WALKER Mr Mainwaring – what's that thing hanging down?

MAINWARING What thing?

WALKER That thing there.

MAINWARING (**Pointing**) What, that thing?

WALKER Yes, that thing.

MAINWARING What's that thing, Wilson?

WILSON I don't know, sir – it doesn't say.

JONES Permission to speak, sir? Perhaps it's the starting handle to a tank.

MAINWARING Yes – yes – possibly. Next slide.

JONES Click.

Picture of Cavalry Private. First Class.

WILSON Cavalry Private. First Class.

PIKE They're very smart, Mr Mainwaring.

MAINWARING I don't want any of that sort of talk, Pike. They're not smart at all – ersatz rubbish – fall to pieces in a few weeks – all for show and not for blow – not like our uniforms, plain – strong – sturdy – dependable – last for ever – made by British craftsmen.

They all look at their battledress.

MAINWARING Carry on, Wilson.

WILSON (**Reading in monotonous voice**) Cavalry serving in reconnaissance units of infantry divisions belong to the...

FRAZER Would you mind asking the sergeant to speak up? I canna hear a word he's saying – he's mumbling – mumbling.

MAINWARING Can't any of you hear?

ALL No.

Mainwaring crosses over to Wilson and whispers in his ear.

MAINWARING How can I possibly hold their attention, Wilson, if you speak in that boring way? You've got a very monotonous voice, you know.

Wilson reacts.

MAINWARING Try and make it go up and down.

WILSON (**Making his voice go up and down**) Cavalrymen serving in reconnaissance units of infantry divisions belong to the infantry arm. Infantry of an armoured division are designated...

MAINWARING All right, Wilson.

WILSON Was that up and down enough, sir?

MAINWARING Yes, all right. Now, you'll notice the dozy expression on his face – so unlike our own keen, alert... (**He notices Godfrey is asleep**) Wake up, Godfrey. Come on – be keen and alert.

GODFREY What... oh, I'm sorry, sir – it's very close in here.

MAINWARING Well, you'll just have to put up with it. You're on active service, remember.

Godfrey reacts.

MAINWARING Now, it's quite on the cards that the first Germans we shall meet will be parachutists – I want to show you several of these . Can we have the first parachutists please, Jones?

JONES Click.

Picture of a 2nd Lieutenant Parachutist in motor vehicle coat. It is upside down.

VERGER It's upside down – you've done it – I knew you'd put one in upside down.

JONES It's not upside down.

MAINWARING Of course it's upside down. It is upside down, isn't it, Wilson?

WILSON Definitely upside down, sir.

MAINWARING How do you know? You're not looking.

WALKER Jonesey could be right, Mr Mainwaring . Perhaps his parachute didn't open and he's landed on his head.

MAINWARING Don't be absurd, Walker. Put it in another way, Jones.

Jones puts it in the right way up.

JONES Click.

WILSON Parachutist 2nd Lieutenant. Parachutists may be expected to appear in overalls of colour suited to terrain and weather conditions.

PIKE Mr Mainwaring, why has he got such tiny little legs?

WALKER He hasn't got little legs – it's his uniform, it's low in the crutch.

MAINWARING Hmm... oh, I wouldn't say it was low – would you, Wilson?

WILSON Just a minute, I'll check. I'd certainly say it was low, sir.

Mainwaring reacts. Wilson returns to seat.

FRAZER Mr Mainwaring – stuffing.

MAINWARING I beg your pardon?

FRAZER Padding for protection.

WALKER In case he lands on iron railings.

JONES That's right, Joe. Don't forget, Mr Mainwaring – they don't like it up...

MAINWARING Thank you, Jones. Yes, you may have a point there, Walker.

GODFREY But all the iron railings have been taken for scrap.

MAINWARING Ah – but the Germans don't know that, Godfrey.

PIKE Where's his gun, sir?

WALKER Perhaps he left it in the plane when he jumped.

MAINWARING Walker, one more word out of you – and I shall order you to leave the lecture. Now, let's get on.

Hodges comes in.

HODGES Good evening, Napoleon.

MAINWARING What is it, Warden?

HODGES I want to have a word with the Verger.

VERGER I'm sorry, I can't see you now, Mr Hodges – I'm standing by to see that there is no incorrect use of the Vicar's apparatus.

HODGES What are you all doing – crouching in here with the blackouts up?

MAINWARING If you must know – I'm giving a lecture.

HODGES Come off it – you're looking at funny photos.

MAINWARING Funny photos!

HODGES Yeah – pin ups – girls with no...

MAINWARING Girls with no... How dare you suggest such a thing? Leave the hall at once.

HODGES I'm not going till I've seen the Verger.

MAINWARING Well, sit down and be quiet until we've finished – you may learn something. Next one.

WILSON German Navy – Admiral of the Line. The number of rings worn denote the rank.

MAINWARING Come on, Jones, let's have the slide.

JONES Sorry, sir – I've got in a bit of a muddle here.

MAINWARING Sort it out quickly.

JONES Yes, sir – yes, sir – it's all right, sir, I've got it now.

MAINWARING Read it out again, Wilson.

WILSON German Navy – Admiral of the Line. The number of rings worn denote the rank.

JONES Click.

Picture of an African giraffe-necked woman, with rings round her neck – she is bare from the waist up.

INTERIOR. SIDE OFFICE. DAY

Mainwaring and Wilson enter.

MAINWARING Close the door, Wilson.

Wilson closes the door.

MAINWARING Now look here, I didn't say anything to you out there just now – because I didn't want to show you up in front of the men.

WILSON I don't know what you're talking about, sir.

MAINWARING I'm referring to that absurd eye glass you were wearing – ridiculous, it makes you look like an advertisement for Sharps Toffee.

WILSON **(Holding it up)** I wear this monocle because I have a weak right eye – it's been bothering me for some time – I went to the opticians a couple of weeks ago, and he recommended it.

MAINWARING Weak right eye, my foot. Why can't you wear glasses like everyone else? Anyhow, sergeants aren't allowed to wear monocles – they're for officers only.

WILSON Show me where it says in Kings Regulations that sergeants aren't allowed to wear monocles.

MAINWARING I don't have to show you. I mean, who ever heard of a sergeant wearing a monocle?

WILSON If it comes to that – who ever heard of an officer wearing arch supports?

MAINWARING **(Rises)** You leave my feet out of this, Wilson.

WILSON Don't go on about my eyes – and I won't go on about your feet.

MAINWARING **(Sits)** Now, look here, don't let's be childish about this . Consider the hazards of wearing a monocle on active service – in your gas mask, for instance. What are you going to do if it falls out of your eye? You can't put it back – it will be rattling about inside.

Wilson reacts.

MAINWARING I can't have a sergeant of mine – with a monocle rattling about inside his gas mask. Besides it could block your air intake. Anyhow, Wilson...

There is a knock on the door.

MAINWARING Come in.

Frazer enters.

MAINWARING What is it, Frazer?

FRAZER Captain Mainwaring, sir – I'll come straight to the point – during the period we have been together, you have wasted hours of our precious time, and tonight's lecture was the last straw.

MAINWARING Now look here, Frazer...

FRAZER Let me finish. **(He takes out a notebook)** I've made a careful note of it all – on November 6th 1940 you wasted three hours giving us a lecture on 'Why the Germans don't play cricket'. On January 28th 1941, you gave us a lecture telling us how Hitler, when he's in a rage, bites the carpet.

MAINWARING It's a well known fact that he does.

FRAZER Maybe – then you proceeded to waste two hours working out a plan on 'How to send him a poisoned hearth rug'. According to my notes, it comes to a total of 438 hours wasted on useless blather. That's how I feel, and I had to come out with it to your face – no offence intended, you understand. That's all.

He rushes out, There is a pause. Mainwaring and Wilson look at each other.

MAINWARING I've… I've… never heard anything like it in all my life. It's rank insubordination.

WILSON Yes, it was rather strong.

MAINWARING Strong! I am sick and tired of Frazer's grumbling – he never stops – he's been a thorn in my side ever since this unit was first formed, every day he grumbles about something. Wait a minute – grumbling! Grumbling!

WILSON I beg your pardon, sir?

Mainwaring crosses to the bookshelf and takes out a Home Guard booklet.

MAINWARING **(Sits)** I've just remembered something I read in this Home Guard Manual last week. Where is it? Ah, here we are, 'Man Management': 'there is a sure cure for this form of unnecessary grousing, but a bad C.O. or N.C.O. may be afraid to try it. It is simply the temporary exchange of rank. Let the grumbler have a free hand to run the section or platoon, and learn for himself that it is not so easy.' Well, I'm not afraid to try it – we'll get the men together and I'll throw out the challenge. That'll soon put paid to Frazer's grumbling.

INTERIOR. CHURCH HALL. DAY

The platoon are drawn up on parade – Mainwaring is addressing them.

MAINWARING And so, in conclusion, I feel that I must say that of late I get the impression that there is, in the ranks, certain lack of confidence in my leadership.

JONES Permission to speak, sir? I wish to make a statement. I look at it this way – an officer is an officer, a sergeant is a sergeant, a lance corporal is a lance corporal and a private is a private.

MAINWARING What's that got to do with it?

JONES I don't know – but I thought I ought to say it.

MAINWARING Now I feel, that it isn't fair to blame the many for the errors of the few.

FRAZER Here, here.

MAINWARING I'm very glad you made that interruption, Frazer, because it just underlines the point I'm trying to make. You're the chief culprit.

FRAZER Me?

MAINWARING Yes – you. When it comes to grumbling and grousing and discontent, you're always at the bottom of it. I've only one thing to say to you, Frazer, and that applies to any of you. **(He turns and looks meaningfully at Wilson)** If you think you can run this platoon any better than I can – you're damn welcome to try for a couple of days – and you can take over now. **(To Wilson)** That's taken the wind out of his sails. **(There is a short pause)** Now, has anyone anything to say to that?

FRAZER Aye, I have.

MAINWARING What is it, Frazer?

FRAZER Give us your pips.

INTERIOR. SIDE OFFICE

Close up of Frazer's finger on the stock book. Pull back to reveal Frazer in Captain Mainwaring's pips with shirt collar and hat. He is addressing Wilson.

FRAZER You can't weadle your way out of it with me – there's a discrepancy – eight yards of four by two missing, and unaccounted for.

WILSON **(About to point to book)** Yes, but if you look at the over all…

FRAZER Stand to attention when you're addressing an officer.

Wilson straightens up.

WILSON Well, perhaps I gave the chaps a bit extra or something.

FRAZER Precisely. Inefficiency and extravagance or even maybe corruption. Well that's it, you're busted.

WILSON I beg your pardon?

FRAZER You heard me – you're busted. Get 'em off.

WILSON Get what off?

FRAZER Those stripes. I want those stripes, Private Wilson, and you can tell yon spiv fella to come in.

WILSON You – you can't treat me in this…

FRAZER You're dismissed. About turn. Left, right, left, right.

Wilson goes out – Frazer follows.

FRAZER You – Walker – in here.

Walker moves quickly into the office.

FRAZER **(Calling after Wilson)** I won't tolerate corruption and nepotism in my platoon. **(He turns back into the office)** You – would you like to be a sergeant?

WALKER What's in it for me?

FRAZER Well, there could be certain side benefits. Mutual advantages.

DRESSING ROOM. CHURCH HALL

This has been used for amateur shows by the scouts, guides, etc. Mainwaring has his eye glued to the door. He sees someone approach and hastily sits down, away from the door. Wilson enters.

MAINWARING **(Casually)** Ah – everything all right, Wilson?

WILSON That Frazer is really going too far.

MAINWARING I'm sure you can handle him.

WILSON He busted me.

MAINWARING He what?

WILSON He busted me. Reduced me to the ranks.

MAINWARING Ah – that's a good sign. Give him enough rope, Wilson, and he'll hang himself. What reason did he give for busting you?

WILSON Oh, some trifling discrepancy in the stores account. Eight yards of four by two – I mean, I ask you.

MAINWARING Well, I've warned you many times, you're far too lackadaisical in these matters.

WILSON Anyway, he told me in the most offensive manner, to get my stripes off, and, and I think you should do something about it.

MAINWARING Very well, I will.

WILSON Thank you, sir.

MAINWARING Give me those scissors.

INTERIOR. SIDE OFFICE

Frazer is dressing down Jones.

FRAZER All those ribbons cut no ice with me, Jones, so you might as well know where you stand from the start. I think you're a woolly minded old ditherer.

JONES **(Outraged)** Woolly minded old ditherer!

FRAZER Aye, well, at least your hearing's sound.

JONES Well, if that's what you think, I'm resigning. I wouldn't soldier under you, not if the King himself asked me. I shall reduce myself down to the ranks with immediate effect from now.

FRAZER Good riddance to you.

JONES **(At door)** And you needn't come round to my shop asking for any sausages, because you won't get none.

Frazer reacts.

INTERIOR. CHURCH HALL

Pike and Godfrey are in a group with the platoon.

GODFREY The trouble is, I don't trust Captain Frazer. Captain Mainwaring is a gentleman, and officers should always be gentlemen.

PIKE Well, I think he ought never to have let Captain Frazer take over, even if it is only for 48 hours.

FRAZER **(Off)** Pike.

PIKE Oh golly.

INTERIOR. DRESSING ROOM. CHURCH HALL

MAINWARING I'm sorry, Wilson, you'll just have to get on parade and soldier on as a private.

WILSON But he'll be rude to me, and I cannot stand people being rude to me. My heart pounds terribly and I have to sit down.

MAINWARING You don't sit down when I'm rude to you.

WILSON Well – I don't take any notice of you.

Mainwaring reacts.

Jones enters.

JONES I'm sorry, Mr Mainwaring – I'd go through fire and brimstone and treacle for you. **(Mainwaring reacts)** But I cannot serve under a common man. I've resigned my non-commission.

Mainwaring reacts.

MAINWARING Sit down, Corporal. There you are, Wilson – he's playing into our hands.

WILSON How do you make that out?

MAINWARING He's turning the platoon against him. No one will serve under him and then, of course, he's done for.

Pike puts his head round the door.

PIKE Uncle Sergeant – shall I tell Mum you'll be round for supper, because Captain Frazer says I can go home now with the good news?

MAINWARING Good news – what good news?

PIKE Captain Frazer says I've got hidden qualities of drive, tenacity and leadership, so he's given me this. **(He shows a stripe on his arm)**

Walker pushes through – wearing his sergeant's stripes.

WALKER Ah – Captain Frazer says Private Wilson and Private Jones can have the rest of the day off to recover, but he expects you both tomorrow at 6.30 sharp. (**To Mainwaring**) Oh, and can he have your gloves and stick?

Mainwaring reacts and rises.

INTERIOR. SIDE OFFICE

Frazer is seated at the desk – Godfrey is standing.

FRAZER Sit down, take the weight off your feet.

GODFREY Thank you.

FRAZER Now, my dear friend, in the past I've said some harsh things to you – all for your own good, mind – but no doubt they hurt.

GODFREY Well – I never thought you meant them unkindly.

FRAZER Precisely – I'm a simple man, I speak my mind and what's in this hard old Scottish heart. But now that I'm in charge, you need have no fears. I sympathise with you.

GODFREY That's very kind of you.

FRAZER If you're feeling off colour, or it's your day for the clinic, don't worry about it. Just don't bother to come in at all. (**This latter phrase with a bite**)

GODFREY Oh – oh that's very understanding of you.

FRAZER But if you do come in, you do what the others do, or take the consequences. So now you know where you stand.

There is a knock at the outside door.

FRAZER Come in.

A Major General Menzies enters – he is 45 to 50 and a Scot – Frazer sees him, sees his red hat and rises.

FRAZER Squad, 'shun. (**He salutes**)

GENERAL Ah, good morning – are you the commander of this unit?

FRAZER Aye, that I am.

GENERAL My name's Menzies – I've taken over the area command.

FRAZER I'm glad they've had the sense to put a Scotsman in charge.

GENERAL Where are you from?

FRAZER The Isle of Barra, it's a wild and lonely place, you understand. The life is hard and so are the men.

GENERAL That's the sort we need these days.

GODFREY D'you think I could go now?

FRAZER Yes, away you go, Godfrey.

GODFREY And thank you for being so considerate… I think. (**He gives a weak salute and goes**)

GENERAL How are things with the unit?

FRAZER Well, to be frank, it's been a terrible day. My sergeant's been on the fiddle, my corporal's incompetent, so I've busted them both.

GENERAL I see. Can you replace them?

FRAZER It's already done.

GENERAL Well, obviously everything's under control here.

FRAZER Aye, it is that.

The general goes to the door and turns.

GENERAL D'you play the pipes, Captain?

FRAZER That I do.

GENERAL I'm planning a highland get-together at H.Q. Officers' Mess, I'd be delighted if you'd join in.

FRAZER It'd be a rare honour.

GENERAL Good – I'll send an invitation. Meanwhile, carry on the good work.

FRAZER Aye, I will, sir.

GENERAL Goodbye, Captain Mainwaring.

General salutes and goes.

FRAZER (**Realising his mistake**) Mainwaring – oh dear – oh dear – oh dear.

INTERIOR. OFFICERS' MESS. DAY

Home Guard colonel is talking to the general over a drink.

COLONEL I'm glad Mainwaring impressed you – he's a good man – but I must say I never knew he played the bagpipes.

GENERAL He certainly does – he told me with his own lips.

COLONEL To tell the truth, I didn't even know he was a Scot. Mainwaring isn't a Scottish name, is it?

GENERAL Perhaps it used to be MacMainwaring and they dropped the Mac.

SUBALTERN Perhaps it wasn't raining.

They both kill him with a look.

COLONEL Go and read a comic or something, boy.

GENERAL Anyway, I thought we could get him and his unit across so that he can pipe in the haggis.

COLONEL My, my, I haven't seen that for years.

GENERAL Precisely, so lay it on, will you?

COLONEL Yes, sir. Captain Mainwaring will pipe in the haggis.

INTERIOR. SIDE OFFICE. DAY

Mainwaring is at his desk, Wilson knocks and enters.

WILSON The men are all waiting in rows, sir.

MAINWARING I presume you mean in ranks. (**He crosses to door. Turns**) How are they?

WILSON Well – we're all rather relieved that things are back to normal and that you're in command again, sir.

MAINWARING Naturally – but I think Frazer's learned his lesson.

WILSON I hope we all have.

Mainwaring goes into hall.

INTERIOR. CHURCH HALL. DAY

MAINWARING Squad, 'shun. (**Jones is late**) Right, stand at ease. Well, now things are back to normal, men, I'm sure you'd like me to thank Frazer for making such a spirited attempt to run the platoon. I'm sure he now realises some of the problems involved and no doubt is very relieved to be a squaddy again.

FRAZER (**About to contradict**) Captain Mainwaring…

MAINWARING No talking in the ranks, Frazer.

WALKER I think Captain Frazer made a very good job of it, considering.

PIKE I'd like to second that.

JONES And I'd like to unsecond it.

PIKE Mind you, I think I prefer Captain Mainwaring to Captain Frazer.

WALKER For some things.

GODFREY He's more gentlemanly than Captain Frazer.

MAINWARING Yes, well, it's all over now and I'm sure we've all benefited from the experience. Now, quite out of the blue, we have received an invitation from Major General Menzies.

FRAZER Menzies!

MAINWARING Pardon?

FRAZER It's pronounced Menzie.

MAINWARING Is it? Good. Well, General Menzies has invited us to take part in the ceremonial piping of the haggis. I think you'll agree that the general is showing us a great honour by selecting us for this ancient ritual.

FRAZER It happened this way, sir. The general was very impressed –

MAINWARING I've told you before, Frazer, I will not have talking in the ranks.

FRAZER Yes, sir.

MAINWARING Now, I want you all to be especially well turned out. Every eye will be upon us.

FRAZER I think you ought to know, Captain Mainwaring –

MAINWARING For the last time, Frazer – stop talking.

FRAZER Very well – but upon your own head be it.

INTERIOR. MESS ANNEXE. DAY

It is a panelled room of an old barracks. There is a small door to the main building and two large, double, panelled doors to the mess dining hall. The colonel of the Home Guard is waiting impatiently in service dress with Sam Brown. There is a knock - a sergeant in a kilt enters.

SERGEANT Escort party outside, sir.

COLONEL Good, show them in.

SERGEANT (**To Mainwaring off**) You may go in, sir.

Mainwaring enters, followed by the platoon.

COLONEL Good evening, Mainwaring.

MAINWARING Sorry we're late, our transport developed a fault. Anyway, I hope the general will forgive us.

COLONEL Unfortunately he's been called to the War Office for a briefing, but he wants us to go ahead. I'll join the other officers, now you've arrived, and the sergeant here will fill you in on the ceremony.

SERGEANT I will, sir.

The colonel goes.

SERGEANT Now, first we need a bearer for this. (**He takes up a round silver salver on which reposes the haggis**)

JONES I would like to volunteer, sir, to bear that – I would enjoy it and consider it an honour also as well.

SERGEANT It should be a sergeant, sir, by rights.

MAINWARING Very well – will you be the bearer, Wilson?

WILSON Yes, sir, I'd absolutely love to.

SERGEANT Then we need two men on the doors, here.

MAINWARING Frazer, Walker.

FRAZER/WALKER Yes, sir.

SERGEANT The escort goes two abreast behind. Now, once inside, it's twice round the table and then present the haggis to the President. Is that clear?

MAINWARING I think so.

SERGEANT I'll go inside and, when they're ready, I'll give you three loud tappies with my pace stick on yon portal. That's the signal for the party to advance with the haggis. Is that plain?

MAINWARING Quite plain, thank you.

SERGEANT Very good, sir – here's the pipes. (**He hands Mainwaring bagpipes**)

MAINWARING Ah, good – is the colonel going to play them in?

SERGEANT No – you are.

MAINWARING Me?

SERGEANT Of course, that's why you're here, isn't it? (**He goes through doors**)

FRAZER Now will you let me speak? It was me the general invited – me because of the way I was handling the platoon.

MAINWARING Indeed.

FRAZER Now you're sunk, Captain Mainwaring, and there's only one thing you can do – let me go in at the head of my platoon – playing the pipes, and let me take the credit I deserve.

Three knocks sound on the door.

FRAZER There go the knocks – they're sounding your doom – nemesis has struck.

MAINWARING Get back in the ranks, Private Frazer.

FRAZER You're a bigger fool than I thought.

Frazer goes back to his place. Mainwaring puts his mouth to his mouthpiece and starts to blow – the warming up sound commences.

WILSON Are you absolutely sure you're doing the right thing, sir?

MAINWARING I was relief manager at Invergeikie for a whole winter. 'Tis a wild and lonely place, you understand. The nights were long and there was nothing else to do.

Playing the appropriate lament, Mainwaring leads the men in.

FRAZER (**As Mainwaring passes him**) Never doubted you could do it, sir – never for a moment, not for a single moment.

SERIES FIVE **EPISODE SEVEN**

Recorded: Friday 23/6/72

Original transmission: Friday 17/11/72, 8.30–9.00pm

Original viewing figures = 16 million

ARTHUR LOWE . . . . CAPTAIN MAINWARING
JOHN LE MESURIER . . . . SERGEANT WILSON
CLIVE DUNN . . . . LANCE CORPORAL JONES
JOHN LAURIE . . . . PRIVATE FRAZER
JAMES BECK . . . . PRIVATE WALKER
ARNOLD RIDLEY . . . . PRIVATE GODFREY
IAN LAVENDER . . . . PRIVATE PIKE
BILL PERTWEE . . . . ARP WARDEN
FRANK WILLIAMS . . . . VICAR
EDWARD SINCLAIR . . . . VERGER
WENDY RICHARD . . . . SHIRLEY
COLIN BEAN . . . . PRIVATE SPONGE
PLATOON . . . . DESMOND CULLUM-JONES, MICHAEL MOORE, GEORGE HANCOCK, LESLIE NOYES, HUGH HASTINGS, EVAN ROSS, HUGH CECIL, FREDDIE WILES, FREDDIE WHITE
WARDENS . . . . CLIFFORD HENSLEY AND HARRY DAVIES
STUNTMAN . . . . TOM ATKINS

THE KING WAS IN HIS COUNTING HOUSE

• PETER FITTON REMEMBERS •

'For me, this episode was a bit of a nightmare in the studio and on location. In the studio, after the bomb had hit the bank, the platoon brought the money back to the church hall to count. Seems simple enough until you appreciate the real problem with props that *Dad's Army* caused the property buyer and myself. Wartime props have not been very well collected and it's much easier finding something for a Victorian piece than getting World War II memorabilia. For example, pencils in the war had no colouring on them so we had to scrape all the colour off modern pencils to achieve the correct look.

'We needed a lot of money to make it look realistic. You can cheat with paper money by putting one note on the top and another on the bottom of any pile and make it look realistic, but if you have to count it in a close-up shot then blank pieces of paper don't look so good. Likewise with coins. Unfortunately for me, the script called for Corporal Jones (who else?) somehow to get the cloth, on which the money was being counted, caught in his trousers. When he got up from the table and moved away, all the hard work of counting was ruined when the money went everywhere. A funny scene, but the money fell all over the studio set and under the audience seating, managing to hide away in some very strange places. Amazingly, I think we were only a few pence out at the end of recording.

'Location work is much harder for everyone because you are away from the safe haven of Television Centre and London, where you can find almost everything round the clock. Also, it isn't easy finding a toilet in the middle of military land, especially when the cast is demanding one.

'We had to build our own little camp with location catering and a honey-wagon (U.S. Air Force slang for a toilet) along with all the other paraphernalia, like dressing rooms, make-up area, an armoury, first aid, crew transport and somewhere dry to go if it rained.

'My most difficult moment came in the last location shot of the episode. Mainwaring and the platoon had put all the money in a laundry basket and Walker had found a horse and cart to transport it to another branch of the bank. Arthur insisted that he drove the horse and cart and didn't want a double; to this day, I don't think he had ever driven such a vehicle before. There was no problem, however, as it was a wide open space. But for one AFM, who was inside the laundry basket, so as money could be scattered across the horizon, it was a very frightening experience. In complete darkness and cramped conditions, driving over rough ground at a speed I hadn't been expecting, proved to be something I shall never forget!'

The King was in his Counting House

INTERIOR. OFFICE. BANK. DAY

Mainwaring is seated at desk – he is on phone.

MAINWARING Yes, Elizabeth… no, Elizabeth… good, that's settled then… I've told them all to be round at the house at eight o'clock tonight… just a few sandwiches and some beer… that should get them all in a convivial mood… you don't think we ought to give them any beer… we've got to give them something to drink, dear… no, of course they won't get drunk and start smashing the house up… my men are not hooligans, Elizabeth. (**There is a knock on the door**) Come in. (**Wilson enters**) What, dear… no – don't wear your fringed dress – it makes you look too much like a flapper. (**Wilson reacts**) No, I shouldn't think they'd mind if you wore your siren suit – after all, Winston Churchill wears one… very well, dear, goodbye.

WILSON Making the final plans for the party tonight, sir?

MAINWARING Yes, just checking to see that the little woman's got everything under control.

WILSON I must say, I'm looking forward to it. Do you know this will be the first time that I've visited your house?

MAINWARING Well, we haven't done much entertaining since the war started – and I thought the time has come for the platoon to get together in civilian clothes and meet on equal terms.

WILSON That's very democratic of you, sir.

MAINWARING Of course, I realise that it's even more difficult for you, Wilson – as your superior here at the bank – and your commanding officer in the platoon – we don't get much chance to meet as equals.

WILSON No we don't, sir.

MAINWARING However, tonight you may call me George.

WILSON Thank you, sir.

MAINWARING And I shall call you Arthur.

There is a knock on the door.

MAINWARING Come in.

Pike enters.

PIKE Here are the letters for you to sign, sir.

He puts the letters on Mainwaring's desk.

MAINWARING Thank you, Pike.

PIKE I'm looking forward to the party tonight, Uncle Arthur.

WILSON So am I. George has just been telling me all about it.

PIKE Who's George?

MAINWARING (**Hissing at Wilson**) I said you could call me George at the party, Wilson – not here.

WILSON I'm sorry, sir – slip of the tongue.

PIKE Can I call you George at the party, Mr Mainwaring?

MAINWARING Certainly not.

WILSON Something's just occurred to me, sir. What's going to happen tonight if the balloon goes up?

PIKE Are we having balloons at the party?

MAINWARING Of course not, you stupid boy. You've no need to worry, Wilson, I've made adequate provision for that – number two and three sections will remain on duty at the church hall. I must say, I'm looking forward to it enormously – all of us, together in civilian clothes – in a nice, happy, relaxed, carefree atmosphere.

INTERIOR. MAINWARING'S HOUSE. NIGHT

The sitting room. Jones, Wilson, Frazer, Godfrey and Pike are standing in a group in front of the fireplace. They are ill at ease. Mainwaring is standing in the middle, also uncomfortable. They are all in civilian clothes.

MAINWARING Yes, well… er… it was nice of you all to come.

WILSON It was nice of you to ask us er… George.

The others all react.

FRAZER Aye… very nice.

GODFREY Er… very nice indeed.

Pause.

PIKE It's a lovely party, Mr Mainwaring.

JONES Yes, I'm enjoying myself, sir – definitely.

MAINWARING Oh please – please – George.

JONES My name's not George, sir – it's Jack.

MAINWARING No, no – I want you to call me George… er, Jack. (**To Wilson**) I say, look at the time, Arthur, Joe's late.

FRAZER He's probably up to some shady business.

MAINWARING Now – now, don't judge him too hastily, Fra…, Jay…, er Jim… er. (**Frazer makes no attempt to help him, but just glares**) Well, my wife will be down in a moment and then we can start on the refreshments.

GODFREY I must say I'm looking forward to meeting your good lady, sir… George.

FRAZER (**Hissing at Godfrey**) Sir George. He hasn't been knighted yet.

The front door bell rings.

MAINWARING I expect that's Joe – let him in, Pike.

PIKE Yes, Mr Mainwaring. **(He goes)**

MAINWARING **(To Frazer)** Well Jay... er James, how's business?

FRAZER I canna complain – I had a lady in today who ordered one of my best oak coffins – her husband dropped down dead – like that. **(He snaps his fingers)** Just about your age and build he was – went out like a light.

The door opens, Pike comes in followed by Walker and a flashy girl in her twenties.

PIKE Joe Walker and lady friend.

WALKER Evening all – this is Shirley.

SHIRLEY Pleased to meet you, I'm sure.

FRAZER **(Muttering to Jones)** Trust Joe to turn up with a tart.

MAINWARING Yes, well er... if you'll excuse me, I'll just go up and see how my wife's getting on. **(As he goes, he draws Walker to one side and whispers to him)** What did you want to bring that girl for, Walker? I told you this was stag.

WALKER Well your missus is going to be here – I thought she might like to meet her.

MAINWARING I hardly think that's likely.

SHIRLEY **(Looking across at them)** What's this? Secret?

MAINWARING Excuse me. **(He goes)**

WALKER Blimey, what's the matter with you all? You look like an undertaker's convention.

SHIRLEY Who are all these old men, Joe? You said it was going to be a lively party.

WALKER Don't worry, luv – it will warm up.

FRAZER **(Looking round)** Well, I must say, I'd have thought he'd have a better place than this – I've never seen such a lot of rubbish – there's nothing here worth twopence.

PIKE This is nice. **(He picks up a small glass bulb with a snow scene inside, which is on the mantelpiece)**

GODFREY We've got one of those at home – they're very pretty – you shake them hard and they make a snow storm.

PIKE What, like this? **(He shakes it)** So it does, look. **(He holds it up)** Look, Uncle Arthur.

WILSON Yes, awfully nice, Frank.

Pike shakes it again – the bottom drops out on to the carpet – he is left with the bulb in his hand.

JONES You've done it now, Pikey – Mr George will be furious.

PIKE What am I going to do, Uncle Arthur?

WILSON I don't know. Why can't you leave things alone?

WALKER **(Crossing to Pike and taking the bulb)** 'Ere, give it to me. **(He crosses to the goldfish bowl and fills it up – he crosses back to Pike and gives it to him)**

PIKE Thanks, Joe. **(He takes it and gets down on the carpet, which has a deep pile. He starts picking at it)**

WILSON What are you doing, Frank?

PIKE I'm trying to pick the snow up.

JONES There's no time for that now – I can hear him coming – quick, put it back.

Pike quickly screws the bottom into the bulb and puts it back on the mantelpiece. The door opens and Mainwaring returns.

MAINWARING Everyone enjoying themselves?

JONES Yes, Pikey and I was having a...

MAINWARING My wife may be a few more minutes – so I think we'll start without her.

He crosses over to the table – on it there are two pint bottles of beer – some wine glasses and a plate of small sandwiches.

MAINWARING Hand the sandwiches round, Arthur.

WILSON Oh yes... right, George.

MAINWARING Beer everyone?

They all nod and he starts to pour. Wilson hands the plate round. After they each take one, there are just three small ones left on the plate.

MAINWARING Don't stand on ceremony – tuck in.

They each finish their sandwiches in two bites.

FRAZER I wish his wife would hurry up and come down – the sooner we get this ridiculous charade over, the better.

WALKER I can't wait to meet her – I wonder what she looks like.

PIKE I've only spoken to her on the phone at the bank – she sounds awfully cross.

JONES Mr Wilson's the only one who's met her.

WALKER What's she like?

WILSON Well she's... er she's... sort of... **(He gestures vaguely – there is a loud knock on the front door)** Answer the door, Frank.

PIKE Yes, Uncle Arthur. **(He goes)**

WALKER Well, go on, tell us.

GODFREY I think it's very caddish to talk about Mr Mainwaring's wife like this – I'm sure she's a charming woman.

WILSON Godfrey's quite right, you'll just have to wait until she comes down.

We can hear Hodges the Warden shouting in the hall.

WILSON What on earth's that?

The door opens and Hodges bursts in, followed by Pike.

HODGES What's going on here?

PIKE We're having a party, Mr Hodges.

HODGES Where's Mainwaring?

WILSON He's upstairs with his wife.

HODGES Oh, it's one of those sort of parties, is it?

WILSON How dare you burst into a private house like this?

HODGES Don't give me that, mate – I saw a light flash from upstairs.

WILSON Why were you hanging about outside the house?

HODGES I wasn't doing anything of the sort.

JONES Yes, it's a funny coincidence that you happened to be passing just at that moment.

PIKE **(Looking up stairs through open door)** They're coming down now.

FRAZER I can't wait to see what this woman looks like.

PIKE Neither can I.

Mainwaring enters.

MAINWARING She's just on her way. **(He breaks off as he sees Hodges)** What do you want, Warden?

HODGES You were showing a light.

MAINWARING If you must know, my wife inadvertently stumbled against it, the blackout curtain.

WARDEN Aye, aye, been at the bismuth.

MAINWARING **(He calls out through the half-open door in a soothing voice)** Come along, dear – we're all waiting.

We hear heavy footsteps coming down the stairs – they all look at each other in anticipation – the steps get nearer – suddenly the sirens go – the footsteps charge down the rest of the stairs along the hall – we hear the back door slam.

MAINWARING **(Shouting after her)** Elizabeth, say hello first. **(He turns back to men)** I'm afraid she's gone down in the shelter.

FRAZER **(To Pike)** Now we shall never know what she looks like.

HODGES Well, I'm off to report to Headquarters. You lot are not going to stand around here with a raid on, are you?

MAINWARING What we do is our own affair – it's probably a solitary plane – the last twitchings of the wounded Nazi beast.

There is a loud explosion – they all dive for the floor – Walker pulls Shirley under the table. There are two more explosions, followed by silence.

INTERIOR. SIDE OFFICE. CHURCH HALL. NIGHT

The Vicar and Verger are squashed under the desk.

VICAR There's not room for two of us under this desk, Verger – this is my hidey hole.

VERGER You wouldn't drive me out in to the fire and tempest would you, Your Reverence?

VICAR I can't stand being squashed with other people in small spaces. Oh, where's Captain Mainwaring? At a time like this he should be here.

INTERIOR. MAINWARING'S HOUSE. NIGHT

Mainwaring, Wilson, Jones, Frazer, Godfrey, Pike and Hodges are all crouching on the floor – Hodges is on the phone.

WILSON Don't you think we ought to get down to the church hall, sir? There's only Private Sponge in charge of the platoon.

MAINWARING I want to find out where those bombs fell –

HODGES Hullo, Gerald – where did that lot come down? **(He gets out his notebook and pencil)** One on the allotments, right – one on the taxi garage – no casualties, right. Where was the third one? I see – that's a bit of luck – good job it was closed – right-oh – I'm coming in now. **(He hangs up)**

MAINWARING Good job what was closed?

HODGES The bank.

MAINWARING The bank!

HODGES Yes – got one right on it.

JONES There's a bomb on the bank – there's a bomb on the bank – don't panic! Don't panic!

MAINWARING Quiet, Jones – come on, we must get down there right away. **(He crosses to the sideboard – opens the drawer, takes out his revolver and straps it on)** Right, Jones – Frazer – Godfrey –Pike – Walker – where's Walker?

Walker pokes his head out from under the tablecloth.

WALKER I'm here, sir.

MAINWARING Come out at once.

WALKER It's not safe out there.

SHIRLEY **(Poking her head out)** It's not safe under here either.

WILSON But there's nothing of any value in the bank, sir.

MAINWARING What are you talking about, Wilson – there's over £96, 000 in the vaults.

WILSON No bomb could get through that concrete, sir.

MAINWARING Let's hope you're right. Come on.

WALKER He's watered it.

INTERIOR. THE VAULTS. NIGHT

The vaults are in ruins – the ceiling is open to the sky – the moon is giving a fair amount of light – money is scattered everywhere. Mainwaring and Wilson are standing side by side. Frazer, Pike, Jones, Godfrey and Walker and Shirley are in a tight group round them – Mainwaring and Wilson are both holding torches – Hodges and two Wardens are clambering over the ruins.

WALKER Blimey, look at all that lovely lolly.

MAINWARING Pike – guard that door.

FRAZER Keep an eye on that hole.

WILSON What are we going to do?

MAINWARING Well, for a start, I'm not having Hodges and his men poking about with all that money lying around. We don't need you, Hodges, you can go.

HODGES **(Clambering over to Mainwaring)** What are you talking about? This is an A.R.P. matter – you shouldn't be here, so clear out.

MAINWARING How dare you? This is my bank and I'm responsible for the money in it. Now, are you going or not?

HODGES No.

MAINWARING Right. **(He draws his revolver)** Come on, out – out.

HODGES How dare you point a gun at me? What do you think we are?

MAINWARING For all I know, you could be looters.

HODGES Looters!

MAINWARING Well, potential looters – and in war time I've every right to shoot you – now, get out.

PIKE That's right, Mr Mainwaring – shoot him.

HODGES All right – all right – come on, men – you haven't heard the last of this, Napoleon **(They go)**

MAINWARING Now, we've got to get all this money together and take it to a place that's secure – where we can keep an eye on it.

JONES Permission to speak, sir? I've got an idea – why don't we gather all the money up and take it to a place that's secure – where we can keep an eye on it?

MAINWARING Thank you, Jones. We'll take it down to the church hall.

WILSON There's just one thing that's occurred to me, George.

MAINWARING We're not at the party now, Wilson.

WILSON I'm sorry, sir – what I was going to say was – what are we going to carry it in?

MAINWARING Yes, that's a problem.

FRAZER I can let you have a box from my funeral parlour, sir – but someone will have to come and help me empty it.

MAINWARING No, I don't think so, Frazer.

GODFREY Er, my sister Dolly always keeps her money in a mattress – perhaps we could get one and pull all the stuffing out.

PIKE I've got an idea, Mr Mainwaring. Why don't we get the curtains and poles out of your office and put all the money in that.

MAINWARING Good thinking, Pike. Go and get them.

Pike goes.

SHIRLEY I've had enough, I'm off.

MAINWARING You're doing nothing of the sort, young lady. You're staying here. I need all the help I can get.

SHIRLEY If I clamber all over this rubble – I'll ladder my stockings.

WALKER Never mind, luv – I'll get you a new pair.

SHIRLEY That's what you said the last time we were on a bomb site together.

INTERIOR. CHURCH HALL. NIGHT

Sponge and the rest of the platoon are gathered in a bunch round the stage, chatting. They have their rifles with them. The Vicar and Verger are talking to Sponge.

VICAR But Captain Mainwaring should be here when there's a raid on.

SPONGE It's no use going on at me, Vicar – all I know is that Mr Mainwaring is giving a party tonight and he's left me here in charge.

VICAR A party at a time like this! What has got into him?

VERGER I've seen this coming on for a long time, your reverence. The power's gone to his head – he's succumbed to the flesh pots.

Vicar reacts. The door opens – Mainwaring, Wilson, Jones and Frazer stagger in. They are carrying two curtain poles – with a curtain slung between full of money. The Vicar and Verger run over to him.

VICAR Where have you been, Captain Mainwaring?

MAINWARING I haven't got time to discuss it now, Vicar – the bank's been bombed. All right, tip it on the floor gently.

They tip all the money in a huge pile – it consists of bundles of notes – loose notes – and a large quantity of copper and silver.

Walker, Pike, Godfrey and Shirley stagger in with a second bundle.

MAINWARING Right, put it on top.

They tip it on top of the pile.

MAINWARING How much money did we have in the vaults, Wilson?

WILSON According to the books, sir – £96, 478 11s 4d.

MAINWARING Right, what we've got to do now, Wilson, is to count it. Perhaps you and the Verger would like to help us, Vicar?

VICAR Certainly not – I wouldn't soil my hands with it.

VERGER That's right, Vicar – drive them out like the money changers in the temple. Fancy suggesting that we should check money on Church property.

JONES Is that why you always count the collection in the bar of The Red Lion?

VERGER How dare you?

VICAR Well, get this money out of here as soon as you can. Come on, Mr Yeatman. (**They both go**) Why do you count the collection in the bar of The Red Lion?

VERGER The landlord helps me – two heads are better than one.

MAINWARING (**To Shirley**) All right, young lady – you can go – I shan't need you any more.

SHIRLEY Blimey – you've got a cheek.

MAINWARING I beg your pardon?

SHIRLEY You're just like all men – you use girls, and when you don't want them any more you cast them off.

MAINWARING See to her will you, Walker?

WALKER Come on, Shirl – I'll walk you to the door.

SHIRLEY (**To Mainwaring**) You old men are worse than the young ones.

MAINWARING (**To Wilson**) I think I shall have a word with Walker about the company he keeps, Wilson.

WILSON I didn't know you were interested in girls, George.

MAINWARING How dare you? And for the last time will you stop calling me by my Christian name.

WILSON I'm sorry, sir, but you started it – I just can't get out of the habit.

MAINWARING Go and tell Sponge that I shall need him and the rest of the platoon to guard this money while we're counting it. Maximum security – do you understand? Maximum security.

WILSON Yes, sir, maximum security.

He goes – Walker returns.

MAINWARING Hurry up, Walker. What have you been doing?

WALKER Well, with all this money about, sir – I thought I'd better search her.

MAINWARING Now, pay attention, men – this money has got to be counted.

WALKER Blimey, that's going to take us all night.

JONES Permission to speak, sir? I should like to volunteer to be a counter, sir – let me be a counter.

MAINWARING Very well, Jones.

Wilson returns.

WILSON I'm afraid we've got a bit of a problem, sir. Sponge is sulking.

MAINWARING What do you mean, Sponge is sulking?

WILSON Well, he and the rest of the platoon say they don't mind doing normal Home Guard duties – but they don't see why they should guard your money.

Mainwaring looks across at them. Sponge and the others are all in a tight group – muttering and looking at him.

MAINWARING What's got into them?

WILSON They're upset because you didn't ask them to the party.

MAINWARING Really, how can they be so childish? Look, tell them I'll give them a party next week.

WILSON Yes, sir. (**He crosses back**)

MAINWARING Right – Jones, you will count the five pound notes.

JONES The five pound notes, yes, sir.

MAINWARING Walker, you will count the pound notes – Godfrey the ten shilling notes – Pike the silver and Frazer the copper.

FRAZER Wait a minute, sir, that's not fair. Why should I count the dirty copper? Why can't I count the five pound notes instead of that old fool. Let him count the dirty copper.

JONES 'Ere, who are you calling an old fool? You get on and count the dirty copper like the officer says.

MAINWARING That will be enough of that. Now, we need something to count it on. Go and get a long trestle table and some blankets… and, Jones.

Frazer, Walker, Godfrey and Pike go.

JONES Yes, sir.

MAINWARING Tell the men to fix bayonets and form a ring of steel round this money.

JONES Right, sir. (**Shouts at Sponge and the rest of the platoon**) Number two and three sections over here. (**They run over**) Right, fix bayonets. (**They fix**) A ring of steel round the money at the double – form! (**The men run into a half circle round the pile of money and face inwards**) Now, if any unauthorised person tries to fondle the money – let 'em have it right up. About turn! (**The men turn outwards**) Ring of steel – stand at ease. (**He salutes Mainwaring**) Ring of steel are now ready, sir.

INTERIOR. CHURCH HALL. NIGHT

There is a long trestle table down the middle of the hall – the rest of the platoon are gathered round it in a half circle with bayonets fixed. At the right end of the table, Jones is counting the five pound notes – next to him, Walker is counting the pound notes – next Godfrey, on the ten shilling notes – a blank space in front of the silver – last Frazer, counting the copper. Starting at Jones, the camera pans along. Mainwaring is watching – Wilson is sitting on a chair, dozing.

JONES 1,555 – 1,560 – 1,565 – 1,570 – 1,580, no, that's wrong, I'll start again. 5 – 10 – 15 – 20 –

WALKER 56 – 57 – 58 – 58. What's this ten bob note doing in here? (**He screws it up and throws it in front of Godfrey**)

MAINWARING This is no time for tomfoolery, Walker –

Pike comes out of the office.

MAINWARING Did you get on to the manager of the Eastgate branch, Pike?

PIKE Yes, Mr Mainwaring – I phoned him up at his home – he was having a party.

MAINWARING Fancy having a party at a time like this! What did he say?

PIKE You can bring the money over to his bank tomorrow morning – and put it in his vaults.

MAINWARING Right – take your place at the silver.

Pike takes his place.

PIKE (**To Frazer**) How are you getting on with your copper, Mr Frazer?

FRAZER Just look at the colour it's turning my hands. (**He holds them out**)

WALKER That's all right, Taff – now they match your face.

FRAZER That does it – Mr Mainwaring, either I count the five pound notes or I'm going home.

MAINWARING Oh, all right, change places with Jones.

JONES That's not fair, sir.

MAINWARING Don't argue.

FRAZER (**Changing places**) Let's see how you like counting the dirty copper.

MAINWARING Wilson, I... (**For the first time he notices that Wilson is asleep**) *Wilson!*

Wilson wakes up.

WILSON I'm sorry, sir – I sort of dozed off.

MAINWARING As chief clerk, this money is just as much your responsibility as mine – now, go and order a taxi to go to Eastgate at nine o'clock tomorrow morning.

WILSON Eight, sir. (**He starts to go**)

MAINWARING Better make it two – one for the money – and the other for the armed escort. Maximum security, Wilson.

WILSON Yes, sir – maximum security. (**He goes**)

Close up of Pike and Jones. Jones is slowly counting the pennies. Pike is counting two shilling pieces expertly by sliding them off the edge of the table into the palm of his hand. Jones stops and looks – he tries it – the coins go on the floor – he tries again.

PIKE You're dropping them all on the floor, Mr Jones.

JONES I can't help it, Pikey.

PIKE Well, tuck the corner of the blanket in your belt – and that will catch them.

JONES That's a good idea. (**He tucks the blanket in his belt**) You're a bright boy, Pikey.

Wilson comes back into the hall.

MAINWARING Have you booked the taxis, Wilson?

WILSON I'm afraid not, sir. One of the bombs fell on the garage and they're both out of action.

MAINWARING Now what are we going to do? I've got to transport this money into Eastgate first thing in the morning.

WALKER I'll get you some transport, sir.

MAINWARING All right, Walker – I'll leave it to you. Well, men, we managed to restore some sort of order out of the chaos – a good night's work. Another hour and we should be finished. Now, we need something to take the money over to Eastgate in.

The money is now in neat piles.

PIKE Mr Mainwaring – there's a big laundry basket full of dirty surplices in the choir room.

MAINWARING Good – Jones, you and Pike go and get it.

JONES Yes, sir – oh there's just one thing – what shall we do with the surplus surplices?

MAINWARING I don't care – go and get it!

JONES Yes, sir, right away – come on, Pikey. (**He walks away from the table – the blanket is still tucked into his belt – all the money crashes on to the floor**)

INTERIOR. CHURCH HALL. DAY

Mainwaring and Wilson are in front of the table – they are just

putting the last of the money into a large laundry basket. Jones, Pike, Frazer and Godfrey are leaning on the table, exhausted. Sponge and the rest of the platoon are sitting in a heap by the stage.

MAINWARING How much does it come to, Wilson?

WILSON £96, 478 11s, sir.

MAINWARING Not bad, only ten and fourpence short. What's the time?

WILSON **(Looking at his watch)** Half past seven.

MAINWARING **(Shouting across at Sponge)** Sponge, you and the men can take the blackouts down and go home – and leave four rifles for the armed escort.

SPONGE Right-oh, Mr Mainwaring. We shall look forward to the party.

Mainwaring does a take.

MAINWARING You know, Wilson – I should think that head office will be very grateful to me for saving this money. It might even mean promotion.

FRAZER Do you no think, Captain Mainwaring – that *we* might have had a little to do with saving the money?

MAINWARING **(Aside to Wilson)** Why does Frazer have to spoil everything by being bolshie?

FRAZER I heard that, and if I'm bolshie, I've a very good reason to be, having to count the money twice. We'd have been away from here hours ago if it hadn't been for a certain old fool.

JONES Don't you cast aspersions, Jock. I couldn't help it – I was just trying to stop my pennies from dropping.

Walker hurries in.

WALKER I've got the transport, Mr Mainwaring.

MAINWARING Right – Pike! Wake up, boy.

PIKE Sorry, Mr Mainwaring.

MAINWARING Get the rifles.

GODFREY Do you think I might be excused, sir? It's been a long night.

MAINWARING Very well – Frazer, Wilson, Jones, Walker take the basket – now stand in together – lift! Left, right, left, right.

EXTERIOR. OUTSIDE CHURCH HALL

A horse-drawn baker's cart is standing outside – Wilson, Pike, Frazer and Jones come into the picture with the basket – Walker is following and Mainwaring is directing them.

MAINWARING Left, right, left, right. Keep in step. **(Mainwaring takes no notice of the cart)** Right, Walker, where's the vehicle?

WALKER **(Pointing)** There.

MAINWARING But that's a horse and cart.

WALKER That's right.

MAINWARING You never said anything about a horse and cart – I assumed you'd get motor transport.

WALKER I hadn't got any petrol – there's a war on, you know. Anyhow, it's very cheap.

MAINWARING How much?

WALKER A fiver.

MAINWARING A fiver! This is absurd. Where's the driver?

WALKER He went off – if you want a driver it's an extra fiver.

MAINWARING **(Purple with rage)** A fiver for a driver! **(He pulls himself together)** Load the basket on, Walker.

Walker, Frazer, Jones and Pike start to load the basket.

WILSON I say, it's rather a pretty horse isn't it, sir. **(Mainwaring climbs up on the cart)** You're not going to drive it.

MAINWARING Certainly I am.

WILSON Do you know how?

MAINWARING For your information, Wilson – my father kept horses.

WILSON **(Puzzled)** Oh, how awfully nice, sir.

A COUNTRY ROAD. DAY

The cart driven by Mainwaring passes at a brisk trot – behind, Wilson, Jones, Walker and Pike are riding abreast on bikes – they all have rifles. Cut to front shot of four riders.

WILSON **(Puffing)** I do wish Captain Mainwaring wouldn't go so fast.

PIKE Mum's going to be furious, Uncle Arthur – me stopping out all night like this. She thought I went to Mr Mainwaring's party.

WILSON Well, you'll just have to tell her it was an all-night party.

WALKER What did he want to drag us along for?

JONES We're the armed escort. You heard what Mr Mainwaring said – he wants maximum security.

WALKER Why, does he think we're going to be attacked by Red Indians?

Several pound notes flutter into their faces.

PIKE **(Pointing)** Uncle Arthur – look!

Cut to rear view of van – pound notes are fluttering out. Cut back to close up of Wilson.

WILSON (**Shouting**) Stop, sir – stop – the money's coming out. (**They all stop and pick up the notes**) Come back, sir – come back.

They all wave and shout 'Stop – come back'.

Cut to front shot of Mainwaring ,unaware of what's happening. Cut back to Wilson.

WILSON It's no use, he can't hear us.

JONES 'Ere – you're the youngest, Pikey – ride after him and make him stop.

Pike jumps on his bike and rides after the van which is now some distance away. Close up of Pike riding furiously with pound notes fluttering round his face.

PIKE Stop, Mr Mainwaring – stop! You're dropping all your money! What am I going to do? I've got to attract his attention. (**He stops and fires his rifle**)

Close up of horse rearing.

Close up of Mainwaring.

MAINWARING Oh no!

Horse turns off the road and takes off at full gallop.

Front shot of Mainwaring pulling on reins.

SILHOUETTE SKYLINE

Shot of cart with showers of notes pouring out of the back – four figures are running behind.

SERIES FIVE **EPISODE EIGHT**

Recorded: Friday 3/11/72

Original transmission: Friday 24/11/72, 8.30–9.00pm

Original viewing figures = 16.5 million

ARTHUR LOWE .... CAPTAIN MAINWARING
JOHN LE MESURIER .... SERGEANT WILSON
CLIVE DUNN.................................. LANCE CORPORAL JONES
JOHN LAURIE .... PRIVATE FRAZER
JAMES BECK .... PRIVATE WALKER
ARNOLD RIDLEY .... PRIVATE GODFREY
IAN LAVENDER .... PRIVATE PIKE

BILL PERTWEE .... ARP WARDEN
BRENDA COWLING .... MRS PRENTICE
FRANK WILLIAMS .... VICAR
EDWARD SINCLAIR... VERGER
COLIN BEAN .... PRIVATE SPONGE
APRIL WALKER .... JUDY, A LAND GIRL
TINA CORNIOLI .... OLIVE, A LAND GIRL
PLATOON .... HUGH HASTINGS, MICHAEL MOORE, FREDDIE WILES,
.... GEORGE HANCOCK, LESLIE NOYES, EVAN ROSS,
.... HUGH CECIL, FREDDIE WHITE, DESMOND CULLUM-JONES
EXTRAS .... (NON-SPEAKING LANDGIRL) AMANDA BISHOP,
.... (HARMONIUM PLAYER) VERA PALMER

All is Safely Gathered In

• BRENDA COWLING REMEMBERS •

'The story of "All is Safely Gathered In" is about the members of the Walmington-on-Sea platoon volunteering to bring in the harvest for an old flame of Private Godfrey. She was a widow whose farm manager had suddenly to go into hospital for an operation, leaving her without the help she needed to gather in the harvest, so she appealed to Godfrey.

'The episode also featured members of the Women's Land Army – young females who were called up to work in agriculture as an alternative to the services (the A.T.S., WAAFS or WRENS). It was important work as the nation had to be fed, and since the German navy surrounded the waters around our coast, preventing the import of food, we had to depend on what we could grow ourselves.

'I played Mrs Prentice, who owned the farm. Dear Arnold Ridley, who played Private Godfrey, seemed to be quite chuffed at being given an old girlfriend as part of the plot! I remember we had a rather sweet fade-out at the end of the episode.

'When I joined the team for filming on location at Thetford, it was a bright autumn morning in October. I was a little nervous about meeting the cast for the first time, but need not have worried because everyone was very welcoming.

'One of my main memories was seeing John Le Mesurier and John Laurie sitting on a bench in the middle of a field waiting to film the thanksgiving harvest festival service. They were shivering with cold and their dressers offered blankets to put round them to keep warm, but they – being the true professionals they were – refused these creature comforts, preferring to suffer proudly in silence.

'It was a great pleasure for me to appear in this episode and, later, I worked with Arthur Lowe again, this time in the series *Potter*.'

All is Safely Gathered In

INTERIOR. SIDE OFFICE

Godfrey is rather agitated and looking at his watch. Jones enters with a small newspaper-wrapped package.

JONES Aren't they here yet?

GODFREY No, it's most unusual for Mr Mainwaring and Mr Wilson to be late. **(He looks at his watch)** My bus leaves at ten past. They won't hold it for you these days.

JONES Well, you just go, Mr Godfrey, and I'll explain to Mr Mainwaring.

GODFREY No, I couldn't do that, he might be upset.

JONES He won't be upset today. **(He opens a desk drawer)** I got four sausages for him and a quarter pound of dripping. I know it's not much, but it's the thought that counts, isn't it? **(He pops the package in the drawer)**

Mainwaring enters, holding a Tommy gun wrapped in an old raincoat. Pike is assisting him as if they are carrying a baby. Wilson is less than interested in the proceedings. He carries the drum mag. and a couple of 20-shot mags.

PIKE Mind you don't bump it, Mr Mainwaring.

MAINWARING Oh, don't be so silly, Pike, it's not that delicate.

WILSON Don't be so fussy, Frank.

JONES Mr Mainwaring, sir, Mr Godfrey here would like to have a…

MAINWARING **(Interrupting)** Not now, Jones. Go and fall the men in, I have important news for them. **(He puts the parcel on the desk)**

JONES But if he doesn't go now, Mr Mainwaring, he might be too late.

MAINWARING Then tell him to go now and get on parade as fast as he can. **(He starts to unwrap the parcel)**

JONES Look, you hang on for five minutes, Mr Godfrey and if Mr Mainwaring hasn't finished with you then, I'll send the Verger to hold it for you.

Godfrey and Jones exit to hall.

PIKE **(Picking up Tommy gun from desk)** Cor, look at that, Mr Mainwaring. A-a-a-a-a-a-a-a-a-a-a. **(He does a gunman act with the Tommy gun)**

MAINWARING Put that down at once, Pike. I carried it here, I'm going to handle it first. **(Mainwaring takes it and shapes up with it)** Ah, beautifully balanced. A devastating weapon, in the right hands.

WILSON I should think it was even more devastating in the wrong hands.

Mainwaring shapes up again.

PIKE **(Making the sound effects)** A-a-a-a-a-a-a-a-a-a-a.

MAINWARING Don't do that, Pike.

PIKE Sorry, Mr Mainwaring.

MAINWARING We'll show this to the troops. Bring the mags, Wilson.

PIKE Let me carry it, Mr Mainwaring.

MAINWARING Go and fall in, Pike. You must control that boy, he thinks it's a game.

INTERIOR. CHURCH HALL

The men are drawn up on parade – Godfrey is on the end. Mainwaring crosses the hall swiftly, holding the gun away from the squad.

MAINWARING **(As he crosses)** Properly at ease, but I know you've all been waiting for it, so here it is. **(He produces the Tommy gun, and swings it into the attack position)**

MEN **(Appreciatively)** Ah….

MAINWARING This is one of the most sophisticated side arms ever produced. It fires 650 rounds of four five ammunition per minute. The drum magazine holds 50 – have you got the drum, Wilson?

WILSON Yes, sir.

MAINWARING Well, hold it up then.

WILSON Certainly, sir. **(He holds up the drum)**

MAINWARING There you are. Sergeant Wilson is holding up the drum. The clip-on magazine holds 20 rounds – show the clip, Wilson.

WILSON Yes, sir. The clip.

JONES Excuse me, sir – is there a detachment for a bayonet?

MAINWARING I'm afraid not, Jones.

JONES Pity.

WALKER You'd soon run out of bullets at 650 rounds a minute, sir – I mean, you only have to touch the trigger and **(he blows a raspberry)** your magazine's empty.

MAINWARING I think it would last a bit longer than that, don't you, Wilson?

WILSON It would be just under two seconds, sir.

JONES We'll time it, Joe. **(He pulls out his watch)** I'll say go, and then I'll say stop.

GODFREY Captain Mainwaring.

MAINWARING Not now, Godfrey.

JONES Right, stand by – go.

Walker blows a raspberry – aided by Pike.

JONES Stop. Now you need a bayonet, sir.

Mainwaring reacts.

FRAZER Just a minute, Captain Mainwaring, that drum thing holds 50 rounds – that will go on longer, something like… **(he blows a five-second raspberry)**

MAINWARING Thank you, Frazer.

PIKE **(Holding up his hand)** Mr Captain Mainwaring – who's going to have it? Please may I.

MAINWARING No, certainly not.

GODFREY Excuse me, Captain Mainwaring.

MAINWARING Not you either, Godfrey.

JONES We ought to take it in turns – General McCully always used to say 'take it in turns'.

MAINWARING General McCully, who was he?

JONES Well, he wasn't very important, he just used to say 'take it in turns', that's about all I remember of him really.

Mainwaring reacts.

WALKER I know, let's have a whist drive, winner has first go.

MAINWARING Certainly not – I will not have the tactical future of this platoon decided on the turn of a card – we'll draw lots.

Godfrey finally decides to take action – he crosses to Mainwaring and salutes.

MAINWARING I'm sorry, Godfrey, I know you're disappointed, but I'm only trying to do the fair thing.

GODFREY May I have three days' holiday?

MAINWARING I beg your pardon?

GODFREY I'd rather like three days' holiday.

MAINWARING Have you gone out of your mind, Godfrey? Hitler is across the Channel, ready to pounce and we're in the front line.

GODFREY I wouldn't ask normally, but it's because of this friend of mine.

MAINWARING Oh yes?

GODFREY It's all very involved.

MAINWARING I'm sure it must be.

JONES Permission to interfere, sir? Mr Godfrey won't speak up for himself, sir, he's too much the gentleman, but my lips are not sealed. I can reveal that at the bottom of all this, sir, there is a woman.

MAINWARING Is this true, Godfrey?

GODFREY Well, yes and no.

MAINWARING Yes and no – what sort of an answer is that?

WALKER It's a bit of each, isn't it?

MAINWARING Don't interrupt, Walker. I think you'd better go in the office, Godfrey.

GODFREY Yes, sir. **(He turns and goes to the office)**

MAINWARING You too, Wilson.

Mainwaring moves to the office, followed by Wilson and Jones.

PIKE Can I look after the Tommy gun for you, sir?

MAINWARING Oh, very well. **(He hands it over)**

PIKE Mr Mainwaring, it's also call the Chicago Piano.

MAINWARING What did you say, Pike?

PIKE It's called the Chicago Piano.

MAINWARING Stupid boy. **(He exits to side office)**

FRAZER **(To Walker)** Yon Godfrey has a weird fey look in his eye. More than likely he's a sex maniac.

INTERIOR. SIDE OFFICE

Mainwaring entering side office, Vicar enters at same time.

MAINWARING Not now, Vicar.

Vicar retreats.

MAINWARING You'd better take notes, Wilson.

WILSON Certainly, sir. **(Wilson picks some paper off the desk)**

MAINWARING Now, Godfrey.

Mainwaring sees Jones standing beside him.

MAINWARING What are you doing here, Jones?

JONES Well, it's like this, sir, Mr Godfrey here is a very retiring man and he won't stand up for himself. I would like to speak for him because I have been privy to his intimate details through things he has told me in continence.

MAINWARING Is that all right with you, Godfrey?

GODFREY Well, I suppose…

JONES Thank you, Mr Godfrey. It all started to commence just before the Boer War. Mr Godfrey here was a dandy young buck of some twenty summers.

WILSON I didn't quite catch that.

MAINWARING Dandy.

WILSON I'm sorry. **(He crosses something out)**

JONES Anyway, Mr Godfrey here lost his heart to a young lady who was in service in a great house nearby – are you listening?

MIANWARING Yes, of course I am.

JONES Now, those days, Mr Mainwaring, wasn't like these days. If you was a serving wench you had to know

your place and mind your peas and onions. You worked from 5.30 in the morning, blacking the grate, to half past eight at night, putting the cat out. You had one Sunday off a month and they give you three and six a week, less laundry. But it was a good life.

MAINWARING Jones, I can't sit here and listen to all this rigmarole.

JONES I'm sorry, Mr Mainwaring – I was disgressing. Seeing her so little, he'd never had a chance to plight his troth, which he would have done, given half a chance, him being a very virile young man, as we all was in those days, me more than most. You're not in a hurry, are you?

MAINWARING Yes, I am, will you please come to the point.

JONES He wants three days' holiday, that's the point.

MAINWARING I know that – look, Jones, please be quiet and let Godfrey speak for himself.

JONES There you are, you see, he won't listen.

MAINWARING Be quiet, Jones. Yes, Godfrey.

GODFREY Well, I wanted three days' holiday to help with the harvest.

MAINWARING That's hardly a holiday, it's very important work, isn't it, Wilson?

WILSON Yes, very important, sir. I didn't get all of what Jones said.

MAINWARING Oh, don't worry about that, I don't think it had anything to do with it.

JONES Oh, yes it did, this serving girl married a farmer and now she's a widow, and it's her harvest he wants to help with.

GODFREY Her foreman has gone to hospital.

JONES For a hernia.

WILSON Hernia.

JONES Left side.

WILSON Left side.

MAINWARING Don't bother with that. Does she have no other form of labour?

GODFREY Only a couple of land girls – I'd like to have helped her, we've kept in touch you know, but I've missed the bus now.

MAINWARING Just a minute, Godfrey. How many acres does she farm?

GODFREY Well, I think there's about a hundred acres of wheat to get in.

MAINWARING This is vital, Wilson, England needs every grain of corn she can grow – that harvest is top priority and we're going to see that it's all gathered in. We'll call for volunteers and Jones will drives us there in the van.

JONES **(To Godfrey)** There you are, you see he wants me now. Two minutes ago he was casting me off like an old acquaintance.

MAINWARING Get the men on parade, Jones.

GODFREY It's most kind of you, Captain Mainwaring. May I phone Mrs Prentice and give her the good news?

WILSON Of course you may, Godfrey.

MAINWARING Right, Wilson, get the nominal role and tick off all the volunteers, and send in Sponge, he's a farmer – he'll be our technical adviser.

Godfrey picks up the phone.

INTERIOR. SMALL CORNER OF OFFICE

The hymn book stand is to be seen, plus the end of a pew or two. The Vicar is sitting – the Verger is by the books.

VICAR Every time I want to use my office, it's packed with people playing soldiers.

VERGER You settle yourself down there, your Reverence. No one will disturb you there.

VICAR Thank you, Mr Yeatman.

The Vicar settles himself and the Verger proceeds to blow the dust off each of the hymn books and to bang the backs together. This happens a couple of times as the Vicar is about to put pen to paper – then the Warden enters.

WARDEN Oh, Vicar – thank the Lord I've found you. I must talk to you.

VICAR Hello, Mr Hodges – I heard you had a narrow escape last night.

WARDEN Narrow escape – it was a miracle. It landed right there beside me. If it had gone off, I wouldn't be here to talk to you now.

VICAR A miracle indeed.

WARDEN It knocked my pint right clean out of my hand – look. **(He shows the mug handle in his hand)** It was a deliverance.

VERGER More like a judgement.

VICAR Go away, Mr Yeatman.

VERGER Yes, sir. **(He goes)**

WARDEN I should have been killed, I was spared – why me? Answer me that – why me – why me – why, why?

VICAR I can't think.

WARDEN I'm just a simple greengrocer. Do you think he's saving me for some great purpose?

VICAR Well, you never know.

WARDEN All my life I've been rotten, but I'm going to turn over a new leaf. I'm going to be kind to everyone, and I'm going to love my enemies, not Hitler, of course, but I'm going to be good to Mainwaring and I'm going to help him with his struggle, because he's a good man at heart, you know.

VICAR I'm sure he is.

WARDEN From now on, I'm going to be right behind him.

VICAR Well, that's marvellous news.

WARDEN Thank you for seeing me, Vicar. I needed your guidance. **(He rises to go)**

VICAR I'm only too glad to help.

WARDEN You've been a rock for me to cling to.

VICAR A pleasure I'm sure.

INTERIOR. BARN

This is used to store miscellaneous farm equipment and general farm rubbish. Mainwaring leads the men in.

MAINWARING Right, stack your kit in the corner and hang on to your rifles. We don't want to be surprised.

PIKE **(With Tommy gun)** They won't surprise me, Mr Mainwaring, I'll fill 'em full of lead. A-a-a-a-a-a-a.

MAINWARING Wilson, how did that boy get that thing? Frazer took first turn.

WILSON I think Frank made some private arrangement.

MAINWARING I will not have private arrangements made on active service.

Mrs Prentice enters. She is a ruddy-faced, grey-haired country woman in the middle sixties.

MRS PRENTICE Colonel Mainwaring, this is kind of you all. I'm sorry it's a bit rough and ready for you, Colonel Mainwaring.

MAINWARING That's quite all right, Madam. All we're concerned with is gathering in the harvest.

MRS PRENTICE Ah, well we've got a bit of a problem there. Mr Yates of Grove Farm was going to thresh it for me, but 'is thresher's broke so 'e's all behind, see.

MAINWARING Don't you have one yourself, Mrs Prentice?

MRS PRENTICE I got one all right, but only my foreman knows how it works.

MAINWARING I'm sure we have enough expertise in our ranks to get the wheels turning, don't you think, Wilson?

WILSON I really don't know. Farming machinery looks so complicated.

MAINWARING Sponge is a farmer, he'll fix it. We'll win through, Mrs Prentice. Rely on us.

We hear the Warden's voice off.

WARDEN Left, right, left, right, halt. That was lovely, absolutely lovely.

MAINWARING What in heaven's name is he doing here?

The Warden enters and salutes.

WARDEN Captain Mainwaring, the Walmington-on-Sea Warden is 'ere to give you help.

MAINWARING I don't think we need them, do we, Wilson?

WILSON No, I suggest you clear off.

WARDEN Don't send me away, Captain Mainwaring, don't spurn me in England's hour of need. We're standing shoulder to shoulder against the common foe. Let them all come, Captain Mainwaring, and you and I will shock them.

Mainwaring reacts.

MAINWARING I see. **(To Wilson)** Does he drink at all?

WILSON I've really no idea.

MAINWARING Watch him, he's up to something. Right, fall in outside in three ranks.

WARDEN That's right, fall in outside. You do as the good Captain says, he's a good man. Fall in outside.

JONES 'Ere, I'm supposed to do all the balling and shouting.

WARDEN Oh I am sorry, Corporal Jones.**(As they both go)** Really, I wouldn't do anything to hurt your feelings, I'm just trying to help the good Captain.

They exit.

WILSON **(On his way out with Mainwaring)** Maybe he has been drinking.

They go out. Godfrey crosses to Mrs Prentice. Taking a small posy of pansies from his Red Cross satchel, he hands them to her.

MRS PRENTICE Oh thank you, Charles. Aren't they lovely?

GODFREY Sorry about last Sunday, my sister Dolly was rather under the weather.

MRS PRENTICE Ah, poor old soul.

GODFREY She's three years younger than I am, you know.

TELECINE: THRESHING AREA

Long shot of area – there is a large old steam engine with smoke coming from its stack – the old threshing machine is hitched up to it and the driving belt is attached. The stacking conveyor is in position, but there is only about three foot of hay stack. Sacks are piled, ready for filling and are attached to the machine. A farm cart stacked with wheat is standing ready for threshing.

Cut to long shot of Mainwaring's platoon arriving. Side by side, march the Wardens with Hodges – there are three of them.

Cut to three land girls by the engine.

JUDY Blimey, what's this then?

Cut to Mainwaring and Wardens.

MAINWARING Platoon, halt!

WARDEN Wardens, halt!

• COLIN BEAN REMEMBERS •

'In the eighth series, made late in 1972, had been one of my moments of glory as "Pte. Sponge" in the episode "All is Safely Gathered In". Earlier that year I had mentioned to Jimmy Perry that in autumn, during the war, I remembered our local Home Guard helping the farmers gather in the all-important harvest. The scene in the wheat field was my very prominent moment!"

'As 'tis said in all the best serial stories "Now read on", the part about the threshing machine still makes me laugh 28 years later.'

(From *Who Do You Think You Are Kidding!*, by Colin Bean)

MAINWARING Right, fall out and gather round.

WARDEN Fall out and gather round like the good Captain says.

Mainwaring moves nearer to machinery.

MAINWARING I don't suppose this is as complicated as it looks. **(He calls)** Sponge!

SPONGE Yes, Captain Mainwaring.

MAINWARING Just select however many men you need for this thing and show them how it works.

SPONGE I don't know how it works.

MAINWARING You don't know… Wilson, I thought you told me Sponge was a farmer.

WILSON Well, he is, I'm sure.

SPONGE I'm a sheep farmer.

MAINWARING He's a sheep farmer – you don't thresh sheep, Wilson, anyone knows that.

WILSON Oh dear, perhaps those land girls know.

MAINWARING Well ask them then.

WILSON Er, excuse me, do you know how this thing works?

ALL No, sorry.

OLIVE We've only been here three weeks.

WILSON Well never mind, you look awfully charming in those uniforms.

MAINWARING All right, Wilson, that'll do.

JONES Excuse me, Captain Mainwaring, I think I know how it works.

MAINWARING Good, well done, Jones. Pay attention everybody. Jones knows how it works.

JONES **(Starts off in loud instructor's voice)** This part here is the engine, and this complication here is the threshing thing. **(To Mainwaring)** I'm not getting too technical for them, am I, sir?

MAINWARING I don't think so, Jones.

JONES Ah good. Well, you toss the stooks in here – whoa, like that – and the engine goes puff, puff, puff, puff, puff, puff over there, and the threshing thing goes jibber, jibber, jibber over here, and while it's going jibber, jibber, jibber, it mashes it all up, you see, and the straw goes upsy-daisy up there, and the grain comes wheedling out of the other end, and then it's all done.

MAINWARING Well, I think we've got the gist of what Jones was saying. Jones' section will run the operation here, the rest of you get on to reaping and gathering.

WARDEN What shall I do, Captain Mainwaring?

MAINWARING Just keep quiet.

WARDEN Yes, Captain Mainwaring.

MAINWARING Now, I need someone up there to load the hopper from the cart.

JONES I'd like to volunteer to be someone up there loading the hopper from the cart.

MAINWARING Good, and you help him, Pike.

PIKE **(With Tommy gun)** And I'll keep everyone covered too. A-a-a-a-a-a-a-a.

GODFREY I usually supervise the grain going into the sacks.

MAINWARING Good. Walker, you look after the straw stack. **(He realises that Walker is missing)** Walker, Walker!

Walker sits up from the middle of the stack with a land girl in his arms.

WALKER Did you call, sir?

MAINWARING See that the straw is well stacked.

WALKER See that it's what?

MAINWARING Well stacked.

WALKER Yes, her name's Judy.

MAINWARING Now, there's the engine to get going. Would you be any good at that, Wilson?

PIKE Mum says you can't even use a tin opener, doesn't she, Uncle Arthur?

WILSON I don't think that's awfully funny, Frank.

MAINWARING Probably true though.

FRAZER I think I have an inkling, sir.

MAINWARING Good – go to it.

WARDEN What about me, Captain Mainwaring? What can I do to help you in your good work?

MAINWARING Oh, look after the horse or something.

WILSON And me, sir?

MAINWARING Oh, you'd better keep tally of the loads and grain.

Mrs Prentice walks up.

MAINWARING It won't be long now, Mrs Prentice, we'll have it running smooth as a sewing machine. Off you go, Frazer.

Mid shot of Frazer moving levers. MCU wheels turning on engine. MCU wheels turning on thresher. Long shot of the rig working, smoke puffing from the engine.

FRAZER **(At the controls)** It's going, I've done it.

JONES **(On cart near hopper)** It's going judder, judder, judder, Captain Mainwaring.

MAINWARING Start loading, Jones.

JONES Yes, sir.

He chucks sheaves into the hopper with a pitch fork. Cuts of the machine working. Straw rising on the conveyor. Cut to Walker and Judy. Walker looks up at the straw about to fall on them – he throws Judy into the stack as it falls down.

WALKER Just saved you from that, didn't I?

JUDY Yeh, now I need saving from something else, don't I?

WALKER You bet. **(He dives on her and kisses her)**

Cut to Mainwaring and Wilson.

MAINWARING Wilson – stop all that.

GODFREY Captain Mainwaring, there's nothing coming through yet.

MAINWARING Isn't there? Load away, Jones.

JONES I'm loading as fast as I can.

GODFREY Maybe I have some kind of constriction in my tubes.

MAINWARING Hmm, I wouldn't have thought so – let me have a look.

Long shot of Jones falling into hopper. Cut to Mainwaring.

MAINWARING It looks all right to me.

Pike joins him.

PIKE I'm sorry to bother you, Captain Mainwaring, but I think you ought to know that Corporal Jones has just fallen in the hopper.

MAINWARING What? Jones, Jones!

Yell from Jones in the hopper.

MAINWARING Frazer – stop the engine.

Mid shot of Frazer throwing levers.

MAINWARING Jones, are you all right? **(He starts to try to clamber on the hopper)**

Walker holds up buttons and a strip of khaki material.

WALKER Hey, Mr Mainwaring, some of this straw's got buttons on.

MAINWARING It's Jones' trousers – Wilson, get him out.

Moans come from inside the hopper, Jones' head and shoulders appear.

JONES Mr Mainwaring, it went judder, judder, judder, judder and tore my trousers off, Mr Mainwaring.

MAINWARING Great Scott, are you all right?

JONES **(Almost in tears)** Mr Mainwaring, I have lost that which I hold most dear.

MAINWARING Oh no. Wilson, give him a hand.

JONES My pocket book with my discharge papers is gone from me.

WALKER **(Holding it up)** It's here, Jonesey.

PIKE **(From about the cart)** It's all right, Captain Mainwaring, he's only lost his trousers.

MAINWARING Then get him out and let's get on with the harvest.

JONES I can't come out in front of all those land ladies.

MAINWARING Get the trousers off that scarecrow.

JONES But I've had a terrible experience.

MAINWARING Oh, get on with it, Jones.

JONES He's not very sympathetic, is he?

MAINWARING Look lively lads, we're holding up the harvest.

Music and montage consisting of short cuts of the following:

Warden with horse

Pike loading stooks

Wilson picking off the sacks which have been loaded in a column marked Saturday

Godfrey and the grain bag

Frazer stoking the fire

Mainwaring and Pike removing a pile of sacks to reveal Walker cuddling Olive

Wilson ticking off total for Sunday

long shot of the team working

two-shot of Mrs Prentice and Godfrey admiring their industry

Pike on the cart throwing a sheaf of wheat over the Warden down below – the Warden is furious – then remembers his new resolution and gives a weak smile and a thumbs up

Mainwaring taking a sandwich from a packet and putting the remainder on the driving belt

Frazer putting the tractor into gear

Mainwaring's sandwiches going round and round the belt pursued by Mainwaring

The hay cart pulling away, revealing Walker with the third girl

Pike suddenly realising that he has lost his Tommy gun – he dives into the haystack and finds it

Jones loading the hopper with his scarecrow trousers on, which are very loose round the waist

Wilson ticking off the total for Monday and then writing in the grand total.

MAINWARING Right, that's it, men, that's the lot.

WARDEN Three cheers for the good Captain.

They all give three cheers.

MRS PRENTICE I've got a real nice harvest spread for you, home-made pasties and potato wine.

The troops give another cheer.

MRS PRENTICE And after that, the Vicar's coming over to bless the harvest.

EXTERIOR. FIELD

Cut to Vicar approaching on his bicycle . He dismounts in the field near the Verger who has set up an altar on bales of hay, with an altar cloth, a couple of candle sticks and an altar ornament, which he is polishing. A small, portable harmonium is in position – the organist is warming up on it. The distant strains of 'We'll Meet Again', sung by the platoon are heard in the background.

VICAR **(Putting his bike against a bale of a tree and getting out his surplus)** Ah, that looks very nice, Mr Yeatman.

VERGER Thank you, your Reverence. I thought the congregation could sit over here. **(He moves to show the pews he has improvised from bales, planks or drums, boxes, etc. Hymn books are on the seats)**

VICAR Excellent. Where are the congregation?

VERGER Still celebrating.

The voices rise to the finale.

VICAR Good heavens, what are they drinking?

VERGER Potato wine. I only tried it once.

VICAR Was it good?

VERGER I got very belligerent.

VICAR Oh dear.

EXTERIOR. FARMHOUSE. FRONT DOOR

MRS PRENTICE **(Voice from inside)** Come on now, the Vicar's waiting for you.

MAINWARING Yes, come on then, outside.

Pike and Frazer emerge.

PIKE My, that potato wine's good stuff, isn't it, Mr Frazer?

FRAZER Show me the man that says it isn't.

The platoon, Wardens and land girls file out, trying to appear steady and sober.

JONES Come on now, my brave lads, let's have some decorum.

Mainwaring and Warden come out together.

WARDEN You're a good man, Captain Napoleon. You can't help being pompous.

Godfrey and Mrs Prentice come out last of all, Godfrey is sober.

MRS PRENTICE My, they have had a lot.

GODFREY I hope they'll be all right, I've never touched it since that night.

TELECINE: FIELD

They file into the congregation positions.

VICAR Hymn 482. All is safely gathered in.

Mrs Yeatman starts up on the harmonium. The congregation start to sing. Reading left to right, they are assembled in the following order: Wilson, Mainwaring, Frazer behind Mainwaring, Warden, Jones, Walker behind Jones, second Warden, Pike. Mainwaring lurches slightly against the Warden.

WARDEN 'Ere, who're you shoving?

MAINWARING You staggered. You can't take your liquor.

WARDEN Who do you think you're talking to, you drunken old snob. **(He pushes Mainwaring)**

FRAZER **(Behind them)** I saw that. **(He shoves Warden)**

MAINWARING I'm quite capable of looking after myself thank you, Frazer. **(He shoves the Warden)**

WARDEN Don't start anything. **(He shoves Mainwaring)**

WILSON Why don't you clear off? **(He shoves the Warden, who stumbles against Jones)**

MAINWARING **(To Wilson)** Leave him alone. **(He shoves Wilson)**

JONES **(To Warden)** Keep to your own place. **(He shoves Warden)**

The second Warden starts to intervene.

WALKER (**Behind them**) Don't you touch that, old man. (**He shoves the second Warden**)

JONES (**To Walker**) Who are you calling an old man? (**He shoves Walker**)

The whole congregation start to shove one another.

VERGER (**Giving Mrs Yeatman a shove**) Keep playing.

MRS YEATMAN Who do you think you're shoving? (**She gives the Verger an almighty shove which sends him flying into the congregation**)

PIKE All right, youz guys, reach for the sky. (**He threatens everybody with his Tommy gun**)

Two Wardens pounce on him. We pull back as the whole congregation starts to shove each other. Mrs Prentice and Godfrey regard it all at a distance. The sun is setting and the scene is otherwise tranquil and idyllic.

SERIES FIVE **EPISODE NINE**

Recorded: Friday 10/11/72
Original transmission: Friday 1/12/72, 8.30–9.00pm
Original viewing figures = 16 million

ARTHUR LOWE .... CAPTAIN MAINWARING
JOHN LE MESURIER .... SERGEANT WILSON
CLIVE DUNN .... LANCE CORPORAL JONES
JOHN LAURIE .... PRIVATE FRAZER
JAMES BECK .... PRIVATE WALKER
ARNOLD RIDLEY .... PRIVATE GODFREY
IAN LAVENDER .... PRIVATE PIKE
BILL PERTWEE .... ARP WARDEN
FRANK WILLIAMS .... VICAR
EDWARD SINCLAIR .... VERGER
HAROLD BENNETT .... MR BLEWITT
TONY HUGHES .... MR BILLINGS
PLATOON .... COLIN BEAN, MICHAEL MOORE, FREDDIE WHITE, GEORGE HANCOCK, HUGH CECIL, DESMOND CULLUM-JONES, FREDDIE WILES, EVAN ROSS, LESLIE NOYES, HUGH HASTINGS.
EXTRA .... (MISS BINNS, CUSTOMER IN BANK) WENDY JOHNSON

WHEN DID YOU LAST SEE YOUR MONEY?

• KEITH ELDRED REMEMBERS •

'One day in 1969 I was contacted by the BBC in my role as Chairman of The Thetford Music & Drama Society. They wanted to know whether I knew anybody in Thetford who would be prepared to act as "extras" in a programme called *Dad's Army*.

'At that time the show was very popular and I was able to say that I would have no difficulty whatsoever in obtaining as many extras as they wanted.

'At first the work was on a voluntary basis, but even so, there was no lack of enthusiastic amateurs eager to participate. Extras were not only obtained from the Drama Society but from many other local organisations, including the golf club, rotary club, scouts, cubs, guides – in fact, extras came from all walks of life in Thetford.

'Sometimes we had individual parts, all non-speaking, of course. I even remember my mother and father rushing backwards and forwards with buckets of water to put out a fire! Sometimes we needed a considerable number of extras for our parades, such as the one at Brandon railway station.

'After a while, our involvement became more regular, and we actually got to know the actors and the many backstage workers very well indeed, particularly the wardrobe mistress who fitted us out in the various costumes needed.

'One day my popularity soared. Due to Equity, Harold Snoad, the then producer, informed me that extras would be paid. This really was not necessary but was much appreciated by one and all. I also received cheques for £5–£6 once every three or four years for the next 20 years for royalties on the videos around the world. My account would show such items as "Performance in New Zealand 1d".

'We had many happy days, and I recall the time when Freddie Trueman was asked to perform in "The Test". It was a bitterly cold October day and we used the cricket pitch on the battle area near Thetford. To get the camera angles right, Freddie was asked to bowl from a most impossible run-up; even so, after much muttering, he bowled one ball and demolished the stumps, and that was all that was required of Freddie in this particular episode. From the extras' point of view, the rest of the day was spent listening to Freddie recounting many stories in the coach.

'I recall one day when travelling in the coach to a location, one of the platoon, I am not sure of his name, was eyeing the long blonde hair of the girl in front of him. On engaging her in conversation, he didn't seem too pleased to find that the blonde hair was a wig and the lady underneath it was probably some twenty years older than he had anticipated.

'I also remember driving John Le Mesurier to Bardwell Village Green in, I think, a Rolls Royce. As he got out of the car, a lady rushed out carrying a glass of gin and tonic, which John gratefully received and, in fact, I think he retired to her house for most of the afternoon. I am told that she probably knew John in his younger days.

'There were many technical triumphs on location, one of which was to make the big wheel operate in "Round and Round Went the Great Big Wheel". This was really quite an achievement and full marks went to the engineers who eventually got it operating as required.

'There was no doubt the whole of the cast of *Dad's Army* were a very friendly lot indeed, and when we travelled to our various locations on the coach, many was the time we would sit with them and chat about their careers – they were always happy to talk to us.

'One of our most sociable occasions was the night the Drama Society invited the cast to attend a party at my house. This was a very happy occasion, and I remember John Le Mesurier sat at my old piano bemoaning the fact that it was out of tune and completely unplayable, and could he please have another gin and tonic.

'James Beck found himself surrounded by many admiring chorus girls and leading ladies of the Drama Society and I think he had a most enjoyable evening. They all signed my visitors' book, and I must say the two pages are a splendid memento of many happy times with *Dad's Army*.

'These times were last remembered when David Croft and Jimmy Perry gave the Thetford Music & Drama Society permission to perform the stage version of *Dad's Army*. I was fortunate enough to be cast as Sergeant Wilson, a part I thoroughly enjoyed and will always remember for the scene in which Wilson plays the piano for the Floral Dance.

'Happy Memories.'

When Did You Last See Your Money?

INTERIOR. THE BANK. DAY

Close up of Pike serving a customer at counter. He pushes the money under the grill towards her.

PIKE Thank you very much, madam.

She takes the money and counts it. Mainwaring appears at Pike's elbow and nods to customer.

MAINWARING Good Morning, Mrs Binns. Everything satisfactory?

MRS BINNS Yes, thank you.

MAINWARING Good day, Mrs Binns.

She nods, picks up the money and goes.

PIKE Bye, bye.

MAINWARING What do you mean 'bye bye'? 'Good morning, madam' is the correct form of address. (**Mainwaring points to counter**) What are those paper clips doing all over the counter, Pike? Gather them up.

PIKE Yes, Mr Mainwaring. (**He picks them up**)

MAINWARING And how many more times have I told you to keep those rubber stamps in the rack?

Mainwaring puts them in the rack.

PIKE Sorry, Mr Mainwaring.

MAINWARING This counter is a disgrace. I've never seen such a mess in all my life. Supposing someone from Head Office came down and saw it like this, they'd have a fit. I run a tidy bank here, Pike, and don't you forget it.

He moves away from the counter – the camera pulls back and for the first time we see that the bank is in ruins. Mainwaring steps over a pile of rubble and moves towards his office. The wall is almost completely down and the door is standing alone in its frame. Mainwaring pushes it open, goes through and closes it behind him. The camera pans to a notice on the counter which reads 'Business as Usual'. Jones enters and comes to the counter.

JONES Morning, Pikey.

PIKE Good morning, Mr Jones.

JONES Morning, Pikey. (**He pushes the takings and paying in book across the counter – he points to notice**) Business as usual – that's the ticket. Take more than a few Jerry bombs to put Mr Mainwaring's bank out of action, eh?

PIKE We're trying to tidy it up as much as we can.

JONES Always remember, Pikey, a soldier's first rule. On active service, keep tidy. I shall never forget when I was in the Sudan, we used to wear little kitbags, just here. (**He indicates his behind**) And some of the lads had odds and ends dangling out. Well, General Kitchener couldn't abide this, he just couldn't stand things dangling. One day, he got us all on parade and he said, 'Boys, I will not have things dangling, remember a tidy mind is a tidy behind, don't be scruffy like the Fuzzie Wuzzies.' Of course, the Fuzzie Wuzzies didn't have any kitbags. Come to that, they didn't have any kit. Just a bit of rag dangling here, and a bit of rag dangling there. **(He indicates)** They had very untidy behinds.

Wilson comes into the picture beside Pike.

JONES Morning, Mr Wilson.

WILSON **(Holding a sheaf of papers)** Morning, Jonesey. Have you got a paper clip, Frank? **(He starts to feel about in a small bowl and upsets it)**

PIKE Mind, Uncle Arthur, I've tidied those up once.

WILSON Well, I only want one.

Wilson takes a clip, pins the papers together and goes to Mainwaring's office door and knocks.

MAINWARING Come in.

Wilson pushes the door. It is stuck.

MAINWARING I said, come in.

Wilson pushes again, he pokes his head round the edge of the door frame.

WILSON It won't open, sir, it's stuck.

MAINWARING Oh, really.

He goes to the door and pulls the handle. It still won't open.

WILSON It must have gone out of true, sir.

Mainwaring comes round the edge of the door frame to the outside.

MAINWARING All you've got to do is to put your shoulder to it, use a bit of effort. You know your trouble, Wilson, you're getting flabby. Now stand back.

Mainwaring puts his shoulder to the door and it flies open. He then shuts the door again.

MAINWARING There you are, Wilson, perfectly simple, just wanted a bit of beef that's all. Well, come in then.

WILSON **(Rattling the door knob)** It won't open, sir.

MAINWARING Oh, come round the side.

Wilson comes round the door frame.

INTERIOR. OFFICE. DAY

The exterior walls are still intact, all the glass is broken in the window behind Mainwaring's desk. Above him is a large tarpaulin, propped up to keep the weather out. There are several holes in it, with buckets underneath to catch the drips.

WILSON I've got all those papers you asked for, sir.

MAINWARING Good, I want to go through them very carefully. **(He takes them)**

WILSON Rather wet in here, isn't it, sir?

MAINWARING Yes, the tarpaulin is full of water from that rain last night.

WILSON Hmmm. **(He reaches up and pokes the tarpaulin. Drops of water fall through on to Mainwaring's desk)**

MAINWARING Don't poke it, you'll only make it worse.

WILSON Sorry, sir.

MAINWARING Why can't you leave things alone? How can I work with water dripping all over my desk?

Wilson takes out his pocket handkerchief and dabs at the desk.

MAINWARING Oh, get out of it, Wilson. **(He reaches under his desk, takes out an umbrella, opens it and holds it over his head)** Now, let's get down to work, shall we? **(A gust of wind blows some of the papers on the floor)** And close that window.

WILSON Yes, sir. **(He moves to the window which is open about six inches and closes it. We can clearly see that all the glass is broken)** Is that better, sir?

MAINWARING No, it isn't.

WILSON **(Picking up the papers)** I don't know why you put up with this, sir. Why don't you move into the stockroom? It's not damaged at all.

MAINWARING Move into the stockroom! **(He gets up and comes round the desk face to face with Wilson. He points to his desk chair)** You see that chair, Wilson?

WILSON Yes, sir.

MAINWARING That is my chair, the manager's chair. **(He taps the desk)** This is my desk, the manager's desk. And this is my office, the manager's office. I didn't become manager overnight, you know, Wilson, it's been a long hard struggle. Office boy, clerk, assistant chief clerk, chief clerk, assistant manager, and manager. It took me 25 years to get to this office, Wilson, and no red-necked, beer-swilling foreigners are going to drive me out of it. Now, what do you say to that?

WILSON Er, do you think I could come under your umbrella, sir?

MAINWARING No, you can't. There's only room for one.

WILSON **(Turning his coat collar up)** But I'm getting awfully damp, sir.

MAINWARING Well, it's your own fault, you shouldn't poke things. **(He sits at his desk)** Now, let's get on with these accounts.

INTERIOR. THE BANK. DAY

JONES ...and I'll tell you another thing about them Fuzzie Wuzzies, Pikey.

PIKE I'm sorry, Mr Jones, I've got to get on with my work. Mr Mainwaring's not in a very good mood this morning. Have you got any more money to pay in?

JONES I'll say I have. **(He takes a small parcel wrapped up in newspaper from a carrier bag)** Five hundred pounds.

PIKE Five hundred pounds!

JONES Yes, you see all us local shopkeepers have been having a collection for a new serviceman's canteen here in Walmington. Last night, the chairman, Dick Humphreys, brought the final amount, £500, round to my shop.

PIKE Why did he give it to you?

JONES I'm the treasurer, I'm paying the money into my account and then tomorrow I shall write out a cheque and present it to the Mayor at the Town Hall.

PIKE Why did you wrap it up like that?

JONES Well £500 is a lot of money. I didn't want to get knocked on the head and robbed. I thought if I wrapped it up like that, people would think it was half a pound of sausages.

PIKE **(Unwraps parcel)** It is a half pound of sausages.

Jones falls.

INTERIOR. OFFICE. DAY

Wilson is holding the umbrella above Mainwaring's head.

MAINWARING Do try and hold that umbrella still, Wilson, I'm getting soaked.

WILSON Well, I'm not exactly dry, sir.

Pike runs through the open wall at the side of the door.

PIKE Mr Mainwaring, Mr Mainwaring, Mr Jones has...

MAINWARING What do you think you're doing, Pike, bursting into my office?

PIKE I'm sorry, Mr Mainwaring, but it's very important, Mr Jones has...

MAINWARING How dare you come through the wall? I've told you before and I'll tell you again, I will not have my staff walking through the wall. Now, go out and come in properly.

PIKE Yes, sir. **(He goes out through the wall and knocks on the door)**

MAINWARING Come in.

Pike puts his shoulder to the door and crashes into the room.

PIKE Mr Mainwaring I've... Mr Mainwaring, don't you know it's unlucky to open an umbrella indoors?

MAINWARING Don't be stupid, Pike. What do you want?

PIKE Mr Jones is lying on the floor outside, he's fainted.

MAINWARING What? **(They all rush out)** Go round.

Pike goes through door.

INTERIOR. THE BANK. DAY

Mainwaring, Wilson and Pike rush through the door. Jones is sitting on the floor, dazed.

MAINWARING Help me up with him, Wilson.

WILSON Come on, Jonesey, you'll be all right.

They prop him up against the counter.

JONES Where am I? **(He realises)** Oh no... I've lost £500, I've lost £500, don't panic, don't panic. I put it somewhere, I know I put it somewhere. **(He feels in his pockets)**

MAINWARING What's he talking about, Pike?

PIKE He was going to pay in £500, but it had turned into half a pound of sausages.

JONES Mr Mainwaring, Mr Mainwaring, oh it's awful.

WILSON Now come on, Jonesey, tell us what happened.

JONES Well, I had the £500 for the canteen, I went to pay it in, but it wasn't.

MAINWARING Wasn't what?

JONES There, it was half a pound of sausages.

Sausages appear under Mainwaring's nose.

MAINWARING When did you last see the money?

JONES In my shop, sir. I wrapped it up in a bit of newspaper.

WILSON You must have picked up the wrong packet.

MAINWARING Yes, that's what happened, you left it in your shop. Now, go back and have a look for it, and I'll see you on parade tonight.

JONES Yes, that's it. Thank you, Mr Mainwaring, I don't know what I'd do without you, sir. You're my maternal support. **(Searching in his pockets)** I'll find it, I'll find it, I know I put it somewhere.

PIKE What shall I do about the sausages?

MAINWARING I'll take charge of those.

INTERIOR. CHURCH HALL. DAY

It is just before evening parade – Frazer, Walker and Godfrey are in a group. During the scene, members of the platoon arrive. It is night and everyone is wearing battle dress.

WALKER Poor old Jonesey, he's in a terrible state. He came into my place 25 times – in and out all day long he was, turned my warehouse upside down.

GODFREY But what I can't understand is, why should he think he'd left it in your place?

WALKER Search me. I kept saying to him, 'You can't have

lost it in here ,Jonesey, you haven't been near the place for weeks.' It didn't make any difference, he kept ferreting around, and muttering – 'I put it somewhere, I put it somewhere. I can't make it out.'

FRAZER I can, the man's gone potty. Mind you, I've seen this coming on for weeks. Jones is senile, and the shock of losing this money has tipped his brain. He's no longer capable of carrying out his duties as a corporal. Now, the question is, who's going to take his place. I'm next in line. I think I'll go and see Captain Mainwaring now.

GODFREY Really, Mr Frazer, I think you're being very heartless.

WALKER Yes come off it, Taff, that's a bit strong.

FRAZER I'm just being practical. There's a war to be fought. We canna stop for mental casualties.

Pike comes in.

WALKER Has Jonesey found that money yet, Pikey?

PIKE Not as far as I know. He's been in and out of the bank all day. He kept crossing backwards and forwards between his shop and the bank, looking on the ground. He nearly got run over twice.

Wilson enters from the side office and crosses to the group.

WILSON Has Jones arrived yet, Walker?

WALKER No, not yet.

WILSON Oh lor! I hope he's all right. (**To men**) Right, would you all be so good as to fall in please. (**They do so**) Come along, three nice neat lines.

Mainwaring appears at the office door.

WILSON Platoon, attention!

MAINWARING Thank you, Sergeant. Platoon, stand at ease.

They do so.

MAINWARING That was very good. Where's Jones?

WILSON I don't know, sir.

MAINWARING We shall just have to start without him, that's all. Now, pay attention, men. We've got a heavy night's duty ahead of us. Private Sponge will take number two section and… (**Jones enters**) …come along, Jones, you're late.

JONES Sorry, Captain Mainwaring. (**As he passes the fire buckets, he looks inside**) No, it's not in there. (**He looks in the others**) It's not in there either. (**He crosses to the office door – starts to open it**) No, it wouldn't be in there.

MAINWARING Hurry up and fall in, Jones.

JONES Yes, sir, yes, sir. It's not behind there. (**He takes his place., muttering and searching in his pockets**) I've put it somewhere, I know I've put it somewhere.

MAINWARING Jones, will you please pay attention?

JONES (**Fumbling through his tunic**) I'm sorry, sir, I'm not feeling myself today.

WALKER (**Aside to Pike**) What's he talking about? He's been feeling himself ever since he came in.

MAINWARING (**To platoon**) Right, men, on the command 'fall out', two and three sections will go out on patrol. Fall out. (**They fall out**) Number one section, gather round.

Jones, Frazer, Walker, Godfrey and Pike gather round Mainwaring and Wilson.

JONES I must apologise for my behaviour, Mr Mainwaring, but I've had a terrible day. Since I lost that money, I've gone all to pieces. I'm not fit for anything.

FRAZER Precisely. May I remind you, Captain Mainwaring, that I'm next in line for his stripe?

MAINWARING That will do, Frazer.

WALKER Can't we help Jones in some way, sir?

MAINWARING I'm going to try and sort it out now, Walker. Sit down, men.

Frazer and Walker get a bench. They all sit in front of Jones, by now the other two sections have left the hall.

MAINWARING Before we go any further, Jones, we're going to find out what you did with that money.

JONES You bring a warm glow of comfort to my heart, Mr Mainwaring.

WILSON You're problem is our problem, Jonesey.

JONES That's right, Mr Wilson, just like the three musketeers. One for one, and two together. United we fall and we stand divided, upright.

MAINWARING Sit down, Jones.

JONES Yes, sir.

MAINWARING Now, pay attention. It's perfectly simple. What we've got to do is to make Jones remember where he put that money.

JONES Permission to speak, sir? If I could remember where I put it, I wouldn't have lost it in the first place, and in the second place, I've been running round all day trying to remember where I put it in the first place. But my mind's a blank! A blank.

FRAZER Can we discuss the question of the stripe now, sir?

MAINWARING Quiet, Frazer.

PIKE Mr Mainwaring, I know how we can make him remember. I saw it in that film *A Man in the Shadows* with Walter Abel and Joan Blondell.

WILSON Yes, we saw that together, didn't we, Frank? It was awfully good. You see, at the start of the film,

Walter Abel was sitting on a bench in the park in the middle of the night.

PIKE That's right, Uncle Arthur, and he kept muttering, 'I can't remember. I can't remember.' And he was searching through his pockets, just like Mr Jones.

GODFREY I saw that film with my sister Dolly, but she made me take her out before the end. She said it was rather near.

Mainwaring reacts.

PIKE Well, as he was sitting there, Joan Blondell came by.

WALKER What was she doing in the park in the middle of the night?

PIKE She was out for a walk. I like Joan Blondell, she's nice.

WALKER If she was in the park at that time of night she can't be very nice.

PIKE Don't you say anything against Joan Blondell, she's my favourite.

MAINWARING Come to the point, Pike.

PIKE Well, she stopped to talk to him.

WILSON That's right, Frank, then she made him go back over everything that he'd done in the previous 24 hours, to try and make him remember.

MAINWARING Remember what?

WILSON I can't remember.

MAINWARING Yes, yes. As a matter of fact, before you started talking all this rubbish about films, I was going to suggest that.

WILSON Were you really, sir?

MAINWARING (**Giving Wilson a glare**) Now, Jones, I want you to tell us calmly and logically everything you did from the moment you received that money yesterday.

JONES Yes, sir, I'll try, sir.

MAINWARING And this time, don't let your brain go off at a tangent.

JONES No, sir, I won't get my brains in a tangle.

MAINWARING Right, start, and keep calm.

JONES Yes, sir. Well, Dick Billings brought the money round to my shop just before I closed last night. It was in five pound notes.

MAINWARING What did you do with it?

JONES I wrapped it up in a bit of newspaper and took it home with me. When I went to bed, I put the money under my pillow.

MAINWARING What happened the next morning?

JONES I woke up (**Mainwaring reacts**) and got out of bed.

WALKER Which side did you get out?

JONES The left side.

WALKER How do you know you didn't get out the right side?

JONES 'Cos the bed's up against the wall. Shut up, Joe, I'm trying to keep calm, I'm trying to keep calm. I washed, dressed and went downstairs. Then I went upstairs again.

WILSON This is probably a silly question, but why did you do that?

JONES To get the money from under the pillow. Please, Mr Wilson, I'm trying to keep calm. I am keeping calm, aren't I, Mr Mainwaring?

MAINWARING You're doing very well, Jones. Be quiet, Wilson.

JONES Then I had breakfast and walked round to my shop, and I still had the £500. I opened the shop, wrapped up the previous day's takings in paper, made out a bank slip for the takings and another for the £500, and put it all in a carrier bag. Then I said to the boy Raymond, 'Mind the shop I'm going to the bank.' I think it's working, Mr Mainwaring.

MAINWARING That's because you're thinking calmly and logically.

JONES Yes, I'm very calm, I'm very calm. Then I walked across the road to the bank. Young Pikey was there, I said 'Good morning', and paid in the takings.

PIKE Yes, that's right, Mr Mainwaring.

MAINWARING What happened next?

JONES It's all coming back, I'm still quite calm. Then I gave Pike the packet with £500 in it. But it wasn't there.

PIKE No, it had turned into half a pound of sausages.

JONES (**Going beserk**) Yes, that's it! I've lost it! I've lost it! Don't panic! Don't panic! I put it somewhere, I know I put it somewhere. I've lost £500! I've lost £500! Don't panic!

INTERIOR. SIDE OFFICE. NIGHT

Mainwaring is at his desk, fast asleep with a blanket round him. His revolver is lying on the desk in front of him. Wilson is asleep, in another chair, also covered in a blanket.

INTERIOR. CHURCH HALL. NIGHT

Close up of pair of stockinged feet pacing up and down. There is a trail of cigarette ends on the floor. We pull back and reveal that it is Jones, muttering and smoking furiously. There is a

table and benches in foreground. On the table is a single candle in a bottle, all the rest of the lights are out. The rest of the platoon are asleep in various positions. Walker comes into the picture with a mug of tea.

WALKER 'Ere you are, Jonesey.

JONES **(Startled)** Aaarrrah!

WALKER It's all right, you silly old duffer, it's only me. I've brought you a mug of char.

JONES Thanks, Joe. **(He takes it and they both sit at the table, Jones puts out his cigarette end)** Have you got a fag on you?

WALKER Blimey, you've already had two packets off me.

JONES I can't help it, Joe.

WALKER **(Giving him a cigarette)** You look terrible.

JONES I feel terrible, I'm ruined, Joe, ruined. I'd give anything to find out where I put that money.

Frazer's face appears out of the gloom behind them.

FRAZER Aaaah!

They both start.

WALKER Stone me, Taff, you nearly gave me a heart attack.

FRAZER Did you say anything?

JONES Yes, Jock, I'd try anything, anything.

FRAZER Very well. **(He slides into the chair opposite Jones and leans across the table)** Come closer.

Jones and Walker lean across the table.

FRAZER When I was in the China Seas, I studied the art of hypnosis.

WALKER Don't be daft, Taff.

FRAZER I tell you, it's true, I've hypnotised many men in my time, and unlocked many terrible dark secrets. It canna fail, but I must have your co-operation.

JONES If it will help me to remember where I put that money, you have my permission to sterilise me.

FRAZER Good. **(He takes a pocket watch out of his pocket and dangles it in front of Jones' face)** Now, concentrate, clasp your hands together, and put them on top of your head. **(Jones does so)** You are going to sleep, you are going to sleep. **(He repeats it over and over again. Cut to the back of the hall. The Verger's face is peering in the gloom)** You are now in a deep sleep, nod your head if you understand me. **(Jones nods)** You can hear nothing but my voice, you can hear nothing but my voice. What can you hear?

JONES **(Far away)** I can hear nothing but your voice.

WALKER Little sir echo.

JONES **(Unclasping his hands, turning and speaking in normal voice to Walker)** Don't muck about, Joe. I'm being hypnotised.

INTERIOR. VICAR'S BEDROOM. NIGHT

The Vicar is fast asleep, the Verger is leaning over him and shaking him.

VERGER Wake up, Your Reverence, wake up.

VICAR What… **(He sits up and puts his glasses on)** Who is it? Oh it's you, Verger. You are a beastly nuisance. How dare you wake me up?

VERGER Your Reverence, you must come at once and exorcise.

VICAR Have you taken leave of your senses, Mr Yeatman? I'm not running about at this time of night.

VERGER You don't understand, sir. There's a horrible black mass in the church hall.

VICAR A horrible black mass of what?

VERGER That Scotsman is carrying out pagan rites on Church property. Oh the blasphemy. You must come at once and exorcise it.

VICAR If you're being silly, Mr Yeatman, I shall get very cross.

INTERIOR. CHURCH HALL. NIGHT

Frazer, Jones and Walker are sitting at the table. Jones is now in a trance.

FRAZER Are you asleep?

Jones nods.

FRAZER Now, tell me everything that happened.

JONES **(In far away voice)** When Dick Billings brought the money, I took it and wrapped it in paper. On the counter was a large chicken.

FRAZER A chicken!

JONES Yes, the boy, Raymond, was going to deliver it to Mr Bluett.

WALKER Blimey, it's working.

FRAZER Sssh! What happened then?

JONES Raymond picked up the chicken, and I said – 'Wait a minute, you've forgotten the giblets'. Then I picked them up and stuffed them in the chicken. I remember now, it wasn't the giblets I picked up, it was the £500.

FRAZER **(Snapping his fingers)** Wake up!

JONES **(Wakes up and jumps to his feet)** It's in the chicken, it's in the chicken. **(He rushes to the office and crashes through the door)**

INTERIOR. SIDE OFFICE. NIGHT

Jones comes through the door.

JONES Mr Mainwaring, Mr Mainwaring, don't panic.

MAINWARING (**Jumping up and grabbing his revolver**) What?

JONES I stuffed the money in Mr Bluett's chicken. (**He rushes out again**)

INTERIOR. CHURCH HALL. NIGHT

Jones rushes out of the office. The Vicar and Verger appear, the Vicar is wearing his dressing gown. Everyone else is waking up.

JONES Wake up, wake up, the money's in the chicken. (**He bumps into the Vicar**)

VICAR What is going on?

JONES I stuffed it, I stuffed it!

VICAR What?

JONES In the chicken!

VERGER Do you hear that, Your Reverence. A chicken! They always use chickens for black rites. We've arrived just in time to stop something very nasty from happening.

EXTERIOR. MR BLUETT'S FRONT DOOR. NIGHT

Mainwaring, Wilson, Jones, Frazer, Walker, Pike and Godfrey arrive at the door. They have their rifles, and Mainwaring, Wilson and Walker are carrying torches.

WILSON But you can't just wake someone up in the middle of the night and ask to examine their chicken.

MAINWARING (**Pressing the bell**) This is an emergency, Wilson. I'm going to sort this out once and for all.

JONES I'm ever so grateful to you, Mr Mainwaring, helping me like this. The next chicken I get in the shop, you can have.

FRAZER What about me? I'm the one who helped you remember.

JONES I won't forget you, Jock.

PIKE My mum would like a chicken.

GODFREY So would my sister Dolly.

JONES You'll have to wait your turn… I'm not made of chickens.

MAINWARING (**His finger still on bell**) What's the matter with him? Why doesn't he answer?

JONES Whatever you do, sir, don't tell him why we're looking in his chicken. I don't want the whole town to know that I've lost the money. They might lose confidence in me.

MAINWARING Leave it to me, I shall be discreet. Why doesn't he open the door?

WALKER (**Looking through letter box**) I think he's coming down the stairs now, Mr Mainwaring.

MAINWARING Now listen, Wilson, I want you to help me out with this, you've got a diplomatic manner.

WILSON I'll do my best, sir. I've never asked anybody to look inside their chicken before.

MAINWARING There's always a first time for everything.

The door opens a few inches on the chain. Mr Bluett's face appears.

BLUETT Who is it?

MAINWARING It's me, Captain Mainwaring.

BLUETT What's the matter? Have the Germans landed?

MAINWARING No, I have to speak to you very urgently. Open the door.

Mr Bluett slips the chain and opens the door.

MAINWARING I understand you had a chicken delivered to you yesterday.

BLUETT Yes, that's right.

MAINWARING Have you eaten it yet?

BLUETT No, and you can't have it back if that's what you want.

WILSON Actually we want to examine it.

BLUETT Have you got a search warrant?

MAINWARING I don't need a search warrant. In the name of the King, I insist on looking at your chicken.

BLUETT What's the King got to do with it?

MAINWARING The defence of the realm. Can we come in please?

BLUETT I'm not having you in my house with your hobnailed boots. You'll wake my wife up. I'll bring the chicken out. (**He closes the door**)

PIKE Do you think he'll let us look inside his chicken?

MAINWARING Oh yes, believe me, Pike, I'm a pretty shrewd judge of this sort of thing.

GODFREY What I can't understand is, how did Mr Jones suddenly remember where he put that money?

FRAZER I hypnotised him.

MAINWARING Hypnotised him! I've never heard such nonsense in all my life. Why didn't you tell me this, Jones?

JONES I was so excited, I forgot.

WALKER Frazer did it very well,Mr Mainwaring. I was there.

MAINWARING Rubbish. If the money's not inside that chicken, Frazer, I shall hold you personally responsible.

Mr Bluett opens the door, he is holding the chicken on a plate.

BLUETT Here's the chicken, so have a good look at it, and let me get back to bed.

MAINWARING Ah yes, that's a nice chicken, isn't it, Wilson?

WILSON Yes, sir, awfully nice.

MAINWARING Actually, it wasn't the outside of the chicken we wanted to look at, it was the inside.

BLUETT What do you want to look inside for?

MAINWARING Well, you see...

JONES **(Whispers)** Don't tell him about the money, sir.

MAINWARING Yes, well er... we are under the impression that the contents of that chicken would provide a canteen for 500 servicemen.

BLUETT You must be barmy. The only way you could do that is to make soup out of it.

MAINWARING You don't quite understand.

BLUETT It would have to be very watery soup. And then they'd only get an egg cupful each.

MAINWARING **(Snatching the chicken)** We must look inside that chicken. It's a matter of life and death. Hold it, Wilson. **(He hands it to Wilson)**

BLUETT But my wife's already stuffed it.

MAINWARING Well, we shall just have to unstuff it.

WILSON It's all sewn up, sir.

MAINWARING Right, Jones, open it with your bayonet.

JONES Yes, sir, yes, sir. **(He gets to work)**

MAINWARING Walker, Pike, hold up those torches so that I can see.

BLUETT I'm not too happy about this.

WILSON Don't you worry, Mr Bluett, we shall leave it exactly as we found it.

HODGES **(Out of vision)** Put those lights out, put those ruddy lights out. **(He comes into the picture)** What's going on 'ere?

BLUETT You may well ask. They knock me up at half past two in the morning, want to take the stuffing out of my chicken and say it's for the King.

HODGES Have you gone mad, Mainwaring?

WILSON Clear off, this is a military matter.

HODGES Don't you tell me to clear off, mate.

JONES It's open, Mr Mainwaring.

MAINWARING Right, hold your hands out everyone.

They all hold their hands out, They are wearing woolly gloves. Mainwaring takes out bits of stuffing and hands them round.

BLUETT You'll get bits off them gloves. I don't want fluff all mixed up with my stuffing!

WALKER Don't worry, they're very good quality army issue.

HODGES What's he doing with a great big chicken like that anyhow? I never get any chickens.

JONES If you must know, it's Mr Bluett's golden wedding anniversary. I let him have it special. Have you found it yet, Mr Mainwaring?

MAINWARING I'm afraid it's empty, Jones.

JONES Oh no. I can't believe it. It's the finish. I'm ruined.

They all look at Frazer.

FRAZER Well, don't all look at me. It's not my fault.

MAINWARING **(Putting the bits of stuffing back and making a mess of it)** Yes, well, I'm very sorry that we disturbed you, Mr Bluett. Give your wife my compliments, and tell her she stuffed it beautifully. **(He hands back the chicken)**

PIKE Mr Mainwaring – please can I have my glove back?

MAINWARING You stupid boy!

INTERIOR. THE BANK. DAY

Mainwaring and Wilson are standing with Jones. Pike is behind the counter.

WILSON We really are dreadfully sorry, Jonesey.

MAINWARING Yes, believe me, if there was anything I could do to help, I wouldn't hesitate.

PIKE You could lend him the money, Mr Mainwaring.

MAINWARING Be quiet, Pike.

JONES There's only one thing, Mr Mainwaring. I must take the honourable way. I've only got an hour before I present the Mayor with the money at the Town Hall. So I shall write out a cheque for £500 from my own money. It's my life savings, but death before dishonour.

Dick Billings comes into the picture, carrying a packet.

BILLINGS There you are, Mr Jones. I've been looking for you everywhere.

JONES I know what you're going to say, Mr Billings, but you needn't worry. I'm going to make it up out of my own money.

BILLINGS What do you mean? I'm talking about the half pound of sausages you served me with the other night. When the wife went to fry them, this is what she found. **(He unwraps parcel – inside is £500)**

JONES Don't panic, don't panic – we've found the money. Where's my sausages?

MAINWARING Aaah.

SERIES FIVE **EPISODE TEN**

Recorded: Friday 17/11/72

Original transmission: Frday 8/12/72, 8.30–9.00pm

Original viewing figures = 18.6 million

ARTHUR LOWE .... CAPTAIN MAINWARING
JOHN LE MESURIER .... SERGEANT WILSON
CLIVE DUNN.................................. LANCE CORPORAL JONES
JOHN LAURIE .... PRIVATE FRAZER
JAMES BECK .... PRIVATE WALKER
ARNOLD RIDLEY .... PRIVATE GODFREY
IAN LAVENDER .... PRIVATE PIKE
BILL PERTWEE .... ARP WARDEN
ROBERT RAGLAN .... COLONEL
EDWARD SINCLAIR.. VERGER
ANTHONY ROYE..................................... MR FAIRBROTHER
MAGGIE DON... WAITRESS
GEOFFREY HUGHES .... BRIDGE CORPORAL
DAVID ROSE.. DUMP CORPORAL
PLATOON.................................. COLIN BEAN, LESLIE NOYES,
.... HUGH HASTINGS, GEORGE HANCOCK
GIRL AT BAR .... LEONNIE JESSEL
GUESTS AT DINNER .... DESMOND CULLUM-JONES, MICHAEL MOORE,
.... FREDDIE WILES, COLIN BEAN, NED HOOD,
.... REX DIAMOND, BOB BLAINE, ARTHUR PARRY,
.... HARRY DAVIES, WILLIAM CURRAN, TONY WEST, SID COSSON

BRAIN VERSUS BRAWN

• PETER FITTON REMEMBERS •

'David Croft is one of the most talented people I ever worked with. He is a writer of prodigious talent, a consummately skilled director of artists and cameras, very good company and possesses a wicked sense of humour. He used to tell me I was the worst AFM he had ever worked with and he never quite achieved his goal for me of writing a whole script with no props in it at all!

'I was privileged to work with him on further series of *It Ain't Half Hot, Mum* and *Are You Being Served?*. I learned so much from him and his co-writers, Jimmy Perry and Jeremy Lloyd, about how to write and how to "do the telly" in general. I will be forever grateful.'

BRAIN VERSUS BRAWN

INTERIOR. BAR AND RECREATION ROOM. NIGHT

The Walmington-on-Sea Rotary Club dinner is being held. The girl behind the bar is pouring sherry, which is being handed round by a waitress. Fifteen or so male guests are assembled, all in dinner jackets with wing collars and stiff-fronted shirts. Mid shot of a notice, which reads 'Peabody Rooms, Walmington-on-Sea Rotarian Dinner'. Mainwaring is taking a small glass of sherry from the tray.

MAINWARING Ah, sherry, thank you very much, quite a treat.

WAITRESS Only one glass each, I'm afraid.

MAINWARING Well, at least we drink it as free men, and not under the Nazi heel.

Wilson joins him.

MAINWARING Ah, Wilson, glad you could join me as my guest. **(Confidentially)** Some of the most influential people in Walmington-on-Sea are here tonight. If you ever intend to get your own branch, you'll have to mingle more in these sorts of circles, you know.

WILSON It was awfully kind of you to invite me.

MAINWARING Not at all, I'd like to see you get on. That's our chairman over there.

The waitress gives Wilson a sherry.

WILSON **(To waitress)** Thank you, my dear, that's most kind of you.

MAINWARING As I was saying, that's...

WILSON What a pretty brooch you're wearing.

WAITRESS Thank you, it was my granny's.

WILSON Was it really? It goes awfully well with the colouring of your hair.

WAITRESS Thank you, sir.

MAINWARING Wilson!

WAITRESS I'll slip you another one when you've finished that.

WILSON That's very sweet of you.

MAINWARING Wilson! Don't bother about the waitress. I'm pointing out our chairman to you. He's over there, looking this way. Ah, I think I've caught his eye. **(Mainwaring nods)** He is the managing director of 'Precision Extrusions', you know.

WILSON Oh really.

MAINWARING Try to ingratiate yourself with him.

A distinguished-looking man ,about Wilson's age, comes up to them.

MAINWARING Ah, Mr Fairbrother, this is my chief clerk, Wilson.

FAIRBROTHER It's Arthur, isn't it?

WILSON That's right.

FAIRBROTHER Good grief, I'm Tony Fairbrother. We were at school together.

WILSON Were we?

FAIRBROTHER We shared a study for three terms.

WILSON So we did.

They shake each other warmly by the hand.

MAINWARING He's been my chief clerk for eight years.

FAIRBROTHER Steven's here, Steven Sebag.

WILSON Steven Sebag?

FAIRBROTHER He's *Sir* Steven now. Come and see him, he's as bald as a coot.

MAINWARING **(Trying to stay in the conversation)** Grass doesn't grow on a busy street, you know.

FAIRBROTHER Excuse us, Mainington.

MAINWARING Yes, of course. It's Mainwaring actually.

Wilson and Fairbrother move away.

FAIRBROTHER **(As they go)** You gave Sebag a beating once, didn't you?

WILSON Actually, I let him off.

Mainwaring is left alone for a second. Another distinguished guest approaches.

MAINWARING Ah, good evening, Mr Bathurst. How's the golf going?

The guest walks straight past him.

MAINWARING Good.

Jones approaches.

JONES Good evening, Captain Mainwaring.

MAINWARING Hello, Jones, nice to see you here again representing the butchers of Walmington-on-Sea.

JONES I'm also representing the athletics society, Mr Mainwaring.

MAINWARING Oh, really?

JONES Yes – Jim Cutter had to go to the Derby and Joan Club.

MAINWARING That's what I like about these gatherings, everyone here represents his profession or craft.

Walker approaches – he wears his dinner jacket with jewel studs and cufflinks.

WALKER Evening, Mr Mainwaring.

MAINWARING What are you doing here, Walker?

WALKER Why shouldn't I be here?

MAINWARING I didn't know that under-the-counter dealing was a profession.

WALKER 'Tis now. Anyway, if it wasn't for me, you wouldn't be supping that sherry, and the chicken croquettes you're going to have would be made of whale meat instead of rabbit.

The colonel joins them.

COLONEL Hello, Joe. Good evening, Mr Jones.

MAINWARING Good evening, Colonel.

COLONEL Sorry, didn't see you, Mainwaring. Are you chaps looking forward to the scheme on Saturday?

MAINWARING Scheme, what scheme?

COLONEL Oh no, of course – none of your chaps are taking part.

WALKER Why aren't we taking part?

JONES Yes, Mr Mainwaring, in what way have we been found to have shortcomings?

COLONEL Well, it was the training major's idea really. He wants to form this sort of Home Guard Commando Unit out of the younger, fitter chaps.

MAINWARING I heard about it.

COLONEL He thought we ought to have a striking force to operate behind the enemy lines. You know the sort of thing – winkling out petrol dumps and blowing them up, etc.

WALKER We sent Pike up to H.Q. for an interview.

JONES Did he get in?

COLONEL No, he couldn't find H.Q.

MAINWARING I Think the whole idea is a complete farce. We're not commandos and we never will be.

JONES Why not, Mr Mainwaring? I can winkle things as well as any of those young chaps, I've always been a good winkler.

MAINWARING We have brains and experience, and local knowledge. Those are our weapons, not muscle and brawn.

COLONEL I must say, I do agree. I was dead against it.

WALKER It's a bit of an insult to the old campaigners, isn't it?

JONES It is, Joe, I feel very spurned.

The noise of a gavel banging is heard and the waitress' voice is heard off.

WAITRESS (**Off**) Take your seats at the table please, gentlemen.

COLONEL We'd better be going in. I suppose you wouldn't like to take part in the scheme and prove your point, would you?

MAINWARING Of course we would, we're game for anything aren't we, Jones?

JONES Always very game, sir.

COLONEL I'll see if I can get the training major to agree. We'll talk about it after dinner.

They move into the dining hall as we fade.

INTERIOR. SIDE OFFICE

Mainwaring has a diagram on a board, Wilson is beside him, Jones' section plus three or four of the platoon are paying attention. We start on a close shot of the end of Mainwaring's stick indicating on the blackboard.

MAINWARING There's where the bomb has to be placed – in or close to the C.O.'s office, which is that hut inside the petrol dump – and this... Have you got it, Wilson?

WILSON Yes, sir.

MAINWARING Well, hold it up.

WILSON The bomb.

MAINWARING ...this represents the bomb that we have to plant.

WALKER I've got a 150 of them if anyone wants to buy them.

MAINWARING Now, Wilson and I did a recce yesterday, and security of this place is absolutely first class. These so-called Home Guard Commandos won't get in there, that's for sure. Brain is what we need.

JONES And ingenuity, sir. Ingenuity is very good for getting people into things.

MAINWARING Quite right, Jones. A platoon of infantry mount guard from here... This (**Indicates the diagram**) is a barbed wire fence, 12 foot high, overhanging at the top and I would say unclimbable.

PIKE Could we put a ladder against it?

MAINWARING I think that might arouse the suspicion of the guards, Pike.

PIKE We could dress up as window cleaners.

WILSON They don't have windows in barbed wire do they, Frank?

PIKE No, Uncle Arthur.

FRAZER Could we not fling it – the bomb – couldn't we fling it?

WALKER That's right, Jock, give it a Highland Fling.

Bit of ad-lib here.

MAINWARING That'll do, Walker. There to there, (**He indicates the wire to the hut**) is a good 35 yards. Corporal

Jones here has tried one or two experiments at throwing it, haven't you, Jones?

JONES Yes sir, I threw it 12 yards at the first attempt, then I grabbed hold of it and whirled myself round like a whirling Dervish – they do it in a trance you know, sir – they do a lot of whirling in trances do Dervishes – I whirled and whirled and I got very dizzy because I wasn't in a trance, and then the handle came off.

MAINWARING Yes, well, I don't think that would work. In any case, we're jumping the gun. Firstly we're going to be dumped somewhere along this road as if we were parachutists.

PIKE Will we have parachutes, Mr Mainwaring?

MAINWARING Of course we won't have parachutes, you stupid boy.

PIKE Well, what's stupid about that? Parachutists have parachutes, don't they?

MAINWARING Don't be impertinent, Pike. We then have to cross the river by this bridge here or by some other means.

GODFREY Captain Mainwaring – I'm rather anxious not to do any swimming.

FRAZER Pontoons, sir, pontoons. We need pontoons, that's what we need – pontoons.

MAINWARING Yes, well, unfortunately we don't have any.

PIKE We could use Mr Frazer's coffins.

MAINWARING If you go on being silly, Pike, I shall send you home.

Pike reacts.

WALKER Captain Mainwaring, why don't we just walk across the bridge?

MAINWARING The bridge and the river bank are being defended by a Company of the Royal West Kents, so frontal attack is not very likely to succeed, unless we create some sort of diversion.

FRAZER Bluff, sir, bluff. We'll have to use bluff, that's what we'll have to use – bluff.

JONES And ingenuity.

GODFREY I don't mind dressing up as a nun.

MAINWARING Thank you, Godfrey.

GODFREY I did it once at a fancy dress ball and everyone said I looked very holy.

WALKER That's it, Pike can be a novice, and Jonesey here can be the Mother Superior.

MAINWARING Walker.

WILSON But surely, sir, we're always reading in the paper about parachutists dressing up as nuns. I think they'll suspect straight away.

JONES Not necessarily, Mr Wilson – that's where the ingenuity comes in. They'll see us walking along the road as a nun crocodile, and the guards will say to themselves – 'Those Home Guard soldiers wouldn't disguise themselves as artificial nuns ecause we would think that they was parachutists. Therefore they must be real nuns, out ventilating themselves in the air' – so they will bless us and let us pass.

MAINWARING I don't think it's a very practical idea, Jones – nuns' habits are not that easy to come by.

JONES Joe here could borrow them.

WALKER Well, it's not easy, Jonesey, I don't do much business with the orphanage.

FRAZER Except for providing the orphans.

WALKER That's libel, that is.

Pike has been whispering to Wilson during the last few sentences.

WILSON Frank here has a suggestion.

MAINWARING Yes, what is it, Pike?

PIKE I don't want to tell it, because you'll say I'm being silly.

MAINWARING Of course I won't; not unless you *are* being silly.

PIKE Well – it's to do with coffins again.

MAINWARING Oh yes?

PIKE Well, why don't we be a funeral? They'd let a funeral across the bridge.

MAINWARING That's quite true, Pike, but it doesn't help us when we get there… (**Points to the enclosure**) because they don't have funerals in petrol dumps.

WALKER Unless it blows up.

MAINWARING Unless it blows up – I shan't tell you again, Walker. The point is this, whatever gets us across the bridge must get us into the petrol dump.

WALKER Captain Mainwaring – there's a shed here, where I store some of my essential supplies. If we could all make our way there, and if you all keep your traps shut, I might be able to help.

MAINWARING I'm sure you could rely on our discretion, Walker.

WALKER One other thing, Captain Mainwaring, you have to keep your hands to yourself. I don't want anyone nicking the stuff. That's how I got it.

MAINWARING Just explain your idea, Walker. Nobody's going to touch your property.

WALKER Well, what we do is this…

INTERIOR. SHED OR BARN

A fire engine is parked in the middle – engine pointing to audience. Various junk is packed around the walls, including tea chests, tins of beans, razor blades, dried egg, etc. There is an adjoining room into which we can barely see. The door of this opens, and Mainwaring emerges. He wears an old fireman's uniform – preferably Victorian – plus the traditional brass, coal-scuttle helmet.

MAINWARING Right, in here, all of you, as soon as you've put on your uniforms. (**Pike enters**) Put your hat on, Pike.

PIKE I can't see with it, Captain Mainwaring. (**He puts it on back to front**)

MAINWARING The other way round, you stupid boy.

Wilson enters.

WILSON They're awfully rough round the neck, aren't they.

MAINWARING You've been mollycoddled too much, that's your trouble.

They start to examine the engine. Frazer enters with Walker.

FRAZER It is a fine machine, how did you come by it, Joe?

WALKER Well, when they re-equipped the fire station, I said I'd give 'em a tenner for it, providing they threw in the helmets. I was going to knock 'em out as flower vases, see.

Jones enters.

JONES Captain Mainwaring, sir, would you clear up a technical point? Should the handles of our axes dangle over our left rump or our right rump?

MAINWARING Left please, Jones.

JONES Thank you, sir. (**In a parade ground voice**) Get your handles over your left rumps! Handles over left rumps!

MAINWARING That'll do, Jones. (**Jones reacts**) Now, gather round quickly while we run over the plan once more.

They assemble, including Sponge and three strong Home Guards. Godfrey is a little late.

MAINWARING Hurry up, Godfrey.

GODFREY I'm afraid there are no buttons on the trousers for my braces.

MAINWARING Can't you wear a belt?

GODFREY I always think trousers hang so much better with braces, don't you?

MAINWARING This is not a fashion show, Godfrey. Right, we leave here at ten past three.

WILSON Thirteen ten.

MAINWARING What did you say?

WILSON Fifteen ten.

MAINWARING That's right. Two minutes later, a fire will be lit outside the wire fence to the petrol dump as a diversion. Now, is that fire taken care of?

WALKER Yes, sir. I dropped a load of old packing cases and a couple of drums of sump oil right near the wire last night.

MAINWARING Good. So at three twelve...

WILSON Fifteen twelve.

MAINWARING Yes, our secret agent will push the barrow of paraffin-soaked straw into that pile and ignite it. Have you taken care of the secret agent, Wilson?

WILSON Yes, sir, I have.

MAINWARING I think at this stage it would be safe to disclose the identity of the secret agent.

WILSON It's the Verger.

MAINWARING It's the Verger – the Verger! Are you out of your mind? You said you were going to arrange for Mrs Pike to do it.

WILSON She couldn't make up her mind what to wear.

MAINWARING But the Verger will get it all wrong.

WILSON I wrote it all down for him and I gave him a ten bob note, so I'm sure he'll be all right.

MAINWARING On your own head be it. Anyway, the fire should help us to bluff our way across the bridge. On arrival at the petrol dump, what do you do, Frazer?

FRAZER My party unloads yon ladder and we put it near the wire.

WALKER Me and Pikey and the rest make a hullabaloo round the fire with hoses.

JONES And while Joe is hullabalooing, I shall shinny up the ladder unseen, and I shall dangle the bomb on the end of this rope, and when Joe's hullabaloo has got very high, I shall sling the bomb on to the hut like a linesman swinging the lead. Not a football linesman, you understand, but a sea-faring linesman. They put a little tallow on the end to see what kind of a bottom they've got. Did you know that, sir?

MAINWARING As a matter of fact, I did.

JONES You might have stopped me.

MAINWARING Yes, thank you, Jones. Now, as this operation depends on split-second timing, we'd better synchronise our watches. (**He takes his pocket watch out**) The time now is exactly, exactly... (**He shakes the watch and listens**) Extraordinary. What time is it, Wilson?

WILSON I left mine at home in case it got wet.

MAINWARING You've no business to leave your watch at home on active service.

FRAZER Joe here has the time.

Walker bares his wrist to reveal eight watches.

WALKER It's seven minutes past three.

MAINWARING Right, stand by at your posts.

PIKE Can I drive the fire engine, Mr Mainwaring? Let me drive the fire engine.

MAINWARING Don't be ridiculous, Pike.

PIKE Well, can I ring the bell then?

JONES I'm ringing the bell.

MAINWARING Get into your place, boy.

Godfrey is struggling to get on to seats at the side.

GODFREY Would somebody give me a hand?

FRAZER What are you talking about? I need a hand myself.

MAINWARING Give them a hand, someone.

Pike and Wilson go to assist Godfrey on to the long side seat.

WILSON Up you go, Godfrey.

Godfrey gets on to the side seat.

WILSON Now you, Frazer.

Frazer mounts beside him.

MAINWARING In you get, Wilson.

Mainwaring helps Wilson into the centre of the front seat.

WILSON Thank you so much, sir, I'm all right now.

Jones helps Mainwaring into the driver's seat.

JONES Upsy-daisy, sir. Let me put my shoulder to you, sir.

MAINWARING I'm all right, Jones. **(Mainwaring gets in)** Hurry up and get in. **(He turns as Jones goes round to the bell seat)** Everybody all right back there? **(There are general 'yeses')** Right, stand by.

JONES **(Trying to mount bell side seat)** Hang on, Mr Mainwaring, don't go yet. I'm not quite at the ready.

MAINWARING **(Getting out himself)** Hold on a minute, Jones.

JONES If you could give me a slight urge when I say 'one, two, three', sir.

MAINWARING Lend a hand from your side, Wilson.

JONES **(Holding up a small, brass fire extinguisher)** Mr Mainwaring, look, a fire extinguisher in case the fire engine catches fire. Firemen are very cautious you know, sir.

MAINWARING Get on with it, Jones. **(Jones is assisted into his seat)** Right, stand by everyone, stand by. **(Mainwaring now has difficulty in getting back into his seat)** Give me a hand, Wilson.

Pike gets down and helps Mainwaring from behind – Mainwaring gets into his seat.

MAINWARING There we are. **(He turns and sees Pike)** Pike, why aren't you on the engine?

PIKE I only got down, sir, to give…

MAINWARING Don't argue, get on at once.

Pike climbs up chuntering.

MAINWARING And no back chat. Now, are we all ready?

ALL Yes.

MAINWARING Right, here we go. **(He is about to reach for the starter)**

JONES **(Ringing the bell like crazy)** Fire, fire, don't panic, don't panic, fire…

MAINWARING Jones, Jones. Stop him, Wilson.

WILSON Jones, you really must be quiet.

MAINWARING Jones.

Jones stops.

JONES Sorry, Mr Mainwaring, I can't hear what you're saying because the bell is so noisy.

MAINWARING Jones, don't touch that bell until I say go.

JONES Ah, very goo,d Mr Mainwaring.

MAINWARING Right, let's get started.

PIKE Mr Mainwaring, Mr Mainwaring.

MAINWARING What's the matter, Pike?

PIKE We can't go yet.

MAINWARING Why not?

PIKE The doors are shut.

MAINWARING We'll open them when we're ready.

WALKER I don't think you ought to start the engine with the doors shut, sir.

JONES No, Mr Mainwaring. Otherwise the gases will come out and we shall breathe them in and then we'll all get sophisticated.

MAINWARING Get down and open the doors, Pike.

PIKE Yes, sir.

Air raid sirens start.

WILSON Hello. Here they come again.

FRAZER It's a good thing. It might distract the guards on the bridge.

MAINWARING Quite right, Frazer, let's go.

JONES **(Ringing the bell)** Fire, fire, don't panic, don't panic, fire.

MAINWARING Stop him.

WILSON Jones, stop, stop.

JONES **(Stopping)** He said go, so I went with my dinger.

MAINWARING Don't ring until we're on the move.

PIKE (Saluting) The door is now open, Captain Mainwaring.

MAINWARING Pike, how many times have I told you to get on your seat?

PIKE I was…

MAINWARING Don't argue. Right, hold on everybody.

Pike climbs on to his seat – Mainwaring presses the self starter – the engine turns over – water from the small, coiled hose spurts over Pike.

PIKE Mr Mainwaring, Mr Mainwaring.

Mainwaring stops, turns round and looks at Pike.

MAINWARING What's the matter, Pike? Why are you all wet?

PIKE Because you squished water all over me.

MAINWARING Don't be ridiculous. **(Mainwaring turns to start the engine again – Pike gets the squirt again)**

WALKER Sergeant Wilson, press that lever forward. It throws the pump out.

MAINWARING Yes, push that lever forward, Wilson, and hurry up about it. **(Mainwaring presses the starter – the engine starts)** Good Lord, it runs well.

WALKER So it should. It's the same petrol they use in Spitfires.

MAINWARING Great Scott.

The engine moves a little bit forward.

JONES We're off. **(He rings the bell like mad)** Fire, fire, don't panic, don't panic, fire!

TELECINE: EXTERIOR. SHED AND ROAD

They are all sitting as follows – Mainwaring is driving, Wilson is next to him, Jones is at the bell. Pike, Frazer, Godfrey, Walker and Sponge are behind them. The fire engine moves swiftly out of the shed and turns on to the road.

TELECINE: EXTERIOR. PETROL DUMP

An open lorry is drawn up – packing cases are loaded on it, and the driver and a regular corporal are just loading on an old oil drum.

CORPORAL That's the lot, and if I could find who dumped 'em, his feet wouldn't touch.

TELECINE: EXTERIOR. ROAD

Medium long shot of fire engine driving along from the front. Jones is ringing the bell.

JONES Don't panic, don't panic, fire, fire ,don't panic. I'm rather enjoying this.

MAINWARING It all hinges now on the Verger.

TELECINE: EXTERIOR. PETROL DUMP

Verger approaching the petrol dump as the lorry drives off – he is pushing a wooden barrow on pram wheels with wooden shafts. He stops and pulls a sheet of paper from his pocket and reads.

VERGER 'Push barrow among pile of packing cases.' **(He looks briefly round for packing cases – he sees the corporal and calls)** Excuse me, have you noticed a pile of packing cases dumped here?

CORPORAL Yeh, he's just driving 'em away.

Cut to lorry disappearing.

CORPORAL Are they yours?

VERGER No, I was just interested in them for a friend. **(He takes the paper out and reads again, Corporal goes to his guard hut – turns and looks mystified)**

VERGER **(Reading)** 'Light paper in the barrow.' **(He lights the paper. The corporal is even more mystified)**

VERGER 'Shout "fire", run to guard room and send for fire brigade.' Fire, fire!

The corporal extinguishes the barrow fire very quickly with the extinguisher.

VERGER Send for the fire brigade.

CORPORAL What for? I've put it out.

VERGER What's your game then?

CORPORAL If it comes to that, what's yours?

VERGER It doesn't say anything about you here. **(Verger indicates the list)** Clear off.

TELECINE: EXTERIOR. ROAD

Fire engine travelling down road.

PIKE There's the bridge straight ahead.

WILSON I don't see any smoke from the Verger. It should be over there.

TELECINE: EXTERIOR. BRIDGE

Three soldiers and a corporal are guarding it.

CORPORAL **(Seeing and hearing distant fire engine)** Ruddy hell.

Long shot of fire engine approaching.

CORPORAL Better check it, lads. There's no telling what those old bastards will get up to.

TELECINE: EXTERIOR. FIRE ENGINE

WALKER Look, sir, the smoke's coming from over there.

MAINWARING The fool! He lit the fire in the wrong place.

WILSON They're stopping us.

MAINWARING I'll deal with this.

TELECINE: EXTERIOR. BRIDGE

Long shot of engine stopping on bridge, Closer shot of corporal at engine.

CORPORAL Just checking to see you've no Home Guards hiding.

MAINWARING Don't be ridiculous, there's a fire. Can't you see?

The corporal opens one of the traps – two hens fly out.

CORPORAL What are those hens doing there?

WALKER Laying eggs. Drive on, driver.

Long shot of fire engine driving through.

CORPORAL **(Mystified for a moment then collecting himself)** Don't stand about, catch them hens.

TELECINE: EXTERIOR. ROAD

Long shot of fire engine approaching the Warden, who is gesticulating in the middle of the road.

WARDEN **(Shouting)** It's over there, it's over there.

MAINWARING **(Braking)** Damn, it's Hodges.

The engine stops.

WARDEN You've been quick, I haven't even sent for you yet.

MAINWARING Get out of the way, Hodges.

WARDEN Mainwaring, what are you doing dressed up as a fireman?

MAINWARING We're on a secret exercise, so let us through.

WARDEN Oh no you don't, that Jerry plane dropped a stick of incendiaries, there's a house on fire round the corner. **(The Warden leaps on the running board)** Drive on.

Long shot of the engine driving on. The engine turns.

TELECINE: EXTERIOR. COTTAGE

The fire engine pulls up at the cottage. Smoke is pouring from an upper floor window. Two bystanders are bringing buckets of water from inside the house. Two Wardens are pumping on a stirrup pump from the bucket and trying to get the jet into the window.

MAINWARING **(Dismounting)** Don't sit there gawping, Pike. Run the small hose out.

Pike leaps down with the nozzle end of the small hose.

MAINWARING Come on, get the ladder off, hoses out.

Frazer and other Home Guards start to get the ladder off.

WARDEN Get a move on, Napoleon, that house'll be burnt down in a minute.

MAINWARING Mind your own business – get the hoses out. **(He turns to go to the back of the engine – Pike is unreeling hose – stops him)** Pike, you're going too fast.

The hose falls clean off the end of the reel.

PIKE **(Holding nozzle and pointing it at window)** Would you mind turning the tap on, Mr Mainwaring?

MAINWARING You've pulled it out of the socket, you stupid boy.

Pike runs back to the engine.

GODFREY **(Still seated)** Captain Mainwaring, I wonder if you'd assist me to the ground?

MAINWARING There's no time for that sort of thing.

WARDEN Hurry up, Mainwaring.

MAINWARING Go away.

Walker runs up to Mainwaring, followed by Jones.

WALKER We've hooked up the hydrant.

JONES Yes, but there's no twiddler.

MAINWARING No what?

JONES It's the iron part, the metal thing like a sardine key, only bigger, that you put in the ground and then you twiddle it, and the water flourishes out.

PIKE **(Now at the engine trap, holding up the hydrant key)** Here it is.

MAINWARING Don't waste time, Pike, take it to the hydrant.

Pike runs to the hydrant.

FRAZER **(At rear controls)** We're all set back here.

MAINWARING Good.

WARDEN **(To Mainwaring)** Why aren't you doing something?

WALKER Here, take this. **(He hands Warden a big hose nozzle attached to the hose)**

MAINWARING And take it over there at the double.

WARDEN Yes, Captain.

GODFREY Captain Mainwaring, I wonder…

MAINWARING Well done, Godfrey, you hang on up there. **(Mainwaring walks quickly round to front of the engine – he sees Wilson)** Wilson, what do you think you're doing there?

WILSON I thought you might want me to start something or stop something – or something.

MAINWARING Stand by to rev up the engine.

Cut to Jones and Pike at hydrant, the large hose is connected and runs between Pike's legs to the engine. Jones is kneeling to locate the hydrant key. Pike is ready to turn.

JONES That's it – twiddle, Pikey.

PIKE All right, Mr Jones. **(Pike turns the key – a jet of water shoots at him from a hole in the hose)**

MAINWARING **(At engine)** Keep turning, Pike.

PIKE I'm getting all wet, Mr Mainwaring.

MAINWARING Don't worry about that.

FRAZER **(At rear of engine)** Standing by this end, sir.

MAINWARING Send the water through, I'll direct the jet. **(Mainwaring moves to join the Warden at the nozzle by the house)**

FRAZER Rev her up, Sergeant.

WILSON Is anything happening?

WALKER **(Moving in beside him)** There's a lever somewhere I think.

Cut to Mainwaring and Warden.

WARDEN **(Holding nozzle)** There's nothing coming through. Tell them to hurry.

MAINWARING Give it to me, it's probably obstructed. **(He looks down the hole)**

Cut to Frazer turning a handle. Cut to Wilson and Walker.

WILSON **(Shoving a lever forward)** There, that's it. Let's go and help them. **(He moves with Wilson to join Captain Mainwaring and Warden)**

MAINWARING **(Still looking through hole)** There's no sign of any foreign body. **(He moves nozzle aside as he calls to men)** Open your valve, Frazer.

The water comes through – the Warden cops it. Mainwaring and Warden struggle to control the jet. Cut to Jones and Pike round the hole leak.

JONES Put your finger in the hole, Pikey.

PIKE You put your finger in it.

JONES No, I'm not going to get all wet.

The main hose is directed on Jones. Cut to Mainwaring and Warden. Walker helps them to get it under control and the jet is directed through the window.

MAINWARING That's it, we'll soon have it out now.

The colonel, in uniform, joins Mainwaring at the nozzle.

COLONEL You're a man of many parts, aren't you?

MAINWARING All this was to enable us to get into the petrol dump. Unfortunately, Hitler spoilt our plan.

COLONEL Never mind, all the Home Guard Commandos got caught and your other plan worked.

MAINWARING Other plan.

COLONEL The training major was actually waiting in the hut to see what happened. You should have seen his face when that parcel arrived on his desk by the twelve o'clock post, and he opened it and found the bomb.

MAINWARING Parcel?

WALKER I posted it yesterday, like Sergeant Wilson said.

Mainwaring looks at Wilson – Wilson smiles.

MAINWARING Ah, well done, Walker.

COLONEL He said it was cheating, but I say it just proves the point, brains very often beat brawn.

MAINWARING Yes, I'll back ingenuity against muscles every time.

The hose gives an urge and starts to get out of control – Mainwaring struggles.

MAINWARING Hang on to it, Warden. Wilson – lend a hand here.

Roll captions as Mainwaring fights with hose.

SERIES FIVE **EPISODE ELEVEN**

Recorded: Sunday 26/11/72

(The *Christmas Night with the Stars* insert was recorded the same evening)

Original transmission: Friday 15/12/72, 8.30–9.00pm

Original viewing figures = 15.4 million

ARTHUR LOWE .... CAPTAIN MAINWARING
JOHN LE MESURIER .... SERGEANT WILSON
CLIVE DUNN .... LANCE CORPORAL JONES
JOHN LAURIE .... PRIVATE FRAZER
JAMES BECK .... PRIVATE WALKER
ARNOLD RIDLEY .... PRIVATE GODFREY
IAN LAVENDER .... PRIVATE PIKE
BILL PERTWEE .... ARP WARDEN
GEOFFREY LUMSDEN .... CAPTAIN SQUARE
FRANK WILLIAMS .... VICAR
EDWARD SINCLAIR .... VERGER
STUART SHERWIN .... REG ADAMSON (JUNIOR WARDEN)
JEFFREY GARDINER .... MR WINTERGREEN
MARJORIE WILDE .... LADY MAGISTRATE
CHRIS GANNON .... MR BONE, THE CLERK OF THE COURT
TOBY PERKINS .... USHER
PLATOON .... COLIN BEAN, HUGH CECIL, LESLIE NOYES, GEORGE HANCOCK, EVAN ROSS, DESMOND CULLUM-JONES, HUGH HASTINGS, FREDDIE WILES, MICHAEL MOORE, FREDDIE WHITE
EXTRAS IN COURT .... PHILIP BECKER, SIMON JUSEL, RICHARD ATTHERTON, EILEEN MATTHEWS, PAT SYMONDS

A BRUSH WITH THE LAW

• COLIN BEAN REMEMBERS •

'Being part of the second line in *Dad's Army* became increasingly and more obviously important as the making of episodes of this TV classic progressed. A number of us were experienced, established theatre artistes, known to either Jimmy or David, and the extent of our role and function was explained to us very clearly (with some professional respect I like to think) at the outset. Even those amongst us who, rather than theatre folk, were professional film and TV supporting artistes were appreciative of this thoughtfulness on the parts of Messrs Croft, Perry and Snoad. We had an important job to do – albeit not starring roles – and they knew (we hoped) that they could rely on us to give supportive performances to the very best of our collective experience and abilities.'

A Brush with the Law

INTERIOR. WARDEN'S POST

Hodges is seated at a table doing some paperwork. Junior Warden enters – he reaches for the phone on the Warden's desk, Hodges stops him.

HODGES Hang on a minute, who are you calling?

JUNIOR WARDEN The wife, I want to tell her I'll be late.

HODGES Sorry, Reg, emergency calls only on this phone.

The phone rings – Warden answers.

HODGES Hello, Frank, thanks for ringing back. Lincoln three fifteen – Farmer's Boy – ten bob each way, okay? Thanks, Frank.

He hangs up – Junior Warden has taken his report book out.

HODGES What have you got?

JUNIOR WARDEN Not bad. Nine forty-five, Miss Samways at the bungalow was showing a light from her bathroom window.

HODGES Very naughty.

JUNIOR WARDEN She was using more than five inches of water an' all.

HODGES Was she?

JUNIOR WARDEN Right up to here it was. (**He indicates above the chest**)

HODGES Yes, well, I'll check that myself before we prosecute. What else?

JUNIOR WARDEN A bad one. Ten thirty-two, the church hall, an uncurtained window and a sixty-watt bulb.

HODGES The church hall – which window?

JUNIOR WARDEN The office.

HODGES Mainwaring! I've got him!

JUNIOR WARDEN I'll say you have. It was shining like a beacon for a whole hour. We had to break in to put it out.

HODGES I've got him, I've got him! Come round to the police station – I'll need a statement. Well done, well done, Reg. (**He starts to take the Junior Warden out**)

INTERIOR. SIDE OFFICE

Wilson is filling in the names on a paper notice on the wall. Mainwaring is standing behind him.

WILSON That's it then, Jones' section patrol the railway sidings and the gasworks.

MAINWARING Good – that does it. Oh and by the way, Wilson, am I hurting you?

WILSON I don't think so.

MAINWARING Well, I should be, I'm standing on your hair.

WILSON It's a very old one, but it always makes me laugh.

MAINWARING I'm trying to tell you to get your hair cut.

WILSON Don't you like it, sir? Mrs Pike says it makes me look like Eden.

The phone rings.

MAINWARING Answer the phone, Anthony.

WILSON (**Crossing to phone**) Yes, sir. (**At phone**) Hello, Sergeant Wilson here. Oh, hello, you're quite a stranger. Yes, he's here. (**He laughs**) Well, we understand him, you know.

Mainwaring reacts. Wilson hands the receiver to Mainwaring.

WILSON It's for you.

MAINWARING Thank you very much – who is it?

WILSON Captain Square.

MAINWARING What's he want? (**Into receiver**) Yes...

Intercut between Square in his office and Mainwaring.

INTERIOR. SQUARE'S OFFICE

SQUARE Ah, Mainwaring, I hope you won't take this the wrong way, but when did you last inspect your platoon's firearms?

INTERIOR. SIDE OFFICE

MAINWARING What is the reason for your inquiry?

INTERIOR. SQUARE'S OFFICE

SQUARE Well, I came across a bunch of your chaps on patrol last night. I thought they looked a bit scruffy, so I had a look at their rifles.

INTERIOR. SIDE OFFICE

MAINWARING You did what?

INTERIOR. SQUARE'S OFFICE

SQUARE My dear fellow, I've never seen anything like it

in all my service. I mean, they practically had birds' nests in them.

INTERIOR. SIDE OFFICE

MAINWARING How dare you inspect my men without my permission?

INTERIOR. SQUARE'S OFFICE

SQUARE It's as well for you I did, they were filthy, old man, filthy. If the colonel got to hear about it he'd have you cashiered, even though you are a civilian.

Mainwaring reacts.

SQUARE Hope you don't mind me mentioning it.

INTERIOR. SIDE OFFICE

MAINWARING I do mind you mentioning it, I find your attitude intolerable.

INTERIOR. SQUARE'S OFFICE

SQUARE There's no need to take that tack!

INTERIOR. SIDE OFFICE

MAINWARING If you ever interfere with my men again I shall give them instructions to arrest you.

INTERIOR. SQUARE'S OFFICE

SQUARE Any more of that sort of talk, Mainwaring, and I shall put the receiver down on you.

INTERIOR. SIDE OFFICE

MAINWARING You're not going to put the receiver down on me, I'm going to put the receiver down on you.

INTERIOR. SQUARE'S OFFICE

SQUARE Oh no you're not.

INTERIOR. SIDE OFFICE

MAINWARING Oh yes I am – hello, hello. **(To Wilson)** He put the receiver down on me.

WILSON My, my, did you have a tiff?

MAINWARING It's all your fault, Wilson. When did you last inspect the men's firearms?

WILSON I think I gave them the once over last week, or was it the week before?

MAINWARING You're a slacker, Wilson.

WILSON A slacker?

MAINWARING Yes, that's what I said, a slacker. And what's more, you look a shambles. Do your collar up and get the men on parade for a rifle inspection.

WILSON Yes, sir.

MAINWARING And do your cuffs up, you're not a day tripper.

Jones enters.

JONES The men are fallen on parade, sir.

MAINWARING Thank you, Jones, fall in.

Jones turns about and goes into the hall again.

MAINWARING You see, Jones has done it for you again. **(Mainwaring follows Jones into hall)**

INTERIOR. CHURCH HALL

MAINWARING **(As he crosses)** Platoon, platoon, 'shun.

The platoon come to attention, Jones isn't quite in position.

JONES Sorry, sir, you caught me on the hop.

MAINWARING Get in your place ,Jones. For inspection – port arms.

PLATOON Up two three, bolt two three, back two three, butt.

JONES **(Still in middle of an about turn)** Two three, two three. What was that you said?

MAINWARING Port arms, Jones.

JONES Ah yes, sir. I was in the middle of abouting turn when you gave the command. Now, let's see, port arms. How does it go? **(He climbs up his rifle)** Up two three, butt two three, thing two three… whoops two three. That wasn't quite right, was it? I'll do it again.

MAINWARING Stay as you are, Jones. **(To platoon)** It's been reported to me that your rifles aren't as clean as they should be – so Sergeant Wilson and I are going to inspect them, Wilson –

Wilson is still in the office –he pops his head out and he is still trying to do up his collar.

WILSON I'm awfully sorry. This hook thing is terribly stiff.

MAINWARING Fall in here, Wilson.

WILSON Yes, sir. **(He starts to cross)**

MAINWARING At the double. **(Wilson jogs into position)** Inspect Jones' rifle.

WILSON Very good, sir. D'you mind if I have a little peep, Jonesey?

MAINWARING You don't do it like that, Wilson – you tap the muzzle and the soldier brings his rifle and foot forward so – 'Sah.' **(He demonstrates the movement the soldiers make)** Watch me carefully. **(He taps the muzzle)**

JONES Sah.

Jones stamps his foot forward and lunges his rifle forward very quickly – Mainwaring is standing too close and is knocked back a few paces.

MAINWARING **(After collecting himself)** Well done, Jones.

WILSON **(Looking down the barrel)** Ah yes, that's awfully good, Jonesey – it really is. You ought to see it, sir.

JONES The British rifle has always been very easy to clear, sir. Before the Lee Enfield we had the Martini Henry, that was a very fine rifle, the Martini Henry.

MAINWARING Thank you, Jones.

JONES We had it right up to the Battle of Ambinmum.

MAINWARING I'm sure you did.

JONES Well, one day, we was having a bit of a battle and the young officer just out from England joined us – 'What's your name?' said the colonel. 'Lieutenant Ffoulkes, sir,' he said, 'and you spell it with two small ffs.' 'You need something to fight with,' said the colonel. 'Will you have a long Lee Enfield or a Martini?' 'Make it a Martini,' says the officer, 'and go easy with the ice.' That's all, sir.

MAINWARING Carry on with the inspection, Wilson.

JONES Excuse me, sir – to appreciate that joke to the full you have to know that Martini is a drink, much patronised by the gentry in high circles.

MAINWARING I did know that, thank you, Jones.

JONES The young officer was confusing that with the martini rifle you see, sir.

MAINWARING I know, Jones.

JONES They had it with ice – the drink, of course, not the rifle.

MAINWARING I'm well aware of that, Jones.

JONES I prefer strong ale myself.

MAINWARING Stop talking in the ranks, Jones.

They move to Walker – Walker places his diamond signet ring in the breach.

WILSON This is marvellous, all sparkling just like fairy land.

MAINWARING What's got into you, Wilson? **(He sees Walker's hand and ring)** Walker, how dare you wear jewellery on active service.

WALKER What's wrong with it? It's real.

MAINWARING See me after parade, Walker.

WALKER It's no good, I can't get you one.

MAINWARING That'll do, Walker.

Wilson moves to Pike.

WILSON That's come up terribly well. How did you manage to get those marks off?

PIKE I put a bit of Harpic down and left it overnight.

MAINWARING Pike, how dare you introduce foreign matter into your rifle.

PIKE It's not foreign, Captain Mainwaring.

MAINWARING You haven't heard the end of this, Pike.

They move to Frazer – Frazer brings his rifle out sharply.

MAINWARING Watch it, Frazer. **(Mainwaring looks down the barrel)** Yes, the barrel's quite good, but I can't say the same for your thumb.

FRAZER Somebody has to grease the hearse.

Mainwaring passes to Godfrey.

GODFREY Good evening.

MAINWARING What do you mean, good evening? Where's your rifle?

GODFREY I don't carry one, sir, I carry the Red Cross haversack.

MAINWARING Oh, of course, I'm sorry, Godfrey.

GODFREY Would you like to inspect my thermometer case?

MAINWARING No thank you, Godfrey. These rifles seem perfectly clean, Wilson.

Enter the Warden with a policeman.

WARDEN That's him, that's him over there.

MAINWARING Go away, Hodges, can't you see there's a parade on?

HODGES Never mind about that. I identify Captain George Mainwaring – that's him – the little fat one with glasses.

POLICEMAN Are you Captain George Mainwaring?

MAINWARING Of course I am.

HODGES Go on, give it to him.

POLICEMAN This is for you.

He hands Mainwaring a summons.

WALKER Blimey, it's a blister.

FRAZER It's a what?

WALKER A blue one, a summons.

FRAZER That's no surprise to me, I always knew there was something shady about him.

MAINWARING What's this about, officer?

HODGES I'll tell you what it's about – a light was blazing from your window for a whole hour, so you're up before the beak.

MAINWARING This is obviously a mistake, I shall get straight on to my solicitor. He'll soon nip it in the bud.

Mainwaring goes towards the office.

FRAZER Mark my words, Mainwaring's for the clink.

INTERIOR. SIDE OFFICE

Wilson has the platoon gathered around him, less Mainwaring.

WILSON Look, there's no getting away from the evidence. The light was on and Captain Mainwaring's responsible for the hall, and so he'll be found guilty.

JONES We can't let it happen, Mr Wilson. We can't let our captain go to the stake and be pilloried.

WILSON It's not as bad as that, Jones.

FRAZER He was the last out. He's guilty, he should suffer.

GODFREY We all left together, I think we're all guilty.

WALKER I look at it this way, every man has his price. Let's get to this beak and straighten him.

WILSON Look, Walker, you cannot bribe magistrates.

WALKER With money no, but with scotch – maybe.

GODFREY One of the magistrates is a lady.

WALKER All right then, knicker elastic.

They all demur.

WALKER You can't get it.

PIKE Maybe there's a crooked district attorney like Warner Baxter.

WILSON Oh do be quiet, Frank.

PIKE It's the only thing I've said.

WILSON Just be quiet.

GODFREY Surely if we tell them we all left together they'll understand.

JONES That's it, Mr Godfrey, we must all tell the same story, even if we purge ourselves.

WILSON Good, well let's decide what we're all going to say.

PIKE And if that fails, perhaps we can rig the grand jury so he beats the rap.

INTERIOR. CALL BOX

Verger on the phone to Warden.

VERGER Is that you, Mr Hodges?

INTERIOR

HODGES Yes.

INTERIOR. CALL BOX

VERGER Is anyone listening?

INTERIOR

HODGES Yes, I am.

INTERIOR. CALL BOX

VERGER Is anyone else listening?

INTERIOR

HODGES Of course not, this is the telephone, not the Albert Hall.

INTERIOR. CALL BOX

VERGER Stay your hand against Captain Mainwaring.

INTERIOR

HODGES Do what?

INTERIOR. CALL BOX

VERGER Stay your hand – don't proceed against him.

INTERIOR

HODGES I'm not proceeding against him, the police are.

INTERIOR. CALL BOX

VERGER Well, I don't think he's done it.

INTERIOR

HODGES What makes you say that?

INTERIOR. CALL BOX

VERGER Somebody else might have left the light on by accident.

INTERIOR

HODGES Listen, Verger, it's taken me months to nail Mainwaring. You keep your trap shut, or somebody might ask why you keep the church stirrup pump in your front hall.

INTERIOR. SIDE OFFICE

The platoon are chanting together.

PLATOON On the evening of the 7th we paraded in the church hall as usual.

JONES Usual.

PLATOON …at 9.45 we all left together and Captain Mainwaring switched out the light in the office.

JONES Nine forty-five.

WILSON Try to keep up, Jones. Now, once again.

PLATOON On the evening of the 7th we paraded in the church hall as usual.

JONES …in the office.

Fade on Jones' face trying to get it right.

INTERIOR. PASSAGE OUTSIDE COURT ROOM

Fade up on Jones' face – he is still trying to get it right.

JONES We all left together and Captain Mainwaring switched out the light in the office. I've got it right.

Pull out to show Wilson, Pike, Frazer, Godfrey and Walker sitting in the passage outside the court room with one or two more of the platoon.

WILSON That's good, Jones, awfully good.

WALKER Now, all do your best to remember it when you get into court, 'cause they try to make you say things you don't mean.

PIKE I won't talk, whatever happens, I won't talk.

Mainwaring enters.

MAINWARING Ah, you're all here, good. I'm very touched that you all turned up for me.

FRAZER I've come to speak the truth.

MAINWARING Good, well, I hope we're all going to do that.

WILSON Your solicitor hasn't arrived yet, sir.

MAINWARING No, I discharged him.

WILSON Oh dear, do you think that was wise?

MAINWARING He wanted me to plead guilty. I won't have that sort of talk, as you well know, Wilson.

JONES That's right, Captain Mainwaring, you go down fighting.

MAINWARING I don't intend to go down at all, Jones, I intend to win.

Hodges comes up to the group.

HODGES I see, all come to say farewell have you?

MAINWARING Just ignore him, Wilson.

WILSON I am doing, sir.

HODGES I'm going in to see the fun. Serves you right if they give you a month. You'll come off your high horse then.

PIKE Uncle Arthur, if Mr Mainwaring gets sent to prison, will mum let us talk to him?

WILSON It won't come to that, Pike.

PIKE Well, she wouldn't let you talk to that lady who was married to the share pusher.

WILSON That was altogether different.

MAINWARING Right, I'm going in now. I shall conduct my own defence and call on each of you in turn to bear witness on my behalf.

FRAZER I shall tell the truth.

Mainwaring reacts.

GODFREY Good luck, Captain Mainwaring. I shall always have most happy memories of you.

WALKER And if you find yourself in the nick, I'll see you get it easy.

MAINWARING You can come in with me, Wilson.

WILSON Won't you be calling me as a witness?

MAINWARING No, you're too vague – the police solicitor would make mincemeat out of you.

They go into court.

WALKER Right, let's go through it again, lads.

PLATOON On the evening of the 7th...

The Verger enters.

VERGER Where's Captain Mainwaring? I must see Captain Mainwaring.

GODFREY I'm afraid he's in court.

VERGER Have they sentenced him yet?

GODFREY I doubt it, he's only been gone a minute.

VERGER Then I may not be too late.

INTERIOR. COURT

Mainwaring sitting himself on the front row beside the police solicitor and his clerk – Wilson is beside Mainwaring.

MAINWARING You sit there, Wilson, then you can hand me the pages of my speeches as I need them.

Mainwaring hands Wilson a file of papers – Wilson looks through them.

WILSON Did you bring sandwiches, sir?

MAINWARING Don't be facetious, Wilson, it doesn't suit you.

Mainwaring sees the clerk of the court enter.

MAINWARING Good morning.

Clerk nods.

MAINWARING (**To Wilson**) That's the clerk of the court.

WILSON Oh, good morning.

MAINWARING Wilson, there's no need for you to say good morning. I'm the one who's being summoned, not you.

CLERK Be upstanding in court. Court rise please.

MAINWARING Get up, Wilson, the magistrates are coming in.

The people in court rise – Wilson, in doing so, drops Mainwaring's papers.

MAINWARING Really, Wilson.

Mainwaring scrambles on the floor for the papers. The magistrates enter – Captain Square is the chairman. Also on the bench are a middle-aged lady and an elderly gentleman.

WILSON (**Seeing Square**) Good Lord. (**He nudges Mainwaring**)

MAINWARING Don't push me, Wilson, give me a hand. (**Mainwaring stands and sees Square**) Good Lord. (**Mainwaring drops the papers again**)

SQUARE Carry on, Mr Bone.

CLERK Captain George Mainwaring.

MAINWARING Yes, that's me.

SQUARE What are you doing there? Are you a solicitor?

MAINWARING No, I'm here to answer the charge.

SQUARE Do you mean you're the accused?

MAINWARING That's right.

SQUARE Well, you shouldn't be down there, you should be up there in the dock.

MAINWARING I'm sorry, I apologise to the court. (**He moves to the dock**)

Cut to the Warden who is further back in the court – the Verger is beside him. The Verger rises.

HODGES Here, where are you going?

VERGER The time is come. I must speak.

HODGES Sit down and shut up. (**He pulls him down into place**)

SQUARE I think, at this stage, that I should point out that the accused is known to me.

LADY MAGISTRATE I'm sure you can be relied upon not to show any favour, Captain Square.

SQUARE I assure you I shall show no favour whatever. You, Mainwaring, have you any objection to your case being heard by me?

MAINWARING (**In the dock**) Well...

SQUARE Good, let's proceed.

CLERK Are you Captain George Mainwaring of 23 Lime Crescent, Walmington-on-Sea?

MAINWARING I am.

SQUARE Of course he's not! He's not a proper captain. He's in the Home Guard – he's Mr Mainwaring, plain Mr, aren't you?

MAINWARING Well, I...

SQUARE Of course he is. Cross that out and read the charge.

CLERK You are charged, under section 23 of the Emergency Powers Act that on the 7th day of September, 10.32 pm in the evening, you caused an unobscured light to be shown at St Aldhelm's Church Hall, in contravention of the said Act. How do you plead?

MAINWARING Not guilty.

SQUARE (**Under his breath**) Damn waste of time. Is anyone appearing for you, Mainwaring?

MAINWARING No, I shall speak for myself, I shall rely on honesty, fair play and the integrity of British justice.

SQUARE I see. Proceed, Mr Wintergreen.

Mr Wintergreen is the police solicitor.

WINTERGREEN I'd like to call Warden Adamson.

CLERK Call Warden Adamson.

PC Call Warden Adamson.

INTERIOR. PASSAGE

Walker is looking through the door which is partly ajar.

PIKE What's happening, Joe?

WALKER They've got one of Hodges' wardens in the box.

FRAZER There's no doubt about it, Mainwaring's done for.

JONES No, he's not. I'm going to speak up for him.

FRAZER That's all he needs.

INTERIOR. COURT ROOM

The Second Warden is in the box, he is embarrassed by the occasion and speaks very quietly.

JUNIOR WARDEN And in order to extinguish it, we were compelled to break in.

SQUARE I didn't quite catch that. Mr Mainwaring, stop chatting with your friends in court.

MAINWARING He's not my friend, he's butting in.

HODGES I was only repeating what he said.

MAINWARING What's it got to do with you what he said? **(He points)** He's the magistrate, not you.

SQUARE Will you both be quiet, please. Have you finished, Mr Wintergreen?

WINTERGREEN Yes, thank you.

SQUARE **(To Mainwaring)** Do you wish to ask the witness any questions?

MAINWARING Yes.

SQUARE What are they?

MAINWARING I don't know.

SQUARE What do you mean you don't know?

MAINWARING Because my papers are down there. **(Pointing to bench)** And I'm up here.

SQUARE Go down and get them then.

HODGES What about the 60-watt bulb then?

MAINWARING He told you to be quiet.

SQUARE Mainwaring, I'm quite capable of maintaining order in my own court thank you very much.

VERGER **(Rising)** Your Grace, I wish...

SQUARE Sit down.

Verger sits quickly.

SQUARE **(To Mainwaring)** Now, have you got your papers?

MAINWARING Yes, thank you. **(He starts to return to the dock)**

SQUARE Where are you going?

MAINWARING Back there in the dock.

SQUARE Stay where you are. You can conduct your case down there, and then go up there for sentence.

Both the other magistrates and the clerk react, and whisper to Square.

SQUARE Oh, oh, I'm sorry. The verdict – slip of the tongue, slip of the tongue.

MAINWARING **(As he settles himself. To Wilson)** Don't sprawl all over the desk, I shall need room to gesture.

SQUARE Carry on, Mainwaring, ask your questions.

MAINWARING Thank you, sir. Now, Mr Adamson. **(He goes through the sheets)** No questions.

Square chucks his pencil down.

SQUARE Back to you, Mr Wintergreen.

WINTERGREEN Call the Reverend Farthing.

CLERK Reverend Farthing.

POLICEMAN Reverend Farthing.

INTERIOR. PASSAGE

JONES Who's on now, Joe?

WALKER The Vicar. Here, wait a minute, you'll never guess who the magistrate is.

JONES Who?

WALKER Captain Square.

FRAZER What did I say! Mainwaring'll do time. It'll be the finish of him.

GODFREY I'm sure Captain Square will behave like a gentleman, and be quite unbiased.

JONES Gentlemen aren't always unbiased you know, Mr Godfrey. Lord Kitchener was a gentleman but he was very biased, especially against the Fuzzie Wuzzies. 'Shoot 'em, lads' – he used to say, and you can't get more biased than that.

INTERIOR. COURT ROOM

The Vicar is in the box.

VICAR I had the hall until five o'clock, and from then on until midnight Captain Mainwaring has it.

SOLICITOR Who then, is responsible for the hall at 10.30 in the evening?

VICAR Captain Mainwaring.

HODGES Here, here. **(To Verger)** We've got him, we've got him.

SQUARE Don't keep calling him Captain Mainwaring, he's not a Captain, he's a bank clerk.

MAINWARING I am not a bank clerk, I'm bank manager.

SQUARE Same thing. Have you any questions for this Vicar chap?

MAINWARING No questions.

SQUARE You did plead not guilty, didn't you?

MAINWARING I did.

SQUARE I see. Carry on, Mr Wintergreen.

SOLICITOR Since the evidence as to the fact of the light showing, and as to the fact of the responsibility has not been challenged, I shall call no further witnesses. The essential elements of the charge would, I submit, seem to be proved.

SQUARE I quite agree. Are you calling witnesses, Mainwaring?

MAINWARING Yes, m'lord.

SQUARE What for?

MAINWARING I intend to show that the light was extinguished by myself. It must therefore have been switched on again by some person, or persons unknown.

Cut to Verger who looks startled.

SQUARE I don't see how that's going to help you, but you'd better get on with it.

MAINWARING I call Corporal Jones.

CLERK Corporal Jones.

POLICEMAN Corporal Jones.

INTERIOR. THE PASSAGE

WALKER That's you, Jonesey – now don't forget, 'On the evening of the 7th…'

JONES **(Saying with Walker)** We paraded in the hall as usual, at 9.45 we all left the hall together and Captain Mainwaring switched out the light.

INTERIOR. COURT ROOM

WILSON I really think you should ask for an adjournment so that you can be properly represented.

MAINWARING Nonsense, I know what I'm doing, I shall call 22 witnesses to show I switched off the light.

WILSON But you're still responsible.

Jones falls into the box, his head emerges over the edge.

JONES On the evening of the 7th, we paraded in the hall as usual.

SQUARE Just a minute, you haven't taken the oath yet.

Court usher hands Jones a bible and card.

USHER Hold the book in your right hand and say the words on the card.

JONES What card?

USHER The card in your left hand.

JONES I see, I hold the book in the right hand, and swear in the left hand.

MAINWARING Get on with it, Jones.

JONES **(Looking at card)** My, my – they do use small print these days, don't they?

SQUARE Repeat after me. **(He says quickly)** I swear by Almighty God, that the evidence I shall give shall be the truth, the whole truth and nothing but the truth.

JONES **(Equally quickly)** I swear by Almighty God, that the evidence I shall give shall be the truth, the whole truth and nothing but the truth.

SQUARE Good, carry on.

JONES On the evening of the 7th…

MAINWARING Just a minute, Jones.

SQUARE Yes, he'll tell you when.

MAINWARING Thank you, m'lord. **(To Jones)** You are Jack Jones, butcher, of 19 High Street, Walmington-on-Sea?

JONES I beg your pardon?

MAINWARING You are Jack Jones, butcher, of 19 High Street, Walmington-on-Sea?

JONES I know I am.

SQUARE So do we. Get on with it, Mainwaring.

MAINWARING Tell the court what happened on the night in question.

JONES Ah, now let me see, on the night of the 45th, we paraded in the light and I put the Captain out together.

WILSON **(Mouthing)** No, Jonesey, on the evening of the 7th we paraded…

SOLICITOR **(Rising)** I must object, not only is he leading the witness, but as far as I know he shouldn't even be here.

MAINWARING I must apologise to my learned friend. Be quiet, Wilson.

SQUARE Look, Mainwaring, I'm the one who tells people to be quiet.

INTERIOR. THE PASSAGE

Frazer is looking through the door.

FRAZER Deary me, it's like watching a man commit suicide.

PIKE Here, what's happened to Joe?

FRAZER No doubt he's deserted the sinking ship.

GODFREY I don't think so, he just said he thought he could fix the magistrate, and when I looked round he wasn't there.

PIKE Mr Godfrey, maybe he's gone to round up a gang of mobsters and rub out the judge.

GODFREY Oh, I do hope not.

FRAZER Wait, he's in the box now.

INTERIOR. COURT ROOM

Walker is in the box.

WALKER Well, it's like this, you see, I came by the hall about twenty minutes after we left and the light was off, and then I see it come on as I was passing.

MAINWARING (**To Square**) This is rather an unexpected turn in the evidence, sir. At what time was this, Walker?

WALKER Well, it's difficult to say.

MAINWARING And why is that?

WALKER Well you see, sir, let's face it, I'm a crook.

MAINWARING Oh, I wouldn't put it quite like that.

WALKER No, for once in my life I must be honest. Everything I do is pretty well against the law, and on this occasion I'd been delivering a couple of illegal bottles of crooked black market whisky to a secret address nearby.

MIX TO PRE-RECORDED SEQUENCE.

EXTERIOR. WINDOW BY NIGHT

Walker approaches, looks round to see that he is unobserved – he then knocks on the window – it is opened and we see Captain Square.

SQUARE Have you got it?

WALKER Course I have.

He hands over two bottles and takes £6.

SQUARE Don't let anyone see you leave.

He gives the thumbs up sign and closes the window.

INTERIOR. COURT ROOM

WALKER Now, if only I could remember the name of the geezer I sold it to, he could verify the time and the truth of what I'm saying.

Cut to nonplussed Square.

SQUARE Just a moment. (**He beckons to his colleagues – they put their heads together and he whispers**) I think an element of doubt seems to have crept into this case. I suggest we stop the proceedings and dismiss the charge.

LADY MAGISTRATE On the contrary, it seems an open-and-shut case to me.

SQUARE Glad you agree. (**Politely**) Captain Mainwaring.

MAINWARING (**Surprised at the change**) Yes.

SQUARE There seems to be a confliction of stories here.

VERGER (**Leaping up**) I can't stay silent any longer, I did it.

HODGES Shut up.

VERGER No – truth must out. I came back after they had all left to do some work.

MAINWARING In my office?

VERGER Yes, Captain Mainwaring, you see I'm writing my memoirs.

HODGES Your memoirs.

VERGER Well, why shouldn't I? Noel Coward did.

SQUARE There you are, I knew I was right. Case dismissed – you leave without a stain on your character, Captain Mainwaring.

WILSON Well done, sir.

FRAZER (**Coming down from door into court with Pike**) I never doubted the outcome for a second, sir.

PIKE It was just like that picture with John Garfield, wasn't it Uncle Arthur.

GODFREY Well done, Captain Mainwaring.

MAINWARING Thank you, men, thank you, and never forget, men, this is what we're fighting for – honesty, fair play and the integrity of British justice.

SERIES FIVE **EPISODE TWELVE**

Recorded: Friday 1/12/72

Original transmission: Friday 22/12/72, 8.30–9.00pm

Original viewing figures = 13.7 million

ARTHUR LOWE .... CAPTAIN MAINWARING
JOHN LE MESURIER .... SERGEANT WILSON
CLIVE DUNN .... LANCE CORPORAL JONES
JOHN LAURIE .... PRIVATE FRAZER
JAMES BECK .... PRIVATE WALKER
ARNOLD RIDLEY .... PRIVATE GODFREY
IAN LAVENDER .... PRIVATE PIKE
BILL PERTWEE .... ARP WARDEN
GEOFFREY CHATER .... COLONEL PIERCE
EDWARD UNDERDOWN .... MAJOR GENERAL SIR CHARLES HOLLAND
MICHAEL KNOWLES .... CAPTAIN STEWART
JEFFREY SEGAL .... THE MINISTER
JOHN CLEGG .... WIRELESS OPERATOR
PLATOON .... COLIN BEAN, HUGH CECIL, DESMOND CULLUM-JONES, MICHAEL MOORE, RICHARD JACQUES, FREDDIE WILES, GEORGE HANCOCK, EVAN ROSS, FREDDIE WHITE, WILLIAM GOSSLING
EXTRAS IN WAR OFFICE .... COLIN THOMAS AND FRED DAVIES

Round and Round Went the Great Big Wheel

• PETER FITTON REMEMBERS •

'This episode was based on a failed military invention that was intended to be radio controlled and set off in the direction of the enemy with a large bomb attached; it was then to be detonated by remote control. It was a good theory but, practically, would only ever work on a flat surface, as any downhill element would cause it to run off in an uncontrolled fashion, while uphill would return it to the sender!

'It was extremely difficult to shoot the location material for this show. The wheel was a huge prop built by Visual Effects, consisting of two metal wheels, about ten feet high, joined together in the centre with a cylinder. It looked a bit like a cotton reel. In the storyline this contraption was to be powered by rockets mounted on the two wheels. This was felt to be too dangerous and it was, therefore, to be powered by a special effects designer concealed in the cotton reel part, operating the device with a converted cycle mechanism!

'*Dad's Army* was reliant on special effects and the team was kept busy on several projects at any one time. Unfortunately the prop hadn't been fully tested before being sent to the location and so, final adjustments were to be made there. There is no need to go into the finer details, but it was thanks only to the skill of the director, cameraman and Visual Effects – and Norfolk being the flattest county – that we got any footage at all.

'It is an old showbusiness adage that you should never work with animals or children as they are basically uncontrollable; to this I would add working with large special effect mobile bomb carriers!'

Round and Round Went the Great Big Wheel

SHOT OF WAR OFFICE, DATE 1941. CAPTION READS 'WAR OFFICE 1941'

SMALL UNDERGROUND ROOM IN WAR OFFICE. DAY

We see close up of a cardboard shoe box with the words 'Top Secret' on the lid. Camera pulls back to reveal several army officers sitting around the talbe, Major General Sir Charles Holland, Colonel Pierce and Captain Stewart, a young guards officer. The other two officers are a lieutenant colonel and major The general pushes the box across to Colonel Pierce.

GENERAL Right, Pierce this is your show, so I'm going to leave you to do all the talking.

PIERCE Thank you, Sir Charles. Now, gentlemen, this is it. **(He takes a model of the secret weapon out of the box. It is a large wheel)** It contains 2000 pounds of high explosive and will knock out an enemy pill box no matter how thick, up to a range of three miles. It's called the High Explosive Attack Device, propelled by Ultra High Frequency. Code name 'Head Pouf'.

Captain Stewart reacts.

GENERAL And you can actually home it on to the target by using radio?

PIERCE I'll show you, Sir Charles. We're here. **(Puts a match box in front of him)** Enemy pill box here. **(Moves a book into position)** We start off **(He runs the model across the table)** It will do anything we want it to do. Go round obstacles, turn left, turn right. **(He demonstrates)** It reaches target, hey presto! And up it goes.

They all murmur.

GENERAL I'm only sorry I shan't be able to be at the demonstration next Saturday. What are you doing about security. This thing's red hot, you know.

PIERCE I'm not going to use any of the usual test ranges. I've picked a deserted aerodrome on the coast, just near a place called Walmington-on-Sea. I'm calling it Operation Catherine Wheel.

GENERAL You'll need quite a few troops to keep the area sealed off.

PIERCE I'm not going to use regulars, I'm using those what do you call them, er... those Home things.

GENERAL Home things? Oh, you mean Home Guards.

PIERCE Yes, that's right. All the locals are used to the Home Guards, and nobody will take any notice. My point is, if we don't make a lot of fuss, we won't attract any attention.

GENERAL Sound thinking, Pierce, very sound.

PIERCE **(Holding up paper)** There are three platoons in the area. The Eastgate under Captain Square, they'll guard the entrances, the Dymwhich under Captain Graham, they'll patrol the perimeter, keep out any snoopers.

GENERAL What about admin, fatigues, cook house and digging the what's-its-names? Who's going to do that?

PIERCE The Walmington-on-Sea platoon, it's run by Captain, er... What's his name, Stewart?

STEWART Captain Mainwaring, he's the local bank manager.

GENERAL What did he say when you asked him to do the fatigues?

PIERCE Haven't told him yet.

STEWART I'm going down to see him today, sir.

GENERAL It's not going to be easy to convince him that his platoon should do all the dirty work.

STEWART I'll talk him into it, sir, give him plenty of soft soap, butter him up.

GENERAL That's right, make him feel important. There's nothing bank managers like better than feeling important.

INTERIOR. OFFICE. CHURCH HALL. DAY

Mainwaring is sitting at his desk, Wilson beside him and Captain Stewart facing him.

STEWART ...and that, Captain Mainwaring, is a brief outline of the test. I don't want to take up too much of your time, after all you're a very important man.

MAINWARING Oh, I wouldn't say I was important, would you, Wilson?

WILSON Not really sir, no.

Mainwaring reacts.

STEWART I see you always back your Captain up, Sergeant.

WILSON I do my best, sir.

STEWART Well, Mainwaring, I've told you what the other Home Guard platoons will be doing at the test, but I haven't said what you'll be doing, have I?

MAINWARING I'm eager to hear, sir.

STEWART **(Shifty)** Well, the fact is I er... er... don't quite know how to put this. You see... er the fact is, there are several things that have to be done, not very pleasant things, and I er... that is to say we... er...

MAINWARING Say no more, sir. What you're trying to tell me is that you want us for special duties.

STEWART That's right, I want you for special duties, yes, special duties.

MAINWARING You can rely on us, sir.

WILSON Exactly what are special duties, sir?

MAINWARING What a question to ask, Wilson. It's top secret, hush hush. We shall find out when we get there.

STEWART Oh yes… er, you'll find out all right. **(Getting up)** Right, Captain Mainwaring, now I want you to get your chaps together and brief them, and don't forget, complete secrecy. Oh, here's a list of things to bring with you. **(He hands him list)**

MAINWARING Thank you, sir. You can trust my chaps, they won't breathe a word to a soul. And may I add how proud and privileged I am, that you have chosen my platoon to carry out these special duties.

INTERIOR. THE CRYPT. NIGHT

The platoon are drawn up in a tight bunch, Mainwaring and Wilson are standing in front. The scene is lit by some candles in milk bottles.

WILSON Platoon, attention.

MAINWARING Thank you, Sergeant. Now, men.

JONES Permission to speak, sir? I wish to apologise for the bunched upness of the men. When you asked us to creep down in the crypt, I did not realise that you intended us to parade here, sir.

MAINWARING That's all right, Jones. **(He lowers his voice)** Now, men, I have asked you down here, because what I have to tell you is highly secret, and I don't want it to be overheard.

FRAZER Captain Mainwaring, would you mind speaking up. I canna hear a word you're saying, you're mumbling, mumbling.

MAINWARING I'm keeping my voice down, Frazer, because what I have to say is secret.

WALKER It will remain secret unless you speak up.

WILSON Allow me, sir. Platoon, attention! Forward shuffle.

They all shuffle forward.

WILSON Halt. **(To Mainwaring)** How's that, sir?

MAINWARING This is ridiculous – get back.

They move back.

MAINWARING Thank you, Sergeant. Now, men, what I have to say must not go out of this crypt, you understand?

They all nod.

MAINWARING On Saturday a new secret weapon is being tested on the disused airfield, and we have been chosen for special duties.

They all gasp.

FRAZER What exactly do we have to do, sir?

MAINWARING I don't know, but Captain Stewart gave me a list of articles to bring, perhaps they'll give us a clue. Read them out, Wilson.

WILSON Right, sir, erm, three knives and three shovels.

MAINWARING Three knives and three shovels, what can we hazard from that?

WALKER I've got it, Mr Mainwaring, it's in case we capture a fifth columnist, we can kill him and then bury him.

MAINWARING Don't start, Walker, what are the other things, Wilson?

WILSON Three bars of soap, three scrubbing brushes, and three buckets.

JONES Perhaps it's a dirty secret weapon, and we've got to clean it.

MAINWARING Oh no, they'd have experts to do that. Anyhow, whatever these special duties are, I'm sure I can rely on you to back me up to the hilt.

ALL Hear, hear.

JONES Permission to speak, sir? I have just been struck by a something deadly.

WALKER Blimey, don't tell me there are scorpions down here.

JONES I look at it this way, sir. **(Puts his hand on his hip)** We are all in possession of highly secret information. Supposing we were captured by enemy agents, how much torture could we stand before we revealed ourselves?

MAINWARING Oh, I think you're going into the realms of fantasy now, Jones.

JONES **(Breaking ranks and closing up to Mainwaring)** Don't start that realms of what's-its-name again, sir. This is vital, we could be tortured, sir, any of us could.

MAINWARING Pull yourself together, Jones.

JONES I'm sorry, sir, but I must awake you to the deadly danger.

MAINWARING Get him back in the ranks, Wilson.

WILSON **(Leading Jones back)** Come on, Jonesey, calm down.

PIKE They might try that torture where they tilt your head back and pour gallons of water into you.

GODFREY Oh dear, I don't think I could stand very much of that.

JONES I should like to volunteer to be tortured, sir, let me be a guinea pig, let me see how much pain I can stand, let me suffer, sir, I demand to suffer.

FRAZER Shut up, you silly old fool. (**He kicks Jones on the ankle**)

JONES Ow. What did you want to do that for? He kicked me, Captain Mainwaring. That hurt that did.

FRAZER I'm sorry, sir, but the corporal was getting hysterical.

MAINWARING All right, Frazer. Will you all please calm down. Now, men, I feel I must warn you that...

WILSON (**Whispering in Mainwaring's ear**) There's someone lurking in the shadows, sir.

MAINWARING Just be nonchalant and change places. Now, men, before we go any further, there are one or two points... (**He whips out his revolver and points it in the corner**) Right, come on out, come on. (**A figure emerges from the shadows**) Get your hands above your head. (**We see that it is Hodes – the platoon react**) How dare you spy on us?

HODGES I wasn't spying, your candles were flickering through the gratings, a Jerry plane could see them for miles, and don't point that gun at me.

WILSON Good Lord, sir, he must have heard everything.

WALKER Blimey, he'll blow the gaff.

HODGES Of course I won't, I happen to be fighting for my country the same as you.

JONES You can't rely on him, sir, a couple of drinks and he's a real blabbermouth. It will be all round The Red Lion before closing time.

MAINWARING You're right, Jones, we can't afford to take any chances.

FRAZER I could screw him down in one of my coffins.

WILSON Don't be silly, Frazer, he'd suffocate.

FRAZER Well, if you're fussy I'll drill some air holes.

PIKE Why don't you shoot him, Mr Mainwaring? Go on, you're entitled to.

MAINWARING Be quiet, Pike. There's only one thing for it, we'll have to take him with us. Meanwhile we'll have to keep an eye on him, and see that he doesn't talk to anyone.

WALKER I can watch him during the day, sir, I'll help him in his greengrocer's shop.

HODGES I'm not having him working in my shop, he'll cheat the customers.

WALKER That will make two of us.

HODGES How dare you?

MAINWARING Hands up.

Warden puts hands up.

GODFREY Excuse me, Captain Mainwaring, I could keep an eye on him at night, sir.

MAINWARING Thank you, Godfrey.

HODGES I'm not sleeping with that old man.

GODFREY I don't snore or anything.

MAINWARING Now you listen to me, Hodges, for eavesdropping on us, you could be prosecuted under the Official Secrets Act, so you'll just do as you're told. For your information, we have been picked for highly secret special duties and that is a great honour and I'm not going to have it ruined by you. Believe me, Mr Chief Warden, you've got to be something very special to be picked for special duties.

INTERIOR. MARQUEE. DAY

It is a medium-sized marquee. Frazer, Walker, Godfrey and Pike are sitting in a row on a bench, peeling potatoes. Mainwaring and Wilson are standing beside them, in the background. Several other members of the platoon are scrubbing down a trestle table. Hodges is lounging on a bench, smoking and reading a paper.

FRAZER Special duties! Bah! (**Throws a potato in water**)

MAINWARING Hoodwinked! That's what we've been, Wilson, hoodwinked. I should have known better than to trust that smarmy Captain Stewart.

WILSON You can't blame him, sir. After all, he's got a job to do.

MAINWARING I'd expect you to stick up for him, Wilson. After all, you both went to public schools.

WILSON I can't help thinking that you've got a bit of a chip on your shoulder about that, sir.

MAINWARING I've no chip on my shoulder, Wilson, but I tell you what I have got – three pips, and don't you forget it.

HODGES 'Ere, Napoleon, I'm glad I came now, I wouldn't have missed this for anything. 'Special Duties', ah well, I suppose someone has to do the cleaning up. Still it's a good job they're not using a troop of cavalry, otherwise you'd really have your work cut out. (**He laughs**)

WILSON If you wish to address Captain Mainwaring, kindly take that filthy cigarette out of your mouth.

MAINWARING (**Quietly**) Thank you, Wilson.

WILSON That's all right, sir, I just won't allow you to be insulted by outsiders.

Mainwaring reacts.

PIKE (**Whispering to Walker**) I'm going to sneak out in a minute, I want to listen to 'Hi Gang' on the wireless.

WALKER What are you talking about, there's no radio round 'ere.

PIKE Oh yes there is, I've brought my portable with me, and hidden it in the van.

Jones enters carrying a shovel.

JONES Mr Mainwaring, now I know what they wanted us to bring the shovels for.

TELECINE: EXTERIOR. AIRFIELD. DAY

Colonel Pierce and Captain Stewart are standing in front of a hangar with the following: Minister and assistant, both dressed in black coat and striped trousers, wing collars, Homberg hats and carrying umbrellas; two boffins dressed in baggy tweeds and five brass hats of various ranks. A low sandbag wall, 5 foot high, has been built just in front of the hangar. There is also a mass of wireless equipment, surrounded by sandbags. It is manned by a sergeant. The secret weapon is standing ready to go.

PIERCE I'm sorry to keep you waiting, Minister, but we're ready to go now.

MINISTER Thank you, Colonel. (**Points**) Tell me, what are two aerial things sticking out?

PIERCE They pick up the radio waves that control it, sir.

MINISTER Amazing. What will they think of next?

INTERIOR. VAN. DAY

Pike and Walker climb into the van.

PIKE Hurry up, Joe, close the door, I don't want Mr Mainwaring to hear.

Pike pulls some sacking off his portable radio, it is quite a big, home-made affair, with earphones.

WALKER Blimey, where did you get that from?

PIKE (**Switching on**) I made it myself, I got the instructions out of *Practical Wireless*.

WALKER You're cleverer than I thought, Pikey.

PIKE As my mum says, I'm not just a pretty face.

WALKER We can't both listen through one pair of earphones.

PIKE Yes we can. You put one to your ear, and I'll put the other to my ear.

They hold the earphones between them.

WALKER I can't hear anything. Are you sure it's working?

PIKE It takes a long time to warm up. I can't wait to hear what Bebe and Ben are up to this week. 'Ere, do you think Vic Oliver really is 85?

TELECINE: EXTERIOR. AIRFIELD. DAY

PIERCE Now, gentlemen, the target is that concrete pill box half a mile away.

Cut to shot of pill box.

PIERCE Are you all ready? Off you go, Sergeant.

SERGEANT Right, sir. (**He twiddles the knobs**)

Cut to the 'weapon'. There is a line of barrels for it to weave in between. The 'weapon' moves off.

PIERCE She's off.

Single bleeps come through on the speaker.

PIERCE Single bleeps, that means forward. Turn left, Sergeant.

The weapon obeys, double bleeps come through.

PIERCE That's two bleeps, she's responding. Turn right.

The weapon obeys, treble bleeps come through.

PIERCE Splendid, splendid, that's three bleeps.

The audience applaud.

MINISTER Excellent, Colonel, excellent.

Suddenly 'Hi Gang' blasts through the loud speakers.

PIERCE What on earth's that? I've never heard it before.

STEWART I have, sir, I heard it on Saturday, it's a repeat of 'Hi Gang'. It was awfully good.

PIERCE What's happening, Sergeant?

SERGEANT I'm getting a lot of interference, sir, I can't make it out.

PIERCE Well get rid of it, man.

'Hi Gang' stops. Rapid bleeps come through the speaker.

PIERCE That's not the signal for left or right. What is it?

SERGEANT I think it's the one for coming towards, sir.

The weapon turns and comes straight for them.

PIERCE Take cover!

They all rush behind the sandbag wall, the weapon rolls towards them. It nearly reaches the wall, turns and goes away.

SERGEANT It's all right now, sir.

They file out from behind the sandbags.

PIERCE It's all right now.

SERGEANT I've got it under control now, sir.

The weapon turns and heads for the wall again.

SERGEANT No, I haven't.

PIERCE No he hasn't. Get back, get back.

They all scramble back behind the wall. The weapon comes towards the wall, veers away and disappears round the edge of the hangar, Pierce and Stewart poke their heads above the wall.

PIERCE Get the transport, quick. We must follow it.

STEWART There isn't any transport, sir. I told the drivers to come after tea. I didn't think you'd want them to see the test.

PIERCE You blithering idiot.

STEWART I've got my motorbike, sir, and Captain Mainwaring's platoon have got their van.

PIERCE Right, get on your bike, go over to Mainwaring, tell him to drive into Walmington, and warn them if that thing reaches the town it will blow it sky high. And then get to the nearest phone and warn G.H.Q. We'll try to get it back here by radio.

INTERIOR. MARQUEE. DAY

Frazer and Godfrey have finished the potatoes.

FRAZER That's the last.

MAINWARING Well done, men. Those are the best potatoes I've seen for many a day.

We hear the roar of a motorbike.

HODGES Don't take any of his soft soap, he's only trying to get round you because he's dropped you in it.

JONES How dare you talk to our officer like that, for two pins...

Stewart rushes in.

STEWART Quick, Captain Mainwaring. I need your help. It's escaped!

MAINWARING What has?

STEWART The secret weapon, it's broken loose and it's going towards Walmington. It could blow the town sky high. You must warn them.

MAINWARING Right, come on, men...

WILSON Wait a minute, sir, we don't know what it looks like.

STEWART It looks like a huge wheel and it contains 2000 pounds of high explosive.

JONES Two thousand pounds of high explosive! Don't panic, don't panic!

MAINWARING Pull yourself together, Jones. Right, men, into the van.

They all rush out.

HODGES The town must be warned by the A.R.P. It's official regulations. I'm coming with you.

TELECINE: EXTERIOR. MARQUEE. DAY

Mainwaring, Wilson, Jones, Frazer, Godfrey, Hodges, Sponge, Hastings and two other privates rush out of the marquee towards the van.

MAINWARING Hurry up, men.

JONES Don't panic, don't panic! We must warn Walmington, warn Walmington.

INTERIOR. VAN. DAY

Pike and Walker are listening to radio.

PIKE Oh I like that bit when he says: 'Not you, mommer, sit down.'

Noises outside.

WALKER Quick, there's someone coming.

They quickly drop the earphones and cover the radio. The back door opens, Frazer climbs in.

FRAZER What are you doing skulking in here? You were trying to get out of peeling those spuds.

WALKER What's going on?

FRAZER Walmington-on-Sea is going to be blown sky high if we don't get there pretty quick.

HODGES (**Pushing Godfrey into van**) Hurry up, Grandad. Get a move on.

GODFREY You are the most rude, common man, I have ever met in my life.

TELECINE: EXTERIOR. MARQUEE. DAY

The van roars off, followed by Stewart on a motorbike.

TELECINE: EXTERIOR. ROAD. DAY

Van travelling along road.

INTERIOR: VAN CAB. DAY

Jones is driving, Mainwaring and Wilson sitting beside him. Pike pokes his head through.

PIKE Mr Mainwaring, what does that secret weapon look like?

MAINWARING What did Captain Stewart say it looked like, Wilson?

WILSON Like a huge wheel, sir.

MAINWARING It's like a huge wheel, Pike. Why do you ask?

PIKE I think it's trying to pass us.

JONES Shall I wave it on, Mr Mainwaring?

MAINWARING Put your foot down, there's 2000 pounds of explosives in it.

JONES Whoa!

TELECINE: EXTERIOR. ROAD. DAY

Long shot of van followed by the weapon travelling along road.

INTERIOR. VAN CAB. DAY

JONES It's following us, Mr Mainwaring. Don't panic, don't panic!

MAINWARING Turn off to the left here, that will fox it.

TELECINE: EXTERIOR. ROAD. DAY

Van turns left, secret weapon follows.

INTERIOR. VAN CAB. DAY

Wilson looking out of cab window.

WILSON It's still following us, it's uncanny.

Walker pokes his head through.

JONES I can't shake it off, Mr Mainwaring, I can't shake it off.

WILSON It seems as if it's being attracted by something in this van.

WALKER Perhaps it's taken a fancy to the spare wheel.

MAINWARING Put your head back in at once, Walker. Turn left again, Jones.

TELECINE: EXTERIOR. ROAD. DAY

Van travelling along road, passes turning on left, carries on. Secret weapon turns off.

INTERIOR. VAN CAB. DAY

Frazer pokes his head through.

FRAZER We've lost it, Captain Mainwaring.

MAINWARING **(Mopping brow)** Phew, thank goodness for that.

WILSON It looked to me as if it was going to blow up at any minute, sir.

JONES Yes, it was very angry, Mr Mainwaring.

MAINWARING Don't be absurd, Jones. How can an inanimate object be angry?

JONES I don't care if it anny anny what's-its-name or not. I think it's got a grudge against us.

WILSON What are we going to do if it blows up, sir?

MAINWARING That's not our problem, Wilson. We were told to get back to Walmington. I know what I'm doing, believe me, we've shaken it off.

TELECINE: EXTERIOR. ROAD. DAY

Van travelling along road. Secret weapon suddenly appears from turning in front of van. Van stops, reverses, weapon follows.

TELECINE: EXTERIOR. ROAD WITH TURNING. DAY

Van travelling backwards along road, secret weapon following. Van backs into turning and stops. Weapon passes turning and stops.

MAINWARING Quick, everybody out, bring your rifles.

They all get out of the van with rifles and creep towards van, Warden lags behind.

WILSON Do you think this is wise, sir?

MAINWARING We've got to try and immobilise it, Wilson.

FRAZER If you ask me, Captain Mainwaring, there are forces at work here, that we know very little about.

WILSON There's 2000 pounds of high explosives in that thing, sir.

MAINWARING Stand by with your first aid kit, Godfrey.

GODFREY Yes, sir, you can rely on me.

JONES **(Fixing bayonet)** You leave it to me, sir, I'll immobilise it. I'll give it a poke with the old cold steel.

MAINWARING For goodness sake, use your head, Jones.

JONES No, sir, I'd rather use the bayonet.

Hodges dodges back behind the van.

PIKE It's gone awfully quiet, Mr Mainwaring.

WALKER Perhaps it's sulking.

Suddenly there is a loud hissing sound. They all drop to the ground. Huge clouds of smoke come from the weapon. Everything is obliterated.

MAINWARING It's all right, keep calm, men, it's only a smoke screen.

FRAZER **(Giving a shout)** Arrh! Careful with that bayonet, you silly old fool.

JONES I can't help it, I can't see where I'm going.

PIKE Ow. He hurt me, Mr Mainwaring.

MAINWARING Unfix your bayonet at once, Jones.

Captain Stewart roars up on his motorbike – the smoke clears.

STEWART What's happening, Mainwaring?

MAINWARING It's all right, sir, it's been following us. We're keeping it under observation.

STEWART Where?

MAINWARING **(Pointing)** There. Good heavens, it's gone!

STEWART Where did all this smoke come from?

MAINWARING The secret weapon.

STEWART That was phase two, it will go into phase three next.

WILSON What's phase three?

STEWART The explosion.

JONES Don't panic, don't panic, it's going up, into phase three, it's going up. We must stop it, Mr Mainwaring.

STEWART I wonder why it tacked itself on to you. Have you got a radio in your van?

Pike reacts – motions to Walker to keep mum.

JONES No, sir, I was going to get a gramophone, but it's difficult to wind and steer at the same time.

MAINWARING Jones! The point is, sir, how can we put it out of action?

STEWART There are two aerials on it, one on the top, and one on the side. If you can chop those off, it's harmless.

JONES Permission to speak? We can do it like Boadicea.

MAINWARING What do you mean, Jones?

JONES You know, with the knives on the chariot wheels. It's perfectly simple, all we've got to do is...

TELECINE: EXTERIOR. ROAD. DAY

Front view of secret weapon, van is coming up behind, it gets close.

JONES **(Voice off)** Open two three, out two three.

A line of rifles with fixed bayonets come out of the side.

JONES Turn two three.

The bayonets are turned so that the cutting edge is sideways.

JONES Step on it, Mr Mainwaring.

The van passes the secret weapon and the bayonets cut off the aerial.

TELECINE: EXTERIOR. AIRFIELD. DAY

Pierce is standing by the sergeant at the radio.

SERGEANT I've made contact, sir, I'm getting a signal.

MAINWARING The point is, how are we going to get after that secret weapon now?

WALKER **(Points to motorbike)** Why don't we use that motorbike. One of us could sit in the sidecar with Frank's portable radio.

MAINWARING Portable radio!

WALKER Yeah, I've just realised, that's what's been

attracting the secret weapon. I'll go and borrow the bike.

MAINWARING **(To Pike)** You stupid boy, why didn't you say anything when the Captain asked us if we had a radio in the van?

PIKE I didn't want to look a fool in front of him.

WILSON **(Patting Pike on shoulder)** That's all right, Frank, we wouldn't want you to look a fool either.

MAINWARING You speak for yourself, Wilson, and stop mollycoddling that boy.

TELECINE: EXTERIOR. AIRFIELD. DAY

Stewart roars up on his bike.

PIERCE What's happening, Stewart?

STEWART Captain Mainwaring's located it, sir, and he's keeping it under observation.

PIERCE **(Getting on bike behind Stewart)** Right, we'd better keep Captain Mainwaring under observation.

TELECINE: EXTERIOR. COTTAGE. DAY

Hodges is sitting astride the bike, Mainwaring behind him, Pike is sitting in the sidecar with his radio. The engine is running.

MAINWARING Now listen to me, Wilson, I'm going to try and lure it back along this road, and up to the aerodrome.

WILSON Right, sir. Don't get too close to it, will you?

HODGES I should have my head examined driving this!

MAINWARING Move off. **(He taps Hodges on his helmet three times, the bike roars off)**

WILSON It was nice of that chap to lend his motorbike. What did you say?

WALKER I just dangled some petrol coupons under his nose.

JONES That's it, dangling, dangling.

GODFREY What's dangling?

JONES I've thought of a way of putting that secret weapon out of action. Joe, go and borrow that bloke's shears. I'll get the tow rope out of the van.

WILSON Whatever you're going to do, Jonesey, I don't think you should.

JONES It's a cinch, sarge. There's a railway bridge just down the road, all we've got to do is…

TELECINE: EXTERIOR. ROAD. DAY

The secret weapon is lurking under some trees. Mainwaring and co. on motorbike come into view. Circle in front of the weapon.

MAINWARING Turn the volume up, Pike.

The weapon rolls towards them, they move off, followed by weapon.

TELECINE: EXTERIOR. RAILWAY BRIDGE. DAY

Close up of Frazer.

FRAZER Here they come.

Close up of Wilson.

WILSON Lower away!

Cut to Jones being lowered on the tow rope from the top of bridge by Sponge, Hastings and two other privates. He has the garden shears in his hand.

WALKER I hope this is going to work, sarge.

WILSON So do I.

GODFREY Oh dear.

Mainwaring and co. on the motorbike appear, followed by the weapon. They go under the bridge, the weapon follows. As it passes, Jones cuts the aerial off. The weapon stops, rolls back clear of the bridge, goes round in a circle, totters, falls and dies. Mainwaring, Pike and Hodges get off the bike and run back. Jones is lowered down. Frazer, Wilson, Walker and Godfrey join them. They all form a circle round the weapon. Jones takes off his hat.

JONES I've killed it, Mr Mainwaring.

Pierce and Stewart roar up on their motorbike.

PIERCE A very promising first test.

MAINWARING Somehow I feel you've got a bit more work to do on it.

WALKER For a start, you've got to stop Bebe Daniels from interfering with you.

Camera pulls slowly back to high-angle shot of dead weapon, surrounded by Mainwaring, Wilson, Jones, Frazer, Walker, Godfrey, Pike, Hodges, Pierce and Stewart.

SERIES FIVE **EPISODE THIRTEEN**

Recorded: Friday 8/12/72
Original transmission: Friday 29/12/72, 8.30–9.00pm
Original viewing figures = 16.6 million

ARTHUR LOWE .... CAPTAIN MAINWARING
JOHN LE MESURIER .... SERGEANT WILSON
CLIVE DUNN .... LANCE CORPORAL JONES
JOHN LAURIE .... PRIVATE FRAZER
JAMES BECK .... PRIVATE WALKER
ARNOLD RIDLEY .... PRIVATE GODFREY
IAN LAVENDER .... PRIVATE PIKE
BILL PERTWEE .... ARP WARDEN
FRANK WILLIAMS .... VICAR
EDWARD SINCLAIR .... VERGER
HAROLD BENNETT .... MR BLEWITT
COLIN BEAN .... PRIVATE SPONGE
JOAN COOPER .... MISS FORTESCUE
ERIC LONGWORTH .... MR GORDON (TOWN CLERK)
CHRISTOPHER SANDFORD .... GERMAN PILOT
PLATOON .... DESMOND CULLUM-JONES, FREDDIE WILES, HUGH HASTINGS, FREDDIE WHITE, HUGH CECIL, GEORGE HANCOCK, EVAN ROSS, LESLIE NOYES, MICHAEL MOORE.
EXTRA IN TEA ROOMS .... MAY GRIMMER

TIME ON MY HANDS

• ERIC LONGWORTH REMEMBERS •

'In May 1972 I was working for ATV at Elstree in an episode of a series called *Lollipop* in which, you may recall, the principals were Hugh Lloyd, Peggy Mount, Rex Garner and Pat Coombs. The two men had joined the Ancient Order of Crows, giving them an excuse for a night out, hence the title of the episode, "Cock-a-Doodle-Don't".

'I was playing the part of Secretary Crow and was dressed in a long, flowing gown which, when I opened my arms, looked like wings and on my head was the head of a crow, with a long, yellow beak. The only snag was the beak, which covered most of my face. As you will appreciate, actors prefer to show their faces in the hope that some director, producer, agent or whoever is watching, will remember them.

'To this end, I devised a cunning plan and whenever I spoke I put my head back to reveal all the salient features, and at the same time nearly dislocated my neck. Four or five months later my agent rang to say he had had a call from the BBC, "They want you to play the town clerk in *Dad's Army*". I nearly forgot to mention, just in case you have forgotten too, that *Lollipop* was written by a gentleman called Jimmy Perry.

'"Time On My Hands" was the episode in question and was the thirteenth and last of the series recorded in 1972. Unlucky for some, but happily I am not by nature superstitious, and the title could not have been more appropriate, as I had been resting for some weeks after a holiday in the West Country.

'Joining the cast of a long-running series is not always a happy experience, as I recall, with one highly successful series, where some of the principals seemed to get bored as the rehearsals went on and amused themselves by sticking lengths of marking tape to people's coat tails. Happily no one got bored whilst rehearsing for *Dad's Army*. Making people laugh is, after all, a serious business, and working with such an accomplished cast was a joy and a privilege.

'I had worked with Arthur before in Granada's production of *Pickwick* on Christmas Day 1963. Jimmy Beck had been a police sergeant to my aged PC in a couple of episodes of *Coronation Street* in 1967, and I had worked with Janet Davies for Yorkshire Television. But here was a challenge to create a character in a series which was well loved and already four years old. Lucky for me, it still had another five years to run, as well as a stage version and a Royal Command Performance.

'I must say it is very comforting in old age to be told, from time to time, that people actually enjoyed your performance. My sincerest thanks to them and all those past and present, who made the making of *Dad's Army*, very happy years.'

Time On My Hands

INTERIOR. MARIGOLD TEA ROOMS. DAY

The shop door and a corner of the tea rooms: it is only necessary to show three tables. The door opens – Mainwaring and Wilson enter in civvies – Mainwaring is wearing his revolver. They both hang up their hats and sit at a table. Miss Fortescue, the owner of the tea rooms, appears.

MISS FORTESCUE Good morning, Mr Mainwaring. Morning, Mr Wilson.

MAINWARING/WILSON Good morning.

MAINWARING The usual please, Miss Fortescue, two coffees and some rich tea biscuits.

MISS FORTESCUE The ration's been cut again, I'm afraid. I can only let you have one and a half biscuits each. Still, I'll let you have an extra lump of sugar to make up for it.

WILSON How awfully kind, thank you.

MISS FORTESCUE We do our best to keep up the morale.

Miss Fortescue goes.

MAINWARING You know, Wilson, I look forward to my morning coffee, it's an oasis in the turmoil of strife. Sitting in here in this typical English setting, one wouldn't know there was a war on. (**He unbuckles his revolver and puts it on the table in front of him**)

WILSON Did you have to bring that great big gun with you, sir?

MAINWARING Great big gun! You talk like some nancy boy, Wilson.

Wilson reacts.

MAINWARING This .38 hasn't been out of my reach day or night since I was issued with it. I take it with me everywhere, everywhere.

WILSON How terribly inconvenient. Don't you get it wet when you're taking a bath?

MAINWARING That's just the sort of flippant remark I'd expect from you, Wilson. But you'd laugh the other side of your face if a Nazi paratrooper came in through that door. What would you say then, 'I'll just run over to the bank and get my rifle"?

The door opens – Walker slides in.

WALKER Morning all.

They both nod.

WALKER Er... have either of you seen young Charlie?

WILSON Who's young Charlie?

WALKER The lad who works for me, I arranged to meet him here.

WILSON We haven't seen anyone, have we, sir?

WALKER Oh, that's a nuisance, er, Mr Mainwaring. (**He lowers his voice and leans over Mainwaring**) I wonder if you'd mind doing me a favour?

MAINWARING What?

WALKER Just go out in the street and keep an eye open in case a copper comes by.

MAINWARING I beg your pardon?

WALKER I've got a few things for Miss Fortescue out in the car, and I want to bring them in.

MAINWARING How dare you? Are you suggesting that I, the manager of Martin's Bank, should act as a look out tout.

WALKER Please yourself, I shall just have to sneak them in through the back door, that's all.

MAINWARING Now, look here, Walker, for the last time I'm warning you, I want nothing whatsoever to do with your black market activities.

WALKER Right, then I'll cancel your order for whisky. (**He slides out of the door**)

Wilson reacts.

MAINWARING The whisky's not for me, you know, Wilson. It's for my wife. Unless she gets it, she makes my life a misery.

WILSON Yes, of course, sir, I quite understand.

Miss Fortescue appears with the coffee.

MISS FORTESCUE Two coffees and three rich tea biscuits. (**She puts down two cups of coffee, a saucer with four lumps of sugar on it, and a plate with three rich tea biscuits on it**)

WILSON Thank you very much.

MISS FORTESCUE Thank you. (**She goes**)

Wilson and Mainwaring each take a biscuit.

MAINWARING I don't approve of black market activities, as you know, I believe in fair shares for all. (**He takes the last biscuit and puts it on his plate**)

WILSON So do I.

Wilson takes the biscuit off Mainwaring's plate – breaks it – takes half himself and puts half back on Mainwaring's plate. Mainwaring reacts. The door opens and Pike comes in with two rifles.

PIKE Come on, Mr Mainwaring, we'd better get over there straight away. (**He hands Wilson his rifle**) Here's your rifle, Uncle Arthur.

MAINWARING What are you talking about, Pike?

PIKE I've just had a phone call from the police.

MAINWARING Don't tell me they've arrested Walker.

PIKE A German pilot has bailed out and landed on the town hall roof.

MAINWARING What… **(He jumps up)**

Jones rushes in through the door, he is in civilian clothes.

JONES Permission to speak, sir? Don't panic, don't panic, there's a Nazi dangling from the town hall clock. He's dangling, sir, he's dangling.

MAINWARING Yes, Jones, we know, we'd better get over there right away.

JONES I'll go back to my shop and get my rifle and bayonet.

MAINWARING Don't bother about the bayonet.

JONES If he stops dangling and comes down, I want to be ready for him. They don't like it up 'em, you know, sir, they…

Walker comes in through the door with a large cardboard box.

WALKER Mind your backs, please. **(To Mainwaring)** I decided to risk it, Mr Mainwaring.

MAINWARING Where's your rifle?

WALKER In the car, why?

MAINWARING Go and get it, we've got to go over to the town hall.

WALKER What are you going to do, shoot the mayor?

MAINWARING Just do as you're told. Come on, we'll pick up Frazer on the way.

TELECINE: EXTERIOR. STREET. DAY

The street below the town hall clock, Hodges, three wardens and a policeman are holding back a crowd of civilians. An old man is standing beside Hodges. They are all looking upwards.

HODGES All right, stand back, stand back, this isn't a side show. Will you stand back? There's nothing to see. What are you making all this fuss about? It's only a German, hanging from a parachute.

EXTERIOR. TOWN HALL CLOCK. DAY

The Nazi pilot is hanging over the edge of the roof, his parachute is caught on a piece of ironwork.

PILOT **(Weakly)** Hilfe! Hilfe!

TELECIN:. EXTERIOR. STREET. DAY

HODGES Will you stand back? If those ropes break, he'll drop right on top of us, it will be a very nasty mess.

OLD MAN Those ropes won't break, them Germans make very good ropes, them Germans do. They make a lot of other things, them Germans, they make er… binoculars, and cameras, and telescopes and bicycles, and air guns, and sewing machines, make very good sewing machines, them Germans.

HODGES Oh shut up, you silly old fool.

Mainwaring, Wilson, Jones, Walker, Frazer and Pike push their way through from the back of the crowd.

OLD MAN Here come our brave lads, give 'em a cheer.

The crowd cheer.

MAINWARING Let us through, please.

HODGES Just a minute, who do you think you're shovin', Napoleon? This is an A.R.P. matter and I'm in charge 'ere.

MAINWARING I don't wish to discuss anything with you, at any time.

HODGES I've got a position of authority in this town and I will not have it undermined. How dare you show me up in front of the townspeople? **(He points to his helmet)** This white helmet means something, you know.

WILSON Yes, it means you're very boring. Now get out of the way. **(He pushes him)**

Mainwaring and the rest push through the crowd and look up.

JONES There he is, sir, just like I said, he's dangling, dangling.

WILSON How are we going to get him down, sir?

MAINWARING We'll think of something.

FRAZER I don't think he's in any position to give us much trouble.

MAINWARING Don't you believe it, Frazer. A wounded jackal is always most dangerous when it's cornered. Come on, men.

They go out of picture.

HODGES **(To old man)** That Captain Mainwaring's got no respect for my white helmet whatsoever.

OLD MAN The German's make very good helmets, make very good boots too.

Hodges gives him a glare and follows Mainwaring.

STUDIO. INTERIOR. TOWN HALL. DAY

The town clerk, Mr Gordon, is standing on the steps. Mainwaring and co. run up to meet him.

GORDON **(North country)** Thank goodness you've come, Captain Mainwaring. You've got to get him down.

MAINWARING We'll do what we can, Mr Gordon.

GORDON As town clerk, I am responsible for the town hall, and I cannot have a German pilot dangling from the roof. I mean, what will the town council say?

MAINWARING How do we get up to the clock tower?

GORDON I'll show you. (**He goes through the doors of the town hall. Mainwaring and co. follow. Hodges runs up the steps.**

INTERIOR. TOWN HALL. DAY

A small corner of the town hall. The town clerk hurries into the picture, followed by Mainwaring and co. The town clerk opens a small door. Inside, we can see the bottom of a wooden ladder.

GORDON That's the way up to the clock tower, but it's not very safe.

MAINWARING What do you mean?

FRAZER Don't you remember, Captain Mainwaring, the staircase was burnt down by a fire bomb last year?

WILSON (**Looking up**) They've rigged up some scaffolding and builder's ladders. The town clerk's right, sir, it doesn't look at all safe.

Godfrey comes into the picture carrying a rubber air cushion.

JONES Hello, Mr Godfrey, where have you been?

GODFREY I was in Timothy Whites when I heard the commotion. Can I be of any assistance, sir?

MAINWARING I doubt it, Godfrey.

JONES (**Pointing to air cushion**) What's that you've got there?

GODFREY It's my sister Dolly's rubber air cushion, I've been to have it repaired.

JONES Didn't they wrap it up for you in the shop?

GODFREY No.

JONES Fancy making you carry it through the streets like that, it's a disgrace.

GODFREY They never wrap things nowadays, I suppose it's the war. I'm afraid all the old standards are going by the board.

JONES You're quite right, Mr Godfrey, they could have put a bit of paper round it.

MAINWARING Jones!

JONES I mean, it's very ingrading carrying it through the streets like that.

MAINWARING Jones, please.

GORDON Mr Mainwaring, may I remind you that there's a German dangling from the town hall roof.

MAINWARING I'm well aware of that fact, Mr Town Clerk. Right, safe or not, we've got to go up those ladders.

WALKER Why bother to go up at all?

MAINWARING What do you mean?

WALKER Why don't we put Mr Godfrey's air cushion at the bottom of the tower, that might break his fall.

MAINWARING One more remark out of you, Walker, and I shall order you to leave the town hall.

JONES Permission to speak, sir? I should like to shin up those ladders. Let me go, sir, let me go first.

WILSON Perhaps Frank ought to go up first, he's the lightest.

PIKE That's not fair, Uncle Arthur, you know I can't stand heights, I'm a martyr to vertigo.

MAINWARING I shall go up first, and that's that.

JONES Mr Mainwaring, I cannot allow you to sacrifice yourself.

Mainwaring has one foot on the ladder, Jones pushes him aside and climbs up. Mainwaring picks himself up.

EXTERIOR. TOWN HALL CLOCK. DAY

The Nazi pilot is still hanging over the edge of the roof.

PILOT (**Struggling weakly**) Hilfe! Hilfe!

INTERIOR. CLOCK. DAY

Through the open arches we can see the pilot hanging. A small trap door is open with the top of the ladder poking through, with a scaffold pole holding it. Above are the works of the clock. Running round the edge is a tunnel, which is covered in. This contains the wooden figures. One of the figures, a horse, is outside the tunnel, at one time it had the figure of a knight on its back, this has been broken off and all we can see are the legs on the side of the horse. Jones comes through the trap-door.

JONES (**Crosses to arch and shouts to pilot**) Don't worry, we will get you in. Stay where you are, whatever you do, don't move.

The pilot gestures weakly. Mainwaring comes through the trap-door. Jones rushes back and helps him through.

JONES He's still there, Mr Mainwaring. What are you going to do?

MAINWARING (**Crossing to arch**) You keep him covered and I'll parley with him.

JONES Right, sir. (**He points his rifle at the pilot**) Now, pay attention, Fritz, the captain will parley with you.

MAINWARING (**Shouting**) Further resistance is useless. In the name of the King, I call on you to surrender.

The pilot gestures weakly, Wilson comes through the trap and crosses to the arch.

WILSON How is he, sir?

MAINWARING If this is a specimen of a crack Luftwaffe pilot, I don't think much of him. He looks like something the cat dragged in, not smart at all, so unlike our own brave R.A.F. lads.

The pilot gestures and shakes his head.

WILSON I wonder how you'd feel if you were dangling 150 feet above the ground.

MAINWARING I don't want any of that sort of talk, Wilson. Look, the man's in a blue funk. (**Shouts**) For goodness sake, pull yourself together.

The pilot shakes his head.

MAINWARING He doesn't even speak English. What's German for 'pull yourself together'?

WILSON I've really no idea, sir.

Frazer and Walker come into the picture.

FRAZER The man looks in a terrible state, enemy or no, you can't help feeling sorry for him.

WALKER Blimey, he looks awful.

WILSON (**To Mainwaring**) How are we going to get him in, sir?

WALKER What we need is some sort of long pole. I've got an idea, Mr Mainwaring, why don't we pull the minute hand off the clock, that should do the trick.

MAINWARING Good idea, Walker, see if you can reach it. Give him a hand, Jones.

JONES Right-oh, Mr Mainwaring.

Walker leans out through the arch, Jones holds him round the waist.

WILSON That's vandalism. You can't desecrate the town hall clock like that, sir.

MAINWARING It doesn't work, it's been at a quarter past three since 1939.

FRAZER Aye, don't forget it's a German clock, sir.

MAINWARING What do you mean?

FRAZER See on this plate. (**Points to brass plate**) Made by Herman Holst, Munich.

MAINWARING That settles it. Pull that hand off, Walker.

JONES It was rather pretty, it used to play nursery rhymes every quarter of an hour and figures used to come out.

WALKER (**Coming down**) It's no use, Mr Mainwaring, I can't reach it.

Pike comes through the trap.

WILSON Where have you been, Frank?

PIKE I had to come up slowly, Uncle Arthur, the ladders wobbled. Is the German still out there?

WILSON Yes.

PIKE Is he fighting you, Mr Mainwaring?

MAINWARING Of course not, you stupid boy.

WALKER There's nothing here to pull him in with, Mr Mainwaring. Perhaps if I lean out I might be able to reach.

FRAZER Can't you lean out any further than that?

WALKER I'm not a flippin' giraffe, you know. If he could swing himself I might be able to grab him.

MAINWARING Yes, that's it. What's the German for swing, Wilson?

WILSON I've really no idea, sir.

MAINWARING You know, Wilson, you're about as much use as a dying duck in a thunderstorm.

WALKER 'Ere, Fritz, swing it, swing it. You know, hot char char.

PIKE Try him with a bit of 'In the mood', Joe, he might understand that.

WALKER Right. (**Sings**) Mr what you call it, are you doing tonight. Hope you're in the mood 'cos I'm feeling just right. (**Pike joins in**) How about a corner with a table for two, where the music's mellow in a gay rendezvous.

They all 'la la' the rest of the tune, the German starts to cry.

PIKE He's crying, Mr Mainwaring.

WILSON I'm not surprised, with that terrible row.

MAINWARING The man's a complete fool, doesn't seem to understand anything.

WILSON Perhaps he prefers classical music, sir. We could try something German.

FRAZER How about Offenbach – The Tales of Hoffman?

WILSON Yes, the Barcarolle, that's got a lovely swing to it.

MAINWARING I refuse to allow my platoon to sing a German song.

FRAZER We've got to get him in somehow, Captain Mainwaring. Right, are you ready boys? All together.

All except Mainwaring, they 'la' the barcarolle. After a few bars, cut to Jones who is examining the scaffold pole holding the top of the ladder.

JONES We can use this pole, Mr Mainwaring.

No one takes any notice, they are all leaning out and singing the Barcarolle. Jones pulls at the pole, it is tied to the top of the ladder with a rope.

JONES If I cut through this rope, I should be able to get it out. (**He takes out his penknife and starts to cut the rope**)

Cut back to Mainwaring and co. – they stop singing.

MAINWARING This is no use, we'll have to go down and get a pole.

Cut back to Jones.

JONES I've got a pole, Mr Mainwaring. (**He has cut through the rope, and is pulling the pole. They all turn**)

MAINWARING No, Jones, don't, you'll...

JONES It's coming!

Jones gives the pole a final tug and it comes away. There is a terrific crash and a cloud of dust as the ladders and scaffolding crash down. They all stare at Jones in silence.

INTERIOR. TOWN HALL. DAY

The door is open, inside we can see a mass of broken ladders and poles. Clouds of dust are coming out. Godfrey and the Warden stare at it.

GODFREY Oh dear, oh dear, oh dear, it's all broken.

HODGES Vandals, hooligans. It took me and my men two days to rig up those ladders.

GODFREY But how are they going to get down now, Mr Hodges?

HODGES I don't know, and I don't care. As far as I'm concerned they can stay up there for ever, and starve. Ruining my ladders like that.

GODFREY I'm sure they didn't mean it.

HODGES Do you know what I'm going to do now? I'm going out in the street and I'm going to give Mainwaring a piece of my mind.

GODFREY But he'll never hear you from the top of the tower.

HODGES Oh yes he will, because I shall shout loud, and when I want to shout loud I can shout very loud indeed. (**He goes**)

GODFREY (**Calling after him**) Don't say anything you'll regret afterwards, Mr Hodges.

INTERIOR. CLOCK. DAY

FRAZER You silly old fool, we'll never get down now, we're marooned, marooned.

JONES Permission to speak, sir? I want to say that I'm very sorry, I did not realise that this pole had things attached to it. I want to make it up to you, sir. Whatever you ask me to do, I will do, no matter how dangerous. I will make any sacrifice necessary in order to regurgitate myself.

Mainwaring reacts.

PILOT Hilfe! Hilfe!

MAINWARING We'll worry about getting down later, let's go and get that Nazi in. I'm fed up with him hanging out there and whining.

TELECINE. EXTERIOR. STREET. DAY

HODGES (**Shouting up**) I've had enough of you, Mainwaring. I hope you stay up there for ever, then I can enjoy the war in peace, because I do enjoy this war, in fact, I never enjoyed anything so much in all my life as being Chief Warden, I love it and you always spoil it.

OLD MAN He won't be able to hear you, you need a megaphone, Germans make very good megaphones, and loud speakers and radios and gramophones, make very good gramophones them Germans.

HODGES Shut up, you old fool.

GODFREY How dare you talk to that old gentleman like that? You're a very common, rude, nasty fellow.

HODGES Don't you start.

The Vicar and Verger come into the picture.

VERGER Hullo, Mr Hodges. (**Points up**) Look, Your Reverence, he hasn't fallen yet, we're not too late, we haven't missed anything.

EXTERIOR. CLOCK. DAY

Mainwaring and co. are leaning out through the arches, holding the pole. The pilot is gripping the other end.

MAINWARING Right, all together, pull.

They pull the pilot towards the parapet, Mainwaring tries to pull one leg over, Walker the other.

FRAZER Careful, Mr Mainwaring, you'll break his leg.

MAINWARING I can't help that, he shouldn't have come in the first place.

WALKER Right, heave, I've got him.

They have now got the pilot's legs over the parapet. He is still hanging backwards on his parachute.

WILSON We can't get him in like this, sir. We've got to release him from his parachute.

MAINWARING How do we do that?

PIKE You see that big buckle, Mr Mainwaring? You give it a quarter turn to the left and then hit it. I saw it in the film *One of our aircraft is missing.*

JONES Permission to speak, sir? I should like to volunteer to give the German a quarter turn and then hit him. Let me do it, sir, let me do it.

MAINWARING Very well, Jones.

Jones reaches out and hits the pilot again.

WILSON Actually, sir, a quarter turn to the left would be on British parachutes, on the Continent they use a left-hand thread.

MAINWARING Yes, that's typically foreign, try turning it to the right, Jones.

Jones reaches out, turns the buckle to the right and starts hitting it.

TELECINE: EXTERIOR. STREET. DAY

VERGER Look, Your Reverence, Jones is hitting the German.

VICAR Where? I can't see.

VERGER There, right across the gargoyles.

VICAR That's not in the Geneva convention.

VERGER No, but it's very near it.

Private Sponge and the rest of the platoon come into the picture at the double.

OLD MAN Here come some more of our brave lads, give 'em a cheer.

The crowd cheer.

SPONGE Halt. (**To Godfrey**) What's happening, Mr Godfrey?

GODFREY Captain Mainwaring's marooned on the top of the tower.

SPONGE Well, we'd better get him down. What do you suggest, Mr Hodges?

HODGES I'm not going to help you, I refuse even to discuss it with you.

VICAR I think I know how to get them down, my good man.

SPONGE How are you going to do that, Vicar?

VICAR By exercising my little skill. Come and help me carry my paraphernalia, Mr Yeatman.

VERGER Very well, Your Reverence.

Jones reaches out, turns the buckle and hits it with his fist. The pilot shouts, nothing happens.

JONES It won't open.

WALKER Try it again, Jonesey.

EXTERIOR. CLOCK. DAY

Mainwaring and co. are hauling the pilot in. As he reaches the ground, he throws his arms around Mainwaring's neck and kisses him.

PILOT Danken, danken.

MAINWARING **(Pushing him away)** Don't start any of those foreign tricks here, go and stand in the corner. Keep him covered, Jones.

JONES Yes, sir. **(To pilot)** Just watch it, the fact that I haven't got a bayonet makes no difference.

Mainwaring takes a piece of paper out of his pocket and writes a note.

MAINWARING Now, what I'm going to do, Wilson, is to throw this note down.

WILSON But that won't go straight down, sir, it will flutter for miles.

MAINWARING What, er… oh yes, just testing you, Wilson.

PIKE **(Taking note)** Give it to me, Mr Mainwaring, this will do the trick. **(He puts the note in an empty beer bottle and throws it)**

TELECINE: EXTERIOR. STREET. DAY

The bottle bursts at the Warden's feet.

HODGES **(Shouting)** Madman! That could have killed me.

GODFREY **(Picking up note)** Look, there's a message in it. **(He hands it to Hodges)**

HODGES **(Pulling a piece of chalk out of his pocket)** Right, now I'll send them a message. **(He starts to chalk on the road)**

INTERIOR. CLOCK. DAY

MAINWARING You could have killed someone, Pike.

PIKE I was just using my initiative.

WILSON Look, sir, Hodges is chalking a reply on the pavement.

JONES What was your message, Mr Mainwaring?

MAINWARING How are we going to get down? What's his message say?

WALKER How are you going to get down.

Pike throws another bottle.

MAINWARING What message was in that, Pike?

PIKE None at all, I was just trying to hit the Warden.

MAINWARING Good, good.

FRAZER Mr Mainwaring, why not have each one of us in turn suggest a way to get down, and then you can pick the best.

MAINWARING I suppose we might as well try, it's better than nothing.

Pike puts up his hand.

MAINWARING Yes, Pike?

PIKE If we could unhook the parachute, one of us could float down on it.

Mainwaring gives him a look of despair.

JONES Permission to speak, sir? If we can unhook the parachute, we could cut it into shreds and then we could plait it and plait it, and keep plaiting it until we have one long rope. Then we could take it in turns to slide down it.

Wilson laughs.

MAINWARING What are you sniggering about?

WILSON I was just thinking, that's a bit of a platitude.

Mainwaring reacts.

FRAZER Mr Mainwaring, I mind the time, many many years ago, in the furtherest point in the Western Isles. Two brave lighthouse keepers were marooned, the stairs had collapsed, and they were cut off. Well, they were up there for two months, and in the end they decided there was only one way to get down.

MAINWARING What was that?

FRAZER To dismantle the lighthouse, brick by brick.

MAINWARING **(Quietly)** That's not a very sensible suggestion, Frazer.

FRAZER Well, maybe no, but you see, they'd been up there so long, they were both quite mad, did you hear what I said, Captain Mainwaring? Mad! Mad! Mad!

There is a long pause while Mainwaring reacts.

MAINWARING **(Quietly)** Your turn, Wilson.

WILSON Well, sir, I can't help remembering a fairy story my dear old nanny used to tell me. It was all about a beautiful princess who was locked in the top of a high tower, and she was rescued by a handsome prince. And, do you know how he did it?

MAINWARING I've no idea.

WILSON Well, you see, he shot an arrow to the top of the tower, and attached to the arrow was a length of silken thread, and attached to the thread was a piece of twine, and attached to the twine was a rope. She pulled them all up and the handsome prince climbed up and rescued her. Wasn't that nice, sir?

MAINWARING I don't think I can stand very much more of this, I feel as if I'm having a very bad dream. **(He turns to Walker)** Please, Walker, please say something sensible.

WALKER Yeah, all right. **(He points)** How about using that rope to get down?

MAINWARING What rope?

WALKER This rope 'ere. **(He crosses over to a large drum with cogs and a handle attached to it. Round the drum is a coil of rope, the end attached to a weight goes through a hole in the floor)** It's got a weight on the end, all we've got to do is to wind it up, drop it through the trap-door, and then wind it down, simple.

The others all react.

MAINWARING Well done, Walker. I'd noticed it ages ago, I was just waiting to see who'd be the first one to spot it. Right, start winding. Give him a hand, Pike.

Walker and Pike start to wind the rope up.

PIKE It ain't half stiff, Joe.

WALKER You're right. **(He looks up)** Oh blimey, no wonder, look there's some sort of brake on. Knock it off, Jonesey.

JONES Right-oh. **(He climbs on to the horse, facing the back, and pulls the lever over)**

WALKER That's better, now we're getting somewhere.

There is a huge whirring sound as the clock starts, the hammer strikes the bell with a huge clang, the picture jars.

WALKER Blimey, we've started the clock.

MAINWARING Quick, Pike, muffle that bell, people will think it's an invasion signal.

Pike grabs Mainwaring's bowler – puts it on the bell. The hammer strikes the bell and goes right through the hat. Pike hands it back. Mainwaring reacts. Suddenly a nursery rhyme starts to play – the horse Jones is on lurches through the doors.

JONES Mr Mainwaring, I'm going out, I'm going out. Don't panic, don't panic.

Mainwaring and co. rush to the arches and lean out, the horse with Jones on its back stops just below the hands of the clock.

WALKER Hang on, Jonesey, and don't look down.

JONES Mr Mainwaring, it's stopped, it shouldn't do that.

WILSON No, of course it shouldn't, it should go right round and in through the other doors.

MAINWARING It's stuck, Jones, you'll have to hang on for a quarter of an hour until the clock strikes again.

JONES But I can't ride, Mr Mainwaring.

WALKER Jonesey, pull the minute hand round a quarter of an hour. That will set it off.

Jones reaches up, turns to face the front of the horse, leans out and pulls the minute hand round a quarter of an hour. The bell strikes.

MAINWARING Stop that bell, Pike. **(He grabs Frazer's top hat and hands it to Pike who holds it in front of the bell, the clapper hits it)**

FRAZER You've ruined it, that hat cost me eight and six in 1911.

MAINWARING It's about time you had a new one.

A nursery rhyme starts to play.

WALKER Hold on, Jonesey, you should come in now. **(He points)** Oh no, look!

A figure of a knight comes out. Figure crosses balcony. Figure sticks Jones.

JONES Mr Mainwaring, he's poking me, he's poking me.

MAINWARING Don't make all that fuss, Jones, it's only a wooden sword.

JONES I know, sir, but I do not like it, I do not like it.

The figures start to reverse back through the doors.

MAINWARING Quick, get him down.

They pull Jones down from the horse.

JONES Oh thank you, sir.

The clock starts to strike, Mainwaring grabs Jones' straw hat.

MAINWARING Pike, do the necessary.

Hat being bashed. The nursery rhyme starts to play, the horse and knight start to move.

WILSON Mind, Jones, for goodness sake, don't get carried out again.

JONES Don't you worry, Mr Wilson, once bitten twice shy.

Figures crossing. The figures move out through the doors. Jones climbs on the track and looks through the doors.

JONES They're wonderful those little figures you know, sir. There used to be a third, I wonder what happened to...

There is a whirring sound and the third figure – the reaper – appears. It chases Jones out.

JONES Oh no! Mr Mainwaring, it's the reaper.

Jones has reached the middle of the rail, the reaper works his scythe at Jones' feet. Jones grabs the minute hand of the clock and jumps as the scythe comes round.

JONES Mr Mainwaring, I'm being reaped, I'm being reaped. What am I going to do, Mr Mainwaring?

MAINWARING You'll have to stay out there with them until they come in.

The figures start to move.

WALKER They're coming now, don't look down, Jonesey, don't look down.

The figures chase Jones through the door. Frazer and Walker help him down.

MAINWARING Now don't go out there again, Jones.

JONES But I didn't go out there on purpose, Mr Mainwaring, they made me, they made me…

MAINWARING That will do, Jones, pull yourself together. Now, during the next two minutes, I want you all to think of a way to get down, and let's hope they'll be a little more sensible than the last lot. Wilson. (**He draws Wilson to the corner of the arch**) And I must say, yours was the most stupid suggestion of them all.

An arrow twangs into the wooden door near Wilson.

WILSON Look at that, sir.

MAINWARING Good heavens.

The arrow has a piece of fishing line and a message attached to it.

WILSON (**Taking the message off the arrow and reading it**) Attached to this arrow is a length of twine, attached to the twine is a length of cord, attached to the cord… Well, well, well, isn't that nice, sir?

Mainwaring reacts.

TELECINE: EXTERIOR. STREET. DAY

The Vicar is standing with a bow in hand, Godfrey, the Verger and Hodges are grouped round him.

GODFREY That was very clever, Vicar. How did you think that up?

VICAR Just an old fairy story my nanny used to tell me.

HODGES Yes, I've heard that you were an expert on fairies.

THE DEADLY ATTACHMENT

SERIES SIX **EPISODE ONE**

Recorded: Friday 22/6/73

Original transmission: Wednesday 31/10/73, 6.50–7.20pm

Original viewing figures = 12.9 million

ARTHUR LOWE .... CAPTAIN MAINWARING
JOHN LE MESURIER .... SERGEANT WILSON
CLIVE DUNN........ LANCE CORPORAL JONES
JOHN LAURIE .... PRIVATE FRAZER
JAMES BECK .... PRIVATE WALKER
ARNOLD RIDLEY .... PRIVATE GODFREY
IAN LAVENDER .... PRIVATE PIKE
PHILIP MADOC........ U-BOAT CAPTAIN
BILL PERTWEE........ CHIEF WARDEN HODGES
EDWARD SINCLAIR........ VERGER
ROBERT RAGLAN .... COLONEL
COLIN BEAN .... PRIVATE SPONGE
PLATOON .... DESMOND CULLUM-JONES, GEORGE HANCOCK, EVAN ROSS, LESLIE NOYES, WILLIAM GOSSLING, FREDDIE WHITE, FREDDIE WILES, ROGER BOURNE, MICHAEL MOORE
POLICEMAN .... RAY EMMINS
NAZI SAILORS .... LES CONRAD, REG TURNER, CLIVE ROGER, DANNY LIONS, ALAN THOMAS, EMMETT HENNESSY, BARRY SUMMERFORD

• PHILIP MADOC REMEMBERS •

'"Was it you who played the U-boat Captain in *Dad's Army?*" Absolute incredulity and amazement in the voice. He was an accountant from the Isle of Man. At this moment he was astride a camel – Bactrian, what else? – on a trek in the Gobi Desert. He glanced over at me as I adjusted myself on my camel in a futile attempt to make my posterior as comfortable as possible on a woefully threadbare blanket. "Yes," I replied. "We do get lucky sometimes."

'This happened quite recently, but many times over the years – though rarely in such an exotic location – the same or similar question has been put to me. I don't think they were doubting my ability to play the Captain necessarily – it was simply dawning on them that they were with someone who had been in the presence of Arthur, John, Clive, Ian and everyone else in that splendid entourage and they were aware that I was the one who failed so prominently in this ever-popular episode.

'From the filming at Thetford, to the rehearsals at Acton and the recording at the BBC, it was, for me, a bewildering joy. I've never been, before or since, on a location where wives have been present in such proactive numbers. Cups of tea, of course – often unsolicited – and chairs to relax in were unfailingly provided by these formidable and caring ladies for their respective spouses – gentlemen who were, as we know, all such splendid individuals, in performance and in reality, a group of people so rich in character that they displayed a bio-diversification all of their own.

'I have to admit that often, when asked to confirm that I was *that* U-boat Captain, I do mention in a belated personal plug, that I have played classical parts too. Nevertheless, despite those feeble claims to profundity, I am convinced that whatever little immortality – who knows? – might, eventually be on offer, it will inevitably and gratefully be linked with the fortunes in the quite unique *Dad's Army*.'

The Deadly Attachment

INTERIOR. CHURCH HALL. DAY

The platoon are drawn up on parade. They are all wearing full equipment and rifles. Mainwaring and Wilson are in front. Mainwaring is holding some papers.

MAINWARING Now, pay attention, men. I have just received a new directive from G.H.Q. regarding Nazi parachutists, and I'll read it to you. **(Reading)** There is a danger that Home Guards might confuse British pilots and air crews who are bailing out, with actual German parachute troops. Not that our chaps get shot down very often, of course, but it can happen. A good point to remember here is the fact that no British plane contains more than six men. So if you see a bunch of parachutists floating down, you count them, and if there are more than six, you shoot them in the air.

PIKE Mr Mainwaring, supposing they're dressed as nuns, do we still count them?

MAINWARING You count them, however they're dressed. On the other hand, it's hardly likely that a whole planeload of real nuns would drop by parachute.

JONES You never know, sir. I look at it this way. Supposing somewhere in occupied France there is a nunnery. And one day the chief nun calls all the other nuns together and she says: 'Look girls, I've had enough of being under their Nazi heels, let us escape to dear old England,' and they all creep out, and they steal a plane, and they fly, and fly, and fly, and when these flying nuns get here, they don't know how to land, so they all jump out by parachute.

MAINWARING I think you're going into the realms of fantasy now, Jones.

JONES But it is a possibility, sir, it is a possibility.

MAINWARING It's a million-to-one chance, but I suppose we should take every precaution.

WILSON Excuse me, sir, if I may be allowed to interject at this point of the discussion.

MAINWARING Hmmm?

WILSON It's really perfectly simple, you see as they float down, the turbulence of the air will cause the habits to rise and we shall be able to see their legs, then we can tell if they're real nuns or not.

MAINWARING A very good point, Wilson, that's it, look at their legs.

GODFREY I don't think I should care to look at nuns' legs, sir. It would be very impolite.

MAINWARING You'd just have to force yourself, Godfrey, this is war.

PIKE Mr Mainwaring, I don't know what real nuns' legs look like, I've never seen them.

WALKER If it comes to that, I don't think anybody has.

FRAZER Hairy ones!

MAINWARING I beg your pardon, Frazer.

FRAZER If they're Nazis, they'll have nasty hairy legs with jackboots on.

WALKER What do we do if the real nuns have got hairy legs with jackboots on.

MAINWARING That will do, Walker. Now: **(Reads)** 'If a Nazi parachutist is floating down with his hands up, would you think this was strange?'

WALKER Not half as strange as if he was floating up with his hands down.

MAINWARING I shan't tell you again, Walker. If he is floating down with his hands up, this does not necessarily mean that he is surrendering, he could have a grenade concealed in each hand, so watch it. **(The phone bell rings)** Answer the phone, Pike.

PIKE Yes, Mr Mainwaring. **(He crosses to the office)**

MAINWARING By the way, Wilson, while we're on the subject of grenades, have you primed our stock of Mills bombs?

WILSON No, sir.

MAINWARING I told you to do it yesterday.

WILSON But it's awfully dangerous, sir.

MAINWARING War is awfully dangerous, Wilson. What would you do if a hoard of Nazi parachutists were to descend on the church hall? Say, 'Wait a minute, while we prime our grenades'? I want those bombs ready for instant use. See to it tonight.

WILSON Yes, sir.

Pike returns.

PIKE You're wanted on the phone, Mr Mainwaring, G.H.Q. It's very urgent.

MAINWARING Thank you. **(He crosses to the door)** Take over, Wilson. **(He goes into the office)**

INTERIOR. SIDE OFFICE. DAY

Mainwaring comes into the office, crosses to the desk and picks up the phone. The colonel is on the other end with a policeman standing behind him.

MAINWARING Good evening, sir. Pike, shut the door. No – the other side, boy.

COLONEL Good evening, Mainwaring. I've got a very important job for you to do.

MAINWARING Excellent. What is it, sir?

COLONEL I've just had a message from the police, a fishing boat has picked up a U-boat captain and seven members of the crew. They're down at the harbour now, locked in the hold.

MAINWARING By Jove, that's good news.

COLONEL I want you to pick them up and take them back to the church hall. I'll send an armed escort over to collect them.

MAINWARING Face to face with the enemy at last, eh, sir? Don't worry, we'll take good care of them.

COLONEL They won't give you much trouble, they've been drifting at sea for two days in a rubber dinghy. Good luck.

MAINWARING Thank you, sir. **(He hangs up, strides to the door and opens it)** Good news, men. After all these months of waiting, we're finally going to get to grips with the enemy.

WALKER **(To Jones)** Blimey, don't tell me we're going to invade France.

INTERIOR. CHURCH HALL. DAY

Wilson hurries over to Mainwaring.

WILSON You're not going to do anything hasty are you, sir?

MAINWARING I've got something very important to say to the men.

WILSON Have you found out what nuns' legs look like?

MAINWARING All right, Wilson. **(To men)** A fishing boat has picked up a U-boat crew, and we're going down to the harbour to collect them.

JONES We're going to collect a U-boat crew. Right, fix bayonets. **(He rushes over to Mainwaring ,waving his bayonet)** I can't wait to get at 'em, Mr Mainwaring. I just can't wait.

MAINWARING Put that bayonet away, Jones, there's plenty of time for that when we get there.

JONES I can't help it, sir, when I get a whiff of action I reach for my bayonet, it's second nature, I tell you, second nature.

MAINWARING Fall the men in outside.

JONES Yes, sir, yes, sir. Fall in outside to collect a U-boat crew, rifles and bayonets at the double.

MAINWARING Wilson – Pike – Wilson, while we're gone I want you and Pike to prime all the grenades.

WILSON If you insist, sir.

MAINWARING I want it done by the time I get back. Right, men, get a move on. **(He follows the men out)**

INTERIOR. SIDE OFFICE. DAY

Later that night in the office. On the desk are seven Mills bombs laid out in a row. Wilson and Pike are standing behind the desk, Pike has a bomb in his hand.

PIKE Okay, you's guys, dis is a show down, share this pineapple amongst you.

WILSON For goodness sake, put that down, Frank.

PIKE Those Chicago gangsters used to call them pineapples, Uncle Arthur. I saw it in that film *Scarface* with Paul Muni.

WILSON I don't care what they called them, they're very dangerous.

PIKE These are quite safe, they haven't got detonators in. Shall I get them? **(He goes to move)**

WILSON Stay where you are, Frank, and don't do anything, I'll get the detonators. **(He crosses to the cupboard, takes out a box gingerly)** This is so risky. **(He opens the box)** There's only two in this box.

PIKE There's some more boxes at the back of the cupboard. Shall I...

WILSON I don't want you to touch them, Frank. **(He pulls a box from the back of the cupboard, and looks at the label)** Hmmm, Dummy Primers, for training purposes only.

PIKE We don't want dummy detonators, they're no good. There's a box of real ones at the back. **(He reaches into the cupboard, Wilson stops him)**

WILSON Wait a minute, Frank. Look, er um, how would it be if we were to put these dummies in the grenades instead of the real thing?

PIKE But Mr Mainwaring said we had to have them ready for instant action. What would we do if the Germans came?

WILSON We could soon change them round, it wouldn't take a moment. We could get it done before the bells had stopped ringing.

PIKE Mr Mainwaring will be awfully cross if he finds out.

WILSON Yes, but somehow I can't help thinking he'll be even more cross, if we all get blown up.

They move to desk.

CHURCH HALL. THE NEXT DAY

JONES Left, right, left, right.

Mainwaring, Walker, Frazer and Godfrey enter, followed by the U-boat captain and seven sailors. The rest of the platoon bring up the rear with fixed bayonets. Jones is milling around waving his bayonet at the prisoners who have their hands on their heads.

JONES Hande hoch! Hande hoch, keep those handies hoch!

MAINWARING All right, Jones, they can put their hands down now.

JONES Right, handies down, handies down.

MAINWARING All right, Jones.

JONES But they're not hoch.

MAINWARING Frazer, get the Lewis gun and set it up on the stage, so that it has a clear sweep of the entire hall.

FRAZER Aye, aye, sir. **(He goes into the office)**

MAINWARING Sponge, Hancock, go and get a step-ladder.

SPONGE Right you are, Mr Mainwaring.

MAINWARING Jones, get those prisoners into a tight group in the middle of the hall.

JONES Yes, sir. **(To prisoners)** At the double, in a tight huddle, into the middle of the hall, move!

Jones and the rest of the platoon push the prisoners into a tight group in the middle of the hall. Wilson and Pike come out of the office.

WILSON You got back then sir, did they give you any trouble?

MAINWARING Not really. **(He lowers his voice)** But they're an ugly mob. You see that captain, you want to watch him, he's a surly brute, he's done nothing else but sneer, and smoke cigarettes.

WILSON I wonder if he's got any to spare, I'm right out of them.

MAINWARING This isn't a cocktail party, Wilson. Did you prime those grenades?

PIKE Well, Mr Mainwaring, we...

WILSON I think I can honestly say, sir, that all the grenades now have detonators in them.

MAINWARING Good, Pike get the Tommy gun.

PIKE Yes, Mr Mainwaring. **(He goes into the office. Jones comes over to Mainwaring and Wilson)**

JONES The prisoners are now in a huddle in the middle of the hall, sir.

MAINWARING Thank you, Jones.

Cut to tight close up of Walker talking to one of the sailors.

WALKER 'Ere, listen, tell your mates that I am in the market for purchasing Nazi daggers, swastikas, badges, signed pictures of Hitler or similar souvenirs. I'll give you a good price. **(The sailor shakes his head)** Oh blimey, you don't speak English, do you? Look, Nazi daggers, see, daggers. **(He makes a stabbing motion at the sailor who jumps back)**

CAPTAIN **(Crossing to Walker)** Get away from my men at once.

WALKER Don't start on me, mate.

MAINWARING Come over here, Walker.

Walker crosses to Mainwaring, Wilson and Jones, who are standing in a tight group away from the prisoners.

MAINWARING How dare you fraternise with the enemy?

WALKER I was only asking them if there was anything they needed.

MAINWARING I'll attend to that. **(He lowers his voice)** Now listen, the armed escort will be here shortly to collect these prisoners, meanwhile we want maximum security, Wilson, maximum security.

WILSON Yes, sir, maximum security.

Frazer comes out of the office with the Lewis gun.

JONES Wooop?

FRAZER Here you are, sir, it's all loaded and ready.

MAINWARING Right, set it up.

Frazer crosses to the stage, puts the Lewis gun on a card table and sits behind it.

JONES Permission to speak, sir? How about cutting their trouser buttons off?

MAINWARING What?

During this speech, the captain moves up quietly to behind Jones.

JONES Well, sir, if we cut their trouser buttons off and they try to run away, it will show at once that they are something unusual. Then a person walking along the street, nonchalant like, will see these men running with their trousers round their ankles, and they will investigate.

CAPTAIN You!

JONES What?

CAPTAIN You don't dare to do anything of the sort, the Geneva Convention clearly states that prisoners of war will not be put in humiliating positions.

JONES **(Gesturing with his bayonet)** You'll be in a humiliating position, mate, if you get this up you.

CAPTAIN Don't threaten me, you silly old fool.

JONES I'm not...

MAINWARING Jones – Jones! That will do, Jones. **(To the captain)** Go back into the middle and speak when you're spoken to.

WALKER Yeah, get back into the huddle.

Pike comes out of the office with the Tommy gun.

CAPTAIN I'm warning you, captain.

MAINWARING Just do as you're told. You see the sort of insolent swine we're up against, Wilson?

WILSON Yes, sir, he has got rather an abrupt manner, but you must make allowances for him, he's probably upset because we sunk his submarine.

SPONGE Where do you want this step-ladder, Mr Mainwaring?

MAINWARING Set it up by the door. Pike get up there with your Tommy gun, then you've got a view of the entire hall.

PIKE You know I don't like going up ladders, Mr Mainwaring, with my vertigo.

MAINWARING Get up there at once, boy.

PIKE **(Starting up the ladder)** It's ever so wobbly.

MAINWARING Get up.

PIKE I've got a note from the doctor.

MAINWARING Do as you're told. Godfrey, where's Godfrey?

Cut to Godfrey dozing in a chair by the door.

MAINWARING Godfrey.

GODFREY **(Waking up)** Did you call, sir? **(He comes over)** I'm sorry, I must have dozed off.

MAINWARING Dozed off! Here we are, guarding a dangerous gang of cut throats and you doze off.

Godfrey reacts.

MAINWARING You're supposed to watch them like a hawk, like a hawk. Hold the ladder.

GODFREY Yes, sir. **(He holds the ladder. The phone rings)**

MAINWARING Take charge, Wilson. **(He goes into the office)**

INTERIOR. SIDE OFFICE. DAY

Mainwaring crosses to the desk and picks up the phone.

MAINWARING Captain Mainwaring.

COLONEL G.H.Q. here, everything all right, Mainwaring?

MAINWARING Yes, sir, I've got the prisoners safe and sound, they're all ready for you to pick them up.

COLONEL I'm afraid the escort won't be able to get over there until tomorrow morning.

MAINWARING Do you mean to say that we've got to look after them all night?

COLONEL Sorry, can't do anything about it. Just give them a blanket each and bed them down. And give them something to eat, of course.

MAINWARING But we've only got our own sandwiches, Colonel.

COLONEL Well send out for some fish and chips.

MAINWARING Send out for...

COLONEL I'll see that you get the money back. Be over about eight in the morning. Cheerio.

MAINWARING **(Hanging up)** Fish and chips! **(He quickly strides to the door and opens it)**

INTERIOR. CHURCH HALL. DAY

MAINWARING Wilson, Jones.

WILSON Yes, sir.

MAINWARING The escort can't get over until the morning, they've got to be here all night.

JONES In that case, I really think we ought to cut their trouser buttons off, sir. **(Drags out his bayonet)** Let me do it, let me do it, sir.

MAINWARING Put that away, Jones. I shall have a word with the prisoners, Wilson.

WILSON But you don't speak German.

MAINWARING Oh, they'll know by the tone of my voice who's in charge, believe me, Wilson, they recognise authority. **(Mainwaring crosses to the prisoners, followed by Wilson and Jones)** Right now, pay attention. **(The prisoners all come smartly to attention)**

WILSON They're awfully well disciplined, sir.

MAINWARING Nothing of the sort, it's a slavish, blind obedience, not like the cheerful, light-hearted discipline that you get with our Jolly Jack Tars. I tell you, they're a nation of unthinking automatons, led by a lunatic who looks like Charlie Chaplin.

CAPTAIN How dare you compare our glorious leader with that non-Aryan clown? **(He takes out a notebook and pencil and writes)** I am making a note of your insults, captain. Your name will go on the list, and when we win the war, you will be brought to account.

MAINWARING You can put down what you like, you're not going to win this war.

CAPTAIN Oh yes we are.

MAINWARING Oh no you're not.

CAPTAIN Oh yes we are.

PIKE **(Sings)** Whistle while you work, Hitler is a twerp, He's half barmy, So's his army. **(The captain crosses to the ladder, the words die on Pike's lips)** Whistle…

CAPTAIN Your name will also go on the list. What is it?

Mainwaring crosses over, followed by Wilson.

MAINWARING Don't tell him, Pike.

CAPTAIN Pike, thank you.

MAINWARING **(Boiling)** Now, look here, I've had just about enough. Tell your men from me that they're going to be here all night, and they'd better behave themselves. Now, get on with it.

The captain shrugs his shoulders.

PIKE **(To Wilson)** Uncle Arthur, I don't think it's fair that my name should be on the list, I was only joking.

WILSON You should be more careful, Frank. You know that the Germans haven't got a sense of humour.

PIKE But you've said much worse things about Hitler. He's said much worse things.

WILSON Quiet, Frank, he'll hear you.

PIKE Do you think if you talked to him nicely, he'll take my name off the list?

During this, the captain is speaking to the prisoners in German.

MAINWARING Have you told them what I said?

CAPTAIN Yes.

MAINWARING Walker!

WALKER Yes, Captain Mainwaring?

MAINWARING Is the fish and chip shop still open?

WALKER I think so, why?

MAINWARING **(Handing him a ten-shilling note)** Go and get some for the prisoners. Jones, Wilson a conference. **(He walks over to Wilson and Jones)**

WALKER **(To captain)** Right, eight cod and chips.

CAPTAIN I want plaice.

WALKER Right, seven cod, one plaice. Who wants vinegar?

CAPTAIN **(In German)** Who wants vinegar?

Four hold up their hands.

WALKER Right, four vinegar. Salt?

CAPTAIN **(In German)** Who wants salt?

Three hold up hands.

WALKER That's three salt. How many without salt and vinegar?

CAPTAIN **(In German)** How many without salt and vinegar?

More hands.

WALKER Two without. Now, let's see if I've got this right.

MAINWARING What do you think you're doing, Walker?

WALKER I was just taking the order.

CAPTAIN And I don't want nasty, soggy chips.

Mainwaring reacts.

CAPTAIN I want mine crisp and light brown.

MAINWARING How dare you? Now, listen to me, I've had just about enough. You'll have what you're given, and if I say you'll eat soggy chips, you'll eat soggy chips.

INTERIOR. CHURCH HALL. NIGHT

Later that night, Jones is sitting behind the Lewis gun on the stage, Walker and Frazer are sitting beside him. Wilson is sitting in front of the stage reading *Picture Post*. Pike is up the ladder with the Tommy gun. Godfrey is sitting on a chair holding the ladder. Mainwaring is walking up and down watching the prisoners,who are sitting on benches in the middle of the hall. The rest of the platoon are sitting in a circle round the prisoners. The Captain is smoking and following Mainwaring with his eyes all the time.

FRAZER Fancy giving those Germans fish and chips, all I've had to eat tonight is paste sandwiches.

JONES You've got to treat prisoners of war properly you know, Jock. I shall never forget when we was in the Sudan, we had a young officer, Captain D'arcy Holdane his name was, and he used to say, 'Boys, always treat them Dervish prisoners well. See that they get plenty of betel-nut. If we treat them well, they'll learn by our example, and treat us well.' Anyhow, a few days later he was captured.

WALKER What happened to him?

JONES They chopped his head off.

FRAZER Look at the time, one o'clock in the morning, you'd think he'd let some of us take it in turns to sleep.

WALKER It's no use, Taff, Captain Mainwaring won't let us take our eyes off them, he's obsessed.

Mainwaring is still walking up and down. Godfrey stops him as he passes.

GODFREY Do you think I could possible be excused, sir?

MAINWARING Certainly not, stick to your post.

PIKE Yes, don't let go of the ladder, Mr Godfrey.

Mainwaring walks back towards the stage. He stops when he gets level with the captain who is watching him like a hawk. He moves and turns again.

MAINWARING (**Waving his hand at the captain**) Don't keep staring at me all the time.

Captain reacts.

MAINWARING Can't you look in another direction. (**Mainwaring walks towards the stage, as he passes Wilson, he pokes him**) Put that down, Wilson. I told you to watch the prisoners.

Wilson reacts. Mainwaring goes up on stage.

MAINWARING Keep them well covered, Jones.

JONES Don't you worry, sir, I'm watching 'em.

FRAZER Yon Captain never takes his eyes off you for a minute, Mr Mainwaring. If you were to ask my opinion, I don't think he likes you very much.

WALKER I wouldn't want to be in your shoes, sir, if he was to turn the tables on us.

MAINWARING There's not much chance of that, Walker.

Hodges and the Verger enter the church hall by the back door.

HODGES Well, I've had a good night tonight. I've booked three houses for showing lights, and we've shared a bottle together, Mr Yeatman.

VERGER By the way, Mr Hodges, not a word to His Reverence, that I keep a bottle in my hidey hole.

HODGES You can rely on me, I'm the soul of discretion, mum's the word. Better go and say goodnight to Napoleon.

Hodges and the Verger enter into the hall.

HODGES Good night, Napoleon. (**Sees the prisoners**) Blimey, what's all this?

MAINWARING They're Nazi prisoners of war, keep away from them.

VERGER You've no right to keep Germans in the church hall, the Vicar will be furious.

MAINWARING Mind your own business.

The captain suddenly clutches his stomach and groans.

HODGES What's the matter with you, mate?

CAPTAIN I feel so ill. (**Groans and slips to the floor**) It's my stomach.

HODGES Give me a hand, Verger.

They both cross to the captain.

MAINWARING Come away from those prisoners at once.

HODGES What are you talking about, can't you see the man's sick?

The captain is groaning and rolling on the floor.

FRAZER He looks bad to me, sir.

WALKER Perhaps it was them soggy chips you made him eat.

Mainwaring crosses down to Wilson.

WILSON I really think we ought to do something, sir.

MAINWARING I don't trust him, Wilson.

WILSON We can't just leave him lying there.

HODGES Well don't stand there, Mainwaring, do something. He's somebody's son you know.

VERGER He's got a heart of stone you know, Mr Hodges.

GODFREY There's some bicarbonate of soda in my Red Cross pack, if that will help.

MAINWARING Stay where you are, Godfrey.

PIKE Yes, don't let go of the ladder, Mr Godfrey.

MAINWARING Keep them well covered, Jones, watch them like a hawk.

JONES Yes, sir, like a hawk.

MAINWARING And you, Pike, I'm going in.

Frazer and Walker come down from the stage with their rifles and bayonets. Mainwaring crosses to the captain who is cradled in Hodge's arms. The captain gives another groan and passes out.

MAINWARING (**Still holding back**) There's something funny here.

HODGES What are you afraid of? They're only a few harmless German sailors.

Mainwaring kneels over the captain.

MAINWARING He seems to be breathing all right.

Suddenly the captain grabs Mainwaring's revolver, gets his arm round Hodges' neck and presses the revolver against it.

CAPTAIN No one move!

MAINWARING You, you...

CAPTAIN (**In German**) Get the machine gun!

Two sailors advance on Jones who picks up the Lewis gun and backs away.

JONES You're not having it, stand back, get back.

WILSON Please be careful, Jonesey.

The two sailors jump up on the stage. Jones backs away, trips, the Lewis gun goes off and blows a hole in the roof. Pike falls off the ladder. Everyone dives for the floor. Clouds of dust and bits of roof fall down.

INTERIOR. CHURCH HALL. NIGHT

Later that same evening, Mainwaring and co. are standing in a tight group facing the door in the middle of the hall. Jones is squatting behind the Lewis gun which is on the card table. Frazer, Walker and Pike are standing beside him with rifles and bayonets. The rest of the platoon are grouped round them (except Sponge, Desmond and Hastings). They all have fixed bayonets. Godfrey is hovering in the background. Mainwaring is in the middle with the Tommy gun. All weapons are pointed at the office door. Wilson comes in from the main doors.

MAINWARING Everything all right, Wilson?

WILSON Yes, sir, I've posted Sponge, Hancock and Desmond outside. They've got the back door and window of the office covered.

MAINWARING That stupid drunken fool, Hodges!

JONES I didn't let them have the gun did I, Captain Mainwaring?

MAINWARING You behaved very well, Jones.

JONES I haven't felt like that since I was in the trenches in 1916. I did do well, didn't I, Mr Wilson?

WILSON You did awfully well, Jonesey.

JONES You behaved well as well, you were very cool.

WILSON Thank you.

FRAZER When they've quite finished this mutual admiration society, perhaps you'd like to tell us what we're going to do now, Captain Mainwaring?

WALKER Yeah, we can't stand here all night.

MAINWARING They've only got one revolver, and they can't get out of the office. Believe me, Walker, we hold all the trump cards.

The office door opens a few inches. They all cock their rifles. A hand comes round the door and waves a white handkerchief. It is the Verger.

MAINWARING Are they surrendering, Verger?

VERGER No, I've got a message from the captain. He says he wants you to take him and his men back to the fishing boat so that they can cross to France.

MAINWARING What!

VERGER If you don't agree to his terms he's going to blow Mr Hodges' head off.

JONES We can't let them escape, sir. If they get back to France they could get another submarine and start sinking our ships again.

WILSON Jones is right, I'm afraid, sir.

WALKER It's one man's life against thousands.

FRAZER A terrible decision you've got to make, Captain Mainwaring, but you must admit you've never liked the man.

MAINWARING Tell him we need time to think it over.

VERGER Right. (**He hurries back to the office**)

INTERIOR. SIDE OFFICE. NIGHT

Hodges is sitting at the desk, the captain is standing beside him with the revolver stuck in Hodges' neck. The rest of the sailors are standing round. The Verger comes in.

CAPTAIN well?

VERGER He's thinking it over.

CAPTAIN I'll give him until dawn.

HODGES What did Mainwaring say?

VERGER I must admit, Mr Hodges, it doesn't look too good for you.

HODGES Oh no!

INTERIOR. CHURCH HALL. NIGHT

In the hall, Mainwaring, Wilson, Jones, Frazer, Walker, Godfrey and Pike are sitting in a group. The rest of the platoon are standing round.

WALKER If only we could get that gun away from him somehow.

JONES Permission to speak, sir? I have an idea. Supposing I was to put on some old clothes, black my face, knock on the door and say I am a chimney sweep. And when I see Mr Hodges, I will say, 'Hello, Fritz,' and they will say, 'Why do you call him Fritz?', and I will say. 'Because he is not British, he is a German prisoner of war who works as an A.R.P. Warden in his spare time.'

MAINWARING Please, Jones.

JONES But it will sow the seeds of doubt in their minds, sir, and while the seeds are being sown, I will jump on the captain, and if the gun goes off, it might not hit Mr Hodges.

Mainwaring gives Jones a look of despair.

PIKE Mr Mainwaring, I saw a film called the *Petrified Forest*. And Humphrey Bogart was holding Leslie Howard by gun point in a cabin all night. And Leslie Howard kept quoting poetry and using long words.

And it didn't half upset Humphrey Bogart. Perhaps you could do the same, sir?

WILSON I missed that film, what happened to Leslie Howard in the end?

PIKE He got shot.

MAINWARING You stupid boy.

GODFREY I saw Freddie Bartholomew, in *David Copperfield*, sir, but there wasn't really anything in that.

MAINWARING Oh all the… wait a minute, *David Copperfield*, Mr Macawber, something's bound to turn up. That's it, we'll play along with them. We've got to go through the town to get to the harbour, someone's bound to raise the alarm. **(Shouts at office)** All right, we agree to your terms. **(To Wilson)** Even if they get to the boat, Wilson, the Navy will blow them out of the water before they've gone a mile.

The office door opens, the captain, with Hodges at gunpoint, comes out of the office. The Verger and the rest of the sailors follow.

CAPTAIN I'm glad you have come to your senses, captain. **(In German to one of the sailors)** Get the machine gun, cover them.

The sailor covers them with the Lewis gun.

CAPTAIN **(To platoon)** Put your rifles down.

They hesitate.

MAINWARING Put them down, men.

They pile their rifles on the floor.

CAPTAIN Get me a hand grenade and a piece of string.

MAINWARING Do as he says, Wilson.

WILSON Yes, sir. **(He goes into the office)**

CAPTAIN **(To sailors in German)** Unload the rifles, take the bayonets off. **(They unload the rifles)**

MAINWARING You won't get away with this, we're bound to be spotted going through the town.

CAPTAIN No one will interfere, captain, because you will be escorting us with empty rifles.

MAINWARING And how are you going to make us do that?

Wilson returns with a Mills bomb and piece of string.

CAPTAIN Very simply. **(He hands the revolver to one of the sailors who holds it against Hodges' neck. He takes the bomb and string from Wilson)** Is it primed?

WILSON Oh yes.

CAPTAIN **(Unscrewing the baseplug)** You don't mind if I make sure.

WILSON By all means.

CAPTAIN **(Looking in bomb)** Good. **(He screws back the base and says to Jones)** You, old man, take off your belt and undo the back of your tunic.

JONES I beg your pardon?

CAPTAIN Do as I say, remove your belt. **(He ties the end of the string to the ring of the pin. Jones takes off his belt and unbuttons the back of his blouse)** Just to make sure that your behaviour is correct, captain, the old man will march in front of me… **(He puts the bomb in the waistband of Jones' trousers)** One false move from you, and I pull the string. **(He buttons up the back of Jones' blouse)**

JONES Don't make any false moves, Mr Mainwaring, or even real ones.

CAPTAIN Seven seconds will give me plenty of time to get clear, but I think it is not enough time for the old man to unbutton his tunic.

FRAZER A terrible way to die.

MAINWARING You unspeakable swine. Now listen to me, I'm the commanding officer here, it's only right that I should have the bomb in my waistband.

JONES I will not allow you to have a bomb in your trousers, sir, don't you worry about me, they can put 20 bombs in my trousers, they won't make me crack.

MAINWARING How can you hope to beat us, you see the sort of men we breed in this country.

CAPTAIN Yes, rather stupid ones.

MAINWARING You can sneer, but you've forgotten one thing, captain.

CAPTAIN What is that?

MAINWARING The Royal Navy, you've got to cross 25 miles of water. You'll never make it.

CAPTAIN I think we will, because all of you will be on the boat with us. **(Points to Godfrey)** We shall leave the old man behind to tell them.

Godfrey reacts.

CAPTAIN Your Navy won't fire on their own people. **(Takes Mainwaring's revolver, empties it, and puts it back in the holster)** So, when we get to France, you will be my prisoners, and then we shall examine the list.

TELECINE: EXTERIOR. STREET. DAY

Next day, the procession is seen marching along. Mainwaring is in front, the Captain is close behind him with the rest of the sailors. They are surrounded by Frazer, Jones, Walker and Godfrey and the rest of the platoon carrying rifles. Wilson and Pike are in the rear. Hodges and the Verger are marching level with Mainwaring.

PIKE Uncle Arthur, if I tell the German there's a dummy

detonator in the grenade, do you think he'll take my name off the list?

WILSON Be quiet, Frank.

The colonel comes round the corner.

WALKER Blimey, sir, look, it's the colonel.

MAINWARING (**Over his shoulder to the captain**) The game's up, now what are you going to do?

CAPTAIN I am not going to do anything, you will bluff your way out.

MAINWARING I refuse to co-operate in any way whatsoever.

JONES Please, Mr Mainwaring, if you don't do as he says, he'll pull the string.

MAINWARING Oh no he won't.

CAPTAIN Oh yes I will.

JONES He says he will, Mr Mainwaring.

They draw level with the colonel.

MAINWARING Platoon, halt.

COLONEL Where on earth are you taking the prisoners, Mainwaring?

MAINWARING The fact is, sir, I...

WALKER We're going for a walk, sir. Captain Mainwaring thought it would be a good idea if we gave them some exercise, they've been cooped up in a submarine for weeks.

COLONEL What on earth's the matter with you, Mainwaring? You're as white as a sheet, you look as if you've seen a ghost.

FRAZER Breath of fresh air will do him the world of good, sir.

GODFREY We're just going down to the harbour, these sailors like a sea breeze.

COLONEL Oh, all right then, I'm on my way to the railway station to pick up the escort for the prisoners. See you later.

MAINWARING Yes, sir, yes, sir. Platoon, by the right, quick march.

They start to move.

COLONEL Wait a minute. Halt!

They halt.

COLONEL You know I'm surprised at you, Mainwaring, your men are usually so smartly turned out. Why isn't Jones wearing equipment and what's that great lump of string hanging down his back?

MAINWARING Where?

COLONEL Here. (**He pulls the string and holds it up. We see the pin on the end of the string**)

MAINWARING Oh no!

Everyone except the colonel, Jones, Wilson and Pike dive for cover and flatten themselves against the wall.

JONES I've got a bomb in my trousers, don't panic! Don't panic!

MAINWARING Get it out, Jones.

He starts to unbutton the back of his blouse. Close up of Hodges holding Verger who has his fingers in his ears.

FRAZER I'll get it, sir, I'll get it.

JONES It's slipped down, Mr Mainwaring!

WALKER Hang on, I'll cut it out.

Frazer thrusts his arm down the back of Jones' trousers.

JONES Save yourself, Mr Mainwaring.

Wilson crosses to the colonel.

WILSON I wonder if I might borrow your revolver, sir?

Mainwaring and Jones are dancing in the road.

JONES Don't panic, sir, don't panic, sir!

COLONEL What the hell's going on?

WILSON I'll explain later. (**Waves revolver at prisoners**) Now listen to me, you German chaps, would you mind just getting up against the wall, with your hands up please.

The prisoners obey.

MAINWARING Jones, wait a minute, it should have gone off by now.

They both stop.

JONES So it should. I've been saved, sir, I've been saved.

Mainwaring crosses to Wilson.

MAINWARING I thought I told you to prime those grenades.

WILSON I did, sir, with dummies.

MAINWARING Why is it you will never... you've saved Jones' life, Wilson.

WILSON Now perhaps you'll agree with me that it's awfully dangerous to keep them primed.

JONES Now that the crisis is past, Mr Mainwaring, would you mind asking Private Frazer to take his arm out of my trousers.

SERIES SIX **EPISODE TWO**

Recorded: Friday 8/6/73

Original transmission: Wednesday 7/11/73, 6.50–7.20pm

Original viewing figures = 12.5 million

ARTHUR LOWE .... CAPTAIN MAINWARING
JOHN LE MESURIER .... SERGEANT WILSON
CLIVE DUNN .... LANCE CORPORAL JONES
JOHN LAURIE .... PRIVATE FRAZER
JAMES BECK .... PRIVATE WALKER
ARNOLD RIDLEY .... PRIVATE GODFREY
IAN LAVENDER .... PRIVATE PIKE
BILL PERTWEE .... CHIEF WARDEN HODGES
ALAN TILVERN .... US COLONEL
FRANK WILLIAMS .... VICAR
EDWARD SINCLAIR .... VERGER
JANET DAVIES .... MRS PIKE
WENDY RICHARD .... SHIRLEY
PAMELA CUNDELL .... MRS FOX
VERNE MORGAN .... LANDLORD
TALFRYN THOMAS .... MR CHEESEMAN
SUZANNE KERCHISS .... IVY SAMWAYS
ROBERT RAGLAN .... COLONEL
BLAIN FAIRMAN .... US SERGEANT
PLATOON .... COLIN BEAN, GEORGE HANCOCK, MICHAEL MOORE, DESMOND CULLUM-JONES, EVAN ROSS, FREDDIE WHITE, FREDDIE WILES, ROGER BOURNE, LESLIE NOYES, WILLIAM GOSSLING
US SOLDIERS .... STEVE KELLY, HUGH ELTON, MICHAEL STEVENS, DOUGLAS ROWE, CLINTON MORRIS, JOHN CANNON, DANNY LYONS

MY BRITISH BUDDY

• PAMELA CUNDELL REMEMBERS •

'This is one of my favourite episodes because there was a line in it that I was struggling to remember. I was getting very worried about it and Clive Dunn said: "Why don't you write it on the palm of your hand, then all you've got to do is put your hand out and read the line?" I thought that was a marvellous idea, but when it came to the actual recording, which is always very nerve-racking, being live in front of an audience, I went to look at the palm of my hand only to find the ink had run with all the perspiration. Luckily, I got the line right anyway.'

BLACK & WHITE
HI BUDDY

My British Buddy

INTERIOR. CHURCH HALL. DAY

The men are drawn up on parade. No equipment or rifles. Mainwaring is addressing them, Wilson is standing beside him.

MAINWARING Men, during the time we have been together, we have had to face some dark times, very dark indeed. In fact there was a time last winter when things were so dark, it was difficult to see ahead.

WALKER You mean when we had the power cuts.

MAINWARING That will do Walker. But now, at last, I'm happy to say, we can see the light at the end of the tunnel. It's a long tunnel, and a very small light, but it's shining brightly for all to see.

PIKE Mr Hodges won't like that, sir.

MAINWARING I'm not referring to the black-out, you stupid boy. I'm talking about the war situation. After our standing alone against the Nazi hordes for two years, I am pleased to tell you that help is at hand.

WILSON That's awfully good news, sir. Who is it, anyone we know?

MAINWARING You should do.

WILSON It's difficult to think who's left. Is it the Portuguese? They're our oldest allies. Somehow I don't think they'll be much help.

MAINWARING Of course it isn't the Portuguese, it's the Americans.

There is a murmur in the ranks.

WALKER Good old Uncle Sam.

MAINWARING As you know, the Americans came into the war a few months ago, and the first consignment is now arriving from the U.S.A.

WALKER Blimey, they've taken their time, the war's been on two and a half years.

MAINWARING I don't want any of that sort of talk, Walker.

PIKE It's just like those Western films, Mr Mainwaring, where the settlers are being attacked by Indians, and the U.S. Cavalry arrived in the nick of time.

MAINWARING I wouldn't say that, Pike, we've been doing pretty well on our own, still it's always an advantage to have a few extra on the team, a second eleven as it were.

FRAZER When can we expect them, sir?

MAINWARING A small advance guard will be arriving in Walmington on Saturday morning. And we must give them a hearty welcome.

WILSON You mean, sort of roll out the red carpet for them, sir.

MAINWARING Precisely, we haven't actually got a red carpet, of course.

WALKER I could get you a roll of American cloth, sir, if that would help.

Mainwaring reacts.

JONES Permission to speak, sir? We must take our American cousins to our bosoms and nurture them, we must take them into our homes.

MAINWARING Exactly, Jones.

PIKE I don't think my mum would like to have a lot of strange Americans in the house.

MAINWARING In time of war, Pike, one cannot afford to choose one's bedfellows.

GODFREY I've got a double bed, sir, I wouldn't mind sharing, if one of them was hard put.

MAINWARING I didn't mean bedfellows in that way, Godfrey.

GODFREY Perhaps it's just as well, sir, I am inclined to get up and walk about rather a lot during the night.

Mainwaring reacts.

WILSON What we want to do, sir, is to show the Americans something typically British.

WALKER How about a display of Highland dancing, sir – you couldn't get more British than that.

MAINWARING Good idea, Walker. How about it, Frazer? You're the president of the Walmington-on-Sea Caledonian Society.

FRAZER That's going to be a bit difficult, sir, I'm the only one in it.

Mainwaring reacts.

FRAZER There used to be two of us, Jock McLean and myself, but when I put the subscription up to five shillings a year, he wouldn't pay – so I threw him out.

Mainwaring reacts.

JONES Mr Mainwaring, sir. I have just been struck by a thought. When I was in the Sudan and we signed a peace treaty with the Fuzzie Wuzzies, General Kitchener thought it would be a good idea to have a get together. So we asked them what they'd like to do, and they said they wanted a spear-throwing competition, but it was a bit difficult.

MAINWARING Oh, why?

JONES They wanted to use General Kitchener as the target.

Mainwaring reacts.

JONES Anyhow, we managed to talk them out of it, and

all of us British soldiers lined up to throw our spears. And the Fuzzie Wuzzies was standing right behind us waiting their turn. I threw mine and I stepped back.

MAINWARING Get to the *point*, Jones.

JONES I did, sir, one of them was holding his spear like that. **(Demonstrates)**

Mainwaring reacts.

JONES I did not like it, sir. Anyhow, the point of my story is this. Why don't we invite them to watch a darts match at The Red Lion.

MAINWARING Excellent, Jones, excellent. An evening at a typically English pub, what could be better?

JONES Oh… well… er, you don't think I'm going into the realms of fantasy then.

MAINWARING Not at all, we'll invite them all to a spear-throwing competition. I mean a darts match, at The Red Lion on Saturday night, you can bring ladies with you, of course.

WALKER I'll bring Shirley, you know her, don't you?

MAINWARING Oh yes, indeed.

PIKE And I'll bring my girl, she doesn't say much but she's nice. And Uncle Art… I mean Sergeant Wilson, will bring my mum, won't you?

WILSON What, oh yes, I suppose so. **(To Mainwaring)** Will you bring your wife, sir?

MAINWARING Oh no, somehow I don't think Elizabeth would do very much for Anglo-American relations. Now, what else can we think of?

WILSON How about a banner stretched across the bar with a message of greeting on it?

WALKER I can get one made up for you, sir.

MAINWARING Can you? Good.

WALKER **(Taking out notebook and pencil)** What do you want to say?

MAINWARING Let me see now, er… how about 'Hullo to our brave American allies… Go to it, and you'll soon be home'?

WALKER You can't have it that long, it will go twice round the bar and across the High Street. I'll cut it down, for a start you don't want all that brave American allies stuff. You don't have to tell Americans they're brave, they know already. We'll just call them Yanks. **(He scratches out)**

JONES And you don't need to tell them where to go, they'll soon find out.

Walker scratches out.

WALKER And there's no need for the 'soon be home', they've only just come into the war. **(He scratches out)**

JONES What have you got left' Joe?

WALKER Yanks, go home.

MAINWARING All right, Walker, just make it a short greeting, and don't spend more than ten shillings.

WALKER Leave it to me, Mr Mainwaring.

INTERIOR. THE RED LION. DAY

Close up of banner hung across the bar with the words 'Hi Buddy' on it. Jones is sitting at a table with Mrs Fox. Wilson and Pike are sitting at another table with Mrs Pike and Ivy Samways. The Vicar and Verger are sitting up at the bar. Frazer and Godfrey are at another table. The rest of the platoon are sitting around and playing darts. Mr Cheeseman – a reporter – is sitting at the bar, he has a camera. Mainwaring and Walker are standing in front of the bar looking at the poster.

MAINWARING 'Hi Buddy' – that's a bit brief isn't it, Walker?

WALKER Well, you said you didn't want to spend more than ten bob. It's snappy and to the point. Yanks like that.

Cut to Jones and Mrs Fox – she is done up to the nines.

JONES I must say you look very nice, Mrs Fox.

MRS FOX Thank you, Mr Jones. I wanted to look my best, Americans are used to all those Hollywood blondes, and we don't want to disappoint them. Do you like my scent?

JONES Lovely.

MRS FOX It's Californian Poppy, I thought it would be appropriate. After all, I said to myself, it's up to us girls to do all we can to make those American boys feel at home, and I fully intend to do my share to help the war effort. As you know, Mr Jones, it's just not in my nature to be mean.

Jones reacts. Cut to Wilson, Pike, Mrs Pike and Ivy.

MRS PIKE Do try and cheer up, Arthur.

WILSON I'm perfectly cheerful, Mavis.

MRS PIKE Oh no you're not. After all, you don't take me out very often, you might at least make an effort.

WILSON It's not that, Mavis, it's just that I never seem to be able to get away from Mr Mainwaring and the others. I'm with him all day at the bank and on parade with him every evening. And then on our one night off, he drags us along to here to meet these Americans. I'd much rather be in some cosy cocktail bar, with perhaps a little Noel Coward playing on the piano.

PIKE I saw Noel Coward in that film *In Which We Serve*, and he's not little, he's quite normal sized.

MRS PIKE I wonder what these American soldiers look like?

PIKE Ivy saw them arrive at the station this morning, didn't you?

IVY **(Very quiet)** Yes, I did.

MRS PIKE I wish you'd ask her to speak up, Frank, I can never hear a word she's saying.

PIKE She says they're very smart, they're all dressed as officers.

WILSON What, even the privates?

PIKE **(To Ivy)** Even the privates?

IVY **(Quietly)** Yes.

PIKE She says yes.

Cut to Mainwaring and Walker.

WALKER I wonder what's happened to Shirley. I'd better go and give her a ring. **(He goes)**

MAINWARING Thank you for making up the darts team, Vicar.

VICAR That's all right, Mr Mainwaring, I'm always ready and eager to help cement Anglo-American relations.

MAINWARING Care for a drink?

VICAR Thank you, scotch please, large one.

MAINWARING Verger?

VERGER Lemon shandy, small one.

MAINWARING **(To landlord)** Half a lemon shandy and a large whisky please.

LANDLORD Sorry, Captain Mainwaring, I can only let you have a single, I'm nearly out of Scotch.

VERGER **(Hissing in Mainwaring's ear)** What a mercy, providence has intervened. You know the Vicar's little weakness, a double this early in the evening and God, I mean, heaven knows what might happen. We don't want the Americans to get the wrong impression of our clergy, do we?

MAINWARING What? **(He looks across at the Vicar)**

Close up of Vicar beaming benevolently. Mainwaring reacts. Shirley comes into the picture and taps Mainwaring on the shoulder.

SHIRLEY Hullo.

MAINWARING What... oh good evening, er Shirley. **(He looks her up and down, she is also done up to the nines)**

SHIRLEY Where's Joe?

MAINWARING He's gone out to phone you.

SHIRLEY I'm sorry I'm late, I was putting my face on.

MAINWARING I beg your pardon?

SHIRLEY I haven't put on too much make up, have I?

MAINWARING Well, er...

SHIRLEY I was trying for the demure look. After all, we don't want those Yanks to get the wrong idea about us English girls, do we?

Mr Cheeseman crosses to Mainwaring.

CHEESEMAN Good evening, Captain Mainwaring?

MAINWARING Yes.

CHEESEMAN My name's Cheeseman, I'm from the *Eastgate Gazette*. I just thought I'd like to take a few pictures of you greeting our American allies.

MAINWARING Excellent.

CHEESEMAN **(Points to Shirley)** This your good lady then?

MAINWARING I beg your pardon?

CHEESEMAN Your wife?

MAINWARING No, she isn't.

SHIRLEY Chance would be a fine thing. **(She laughs, crosses and sits with Mrs Fox)**

MAINWARING **(Beckons to Wilson)** Wilson, a word please.

CHEESEMAN This will be one of a series of articles I'm doing for the *Gazette*, it's entitled 'The Doughboy meets the Tommy'.

Wilson comes into the picture.

CHEESEMAN I'll see you later then, Mr Mainwaring. **(He starts to move away, Mainwaring grabs him)**

MAINWARING **(Whispering)** Er, give me the wink when you're going to take the photograph.

CHEESEMAN Eh?

MAINWARING Just so that I can remove my spectacles.

CHEESEMAN Right-oh, boy.

Mainwaring reacts.

MAINWARING Now look, Wilson, when these Americans arrive, I want you all to line up, and then I'll say a few appropriate words.

WILSON You're not going to be too formal are you, sir?

MAINWARING No, of course not, that's the whole point. Apparently there's some sort of colonel in charge of them, the question is, how am I going to greet him?

WILSON Well, he'll probably say, 'Howdy, partner, put it there.'

MAINWARING What?

WILSON 'Howdy partner, put it there.'

MAINWARING Put what, where?

WILSON His hand in yours, sir.

MAINWARING Eh!

WILSON You shake hands.

MAINWARING Don't be absurd, Wilson, a colonel in the American army wouldn't say, 'Howdy partner, put it there'. You and that boy Pike see far too many American films.

Hodges enters and comes up to the bar.

HODGES Evening, Napoleon. Evening, Vicar.

VICAR Good evening, Mr Hodges, so nice of you to make up our little darts team.

HODGES That's all right, always ready to give the Home Guards a thrashing. **(To Mainwaring)** What time do we kick off?

MAINWARING Nine o'clock.

HODGES Why do we have to wait till then?

MAINWARING We're putting on this darts match for the benefit of the Americans.

HODGES Oh blimey, I hate blooming Yanks, loud-mouthed overbearing lot, can't stand 'em. **(Bangs on counter)** Let's have some service please.

Walker hurries in.

WALKER They're here, Mr Mainwaring!

MAINWARING What?

WALKER The Yanks, two jeep loads of 'em.

MAINWARING Jones, get the men lined up.

JONES **(Jumping to his feet)** Yes, sir, yes, sir.

MAINWARING Informally.

JONES Line up, informally, at the double.

Jones, Pike, Walker, Frazer, Godfrey start to line up, Mrs Fox and Shirley are amongst them.

JONES Not you, Mrs Fox.

MRS FOX I don't want to be left out, you know.

WALKER Go and sit down Shirley.

SHIRLEY I'm sure those Yanks would rather meet us, than all these old men.

MAINWARING Will you please sit down, ladies.

SHIRLEY **(To Mrs Fox)** Blimey, don't tell me we've put all this lot on for nothing.

They both go and sit down. Jones, Frazer, Godfrey, Pike and Walker are now standing in a line by the door. The rest of the platoon are standing behind them.

MAINWARING **(Pushing Wilson in position)** Stand there, Wilson, just a minute. **(He walks down the line to Mr Cheeseman who is at the bar getting his camera ready)** When are you going to take the photograph?

CHEESEMAN As soon as they come in.

MAINWARING Good. **(He takes his glasses off, puts them back in his pocket and hurries back up the line. He barges straight into Pike)** Don't stand in the way, boy.

Mainwaring takes up his position beside Wilson. The door opens and Colonel Shultz comes in, he is a large, thickset man in his early forties. He is followed by a sergeant and six privates. Mainwaring advances on one of the privates and grabs his hand.

MAINWARING On behalf of the people of Walmington-on-Sea, may I...

Wilson steers him towards the colonel.

WILSON This is the colonel, sir.

MAINWARING What? Oh, yes.

SHULTZ Howdy partner, put it there.

He grabs Mainwaring's hand.

MAINWARING What?

WILSON I told you so.

CHEESEMAN Can you turn your head a little more this way please, Captain Mainwaring?

MAINWARING Certainly. **(Still holding the colonel's hand, he turns his face towards the camera and gives a sickly grin. The flash goes off)** I'd just like to say a few words of welcome to your men, Colonel.

SHULTZ Sure, go ahead.

Mainwaring steps back on Pike's foot.

MAINWARING **(Hissing at Pike)** Don't keep getting in the way, Pike.

WILSON **(Whispering in his ear)** Hadn't you better put your glasses on, sir.

Mainwaring gives him a glare and puts his glasses on.

MAINWARING On behalf of the people of Walmington-on-Sea, may I bid you welcome, and congratulate you upon entering the war.

WALKER **(Aside to Pike)** At last.

SHULTZ Thanks a lot. My name's Shultz, Colonel Shultz.

Mainwaring reacts to Wilson.

MAINWARING My name's Mainwaring, Captain Mainwaring. May I introduce my sergeant, Sergeant Wilson.

WILSON **(Shaking hands)** How awfully nice to meet you, did you have a jolly trip over?

SHULTZ Oh, it was very jolly, except for one thing.

WILSON What was that?

SHULTZ Those beastly Krout submarines that kept firing torpedoes at us.

WILSON How awful!

Mainwaring and Wilson exchange looks, they are not quite sure how to take this.

MAINWARING Yes, quite, er... Now, while you're here, you're our guests, and we want you to make yourselves at home.

SHULTZ **(To his men)** Okay, boys, you heard what the captain said, relax, make yourselves at home.

The sergeant and two privates go straight over and sit with Mrs Pike, the other four privates sit with Shirley and Mrs Fox. Mainwaring and co. react.

MAINWARING Yes, well er… perhaps you'd like to meet some of my men. This is Lance Corporal Jones.

SHULTZ Howdy.

JONES I'm pleased to meet you, sir, I had the honour of serving with the Americans in France in 1917. They used to call us Limeys, you know why that was, don't you?

SHULTZ Can't say I do.

JONES Well, sir, in times of old on British ships, the sailors used to get all scurvy and mingy, and one day the captain called them all together and he said, 'Listen, boys, I'm fed up with you all crawling about, looking scurvy and mingy.' So every evening he made them all line up and drink lime juice. Now, there was an American in the crew, and he refused to drink it and he told the captain what to do with his lime juice, and the captain got very cross, and ordered him to be flogged. They used to do a lot of flogging in them days, sir. As he was being flogged, the captain said, 'Why won't you drink your lime juice like these brave British lads 'ere?' And the American said, 'they're nothing more – ow – than a lot of – ow – crawling limeys – ow.' The 'ow' was him being flogged, you understand, anyhow, hence the expression, Limeys.

SHULTZ You don't say.

JONES Yes I do, I've just told you.

Cut to Wilson who has crossed over to Mrs Pike, she is deep in conversation with the American sergeant.

WILSON **(Hissing in Mrs Pike's ear)** Look, what's going on Mavis?

MRS PIKE The sergeant here is being ever so nice, he says I'm the perfect English Rose.

U.S. SERGEANT You sure are, sister.

WILSON Now, look here, you haven't even been introduced to this lady.

U.S. SERGEANT Listen, buddy, why don't you take a powder?

WILSON Take a powder?

MRS PIKE I do believe you're jealous, Arthur.

MAINWARING Wilson!

Wilson hurries back to Mainwaring.

MAINWARING **(Pointing to Frazer)** And this is Private Frazer.

SHULTZ Howdy.

FRAZER **(Grabbing his hand)**

Now's the day, and now's the hour.

See the front O'battle lour.

See approach proud Hitler's power

chains and slavery.

Who will be a traitor knave.

Who can fill a coward's grave.

Who's so base as be a slave.

Let him turn and flee.

There is a pause.

SHULTZ I see you're running an international unit here, Captain, I don't know what lingo that was, but it sounded great. What part of the world does this old timer come from?

FRAZER Scotland! And that was no a foreign language, that was a war greeting by Robbie Burns – brought up to date by me.

SHULTZ Goddammit, what do you know.

MAINWARING What indeed! **(Moving on to Godfrey)** This is Private Godfrey.

GODFREY Good evening, I'm afraid my sister Dolly couldn't come tonight, a touch of rheumatics. But she's sent you some of her upside-down cakes. **(He hands the colonel a small box)**

SHULTZ Gee thanks. **(To Mainwaring)** You've certainly got some veterans in your outfit, captain. I didn't know that the British Army took them so old.

WILSON Well, of course, we're not real soldiers.

MAINWARING What are you talking about, Wilson, of course we're real soldiers.

WILSON But we're not, sir, we're Home Guards.

SHULTZ What are Home Guards?

WILSON Well, we're sort of part-time soldiers, Mr Mainwaring's a bank manager, I'm his chief clerk and the others are shopkeepers. We were formed to protect the town against German parachute troops and things.

SHULTZ Well you don't have to worry any more, we'll do all the defending there is to do around here. You old timers can just relax and take it easy.

GODFREY How kind.

MAINWARING **(Bristling)** Now look here, Colonel…

Wilson grabs Mainwaring by the arm and pulls him towards the bar.

WILSON Shall we all go over to the bar and have a drink, sir?

They all move over to the bar. Walker taps the colonel on the shoulder.

WALKER 'Ere, listen, Colonel, anything you want, razor blades, petrol coupons, elastic, just let me know.

SHULTZ You're wasting your time, buster, we don't need a thing, we brought it all over with us. (**He moves to the bar**)

WALKER Blimey.

JONES Joe, we've got to do something quick, look what's happening to our girls.

Cut to Shirley and Mrs Fox. There is an American soldier sitting each side of them, with their arms round them.

SHIRLEY (**Chewing gum**) Who'd have thought it, fancy you being a cowboy. I expect quite a lot of you are film stars as well.

The soldier nods.

MRS FOX Oh I like these Americans, they're such nice, clean-cut boys, and so generous.

Walker and Jones come into the picture.

SHIRLEY (**To Walker, pointing to U.S. soldier's medals**) 'Ere, Joe, look at all his medals, he's got that one for sharp shooting, and that one for good conduct. Not too good I hope. (**She giggles**)

JONES (**Hissing in Mrs Fox's ear**) I'm ashamed of you, Mrs Fox, you're old enough to be his mother.

MRS FOX If it comes to that, you're old enough to be my father.

Jones reacts.

JONES (**To Walker**) What are we going to do, Joe?

WALKER Search me, they don't want to buy anything, and they've pinched our girls. If you ask me, the war's taken a very nasty turn.

Cut to Mrs Pike and Ivy with the U.S. sergeant and two privates. Pike is hovering in the background. He hisses in Ivy's ear.

PIKE Ivy, you're supposed to be with me.

IVY Oh, go away, Frank.

PIKE What?

IVY I said go away.

PIKE Mum, mum.

MRS PIKE What's the matter?

PIKE He's got his arms round her, make him let go.

MRS PIKE Don't be silly, Frank.

PIKE I shall never speak to you again, Ivy. (**He stamps away towards the bar**)

Cut to bar, Mainwaring is handing the colonel a pint of beer, Walker, Wilson, Jones, Frazer and Godfrey are standing beside him, Pike joins them.

MAINWARING There you are, Colonel, a drop of real English beer.

CHEESEMAN Captain Mainwaring.

MAINWARING Right. (**He takes off his glasses, still holding the mug, he gives a sickly grin, the flash goes off**)

SHULTZ (**Taking mug**) Thanks. Well, bottoms up. (**He drinks and chokes**)

MAINWARING I bet you've never tasted anything like that before.

SHULTZ It's warm!

MAINWARING (**Touching the glass**) It seems quite cold to me.

SHULTZ It tastes like tub water that's come through the fawcet.

PIKE Oh no, he didn't have to force it, he just turned the tap on and out it came.

SHULTZ What did you say, kid, are you having me on?

PIKE Having you on what?

WILSON Perhaps you'd like to try something else, sir.

SHULTZ Okay, I'll have a highball.

MAINWARING Yes, of course. (**To landlord**) Er, do you have a...

Pike mimes.

MAINWARING Do you have a highball?

LANDLORD What's that?

SHULTZ Scotch on the rocks.

LANDLORD Sorry, no scotch.

SHULTZ What sort of joint is this? No scotch, warm beer. Is this your typical English hospitality?

WILSON I'm very sorry, but we have been fighting a war for two and a half years and things are in rather short supply.

SHULTZ What do you mean by that remark?

WILSON Er... nothing really.

Hodges comes into the picture.

HODGES Hull, Colonel, my name's Hodges. I met your lot when they came out to France in 1917 under General Perishing.

SHULTZ You mean General Peshering.

HODGES I knew it was some perishing general. You'll notice I said 1917, the war, as we all know, started in 1914. And now you're going to win this war for us. Well, better late than never, after all it's only been on for two and a half years. I suppose that's an improvement on last time.

CHEESEMAN (**Signals to Mainwaring**) Captain Mainwaring.

MAINWARING Oh, right. (**Mainwaring takes off his glasses**)

SHULTZ What did you say, buster?

HODGES I said you're improving, this time you've only waited two and a half years instead of three.

Colonel draws back fist.

CHEESEMAN Hold it!

The flash goes off.

INTERIOR. SIDE OFFICE. DAY

Close up of newspaper, the headline read, 'The Doughboy Meets The Tommy'. There are three photos on the page. The first one shows Mainwaring shaking hands with the colonel, underneath are the words '7 o'clock', the next one shows Mainwaring giving the colonel a pint of beer, in the background are Wilson, Jones, Walker, Frazer and Pike. Underneath the words 'Ten minutes past 7'. The third one shows the colonel's fist in Mainwaring's eye, Hodges' face is beside Mainwaring's. Wilson is in the background – underneath is 'A quarter past 7'. Pull back to reveal Wilson reading the paper. Mainwaring is on the phone to the colonel. Mainwaring has a black eye.

MAINWARING I assure you, Colonel, that it was in no way our fault. Hodges made an insulting remark, the American went to hit him. Hodges dodged and I got hit instead. My men were not to blame in any way.

COLONEL I realise that, Mainwaring, but the fact remains that a photograph of you brawling with an American colonel, is on the front page of every newspaper. The German propaganda machine will have a field day with this. The Americans are only in the country a few hours, and there's a fight with British troops, it will be all round the world. Well, we're going to nip it in the bud.

MAINWARING What do you want me to do?

COLONEL I'm sending that reporter over there today. I want you to ask the American colonel round, and make a public apology to him. I want a photograph of you two shaking hands, I'll see it gets in tomorrow's papers.

MAINWARING You mean I'm to be the scapegoat.

COLONEL I'm afraid so. That's one of the penalties of wearing pips on your shoulder, sometimes you have to take the can back even if it's not your fault. See to it.

MAINWARING Very well, sir. **(He hangs up)**

WILSON **(Showing him the paper)** Quite a spread, eh, sir.

MAINWARING It's a terrible disgrace, I shall never live this down.

WILSON It's rather a good one of me, don't you think?

Mainwaring reacts.

WILSON I wonder if I wrote to the paper they'd let me have some prints.

There is a knock on the door.

MAINWARING Come in.

Jones, Walker, Frazer, Godfrey and Pike enter.

JONES Permission for you to receive a deputation, sir?

MAINWARING Yes, Jones.

JONES We want to say how sorry we are about last night, and to assure you that it was not our fault.

MAINWARING I realise that, Jones, and so does G.H.Q. All the same, I've got to make a public apology to that American colonel.

JONES You mean you're going to be the scapegoat.

MAINWARING Yes. However, if I've got to take the blame in public, I'm going to make sure that G.H.Q. realises that we were in no way responsible. I'm going to make a report out that will completely clear us of any blame. **(He picks up a pen)** I want you all to tell me in your own words what happened. We'll start with you, Sergeant.

WILSON Well, sir, when the fight started I thought I'd get out of the way, so I dived under a table.

WALKER That was after he'd thumped the American sergeant.

MAINWARING What!

WILSON I'm sorry, sir, I only tapped him a couple of times. He'd been getting on my nerves all the evening, he was being far too familiar with Mrs Pike.

PIKE Mum was furious, when Uncle Arthur got home she wouldn't let him in, and he had to spend the night in the tool shed.

WILSON Frank!

MAINWARING I see, what about you, Jones? That's a nasty bump you've got on your forehead, which American did that?

JONES None of them, sir, it was Mrs Fox.

MAINWARING Mrs Fox!

JONES Yes, she didn't like my attitude to one of the Yanks.

MAINWARING Why, what were you doing?

JONES Banging his head on the floor, sir. I had him in a deadly Dervish death grip.

MAINWARING Frazer.

FRAZER Ah well, sir, I just gave one of them a wee push, nothing more you understand, sir, just a push. You see, he'd knocked my glass of whisky out of my hand, and no true Scot will tolerate that. It was just unfortunate that he collided with the bottle that Walker was holding.

WALKER Ah, I can explain that, Captain Mainwaring, you see, when the fight started I thought I'd calm things down, so I tried to get a sing song going. And I was conducting like that, and it just so happened, that I had a bottle in each hand.

Mainwaring takes his glasses off and blows hard.

MAINWARING What about you, Pike? I don't suppose you did anything violent.

PIKE Oh yes I did, sir, I must confess, I lost my temper. Those two Yanks were clinging to my Ivy.

Mainwaring reacts.

PIKE They wouldn't take their arms away, and my mum wouldn't do anything about it. So I thought I'd be a man and stand up for myself.

MAINWARING What did you do?

PIKE I went up to them and I went… **(He puts his hands to his nose and blows a raspberry)**

Mainwaring reacts.

PIKE Then one of them chased me round the bar until Mr Godfrey hit him on the head with a chair.

MAINWARING You, Godfrey!

GODFREY Well, he'd trodden on my sister Dolly's upside-down cakes, sir.

MAINWARING Under the circumstances, I think we'd better let sleeping dogs lie. **(He screws up the paper and throws it in the basket)**

WILSON We were provoked you know, sir.

MAINWARING I must admit, I didn't like that colonel's attitude from the start, calling us old timers, telling us to take it easy and he'd do all the defending there was to do round here. There are 30 crack Nazi divisions poised across the Channel, 25 miles away, ready to mount their spring offensive, and he's telling battle-scarred veterans like us to take it easy and they'll do the defending – them! A bunch of American greenhorns.

WILSON Actually, sir, it's tinhorns.

MAINWARING I don't care if it's tinhorns, or greenhorns, or ice cream horns, they know nothing about war whatsoever.

Colonel Shultz enters with Mr Cheeseman, the colonel is carrying a box.

SHULTZ Sorry to crash in on you like this.

Mainwaring gets up.

SHULTZ That's all right, captain, relax. I just want to apologise for what happened last night, I never realised what you guys have been through, what with all the bombing and food shortages and the like. And I want to make it up to you, I've brought some scotch and some candy. **(He puts the box on the desk and takes out two bottles of whisky)**

WILSON That's awfully generous of you, sir.

SHULTZ Forget it, now what I want to do, captain, is to apologise to your men, and this press guy is going to take a photo.

MAINWARING Actually, I was going to apologise to you.

SHULTZ What for? It wasn't your fault, I can't let you do that. As you British say, it wouldn't be cricket, so if you'll get your men together, captain, I'd be beholden to you.

MAINWARING Very well, if you insist. Jones. fall the men in.

JONES Right **(To colonel)** This way, sir.

SHULTZ I'm right behind you, old timer.

WALKER Give you two quid for the lot.

MAINWARING No.

WALKER Two ten then.

MAINWARING Go away.

WILSON **(Pointing to bottles of whisky)** I rather like the look of that whisky, nice man Colonel Shultz. **(He moves to the door. Mainwaring stops him)**

MAINWARING Just a minute, Wilson, Shultz is a German name, isn't it?

WILSON That's right, sir.

MAINWARING Well what's a German doing in the American army?

WILSON There are quite a lot of people with German names in America.

MAINWARING Oh, the whole thing's getting out of hand, people fighting on our side with German names, it was much better when we were on our own. At least we knew who was who and what was what.

INTERIOR. CHURCH HALL. DAY

JONES Right, men. Fall in.

SHULTZ Don't bother with all that, just gather round me in an informal group.

JONES Right, in an informal group, at the double, round the colonel, gather.

The platoon gather round the colonel, Jones, Walker and Pike are together. Mainwaring and Wilson come out of the office, Wilson stands beside Pike.

SHULTZ Men, I just want to say how sorry I am about last night and as a peace offering I've brought you some chocolate bars, perhaps you'd like to help me distribute them, captain.

MAINWARING Certainly.

SHULTZ My men would be here to apologise in person, but we're having a Ladies Night in the mess, and they're fixing the place up.

Shultz and Mainwaring start to hand out the chocolate.

WILSON **(To Pike)** A Ladies Night in the mess. Frank, when we went home to tea, did you notice that your mother was wearing her party frock.

PIKE Yes I did, Uncle Arthur.

WILSON I thought it was funny, just to make toast in.

PIKE When I rang up Ivy to ask her to meet me after parade, she made an excuse. I knew she was lying 'cos I could hear every word she said.

WALKER Wait a minute, Shirley told me she couldn't come out tonight because her hair was in a bit of a mess, now I know which mess.

Mrs Fox appears in the doorway.

MRS FOX Yoo hoo, Colonel, I'm all ready.

SHULTZ Be right with you, honey, just wait outside in the jeep.

Jones reacts.

CHEESEMAN Ready for the photograph, gentlemen?

MAINWARING Right. **(He takes off his glasses)**

JONES Excuse me, Colonel, is it true, that in the last war, the only things the Americans charged was ten per cent on the money they lent us?

SHULTZ What was that, old timer?

Cut to single of Cheeseman.

CHEESEMAN Hold it! **(The flash goes off)**

Cut to photo of Shultz's fist in Mainwaring's other eye. Jones is beside Mainwaring.

SERIES SIX **EPISODE THREE**

Recorded: Friday 29/6/73
Original transmission: Wednesday 14/11/73, 6.30–7.00pm
Original viewing figures = 13.1 million

ARTHUR LOWE . . . . CAPTAIN MAINWARING
JOHN LE MESURIER . . . . SERGEANT WILSON
CLIVE DUNN . . . . LANCE CORPORAL JONES
JOHN LAURIE . . . . PRIVATE FRAZER
JAMES BECK . . . . PRIVATE WALKER
ARNOLD RIDLEY . . . . PRIVATE GODFREY
IAN LAVENDER . . . . PRIVATE PIKE

BILL PERTWEE . . . . CHIEF WARDEN HODGES
FRANK WILLIAMS . . . . VICAR
EDWARD SINCLAIR . . . . VERGER
WILLIAM MOORE . . . . STATION MASTER
FREDDIE EARLLE . . . . HENRY (ENGINE DRIVER)
RONNIE BRODY . . . . BOB (ENGINE FIREMAN)
FRED MCNAUGHTON . . . . MAYOR
SUE BISHOP . . . . TICKET COLLECTOR
BOB HORNERY . . . . CITY GENT
PLATOON . . . . COLIN BEAN, DESMOND CULLUM-JONES, GEORGE HANCOCK, EVAN ROSS, LESLIE NOYES, WILLIAM GOSSLING, FREDDIE WHITE, MICHAEL MOORE, FREDDIE WILES, ROGER BOURNE

THE ROYAL TRAIN

• FRANK WILLIAMS REMEMBERS •

'I suppose every fan of *Dad's Army* has a favourite episode. For someone like myself who took part in the series, one's choice is influenced by a number of personal memories. So, why is "The Royal Train" mine?

'"The Royal Train" contains some classic moments. Pike's insistence on having his turn with the Tommy gun, Wilson's ineffectual search for a red carpet, Mainwaring going down the train looking for the King, and his subsequent heroic climb along the roof of the train with the ever-loyal Corporal Jones "assisting" him, are all wonderfully typical of the characters.

'When a crisis occurs and the station staff are clearly unable to cope, Mainwaring characteristically takes charge. The ensuing chase, accompanied by the *Dick Barton* signature tune, as the Warden, Vicar and Verger together with the mayor pursue and are then pursued by the train, is a scene in the great tradition of British comedy.

'Filming it had its worrying moments and at one point the train seemed to be getting perilously close to us. We were not sure that the driver could see us and I seem to remember Bill Pertwee suggesting that if it got any nearer we'd be advised to jump clear. At the speed we were going, this was clearly not a realistic option. In the end, of course, all was well. The train driver may not have been able to see us, but he was in walkie-talkie communication with the director, who from his vantage point behind the camera, could see everything, and so we emerged unscathed. A bonus at the end of the days of filming was a ride on the footplate of the engine, watching the coal being shovelled in by one of the dedicated railway enthusiasts who keep this line running.

'At the end of the episode the whole cast lines up and, fully clothed, is drenched with water. Hard work pumping the trolley, risking one's life being pursued by a train and then finally being soaked in cold water – this would not be everyone's idea of a good time. So why do I remember it with such affection? Well, as I said, it was fun!'

THE ROYAL TRAIN

SIDE OFFICE

The Tommy gun is on the desk. Wilson is being brushed down by Jones.

JONES That's better, Mr Wilson. The hairiness of the serge is lying now all in one direction. We can't have you going on a highly important parade with your serge hairiness going in all different directions.

WILSON Thank you, Jones. I'm sure you've made it look delightful.

JONES Have you any notion what the parade's for, Mr Wilson?

WILSON Not the foggiest, Jones. We just have to be at the station. Captain Mainwaring will then open the sealed orders, oh, and we have to be very smart.

JONES In that case, Mr Wilson, you'd better do up your cuffs and your collar.

Enter Mainwaring.

MAINWARING Morning, Wilson. Morning, Corporal.

JONES Morning, sir.

MAINWARING I'm not late, am I?

WILSON No, sir.

Mainwaring puts a bottle of pills on the desk.

MAINWARING I had to pop into the chemist – for Mrs Mainwaring – and, of course, they made me wait.

WILSON Oh dear, nothing serious I hope.

MAINWARING No – not really. She doesn't sleep that's all. It's the raids.

WILSON We haven't had any lately.

MAINWARING No, but she imagines them just the same. She's a very highly strung woman, you know.

WILSON So you've said.

MAINWARING The slightest noise and she'll toss and turn until sunrise. The lid blew off the dustbin last night and before you could say Jack Robinson she was under my bunk with her gas mask on.

Wilson and Jones react.

MAINWARING It took me twenty minutes to persuade her to come out. Then, of course, she had fluff all over her night gown and I started to brush it off and – ooh, there was a terrible set to.

WILSON Couldn't you get her some sleeping tablets or something?

MAINWARING That's precisely what I have done. (**He indicates the bottle**) The doctor says these'll put her out like a light.

JONES We didn't have none of those modern medications when we was in the Sudan. We only had cascara and bicarbonate of soda.

WILSON I don't think they'd be much help to Mrs Mainwaring, Jones.

JONES You're quite right, Mr Wilson. Neither of them was much good for making you sleep. They was good for making you run and belch though.

Mainwaring reacts.

JONES We did a lot of running and belching when we was in the Sudan.

MAINWARING Yes – I'm sure you did, Jones.

Enter Pike.

PIKE Pardon me, Mr Mainwaring – do we know what the parade's for yet, sir?

MAINWARING No, Pike. Not until we get to the station and I open the sealed orders. (**He taps his map pocket which contains the sealed orders**)

PIKE In that case, sir, we'd better be on the safe side and take the Tommy gun. And I'd better carry it because I haven't had it for three weeks and two days and it's my turn again today. Thank you. (**He grabs for the gun and in doing so he knocks the pills on to the floor. The bottle breaks**)

MAINWARING What are you doing, you stupid boy?

PIKE I'm sorry, Mr Mainwaring.

MAINWARING Look, you've broken the bottle.

PIKE Don't worry, sir. I'll pick it all up.

MAINWARING Careful – they cost 13 shillings.

JONES They've got broken glass in them, Mr Mainwaring, Mrs Mainwaring mustn't have broken glass, sir – it's deadly. It can mean instant death.

MAINWARING Yes, well we'll dust them over.

Jones reacts.

MAINWARING Find an envelope or something, Wilson.

WILSON There's a bottle in the top left drawer, I think. (**He looks**) It's the Vicar's, but I don't suppose he'll mind. (**He finds it**) Yes, here it is.

MAINWARING Thank you, Wilson. (**Sees bottle**) It's got a few pills in it.

WILSON They'll only be saccharin, sir – it says it on the bottle. Saccharin – use one tablet per lump of sugar. (**Wilson empties the few tablets**)

MAINWARING Saccharin. Rather go without sugar myself.

WILSON Well, it won't do any harm to Mrs Mainwaring, sir. In fact, it might even sweeten her nature.

MAINWARING Get the men on parade, Wilson.

Mainwaring and Pike put pills into the bottle.

FILM: LONG SHOT OF STATION

The platoon, led by Mainwaring, approach the station and enter.

MAINWARING Left, right, left, right, right wheel. Left, right, left, right, right wheel.

They wheel from the platform into the waiting room.

STUDIO. THE WAITING ROOM

They march into the waiting room. It is the usual sparse Victorian or Edwardian waiting room for a small station. Just off it is a small side room – about 6 foot square – which the station master, porter and ticket collector use to put their coats, lunch boxes, etc. and to make tea on the gas ring. Frazer sings. Frazer is in this small room, boiling the kettle. There is a hatchway between the room and the main waiting room. Frazer hears the platoon entering the waiting room.

MAINWARING **(Out of vision)** Squad, halt!

Frazer raises the lid of the kettle to see if the water is boiling and then pours the water into a large tea pot.

MAINWARING **(Out of vision)** Fall out.

Frazer goes to the hatch – opens it.

FRAZER Captain Mainwaring, sir. **(He salutes. Mainwaring reacts)**

MAINWARING Yes, Frazer?

FRAZER Your tea's on the brew, sir.

MAINWARING Well done, Frazer. **(Looks at his watch)** Pay attention, men. We have a minute or two before the time appointed for me to open the sealed orders, so we'll have our tea break now.

WALKER And before you get stuck into it, it's threepence a cup. Tea's getting very hard to come by.

They move to the hatch. Walker goes into the room to help Frazer.

FRAZER Before you start collecting the money, Joe, there's no milk or sugar.

WALKER Couldn't Mike let you have any?

FRAZER It hadn't arrived.

WALKER Not to worry. **(He moves to a cupboard in the little room. He tries it – it is locked. He gives four thumps in carefully selected places and it springs wide open. He takes out a milk bottle and a sugar bowl)**

FRAZER Joe Walker, you'll burn in the devil's own personal furnace.

WALKER Look, who got it for them in the first place?

Jones goes up to Mainwaring and Wilson.

JONES Captain Mainwaring, sir, Mr Wilson, I've been worrying my brain box about why we've been sent to this station, and I think I've hit it.

MAINWARING Oh yes.

JONES Well, sir, where there's stations there's trains – you must admit that, Mr Wilson.

WILSON Yes, you're quite right there, Jones.

MAINWARING Is this leading us anywhere, Corporal?

JONES Well, sir, when they decided not to have the last war going on any longer, the German generals all come along in a train and surrendered. They've ended a lot of wars like that, you know, sir – since they've had trains. I think the generals like the conveniences of them.

Mainwaring reacts.

JONES So do you think, sir, that Hitler might be coming to surrender?

MAINWARING I don't think it's very likely, Jones.

JONES But you said yourself, sir, that he's in a bad way.

PIKE Captain Mainwaring, when you've read the sealed orders, will you have to eat them?

MAINWARING What on earth for?

PIKE So they don't fall into the hands of spies or quislings?

JONES I would like to volunteer to eat your sealed orders, sir. I would consider it a great honour.

MAINWARING Oh, do be quiet, Jones. Wilson, in about thirty seconds it'll be time to open the orders. I don't want anyone looking over my shoulder. I think I shall use that side room.

WILSON Good idea, sir. **(He moves to it)** Walker, Fraser, I wonder if you'd mind vacating this room – Captain Mainwaring wants to be alone.

GODFREY Captain Mainwaring, what time do you think we might be free?

MAINWARING Why do you ask?

GODFREY Well – Evelyn Laye is on the Forces programme at 8. I saw her in 'Bitter Sweet', you know. I was most taken with her.

MAINWARING I'm sorry, Godfrey. We're on active service. I can't release you from duty just because Evelyn Laye is on the wireless.

GODFREY Jessie Matthews is on as well.

Mainwaring reacts.

WILSON The room is clear, sir.

MAINWARING **(As he's crossing)** Right, stand by, everyone.

(They enter)

MAINWARING I'm going to open the sealed orders.

JONES **(Shouting)** Pay attention, there. The officer is about to open the sealed orders. Absolute silence while the officer opens the sealed orders. I've got complete silence now, sir.

MAINWARING That's enough, Jones. **(Shuts trap)**

Jones reacts.

MAINWARING Right – here goes. **(He puts his hand into his pocket to take out the orders. They stick. He tries a couple of times)**

WALKER **(To Fraser)** I think the sealing wax has gone sticky.

WILSON Are you all right, sir?

MAINWARING It's your blasted bottle – here, hold this. **(He hands Wilson the bottle, then he hands a large map)** That's the map. Don't lose it, we might need it. Here we are. **(He takes out a large folded envelope, sealed with red wax. Wilson is standing behind him)**

MAINWARING Wilson – outside.

WILSON I won't look.

MAINWARING Outside.

WILSON Yes, sir. **(Wilson puts the map and the bottle on the side table and goes out)**

Mainwaring sees Walker – he shuts trap. He opens orders and reads.

MAINWARING Ah.

JONES What is it Mr Mainwaring? Tell us what it is. I can't stand the suspicion. He's gone. He's gone. **(Goes back to place)**

MAINWARING This really is most exciting news. Listen carefully.

JONES Listen carefully. The officer is about to divest himself of the secret orders, and it's very exciting. Listen carefully.

MAINWARING Gather closer.

They all gather closer.

MAINWARING I don't want to talk too loud, this secret must not be known by anybody outside this room. Twenty minutes from now a train will pass through this station…

JONES There you are. What did I say? I knew it had to do with trains.

MAINWARING It will contain the person of His Majesty, King George the Sixth.

FRAZER King George the Sixth.

GODFREY God bless him.

WALKER What's he coming here for? They're not having the Rotary dance till Saturday.

MAINWARING He will simply be passing through on the royal train, camouflaged of course.

WILSON Do you mean the train's camouflaged or the King's camouflaged?

Mainwaring looks at him.

WILSON The train's camouflaged.

MAINWARING Our function is twofold. Firstly, no unauthorised person must go near the train. Secondly, we will form a guard of honour on the platform and give the royal salute as the train steams by. Of course, this is a great honour and also absolutely secret. Not a living soul must get the slightest inkling of what's happening.

Warden enters.

WARDEN Has he been through yet?

MAINWARING Who?

WARDEN The King.

MAINWARING How did you know about that?

WARDEN **(Tapping his warden's hat)** That's not a vanilla ice, you know. I'm very important. Back in two minutes. **(He goes)**

MAINWARING What do you make of that, Wilson? How did he find out?

WILSON Perhaps he was told in case there was an air raid.

JONES Shall I fall the men in on the platform, sir, so that we have a quick practice?

MAINWARING Yes, Jones. No, wait a minuet. That might give the game away to anyone who was passing by.

FRAZER We could do it here if we squeezed up close.

MAINWARING Yes, fall in here, quick as you can. Listen, I shall give the word of command in a very low voice. At all costs nobody must suspect that the King is on that train.

Enter station master with girl ticket collector. They pass through to the side office. As he goes he addresses Mainwaring.

STATION MASTER It's been one of those days, hasn't it? (**He grabs his overcoat**)

MAINWARING Squad…

STATION MASTER The King coming, me without me bowler and her with gravy down her tunic. Come on, Freda, we've got ten minutes to get you home, sponge you down and back on that platform. (**He rushes out again**)

MAINWARING Being the station master, of course, he would have to be in possession of all the facts.

The squad have fallen in at the slope.

MAINWARING Present arms!

ALL One, two, three. One, two, three. One.

Pike does the drill with a Tommy gun.

MAINWARING Pike, you know perfectly well you don't present arms with your Tommy gun, you stupid boy.

PIKE Why not?

MAINWARING Just stand in the attention position.

PIKE What, like this?

MAINWARING That's right. And take that silly scarf off.

PIKE Mum said I looked ever so peaky this morning.

MAINWARING Take it off.

Pike takes off scarf.

MAINWARING Slope arms.

ALL One, two, three. One.

MAINWARING Try to get with the rest, Jones. Present arms.

ALL One, two, three. One, two, three. One.

PIKE Uncle Arthur, I can't just stand here while they're doing all that. The King'll think I'm rude.

WILSON It's perfectly all right, Frank.

PIKE Well, couldn't I show it to him, like this. (**He holds the Tommy gun out**)

MAINWARING Stand to attention, Pike.

PIKE I feel a fool, that's all.

GODFREY I'm slightly at a loose end too, sir. Do you think perhaps I ought to wave?

MAINWARING Silence in the ranks, Godfrey.

Godfrey reacts.

MAINWARING Slope arms.

Pike stamps his foot.

MAINWARING If I have any more trouble from you, Pike, I shall take that away from you and send you back home.

WALKER Excuse me, Captain Mainwaring, some of them trains go through at 60 miles an hour. By the time you've said 'Present Arms' and we've done it, the King'll be halfway to Eastgate.

JONES Joe's quite right, sir. We ought to do it more swiftly. We are all waiting here on our tender hooks, when suddenly you espy the train. (**He shouts and makes them move very rapidly**) One, two, three. One, two, three. There goes the King. One, two, three. One. Something like that, sir.

Mainwaring reacts.

PIKE It doesn't make any difference to me what speed you do it. I just stand here like a banana.

MAINWARING You won't get another warning, Pike.

WILSON I think Jones and Walker may have a point. We ought to do it quicker.

FRAZER Aye – but if the train comes through at a crawl, we could be stood there till our bones set. Some of these old ones are not up to it.

MAINWARING Well, perhaps the solution is to have two versions. I shall say 'Slow Present Arms' or 'Quick Present Arms'. We'll try it. 'Quick Present Arms!'

They present arms very quickly, shouting, 'One, two, three. One, two, three. One.'

MAINWARING No – that won't do at all. There's no precision. Slope arms again.

The Vicar, wearing his university robes, enters… followed by the Verger, the Warden and Alderman Bickerstaff, the mayor. Bickerstaff wears his chain of office and his cocked hat, and red cloak.

VICAR Have we missed him?

MAINWARING What are you doing here?

VICAR I represent the church. This is Alderman Bickerstaff, he represents the council.

WARDEN And I represent the A.R.P.

VERGER I'm a sightseer.

MAINWARING We can't have sightseers at the station.

VERGER Why not? He's just as much my King as he is yours, you know.

A train whistle sounds.

MAINWARING He's here.

General chaos.

MAINWARING Outside everybody. Line up along the platform.

JONES The King's here. Don't panic. Line up on the platform for the King.

They all rush out.

FILM: STATION PLATFORM

It is littered with the usual station luggage, railway trolleys, milk churns, baskets of pigeons, packing cases, etc. etc. The platoon start to line up.

MAINWARING Quickly into line. Dress by the right.

They line up in order – Mainwaring, Wilson, Jones, Walker, Pike, Godfrey. Wilson now carries a rifle.

JONES Into line like the officer says. Dress by the right for the King.

Hodges, the Vicar and the Verger line up in front of Mainwaring.

MAINWARING All civilians to the rear, please.

JONES That's right. All civilians to the rear.

WARDEN Don't you shove me, mate.

VERGER Yes, and don't shove His Reverence either.

They move behind.

MAINWARING Squad, 'shun. Slope arms.

ALL One, two, three. One, two, three. One.

They all come to attention. Long shot of train coming into view.

MAINWARING Here it comes. Chins in, chests out.

WILSON It's coming rather slowly.

MAINWARING We'll do the Slow Present – pass it on.

WILSON We'll do the Slow Present – pass it on.

JONES We'll pass on the Slow Present – we'll present the slow do.

Long shot of train pulling slowly into the station. It consists of the engine, one carriage and one flat wagon.

WALKER It's slowing up, sir.

MAINWARING Slow Present Arms.

ALL One, two, three. One, two, three. One.

Mainwaring salutes.

WALKER I think it's going to stop.

JONES It's going to stop, Mr Mainwaring.

MAINWARING Hold the Present.

JONES Mr Mainwaring – perhaps it isn't a corridor train and the King wants to get out and have a –

MAINWARING That'll do, Jones. It's definitely stopping, Wilson. Get some red carpet.

WILSON Where on earth am I going to find red carpet?

MAINWARING Don't argue. Just do as you're told – get some red carpet.

Wilson chunters off into the buildings. Cut to train about to stop.

WALKER It doesn't look like a royal train.

PIKE Perhaps that's the camouflage.

Cut to train stopping. Henry and Bob, the two drivers, get down, opposite Mainwaring. Henry carries the small brake wheel.

HENRY War or no war, it's a damned disgrace.

BOB I'd complain to steam maintenance.

HENRY I'm going to, don't you worry. (**He pushes between Mainwaring and Jones**) Excuse us, mate.

They go towards the waiting room.

STUDIO. WAITING ROOM

Henry and Bob are in the side room. Henry picks up the phone.

HENRY See if you can squeeze one out of that pot, while I give 'em an earful. (**He shows Bob the centre of the wheel**) Look at that. There's hardly any grip at all.

BOB (**Pouring the tea**) Couldn't you pack it with a bit of paper?

HENRY You don't pack brake wheels with bits of paper, lad. (**Into receiver**) Hallo, I want George Marshall on this phone, at once, in person.

BOB They seem to have done for the sugar. (**He picks up the bottle and reads**) Saccharin, ever tried it?

HENRY No, but it's better than nothing, I expect.

BOB How many lumps?

HENRY Four.

BOB Same as me. (**He reads**) One tablet for each lump.

We see the pills going into the mugs. Enter Wilson.

WILSON Excuse me, you don't happen to have a bit of red carpet, just a few feet would do.

BOB Sorry, mate.

WILSON I didn't think you would. (He goes out)

HENRY Is that you, George? Henry Burstall here. You know the square boss on the steam brake wheel. Well, I've got one here that's round.

FILM: PLATFORM

The platoon are all at the Present position.

JONES Captain Mainwaring, I think this is a rum do.

WALKER The King wouldn't travel on that, it's too scruffy. Look at it.

MAINWARING That may be part of some master plan to which we're not privy.

GODFREY Captain Mainwaring.

MAINWARING Stay where you are, Godfrey. I'm going to see if I can find an equerry.

They all remain rigidly at the Present. Mainwaring approaches the first compartment.

MAINWARING Are you there, Your Majesty?

It is empty, he goes to the next compartment.

MAINWARING Anyone there?

It is empty, we see the reverse of Mainwaring as he moves to the third compartment.

MAINWARING Your Majesty? (**He moves to the fourth compartment. A man in a city suit sits reading his paper – it is held up so we can't see his face. Mainwaring opens the door and coughs**) Your Majesty?

MAN (**Putting down paper**) I beg your pardon?

MAINWARING Sorry – wrong person.

Wilson moves behind Mainwaring, carrying a roll of matting.

WILSON I'm afraid this is the best I could find. (**He unrolls it and reveals 4 foot of very tatty coconut matting**)

The station master, now in a bowler, runs on to the platform with the ticket collector, now in a sponged jacket. He sees the train.

STATION MASTER What's all this rubbish doing here?

TICKET COLLECTOR That's the Snettlefold stopping train.

The Warden joins them.

WARDEN Of course it is. That's the Snettlefold stopping train. The King's not on that.

STATION MASTER Who left it here then?

JONES (**Joining**) The driver went into the office.

STATION MASTER I bet it's that Henry Burstall. Henry – you're stopping the King.

MAINWARING Shush – that's supposed to be a secret.

The station master, ticket collector, Mainwaring and the six move towards the waiting room, followed by the Vicar, Verger, Warden and mayor.

STATION MASTER (**Calling as he goes**) Henry, get this lot shifted on to the siding. You're stopping the King.

STUDIO. WAITING ROOM

The two train drivers are happily asleep.

STATION MASTER Henry – did you hear what I said? (**He spots them asleep – crosses and shakes them**) Henry, give over snoring while I'm talking to you.

MAINWARING They're dead drunk.

WILSON (**Holding up bottle**) I think they've had your pills, sir.

FRAZER They've passed out cold.

STATION MASTER The King can't come through with that lot stuck there.

JONES Can't we push it out of the way?

WALKER Yeah – us and two elephants.

PIKE (**Whispering**) I can drive Mr Mainwaring.

STATION MASTER We'll have to get a driver down from Snettlefold. (**He goes to the phone**)

MAINWARING That'll take half an hour. What's the King going to do, stuck here for half an hour?

GODFREY Shall I run to my sister Dolly and tell her to put the kettle on?

PIKE I can drive it, Mr Mainwaring.

MAINWARING What's that, Pike?

PIKE I learned how at the Schoolboys' Exhibition. There's nothing to it.

WILSON (**Looking at station master**) I don't suppose he'd let us.

MAINWARING We won't even ask him. Outside all of you.

They move out.

STATION MASTER Hello – hello, Brian. This is Walmington. We've got a right to-do here, I can tell you. Can you send me up a driver?

WARDEN (**Tapping station master on shoulder**) Here, do you know what's happening?

STATION MASTER Give over. I'm on to Snettlefold for a driver.

WARDEN Well, you won't even have a train, mate, Mainwaring's lot are going to shift it.

STATION MASTER Now look here, Brian, I haven't time for a lot of argy-bargy.

STUDIO. CAB OF ENGINE

The seven are climbing aboard.

MAINWARING There's no need for all of you.

FRAZER I'd not miss this for £3.

WALKER You'll need me to switch the points at the siding.

MAINWARING Right, off you go, Pike.

PIKE Aye aye, sir. Full steam ahead. (**Pulls the whistle a couple of times and then moves the main control**)

WILSON I somehow feel this is not an awfully good idea.

MAINWARING Stop being a wet blanket, Wilson, and put some coal on.

Train moves.

FRAZER We're on the shift.

WILSON Do we have a pair of tongs.

MAINWARING Get a shovel man!

FILM: PLATFORM

The station master, ticket collector, the Vicar, Verger, Warden and Mayor run out of the waiting room on to the platform. The train is just moving.

STATION MASTER Here. Where are you going with that train?

WARDEN There you are. I told you.

STATION MASTER They've no business to do that. Come back. Stop.

VERGER (**Holding up brake wheel**) Do you think they need this?

STATION MASTER That's the steam brake wheel. It ought to be on the brake.

WARDEN (**Pushing Verger**) What are you doing with it?

VERGER Don't you push me.

WARDEN Why don't you leave things alone.

VERGER He pushed me.

VICAR Stop bickering. Is it an important piece?

STATION MASTER I'll say. Without that they can't stop.

VICAR Can't stop?

WARDEN Come on then, get after them.

Verger, Vicar and Warden run after the train.

STUDIO. CAB OF TRAIN

JONES I'm enjoying this, Mr Mainwaring.

• PETER DAY REMEMBERS •

'For this, we went to a location between Sheringham and Weybourne in Norfolk. Whilst there, we filmed a real train and from that we could build a replica of the cab in the studio. I managed to get hold of some real gauges and made some levers by referring back to the pictures of the real cab.

'The cab was then placed on a rocker base and square platform with huge springs. Then, by projecting a blue background and having people jumping on the corners of the platform, we gave the impression it was moving along.'

MAINWARING You know, Wilson, I've always wanted to drive a train since I was quite a little lad. Give it a bit more, Pike.

PIKE Yes, Mr Mainwaring.

WALKER Mr Mainwaring, The Warden, the Vicar and the Verger are chasing after us like mad things.

MAINWARING Oh they probably wanted a ride, too.

WALKER That's far enough, Captain Mainwaring.

MAINWARING Right, hold it there, Pike.

PIKE Captain Mainwaring, there ought to be a little wheel there.

MAINWARING I shouldn't worry about the technical details, Pike, just stop the train.

PIKE I can't. The little wheel works the brake.

MAINWARING You stupid boy, I thought you said you knew how to drive the thing.

PIKE I can't stop it without the brake, can I?

MAINWARING Don't start using that tone of voice.

Mainwaring moves the main lever over to the other side.

PIKE Don't do that, that makes it go faster.

WILSON How do we stop it, Frank?

PIKE We can't.

JONES We can't stop the train. Don't panic, we can't stop the train.

FILM

Warden, Vicar and Verger arrive at the hand cart. Long shot of train receding.

VICAR We'll never catch them like that.

VERGER They can't stop the train without this.

WARDEN Come on – give me a hand.

They start to mount the hand cart.

STUDIO. CAB

WILSON Surely if we turn the power off we'll just slowly stop.

MAINWARING That's right – turn the power off. (**Moves the regulator right over again**)

PIKE That's turning it on – we're going faster.

WALKER It will freewheel. Anyway – it's downhill all the way to Snettlefold.

GODFREY Supposing there's another train on the line.

FRAZER The Warden's following us – on a wee bogey – look.

FILM

Warden, Verger and Vicar are pumping along on the hand cart. The Verger is brandishing the wheel.

WARDEN Come on, pump.

MAYOR I can't pump in my regalia.

STUDIO. CAB

FRAZER The Verger – he has the brake wheel in his hand.

MAINWARING If there's a train standing at Snettlefold and we smash into it, there could be hundreds killed and injured. I'm going back along the train to see if I can get that wheel.

GODFREY There's no corridor.

MAINWARING Then I'll go over the roof. (**He starts to climb towards the back of the engine**)

JONES I cannot let you go alone, sir. I must come with you to give you assistance and to steady you. Wer – er… (**He stumbles**)

MAINWARING You're in charge here, Wilson.

WILSON Oh good.

Mainwaring starts to climb with Jones.

GODFREY Captain Mainwaring, oughtn't you to have a scarf or something? It's very nippy in the wind.

FILM

Warden, Vicar and Verger are pumping hard.

WARDEN Come on – put your backs into it.

VERGER Don't you push me – he's pushing me again, Your Reverence.

VICAR Oh get on….

STUDIO. CAB

WILSON Whatever you do, Frank, keep it steady.

STUDIO. ROOF OF CARRIAGE

Mainwaring and Jones are crawling along.

JONES Captain Mainwaring, you'll be much safer if you hold my hand.

MAINWARING Go back, Jones.

JONES I go where you go, Mr Mainwaring. It's very slippery, isn't it? Someone ought to tell them, you know. It's very dangerous having the roof so slippery. Wer-err… (**The train lurches and he nearly falls. Mainwaring grabs him**)

MAINWARING Be careful, Jones.

JONES You saved my *life*, Captain Mainwaring. I'll never forget that.

MAINWARING Come on, Jones.

JONES Mr Mainwaring.

MAINWARING Yes, Jones.

JONES Keep away from the edge.

FILM

VICAR I do believe Captain Mainwaring's crawling along the top.

WARDEN You keep pumping, mate – that's all you've got to do. If we get close enough, I'll chuck it.

STUDIO. CAB

Frazer is leaning out.

WILSON Can you see what's happening, Frazer?

FRAZER I think they're getting nearer.

FILM

Mainwaring and Jones move from the front to the rear of the flat wagon. Long shot of train with Mainwaring and Jones on flat wagon being pursued by hand cart.

FILM

Cut to Jones and Mainwaring. Mainwaring cups his hands.

MAINWARING Throw it!

FILM: HANDCART

WARDEN Keep pumping and I'll chuck it.

Warden moves to the front of the handcart, the pump handle catches him repeatedly on the backside as he poises himself to throw. He throws.

FILM

Mainwaring catches it.

MAINWARING Got it!

JONES Well caught, Mr Mainwaring. Now all we've got to do is to get it back to the end that puffs.

They move back to the front end of the flat truck.

FILM

WARDEN All right, you can ease up now.

STUDIO. CAB

WILSON Frank, I've been thinking. That great big lever there must do something.

PIKE It makes it change gear to go faster, or go backwards.

WALKER Here, if we can put it in reverse – wouldn't that stop it?

PIKE It might do.

GODFREY Or perhaps make it blow up.

WILSON If we're likely to run into the train at Snettlefold I think we ought to try.

PIKE Right – here goes.

Pike pulls the lever hard over. There is a huge sound.

STUDIO. ROOF

Jones and Mainwaring are crawling along. Jones falls over Mainwaring – Mainwaring grabs him.

JONES You saved my life *again*, Captain Mainwaring. Where would I be without you, sir?

MAINWARING What the hell are they doing in front?

STUDIO. CAB

PIKE It's stopping, Uncle.

WILSON Well done, Frank.

FILM

The wheels lock and spin in reverse. Cut to Warden and co. who are stationary.

VERGER They're stopping.

VICAR They can't have got the brake wheel back yet.

WARDEN They're stopping anyway.

VICAR Perhaps they used some other sort of lever.

Cut to long shot of train going backwards.

WARDEN You're dead right. They've used reverse, it's coming towards us.

VICAR Are you sure?

WARDEN Course I'm sure. Well, don't gawp. Start pumping.

Cut to long shot of train approaching. Long shot of handcart from train's point of view. They are pumping like mad.

STUDIO. WAITING ROOM

STATION MASTER I can't understand it. Snettlefold should have seen them come by long ago, and phoned us.

TICKET COLLECTOR Perhaps they've stopped?

STATION MASTER How can they without the wheel?

Train whistle is heard off.

STATION MASTER Blimey, they're coming back. We've got to get them into the siding.

They run out.

FILM

Long shot of handcart. Long shot of train. Long shot of point

lever. Station master and ticket collector run to it and move it over.

STUDIO. DRIVER'S CAB

Mainwaring and Jones clamber into the cab.

GODFREY Take my hand, Captain Mainwaring, I'll steady you.

WILSON Do be careful, sir. All this is awfully dangerous.

MAINWARING **(Handing the wheel over)** There it is, Pike – get it on.

Pike takes the wheel, replaces it and starts to turn it.

FILM

Long shot of handcart swinging on to siding. Mid shot of ticket collector and station master watching. Long shot of train swinging on to siding. Mid long shot of train wheels locking. Mid long shot of ticket collector and station master. They hear another train whistle.

STATION MASTER Blimey – that'll be the King.

Cut to Vicar, Verger and Warden, dismounting.

WARDEN **(Breathlessly and shaking his fist at Mainwaring)** You ruddy hooligans – you nearly killed us.

VICAR **(Exhausted)** Speaking for myself, I think it's quite possible that he has.

Cut to side of train. The six are running towards the rear. Mainwaring is the last to dismount from the engine. Distant whistle blows again.

JONES The King's coming, Mr Mainwaring. The King's coming.

MAINWARING Right. Line up – smarten yourselves up.

They line up. Opposite them in the centre of the empty line is a refilling trough – this is a long trough about 1' wide, 8" deep, used for refilling trains that are on the move.

WALKER **(Seeing the trough)** Hey, Pikey, what's that?

PIKE Oh, that's where the engine picks up water when it's going along. They lower a sort of scoop thing down and spray flies everywhere.

WALKER If we stand here, we're going to get soaked.

PIKE Oh yes. Uncle Arthur – I think you ought to tell Mr Mainwaring… **(The whistle goes again)**

WILSON Just line up, Frank.

• JIMMY PERRY REMEMBERS •

'The end of the episode, when the water gets scooped up and sprayed all over the platoon, was initially filmed on location. But when we saw the results back at Television Centre, it hadn't really worked because you could hardly see the water.

'To put the matter right, my suggestion was accepted and instead of travelling back to Norfolk, we painted a background like the railway carriage we'd used on film, stood everybody in front of it, and one by one, in close up, we threw a bucket of water in their faces. It was recorded in someone's back garden and worked well.'

PIKE But we're going to get all wet. Mr Mainwaring, we're going to get all wet.

MAINWARING A drop of rain won't hurt you, boy. Here they come. Royal Salute – Present Arms.

ALL One, two, three. One, two, three. One.

They present arms. Long shot of train approaching, fast. Shot through the wheels as train goes thundering past with much spray. Various shots of the six, and the Warden, the Vicar and the Verger doused with water.

SERIES SIX **EPISODE FOUR**

Recorded: Friday 15/6/73

Original transmission: Wednesday 21/11/73, 6.50–7.20pm

Original viewing figures = 11.6 million

ARTHUR LOWE .... CAPTAIN MAINWARING
JOHN LE MESURIER .... SERGEANT WILSON
CLIVE DUNN................................ LANCE CORPORAL JONES
JOHN LAURIE .... PRIVATE FRAZER
JAMES BECK .... PRIVATE WALKER
ARNOLD RIDLEY .... PRIVATE GODFREY
IAN LAVENDER .... PRIVATE PIKE
FULTON MACKAY .... CAPTAIN RAMSEY
BILL PERTWEE................................ CHIEF WARDEN HODGES
EDWARD SINCLAIR... VERGER
ALEX MCAVOY .... SERGEANT
PAMELA MANSON .... NAAFI GIRL
CY TOWN .... MESS STEWARD
PLATOON .... COLIN BEAN, DESMOND CULLUM-JONES,
.... GEORGE HANCOCK, MICHAEL MOORE,
.... LESLIE NOYES, FREDDIE WHITE, FREDDIE WILES,
.... WILLIAM GOSSLING, EVAN ROSS, ROGER BOURNE.
EXTRAS .... (SOLDIERS) COMPTON COLSON, JACK BLADES,
.... CLIVE PORTER, HARRY WILKES, MERVIN EVANS,
.... SID SMITH, NELSON BISHOP, DAVID LANGLEY,
.... JOHN KERRIDGE, TONY MAXEY

We Know Our Onions

• JO AUSTIN REMEMBERS •

'A strike prevented most of the studio scenes being recorded at Television Centre, so we shot them on location at Preston Barracks, Brighton. Filming there was amazing because it was totally different to our normal situation. We were let loose in a town renowned for entertainment, so not too many evenings were spent in the hotel other than to plot where would be "hit" that night.

'The hotel we stayed in was a very smart one, on the front, much used for conferences and other such events. It had a welcome board in the foyer, which greeted us with the usual message on arrival

'Bill Pertwee, the chief prankster and loudest member of the gang, was intrigued with this and came in one night when the foyer was deserted apart from him and his henchmen. The nightporter was occupied elsewhere, so Bill altered the next day's welcome board into a rather rude message, which went unnoticed till the first PR staff came on duty the next morning. Fortunately we'd left for filming at the usual crack of dawn so all was over when we got back that evening!'

We Know Our Onions

FILM: EXTERIOR. OUTSIDE CHURCH HALL. DAY

Jones' van is standing in the road. attached to the back by a tow bar is a 'Smith gun'. Mainwaring, Wilson and Jones are standing by the gun. The rest of the platoon are lined up in two ranks behind the gun. Frazer, Godfrey and Pike are in the front rank. They are all wearing full equipment and carrying rifles. Pike has the Tommy gun.

JONES A very impressive weapon, sir. When those Nazi paratroopers get a load of this, you won't see their heels for dust.

WILSON Did we have to drag this great gun along with us, sir, it's an awful fag.

MAINWARING An awful fag! We're on active service, Wilson. This gun plays a very important part in these efficiency tests we're going on today. The orders clearly stated, bring the Smith gun.

JONES (**Who is holding some papers**) That's right, sir. It says here, bring sandwiches and the Smith gun.

MAINWARING Get the men aboard, Jones.

JONES I can't do that, sir, the van's locked and Walker's got the key.

MAINWARING Well go and get him, and hurry, it's getting late.

JONES Hurry, yes, sir. (**He goes**)

MAINWARING Godfrey.

GODFREY (**Coming over**) Yes, sir.

MAINWARING Did you get the cover made for the gun.

GODFREY Yes, sir, it's in the cab, my sister Dolly was working on it till midnight.

MAINWARING Right, go and get it and put it on. Frazer, give him a hand.

FRAZER Aye, aye, sir.

STUDIO. SIDE OFFICE

JONES Joe, Joe, Mr Mainwaring wants the key for the van, he's in a hurry to get off. Joe! Where's he gone? (**Phone rings – Jones picks up receiver**) Jack Jones, the butcher.

HODGES I don't want you, I want Joe Walker.

JONES He's not here.

HODGES Listen to me, mate, I don't want any excuses, I want my onions, do you hear me? I want my onions.

JONES What are you shouting for?

HODGES I'm not shouting! I gave him 50 quid in oncers for half a ton of onions, he said he'd bring them round to my shop yesterday. Where are they?

JONES Don't ask me.

HODGES Tell him to bring them round at once.

JONES He can't, we're going away for the weekend.

HODGES Going away for the weekend!

JONES Yes, on a Home Guard efficiency test.

HODGES Listen, I'm coming round there now, and if I don't get my onions, there won't be anything left of him to test. (**Hangs up**)

Jones crosses to hall door and opens it.

JONES Hurry up, Joe, Captain Mainwaring wants the key to his van.

FILM. OUTSIDE CHURCH HALL. EXTERIOR. DAY

Mainwaring and Wilson are standing at the front of the van.

MAINWARING Look at the time, Wilson, we shall never get off today at this rate.

Frazer comes into the picture.

FRAZER We've put the cover on the gun, sir. Would you like to come and have a look at it?

MAINWARING Thank you, Frazer.

Mainwaring and Wilson follow Frazer round to the back of the van. The cover is on the gun, it is made of flowered chintz with a frill round the bottom. Pike and Godfrey are standing by the gun.

MAINWARING What's this, Godfrey?

GODFREY My sister Dolly made it from an old chair cover.

MAINWARING We can't have this, Wilson, it will make us look like a lot of pansies.

WILSON His sister has taken a lot of trouble. Don't hurt his feelings, sir.

MAINWARING Yes, well, it's very nice, Godfrey, but I don't think we need it, it doesn't look as if it's going to rain.

Walker and Jones come into the picture. Godfrey takes the cover off the gun.

MAINWARING Come on, Walker, unlock the van.

WALKER Ah, well, that's a bit difficult you see, sir.

MAINWARING Have you got the key?

WALKER (**Taking the key out of his pocket**) Yes, I've got the key, but that's not the point...

MAINWARING Oh, give it to me. (**He snatches the key and starts to unlock the van door**) And if you've been up to any monkey business, Walker, I shall come down on you like a ton of bricks. (**He pulls open the door, a shower of onions knocks him over**)

JONES (**Rushing over and helping Mainwaring up**) Captain Mainwaring, sir, you're all onioney.

WALKER Those onions don't belong to me, sir, I was going to deliver them to a customer.

MAINWARING How dare you? I shall speak to you later. Come on, Wilson, we must get off.

WILSON Hadn't we better unload the onions first, sir?

MAINWARING We haven't got time, we're late enough as it is. Right, Jones, get the men aboard, tell them to climb on top of the onions.

JONES Right men, at the double, on top of the onions, climb!

The platoon start to embark.

MAINWARING Come on, Jones, get in the cab, we're ready to move off. (**He goes to the cab**)

JONES (**Following him**) Yes, sir, ready to move off, sir.

PIKE (**To Wilson**) Uncle Arthur, I can't travel on top of those onions, I shall cry my eyes out.

WILSON Oh don't be so namby pamby, Frank, get aboard.

PIKE I shall tell Mum. (**He gets aboard**)

MAINWARING Wilson.

WILSON Coming, sir.

Hodges roars up in his greengrocer's van. The Verger is with him. He gets out, followed by the Verger with a basket.

HODGES 'Ere, where are you going with my onions? Pick 'em up, Mr Yeatman.

VERGER Yes, Mr Hodges. (**He picks the onions up off the ground and puts them in the basket**)

HODGES I want my onions.

They slam the doors of the van in his face. He hammers on the doors.

HODGES Do you hear me? I want my onions.

The van moves off over his foot.

HODGES Oh my foot! Hooligans! (**Hodges gets up and pushes the Verger about**) Come on – we'll follow them.

They scramble in the van and roar off.

STUDIO. OUTSIDE EXAMINATION ROOM. DAY

Close up of notice on door which reads 'Home Guard Efficiency Tests'. Mainwaring, Wilson, Jones, Frazer, Walker, Godfrey and Pike are sitting on a bench outside the door. Pike is crying.

MAINWARING For goodness sake, stop sniffling, boy.

PIKE I can't help it, Mr Mainwaring, it was those onions.

MAINWARING Haven't you got a handkerchief?

PIKE No.

MAINWARING Give him a handkerchief, Wilson.

WILSON (**Handing Pike his handkerchief**) You know, I really don't think we ought to have come on these efficiency tests, sir, it's asking for trouble.

MAINWARING Nonsense, besides, we couldn't very well get out of it, all the other Home Guard units in our area have been, and if we'd have funked it, it would have looked as if we hadn't got any confidence in ourselves.

JONES I have every confidence in ourselves, Captain Mainwaring.

MAINWARING I'm glad to hear it, Jones.

JONES And I have confidence in you, sir, because I know that you have confidence in yourself. And you have confidence in yourself, because you have confidence in us, and even if you hadn't got any confidence in us, you wouldn't show it, and that's what gives me confidence.

FRAZER (**Rolling his eyes**) Well it doesn't give me any confidence.

MAINWARING Don't roll your eyes in that manner, Frazer. I keep telling you about it. Now listen, men, if we pass these tests with flying colours we shall get 12 stars, and I very much want us to be a 12-star platoon, because if we're a 12-star platoon, you know what that means, don't you?

WALKER Yeah, we get a mention in the AA book.

MAINWARING Watch it, Walker, you're on very thin ice.

PIKE Excuse me, Mr Mainwaring, the Warden and the Verger are at the window.

Cut to Hodges and the Verger making faces at the window.

MAINWARING How dare they follow us here?

WALKER You leave it to me, sir, I'll sort 'em out. (**He crosses to the sash window and opens it**) What do you want?

HODGES You know perfectly well what I want, I want my onions.

VERGER Yes, he wants his onions.

WALKER I can't come now, we're just going in for the test.

HODGES I'm not hanging about here all day.

MAINWARING Tell them to go away, Walker.

WALKER They won't budge.

MAINWARING Just shut the window.

Walker shuts the window on the Warden and crosses back.

MAINWARING Now, the important thing to...

PIKE They're still there, Mr Mainwaring.

MAINWARING Oh, really! (**He gets up, crosses to the window and taps on the pane**) Go away, clear off. (**He crosses back**

and sits down) Now, as I was saying, we've got no idea what's going to take place in that room, but whatever it is, I'm relying on you men to keep on your toes.

WILSON Last week I had a drink with a sergeant in the Eastgate Home Guard, and it turned out that his people knew my people some years ago, he was an awfully nice chap.

MAINWARING We're not interested in your social life, Wilson.

WILSON Oh, all right then, I won't bother to tell you.

MAINWARING Tell us what?

WILSON You see he'd been on one of these tests.

MAINWARING Well, why didn't you say so in the first place? Right, listen to Sergeant Wilson everybody. **(Pause)** Well, get on with it, Wilson.

WILSON What, oh yes, well you see he was a bit cut up because he'd arranged to play golf that weekend... he and Tubby Glossop had arranged to play a few holes at...

MAINWARING Tell us about the tests!

WILSON Oh, the tests, well, when you get in the room, they fire all sorts of questions at you, and at the end, the officer goes out and leaves you alone. Then someone comes in the room in disguise and plants a bomb.

MAINWARING Well done, Wilson. Right, men, when the officer leaves the room, I'll tip you the wink, then whoever comes into the room, we'll jump on them.

WILSON Another thing they do, sir, as soon as you get in the room, they search you for weapons.

JONES Don't worry, sir, I've come prepared. **(He takes out a length of yellow silk with a knot in the end)**

WALKER What's that, Jonesey?

JONES It's a rumal.

FRAZER A terrible weapon.

PIKE What's a rumal?

JONES A thugee scarf, used by the thugs in India to strangle their victims. They used to do a lot of strangling in them days, sir, a lot of strangling.

MAINWARING I don't think we shall need that, Jones.

JONES You never know, sir, now you see that knot in the end, there should be a silver rupee in there but I've put a half-crown in instead, it's just as good. Now, you creep up behind the victim and you whip the scarf round his neck, the weight of the coin carries it round, then you tighten it. It doesn't half make their eyes water.

MAINWARING Put it away, Jones.

The door opens and Captain Ramsey comes out. He is a tall, thin, intellectual Scot. He is slightly mad. Mainwaring and co. jump up.

RAMSEY Good morning, my name is Ramsey and I'm in charge of the tests, and I must warn you before you enter that room that once inside, anything can happen. Are you prepared for the worst?

MAINWARING Yes, sir, we're prepared for the worst.

RAMSEY **(To Pike)** What are you crying for laddie?

PIKE I'm not crying.

RAMSEY Yes you are, you're a coward. I hate cowards.

WILSON It's the onions you see, sir.

RAMSEY Rubbish. One of your men crying, and one of them talking rubbish, that's not a very good start is it, captain? What is it?

MAINWARING It's not a very good start.

RAMSEY All of you together. What is it?

ALL It's not a very good start.

RAMSEY Right, in you go. Left, right, left, right.

Mainwaring, Wilson, Jones, Walker, Frazer, Pike and Godfrey double into the room.

STUDIO. EXAMINATION ROOM. DAY

In the centre of the room are three small school desks. At the back is a bench, and there is a blackboard in front of the desks. There is a sash window at the back of the room. A regular army sergeant is standing in the middle of the room. Mainwaring and co. enter at the double.

RAMSEY Left, right, left, right. Halt. Right, Sergeant, search them for weapons. Now, during the time you are in this room you are under battle conditions. If you pass this part of the test you get four stars. My sergeant and I can be anything. A Gestapo officer, a British Naval Officer, anything. Have you searched them, Sergeant?

SERGEANT Yes, sir, nothing.

RAMSEY Right, over here.

The sergeant crosses to Ramsey and whispers in his ear.

JONES **(To Walker)** Blimey, Joe, for a minute I thought that sergeant was going to comprehend my rumal.

RAMSEY Right, the captain, sergeant and corporal sit at the desks, the rest of you on the bench, move.

FRAZER I wish this fellow would talk the King's English.

Mainwaring, Wilson and Jones sit at the little desks. Walker, Frazer, Godfrey and Pike sit on the bench.

RAMSEY Now, I want you to be alert and on your toes at all times. What do I want?

ALL Alert and on our toes at all times.

RAMSEY Stand up.

They stand.

RAMSEY Sit down, too slow. Stand up, sit down.

Mainwaring has a bit of difficulty with the small desk and hurts himself.

RAMSEY Up, down, up, down.

GODFREY Excuse me, sir, I think I missed one. Shall I stand up and sit down again?

RAMSEY Keep sitting, now the first part of this test is for officers and N.C.O.s only. I will ask three questions, and you four at the back will criticise your leaders when I ask for comment. What will you do?

ALL We will criticise our leaders.

RAMSEY You, Corporal.

JONES Yes, sir, yes, sir.

RAMSEY When I blow my whistle I am a Gestapo officer. What am I?

JONES (**Confused**) Well, you're a, you're a...

RAMSEY Come on, man.

JONES Sorry, sir. You're getting me a bit confused.

RAMSEY I'm a Gestapo officer. What am I?

JONES Geste officer arpo, I mean a Gestapo officer.

RAMSEY Right. (**Turns his back on Jones, and writes 'Question One' on the blackboard. As quick as a flash, Jones gets up and whips the 'thug' scarf round the captain's neck**) What are you doing? Get him off!

Mainwaring jumps up and pulls Jones off. The sergeant helps him.

MAINWARING Control yourself, Jones.

RAMSEY Are you mad, Corporal?

MAINWARING He's very keen you know, sir.

RAMSEY (**To Mainwaring**) Take him back to his place, captain.

JONES You said you were a Gestapo officer, I was just being alert, sir.

RAMSEY I'm not a Gestapo officer until I blow my whistle.

FRAZER Somehow I don't think we're going to get those 12 stars.

RAMSEY (**Blows whistle**) Now I'm a Gestapo officer.

WILSON Er yes?

RAMSEY What are you doing in France?

WILSON I'm not in France.

RAMSEY Yes you are, you were dropped by parachute. I captured you, and I'm now interrogating you.

WILSON Oh all right, what do you want to know?

RAMSEY You're not supposed to tell me anything. Now what are you doing in France?

WILSON I don't know.

RAMSEY You were trying to blow up a munitions factory.

WILSON All right, I was trying to blow up a munitions factory.

RAMSEY So, you admit it?

WILSON Oh really, this is absurd.

RAMSEY I'll show you how absurd it is, right, now I'm putting matches under your fingernails, now I'm setting light to them. (**He mimes**) They're burning down, now they've reached your fingers, you're in agony, how do you like that?

WILSON Well to be absolutely honest, it's not really bothering me very much.

RAMSEY (**Pointing at Pike**) Comment!

PIKE I think he's being very brave.

RAMSEY Rubbish, watch my rear, Sergeant.

SERGEANT Yes, sir.

Ramsey turns his back on them and writes 'Question Two' on the blackboard. When he has finished he whispers to the sergeant. During this, Hodges and the Verger appear and flatten their faces against the window. Hodges gestures at Walker who mouths 'clear off'. Hodges reacts and presses a sheet of paper against the window, on it are written the words 'I want my onions'. Ramsey turns, Hodges and the Verger dodge down.

RAMSEY Right, next question. (**Points at Mainwaring**) Captain!

MAINWARING Yes, sir. (**Gets up and has difficulty with the desk. He hurts himself again**)

JONES Permission to speak, sir? (**Jumps up**)

RAMSEY Yes?

JONES In what capacity are you asking the question, sir, are you a Gestapo officer or what?

RAMSEY I'm not anyone, I'm me.

JONES Shouldn't you blow your whistle, sir?

RAMSEY What for?

JONES Last time you said I'm not a Gestapo officer until I blow my whistle. Then you blew it and you said, 'Now I'm a Gestapo officer'. This time you should say, 'I'm not me until I blow my whistle'. Then you should blow it and say, 'Now I'm me'.

RAMSEY I don't need to say when I'm me, they know who I am. Sit down!

JONES (**To Wilson**) He should blow his whistle and say who he is.

RAMSEY (**Shouting**) All right. (**He blows whistle**) Now I'm me. Satisfied?

JONES Thank you, sir. Now he's him.

RAMSEY Now then, captain, you are in a balloon, travelling over enemy territory with your men here. The

balloon is losing height, and you have to push one of them out. Which one will you choose?

MAINWARING Ah, that's a tricky one, sir, I think I should call for a volunteer.

RAMSEY You can't do that, you must make a decision and choose one. What must he do?

ALL He must make a decision and choose one.

MAINWARING Well, I should prefer to throw myself out, but of course I am more valuable, so I'm very much afraid that it would have to be Private Godfrey.

RAMSEY **(Pointing at Frazer)** Comment!

FRAZER Sound common sense.

RAMSEY **(Pointing at Pike)** Comment!

PIKE Well, whoever was thrown out, it certainly shouldn't be me. I've got my whole life before me, I haven't done anything, no living at all.

WALKER All the more reason why you should be the one, after all, what you've never had you don't miss.

JONES Mr Godfrey is a fine man, sir, and if I was the officer I couldn't throw him out. I'd order the sergeant to do it.

WILSON Excuse me, sir, if the balloon's losing height, all we've got to do is to wait until it reaches the ground, then Godfrey could step out.

GODFREY Thank you, Mr Wilson.

WILSON Don't mention it, my dear fellow.

RAMSEY **(Blowing hard)** Right, now if you'll excuse me, my sergeant and I will leave the room for a short while.

GODFREY Er, may I leave the room with you.

RAMSEY No, you may not.

Ramsey and the sergeant go.

MAINWARING Right, men, gather round. Now remember what Sergeant Wilson's friend said, when the officer leaves the room, someone comes in disguised with a bomb.

STUDIO. OUTSIDE EXAMINATION ROOM

RAMSEY I tell you they're mad, Sergeant, stark, staring mad, the lot of them.

SERGEANT They are a bit odd, sir. How many marks are you going to give them?

RAMSEY Marks! I'd like to mark that silly old fool of a corporal for life.

A NAAFI girl with long blonde hair comes into the picture, she is pushing a tea trolley with an urn and tea cups on it.

GIRL Shall I take their tea in to them now?

RAMSEY You might as well, give me a cup first, I need it.

STUDIO. EXAMINATION ROOM

MAINWARING Right, men, whoever comes in that door, grab them and we'll get rid of that bomb. We shall get four stars for this, as sure as eggs are eggs.

The NAAFI girl comes in backwards with the tea trolley.

GIRL Tea's up.

MAINWARING Right, grab him!

Walker, Jones and Frazer grab the girl.

WILSON It's a girl, sir.

MAINWARING Rubbish, get that wig off.

GIRL You old ones are worse than the regulars.

PIKE The bomb must be in this tea urn.

MAINWARING Get rid of it, Pike!

PIKE Yes, Mr Mainwaring. **(He picks up the tea urn and hurls it through the window. There is a crash and a scream. We see Hodges and the Verger on the grass with tea over them)**

HODGES You flipping hooligans!

VERGER Mr Hodges, would you mind turning the tap off please, it's going all over my vestments.

STUDIO. YARD. DAY

A high brick wall backing and the corner of a building with a door in it. In the centre of the yard is a wire fence 6 foot high. Beside the fence are three oil drums (empty), large, medium and small. An 8-foot ladder and two 8-foot builders planks, a coil of rope, two 8-foot steel scaffolding poles and a football. The platoon are drawn up in three ranks, with Mainwaring and Wilson in front. They are just wearing webbing equipment with bayonets. Captain Ramsey is addressing them. His sergeant is standing beside him.

RAMSEY Right, this is phase two of the test, if you pass this you get four stars. Now, Captain Mainwaring, you've got to get all your men over this electric fence, using only this equipment. If you touch the fence, an alarm will go off and you have to start again. Any questions?

PIKE Excuse me, sir, is it a hypothetical electicityfied fence, or a real electricityfied fence?

RAMSEY It's a hypothetical electric fence, but there's a small charge running through it just to give the test a hint of zest. It won't hurt you, just give you a wee shock. Right, Captain Mainwaring, you've got three minutes to appreciate the situation then I shall blow my whistle and you have half an hour to complete the test. Off you go!

MAINWARING Thank you, sir, now pay attention.

They gather round Mainwaring.

MAINWARING Right, men, this is a tough one, but we can crack it. Now, I suggest that we all think hard for a minute, and then I want ideas thick and fast. Right, go.

Close up of Wilson, Jones, Frazer, Walker, Godfrey and Pike, thinking hard.

MAINWARING Times up. Wilson?

WILSON Well er… er.

MAINWARING Frazer?

FRAZER If we could er… er… no, that wouldn't work.

MAINWARING Pike?

PIKE I'm not ready yet, Mr Mainwaring.

MAINWARING Jones?

JONES Acrobats, sir.

MAINWARING What?

JONES I've seen it done in a circus, sir. If we put one of those planks on a small oil drum, I will stand on the end, then if Private Walker jumps on the other end it will levitate me over the wire.

WILSON He'll break his neck, sir.

MAINWARING It's far too dangerous, Jones.

JONES Let me do it, sir. Let me do it.

Ramsey blows his whistle.

RAMSEY Right, start.

JONES I won't go up too high, sir, just enough to clear the fence. I'm very agile, sir.

MAINWARING All right, Jones.

JONES Thank you, sir. Right, Private Frazer, Walker, Pike give me a hand.

They put one of the planks across a small drum, Walker climbs up on a large drum, Jones stands on the end of the plank.

MAINWARING You've got to admire Jones, you know, Wilson, I like to see his guts.

WILSON You probably will, sir, all over the yard.

JONES Ready, Mr Mainwaring. Right, Joe get ready to jump.

WALKER I hope you know what you're doing, Jonesey.

JONES Don't argue, right ready, jump!

Walker jumps on to the plank. It breaks in the middle.

MIx to the three oil drums piled on top of each other. At the top is the football, the ladder is balanced on top of the ball, Mainwaring and co. are holding one end of the ladder.

MAINWARING Ready, Jones?

JONES All ready.

They lower the ladder, Jones clings to it, they slowly lever him round.

JONES I'm nearly over, sir.

The bottom of his bayonet catches the fence, sparks fly, a siren and bells go off.

MAINWARING Start again.

Mix to four members of the platoon holding the ladder upright. The plank is pushed through the ladder. Walker, Frazer and Pike are holding the end. Jones is crawling along the plank.

MAINWARING Take it easy, Jones.

JONES Don't worry, sir, I'm nearly over. Whoa! **(He falls round the end of the plank and touches the fence, sparks fly, the siren and bells go off)**

MAINWARING Right, start again.

They get Jones down.

RAMSEY **(Blowing his whistle)** Time's up, Mainwaring.

MAINWARING Can't we have an extension, sir, we've nearly got it licked.

RAMSEY Oh, all right.

Mix to the platoon in two lines, holding the poles which are stretching across the fence. Jones is crawling across.

JONES I think I'm going to make it this time, Captain Mainwaring.

WILSON **(To Mainwaring)** Perhaps one of us should say a little prayer, sir?

JONES I'm nearly over, whoa! **(He slips and touches the fence, sparks, sirens, etc.)**

MAINWARING Right, start again.

STUDIO. OFFICERS MESS. NIGHT

Ramsey is drinking at the bar, a steward is behind the bar. Suddenly we hear the sirens and bells.

MAINWARING **(Out of vision)** Right, start again.

Ramsey reacts. Mix to close up of clock over bar at twelve o'clock. Pan down to Ramsey.

RAMSEY Same again please.

STEWARD Sorry, sir, I've got to close the bar, it's midnight.

RAMSEY Ah well, I'll away to my bed.

EXTERIOR. YARD. NIGHT. STUDIO

It is pitch dark, we can't see anything.

MAINWARING Are you across yet, Jones?

JONES Nearly, sir.

The door opens, Ramsey appears.

JONES Look out, Whoa!

Sparks reflect in Ramsey's face, sirens and bells.

MAINWARING Right, start again.

RAMSEY (**Wearily**) Good night to you, Mainwaring. (**He closes the door**)

FILM: BATTLE RANGE. EXTERIOR. DAY

The van is parked in a field, the platoon are lined up beside it. The 'Smith gun' has been unlimbered and is pointing in the direction of a wooded copse two hundred yards away. Mainwaring and Wilson are standing in front of the platoon. Captain Ramsey is addressing them, his sergeant is with him. Everyone except Ramsey and his sergeant are wearing battle order with camouflage in their steel helmets.

RAMSEY This is the third and final phase of the test, if you pass this you get four stars.

JONES Permission to speak, sir?

RAMSEY Yes?

JONES May I be so forward and presumptuous looking as to ask how many stars we have enquired so far?

RAMSEY In the first test nothing, in the second test I've given you one star for perseverance, in spite of the fact that you kept me awake half the night.

MAINWARING Ah well, one's better than nothing, sir.

RAMSEY Rubbish, you haven't done very well. What haven't you done?

ALL We haven't done very well.

RAMSEY Confession is good for the soul, captain. (**He sees Pike who is crying**) I do believe that boy's crying again.

PIKE I'm not crying.

RAMSEY Yes you are, you're a coward, a coward.

WILSON I told you before, sir, it's the onions.

RAMSEY Rubbish.

PIKE I'm not a coward, I've done all sorts of brave things. I've even taken dead mice out of traps.

MAINWARING Quiet, Pike.

RAMSEY Right, now this is the test – concealed in that copse over there are a body of my men. I will blow my whistle and you will prepare yourselves. At the end of 15 minutes I will blow the whistle again and my men will advance. You will then fire three dummy bombs at them and they will retreat.

MAINWARING That seems straightforward enough, eh, Wilson?

WILSON Yes indeed, sir, it couldn't be more straightforward.

RAMSEY Right, Sergeant, give them the charges.

SERGEANT Yes, sir. (**He hands the charges to Wilson**) Three charges.

MAINWARING Where are the dummy bombs, sir?

RAMSEY Ah, that's the interesting part of the test, I'll show you. Follow me. **(He walks off)**

MAINWARING Right, platoon, attention, by the right, quick march. Right wheel.

FILM: A HEDGE. EXTERIOR. DAY

The hedge parts. Hodges' and the Verger's faces poke through.

VERGER There are your onions, Mr Hodges.

HODGES I can't wait to get my hands on them, there'll be a queue outside my shop tomorrow morning a mile long. Come on, we'll go and get the van.

FILM: ANOTHER PART OF THE RANGE. EXTERIOR. DAY

Mainwaring and co. are standing in front of the fence used in phase two. All the equipment – poles, ladders, drums, etc. are piled beside the fence. Ramsey is pointing to the fence.

RAMSEY Now then, gentlemen, I think you're all familiar with this fence.

MAINWARING Excuse me, sir, where are the dummy bombs?

RAMSEY There. **(He points to a pile of bombs behind the fence)** Now, when I blow my whistle, captain, you and your men will double over here from the gun, get over this fence, collect the bombs and get back again. If you touch the fence, you start again. My sergeant and I will be here all the time to see that you don't take any short cuts.

WILSON **(To Mainwaring)** Oh Lor', we're not going all through that again, are we, sir?

WALKER **(To Frazer)** Blimey, if we couldn't get over that fence in five hours, we're certainly not going to do it in 15 minutes.

FRAZER I said the whole weekend would finish in disaster.

RAMSEY You then double back to your gun with the bombs, and wait for my signal to fire. Is that clear, captain?

MAINWARING Yes, sir, very clear indeed.

FILM: BATTLE RANGE. EXTERIOR. DAY

Hodges' van draws up beside Jones' van. Hodges' and the Verger get out.

HODGES Come on, hurry up.

VERGER Do you think we ought to take these onions without permission, Mr Hodges?

HODGES What are you talking about, I've paid for these onions. **(He opens the doors of the van)** They're mine. Shut up and hold your frock out.

The Verger picks up the ends of his cassock, Hodges piles the onions into it.

VERGER I don't think the Vicar would approve of me using holy vestments to carry onions in.

HODGES Stop nattering, you old woman – come on, get a move on. **(Hodges holds the end of the cassock and they run to his van and tip the onions in)**

FILM. FIELD. EXTERIOR. DAY

Mainwaring and co. are marching back to the van.

WILSON Don't you think it would be a good idea if we just got in the van and drove home?

MAINWARING I refuse to give in until the final whistle blows.

JONES Couldn't we dig a tunnel under the fence, sir?

WALKER What, in 15 minutes? Don't be daft.

FRAZER **(Pointing)** Look, sir, the Warden and the Verger are messing about with our van.

MAINWARING Damn cheek! Right men, at the double forward.

They all run.

FILM: BATTLE RANGE. EXTERIOR. DAY

Hodges is loading onions into the Verger's cassock.

HODGES Hold it still, hold it still.

Mainwaring and co. come into the picture.

WILSON Look her, how dare you mess about with our van?

HODGES I'm only taking what's mine.

JONES We're on a 12-star test.

HODGES If you don't get out of my way, mate, you'll see more than 12 stars.

MAINWARING Oh come away, don't bandy words with him, we've got more important things to do. Come on, follow me. **(He moves back to the gun, the others follow)**

HODGES See what I mean, stand up to him and he's like a pricked balloon.

VERGER You've got a masterful personality, Mr Hodges.

WILSON There goes the first whistle, sir, we've got 15 minutes.

PIKE We'd better get down to the fence, Mr Mainwaring.

MAINWARING Now wait a minute, men, there must be some way. We must all think.

FRAZER Mr Mainwaring, it's just occurred to me, this is a smooth-bore weapon, we can fire anything from it.

PIKE In that film *Captain Blood* with Errol Flynn, they fired grape shot from the cannons.

WALKER That's right, we've got the charges, all we need is some bits of old iron and nuts and bolts.

MAINWARING We haven't got any nuts and bolts.

WALKER We can take some bits off Jonesey's van.

JONES How dare you? You're not taking my van to pieces.

GODFREY Captain Mainwaring, sir, if we fire bits of iron at the people who are attacking, it will make holes in them and spoil them.

WALKER Yes, and it will kill them as well.

MAINWARING Of course it will, the whole idea's absurd.

WILSON You know it's just occurred to me, sir, what we need to fire from that gun is something that's hard but not lethal.

MAINWARING We haven't got anything that's hard and not... wait a minute!

They all look at Hodges loading the onions.

ALL Onions!

MAINWARING Come on.

They all rush over to the van.

VERGER That's the last lot, Mr Hodges.

HODGES You took long enough about it.

MAINWARING We want those onions.

HODGES Well you're not having 'em.

MAINWARING In the name of the King, I demand those onions.

HODGES You can demand as much as you like, you're not having 'em.

MAINWARING We'll buy them off you.

HODGES You can't, you're not registered with me.

JONES Well you're registered with me, and if you don't sell us those onions, you've had it for kidneys.

HODGES All right, shilling a pound.

WALKER I sold them to you for fourpence.

HODGES That's your hard bun.

MAINWARING Right, we'll have 20 pounds.

HODGES That will cost you a quid.

There is a set of greengrocer's scales in the van. He starts to weigh up the onions.

HODGES Hold your dress out, Mr Yeatman.

• PETER DAY REMEMBERS •

'We built a Smith gun from photo reference obtained from the Imperial War Museum, a very useful source for *Dad's Army* props. Plywood on wooden formers was used, while a steel shaft was placed through the centre. Everything else was cardboard tubes and nuts and bolts, but it was strong enough to cope when we fired a small gunpowder charge, which made a flash and created a puff of smoke.

'The platoon set up and fired the gun, supposedly filled with onions. We simply fired a small gunpowder charge remotely, in the empty gun barrel, while the entire film crew stood out of camera shot hurling onions on cue – and a good cry was had by all!'

MAINWARING Lend me a pound, Wilson.

FILM: ANOTHER PART OF THE RANGE. EXTERIOR. DAY

Ramsey and the sergeant are standing by the fence.

SERGEANT It looks as if they've funked the test, sir.

RAMSEY What can you expect from a bunch of softies like that?

FILM. BATTLE RANGE. EXTERIOR. DAY

Pike is tipping the last few onions down the barrel of the gun.

MAINWARING That's enough, Pike. Hurry up, Verger!

The Verger dumps a load of onions beside the gun.

MAINWARING Range two hundred yards.

WILSON Two hundred yards, right, sir.

MAINWARING Load the charge.

They elevate the gun.

JONES My charge is loaded, sir.

MAINWARING Stand by to fire.

Ramsey and the sergeant come into the picture.

RAMSEY So you're backing out are you, Mainwaring? I shan't even give you one star now.

MAINWARING We're not backing out of anything.

RAMSEY What are you talking about man, you've no ammunition, and I'm due to blow the whistle in 30 seconds.

MAINWARING Go ahead and blow it.

RAMSEY There's no point.

MAINWARING Oh give it to me. **(He snatches the whistle and blows hard)**

Cut to ten regular soldiers emerging from the copse. They spread out in a line and advance across the open ground. They are wearing steel helmets, equipment, and carrying short Lee Enfield rifles.

Cut to Mainwaring and co.

MAINWARING Fire!

The gun fires a shower of onions.

Cut to the soldiers. A shower of onions lands amongst them.

Cut to Mainwaring and co.

MAINWARING Fire!

The gun fires.

Cut to the soldiers. More onions land on them, they dodge about.

Cut to Mainwaring and co.

MAINWARING Fire!

The gun fires.

Cut to the soldiers. More onions, they break and run.

Cut to Mainwaring and co. They all cheer.

MAINWARING Well done, men. **(To Ramsey)** I think we've achieved the object of the exercise, sir.

RAMSEY I take my hat off to you, Mainwaring, that's the best bit of initiative I've seen in this whole war. I'm going to give you 12 stars.

MAINWARING Do you hear that? We're a 12-star platoon.

The men cheer. Hodges and the Verger push their way through.

MAINWARING Just a minute, where do you think you're going?

HODGES I'm going to pick those onions up.

MAINWARING You'll do nothing of the sort, they belong to us. Come on, men.

They all rush towards the onions.

The Honourable Man

SERIES SIX **EPISODE FIVE**

Recorded: Sunday 8/7/73

Original transmission: Wednesday 28/11/73, 6.50–7.20pm

Original viewing figures = 12.1 million

ARTHUR LOWE .... CAPTAIN MAINWARING
JOHN LE MESURIER .... SERGEANT WILSON
CLIVE DUNN.................................. LANCE CORPORAL JONES
JOHN LAURIE .... PRIVATE FRAZER
JAMES BECK .... PRIVATE WALKER
ARNOLD RIDLEY .... PRIVATE GODFREY
IAN LAVENDER .... PRIVATE PIKE
BILL PERTWEE.................................. CHIEF WARDEN HODGES
FRANK WILLIAMS .... VICAR
EDWARD SINCLAIR.................................. VERGER
ERIC LONGWORTH .... TOWN CLERK
JANET DAVIES.................................. MRS PIKE
GABOR VERNON .... RUSSIAN
HANA-MARIA PRAVDA.................................. INTERPRETER
ROBERT RAGLAN .... COLONEL
PAMELA CUNDELL.................................. MRS FOX
FRED MCNAUGHTON.................................. MAYOR
PLATOON..................... COLIN BEAN, DESMOND CULLUM-JONES,
.... MICHAEL MOORE, GEORGE HANCOCK, EVAN ROSS,
.... LESLIE NOYES, WILLIAM GOSSLING, FREDDIE WHITE,
.... FREDDIE WILES, ROGER BOURNE
OTHER EXTRAS .... LEILA FORD AND EILEEN MATTHEWS
BAND.................................. THE NEWMARKET TOWN BAND

• JIMMY PERRY REMEMBERS •

'The story of how David Croft and I got together, and how the series became a national institution has been written so often that legends have grown up around it, some of them are completely untrue. One that persists is that David and I changed the parts of Captain Mainwaring and Sergeant Wilson around and that John Le Mesurier was originally going to play the officer – this is completely incorrect. The true story is very simple: we cast Arthur Lowe as the officer long before casting the part of the sergeant. The then head of comedy [at the BBC] was Michael Mills. Michael had been a lieutenant-commander in the navy during the war and always behaved as though he was on the quarterdeck in a force ten gale. "I got you Sergeant Wilson!" he shouted. "It's John Le Mesurier." And that was it.'

The Honourable Man

THE CHURCH HALL

It is set out for a meeting, with a long table, at which are sat Mainwaring, Frazer, Walker, Godfrey, Vicar, Warden, Mrs Fox and the town clerk. Pike is sat on a chair by the office door. All are wearing civilian suits. The town clerk is in the centre. Mainwaring is next to him and there is an empty chair beside them. Everyone is talking. The town clerk bangs the table.

TOWN CLERK Right. Can I call the meeting to order? I've got you gathered as a General Purposes Committee to discuss the arrangements for the visit of this Russian chap to Walmington-on-Sea. Now as town clerk, it has fallen to my lot to find a suitable man to co-ordinate and mastermind our arrangements. Everyone I've talked to is of the same opinion. There's one man, and he's one who's outstandingly suitable to get his teeth into this sort of do and I'm going to ask him – with your approval, I'm sure – to take the chair, Captain George Mainwaring.

All – except the Warden – applaud and say 'hear hear'. Mainwaring moves into the centre chair – town clerk moves to the spare one.

MAINWARING Mr Town Clerk – ladies and gentlemen.

WARDEN Just a minute. Why do we have to have him as a chairman? Russians don't want officers and bank managers and all that snobbish rubbish.

TOWN CLERK Well, from the enquiries I've made around the town it seemed to me that Captain Mainwaring was the best choice.

WARDEN Well, I don't agree. I think we ought to have an ordinary bloke – a greengrocer or somebody else.

TOWN CLERK Do we know a greengrocer?

WARDEN Yes… me.

MAINWARING If there's any dissent, I'd gladly stand down.

TOWN CLERK Well, the simplest thing is for you to vacate the chair, then I'll take the chair and we'll take a vote.

WARDEN Hear hear.

Mainwaring and town clerk change chairs.

WALKER Stand by for a quick game of musical chairs.

TOWN CLERK Now – all in favour of Captain Mainwaring taking the chair raise their hands.

All except the Warden raise their hands.

TOWN CLERK Against?

Warden raises his hand.

TOWN CLERK Carried. Captain Mainwaring take the chair which I shall now vacate.

They both stand and move. Walker hums. Mainwaring reacts.

MAINWARING Mr Town Clerk – ladies and gentlemen.

WARDEN You said that already.

MAINWARING Order please. We are here assembled to honour the Russian worker Vladislov Vladis… well, it doesn't matter what his name is. The point is, he's a hero of the Soviet Union. That doesn't mean he's brave. What it does mean is that his team have made 5,723 tanks.

WALKER Which means he's been busy.

MAINWARING Precisely. And he's visiting, among other cities, Walmington-on-Sea. Now, what form…

Wilson enters from the side office.

WILSON Oh – I'm awfully sorry, I thought it was half past.

MAINWARING Come and sit down, Wilson. This is Wilson, he's my chief clerk and also my sergeant.

WILSON I was sure you said half past.

MAINWARING I said quarter past… you don't listen.

Wilson sits down beside Mainwaring.

WALKER We just had the best bit – Hodges tried to give Mainwaring the elbow.

WILSON Oh, I'm sorry I missed that.

MAINWARING Now – as I was saying – what form…

Jones enters from the rear.

JONES Evening, everybody. Sorry I'm late. It's been one of those days. You see I had a batch of sausage skins which was very diaphanous. They were all right when I filled them, but when the ladies cooked them, the heat caused them to splurge. Well, the ladies don't like that sort of thing, you know. It's obnoxious to them.

MAINWARING Please sit down, Mr Jones. As I was about to say, what form should our welcome to Mr er, er – this Russian take?

FRAZER **(Rising)** I've been giving the matter most careful thought and I'm prepared to offer him a voucher worth £10 towards the cost of a funeral.

Mainwaring reacts.

WALKER Blimey. He won't be able to take advantage of it unless he pegs out.

FRAZER That's a risk I'll have to take.

MAINWARING Well – that's a good start, I'm sure, but I was talking about the broader aspect of welcome.

MRS FOX Well, I'm representing the W.V.S. and I think we should try not to be all British and reserved. I think we should smile a lot.

MAINWARING Yes – well, that would be very nice.

GODFREY Personally, I've never had much sympathy for Reds. I don't think we should go too far.

MAINWARING Well, as you know, there was a time when I felt very much the same about bolshies and their like. But let's not be prejudiced – they can't be all that bad otherwise they wouldn't be on our side.

WILSON Why don't we give him the Freedom of Walmington.

PIKE That's right, and we could let him go into the pictures for nothing.

WALKER He's only going to be here for a couple of hours.

PIKE They could put on a Mickey Mouse and a Donald Duck.

This is greeted with general derision.

MAINWARING Excuse me a moment. **(He crosses to Pike)** Pike, you're not on this committee – you're here as a messenger boy.

PIKE I was only trying to be helpful.

MAINWARING If you say another word, I shall make you wait in the office with the door shut.

Pike reacts. Mainwaring returns to his place.

MAINWARING I'm sorry about that. I think Wilson has a very good suggestion. The question is – what form should the Freedom take?

TOWN CLERK How about a parchment scroll… tied up with red ribbon. They're very nice, they are.

WALKER Now parchment isn't at all easy, but I think I know where I can lay my hands on some.

WILSON What about a key?

MAINWARING Better still.

WALKER Wood or cardboard – easy. Brass could be a problem.

MAINWARING Let's have a wooden key then. We'll arrange some sort of ceremonial presentation, the mayor can say a few short words and then I, as chairman of the committee, will hand it over to him.

WARDEN Got yourself in there quick enough, didn't you?

JONES Mr Mainwaring, why don't we have the town band playing Russian music and I will dress up as a Cossack and do cobblers.

MAINWARING I beg your pardon, Jones?

JONES Cobblers, sir. They are the very highly difficult kicking and crouching steps which Cossacks do – they do a lot of kicking and crouching, Cossacks do. They crouch down in this fashion. **(He demonstrates)** Then they kick out their legs, so – hi hi. **(He subsides on to his backside)** I'll have to practise of course.

MAINWARING Yes, well… the Home Guard will parade, of course. I don't suppose the Wardens will want to bother.

WARDEN Oh yes they will. You're not keeping us out of it.

WALKER Captain Mainwaring, I dare say Sergeant Wilson will give a demonstration of acrobatic motorcycle riding.

The Home Guard members laugh.

MAINWARING That's a joke at the expense of my sergeant, I'm afraid. We have a motorcycle in the platoon but so far we haven't persuaded him to mount it.

WILSON They're such noisy things.

FRAZER Music, that's what we need. Music. The band playing and the choir singing 'The Red Flag'.

VICAR I assure you my choir is not going to sing 'The Red Flag'.

GODFREY I quite agree.

WARDEN You should have heard what they were singing behind the scout hut last night. It would have made your hair stand on end. **(He sees the Vicar's head)** Beg pardon.

WALKER Why not have them la-la it.

VICAR I think that would be rather silly.

MAINWARING Yes, well – one way or another it's all taking shape. I shall go ahead and co-ordinate these various suggestions and I feel sure that, as usual, Walmington will rise to the occasion.

PIKE And bore the pants off everybody.

Mainwaring points.

PIKE I'm going.

BANK. MAINWARING'S OFFICE

Mainwaring is on the phone.

MAINWARING I'm sorry, Mr Livings. War or no war you cannot issue a cheque for £32… Yes, but you've only got one and fourpence in your account… Well you'd better come in and see me.

Pike enters with the mail during this conversation.

MAINWARING Ask Wilson to step in, Pike.

PIKE He's not back from lunch yet, Mr Mainwaring.

MAINWARING Not back from lunch – it's twenty past two. Tell him I want to see him the second he gets in.

PIKE Mr Mainwaring, can I have Sergeant Wilson's turn with the motorbike again this evening?

MAINWARING Certainly not, Pike. That bicycle is issued for the platoon sergeant and he's jolly well going to knuckle down and learn to ride it.

PIKE Mum says if he comes home with his face scratched and his arm in a sling, she'll give him what for.

MAINWARING Look, Pike, who's running this platoon – me or your mother?

PIKE Well, he's more frightened of Mum.

MAINWARING Is he indeed.

PIKE Oh, here's the twelve o'clock post – it came at five past two. And someone's playing a joke on Uncle Arthur – look. **(He reads)** The Honourable Arthur Wilson.

MAINWARING Let's see. The Honourable Arthur Wilson. Private.

PIKE Does that mean he isn't a sergeant any more?

MAINWARING It's a private letter, you stupid boy. He knows jolly well I don't approve of personal correspondence being sent to the bank.

Knock. There is a knock at the door and Wilson enters.

WILSON Did I leave my bunji here?

MAINWARING Your what?

WILSON My bunji. My rubbing out thing.

MAINWARING **(Ignoring him)** Come in, Wilson. **(He chucks the envelope in front of him)** Would you kindly ask your friends to keep their practical jokes out of my bank.

WILSON That wretched solicitor. I told him not to use the title on my letters. Blast.

MAINWARING What are you talking about?

WILSON Still, it's all round the town, it seems. I suppose you were bound to find out sooner or later. **(He turns to leave)**

MAINWARING Wilson, I haven't finished talking to you.

WILSON Oh, haven't you? Sorry, sir.

MAINWARING Now, are you trying to tell me that this isn't a joke?

WILSON No, I'm afraid. Anything but.

MAINWARING And you really are the Honourable Arthur Wilson?

WILSON Silly, isn't it?

Pike gawps.

MAINWARING Pike, leave the room.

PIKE Yes, Mr Mainwaring.

Pike goes out quickly.

MAINWARING Now, would you mind explaining yourself, Wilson.

WILSON It's just that this uncle of mine died and he didn't have any children so my side of the family all moved up one, so to speak. So now I'm Honourable.

MAINWARING Well, bless my soul.

WILSON There's no reason why it should make any difference to us.

MAINWARING You can bet your bottom dollar it won't make any difference – and you needn't think you can start rolling in twenty minutes late after lunch. Where have you been?

WILSON I popped up and had a bite at the golf club.

MAINWARING Who took you to the golf club?

WILSON I'm a member.

MAINWARING You're a member? Since when?

WILSON Well, they heard about this title thing and they asked me if I'd join.

MAINWARING I've been trying to get in that golf club for years.

WILSON Yes, I believe they're awfully particular.

MAINWARING You don't even play.

WILSON No, but I shall enjoy the food. Do you know – they managed to find some smoked salmon at lunch time.

MAINWARING Smoked salmon at the golf club. All I got was a snoek fishcake at the British Restaurant. **(Mainwaring looks at him)** The Honourable Arthur Wilson. **(He looks again)** Of course, you being a member of the aristocracy explains a lot about your character, you know.

WILSON Really?

MAINWARING Oh yes. They're an ambling, woolly minded lot.

WILSON Not all of them, surely?

MAINWARING Practically to a man. It's all those centuries of in-breeding.

The door flies open. Mrs Pike hurries in.

PIKE **(Close behind her)** Mum, you mustn't come in, they're busy.

MRS PIKE Oh Arthur, is it true that you're Honourable?

WILSON Oh really, Mavis.

MRS PIKE Frank just phoned me. I knew you could do it. **(She throws her arms round him and kisses him)**

WILSON Mavis, please.

MAINWARING Pike, how dare you use the bank telephone for an improper purpose?

MRS PIKE Will you wear one of those uniforms with velvet knee breeches?

WILSON Don't fuss, Mavis.

MAINWARING Mrs Pike, will you please leave my office.

MRS PIKE I'm sorry, Mr Mainwaring. But I just had to

touch that noble face. (**She moves to the door and pauses**) It's not going to make any difference is it, Arthur?

WILSON Of course not, Mavis. Please go home.

PIKE Difference to what, Uncle?

She goes, followed by Pike.

WILSON I'm sorry about that.

MAINWARING Don't apologise. And you're quite right, Wilson. It's not going to make any difference. I'm still the manager and you're still the clerk, I'm still the officer and you're still the sergeant. So pull your socks up and get on with your work at the bank.

WILSON Yes, sir. (**He moves to the door, Pike meets him in the door**)

PIKE Mr Mainwaring, the area manager is on the telephone. He's been hanging on for quite a while but I didn't put him through because you were talking to the Honourable Uncle Arthur. (**He goes quickly**)

Mainwaring picks up the phone.

MAINWARING Hullo, Mainwaring here. Sorry to have kept you waiting, I was in conference with my chief clerk. Yes, that's right, Wilson – well it's the Honourable Arthur Wilson, actually. Yes, I pick my staff with great care, you know.

MAIN HALL

They are now in uniform. Jones, Walker, Frazer, Godfrey and Pike are chatting before the parade.

JONES Of course, when I was a regular soldier we had a lot of officers who were Honourable – well, at least they were called Honourable. They used to stand in a haughty manner, as if they had a smell under their noses, but I'll say this for them, they was very good at keeping stiff upper lips.

JONES We had one officer at the Battle of Omdurman who had his head blown off, but his upper lip was stiff as cardboard.

WALKER I'm going to invite him to be on the board of my company – Directors Joe Walker and the Honourable A. Wilson. It's good to have an Honourable on the note paper, it's the best con you can get.

PIKE It hasn't changed him a bit. He still calls me Frank like he was an ordinary, common person.

FRAZER It won't change him. He was a fool before and he's a fool now.

GODFREY I used to serve one or two Honourables when I was in the Army and Navy Stores – they were just ordinary people like any other customers, the only difference was you couldn't get the money.

Enter Mainwaring and Wilson.

MAINWARING Right, fall the men in, Corporal Jones.

JONES Yes, sir. Fall in in three ranks like the officer says. Look sharp about it.

MAINWARING Settle down.

JONES Permission to speak, sir?

MAINWARING Yes, Jones.

JONES Could you settle a small technical discussion, sir?

MAINWARING What is it, Jones?

JONES Do we address Sergeant Wilson as the Honourable Sergeant Wilson or Sergeant the Honourable Wilson?

Mainwaring reaacts.

WILSON Look – please, I don't want any fuss, I just want to be like an ordinary sergeant.

MAINWARING I think that would suit us all, Wilson.

PIKE And please, sir, can I ride the motorbike on Saturday morning before the ceremony instead of Uncle Sergeant the Honourable Wilson?

MAINWARING No, I'm sorry, Pike.

WILSON I'd be quite happy to give up my turn if Frank wants it.

MAINWARING Prefer a Rolls Royce would you?

WILSON It's not that – I just don't have any rapport with that sort of device.

MAINWARING Latin phrases don't impress me, Wilson. The motorcycle is for you and you are going to ride it. Now, I've been doing some research into the way these Russian chaps show appreciation. They don't cheer like we do but apparently they applaud, and so I think that's what we ought to do.

WALKER Yes – but Mr Mainwaring, if we present arms and then clap hands there won't half be a lot of blue toes around the platoon.

MAINWARING I don't have to be told that, thank you, Walker.

WILSON Why don't we ground arms – then we can clap away till the cows come home.

MAINWARING That's just what I was about to say.

JONES We haven't done any grounding of late, sir. Could we do it and then we can all get familiar?

MAINWARING Good idea, Jones. Squad, 'shun. Ground arms.

They do so, calling 'One, two, three, up'. On 'up' Jones and Frazer fail to rise.

MAINWARING Help them up, somebody.

FRAZER I wasn't stuck. I was waiting for Jones here.

JONES My joints have become asphyxiated, sir.

MAINWARING Right, let's get on. Applause for the Russian hero – begin.

They all start to clap.

WALKER Encore. (**He whistles**)

MAINWARING Stop! (**They do so**) I don't want any of that, Walker. (**Walker reacts**) This isn't a football match. Once more – begin.

They applaud. The town clerk enters from the side office.

TOWN CLERK Oh, thank you very much, gentlemen. Can I have a word with you, Captain Mainwaring?

MAINWARING Yes, certainly. (**To Wilson**) Carry on, Wilson.

TOWN CLERK (**To Wilson**) Good evening, sir.

WILSON Good evening. How nice to see you.

MAINWARING (**At door**) Wilson, practise the whole manoeuvre for a minute or two.

WILSON Certainly, sir.

Mainwaring and the town clerk go into the side office.

MAINWARING How can I help you?

TOWN CLERK Now, I hope you won't take this... amiss, but we feel that since Mr Wilson has come into a title – and we haven't any other titled people in Walmington – well the Honourable Arthur ought to present the key.

MAINWARING Oh no, no, I couldn't allow that. Let's be quite clear about this. I'm presenting the key and that's an end to the matter.

TOWN CLERK The mayor said he hoped you wouldn't take it the wrong way.

MAINWARING You can tell the mayor – and the corporation – that I'm not going to take it at all. This interview is now at an end.

TOWN CLERK Oh, I see, well if you feel like that...

MAINWARING I do. Good evening. (**Mainwaring goes to the hall. Under his breath**) Damned impertinence.

WILSON Ah, glad you came. I've changed the drill a little bit. What do you think about this? Russians welcome.

They bend their knees, place the rifles between them, grip the rifles with their knees and applaud.

MAINWARING Now look here, Wilson, when I want you to re-write the drill book, I'll let you know. Let's get down to the part of the ceremony where I hand over the key. (**The phone rings in the office**) Answer that, Pike.

Pike goes.

FRAZER Captain Mainwaring, why are you handing it over? I think the Honourable ought to do it.

Mainwaring reacts.

GODFREY I don't agree. Captain Mainwaring always does this sort of thing with great dignity.

WALKER Mind you, I think there's a lot to be said for a change.

JONES Well, I look at it this way. Sergeant Wilson may have the three stripes on his noble arm, but you have three pips on your common shoulder. So it's one up to you, Mr Mainwaring, even if you are common, because you have a better insignia –

Mainwaring reacts.

JONES And that is how it should be, because that is the status quo.

MAINWARING Now, look here, all of you...

The Verger enters with the Vicar. He addresses Wilson.

VERGER Excuse me, my lord. (**He does a curtsey**)

Mainwaring reacts.

VERGER Can His Reverence have an audience with you?

MAINWARING What is all this?

VICAR It's just that I wondered if the Honourable Arthur will consent to join the parish council and also will he approve a crest to put on his private pew?

MAINWARING How dare you come in here while I'm holding a parade?

Pike enters.

PIKE Captain Mainwaring, it's the phone. It's the Civil Defence Authorities and it's very urgent.

MAINWARING Right. Jones, take the parade. Wilson, come with me. I don't trust you out of my sight. (**To the Vicar, as he passes**) I'll deal with you later.

Mainwaring and Wilson cross into the office.

WILSON (**As he goes**) It really is most awfully kind of you to ask me.

MAINWARING Wilson.

SIDE OFFICE

They go into the office. Mainwaring picks up the phone.

MAINWARING Yes?

Cut to Warden.

WARDEN Hodges here. Now look here, Mainwaring, I represent the breakaway committee.

Intercut between Mainwaring and Warden.

MAINWARING Breakaway from what?

WARDEN From you, mate. You think you run this town. Well, we're not having it any more. We want the sergeant to present the key.

MAINWARING Just hold on one minute, will you? **(He covers the mouthpiece)** Wilson, tell this man once and for all that you are not presenting that key.

WILSON Aren't I?

MAINWARING Tell him.

WILSON **(Taking the phone)** Once and for all I am not presenting that key.

MAINWARING **(Snatching the phone back)** Good day to you. **(He puts the phone down and rounds on Wilson)** You've engineered all this, haven't you?

WILSON Believe me, I wish it had never happened. I didn't ask to belong to the golf club, I don't want to go to church, I'm getting begging letters and Mrs Pike wants me to buy a pipe, a tweed hat and a Labrador. Life just isn't worth living any more.

MAINWARING Don't give me all that soft soap. You're revelling in it. Anybody would. Why, if I had that title, I'd be on the board of directors of this bank, not managing a tinpot branch with a crackpot clerk.

Wilson reacts.

MAINWARING Well, from now on just watch your step, Wilson. Remember Jones' words.

WILSON Which particular words did you have in mind?

MAINWARING I've got three of these and you've only got three of those. I'm presenting that key. And do you know what you're going to do? *You're* going to ride that motorcycle. And I'm going to supervise you – in person. And I'll tell you when you can smoke.

FILM: OUTSIDE THE HALL

Walker is tinkering with the motorcycle, which is a mid-thirties model.

WALKER There you are – with a full tank, very nearly.

PIKE Captain Mainwaring, if he falls off and breaks his leg, can I have it for a bit please?

MAINWARING Do be quiet, Pike. Why is he taking so long?

FRAZER He's putting on his protective clothing, sir.

Cut to Wilson emerging. He wears old overalls, large leather driving gloves, flying helmet and goggles. He is attended by Jones.

WALKER Blimey – Amy Johnson.

MAINWARING Right, get him on.

Wilson climbs on to the bike.

MAINWARING You've time for a good one-hour spin before you need to get ready for the ceremony.

WILSON Wouldn't ten minutes be enough?

MAINWARING Just get on with it.

JONES Now remember – squeeze the clutch with your left hand, kick upwards on to the gear with your right foot, like this, rev up with your right hand by doing this sort of motion, thrum thrum, thrum thrum, and then let out the clutch with your left hand, like you was unsqueezing a lemon.

Wilson revs up and shoots off. They watch him go.

GODFREY Do you think I should follow on a bicycle with this? **(He holds up the Red Cross bag)**

MAINWARING No, it's time he learnt to fend for himself.

Cut to long shot of Wilson zig-zagging along a country road. Mid long shot of the Vicar cycling along a road. The motorcycle comes along the road and wobbles very close to the Vicar, causing him to ride off the road into a tree. The motorcycle wobbles away.

VICAR Oh, you silly man!

Cut to long shot of Wilson heading across fields. Long shot of road, a staff car – preferably an army Humber – is progressing. Wilson comes out of the farm gate, turns into the same direction as the car and then goes into a ditch. The driver stops and gets out to help him, closely followed by the Russian and his interpreter.

FILM: LONG SHOT OF SCENE OF CEREMONY.

This should preferably be in an attractive village green setting. There is a small platform with the canopy decked in bunting and flags. The ceremonial key is on the table, with a microphone. The mayor, Mrs Mayor, Mrs Fox, the Vicar are seated. There are chairs for the Russian, the interpreter, Mainwaring, the colonel and the town clerk. The Home Guard are drawn up, so are about a dozen nurses, ten wardens. The town band is at the ready. Mainwaring is adjusting Pike's belt.

PIKE If you've killed my Uncle Arthur, Mum'll never let you hear the end of it.

MAINWARING Silence in the ranks, Pike.

WALKER It's not like him not to telephone, or something.

The colonel and the town clerk approach Mainwaring.

TOWN CLERK Is everything ready, Captain Mainwaring?

MAINWARING Of course. Everything will go like clockwork.

TOWN CLERK I hope that I didn't offend you by suggesting that the Honourable Arthur Wilson should do the handing over.

They stroll towards the band.

MAINWARING I'm not a vindictive man, Mr Town Clerk.

COLONEL Where is Wilson?

MAINWARING He hasn't returned from his motorcycle training yet. He has his good points but he's not one hundred per cent reliable, you know.

COLONEL Who'll command the platoon while you're performing the ceremony?

MAINWARING Corporal Jones.

COLONEL Will he be all right?

MAINWARING Oh yes, a first class man.

COLONEL That looks like the staff car.

Cut to long shot of the same staff car approaching. It contains the Russian, female interpreter, Wilson, driver and official.

MAINWARING Stand by, everyone.

Right behind them the band starts up with 'The Red Flag'.

MAINWARING Not yet. Wait until the car door opens.

Long shot as the car stops. Mid long shot of Jones and the platoon.

JONES Number One Platoon – ground arms!

They ground arms. Two hands readily assist Frazer and Jones to rise.

JONES Clapping and greeting the Russian visitor – begin.

They applaud. The band starts up 'The Red Flag'. The driver opens the car door, and the Russian, the interpreter and the official, escorted by Mainwaring, move to the dais. This takes one chorus, by which time they are all seated. The band starts the second chorus. Warden follows Mainwaring up steps.

MAINWARING Not you! **(Waving them to desist)** That'll be quite enough of that. **(He moves to his place)**

TOWN CLERK Pray silence for the mayor of Walmington-on-Sea.

Everybody applauds.

MAINWARING **(Aside to colonel)** He's promised to be very brief.

MAYOR Mr Vladislovski – on behalf of Walmington-on-Sea – welcome. **(He sits down)**

COLONEL He kept his promise.

INTERPRETER **(In Russian)** Welcome.

The Russian shrugs his shoulders. Mainwaring rises.

MAINWARING Mr Vladislovski. You and I are united in our common struggle although we live poles apart.

WALKER **(To Jones)** He would have to mention the Poles.

Interpreter translates what Mainwaring has said into Russian.

MAINWARING We greet you as a brother in arms and we are honoured to present to you…

The interpreter starts translating.

MAINWARING Look, I haven't finished the sentence yet. We are honoured to present to you this key, which symbolises the Freedom of Walmington-on-Sea.

The Russian pushes away the key and rises.

RUSSIAN **(In Russian)** I represent the workers of the Soviet Union.

INTERPRETER **(Immediately after him)** I represent the workers of the Soviet Union.

Mainwaring and co. applaud.

MRS FOX Hear, hear.

RUSSIAN & INTERPRETER You people sitting here are not workers. Your faces are soft, your hands are soft. You are bourgeois middle class.

MAINWARING **(To colonel)** Damned cheek.

RUSSIAN & INTERPRETER And you honour me. Better you should honour your own workers.

He moves off swiftly with the interpreter towards the car. Mainwaring ,at a loss, moves after him with the key. Followed by the town clerk, the mayor, the colonel and all on the dais.

MAINWARING **(To band leader)** Play the music.

They strike up 'The Red Flag'. The Russian opens the door and drags out Wilson, who is in his overalls, distinctly grubby, but without the helmet and gloves. The band fade off.

RUSSIAN & INTERPRETER Here is a man in the uniform, not of an officer, an imperialist, but of a slave worker.

WILSON Sorry I'm late.

RUSSIAN & INTERPRETER He has the dirt of the worker on his hands, he has the sweat of the worker on his brow, he shall have your honour.

He grabs the key and hands it to Wilson.

WILSON I say. Thank you so much. **(To Mainwaring)** Awfully kind of you, sir.

The interpreter and the Russian get into the car, slam the door and it drives off. The band start up 'The Red Flag' again.

MAINWARING **(Yells at them)** Oh, shut up!

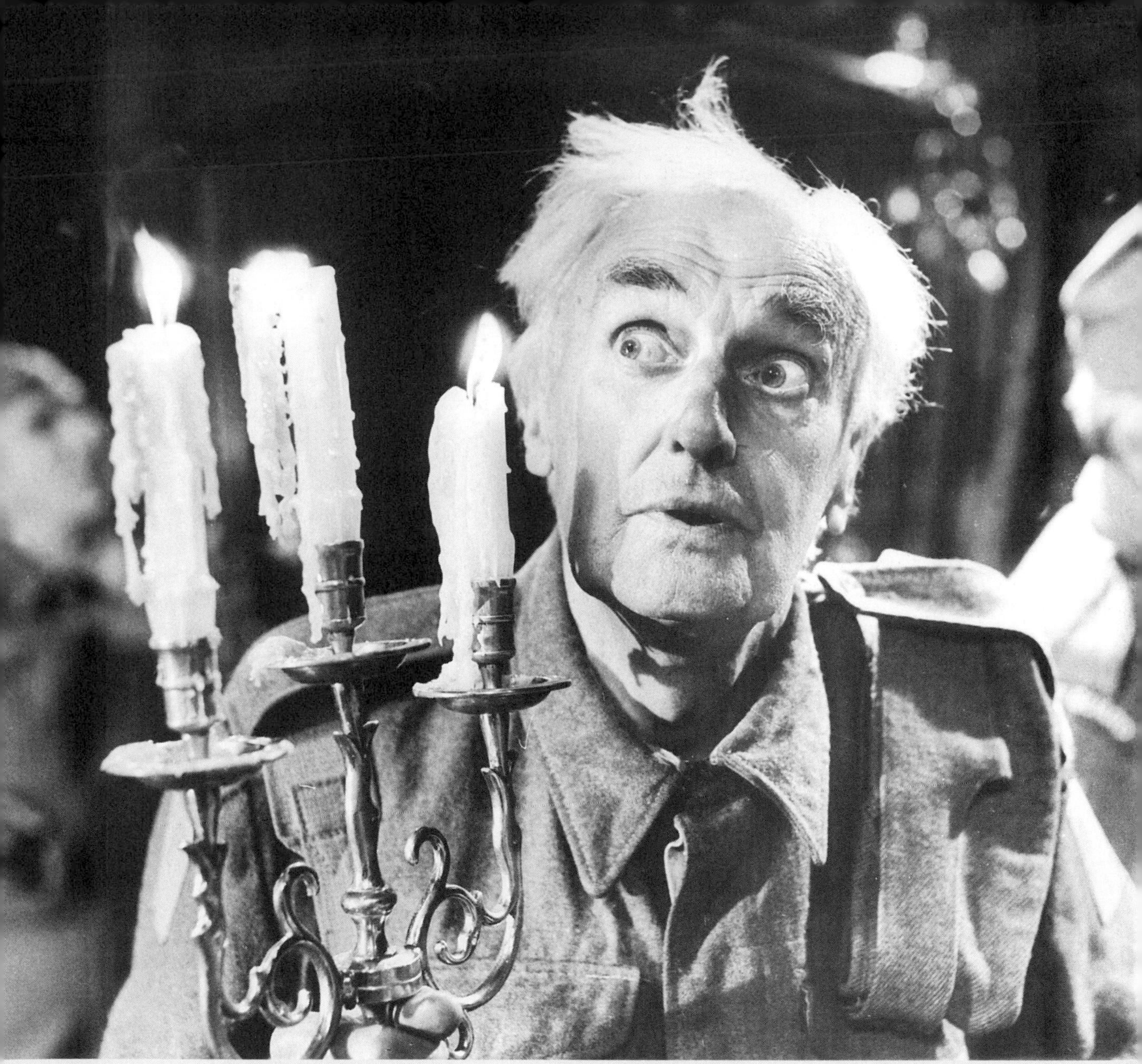

Things That Go Bump in the Night

SERIES SIX **EPISODE SIX**

Recorded: Sunday 15/7/73

Original transmission: Wednesday 5/12/73, 6.50–7.20pm

Original viewing figures = 12.2 million

ARTHUR LOWE .... CAPTAIN MAINWARING
JOHN LE MESURIER .... SERGEANT WILSON
CLIVE DUNN................................ LANCE CORPORAL JONES
JOHN LAURIE .... PRIVATE FRAZER
JAMES BECK .... PRIVATE WALKER
ARNOLD RIDLEY .... PRIVATE GODFREY
IAN LAVENDER .... PRIVATE PIKE
JONATHAN CECIL................................ CAPTAIN CADBURY
COLIN BEAN .... PRIVATE SPONGE
PLATOON .... GEORGE HANCOCK (PRIVATE HANCOCK)
.... AND DESMOND CULLUM-JONES (PRIVATE DESMOND)

• JOHNATHAN CECIL REMEMBERS •

'It is now hard to believe but I nearly passed up the opportunity of appearing in *Dad's Army*. I had just played two important London theatre roles and, devoted as I was to the series, my impression was that its guest parts were very small.

'It was my late father – David Cecil, the writer and academic – who decided me: "You must be in *Dad's Army*. It's the best thing on television!"

'And when the script arrived I was, of course, delighted with dotty Captain Cadbury. Oddly enough, I didn't find the regulars' lines especially funny on the page. It was only when I heard them spoken by their characters that I appreciated David and Jimmy's unique talent in writing for specific actors.

'On my first day's filming I plunged straight into the barmy pep talk to the bloodhounds. I shall always be grateful to Arthur Lowe for suggesting a cut-away shot of him and John reacting to me as if to ask, "What have we here?"

'This helped to establish my character instantly, and a great *Dad's Army* delight was how everybody helped each other. The regulars – disparate as they were – all found each other hilarious. Time after time in rehearsal Mainwaring's pomposity convulsed everyone – including Arthur.

'It was difficult to get the bloodhounds – docile creatures – to chase us, and when they finally set off it was in quite the wrong direction. As they vanished over the horizon, dear John Le Mesurier murmured to me in his best languid Wilson tones: "This doesn't seem to be an entire success." The actor and his role were near-identical.

'Looking back over some forty years in television, theatre and films I don't think I have ever had more fun than in that brief time I spent with the wondrous team of *Dad's Army*.'

Things That Go Bump in the Night

TELECINE: EXTERIOR. COUNTRY ROAD. NIGHT

A rough, country road. Jones' van lurches into sight. It is raining very hard with thunder and lightning. In the background are the gates of an old country house. If possible, we see the drive leading up to a Tudor house. The van stops outside the gates.

INTERIOR. STUDIO. INSIDE THE VAN. NIGHT

Jones is driving. Mainwaring is sitting beside him, and Wilson is sitting on the left, holding a map. He is peering at it with a torch.

MAINWARING Where are we, Wilson?

WILSON Well, according to my calculations, we should be outside Jones' butcher's shop in the High Street.

MAINWARING You mean you're lost, Wilson. (**Blows his nose, he has a slight head cold**)

WILSON I wouldn't say that I was the only one that was lost, I think we all are.

MAINWARING (**Gives Wilson a glare**) How much petrol have we got left, Jones?

JONES (**Looking at dial**) About half a gallon, sir.

MAINWARING Half a... Walker!

Walker's head appears at the hatch with Pike and Frazer.

WALKER Yes, Captain Mainwaring.

MAINWARING I thought you filled the tank up yesterday?

WALKER So I did.

MAINWARING Well, why is it empty?

WALKER Ah, well... you see, I had a customer who wanted four gallons urgent, so I took some out.

MAINWARING How dare you tamper with my fuel?

WALKER You didn't pay me for it. You know my terms, cash on delivery.

MAINWARING Take his name, Wilson.

WILSON Yes, sir.

WALKER Walker.

Wilson writes Walker's name on the window with his finger. Mainwaring sneezes.

JONES That's a nasty cold you've got, sir, you should be in bed.

MAINWARING Never mind about that, the point is we can't sit here cooped up in this van all night, we'd better go up to the house and get some help.

JONES You're not going out in this pouring rain, with that cold of yours, Mr Mainwaring, you'll catch pneumonia.

MAINWARING Don't talk rubbish, now let me out. (**Mainwaring starts to move, Jones grapples with him**) What are you doing?

JONES I must restrain you, sir, I will not allow you to catch pneumonia.

MAINWARING Nonsense, drop of rain won't hurt me.

FRAZER Jones is right, sir, I knew a man once, just about your age and build he was, had a slight head cold and he got caught in the rain. Five days later I was screwing the handles on his coffin.

WALKER I know how to get you up to that house without getting wet, Mr Mainwaring. Hang on a tick.

TELECINE: EXTERIOR. COUNTRY ROAD. NIGHT

Walker and Frazer come round from the back of the van. Above them is a tarpaulin about 8 feet square. It is supported at each corner by Sponge, Hastings, Desmond and Pike. They have their bayonets on their rifles and these are stuck through the tarpaulin. They shuffle round to the door of the cab.

WALKER Right, Mr Mainwaring, you can get out. Come on, Jonesey – get down.

Jones gets down.

JONES It's all right, Mr Mainwaring, you won't get wet, Joe has rigged up a great big cantaloupe. Come on, sir, I'll help you down. Hold it steady, Pikey.

PIKE I am holding it steady.

JONES No you're not, you're joggling it, and it's dripping on Mr Mainwaring, don't get any drips on the officer. (**He paws Mainwaring**)

MAINWARING Stop mauling me about, Jones.

JONES I must protect your welfare, sir, I will not have you having pneumonia.

MAINWARING Get down, Wilson.

WILSON Just coming, sir. Isn't this nice? How awfully clever of you, Walker.

They are all standing in a tight bunch.

JONES Now, if we all walk in a line close together we won't get wet. You get in the front, sarge, that will stop the drips going on Mr Mainwaring. (**He pushes Wilson into position**) And you get behind him, sir and put your arms round his waist. (**He pushes Mainwaring**)

MAINWARING Now, just a minute, Jones, I am in command here, and I give the orders.

JONES I assure you, sir, I have no intention of uslurping your officership, but I must keep you dry.

WILSON Better do as he says, sir, after all we don't want to get wet. I don't mind you putting your arms round my waist.

JONES Right, Joe, you get behind Mr Mainwaring. Jock, you put your arms round Joe. **(He pushes them about)**

FRAZER I don't like this very much.

JONES And I'll put my arms round you. **(He gets behind Frazer)**

FRAZER Now I'm certain I don't like it.

JONES Are we all ready? And don't forget to keep in step. By the left, quick march. Left, right, left, right…

They shuffle forward.

WILSON I feel rather like the Emperor of China in *Aladdin*.

WALKER I feel like I'm at a Jewish wedding.

MAINWARING Just a minute.

JONES Halt. Are you getting drips on you, sir? I told you not to joggle it, Pike.

PIKE I'm not joggling it.

MAINWARING Where's Godfrey?

FRAZER He's in the back of the van, sleeping like a baby.

MAINWARING We'd better go and get him.

JONES Right, sir. By the left, quick march, left, right, left, right, right wheel, right wheel.

They shuffle round in a crocodile towards the back of the van. Walker makes a noise like a railway train.

MAINWARING That will do, Walker.

TELECINE: EXTERIOR. FRONT DOOR. NIGHT

Mainwaring and co. shuffle into the picture. There is a flash of lightning and a heavy clap of thunder. The tarpaulin has a lot of water in the top.

JONES Halt!

WILSON Well, sir, we made it, and we're as dry as a bone.

MAINWARING I suppose you're right, well done, Jones, Walker. We should be grateful that none of us have got wet. All right, Pike, ring the bell.

PIKE Yes, Mr Mainwaring.

Pike lowers his rifle, all the water in the tarpaulin pours on top of him.

MAINWARING Don't play the fool, Pike.

PIKE You told me to ring the bell, I'm wet through. Look! **(He shakes his tunic)**

MAINWARING Well, don't shake it all over me.

JONES Yes, stop shaking it all over Mr Mainwaring.

MAINWARING Knock on the door, Wilson.

WILSON Right, sir. **(There is a huge brass knocker on the door. He knocks and the door swings slowly open with a creak)** Look, sir, it's open.

MAINWARING Well, let's get in, I'm not standing out here in the pouring rain.

WILSON But we can't walk into a strange house without being invited.

Mainwaring goes in. The rest troop after him.

INTERIOR. HALL. NIGHT

A large, oak-panelled hall, with several doors leading off. On the right is a staircase. On the stairs are three tabards hanging on poles. The only furniture is a heavy oak chest, with two four-arm candelabras on it. On the floor is a bearskin with the head on. Mainwaring and co. come into the picture.

MAINWARING **(Striking match)** Hello – hello – anyone at home? Turn the lights on, Wilson.

WILSON Right. **(He flicks his lighter and crosses to the light switch)** They don't work, sir.

MAINWARING Light those candles, Walker. Hello, is there anyone about? **(Silence)** Now listen, all keep absolutely quiet, so that we can hear if anyone answers. Hello! **(Silence except for Pike's teeth chattering)** I told you to keep quiet, Pike.

PIKE I can't help it, I'm freezing.

WILSON I really think he ought to get those wet clothes off, sir.

PIKE What am I going to put on? I'm not standing around naked.

Jones' mouth moves.

MAINWARING Eh?

Jones mimes.

MAINWARING I can't hear a word, come here.

JONES Permission to speak, sir? He could wear one of those flag things. **(Points to the tabards)**

MAINWARING Good idea, get one down. Give him a hand, Walker. Right, boy, take your clothes off.

PIKE I don't like to.

WILSON Now come on, Frank, do as you're told.

PIKE Oh, all right, but don't look. Don't look.

They all turn their backs on him so that he is hidden from the view of the audience. Mainwaring draws Wilson aside.

MAINWARING You know, Wilson, I think that boy's going soft in the head. And the way you mollycoddle him only makes him worse.

WILSON Well, I feel sort of responsible for him, sir. If I don't look after him, Mavis – that's Mrs Pike – goes round with a miserable look on her face all the time, and, you know, I just can't stand people looking miserable.

Mainwaring reacts, Frazer comes into the picture holding a candelabra.

FRAZER **(Rolling his eyes)** Captain Mainwaring, can you no feel a strange atmosphere in this house. I tell you there's something amiss, something strangely amiss.

MAINWARING Oh, stop rolling your eyes like that, Frazer, and pull yourself together. There's obviously a perfectly logical explanation for all this.

During this dialogue Walker and Jones have taken down the tabard, Pike has put it on. He pushes his way through the men and we see him for the first time. The tabard comes just above his knees and it is open at the sides. He is just wearing his underpants, boots and socks.

PIKE I don't half feel silly, Mr Mainwaring.

WALKER I think he looks quite a card.

GODFREY Personally, I think it looks rather nice.

WALKER I bet it ain't half draughty round the how's your father.

PIKE I'm freezing to death, Mr Mainwaring.

MAINWARING For goodness sake, stop whining, Pike, we shall just have to improvise. **(He picks up the bearskin and puts it on Pike)** This will keep you warm. Now, come on, we'd better explore the house.

PIKE Mr Mainwaring – Grrh!

MAINWARING Stupid boy. **(He picks up one of the candelabras. Frazer picks up the other. They all cross over the hall. They try door)**

MAINWARING We'd better try upstairs.

Suddenly there is a terrible howl of a dog. They all freeze in a tight group. There is a second howl.

JONES Permission to whisper, sir? There's something horrible about.

MAINWARING It's only a dog. Come on.

They move to foot of stairs. They reach first landing.

FRAZER That's no ordinary dog, it's a hound.

MAINWARING A hound.

There is a whole chorus of howls.

FRAZER A whole pack of them.

JONES There's a whole pack of horrible hounds, don't panic, don't panic.

MAINWARING Quiet, Jones.

GODFREY I really think we ought to get back in the van, I just don't get on with dogs, even little dogs, they upset me. My sister Dolly had a Pekinese once, it used to jump up at me an awful lot. In the end I had to order it to leave.

MAINWARING Those dogs are outside somewhere, they can't harm us. Come on, we're going upstairs. **(He leads**

the way, holding the candelabra, followed by Wilson, Jones, Pike, Walker, Frazer and Godfrey, Sponge. Hancock and Desmond bring up the rear, carrying their rifles. Walker is carrying Pike's rifle)

INTERIOR. LANDING OUTSIDE BEDROOM DOOR. NIGHT

Mainwaring and co. creep along. Mainwaring opens the bedroom door, it creaks back, they go in.

INTERIOR. BEDROOM. NIGHT

A large, oak-panelled room. It is furnished with a large, four-poster bed, single bed in corner, a wash stand with large basin

and jug on it, large Chesterfield and rocking chair by the fireplace. There is a warming pan hanging on the wall and a fire is burning brightly in the grate. Mainwaring and co. come into the room.

MAINWARING Anybody here? **(He holds up the candelabra)** This really is most strange, Wilson, the house must be empty.

WILSON Whoever was here must have left suddenly, look, the fire's still burning.

FRAZER **(Rolling his eyes)** The question is Captain Mainwaring, what made them leave? An old house – the fire still burning in the grate and nobody about. Nothing except the wind and rain and those ghostly hounds howling, howling, howling. Why are they howling? Are they of this mortal world or are they the hounds of hell?

MAINWARING I told you to stop rolling your eyes. All right, Pike, dry your clothes by the fire.

PIKE Yes, Mr Mainwaring. **(He crosses to the fire and spreads out his clothes)**

MAINWARING Now, pay attention, men, it's quite on the cards that this storm may last all night. We don't know where we are, and we haven't got any petrol. So we shall just have to make the best of a bad job, and settle down here for the night. I'll take this bed. **(He crosses to the single bed, takes off his hat and belt. The men all stare at him in silence. He sits on the bed and takes off his boots and gaiters)**

MAINWARING **(He gestures to them)** Make yourselves comfortable, men.

WILSON Where am I going to sleep, sir?

MAINWARING **(Pointing to the four-poster)** In that bed.

WILSON Well, where are the others going to sleep?

MAINWARING In that bed with you.

WILSON But that's absurd.

MAINWARING **(Lowering his voice and hissing at Wilson)** You know, Wilson, you really are the most selfish man I have ever met. What gives you the right to think that you should have a bed to yourself?

WILSON Well, I err...

MAINWARING That's settled then. Right, five of you can sleep in that bed with Sergeant Wilson. N.C.O.s at the top, other ranks at the bottom. **(Wilson reacts)** The other two can sleep on the settee. Right, settle down.

He sneezes, pulls back the covers and starts to get into bed.

JONES Stop.

He rushes around the room and grabs Mainwaring.

MAINWARING What are you doing?

JONES You can't get in that bed, sir, those sheets are damp. I will not allow you to have pneumonia.

MAINWARING Nonsense.

JONES **(Pushing him on the bed)** You sit there, sir, I'll warm it up.

WALKER What are you going to do, Jonesey?

JONES **(Crossing to the wall and taking down the warming pan)** I'm going to do what those young serving wenches did in days of yore. **(He picks some hot coals out of the fire with the tongs and puts them in the pan)** When they used to warm the bed up for the master.

WALKER I don't think Mr Mainwaring would want to cuddle you all night.

MAINWARING That will do, Walker. This really isn't necessary, Jones.

JONES Let me be the best judge of that, sir. **(He puts the warming pan in the bed)**

MAINWARING Right, get into bed everyone.

Sponge, Hancock and Desmond are standing in a tight group, muttering.

MAINWARING What are you muttering about Sponge? You know how I hate mutterers.

SPONGE We don't see why we should sleep at the bottom of the bed. Can't we toss for it?

MAINWARING Certainly not, now do as you're told and get into bed.

Smoke starts to drift up from the bed.

JONES Look at that steam, Mr Mainwaring, see, I told you the sheets were damp.

MAINWARING You're right, Jones.

WILSON Excuse me, sir, I don't think that's steam, it looks like smoke to me.

MAINWARING What!

WALKER Blimey, the bed's on fire!

MAINWARING Get some water quick.

Walker dashes over to the wash stand, pours the jug of water into the basin. Mainwaring grabs the basin. Walker hands the jug to Pike.

WALKER 'Ere, Pikey, go and get some more water, quick!

Pike drops the bearskin, grabs the jug and rushes out. Mainwaring throws the water on the bed.

MAINWARING Of all the stupid, idiotic things to do, Jones.

JONES I'm sorry, Mr Mainwaring, I was only trying to warm you up.

MAINWARING The bed's wet through. Now where am I going to sleep?

WILSON **(Pointing to the four-poster)** In that bed, sir, Officers and N.C.O.s at the top, other ranks at the bottom.

Mainwaring reacts.

INTERIOR. LANDING. NIGHT

Pike rushes along the landing with the jug of water clutched to his chest.

INTERIOR. BEDROOM. NIGHT

MAINWARING Shut that door, Frazer, it's draughty enough in here as it is.

FRAZER Aye aye.

INTERIOR. LANDING. NIGHT

PIKE I've got it… **(He reaches the door, it slams in his face breaking the jug. The water goes all over him)** Oh, Mr Mainwaring, I'm all wet again.

INTERIOR. BEDROOM. NIGHT

Pike is sitting in the rocking chair, he has a sheet round him with the bearskin on top. He is sucking his thumb, rocking and shivering. He gets up and crosses to the four-poster. Wilson, Jones, Walker and Mainwaring are asleep at the top, at the bottom Sponge, Hancock and Desmond.

PIKE **(Whispering)** Uncle Arthur. **(He leans right over Wilson, the bear's head is just above his own and he sticks it right in Wilson's face. He shakes Wilson)**

WILSON **(Waking up)** Arrah.

PIKE It's all right, it's only me.

WILSON Go back to sleep. **(He closes his eyes)**

PIKE Uncle Arthur.

WILSON What?

PIKE Can I come into bed with you please?

WILSON You'd better ask Mr Mainwaring.

PIKE **(Shaking Jones)** Mr Jones, ask Mr…

Jones wakes up and sees the bear's head.

JONES **(Waking up)** Oh no – it's a horrible hound, it's a horrible hound.

PIKE It's only me, Mr Jones.

JONES Oh blimey, I thought my end had come.

PIKE Ask Mr Mainwaring if I can come into bed.

JONES **(Shaking Joe)** Wake up, Joe.

WALKER What's the matter?

JONES Ask Mr Mainwaring if Pikey can come into bed with us.

WALKER **(Shaking Mainwaring)** Captain Mainwaring.

MAINWARING **(Opening his eyes)** Yes.

WALKER Can Frank come into bed with us?

MAINWARING Certainly not, there's no room. **(He goes straight back to sleep)**

WALKER **(To Jones)** He says there's no room.

JONES **(To Wilson)** He says there's no room.

WILSON **(To Pike)** He says there's no room.

PIKE All right, I heard.

WILSON I'm sorry, Frank, if it was up to me I'd let you in, but he's the officer.

PIKE Well come with me to the bathroom, I've got to wash my hands and clean my teeth. You know Mum won't let me go to bed without washing my hands and cleaning my teeth.

WILSON But you haven't got a toothbrush.

PIKE Well, I'll just rinse my mouth out. You've got to come with me, I'm not going on my own.

WILSON Oh really.

PIKE If you don't come I'll tell Mum.

WILSON Oh all right. **(Gets out of bed and picks up the candelabra. Pike drops the bearskin and wraps the sheet tightly round himself. They go out of the room. Cut to Godfrey and Frazer on the Chesterfield, Frazer is asleep)**

GODFREY **(Shaking him)** Mr Frazer.

FRAZER What's the matter?

GODFREY I've got to go to the little boy's room, would you mind coming with me please?

FRAZER Nothing would make me move from this room. There's too many unnatural causes.

GODFREY Well, I'm worried about natural causes.

FRAZER No!

Godfrey gets up, picks up the candelabra and crosses to Mainwaring and shakes him.

MAINWARING **(Opening his eyes)** Yes?

GODFREY I wonder if you'd mind accompanying me to the bathroom, sir?

MAINWARING Certainly not. **(Mainwaring goes straight back to sleep)**

Godfrey moves to Jones. Jones grabs him.

GODFREY Will you accompany me to the bathroom?

JONES **(Opening his eyes)** I'll come with you, Mr Godfrey.

GODFREY Oh thank you so much, I'm very grateful.

Jones gets out of bed, picks up a bayonet from the pile of kit.

JONES I'll take this with me, and if we meet one of those horrible hounds I'll let him have it right up.

INTERIOR. CORNER OF PASSAGE. NIGHT

Pike wrapped in the sheet, behind him Wilson is holding the candelabra. They creep towards the corner. From the other direction we can see Jones and Godfrey, Jones is holding a bayonet, Godfrey, the candelabra. The two pairs creep towards each other. Jones comes round the corner and comes face to face with Pike wrapped in the sheet.

INTERIOR. BEDROOM. NIGHT

Close up of candles burning, pan round the room. They are all asleep.

INTERIOR. HALL. NIGHT

Close up of bottom of door, it opens slowly with a creak. A shaft of light from the torch shines on a pair of wellington boots. The boots come through the door, move across the hall and mount the stairs. They go up, the stairs creak.

INTERIOR. BEDROOM. NIGHT

Pike wakes up, he crosses to the bed and shakes Wilson.

PIKE Wake up, Uncle Arthur.

WILSON **(Opening his eyes)** Oh, for goodness sake, go back to sleep, Frank.

PIKE I can hear someone coming up the stairs. Listen.

WILSON You'd better wake Captain Mainwaring up.

INTERIOR. STAIRS. NIGHT

The boots continue up the stairs, and reach the top, they pause and go along the landing towards the bedroom door.

INTERIOR. BEDROOM. NIGHT

Mainwaring is standing at the bottom of the bed clutching his revolver, the others are gathered round him in a tight group clutching rifles and bayonets.

WILSON Whatever it is, sir, I think it's coming towards this room.

JONES It can't be a horrible hound, the footsteps are too heavy.

MAINWARING Quiet, blow those candles out.

They extinguish the candles. The door handle slowly turns and the door opens, a bony hand comes round the edge and reaches for the light switch. The room is flooded with light. Captain Cadbury, a tall, thin, silly ass about 25, is standing in the doorway.

CAPTAIN CADBURY I say, what are you doing in my bedroom?

INTERIOR. KITCHEN. DAY

Mainwaring, Wilson, Jones, Walker, Frazer, Godfrey, Sponge, Hastings and Desmond are standing round a long table with Captain Cadbury drinking tea, laughing and chatting.

WILSON Well, I must say, sir, you gave us quite a fright last night.

CADBURY Sorry about that, if the storm hadn't put the lights out of action, I wouldn't have been outside tinkering with the generator when you arrived.

MAINWARING So those were your dogs we heard?

CADBURY Yes, the storm must have upset them.

JONES What do you use them for, sir?

CADBURY This is a dog training school, we train tracker dogs for the War Department.

FRAZER I knew it was something of that description.

CADBURY We're a bit slack at the moment, so I've given the rest of the staff weekend leave.

The door opens, Pike comes in. He is dressed in a tatty German uniform.

WALKER Blimey, look what the cat's dragged in.

WILSON What on earth are you dressed like that for, Frank?

PIKE My uniform's still wet, the captain lent me this.

CAPTAIN It was the only thing I had I'm afraid, it's an old German uniform we use for training.

MAINWARING Well we'd better go and get that petrol.

CADBURY I'll show you the way, it's only about a mile if we take a short cut across the fields. Sorry I haven't got a can, but there's stacks of empty gin bottles in the yard.

MAINWARING We'd better take plenty, we'll carry one

each. Right, men, brisk walk across the fields will do us the world of good. You'd better stay here, Godfrey.

GODFREY I'd rather come with you, if you don't mind, sir, I don't want to be left alone with those dogs.

TELECINE: EXTERIOR. YARD. DAY

Five large dogs are growling and barking in a wire pen. Captain Cadbury, followed by Mainwaring and co. carrying a gin bottle each, come into the picture. The captain talks to the dogs as if they were soldiers.

CADBURY Quiet! Settle down at once.

The dogs all stop barking.

MAINWARING You seem to have them well under control, sir.

CADBURY These are only half-trained raw recruits. The fully trained batch left yesterday. They're not a bad bunch really, except for that one. **(He points to the largest dog who has a surly look on his face)** Prince 439, he's a troublemaker, upsets the others. You, 439, stand to attention when I'm talking to you. **(Dog snarls)** Absolute slacker, failed the course three times, had him on a charge twice. If he fails this time he'll be out on his ear. You know how it is, if you get one rotten apple in the barrel.

MAINWARING Quite, sir. Fall the men in, Sergeant.

WILSON Right, sir. Fall in.

The men fall in, in a single line.

WILSON Excuse me, sir, do you want us to carry our gin bottles at the slope?

Mainwaring gives him a glare.

TELECINE: EXTERIOR. A FIELD. DAY

The men are marching in a single line with Jones at the back. Mainwaring, Cadbury and Wilson are walking beside them.

WILSON **(To Captain)** It's a really lovely morning, isn't it, sir?

CADBURY Absolutely first class.

MAINWARING What exactly are those dogs of yours for?

CADBURY They're trained to track down German parachutists.

WILSON You must have quite a way with dogs.

CADBURY Not really, I'm scared stiff of them, I don't have anything to do with the training, I just run the admin. **(We can hear the dogs barking in the distance)**

MAINWARING Open the gate, Walker.

JONES Those dogs of yours have certainly got loud voices, sir.

CADBURY Yes, they carry for miles.

MAINWARING What happens when the dogs have tracked down a parachutist?

CADBURY They hold him until the troops arrive. That is when they're fully trained. At the moment they've only completed half the course, the tracking bit.

WILSON What's the second half of the course?

CADBURY The holding, that's the most difficult part. We have to train them not to tear the victim to pieces.

GODFREY Captain Mainwaring, can we stop for a minute please?

MAINWARING Oh really, Godfrey, all right.
Section, halt.

They all stop.

FRAZER You silly old fool, you should have stayed behind, I knew you wouldn't be able to keep up.

MAINWARING That will do, Frazer.

The dogs get louder.

WALKER Those dogs are definitely getting louder, sir.

WILSON I think Walker's right.

MAINWARING Quiet, listen.

More dogs.

CADBURY They must have got out. I bet it's that troublemaker, Prince.

WILSON They won't come after us, will they?

CADBURY I don't see why they... Oh Lord... **(Points to Pike)** That uniform, the boy's wearing, it's soaked in aniseed.

MAINWARING Aniseed! Get it off Pike.

PIKE I'm not going to...

MAINWARING Don't argue, get it off. **(He grapples with Pike)**

CADBURY Now you're covered in the stuff, Mainwaring.

Mainwaring quickly jumps back.

MAINWARING Can't you control those dogs?

CADBURY Of course I can't.

JONES The horrible hounds are after us, and he can't control them, he can't control them. Don't panic!

MAINWARING What are we going to do?

CADBURY There's only one thing we can do.

MAINWARING What?

CADBURY Run!

PIKE What's aniseed?

TELECINE: EXTERIOR. A FIELD. DAY

The five dogs are running in full cry.

TELECINE: EXTERIOR. A FIELD. DAY

Mainwaring and co. are running, Godfrey is trailing behind.

MAINWARING Keep up, Godfrey.

GODFREY **(Stopping)** It's no use, Mr Mainwaring, I can't go another step.

They all stop.

JONES What are we going to do, sir? We can't leave poor old Mr Godfrey here to get torn to pieces by those horrible hounds.

Walker points to a stack of hurdles.

WALKER 'Ere, why don't we put him on one of those sheep things and drag him along?

MAINWARING Well done, Walker. Sponge, Desmond, get one of those sheep things.

TELECINE: EXTERIOR. HEDGE. DAY

The dogs burst through the hedge.

TELECINE: EXTERIOR. FIELD. DAY

Long shot of Mainwaring and co. running, Godfrey is being dragged behind on a hurdle.

TELECINE: EXTERIOR. GATE INTO FIELD. DAY

The dogs come through the gate.

TELECINE: EXTERIOR. STREAM. DAY

The men are all sitting on the ground taking off their boots.

MAINWARING Hurry up with those boots – put them on the hurdle.

WILSON Aren't you going to get your boots off, sir?

MAINWARING No, I'm not getting my feet wet with this cold of mine.

JONES That's right, sir, you don't want to catch pneumonia, as well as getting torn to pieces.

MAINWARING You can carry me on the hurdle – Godfrey can walk that little bit.

They all put their boots on the hurdle and pick it up. Godfrey and Mainwaring get on it. Wilson, Jones, Walker, Sponge, Hastings, Desmond and Cadbury pick it up and start to wade across the stream. Pike follows.

MAINWARING Not you, Pike, you cross the stream lower down.

PIKE Why do I always have to be the one that…?

MAINWARING Don't argue, boy, do as you're told. It will put the dogs off the scent.

Pike runs about fifty yards downstream and starts to cross.

MAINWARING Hurry up, Wilson, get a move on.

WILSON These stones are awfully sharp under the feet, sir.

JONES Don't joggle it, don't joggle the officer.

There is a loud splash, cut to Pike, he is standing up to his waist in water.

PIKE Mr Mainwaring, I'm all wet again.

Cut back to close up of Mainwaring.

MAINWARING Stupid boy.

TELECINE: EXTERIOR. BUSHES ON TOP OF SLOPE. DAY

They are all putting their boots on, looking down on the stream about a hundred yards away. Pike is wringing the water out of his uniform.

WILSON Did he have to get all wet like this, sir?

MAINWARING It was the only thing we could do. Dogs cannot follow a scent across water, any fool knows that, eh, Captain?

CADBURY Absolutely.

MAINWARING Believe me. I'm a pretty shrewd judge of these things, Wilson.

Cut to the river, the dogs reach the bank, don't hesitate and run straight across. Cut back to Mainwaring.

MAINWARING Run!

TELECINE: EXTERIOR. WOODS. DAY

There are several large trees with low-hanging branches, under one of the trees is a tiny woodsman's hut with no windows, just a door and a sliding shutter in the roof. Mainwaring and co. run into the picture, Mainwaring opens the door of the hut.

MAINWARING Quick, Frazer, Godfrey, Wilson inside. The

rest of you up the trees. **(He follows them in and slams the door. Sponge, Hastings and Desmond get up tree. Walker, Pike and Cadbury get up the one above the hut)**

JONES **(Trying to open door of hut)** Mr Mainwaring, Mr Mainwaring.

MAINWARING **(Out of vision)** You can't come in.

JONES Please open the door, sir.

MAINWARING **(Out of vision)** There's no room, you'll have to get up a tree.

JONES I can't climb trees at my time of life, sir. **(He sees the dogs)** Whoa!

WALKER Quick, Jonesey, up here! **(He hangs down to help Jones who grabs a branch)**

JONES I can't climb trees, Joe.

The leading dog jumps up. There is a tearing sound. Jones is propelled into the tree.

WALKER You can now.

The dogs are all jumping up at the tree and barking.

CADBURY I thought so.

WALKER What?

CADBURY It's that troublemaker, Prince, he's behind it all. **(Shouting down at the dog)** You've had your chips this time, 439. **(Close up of 439 snarling)** You'll be on a fizzer in the morning, and I'll have you out of the camp so fast your feet won't touch the ground.

Dog 439 leaps up. Mainwaring opens the shutter and shouts through it.

MAINWARING Jones, are you there?

JONES Yes, sir, I'm here, well almost all of me. I have to report I've suffered damage in unknown parts.

MAINWARING Stay where you are, I'm going for help. **(He closes the shutter) (Out of vision)** Right, men, lift!

The hut starts to move away.

WILSON **(Out of vision)** Do you think this is wise, sir?

MAINWARING **(Out of vision)** Don't argue, Wilson, keep walking.

The hut moves off with the dogs snapping round it. It goes round in a circle, comes back and bashes into the tree. The shutter opens and Mainwaring's face comes into view.

MAINWARING Look where you're going, Wilson.

CADBURY Captain Mainwaring, if the boy takes his clothes off and throws them to the dogs, that might keep them busy while we sneak away.

MAINWARING Good idea. Right, Pike, take your clothes off and throw them to the dogs.

PIKE No, I won't.

MAINWARING Do as you're told, or you'll be on a charge.

PIKE **(Taking his tunic off)** I'm fed up, fed up, in the past 24 hours I've been soaked to the skin three times, frightened out of my wits, and nearly torn to pieces, and now I've got to walk around naked. **(He starts to take his trousers off and stops)** Don't look. **(Jones, Walker and Cadbury turn their backs. Pike throws the clothes as far as possible away from the tree. The dogs pounce on them and tear them to pieces)**

JONES Blimey, Joe, look, they're tearing that uniform to pieces.

WALKER Good job Pikey wasn't in it.

MAINWARING **(Face through shutter)** Now, all get down and walk away as calmly as possible.

They all get down from the trees. Pike is wearing two gas masks. One in front and the other behind.

JONES **(Knocking on door and whispering)** You can come out now, sir.

The door handle rattles, the door won't open.

MAINWARING **(Out of vision)** It's stuck, give me a hand, Wilson. Come on, push.

WILSON **(Out of vision)** I'm pushing as hard as I can.

FRAZER **(Out of vision)** Ow, that was my foot you trod on.

GODFREY **(Out of vision)** Captain Mainwaring, I must get out quite soon. I'm getting claustrophobic.

MAINWARING **(Out of vision)** This is no use, come on, lift.

The hut moves away, followed by the men.

MAINWARING **(Out of vision)** Now, walk slowly and when I say run, run.

They walk slowly.

MAINWARING **(Out of vision)** Right, run!

They all run, the hut falls over.

TELECINE: EXTERIOR. ROAD. DAY

The men are marching along. Wilson, Cadbury and Mainwaring in front.

MAINWARING Left, right, left, right. **(Shouting back over his shoulder)** Swing those arms, Pike.

Cut to single of Pike in rear, he is wearing a potato sack, with his arms inside. It is tied up tight round his neck.

SERIES SIX **EPISODE SEVEN**

Recorded: Sunday 22/7/73

Original transmission: Wednesday 12/12/73, 6.50–7.20pm

Original viewing figures = 11.5 million

ARTHUR LOWE .... CAPTAIN MAINWARING
JOHN LE MESURIER .... SERGEANT WILSON
CLIVE DUNN.................................. LANCE CORPORAL JONES
JOHN LAURIE .... PRIVATE FRAZER
ARNOLD RIDLEY .... PRIVATE GODFREY
IAN LAVENDER .... PRIVATE PIKE
BILL PERTWEE.................................. CHIEF WARDEN HODGES
FRANK WILLIAMS .... VICAR
EDWARD SINCLAIR.................................. VERGER
SUSAN MAJOLIER.................................. NURSE
LINDSEY DUNN .... HAMISH, THE SMALL BOY
PLATOON .... COLIN BEAN, DESMOND CULLUM-JONES,
.... GEORGE HANCOCK, MICHAEL MOORE,
.... LESLIE NOYES, EVAN ROSS, FREDDIE WHITE,
.... FREDDIE WILES, WILLIAM GOSSLING.
ASSISTANT WARDEN .... JIMMY MAC

Jimmy Beck became ill after 'The Recruit' was written, but before the episode was recorded. The original script for this episode, in which Walker appears, can be read in *The Complete A–Z of Dad's Army*.

The Recruit

• JO AUSTIN REMEMBERS •

'During my time on the series Jimmy Beck died, which was totally traumatic for all of us, all the more so because this was the one unit where we got to know all the wives of the actors as most of them used to join us at weekends. We felt so much sympathy for Kay Beck. While Jimmy was still alive but on life-support machines, we had two more studio recordings and naturally the audiences wanted news. We could hardly tell them the truth that it was just a matter of time so had to keep up a façade of 'slight improvements' in his condition. It was very difficult for the cast – particularly for Arthur Lowe who was very close to Jimmy.

'When it came to recording "The Recruit" David phoned me Saturday evening, the night before the recording, to say Jimmy wouldn't be able to make it. That evening him and Jimmy Perry had to rewrite the script, reallocating the lines they had written for Walker. David asked if I could arrive at Television Centre early on the Sunday because he wanted me to retype the scripts. It was very sad.'

THE RECRUIT

A PRIVATE WARD. WALMINGTON COTTAGE HOSPITAL

Mainwaring is in the only bed, with a small cage under the bedclothes over his feet. He is reading the paper. A young nurse enters.

NURSE How are they feeling now, Mr Mainwaring?

MAINWARING They're throbbing from time to time, but I'm just grinning and bearing it.

NURSE Well, we've got some visitors to cheer you up.

MAINWARING Not Mrs Mainwaring?

NURSE No – it's two gentlemen. **(Calls through the door)** You can come in, he's quite respectable.

Jones puts his head round the door. He is in his civilian clothes.

JONES Can I do you now, sir?

MAINWARING Come in, Jones.

Jones enters, Wilson follows, he is in his bank suit.

MAINWARING Hello, Wilson.

NURSE You can stay till the bell goes.

WILSON **(To her)** Thank you. It was very sweet of you to show us the way.

NURSE That's quite all right, sir.

WILSON And that uniform does suit you most awfully well.

NURSE Thank you, sir.

MAINWARING Thank you, nurse.

WILSON It's that belt – it makes your waist look absolutely tiny.

Nurse reacts.

MAINWARING That'll be all, nurse.

The nurse goes.

MAINWARING They have work to do, Wilson – tending the sick. They've no time to stand around listening to all that Ronald Colman stuff.

Wilson reacts.

JONES I brought these for you, sir.

He presents a small tissue-covered basket, tied with ribbon.

MAINWARING That's very kind of you. Make yourself at home.

Wilson sits on the only chair, Jones sits on the bed and gets up suddenly. Mainwaring removes a revolver from under the pillow.

JONES Hitler's not going to catch you bending, is he ,Mr Mainwaring?

MAINWARING Quite right, Jones. I have to hide it from matron of course. **(He has opened the package)** Great Scott – grapes. I haven't seen them since 1939. **(He takes one and eats it)**

JONES Well, they're not real grapes, sir. We impersonated them out of electric light flex and shaved gooseberries.

MAINWARING **(Who has just bitten a gooseberry and got the sour taste)** I see what you mean.

JONES The gooseberry fur gave us a bit of bother, and then Mr Frazer found a bit of very, very fine glasspaper what he finishes his ten-guinea coffins with and that seemed to answer.

MAINWARING Well, it was very thoughtful of you, Jones. As a matter of fact, I have received some fruit from Mrs Mainwaring.

Wilson picks up an apple, from the side table, to which is attached a label.

WILSON Is this it, sir?

MAINWARING Yes, that's right.

WILSON **(Reading)** 'Get well soon' – isn't that nice?

Mainwaring reacts.

JONES There's something on the back.

WILSON **(Turns over the label)** The Anderson shelter is leaking again.

MAINWARING It'll have to wait till I get back, I'm afraid.

WILSON How is the operation?

MAINWARING Ah, I wanted to talk to you about that – in private. I wonder if you'd mind popping out of the room for a moment, Jones.

JONES Who, me, sir?

MAINWARING Yes, Jones. I have something rather personal to say to Sergeant Wilson.

JONES Of course, sir. **(Goes to door – they wait for him)**

MAINWARING Now, Wilson, I've asked Jones…

JONES I shall be just outside, not quite in earshot.

MAINWARING Thank you, Jones.

Jones goes and closes the door.

MAINWARING Now, Wilson, I asked Jones to pop out because I thought you ought to see my feet.

WILSON **(After some thought)** Why?

MAINWARING I think you should understand the full implications of this whole affair. **(Mainwaring throws off the blanket and takes his feet out of the cage to reveal two bandaged big toes)**

WILSON My my.

MAINWARING Now it's my contention, Wilson, that this is due entirely to active service.

WILSON What? Ingrowing toenails?

MAINWARING There's no doubt about it at all. It's those long hours on duty – they'll never be the same again, you know.

WILSON Are you going to try for a disablement pension?

MAINWARING Oh no, nothing like that – but mark my words, it's all that standing about that's done it.

WILSON You do an awful lot of sitting about as well – have you had any trouble there?

MAINWARING You have a very coarse streak, Wilson. You got it at that public school, I suppose.

WILSON I'm sorry, sir.

MAINWARING I'm simply alerting you to my condition so that you can be on guard against it yourself and on behalf of our troops.

WILSON I'll watch it very carefully.

Mainwaring puts his feet back under the cage.

MAINWARING I shall never mention it again. Come in, Jones.

Jones enters.

JONES I didn't hear a word, sir.

MAINWARING (**Tapping the newspaper**) I'm glad to see our lads are doing so well in the desert. Those Eyeties are no match for Tommy Atkins, eh, Jones?

JONES That's because we've been going in with the cold steel a lot, sir. Those Wops are not used to it, you know, sir. Well, some people never get used to it. I mean, it stands to reason – when you get a great big grenadier guardsman going wher-er wher-er up you like that, very few take kindly to it.

MAINWARING Yes, all right, Jones. How's the platoon, Wilson?

WILSON Oh they're getting along swimmingly.

MAINWARING Really?

WILSON We miss you, of course.

MAINWARING Yes, you're bound to. Unfortunately it looks as if I shall be stuck here for another four days.

JONES Well, don't you fret yourself, Mr Mainwaring. Mr Wilson here is making us carry on as if your invisible presence was with us like a guiding star, only he don't go in for so much bull.

MAINWARING I'm not in favour of bull, Jones, as anyone will tell you. The thing is – are you maintaining discipline?

WILSON Oh yes, sir – I am keeping discipline really rather well – in my own style.

MAINWARING I sincerely hope you are. There's only one way to run an army, Wilson, you must have obedience – instant, unthinking obedience.

SIDE OFFICE

Frazer, Godfrey, Pike and Jones are sitting round the desk where Wilson is sitting in Mainwaring's seat. They are all talking at once.

WILSON Please. Please – one at a time.

GODFREY I'm sorry, Mr Wilson, but I'm afraid I have to say I think you've done the wrong thing.

WILSON I do wish you wouldn't nag so, I've got a terrible headache coming on.

FRAZER The whole idea's doomed – doomed from the start! You can't have vicars in the army. They don't mix, it's like oil and vinegar.

GODFREY It makes very good salad dressing.

PIKE What does?

GODFREY Oil and vinegar – as long as you put the oil in first, or is it the vinegar?

FRAZER Look, I'm not talking about salad dressing. I'm simply saying that when young Arthur here let the Vicar and the Verger join the platoon, he made an idiot of himself – didn't you, son? Admit it, admit it!

WILSON But, Jock, what else could I do? (**He picks up a newspaper**) The story's all here – lots of clergymen have joined.

FRAZER Mark my words, that Verger's a Jonah. He's a face like a sour prune.

GODFREY If Mr Mainwaring had been here I'm sure it wouldn't have happened.

WILSON Well, he isn't here – and he won't be here for another three days. I just wish you wouldn't all go on at me so.

PIKE I think Uncle Arthur did right. Vicars are a good thing sometimes. Look at Spencer Tracy – James Cagney was going to the chair and Spencer Tracy told him to behave like a coward so the dead-end kids wouldn't think he was a hero – and in the end he went shouting and screaming and carrying on something awful – so he died all yellow.

GODFREY Wasn't that Charlie Chan?

JONES We had a padre when I was with Lord Kitchener. He was a hard man Kitchener was and he did a lot of cursing and swearing, and the padre was forever begging him to turn from his evil habits. Anyway, the night before the Battle of Omdurman, he lined us all up and give Kitchener and the rest of us a drum head service. Well, next day, just before the battle was due to start, Kitchener grabbed hold of his binoculars and there on the horizon he saw forty thousand Dervishes chasing towards us. 'Oh my God', he says, and the padre was all smiles, cos he thought he'd done a good job on him.

WILSON Well, it's no good going on and on about it – it's done.

GODFREY **(Looking at watch)** And it's very nearly half past.

WILSON There you are, you see. You really are very naughty all of you. You've kept me chatting here and we should be on parade or something. Now come along, all of you.

Enter the Vicar in Home Guard uniform with dog collar underneath. They start to move towards the hall.

VICAR Sorry I'm late – the confirmation class went on and on and on. Have I missed anything?

WILSON No – we're just going on parade now.

VICAR Oh how very exciting.

The Verger enters in uniform with his usual flat hat. He carries the Vicar's belt.

VERGER You left your belt in the vestry, Your Reverence.

VICAR Oh dear, clumsy me.

WILSON Well, if you're both ready I think we can start.

VICAR Oh goody goody.

Wilson moves into the hall, Vicar turns to the Verger.

VICAR Private Yeatman – hat.

The Verger substitutes a forage cap for his cap.

CHURCH HALL

WILSON **(In hall)** Now, just stand at the end here and try to follow the others, and we'll see how we get on.

Wilson takes up position camera right. Reading right to left they are lined up Jones, Pike, Godfrey, Frazer, Vicar, Verger. Pike carries a violin case.

WILSON Squad. Squad. 'shun! **(Jones, the Vicar and Verger are late)** Stand at ease. **(The same thing happens)** That wasn't awfully good. You see, the general idea is to try to do it all together. Now, let's try again. Squad, 'shun!

There is some improvement.

WILSON Stand at ease. That was quite a lot better.

Mainwaring has entered from the rear door. He comes between Wilson and the platoon. He walks on two sticks and he wears a pair of canvas gym shoes with the toes cut off.

MAINWARING Oh no it wasn't. It was an absolute shambles.

PIKE Ooh look – Hopalong Cassidy.

WILSON We didn't expect you for another three days.

MAINWARING Obviously. Beds were needed for some urgent cases, so I discharged myself and, by the look of things, it's just as well.

JONES Good to see you firmly in the saddle again, sir.

MAINWARING Thank you, Jones.

JONES Even if you are a bit doddery on your pins.

MAINWARING I think I'd better inspect the men, Wilson.

WILSON Yes, sir. Squad...

MAINWARING Wilson.

WILSON Squad...

MAINWARING Wilson – stand further away from my feet.

WILSON I'm sorry, sir. Squad. 'shun!

MAINWARING **(Moving to Jones)** Very smart as usual, Jones.

JONES Thank you, sir. I always try to be smart and very alert, sir. Even though I'm talking to you now, my eyes are darting everywhere, hither and thither in case there should be a lurking danger, and if I detect one little bit of peril, I'm on to it before you can say wher-er-er. **(He grabs Pike by the throat)**

PIKE Aaah. Let go.

JONES What's your game then – what's your game? You moved.

MAINWARING Put him down, Jones.

JONES He moved and I detected him.

PIKE Please, Mr Mainwaring, can I stand next to someone else?

MAINWARING Stay where you are, Pike. **(He sees the violin case)** What's that?

PIKE A violin case, Mr Mainwaring.

MAINWARING A violin case. How dare you come on parade carrying a violin? Take this man's name, Sergeant. **(He turn to Wilson)** Would you please keep away from my feet.

PIKE Mr Mainwaring, I'm not carrying a violin inside it. I'm carrying a Tommy gun like Edward G. Robinson did in *Scarface*. I can whip it out in a second.

MAINWARING Did you know about this, Wilson?

PIKE **(Whipping out the Tommy gun while Mainwaring is looking towards Wilson)** A-a-a-a-a-a-a-a-a...

MAINWARING Pike! My feet!

PIKE I'm sorry, Mr Mainwaring.

MAINWARING **(To Pike)** Don't bring that on parade any more and you'd better see me in the office after. **(He is about to pass Walker and then sees the empty place)** Just a minute. Where's Walker?

PIKE He asked me to leave a note in his place.

MAINWARING **(Mainwaring looks down and sees an envelope on the floor)** Leave a note! Pick it up, Wilson.

WILSON **(Does so)** It says 'Captain Mainwaring, Personal'. **(Starts to open it)**

MAINWARING Give it to me. **(Takes out letter and gives envelope to Wilson)**

WILSON **(Smelling envelope)** What an unusual perfume. **(Sniffs again)** Petrol.

MAINWARING **(Reads letter. Two £1 notes are pinned to it)** 'Dear Cap, Thanks for letting me off. Had to go up to the Smoke for a few days to do a deal. I think I can swing it for a grand, but I shall have to drop the geezer a pony. On the other hand I may cop it for a bit under the odds in which case I'll have to sweeten him with a monkey and half a bar for his nippers. P.S. Here's a couple of oncers for your trouble.' How dare he try to bribe me? **(Screws up notes. He is about to throw them away, but puts them in his pocket)** As soon as he gets back I want to see him in my office.

WILSON There's going to be quite a queue, isn't there?

MAINWARING That's quite enough from you, Wilson. **(He turns to Godfrey)**

GODFREY Good evening.

MAINWARING **(Seeing a small piece of white paper in Godfrey's hat band)** Godfrey – there's a small piece of white paper in your hat band.

GODFREY Yes, sir. It's for the sun.

MAINWARING The sun?

GODFREY Yes – I have a rather sensitive nose and since Sergeant Wilson wouldn't let me wear my panama hat on parade, I thought this was the next best thing. **(He places the piece of paper over his nose and secures it in position with a pair of sunglasses)**

MAINWARING **(Turning to Wilson)** Words fail me!

WILSON Perhaps he'd better see you in the office.

MAINWARING At least you look normal, Frazer.

FRAZER Thank you, sir. The wee moose will be gone from my pocket by the morrow.

MAINWARING The what?

FRAZER The wee moose. **(He puts his hand into the top pocket of his jacket and takes out a small mouse)** I didna want to leave her alone. Her bairns are due.

MAINWARING A pregnant mouse, nose shields, violins – I'm away for a few short hours and you allow the whole unit to crumble before your eyes, Wilson. **(He turns and sees the Vicar)** What's this?

VICAR I've joined your happy band.

VERGER Where His Reverence goes – there goest I.

MAINWARING If this is your idea of a joke, Wilson, it's a very bad one.

WILSON They asked to join and I saw no reason to stop them.

MAINWARING All three of you had better follow me.

SIDE OFFICE

They march into the side office.

MAINWARING Now – what's all this tomfoolery?

VERGER Don't you call His Reverence a Tom Fool.

WILSON Look, it's all in the paper.

MAINWARING I've read all that rubbish.

WILSON Well, they asked to join – so I signed them up.

VICAR It was a spontaneous thing – I'm rather like that, you know. I've been wrestling with my conscience for some time.

VERGER It's been agony. He was wrestling night and day – I can vouch for that.

VICAR Thank you, Mr Yeatman. Finally, I asked myself – could I stand by and watch my wife being raped by a Nazi? No, I said to myself, I couldn't.

MAINWARING But you're not married.

VICAR I have a very vivid imagination. So, with the example of all those other clergy before my eyes, I knew that my place was at your side.

MAINWARING I don't want you at my side.

WILSON I'm afraid it's too late to do anything now.

MAINWARING Are these the papers?

WILSON I think so.

MAINWARING Well, I'll show you if it's too late or not. **(He is about to tear them)**

VERGER Don't you dare destroy His Reverence's particulars.

WILSON It won't help very much anyway – they're only duplicates.

MAINWARING Very well, if that's the way the land lies – soldiers you are and soldiers you will be. You'll both parade tonight with Jones' patrol and we'll show you what army life is all about. And we won't spare you, I promise you that. You'll find no pulpit to lean on here.

EXTERIOR. COMMAND POST

This is a sandbagged hut, about 15 foot by 10 foot. It is set at the entrance to a factory or gasworks. Jones leads the section on, including the Vicar and the Verger. The air raid siren is just finishing.

JONES Left, right, left, right, halt. Private Pike, Private Vicar and Private Verger, stand fast, the remainder into the guard room. Fall out.

They do so.

JONES **(To Vicar, Verger and Pike)** You'd better put your tin

hats on in case a bomb drops. Now then, Private Vicar, Private Pike and myself are going to demonstrate to you the correct proceedings for military soldiers guarding things on century. First of all, you will be on the look-out for parachuters, saboteurs and enemies of the realm. When you see any of these approaching your person, you will challenge them in the aforesaid manner. Show them, Private Pike.

PIKE Halt – who goes there?

JONES That was very good. You do it just like that.

PIKE Can I go in now? Cos it's chilly and I haven't got my muffler.

JONES You don't want to bother about mufflers, lad, you're a soldier now. **(He sneezes)** There is a nip in the air, isn't there. Never mind – we won't be half a tick. Now, Private Vicar, you do what Private Pike just done.

VICAR Halt – who goes there?

JONES He won't be coming up from down there. Yes – well, you want to say it a bit more fierce, like you was a rough, devil-may-care, brutal sort of person.

VERGER I thought he did it very well.

JONES I'm not asking you – silence in the ranks.

VERGER I'm not frightened of you, you know. You don't impress me at all.

VICAR Be quiet, Mr Yeatman.

JONES If he starts making trouble he'll be on a fizzer under Section 40 – that's Conduct to the Military Discipline Prejudice.

PIKE Can we do the next bit?

JONES Yea. Yea. What's next?

PIKE On being challenged with 'Halt – who goes there?', the parachutist or saboteur says 'Friend', whereupon you shout 'Advance friend and be recognised'.

JONES Yea – well, go on and do that.

VICAR Advance friend and be recognised.

JONES Yes, but you mustn't say it so friendly. You're asking them if they're friendly, but you don't want to be friendly yourself.

VICAR Supposing he advances and I don't recognise him.

VERGER Well, if you didn't know him, he'd know you. Everyone knows His Reverence – and respects him.

JONES Well, there's a lot more to it, but you'll pick it up as you go along. If you have any bother, you send for the guard commander – that's me – and if I have any trouble or if anyone shoots you or anything like that, I say 'Turn out the guard' and we'll all come and give you a hand. Come on, let's get inside the warm.

They go to command post.

INSIDE THE COMMAND POST

FRAZER Look at this. Two shillings for a packet of 20 cigarettes. It's daylight robbery.

GODFREY I know – the world's gone mad. Do you know, I can remember when I was a young man, us young blades thought we would have a night out. So we all went up to London, saw the show at the Gaiety, then had a top-hole four-course dinner with wine, and sailed home in a hansom cab – and we still had change from five shillings.

FRAZER You know your trouble, Godfrey – you've always been a spendthrift.

JONES Mind you – prices are not all that bad. Pikey and I were in the Rosemary Café at Eastgate the other day and we had brown windsor soup, whale meat cutlets, swedes and mashed potatoes, tapioca pudding and a cup of tea – ninepence. Mind you, it wasn't very good.

PIKE I was sick afterwards.

EXTERIOR. COMMAND POST

VERGER Your Reverence – somebody is making an approach.

VICAR Where?

VERGER Over there. I can just see something through the murk.

VICAR Oh dear. Will you do it or will I?

VERGER Don't worry yourself, sir. I'll take care of it. Halt – who goes there?

SMALL BOY What did you say?

VERGER I said – halt – who goes there?

SMALL BOY Adolf.

VICAR What did he say?

VERGER I think he said Adolf.

VICAR Did you say Adolf?

SMALL BOY That's right.

VICAR Adolf who?

SMALL BOY Adolf Hitler.

VERGER I think it's a cheeky young boy, sir, and he's having us on.

VICAR Come here, little boy.

The boy approaches.

VICAR If you don't behave properly, you'll be in serious trouble for disobeying army orders.

SMALL BOY Go on – you're not proper soldiers. You're an

old Vicar and he's your old Verger. I'm not taking any notice of you.

VICAR I'll give you one more chance. Say it again, Mr Yeatman.

VERGER Halt – who goes there?

SMALL BOY Adolf Hitler.

VICAR We'd better send for Mr Jones.

VERGER I could clip his ear for him.

VICAR No – no violence. We'll send for Mr Jones. Turn out the guard, turn out the guard.

INTERIOR COMMAND POST

JONES Come on, lads. The Vicar's in trouble. Turn out the guard. Turn out the guard.

EXTERIOR. COMMAND POST

The Verger has hold of the boy. The section rushes out.

JONES Where are they? Where's the enemy? Fix bayonets.

VICAR Mr Jones, I said 'Halt – who goes there?' – just as you told me – and he positively refuses to say 'friend'.

JONES Who does?

VICAR This little boy.

FRAZER Have you turned us out for him?

VICAR He's supposed to say 'friend' – you said so yourself.

JONES I know him – he's a cheeky little monkey. He runs into my shop when it's full of people and shouts 'Sainsbury's'.

PIKE Yea, and he runs into our bank and shouts 'National Provincial'.

SMALL BOY You can't do anything about it – you're not proper soldiers.

JONES Oh – aren't we? I'll show you. Bring him inside.

VERGER You heard what the corporal said. Gert inside. **(He swipes him one)**

SMALL BOY Here – he hit me. You're not supposed to do that – it's against the Geneva Convention.

VERGER Yes – and so's that. **(He swipes him again)**

INTERIOR COMMAND POST

JONES You come in here, young feller-me-lad.

SMALL BOY He hit me, the great big bully. I'll tell my uncle on you.

FRAZER Now listen to me, sonny boy – I'm going to talk to you in your own language. We'll have no more of your filthy Gorbals backchat – behave yourself or you'll be handed over to the police.

JONES That's right – for not compiling with lawful army things what we're telling you to do.

Mainwaring enters.

MAINWARING What's going on here? Why is nobody on guard.

JONES We've detained a suspect, sir, and we're just interrogating him.

MAINWARING A suspect! Where is he?

JONES There. **(He points to the boy)**

WILSON He doesn't look very suspicious to me.

VICAR He said his name was Adolf Hitler.

MAINWARING I shouldn't set too much store by that if I were you, Vicar. Go away, little boy, and in future don't be cheeky.

SMALL BOY He hit me. I want an apology.

MAINWARING Just run along or my sergeant'll put his belt across your backside.

WILSON Who, me?

SMALL BOY So that's how it is, is it? Assault, battery and threats and foul language. My uncle will have the law on you.

MAINWARING See him off, Wilson.

WILSON I wish you'd stop talking to me as if I was a Labrador.

VERGER Go on you little perisher. **(Chases the boy off)**

SMALL BOY I'll tell my uncle, I'll tell my uncle.

MAINWARING Right, in case there is any follow up to this incident, I want a full report from you all as soon as Sponge's section relieves you.

SMALL WARDEN'S POST

The Warden and the Assistant Warden are listening to the boy recounting the incident.

SMALL BOY Anyway, Uncle. I was just having a little joke with them when this great big Home Guard fetched me one across the lugs.

WARDEN Go on. Go on, Hamish.

SMALL BOY Then he did it again and then they all set on me.

WARDEN Pushing and shoving and punching?

SMALL BOY That's right. Then the officer – old sour face.

WARDEN You mean Mainwaring?

SMALL BOY That's him – he told his sergeant to give me a whipping – so I ran away in terror.

WARDEN If there's one thing that makes my blood boil, it's cruelty to innocent children.

SMALL BOY They was cruel – very cruel.

WARDEN You come with me. I'll settle Mainwaring's hash.

SMALL BOY Are you going to fight him?

WARDEN Well, we'll see what happens.

CHURCH HALL

Wilson is sitting at a table, writing. The section are lined up.

FRAZER He was a young monkey – he deserved a skelping.

MAINWARING Well if you've got it all down, Wilson, I'll sign it and then you can put it on the file, but if I'm any judge of these sort of things, we'll hear no more about it.

Enter Warden.

WARDEN Right, Mainwaring, get your jacket off and come outside.

MAINWARING What are you talking about? How dare you come barging in here like that?

WARDEN Come in here, Hamish. (**Little boy enters**) Now, just you repeat what you told me.

SMALL BOY (**Pointing at the Verger**) That's the one – he hit me time and time again. (**Points at Jones**) And he pointed a bayonet at me. And that fat pompous one said, 'Just run along or my sergeant will put his belt across your backside'.

WARDEN Just about your mark, isn't it, Mainwaring – bullying little boys. (**Squaring up**) Now, have a go at someone your own size. Come on, try hitting me.

MAINWARING Hold my glasses, Wilson.

JONES Don't you tangle with him, Mr Mainwaring, not in your crippled state. Let me do it for you.

FRAZER Here, hold my rifle, Pike, come on – put 'em up.

WARDEN Oh that's sporting, that is. Nine of you against one.

PIKE It's only eight, I'm not feeling very well.

WARDEN Well, that settles it. I'm bringing charges. I'm having you all up in court. You'll hear a few home truths there.

SMALL BOY They're a laughing stock, aren't they, Uncle?

WARDEN Course they are.

SMALL BOY Playing at soldiers – that's all they do.

WARDEN That's right – playing at soldiers.

SMALL BOY (**Pointing at Jones**) And his sausages are all bread.

JONES They're not all bread – you can't get the meat.

WARDEN Go on – tell them, tell them.

SMALL BOY You should hear me and my mates laugh when you go on church parade. (**Points to Godfrey**) His hobbling around with his Red Cross handbag.

WARDEN That's it – tell them, tell them.

SMALL BOY They're almost as funny as the Wardens.

WARDEN That's right, almost as funny as... What did you say?

SMALL BOY (**Carried away**) You with your white hat and your flat nose – and your 'left, right, left, right, halt'.

WARDEN You cheeky little whipper-snapper, you wait till I get my hands on you. (**Starts to chase him out**) I'll give you flat nose.

The platoon laugh and jeer.

MAINWARING Well, that's probably the end of that. But I think one thing is very clear. If you, Vicar, and you, Verger, had dealt with this in the proper military manner in the first place – this incident would not have occurred.

VICAR Oh, I see, it's all my fault, is it?

VERGER It's His Reverence's fault, is it?

VICAR Well, as far as I'm concerned, it just goes to show how very silly the whole thing is. I'm just fed up to the teeth with the lot of you. (**Crosses to Mainwaring**) You can keep your silly gun. (**Hands each item to Mainwaring**) And your silly hat. And your silly tunic. (**Moves to the door**)

VERGER What about the silly trousers?

VICAR I'll send those round in the morning. Come along, Mr Yeatman.

Warden dashes back in.

WARDEN Here, come on, quick. There's a stick of incendiaries dropped across the High Street. We'll have the whole town on fire in a minute.

MAINWARING Right, get the sand buckets. Frazer – stirrup pump. Pike – two buckets of water – move, all of you.

They all dash for the various items. Wilson bumps into Mainwaring.

WILSON Sorry, sir – did I tread on your feet?

MAINWARING Oh, don't worry about that – there's a war on.

SERIES SEVEN **EPISODE ONE**

Recorded: Sunday 27/10/74
Original transmission: Friday 15/11/74, 7.45–8.15pm
Original viewing figures = 14.1 million

ARTHUR LOWE .... CAPTAIN MAINWARING
JOHN LE MESURIER .... SERGEANT WILSON
CLIVE DUNN.................................. LANCE CORPORAL JONES
JOHN LAURIE .... PRIVATE FRAZER
ARNOLD RIDLEY .... PRIVATE GODFREY
IAN LAVENDER .... PRIVATE PIKE
BILL PERTWEE.................................. CHIEF WARDEN HODGES
FRANK WILLIAMS .... VICAR
EDWARD SINCLAIR... VERGER
PAMELA CUNDELL.. MRS FOX
HAROLD BENNETT.. MR BLUETT
OLIVE MERCER.. MRS YEATMAN
FELIX BOWNESS .... DRIVER
COLIN BEAN .... PRIVATE SPONGE
PLATOON............... DESMOND CULLUM-JONES, GEORGE HANCOCK,
.... EVAN ROSS, LESLIE NOYES, FREDDIE WHITE,
.... FREDDIE WILES, HUGH CECIL, ROGER BOURNE,
.... MICHAEL MOORE
AUNTIE ELSIE .... NELLIE GRIFFITHS

EVERYBODY'S TRUCKING

• ANNIE OGDEN REMEMBERS •

'Filming in Norfolk was hard work during the day but a lot of happy socialising took place in the evenings at The Bell Hotel in Thetford. We had a wonderful make-up lady called Sylvia Thornton; she was wickedly funny and often after a meal in the hotel she would have us all rocking with laughter with an impression or a funny song.

'One of my responsibilities on filming was to get all the props assembled and make sure they got to the location in one piece and on time. Things didn't always go to plan.

'During "Everybody's Trucking" we were filming with the platoon on the quiet country roads outside Thetford when, each time the camera rolled, a great roar was heard in the sky and a jet would streak overhead. It became clear to John Gatland [film sound] and David Croft that we wouldn't be able to continue. So Bob Spiers took the initiative: he jumped into his car and drove to the American air base, which was nearby. Twenty minutes later he was back and the skies were quiet. Bob had explained our problem to the Commanding Officer who had laughed and said: "Gee, that's no problem. I'll bring the boys down – they were just bored and went up for a spin." Problem solved.'

Everybody's Trucking

THE CHURCH YARD. EXTERIOR. DAY

Jones' van is parked centre. The front towards camera. Jones, Frazer, Godfrey, Pike and the platoon are standing around waiting for Mainwaring. The van has been newly painted and is looking very smart.

PIKE It looks very posh, Mr Jones.

JONES Well, you have to look after things these days, don't you, Pikey boy? I mean, they don't make vans like this any more. So you have to nurture them with craftsmanship and oil and things. **(He points to the lettering)** That's real gold leaf, that is.

FRAZER Vanity, pure vanity. He just wants to bandy his name all over the town – like he was a tin of baked beans.

Jones reacts.

GODFREY I think it looks very jolly. It'll cheer people up as it goes along the road, even though there isn't any meat in it.

Jones reacts. Enter Mainwaring and Wilson from the door to the side office. Mainwaring holds a clipboard.

MAINWARING Wilson, gather the men round with their secret signs. This is very confidential. **(Mainwaring consults his clipboard. Wilson goes up to Godfrey and speaks very quietly to him)**

WILSON Would you mind gathering round Captain Mainwaring. **(He goes to a group and whispers)**

WILSON Gather round Captain Mainwaring, please. **(He goes up to Pike and whispers in his ear. Mainwaring sees what's going on)**

MAINWARING Wilson.

Wilson moves behind the van to whisper to some of the platoon.

MAINWARING Wilson!

Mainwaring crosses to the back of the van where Wilson was last seen.

MAINWARING Wilson, where are you?

Wilson appears round the front of the van.

WILSON **(Still whispering)** Did you want me, sir?

MAINWARING What are you doing?

WILSON You told me to gather the men round confidentially.

MAINWARING Look. **(Tapping clipboard)** What I have to say is confidential, not the fact that they have to gather round.

WILSON I'm sorry, sir.

MAINWARING Pay attention, everybody.

PIKE Excuse me, sir, Mr Jones has just had his van done up. Don't you think it looks nice?

MAINWARING Don't interrupt, Pike, or you'll be sent home.

Pike reacts.

MAINWARING Now, what I'm about to say is very highly confidential.

WILSON It does really look awfully nice.

MAINWARING I beg your pardon?

WILSON Jones' van. He's made a marvellous job of it, hasn't he?

MAINWARING **(Looking)** Yes. Now, this area has been selected...

PIKE **(Interrupting)** Will Sergeant Wilson get sent home if he interrupts any more?

MAINWARING I shan't tell you again, Pike.

Pike reacts.

MAINWARING As I was saying, this area has been selected for the divisional scheme, and the broad plan is as follows. **(He puts his foot on the running board to rest the clipboard on his knee while turning over a page. As he does so ,the running board falls off)**

JONES Mr Mainwaring, you've broken my running board. **(He goes to put it back)**

MAINWARING Leave it where it is. We'll deal with it later.

JONES You shouldn't have done that, Mr Mainwaring.

MAINWARING Be quiet and go back to your place, Jones.

JONES **(To platoon)** He put his great heavy leg on it.

PIKE Better be quiet, Mr Jones, or he'll send you home. He's in one of his moods.

MAINWARING Three battalions of regular troops will move into this area around Walmington and Eastgate, and will defend it in depth. Our task is a vitally important one. We are to signpost the area so the units reach their correct destinations. **(He takes a piece of chalk from his clipboard)** Now, the axis of advance is down the Clayton Road, thus. **(He chalks a vertical line down the side of Jones' van, across the lettering)**

JONES Don't do that, Mr Mainwaring.

MAINWARING Don't fuss, Jones, it'll soon come off. **(He licks his finger and rubs. Some of the lettering peels away)**

JONES You're making it worse, Mr Mainwaring. **(Mainwaring rubs it with his cuff)** Please don't do that to my van, Mr Mainwaring, you're desecrating it.

MAINWARING Oh, you can soon retouch that. Now, of course, all signposts have been removed, so without our help, the whole convoy could finish up in chaos. That is why you were told to prepare the secret signs to guide them. Now, who has the signpost for Walmington?

Pike holds up a wooden sign saying Walmington followed by a hand with a pointing finger. The hand is painted very realistically.

WILSON That's very good, Frank. The hand is absolutely lifelike. Don't you think so, sir?

MAINWARING Yes, well done, Pike.

GODFREY It has dirty finger nails. I don't like that sort of thing.

FRAZER There's just one thing. It points the wrong way.

MAINWARING What do you mean?

FRAZER When you come down yon road, Walmington is to the left.

MAINWARING Ah. I was wondering who'd be the first to notice that.

PIKE Well, that's easily solved isn't it. (**He turns the sign upside down**)

MAINWARING Stupid boy.

PIKE All they have to do is stand on their heads, sir.

MAINWARING Don't be impertinent, Pike.

JONES It's very simple, sir. (**He takes the sign**) We put it up thus wise. (**He shows Mainwaring the blank side**) Now, a body of men on seeing a sign with nothing on it will find it intriguing and wonder to themselves if there's nothing on the other side as well.

Mainwaring reacts.

JONES But when they come round the other side it will point the right way and we will win the war.

MAINWARING Where's the Eastgate one?

GODFREY (**Holds up a sign on which is drawn a Chinaman and a gate and an arrow**) Er, this is it, sir.

MAINWARING What's that?

GODFREY You said it was secret, so I did the thing in code. (**He points**) The Chinaman for east and gate for gate. Eastgate.

MAINWARING It doesn't look much like a Chinaman to me. Anyway – it's not a very good idea, Godfrey.

Godfrey reaacts.

PIKE Send him home, Mr Mainwaring.

MAINWARING Now, you will each be dropped off the van to fix your notice and then, as soon as the convoy has passed, you will destroy it.

WILSON Destroy the convoy?

Mainwaring kills him with a look.

WILSON Destroy the notice.

JONES Do we have to eat it, sir?

GODFREY I hope not, my new dentures are hardly up to it.

MAINWARING You will destroy it by fire.

FRAZER Suppose it's raining and they don't light.

MAINWARING War is fraught with hazard, Frazer. Now, you will be dropped off the van one by one and I shall give the signal like this. (**He raps the side of the van twice with his stick**)

JONES Mr Mainwaring, do you mind not striking my van in the aforesaid manner?

MAINWARING Don't keep on fussing, Jones. There's a war on, you know.

JONES There's no need for you to spoil my van. That's up to Hitler, isn't it?

MAINWARING Now, it's quite on the cards that during the exercise you will have to take the van across country and, of course, we could get stuck. Now, this is nothing to worry about as long as we are prepared. Jones, get into the van and pretend you're driving along and then you get stuck.

JONES You won't have to hit it again will you, Mr Mainwaring?

MAINWARING Get into the van, Jones. (**Jones starts to climb in**) Now, the sort of materials you should carry with you are: one – (**He points to these items that are standing against the wall**) sawdust, two – old sacks, three – planks, and four – a length of rope. With these and a bit of brute force you should be able to overcome any hazard.

JONES Dimmer, dimmer, dimmer, dimmer, dimmer, I'm driving along, sir. Dimmer, dimmer,

dimmer, dimmer, dimmer. Oh dear, I think I'm stuck. Whur, whur, whur.

MAINWARING Good, Jones. Switch off, the wheels are spinning. What do we do?

FRAZER Sawdust, sir, or straw to give a grip, and, of course, a wee push.

MAINWARING Good. Now take up your pushing positions.

The platoon move to various positions round the van. Pike to the rear of the back wheel.

MAINWARING I shall supervise from here. (**He puts his hand on the side lamp in front of Jones. It comes loose in his hand**)

JONES Don't do that please, Mr Mainwaring. You've made it dangle.

MAINWARING You really should look after your van better than this – it's falling to pieces. Get back in the van. Sawdust, Wilson.

WILSON Pardon, sir?

MAINWARING Sawdust, Wilson.

PIKE Over there, Uncle.

WILSON Well, what about it?

MAINWARING Put it under the wheels, Wilson. And don't dawdle, Wilson. There's a lot of ground to cover.

Wilson sprinkles some near the wheel.

WILSON Like this, sir?

MAINWARING You need more than that, man.

WILSON (**Pouring the whole sack**) Is that better?

MAINWARING Good. That's much more like it. Clear it up, Pike.

PIKE He just chucked it down.

MAINWARING Do as you're told, boy.

Pike reacts.

MAINWARING Now, that will get you out of mud and soft ground and, of course, it'll do just as well if you throw down straw.

PIKE He's not going to throw down straw, is he?

MAINWARING Sacking will sometimes do the trick and, of course, one should always carry a few planks. Now, there's one little wrinkle that's worth knowing if you have to deal with a lot of ice. Lower the pressure of the rear tyres. Now, this is very easily done. You merely (**He demonstrates**) push the valve needle down and allow a little air to escape. (**He stands up, air still hisses out**)

JONES Mr Mainwaring, what are you doing to my van?

MAINWARING The valve's stuck, that's all. Give it a kick, Wilson.

Wilson kicks they tyre gently. The hiss continues.

MAINWARING Not like that. The plunger needs shaking up. (**Mainwaring gives the tyre a good kick. The hiss continues**)

JONES Mr Mainwaring, you're spoiling my van.

MAINWARING By Jove, it's a stubborn one. (**He continues to kick**)

Frazer, Pike and the others start to join in, kicking the tyres and banging the sides.

JONES Leave my van alone. Leave it alone. Go away, all of you.

Fade as the tyre goes flat.

COUNTRY ROAD. EXTERIOR. DAY

Long shot of van progressing along country road, left to right.

INTERIOR OF FRONT OF VAN. EXTERIOR. DAY. STUDIO

Mainwaring is on the left, Wilson in the middle, Jones is driving. Frazer and Pike are looking through the trap.

MAINWARING Right. First signposter, stand-by.

FRAZER He's standing-by, sir.

MAINWARING Stand-by to tick him off the list, Wilson. (**He turns to call through the hole**) Now, this is a great honour and a great responsibility. One sign wrong and we could ruin the whole divisional scheme.

FRAZER There's the turning.

MAINWARING Right. Stop, Jones.

COUNTRY ROAD. EXTERIOR. DAY

Long shot of van stopping.

INTERIOR. FRONT OF VAN. EXTERIOR. DAY

MAINWARING First signposter out. (**He bangs his stick twice on the side of the van**)

JONES Mr Mainwaring, please don't start spoiling my van again.

MAINWARING Don't be absurd, Jones, I must give the signal to the men.

JONES Couldn't you make some other sort of noise, sir. One that doesn't spoil my van.

PIKE Why don't you toot your hooter?

MAINWARING Good suggestion, Pike. (**Calls to men at back**) We'll toot the hooter when we want you to disembark. Is that clear?

FRAZER (**To back of van**) He's going to toot his hooter when he wants you to disembark.

PIKE I get some good ideas sometimes, don't I?

GODFREY Captain Mainwaring, the first man has alighted safely.

MAINWARING Good. Drive on, Jones.

COUNTRY ROAD. EXTERIOR. DAY

As the rear of the van is seen to drive away. A member of the platoon takes up position by a turning and holds up his sign, which reads 'Little Barstead'. Long shot of van driving along lane. Long shot of van in another lane by a junction. It comes to a halt.

INTERIOR. FRONT OF VAN. EXTERIOR. DAY

MAINWARING Right, Jones, signal the last one out. Tick him off the list, Wilson.

Jones pushes the horn. Nothing happens.

JONES Mr Mainwaring, the hooter isn't tooting.

MAINWARING Give it a good hard push. (**He leans across and bangs his hand on the horn. It sticks in the on position. They bash it more. It falls off the note and slides down to silence**)

JONES You've broken my horn, Mr Mainwaring. If you go on like this, I won't have anything left.

MAINWARING Never mind, Jones, you're helping the war effort.

PIKE Mr Mainwaring, the last signposter just dropped off the back.

MAINWARING Good. Turn round, Jones. We'll go back to the crossroads and wait for the convoy to pass through, and then we can pick everybody up again.

Jones starts to turn the van.

COUNTRY ROAD. EXTERIOR. DAY

Long shot of van returning along the road, right to left. Long shot of steamroller with organ trailer in the centre of a narrow road adjacent to a telegraph pole and a telephone box. It completely fills the road. Long shot of van approaching and stopping from head on position.

MAINWARING (**From the van**) Get out of the way.

JONES It's been left alone and uncared for, sir.

MAINWARING We'll go and investigate.

Jones, Mainwaring and Wilson get out of the van. Pike and Frazer get out of the back. They approach the steamroller.

WILSON There's nobody with it.

MAINWARING I can see that, Wilson.

PIKE Captain Mainwaring, perhaps the driver's gone into a field to have a…

MAINWARING That'll do, Pike.

FRAZER Captain Mainwaring, does it not put you in mind of the *Marie Celeste*? She was found abandoned in the midst of an empty ocean – food on the table, wine in the glass, not a human soul aboard, dead or alive – only the creaking of the rigging and the eerie cry of the birds. Cor, cor! Cor, cor! Does it not strike you, Captain Mainwaring? Do you not see the connection?

MAINWARING No, not really.

GODFREY Captain Mainwaring, there's a note here. (**Godfrey holds up a note**) It says – gone to get some coal.

MAINWARING Well, we can't wait here. He might have gone for miles. We'll drive round. Back in the van, everyone.

WILSON (**As they go toward the van**) There's been rather a lot of rain lately – are you sure we won't bog down?

MAINWARING Nonsense, Wilson. The ground's as firm as a rock. Anyone can see that. Everybody on the van.

Mainwaring and Wilson start to climb into the van.

WILSON In that case, wouldn't it be wiser for us all to stay off the van to lighten the load?

MAINWARING You know, you're not very scientific, Wilson, are you? Anybody knows that extra weight gives more traction to the driving wheels. Do use your common sense. Drive on, Jones.

They drive off the road. The wheels spin. Jones struggles. Mainwaring looks worried. They stick.

PIKE (**From hole in the roof**) Captain Mainwaring, we're stuck.

MAINWARING Right. Everybody off. Pushing positions.

They climb off.

WILSON (**As they climb off**) Do you think that some of them should stay on so as to give more traction to the wheels, sir?

MAINWARING Don't be flippant, Wilson. And try not to look so miserable.

WILSON (**Giving a wan smile**) Is that better?

MAINWARING Hardly.

FRAZER We're ready in our pushing positions, sir.

GODFREY Er, Captain Mainwaring, would it be in order if I only push with one hand. I've a touch of rheumatism in the shoulder. My sister makes me sit by the window during breakfast and the draught cuts right across to the door.

MAINWARING If you're not fit enough for front-line action, Godfrey, you shouldn't come at all.

GODFREY I didn't want to disappoint you.

MAINWARING Right, stand by to push. Away you go, Jones.

JONES Dimmer, dimmer, dimmer.

MAINWARING Jones, Jones, this isn't an exercise. It's the real thing. Let in the clutch.

JONES Sorry, Mr Mainwaring. I don't know what I was thinking about. (**Jones lets in the clutch**)

MAINWARING Push.

They push. The wheels spin. Pike, behind the rear wheel, gets showered in wet mud.

PIKE Mr Mainwaring. Stop! Mr Mainwaring!!

MAINWARING What are you playing at, Pike? Look at the mess you've made of your uniform.

FRAZER **(With a bag of sawdust)** Should we not be using the sawdust, Captain Mainwaring?

MAINWARING Of course we should. Shove it under the wheel.

Frazer empties the bag.

MAINWARING Now, all push when I give the word. Jones, let out the clutch on my signal.

WILSON Do you think perhaps Pike should stand back this time?

MAINWARING Certainly not. If you keep molly-coddling that boy, he'll finish up a complete nancy. Get in your place, Pike.

Pike takes his place again.

MAINWARING Right, stand-by. Push.

He signals to Jones. They all push. Jones lets in the clutch. The wheels spin and eat up the sawdust.

MAINWARING We nearly got it that time.

PIKE I got it all right.

Long shot of warden approaching in his vegetable van. He stops. The man comes from crossroads, i.e. in the opposite direction to the platoon van.

WARDEN Hello. Stuck in the mud, are we? **(Crosses towards them)**

MAINWARING Ignore him, Wilson. I don't want you to lose your temper with him.

WARDEN Dear, oh dear. Playing at mud pies are we? You wait till Mummy sees you.

MAINWARING Right. One more go and we'll be clear.

PIKE Please can I push somewhere else, Mr Mainwaring?

MAINWARING Stay where you are, Pike. Stand by, Jones.

FRAZER **(To Warden)** Go on, daddy – give us a push. Help the war effort.

WARDEN It's no good just pushing it. You've got to lift the back at the same time.

PIKE Come and lift at the back next to me, Mr Hodges.

WARDEN I'm not standing there. All the mud and stuff will come flying. **(He stands by Jones)**

Wilson goes round to Jones at the other side.

WILSON Jonesey, try reverse and see if we can come out the way we came in.

JONES That's a good idea. Why didn't I think of that? **(He puts the gear into reverse)**

MAINWARING Right, one, two, three – lift. **(He signals to Jones. Jones lets in the clutch. The wheels spin in reverse. The Warden is showered with mud)**

WARDEN Stop, stop.

MAINWARING Stop. It's no good.

Jones gets out of van.

WARDEN You're telling me it isn't. Look what you've done, you ruddy hooligans.

MAINWARING You'd better try the planks. Get the planks out.

GODFREY The planks don't seem to be here, sir.

MAINWARING The planks are not there! Put somebody on a charge, Wilson.

PIKE Captain Mainwaring, we could take the doors off the van and use those.

MAINWARING Good idea. Jones, give me a screwdriver.

JONES You can't do this, Mr Mainwaring. You can't have my doors.

MAINWARING It won't do them any harm.

JONES I have no wish to insubordinate or mutinous in my manner, Captain Mainwaring, but I have to stand up and boldly defy you and even threaten you with blackmail.

MAINWARING What are you saying, Jones?

JONES I shall cancel your offal, sir, and put your name on my sausage blacklist.

MAINWARING Now steady on, Jones.

JONES I have a blacklist, sir, of certain people who I will not supply with sausages and I shall put your name on that list. I'm sorry, Mr Mainwaring, I never thought I would utter these words to you, but you have driven me to it.

FRAZER Why don't we ask yon Warden feller to give us a wee bit tow.

MAINWARING Good idea.

WILSON If I may say so, sir. I think we should be very diplomatic with him.

MAINWARING Of course I will. **(He moves off calling)** Hodges, come here.

WILSON That should have done it.

MAINWARING **(To Hodges)** Be good enough to give us a tow, would you?

WARDEN Me give you a tow? What have you ever done for me?

MAINWARING There's a large military convoy coming up this road. We are responsible for seeing that it gets to its destination.

WARDEN That's your hard bun, isn't it?

MAINWARING Very well. In the name of the King, I requisition your vegetable van.

WARDEN Oh no you don't. There's a load of logs on that van for the Warden's Post and I'm going to deliver them. If you don't like it, you know what you can do. **(Goes towards his van)**

PIKE Why don't you shoot him, Mr Mainwaring?

MAINWARING Be quiet, Pike.

PIKE Go on, you've got the authority.

MAINWARING I said be quiet, Pike.

PIKE Look, he's trying to drive round. **(Shouts to Warden)** You'll get stuck the same as we did.

WARDEN **(From the van which he is backing on to the field)** Oh no I won't, you dopey-looking thing.

PIKE Who are you calling a dopey-looking thing?

WARDEN I won't get stuck because I've got it up here. **(He taps his head)** I'm going to back round. Then the driving wheels will be leading like they do in a four-wheel drive. **(He taps his head again)** Here's where you need it, sonny. **(He backs the van)**

Cut to Mainwaring, Wilson and Pike.

PIKE You could shoot him, Uncle Arthur.

WILSON Go away, Frank.

PIKE You heard him. He called me a dopey-looking thing. You're not going to stand for that, are you?

WILSON Yes, I am.

PIKE Well, I'll tell Mum. She'll soon go round to his shop and give him what for.

WARDEN **(Backing the van)** See, all you have to do is use your loaf. **(He gets stuck, the wheels spin)**

WARDEN Well, don't just stand there, give me a push.

WILSON Do we help him, sir?

MAINWARING No. Just come away.

They turn and walk away.

Cut to a bus coming along the road from the crossroads, i.e. the same way as the Warden's van. It's full of old age pensioners in paper hats. They are escorted by the Vicar and include Mrs Yeatman and Mr Bluett.

Cut to Mainwaring. The group by the van are poised for another push.

FRAZER Look, perhaps they'll give us a hand.

The bus halts. The Vicar puts his head out of the window.

VICAR Are you stuck, Mr Mainwaring?

MAINWARING Well – only slightly. We'd welcome a few willing hands to give us an extra push, though.

MR BLUETT Come on, boys and girls. They need a bit of a push.

The OAPs start to disembark. They are very infirm, and are supported by sticks, umbrellas and each other.

MAINWARING We'll soon be out now.

We see the decrepit file crossing from the bus.

WILSON I don't think they're going to be very much help, sir.

MAINWARING Oh, this won't do at all. **(He shouts)** We'll manage thank you, go back on again.

MR BLUETT Right, boys and girls, back on the bus.

DRIVER **(Shouts)** Tell you what, I'll just come near enough to tie the rope on, then I'll reverse and pull you out. The ground's all right here. Everybody off.

MR BLUETT Come on, boys and girls, everybody off.

VICAR I'm terribly sorry about this, Mr Bluett. It seems a very strange way to spend your annual party.

MR BLUETT It's better than sitting in that draughty church hall and listening to those boring old songs.

VICAR You said you liked my songs.

Cut to driver.

DRIVER Right. Here we go.

GODFREY Shall I nip up on to the back of the van, sir, and get the towrope?

MAINWARING Good idea, Godfrey.

WILSON Won't he get stuck, sir?

MAINWARING He's very keen, you know.

WILSON I mean the bus, sir, won't the bus get stuck?

MAINWARING I'm just about fed up with your pessimistic attitude, Wilson. Anyone can see that the ground there is perfectly sound. The driver knows what he's doing.

PIKE Captain Mainwaring, I thought you ought to know – the bus is stuck.

Cut to the Warden's motorcycle and sidecar, which the Verger is driving, Mrs Fox is in the passenger seat. It is coming from the town, i.e. head on to the bus and the same way as the butcher's van. Cut to Mainwaring and Wilson. Frazer approaches.

FRAZER Captain Mainwaring, I suppose you realise the convoy will be coming down that road fifteen minutes from now.

MAINWARING **(Looking at his watch)** By Jove, you're right, Frazer.

FRAZER Lorries will be piled up for a mile or more. Chaos it'll be, sheer chaos. And you're responsible... you'll be a laughing stock, a laughing stock. I just thought you ought to know.

WILSON We could divert them at the crossroads, sir.

JONES Let me divert them at the crossroads, sir, I should like to volunteer to do that.

MAINWARING It's five miles away – it would take you an hour even if you ran.

FRAZER Which he can't.

PIKE Look, sir. You could get a lift on that motorcycle.

They see the motorcycle and start towards it.

Cut to motorcycle. It stops.

MRS FOX Look, it's Captain Mainwaring and lots of people.

VERGER Oh no. Hide.

MRS FOX I can't hide in this.

VERGER Pretend we haven't noticed them.

The Warden joins them.

WARDEN What are you doing with my bike? How dare you?

VERGER It's not your petrol. I pinched it from the Vicar.

Jones arrives.

JONES **(To Mrs Fox)** What are you doing, gallivanting with him?

MRS FOX I've got nothing to be ashamed of. Mr Yeatman said he'd take me to pick bluebells.

MRS YEATMAN That's my husband you've got. **(To Mr Yeatman)** You said you was going to be all day, repairing the organ.

VERGER But what about you? You said you had to go to an affair at the W.V.S.

MR BLUETT I take full responsibility.

MRS YEATMAN **(To Mr Bluett)** Norman!

MR BLUETT I don't care. Let the world know. It's been five years of heaven, but now we must face the music.

VICAR Mr Yeatman, I have to warn you that if something has been going on, I may have to reconsider your position in the church.

VERGER Oh the scandal, the pointing fingers, the wagging tongues. Tittling, tattling, tittling, tattling.

JONES There aren't no bluebells this month.

MAINWARING Look – you'll have to sort this out some other time. In the name of the King, I requisition this motorcycle. **(He pushes the Verger off)**

WARDEN Oh no you don't. I'm going to get a tractor to tow me out.

Mrs Fox climbs out.

MAINWARING Then you can drop me at the crossroads.

WARDEN Al lright – start bumping.

He steers the motorcycle on to the field.

MAINWARING What are you talking about?

WARDEN Bump up and down to get us through the mud. You've seen them in the scrambles, haven't you?

MAINWARING Pike, get in and bump.

Pike climbs into the sidecar. The Warden endeavours to drive across the mud. Cut to Frazer and Godfrey.

FRAZER Yon Mainwaring shouldn't be doing that at his time of life.

GODFREY In the ordinary course of events we'd all be sitting by the fire, reading something.

WARDEN Go on – bump up and down. Bump, bump.

MAINWARING Pike – Bump.

PIKE I am bumping.

They stick in the mud.

WARDEN What's the matter with you? Why don't you keep bumping?

MAINWARING **(Breathless)** I am bumping.

Cut to Wilson and Sponge.

SPONGE Come on, Sergeant Wilson. We can manhandle it.

They all run to the bike.

FRAZER We'll manhandle it, sir. **(Mainwaring and the Warden get off)** Go on – one – two – three – lift.

They lift the bike bodily and take it towards the road. Cut to Godfrey. He stands where the bike was.

GODFREY Captain Mainwaring, you've left a little bit behind.

Cut to the front and sidecar wheels which remain upright in the mud at Godfrey's feet.

WARDEN You ruddy hooligans. You've ruined my bike.

JONES You know, Mr Mainwaring, you are very heavy handed with vehicles. You should cherish them more and they would respond likewise.

WILSON Why don't we use the steam engine to pull us out?

MAINWARING Because, Wilson, there is no coal.

WILSON Mr Hodge's van is full of logs.

MAINWARING I was wondering how long it was going to take you to think of that. Get the wood out of Hodge's van.

WARDEN You're not having my wood and that's final.

PIKE You really ought to shoot him, Mr Mainwaring.

WILSON Oh do be quiet, Frank.

PIKE We could rub him out, then he wouldn't keep stopping us doing things we want to do.

MAINWARING Get the wood on to the fire, Frazer.

FRAZER Aye, aye, sir.

MAINWARING You know how to drive. Get the roller in position. Pike disconnect the trailer.

Mid long shot of the wood being unloaded. Wood is put on

the fire. Frazer blows the whistle and turns the steering wheel. Pike disconnects the trailer. He throws a lever and the organ on the trailer starts to play.

MAINWARING Stop that, Pike.

PIKE I can't stop it, Mr Mainwaring.

MR BLUETT Come on, boys and girls – let's have a bit of a sing-song.

The OAPs start to sing and dance.

MAINWARING Get the steamroller moving.

GODFREY **(To Mainwaring)** Captain Mainwaring, I've just been thinking. My sister Dolly's Auntie Ethel has a cottage at the crossroads. I could telephone her from that telephone box. She could divert the convoy. She's only little, but she's very determined.

MAINWARING That might be our best chance of all. Don't you think so, Wilson?

WILSON It might be our only chance.

MAINWARING Make the call, Godfrey. Here's twopence.

Cut to Jones who is giving directions for the moving of the engine towards the phone box.

JONES Bit more. Bit more – right, that's enough. That's enough. **(The engine rolls on)** That's enough.

Frazer struggles with the engine but it moves on. It flattens the box as Godfrey approaches with his twopence. The roller passes over the box, leaving the phone between the front and rear rollers. Jones picks up the phone and listens.

JONES Hello. **(To Mainwaring)** I think the line's out of order, Captain Mainwaring.

Pike points to the wires that are down on the telegraph poles.

PIKE The wires are down, Mr Mainwaring.

WARDEN You've really done it now, haven't you? That convoy will come piling up on the road and there's nothing you can do about it.

MAINWARING Don't you believe it. My men will join those together in no time at all. Where there's a will, there's a way.

Mix to close shot of Pike. He holds a large poker and a shovel at arm's length. The telephone wires are attached to these and run over his shoulder.

PIKE A bit more – a bit more.

Cut to close shot of Jones. He holds two bayonets at arm's length. The other two wires are attached in a similar manner.

JONES A bit more – a bit more.

Long shot reveals that Jones is sat on the canopy of the steamroller, which is backing up towards Pike, who is sitting on the roof of the organ. They meet.

PIKE Contact.

JONES Go ahead, Captain Mainwaring.

Cut to Mainwaring, Wilson, Godfrey.

MAINWARING Put the twopence in, Wilson.

Wilson inserts twopence into the box which is buried in the ground.

MAINWARING Over to you, Godfrey.

GODFREY Ah, good morning. Could you connect me to Walmington-on-Sea 302.

Mix to sign written on a tablecloth which reads 'Decoy diversion'. There is an arrow pointing to the left. Pull back to reveal a little old lady, holding the sign. As we pull further back we see she is sitting on a step-ladder in the middle of a deserted crossroads. Pull back as far as possible.

SERIES SEVEN **EPISODE TWO**

Recorded: Tuesday 7/5/74

Original transmission: Friday 22/11/74, 7.45–8.15pm

Original viewing figures = 16.4 million

ARTHUR LOWE .... CAPTAIN MAINWARING
JOHN LE MESURIER .... SERGEANT WILSON
CLIVE DUNN.................................... LANCE CORPORAL JONES
JOHN LAURIE .... PRIVATE FRAZER
ARNOLD RIDLEY .... PRIVATE GODFREY
IAN LAVENDER .... PRIVATE PIKE
BILL PERTWEE.................................... CHIEF WARDEN HODGES
TALFRYN THOMAS.................................... MR CHEESEMAN
FRANK WILLIAMS.................................... VICAR
EDWARD SINCLAIR.................................... VERGER
ERIC LONGWORTH .... TOWN CLERK
HAROLD BENNETT.................................... MR BLUETT
ARNOLD PETERS.................................... FIRE OFFICER DALE
JAY DENYER .... INSPECTOR BAKER
ROBERT MILL.................................... CAPTAIN SWAN
COLIN BEAN .... PRIVATE SPONGE
PLATOON.................................... GEORGE HANCOCK, MICHAEL MOORE,
.... DESMOND CULLUM-JONES, FREDDIE WHITE,
.... EVAN ROSS, LESLIE NOYES, ROGER BOURNE, HUGH CECIL

A Man of Action

• ANNIE OGDEN REMEMBERS •

'For most of 1974–75 I worked as an AFM [Assistant Floor Manager] on 13 episodes of *Dad's Army*. It was, without doubt, the happiest time in my television career and I owe thanks to Bob Spiers for getting me the job. Bob was David Croft's production manager at the time and he persuaded David that a long-haired, short-legged, little lady would be able to cope with a bunch of elderly and irascible thespians. They were charm itself.

'I was the first female AFM they had used on the programme and they treated me like a princess. On location in Thetford one summer, Jo Austin, who was then the production manager, had put a "Be Nice to Annie Day" in the schedule on the date of my birthday. Arthur and the boys couldn't have been kinder. I got a cake, flowers, and cards which I still have to this day.'

A Man of Action

EXTERIOR. OUTSIDE PARK GATES. NIGHT

Park gates, behind which we can see bushes and trees. Jones and Pike are sitting on a park bench. Jones is eating.

PIKE I ain't half hungry, Mr Jones.

JONES You're always hungry, boy. I'll just finish this and then we'll report back to the church hall.

PIKE You know, I was thinking, I wonder if we'll ever get any bananas again.

JONES Of course we will, when the war's over.

PIKE I used to love a big plate of bananas and cream, all mashed up with plenty of sugar. I'd take a big mouthful and press it with my tongue through the gaps in my teeth. (**Teeth business**)

Jones reacts.

PIKE Did you like pressing bananas and cream through the gaps in your teeth, Mr Jones?

JONES No, but I don't mind doing it with blancmange.

PIKE And jelly?

JONES Yes, jelly's all right, but not bananas, not at my age with this upper set, it's too risky.

PIKE What about chocolate cream?

JONES Lovely. I'll tell you something, talking of chocolate, when I was out in South Africa during the Boer War, it was Christmas, 1900, and old Queen Victoria sent each one of us lads a tin box with a slab of chocolate in it. And, do you know, I never touched that chocolate. I kept that tin unopened all through the Boer War, all through the 14–18 War, I never let it out of my sight, until I had to go into hospital, and I gave it to an old pal of mine, Charlie Higgins, to look after.

PIKE Did you ever eat the chocolate, Mr Jones?

JONES I never opened that tin for 35 years. Until, one day, I said to myself, I fancy a bit of chocolate.

Pike reacts.

JONES And I opened the tin, it was full of sand. Charlie Higgins had eaten that chocolate while I was in hospital. But I got my revenge.

PIKE What did you do?

JONES Every year after that, at the Old Comrades Association get together, I used to look Charlie full in the face and sing: 'Comrades, Comrades, ever since we were boys, Sharing each other's sorrows, Sharing each other's chocolate.'

Pike reacts.

JONES Old Charlie used to go all red and look on the floor. Mind you, it didn't rhyme. But it did the trick.

PIKE Funny you should say that, Mr Jones. When I was a kid, I was out shopping with my mum, and we were passing this very spot and I asked her to buy me a bar of chocolate. She said no, so I thought I'd give her a scare, and do you know what I did? I stuck my head through those railings, and pretended I couldn't get it out.

JONES What did your mum do?

PIKE She got in a terrible state, she was going to send for the fire brigade, then I pulled my head out and laughed. She didn't half give me one.

JONES Kids do that, you know, they're always getting their heads stuck in railings.

PIKE I said, 'I want a bar of chocolate', and I stuck my head through like this. (**Pike sticks his head through the railings**)

JONES Come on, Pikey, we'd better report back to the church hall.

PIKE Mr Jones.

JONES What's the matter?

PIKE I can't get my head out.

JONES This is no time for playing about. Come on, Mr Mainwaring will wonder what's happened to us.

PIKE I tell you I'm stuck.

JONES Oh, blimey! (**Starts to pull at Pike**)

PIKE Ow! Ow! It won't come out. I can't understand it, it came out all right last time.

JONES How old were you when it happened?

PIKE Twelve.

JONES Twelve! Your head's grown since then.

PIKE I didn't think heads did grow. What am I going to do, what am I going to do?

JONES Don't panic, don't panic, I'm going to ring up Mr Mainwaring. Now, you stay there, and don't move. Whatever you do, don't move, and don't panic.

INTERIOR. OFFICE. CHURCH HALL. NIGHT

Mainwaring is sitting at his desk, Wilson is standing in front.

WILSON Well, all I can say is, sir, that I think you're making a big mistake.

MAINWARING Oh you do, do you?

WILSON I mean, it's asking for trouble. I can't understand why you agreed to do it in the first place.

MAINWARING Because I don't want to offend the press.

And when the editor of the *Eastgate Gazette* rang me up and said he wanted to do a featured article every week on this platoon, naturally I jumped at it.

WILSON But if this reporter who's writing the articles is going to be a temporary member of the platoon, he'll be here all the time.

MAINWARING Exactly. It was my idea – if he's one of us, he'll be able to write the articles from first-hand knowledge, see everything that goes on from the inside.

WILSON Isn't that rather dangerous, sir?

MAINWARING What do you mean, dangerous?

WILSON Well, if he's here all the time, how are you going to cover up your mistakes?

MAINWARING I'm going to pretend I didn't hear that remark, Wilson.

There is a knock at the door.

MAINWARING Come in.

Frazer enters with two cups of cocoa.

FRAZER I've brought you some cocoa, sir.

MAINWARING Thank you, Frazer.

FRAZER Yon reporter feller's outside.

MAINWARING Good. Send him in.

FRAZER Captain Mainwaring, I may have said some harsh things in the past, but I want to say here and now, that I admire your courage.

MAINWARING I don't quite understand, Frazer.

FRAZER I think you're a very brave man, captain, to let that reporter watch your every move. You're either very brave or you're a, er…

MAINWARING What?

FRAZER Nothing, nothing at all. Yes, Captain Mainwaring, I have to admire you. At the same time, I can't help thinking you're taking a terrible risk. That's all. (**He quickly goes**)

MAINWARING What do you suppose he meant by that, Wilson?

WILSON (**Round the head of desk**) I've really no idea, sir.

There is a knock at the door. Godfrey, Frazer and Cheeseman enter. Cheeseman has a camera and Godfrey a tape measure.

GODFREY Mr Cheeseman, from the *Eastgate Gazette*, sir.

CHEESEMAN Good evening, Captain Mainwaring.

MAINWARING Good evening, Mr Cheeseman. All ready to start work?

CHEESEMAN Oh yes indeed, yes, yes.

MAINWARING Now, while you're with us, you will be a temporary trainee recruit. Have you measured him for his uniform, Godfrey?

GODFREY No, not yet, sir, you see we've only got one spare uniform.

MAINWARING Well, measure him for that one.

CHEESEMAN Now, I'm going to call this first article, 'Captain Mainwaring, a Man of Action'.

MAINWARING An excellent title, eh, Wilson?

WILSON Yes, sir, it should look awfully good in print.

FRAZER Aye, Captain Mainwaring, a man of action?

MAINWARING There's no question mark after the title.

CHEESEMAN Now, how about a photograph? (**He takes out his flash**)

WILSON What an awfully good idea. Do you want me sitting or standing? Something like this. (**He moves in beside Mainwaring**)

MAINWARING (**Pushing him away**) You're not in this, Wilson, it's for officers only. (**He sits**) Now, how about one of me, sitting at my desk, working?

CHEESEMAN Oh yes, yes, indeed. That's good.

MAINWARING (**Takes off glasses and picks up a pen**) Now, do you think I ought to keep my gloves on?

WILSON You'll look rather strange writing in gloves, sir.

Mainwaring gives him a glare and takes his gloves off.

MAINWARING This pen isn't very good. Lend me your gold fountain pen, Wilson.

WILSON You know I don't allow anyone to use my pen, sir, it spoils the nib.

MAINWARING I'm not going to use it, I just want to hold it.

WILSON (**Handing over pen**) Well, keep the top on.

MAINWARING Don't be absurd, Wilson, how can I have a photograph taken writing with a pen with the top on. Now, I think I ought to be on the phone.

CHEESEMAN Oh yes, indeed, that's good, get on the phone.

MAINWARING (**Picks up the phone**) How's this?

CHEESEMAN Oh yes, that's good, that's very good, yes.

FRAZER (**Aside to Godfrey**) Is there no end to the conceit of the man?

GODFREY I think he looks rather noble.

MAINWARING How's this, rather Churchillian I think.

CHEESEMAN Oh yes, indeed, very Churchillian, yes.

INTERIOR. TELEPHONE BOX. NIGHT

Jones is on the phone.

JONES Hullo, hullo, Mr Mainwaring. Permission to speak, sir?

Cut to office.

MAINWARING Jones? Is that you? What are you doing on the phone? Get off at once, I'm having my photograph taken on it.

Jones reacts.

CHEESEMAN Is there something wrong, Captain Mainwaring?

MAINWARING Wrong, certainly not, just one of my patrol phoning in. The whole thing works like a smooth, well oiled machine. **(To Cheeseman)** Excuse me, you'd better let me have your report, Jones.

Cut to phone box.

JONES Private Pike has got his head stuck in the park gates, sir.

Cut to office.

MAINWARING Yes, yes, I see.

Cut to phone box.

JONES Didn't you hear what I said, sir? Young Pike has got his head stuck in the park gates.

Cut to office.

MAINWARING **(Gives Cheeseman a sickly smile)** Good, good, excellent.

Cut to phone box.

JONES What's good about it? I don't understand. What am I going to do?

Cut to office.

MAINWARING Can't you remove the obstacle?

Cut to phone box.

JONES I've tried pulling him out, but it's his ears, you see, it's his ears, they're in the way.

Cut to office.

MAINWARING Yes, yes, I see, yes.

CHEESEMAN Are you sure nothing's wrong?

MAINWARING No, no, just a routine matter, one of my patrols is hung up. Something is exposed, that, er, shouldn't be exposed. Do you hear that, Jones, it shouldn't be exposed, cover it up, camouflage, camouflage. I'll be over as soon as I can. **(Hangs up)**

Cut to phone box.

JONES Yes, sir, cover him up, camouflage, camouflage.

Cut to office.

WILSON What is it that's exposed, sir, that shouldn't be exposed?

MAINWARING You should know better than to ask questions like that in front of a civilian, Wilson. I'm going down to investigate. Come on. **(Rise)**

CHEESEMAN I'll come with you.

MAINWARING You can't do that, you're a civilian. You see, the thing that's exposed, and has got to be covered up, is highly secret.

CHEESEMAN But I'm not a civilian, I'm a member of the platoon.

MAINWARING No you're not, you're not a member of the platoon until I've sworn you in.

CHEESEMAN Can't you swear me in now?

MAINWARING There's no time, you stay here and I'll swear you in when I get back.

CHEESEMAN Oh yes, yes, right-oh, boyo, you can swear me in when you get back, and then you can tell me what you've got to cover up.

FRAZER **(Aside to Godfrey)** I could tell him what Mainwaring's got to cover up, it's another one of his mistakes.

EXTERIOR. OUTSIDE PARK GATES. NIGHT

Pike is nearly covered with the branches of a bush. Jones is hacking down some more branches just inside the park gates.

PIKE Why are you covering me up, Mr Jones?

JONES I don't know, I'm just carrying out orders. Mr Mainwaring said you had got to be camouflaged. **(He stacks some more branches against Pike)**

PIKE Ow, ow, that hurt. Couldn't you use a bush that hasn't got prickles in it?

Mainwaring, Wilson, Frazer, Godfrey and Sponge run into the picture.

MAINWARING Where is he, Jones?

PIKE I'm under here, Mr Mainwaring.

Mainwaring pulls the branches aside.

PIKE I'm sorry, Mr Mainwaring.

MAINWARING You... you stupid boy. **(Stands perplexed)**

WILSON Good heavens, why on earth didn't you tell us in the office that Frank had got his head stuck in the railings, sir?

MAINWARING Because I didn't want that reporter to know. If he had put this in his newspaper article, I'd have looked a complete fool.

JONES Why did you ask me to camouflage him, sir?

MAINWARING Because if any passers by had seen him, we'd be the laughing stock of the whole town.

The sirens go.

MAINWARING Put your steel helmets on, men.

They all do so.

WILSON Hadn't we better get under cover, sir?

PIKE What about me, Uncle Arthur?

MAINWARING Be quiet, boy, and put your steel helmet on.

Pike takes his helmet off his shoulder.

MAINWARING Now the question is, how are we going to get him out?

FRAZER I could run back to my workshop and get a hacksaw.

WILSON It will take hours to saw through those bars. Why don't we send for the fire brigade?

MAINWARING There's an air raid on, Wilson, they've got more important things to do, besides I keep telling you, I don't want anyone to know. **(To Pike)** I said, put your helmet on, Pike.

PIKE **(Struggling)** I can't get it through the bars.

MAINWARING Turn it sideways.

PIKE How can I see which is sideways, I haven't got eyes at the back of my head.

MAINWARING Don't use that tone of voice to me, Pike. Jones, put his steel helmet on for him.

JONES Yes, Mr Mainwaring. **(He takes Pike's helmet and goes behind the gate)**

GODFREY Excuse me, sir, I have a jar of Vaseline in my first aid bag. If we smear it round his head, he might slip through.

MAINWARING An excellent idea, Frazer. Wilson, help Godfrey to grease Pike's head.

They both start to grease Pike's head.

MAINWARING What are you fiddling about for, Jones?

JONES Every time I put his helmet on sir, it drops off.

PIKE Ow, that's cold. What is it?

WILSON It's only Vaseline, Frank.

MAINWARING Don't dab at it like some nancy boy, Wilson, smear it on, smear it on.

WILSON I am smearing it on.

PIKE I don't want my head greased. I shall tell Mum, Uncle Arthur.

WILSON Oh, do be quiet.

FRAZER Don't be such a soft Jessie.

GODFREY We've used the whole pot, sir.

MAINWARING Sponge, grab his legs and bring your full weight to bear.

SPONGE **(Flexing his muscles)** Yes, Captain Mainwaring, my full weight.

MAINWARING The rest of you get what purchase you can. **(They all grab Pike)** Now, pull.

They all pull.

PIKE Ow, ow. You're pulling my head off.

WILSON I don't think it's working, sir.

MAINWARING Don't give up. Come on, try again. Pull, pull.

There is a loud explosion, they all dive for the ground. Mainwaring, Wilson and Jones all have their heads close together.

MAINWARING That was too heavy for a bomb.

WILSON I think it was a land mine, sir.

JONES Thank goodness. I thought it was Pike's head exploding.

FRAZER We've got to get this boy under cover, sir.

MAINWARING **(Getting up)** I quite realise that, Frazer. Right, Wilson, Jones, Frazer, Godfrey, Sponge. O Group **(They all gather round Mainwaring, just out of earshot of Pike)** – now, we've got to get Pike's head out of those railings. Any suggestions?

JONES Permission to speak, sir? I look at it this way, drastic times call for drastic measures. The only thing that's stopping us from getting Pike's head out of those railings is his ears. Why don't we remove the obstruction?

MAINWARING What do you mean?

JONES Cut them off.

WILSON Oh for goodness sake, Jones.

JONES We needn't cut them both off, we could cut off one and try it.

MAINWARING Don't talk rubbish, Pike can't walk around for the rest of his life without any ears.

JONES That's better than walking around without any head.

PIKE You're talking about me, aren't you? What are you saying?

MAINWARING Mind your own business, boy, eavesdroppers never hear good of themselves.

WILSON Wait a minute, sir, I think I've got it. Look, why don't we lift the gate off its hinges, then we can march back with it to the church hall.

MAINWARING Yes, yes, well done, Wilson, I was waiting to see who'd be the first one to spot that. Right, come on, men, we'll get this gate off.

They all gather round the gate.

MAINWARING Right, are you ready? Lift.

PIKE Ow, ow, you're strangling me.

MAINWARING Don't go up with the gate, you stupid boy, as we lift it, you slide down. Right, lift.

WILSON I think it's coming, sir.

They lift the gate – it comes off its hinges.

MAINWARING Right, we'll get back to the church hall as quickly as possible, and let's hope no one sees us. By the left, quick march, right wheel, right wheel. Keep in step, Pike.

INTERIOR. CHURCH HALL. NIGHT

The rest of the platoon are standing around, Mainwaring and co. come in with the gate. They have a slight difficulty getting it through the doors.

JONES Right hand down, that's it, don't juggle the private.

PIKE Ow, ow.

MAINWARING **(To platoon)** All right, men, nothing to worry about, stand by for orders.

They get the gate in the middle of the hall.

MAINWARING Put it down, gently.

PIKE Ow, ow.

WILSON That gate weighs a ton, it's nearly pulled my arms out of their sockets.

PIKE What do you think it's done to my head?

WILSON Oh, stop grumbling, Frank.

MAINWARING Yes, stop grumbling, Pike.

FRAZER We can't stand here holding this gate all night, Captain Mainwaring.

JONES Permission to speak, sir? Why don't we get two long ropes and hang the gate from that beam? Then we won't have to hold it.

MAINWARING Good idea. Sponge, get two long ropes.

SPONGE Yes, Captain Mainwaring, two long ropes. **(He goes)**

JONES The Fuzzie Wuzzies used to do that to their prisoners in the Sudan. Hang them up in the sun, with nothing to drink.

PIKE I don't want to be hung up, with nothing to drink.

MAINWARING You'll do as you're told, boy.

GODFREY Captain Mainwaring, I don't mind bringing him a glass of water from time to time.

There is the sound of raised voices in the office.

WILSON There's someone in the office, sir.

The office door opens, Cheeseman comes out, he shouts back into the office.

CHEESEMAN Oh yes, yes, right-oh... **(He sees Mainwaring)** It's a good job you got back, Captain Mainwaring, there's a... hullo, what's this?

MAINWARING This, er... this is Private Pike.

CHEESEMAN Hello, how are you? What's he doing with his head stuck in a gate?

MAINWARING That's a very good question, but I can't answer it, it's highly secret.

CHEESEMAN You can tell me.

MAINWARING Not until you're sworn in.

CHEESEMAN Well, swear me in now.

MAINWARING There's no time. **(More uproar in the office)** What's going on in the office?

CHEESEMAN The Chief Warden is holding an emergency meeting.

MAINWARING How dare he? I'll soon put a stop to that. Come on, Wilson.

WILSON I don't think we ought to interrupt if it's a private meeting, sir.

MAINWARING What are you talking about? That's my office, come on. **(He strides towards the office, followed by Wilson)**

INTERIOR. SIDE OFFICE. NIGHT

The Vicar is sitting at his desk, the Verger is standing behind him, Hodges is banging the table and shouting at the police inspector and fire officer. Everyone is talking at once.

HODGES If everyone talks at once, we won't get anywhere...

Mainwaring and Wilson enter.

HODGES There you are, Napoleon. Where have you been? Don't you know there's an emergency on?

MAINWARING How dare you use my office without my permission?

VICAR This happens to be my office, Captain Mainwaring.

VERGER That's right, this happens to be His Reverence's office.

MAINWARING It's also my office.

HODGES It's also my office, and I'm holding an emergency meeting.

MAINWARING Emergency, what emergency?

VICAR Do you mean to say you haven't heard? Oh, you know Inspector Baker and Fire Officer Dale?

Baker and Dale both nod.

WILSON How awfully nice to meet you again. It was fun last night, Connie wears awfully well, don't you think?

MAINWARING Wilson! Never mind about Connie. Now, what's happened?

HODGES A land mine has dropped on the railway line, just outside the town.

BAKER Fortunately no one was hurt, but it's destroyed a hundred yards of railway track.

HODGES Yes, and it's cut off the town's gas and water supplies.

DALE If those Jerry planes drop any fire bombs, we've had it.

MAINWARING This is damned serious. (**He crosses to the phone**) I'm going to get on to G.H.Q.

HODGES You can't do that, the telephone lines are down as well.

The side door bursts open and Mr Gordon the town clerk comes in.

GORDON I've just heard the news, no gas, no water and no telephones, the town's cut off, we're marooned, marooned. What are we going to do?

MAINWARING All right, Mr Town Clerk, there's no need for panic.

GORDON I'm not in a panic, but somebody's got to do something. (**Shouting at him**) What are you going to do?

They are all shouting at once. Mainwaring draws Wilson downstage.

MAINWARING Wilson.

WILSON Yes, sir.

MAINWARING Something's got to be done.

WILSON It certainly has, sir.

MAINWARING There's only one thing for it, I shall have to take charge.

WILSON Yes, sir, I quite agree.

MAINWARING That's just the sort of remark I'd expect you to make, I don't... what did you say?

WILSON I said, I quite agree. If you don't take charge, God knows what's going to happen to this town. I'm right behind you, sir.

MAINWARING Thank you, Wilson. (**He shakes his hand**)

WILSON Don't mention it, sir.

MAINWARING Get Jones, Frazer and Godfrey in here at the double, rifles and bayonets.

WILSON Right, sir. (**He strides to the door, wrenches it open and bawls**) Jones, Frazer and Godfrey in here at the double, rifles and fixed bayonets. (**Back to Mainwaring**) How's that, sir?

MAINWARING I can hardly believe it, Wilson. Is this really you?

WILSON It's me all right. You see, when the occasion demands, I can bawl and shout just like you.

Jones, Frazer and Godfrey enter, followed by Cheeseman.

MAINWARING (**Points to the Vicar**) I'm sorry to have to do this, Vicar. Jones, Frazer, clear my desk.

FRAZER Right, sir.

VERGER How dare you threaten His Reverence with a bayonet?

JONES I'm threatening you as well, mate, clear off.

VICAR Better humour them, Mr Yeatman, it's quite obvious Captain Mainwaring has gone mad. (**He moves away from the desk**)

Hodges, with the town clerk in the centre, are still arguing.

MAINWARING Wilson, Jones, Godfrey, Frazer, get behind me in a tight group.

JONES Right, into a tight group behind the captain, at the double.

Wilson, Frazer, Jones and Godfrey get behind Mainwaring.

MAINWARING Not as tight as that Godfrey. Right, get their attention, Frazer.

FRAZER Aye, aye, sir. (**He goes a blood-curdling war whoop – there is silence**)

WILSON Attention, please, Captain Mainwaring has an announcement to make.

MAINWARING Gentlemen, this town is now under martial law.

Dale and Baker react.

HODGES What's that mean?

MAINWARING Martial law, law enforced by military authorities in times of danger or emergency. I'm taking over.

HODGES He's been leading up to this for years, and he's finally done it. Well, you're not getting away with it, Napoleon. Inspector, arrest that man.

BAKER You can't do this, Captain Mainwaring. If anyone should take charge, the police should. Where's your authority?

Mainwaring takes out his revolver and lays it on the table.

MAINWARING That is the symbol of my authority, I've got 15 fully armed men behind me, what have you got?

BAKER Well there's me, and my sergeant, and two constables.

DALE Yes, Dick and George.

CHEESEMAN You certainly are a man of action, Captain Mainwaring. I'm right behind you, boyo, ... the power of the press, remember, the power of the press, oh yes, indeed, oh yes.

MAINWARING Thank you, Mr Cheeseman. Wilson, bring a notebook and pencil. The rest of you, follow me. (**He puts his revolver back in its holster and strides towards the door**)

INTERIOR. CHURCH HALL. NIGHT

The park gate is hanging from the ceiling, Pike is sitting on a chair. Mainwaring comes in.

MAINWARING Right, pay attention, everyone. This town is now under martial law.

GORDON Stop him, someone, we can't let him take over the town. He's a tyrant. **(Points to Pike)** Look at the way he punishes his men.

PIKE I'm not being punished, I just got my…

MAINWARING Be quiet, Pike. Right, Wilson, Jones, Frazer, Godfrey, take these orders down and then get on your bikes and shout them out around the town. You first, Wilson, start writing.

WILSON Ready, sir.

MAINWARING This town is now under martial law. **(Wilson repeats)** All looters will be shot on sight.

WILSON All looters will be shot on sight.

GORDON As town clerk, I demand that someone stops him. He's behaving like some dictator in a South American Banana Republic.

PIKE Does that mean we're going to get bananas again, Mr Mainwaring?

MAINWARING No, you stupid boy. Right, Jones, you're next.

JONES Yes, sir, yes, sir.

MAINWARING The gas and water supplies.

JONES Gas and water supplies.

MAINWARING I'm just telling you they've been damaged so there's a danger of cholera. No water to be drunk unless boiled.

JONES No water to be drunk unless boiled.

WILSON How are they going to boil it without gas, sir?

MAINWARING That's their business.

JONES That's their business.

MAINWARING No, Jones. No one to take a bath without a permit.

JONES No one to take a bath without a permit.

MAINWARING Jones, you'll be in charge of all water permits.

GODFREY Excuse me, sir, I wonder if…

MAINWARING Quiet, Godfrey. Right, Frazer, you're next. All rumour mongers will be imprisoned, all defeatists will be imprisoned, anyone not obeying orders of the military will be imprisoned.

FRAZER Anyone not obeying orders of the military will be imprisoned.

BAKER We've only got two cells.

GORDON I've never heard anything like it. I'm going to see the mayor about this. **(He goes)**

MAINWARING No gathering of more than five persons.

Frazer repeats.

VICAR But I always have at least ten in my congregation.

VERGER Nine, Mrs Fletcher's in hospital expecting her fifth.

HODGES He'll stop that, given half a chance.

Mainwaring reacts.

MAINWARING Take the Warden's name. Here's another one for you, Jones. No alcoholic beverages to be sold without permission from me.

FRAZER This is most undemocratic.

MAINWARING You'll be in charge of the liquor permits, Frazer.

FRAZER I'm right behind you, captain.

MAINWARING Right, Wilson, when you and Jones and Frazer have shouted those messages round the town, come back here and await further orders. I'm going to set up my headquarters at the town hall.

WILSON Why the town hall?

MAINWARING Because whoever holds the town hall, holds Walmington-on-Sea. Right, men, follow me, we march on the town hall.

INTERIOR. CHURCH HALL. NIGHT

Pike is sitting with his head through the railings, Godfrey is holding a mug of tea for him to drink.

PIKE Mr Godfrey, I don't think I can stand much more of having my head stuck in here.

GODFREY You must be brave, Frank, and hold on a little while longer.

PIKE Well, someone will have to do something soon, quite soon.

GODFREY I know how you feel only too well, and you have my deepest sympathy.

We hear Jones' voice.

JONES **(Out of vision)** No one to take a bath without a permit.

Wilson, Jones and Frazer enter.

JONES No one to take a bath…

WILSON Please, Jones, that's enough, you can stop now, we're here.

FRAZER I never knew you had such a loud voice, Sergeant Wilson, I could hear you four streets away.

WILSON I felt rather like a rag-and-bone man.

PIKE Uncle Arthur, have you thought of a way to get me out of here yet?

WILSON Don't keep moaning all the time, Frank, I'm working on it, I'm working on it.

Mr Bluett enters with his overcoat over his pyjamas.

BLUETT Excuse me.

JONES Hullo, Mr Bluett, what brings you out at this time of night?

BLUETT I was going to take a bath, and I'd just got one foot in, when I heard this voice shouting that I'd got to have a permit.

WILSON Well, Mr Bluett, I don't really think...

JONES Of course he's got to have a permit, what do you think I've been shouting me head off for?

FRAZER This whole thing has assumed ridiculous proportions.

BLUETT Well, make your mind up, the water's getting cold.

JONES The trouble is, you see, I haven't got any bath permits just at the moment. 'Ere, wait a minute. **(He takes a notebook out of his pocket and writes)**

BLUETT The wife usually gets in after me, does she have to have a permit as well?

JONES No, no, one's enough, here you are. **(Reads)** I give you permission to have a bath, yours sincerely Jack Jones, Lance Corporal. **(He tears it out and hands it to Bluett)**

BLUETT Who do I give it to?

JONES Ah, that's a point. You'd better give it back to me. **(He takes it back)**

BLUETT That's all right then, I'm very law abiding, I always obey all the rules. **(He points to Pike)** I wouldn't want to end up being punished like him. Good night all. **(He goes)**

FRAZER I knew it, the whole affair has become a complete farce.

Mainwaring and the rest of the platoon enter with Cheeseman.

WILSON You're back early, sir, I thought you were going to take over the town hall.

MAINWARING It was closed, doesn't open until nine o'clock in the morning.

CHEESEMAN I've got a nice picture of Captain Mainwaring knocking on the door, and the town clerk going like that through the letter box. **(He gives the V sign)**

MAINWARING I shall deal with him first thing in the morning.

PIKE What about me, Mr Mainwaring?

MAINWARING Be quiet, Pike, you'll be attended to, all in due course.

Pike reacts.

FRAZER Captain Mainwaring, I feel it's my duty to point out to you that you're behaving in an undemocratic and unconstitutional manner, by usurping the power of the land.

WILSON I think Frazer's right, sir, all this threatening to shoot people, you really are going too far, I mean, you're behaving like a dictator.

MAINWARING I am not behaving like a dictator, Wilson, I'm just asking people to do as they're told.

JONES That's right, Captain Mainwaring, at a time like this you've every reason to uslurp the power of the land, and to carry out a coup de tart.

MAINWARING Someone has to take charge in this emergency, and that someone is me. Of course, as soon as I consider that the civil powers are able to take over, I shall relinquish all control. In the meantime everyone will have to knuckle down. It's for their own good.

Captain Swan enters.

SWAN Good evening, I'm Captain Swan.

MAINWARING How do you do, I'm Captain Mainwaring.

SWAN I've been sent across from G.H.Q. to take over control and distribution of all essential services.

MAINWARING Do you mean you are putting the town under martial law?

SWAN I suppose you might call it that. I've got a notice here about it, all the usual rubbish on it. Illegal assembly, looting and all that sort of thing.

MAINWARING But I've done all that, I've put myself in complete control.

SWAN In that case, all I've got to do is to take over from you. Where's your office?

FRAZER **(Pointing)** Over there.

SWAN Thanks. **(To Mainwaring)** Don't mind if I borrow your desk, do you? **(He walks over to Mainwaring's office, Mainwaring and co. follow, he slams the door in man's face)**

MAINWARING But this is monstrous, it's undemocratic, it's unconstitutional, it's against everything we're fighting for. I shall get straight on to my MP.

WILSON I shouldn't worry, sir, all you've got to do is knuckle down. It's for your own good.

SERIES SEVEN **EPISODE THREE**

Recorded: Sunday 27/10/74

Original transmission: Friday 29/11/74, 7.45–8.15pm

Original viewing figures = 14.4 million

ARTHUR LOWE .... CAPTAIN MAINWARING
JOHN LE MESURIER .... SERGEANT WILSON
CLIVE DUNN .... LANCE CORPORAL JONES
JOHN LAURIE .... PRIVATE FRAZER
ARNOLD RIDLEY .... PRIVATE GODFREY
IAN LAVENDER .... PRIVATE PIKE
BILL PERTWEE .... CHIEF WARDEN HODGES
TALFRYN THOMAS .... PRIVATE CHEESEMAN
EDWARD SINCLAIR .... VERGER
ROBERT RAGLAN .... COLONEL
ROBIN PARKINSON .... LIEUTENANT WOOD
ERIK CHITTY .... MR CLERK
RACHEL THOMAS .... THE MOTHER SUPERIOR
MICHAEL SHARVELL-MARTIN .... LIEUTENANT
VERNE MORGAN .... FARMER
JOY ALLEN .... LADY WITH THE PRAM
PLATOON .... COLIN BEAN, GEORGE HANCOCK,
.... DESMOND CULLUM-JONES, MICHAEL MOORE,
.... FREDDIE WHITE, FREDDIE WILES, EVAN ROSS,
.... LESLIE NOYES, ROGER BOURNE, HUGH CECIL
NUN (NON-SPEAKING) .... BELINDA LEE

GORILLA WARFARE

• DEREK WARE REMEMBERS •

'Doubling for Clive Dunn as a passenger in the sidecar of a period military motorcycle sounded like a piece of cake. Fellow stuntman Stuart Fell was assigned as a double for Captain Mainwaring and after a couple of establishing shots of Arthur Lowe at the handlebars we were to take over, racing around country roads with a professional "skin" actor dressed up in a very realistic gorilla costume.

'However, once he got the "bit between his teeth", Stuart came up with a few ideas that were not in the script, such as going round corners on two wheels and jumping off a small ramp. The production crew were delighted to go along with all suggestions as long as no damage was inflicted on the period bike and sidecar, which had probably cost more to hire than those it was transporting altogether. The sidecar was extremely confined and I was getting buffeted all over the place. After tearing across a newly ploughed field, the up-and-down bumping effect causing great bursts of merriment from viewers nationwide when it was shown, I sustained heavy bruising to the left-hand side of my ribs and two hair line fractures on the right. No one was happier than I when the climactic shot caused me to somersault out of the sidecar into a patch of welcoming soft mud, and on the cry of "Cut! That's a wrap..." I retired to the nearest hostelry for a large scotch. Or maybe it was three...'

2
1

GORILLA WARFARE

EXTERIOR. CHURCH HALL. DAY

Several members of the platoon are standing around, others are arriving. Mainwaring is reading a map, Pike arrives, he is wearing his scarf, he salutes. Everyone wears full equipment.

PIKE Good afternoon, Captain Mainwaring, I'm really looking forward to this weekend exercise.

MAINWARING How many times have I told you not to come on parade wearing that scarf, boy?

PIKE My mum made me put it on, if we're sleeping out all night, she doesn't want me to catch cold.

MAINWARING You won't come to any harm in this weather, it's midsummer.

Wilson comes into the picture, he is carrying a suitcase.

WILSON Hullo, sir.

MAINWARING What have you got in that suitcase?

WILSON Just a couple of rugs, and my pyjamas and things.

PIKE One of the rugs is for me, Mr Mainwaring. Mum made him put them in.

MAINWARING Rugs and pyjamas on active service? I never heard anything like it in all my life. (**He moves close to Wilson**) Now, look here, Wilson, as my sergeant you're supposed to set an example of toughness, you're supposed to... (**He starts to sniff**) Are you wearing scent, Wilson?

WILSON Scent?

MAINWARING Yes, scent.

WILSON I just put some eau-de-Cologne on my face after I shaved.

MAINWARING You put scent on your face after you shave? I've never heard of such a thing.

PIKE Mum likes it, she says he smells ever so nice.

MAINWARING Be quiet, Pike. I can't think why I haven't smelt it before.

WILSON I only use it at the weekends, sir, it's so hard to get.

MAINWARING A good job too, that's the sort of thing you'd expect a foreigner to do, some dago or other, but not an Englishman.

WILSON Oh really, sir?

MAINWARING You're decadent, that's what you are, Wilson, decaden. You'll be wearing suede shoes next. You'd better wash it off before anyone smells you.

Frazer comes into the picture.

MAINWARING You don't catch Frazer, stinking of scent, er... (**Mainwaring sniffs**) What's that smell?

FRAZER Just a wee drop of embalming fluid behind my ears.

Mainwaring reacts.

FRAZER It keeps the mosquitoes away.

Godfrey comes into the picture. He is carrying a pink eiderdown, tied up with string, over his shoulder.

GODFREY Good afternoon, sir.

MAINWARING What are you doing with that eiderdown, Godfrey?

GODFREY As we're sleeping out, my sister Dolly thought it would keep me warm.

MAINWARING You can't move swiftly across country, loaded down with that.

FRAZER He could'ner move swiftly across country stark naked.

Godfrey reacts. Jones and Cheeseman enter, Cheeseman is carrying a tripod and plate camera, and is in uniform.

JONES All present and correct, sir, and raring to go.

MAINWARING Just a minute. What's all this?

CHEESEMAN So everyone knows what I do.

MAINWARING What?

CHEESEMAN War correspondent.

MAINWARING Take it off, and you can't bring that camera with you, Cheeseman.

JONES He's just been taking my photograph, sir, he's featuring me in one of the articles he's doing for the *Gazette.*

CHEESEMAN Oh yes indeed, how's this for a title, 'Corporal Jones Battle Scarred Veteran'?

JONES When he says battle scarred veteran, that doesn't mean that I'm all mangled and mingy, I'm mentally scarred, you see, sir.

FRAZER You mean you're barmy.

JONES No, I am not barmy. Now, look here, Private Frazer...

MAINWARING That will do, Sergeant!

WILSON Yes, sir.

MAINWARING For goodness sake, fall the men in, we've wasted enough time as it is.

WILSON Fall in, in three ranks.

The men fall in, Cheeseman still has his camera.

MAINWARING Not with the camera, Cheeseman.

CHEESEMAN Oh yes, sorry. (**He hands it to Wilson and falls in**)

MAINWARING Get rid of it, Wilson.

WILSON Where?

MAINWARING Oh, give it to me.

Wilson thrusts the camera at Mainwaring, the cloth goes over his head.

WILSON Platoon, attention! All present and correct, sir.

Mainwaring comes out from under the cloth and adjusts himself.

MAINWARING **(Coldly)** Stand at ease. Thank you, Sergeant. Now, pay attention, men. For the purpose of this exercise, we are a patrol of commandos behind the enemy lines. And our job is to rendezvous with a highly important secret agent, who has been dropped by parachute. We then escort the secret agent to a secret destination.

JONES Permission to speak, sir? I should like to volunteer to be the highly important secret agent.

MAINWARING Thank you, Jones, but I have already decided who is going to be the highly important secret agent.

WILSON It wouldn't by any chance be you, sir, would it?

MAINWARING Yes, how did you know?

WILSON Oh, just a guess.

PIKE Are you really going to drop out of an aeroplane by parachute, Mr Mainwaring?

MAINWARING Of course not, you stupid boy, it's a hypothetical parachute.

JONES I shouldn't use one of them, sir, they're not safe.

PIKE He's just pretending, Mr Jones.

JONES You mean he's not going to use a parachute at all?

MAINWARING Now, our task is to avoid being spotted from the air as we move across country, so we shall use camouflage. Now, G.H.Q. in their turn will endeavour to capture our secret agent...

FRAZER Who is highly important.

MAINWARING **(Giving Frazer a glare)** ...they will do this by trying to divert us from our task, by the use of counter agents. Now, we've... **(He notices that Wilson has his face turned to the sun with his eyes closed)** What are you doing, Wilson?

WILSON Oh I'm sorry, sir, it's such a beautiful day, I thought that while you were chatting away I'd take advantage of this sun, and try to get a bit of a tan.

PIKE Mum said he was looking ever so pale at breakfast.

There is a pause, Mainwaring draws Wilson down stage.

MAINWARING Wilson, I don't know if it's your age or what, but your behaviour is getting more peculiar every day, and if you go on like this much longer, we shall have, to have a very serious talk. **(He turns back to the men)**

FRAZER Captain Mainwaring, how will we know who these counter agents are?

MAINWARING We won't, they will be in all sorts of disguises, so in order to be on the safe side, we'll assume everyone we meet is a counter agent, and ignore them.

JONES Permission to speak, sir? How important are their counter agents, are they just important, or highly important?

MAINWARING That's not important, Jones.

GODFREY Oh, I'm sure you'll be the most important one, Captain Mainwaring.

CHEESEMAN Oh yes indeed, no one more important than you, Captain Mainwaring.

JONES We had an important secret agent in the Sudan, sir, until them Dervishes got hold of him. He wasn't very important after that. I wouldn't want that to happen to you, sir.

MAINWARING Don't you worry about that. Wilson, tell them what happened to the Eastgate platoon last week.

WILSON What?

MAINWARING Tell them what your friend Freddie Buckmaster told you.

WILSON Well you see, it appears that the Eastgate platoon did this exercise last week, and Captain Square made himself the highly important secret agent.

MAINWARING He would, pompous ass.

WILSON And they'd only been going an hour when he was captured.

MAINWARING That's right, he made a complete mess of it.

They all cheer and jeer.

INTERIOR. INSIDE OFFICE WINDOW. DAY

Hodges and the Verger are looking out into the yard.

VERGER Look at that, Mr Hodges, laughing and sneering at poor old Captain Square and the Eastgate platoon.

HODGES Hooligans, that's what they are.

VERGER You don't mind helping Captain Square then? There's a fiver in it for us.

HODGES I'd do it for nothing, any enemy of Mainwaring's is a friend of mine.

MAINWARING **(Out of vision)** Right, men, get ready to move off, load up!

HODGES Now, remember what Captain Square said, we've got to make sure that Mainwaring's mob, are spotted by that aeroplane.

TELECINE: COUNTRY ROAD. EXTERIOR. DAY

Jones' van is parked off the road, Mainwaring is standing with Wilson, Jones, Frazer, Pike, Godfrey and Cheeseman. The rest of the platoon are getting out of the van. They are all heavily camouflaged.

MAINWARING Now, I'm going to put everyone in the picture, Wilson. Jones, get the men together for a short brief.

JONES Right, sir. At the double, gather round the captain for your short briefs.

MAINWARING Now, listen carefully, men, I am the highly important secret agent, and I have just been dropped by parachute. Now, we must be on our guard, against G.H.Q. counter agents, and, as we don't know what sort of disguises they'll be using, we'll ignore everybody that we don't know personally. Is that clear? Get ready to move off.

TELECINE: ROAD. EXTERIOR. DAY

An Austin 7 is parked by the road with the bonnet up. Two nuns are looking in the engine. The platoon come into the picture, Mainwaring in front with Wilson. Jones, Frazer and Pike are heading the three files.

WILSON Look at those poor nuns, sir, their car's broken down.

MAINWARING Rubbish, they're obviously counter agents, disguised as nuns. You'd think they'd use something more original than that. (**Shouts back over his shoulder**) Ignore those nuns, men.

JONES 'Ere, Pikey, they don't look like secret agents to me.

PIKE Of course they don't, if they looked like secret agents, they wouldn't be secret.

FRAZER They're not counter agents, they've got women's faces.

CHEESEMAN Perhaps they're effeminate secret agents.

FRAZER Nonsense. Hey, Captain Mainwaring, they've got women's faces.

MAINWARING I don't care what sort of faces they've got. Just keep going.

They draw level with the nuns.

MOTHER SUPERIOR I say, our car's broken down, could you gentlemen give us some assistance please.

MAINWARING Take no notice.

MOTHER SUPERIOR Please help us.

WILSON We're being awfully rude, sir.

MAINWARING Look to your front, Wilson.

They march past.

MOTHER SUPERIOR Please, please. You know, Sister Mary, since this Nazi parachute scare, life is becoming quite unbearable.

TELECINE: COUNTRY ROAD.EXTERIOR. DAY

Woman pushing pram with hood up. Mainwaring and co. come into the picture.

MAINWARING Hullo, there's another one.

WILSON Another what, sir?

MAINWARING A counter agent, I'll lay you a pound to a penny there's a wireless receiver in that pram.

WILSON Oh really, sir?

MAINWARING I'm not taking any chances, Jones.

JONES Yes, sir.

MAINWARING When I give the order, surround that pram.

JONES Right, you heard what the officer said, boys. When he gives the word, surround the pram. Shall we fix bayonets, sir?

MAINWARING I don't think that will be necessary.

They draw level with the woman.

MAINWARING Now! (**He draws the revolver, points it at the woman**) Get back.

Woman backs away with her hands up – the rest of the platoon surround the pram.

MAINWARING Search the pram, Wilson.

Wilson puts his hands in the pram.

MAINWARING Is there a wireless set in there?

WILSON If there is, the battery's leaking. (**He holds up bottle, loud screams from baby**)

TELECINE: HEDGE. EXTERIOR. DAY

Mainwaring and co. are crouching beside the hedge, behind which is open country dotted with bushes. About three hundred yards beyond this are thick woods. A small spotter plane swoops low over the field and climbs away.

MAINWARING We've got to get across that field and into those woods, without being spotted by that plane.

The plane turns, and flies back across the field.

MAINWARING Here is comes again, keep down.

JONES How will we know if the plane spots us, sir?

MAINWARING If it does see us, it will drop bombs of yellow dye, right. It's all clear, come on!

TELECINE: COUNTRY ROAD. EXTERIOR. DAY

Mainwaring and co. are moving across in extended order. We hear the sound of the plane.

MAINWARING Here it comes, men. Crouch down and freeze.

They all crouch down and freeze, the plane swoops over.

MAINWARING It didn't spot us. Well done, men.

TELECINE: FIELD. EXTERIOR. DAY

Hodges and the Verger are crouching behind a bush.

VERGER They haven't been spotted so far, Mr Hodges.

HODGES They soon will be. Quick, spread that sheet out.

They quickly spread the sheet out on the ground. We hear the sound of the plane.

HODGES Here it comes.

They both shout and jump up and down. Aerial or high-angle shot of sheet. On it are painted the words 'there they are' and an arrow. Hodges and Verger are waving their arms. Close up of Hodges.

HODGES Over there! (**Points wildly**) Over there! He's bound to spot 'em, he can't miss, he can't…

We hear the roar of the engine. A paper bag hits Hodges on the head and covers him in yellow dye.

TELECINE: FIELD. EXTERIOR. DAY

Mainwaring and co. are half way across the field, a man in a white coat runs towards them from behind.

MAN I say, wait!

WILSON (**Looking back**) I think somebody's calling you, sir.

JONES He's probably one of those counterfeit agents, sir.

MAINWARING Quite right, Jones. Take no notice, men.

WILSON But he'll attract the attention of the plane.

MAINWARING What a blessed nuisance. (**Shouts**) Right, freeze, and crouch down. (**Mainwaring turns, crouches down and faces the man who is about twenty yards away**)

MAINWARING What do you want?

MAN I must speak to you.

MAINWARING Well, don't come any nearer. Pretend you're not talking to us.

The plane swoops over.

PIKE Look, Mr Mainwaring, he's got officer's clothes on under that white coat.

The man is wearing a khaki shirt, tie and battledress trousers under his white coat.

FRAZER It looks very suspicious to me.

JONES I think he *is* one of them counterfeit agents, sir.

WILSON Oh really, he can't be, he's too much of a gentleman.

MAINWARING There are no gentlemen in war, Wilson, only them or us.

MAN Are you listening?

MAINWARING Yes, get on with it, and don't look at us when you're talking.

Man looks down and up as he's talking.

MAN I work for an experimental laboratory that's run by the war office. We train animals for secret war work.

MAINWARING A likely story. (**Shouts to man**) What sort of animals? Monkeys, I suppose.

MAN That's right, one of them's escaped, it's not really a monkey, it's an ape, a gorilla. Watch out for it, it's dangerous. (**He goes**)

JONES Don't panic! Don't panic! There's a loose gorilla about… Wait a minute, if he's a counterfeit agent, he's just telling us that to divert us from our purpose.

MAINWARING Exactly.

• JIMMY PERRY REMEMBERS •

'In this episode, Hodges and the Verger try to show the pilot of a plane where Mainwaring and his men are hiding, but they come a cropper when the plane drops dye where they're standing instead. For the scene in which Hodges gets covered in the liquid, we used custard, dropped from a high ladder. I remember Bill got quite a lot of it in his ear and had to go to the local hospital just to get it checked.'

GODFREY All the same, I think we ought to be careful, sir. I don't think I could stand the shock of coming face to face with a hairy ape. (**He turns and is face to face with Frazer**)

FRAZER Rubbish! Sheer rubbish!

WILSON I must say, sir, that's the most absurd story I've ever heard in my life.

MAINWARING Of course it is. G.H.Q. must think we're a bunch of idiots.

PIKE He might be telling the truth, Mr Mainwaring. Gorillas are ever so intelligent, I saw one in that film *The Hairy Ape*. Perhaps they're training them to fight the Germans.

MAINWARING Don't talk piffle, boy. If there are any gorillas within a thousand miles of here, I'll eat my hat. (**He gestures**) Forward!

The line moves forward, the camera pans along the line of heavily camouflaged figures. The end one looks like a bush. We see a pair of gorilla's legs sticking out.

TELECINE: EXTERIOR. WOODS. DAY

Mainwaring and co. come into the woods.

MAINWARING Halt. Right, fall out for a smoke, and take your camouflage off.

WILSON I must say, sir, we've done awfully well. That plane never spotted us once.

MAINWARING Believe me, G.H.Q. will have to get up pretty early in the morning to catch me out. Gorilla indeed.

Jones and Frazer are sitting on the ground in front of a bush, Jones takes out a packet of cigarettes, pulls out two, puts one in his mouth and holds the other with his left hand.

JONES Fag, Jock?

FRAZER Ta. (He holds his right hand out. Jones looks down at his right-hand pocket, as he puts the packet away. The gorilla's hand comes through the bush and takes the cigarette out of Jones' hand and puts it into Frazer's. Frazer takes it. He is looking down at his boot as he removes a bit of camouflage with his left hand)

TELECINE: EXTERIOR. WOODS. DAY

Hodges and Verger are sitting on a tree stump. The Verger is dabbing at Hodges' uniform with his duster.

HODGES Stop dabbing at it like that, you'll only make it worse.

VERGER I'm sorry, Mr Hodges, I'll pay for it to be cleaned.

HODGES I'm fed up, fed up with Mainwaring always making a monkey out of me. Come on. (He gets up)

VERGER No one's trying to make a monkey out of you, Mr Hodges.

HODGES Oh, shut up.

They move off. We see the back view of the gorilla as he comes through the bushes and follows them.

TELECINE: EXTERIOR. WOODS. DAY

Back view of Verger and Hodges – camera pulls back, we see the gorilla following them. Verger turns – sees gorilla, taps Hodges on the shoulder.

HODGES Get off.

Verger gives a strangled moan.

HODGES What's the matter with you. (Hodges turns, they both freeze, pause, then run – gorilla follows)

TELECINE: EXTERIOR. WOODS. DAY

Mainwaring and co. are marching along in patrol order.

MAINWARING (Shouting back over his shoulder) Keep up, men, we're doing well.

FRAZER Captain Mainwaring, I can hear voices, voices.

MAINWARING Halt!

We hear Hodges and the Verger calling for help.

FRAZER There they are again, ghostly voices.

MAINWARING Oh, stop rolling your eyes, Frazer.

WILSON He's right, sir, I can hear them as well. Listen.

More cries of help.

WILSON There it is again, someone's in trouble.

JONES Permission to speak, sir? It could be some of them counterfeit agents, trying to divert us from our purpose.

WILSON Look, sir, if it is a trap, you're the one they're after. You stay here and I'll go and see what it is.

MAINWARING Oh all right, take Jones' section with you.

JONES (Shouting suddenly) At the double, a ring of steel, round the captain, form!

The rest of the platoon form a tight ring round Mainwaring, facing outwards.

MAINWARING What are you doing, Jones? What are you doing?

JONES I'm just making sure that while we're gone nobody lays their dirty hands on you, sir.

WILSON (Peering over the men at Mainwaring) Are you all right in there, sir?

MAINWARING Get on with it, Wilson.

TELECINE: EXTERIOR. WOODS. DAY

Hodges and the Verger are up a tree. Wilson, Jones, Frazer, Pike and Cheeseman run into picture.

HODGES/VERGER Help! Help!

PIKE Oh look, Uncle Arthur, it's only Mr Hodges and the Verger.

JONES How dare you divert us from our purpose?

WILSON Come on, let's get back.

HODGES Please don't leave us.

VERGER Yes, don't leave us.

They clutch each other.

HODGES It was a monster! Horrible! And hairy!

VERGER Yes, horrible and hairy!

INTERIOR. BARN. NIGHT

Door opens. Gorilla comes in, looks around, we hear voices, gorilla dives under pile of straw. Mainwaring and co. enter with farmer. They carry hurricane lamps.

FARMER Wel,l you should be warm and cosy here for the night.

MAINWARING Thank you, it was very kind of your wife to give us that delicious supper.

WILSON I must say, I haven't tasted eggs and bacon like that for years.

JONES Yes, it was a real meal.

MAINWARING I really think we ought to pay you something for…

FRAZER (**Quickly pushing the farmer towards the door**) Good night to you, thank you very much.

FARMER Good night then.

Hodges and the Verger come in.

FARMER There's two more gentlemen to join you. (**Goes**)

MAINWARING What do you want, Hodges? I'm sick and tired of you following us about all the time.

WILSON Yes, why don't you go home?

HODGES We daren't, not with that monster about.

MAINWARING Rubbish.

JONES If you ask me, sir, they're up to something.

HODGES (**Grabbing Wilson**) Please let us stay, Sergeant Wilson, please, please.

WILSON Just stop pawing me.

MAINWARING If you must stay, get over there in the corner and keep quiet.

HODGES Oh thank you, Captain Mainwaring, sir. We won't give you any trouble.

VERGER No, we won't give you any trouble.

They both go into a corner and settle down in the straw.

MAINWARING What's the matter with them? I've never seen Hodges grovelling like that before.

WILSON I know, sir, it's quite disgusting. (**He starts to settle down in the straw where the gorilla is hiding**)

MAINWARING Settle down.

PIKE Uncle Arthur, I don't think Mum would like us to sleep in that straw. It could have crawly things in it.

WILSON Oh really, Frank, a little spider won't hurt you. It's really awfully cosy. (**He snuggles up against the gorilla, Pike settles down beside him**)

PIKE It's not bad, is it? Not like straw at all, it's all soft and warm.

WILSON Straw always gives off a certain amount of animal heat.

They are now lying down in the following order – Frazer, Mainwaring, Wilson, Pike, Jones, Godfrey and Cheeseman.

JONES You all right, Mr Godfrey?

GODFREY Yes, I must say this straw is extremely comfortable.

CHEESEMAN Yes, it's real cosy, better than a feather bed.

GODFREY You don't think there's anything in that story about the escaped gorilla, do you?

JONES Of course not, Mr Godfrey.

CHEESEMAN What a story it would make for the *Gazette* if it were true. I can see the headlines now: 'Mad Gorilla Terrorises Countryside'. Oh yes indeed.

JONES Talk about me going into the realms of fantasy. For a start, a gorilla wouldn't last five minutes in this climate, it's too cold. They come from Africa, they need tropical heat. I mean, it would be all right if it were in here, 'cos it's nice and warm, but it's not in here, is it? And it couldn't stand running about outside in the cold night air.

CHEESEMAN Oh no, it wouldn't do any good at all out there, no good at all.

GODFREY Thank you, Mr Jones, you're a great comfort.

JONES Not at all, Mr Godfrey, I'm just talking plain common sense. Now, you go to sleep.

PIKE Uncle Arthur?

WILSON What is it, Frank?

PIKE Tell me a story.

WILSON Really, Frank, you're too old for that sort of thing.

PIKE You used to tell me stories, why have you changed?

WILSON You're grown up now.

PIKE Mum says you tell her stories and it's always the same one.

WILSON Oh go to sleep, Frank.

MAINWARING What's that boy want, Wilson?

WILSON He wants me to tell him a story, sir.

MAINWARING I can't help thinking he's slightly retarded.

WILSON It's his mother, you see, sir, she spoils him to death.

MAINWARING Yes, she's been a widow far too long. What that boy needs is the firm hand of a father.

WILSON I quite agree. Wish I could find somebody.

FRAZER Captain Mainwaring, did you no hear the story of the old empty barn?

MAINWARING No.

FRAZER Would you like to hear the story of the old empty barn?

MAINWARING It will put us in a good mood before we go to sleep. Pay attention, everyone, Private Frazer is going to tell us the story of the old empty barn.

FRAZER The story of the old empty barn – well, there was nothing in it. **(He starts to cackle)** Did you hear what I said? Nothing, nothing. That's all, good night.

MAINWARING You know, Wilson, over the years that I've got to know the members of this platoon, I've grown fond of them, but I can't help thinking sometimes, that I'm in charge of a bunch of idiots.

INTERIOR. G.H.Q. COMMAND POST. NIGHT

Sandbag walls, colonel is sitting at small table with field telephone etc. He is talking to the man we met in the field with the white coat on. He is now wearing battledress, he is a lieutenant.

COLONEL **(Looking at map)** Captain Mainwaring's platoon seem to be doing very well.

LIEUTENANT Lieutenant Wood and I have got a pretty elaborate scheme to upset them, but we haven't had much luck so far.

COLONEL Don't underestimate Mainwaring. He's got a lot of guts and he's very tenacious. Where are they now?

LIEUTENANT They're spending the night in a barn. **(Points to map)** Just here. Lieutenant Wood is keeping an eye on them.

INTERIOR. BARN. NIGHT

Mainwaring and co are fast asleep, Gorilla gets up from straw, shakes himself, and creeps towards door. He trips over Hodges and falls on top of him. Hodges and Verger wake up, try to scream – nothing comes out. Gorilla gets up quickly and rushes out of the door.

INTERIOR. COMMAND POST. NIGHT

Colonel is at table, lieutenant enters.

LIEUTENANT He's here, sir.

COLONEL Well, get him in.

LIEUTENANT **(Calling through door)** Come in, old boy.

Gorilla comes in and salutes.

COLONEL Oh for goodness sake, take that silly mask off. Of all the mad-brained ideas, this takes the biscuit.

WOOD **(Taking off mask)** It seems to be working, sir.

LIEUTENANT We've still got tomorrow morning, sir.

COLONEL Have you found out who the highly important secret agent is?

WOOD Yes, sir, it's Captain Mainwaring.

COLONEL Well, you've only got until 11.00 hours to lure him away from his men and capture him.

WOOD Don't you worry, sir, I'll capture him if it's the last thing I do.

COLONEL Well, you've only got until 11.00 hours to lure him away from his men and capture him.

TELECINE: EXTERIOR. OUTSIDE BARN. DAY

Mainwaring and co. are in a group, Frazer is holding the map.

MAINWARING What's the time, Wilson?

WILSON Half past eight, sir.

MAINWARING Now, you have to deliver me, the highly important secret agent, to G.H.Q. by 11.00 hours. Let's have a look at the map, Frazer.

FRAZER I've worked the route out, sir. We follow this road here, through the woods, pick up this road here, follow it till we get to the bridge, bear right, keep straight on and that will bring us to G.H.Q.

MAINWARING That's miles out of our way. **(Points to map)** All we've got to do is to take a direct route across country.

WILSON But we might get lost.

Mainwaring takes out compass.

MAINWARING I shall use the compass.

WILSON Do you think that's wise, sir?

MAINWARING I'm quite capable of using a compass, Wilson. Now, watch this and you might learn something. I take a bearing. **(Looks through compass then looks at map)** Yes... yes. All we've got to do is to go on a bearing of 94° and that will take us straight to G.H.Q.

TELECINE: COUNTRY ROAD. EXTERIOR. DAY

Long shot of Mainwaring and co. in group, looking at map. Pan in.

MAINWARING Well, I may have been a few degrees out.

FRAZER One hundred and eighty degrees, to be precise. We're right back where we started.

JONES What are we going to do, sir? We've only got half an hour to deliver you to G.H.Q.

They all talk at once.

MAINWARING All right, all right, quiet. **(Points to map)** G.H.Q. is only five miles away, it's a direct road.

WILSON But we'll never make it in half an hour, sir.

MAINWARING Yes we will, we'll use the van.

WILSON But you're not allowed to use our transport.

MAINWARING **(Points to Hodges' motorbike)** I'll use that motorbike, that's not ours.

WILSON Yes, but...

MAINWARING Don't split hairs, Wilson, I am the highly important secret agent and there's nothing to stop me using my initiative and commandeering that motorbike. You can follow in the van. Jones, get the men aboard.

JONES Yes, sir. Right, you heard what the officer said, embark! Embark!

The men scramble aboard the van.

MAINWARING Wilson, you drive the van. Jones, come with me.

JONES Yes, sir, yes, sir.

Mainwaring and Jones run to the motorbike, Wilson, Frazer and Pike get in the front of the van, Godfrey and Cheeseman in the back. A small car comes into the picture, it contains Hodges, the Verger and Mr Clerk. They get out and run towards Mainwaring.

HODGES Oi, where are you going with my motorbike?

MAINWARING I'm commandeering it. Get out of the way.

CLERK **(Thrusting small cardboard box at Mainwaring)** Here it is.

MAINWARING What?

CLERK It's a hypodermic syringe.

MAINWARING What on earth for?

CLERK To inject the gorilla with. It won't hurt it, just put it to sleep.

MAINWARING Are you mad?

HODGES No, he's from the RSPCA. I telephoned him about the escaped gorilla.

CLERK When you've put it to sleep, send for us, we'll do the rest.

JONES He's another of those counterfeit agents, Mr Mainwaring. They don't give up trying, do they?

Mainwaring throws the box into the sidecar.

MAINWARING I've never heard such rubbish.

JONES Yes, even if there was a gorilla, how could we get close enough to inject it?

CLERK That's your problem, I'm a very busy man. Good luck. **(He goes)**

The platoon are all inside the van with the doors shut. Wilson, Pike and Frazer are in the cab. The motorbike and sidecar are behind the van.

JONES Nuns, escaped gorillas, they've really tried everything, sir.

MAINWARING And none of it's worked.

Wilson leans out from the driving seat.

WILSON All ready, sir?

MAINWARING We'll go on ahead, Wilson. You follow us.

WILSON Right, sir.

MAINWARING We're using your motorbike, Hodges. You can follow in the van.

HODGES Now look, Napoleon...

MAINWARING I don't know what your game is, but you're obviously doing your best to ruin our chances of completing this exercise. How you expected us to swallow that story of the escaped gorilla is beyond my comprehension.

Suddenly Hodges and the Verger freeze and slowly raise their hands.

JONES They're trying something else now, Mr Mainwaring.

The gorilla appears behind Mainwaring and Jones with a revolver in his hand. Hodges and the Verger pointing weakly, Mainwaring and Jones turn and see the gorilla. Cut to cab of van.

WILSON Where did you say G.H.Q. was, Frazer?

FRAZER Just down the road here.

Wilson and Frazer are both looking at the map. The motorbike roars past. Mainwaring driving, Jones in the sidecar and the gorilla on the pillion. Only Pike sees them.

PIKE Uncle Arthur, Mr Mainwaring has just gone by with a monkey on his back.

TELECINE: EXTERIOR. ROAD. DAY

Long shot of motorbike.

JONES Don't panic Mr Mainwaring, don't panic!

TELECINE: EXTERIOR. ROAD. DAY

Long shot of van – Hodges is driving.

TELECINE: EXTERIOR. ROAD. DAY

MAINWARING Quick, Jones, get that hypodermic syringe and stick it in him.

JONES Yes, sir, yes, sir, stick the syringe in the monkey. **(Jones takes the syringe out of the box and waves it about)**

• STUART FELL REMEMBERS •

'I remember filming the scene where I'm driving the motorbike and sidecar around the place just before it eventually crashes. It was a vintage bike, and with it being attached to a sidecar and with two passengers as well, it was very heavy. It was fine going round the roads but when we actually got to a very muddy field with long grass, I remember thinking that one of our problems, as well as the actual stunt, was going to be making sure the clutch didn't burn out on us while we tried getting it up to speed in the long grass. If it had, we wouldn't have had a bike to finish off the shoot that day, and would probably have experienced great difficulty getting the bike repaired. Fortunately we completed the filming in one take.

'It was a potentially dangerous stunt because we had a monkey on the back! A professional skin artist was wearing the monkey's outfit for the scene, but he also had to act right up to the point of impact. I found a big hole to run the bike into, and we put some sandbags in to help the bike come to an abrupt halt, giving us the impetus as the bike lifted at the back and threw us all off. Having been a gymnast in the past, I was able to do a very clean somersault over the handlebars. Derek Ware, who was in the sidecar, knew exactly where I was going to land, so he, being a professional, made sure that he went in another direction. We all walked away unscathed and, if I remember rightly, the costume I wore was nice and bulky, bearing in mind I was doubling for Arthur Lowe, so I was able to apply lots of padding.

'It was a great privilege to have been associated with the programme.'

MAINWARING Ow! That was me you stuck it in.

JONES Sorry, sir, the monkey won't keep still.

TELECINE: EXTERIOR. ROAD. DAY

Van moving along.

TELECINE: EXTERIOR. ROAD. DAY.

Longn shot of motorbike swerving. It goes off the road, gorilla falls off. Mainwaring is slumped over handlebars. The van comes into the picture and stops. Jones scrambles out of the sidecar, picks up the revolver and threatens the gorilla. Wilson and the others get out of the van and run over to Jones.

JONES (**Waving revolver**) Get back! Get back!

The gorilla has his hands up.

WILSON Good heavens, there was an escaped gorilla after all.

PIKE See, I was right, Uncle Arthur, they were training them to fight the Germans.

FRAZER I still canna believe it.

CHEESEMAN Oh, what a story this is going to make for the paper.

GODFREY I don't think we ought to get too close, it looks awfully fierce.

PIKE Perhaps we ought to shoot it, Uncle Arthur.

GORILLA No, don't shoot! Whatever you do, don't shoot!

JONES That's funny, I thought gorillas came from Africa. Why is it talking English?

GORILLA (**Tearing off his mask**) I am English.

WILSON Who are you?

GORILLA Lieutenant Wood, and it didn't work.

The Austin 7 comes into the picture, with the two nuns in it. The colonel is driving.

COLONEL (**Getting out**) Thanks for the lift, ladies.

MOTHER SUPERIOR Don't mention it. It's such a change to meet someone who thinks we're real nuns.

COLONEL Congratulations, chaps, you've completed the exercise successfully.

They all cheer.

COLONEL Now, all I've got to do is to get the report of the highly important secret agent. Where is he?

WILSON Over there, sir.

Cut to Mainwaring lying in the sidecar, drunk.

MAINWARING Tiptoe, through the tulips…

The Godiva Affair

SERIES SEVEN **EPISODE FOUR**

Recorded: Sunday 3/11/74

Original transmission: Friday 6/12/74, 7.45–8.15pm

Original viewing figures = 13.8 million

ARTHUR LOWE .... CAPTAIN MAINWARING
JOHN LE MESURIER .... SERGEANT WILSON
CLIVE DUNN.................................. LANCE CORPORAL JONES
JOHN LAURIE .... PRIVATE FRAZER
ARNOLD RIDLEY .... PRIVATE GODFREY
IAN LAVENDER .... PRIVATE PIKE
BILL PERTWEE.................................. CHIEF WARDEN HODGES
TALFRYN THOMAS .... PRIVATE CHEESEMAN
FRANK WILLIAMS .... VICAR
EDWARD SINCLAIR.. VERGER
JANET DAVIES.. MRS PIKE
PAMELA CUNDELL.. MRS FOX
ERIC LONGWORTH .... TOWN CLERK
PETER HONRI .... PRIVATE DAY
ROSEMARY FAITH .... WAITRESS
COLIN BEAN .... PRIVATE SPONGE
GEORGE HANCOCK .... PRIVATE HANCOCK
PLATOON.................. MICHAEL MOORE, DESMOND CULLUM-JONES,
.... FREDDIE WHITE, FREDDIE WILES, EVAN ROSS,
.... LESLIE NOYES, ROGER BOURNE, HUGH CECIL
YOUNG GIRLS...................... PENNY LAMBIRTH, YASMIN LASCELLES,
.... ELAINA GRAND, BELINDA LEE

• ERIC LONGWORTH REMEMBERS •

'Fleshings! A word not in common use in the English language, I think, and briefly described in the Concise English Dictionary as "actor's flesh-coloured tights". Nothing to get excited about there, you might say. Nothing, that is, until you conjure up the one and only Mrs Fox, to give substance to the word, and if you add the fact that she would also be wearing long golden tresses and riding on a horse, then the mind boggles. First seen in 1974, "The Godiva Affair" ranks as my favourite of the eight episodes I had the pleasure of appearing in.

'At a *Dad's Army* convention at Bressingham in May 2000, after the question "Can I have your autograph please?", was added "Will you please say 'fleshings'?". This was followed up at another event at Bristol in October 2000. I obliged, but not before I had explained it was not an easy word to say, until I had conjured up in my mind's eye, that entrancing figure, with tresses flowing in the wind, trotting down the street in Walmington-on-Sea. Of course, I was deluding myself, if not my audience. I must confess I was not thinking of Mrs Fox at all, but of the real flesh-and-blood Pamela Cundell, with or without "fleshings" and with no sign of long golden tresses. Pamela could come into a rehearsal room on a dreary wet summer's day and with her radiant presence transform the scene just as she does today at our reunions.

'Where was I? Oh yes, I've just remembered, it was back in 1977, when touring with Arthur and his wife Joan in *Laburnum Grove* that I discovered he made a charge for his autograph. One shilling (five pence to you) if my memory serves me right, in aid of the RNLI, all entered up in a little black book. What, I wonder, is the right amount to charge for uttering that thought-provoking word today, and to which charity should the proceeds go? What about Denville Hall, Home for Retired Actors? Who knows, they might let me enrol at a reduced rate when I retire and maybe there will be a room for Pamela, too. That would be very nice, very nice indeed.'

The Godiva Affair

INTERIOR. CHURCH HALL. DAY

Mainwaring is talking to Private Hancock, who has a rifle and fixed bayonet.

INTERIOR. SIDE OFFICE. DAY

MAINWARING Right, Hancock, you are to stay on guard outside this door and let no one through. Understand?

HANCOCK Right, sir, let no one through.

MAINWARING Maximum security, is that clear? Maximum security.

HANCOCK Yes, Captain Mainwaring, maximum security.

Mainwaring goes through the door into the hall.

INTERIOR. CHURCH HALL. DAY

Mainwaring comes through and locks the door.

MAINWARING Right, men, this is top secret. Put the black-outs up. Private Woods and Meadows, on guard outside the main doors, no one is to enter, I don't care who they are.

Woods and Meadows go out through the main doors, the rest of the platoon, put up the black-outs.

MAINWARING **(Knocking on office door)** All clear out there, Hancock?

HANCOCK All clear, sir.

Mainwaring comes down to the centre of the hall.

MAINWARING All clear, Jones?

JONES **(Out of vision)** Right you are, sir.

The door at the side of the stage opens. Jones, Frazer, Pike, Godfrey, Cheeseman and Sponge file on. They are dressed as Morris dancers.

MAINWARING Excellent turn out, men, excellent.

JONES Permission to speak, sir? Aren't you going to put on your attire?

MAINWARING Not at the moment, I'll just wear the hat. **(Mainwaring gets bowler hat with ribbons on)**

MAINWARING Now, pay attention. The reason I have taken all these precautions to keep this a secret, is because I don't want us to look like a bunch of idiots. **(He puts on the bowler hat)**

Reaction.

MAINWARING No one must see us until we get this dance perfect.

FRAZER Captain Mainwaring, if I can have a word? As a Scot, I must say that I object to wearing these pansy Sassenach clothes.

JONES They are not pansy, this is our English national dress.

FRAZER English national dress, rubbish! Cricket clothes, with bells and ribbons on!

MAINWARING All right, Frazer, you can sneer, but if you care to work it out, it's a costume that sums up the English character pretty well. Clean white cricket flannels that stand for fair play and sportsmanship. The bowler hat that stands for respectability and clear thinking. And the ribbons and bells for just a touch of frivolity.

GODFREY Beautifully put, Captain Mainwaring.

JONES General Kitchener liked a touch of frivolity, sir, he used to wear great long…

MAINWARING All right, Jones, we've no time for that now.

JONES Pity, it was a good story.

MAINWARING **(Shouts)** Hurry up, Wilson.

WILSON **(Out of vision)** Do you think someone could open the door for me, sir?

MAINWARING Go and help him, Pike.

PIKE Yes, Mr Mainwaring. **(He crosses to the door)**

MAINWARING Now, I don't want to take too long over this rehearsal, we've got a full training programme ahead of us tonight. Private Day.

DAY Yes, Captain Mainwaring.

MAINWARING Stand by with your concertina.

DAY Right. **(He plays chord)**

MAINWARING Good.

Wilson comes through the door, wearing a hobby horse with a skirt and little legs which are the wrong way round. He has some trouble getting through the door.

WILSON This really is most awkward, sir.

MAINWARING You'll soon get used to it.

JONES Permission to speak, sir? Sergeant Wilson is not looking like a normal man, his little legs are going in the wrong direction.

MAINWARING Do try and sort yourself out, Wilson.

He pulls the legs the right way round.

MAINWARING As you know, men, we only need another £2000 to reach our target, which is to buy a Spitfire. Now, during the whole of next week everyone in Walmington-on-Sea will be doing their utmost to raise the money. The grand climax will be the procession next Saturday afternoon. That is when we will perform our dance. Sergeant Wilson will collect the money from the crowd.

WILSON I don't think I like the idea of asking strangers for money.

MAINWARING It's perfectly simple. All you have to do is to gallop the horse. Try to make it look as lifelike as possible. Then you weave in and out of the dancers, then you weave round the edge of the crowd, pull open the horse's mouth for them to put the money in while you're doing it and make jocular remarks.

Wilson reacts.

WILSON What sort of jocular remarks?

MAINWARING Oh, I don't know, you could say, 'Har, har, har, give till it hurts, har, har, har'. Try that.

WILSON Har, har, har, give till it hurts, har, har, har.

Mainwaring reacts.

JONES If we're going to collect £2000, he'll have to be a bit more jocular than that, sir.

GODFREY I don't think he can afford to be too jocular, otherwise people will think he's being over familiar.

Mainwaring reacts.

PIKE I've got it, why can't he say, 'We need Spitfires to beat the hum, put money in my mouth and it goes to my tum'?

CHEESEMAN Oh that's clever, boyo, that's really good.

FRAZER Rubbish. All he's got to do is to wave his stick at the crowd and shout, 'Give us some money or I'll bash you on the head'.

WILSON Oh really, sir, couldn't you get someone else to do the horse?

MAINWARING No, you are going to do the horse, and that is an order, Wilson. Right. Form up, Sponge – give the book to Sergeant Wilson.

They form up in two lines facing each other. Frazer opposite Jones, Pike opposite Godfrey, and Sponge opposite Cheeseman.

MAINWARING Now, where did we get to last time?

JONES I was having trouble with my whiffling, sir.

MAINWARING Oh yes, whiffling. Now, I think it is very important that we should fully understand the meaning of these movements. Read out the bit about whiffling, Wilson.

WILSON Whiffling, whiffling. The movements with the whiffling stick represent frightening the evil spirits away.

PIKE Away from what, Mr Mainwaring?

MAINWARING This is a fertility dance, Pike.

GODFREY I don't think my sister Dolly would approve of that sort of thing, sir.

FRAZER Ah, you silly old fool, the whole idea of this dance is to encourage the crops to grow. It's danced every spring by the young, fertile men of the village.

JONES Well, there's not much point in us doing it.

FRAZER You speak for yourself.

MAINWARING All right, that will do.

JONES Permission to speak, sir? I do not want to stand opposite Private Frazer when he is whiffling.

MAINWARING Why not?

JONES Well, sir, I have faced whirling Dervishes, and I have faced charging Fuzzie Wuzzies, but I do not want to face Private Frazer when he is waving his whiffling stick. He has a mad look in his eyes.

FRAZER Mad, mad, my eyes are perfectly sane. Captain Mainwaring, would you say that I had mad eyes?

MAINWARING Well er…, no…, not really mad.

FRAZER There you are.

MAINWARING What's next, Wilson?

WILSON The bean sprouting.

MAINWARING Ah yes, the bean sprouting. Come here, Pike. Now, you tap twice on the ground, so. **(He taps Pike's stick)** Then you shout, 'Woa!' and leap up in the air. This represents the beans growing.

PIKE How high do you want us to leap, Mr Mainwaring?

MAINWARING As high as a bean grows.

CHEESEMAN I had some last year that grew to 8 feet.

GODFREY I don't think I could quite manage that, sir.

SPONGE I can leap high, Mr Mainwaring. How's this? **(He shouts 'Woa!' Gives a terrific leap in the air and lands with a crash)**

MAINWARING Yes, yes.

WILSON I think we ought to be a bit careful, sir, the Vicar's got dry rot in the hall.

MAINWARING Perhaps you're right, Wilson, we won't do the leap. Now, we'll go through the whole thing from the start. Ready, Private Day?

DAY Ready, sir. **(He gives a blast on his concertina. They close on Mainwaring)**

MAINWARING Oh, just before we start, I'd better make sure that your bells are working properly. Left legs.

They all shake their left legs.

MAINWARING Right legs.

They shake their right legs.

MAINWARING Can't you make any more noise than that, Godfrey?

GODFREY A touch of rheumatics, I'm afraid, sir.

MAINWARING **(Giving Godfrey a look of despair)** Right. Off we go.

JONES **(Silent mime)** One, two, three, four.

FRAZER Five, six, seven, eight.

They move back. They move forward. They circle clockwise. They circle anti-clockwise. Whiffling. beansprouting. Beansprouting. waffling and finish.

MAINWARING Excellent, men, I'm very proud of you. Right now, take a break and change into your uniforms. Jones.

JONES Yes, sir.

MAINWARING **(Taking him aside)** Now look, Jones, what's the matter with you? All that nonsense about Frazer hitting you with his stick, that's not like you at all.

JONES I know, sir, I'm afraid I cannot cover it up any longer, I am in a highly nervous state.

MAINWARING What's the matter?

JONES Well, sir, it's er… **(He lowers his voice)** It's er, very personal.

MAINWARING Have you got trouble at home?

JONES No, sir, I've got trouble away from home.

MAINWARING You'd better come in the office.

JONES Can Sergeant Wilson come as well, sir?

MAINWARING Why?

JONES 'Cos he's a man of the world.

MAINWARING Oh very well. Wilson.

WILSON Sir?

MAINWARING Office.

WILSON Do you want me to walk or gallop?

MAINWARING Just get in the office!

INTERIOR. SIDE OFFICE. DAY

Mainwaring and Jones come in, Wilson follows.

MAINWARING Sit down, Jones.

JONES Thank you, sir, thank you. **(He sits, Mainwaring sits behind the desk. Wilson stands at the top of the desk. The horse's head goes right across the desk)**

MAINWARING Now, Jones.

The horse's head is blocking his view of Jones.

MAINWARING Get that thing off the desk, Wilson.

WILSON I'm sorry, sir, I can't help it, it sort of sticks out.

MAINWARING Well, take it off.

Wilson takes off the horse.

MAINWARING Now, come along, Jones.

JONES This really is very delicate, sir, you see it's er... Mrs Fox.

MAINWARING Mrs Fox?

JONES Yes, sir, she's a widow lady, and we both have a certain arrangement. For some time now we've been walking out.

MAINWARING Walking out where?

JONES All over the place. You see, I take a couple of chops round to her house every Saturday night, she cooks them and we have supper together.

MAINWARING I see. (**He looks at Wilson**) You're not the only member of this platoon who has that arrangement with a widow, Jones.

WILSON Really, sir, that was a bit below the belt.

JONES There is nothing between Mrs Fox and myself, sir, it is purely a Teutonic arrangement.

Mainwaring reacts.

JONES As I said, every Saturday night we have supper together, and listen to 'In Town Tonight'. Then, when the announcer says, 'Carry on, London', I go home.

MAINWARING I really don't see what this has got to do with me, Jones.

JONES Well, sir, just lately, her affections have been taken by another.

MAINWARING Who?

JONES Mr Gordon, the town clerk.

WILSON What, that silly old bald-headed duffer? (**He laughs and breaks off as Mainwaring gives him a glare**) I er... don't mean that he's a silly old duffer because he's got a bald head, he'd be a silly old duffer even if he had a full head of hair.

MAINWARING All right, Wilson, all right.

JONES Everyone knows that he is a roué and a philanthropist.

Mainwaring reacts.

JONES Her head has been turned by the gay life that he is showing her. Old time dancing at Pevensey Bay, and trips into Eastgate. What can I offer her? I'm just a simple butcher.

MAINWARING But I really don't see what I can do, Jones.

JONES I want you to speak to her for me.

MAINWARING But I couldn't possibly...

JONES You must, sir, you must. (**He rises. He hands Mainwaring a piece of paper**) Here, I've written down her telephone number. Don't spread it around.

MAINWARING Yes, but...

JONES Please speak to her, sir, otherwise I shall be a broken man, and what use is a broken lance corporal to you? (**He goes**)

WILSON What are you going to do, sir?

MAINWARING I don't know, I suppose I could speak to her. I think perhaps I ought to point out what sort of man this town clerk is. I'll give her a ring and arrange to meet her.

INTERIOR. FRAZER'S HOUSE. NIGHT

Frazer is on the telephone, he is in his dressing gown.

FRAZER Hullo, hullo, Godfrey, son, are you there?

INTERIOR. GODFREY'S COTTAGE. NIGHT

Godfrey is also in his dressing gown.

GODFREY Yes, I'm here. I was just having my hot milk before going to bed.

FRAZER Well, it's happened, I knew it would some day.

GODFREY What has?

FRAZER Mainwaring has succumbed to the lure of the flesh.

Godfrey reacts.

FRAZER Did you hear what I said, Godfrey, son, the flesh, the flesh!

GODFREY Oh please, don't keep repeating that word, my sister Dolly might hear you. Anyhow, Mr Frazer, I refuse to believe a word of it.

FRAZER I tell you, I heard it with my own ears. It just so happened that I was passing the office door, and I heard him speaking to this woman.

GODFREY Er… what woman?

FRAZER Mrs Fox, that fine big widow woman.

GODFREY But Mr Mainwaring is a pillar of respectability.

FRAZER It's men like him that are the worst, always looking down his nose at other people, and all the time inside, lust, lust, sheer naked lust.

Godfrey reacts.

FRAZER I tell you, the fires of hell are lying in wait for him, he's doomed, doomed.

GODFREY I think the whole thing's nonsense.

FRAZER Nonsense, is it? I heard him arrange to meet this woman at the Marigold Tea Rooms tomorrow morning at 10.30. If you don't believe me, come and see for yourself.

GODFREY Very well, I'll come just to prove that you're wrong.

FRAZER Right, I'll see you there, and don't forget, it's your turn to pay for the coffee.

Godfrey reacts.

INTERIOR. TELEPHONE BOX. NIGHT

Cheeseman is on the phone, he is in civilian clothes.

CHEESEMAN Hullo, hullo, listen, Pikey I've got to speak to you. It's very important, boyo.

INTERIOR. FRANK'S HOUSE. NIGHT

Pike is on the other end of the line, he is in his pyjamas and dressing gown.

PIKE What do you want to ring me up at this time of night for? Mum's furious.

Mrs Pike comes into the picture.

MRS PIKE Who's that on the phone, Frank, it's not a girl, is it?

PIKE No, Mum, it's Mr Cheeseman.

MRS PIKE How dare he ring you up in the middle of the night? Tell him to go away.

PIKE It's only ten o'clock, Mum.

MRS PIKE I don't care, you should be in bed, and don't forget to clean your teeth. **(She goes)**

PIKE Mum says I've got to go to bed, and clean my teeth.

CHEESEMAN Oh yes. Clean your teeth. They're very important. I just want a bit of information. What time does Mainwaring go for his morning coffee?

PIKE Ten thirty every morning at the Marigold Tea Rooms, regular as clockwork, why?

CHEESEMAN Well, I have it from a very reliable source, that Captain Mainwaring is meeting a certain lady there.

PIKE Oh no, Mr Mainwaring doesn't know certain ladies, he's married.

CHEESEMAN Well, she's not so much a lady see, she's sort of… well, you know, very much. **(He gestures with his hands)**

Pike reacts.

CHEESEMAN Anyhow, I write this gossip column for the *Eastgate Gazette*, 'Whispers from Walmington', oh yes indeed, I can see it now. What certain local bank manager's name is linked with a mysterious widow lady?

PIKE I'm sure you've got it all wrong.

CHEESEMAN My information is that he's besotted with this woman, boy, besotted.

PIKE Hey, like in that film *Rain*, this clergyman was besotted with a girl called Sadie Thompson. Well, being a clergyman, he wasn't allowed to be besotted, so in the end he walked into the sea. Here, you don't think Captain Mainwaring will walk into the sea, do you? If he does, he'll have to walk miles, tomorrow morning, the tide's out.

INTERIOR. MARIGOLD TEA ROOMS. DAY

Frazer and Godfrey are sitting at a table in the corner, they are both dressed in civilian clothes. Cheeseman is sitting at another table behind a newspaper, also in civilian clothes. There are two booths, Jones is sitting in one, behind a newspaper. He is wearing balaclava, bowler hat and mac.

GODFREY I'm sorry, Mr Frazer, Mr Mainwaring is a respectable married man. I refuse to believe that he's capable of such a thing.

FRAZER You know your trouble, Godfrey, you live in a fool's paradise, I tell you…

Mainwaring and Wilson enter.

FRAZER Whist, here he is.

Mainwaring nods at Frazer and Godfrey.

MAINWARING I had hoped that we'd have the place to ourselves.

WILSON I shouldn't worry, sir, no one knows why you're meeting Mrs Fox.

MAINWARING All the same, it doesn't do for a man in my position to be seen in a public place with a flashy woman like Mrs Fox. In a small town like this, tongues wag you know, tongues wag.

WILSON I'm sure no one's the slightest bit interested, sir.

Frazer, Cheeseman and Jones looking.

WILSON Where shall we sit? (**They move to a table**)

MAINWARING I shall sit here. (**Points to booth**) You go and sit on your own.

Wilson reacts. Mainwaring starts to sit.

JONES Psst, psst, Mr Mainwaring.

MAINWARING Good morning, is that you, Jones?

JONES You won't let me down, will you, sir?

MAINWARING Why on earth are you dressed like that?

JONES I'm in disguise, sir, I don't want anybody to recognise me.

Mainwaring reacts. Mrs Fox enters. Jones disappears.

MRS FOX Yoo hoo! Morning, Mr Frazer, Mr Godfrey, morning, Mr Wilson.

They all react.

MRS FOX Hullo, Mr Mainwaring, sorry I'm late.

MAINWARING Please sit down, Mrs Fox.

MRS FOX I'm usually on time when I meet a gentleman friend, but today I...

MAINWARING Sit down, please. (**He pushes her into the booth**)

FRAZER Did you see that, Godfrey! Did you see the way he handled her?

MRS FOX (**Settling down**) Well, this is cosy.

Waitress comes to the table.

WAITRESS Good morning, sir.

MAINWARING Ah, good morning, two coffees please.

WAITRESS Aren't you having coffee with your friend Mr Wilson this morning?

MAINWARING No, I'm having coffee with my er... this lady here.

WAITRESS I see. (**She giggles and goes**)

Mainwaring reacts. Pike comes in.

MAINWARING Now, Mrs Fox, I have er... asked you to meet me here today because...

Pike's head comes over the top of the booth.

PIKE Excuse me, Mr Mainwaring.

MAINWARING What do you want, boy?

PIKE Mrs Mainwaring's on the phone.

MAINWARING What! Oh, yes, well, tell her I'll ring her back later.

PIKE Ring her back later, right. Hullo, Mrs Fox.

MRS FOX Hullo, dear.

Pike goes.

MAINWARING Well now, Mrs Fox, I've asked you to meet me here today, because I have to speak to you on a very delicate matter.

MRS FOX **(Leaning forward)** Yes.

MAINWARING I find these things concerned with emotions, very difficult to discuss.

MRS FOX You needn't be shy with me, Mr Mainwaring.

MAINWARING Well now, the fact is, Mrs Fox, you are a very attractive woman.

WAITRESS Two coffees. **(She puts them on the table)**

MAINWARING Thank you. **(Waitress giggles)**

Mainwaring reacts.

MAINWARING Well, now – what was I saying?

MRS FOX How attractive I was.

MAINWARING Yes, well you are, particularly to older men.

MRS FOX You're very attractive too, Mr Mainwaring.

MAINWARING Yes, yes, well that's got nothing to do with it.

MRS FOX Oh, but it has.

MAINWARING Well – we won't argue over that. What I'm trying t say is, you have had Mr Jones as an admirer for some years, and now, of course, you have another.

MRS FOX Oh, Mr Mainwaring. **(She grabs his hand)**

FRAZER Did you see that! Did you see!

GODFREY Oh dear, perhaps we'd better go.

Cheeseman writing, Wilson looking, Mainwaring snatches his hand away.

MAINWARING I realise, of course, that being a public figure, this other man must seem very attractive to you.

MRS FOX Oh, he does.

MAINWARING Jones, on the other hand, is just a simple butcher, but he is a fine figure of a man, Mrs Fox, a full head of grey, distinguished hair.

Jones reacts.

MAINWARING Your other admirer is, not to put too fine a point on it, bald.

MRS FOX Well, you know what they say about bald-headed men, Mr Mainwaring.

MAINWARING What do they say?

Pike comes in.

MAINWARING The point is, Mrs Fox, Jones is a very loyal member of my platoon and I don't want him hurt.

MRS FOX We won't hurt him, Mr Mainwaring.

MAINWARING We!

MRS FOX He can have Mondays and Saturdays, and you can have Tuesdays and Fridays.

MAINWARING Madam, I'm talking about Mr Gordon the town clerk.

MRS FOX Well, he can have Wednesdays.

PIKE Excuse me, sir.

MAINWARING What is it, boy?

PIKE Mrs Mainwaring is on the phone again, I told her you were busy having coffee with Mrs Fox, but she insists on speaking to you.

MAINWARING You stupid boy.

INTERIOR. SIDE OFFICE. DAY

MAINWARING I tell you, Wilson, I've never had such a shock in all my life. That woman, that dreadful woman, actually thought that I had amorous intentions towards her.

WILSON How awfully embarrassing for you, sir.

MAINWARING And on top of everything, when my wife phoned up, that stupid boy, Pike, told her I was having coffee with Mrs Fox. There was hell to pay when I got home, Elizabeth refused to listen to my explanations, and look what she did to my tie. **(He pulls his tie out, it has been cut short at the ends)**

Wilson reacts.

MAINWARING She rang me up 12 times at the bank today. Now, if she rings tonight, I want you to tell her I'm not here, you understand?

WILSON Yes, all right, sir.

Jones comes in.

JONES Evening, Mr Wilson, evening, sir. I want to thank you for speaking to Mrs Fox. I'm sure you had a great effect on her.

WILSON Yes, he really did.

Frazer, Pike, Godfrey, Cheeseman and several other members of the platoon enter, Frazer is carrying the Lewis gun.

FRAZER We can't get into the hall, sir, the doors are locked.

PIKE Mr Hodges shouted at us to go away.

MAINWARING As if I haven't got enough to put up with as it is. (**He crosses to the office door, it is locked**)

MAINWARING It's locked, Wilson.

WILSON It is Hodges' night to have the hall, sir.

MAINWARING I know that, but there's no need for him to lock the door. All right, Frazer, put the Lewis gun on the desk. I'll start the lecture. (**He crosses to the desk**) Now my subject tonight, men, is stripping down.

INTERIOR. CHURCH HALL. DAY

The Vicar, Verger and town clerk are sitting at a table in the middle of the hall. Hodges is standing by a hobby horse in front of the table.

HODGES All right, girls, you can come out.

Four girls in swimming costumes come through the door at the side of the stage.

HODGES Line up, girls.

They line up.

HODGES Right, what do you think, Mr Town Clerk?

GORDON Oh, they're very nice, they are.

VERGER I quite agree with you. What do you think, Your Reverence?

VICAR Look, can we get on please, I've got a very busy evening ahead of me.

Hodges crosses to the Vicar, nudges him and leers.

HODGES (**Whispering**) I wouldn't mind having a busy evening with this lot, eh!

VICAR Just explain to the girls what we want, Mr Hodges.

HODGES Right, now, girls, as you know, we have got you here tonight so that we can choose one of you to play the part of Lady Godiva in the procession next week.

GORDON Can we have the first girl on the horse, please?

HODGES Right, girls. On the horse.

Girls move to horse.

INTERIOR. SIDE OFFICE. DAY

Mainwaring and the rest of the platoon are gathered round the Lewis gun on the table. Pike and Wilson are by the door, Pike has his eye to the keyhole.

MAINWARING Right, Jones, I want you to show the men how to strip the Lewis gun down in two minutes, and I shall time you. Are you ready?

JONES Yes, sir, yes, sir.

MAINWARING (**Looking at his watch**) Strip!

Jones starts on the gun, Pike straightens up and whispers in Wilson's ear.

PIKE Uncle Arthur, the hall's full of naked girls.

WILSON Don't be stupid, Frank, pay attention to the lecture.

PIKE It's true. Look for yourself.

He pushes Wilson down to the keyhole.

WILSON Good heavens!

PIKE Shall we tell Mr Mainwaring?

WILSON Well, I er…

The phone bell rings.

MAINWARING Answer the phone, Sergeant.

WILSON Yes, sir.

MAINWARING Hurry up, Jones, you've only got another 30 seconds.

Wilson picks up the phone.

WILSON Hullo, oh good evening, just a minute. (**He puts his hand over the mouthpiece. Whispers to Mainwaring**) It's Mrs Mainwaring, sir.

MAINWARING I told you to tell her I'm not here.

WILSON Sorry, sir. (**Into the phone**) I'm afraid he's not here.

Mrs Fox suddenly appears.

MRS FOX (**In loud voice**) Yoo hoo, Mr Mainwaring, I'm here.

MAINWARING Oh no. (**He grabs the phone and hangs up**) How dare you burst in on my lecture?

MRS FOX Sorry, just on my way to the hall, excuse me, boys. (**She pushes her way through the crowd, she is carrying a small case. She knocks on the door**) Let me in, Mr Gordon, I'm here.

Gordon opens the door.

GORDON Good evening, my dear, you're just in time, come in.

JONES Mr Mainwaring, Mr Mainwaring, he's at it again. What's he doing?

MAINWARING I'll soon find out. (**He goes into the hall followed by the others**)

INTERIOR. CHURCH HALL. DAY

MAINWARING (**Beside himself**) What is the meaning of this?

HODGES Buzz off, Napoleon, this is my night to have the hall.

MAINWARING How dare you, how dare you have naked girls in my H.Q.?

CHEESEMAN Oh I wish I had my camera here, yes indeed.

MAINWARING I'm appalled at you, Vicar. Don't keep staring at them, cover them up. Come away, boy.

VICAR Don't be absurd. All this fuss over a few silly girls.

VERGER Yes, if the Vicar wants to have silly girls in his hall, that's his affair.

MRS FOX Shall I change into my swimming costume now, Mr Gordon?

FRAZER I don't think I could stand the shock.

GORDON Yes, my dear, go and get changed.

JONES Mr Mainwaring, stop him, stop him.

MAINWARING Be quiet, Jones. I demand an explanation, Hodges.

HODGES Keep your hair on, we're just choosing a girl to play the part of Lady Godiva in the procession next Saturday.

MAINWARING Lady Godiva!

HODGES Yes, and it's much better than your silly Morris dancing.

JONES Our Morris dancing is not silly.

MAINWARING Now, Mr Town Clerk, do I understand that one of those young ladies is going to ride... er... bare through the streets of Walmington-on-Sea?

GORDON Yes, it's a tribute to the brave city of Coventry. The girl won't be bare, of course, she'll wear fleshings.

MAINWARING Fleshings!

WILSON Yes, they're all-over body tights and perfectly respectable.

MAINWARING All-over body tights!

HODGES Yes, lovely, we're not living in Victorian times, you know.

MRS FOX Can I have a word with you please, Mr Gordon?

GORDON Certainly, my dear.

She whispers in Gordon's ear.

JONES Mr Mainwaring, Mr Mainwaring, he's doing it again, Mr Mainwaring, stop him, stop him.

MAINWARING Will you be quiet, Jones? Now look, Mr Gordon, I've had just about...

GORDON Now wait a minute, Captain Mainwaring, I think we have the solution. You don't want one of those young girls as Lady Godiva. Now, it's just been pointed out to me that Lady Godiva Leofric was, in fact, a woman of more mature years. So, in the course of historical accuracy, I suggest that Lady Godiva should be Mrs Fox.

Uproar from girls.

GORDON Quiet please. Mrs Fox will be perfectly respectable, covered from top to toe in fleshings, and wearing a wig of long golden tresses.

FRAZER You'll never cover her with golden tresses, you'll need a bell tent.

INTERIOR. SIDE OFFICE. DAY

Mainwaring is on the phone.

MAINWARING Yes, Elizabeth... no, Elizabeth, I keep telling you, I did not have anything to do with choosing Mrs Fox to play the part of Lady Godiva.

Wilson comes in.

MAINWARING Yes, dear... no, dear. It was the town clerk's decision, he thought it would be better for the part to be taken by a woman of more mature... well, ample proportions... Yes, dear, I realise that you are more ample than Mrs Fox.

Wilson reacts.

MAINWARING But then you're not Lady Godiva, are you... Hullo, hullo, dear. (**He hangs up and gives Wilson a sickly grin**) Just chatting to the little woman.

WILSON Oh, what little woman?

MAINWARING My wife, of course.

Jones come in.

JONES I've lost her, Mr Mainwaring. Since the town clerk chose Mrs Fox for Lady Godiva, her head's been turned completely, right round.

WILSON I'm sorry, Jonesey.

MAINWARING This is what happens, Wilson, when women come into men's affairs. The whole platoon has been thrown completely sideways.

Pike and Mrs Pike come in.

PIKE You can't come in now, Mum, we're just going to start the parade.

MRS PIKE Oh get out of the way, Frank. (**She nods to Mainwaring**) Arthur, what's this I hear about Mrs Fox being chosen as Lady Godiva?

WILSON It was really nothing to do with me, Mavis.

MRS PIKE You were there.

WILSON Well, I was only sort of standing around.

MRS PIKE A woman like Mrs Fox! I'm much slimmer than she is. I mean, what's wrong with my figure?

WILSON Er, nothing.

MRS PIKE And I've got nice legs haven't I, haven't I got nice legs?

WILSON Yes, awfully nice.

MAINWARING You wouldn't want to be Lady Godiva, Mrs Pike.

MRS PIKE But I would have liked to have been asked.

MAINWARING Now, Mrs Pike, consider how your son here would have felt, seeing his mother riding through the streets clad only in…

PIKE Fleshings.

MAINWARING Well, I know how I would have felt if it had been anyone close to me. So, my advice to you is to let sleeping dogs lie.

INTERIOR. MARIGOLD TEA ROOMS. DAY

Mainwaring and co. are waiting in the shop, all the blinds are down. They are dressed as Morris dancers.

MAINWARING Right, men, are you all ready? Now, as soon as the procession has gone past, Jones will open the door, we will burst out of the tea rooms into the street and perform the dance.

GODFREY I'm not awfully good at bursting out of tea rooms, Mr Mainwaring.

MAINWARING You'll just have to do the best you can, Godfrey.

Sound of a band and crowds cheering.

PIKE (**Pulling the blind aside**) Here comes the procession now.

MAINWARING Good. Stand by. (**Wilson hits Mainwaring with the horse**) And get that horse out of the way, Wilson.

WILSON I can't help it, sir, it's terribly heavy.

MAINWARING Well, go round there, and rest it on the counter.

There is a banging on the back door.

MAINWARING Who's that?

WAITRESS There's someone at the back door, Mr Mainwaring. Don't they know we're closed.

More banging.

WAITRESS All right, all right, I'm coming. (**She goes to the back door**)

MAINWARING And don't forget, Wilson, I expect you to collect as much money as you can. Har, har, har, give till it hurts, right?

WILSON Yes, sir.

Mrs Fox bursts in, she is wearing a coat and her hair is all over the place.

JONES Mrs Fox, what's happened?

MRS FOX (**In tears**) It was terrible, terrible.

• ANNIE OGDEN REMEMBERS •

'A funny memory relates to "The Godiva Affair". The men had to dress up as Morris dancers and John Le Mesurier wore a horse costume. He had to climb into it to give the loose appearance that he was riding it. However, David wanted the horse to have little legs which hung down either side, so to help out I made a little pair of yellow felt legs, which looked very silly when attached. But they gave us and the audience a jolly good laugh.'

JONES Now, don't you upset yourself. (**He puts his arm round her**) There, there, you're safe with your little Jack. Just tell me what's the matter?

The music gets louder.

MAINWARING There's no time for all that, Jones.

MRS FOX I was going to change in a room in the town hall, and I left my fleshings and wig on a chair. Well, I went out for a minute and when I got back they were gone, gone. (**More tears**)

FRAZER So, it doesn't look as if we're going to get a Lady Godiva after all.

MAINWARING Never mind, it's up to us now. (**He pulls Jones away from comforting Mrs Fox**) That's enough of that, Jones, get ready to open the door. (**He pushes Jones towards the door**)

PIKE (**Pulling the blind aside**) Hey, Mr Mainwaring, there is a Lady Godiva.

Jones goes to look.

WILSON Oh Lord, not Mavis.

MAINWARING (**Pushing to the door**) You really should keep that woman under control, Wilson.

JONES No, Mr Mainwaring, don't look, sir, please don't look.

MAINWARING Get out of the way, Jones. (**He pulls the blind to one side, looks, gives a low moan and faints into Jones' arms**)

PIKE Hey, it's Mrs Mainwaring.

JONES (**Cradling Mainwaring in his arms**) Speak to me, sir, speak to me. Poor Mr Mainwaring, he'll never get over it.

FRAZER Aye, and neither will the horse.

SERIES SEVEN **EPISODE FIVE**

Recorded: Sunday 17/11/74

Original transmission: Friday 13/12/74, 7.45–8.15pm

Original viewing figures = 14.4 million

ARTHUR LOWE .... CAPTAIN MAINWARING
JOHN LE MESURIER .... SERGEANT WILSON
CLIVE DUNN.................................. LANCE CORPORAL JONES
JOHN LAURIE .... PRIVATE FRAZER
ARNOLD RIDLEY .... PRIVATE GODFREY
IAN LAVENDER .... PRIVATE PIKE
BILL PERTWEE.................................. CHIEF WARDEN HODGES
TALFRYN THOMAS .... PRIVATE CHEESEMAN
FRANK WILLIAMS .... VICAR
EDWARD SINCLAIR... VERGER
ROBERT RAGLAN .... COLONEL
ERIC LONGWORTH .... TOWN CLERK
FRED MCNAUGHTON... MAYOR
MAVIS PUGH .... LADY MALTBY
JOHN HART DYKE .... FRENCH GENERAL
DONALD MORLEY .... GLOSSIP
PLATOON .... COLIN BEAN, GEORGE HANCOCK,
.... MICHAEL MOORE, FREDDIE WHITE, FREDDIE WILES,
.... ROGER BOURNE, EVAN ROSS, LESLIE NOYES,
.... DESMOND CULLUM-JONES, HUGH CECIL

THE CAPTAIN'S CAR

• JOHN HART DYKE REMEMBERS •

'I think I have had a very lucky theatrical life – I hesitate to use the word "career"! – because I have rarely been out of work. I have been given some wonderful parts to play, I have seen a great deal of the world while working (which I am sure I would not have done had I not been an actor), but above all I have met and worked with so many marvellous people and consequently have had numberless happy times. Many of these people have become firm friends – friendships that date back to when I started in the business, almost fifty years ago. Among those happy times I like to count a very brief-seeming 36 hours as some of my happiest – the very short time I spent playing the French General in *Dad's Army*.

'I first met Jimmy Perry in 1960, when he was running Watford's Palace Theatre as a weekly rep. Over the next four years I think I appeared in about fifteen plays for him there, the last in 1964. I didn't see Jimmy again until 1974 – and this is where luck came in again. In May of that year I was just coming to the end of the run of *The Constant Wife* with Ingrid Bergman at the New Theatre (now renamed The Albery), and on one Thursday afternoon between the matinée and the evening show I was taking my customary walk down St Martin's Lane for a bit of fresh air and who should I bump into, quite by chance, but Gilda Perry, Jimmy's wife, with whom I had appeared in so many of those plays at Watford. After some usual thespian (not luvvie) greetings, questions and answers, Gilda invited me home for a cup of tea (down the road in Westminster), with the added throwaway, "Jimmy must have something for you in his next episode." After a very welcome reunion over a cuppa with Jimmy, he suddenly said: "Do you speak French?" When I replied "Well, a sort of schoolboy French", he said, "How would you like to play a sort of General de Gaulle in my next episode?" And that's how I got the job! You can imagine how happy I was.

'The location for my brief appearance in "The Captain's Car" was Thetford Town Hall in Norfolk. The day of shooting was a Sunday, so I travelled up to Thetford on the afternoon before with some apprehension (always nervous about starting a new job, and *Dad's Army* was by now very popular and I felt flattered to be involved), but with not a little anticipation also, for I knew I would be seeing old friends again. Actually, the whole cast and crew were welcoming and friendly, but it was particularly lovely to see Frank Williams and Colin Bean (Private Sponge) again, both of whom I knew from Watford days. Dear Arnold Ridley also took me under his wing, as he had done several years before at Wimbledon Rep, where I had appeared, with him, in two of his own plays: *The Ghost Train* and *Easy Money*. We had also performed together in *The Rainmaker*, playing father and son. I remember we all had a very convivial evening at the hotel where we stayed – but not a late night, though, for we were all up bright and early for a hard day's shoot.

'Everything was so highly organised by Jimmy and David Croft, and we worked steadily through the day with no apparent problems. I don't recall a lot of rehearsal, we just got on with it – we did, of course, have breaks between "takes", when we had a lot of chat and a lot of laughs: John Laurie and John Le Mesurier were particularly kind to me, I remember, and were even complimentary about my French accent – though I can't think why for when I eventually saw the finished article I think it left something to be desired – I know that my French schoolmaster would have said something of the sort!

'I remember throughout the day there was quite a large public audience in the square outside the town hall and they were most appreciative of our efforts, especially when we reached the kissing sequences! I don't recall any actual remarks from them, or catcalls and the like, but I wonder how they would have reacted if we had been filming all that today! I think I apologised to Bill Pertwee for making a mess of his face – after all, it was in pursuit of a laugh! I hadn't met him before and I was anxious about that piece of business. Subsequently we have become good friends – that's what is so wonderful about our business. I did a tour of *See How They Run* with Bill's son, Jonathon, which Bill saw and later on I took over from Bill in a Ray Cooney farce *It Runs in the Family* at The Playhouse Theatre.

'To complete the friendliness from the whole cast that day, I was given a lift back to London by Robert Raglan, whom I had only just met, but by the time we reached town I felt as though I had known him all my life.'

The Captain's Car

SIDE OFFICE. DAY

Wilson is sitting at Mainwaring's desk. He is making out a sign. Enter Mainwaring.

WILSON Good evening, sir.

MAINWARING Wilson, don't sit at my desk when I'm not here.

Wilson gets up and moves round.

WILSON I was just writing out a notice.

MAINWARING What you're doing is neither here nor there. I've told you before, I do not like you sitting at my desk in my absence.

WILSON What am I to lean on?

MAINWARING Really, Wilson, as an NCO, you really are supposed to show a little bit of initiative. Write on your knee, man. (**Mainwaring looks at the papers on his desk. Wilson sits at the seat opposite and continues to write on his knee. Mainwaring looks up**)

MAINWARING And I don't think I gave you permission to sit down.

WILSON (**Getting up**) I'm sorry, sir.

MAINWARING We are in the Army, you know.

WILSON Yes, sir.

MAINWARING I'm an officer and you're supposed to be a sergeant.

WILSON Yes, sir.

MAINWARING Well, just remember it. (**He leans back in the chair and it collapses. Wilson helps him up**)

WILSON That was the notice I was making out. 'Do Not Lean Back In This Chair'.

Mainwaring reacts.

WILSON Oh, and there was a phone message – The French general is definitely coming.

MAINWARING Who said so?

WILSON The colonel. (**He finds the paper**) Here, it is. 'Visit of French general, confirmed. A unit of the Home Guard to provide guard of honour at town hall.'

MAINWARING Well, I hope it's not us. Damned red tape. Don't they realise we're front-line troops. Anyway, I've never had much time for the French.

WILSON Surely they're very fine soldiers.

MAINWARING Only up to a point.

Wilson reacts.

MAINWARING They were never much good after lunch, you know.

WILSON Weren't they?

MAINWARING Oh no. All that wine and garlic is very debilitating.

Wilson reacts.

MAINWARING All they think about is chasing women, 'Come with me to the Casba' – and all that sort of thing.

WILSON I suppose you could say they're emotional.

MAINWARING Well, look at all that sloppy kissing they get up to. They can't even pin a medal on a chap without kissing him.

WILSON If you were picked as the guard commander, you'd probably get one.

MAINWARING A medal?

WILSON No. A kiss.

MAINWARING I assure you that I'm not having any of that sort of thing.

Enter Jones, he salutes.

JONES Captain Mainwaring. There is a lady outside wishes to have an audience with you, and when I say a lady, I don't mean a woman, although, of course, she is a woman because otherwise she couldn't be a lady, which she is, because the name in which she rejoices is Lady Maltby.

MAINWARING Lady Maltby, what does she want?

JONES She didn't give me any confidence about that, sir. Lords and ladies very rarely do, you know, sir. When we was in the Sudan, Lord Kitchener never gave any of us any confidence.

MAINWARING Better show her in, Jones.

Jones goes out.

MAINWARING Now, do your collar up, Wilson. And as soon as you've paid your respects to her ladyship, you can withdraw. She'll probably only want to deal with officers.

Wilson reacts. Jones re-enters.

JONES Her ladyship – Lady Maltby.

Lady Maltby enters.

MAINWARING Your ladyship, this is indeed an honour, I am Captain Mainwaring.

LADY MALTBY I've heard about you.

MAINWARING This is just my sergeant – he's going.

LADY MALTBY Arthur – how nice to see you.

WILSON My dear Angela – you're looking marvellous. It really is good to see you.

They embrace.

JONES Mr Mainwaring. She seems to have confidence in Mr Wilson. I think they've met previous.

LADY MALTBY **(To Jones)** I seem to know your face.

JONES Yes, your ladyship, I have been purveying meat to your establishment ever since 1933, when his late lordship fell out with Sainsbury's.

LADY MALTBY Of course, you're Mr Jones. Well, there'll be one book extra this week – my son is home on leave.

JONES Ah well, I can do you chops or a nice bit of shin.

LADY MALTBY Perhaps you'll talk it over with the cook.

JONES We'll put our heads together, your ladyship, never you fear.

MAINWARING That'll be all, Jones.

JONES Yes, sir. Right, sir. **(He salutes and goes)**

LADY MALTBY Arthur, it is good to see you again.

WILSON So, Nigel's coming home. How is he?

LADY MALTBY He got married, you know.

WILSON Yes Auntie Lettice told me.

LADY MALTBY And now he's with the Blues, foolish boy.

WILSON Is he really? My grandfather was in the Blues.

MAINWARING Yes, well I'm sure Lady Maltby hasn't come here to discuss your family affairs, Wilson.

LADY MALTBY You must forgive us, but it's been so long since dear Arthur and I had a chinwag. I really came here to talk about my car.

MAINWARING Oh, yes.

LADY MALTBY Well, I can't get petrol for it and it just sits there in the garage, so I thought someone should use it to help the war effort – and then I can have it back when we've won.

MAINWARING I see – so what kind of a car is it?

LADY MALTBY Oh, just an ordinary sort of Rolls.

Mainwaring reacts.

LADY MALTBY Now, the thing is, who would make the best use of it, the Home Guards or the Wardens?

MAINWARING Definitely the Home Guard.

LADY MALTBY I'm glad you think so. That Mr Hodges seemed awfully common – and I know Mr Jones and, of course, Arthur is such a dear.

Mainwaring reacts.

LADY MALTBY And I'm sure you're very nice when one gets to know you.

MAINWARING Yes – well. We would take awfully good care of it. My men are very reliable. I'm very particular who I have in my platoon. Every man is hand picked.

The door opens and Frazer storms in.

FRAZER We're all lined up there waiting and if you're going to be much longer we're all off home. I just thought you ought to know. **(He goes)**

MAINWARING He's a rough diamond – but underneath he's pure gold – just the man to have beside you in a scrap.

WILSON What would we actually do with the Rolls Royce, sir?

MAINWARING I shall use it as a staff car.

WILSON But it's all sort of shiny and Rolls Roycey.

LADY MALTBY You can camouflage it, as far as I'm concerned.

MAINWARING There you are, you see.

WILSON But, I mean – a large Rolls Royce – won't it look a bit silly?

MAINWARING What do you mean?

WILSON I suppose you could sit on a cushion.

Mainwaring reacts. Pike enters quickly from outside the door – he carries a bucket and a shovel.

PIKE Sorry I'm late, Captain Mainwaring. Carter Patterson's horse went down the street so I bought some for you to put on your roses.

MAINWARING Get out, Pike.

PIKE I'll leave it outside in the bucket. **(He goes)**

MAINWARING A new recruit. We haven't kicked him into shape yet.

LADY MALTBY **(Rising)** I'll tell Glossop to drive it round on Saturday.

MAINWARING That really is most generous of you, your ladyship.

WILSON Yes, Angie – you're an absolute brick.

LADY MALTBY **(To Wilson as she goes)** And you must pop round and have a drink.

WILSON I'd love to.

LADY MALTBY And we must ask Captain Fanshaw…

MAINWARING **(Interrupting)** Mainwaring. I'd be delighted, I'm sure.

LADY MALTBY We must ask Captain Mainwaring to let you off one evening.

MAINWARING Delighted, your ladyship.

She goes.

WILSON Isn't she a sweet person?

MAINWARING I think it's pathetic.

WILSON What is?

MAINWARING The way you kowtow to her just because

she has a title. It doesn't cut any ice with me ever, I can assure you. And you can tell that to your Auntie Lettice.

The Warden enters.

WARDEN Where is he? Where is he? You've done it, haven't you, Mainwaring?

MAINWARING How dare you barge into my office?

WARDEN Never mind about that. She was thinking of giving me that car. Now you've stuck the sherbet in and put her off me.

MAINWARING We didn't put her off you.

MAINWARING It just so happens we know her ladyship very well socially.

WARDEN Well, I tell you one thing – me and my lads is providing half the guard of honour for the French general, and I hope you're not providing the other half, because I don't want to be stuck opposite your ugly mug.

MAINWARING If you're going to be there, I shall refuse to parade.

WARDEN You better watch it, mate. And there's another thing – from now on, you mind your step. If I see a chink of light from this hall – or if you shine a torch or if you leave as much as a bicycle without immobilising it – I'll have you.

MAINWARING I don't have a bicycle.

WARDEN Then you better immobilise your crutches. **(He goes)**

WILSON What an awful fellow he is.

MAINWARING What do you expect? He shouldn't be Chief Warden. He's a greengrocer.

WILSON So was Lord Maltby.

MAINWARING Was he? I expect he was in a very big way of business.

WILSON Oh, yes. It's not what you know or who you know, it's how much of it you have.

MAINWARING I don't want any of that Bolshie nonsense. Fall the men in, Wilson.

WILSON **(Going into hall)** Yes, sir.

CHURCH HALL. INTERIOR. DAY

WILSON Fall in, you chaps. Three nice tidy rows.

MAINWARING Squad, 'shun. Stand at ease. Right. Pay attention. I am proud to announce that another vehicle has been added to our battle fleet. It is a Rolls Royce staff car.

PIKE Can I drive it, Captain Mainwaring?

MAINWARING Certainly not.

PIKE Well, bags first ride in it then.

MAINWARING Be quiet, Pike.

GODFREY Rolls Royces are very comfortable. I went to a wedding in one and you could give the driver instructions through a speaking tube. I didn't, of course – it wasn't my car.

MAINWARING Godfrey, silence in the ranks.

JONES They're very reliable too, sir. General Kitchener had one in France in 1914. General French also had one. When I say General French I don't mean a French general. I mean General French who was an English general. A lot of people get confused about that, but he's got nothing to do with it anyway, because the man I'm talking about was General Kitchener and he was very worried about recruiting because a lot of soldiers was getting killed and he thought he was going to run out of them, so he was getting into his Rolls Royce one day when he noticed the dashboard was all mangy. He turned to his driver and he said, 'Driver – why is my dashboard all mangy?'. And the driver said, 'Well, sir, this foreign mahogany is no good in these parts. We want a good old English wood – we need yew.' 'That's it,' says the general – that's the slogan I've been looking for. 'Your country needs you.' **(Jones points)** That story is not generally known, sir.

MAINWARING Thank you, Jones.

JONES He never ran short of soldiers after that, sir. No matter how many he used up.

Enter the colonel. Mainwaring sees him.

MAINWARING Platoon. Platoon, 'shun. **(Mainwaring salutes)**

Colonel salutes back.

COLONEL Right, stand your men at ease, Captain Mainwaring.

MAINWARING Stand at ease.

COLONEL I thought you'd be interested to know that you've been selected to provide the guard of honour outside the town hall for the visit of the French general.

MAINWARING Thank you, sir. It's a great honour. **(To platoon)** You see the reward you get for being smart.

CHEESEMAN Yes. Another hour's cleaning and blancoing.

COLONEL You've also been chosen because of the person who has to make the speech before the general's departure.

MAINWARING Oh, yes, of course.

COLONEL It has to be in French.

MAINWARING Well, I suppose I could practise a bit.

COLONEL Your sergeant speaks French. So he's the obvious choice.

MAINWARING Not all that obvious, I would have thought. Do you speak French, Wilson?

WILSON Well, what you might call 'un petit peu'.

MAINWARING Personally, I'm very much against these parades. They take us away from valuable training.

COLONEL I'm afraid I've been asked by Area to make it as smart an occasion as possible.

MAINWARING I don't see how it's going to be smart if we have those Wardens sprawling about all over the steps.

JONES Quite right, sir. We should provide the whole guard comprehensively.

COLONEL Well – I must say, the Wardens will make it look a bit of a shambles. Very well. I'll fix it with the mayor and town clerk. Your platoon will provide the whole guard of honour.

MAINWARING Thank you, sir.

PIKE And Uncle Arthur will make a French speech.

FADE UP FILM. OUTSIDE TOWN HALL

Rolls Royce hiccups to a standstill. Chauffeur gets out and goes into town hall. Cut to side office.

SIDE OFFICE. STUDIO

Wilson is writing his speech in the chair opposite Mainwaring's. Pike is sweeping the office.

WILSON Mon general – nous autres à Walmington-sur-mer.

Phone rings.

WILSON Answer that, Frank, will you?

Pike picks up the phone.

PIKE Home Guard.

Cut to Glossop. He is by a wall phone in the town hall.

TOWN HALL. STUDIO

GLOSSOP Good morning. Glossop here. Lady Maltby's chauffeur.

PIKE Oh yes, Mr Glossop.

GLOSSOP I'm on the way to the paint shop to get Lady Maltby's Rolls camouflaged for Captain Mainwaring and I'm afraid I've run out of petrol.

PIKE Oh dear. Where are you?

GLOSSOP Outside the town hall.

PIKE You stay there and we'll come and give you a push.

GLOSSOP All right then. **(He puts the receiver down)**

PIKE Come on, Uncle Arthur. Captain Mainwaring's Rolls is stuck outside the town hall. You and the chauffeur can push it and I'll steer.

Pike starts to write a note.

WILSON What are you talking about, Frank? We can't push a great big car like that.

PIKE Course we can. You're ever so muscular – Mum's always saying so.

WILSON But it's enormous.

PIKE All right. If I find some petrol, can I drive it?

WILSON I don't suppose the chauffeur will let you.

PIKE You could make him. You could commandeer it. It's ours anyway.

WILSON Ring back and say we can't do anything.

PIKE I can't – I don't know his number. Come on, Uncle Arthur.

WILSON But what about Captain Mainwaring?

PIKE I've written him a note. Come on, Uncle.

WILSON **(Going to Pike)** Really, Frank – you always want to do things in such a hurry.

They go out.

MIX TO FILM. OUTSIDE

Mid long shot of Warden's sidecar and motorcycle. Pike and Wilson come into shot.

PIKE Look, Uncle. That's Mr Hodges' bike. I bet he's got petrol in that.

WILSON But you can't take that. It's stealing.

PIKE No it's not, you can commandeer it. Anyway, it's only the Warden. Look – there's a tin in the back. We can put it in that. **(He pulls out a cut off petrol can from the sidecar and hands it to Wilson. He takes the cap off the petrol tank.**

WILSON That's all very well, but how are we supposed to get it from there **(indicating tank)** into this **(indicating tin)**?

PIKE Oh, you are silly, Uncle Arthur. We pour it in, of course. **(He goes to the sidecar and starts to tip the bicycle)** Well, come on, give me a hand.

Wilson moves round to do so.

CUT TO STUDIO. SIDE OFFICE

MAINWARING (**Voice off**) Wilson, Wilson.

Frazer enters, followed by Mainwaring and Jones.

FRAZER He's not in here, sir.

JONES I thought I saw him with Pike, going up the road – in a furtive sort of way, sir.

FRAZER They've left a note, sir.

MAINWARING What does it say?

FRAZER 'Rolls broken down by town hall. Gone to help.'

MAINWARING What help can Wilson possibly give? (**Mainwaring looks at his watch**) It's due at the paint shop for camouflaging. Jones, take your van and a rope and go to the town hall and give them a tow to the paintshop.

JONES Right. Come on, Jock.

CHEESEMAN I'll come too. There might be a story, you know. Traffic chaos in Walmington. Vital supplies delayed.

FRAZER Have you no regard for the truth, man?

CHEESEMAN Don't insult the press, boyo. Vital supplies will be delayed. Jones here will be late with his deliveries.

CUT TO THE ROLLS OUTSIDE THE TOWN HALL. FILM

Pike, Wilson and Glossop are standing by it. Pike is pouring petrol from the can into the tank.

PIKE There is it. You've got the last drop. Now can I drive it?

WILSON Don't be silly, Frank.

PIKE Well, can I have a ride in the back then.

WILSON Oh, get in. I'm sure Glossop will drive us round to the paintshop.

Pike and Wilson get in. Glossop drives the car off. Cut to mayor's Rolls Royce. It approaches and stops. The town clerk comes from the town hall as the chauffeur holds the car door for the mayor (mayor is wearing his mayoral robes).

TOWN CLERK I'm that glad you've come.

MAYOR What's up, Claude?

TOWN CLERK The mace isn't fit to be seen and Roger can't clean it 'cos he's laid up with his old trouble.

MAYOR Well, what am I supposed to do about it?

TOWN CLERK Sam here can give it a rub over. Come on, Sam. Look lively.

All three move up the steps into the town hall. Jones' van draws up in front of the mayor's rolls. Sponge and a couple of others dismount with Cheeseman.

JONES Right, lads. Get the rope out and tie it round the front axle and we'll tow it round to the paintshop.

Frazer and Jones stay in the cabin.

FRAZER Hold on. Hold on. How much is Mainwaring paying for the camouflaging job?

JONES Eight pounds, I think.

FRAZER I have a spray gun in my workshop. I use it for touching up the hearse. I'll do it for £7. After all – it's only dirty old brown and green paint.

JONES I don't think Mr Mainwaring would like that.

FRAZER We're saving money – and it's the platoon funds.

JONES All right then, Jock.

CHEESEMAN (**At the rope**) Oy, Jones the Butcher, it's all attached and at the ready.

JONES You drive that one, Sponge.

Jones drives the van off, towing the mayor's car.

MIX TO CHURCH HALL. STUDIO

Mainwaring is at his desk. Godfrey enters from the outside door.

GODFREY There's still no sign of them, Captain Mainwaring.

MAINWARING I can't understand it. They've all been gone for a couple of hours and I wanted to carry out a final briefing for the general's parade. Well, keep looking out.

GODFREY I'm getting a little chilled. One loses heat, you know, with just standing about.

MAINWARING Well, jump up and down then.

Godfrey reacts. The Warden bursts in holding a piece of paper.

WARDEN You've gone too far this time, Mainwaring. Your hooligans have pinched my petrol.

MAINWARING I'm sure they've done no such thing.

WARDEN Oh yes they have – and they didn't even siphon it. They poured it out – like my bike was a ruddy teapot – and left it on its side.

MAINWARING My men don't do that sort of thing.

WILSON What's this then? (**Reads note**) 'Petrol requisitioned, F. Pike.'

MAINWARING That's not how you spell requisitioned.

WARDEN Well, that proves it then – and you needn't think you've got me off that parade. I'm appealing to the Home Secretary. Herby Morrison will sort you out, mate.

Pike bursts in, followed by Wilson.

PIKE We've got the Rolls, Captain Mainwaring. We've got it.

WILSON Don't get so excited, Frank.

PIKE The paintshop did it right away and I rode in the back and waved to everyone and pretended I was a field marshall.

WARDEN Never mind about all that. What are you going to do about this?

MAINWARING I'm too busy to argue with you now. I'm going to inspect my new staff car.

CUT TO EXTERIOR OF HALL. FILM

The Rolls Royce, with brown or green camouflaging in two tones, is outside. Mainwaring comes out, followed by the Warden, Wilson and Pike.

MAINWARING Look at that, Wilson.

WARDEN You shouldn't have it by rights. She'd have given it to me if you hadn't shoved your oar in.

MAINWARING It's magnificent, isn't it, Wilson? Look at that craftsmanship – British throughout. Show me a French car that can possibly match that.

PIKE Or a Yankee car.

MAINWARING Or indeed as you say, Pike – a Yankee one.

WILSON I must say it looks awfully good as a staff car.

MAINWARING Good! I'll say it looks good – I bet there isn't another one like it in the entire British Isles.

Cut to long shot of the mayor's car approaching. It also is camouflaged. It is driven by Jones with Frazer beside him. Jones honks the horn. Mainwaring looks up.

MAINWARING Great Scott, what's that?

PIKE It's twins.

Cut to Jones' Rolls stopping.

JONES Look, Mr Frazer. He's got another one.

FRAZER That's typical Mainwaring – one on and one in the wash.

MAINWARING Wherever did you get that car, Wilson?

WILSON Outside the town hall with Angela's chauffeur.

MAINWARING Then where did that one come from, Jones?

Godfrey approaches from the hall.

GODFREY I'm sorry to trouble you Captain Mainwaring, but the town clerk is on the telephone. He wants to speak to you rather urgently. It seems the mayor has lost his Rolls Royce.

Mainwaring turns towards the office.

PIKE Uncle Arthur, do you think the mayor will be cross with Captain Mainwaring for putting dirty brown paint all over his Rolls Royce?

CUT TO TOWN CLERK ON PHONE IN HIS OFFICE. STUDIO

TOWN CLERK Well, it's like this Mr Mainwaring. It looks as if it's been stolen. And I'm in a bit of a flummox to know what's right to do about it.

MAINWARING (**Inside office**) Have you told the police?

TOWN CLERK No, I didn't think it was wise.

MAINWARING Quite right.

TOWN CLERK You see. I left the window open and took the chauffeur away – so I'm responsible that it wasn't immobilised. Well, you've got to immobilise them – you can get three months for not doing that. So, I'd just as soon the police didn't get word of it. And I thought seeing you've got a lot of men, you could send them out and search for it and you might come across it.

MAINWARING Yes, I might be able to help you.

TOWN CLERK Oh, thank you, Mr Mainwaring. Is there anyone else I ought to inform?

MAINWARING No – leave it entirely in my hands.

TOWN CLERK You'll have to look sharp. That car has to be outside the town hall at three o'clock for the French general.

MAINWARING Never fear. It will be there. (**He puts the phone down**) (**To Wilson**) Of all the blundering fools, Wilson.

WILSON It's nothing to do with me – I didn't touch the mayor's car.

MAINWARING If you hadn't taken away Lady Maltby's car without my orders.

WARDEN And with my petrol.

MAINWARING You be quiet.

CHEESEMAN I'll tell you one thing, boyo. If I get a picture of the mayor's face when he sees his lovely Rolls Royce covered in dirty brown paint – I'll have it in every paper in the country.

JONES Do you think you could spray it black again, Jock.

FRAZER What's the hour?

JONES Twelve o'clock.

FRAZER Three hours – I could try.

MAINWARING Good man, Frazer.

FRAZER For £10.

MAINWARING Just you have that car outside the town hall

by three o'clock. With any luck, nobody will be any the wiser.

WARDEN Oh yes, they will – because I'm going to split.

PIKE Sneak.

WARDEN You can call me what you like, mate – but unless you let my lads parade on those steps, I'm going to tell the mayor what you done with his motor.

JONES Well, as General Kitchener used to say, sir, he's got us by the Fuzzie Wuzzies.

MAINWARING Yes, very well. You can come on the parade.

JONES General Kitchener used to use that expression because the Fuzzie Wuzzies had short curly hair, so when he said they got them by the Fuzzie Wuzzies – what he really meant was 'They've got us by the short…'.

MAINWARING Yes, I think you've made the point, Jones.

JONES Don't be like that. I'm only trying to make the war a bit more cheerful.

FADE UP FILM: EXTERIOR TOWN HALL

The Home Guard line one side of the entrance. The Wardens are opposite them on the other side of the entrance. One of the Wardens holds a standard on which flies the Tricolour. Jones holds the Union Jack. The choir is on parade in surpluses in the charge of the Vicar. The Verger is in charge of one boy scout or boy's brigade bugler. The Verger is dressed as a sea scout. There are also a few bystanders. They are just arranging themselves. Cheeseman has a camera with an old time flash powder attachment. Cheeseman is indicating to Mainwaring.

CHEESEMAN Sorry about this, boyo – can't get the flash bulbs, you know. Not one to be had in the town.

MAINWARING Try not to be too obtrusive. (**Mainwaring sees Wilson, who is reading his notes, which are rather long**) You're not saying all that, are you?

WILSON No – it's mostly crossings out. I changed my mind a lot.

MAINWARING Keep it short – otherwise it'll be very boring.

WILSON On the other hand, if the car hasn't arrived, I may have to keep it going for a bit.

CHEESEMAN Don't worry, Mr Mainwaring, I'll get one of you and the general, like you said.

MAINWARING Good man. (**Mainwaring looks at his watch**) Frazer's cutting it damn fine.

PIKE That's Mr Frazer coming round the corner, sir.

Long shot of mayor's car, now painted black, coming round corner.

MAINWARING By Jove – he's made a magnificent job of it.

WARDEN (**To Mainwaring**) Here – I just want you to know that when you bawl out all that rubbish about attention and present arms – my lads won't take the slightest bit of notice.

MAINWARING You'll make the whole parade a complete shambles.

WARDEN All right then, I'll bawl out attention and present arms and your lot can take notice of me.

MAINWARING Certainly not.

VICAR (**Joining Mainwaring with Verger**) Do you want the bugler to play before the salute or during the salute?

MAINWARING He should play while my men are at the present – and then the choir should sing the 'Marseillaise'.

VICAR Is that clear, Mr Yeatman?

VERGER You give me a nod, Your Reverence, and I'll tip him the wink.

Town clerk comes to door.

TOWN CLERK He's coming down the back passage now.

MAINWARING Places everybody.

Frazer comes up to Mainwaring.

MAINWARING Everything all right, Frazer?

FRAZER There's just one thing, sir.

MAINWARING Tell me after.

FRAZER It'll be as well for you to know.

MAINWARING He's coming – fall in.

Frazer falls in.

PIKE (**To Frazer**) How did it go, Mr Frazer?

FRAZER Fine but for one thing. I could not get any quick-drying paint.

PIKE Is it still tacky?

FRAZER Oh no – it's not tacky.

PIKE Good.

FRAZER Just plain wet.

Mainwaring is now at the top of the stairs with the Warden. The Vicar is beside him.

MAINWARING Here he comes. Squad, 'shun.

WARDEN Wardens, 'shun.

They boy bugler blows one note, the Verger clips his ear.

VERGER Shut up.

VICAR (**Stage whisper**) I didn't give the nod.

VERGER It was him. (**To boy**) Wait till I say.

General appears with mayor and colonel and macebearer.

MAINWARING No. 1 Platoon, B Company!

WARDEN Not the Wardens.

MAINWARING General salute, present arms.

They do so.

WARDEN Walmington-on-Sea Wardens, present pumps.

They hold their stirrup pumps out.

VICAR Now, Mr Yeatman.

Verger nudges the boy who plays 'Come to the Cook House Door'.

MAINWARING That's 'Come to the Cook House Door'.

VICAR He doesn't know 'The Last Post'.

The Vicar then leads the choir into the 'Marseillaise'.

MAINWARING Look at him – the man's blubbing!

JONES Well, it's very sad, Mr Mainwaring.

The choir stop in the middle of a phrase.

MAINWARING Is that all?

VICAR There just wasn't time to learn the rest.

MAINWARING Oh well, really.

VICAR They're only little boys, you know.

MAINWARING No. 1 Platoon, B Company.

WARDEN Not the Wardens.

MAINWARING Slope arms.

They do so.

WARDEN Wardens – order pumps.

They bring their pumps down beside their feet.

MAINWARING Go on, Wilson.

WILSON Mon cher Général. Nous autres à Walmington-on-Sea sommes très honorés de votre visite. Nous vous souhaitons bon voyage et un retour et victorieux dans votre France bien-aimée.

JONES **(During the speech)** What's he saying, Mr Mainwaring?

MAINWARING Just the usual trite rubbish.

PIKE You've got to hand it to Uncle Arthur – it's like Mum says, he can do nearly anything if he gets the urge.

Godfrey wipes away a tear as Wilson finishes. There is applause.

GENERAL Mes amis, mes chers camarades d'armes. Je ne puis parler. Mon coeur déborde. Mais... merci.

He kisses Wilson. He kisses the town clerk and the mayor. The Vicar purses his lips but the general passes him and kisses Mainwaring. He then goes towards the car.

WARDEN Here, hang on – don't I get a kiss?

The general is by the car. He turns.

CHEESEMAN Hey, General boyo. Hold it. **(Cheeseman takes his photograph. There is a very large flash. The general stumbles back against the car. His hands behind him)**

Mid close up of general's hands going on to the west black surface.

GENERAL **(To Warden)** Pardon, mon brave. Mille fois pardon. **(He takes the Warden's face in his two hands and kisses him, leaving large black hand marks)**

SERIES SEVEN **EPISODE SIX**

Recorded: Sunday 10/11/74

Original transmission: Monday 23/12/74, 8.00–8.30pm

(This programme was originally planned for transmission on 6/12/74)

Original viewing figures = 15.8 million

ARTHUR LOWE . . . . CAPTAIN MAINWARING
JOHN LE MESURIER . . . . SERGEANT WILSON
CLIVE DUNN . . . . LANCE CORPORAL JONES
JOHN LAURIE . . . . PRIVATE FRAZER
ARNOLD RIDLEY . . . . PRIVATE GODFREY
IAN LAVENDER . . . . PRIVATE PIKE
BILL PERTWEE . . . . CHIEF WARDEN HODGES
TALFRYN THOMAS . . . . PRIVATE CHEESEMAN
FRANK WILLIAMS . . . . VICAR
EDWARD SINCLAIR . . . . VERGER
HAROLD BENNETT . . . . MR BLUETT
PAMELA CUNDELL . . . . MRS FOX
JANET DAVIES . . . . MRS PIKE
OLIVE MERCER . . . . MRS YEATMAN
DAVE BUTLER . . . . FARMHAND
PLATOON . . . . COLIN BEAN, GEORGE HANCOCK, EVAN ROSS, LESLIE NOYES, MICHAEL MOORE, FREDDIE WHITE, FREDDIE WILES, HUGH CECIL, ROGER BOURNE, DESMOND CULLUM-JONES
OAPS . . . . HEATHER GRAHAM, DAPHNE DAY, NELLIE GRIFFITHS, DORIS LITTLEWOOD, CONSTANCE MYERS, WYNN MCCLOUD, VERA WALDEN, CORALIE WILSON, GILLY FLOWER, EILEEN MATTHEWS, RUBY BUCHANAN, MARGI YOUNG, MERRELL HOBSON, CHARLES ADEY GRAY, VERNON DRAKE, WALTER GOODMAN, DAVID JAY GRAHAM, FRANK LITTLEWOOD, JIMMY MAC, JOHN TUCKER
WALK-ON (LAND GIRL AT TURKEY FARM) . . . . JILL HOPE

TURKEY DINNER

• ANNIE OGDEN REMEMBERS •

'Filming for "Turkey Dinner" had its problems, not least the fact that we all had a very muddy day out at a turkey farm. Also, there is only one drawback to filming fowl: they won't stay where you want them.

'As it was, we got our shots as more and more food was thrown down to entice them into the right place for the camera. They certainly fattened themselves up that day.'

WAR DEPARTMENT

TURKEY DINNER

SIDE OFFICE

Mainwaring is sitting at his desk, writing. On the door is a sign, painted in white, on a piece of board about two-thirds the width of the door and eight or ten inches deep. It is hinged at the bottom and held in position by a clasp at the top. On the board is written: 'War Department Captain G. Mainwaring, H.G. O.C. No.1 Plt. B Coy". Mr Bluett carries a small pot of paint and a couple of signwriters' brushes.

BLUETT There it is. How do you like it?

MAINWARING **(Looking at sign)** Oh yes. That's better.

WILSON **(Behind Bluett)** Hasn't he done it well, sir?

BLUETT I can't make his name any bigger, or it won't go on the board.

MAINWARING That'll do very adequately.

BLUETT Mind you, I could do it in long thin letters, but it wouldn't be right.

MAINWARING I don't see why not.

BLUETT No, I like the letters on the front of the door to be in keeping with the person who's sitting behind the desk inside – so I've done little short fat letters.

MAINWARING Thank you very much, Mr Bluett.

BLUETT It seems a rum way to spell Mainwaring, but I suppose you know best.

Bluett puts his paint pot on the desk.

WILSON The men are ready for inspection, sir.

MAINWARING **(Indicating his work)** I'll finish that later. It's my speech for the Rotary Club. I'm guest speaker, you know.

WILSON Are you really, sir? How exciting for you.

MAINWARING Are the men in good heart, Wilson?

WILSON No, sir. As a matter of fact, they seem to be a bit quiet.

MAINWARING I'll soon put that to rights. I've been reading a book called *Great Leaders of Men*. They all had one thing in common, you know. Before going into battle, they would tell the men a joke.

WILSON We're not going into battle, are we?

MAINWARING We're in the front line every minute of our lives, Wilson. **(Mainwaring goes into the hall, where the men are lined up. Godfrey is sitting by the stage)**

HALL

MAINWARING Squad, 'shun, stand at ease.

GODFREY **(Getting up and crossing to his place)** I'm sorry. I didn't know you were starting.

JONES I told Mr Godfrey to sit down for a minute or two. He goes a bit giddy if he stands around too long.

MAINWARING Right – now, pay attention. As we have a long night ahead of us, I thought I'd lighten the proceedings by cheering you up with a little anecdote. When I have finished, you have my permission to laugh in the ranks.

GODFREY How nice, sir. **(He smiles)**

MAINWARING Don't anticipate me, Godfrey, wipe that smile off your face.

GODFREY I'm sorry, sir.

MAINWARING Now, it appears that there were three British soldiers, a Welshman, an Englishman and a Scotsman.

FRAZER Just a minute, Captain Mainwaring, I hope it's not another of those stupid jokes about kilts. May I say, as a Scot, that I am sick and tired of being used as a butt for silly Sassenach jokes. We Scots don't make jokes about bowler hats. And another thing…

MAINWARING Quiet, Frazer. This has got nothing to do with kilts. Where was I, Wilson?

WILSON A Welshman, an Englishman and a Scotsman, sir.

MAINWARING Oh yes. Now, these three Tommies were sitting in the mess hall, and the Scotsman said to the Englishman, 'Pass the semolina pudding,' and the Englishman said, 'No, I won't'. Then the Scotsman said, 'Why not?'. To which the Englishman replied, 'Because King's Regulations specifically state: Never help another soldier to desert'.

There is a blank silence from the men.

MAINWARING It's all right, you can laugh.

They all laugh half-heartedly.

MAINWARING Yes, I thought you'd all enjoy that. **(To Wilson)** That's put them in a good mood, eh, Wilson?

WILSON Yes, sir, cheered them up no end.

MAINWARING **(Whispering)** A good tip on handling men, Wilson, always know when to unbend.

WILSON Yes, sir, I'll remember that.

CHEESEMAN What happened to the Welshman?

WILSON Perhaps he didn't like semolina.

Platoon laugh. Mainwaring reacts.

JONES Permission to speak, sir?

MAINWARING Yes, Jones.

JONES I hope you don't think that because we didn't laugh very much we was casting aspersions at your joke-telling. It wasn't that at all, sir.

PIKE No. You told it quite well, Captain Mainwaring.

CHEESEMAN Very good it was. I shall write it down after parade and send it to Radio Fun. They give half a crown for a joke like that, or five bob if it's a good one.

Mainwaring reacts.

JONES It's just that at the moment, sir, we're not much in the mood for merriment and horseplay.

MAINWARING Come come, Jones, that's not like an old soldier. Tommy Atkins was always one for a laugh – even when he was up to his neck in mud.

JONES Oh yes, sir, you're right there. We did a lot of laughing in mud in the last war. We was doing it nearly all the time, except when we was shot.

Mainwaring reacts.

JONES But tonight is different, sir. We have been wrestling with our consciences, sir, over an incident what happened last night and my section would like to go into a private place with you, sir, and reveal something.

MAINWARING I see. Well, I'm sure after parade will be soon enough.

FRAZER Quite right, sir. I would like to say here and now that he's making a flagpole out of a matchstick, and bringing you into it is only going to make things ten times worse.

PIKE It's only fair, Mr Frazer. Captain Mainwaring's the one that'll be court martialled.

MAINWARING Court martialled? Right, Jones' section – follow me into the office. And you, Wilson. (**Mainwaring crosses to office**)

WILSON (**To Pike**) What on earth have you all been doing, Frank?

PIKE Look, if I tell you, promise you won't tell Mum.

WILSON Of course not.

PIKE Well – no, I'd better not. It's a secret.

OFFICE

MAINWARING (**In office, joined by the others**) Right, settle down all of you. Now, what's it all about?

JONES Well, it's like this, sir. It was very cold on patrol last night, wasn't it, lads?

They all agree.

JONES And I know you wouldn't want us to catch a chill, so I took my lads to The Horse and Groom, and made sure they all had a tot of rum inside them. I knew you'd have done the same, sir, if you'd been in my position.

MAINWARING I doubt it, Jones. You know my views on alcohol.

JONES Well, sir, we'd only been back on patrol for ten minutes when Mr Cheeseman here started shivering.

CHEESEMAN You know what it's like, boyo, when you have the nadgers. You shiver all over, don't you?

JONES Well, I knew you wouldn't want anything to happen to a guest in the platoon – especially a newspaper press correspondent reporter – so we took him into The King's Head. Well, it was just as well we did, because by the time he'd downed a couple, he was right as ninepence.

PIKE I only had one in there, Captain Mainwaring.

JONES Well, we came out of The King's Head, and as we was passing The Goat and Compasses, the landlord come out and said he'd heard something rumbling down below. Well, I sent two men down below with hand grenades, and the rest of us stood by to give them covering fire.

MAINWARING Whereabouts?

JONES Two in the saloon bar and the rest in the snug.

MAINWARING You did right to tell me about it, all of you, but if you promise never to let it happen again, I'll overlook it just this once.

FRAZER The man's not finished.

MAINWARING You mean there's more?

JONES Yes, sir. You see – when we come out of there, it got a bit embarrassing.

WILSON If it's embarrassing, I'm sure you don't want to hear it, do you, sir?

MAINWARING Yes, I certainly do. Go on.

GODFREY It was I, sir. I started to get rather embarrassing.

MAINWARING You, Godfrey?

GODFREY I'm afraid so, sir. I started to sing, rather raucously.

PIKE It was a song about a monk.

MAINWARING Yes – well I'm glad it was a religious song.

FRAZER This one was not religious.

PIKE It was about a monk of high renown, Mr Mainwaring.

MAINWARING I see.

PIKE I didn't know high renown monks were all wicked like that.

WILSON That's enough, Frank.

MAINWARING I'm flabbergasted to think you should even know such a song, Godfrey.

GODFREY I heard it quite a lot in the last war, sir, when I was sitting in the mud.

MAINWARING I hope nobody heard you.

JONES Well, that's the next bit, sir.

MAINWARING I see. Go on.

JONES It gets even more embarrassing.

WILSON I'm sure you won't want to hear any more if it gets more embarrassing.

MAINWARING Stop interrupting, Wilson.

JONES Well, we knew you wouldn't want Mr Godfrey to make an exhibition of himself, so we took him inside to sober up.

PIKE Inside The Red Lion.

FRAZER While he was sobering up, the rest of us hardly had anything to drink at all – did we? Hardly anything at all.

JONES No – it was afterwards that it got more embarrassing.

WILSON Are you sure you want to hear about it, sir?

MAINWARING Do be quiet, Wilson.

JONES Well, sir. Someone come in and said they could hear something going on in a haystack. In a jocular fashion, I said that lots of things go on in haystacks.

CHEESEMAN Aye – like Bronwen Jones, that fat Welsh girl who used to wash up the glasses on Saturday nights… she spent half her life in that haystack. They used to call her the welcome in the valley.

WILSON Quiet, Cheeseman.

JONES Well, sir – all jocular thoughts was suddenly wiped from my mind as I realised that I was a soldier and it was my duty to investigate.

MAINWARING I'm glad somebody came to their senses at last.

JONES It sobered me up in a flash, sir – not that I was drunk – but the thought of encountering a fierce German parachuting stormtrooper, possibly disguised as a nun, sent a cold shiver down my spine. I rallied my men, and we went out into the murky night with our bayonets fixed.

PIKE I wasn't frightened this time. I think rum and whisky and cider give you courage, don't you, Mr Frazer?

FRAZER Wheesht, you fool.

JONES We was crossing a field near the haystack when all at once something flutters up. I was very alert by now, sir, and my reflexions was very quick. All of a sudden, I raised my rifle and shot it.

WILSON Good heavens. Don't tell me you shot Bronwen Jones?

JONES No, sir. It was an enormous great turkey. It's plucked and in my fridge.

MAINWARING I can't believe my ears. To think that my troop should go on a drunken rampage from pub to pub just like those comic stories told by that chap on the wireless.

PIKE Robb Wilton, sir. **(He does impression)** The day war broke out…

MAINWARING Be quiet, Pike. You should all be on a charge – and as for you, Pike, you're getting much too cheeky. I shall certainly have a word with your mother.

PIKE That's not fair. I'm being victimised because of my youth. Why don't you have a word with Mr Jones' mother?

JONES You leave my mother out of this. My mother has gone to another place.

PIKE I'm sorry, Mr Jones.

JONES Angmering.

MAINWARING How many people know about this?

JONES Very few, sir, she don't have many friends.

MAINWARING About the rampage.

FRAZER Only us. I say we should eat the turkey and hold our tongues.

MAINWARING Oh no. There's only one place that bird could have come from. The North Berrington Turkey Farm. You're all going to apologise to Mr Boggis personally, and you're going to pay for that turkey.

FILM. TURKEY FARM

Two hundred or so turkeys are in a compound, farmyard or small field. A farmhand is in the middle, putting water into a trough. Mainwaring and Jones' section approach.

MAINWARING Excuse me – is Mr Boggis about?

FARMHAND It's Wednesday.

MAINWARING What did he say?

WILSON He said it was Wednesday.

MAINWARING We'd better humour him, I suppose. I wonder if it's possible for us to see your master?

FARMHAND I just told you – it's Wednesday.

MAINWARING The man's obviously a fool.

PIKE Wednesday's market day – he'll have gone to market.

WILSON Has he gone to market?

FARMHAND That's right – it's Wednesday.

MAINWARING This is getting us nowhere. Have you lost a turkey?

FARMHAND **(Looks round, counts about three)** Hard to say, isn't it? **(He wanders over towards them)**

MAINWARING My men have accidentally killed one, and we feel sure it must have come from here. So we wish to pay for it. **(Holds up envelope)** Would you give this money to Mr Boggis when he returns, and ask him to accept our apologies.

FARMHAND Oh no, Mr Boggis wouldn't want me to take money. It might not be his turkey.

MAINWARING Nobody else in the district keeps them, so it must be yours.

FARMHAND That wouldn't be good enough for Mr Boggis – not unless he knew one of ours was missing.

MAINWARING How many should there be?

FARMHAND Two hundred and ten.

JONES **(Starts to count)** One – two – three – four – five – six – keep still. One – two.

MAINWARING That's no good. It'll take years.

PIKE We could count 30 each.

MAINWARING Good idea. Pay attention, all of you – we're going to count 30 turkeys each.

All start to count, except Wilson.

MAINWARING Get on with it, Wilson. You are in this platoon, you know.

WILSON Excuse me, sir. How do we know we're not counting the same turkeys?

MAINWARING Took you a long time to spot that, didn't it?

JONES Captain Mainwaring, why don't we all put a little dab of paint on each one we count?

FARMHAND Mr Boggis wouldn't like that. He don't like people painting his turkeys.

GODFREY Captain Mainwaring., my sister Dolly has hundreds of pickle jar rings. If we put one on each turkey, we'd soon know which ones we'd counted.

MAINWARING That's a very good idea, Godfrey.

GODFREY Shall I nip and get them?

MAINWARING Yes, do that.

Mix to Mainwaring and group. They each hold a bunch of large rubber rings.

MAINWARING Now, you each have 30 rings. On the command 'Move' you will each start placing one ring on each turkey. If there's a ring left over, then we know there's a turkey missing. Right – move.

The seven start to place rubber rings on the necks of the turkeys. A land girl comes along with a bucket, and starts throwing grain to the birds. They start to peck, so their heads go down.

MAINWARING No, no – don't do that!

JONES All their heads are not up, sir. We can't put the rings on.

WILSON I suppose we'll just have to wait till the turkeys finish lunch.

STUDIO. SIDE OFFICE

Mainwaring and Wilson.

MAINWARING All the rings were used up, so obviously it didn't come from there. The question is, what do we do next?

WILSON Jones shot it. I suppose it rightfully belongs to him.

MAINWARING Not at all. Whatever happens, he mustn't profit from that disgraceful drunken affair. Besides, he was on duty, in one of my uniforms, with one of my rifles, and he used one of my bullets.

WILSON Does that mean you're bagging it?

MAINWARING I'm certainly not bagging it – not all of it.

WILSON In that case, I bags it.

MAINWARING Oh no you don't. Anyway, I bagged it first.

WILSON You said you didn't want it. And anyway, you didn't say the word bags, so it doesn't count.

MAINWARING Don't start that public school cheating with me, Wilson.

WILSON I bags first, that's all.

MAINWARING No you didn't, I bagged first.

There is a knock on the door. Jones enters.

JONES Captain Mainwaring., me and my men have just been having a heart-to-heart think, and we want to say that we are very askanced at what we have done and we've come to the conclusion that with our ill-gotten gains, we ought to give a turkey dinner to the old-aged pensioners.

MAINWARING Do you hear that, Wilson? Trust our lads to turn up trumps in the end.

WILSON It does seem – on the face of it – quite a good idea.

MAINWARING It's a capital idea. It'll be a night to remember. We must organise it properly. Wilson – form a Turkey Dinner General Purposes Committee – I'll be chairman.

MAIN HALL. DAY

All the platoon present are in their civvies clothes. Mainwaring, and Jones' section are sitting round trestle tables. Also present are the Vicar, Verger, Mr Bluett, Warden, Mrs Pike, Mrs Yeatman and Mrs Fox. Mainwaring is on his feet.

MAINWARING Now, in order to speed our deliberations, I have made a shortlist of the various elements that have to come together to make a successful turkey dinner.

WARDEN Trust him to make it long winded.

MAINWARING First of all, there's the turkey, which Mr Jones' section has provided.

WARDEN I heard about that – what did you do? Fix bayonets and charge?

JONES Don't you start. You're a troublemaker, you are.

WILSON Yes – why is he here at all?

VICAR Mr Hodges had booked the hall for this evening. It's only because he released it that you can have this function at all.

VERGER **(Rises)** I think we ought to propose a vote of thanks to Mr Hodges. Don't you, Your Reverence?

VICAR No, I don't – and please sit down, or we'll be here all night.

MAINWARING Now, when times were different, turkey dinner would also include sausages, bacon, vegetables, roast potatoes, bread sauce and last, but not least, gravy.

BLUETT Did you save the giblets? Makes lovely gravy, giblets does – with a pinch of salt.

MAINWARING I'm sure we saved the giblets.

JONES Of course I saved the giblets.

WARDEN Let's all give a vote of thanks to Mr Jones for saving the giblets.

JONES **(Standing)** Now look here, Mr Hodges.

MAINWARING Jones, don't take any notice of him.

PIKE Uncle Arthur – what are giblets?

WILSON Oh, Frank. It's the inside of the turkey – the liver, kidneys, and gizzard – all that sort of thing.

PIKE I don't want gravy made out of that.

MRS PIKE Don't be silly, Frank. You've had it dozens of times.

PIKE I wouldn't if I'd known.

GODFREY My sister won't boil the giblets. She says the smell makes the Pekinese too excited.

CHEESEMAN My cat's like that with kippers, you know.

MRS YEATMAN Can we get on?

MAINWARING Yes, I quite agree. Don't let's get tied up with giblets at this stage. Now, first we have to select a volunteer to cook the bird.

JONES **(Rise)** I look at it this way, sir. Knowing what a good cook you say Mrs Mainwaring is, I feel the honour should fall to her lot.

WILSON Could you ask Mrs Mainwaring if she'd volunteer, sir?

MAINWARING No, I don't think that would be a very good idea, really. She doesn't have the experience of anything quite so large. There's only ever been the two of us, you know.

WARDEN Well, we've got a week – she could start with a pigeon and work her way up.

Mainwaring reacts.

PIKE My mum could cook it. She can cook anything – can't she, Uncle Arthur?

Wilson is silent.

MRS PIKE Well, answer the boy.

WILSON Of course she can, Frank.

JONES Mrs Fox is the finest cook I ever come across. Haven't I always said you're the finest cook, Mrs Fox?

MRS FOX Well, you've always been very nice about my dumplings.

MAINWARING Well, perhaps we should put it to the vote. All in favour of Mrs Pike cooking the turkey –

Pike, Godfrey, Cheeseman, Mr Bluett and Warden raise hands.

MAINWARING **(Counts)** Five. Now, all in favour of Mrs Fox.

Jones, Frazer, Mrs Yeatman, Vicar and Verger raise hands.

MAINWARING Five. In that case, I give the casting vote to Mrs Fox.

There is applause.

MRS PIKE **(To Wilson)** That's very nice, isn't it. You didn't put your hand up, did you?

WILSON I didn't want you to have all that trouble, Mavis.

PIKE That's a nice way of thanking you, isn't it, Mum. She give you her egg for breakfast this morning.

WILSON Look, Mavis –

MAINWARING Wilson, please address your remarks through the chair.

WILSON Through the chair – I didn't know it was Mrs Pike's egg.

MRS YEATMAN Can we get on?

MAINWARING I quite agree. We're doing very well – Mrs Fox is very kindly going to cook the turkey.

MR BLUETT Don't make it dry, will you? My pensioners don't like it dry.

VERGER Turkey can be very dry. I second that.

VICAR Be quiet, Mr Yeatman.

JONES When I was in the Sudan, we cooked an ostrich once. That wasn't dry, because we boiled it, in General Kitchener's bath. Next day, when the general came to do his ablutions, he sent for his batman, and he said, 'Come here, my man. What's this ring of dirt round my hip bath?' And the batman said, 'That's not dirt, sir, that's ostrich fat'. And he give him seven days' field punishment for impertinence – but it was the truth, wasn't it – doesn't do to tell the truth sometimes. It doesn't do to tell the truth.

MAINWARING Thank you, Mr Jones. Now, what comes next?

FRAZER Captain Mainwaring – stuff it.

MAINWARING I beg your...

FRAZER Stuff it. You'll need to stuff it. With parsley and thyme – or chestnuts.

WARDEN Chestnuts are out of season – every fool knows that.

MAINWARING Parsley and thyme it is, then. Perhaps Mrs Pike would undertake that side of the operation.

MRS PIKE Of course. If Mr Wilson thinks I'm good enough.

WILSON I'm sure you'll do it beautifully, Mavis.

MAINWARING Good – that's decided then.

VERGER My wife makes very taste parsley and thyme stuffing.

MAINWARING We've already decided that Mrs Pike will take care of it.

MRS YEATMAN It's not what you know, it's who you know.

JONES Big animal, an ostrich. I fed my section off the parson's nose.

MAINWARING Jones.

CHEESEMAN You want bread sauce, boyo. Makes turkey go down a fair treat, it does – oh yes indeed.

BLUETT Especially if it's dry.

MRS FOX It's not going to be dry.

JONES Mrs Fox makes a lovely bread sauce.

MRS YEATMAN Is she going to do it all then?

MAINWARING I think it would be an excellent idea if Mrs Yeatman made the bread sauce.

GODFREY I don't think we should have too much onion in the bread sauce. Onions are not good for old people.

WARDEN Make 'em excited, do they – like the Pekinese?

JONES Don't you get clever with Mr Godfrey here. He's a very wise man.

WARDEN There's another thing. Is old Jones here serving turkey as a Home Guard, or eating it as a pensioner?

JONES I've had enough of you. Get your coat off, come outside.

MAINWARING Jones – stop him – sit down.

They sit Jones down.

MAINWARING If I have any more of this, Mr Hodges, I shall ask you to leave.

WARDEN In that case, I'll have my hall back.

MAINWARING Now – everyone except Mr Bluett will, of course, be serving. I shall supervise, but I shall be leaving a little early, as on that night I am guest speaker at the Rotary dinner.

PIKE **(To Wilson)** So that's why you sent the tickets back, Uncle Arthur.

WILSON Frank!

MAINWARING But, of course, we cannot serve the meal until we've cooked it, so let us not leap ahead too fast.

WARDEN Too fast? At the rate you go, you'll only be half way through talking before it's time to put it in the oven.

MAINWARING Let us turn our attention to the gravy.

BLUETT Giblets make lovely gravy.

VERGER You've already said that, you silly old fool.

JONES There's no call to be offensive to Mr Bluett, just 'cos he's getting a bit past it.

VERGER He's not past it. He's anything but past it.

VICAR Now now, Mr Yeatman. Don't let's bring family squabbles into it.

Verger and Mrs Yeatman react.

MAINWARING No indeed. Let's stick to the gravy.

CHEESEMAN My wife makes very good gravy, you know. She burns everything else to a cinder, but you never tasted gravy like it. Life has its little compensations.

WILSON Can we get on?

MAINWARING We are getting on, Wilson. We'll put Mrs Cheeseman down for the gravy. Which brings us to the vegetables. Now, as I see it, vegetables pose a rather larger problem, not only because of availability, but also because of the greater bulk of material to be firstly prepared – secondly cooked – thirdly kept warm – and finally, served.

Fade as he drones on.

SIDE OFFICE

Mrs Fox accepts plate from Frazer.

MAIN HALL

Mrs Fox enters with plate.

SIDE OFFICE. INTERIOR. EVENING

Mainwaring carves on to plates.

MAINWARING (**Carving**) You're giving too much, Wilson. It won't go round.

WILSON According to my calculations, there's only four more to serve.

MAINWARING Don't splash – I don't want to get anything on my tails.

WILSON The way you've covered yourself up, I don't think there's much chance of that.

CHEESEMAN (**Passing a plate to Godfrey**) There you are, boyo.

GODFREY There's far too much onion, in spite of my warning.

FRAZER Aye, and the gravy's too thick. When I was a wee lad, my mother made thin, weak gravy and my father belted us with a tawse – but it made men out of us.

The Warden goes up to Mainwaring for another plate. He is chewing.

WARDEN Hurry up – the first ones'll be finished before the last ones are served.

MAINWARING Are you eating?

WARDEN What if I am?

MAINWARING This is for the pensioners of Walmington – not you.

WARDEN It was only a bit of skin.

Jones brings a plate back.

JONES Captain Mainwaring – this is Mr Bluett's.

MAINWARING What's the matter with it?

JONES He says, can you put it through the mincer?

MAINWARING We don't have a mincer – cut it up for him.

Pike joins them.

PIKE Captain Mainwaring – one or two of them are asking what happened to the parson's nose.

MAINWARING I can't be bothered with details like that – I have 32 meals to serve.

Pike goes.

MAINWARING (**To Wilson**) As a matter of fact, the parson's nose is missing, but I thought it best to turn a blind eye.

WILSON I cut it off and hid it underneath.

MAINWARING You did what?

WILSON I cut it off and hit it underneath.

MAINWARING What in heaven's name for?

WILSON I thought you and I might share it – after they've all gone – in here.

Mainwaring reacts. Mainwaring looks under turkey.

MAINWARING I don't think I'll ever get to understand you, Wilson.

Vicar enters.

VICAR Captain Mainwaring, this whole affair is not well organised at all. They all started to eat as soon as their plates arrived.

MAINWARING Of course they did, otherwise it would have got cold.

VICAR Well, it's not right. Before I started to say 'For what we are about to receive', half of them had received it.

MAIN HALL. INTERIOR. EVENING

Cut to hall. Mr Bluett rises.

BLUETT Here – I'm not having this. (**Points to neighbour's plate**) He's got all white meat, and I haven't got any.

JONES We'll soon put that to rights, Mr Bluett. (**He spoons some of the white meat on to Bluett's plate**)

BLUETT I'm not going to eat that – it's been on his plate.

Mrs Fox joins.

MRS FOX Mr Jones, Mrs Garstang says, have we got anything else, because she doesn't eat turkey.

JONES Well, if she don't like turkey, she shouldn't come to a turkey dinner, should she?

SIDE OFFICE. INTERIOR. EVENING

MAINWARING That's the last. (**Starts to take off apron**)

WILSON My, my, you do look smart, sir.

MAINWARING Well, I am guest speaker, you know. I don't think we should lower our standards just because there's a war on. Oh, by the way, Wilson, before I go, I think I ought to say a few words of welcome to the pensioners.

WILSON Don't you think you should let them digest their turkey first?

MAINWARING No. That would make me late for the Rotary dinner.

MAIN HALL

Mainwaring moves into the main hall, followed by Wilson. He greets various people.

MAINWARING Good evening, Mrs Sanger. Good evening, Mr Stanley.

BLUETT There's not enough salt in the gravy. **(Turns to Mainwaring)** Here, can I have some salt please, waiter?

Pike comes up to Mainwaring.

PIKE Captain Mainwaring, Mr McCully says, are there any seconds? **(He puts the plate into Mainwaring's hand. There is some gravy on the side of the plate which makes a mark about an inch long on Mainwaring's shirt)**

MAINWARING You stupid boy – look what you've done.

PIKE I'm not stupid. Whoever put the gravy on the edge of the plate was the one that was stupid.

MAINWARING It's the only shirt I have.

WILSON There's some blotting paper in the office – that'll probably take it off.

They move into the office.

PIKE **(Following)** I'm very sorry you've got gravy on your dickie, Mr Mainwaring, but I wasn't stupid.

SIDE OFFICE

MAINWARING This is not a dickie, Pike.

WILSON **(Having obtained blotting paper)** Just try this.

MAINWARING Careful, Wilson.

WILSON There – that's much better. It hardly notices at all.

Jones enters.

JONES Oh dear, Mr Mainwaring, you've got a little mark on your dickie.

PIKE It's not a dickie, Mr Jones. He just said so.

JONES Just a minute, sir. A little dab of white enamel will just cover that little spot, so it don't obtrude.

Warden opens the door. He carries an empty gravy boat.

WARDEN Hey – more gravy wanted for the far table.

PIKE Shan't be a second. **(He takes the gravy boat and refills it)**

JONES **(Taking tin of paint in his left hand and brush in his right)** This won't take a second, sir.

MAINWARING Do it very carefully, Jones.

Jones carefully puts white paint on the mark. In doing so, he presses the tin in his left hand against Mainwaring's jacket, leaving a white paint mark.

JONES There – you can't see that, can you?

MAINWARING No – well done, Jones.

FRAZER **(Pointing to white paint mark on jacket)** Look!

MAINWARING Jones – really.

JONES Anyone got any black paint?

MAINWARING This is impossible. How can I possibly get to my feet as guest speaker with paint all over my tails?

WILSON I have one at home, sir.

PIKE That wouldn't fit, Uncle Arthur. Not anyone as round as Mr Mainwaring.

GODFREY I think I have the answer, sir. Why don't you pretend you have hurt your arm, and make a sling with your scarf?

FRAZER That's a good idea, sir. It'll cover up the mark a treat.

JONES Just try it, Mr Mainwaring. **(He helps Mainwaring into the scarf)** It'll make you look very brave during your speech-making.

WILSON Jones is right, sir. And if you wince a bit now and then, you'll get twice the applause in the end.

FRAZER That does it, sir. Nobody will ever know.

JONES And you look very brave, Mr Mainwaring.

MAINWARING Well, I'm most angry, of course. But I think it's typical of our lads, Wilson, to show such ingenuity and resourcefulness in an emergency. Help me into my coat, Wilson.

Wilson gets the coat. Puts Mainwaring's hat on Mainwaring's head.

GODFREY Good luck, sir.

FRAZER Aye – good luck, sir – and don't worry, you look fine.

PIKE Yes – good luck, Mr Mainwaring – and I wasn't a stupid boy, was I, sir?

MAINWARING No, Pike – I'm sorry.

WARDEN **(Off)** 'Ere – are you bringing that gravy or aren't you?

Warden opens the door suddenly. The door hits Pike. Pike deposits contents of gravy boat over Mainwaring.

MAINWARING You stupid boy.

RING DEM BELLS

SERIES EIGHT **EPISODE ONE**

Recorded: Thursday 3/7/75

Original transmission: Friday 5/9/75, 8.00–8.30pm

Original viewing figures = 11.3 million

ARTHUR LOWE .... CAPTAIN MAINWARING
JOHN LE MESURIER .... SERGEANT WILSON
CLIVE DUNN.................................. LANCE CORPORAL JONES
JOHN LAURIE .... PRIVATE FRAZER
ARNOLD RIDLEY .... PRIVATE GODFREY
IAN LAVENDER .... PRIVATE PIKE
BILL PERTWEE.................................. CHIEF WARDEN HODGES
FRANK WILLIAMS .... VICAR
EDWARD SINCLAIR.................................. VERGER
JACK HAIG .... MR PALETHORPE, THE LANDLORD
ROBERT RAGLAN .... COLONEL
FELIX BOWNESS.................................. SPECIAL CONSTABLE
JOHN BARDON .... HAROLD FORSTER
HILDA FENEMORE.................................. QUEENIE BEAL
JANET MAHONEY.................................. DORIS, THE BARMAID
ADELE STRONG .... LADY WITH UMBRELLA
PLATOON .... COLIN BEAN, GEORGE HANCOCK, MICHAEL MOORE,
.... DESMOND CULLUM-JONES, FREDDIE WHITE,
.... EVAN ROSS, LESLIE NOYES, ROGER BOURNE,
.... FREDDIE WILES, HUGH CECIL

• FRANK WILLIAMS REMEMBERS •

'For me, the abiding memory of working in *Dad's Army* revolves around the location filming. In retrospect, those days spent in and around Thetford have an idyllic quality. David Croft had a reputation for being lucky with the weather and so he was. The memory seems to be of endless sunshine, not always completely welcome as the cast sweltered in uniforms and other heavy wartime clothing. Of course the location filming was hard work but it was also fun, and relaxing in the evening at The Bell Hotel over dinner was always a happy occasion.'

Ring Dem Bells

INTERIOR. CHURCH HALL. DAY

The men are standing around waiting for the parade to start. Jones, Frazer, Pike and Godfrey are sitting on the steps of the platform.

PIKE I ain't half excited, I'm so excited, I couldn't eat a thing at tea time. My mum could hardly believe her ears when I told her I'm going to be a film star.

FRAZER Rubbish, sheer rubbish.

PIKE I'm going to play my part like Ronald Colman, in that film *Under Two Flags* – I think I shall put a moustache on.

FRAZER Whist, laddie, is there no end to your stupidity? It's not going to be shown in any cinema, it's just a cheap training film, made for the Home Guard.

JONES When we was fighting the Fuzzie Wuzzies out in the Sudan, we never had no films.

GODFREY Surely they hadn't been invented then?

JONES That's why we never had any. Mind you, General Kitchener was very fond of his magic lantern, he used to lend it to the soldiers to stiffen up morals. Well, one night, they was having a show, and they hadn't got a screen, so they was shining the light on the side of Captain Spencer's tent. Well, General Kitchener was passing the back of the tent with his batman at the time, 'Good heavens my man, he said to his batman, I do declare those magic lantern pictures are moving'. 'That's not a slide, sir,' quoth the batman, 'that's Captain Jackson and a native girl.He's paying her for doing his washing.'

INTERIOR. SIDE OFFICE. DAY.

Mainwaring is looking in the mirror on the wall.

MAINWARING Men of the Home Guard, we are facing a cunning and ruthless enemy. Men of the Home Guard, we are… mmm, I wonder which is my best side. (**He picks up a small bit of broken mirror from the shelf and holds it up so that he can see his profile**) Men of the Home Guard, no. (**He turns the other way**) Mmm, perhaps it would be better with the hat off. (**He takes off his hat and turns both ways**) No perhaps not.

Wilson enters.

WILSON Good evening, sir.

MAINWARING Tell me, Wilson, which do you think is my best side?

WILSON Well, sir, your nose does look a little red from this side, turn the other way. (**Mainwaring turns**) Yes, it looks a bit red from this side as well, I don't think you've got a best side.

MAINWARING (**Coldly**) Really.

WILSON What I'm trying to say, sir, is that one side's no better than the other, I mean no worse than the other, I mean they're both the same.

MAINWARING All right, Wilson, all right.

WILSON I shouldn't worry, sir, they can do wonders with make up.

MAINWARING Make up, do you mean lipstick and powder?

WILSON Well, sort of.

MAINWARING I'm not having that muck on my face.

WILSON It does help to accentuate the good points. In your case, it would bring out the firm, craggy line of your jaw.

MAINWARING Do you really think so, craggy, eh. Well, perhaps I might let them put on a little, purely for technical reasons, you understand?

WILSON Yes, of course, sir. It might also take away your double chin.

MAINWARING They want men in this film, Wilson, not a lot of painted nancy boys.

WILSON I'm surprised they didn't have proper actors. Jack Buchanan could play my part very well.

MAINWARING Yes, you rather fancy that you look like Jack Buchanan, don't you, Wilson?

WILSON Well, I er…

MAINWARING Believe me, you are nothing like him whatsoever, either in speech or looks.

Pike comes in, he has a small ,thin moustache painted on his lip, his eyes are half closed.

PIKE Excuse me, Mr Mainwaring, the colonel's here with the film people.

MAINWARING Good.

PIKE He doesn't look a bit like a film producer, I thought he'd be wearing riding breeches and carry a whip like Eric Von Stroheim.

MAINWARING You stupid… what's the matter with your eyes, boy?

PIKE Nothing, Mr Mainwaring.

MAINWARING You've got a dirty mark on your lip. Wipe it off. (**He goes**)

PIKE I was only trying to look like Ronald Colman. Don't you think I look like him, Uncle Arthur?

WILSON Not really, Frank, no.

PIKE Well, I think I look more like Ronald Colman, than you look like Jack Buchanan.

INTERIOR. CHURCH HALL. DAY

The men are drawn up to attention, the colonel is waiting with Harold Forster, the production assistant, a thin, sharp man with glasses and a baggy suit, and Queenie Beal, the costume lady, wearing a head scarf,with a cigarette dangling out of her mouth. Mainwaring enters and salutes the colonel.

MAINWARING Good evening, sir.

COLONEL Evening, Mainwaring.

JONES Permission to speak, sir? As you were not here, in your absence, I took the liberty of falling the men in for inspection by the colonel, and the film people.

MAINWARING Thank you, Jones.

JONES You did want the men to be looked at by the film people, didn't you, sir?

MAINWARING Yes, Jones, thank you.

JONES I mean, they do look all right for the film people to look at, don't they, sir?

MAINWARING Yes, yes, just so that they can get an all-round picture of the platoon.

JONES Right, sir, right, sir, about turn. About turn – about turn.

The platoon turns, they now have their backs to Mainwaring.

MAINWARING What are you doing, Jones, what are you doing?

JONES You said they wanted an all-round picture of the men, sir.

MAINWARING All right, Jones. (**To the platoon**) About turn.

The platoon turn back. Jones' business. Mainwaring reacts.

MAINWARING (**To colonel**) He's very keen, sir, very keen. (**Wilson and Pike come in from the office**) Fall in, Pike.

Pike continues.

MAINWARING Pike – fall in.

COLONEL Now, Mainwaring, these are the people from the Crown Film Unit. This gentleman is the production assistant, Mr Forster.

FORSTER Hullo, squire.

Mainwaring reacts.

FORSTER This is Mrs Beal, our costume lady.

MRS BEAL Hullo, dear, just call me Queenie.

MAINWARING (**Coldly**) How do you do? This is Sergeant Wilson.

MRS BEAL Hello, dear.

WILSON How awfully nice to meet you.

MAINWARING I don't understand, sir. We don't need costumes, we've got our own uniforms.

COLONEL Well actually, Mainwaring, you won't be Home Guards, you're playing the Nazis.

MAINWARING Nazis! I'm not having my men blazoned all over the screen in German uniforms.

FORSTER Nothing to worry about, squire, all your stuff will be in what we call long shots, in the distance.

MAINWARING In the distance!

FORSTER Yes, on the screen you won't be much bigger than that. (**Indicates six inches**)

WILSON You won't have to worry about make up, will you, sir?

Mainwaring reacts.

MAINWARING Is that all we have to do?

FORSTER That's all, squire.

COLONEL The rest of the film is being done at the Gaumont British Studios. The captain and the sergeant are being played by actors giving their services for nothing. Jack Hulbert's playing the captain, and Jack Buchanan the sergeant.

Mainwaring reacts.

WILSON Well, well, fancy that, sir, Jack Buchanan's playing the sergeant.

Mainwaring reacts.

MRS BEAL Yes, I measured him for his uniform yesterday. Lovely bloke he is, just like you, sarge, you're a dead ringer for him.

FORSTER Right, who are we going to have for the officer?

MAINWARING I shall be the officer, of course.

COLONEL I'm sure Captain Mainwaring will make an excellent German officer.

FRAZER (**Aside to Pike**) He couldn't make a worse mess than he does as a British officer.

FORSTER Run your tape over him, Queenie.

Mrs Beal advances on Mainwaring with a tape measure.

MRS BEAL Get your arms up, dear. (**She measures Mainwaring's chest**) Oh dear – (**Then his waist**) Oh no –

FORSTER It's ridiculous.

MRS BEAL (**Measures Mainwaring's hips**) No, I couldn't do him, dear, and look at those feet, I've never seen such tiny feet, I haven't got any Jackboots that size, tiny, he's got girl's feet.

MAINWARING Well, couldn't you get a uniform made for me?

MRS BEAL We couldn't even get one made for Conrad Veidt. There is a war on, you know.

FORSTER Sorry, squire, but it's like this – we've only got two officers' uniforms, it's a question of getting the men

to fit the uniforms. Have a look round, Queenie. Excuse me.

Mrs Beal starts to measure the men.

MAINWARING **(To colonel)** May I have a word with you please, sir?

COLONEL Yes, of course. **(He takes Mainwaring aside)**

MAINWARING Now look, sir, I refuse to have anything to do with this.

COLONEL Don't be difficult, Mainwaring, your men have got to play the Germans, and that's an order. However, I respect your feelings, so you needn't take part in it, just stay on the touchline and look after your men.

Mrs Beal pulls Wilson and Pike down to Forster.

MRS BEAL I've got your two officers, dear, this one and this one. Oh, he does look like Jack Buchanan, he'll make a lovely officer. Now, who's going to be the sergeant? **(She advances on Jones with the tape)** Come on, sonny boy, get your arms up.

INTERIOR. CHURCH HALL. DAY

The men are standing around dressed as Germans. Jones, Frazer and Godfrey are standing together. They are all wearing Nazi steel helmets. Jones is dressed as a sergeant.

FRAZER I feel a right Jessie, dressed up in these absurd clothes. I notice Mainwaring got out of it, just because he couldn't be an officer. Sheer childishness. Why shouldn't he look a fool just like the rest of us?

GODFREY I don't think you look a fool, Mr Frazer, that helmet makes you look like an eagle.

FRAZER **(Moving his head in jerks)** Rubbish.

JONES General Kitchener would turn in his grave if he saw me dressed like this. He couldn't abide the Hun uniform, Hun helmets are just like saucepans he used to say. I shall never forget they brought a German prisoner to him one day, and as this German was grovelling in front of him, the general fixed him with a cold look. 'How dare you grovel in front of me with that saucepan on your head, my man? Take it off at once', he expurgated. 'I cannot get it off, mein general,' said the grovelling German, 'it is stuck.' 'Well,' said General Kitchener, jocular like, 'if that saucepan is stuck , the best thing you can do is to go and boil your head.' He could be very witty at times.

Godfrey and Frazer react.

INTERIOR. SIDE OFFICE. DAY

Wilson enters. Pike enters.

PIKE **(In German accent)** You swines. We are the masters now. You have just five seconds to tell me your plans, otherwise, kaput. I like being an officer, don't you like being an officer, Uncle Arthur?

WILSON **(Looking in mirror)** Well, I must admit these uniforms are very smart. **(He tilts his hat)** They certainly do something for one.

PIKE I think we ought to strut and swagger, shall we try strutting and swaggering?

WILSON How do you mean?

PIKE Like this. **(He struts up and down hitting his breeches with his gloves)**

WILSON That's awfully good, Frank.

PIKE You try Uncle Arthur.

WILSON Somehow I don't think strutting and swaggering is quite my style.

PIKE Well, do a goose step then. Go on.

WILSON Like this? **(He does it half-heartedly)**

Mainwaring comes in.

PIKE He was very good, no, Mr Mainwaring?

MAINWARING Get on your feet, boy. I'm beginning to wonder where your loyalties lie, Wilson.

WILSON Oh really, sir, it's just that this uniform, just sort of er... lends itself to any figure.

MAINWARING The sooner we get this nonsense over, the better. Fall the men in.

INTERIOR. CHURCH HALL. DAY

Wilson, Mainwaring and Pike come in.

WILSON Right, fall in, three ranks.

They fall in, except Pike who stands beside Mainwaring.

MAINWARING Fall in, boy.

Pike stands still.

MAINWARING Didn't you hear me? Fall in.

PIKE I'm an officer, Captain Mainwaring. I'm not going to fall in with the privates. All officers should be treated with respect, whatever their nationality. It says so in the Geneva Convention.

MAINWARING If you don't stop playing the fool, Pike, you'll be sent home. Now, fall in. Right, pay attention, men.

JONES Permission to speak, sir? I wish to unvolunteer to be a German sergeant. All my life I have wanted these two extra stripes, but I feel this is too high a price to pay.

FRAZER And I think it all wrong that I should have to wear this ludicrous helmet.

MAINWARING I appreciate your feelings, men, but we have been ordered to take part in this film and we shall just have to get on with it.

GODFREY Excuse me, sir, my uniform has got the name 'Bermans' inside, I hope it's been cleaned, you never know where those Germans have been.

MAINWARING Don't worry, Godfrey, they're not real uniforms, they're theatrical costumes.

PIKE Mr Mainwaring, how will people know we're Home Guards dressed up as Nazis, and not real ones.

MAINWARING That's a good point Pike, the colonel has given me instructions for strict security. No one must see you, so you will all stay inside the van, and I will drive you there, and back.

TELECINE: EXTERIOR. EDGE OF FIELD. DAY

The van approaches along the road, pulls up and stops. Mainwaring gets down, looks round and bangs on the side of the van.

MAINWARING All clear, you can come out.

The back door opens, Pike jumps down, he has a monocle in his eye.

PIKE **(In German accent)** Raus, raus, come on, at the double, move, move.

MAINWARING Stop playing the fool, boy, and take that stupid thing out of your eye.

Wilson crosses to Mainwaring.

WILSON Are you sure this is the right place, sir?

MAINWARING Of course I'm sure, Wilson.

WILSON But it's deserted, shouldn't there be lots of cameras and lights and things like that?

MAINWARING These film people are always late. They're very unreliable, spend most of the day lounging around and drinking cocktails. **(Shouts)** Lance Corporal Jones.

JONES Yes, sir, yes, sir.

MAINWARING Tell the men they can eat their sandwiches.

JONES Right, sir, do like the officer says, eat your sandwiches.

PIKE **(To Wilson)** Uncle Arthur, I don't think we ought to eat our sandwiches with the men.

WILSON Why not?

Harold Forster draws up on a motorbike.

PIKE Well, we're officers, let's you and I go away somewhere and eat them on our own.

WILSON Oh don't be absurd, Frank.

Harold crosses to Mainwaring.

FORSTER Hullo, squire, sorry about this, but the filming's been postponed until next week.

MAINWARING Postponed!

FORSTER Yes, spot of bother with Jack and Cis.

MAINWARING Jack and Cis?

WILSON Jack Hulbert and Cicely Courtneidge, sir.

FORSTER They're doing a new show next week, so we're filming all Jack's stuff this week.

FRAZER Do you mean to say we've been shut in that van on a hot day like this, in these stupid uniforms, just because two…

MAINWARING All right, Frazer.

FORSTER Sorry, squire, but Jack insists on being with Cis, and Cis insists on being with Jack, they're always together.

GODFREY Yes, they're inseparable. I was reading in the newspaper only last week that they're the happiest couple in showbusiness.

JONES I read that too, Mr Godfrey. Jack the boy, eh? **(Sings)** Oh the flies crawl up the window…

MAINWARING Be quiet, Jones. **(To Forster)** Do you realise that we are fighting a war upon which the whole future of civilisation depends, that at this moment the entire might of the German Army is poised across the Channel ready to strike, and you have dragged us, front-line troops, out here on a fool's errand, because Cis insists…

FORSTER Sorry, squire, mustn't upset the stars, you know. See you next week. **(Goes)**

MAINWARING This is outrageous, Wilson, I'm going to phone up G.H.Q. at once.

WILSON What a pity, we're not going to do any shooting today.

MAINWARING Shooting?

WILSON That's right, shooting. It's the technical term for filming, still, if Jack and Cis…

MAINWARING **(Coldly)** Get back in the van, Wilson.

EXTERIOR. ROAD. DAY

Van approaching. Pike is giving the Nazi salute out of the top. Van stops, Mainwaring gets out.

MAINWARING **(Shouting to Pike)** This is not a game, boy. Get back inside.

TELECINE: EXTERIOR. OUTSIDE PUB. DAY

The van draws up outside the pub. Across the road is a phone box. Wilson and Jones poke their heads through the hole behind the driver's seat.

MAINWARING Now listen, Wilson, I'm going across to that phone box to ring up G.H.Q. Whatever you do, don't get out of the van. I don't want anybody to see you in those uniforms.

WILSON But it's like an oven in here, sir.

JONES Mr Godfrey is looking very pale, sir, he must have some fresh air.

MAINWARING Well, open the back door of the van a few inches, and push his face against the crack. I shan't be long. **(Mainwaring gets out and crosses to the phone box)**

Cut to the back of the van, the door opens a few inches and Godfrey's nose appears.

JONES How's that, Mr Godfrey?

GODFREY A little better, thank you.

FRAZER What about me? I want some fresh air as well.

JONES Well you can't have any – you heard what Mr Mainwaring said, no one must see us in these uniforms.

FRAZER Rubbish.

The door is pushed open from the inside and swings right back.

JONES How dare you disobey an order, Private Frazer? You've exposed us to the whole world.

FRAZER Nonsense, there's not a soul about.

PIKE Uncle Arthur, that pub looks nice. I'm awfully thirsty, I couldn't half do with a drink.

WILSON So could I, Frank, but Captain Mainwaring said we mustn't get out of the van.

PIKE Mr Mainwaring's only a Home Guard officer, we're the officers of the Germans.

WILSON Yes, I suppose we are.

PIKE Well, let's go in and have a drink then, come on, nobody will see us, come on. **(In German accent)** In ze pub for ze drink, raus, raus.

INTERIOR. BAR. DAY

Pike, Wilson, Jones, Frazer and Godfrey come in, followed by the rest of the platoon. The bar is deserted.

PIKE It's all right, Uncle Arthur, there's nobody about.

JONES We shouldn't be doing this, you know, Sergeant Wilson.

WILSON What are you having?

JONES I'll have a pint.

WILSON We'll just have a quick drink and then we'll get back in the van. Captain Mainwaring will probably be on the phone for ages.

PIKE Right, I'll order the drinks. **(Bangs the bell on the bar)**

GODFREY I really don't think anyone could possibly mistake us for Nazi paratroopers, we're far too old.

JONES Of course we are, Mr Godfrey, I never thought of that. You know you're a very wise man.

The landlord comes through a curtain at the end of the bar.

LANDLORD Good morning, gentlemen, what will it… **(Takes in the uniforms)**

PIKE **(In German accent)** Ach, good day, mein host, 16 shandys, mid der ginger beer.

Landlord reacts.

LANDLORD Er… pints or halves?

PIKE Pints.

LANDLORD Er… yes ,of course, excuse me. **(Goes through the curtain at the end of the bar)**

WILSON Don't play the fool, Frank, I'm very hot and very tired.

Landlord comes through the other side of the curtain.

LANDLORD Doris.

DORIS Yes, Mr Palethorpe.

LANDLORD I've got 16 Nazis out there, and they want 16 shandys.

DORIS Well, it's a hot day, they're probably thirsty.

LANDLORD Didn't you hear me? They're Nazis.

DORIS Don't be daft.

LANDLORD Look for yourself.

Doris peeps through the curtains.

DORIS They're not Nazis, they're a lot of old men.

LANDLORD Don't be stupid, they're only disguised as old men so that they won't look like Nazis.

DORIS Well, if they don't want to look like Nazis, why are they wearing Nazi uniforms?

LANDLORD Look, don't argue. Go and rouse the village and tell the police. **(He goes back through the curtains)** Well, gentlemen, nice weather for the time of the year.

EXTERIOR. PUB. DAY

Mainwaring comes out of the phone box. Crosses to the van, sees the door open, looks in.

MAINWARING Wilson, Jones? **(Looks towards the pub)** I thought as much. **(He goes towards the pub)**

INTERIOR. BAR. DAY

Mainwaring comes in.

MAINWARING (To Wilson) What do you think you're doing, Wilson?

WILSON Well actually, sir, we were rather thirsty, so we thought we'd have a drink.

MAINWARING You'll give the whole game away, they'll think we're Germans.

Landlord comes back through the curtains, Mainwaring leans across the counter and lowers his voice.

MAINWARING Now, look here, landlord. You may think this is all rather odd, seeing us dressed as Germans. Of course, I don't have to tell you we're not Germans, all the same, I wouldn't breathe a word of this to anyone, they might get the wrong idea. (**He laughs weakly**) You do understand, don't you?

Landlord nods.

MAINWARING Right, outside, men.

PIKE Outside, move, raus, raus.

EXTERIOR. PUB. DAY

Mainwaring and co. come out of the pub.

MAINWARING Get in the van, quickly, before anyone sees you.

Policeman, barmaid and small group of villagers peep round side of pub. Landlord comes out of door and crosses to the policeman.

LANDLORD Well, go on, do something. They'll get away.

POLICEMAN What do you expect me to do?

LANDLORD You're a special constable, arrest them.

POLICEMAN What all of 'em?

DORIS Arrest that British officer then, he's a quisling, a collaborator.

POLICEMAN Well, I er...

LANDLORD Go on. (**Pushes him**) Go and speak to him.

TELECINE: EXTERIOR. OUTSIDE PUB. DAY

Mainwaring closes the back door of the van and walks round to the front. The policeman approaches, with the landlord and Doris pushing him. The rest of the villagers approach cautiously from behind.

POLICEMAN Excuse me, sir, can I have a word with you?

MAINWARING What is it, officer?

POLICEMAN I'd like to ask you a few questions.

MAINWARING Yes?

POLICEMAN May I ask what you're doing with a butcher's van full of Germans?

MAINWARING Ah yes, well, I can assure you, officer, they're not Germans.

Pike pokes his head out of the top of the van and waves his Tommy gun.

PIKE (**In German accent**) Schwein hund! Get out of the way at once, do you hear me, donner and blitzen!

MAINWARING Get inside at once, boy, I shan't tell you again. (**To policeman**) Youthful high spirits, you know.

An old lady detaches herself from the crowd, pushes the policeman out of the way and advances on Mainwaring, waving her umbrella.

OLD LADY I'm not afraid of 'em, even if you are. (**To Mainwaring**) You quisling, traitor.

MAINWARING Madam, I am not a...

OLD LADY Collaborator! You're a disgrace to that uniform, take it off, take it off! (**She starts to hit Mainwaring with her umbrella. The rest of the crowd gather round shouting**)

ALL Quisling! Traitor!

Mainwaring fights his way into the cab of the van.

MAINWARING You don't understand, I tell you, I'm Captain Mainwaring...

The crowd are all round the van, booing, shouting and hitting it. Jones' face appears through the hole behind the driver's seat.

JONES Mr Mainwaring – there's somebody knocking on the side of the van.

Mainwaring drives off.

DORIS (**To policeman**) You let 'em get away!

The crowd are all shouting at the policeman.

POLICEMAN All right, all right, calm down. I shall take charge of this, we must warn England. (**To landlord**) Mr Palethorpe, they're making for Walmington-on-Sea. Phone up the Home Guard there and tell them, I'll ring up the superintendent at the Eastgate police station.

INTERIOR. SIDE OFFICE. DAY

The Vicar is sitting at his desk writing, Hodges and the Verger are standing by the desk, the Verger has a small book in his hand.

HODGES (**Pointing at book**) Look, it clearly states there, that I have the booking for the hall every Thursday night. Why has it been changed and given to Mainwaring?

VERGER Mr Mainwaring told me he'd spoken to you, Mr Hodges.

HODGES He never said a word to me.

VERGER (**To Vicar**) What shall I do about it, Your Reverence?

VICAR You'll have to sort it out yourself, Mr Yeatman.

Don't worry me, I'm trying to write my sermon.

HODGES As soon as Mainwaring gets back, I'm going to have a few words to say to him.

The phone rings.

VICAR Answer the phone, Mr Hodges.

Hodges picks it up.

HODGES Hello.

LANDLORD Is that the Walmington-on-Sea Home Guard?

HODGES They're not here.

LANDLORD I've got an urgent message. There's a party of Nazi paratroopers on their way.

HODGES Who are you?

LANDLORD The landlord of The Dog and Fox. Did you hear what I said, a gang of Nazis, led by a British officer, he's a quisling. Tell the Home Guard, warn England. (**He hangs up**)

HODGES Blimey!

VERGER What's the matter, Mr Hodges?

HODGES The landlord of The Dog and Fox, sounds as if he's had a skinful. He was babbling something about some German troops led by a British officer.

VICAR Oh dear, the evils of drink.

VERGER Yes indeed, Your Reverence.

We hear the sound of the van drawing up outside the church hall.

MAINWARING (**Out of vision**) Right, fall in, men.

HODGES There's Mainwaring now. I'm going to sort out the booking of this hall once and for all. Come on, Vicar.

VICAR I'm trying to write my sermon.

HODGES (**Grabbing him**) Look, it's your hall.

VICAR Stop handling me, Mr Hodges, you know I can't stand that sort of thing.

TELECINE: EXTERIOR. CHURCH HALL YARD. DAY

Hodges, the Vicar and the Verger come round the side of the building. They stop dead in their tracks. Cut to rear view of the platoon in German uniforms. Cut back to Hodges and co. They run to the edge of the building, their three faces come round the corner.

HODGES Ger... Ger... Germans!

Cut to rear view of platoon, Mainwaring appears in front of the platoon and walks to side so that he can be clearly seen by Hodges and co.

MAINWARING Now, pay attention, men, I'm sure you're all as disappointed as I am that we didn't get a chance to do any shooting today.

Cut to reaction of Hodges and co. Cut back to Mainwaring.

MAINWARING Let's hope we have better luck next week. Meanwhile, I must impress on you how secret this is. I don't want any repetition of what happened at that public house this morning. No one must see us in these uniforms, so keep them hidden until we need them for shooting.

Cut back to Hodges and co.

VICAR I can't believe my eyes.

HODGES That landlord wasn't drunk, it's Mainwaring! He's a quisling! A traitor!

VERGER Oh no, they'll shoot us.

HODGES Yeah, they'll shoot us.

VICAR We must sound the alarm.

HODGES Th... th... that's it, the church bells.

TELECINE: EXTERIOR. CHURCH YARD. DAY

Long shot of Hodges and co. running through tombstones.

INTERIOR. BELL TOWER. DAY

Hodges and co. rush in.

VICAR Quick, lock the door, Mr Hodges.

Hodges locks and bolts the door.

VERGER What peal shall we do, Your Reverence?

VICAR Oh, you stupid fellow, just ring the bells.

VERGER Yes, but...

HODGES (**Pushing him and grabbing the rope**) Stop arguing, just pull the rope.

STUDIO. INTERIOR. CHURCH HALL. DAY

MAINWARING Right, that's all, men. Dismiss.

The men fall out, suddenly we hear church bells.

WILSON Good heavens, church bells.

JONES It's the invasion signal, the Germans are coming, don't panic, don't panic!

MAINWARING Pull yourself together, Jones.

WILSON Someone must have seen us in these uniforms, and thought we were real Germans.

MAINWARING The whole countryside will be up in arms. Quick, we must stop them. Come on, men.

They all rush to the church.

INTERIOR. BELL TOWER

The three are ringing the bells.

EXTERIOR. DOOR OUTSIDE BELL TOWER. DAY

Mainwaring and co. rush into the picture. Mainwaring tries to open the door.

MAINWARING It's locked. (**He bangs on the door and shouts**) Stop ringing those bells.

JONES (**Banging on the door with his rifle**) We're not real Germans.

MAINWARING Break the door down.

They all bang on the door with their rifle butts.

INTERIOR. BELL TOWER. DAY

VICAR They're trying to get in, ring louder.

EXTERIOR. OUTSIDE BELL TOWER. DAY

MAINWARING (**To the men**) Stop, stop, this is no good.

WILSON They can't hear us, sir, it's the sound of the bells.

MAINWARING I know, Wilson, I know.

FRAZER Any minute now bombs and shells will come raining down on us, we're doomed! Doomed!

MAINWARING Pike, go and ring up G.H.Q. Tell them it's a false alarm.

PIKE Yes, Mr Mainwaring. (**He goes**)

JONES Permission to speak, sir? Why don't you shoot the lock off?

MAINWARING Good idea, Jones. (**He draws his revolver**)

WILSON But if you do that, sir, you might hit the people who are ringing the bells.

MAINWARING Well done, Wilson, I wondered who'd be the first to spot that.

Wilson goes.

GODFREY Why don't you put a note under the door, sir?

MAINWARING Well done, Godfrey. Jones, take a note.

JONES Yes, sir, yes, sir. (**He pulls a paper and pencil out of his pocket**)

MAINWARING Stand clear, I am going to shoot the lock off.

JONES ...shoot the lock off, yours sincerely, Jack Jones, Lance Corporal.

MAINWARING Put it under the door.

JONES Yes, sir, yes, sir. (**He pushes it under the door**)

FRAZER Hold on, hold on a minute, Captain Mainwaring. If you shoot the lock off, we'll have to pay for the damage.

MAINWARING Get out of the way, Frazer. Right, stand back. (**He shoots the lock, the bells stop and there is silence. Mainwaring tries to open the door**) It still won't open.

We hear Wilson's voice from the other side of the door.

WILSON Just a minute, sir.

There is the sound of bolts being drawn. Wilson opens the door.

WILSON It was bolted, sir.

MAINWARING How did you get in, Wilson?

WILSON I came through the vestry, sir.

They all go in.

INSIDE BELL TOWER. DAY

Mainwaring and co. come in.

WILSON There doesn't appear to be anybody here, sir.

JONES (**Pointing up**) Look, Mr Mainwaring.

They all look up. Hodges, Vicar and Verger are clinging to the bell ropes about eight foot up.

HODGES You... You... flippin' hooligans.

Pike comes in.

PIKE I got on to G.H.Q., Mr Mainwaring. I spoke to the brigadier in person.

MAINWARING What did he say?

PIKE There were three battalions of Coldstream Guards and an armoured division on the way, but he managed to stop them.

MAINWARING Well done, Pike.

PIKE The whole of the south coast is on red alert, and he wanted to know what blithering idiot was responsible. So I made an appointment for you to see him at half past nine in the morning.

MAINWARING You stupid boy.

Mainwaring and Pike react.

SERIES EIGHT **EPISODE TWO**

Recorded: Friday 6/6/75

Original transmission: Friday 12/9/75, 8.00–8.30pm

Original viewing figures = 12.6 million

ARTHUR LOWE .... CAPTAIN MAINWARING
JOHN LE MESURIER .... SERGEANT WILSON
CLIVE DUNN.................................. LANCE CORPORAL JONES
JOHN LAURIE .... PRIVATE FRAZER
ARNOLD RIDLEY .... PRIVATE GODFREY
IAN LAVENDER .... PRIVATE PIKE
BILL PERTWEE.................................. CHIEF WARDEN HODGES
FRANK WILLIAMS .... VICAR
EDWARD SINCLAIR... VERGER
JANET DAVIES .... MRS PIKE
ERIC LONGWORTH .... TOWN CLERK
FREDDIE EARLLE.................................... ITALIAN SERGEANT
TIM BARRETT... DOCTOR
COLIN BEAN .... PRIVATE SPONGE
FRANKIE HOLMES .... FISH FRYER
PLATOON........................ GEORGE HANCOCK, MICHAEL MOORE,
.... DESMOND CULLUM-JONES, FREDDIE WHITE,
.... EVAN ROSS, LESLIE NOYES, ROGER BOURNE,
.... FREDDIE WILES, HUGH CECIL

WHEN YOU'VE GOT TO GO

• ANNIE OGDEN REMEMBERS •

'Food is the bugbear of every AFM. "When You've Got to Go" was a big headache for me regarding hot fish and chips. In the rehearsal room, I had to offer the actors something that approximated fish and chips with which to rehearse. It couldn't be hot because we didn't have the facilities, and the plates at my disposal were cracked and dirty. So I think I gave them crisps and cold ham.

'I remember that was the only time that David Croft got cross with me – over the rehearsal food. And I didn't like it! When we came to do the recording in the studio, the designer had installed into the chip shop set a wonderful period fish-fryer; but, of course, it didn't work and was very cold. What I had to do was order freshly cooked fish and chips from the BBC canteen, keep them in a hot trolley until they were needed and then, at the last moment, transfer them to the old fish and chip fryer for the actor Frankie Holmes to serve to Pike and the others. Even then I think the chips had gone cold. Poor Ian.'

When You've Got to Go

MRS PIKE'S SITTING ROOM

Mrs Pike and Wilson are sat at the table. Pike's place is set but he is absent. Wilson is toying with a piece of pie and reading the evening paper, which is folded beside his plate.

MRS PIKE Don't you like it then?

WILSON Yes, it's lovely – absolutely lovely.

MRS PIKE I queued up for hours for it.

WILSON It's beautiful. I'm really awfully fond of veal and ham pie.

MRS PIKE If there's one thing I can't stand, it's people who push their food around on their plates.

WILSON I just want to see what I'm eating. (**He starts to sugar his tea**)

MRS PIKE You've already had one spoonful of sugar.

WILSON Oh yes, I'm sorry.

MRS PIKE Of course, the whole thing's a farce.

WILSON Oh I don't know, I think we get on rather well.

MRS PIKE I'm talking about Frank. It's a farce that he should waste a whole day going for his medical.

WILSON He had to be called up sooner or later.

MRS PIKE But they couldn't possibly take him – not with his chest. If he doesn't wear his scarf he gets croup and then I'm up all night.

WILSON Perhaps he could wear his scarf under his uniform.

MRS PIKE Can you see him doing that? He's like you – he won't be advised. Look what happened when I tried to cure his sinus.

WILSON He just didn't like sleeping with a hot water bottle on his face.

MRS PIKE There you are then. And what about his weak ankles. The slightest thing and over he goes.

WILSON I hadn't noticed that.

MRS PIKE Why do you think I spend hours holding ice packs on his feet?

WILSON I've often wondered.

MRS PIKE On top of that, there's his nerves.

WILSON Yes, that face thing is getting rather worrying.

MRS PIKE Face thing – what face thing?

WILSON Well, he's been doing it ever since his papers arrived.

MRS PIKE Doing what?

WILSON This. (**He raises his eyebrows and drops his jaw to stretch his face muscles**)

MRS PIKE That's his age – all boys do that.

Wilson reaches for a packet of cigarettes.

MRS PIKE How many times have I told you not to smoke during meals?

WILSON I've finished.

MRS PIKE You don't eat enough to keep a fly alive. It beats me where you get your energy from.

Wilson reacts.

PIKE (**Out of vision**) I'm back.

MRS PIKE He's back. Thank goodness, I was worried to death.

Pike appears in the doorway.

PIKE Hullo, Mum. (**He makes the face**)

MRS PIKE And about time too. You're due on parade in ten minutes. Now, sit down there and don't bolt your tea.

PIKE (**Pleased with himself**) Don't you want to hear how I got on?

MRS PIKE What have you been doing? It can't have taken them more than five minutes to decide about you.

PIKE I was there all day. I've passed. I'm A1.

MRS PIKE A1. Oh no. (**She dissolves into tears**)

WILSON Now, Mavis, don't upset yourself.

MRS PIKE It's a mistake. I should have gone with him. Did you tell 'em what I told you.

PIKE Yes, and the doctor said there was nothing the matter with me that couldn't be put right with fresh air, exercise and good food.

MRS PIKE Good food. Good food. I gave him my egg this morning, didn't I? Tell him, Arthur, tell him I gave him my egg.

WILSON She gave you her egg, Frank.

PIKE Thank you.

MRS PIKE You'll have to go and see them. They're not having him for a soldier.

PIKE No, they're not – I've asked to be put in the R.A.F.

MRS PIKE You – in an aeroplane – you get dizzy standing on a chair.

PIKE I told them I'd like to be a Spitfire pilot and the officer said I'd better be an ordinary aircraftsman for a bit and then they'd see how I got on. Just think – I'll be the second of the few.

MAIN HALL

The platoon is on parade – less Jones.

MAINWARING Platoon, 'shun! Stand at ease.

They all 'shun together.

MAINWARING Where's Jones?

FRAZER He's not here, sir. He's absent. You should mark him absent – without leave.

MAINWARING Right, that'll do, Frazer. Now, in a few weeks' time, we shall be losing one of the loyalest members of our platoon – Private Pike.

Cut to Pike, who pulls his face.

MAINWARING Young Frank Pike has been with us since the first day we were formed and through our darkest days he has given devoted service and always been ready with a cheerful quip.

Cut to Pike, who repeats his face.

MAINWARING Well, (**To Wilson**) Wilson – why does he keep doing that?

WILSON What, sir?

MAINWARING (**He makes the face**) That.

WILSON I think it's his age, sir. All boys do it.

MAINWARING Not the ones I know. Now, to mark the occasion of his departure…

Enter Jones from the side office. He holds up a bandaged finger of his right hand.

JONES (**Moving to his place**) Sorry I'm late, Mr Mainwaring, I had a bit of a crisis at the shop.

MAINWARING Right, settle down, Jones.

JONES Don't you want to know what the crisis was?

MAINWARING You cut your finger.

JONES Who told you?

FRAZER You've been marked absent without leave.

JONES Well, I had to go to hospital. It's one of the hazards of my profession, Mr Mainwaring.

MAINWARING Well, you're here now anyway.

JONES Mr Mainwaring, you don't have to worry about it being my trigger finger. I'm amphibious.

MAINWARING Good.

JONES And it doesn't stop me using the old cold steel. I can still shove it right up.

MAINWARING Right – that'll do, Jones. Now where was I, Wilson?

WILSON We were discussing what to do about Pike.

MAINWARING Ah yes. Leave the room, Pike.

PIKE Why, what have I done?

WILSON It's all right, Frank. We're going to talk about ways of celebrating your departure.

PIKE Oh, I'll go then. (**He goes to the office door**) I'll wait in here. (**He makes the face again**)

MAINWARING You must have a word with his mother about that. These things sometimes indicate a deep-seated disorder, you know.

FRAZER Captain Mainwaring, as you say, he's been a good lad, so I suggest we have a voluntary collection – maximum sixpence.

GODFREY Couldn't we buy him a pen knife. I had a pen knife when I was his age. I used to do all sorts of things with it. I used to whittle.

MAINWARING Yes. What do you think, Wilson?

WILSON Well, I know him pretty well.

FRAZER Aye – you know his mother pretty well, too.

MAINWARING Don't let's start being personal, Frazer.

GODFREY I think it's very nice the way Sergeant Wilson looks after Mrs Pike. He's a true gentleman.

JONES We had an officer once who used to look after three ladies. He was a gentleman. He wasn't very true though.

MAINWARING Don't let's get diverted. You were about to make a suggestion, Wilson?

WILSON Well, I know what Frank likes and I think we should give him a farewell supper at the Fish and Chip Restaurant.

MAINWARING A capital idea. Do you all agree?

They agree.

MAINWARING Good. (**He calls**) Pike, you can come in.

Pike comes in very quickly.

MAINWARING We've decided what to do for your surprise farewell.

PIKE Oh good – I like fish and chips.

Mainwaring reacts.

SANDBAGGED OBSERVATION TRENCH,
OR IMPLACEMENT. STUDIO. DAY

Pike and Jones are on guard with steel helmets and rifles. The drone of an aeroplane can be heard.

PIKE Is that one of theirs or one of ours?

JONES That's one of theirs. You can tell from the coming and going hum. (**He demonstrates**)

PIKE Makes the back of your neck go goosey, doesn't it. (**Makes the face again**)

JONES Pikey, you're not worried about joining up, are you?

PIKE No, not really.

JONES You don't want to worry about that – not in these modern times. The first day I joined up they shaved all me hair off and washed me all over with carbolic. Then they give me a bowl of cold, fatty soup, a prickly horse blanket and I cried myself to sleep.

PIKE Did you? **(He makes the face three times)**

JONES It's different now though, I expect.

PIKE Yeah – I expect it is.

JONES One thing won't have changed though – and that's the comradeship.

PIKE No, that won't have changed.

JONES You've got to learn comradeship, Pikey boy.

PIKE Yeah, I'll have to learn that.

JONES If someone nicks your kit – you nick someone else's. Always be first in the queue when the grub's up – then you can gobble up quick and go round a second time and have some more. And never volunteer for anything. And look after number one – and if someone puts you in it, make sure you put them in it.

PIKE Yeah, that's right.

JONES That's the best thing about the Army, is the comradeship.

PIKE Yeah, I'm looking forward to it. **(He makes the face again)**

SIDE OFFICE. DAY

Mainwaring, Wilson, the town clerk, Vicar and Verger are present.

TOWN CLERK Well, it's like this, Mr Mainwaring, the blood donor people will be taking this church hall for two days.

VERGER His Reverence has agreed.

VICAR Mr Mainwaring knows that, Mr Yeatman.

TOWN CLERK Well, of course, blood's very important in times such as this and I want to be sure we get a good turn out, so the point is this – how much of the stuff could you manage – not personally – but as a group?

MAINWARING Well, let me see – there's the platoon – and some of their relations no doubt – put us down for 50.

WILSON Fifty pints. Isn't that rather a lot?

MAINWARING What are you talking about, Wilson? There's 20 in the platoon – we'll only have to rustle up another 30.

Warden enters without knocking.

WARDEN Hullo, what's this – a mother's meeting?

MAINWARING Would you mind not barging into my office without knocking.

WARDEN What do you mean, your office? It's my office as well, you know.

VICAR May I remind you that first and foremost, it is my office.

WARDEN **(To town clerk)** You've told him, have you?

TOWN CLERK Oh no. **(To Mainwaring)** The Warden's group will be doing their donoring on the first day – oh – and they give a certificate to each group to put on the wall. It's sort of parchment like with a red seal and a bit of ribbon – they look very nice.

WARDEN Yes – and my certificate's going to be up there on that wall. 'Chief Warden Hodges' group donated 50 pints'.

MAINWARING In that case my certificate will be above it – 'George Mainwaring, 100 pints'.

WILSON Aren't you being rather hasty, sir?

MAINWARING Leave this to me, Wilson.

WARDEN Where are you going to get 100 pints?

MAINWARING For that matter, where are you going to get 50?

WARDEN I'll get 'em through my shop. Anyone who signs on will get a pound of onions.

MAINWARING Very well, if that's your game – Jones will give sausages.

WARDEN He can't – they're rationed.

MAINWARING Well, he'll give dripping or something – anyway, the sort of people I recruit won't need to be bribed.

VICAR My entire congregation will throw its weight right behind this scheme, and in order to be quite fair, I shall divide them equally between you both.

VERGER That'll be three each.

WILSON And we'll toss for the organist.

Mainwaring reacts.

MAIN HALL

Mainwaring is sitting at a trestle – Wilson is beside him. The platoon are sitting or standing around. Pike is at the table.

MAINWARING Have you ever had jaundice?

PIKE I don't think so.

MAINWARING Brucellas?

PIKE What's that?

MAINWARING Put down no.

PIKE I get croup and Mum says my ankles are a bit wonky and if I stand on anything high I get verdigris. Apart from that I'm fit as a fiddle. **(He pulls his face again)**

MAINWARING Mark him down as a donor, Wilson. Right, that's all, Pike.

Pike leaves.

MAINWARING What's the score, Wilson?

WILSON **(Reading)** Let me see. Godfrey, Jones, Frazer – that's three. **(Looks down the list)** Four, five, six, seven, eight, nine. Nine not eligible because they're over age – jaundice two, one on pills. Godfrey's on pills, so that's twice you can't have him.

MAINWARING Don't count them more than once or we'll get into a terrible muddle.

WILSON Two with colds and Private Elgood. **(He whispers to Mainwaring)**

MAINWARING Yes. Well, that just leaves you and me and Pike.

WILSON I'm afraid you'll have to count me out.

MAINWARING Why is that?

WILSON I'm a little bit anaemic.

MAINWARING Absolute nonsense.

WILSON No – it's true. I had a word with my doctor this morning and he said far from giving it, I should be having it.

MAINWARING I think you're just trying to wriggle out of it because you're afraid.

WILSON On the contrary. I've been a donor lots of times. It just happens that at the moment I'm a little run down because I've been overdoing things.

MAINWARING You haven't been overdoing anything while I've been around.

WILSON The fact remains that you're rather short of your target – 98 pints short.

MAINWARING This is disaster, Wilson.

WILSON I did say you were being a bit hasty.

Jones, Frazer, Godfrey approach the table.

JONES Captain Mainwaring, desperate times call for desperate doings. Could we falsificate our ages?

GODFREY I'm sure we'd pass for 65 – some of us.

Mainwaring reacts.

FRAZER We could put the black-outs up and have one wee candle and say we were trying to save electricity.

MAINWARING No, I'm sorry, I couldn't be a party to that. But what a marvellous spirit we have here, Wilson.

WILSON Absolutely marvellous.

MAINWARING I'm going to talk to the men. **(He starts to climb on the chair)** Help me up, Wilson. **(He falls)**

Mainwaring recovers from fall.

WILSON One step at a time, sir.

MAINWARING Now, pay attention, men.

JONES Pay attention to the officer. The officer wants attention paying to him. The men are paying attention, sir.

MAINWARING Thank you, Jones.

JONES Do you want them to stand to attention while they're paying attention, sir?

MAINWARING No, thank you, Jones.

JONES No, don't bother with any of that.

MAINWARING The honour of the platoon is at stake. I won't conceal the facts, but through no fault of our own, we're short of our target.

WILSON Ninety-eight pints short.

Mainwaring reacts.

MAINWARING Well, the details don't matter. The point is – we've seen dark times before, but together we've triumphed. It's up to every one of us to comb the highways and byways and to call upon our friends, our loved ones and our relations, to…

WILSON Rally to our bottle cry.

MAINWARING Rally to our bottle cry… battle cry. Rally to our cause. I do wish you wouldn't do that, Wilson.

FRAZER Excuse me, Captain Mainwaring, will Mrs Mainwaring be rallying to the cause?

MAINWARING **(Deciding to ignore Frazer)** And I am sure with our combined efforts, that certificate is as good as on the wall now.

JONES **(Quietly to Frazer)** Mr Frazer, I don't think Mrs Mainwaring is going to do much rallying.

MAIN HALL. DAY

Empty beds are lined up ready for customers. Six nurses await events. One of them is a sister. The doctor is at a table with his papers. Pike and Mainwaring have just finished and have their left sleeves rolled up with a bandage round their forearms, they carry their coats over their shoulders.

PIKE I didn't know it was happening. It didn't worry me a bit. **(Pulls his face)**

MAINWARING Yes. It's the least one can do to help the war effort.

Godfrey enters.

GODFREY I'm sorry, Captain Mainwaring, but there's no sign of anyone else.

MAINWARING Thank you, Godfrey. I can't understand it. It's not like Jones to let me down.

PIKE He went off with ten men with fixed bayonets.

Doctor joins.

DOCTOR Really, Captain Mainwaring, this is too bad. I have all these nurses standing by for a 100-pint operation, and so far I have you, the boy and the Vicar.

MAINWARING I'm sorry, doctor, but I'm sure there'll be more in a few minutes.

DOCTOR Well, I sincerely hope so. I could have gone to another town.

MAINWARING (**To Vicar**) What happened to your three that you promised me?

VICAR Well, the flesh is weak, Captain Mainwaring, and they haven't seen any onions for a month.

MAINWARING This is most awkward, Wilson.

WILSON I know it is, sir, I feel very deeply for you.

MAINWARING Surely you could help out.

WILSON I'm terribly sorry, sir.

MAINWARING You're very selfish, you know, Wilson. You can see what an embarrassing situation I'm in.

WILSON Couldn't you and Pike go round again?

Mainwaring reacts.

PIKE (**Joining**) I'm sure Mum would have come along but, of course, she's very upset at losing me. I'm all she's got. That's why she acted a bit strange when Uncle Arthur asked her.

MAINWARING (**To Wilson**) You did ask her then?

WILSON Oh yes. (**He moves towards the office**)

PIKE At breakfast – I think she was going to say yes and then Uncle Arthur happened to mention that the porridge had a burnt taste so she poured it in his homberg hat and wouldn't talk to him again.

MAINWARING Really?

PIKE Strange are the ways of women, aren't they, Mr Mainwaring?

MAINWARING Oh yes, indeed. Take my advice, Pike. If you ever marry, deal very firmly with your wife from the outset.

PIKE Start as you mean to go on, eh?

MAINWARING That's right.

PIKE I'll remember that, Mr Mainwaring.

MAINWARING Good lad.

PIKE Is Mrs Mainwaring coming?

Mainwaring stares at him and doesn't reply.

PIKE I said is Mrs Mainwaring coming? (**He pulls the face again**)

MAINWARING You'll have to do something about that habit of yours, you know, Pike.

PIKE What habit?

MAINWARING This. (**He does it**)

PIKE What?

MAINWARING This. (**He does it again**)

PIKE Do I do that?

MAINWARING At the end of practically every sentence, you go. (**He does it again**)

PIKE Oh, how awful. Thank you for telling me, Mr Mainwaring. (**He does it**)

WILSON (**Joining**) Excuse me, sir, I was noticing you talking to Frank just then and I think you're picking up that face thing, because at least three times, you went. (**He makes the face**)

MAINWARING I was simply explaining to the boy… (**He is interrupted by the entrance of the Warden**)

WARDEN Blimey – it looks a bit quiet. You couldn't move in here yesterday. Let's have a look at the score. (**He looks at the doctor's list**) Hodges, fifty. Mainwaring, three. (**He laughs**)

MAINWARING Ah well, most of ours haven't arrived yet.

DOCTOR Well, I sincerely hope they come soon.

WARDEN Go on, admit it, Mainwaring, you've lost.

DOCTOR There is one consolation, Captain Mainwaring, from my preliminary tests, it seems that Private Pike comes from an extremely rare group. You won't find one in ten thousand like him.

WILSON Well done, Frank.

PIKE Do you hear that, Mr Mainwaring, I'm one in ten thousand.

WARDEN I always said he wasn't normal.

MAINWARING Don't insult this boy. He's going to serve his country.

WARDEN Blimey, they must be scraping the barrel.

DOCTOR Give me your call-up details and I'll notify your unit in case they're interested. Right, start packing up, sister. We'll get over to our next collection point.

Godfrey enters.

GODFREY Excuse me, Captain Mainwaring.

MAINWARING Very well, Godfrey, but don't be long.

GODFREY No, Captain Mainwaring, the yard's full of people.

MAINWARING Well, use the one by the vestry.

GODFREY Mr Jones has brought them, sir.

JONES (**Entering**) I've done it, Captain Mainwaring, I've done it, I've brought you 97 pints.

MAINWARING What are you talking about, Jones?

JONES (**Calling off**) Mr Frazer – bring in the sergeant.

Frazer ushers in an Italian sergeant at bayonet point.

FRAZER Go on with you. Get in there and salute the officer. Salute, compri?

ITALIAN SERGEANT What for you sticka me with the bayoneti? I no make de trouble. Me buddy buddy friends.

MAINWARING What's going on, Jones?

JONES Well, sir, I went down to the Italian prisoner of war,

P.O.W. camp, and had a word with the guard and gave him a bit of fillet steak and he let me take 80 men to be volunteers for your donoring list.

WARDEN 'Ere, I object. That's not fair, that's enemy blood.

MAINWARING Of course it's fair – they started it.

ITALIAN SERGEANT Hey – what you talk about Henemy. I no henemy. I sit at home – I minda my business – Trattoria Paesana – very good food – I cooka myself. Then one day they come and they say – you, you gotta fight – you gotta go bang bang – we is not to blame, Capitano. It is the Signori Adolf Hitler – they is to blame.

MAINWARING Your government should be more careful who they have as friends.

ITALIAN SERGEANT Friends, friends – you one to talk. What about the Stalins?

MAINWARING That'll be enough of that.

The Verger enters.

VERGER 'Ere, there's 80 Eyeties in the church yard. His Reverence will have a fit.

VICAR I'm here, Mr Yeatman, and I'm not given to having fits.

WARDEN Anyway, even with cheating you've only got 83 pints. I've still won. I've reached my target.

JONES Oh no you haven't won. I've got 17 nuns as well.

VERGER I was coming to that. There are 17 nuns in the yard as well, Your Reverence, and they're Roman Catholics.

VICAR Nuns usually are, Mr Yeatman.

PIKE Are they real nuns, Mr Jones, or Nazi parachutists?

JONES They're real nuns, of course.

MAINWARING Obviously they're real ones. Don't be a fool, Pike. Take his name, Wilson.

Wilson reacts.

JONES You see, when I picked up the Italian P.O.W. prisoners, these nuns were administering to their needs with balaclava helmets and thick socks and such like – because they're Catholics you see –

FRAZER And 83 and 17 is 100.

MAINWARING Well done, Jones. There you are, doctor, we've fulfilled our target.

DOCTOR Good show. Get weaving, sister.

MAINWARING Show them in, Jones. Ladies first.

JONES Right, you heard what the officer said – this way for the donoring. Nuns first, Eyeties second.

As Jones shouts his instructions, four nuns enter and the Italian sergeant is taken off by Frazer.

SMALL DINING SECTION OF A FISH AND CHIP SHOP

The platoon is present. The Warden is in a corner. Most of them have their fish and chips in a newspaper, except for Pike, Jones and Wilson who have plates. The fryer is handing out the remaining packets. Frazer is negotiating.

MAINWARING **(Sitting down)** Ah well, this is very nice, isn't it?

WILSON Yes, Frank and I come here if anything goes wrong with the cooking arrangements at Mrs Pike's.

MAINWARING I see.

FRAZER There we are. That's three cod and two, and one plaice and two. **(Hands over a pound)** One pound – I'll need eight shillings and ten pence change.

GODFREY Haven't you got yours, Captain Mainwaring?

MAINWARING No – mine was the fillet of plaice and two pennyworth of fried potatoes.

FRAZER Hold on – here it is. **(He plonks the paper down in front of Mainwaring)**

MAINWARING Oh, thank you.

JONES You must have a plate, Mr Mainwaring. It is not seemly for officers to eat their fish and chips from the paper.

MAINWARING Oh – well that would be rather nice.

JONES A plate for Mr Mainwaring.

FRAZER Don't bother the man – he's counting the change.

FRYER Sorry – haven't got plates for everyone. There's a war on.

JONES You have mine, Captain Mainwaring. **(He puts the plate in front of Mainwaring)** No – that's no good. You're plaice and two and I'm rock and two. Hang on. **(He proceeds to put Mainwaring's plaice on his plate and his own fish on the paper)** There we are. No – that won't do because I've had half a dozen chips. There. **(Suiting the action to the words)** There's my chips on the paper and there's your chips on the plate.

GODFREY Do you want a gherkin or a pickled onion, Mr Mainwaring?

MAINWARING No – this will suit me admirably, thank you, Godfrey.

GODFREY I never have them either.

Pike could pour some raspberryade into Mainwaring's glass.

PIKE Have some raspberryade, Mr Mainwaring.

MAINWARING That'll be sufficient, thank you, Pike.

PIKE Go on – there's plenty. It's all paid for – or would you prefer lime fizz?

MAINWARING No, I'm quite content, thank you. **(Aside to Wilson)** Wilson, why are we drinking raspberryade?

WILSON Well, Frank likes it and after all, it is his party.

MAINWARING I'm glad we're in uniform. It wouldn't do for my customers to see me in here.

The Warden approaches.

WARDEN Hello, Mainwaring. Eating with the poor people are we?

WILSON Do you mind going away – this is a private party.

WARDEN What are you talking about? I'm a regular, I come in here the same time every Thursday.

MAINWARING Take no notice of him, Wilson. (**He smells his clothes**) I'll have to go for a long walk after this. If Mrs Mainwaring smells fish and chips on my clothes, she'll have a fit. (**He takes the salt cellar**) She has a very sensitive nose, you know. I smoked a cigarette once and she tried to keep me out of the drawing room for three days. I didn't stand for that, I can tell you. Look here, I said, if that was her attitude, I'd keep out of the drawing room for a week.

WILSON You seem to be having some difficulty with the salt.

PIKE Allow me. (**He grabs it. It is a large tin salt cellar. He unscrews the top**) It's the sea air that does it. (**He stirs it round with Mainwaring's fork**) There, how's that?

MAINWARING I'm sure it's much improved.

The fryer puts his head through.

FRYER Here, you're not going to be long, are you? I've got a queue a mile long outside.

FRAZER You've got our money – now hold your peace.

MAINWARING Wilson, we'd better have the speeches and go.

JONES Right. Charge your glasses, gentlemen. (**He starts to pour more raspberryade for Mainwaring**) Charge your glasses, Mr Mainwaring.

MAINWARING No – I have sufficient, thank you.

JONES Oh and Mr Mainwaring. We thought that since Mr Wilson is more closely connected with Frank than what you are, he ought to make the speech.

MAINWARING Yes, good idea. But don't go on too long, Wilson, it gets very boring.

WILSON I'll remember that.

JONES Then you've got to reply, Pikey.

PIKE Well, before I say anything – could I have another cod and chips?

JONES Of course you can. One more cod and chips for Pikey.

SPONGE One more cod and chips coming up.

JONES My lords, ladies and gentlemen. Pray silence for Sergeant Wilson.

They applaud.

WILSON Well – ladies and gentlemen, this is a sort of dual celebration. Firstly, we have to congratulate Captain Mainwaring for his noble effort in the Blood Donor Scheme.

WARDEN It was a fiddle. You had a load of nuns and wops.

WILSON Anyway. The town clerk has sent you this certificate. (**He hands Mainwaring a rolled up certificate**)

WARDEN You ought to send it to Mussolini – or the Pope.

The platoon shout him down.

WILSON Secondly, we all want to wish God speed and good luck to one of our fellow soldiers, Private Frank Pike.

They applaud.

WILSON Frank, you've been a good soldier and a loyal and reliable member of the platoon. We shall always remember you.

They applaud and say 'speech'.

PIKE Just a minute – I've got six more chips to finish.

FRAZER Get on with it, lad.

GODFREY You take your time, Frank.

PIKE (**Rising**) Well, ladies and gentlemen. Thank you for the fish and chips supper. I'm not going to make a long speech, but I've got a funny story to tell you.

FRAZER Good – I like funny stories.

GODFREY I hope it's not going to be coarse.

PIKE You know some of us gave blood for this certificate. (**He picks up the certificate and it drops in Mainwaring's chips**) Oh, sorry, Mr Mainwaring – well, it turned out that mine is ever so rare, so the doctor wrote to the R.A.F. about me. Well, they said, if I got wounded they wouldn't have anything to transfuse me with.

FRAZER If you don't mind me saying, lad – this story's not very funny so far.

PIKE Well, the funny thing is – they won't have me. I'm not going.

MAINWARING Not going.

Pike reacts.

MAINWARING When did you hear this?

PIKE Yesterday.

MAINWARING Yesterday. Well, why didn't you tell us?

PIKE Well. No one's ever given a dinner in my honour before – I like fish and chips and I didn't want to miss them.

MAINWARING You stupid boy.

Is There Honey Still For Tea?

SERIES EIGHT **EPISODE THREE**

Recorded: Thursday 26/6/75

Original transmission: Friday 19/9/75, 8.00–8.30pm

Original viewing figures = 12.8 million

ARTHUR LOWE .... CAPTAIN MAINWARING
JOHN LE MESURIER .... SERGEANT WILSON
CLIVE DUNN .... LANCE CORPORAL JONES
JOHN LAURIE .... PRIVATE FRAZER
ARNOLD RIDLEY .... PRIVATE GODFREY
IAN LAVENDER .... PRIVATE PIKE
BILL PERTWEE .... CHIEF WARDEN HODGES
GORDON PETERS .... MAN WITH THE DOOR
ROBERT RAGLAN .... COLONEL
CAMPBELL SINGER .... SIR CHARLES RENFREW MCALLISTER
JOAN COOPER .... DOLLY
KATHLEEN SAINSBURY .... CISSY
PLATOON .... COLIN BEAN, DESMOND CULLUM-JONES,
.... EVAN ROSS AND GEORGE HANCOCK
WALK-ON .... JIMMY MAC

• ANNIE OGDEN REMEMBERS •

'Human error is one thing, but nature brings its own problems, too. When we were filming "Is There Honey Still For Tea?" the tea table was set in the garden of an old and very pretty cottage, although the designer – Robert Berk – had to enhance the flowers in the garden with a few old world roses of his own!

'The upside-down cake, the sandwiches and all the tea things looked lovely, until the wind got up – and what a wind it was. It whipped up the table cloth and made the tea cold. In fact, we spent longer on that scene, because of the wind, than David would have liked.'

Is There Honey Still For Tea?

INTERIOR. BANK. DAY

Wilson is sitting behind the counter with his head in his hands. Pike is standing beside him writing with a scratchy pen in a ledger.

PIKE Aren't you feeling well, Uncle Arthur?

WILSON I've just got a bit of a headache, that's all – must you make all that noise, Frank?

PIKE I've got to enter up the ledger, you know how fussy, Mr Mainwaring is.

WILSON Well, can't you do it a bit more quietly, use another nib or something?

PIKE This is the only nib I've got. They're very difficult to get, there is a war on, you know. Anyhow, if you've got a headache, it's your own fault. By the time we've finished supper it's always so late, and you never leave our house until I've gone to bed, then you're back early for breakfast before I'm awake.

WILSON You know I have to come round to your house for all my meals, Frank. Your mother keeps my ration book.

PIKE What I can't understand is, I never hear you leave and I never hear you come back in the morning.

WILSON Well, I let myself in and out very quietly.

PIKE You don't do anything else quietly.

WILSON Oh, do stop, Frank. Just stop it, stop it.

PIKE You know your trouble, Uncle Arthur, you're not getting enough sleep. Well, tonight I'm not going to bed until you go home. I shall push you out of the door, if necessary. It's for your own good. **(He blots ledger and bangs it shut)**

Wilson winces. Mainwaring enters with two men carrying a large plywood case.

MAINWARING Morning, Wilson. Morning, Pike.

PIKE Good morning, Mr Mainwaring.

WILSON What have you got there, sir? **(He comes round to the front of the counter)**

MAINWARING A new door for my office.

WILSON How awfully nice, sir.

MAINWARING Do you realise, Wilson, it's three months since this bank was bombed? I can't tell you how many applications I've put in for a new door, confounded red tape.

Pike climbs on to bank counter.

MAINWARING Get down, Pike. Have you got the name plate?

PIKE Yes, Mr Mainwaring, it's in the drawer. **(He takes the name plate out of the drawer and gives it to Mainwaring. It is wrapped in tissue paper. Pike comes round to the front of the counter, Mainwaring unwraps the name plate)**

MAINWARING **(He rubs the name plate on his sleeve)** Look at that, Wilson. My name in gleaming gold letters. I can't wait to see it back in its rightful place, on my office door.

WILSON It's rather a plain door, isn't it, sir?

MAINWARING This isn't the actual door, Wilson. The door's inside. They probably put it in a case to protect the panelling.

WILSON Oh, I see.

MAINWARING They'd hardly give me, the manager of the bank, a door made of plywood. Do use your intelligence.

The men pull the door out of its case.

MAINWARING Right, take the paper off.

FIRST MAN What paper? This is the door.

The door is a light wooden frame covered in tar paper.

MAINWARING But it's made of paper.

FIRST MAN That's right, tar paper to be exact. Standard government issue to replace doors in bombed offices.

MAINWARING I can't screw my name plate on a paper door.

PIKE You could stick it on, Mr Mainwaring.

MAINWARING Be quiet, boy, and get back behind the counter. This is monstrous, I shall complain to head office.

Pike goes behind the counter.

FIRST MAN Look, mate, it's no use going on at me . Do you want us to put the door up or not?

MAINWARING Oh, very well, get on with it.

The men start to hang the door.

MAINWARING **(To Wilson)** How am I supposed to see important clients in an office with a paper door?

WILSON Well, they have paper doors in Japan.

MAINWARING What's that got to do with it?

WILSON I don't know really.

MAINWARING And how are people going to knock on it?

WILSON You could put up a notice 'Don't knock, cough'.

MAINWARING I'm not having people coughing and spluttering outside my door. Wait a minute. **(He crosses to the door, there are several small holes in it)** There are holes in it.

FIRST MAN Don't worry, I'll soon fix that, guv'nor. **(He crosses to Pike)** Got any stamp paper?

PIKE Yes, sure. **(He takes down the stamp book, takes out a sheet of stamps, tears off some white margin paper and hands it to man)**

FIRST MAN Ta. **(He crosses back, tears off two bits of paper, licks them and sticks them over the holes)** There you are, guv'nor, as good as new.

MAINWARING I can't have white spots all over my door.

FIRST MAN Fussy little fellow, aren't you? **(He reaches up, and runs his finger along the top of the counter partition, spits on it and rubs it on the white bits)** That suit you?

MAINWARING **(Giving man a glare)** Come in the office, Wilson.

They both go into office.

INTERIOR. OFFICE. DAY

Mainwaring and Wilson come into the office, they both stand close to the door. Mainwaring hangs up his hat and gas mask.

MAINWARING I must have a word with those cleaners, Wilson.

Pike opens the door and puts his head round.

PIKE Excuse me, Mr Mainwaring, the colonel's hear to see you.

MAINWARING Tell him I shan't be a minute.

PIKE Yes, Mr Mainwaring. **(He closes the door)**

MAINWARING And while we're on the subject of tidiness, isn't it about time you got your hair cut.

WILSON I never seen to be able to get round to it.

MAINWARING I know you think you look like Anthony Eden, but you are my chief clerk, and my sergeant…

A small round burn appears in door, it starts to smoulder.

WILSON Good heavens, sir, look at that.

Mainwaring opens the door, the colonel is standing outside, chatting to Pike. He is holding a cigarette in a holder.

COLONEL Morning, Mainwaring.

MAINWARING You've set my door on fire.

COLONEL Oh dear.

PIKE Excuse me. **(He rushes into the office, grabs the water carafe on Mainwaring's desk, takes a swig, rushes back and spits the water on the smouldering hole. It goes out)**

WILSON Well done, Frank.

COLONEL That was very quick thinking, young man.

PIKE **(Beaming)** Thank you, sir.

MAINWARING What about the hole in my door?

COLONEL Just stick a bit of paper over it.

PIKE Shall I get the stamp book, sir?

MAINWARING Get out, boy.

Pike goes.

MAINWARING Sit down, Colonel. **(Mainwaring sits at his desk, the colonel in front of him. Wilson stands beside Mainwaring)**

COLONEL I'm sorry to barge in like this, but I'm afraid I've got some bad news. It's about Godfrey.

MAINWARING I hope you're not going to tell me he's too old to stay in the platoon. Godfrey may be getting on a bit, but he's very useful to us, he's a sort of father figure for the younger men to lean on.

WILSON As long as they don't lean on him too heavily.

MAINWARING I meant emotionally. Anyhow, when the bullets start flying you won't find Godfrey throwing himself in a funk hole.

WILSON Well certainly not quickly, with his rheumatics.

Mainwaring reacts.

COLONEL Don't worry, it's nothing to do with his being in the Home Guard. He lives at Cherry Tree Cottage, doesn't he?

MAINWARING Yes, that's right.

WILSON It's a delightful little place, thatched roof, white fence, and a garden full of hollyhocks and roses. It's just like a picture on a chocolate box. You know, whenever I pass that lovely little cottage I stop and I say to myself, 'This is what we're fighting for'.

MAINWARING I couldn't have put it better myself, Wilson.

WILSON Thank you, sir.

COLONEL It is what we're fighting for, but unfortunately it's got to come down.

MAINWARING Come down!

COLONEL Yes, a new aerodrome is being built, and Godfrey's cottage will be right in the middle of it.

MAINWARING Can't anything be done?

COLONEL I'm afraid not, it's vital for the war effort, he'll get compensation, of course. I thought that it would be better that you should tell him yourself, so that he won't get such a shock, when he gets the official notice. **(Gets up)** Well, I won't take up any more of your time. Cheerio. **(He goes)**

MAINWARING What are we going to do, Wilson?

WILSON He's lived in that cottage with his two sisters for donkey's years.

MAINWARING How on earth am I going to tell him? We'd better get Jones and Frazer over here. **(He calls)** Pike! Pike!

Cut to outside the door, Pike runs to the door, grabs the handle, it comes away in his hand, he looks through the burn hole.

PIKE Mr Mainwaring, I can't get in… never mind. **(He puts his arm through the hole. Cut to the other side of the door, his hand reaches through to the handle and he opens the door. He comes in)**

MAINWARING How dare you put your arm through my door, Pike.

PIKE (Holding up the handle) **I'm sorry Mr Mainwaring, the handle came off.**

MAINWARING **(Pointing to the torn paper)** You've torn it.

PIKE It's not my fault, if they gave you a paper door with rotten old handles on it.

MAINWARING Don't you use that tone of voice to me, boy. Now run across the road and get Jones and Frazer over here at the double.

PIKE Yes, Mr Mainwaring. **(He goes)**

Mainwaring closes the door.

MAINWARING Look at that, Wilson, the door's only been up a few minutes, and it's already in ruins.

Pike's face appears at the hole.

PIKE Excuse me, Mr Mainwaring.

MAINWARING What is it now?

PIKE Mr Jones is here, he's at the counter now, paying in his takings.

MAINWARING Well, ask him to come in, and then go and get Frazer.

PIKE Yes, Mr Mainwaring. **(He goes)**

MAINWARING If only I could do something to help Godfrey. I feel very deeply about this, Wilson, very deeply.

WILSON Then why don't you lend him the money to buy another cottage?

MAINWARING Ah… I'm afraid I cannot allow my personal feelings to interfere with my position as bank manager.

Jones' face appears at the hole.

JONES Good morning, Mr Mainwaring, did you want to see me?

MAINWARING Yes, just a minute, I'll let you in. **(Mainwaring crosses to the door, grabs the handle, it comes off in his hand)**

MAINWARING Cheap rubbish. **(He shouts through the hole)** The handle's come off, Jones.

JONES Don't worry, I'll put my shoulder to it.

MAINWARING No don't do that, Jones, it's made of…

Pike puts his head through door.

INTERIOR. OFFICE. DAY

Mainwaring is sitting at his desk, Wilson and Pike are standing beside him. Jones and Frazer are sitting in front of the desk. They are wearing their butcher's and undertaker's sets.

MAINWARING Well, that's the whole thing in a nutshell, Godfrey's cottage has got to come down, and the colonel's asked me to break the news to him.

FRAZER At his age, the shock could quite easily kill him, and you'll be responsible. Did you hear what I said, Mr Mainwaring? You'll be responsible.

MAINWARING All right, Frazer.

JONES Couldn't we move Mr Godfrey's cottage, sir?

MAINWARING Move it?

JONES Yes, we could take it to bits and put it together in some other place, be all right, all we've got to do is to number each brick and tile.

FRAZER The roof is made of thatch, you canna number that.

JONES Well, we could cut it in slices and roll it up, so long as we didn't do it on a windy day.

MAINWARING I think you're going into the realms of fantasy now, Jones.

PIKE He's not, Mr Mainwaring. In that film *The Ghost Goes West*, with Robert Donat and Jean Arthur, an American millionaire took a whole castle from Scotland to California.

The phone rings.

MAINWARING (**Wearily**) Answer it, Wilson.

FRAZER I saw that film rubbish, the kilts hung too far below the knees.

WILSON (**Picking up the phone**) Hullo, Martin's Bank. Oh hullo, Raymond... yes... yes... just a minute. Jones, it's your boy, Raymond, he says will you hurry up because the offal queue is getting rather impatient.

JONES Tell him I won't be long.

WILSON (**Into phone**) Hullo, he says he won't be long.

MAINWARING Can we get on please, now, Jones, Frazer...

WILSON I'll tell him, goodbye. (**He hangs up**) Excuse me, sir, er, Jones, your boy, Raymond, says that Frazer's boy, Heathcliffe, has told him to move the offal queue away from the front of Frazer's shop.

JONES Is that true, Mr Frazer?

FRAZER Aye, I told him to get them shifted.

JONES How dare you interfere with my offal queue?

FRAZER They've no right to queue up in front of my shop. I don't want a lot of fat women gawking in my window, and arguing about their points.

Mainwaring reacts.

JONES My offal queue does not want to look in your rotten window, it's only got an old urn, or a bit of old velvet in it.

FRAZER It's better than your window, all you've got in it is two plaster pigs with stupid expressions on their faces.

JONES It's not my fault I can't get any meat.

MAINWARING Look, Jones, Frazer, I know we're all very busy, so will you please just give me your attention for two minutes. As you know, the colonel has asked me to tell Godfrey, but I... (**Looks at Wilson**) that is, we... er thought it would be better if you, Jones, or you, Frazer, told him – after all, you're both his contemporaries.

FRAZER You mean you're trying to wriggle out of it.

JONES Mr Mainwaring is not trying to wriggle out of it. May I remind you that Mr Mainwaring is not only a bank manager, but he is also our commanding officer and a gentleman... 'Ere, wait a minute, those two little plaster pigs that I've got in my window have not got stupid expressions on their faces, they've got happy, laughing faces.

FRAZER You talk more tripe than you sell...

Jones and Frazer continue to argue.

MAINWARING Oh, this is no good, Wilson. You and I will just have to go to Godfrey's cottage tomorrow afternoon and tell him straight out. You'd better come too, Pike. We must grasp the nettle.

PIKE Mr Mainwaring, there aren't any nettles in Mr Godfrey's garden, he's very proud of it.

Mainwaring reacts.

GODFREY'S COTTAGE

Exterior shot of the cottage. Pick up Mainwaring, Wilson and Pike approaching. They are all wearing their bank clothes.

MAINWARING Now, we don't want to hurry this, Wilson. We've got to pick exactly the right moment to tell Godfrey.

WILSON How will we know when the right moment is?

PIKE In the film *Dangerous Moonlight*, Anton Walbrook had to tell his girlfriend that he was leaving Poland for ever, so he played the piano to take her mind off it. Uncle Arthur could do that, he plays the piano ever so well.

Mainwaring gives Pike a look. They reach the garden gate, behind it is a large rose bush.

WILSON Oh look, sir, what beautiful flowers.

Godfrey's face appears over the top of the bush, he is cutting some roses.

GODFREY Hullo, Mr Mainwaring, Mr Wilson, Frank.

PIKE Afternoon, Mr Godfrey, Mr Mainwaring's got something to tell you.

MAINWARING (**Shouting Pike down**) We were just passing, Godfrey, so we thought we'd drop in and say hullo.

GODFREY How awfully nice of you, sir, you're just in time to join us for tea. (**He calls to Cissy and Dolly**) Cissy, Dolly, look who's come to tea.

Cut to Cissy and Dolly, they are fussing round a small Victorian table with a lace tablecloth on it. It is beautifully laid for tea. Round it are three small, Victorian, hooped-back chairs with padded seats.

DOLLY Isn't that nice, Cissy? It's Mr Mainwaring and his friends.

CISSY We'd better get some more chairs, Dolly.

DOLLY Yes, more chairs.

They both go into the cottage.

GODFREY What were you going to tell me, Mr Mainwaring?

MAINWARING Er... I was going to tell you, Godfrey, that I have never seen such beautiful roses.

GODFREY They are lovely, aren't they? Do you know this rose bush was planted by my father over fifty years ago? **(He stoops down and picks a rose out of the basket)**

WILSON **(Whispering to Mainwaring)** Tell him quickly, and then we'll go.

MAINWARING **(Hissing back)** We can't go now, we've been asked to tea.

Godfrey straightens up, holding a rose.

GODFREY Look at that, isn't it a picture? You know, often I say to my sisters, it doesn't matter what Hitler does, this cottage and this garden with its beautiful roses will always be here. It's what we're fighting for, isn't it? Come along. **(He turns and walks towards the tea table. Mainwaring looks sick)**

PIKE Mr Mainwaring, are you going to tell him now, or during tea?

MAINWARING Er... during tea.

They go through the gate towards the tea table.

DOLLY Come and sit down everyone. You sit there, Mr Wilson.

WILSON Thank you so much. How pretty the table looks.

PIKE Mr Mainwaring, shall I sit next to Mr Godfrey in case he faints when you tell him.

MAINWARING Be quiet, boy, and sit down.

CISSY Milk, everybody?

They all nod, Cissy pours the teas. Dolly hands them round.

GODFREY I hope you like this tea, it's made with water from our own well, that's what makes it taste so special. **(He hands Pike a plate of bread and butter)** Tuck in, Frank.

PIKE Thanks, Mr Godfrey. **(He takes a slice)**

GODFREY **(Offering plate to Mainwaring)** Bread and butter, sir?

MAINWARING No thank you, Godfrey, I'm not hungry.

DOLLY **(Hands him a plate of upside-down cakes)** You must have one of my upside-down cakes, Mr Mainwaring.

MAINWARING Oh, all right, thank you. **(He takes one)**

During this, Wilson has spread his bread with raspberry jam. He takes a bite.

WILSON Umm, this bread and raspberry jam is simply delicious.

CISSY I bake the bread in our old brick oven, that's what gives it that lovely crusty taste.

DOLLY And I make the jam from our own raspberries.

GODFREY We're almost self sufficient here, this cottage and garden give us all we need.

PIKE **(Whispering to Mainwaring)** Mr Mainwaring, it's during tea, are you going to tell him now?

MAINWARING After tea, Pike.

Long shot of tea party. Close up of tea being poured. Close up of Pike eating. Close up of Mainwaring looking uncomfortable.

WILSON You know it's awfully nice the way the sun brings out the lovely colour of that wall.

GODFREY Yes, the whole place has a sense of permanence. My sisters and I always say, this cottage stands for England.

PIKE **(Whispering to Mainwaring)** It's after tea, Mr Mainwaring, you can't wait any longer, you've got to tell him.

MAINWARING You're right, Pike. **(He clears his throat)** The fact is, Godfrey... the fact is... that er... Wilson has something to say to you.

WILSON Me, sir, I can't...

MAINWARING **(Hissing at him)** Get on with it, that's an order.

GODFREY **(Beaming at Wilson)** Yes, Mr Wilson?

WILSON Erm... erm... do you think I might have another upside-down cake?

TELECINE: EXTERIOR. COUNTRY LANE. EVENING

Rear shot of Mainwaring and Wilson walking away from camera. Pike is just a bit behind them with his hands in his pockets.

MAINWARING You know your trouble, Wilson, you've got no guts.

WILSON It wasn't my fault, sir.

MAINWARING I made it perfectly simple for you, and all you could say was, 'Can I have another upside-down cake?'

WILSON Well, I wanted another upside-down cake.

PIKE **(Spraying imaginary Tommy gun)** Ah... ah... ah... ah.

MAINWARING Stop playing the fool, you stupid boy.

Pike kicks the dust and sulks.

EXTERIOR. SHELTER ON SEA FRONT. NIGHT

Jones and Frazer are sitting in shelter, they are wearing uniforms, steel helmets, equipment and rifles.

JONES You know Jock, Mr Mainwaring was very complimentary to me. He asked my advice, you see, he went round to Mr Godfrey's cottage on Saturday afternoon to tell him, but as Mr Godfrey's two sisters were there, he thought the shock would be too much for them. I quite agreed with him and I told him that I thought it would be much better if Mr Godfrey was alone when we told him.

FRAZER We?

JONES Pardon?

FRAZER We – when we told him –

JONES And Mr Mainwaring was very grateful for my advice, he said he'd give us a couple of minutes and then he'd send Mr Godfrey out with the tea.

FRAZER Oh, man, have you not got enough sense to see that Mainwaring has left you and me holding the baby?

JONES That's not fair. Mr Mainwaring thought that as the senior members of the platoon, it would be more tactful coming from us. You will back me up, won't you?

FRAZER Aye, I'll manoeuvre the conversation round to it.

JONES That's right, you…

Godfrey appears with a flask of tea and a tin of cakes, he is in uniform.

JONES Hullo, Mr Godfrey, what brings you out here?

GODFREY Mr Mainwaring thought you might like a nice hot cup of tea, so he asked me to bring it out personally.

JONES That's nice, just put it down on the seat. (**He draws Frazer on one side**) We'd better get it over and done with. You start to manoeuvre the conversation round.

FRAZER Godfrey, son, Jones here has got some bad news. (**To Jones**) How's that? Well, it's my turn to patrol down to the end of the promenade.

JONES (**Grabbing him**) Don't leave me, Jock.

FRAZER Sorry, the war comes first.

GODFREY Don't you want a cup of tea?

FRAZER I'll have it when I get back. Cheerio. (**He goes**)

GODFREY What's the bad news, Mr Jones?

JONES What… oh… well, I'll come to that in a minute, let's sit down and have a nice cup of tea.

They both sit, Godfrey hands Jones a cup of tea.

JONES Thank you, the cup that cheers, eh? Well now,Mr Godfrey, the point is, at a time like this we're all fighting for our lives, our very existence even, and we've all got to make sacrifices. Take Mr Mainwaring, for instance, he's got to make sacrifices, and what a fine man he is. I'd put my right hand in the fire for him any time. I don't mean I'd put it in a real fire, of course, it wouldn't do any good if I was to go around all over the place sticking my hands in fires, that wouldn't help Mr Mainwaring, would it? No, I'm speaking meta… meta… er…. metaphor, metaphysically, you understand. Where was I? I've lost my thread now.

GODFREY About the sacrifice Mr Mainwaring is making?

JONES Well, he is, they've given him a paper door. Fancy, a man of his status, having to sit in an office with a paper door, and what's worse, I tore it. It's the same with houses, I mean, if some highly important person comes along, nonchalant like, and says to me, 'I have got to knock down your house for the war effort', then I've got to let them do it.

GODFREY Oh dear, I'm so sorry, they're going to knock down yours as well, are they?

JONES No, they're not knocking my house down, 'ere, wait a minute, what do you mean, as well?

GODFREY As well as my place.

JONES You mean you know?

GODFREY Yes, we were told officially yesterday. I was going to speak to Mr Mainwaring about it, but I didn't want to upset him.

JONES What are you going to do, Mr Godfrey?

GODFREY We'll manage. Dolly and Cissy are going to stay with some friends, and we're putting our furniture into store.

JONES Where will you go?

GODFREY I'll find a room somewhere.

JONES You'll do nothing of the sort, you'll come and stay with me.

GODFREY Oh, I couldn't do that.

JONES Why not, I'd be glad of your company, we'd get on wonderfully well together. After parade, we'll go home and have a nice glass of stout each.

GODFREY I don't like stout.

JONES Oh, don't you? Well, you could have something else to drink, then we could have a nice bit of cheese on toast.

GODFREY Toasted cheese gives me shocking indigestion.

JONES Well, then, we could listen to the wireless together, you like listening to the wireless, don't you?

GODFREY Yes, very much indeed.

JONES That's all right then, we'll sit and listen to the forces programme, and have a good laugh. I like the forces programme.

GODFREY I always listen to the Home Service.

JONES Oh… well, we'll listen to that, be all right, you'll see.

INTERIOR. FRAZER'S HOUSE. NIGHT

Frazer is on the phone. He is wearing his dressing gown.

FRAZER Hello, operator, I want to make a trunk call to London.

INTERIOR. SIR CHARLES MCALLISTER'S BEDROOM. NIGHT

Sir Charles is in bed asleep. He is a man in his early 60s. The phone on the beside table rings. Sir Charles wakes up and picks up the phone.

FRAZER Hullo, is that Sir Charles?

SIR CHARLES Yes.

FRAZER The Sir Charles Renfrew McAllister?

SIR CHARLES Speaking.

FRAZER My name's Frazer, James Frazer.

SIR CHARLES What the hell do you think you're doing, ringing me up in the middle of the night?

FRAZER It's quiet, peaceful, and it's cheaper.

SIR CHARLES What do you want?

FRAZER Are you the minister in charge of building the new aerodrome at Walmington-on-Sea?

SIR CHARLES Look, if you're after a building contract, there's nothing doing.

FRAZER No, it's not that.

SIR CHARLES What do you want then?

FRAZER I just want you to shift the aerodrome a wee bit.

SIR CHARLES Are you mad?

FRAZER I was reading in the papers that you got a knighthood recently, and that you come from a very old Scottish family that can trace its origins back to Robert the Bruce.

SIR CHARLES You haven't woken me up to discuss my ancestors.

FRAZER No, I've woken you up to say, you couldn't possibly be the laddie of the same name whose father kept the fish and chip shop on the lonely isle of Barra, who was expelled from school for cheating, got that wee girl Maisie McIntosh into trouble, and got the sack from the draper's shop in the High Street for getting his fingers caught in the till. That wasn't you, was it?

SIR CHARLES Certainly not.

FRAZER That's all right then, in that case, you won't object to me telling the story to a certain society magazine. I've got the phone number right here in front of me.

TELECINE: EXTERIOR. GODFREY'S COTTAGE. DAY

Jones' and Hodges' vans are drawn up outside. The platoon are loading Godfrey's furniture into it. Godfrey and his two sisters are sitting on a packing case looking very forlorn, he is wearing his civilian clothes, everyone else is in uniform. Pike crosses to Hodges' van carrying a chair. He stops to talk to Jones.

PIKE Look at poor old Mr Godfrey and his sisters, I feel ever so sorry for them.

JONES Yes, war can be very cruel, Pikey.

WILSON We've nearly finished the loading, sir.

MAINWARING Thank you, Wilson, this is a very sad day. I wrote to the minister in charge of building the airfield, pointing out all the facts, but I never got a reply. We're all in the hands of these petty bureaucrats, faceless men.

Pike starts to load the chair on to Hodges' van.

HODGES Don't load any more on my van, you'll break the back axle.

PIKE Mr Mainwaring told me to put it in. (**He puts it in the van**)

HODGES And I'm telling you to take it out, you soppy looking boy. (**He takes it out**)

PIKE Don't you call me a soppy looking boy. (**He puts it back**)

HODGES I'm going to have a word with Mainwaring about this. (**Crosses to Mainwaring**) Look, Napoleon, I can't take any more on my van, and I want my money now.

MAINWARING The agreement was that you would be paid £2 from the platoon fund, when you've finished the job.

HODGES Well, I want my two quid now.

Frazer's hearse appears. Frazer is driving with a small man beside him, Frazer is wearing his undertaker's clothes.

PIKE Shoot him, Mr Mainwaring, go on – you're entitled.

MAINWARING Be quiet, Pike.

WILSON It's a pity Frazer didn't arrive a bit earlier, sir. We could have used his hearse instead of Hodges' van.

Frazer runs towards Mainwaring with the small man.

FRAZER Hold on, Mr Mainwaring, hold on.

MAINWARING What is it, Frazer?

FRAZER (**Grabbing small man**) This is Mr Blackwell from the town hall, they're going to move the aerodrome.

JONES Poor old Mr Godfrey won't have to get out of his home after all.

MAINWARING This is good news.

JONES Yes, now I shall be able to listen to the forces programme. I'll tell Mr Godfrey.

Frazer grabs the plans from the small man.

FRAZER They're moving the whole aerodrome 200 yards further north.

WILSON So Godfrey's cottage won't be in the middle.

FRAZER No, just on the edge.

MAINWARING Right men, unload the vans.

HODGES 'Ere, what about my two quid?

MAINWARING The agreement was that you'd get paid when the job was done. Well, the job has not been done.

HODGES You chiseller, I want my two quid.

WILSON Do you mind not raising your voice.

HODGES **(Shouting)** I want my money.

MAINWARING Just come away, Wilson.

TELECINE: EXTERIOR. GODFREY'S GARDEN. DAY

The tea table is laid, Godfrey, Cissy, Dolly, Mainwaring, Wilson, Jones, Frazer and Pike are having tea. They are all wearing civilian clothes.

WILSON Isn't this nice, sir, a bit different to the last time we had tea with you, Godfrey, when Mr Mainwaring was wondering how he was going to break the news to you.

• DAVID CROFT REMEMBERS •

'I remember the wind machine we had to use in this episode made a terrible noise, and we had problems trying to make Frazer's hat blow off, so ended up tying a piece of nylon string on it and pulling it at the required moment.'

MAINWARING Quite so, Wilson. It must have been my letter to the minister that did it.

FRAZER No doubt about it, Mr Mainwaring, no doubt at all.

MAINWARING What was his name?

FRAZER Sir Charles Renfrew McAllister, a fine man, they say he can trace his ancestors back to Robert the Bruce.

GODFREY I'm very grateful, Mr Mainwaring. If it hadn't been for you, our peaceful little world would have come to an end.

There is a terrific roar of planes, hats fly off, table napkins, etc. fly all over the place.

SERIES EIGHT **EPISODE FOUR**

Recorded: Thursday 10/7/75
Original transmission: Friday 26/9/75, f8.00–8.30pm
Original viewing figures = 14.6 million

ARTHUR LOWE .... CAPTAIN MAINWARING
JOHN LE MESURIER .... SERGEANT WILSON
CLIVE DUNN.................................. LANCE CORPORAL JONES
JOHN LAURIE .... PRIVATE FRAZER
ARNOLD RIDLEY .... PRIVATE GODFREY
IAN LAVENDER .... PRIVATE PIKE
BILL PERTWEE.................................. CHIEF WARDEN HODGES
FRANK WILLIAMS .... VICAR
EDWARD SINCLAIR.. VERGER
HAROLD BENNETT.. MR BLUETT
COLIN BEAN .... PRIVATE SPONGE
PLATOON .... GEORGE HANCOCK, DESMOND CULLUM-JONES,
.... MICHAEL MOORE, FREDDIE WILES, LESLIE NOYES,
.... HUGH CECIL, FREDDIE WHITE, ROGER BOURNE, EVAN ROSS
EXTRAS .... JOHN DANIELS, BRIAN SMITH, ALLAN BRENNAN,
.... TERRY KELLY, ANTHONY BROWN, SPENCER BRADLEY,
.... PAUL PRESTON, JOHN CLARK, ANDREW BYSOUTH,
.... PAUL WALKER, TIMOTHY BALL, RAE PARISH

COME IN, YOUR TIME IS UP

• PETER DAY REMEMBERS •

'For this episode, we fitted a "flip-up" arrow on the face of the dinghy, which you couldn't notice. When the arrow was supposed to strike the dinghy, a string was pulled which released a catch, allowing the arrow to spring up and give the impression it had been fired into it. As we couldn't wait forever for the dinghy to sink, we fitted a large grease-sealed panel in the bottom. When this was slid open, the dinghy rapidly filled with water, and the effect was achieved, leaving the German airmen floundering in the lake.

'We didn't really rehearse, I just showed everyone concerned what to do; there was a rescue boat on standby, just in case anything went wrong, but the dinghy wasn't too far away from the shore.'

HOME GUARD
CP
I

Come In, Your Time is Up

EXTERIOR. VICAR'S GARDEN. DAY

Mainwaring and Wilson are standing on the lawn.

MAINWARING Look at the time Wilson. Did you give Jones my instructions?

WILSON Yes, sir, I told him to wait outside the church hall until all the platoon arrived and then bring them down here.

MAINWARING This evening's parade has been a complete mess up.

Mr Bluett enters.

MR BLUETT Good evening, can I help you?

MAINWARING No thank you, I'm just waiting for my men.

MR BLUETT I don't want any help with the garden, I always do the Vicar's garden on my own.

WILSON We're not doing any gardening, Mr Mainwaring is going to give a lecture.

MR BLUETT **(Pointing to Mainwaring)** He's not qualified to give a lecture on gardening. I've seen his garden, it's in a terrible state.

MAINWARING I am not giving a lecture on gardening, Mr Bluett.

MR BLUETT Well who is then? **(To Wilson)** You?

WILSON Of course not.

MR BLUETT Well, don't look at me, I'm not giving a lecture on gardening. Mind you, I could, but I've got to spray the Vicar's greenfly.

MAINWARING I don't want anyone to give a lecture on gardening.

MR BLUETT Mind you, I could give lectures on lots of things, woodwork, cleaning out gutters, bicycle repairs. I could give a good lecture on bicycle repairs.

MAINWARING Yes, thank you, Mr Bluett.

MR BLUETT Keeping chickens, restoring old picture frames, that's a dying art, restoring old pictures frames, I could give a good lecture on that.

Jones marches the platoon into the garden.

JONES Left, right, left, right.

BLUETT 'Ere, I'm not having them tramping on my lawn, they'll cut it to pieces. I'm going to see the Vicar about this. **(He goes)**

MAINWARING Go with him, Wilson, we don't want any trouble.

WILSON Right, sir. **(He follows Bluett)**

Bluett crosses to the windows of the Vicar's study, which are open, and calls inside.

MR BLUETT Mr Farthing, Mr Farthing.

The Vicar's head appears at the window.

VICAR What's the matter, Mr Bluett? I'm trying to write my sermon.

Wilson comes into the picture.

MR BLUETT Captain Mainwaring has got a lot of men on your lawn, and he wants me to give them a lecture on gardening.

WILSON My dear fellow, you've got it all wrong, the Vicar did give us permission to use his garden.

MR BLUETT You don't want lots of men in your garden, Vicar.

VICAR I did give them permission, Mr Bluett.

BLUETT Yes, but…

VICAR I don't mind having a lot of men in my garden.

MR BLUETT They'll tramp all over the flower beds.

VICAR I'll keep an eye on them, I can see quite clearly from my desk, I'll see that they don't do anything improper.

WILSON We're not going to do anything improper, Vicar.

VICAR Well, just see that they don't, after all, I've never had a lot of men in my garden before, I don't know what to expect. **(He goes in)**

Mainwaring and platoon are sitting on the lawn.

MAINWARING Now, pay attention, men, I'm sorry about this slight mix-up, but Hodges the Warden is using the church hall, and the sea scouts are using the church yard.

Wilson comes back into the picture.

MAINWARING What did the Vicar say, Wilson?

WILSON He says it's all right, as long as we don't do anything improper.

Mainwaring looks at Wilson. Mainwaring looks at Bluett.

MAINWARING What's he mean by that?

WILSON I don't know, sir. He says he's never had a lot of men in his garden before.

MAINWARING Hasn't he? Hmm, I see. Now, the subject of my lecture today is field craft. We have just been issued with a number of two-man bivouac tents. Hold it up, Wilson.

WILSON **(Holding up tent)** A two-man bivouac tent.

MAINWARING Now, the best way to try out these tents is by going on a weekend camp, and I thought the right time to do this would be…

FRAZER At the weekend.

MAINWARING **(Coldly)** Thank you, Frazer.

JONES Permission to speak, sir? When you say that is a two-man tent, it may be all right for two tiny men, but not for two tall men, or two fat men. I mean, what about a big man like Private Sponge here?

SPONGE Yes, I'm very big, I'd need a tiny man to share with me.

JONES And you're big, Mr Mainwaring, you'd need a tiny man, and so would Sergeant Wilson, and so would you, Mr Godfrey.

MAINWARING All right, Jones.

JONES But we're going to run out of tiny men, sir.

GODFREY I'm sure I could find a tiny man to share with me.

JONES There aren't enough tiny men to go round, Mr Godfrey.

MAINWARING Jones, please, I will sort out the sleeping arrangements.

FRAZER Aye, and while you're at it, I don't want to sleep with Jonesey here, he counts in his sleep.

JONES Well, I can't help it, when you've been counting coupons all day, it's difficult to get your brain back to normal.

FRAZER In your case, I'd say it was impossible.

JONES Now don't you start, Jock.

FRAZER Anyhow, I'm not fussy, I'll sleep with Sergeant Wilson.

PIKE Oh no, Mr Frazer, I always sleep with Uncle Arthur. I mean Sergeant Wilson.

MAINWARING Be quiet, Pike, or you'll be sent home.

Pike reacts.

MAINWARING Now, the whole advantage of these tents is that it only takes a minute to put them up. I'll just show you. **(He picks up the two poles)** Bang these in the ground, Pike.

PIKE **(Taking the poles)** Yes, Mr Mainwaring. **(He takes out his bayonet and starts to bang one of the poles)**

MR BLUETT 'Ere, you can't bang poles in the Vicar's lawn.

MAINWARING It will only make a little hole.

Bluett runs across to the study windows.

MR BLUETT Mr Farthing, Mr Farthing.

VICAR What is it?

MR BLUETT They're banging poles in your lawn.

VICAR Oh, really? **(Shouting to Mainwaring)** You're behaving in an improper way, Captain Mainwaring. No holes in the lawn, please.

MR BLUETT You heard what the Vicar said, no holes in the lawn.

MAINWARING This is absurd. How can I give a lecture under these conditions?

WILSON Look, sir, why don't you get someone to just hold the poles, then you won't have any holes?

MAINWARING Good thinking, Wilson. Pike – you hold one, Jones – you hold the other.

JONES Hold the pole, yes, sir, yes, sir.

Jones and Pike lie flat on their faces, holding the poles.

MAINWARING (**Picking up one end of the tent**) Grab the other end, Wilson.

Wilson picks it up.

MAINWARING Now, once the poles are in the ground, you just throw the tent over them, bang in the pegs, and it's done. Simple as ABC, I'll show you. Right, Wilson.

They throw the tent over the poles, the whole thing collapses flat on the ground, with Jones and Pike underneath.

MAINWARING Ah, yes, well, you get the general idea. Pike!

Pike's head appears from under the canvas.

MAINWARING Clear it up, boy.

Pike reacts. Jones and Pike clear away the tent.

MAINWARING Now, the next stage of field craft I want to deal with is living off the land. Get it out of the box, Wilson.

WILSON Get what out?

MAINWARING In the box.

WILSON Oh yes, of course. (**Wilson takes an old hairbrush out of the box**)

MAINWARING Now, I want you to imagine that the Germans have landed and we have been cut off from all supplies. We are starving, so we must comb the land for food.

FRAZER With a hairbrush.

MAINWARING With a… Tell them what that is, Wilson.

WILSON This is a hedgehog.

Mainwaring reacts.

PIKE Mr Mainwaring.

Mainwaring crosses.

PIKE Why do you want Sergeant Wilson to brush his hair with a hedgehog.

MAINWARING We are going to eat the hedgehog.

GODFREY I don't think I could bring myself to eat a poor little hedgehog, sir.

MAINWARING This is war, Godfrey. It's either the hedgehogs or us.

WILSON Excuse me, sir, how do you know that you can eat hedgehogs? I mean, have you ever eaten one?

MAINWARING Not personally, no, but it's a well known fact that hedgehogs make very good eating. Gypsies eat them all the time.

JONES Permission to speak, sir? That's a point, supposing we have had our supplies cut off, and you say nonchalant-like, boys, we'll have hedgehogs for dinner today, and we look around, and we can't find any, because the gypsies have eaten them all previous?

MAINWARING Believe me, Jones, there's always enough hedgehogs to go round. The countryside's teeming with them.

FRAZER Not at this time of year.

Mainwaring gives Frazer a look.

MAINWARING Now, having caught the hedgehog, we're going to cook it. Here's a little wrinkle that's well worth knowing. Come here, Pike.

Pike crosses to Mainwaring.

MAINWARING Hold your hands out in front of you.

Pike does so, Mainwaring picks up a tin and tips a lump of mud into Pike's hands.

PIKE Mr Mainwaring, why did you tip that lump of mud into my hands?

MAINWARING All in good time, boy. (**He takes the brush from Wilson and plonks it on the lump of mud**) Now, you cover the hedgehog in the mud. Get on with it, Pike.

PIKE But, Mr Mainwaring.

MAINWARING Do as I say.

Pike covers the brush in mud.

MAINWARING Now, you roll it into a ball, pop it in the hot embers of the fire, until the mud is baked hard, break off the mud, all the bristles come away, and it's done to a turn. Get the idea? Clear it up, Pike.

PIKE Look at the mess I'm in. My mum will be furious.

MAINWARING Stop fussing, boy. Wilson, start building the fire.

WILSON Right, sir. (**He picks up the piece of corrugated iron, puts it on the lawn**)

MAINWARING Give him a hand, Jones.

JONES Yes, sir, yes, sir.

They start to build a fire of twigs, etc. All this time, Mr Bluett has been spraying the roses. He rushes over to the study windows.

MR BLUETT Mr Farthing, Mr Farthing.

The Vicar's head pops out.

MR BLUETT They're setting fire to your lawn.

MAINWARING (**Shouting to Vicar**) It's all right, Vicar, we're not going to light the fire, just a demonstration.

VICAR Mr Bluett, if you disturb me just once more, I

shall get very cross. In future, if Captain Mainwaring does anything he shouldn't do, deal with it yourself.

Cut back to Mainwaring, the fire is now built.

MAINWARING Now, here's another little tip on lighting the fire. If the wood is damp, you can get it going quickly by pouring some rifle oil on it, so. **(He takes a bottle out of his pocket and pours it on the fire)** If there is a strong wind blowing, you can get over this by striking three matches at once. Come here, Pike. **(He hands a box of matches to Pike)** Now, whatever you do, don't light the fire, I just want you to go through the motions. Put three matches together and strike them.

Pike kneels down and strikes the matches. They flare up.

PIKE Ow. **(He drops them into fire, it flares up)**

MR BLUETT I'm not having that. **(He grabs the bucket of soapy water and throws it. Most of it goes over Pike)**

PIKE I'm all wet, Mr Mainwaring.

MAINWARING You stupid boy.

TELECINE: EXTERIOR. CAMP. DAY

It is on the edge of the river. Long shot of camp. Nine two-man tents have been set up in a line. Mainwaring is taking the platoon for P.T. They are all stripped down to their battledress trousers and vests, they are doing jumping and arms astride. The van is parked in background.

MAINWARING One, two, three, four, one, two, three, four. Keep it up, men, keep it up.

The camera pans to Frazer and Godfrey, who have set up a small field kitchen and are cooking the evening meal. Frazer tips some potatoes into the boiling water.

FRAZER That's the lot, put the salt in, Godfrey, son.

GODFREY **(Starts putting in the salt a pinch at a time)** I'll put in 17 pinches, that's a pinch for each man.

FRAZER Don't be so mamby pamby, just tip it in. **(He grabs the salt and tips it in)**

Cut back to Mainwaring.

MAINWARING Right, halt.

They stop, Mainwaring is very out of breath.

MAINWARING This is the life, eh, men? Feel that fresh air in your lungs. This will give us an appetite. Right – deep breath in, running on the spot, commence. **(He starts running on the spot)** Keep them at it, Wilson, I'm going to see how the supper's getting on. **(He trots across to Frazer and Godfrey)**

FRAZER Here comes Mainwaring, poking his nose in. Will you look at him? He's gone purple. If he keeps this up, he'll burst a blood vessel.

Mainwaring reaches them.

MAINWARING **(Still running on the spot)** How's the rabbit stew coming on?

GODFREY It will be ready in about half an hour, sir. We've just put the potatoes on.

MAINWARING **(Still running)** Good, good. I hope there's enough to go round, we're all starving.

FRAZER Oh, aye, there's plenty. It's a good job we didn't have to rely on hedgehogs, I haven't seen a single one. I wonder where the fellows must be hiding?

MAINWARING All right, Frazer, just get on with the cooking. **(He trots back to the platoon, shouting as he runs)** Keep it up, men. One, two, three, four. **(He reaches the platoon)** Right, rest, deep breath, hands on hips, trunk circling – commence.

Hodges' van appears in the distance and drives across the grass to the camp. Hodges is driving ,with the Vicar and Verger sitting beside him.

WILSON **(Stops doing exercise)** Just a minute, sir. **(He is panting hard)**

MAINWARING Keep up, Wilson, don't stop.

WILSON Look, sir, it's Hodges.

MAINWARING What! **(Stops)** All right, men, rest.

The platoon stops.

MAINWARING How dare he disturb us? We'll soon put a stop to that. Come on, Wilson, at the double. Jones, to me at the double.

JONES To you at the double, yes, sir, yes, sir.

Mainwaring runs towards the van, followed by Wilson and Jones.

MAINWARING **(Standing in front of the van, holding his hand up)** Stop! Stop! **(The van stops)** Turn back, turn back at once.

Hodges gets out of the van.

HODGES What's the matter with you, Napoleon? Have you gone mad?

The Vicar and Verger get out of the van, the Verger is wearing his sea scout uniform, the Vicar is wearing sports clothes.

MAINWARING Clear off at once, we're camping here.

HODGES Oh no you're not, the Vicar's camping here, aren't you, Vicar?

VICAR That's right, I'm camping here, Captain Mainwaring.

VERGER And you've no right to interfere with the Vicar's camping.

JONES Don't you start, you're a troublemaker.

WILSON **(To Mainwaring)** It seems a bit odd, sir, three grown men coming out camping.

HODGES I'm not doing any camping, I've just given them a lift out here.

WILSON Even more odd.

VICAR Get the boys out of the van, Mr Yeatman.

VERGER Yes, Your Reverence. (**He blows his whistle and ten sea scouts pour out of the van and form up in a line**)

VERGER Do you wish to inspect the boys now, Your Reverence?

VICAR No, you carry on and inspect them, Mr Yeatman.

VERGER Right you are. (**He gives the scout salute and crosses to the line of boys**)

WILSON They're awfully smart, don't you think, sir?

MAINWARING (**Giving Wilson a glare**) Now, look, Vicar, I am in charge of a bunch of highly trained men on active service, how do you expect me to maintain discipline with a lot of boys mucking about all over the place?

VICAR For your information, Captain Mainwaring, my boys do not muck about all over the place, they are also very highly disciplined.

HODGES Yeah, that's right, you tell him, Vicar.

Wilson starts to snigger.

MAINWARING What are you sniggering at, Wilson?

WILSON Well, the thought's just occurred to me, sir. If we had been having hedgehogs for supper, and the scouts had decided to have them for supper as well, there wouldn't have been any left for them, because we'd have eaten them all.

TELECINE: EXTERIOR. CAMP. DAY

Mainwaring and co. are sitting in front of the tents finishing their supper. The scouts have pitched their camp, it consists of two bell tents and a small pole with a union jack on it.

JONES That was a very nice rabbit stew, very tasty, very sweet.

PIKE I thought the potatoes were a bit salty.

FRAZER You can blame Godfrey for that. He cooked them, I just cooked the stew.

WILSON You know, it really is a beautiful evening, sir.

• ROBERT BERK REMEMBERS •

'By series eight, when I started work as production designer on *Dad's Army,* all the main sets were well established. However, one item which was both a challenge and also great fun, was the pirate raft in "Come In, Your Time is Up".

'I'd had the raft, which floated on six 40-gallon oil drums, made by prop makers at Shepperton Studios and was very pleased with the result, but to keep it stationary in the middle of the lake, as required for some of the sequences, was the problem. Armed with over a mile of black Terylene rope, we ran a line from the far bank to the centre of one side of the raft, and two more from bow and stern to our side of the lake. When, at last, the raft was secured immovably in the best position, and at the appropriate angle to the camera, the cast were ferried out to it. Arthur, who at that time owned the 100-foot Victorian steam yacht, *Amazon*, was first aboard and, standing in the stern with the tiller under his arm, immediately took command.'

VICAR My mind is made up. This is a free country and we're entitled to camp where we like. (**Points**) And we shall camp over there. Mr Yeatman, back in the van.

VERGER Aye, aye, sir. (**He salutes and blows his whistle**)

The boys all file back into the van.

VICAR Right, Mr Hodges, forward!

They get back in the van. The van drives off.

MAINWARING What are we going to do, Wilson?

JONES Permission to speak, sir? Why don't we take the platoon with fixed bayonets and run 'em off?

MAINWARING We're not savages, Jones. Come on, let's go and have supper.

MAINWARING Yes, it's a pity about those scouts. Here we are, a bunch of comrades, camping out together under the stars, and it's spoilt by those kids swarming all over the place.

The Vicar and Verger come out of one of the tents.

VICAR Right, Mr Yeatman, get them out.

VERGER Aye, aye, sir. (**He blows his whistle**)

MAINWARING Now what are they up to?

The scouts swarm out of the tents, and line up. They are all dressed as pirates.

GODFREY Oh look, sir, they're going to play pirates. How nice.

VICAR Right, boys, down to the water and hoist the jolly roger.

The boys all cheer and run down to the water's edge where there is a large raft mounted on petrol drums. It has a mast in the centre with a square rigged sail – the skull and crossbones are painted on it. They swarm on the raft and hoist the sail.

MAINWARING This is absurd.

Hodges crosses over to them.

HODGES Well, I'm off now. Enjoy your weekend camp.

MAINWARING You did this deliberately, Hodges. You drove those boys out here to upset our camp.

HODGES Don't be such a spoilsport, they're nice kids, why shouldn't they enjoy themselves?

The Vicar crosses over to them.

VICAR Goodbye, Mr Hodges, thanks for the lift.

HODGES Don't mention it, Vicar. I like to see young lads enjoy themselves.

He crosses to his van. The boys are paddling the raft out to the middle of the river and singing, 'What shall we do with a drunken sailor'.

MAINWARING This is hardly helping the war effort, Vicar.

VICAR On the contrary, Captain Mainwaring, we're having a practice for next Saturday. The boys are taking the raft down to the town to collect money for the Spitfire fund.

All this time Hodges has been trying to start his van. He lets out a howl of rage., jumps down and starts kicking the tyres.

HODGES Flipping kids, flipping kids.

WILSON I think Hodges is having a fit, sir.

Hodges charges over to the Vicar.

HODGES It's all your fault, Vicar. You and your soppy boys.

VICAR What's wrong?

HODGES I've run out of petrol!

VICAR That's hardly my fault.

HODGES Of course it's your fault, if I hadn't wasted petrol driving you and your silly kids out here to this silly camp, I wouldn't have run out.

VICAR You'll just have to spend the night out here, that's all.

HODGES I'm not sleeping in a tent with rotten kids crawling all over me all night. I want to go home!

VICAR You can sleep in the other tent with the Verger and myself. There's plenty of room, we sleep with our feet to the pole.

HODGES You know what you can do with your pole.

VICAR How dare you, Mr Hodges?

MAINWARING Just come away, men.

TELECINE: EXTERIOR. CAMP. NIGHT

Pan along row of tents. Assorted snores come from them. Cut to Frazer on guard, leaning against the van, smoking his pipe. Faint sound of gunfire, Frazer reacts, more gunfire. He hurries to Mainwaring's tent.

FRAZER Captain Mainwaring, Captain Mainwaring. (**No answer**) Captain Mainwaring, ach.

There is a bulge at the side of the tent, Frazer prods it with his boot, noises from inside, Mainwaring's bleary face appears.

MAINWARING What are you doing, Frazer?

FRAZER Trying to wake you up. Listen.

MAINWARING What?

FRAZER Can you no hear it, there? Gunfire!

More gunfire.

MAINWARING You're right, turn out, turn out. Wilson, Jones, Pike.

FRAZER Listen, sir, I can hear a plane.

MAINWARING It's coming this way.

Pike comes out of his tent with a blanket wrapped round him, he is dragging Wilson.

PIKE Come on, Uncle Arthur, hurry up.

WILSON Don't pull me about, Frank, I'm coming.

Jones comes out of his tent. They all group round Mainwaring.

JONES What is it, Mr Mainwaring?

MAINWARING Quiet, everyone, listen.

The sound of the plane gets nearer.

PIKE (**Points up**) Look, Mr Mainwaring, it's on fire.

MAINWARING Is it one of ours, Wilson?

WILSON No, sir, it's German.

Cut to reverse of German bomber on fire. Cut back to Mainwaring and co. The noise roars overhead and fades in the distance.

MAINWARING Did you hear an air raid siren, Frazer?

FRAZER No, sir, not a thing.

MAINWARING It's probably a lone raider trying to get back to France.

JONES They'll never make it, sir.

The engines die away.

MAINWARING I wouldn't like to be in their shoes. Well, there's nothing we can do. All right, men, back to bed. Well done, Frazer.

TELECINE: EXTERIOR. CAMP. DAY

Long shot of camp asleep. Cut to Hodges asleep in the cab of his van. He wakes, gets out of the cab, scratches and yawns. A boy scout comes out of one of the tents with a bugle. Hodges runs across and stops the boy as he is putting the bugle to his lips.

HODGES Do you want to earn sixpence?

The boy nods.

HODGES Don't blow it here – come with me. (**He hurries the boy over to Mainwaring's tent**) Right, blow it here, and I'll give you sixpence. (**He gives the boy sixpence and runs off. The boy blows reveille. Mainwaring's face appears through the tent flap**)

MAINWARING Go away, boy. (**He drags himself out of the tent, yawns, looks around and puts his glasses on. He looks at the river, does a take**) Good heavens. (**Grabs a pair of field glasses out of his tent and looks through them**)

Cut to reverse. Three German airmen are sitting in the rubber dinghy, in the middle of the river.

MAINWARING Sergeant Wilson, Lance Corporal Jones, turn out the guard, turn out, rifles and bayonets at the ready.

The men pour out of the tents. Wilson and Jones run to Mainwaring.

WILSON What on earth's the matter, sir?

MAINWARING (**Pointing**) Look.

WILSON Who are they?

MAINWARING They're Germans. Of course, they must have parachuted from that plane last night.

JONES Don't panic, don't panic, there's some Germans on the water, there's some Germans on the water!

MAINWARING Pull yourself together, Jones.

JONES I'm sorry, sir, it's just the sight of those Nazi uniforms, they get my blood up. (**Fixing his bayonet**) Let's go and get 'em, sir.

MAINWARING You're right, Jones.

WILSON I don't think even you can walk on the water, can you, sir?

MAINWARING (**He gives him a glare**) Give them a shout, Pike. Tell them to come in at once.

PIKE Yes, Mr Mainwaring. (**Shouts**) Hey, Mr Mainwaring says you've got to come in at once.

JONES With their hands up, Pikey. Hande hoc, hande hoc.

PIKE (**Shouting**) With your hands up, hande hoc, hande hoc.

FRAZER They're not taking a blind bit of notice, sir.

GODFREY Oh dear, you don't think they're dead do you?

FRAZER Of course not, they're sitting upright.

WILSON Why bother with them, sir. Why not just let them sit out there, they'll have to come in sooner or later.

MAINWARING Do use your intelligence, Wilson. As soon as it's dark ,they could slip ashore, and we'd have to comb the entire countryside for them. Right, they've asked for it. (**Shouts across to Vicar**) Get your boys out of the way, Vicar, there's going to be some shooting.

VICAR Come on, boys, into the trees.

VERGER Yes, come on, boys, into the trees.

VICAR You stay here, Mr Yeatman, Captain Mainwaring might need you.

He ushers the boys off.

MAINWARING Frazer, fire a shot over their heads.

FRAZER Right, sir. (**He fires, nothing happens, the Germans take no notice**)

WILSON They haven't moved a muscle. You've got to admire their courage.

MAINWARING I don't want any of that sort of talk, Wilson, they're just stupid.

PIKE Mr Mainwaring, if they won't come to us, why don't we go out to them, and make them surrender. We can use the scouts' pirate raft.

MAINWARING Good thinking, Pike. Frazer, Godfrey, you stay here. The rest of you, come with me.

WILSON How are we going to make them understand? None of us speak German.

VERGER Mr Hodges speaks German. (**He points to Hodges, who all this time has been skulking in the background**)

MAINWARING How do you know?

VERGER He told me. In the last war he was a guard at a prisoner of war camp.

MAINWARING (**Shouting to Hodges**) Hodges, over here at the double.

HODGES (**Shouting back**) And you know what you can do.

MAINWARING Go and get him, Jones.

JONES Right, sir. (**He runs up to Hodges with his bayonet**)

MAINWARING Come on, down to the raft.

They all move down to the raft.

JONES (**To Hodges**) You heard what the officer said. Come on, at the double.

WILSON What are going to do if the Germans are armed, sir?

MAINWARING Oh, we have overwhelming firepower, Wilson, we'll blast them out of the water.

Wilson and Pike climb on the raft. The sail is down. Jones comes down, prodding Hodges with his bayonet.

MAINWARING Right, Hodges, get on the raft. We need you as interpreter.

HODGES I'm not getting mixed up in this, I'm a civilian non-com.

MAINWARING (**Drawing his revolver**) You are now under my orders on active service, and you'll do as you're told.

JONES Yes, get on the raft.

They all get on.

PIKE Why don't you shoot him, Mr Mainwaring? You've got every right.

MAINWARING Be quiet, Pike. Right, shove off. (**He hands a paddle to Hodges**) Start paddling. You take the other one, Jones.

JONES Yes, sir, yes, sir.

MAINWARING Up the front, Pike, keep them covered.

The raft moves slowly towards the rubber dinghy. Hodges and Jones are paddling, Mainwaring, Wilson and Pike are up the front, keeping the Germans covered.

WILSON I don't know what's the matter with them, sir. They're just not taking any notice of anything.

MAINWARING I've never seen three such surly looking brutes.

Cut to the Germans in the dinghy. They are sitting silently in a circle facing inwards. Cut back to Mainwaring. The raft is about ten feet away from the Germans.

MAINWARING That's close enough. Watch them, Pike.

PIKE Yes, Mr Mainwaring. (**He holds his Tommy gun at the ready**)

MAINWARING (**Pushing Hodges forward**) Tell them to surrender in the name of the King.

HODGES (**Shouting at the top of his voice in terrible German**) Ergeben sich in der name von den Konig.

The Germans put their hands up.

WILSON They seemed to understand that, sir.

MAINWARING Tell them to come in, Hodges.

Cut to Frazer and Godfrey on the shore.

GODFREY What's happening, Mr Frazer? Are the Germans being awkward?

FRAZER (**Looking through field glasses**) They're just sitting there with their hands up. Mainwaring keeps shouting at them to come in, but they're not taking a blind bit of notice.

Cut back to raft.

MAINWARING Tell them again, Hodges.

HODGES Kommen sie herein!

JONES I don't think they want to come in, sir.

MAINWARING They're sulking. If it's one thing I can't stand, it's sulking Nazis.

PIKE Why don't we just shoot them?

MAINWARING Don't be absurd, Pike. We're British, we can't shoot men with their hands up, and they know it.

PIKE Well, we could shoot the rubber dinghy and sink it.

MAINWARING We can't do that either, the bullets will go right through and hit them. That's the penalty one pays for being a sporting nation and playing a square bat.

WILSON It's really quite simple, sir, all we've got to do is to attach a rope to the dinghy and tow it to the shore.

MAINWARING Well done, Wilson, I wondered who'd be the first one to spot that. (**Picks up rope**) Jones, tie that rope to the mast.

JONES Yes, sir, yes, sir. (**He attaches the rope. Mainwaring hands the other end to Hodges**)

MAINWARING Right, Hodges, when we get close enough, tie this to the dinghy.

HODGES Now, look...

MAINWARING Do as you're told. Right, men, forward, bit more, bit more.

Hodges reaches right out with the rope, he puts his hand on the dinghy, the Germans suddenly pick up paddles and pull the dinghy away. Hodges goes into the water.

MAINWARING Get him in, men.

Hodges grabs at the raft, his hand grips the cap of one of the petrol drums. As they pull him over the side of the raft, the hole goes underwater.

PIKE Mr Mainwaring, the petrol drum is filling with water, we're sinking.

MAINWARING Good, what! Quick, back to the shore.

TELECINE: EXTERIOR. CAMP. DAY

Mainwaring, Wilson, Frazer and Godfrey are standing in a group. Hodges has his jacket off and a blanket round him. He is shivering. Jones is holding a gas mask in his hand.

MAINWARING I tell you it won't work, Jones. You're going into the realms of fantasy again.

JONES Let me do it, sir, let me do it. I just put this gas mask on. (**He pulls the end of the pipe off the filter**) Attach this end of the pipe to a little raft with camouflage on it, then I can swim underwater and breathe through the pipe. When I get near the German dinghy, I dive under and pierce it with my bayonet, and it sinks.

MAINWARING What do you think, Wilson?

WILSON I think he'll drown, sir.

JONES I'll show you. (**He puts on his gas mask, mimes swimming, pulls out his bayonet and gestures upwards. All the time we can hear his voice mumbling**)

MAINWARING What did you say, Jones?

JONES (**Taking off his mask**) They don't like it up 'em, sir, they do not like it up 'em.

FRAZER It's worth a try, sir. After all, what have we got to lose?

MAINWARING All right, let's get on with it.

Pike runs into the picture, he is carrying a long, thin thing, wrapped in cloth.

MAINWARING Come on, Pike, where have you been?

PIKE Sorry, Mr Mainwaring, I just borrowed something from one of the boy scouts.

MAINWARING This isn't a game, Pike, we're dealing with three vicious Nazi thugs. Come on, get your coat on, Hodges.

HODGES (**Shivering**) Now... lo... lo... look.

MAINWARING Stop making all that fuss.

EXTERIOR. CAMP. DAY

The raft is moving towards the German dinghy. The sail is up.

MAINWARING Keep the raft facing them, Pike, so that they can't see what we're up to.

PIKE Yes, Mr Mainwaring.

Mainwaring, Wilson, Jones and Hodges are behind the sail, so that they are hidden from the Germans. Jones is dressed in a vest and long johns, with a belt round his waist.

MAINWARING Are you ready, Jones?

JONES Yes, sir.

MAINWARING Good luck. (**They shake hands**) You're a brave man, I shan't forget this.

WILSON Good luck, Jonesey, don't forget your bayonet. (**He hands him a bayonet**) Where are you going to put it?

JONES I'll grip it in my teeth.

MAINWARING You'll be wearing a gas mask.

JONES Oh, yes. (**He puts it in his belt and puts on the gas mask. Wilson holds the end of the pipe, which is attached to a small piece of wood, covered in a bunch of leaves. They lower him into the water. He goes under, the leaves move away from the raft**)

MAINWARING There's no doubt about it, Jones has got guts. I sometimes wonder what we'd do without him.

WILSON If this goes wrong, we might have to.

The bunch of leaves suddenly turns and comes back towards the raft.

HODGES He's turning round.

MAINWARING What's he coming back for?

The leaves go round in a circle and disappear.

WILSON He's under the raft.

MAINWARING Can you see him? Jones! Jones!

WILSON He can't hear you, sir.

The bayonet comes up through a crack in the boards, Hodges is bending down, looking in the water, it catches his backside.

HODGES Ow! (**He leaps right out into the water**)

Jones' head appears and he takes off his mask.

JONES (**Gasping for breath**) I got 'em, I got 'em. Mr Mainwaring, what are you doing in the Germans' boat?

Wilson and Mainwaring pull Jones on to the raft.

MAINWARING You came up under our boat, Jones.

JONES Sorry, sir, I must have taken the wrong turning.

Pike pokes his head round the sail.

PIKE Mr Mainwaring, the Germans have got Mr Hodges.

MAINWARING What!

The Germans are pulling Hodges into the dinghy, one of them raises a revolver and shoots at the raft.

MAINWARING Get down.

More shots.

WILSON They're shooting at the petrol drums, they're trying to sink us.

MAINWARING The swines, that settles it. (**He draws his revolver**) Let them have it, men.

Jones raises his rifle.

WILSON Don't do that, sir, you'll hit Hodges.

MAINWARING Why is that blasted man always in the way?

PIKE Excuse me, Mr Mainwaring, would you mind getting out of the way, please. (**He is holding a large bow and arrow. He takes aim and lets fly**)

PIKE One more for luck. (**He shoots again. Cut to the dinghy with two arrows sticking out of it. It starts to deflate**)

MAINWARING Well done, Pike.

WILSON We'd better warn them, sir. What's the German for 'Can you swim'?

MAINWARING I don't know. (**Shouts**) Hodges, ask them in German if they can swim.

HODGES I don't care about them, I'm the one who can't swim, you flippin' hooligans.

SERIES EIGHT **EPISODE FIVE**

Recorded: Friday 30/5/75

Original transmission: Friday 3/10/75, 8.00–8.30pm

Original viewing figures = 14.3 million

ARTHUR LOWE .... CAPTAIN MAINWARING
JOHN LE MESURIER .... SERGEANT WILSON
CLIVE DUNN.................................. LANCE CORPORAL JONES
JOHN LAURIE .... PRIVATE FRAZER
ARNOLD RIDLEY .... PRIVATE GODFREY
IAN LAVENDER .... PRIVATE PIKE
BILL PERTWEE.................................. CHIEF WARDEN HODGES
FRANK WILLIAMS .... VICAR
EDWARD SINCLAIR.. VERGER
JANET DAVIES.. MRS PIKE
RONNIE BRODY .... MR SWANN
COLIN BEAN .... PRIVATE SPONGE
NATALIE KENT .... MISS TWELVETREES
PLATOON........................ GEORGE HANCOCK, MICHAEL MOORE,
.... DESMOND CULLUM-JONES, FREDDIE WHITE,
.... EVAN ROSS, LESLIE NOYES, ROGER BOURNE,
.... FREDDIE WILES, HUGH CECIL

HIGH FINANCE

• ROBERT BERK REMEMBERS •

'One off-the-set incident I remember took place in The Bell Hotel, Thetford. John Le Mesurier, Jimmy Perry and Bill Pertwee were in the bar when a member of the public mistook John for Robert Dougall, the late BBC newsreader, and asked what brought him to Norfolk. John, knowing Robert was a keen bird watcher, pretended to be him, explaining at great length how a particular bird had been seen nearby and he had come to try and see it. Jimmy, who quite rightly thought *Dad's Army* was one of the best programmes ever, couldn't understand why John didn't tell the truth, and was silently smarting with indignation. Meanwhile, Bill, always a bit of a joker, was bubbling and almost exploding with delight.'

HIGH FINANCE

INTERIOR. BANK OFFICE. DAY

Wilson is fiddling with the sandbags which are stacked against the window. Mainwaring is by the filing cabinet.

MAINWARING What are you doing, Wilson?

WILSON Just tidying up the sandbags, sir. (**He plonks one on Mainwaring's desk**)

MAINWARING Get it off my desk.

WILSON Sorry, sir. (**He takes it off, and spills some of the sand on the floor**)

MAINWARING Watch what you're doing, Wilson, you're spilling sand on the floor.

PIKE Mr Mainwaring –

MAINWARING What is it, Pike?

PIKE I've got Mr Jones in the bank. He's just paid in his takings,£15 6s 4d, and he's presented this cheque for £3 2s 6d. (**He hands Mainwaring the cheque**)

MAINWARING Ask him to come in.

PIKE Yes, Mr Mainwaring. (**He goes**)

WILSON I'd better go then, sir.

MAINWARING No, this is a very delicate matter, I want you here. You stay where you are.

WILSON Right, sir. (**He makes a crunching sound with his feet**)

MAINWARING And stop making that crunching noise.

WILSON I can't help it, sir, it's the sand on the floor.

MAINWARING Well, go and stand somewhere else.

WILSON You told me to stay where I was.

Mainwaring gives him a look, Wilson moves away, Pike comes in with Jones.

MAINWARING Mr Jones.

JONES Yes? Oh, good morning, Mr Mainwaring. Morning, Mr Wilson.

WILSON Morning, Jonesey.

MAINWARING Pike, bring in Mr Jones' statement.

PIKE Yes, Mr Mainwaring. (**He goes**)

MAINWARING Sit down please, Jones. Now then, this cheque you've just presented for £3 2s 6d.

JONES Yes, sir, that's for my staff wages. I know it's a lot of money, but if you don't pay your staff well, you can't keep 'em these days.

MAINWARING I'm afraid I can't cash it, Jones.

JONES Why not?

MAINWARING Insufficient funds.

JONES Well, can't you get some more?

MAINWARING No, Jones, you have insufficient funds to meet this cheque.

JONES Then give me back my £15 6s 4d I've just paid in.

MAINWARING I can't do that. As you say, you've just paid it in.

JONES It's my money, I want it back.

MAINWARING The only way you could get it back would be to write out a cheque.

JONES Then I'll write out a cheque.

MAINWARING I couldn't cash it, you've got insufficient funds.

JONES I don't understand.

MAINWARING Didn't you get a letter from the bank?

JONES What bank?

MAINWARING This bank.

Pike comes in with a small tray, with a cup of coffee and a bowl of sugar on it. He also has Jones' statement.

PIKE Here's Mr Jones' statement, and I've brought your coffee.

MAINWARING Thank you. (**He takes the statement and some cancelled cheques. Pike moves round desk. Pike puts the tray on the desk, he crunches as he moves**)

MAINWARING Don't crunch about, boy.

PIKE I can't help crunching, Mr Mainwaring, it's the sand on the floor.

MAINWARING Well, sweep it up.

Pike crosses and chunters.

MAINWARING Pike! Watch it!

Pike reacts.

JONES Wait a minute, I tell a lie. (**He pulls a letter out of his pocket**) I did get a letter from the bank on Tuesday.

MAINWARING Why didn't you open it?

JONES Well, I was just going to, when I got an urgent delivery of offal, and it drove it clear out of my mind – well, you've got to concentrate when you get an urgent delivery of offal, you know. I'll just have a look at it.

MAINWARING You needn't bother, I'll tell you what's in it.

JONES Don't do that, Mr Mainwaring. If it's a letter from the bank addressed to me, it's private.

MAINWARING I wrote it, Jones.

JONES Oh yes – of course.

MAINWARING What are you doing, Pike?

PIKE Sorry, Mr Mainwaring.

Mainwaring bangs his knee.

MAINWARING You stupid boy. The fact is, for several months, you have had an overdraft of £50, and it's not getting any less. I'm afraid I can't let it go on any longer.

JONES I'm sorry to retiterate myself, but what about the £15 6s 4d I've just paid in?

MAINWARING The cheque here, that you paid to United Meat Supplies, has just been presented, so that takes care of that. That is right, isn't it, Pike?

Pike straightens up. As he leans across Mainwaring to look at the cheque the sand tips into the sugar bowl.

PIKE Yes, Mr Mainwaring.

MAINWARING So you see, Jones, we have a problem. **(Mainwaring puts two spoonfuls of sand in his coffee and stirs. He hands Wilson some cheques)** We'll just go through these cheques, Wilson.

WILSON Right, sir.

Mainwaring sips his coffee.

MAINWARING Hmm, this is a nice cup of coffee, Pike.

PIKE Thank you, Mr Mainwaring.

MAINWARING The Germans don't get coffee like that. What's that stuff they drink called, Wilson?

WILSON According to the papers, it's ersatz coffee, made from acorns, sir.

MAINWARING Acorns, eh, and we're drinking stuff like this. It's what we're fighting for, you know. All right, Pike, you can take it away. It must have been the brown sugar that made it taste so nice.

PIKE Brown… **(He realises and quickly whips the tray away)** Yes, Mr Mainwaring. **(He moves to door. He looks at Mainwaring)**

Mainwaring reacts. Pike goes out and giggles.

MAINWARING How that boy got a school certificate, I'll never know. What's the first cheque, Wilson?

WILSON It's a bit difficult to read, sir, it's got a brown stain on it.

JONES That's a liver stain.

MAINWARING How do you explain that, Jones?

JONES Well, liver always leaves a brown stain, sir.

MAINWARING Oh, this is no use. **(He takes the cheques back)** The point is, Jones, your affairs are in a terrible mess.

JONES Being a butcher is a messy business, Mr Mainwaring. I mean, not all the cheques have got liver stains on them – some of them are quite ordinary stains.

MAINWARING Look, Jones, can you pay off this £50 overdraft?

JONES No.

MAINWARING Have you got any sort of security?

JONES No.

MAINWARING Then you're becoming insolvent.

Jones reacts.

MAINWARING What can you do about it?

JONES I can keep the cheques separate from the meat.

MAINWARING This has got nothing to do with liver stains, Jones. Look, I'm sorry to have to tell you this, but the bank cannot honour any more of your cheques until this overdraft is paid off.

JONES You wouldn't do this to me, Mr Mainwaring.

MAINWARING It's not me that's doing it, Jones, it's the bank. I am merely the servant of the bank, carrying out the policy of the bank. Isn't that right, Wilson?

WILSON Yes, sir, merely a servant.

Mainwaring looks. Wilson smiles.

MAINWARING Now, if you'll excuse me, Jones, I'm very busy.

JONES **(Getting up)** Yes, thank you, Mr Mainwaring, you've been very helpful, I'll go back to my shop and have a think. Yes, that's what I'll do, I'll go and have a think. **(Jones goes)**

WILSON Aren't you being a bit hard on him, sir?

MAINWARING You don't think I enjoy this sort of thing, do you?

WILSON I've really no idea.

MAINWARING Look, if I were to give Jones an overdraft with no security, people would say I'd done it because Jones is a member of my platoon. I'd have every Tom, Dick and Harry knocking on my door for a loan. There is a war on, money's short.

WILSON All the same, it would be terrible, if Jones were to go bankrupt.

MAINWARING I realise that, Wilson, but what can I do?

WILSON You know, sir, every morning I walk up the High Street to work, and as I pass those little shops, a sort of warm, friendly atmosphere comes wafting out, even from that terrible man, Hodges' greengrocers. Then, I sort of stroll on, and I pass Frazer's funeral parlour, and before I cross the road to the bank, there's Jones' butcher's shop, gleaming white tiles, and Jones inside, wearing his straw hat and striped apron, giving me a cheery wave. And I say to myself, this is my town, and it sort of sets me up for the day.

MAINWARING You know, I envy you, Wilson.

WILSON In what way, sir?

MAINWARING Yes, I wish I could afford to be sentimental, but I can't. However, I see your point, so as soon as the bank closes, we'll go over to Jones' shop, and try and sort this mess out.

WILSON That's awfully nice of you, sir.

MAINWARING I'm not a hard man, Wilson, but some of us are born leaders, and others are born to be led. As commanding officer of the platoon, I have to make decisions that could be a matter of life and death. And, as manager of this bank, I have to make decisions that involve thousands of pounds. I only wish I had time like you, Wilson, for the simple things of life, but I have to take the whole burden… Good heavens, I've just remembered, it's Tuesday.

WILSON Tuesday?

MAINWARING Yes, rock cakes.

WILSON Rock cakes?

MAINWARING Today is the day they have rock cakes at the Marigold Tea Rooms.

WILSON We'd better get over there quickly, otherwise they'll all be gone.

MAINWARING Good thinking, Wilson. Quick, while I'm ringing up Jones, you run across to the Marigold Tea Rooms. Order two coffees and two rock cakes.

WILSON Right, sir. **(He takes his hat off the peg and moves to the door)**

MAINWARING And, Wilson.

WILSON Yes, sir?

MAINWARING Don't take the one with all the fruit in.

INTERIOR. JONES' SHOP. DAY

Jones is wiping down the counter, there is a knock on the door, he crosses and unlocks it. Mainwaring, Wilson and Pike enter.

JONES I'm ever so grateful for you coming round here to help me, Mr Mainwaring. When I left the bank today, I was a broken man. Then I got your phone call and I realised that I was not alone in my trouble.

MAINWARING We'll do our best to help, Jones. And we're a pretty formidable team, you know, the entire financial brains of my bank.

Pike is sucking his thumb.

MAINWARING Take your thumb out of your mouth, boy. Now, where are your books and things?

JONES Over here in the cash desk, sir. **(He leads the way to the cash desk, and opens the door. It is about five feet high, and has a small opening in the front for paying money in)**

MAINWARING Come on, Wilson, let's get on with it.

They both squeeze into the cash desk and shuffle around.

MAINWARING Oh, this is no good. Go out, Wilson.

Wilson goes out.

MAINWARING I can't work on the books in this mess. What's this? **(He hands Jones a cardigan)**

JONES That's Mrs Johnson's cardigan, sir. There's a nasty draught when I open the door of the cold room. You can put it on if you like.

MAINWARING No, thank you. **(He hands out some knitting)** Take this.

JONES That's Mrs Johnson's knitting.

Mainwaring hands out a tin.

JONES That's her bismuth tablets. Well, I'll leave you to get on with it.

MAINWARING Jones.

JONES Yes, sir. **(He puts his head down to the opening)**

MAINWARING Jones. **(He pokes his head over the top)** Where are you?

JONES Here, sir.

Mainwaring puts his head to opening. Jones looks over the top. Mainwaring's head comes up.

MAINWARING Open the door please.

Jones opens the door. Mainwaring has a flypaper stuck to his hat.

JONES That's Mrs Johnson's flypaper, sir. She's very hygienic you know – well, you've got to be hygienic in a butcher's shop.

MAINWARING **(To Pike)** I don't care whose it is – get it off, boy.

PIKE Yes, sir. **(Pike takes hat and goes to counter. He is about to scrub the hat)**

MAINWARING Not with that, boy! Look, Jones, get everything out on the counter. Then I can sort it out.

PIKE I'll cut it.

Jones reacts.

PIKE I missed.

JONES Right, Mr Mainwaring. **(He goes into the cash desk)**

Mainwaring notices Wilson staring at his head. He takes off the hat and shouts.

MAINWARING Pike –

Pike appears.

MAINWARING I'll stop that out of your wages!

Pike smiles weakly.

MAINWARING I want the invoice book, the cashbook, the ledge, the daybook, petty cash book and the post book.

Jones hands him an exercise book.

JONES Here it is, Mr Mainwaring.

MAINWARING Is this all you've got?

WILSON There's several sections in it, sir.

MAINWARING **(Pointing to page)** What's this?

JONES Don't take any notice of that, that's a mistake.

He tears the page out, crumples it up and throws it on the floor.

MAINWARING Get the rest, Jones.

JONES Yes, sir, yes, sir. **(He goes back into the cash desk)**

MAINWARING **(To Wilson)** In all my years as a bank manager, I have never seen such slapdash methods.

Wilson is looking through the book.

WILSON It seems to work, sir. See, it does balance. Seventeen pounds, fourteen and twopence.

MAINWARING That's not the point, Wilson, it's not the proper way to do it.

Jones comes out of the cash desk with an armful of stuff, and dumps it on the counter. There is a shoebox, several books of cheque stubs, and several spikes with papers, bills, etc. on them.

JONES That's the lot.

Mainwaring picks up two books of cheque stubs and hands one to Wilson.

MAINWARING Have a look through these, Wilson.

WILSON Right, sir.

Mainwaring hands another one to Pike.

MAINWARING Look through that one, Pike.

PIKE Yes, Mr Mainwaring.

WILSON This cheque is dated 1491, Jones.

JONES **(Looking)** Oh yes, I got it the wrong way round, it should be 1941. I was in a bit of a tizz that day.

MAINWARING What are these figures, Jones?

JONES Just the usual pounds, shillings and pence, sir.

MAINWARING No, the little man on the back of these cheque stubs.

JONES That must be the boy, Raymond, sir. He's always larking about.

PIKE **(Taking the cheque stubs)** I'll show you how it works, Mr Mainwaring. It's good, look. **(He flicks through the stubs)** Now the little man's running along, now the little man's jumping in the air, now he's going over the fence, and he's landed on the ground. Look, Uncle Arthur.

WILSON Oh yes, that's rather sweet, Frank.

PIKE See, he's running along, now he's jumping…

MAINWARING **(Snatching the book)** All right, Pike, this isn't a game. There's only one thing for it, Jones, I shall have to take all this stuff home, and do a complete audit. I shall want something to put it in.

JONES I'll get you a carrier bag, sir.

PIKE This will do, Mr Mainwaring. **(He picks up the shoebox, takes off the lid, there are hundreds of coupons inside, Pike tips them on the floor)**

JONES No, Pikey! Those are my coupons, it took me hours to count that lot.

Pike reacts.

MAINWARING You stupid boy!

Pike reacts.

INTERIOR. CHURCH HALL. NIGHT

Jones, Frazer, Godfrey and Pike are sitting on the steps. The rest of the platoon are standing round, they are all in uniform.

JONES Mr Mainwaring was very helpful, but I'm worried to death about it, he told me I was insolvent, and he took all my books away to do a complete audicredit.

FRAZER Are you mad? Letting Mainwaring poke his nose into your affairs. Once that bank's got their hands on you, they'll squeeze you, and squeeze you, you're doomed, doomed.

GODFREY I don't agree. Mr Mainwaring would be the first person I'd go to if I were in trouble.

FRAZER He wouldn't have been in trouble if it hadn't been for Mainwaring. He's a vulture, you should have come to me for help, Jonesey.

JONES Will you lend me 50 quid, then?

FRAZER Well, er… you know the old saying, lend money and you lose a friend, and you're a very dear friend of mine, Jonesey.

GODFREY I wish I could help, but I've just lent some money to somebody else.

JONES Well, if I go on like this, I'll end up in Queer Street.

PIKE Perhaps they haven't got any butcher's shops there, Mr Jones.

INTERIOR. OFFICE. NIGHT

Wilson is pinning a notice on the board, Mainwaring comes in, they are both in uniform.

WILSON Hullo, sir, you're late.

MAINWARING I've only just finished sorting out Jones' books. **(He puts a brown paper parcel on the desk)** His affairs are in a terrible state, I still can't find out where that £50 has gone. We'd better get him in.

WILSON I'll give him a shout.

MAINWARING I don't want the others to know, we must be discreet about it, I'll get him. Have a look at that balance sheet I made out. **(He goes out of the door)**

INTERIOR. CHURCH HALL. NIGHT

Mainwaring comes out of the office door, and crosses over to Jones. They rise.

MAINWARING **(Whispering)** Would you mind coming into the office, Jones?

JONES What, Mr Mainwaring?

MAINWARING **(Mouthing)** The office, I want to speak to you.

FRAZER If it's about you making him bankrupt, we all know.

JONES Permission to speak, sir? Could the others come as well, please. They might be able to help.

MAINWARING Oh, very well, into the office all of you. Private Sponge.

SPONGE Yes, Captain Mainwaring.

Jones, Frazer, Godfrey and Pike cross to the office.

MAINWARING I'm leaving you in charge, Sponge, and don't disturb me unless something vital happens.

SPONGE What sort of vital?

MAINWARING When it's time to bring in the tea. **(He starts to follow the others into the office. Mr Swann comes in the main door, he is a small, meek man, he hurries across to Mainwaring)**

SWANN Excuse me, Mr Mainwaring?

MAINWARING Yes?

SWANN I'm Mr Swann, I keep the grocer's shop in the High Street. I tried to reach you at the bank today, I must speak to you, it's very important.

MAINWARING What is it?

SWANN Not in front of all these people, it's very embarrassing.

MAINWARING If you're embarrassed, the best thing you can do is to pull yourself together. I've got an important meeting, excuse me. **(Goes into the office)**

Swann reacts. Mainwaring looks again.

SWANN **(To Sponge)** It's embarrassing for him, not me.

INTERIOR. OFFICE. NIGHT

The others are standing around, Mainwaring comes in and sits at his desk.

MAINWARING I'll be as brief as possible, gentlemen. The fact is, Jones is insolvent. Now, I have made out a balance sheet, and, as my chief clerk, Sergeant Wilson will give you the facts. Get on with it, Wilson.

WILSON Right, sir. Well, Jones, it appears from this balance sheet which Mr Mainwaring has done, rather beautifully, I think, that your business is just ticking over. The only snag is the £50 overdraft that you owe the bank.

MAINWARING So, we've all got to rally round and see how we can get you out of this mess, Jones. Now, in this discussion, I shall be wearing three hats. One as your bank manager, one as your commanding officer and one as your friend.

FRAZER Heaven help us all.

GODFREY Excuse me, sir, what sort of hat will you be wearing as his friend?

MAINWARING It's a hypothetical hat, Godfrey. Now, the first thing we've got to do, Jones, is to examine your assets.

JONES Permission to speak, sir? Are you now wearing your commanding officer's hat, your bank manager's hat or your friendly hat?

MAINWARING My bank manager's hat.

JONES Just so long as I know, sir. It's a bit difficult without the actual hat.

PIKE Mr Mainwaring, shall I run to your house and get your bowler hat?

MAINWARING Quiet, Pike, or you'll be sent home. Read out the assets, Wilson.

WILSON Well, there's the van, sir.

MAINWARING That's worth £10, put it down.

Jones reacts.

WILSON Right, sir, £10.

FRAZER Hold on, Captain Mainwaring, if we sell Jones' van, the platoon won't have any transport.

MAINWARING Good point, Frazer, we'll buy it off him. Put down £9, Wilson. What's next?

WILSON The chopping blocks.

MAINWARING Ah yes, the chopping blocks.

FRAZER We could cut them up and sell them for firewood, that should bring in about £3.

JONES 'Ere, just a minute.

MAINWARING Quiet, Jones, put down £3, Wilson. Next?

WILSON The scales.

MAINWARING Two pounds. What's next?

WILSON That's all, sir. It comes to £14.

MAINWARING Well, that's not too bad, if we sell all your assets, we could pay off nearly a third of your debt.

JONES But if I do that, I shan't have any business left.

MAINWARING **(Sharply)** I'm trying to help, Jones. I'm speaking as your friend.

JONES You don't sound very friendly.

MAINWARING Well, what do you suggest?

JONES I don't know, I just can't bring myself to squeeze those poor little orphans.

MAINWARING Squeeze an orphan?

JONES Well, sir, I supply all the meat to the orphanage, and for the past three months, they haven't paid any of my bills. Here. **(He takes some bills out of his pocket and hands them to Mainwaring)** They come to £50 exactly.

MAINWARING Really, Jones, this is the limit. I spent hours of my precious time trying to find out where this money had gone.

JONES I'm sorry, Mr Mainwaring, I should have told you, but I can't see those little orphans starve. They haven't got any mothers and fathers, you know.

MAINWARING I know what an orphan is, Jones.

GODFREY The Vicar is one of the trustees of the orphanage, Mr Mainwaring, perhaps he can help.

MAINWARING Good idea, Godfrey. Pike, go and get the Vicar.

PIKE He won't want to be disturbed at this time of night, Mr Mainwaring.

MAINWARING Nonsense, it's only half past nine. Go and get him at once.

INTERIOR. OFFICE. NIGHT

Mainwaring is sitting at his desk. Wilson is standing beside him. Jones, Frazer, Godfrey and Pike are standing in front of the desk. The Vicar is sitting, with the Verger standing behind him.

VICAR I hope, Mr Mainwaring, that what you have to discuss with me about the orphanage is important. I strongly object to being dragged out of my bed in the middle of the night.

MAINWARING It's not even dark yet, Vicar.

VICAR That's got nothing to do with it, one hour's sleep before midnight is worth two after.

VERGER That's right. His Reverence must have his eight hours.

JONES What's he doing here? I don't want him poking his nose into my affairs, he's a troublemaker.

VERGER I am not a troublemaker, I'm here in my capacity.

VICAR Mr Yeatman is the treasurer to the orphanage, he assists me in every way.

JONES No wonder my bills haven't been paid, he's on the fiddle.

VERGER How dare you?

MAINWARING Quiet, Jones. The fact is, Vicar, Mr Jones is in severe financial trouble because the orphanage has not paid his meat bills for several months. He's owed £50.

VICAR It's not my fault, it's Miss Twelvetrees.

MAINWARING Miss Twelvetrees?

VICAR I haven't had a cheque from her for five months.

INTERIOR. BANK OFFICE. DAY

Mainwaring is sitting at his desk, Miss Twelvetrees is sitting opposite, she is a small bird-like lady.

MAINWARING This is a very delicate situation for me, Miss Twelvetrees. Now, I don't wish to pry into your affairs in any way, but one of my clients is in danger of going bankrupt, and I must help him. I understand you make a donation to the orphanage every month, but they haven't received anything from you for some time.

MISS TWELVETREES That's right, Mr Mainwaring, you see I own a small shop in the High Street, and I donate the £10 a month rent to the orphanage, but for the past five months I've received nothing.

MAINWARING So you're owed £50. Have you asked for the rent?

MISS TWELVETREES Yes, several times, but my tenant is such a kind, religious man, that I don't want to press him too hard. You see, he's so very poor.

INTERIOR. BANK OFFICE. DAY

Mainwaring is on the phone, Wilson is standing beside him.

MAINWARING What's this I hear about you being poor?

Cut to Frazer on phone.

FRAZER Well, I am poor, very poor indeed.

MAINWARING What about this £50 rent you owe Miss Twelvetrees?

FRAZER I just got a wee bit behind, that's all. I had the £50 all ready to pay her, but I lent it to somebody else.

MAINWARING Who?

FRAZER Mind your own business, and don't go poking

your nose into my affairs. You're not squeezing me like poor old Jonesey, that's all. See you on parade. **(He hangs up)**

MAINWARING I've never seen such a web of intrigue in all my life, Wilson. I'm going to unravel it, if it's the last thing I do.

INTERIOR. CHURCH HALL. DAY

A long trestle table is set up. Jones is sitting at the far end, the rest of the platoon are sitting in the following order, from Jones: Verger, Vicar, Miss Twelvetrees, Frazer, Godfrey, Warden, Pike and Wilson. They are all in uniform. Wilson is addressing the meeting.

WILSON Thank you very much for coming here today, ladies and gentlemen. Mr Mainwaring won't keep you long.

HODGES What's all the mystery?

WILSON Mr Mainwaring will tell you when he gets here.

HODGES Well, he'd better hurry up, I haven't got all day, you know. I'm on duty in half an hour.

PIKE Uncle Arthur, has Mr Mainwaring found out what's happened to the £50?

WILSON I think so, Frank.

PIKE It's ever so exciting, it's just like that film *Charlie Chan Investigates*. You see, there was this weekend party at a big country house, and one of the guests was murdered. Well, at the end of the film, Charlie Chan got them all into the drawing room and he said: **(Doing impersonation)** 'One of you in this room is the murderer, and very soon I shall reveal his identity'. Here, do you think Mr Mainwaring will do it like a Chinaman? 'Ah so.'

WILSON Oh, don't be absurd, Frank.

Mainwaring enters, goes to the head of the table and takes some papers out of his briefcase.

MAINWARING Ah so.

PIKE See – I told you so. **(Makes face at Mainwaring)**

Mainwaring gives him a look.

MAINWARING Thank you very much for coming here today, ladies and gentlemen. I won't keep you long.

HODGES **(Pointing to Wilson)** He's just said all that, Napoleon, get on with it.

MAINWARING Very well, I'll come straight to the point. Yesterday Mr Jones informed me that he could not pay the bank the £50 he owed, because he in turn was owed the money by you, Vicar. You were unable to pay him because you were owed the money by Miss Twelvetrees. She was unable to pay because she was owed the money by you, Frazer. You couldn't pay because you had lent the money to someone else, and that someone else was... **(Points)** You, Godfrey.

GODFREY Oh dear.

MAINWARING And Godfrey in turn had lent the money to Sergeant Wilson.

WILSON Is all this necessary, sir? It's awfully embarrassing.

MAINWARING There's no need for any of you to feel ashamed, you all acted from the best possible motives. The point is, what did Sergeant Wilson need the £50 for? I now come to the missing factor x, which is... **(Points)** You, Hodges.

HODGES What are you talking about?

MAINWARING I intend to show, that by your greed and profiteering, you are responsible for this whole miserable affair.

HODGES Very clever, Mainwaring, and just how do you intend to prove it?

MAINWARING I'll show you. **(He crosses to the door)**

PIKE **(To Wilson)** I knew Mr Hodges would turn out to be the murderer.

WILSON Quiet, Frank.

(Mainwaring crosses to the office door and opens it)

MAINWARING Come in, Mrs Pike.

Mrs Pike comes in.

MAINWARING Sit down, please.

HODGES What's she doing here?

MAINWARING You'll find out soon enough.

Mrs Pike sits between Godfrey and Hodges.

MAINWARING Now, Mrs Pike, repeat exactly what you told me earlier on.

MRS PIKE Well, Mr Hodges is my landlord, and about a year ago, he said he was going to increase the rent on my house from a pound a week to £2. I told him I couldn't possibly afford it, and he told me not to worry, I could owe it to him. Then... then... **(She starts to sob)** Last week he asked me to have a drink with him at The Red Lion, and he told me that I owed him £50 back rent, but he'd forget all about it if I was nice to him.

WILSON **(To Mainwaring)** Excuse me, sir. **(He gets up, crosses to Hodges)** Would you mind standing up? **(He knocks him on the floor, crosses back and sits down)**

WILSON It's all right, sir, carry on.

Frazer and Godfrey help Hodges up.

HODGES Are you mad? That's criminal assault, I'm going to sue you, I'm going to...

MAINWARING Sit down, Hodges, and stop making all that fuss, it was only a little tap.

HODGES **(Holding his jaw)** A little tap!

MAINWARING Go on, Mrs Pike.

MRS PIKE I just told Arthur… I mean Sergeant Wilson, that I needed the £50 for back rent.

MAINWARING The best thing you can do Hodges, is to give that £50 back to Mrs Pike. You'd no right to increase her rent, and you know it.

HODGES I'll do nothing of the sort, it's my property and I'll charge what I want for it.

JONES Oh no you won't, I'll report you to the Chamber of Commerce. You'll get chucked out on your ear for this.

FRAZER As a member of the Chamber of Commerce, I second that.

GODFREY And I third it.

FRAZER You're not a shopkeeper, shut up.

HODGES All right, all right, I'll pay it back.

PIKE Well, go on, give it to Mum now.

HODGES I don't carry £50 around with me.

Mainwaring takes a packet of notes out of his pocket and throws it on the table.

MAINWARING There's £50, you can give me a cheque.

HODGES I haven't got a cheque.

MAINWARING I have. **(He takes a cheque out of his wallet)** I've made it out, cash to your account, all you've got to do is sign it. **(He takes out his pen and offers it. Hodges crosses and takes it)**

HODGES **(Signing)** All right, you can sneer, but I've admired Mrs Pike for years, and she won't even look at me. Treats me like dirt, just because she's besotted with him. **(Points to Wilson)**

PIKE Hit him again, Uncle Arthur.

WILSON Do you want another one?

HODGES Er… no.

WILSON Then sit down.

MAINWARING **(Handing Hodges the notes)** There's the £50, Hodges.

HODGES **(Handing it to Mrs Pike)** There you are, Mavis. **(Wilson starts to rise)** I mean, Mrs Pike, er… sorry.

MRS PIKE **(Handing it to Wilson)** Here you are, Arthur, thank you.

Wilson takes the money and crosses to Godfrey.

WILSON Here you are, Godfrey, my dear fellow.

GODFREY Thank you. **(Hands money to Frazer)** And thank you, Mr Frazer.

FRAZER Don't mention it, Godfrey, son. **(Hands money to Miss Twelvetrees)** Your money, dear lady.

MISS TWELVETREES Thank you, Mr Frazer, you're such a kind, honest, religious man. **(Handing money to Vicar)** Here you are, Mr Farthing.

VICAR Thank you, Miss Twelvetrees, and here's your £50, Mr Jones. **(He hands the money to Jones. The Verger snatches it back)**

VERGER Just a minute, Your Reverence, I'm the treasurer, it's my job to give Mr Jones the money. Here you are, Mr Jones. **(He hands it back to Jones, who crosses and hands it to Mainwaring)**

JONES There you are, Mr Mainwaring – now we're all square.

MAINWARING Thank you, Jones.

Mr Swann comes in.

SWANN I must speak to you, Mr Mainwaring.

MAINWARING What?

SWANN Remember me, Swann, the grocer?

MAINWARING What do you want?

SWANN It's a bit embarrassing – in front of all these people.

MAINWARING You're far too sensitive – spit it out.

SWANN Can't we go somewhere private?

MAINWARING No – come on – out with it.

SWANN All right then, your wife hasn't paid her grocery bill for six months – it comes to £50.

MAINWARING Fifty…

SWANN I'll take it now. **(Pointing to money)** How much have you got there?

PIKE Fifty pounds, Mr Swann.

SWANN Thanks. **(Takes the money)** I'll send the receipt on. **(Goes)**

MAINWARING Wait a minute, that money belongs to the bank.

WILSON Don't worry, sir, just treat it as a loan, and give yourself an overdraft.

Mainwaring reacts.

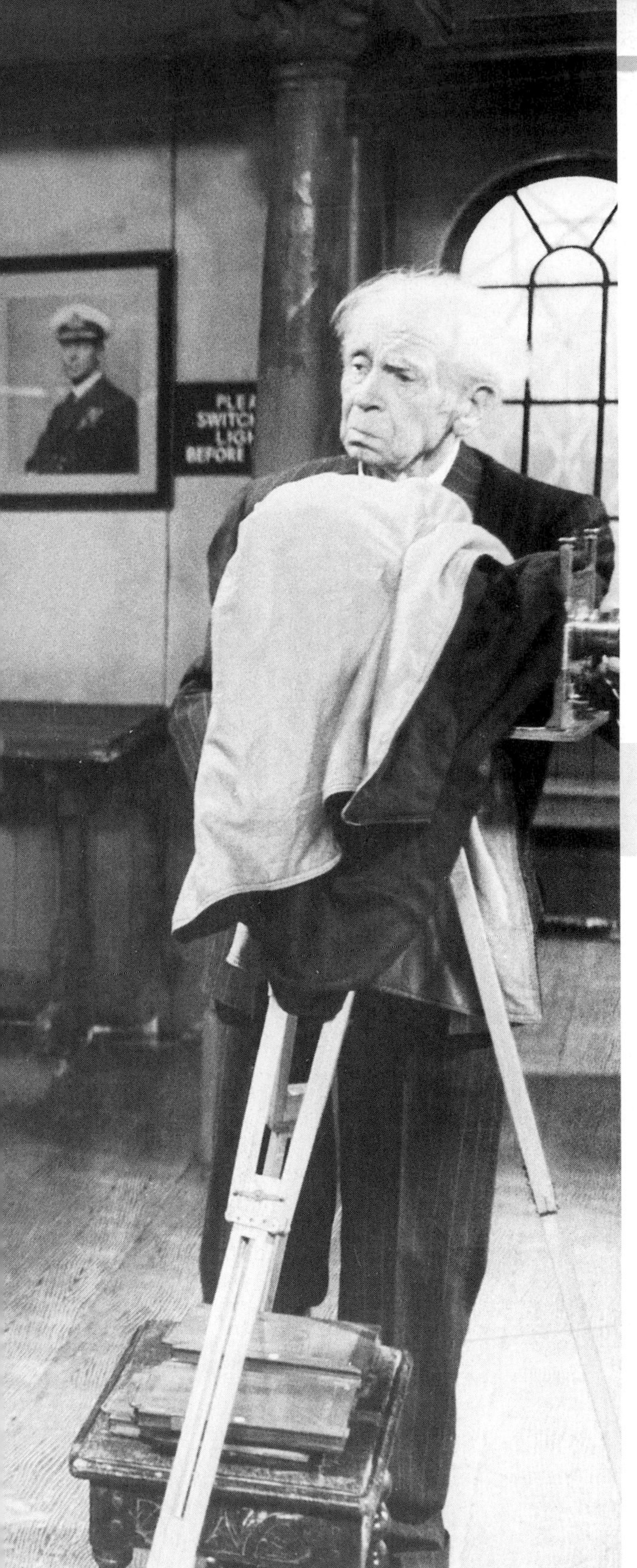

SERIES EIGHT **EPISODE SIX**

Recorded: Thursday 17/7/75

Original transmission: Friday 10/10/75, 8.00–8.30pm

Original viewing figures = 15.5 million

ARTHUR LOWE	CAPTAIN MAINWARING
JOHN LE MESURIER	SERGEANT WILSON
CLIVE DUNN	LANCE CORPORAL JONES
JOHN LAURIE	PRIVATE FRAZER
ARNOLD RIDLEY	PRIVATE GODFREY
IAN LAVENDER	PRIVATE PIKE
BILL PERTWEE	CHIEF WARDEN HODGES
FRANK WILLIAMS	VICAR
EDWARD SINCLAIR	VERGER
PETER BUTTERWORTH	MR BUGDEN
HAROLD BENNETT	MR BLUETT
GABOR VERNON	POLISH OFFICER
COLIN BEAN	PRIVATE SPONGE
BILL TASKER	FRED
MICHAEL BEVIS	THE POLICE SERGEANT
PLATOON	DESMOND CULLUM-JONES, MICHAEL MOORE, GEORGE HANCOCK, LESLIE NOYES, HUGH CECIL, FREDDIE WILES, FREDDIE WHITE, ROGER BOURNE, EVAN ROSS

THE FACE ON THE POSTER

• ANNIE OGDEN REMEMBERS •

'On the morning we were due to shoot scenes for "The Face on the Poster", I realised I had forgotten (or thought I had) to book the armourer. He was the man responsible for all the rifles, pistols, etc. The arms didn't go anywhere without him. As we were due to shoot a scene with the rifles that morning, I knew I had made a serious blunder and feared the wrath of David. My heart took a dive, along with my stomach. David Croft is a lovely, friendly, amusing man and a real professional, but he always expects the highest standards from his crew, so I didn't think he was going to be amused.

'I ran to a phone box (no mobiles or faxes then), rang London and, thank goodness, the armourer was there. Poor man. He said it was his fault: I had told him but he'd forgotten, so he'd set off for Norfolk right away. Panic over. That taught me always to double-check everything. He arrived in time and David was none the wiser – until now!'

The Face on the Poster

SIDE OFFICE

Mainwaring is writing, Wilson knocks and enters.

MAINWARING Ah, Wilson. Come in, sit down.

WILSON Thank you, sir. Still doing paperwork, I see.

MAINWARING **(Indicating paper)** Well, this concerns you particularly. The officers have been asked to send confidential reports on their sergeants.

WILSON Oh, really.

MAINWARING Now, I want to be absolutely fair, so here's a copy of what I've written about you. **(He hands Wilson a sheet of paper)** We'll go through it together and then you can countersign it, then you'll know I'm not doing anything underhand.

WILSON I'm sure you're not.

MAINWARING **(Reading)** Conduct – good.

WILSON Thank you, sir.

MAINWARING This is military conduct you understand. It has nothing to do with your private life.

WILSON **(Mildly amused)** I see.

MAINWARING Next – appearance. Now, I found this very difficult.

WILSON Oh indeed – why was that?

MAINWARING Well, I've known you many years – you're my chief clerk – in fact you're almost a friend. At the same time, as your commanding officer, I must be fair and impartial. So, you see what I've put down.

WILSON **(Reading)** Could do better. **(To Mainwaring)** How could I do better?

MAINWARING Well, look at you. Hair untidy, collar undone, cuffs undone.

WILSON But it's so much more comfortable. And I always do them up if anybody important is coming.

MAINWARING It's not only that, Wilson, your whole bearing is slack. You don't even stand like a soldier.

WILSON Don't I really? I had no idea.

MAINWARING **(Standing)** It's perfectly true, I assure you. You frequently stand like this. **(He stands with his arm slightly bent and his hand low down on his hip)**

Wilson laughs.

MAINWARING It's nothing to laugh about, Wilson. It only needs another couple of inches... **(He shifts his hand further up)** ...and you'll look like one of those nancy boys.

WILSON Well, I'm not a nancy boy.

MAINWARING We all know that. But the fact remains, you're supposed to stand like that. **(He shows him the correct position for attention)**

WILSON Anyway, I'm terribly sorry if I don't look smart enough. The last thing in the world I want to do is to upset you.

MAINWARING You're not upsetting me, Wilson. We're supposed to be soldiers, and there's a war on.

WILSON Of course, I'd forgotten. **(He reads on)** Parade ground manner – room for improvement. **(He laughs rather more than before)**

MAINWARING I'm glad you find it funny.

WILSON I'm sorry – it's just that it all sounds rather like a headmaster's end-of-term report.

MAINWARING I wouldn't know about that. We didn't have any of that public school nonsense at the school I went to. If you didn't pay attention, you got a clip on the ear. You jolly soon paid attention then, I can tell you.

WILSON **(Reading on)** General alertness – could do better. **(He laughs even more)**

MAINWARING I should take this seriously if I were you, Wilson. This could affect your entire Home Guard career.

WILSON I'm sorry, sir, I promise I'll try not to laugh any more.

MAINWARING I'm doing my best to let you down lightly. Do you know what I should have put under General Alertness? I should have put dozy.

WILSON Dozy?

MAINWARING Yes – dozy. You walk around in a dream. **(He grabs the paper knife, leaps up and, with a snarl,points it at Wilson's throat. Wilson is completely unmoved)**

WILSON Are you all right, sir?

MAINWARING There you are, you see. You took no notice – I could have been a Nazi about to cut your throat.

WILSON But you're not. You're you – waving a paper knife around.

MAINWARING **(Sitting)** You're throwing away great opportunities, Wilson. Strictly between you and me, big changes are in the wind. This little band of ours may grow to three times its size. These three pips of mine may become a crown.

WILSON You – a major?

MAINWARING Oh yes, indeed. I intend to increase our platoon to a company – and you would be in line for company sergeant major or even a second lieutenant.

WILSON But where are all the extra men coming from?

MAINWARING I intend to take time by the forelock there. You know what C.B. Cochrane used to say? Early to bed, early to rise – no jolly good if you don't advertise. I'm going to start a recruiting campaign.

Jones enters.

JONES **(Salutes)** Permission to speak, Captain Mainwaring?

MAINWARING Yes, Jones.

JONES It's falling in time, sir. Now, half the men are in the hall and half the men are in the yard. Now, would you like those in the yard in the hall or those in the hall in the yard?

MAINWARING In the hall, please, Jones.

JONES **(Speaking into the hall)** Those in the hall, fall in in the hall. **(Goes to the yard door)** Shan't be a minute, sir. **(Through the door)** Those in the yard fall in in the hall. **(He steps back into the corner to salute)** They're carrying out your orders at the double, sir.

Pike enters from the hall and pushes Jones further into the corner with the door.

PIKE Mr Jones – half of the men are in the yard.

Sponge and five more men enter from the yard, thus trapping Jones behind the second door.

SPONGE Excuse me, sir – we've got to fall in in the hall. **(To the men)** Fall in in the hall. **(They move through)**

MAINWARING Look – there's no need to come through this way.

JONES **(From behind the door)** You heard what the officer said. Fall in the other way.

SPONGE Right. Fall in the other way.

PIKE **(In the hall)** He wants us in the yard now.

They start to move through the office into the yard to cries of 'fall in the other way'.

JONES **(Appearing over the top of the door and saluting)** They're falling in the other way, sir.

Mainwaring reacts.

MAIN HALL

Mainwaring is addressing the platoon.

MAINWARING Well, that's the target – to treble our strength. Now, quite apart from persuading anyone we know personally to join us, I think a poster round the town would be a great help.

JONES I think we should do like Kitchener did, sir. The Home Guard needs you. **(He points)**

MAINWARING How remarkable. I thought the same, Jones. I don't have any suitable pictures, but I could get some taken.

FRAZER Now hold on, hold on. I don't think we should have an officer's picture at all.

MAINWARING Oh really, why not?

FRAZER It's not officers we need – it's men.

PIKE We ought to have a picture of Uncle Arthur.

WILSON Thank you very much, Frank, but I wouldn't want that.

MAINWARING No, I quite agree.

Wilson is standing with his hand on his thigh. Mainwaring draws attention to Wilson's pose.

WILSON I'm sorry, sir.

PIKE But Mum thinks he's ever so good looking. She says he's got piercing eyes and a granite jaw.

GODFREY My sister Dolly always says that beauty is in the eye of the beholder.

MAINWARING There's no need to be rude, Godfrey.

Godfrey reacts.

JONES Captain Mainwaring, why don't we vote in a secret ballet. **(Mainwaring reacts)** And whoever wins can have their picture on the poster.

WILSON That seems an excellent idea, don't you think so, sir?

MAINWARING Well, it's a compromise, I suppose.

FRAZER Whatever happens, we'll need a photo. I know a fine photographer who works very cheap.

MAINWARING Good – well, lay that on, Frazer - and Wilson, organise a secret ballot.

MAIN HALL

The Vicar is standing beside a trestle table. The Verger is beside him. A box is before them. In front of the Verger are several piles of voting papers. The platoon are standing the other side of the table.

VICAR All the votes have now been counted in the secret ballot and I shall now ask Mr Yeatman to hand me the result. Hand me the result, Mr Yeatman.

VERGER Here it is, Your Reverence.

VICAR **(Reading)** Captain Mainwaring has one.

They all applaud.

WILSON Congratulations, sir.

MAINWARING Very gratifying, I must say.

VICAR Just a minute, Captain Mainwaring. I'm announcing the result in reverse order. Captain Mainwaring has one vote.

WILSON I thought we'd all agreed not to vote for ourselves.

GODFREY I voted for Captain Mainwaring.

MAINWARING Thank you, Godfrey.

FRAZER Crawler.

VICAR Pike – two.

PIKE Thanks, Uncle.

VICAR Sergeant Wilson has four.

PIKE Well done, Uncle.

WILSON Frank, do be quiet.

VICAR Lance Corporal Jones – ten.

VERGER (To Vicar) Lance Corporal Jones is the winner.

VICAR I had managed to work that out for myself, thank you, Mr Yeatman. Lance Corporal Jones is the winner.

They all congratulate Jones.

JONES It's been a fair fight and I'm very happy with the result.

FRAZER What time do we come round for the sausages?

SIDE OFFICE

Wilson is sketching something on a foolscap size piece of white card. Pike enters.

WILSON Ah, Frank. Has Jonesey turned up to have his photograph taken yet?

PIKE No – but the photographer's here and he's getting everything ready.

WILSON Oh good.

PIKE Uncle Arthur – I think you ought to come and have a look.

WILSON Whatever for?

PIKE Well – it's not very modern.

WILSON Oh, I'm sure it'll be all right.

PIKE Please come and have a look, Uncle.

WILSON **(Rising and taking his card with him)** Really, Frank, you do make a fuss.

They move towards the hall.

MAIN HALL

A sheet has been hung up as a backcloth. In front are a couple of palms in pots. Centre is a stone bench with a fur rug on it. One empty stone plinth stands prominently beside it. Mr Bluett is concealed under the cloth of an old-fashioned plate camera on a tripod. Godfrey enters with an aspidistra covered in a cloth.

GODFREY Where do you want this, Mr Frazer?

FRAZER What is it?

GODFREY Sister Dolly's aspidistra. She said I had to be most careful not to let it be exposed to any draught.

FRAZER Shove it on the column.

Pike and Wilson are looking at the set up.

PIKE That's where Mr Jones is going to be snapped. It'll be like the one of my grandpa on mum's whatnot.

WILSON Yes, Frank, I do see what you mean. Where's the photographer?

MR BLUETT **(Under the cloth)** I'm under here. **(He emerges)** Good afternoon.

WILSON Hello, Mr Bluett. I didn't know you did this sort of thing.

BLUETT Oh yes. I had the concession on the West Promenade for years. I used to say 'Hold still my jolly holidaymakers', then I used to go click – dip it in the little tank and give it to 'em all wet for two bob.

FRAZER Aye – and it didn't fade until they got home a week later.

BLUETT Well, it was just a bit of holiday fun, wasn't it? This one won't fade.

WILSON Don't you think perhaps the background is the teeniest bit old fashioned.

FRAZER It'll fit Jones' face.

GODFREY I like it. I think it's very good class and genteel. I hate all those modern chromium-plated things.

Enter Jones. He is in his red jacket with medals and he carries his spiked hat.

JONES All right then, where do I stand?

BLUETT Over there please, Mr Jones.

PIKE Uncle Arthur, Mr Mainwaring's not going to like this – and he'll blame you.

WILSON Well, it's nothing to do with us, Frank.

PIKE You ought to assert yourself. Mum's always saying so and she's quite right.

WILSON Don't interfere, Frank.

JONES I want a very serious and grim picture like Lord Kitchener had. How about this? **(He points and looks grim)**

BLUETT **(Imitating the pointing of the hand)** Well – you'll have to keep that hand absolutely still for six seconds.

JONES Six seconds. I'm not keeping my hand still for six seconds.

BLUETT I don't blame you. I doubt if I could do it myself.

FRAZER Can you no use flash?

BLUETT No, I can't get the bulbs.

FRAZER What about flash powder?

BLUETT I tried it at a wedding once, and I must say the picture had a lovely quality, but the hall burnt down.

Frazer reacts.

JONES (**Putting his hand on his hip**) I'll have it like this. I can look like this for six seconds easy.

BLUETT Right – is everybody ready?

WILSON Take a deep breath and try to keep absolutely still, Jonesey.

BLUETT Now. (**He removes the cap from the lens**) One, two, three, four, five.

Jones sneezes.

BLUETT Oh, what a pity.

FRAZER Never mind – we'll do another one. There's no extra charge, is there?

BLUETT No – no extra charge. Hang on while I put in another plate.

JONES Mr Wilson – do you think I should have one without my spectacles? Kitchener never wore spectacles when he was being photographed. Come to think of it, he didn't wear spectacles when he wasn't being photographed.

PIKE Captain Mainwaring's not going to like it either way.

WILSON Do be quiet, Frank. I think without the spectacles might be better.

JONES Right. (**Takes them off**) How's this then?

FRAZER It's fine – as long as you hold still.

BLUETT Right, I'm ready.

WILSON Deep breath.

BLUETT Now. (**He takes off the lens cap**) One, two...

Cut to close shot of Jones. We hear a fly buzzing. His eyes follow the fly.

FRAZER Och – we can't have that.

BLUETT No, that's no good. His eyeballs will look like fuzzy prunes. One more for luck.

FRAZER Still no extra charge?

BLUETT No, but this is the last one.

FRAZER Do you hear that? You've got to hold still you old fool.

JONES (**Rising**) Don't you start on me. I'm a lance corporal. You mustn't call me a silly old fool. You can go on a fizzer for prejudice conduct.

FRAZER Sit down, shut up and hold yourself still.

BLUETT Now. (**He takes the lens cap off**) One, two, three...

Mainwaring enters from office.

JONES Squad, 'shun. (**Jones stands up**)

BLUETT You're making a monkey out of me. (**He goes under the cloth**)

MAINWARING What's going on, Wilson?

WILSON We're taking the photograph for the poster.

MAINWARING Oh, I see – who's the photographer?

BLUETT (**Head out**) It's me, Mr Mainwaring.

MAINWARING It's Mr Bluett, isn't it?

BLUETT That's right.

WILSON (**Aside**) Frazer fixed it – he works very cheaply.

BLUETT It's very artistic – come and have a look.

Mainwaring goes to the camera and looks through.

BLUETT It's upside down, but you soon get used to it.

MAINWARING (**Under the cloth**) I can't see you, Jones. Wave your hand.

Jones does so.

JONES Here I am, Mr Mainwaring.

MAINWARING (**Emerging and looking**) Oh no, I'm sorry, this won't do at all. (**He crosses to Wilson**) The whole thing looks ridiculous, Wilson.

PIKE I told you, didn't I?

WILSON Be quiet, Frank.

JONES Would it be better if I wore my hat, sir?

MAINWARING No, it's not your fault, Jones. Sergeant Wilson's whole conception is quite wrong.

WILSON It's not my conception. In fact, I was doing this little sketch in the office, and what I think we need is something like this. (**He points to the sketch**) 'You' – then Jonesey's face 'need a new hat' – and then we have a picture of a tin hat with 'Home Guard' on it. Then at the bottom 'Join the Home Guard today'.

MAINWARING That's very good, Wilson. We don't need all this paraphernalia. (**He indicates the photo set up**) All we need is Jones' face.

PIKE Well, that's easily done. Come round here, Mr Jones. (**He takes out his bayonet and goes round behind the sheet**)

WILSON (**To Bluett**) Could you come closer, Mr Bluett? We only need Jones' face.

Bluett starts to move his tripod nearer. Pike rips a hole in the sheet and sticks his head through.

PIKE How's this?

BLUETT Here – that sheet come off my bed.

FRAZER You can soon stitch it up.

BLUETT My wife will play merry hell when I take that home.

Jones puts his head through.

JONES Captain Mainwaring, do you prefer me with the glasses on or glasses off?

MAINWARING On, I think, please, Corporal.

Jones glasses business.

MAINWARING Right, are you ready, Mr Bluett?

BLUETT I'm ready. The trouble is, he can't keep still. I never knew anyone like him.

JONES I can keep just as still as you can keep still.

BLUETT Well, I don't have to keep still.

JONES Yes, well, I'll keep still this time, no matter what happens.

MAINWARING Right. Put your expression on, Jones.

Jones does so.

MAINWARING Go.

BLUETT One, two, three, four, five, six...

JONES There you are, I kept still.

MAINWARING You did indeed, Jones, well done.

BLUETT That was a very good one.

PIKE No it wasn't. You forgot to put the plate in.

BLUETT Damn. One more for luck.

PRINTER'S OFFICE

This is an outer office with a counter. The printing press is in the room behind the counter. Another printing press is heard operating through the door. The place is in chaos. The printer, Mr Bugden, wears an ink-stained apron and a green eye shade. He is on the phone. Fred, his young assistant, is by the printing machine. A police sergeant waits on the other side of the counter to talk to Mr Bugden.

BUGDEN **(Into phone)** I'm sorry – I'm not taking any more orders for printing wedding stuff. I'm only taking war work. **(He puts the phone down) (To assistant)** Fred, take your sandwiches off that machine, you'll have crumbs all over the type.

FRED **(Pointing to inside room)** Mr Bugden – that one's slowing down again.

BUGDEN Aye up, so it is. **(He rushes into the other room and we hear several bangs. The machine picks up speed, he returns)** You can't get the parts, you know. Now, where were we?

SERGEANT Well, there's this escaped prisoner of war poster. **(He hands the picture of the prisoner of war across with the copy)**

BUGDEN Oh yes, I remember. I wouldn't like to meet him on a dark night. How many do you want?

SERGEANT Well, say 50.

BUGDEN I'll do 'em soon as I can. Shove it over there. **(He indicates a pile of paper)**

SERGEANT Be all right here, will it?

BUGDEN That's it. You'll have 'em the day after tomorrow.

SERGEANT So long then. **(He exits)**

Phone rings again. Bugden picks it up.

BUGDEN Hello. **(To sergeant exiting)** Take care of yourself. **(To phone)** No, I'm sorry, I'm only doing war work. I can't do visiting cards. Well, you'll have to tell them who you are. **(Puts phone down)**

BUGDEN Look livel,y Fred. The big one'll be running dry.

FRED Oh heck. **(He runs into the side room)**

WILSON Good morning, Mr Bugden. I spoke to you on the phone.

BUGDEN Oh aye – you're the one with the posh voice. What was it you wanted?

WILSON This is the rough idea. **(He hands over his sketch and the cut out photograph of Jones)**

BUGDEN You need a new hat. I'm sorry, I can't take hat adverts. I'm only doing war.

WILSON Ah – well, it's a war hat. The Home Guard, you see.

BUGDEN Oh – well, I suppose Home Guard counts as war.

WILSON And this is the picture.

BUGDEN Well, you can't have many – it's the ink, you see – you can't get it.

WILSON Can't you really?

BUGDEN No – and you can't get the paper either.

WILSON That must make life awfully difficult for you as a printer.

BUGDEN Oh, it's murder. 'Ow about 50, the day after tomorrow.

WILSON Excellent. What shall I do with it?

BUGDEN Shove it over there. **(He indicates the same pile)**

Fred shoves his head through the outer door.

FRED She's playing up again.

BUGDEN Have you hit her?

FRED Well, I didn't like – not without you saying.

BUGDEN You daft ha'p'orth – you'll never learn.

They rush into the side room and start banging as Wilson puts the paper and picture on the pile.

• JO AUSTIN REMEMBERS •

'This was the first *Dad's Army* filming that I had set up as Production Manager, and every time I see the door of the Polish Club, I remember the fantastic house behind the rather bland front door, which was never seen on screen.

'The first day of location filming was kept as easy as possible with no great distances to travel from our base in Thetford, so Annie Ogden and I were driving around the town looking for a quiet street (for Clive Dunn to be chased down), and having found a neat cul-de-sac very close to the hotel, we then checked out a smart but unassuming door which she had spotted at the top end. The owners of the house invited us in and we just gasped at the interior – it was gorgeous. A huge hall open to the top floor with an elegant gallery running round the upper floors. The gardens at the rear were to die for – a huge oak tree, several hundred years old, and at the top end of the lawns a bridge over the river leading to a smaller garden. I think they had a stretch of fishing rights. The house had been in the family for years and I expect it remains so. They very kindly invited us in again after we had finished filming so that David and Jimmy could also see inside – I seem to remember all of us sitting in that wonderful garden drinking tea on a hot, sunny day and not wanting to leave. The owners were as charming as their property.'

SIDE OFFICE

Godfrey, holding a rolled up poster, is knocking at the office door. Mainwaring is in the office with Wilson, Frazer is cleaning the windows.

MAINWARING come in.

GODFREY Ah, Captain Mainwaring. The printer has sent round a sample of the poster.

MAINWARING Ah good. Let's see it. It's a very striking layout you devised, Wilson.

The poster is unrolled. It is Wilson's layout with the picture of the Nazi escaped prisoner of war in place of Jones.

WILSON It's not an awfully good likeness, is it?

FRAZER That's not Jones. That's a Nazi.

MAINWARING Can't I trust you with anything, Wilson? **(He picks up the phone)**

PRINTER'S OFFICE

Bugden is on the phone.

BUGDEN What do you mean the wrong picture. Fred, where's that Home Guard poster?

FRED Here it is.

BUGDEN You dozy arbuckle. That's the escaped prisoner of war. Where's the other one?

Fred shows the prisoner of war poster with Jones' face.

BUGDEN You've been and mixed 'em up. **(To phone)** We'll sort it out and see you get the right one.

MAINWARING Thank you very much.

BUGDEN **(Putting phone down)** You'll have to tear up the lot.

FRED I can't. I give these... **(Indicating P.O.W. poster)** ...to the bill poster last night.

BUGDEN They'll be all over town by now. You know, you're going to ruin my business.

Fred reacts.

BUGDEN Aye up, there she goes again.

EXTERIOR. STREET

Jones in civilian clothes, clutching a paper bag with half a dozen eggs in it, is walking with Pike.

PIKE What have you got there Mr Jones?

JONES Half a dozen eggs, Pikey.

PIKE Can I have one?

JONES No. I'm going to give them to Mrs Prosser. I look after her from time to time, but there's nothing in it. She's 83. **(He stops)** She's meeting me here, so you'd better be running along.

They are outside a building on which is a sign which reads 'Free Polish club' – the club being in smaller letters.

PIKE **(Pointing to the sign)** Ooh look. They're giving away Free polish.

JONES That's Free Polish. It's a club for Polish foreign soldiers.

PIKE Shall I wait with you?

JONES No – you run along.

PIKE Can I have an egg then?

JONES Oh – all right. **(He gives him one)**

PIKE Thanks. Bye bye.

Pike goes. Jones turns and sees the poster on the wall. It reads 'escaped prisoner of war', followed by Jones' face. Then 'this man is dangerous'. In a smaller box it reads 'notify your nearest police station or military headquarters'. Jones sees the picture. A Polish officer comes out of the club in the Polish officer's uniform with jack boots and swagger cane. He notices the poster. In halting English he reads.

POLISH OFFICER Escaped prisoner of war. This man is dangerous. Ugly-looking swine. **(He looks at Jones. Jones looks at him. Jones starts to whistle. Jones starts to walk up the street. Polish officer follows him, keeping in step. Jones stops. Polish officer stops. Jones moves on. Polish officer moves on. Jones quickens his pace, Polish officer quickens his pace. Jones runs)**

POLISH OFFICER Stop or I shoot. **(He fires his revolver into the air)**

Jones falls over. The eggs break.

OFFICE OF POLISH PRISONER OF WAR CAMP COMMANDANT

Jones is sitting, guarded by two Polish privates.

POLISH OFFICER If you had been here in my camp, my friend, you would not have escaped so easily. Now, who are you?

JONES I keep telling you – my name is Jack Jones.

POLISH OFFICER **(Banging the desk with his swagger cane)** Lies, lies, lies.

JONES It's the truth. I'm a butcher. I'm a purveyor of high quality meat to the gentry, families waited on daily.

POLISH OFFICER Lies, lies, lies. **(Banging the desk again)**

JONES You're not half making a mess of your desk. It's a nice bit of mahogany and you're not taking care of it.

POLISH OFFICER Silence!

JONES Sorry.

POLISH OFFICER Now, I shall ask the question a different way. **(He points to the picture on the poster)** Who is that?

JONES That's me.

POLISH OFFICER So, you admit it?

JONES Me – Jones the butcher.

POLISH OFFICER **(Putting the cane under his nose)** You try to be funny with me and it will be very very bad for you.

JONES Do you mind if I get on the phone to my solicitor?

POLISH OFFICER Silence!

JONES You're not supposed to talk to me like that. I'm treasurer of the Darby and Joan Club.

POLISH OFFICER Where did you get that moustache?

JONES My moustache? I've had it ever such a long time.

POLISH OFFICER Concealed in your bunk, eh. It is false – admit it. **(He seizes the moustache and pulls)**

JONES **(Yells)** 'Ere, you wait till I tell Mr Mainwaring what you've done. He'll have you on a fizzer.

Phone rings. Polish officer answers it.

POLISH OFFICER Ah, major. Thank you for ringing back. I have your escaped prisoner. You had better please pick him up because I do not want him teaching my prisoners bad habits. Not until Wednesday week, eh. Very well. I shall keep him here and we shall make him very welcome. **(To the guards)** Put him in the compound with the others.

MAIN HALL

Enter Warden. He crosses quickly. He has the poster with him.

WARDEN Where's Mainwaring? I can't wait to see his face when he claps eyes on this. **(He barges into the office)**

OFFICE

The same crowd as before are there, including Pike.

WARDEN Here, Napoleon, look at this – I tore it off a wall. **(He shows Jones' P.O.W. poster)**

MAINWARING Great Scott! Wilson, you've mixed up the photographs.

WILSON It was nothing to do with me.

MAINWARING Can't you get anything right?

Bluett enters from the outside door.

BLUETT Excuse me. I don't know if it's any interest to you, but I was in the town half an hour ago and I see Mr Jones driven off in a truck by a lot of Polish soldiers – I expect you know about it, but I just came to make sure.

WARDEN **(Laughing)** Oh, that's good. Those Poles run one of the prisoner of war camps. They'll have seen that notice and carted him off.

MAINWARING Wilson, we've got to get him out of there.

WARDEN What are you going to do – dig a tunnel?

MAINWARING Right, into Jones' van and we'll drive down there straight away.

FRAZER Hold on, hold on – Jones has the key.

PIKE We could push.

WILSON Don't be silly, Frank.

WARDEN I'll drive you in my delivery van. I wouldn't miss this for the world.

They start out of the door.

TELECINE: PRISONER OF WAR CAMP COMPOUND

Jones, dressed as a German P.O.W. is standing in a group of five German P.O.W.s behind the wire.

JONES It's all a mistake, you know, I shouldn't be here. They don't listen to you, them Poles.

P.O.W. spits. Cut to long shot of Hodges' van arriving.

JONES Mr Mainwaring, Mr Mainwaring, I'm over here.

Mainwaring and the section with Hodges approach the wire.

JONES They won't let me out, Mr Mainwaring. These here won't speak to me and him in there won't listen to me.

MAINWARING Don't you worry, Jones. We'll have you out of there in a jiffy. (**He sees the Polish soldier on the guard tower**)

MAINWARING Hey, you. Get me your commanding officer – and look sharp about it.

The soldier slowly levels his rifle at Mainwaring.

WILSON I think it might pay to be rather tactful.

MAINWARING Damned impertinence. I'll soon put him in his place.

WARDEN Go on, Napoleon, you tell him.

MAINWARING Hey you. Put that gun down and listen to me.

Soldier cocks the rifle.

COMMANDANT'S OFFICE

Mainwaring and the section, less Jones, are standing in front of the Polish officer. The Warden is with them.

POLISH OFFICER I think it would be a good thing if you do not beat any more about the bushes.

WILSON Captain Mainwaring wasn't intending to beat about the bushes. He's not like that at all.

MAINWARING Don't apologise to him, Wilson. He's the one who's in the wrong.

POLISH OFFICER You are the one who is wrong. You have no papers.

WILSON Yes, we're awfully sorry about that.

MAINWARING Oh no we're not. I don't need papers. I'm not some foreigner. I'm British. What's more, everybody in this area knows me.

POLISH OFFICER I do not know you.

MAINWARING Look, I've had about enough of this.

WILSON Steady on, sir.

MAINWARING Quiet, Wilson. I'll phone up my commanding officer and I don't mind telling you that when he hears about this, your feet won't touch. (**He goes to pick up the phone. The Polish officer puts his stick across it. Mainwaring reacts**)

POLISH OFFICER It will not be necessary for you to phone anybody.

MAINWARING That's better. (**To Wilson**) You see, they climb down as soon as you call their bluff. Now, I insist that you release my colleague.

POLISH OFFICER (**Tapping poster**) So, this man is your colleague. That is very interesting.

TELECINE: PRISONER OF WAR CAMP COMPOUND

The section and the Warden are in P.O.W. uniform behind the same barbed wire.

JONES You're a fine gallant man, Captain Mainwaring. I always said that through thick and thin you'd stand by your comrades, and you have.

FRAZER It wasn't gallantry, it was sheer stupidity.

PIKE Mr Mainwaring, do you think Mum will be allowed to send me a Red Cross parcel?

MAINWARING Go away, Pike.

GODFREY I wonder what time they serve dinner?

WARDEN It'll be fatty soup. They always have fatty soup in these places. I can't stand fatty soup.

MAINWARING Steady now – don't lose control.

Wilson starts to laugh.

MAINWARING What do you find so funny, Wilson?

WILSON It was just a thought. Do officers have confidential reports?

MAINWARING Oh yes – it's the same for everyone.

WILSON I wonder what the colonel will say on yours when he hears about all this?

MAINWARING Wilson, you're doing it with both hands now.

Wilson is standing with both hands on his thighs.

My Brother and I

CHRISTMAS SPECIAL

Recorded: Friday 23 & Saturday 24/5/75

Original transmission: Friday 26/12/75, 6.05–6.45pm

Original viewing figures = 13.6 million

ARTHUR LOWE .... CAPTAIN MAINWARING
JOHN LE MESURIER .... SERGEANT WILSON
CLIVE DUNN................................ LANCE CORPORAL JONES
JOHN LAURIE .... PRIVATE FRAZER
ARNOLD RIDLEY .... PRIVATE GODFREY
IAN LAVENDER .... PRIVATE PIKE
BILL PERTWEE................................ CHIEF WARDEN HODGES
FRANK WILLIAMS .... VICAR
EDWARD SINCLAIR.. VERGER
PENNY IRVING... CHAMBERMAID
ARNOLD DIAMOND .... MAJOR-GENERAL
COLIN BEAN .... PRIVATE SPONGE
PLATOON .... DESMOND CULLUM-JONES, GEORGE HANCOCK,
.... MICHAEL MOORE, FREDDIE WHITE, EVAN ROSS,
.... LESLIE NOYES, ROGER BOURNE, FREDDIE WILES, HUGH CECIL

• BILL PERTWEE REMEMBERS •

'This episode was one of the best in the series. Arthur Lowe's performance as Mainwaring *and* his inebriated brother was wonderful. The brother, a travelling salesman of carnival novelties, was the complete opposite of Mainwaring's organised and slightly pompous style: he's full of fun and jolly japes, particularly when he's had a drink or two.

'The portrayal of the brother gave Arthur scope for his comic genius. I had a particularly privileged view of Arthur's performance in this episode because I was behind the camera for most of it, giving him his eye line and cues for whichever character he was playing. If he was George Mainwaring I was being his brother, Barry, and vice versa. It really was a great education to watch the little added subtleties and thoughtful touches that Arthur brought to both characters. I always admired his performances but I think those in "My Brother and I" were just wonderful.'

My Brother and I

MAIN HALL. DAY

The platoon, less Frazer and Wilson, double in, led by Mainwaring. They are all exhausted – Mainwaring most of all.

MAINWARING Come on – keep it up. Double mark time – up, up, up, up. Get 'em up, Godfrey. Platoon, halt. Steady now – stand up straight. Stand still, Jones.

JONES I'm sorry, Mr Mainwaring. My spirit is willing, but my body's slung it in.

MAINWARING You'll have to run a jolly sight faster than that if Hitler comes. **(Staggers himself)** Platoon – stand at ease. Now, before we fall down – out – **(He is gasping for breath)** – there are… one… or two… things… I want to say to… you.

PIKE I think you'd better sit down a bit, Captain Mainwaring.

MAINWARING No, I'm quite all right. I'd better get my notes. **(Mainwaring staggers towards the office)**

JONES Can I give the men a bit of a breather while you're getting them?

MAINWARING Yes, very well. If you think they need it. **(Goes into office)**

Platoon break up.

SIDE OFFICE. CHURCH HALL

Wilson is sitting down reading *The Hotspur*. Mainwaring staggers to his desk and collapses.

WILSON Are you all right, sir?

MAINWARING **(Still breathless)** Yes, perfectly all right. Those men, Wilson – they're badly out of condition.

WILSON Are they, sir?

MAINWARING Definitely. You'll have to take them on a series of cross-country runs.

WILSON I shall enjoy that.

MAINWARING What's that in your hand?

WILSON *The Hotspur*.

MAINWARING *The Hotspur*! Really, Wilson – I left you behind to answer the telephone. If you want to pass the time there are plenty of training pamphlets. You don't have to resort to schoolboy comics and penny dreadfuls.

WILSON Actually, I was reading this. **(He holds up a sheet of paper)** It's in young Frank's writing.

MAINWARING Give it to me.

WILSON **(Handing it over)** It's a sort of article about the Home Guard. I found it rather amusing.

MAINWARING **(Reading the first paragraph swiftly)** Amusing? I think it's disgraceful. I'm going to nip this sort of thing in the bud once and for all. Fall the men in, Wilson.

WILSON Yes, sir. **(He goes swiftly into hall)**

Mainwaring rises and staggers.

CHURCH HALL

WILSON Right – fall in, everybody.

JONES Fall in like the sergeant says – you heard the sergeant. Fall in. Fall in. The men are fallen in, sir, like the sergeant says.

MAINWARING Thank you, Jones. Squad, 'shun.

They do, Jones is late.

MAINWARING Stand at ease. Hurry up, Jones.

Jones stands at ease.

MAINWARING Good.

Jones reacts.

MAINWARING Pay attention. Now, Private Pike – what is this?

PIKE Here, where did you get that?

MAINWARING Never mind where I got it. What is it?

PIKE It's an article I'm writing for a competition. How did you get hold of it?

WILSON You left it in your *Hotspur*, Frank.

PIKE You've no business to touch my *Hotspur* – I haven't read it yet.

JONES Permission to speak, sir? I'm supposed to have Private Pike's *Hotspur* before Sergeant Wilson.

WILSON I only glanced at it, Jones.

JONES I always have it after Pike.

MAINWARING Quiet. Wilson, I want you to read it.

WILSON What? *The Hotspur*?

MAINWARING No, no, the article. Read it out loud.

PIKE That's not fair, it's private.

MAINWARING Silence in the ranks. Carry on, Wilson.

WILSON **(Reading)** 'My name is Frank Pike. I am a private in the Home Guard.' That should be g-U-a-r-d, Frank.

MAINWARING Never mind about the spelling, read on.

WILSON 'Me and the lads will soon spot any parachutists who land in our district, especially if he lands in a pub. The other night we started at The Dog and Partridge and we made sure there were no parachutists in 11 pubs in two hours. By that time we were all soozled.'

PIKE Sozzled.

MAINWARING Quiet, Pike.

WILSON 'The sergeant is my Uncle. I can do what I like with him'.

MAINWARING Disgraceful.

WILSON 'The officer is a bit of an old...'.

MAINWARING Right – we've heard enough. Now, I'm not going to go into your shameful conduct in writing this, Pike. You've let the side down and I expect you feel pretty rotten about it. I don't doubt also that your mother will have plenty to say when I tell her. What concerns me is the subject. This is the sort of story about the Home Guard we get from the comedians on the wireless.

Wilson laughs. Mainwaring reacts.

MAINWARING It's not true. My unit is a hand-picked body of ruthless fighting men.

Godfrey reacts.

MAINWARING During the time I've been in command, I've tried to set an example of sobriety and devotion to duty. I don't want to hear any more tales of spongers, drunkards and four-ale bars.

GODFREY Captain Mainwaring, I usually wait outside.

Mainwaring reacts.

JONES Permission to speak, sir? You shouldn't be too downcast and trodden about what young Pike has written. Since days of yore – soldiers and drink have always gone together like chalk and cheese.

MAINWARING That's no excuse for my men to go swilling around in beer.

JONES When we was in the Sudan, we used to drink arak. Half a pint of that and you didn't know whether you was coming or going. Mind you, we didn't do much coming and going, so it didn't matter a lot.

MAINWARING Well, let me make it quite clear – I don't want ever again to hear of troops under my command drinking. Now, the Home Guard officers in this district are giving a sherry party for local dignitaries and the officers of surrounding units. I've offered to be the host, and the offer has been accepted. We shall use this hall, and Jones' section will volunteer to provide stewards, etc. Er, Jones – bring your section into the office.

Jones' section start to move towards the office.

MAINWARING Sponge – your men will patrol from the gasworks to the Novelty Rock Emporium – and no drinking, mind.

SPONGE Not a drop will touch our lips, Captain Mainwaring.

MAINWARING Right – move.

Sponge's lot prepare for patrol.

SIDE OFFICE

Cut to office. The rest are assembled. Mainwaring enters.

MAINWARING Right – are we all here?

WILSON Frazer isn't back yet. He's gone to Eastgate to see a client.

PIKE Mr Croxton.

MAINWARING I see. He'll probably be delayed some time. Mr Croxton is a bit of a chatterbox.

JONES He won't do much chatting in the box Mr Frazer's going to put him in.

Mainwaring reacts.

JONES He might rattle a bit.

MAINWARING I don't think that joke's in very good taste.

Jones reacts.

MAINWARING Wilson, put Frazer down as a steward. He can hand round drinks. You can be on the door, Jones.

JONES Yes, sir – I shall be on the door and I shall find out the names of the guests and tell them who they are – not the ones who've just given me their names, of course – they already know who they are – I shall tell the ones standing around who the other ones are.

MAINWARING Yes, all right, Jones.

GODFREY I could look after the cloakroom and coats and things.

MAINWARING Yes, good idea, Godfrey.

PIKE Can I serve the drinks, Mr Mainwaring?

MAINWARING No – you can hand round the cucumber sandwiches. You're too young to handle alcohol.

Pike reacts.

WILSON What would you like me to do, sir?

MAINWARING Oh just try and be pleasant.

Wilson reacts.

JONES Why don't you have Sergeant Wilson playing a little light music on the piano? That would be pleasant.

WILSON No, I don't think I'm good enough.

PIKE Don't you believe him, Mr Mainwaring. Mum says he has a touch just like Jack Penfold.

MAINWARING Who's Jack Penfold?

PIKE Jack Penfold used to play at the Peabody Rooms.

GODFREY I think that Sergeant Wilson's playing would add a lot of tone to the occasion.

MAINWARING Yes, very well then. You play the piano, Wilson.

WILSON Very well, sir.

MAINWARING Only not very loud.

Enter Warden, Vicar and Verger.

WARDEN 'Ere – what's all this I hear about you wanting the hall on Wednesday? It's my time and I need it for training.

MAINWARING I need it for an essential military purpose.

WARDEN Essential military purpose? You're just having a booze up.

MAINWARING It is not a booze up.

WARDEN Well, it's my night and I'm going to exercise my prerogative.

VICAR I'm afraid it *is* his night, Mr Mainwaring.

VERGER He's within his rights, and that's a fact.

VICAR I'll deal with this, Mr Yeatman.

MAINWARING It's essential that I have it, Vicar. I'm having this most important liaison meeting with army officers and local civic dignitaries.

WARDEN Local civic dignitaries? I haven't been invited. I'm not just a nobody, you know – I'm a bigwig around here.

VICAR **(Hinting broadly)** I'm sure you had every intention of inviting Mr Hodges, didn't you, Mr Mainwaring?

MAINWARING Well, yes, I suppose so. Of course.

WARDEN Oh good – I like a party – any women?

MAINWARING Certainly not.

WARDEN Well, never mind – we'll be able to have a few jars and a bit of a knees up, eh?

MAINWARING Bit of a knees up? This is a dignified social occasion.

JONES With musical cocktails and cucumber sandwiches.

WARDEN Cucumber sandwiches? They make you belch, don't they? Oh well, never mind – thanks for the invite, and you can have the hall. **(He goes)**

VICAR Well, thank goodness that's settled. I hope you have a very good evening.

VERGER His Reverence hasn't had an invite yet.

MAINWARING Ah no – well you're invited, of course.

VICAR Thank you, Mr Mainwaring – I shall look forward to it. **(He goes, followed by the Verger)**

MAINWARING Well, that's all settled then. Take your section, Jones, and continue with normal training.

JONES Yes, sir. My section, to continue normal training, in the hall – go.

GODFREY **(Before he leaves)** My sister Dolly makes very nice cucumber sandwiches – very dainty and moist. Shall I ask her to do some?

MAINWARING Thank you, Godfrey.

GODFREY Oh good, she will be pleased. **(Goes)**

MAINWARING A fine man that, Wilson. They all are. There's nobody I'd rather have beside me when the balloon goes up.

WILSON Weren't you a little hard on them about pubs and drink and so forth?

MAINWARING Oh no. I feel very strongly about it. I suppose it's the way I was brought up. My father was a member of the Master Tailor's Guild, you know.

WILSON Don't they drink while they're sewing?

MAINWARING Well, he would take a glass of sherry on festive occasions just to join in the fun. But all the family were the same. They all knew when to stop.

RAILWAY COMPARTMENT ON THE MOVE

The train is slowing. Barry Mainwaring is sitting in a corner, a fag droops from his lips. His mouth is dry – he fancies a drink. He takes out a flask. He has a quick look up and down the corridor and then takes a quick swig. He burps.

BARRY MAINWARING That's better.

The train halts.

VOICE OFF Eastgate. Eastgate.

The door opens. Frazer, in his full funeral regalia, gets in and sits opposite Barry. Barry regards him sardonically. Frazer sits.

BARRY MAINWARING Been to a funeral then? **(He laughs at his own joke)**

FRAZER I happen to be an undertaker.

BARRY MAINWARING Are you? You've got the right sort of mush for it.

FRAZER I've also got the right sort of fist to flatten that red nose of yours.

BARRY MAINWARING Don't be like that. **(Offers flask)** Have a drink.

FRAZER Certainly not.

BARRY MAINWARING It's real scotch.

FRAZER I never touch it when I'm going on a professional call.

BARRY MAINWARING Pity – it reaches the spot, I can tell you. **(He drinks)** Come on, change your mind.

FRAZER Well, truth to tell – I'm coming back from a professional call, so I'll accept your offer. (**He grabs the flask eagerly**) Schlans.

BARRY MAINWARING And you. You mustn't mind me. I say what I think. Speak the truth and shame the devil, that's me. Besides, in your trade, you need a miserable, sour-looking face.

FRAZER I do indeed. (**Swigs the flask again**)

BARRY MAINWARING You look right for an undertaker. In my line, I need a happy face. I'm a traveller. (**Takes flask back**) I don't travel in scotch either.

FRAZER There wasn't much in it.

BARRY MAINWARING Damned sight less now. Guess what I'm in?

FRAZER I've no idea.

BARRY MAINWARING (**Offering his hand**) Put it there.

FRAZER Oh – how do you do?

Barry has a handshake vibrator in his hand which buzzes.

FRAZER Aah!

Barry creases himself with laughter.

BARRY MAINWARING You've got it – jokes, carnival novelties.

Frazer reacts. He offers his lapel rose to smell.

BARRY MAINWARING Smell that.

Frazer does so and receives a squirt of water in the face. Barry again falls into hysterics. Frazer reacts.

BARRY MAINWARING That caught you! (**He offers his hand again**) Mainwaring's the name – Barry Mainwaring.

FRAZER Mainwaring. Could it be your father was a master tailor in Eastgate?

BARRY MAINWARING My dad a master tailor? That's a good one. He kept a little draper's shop in East Street with workmen's trousers hanging up outside.

FRAZER Is that the truth? Would you be any relative then of George Mainwaring, the bank manager?

BARRY MAINWARING You mean old Po-Face?

Frazer reacts.

BARRY MAINWARING He's my brother.

FRAZER You don't say.

BARRY MAINWARING I'm on my way to see him. I haven't worked the south coast for about fifteen years. All my trade's up in the north, so I thought I'd drop by and give him a surprise.

FRAZER He'll be pleased to see you, no doubt.

BARRY MAINWARING I shouldn't think so – not when he knows why I've come.

FRAZER I see. I've no wish to pry into your private affairs, you understand, but why is that?

Barry rises. He goes into corridor. He looks out. He returns.

BARRY MAINWARING Well, I'll tell you. **(Beckons)** Listen. When my old dad died – I'd been looking after him – right up to the finish. Well, he didn't leave much because he liked a drop himself on the quiet.

Frazer reacts.

BARRY MAINWARING Anyway, I always admired the gold half-hunter he used to wear on a chain in his waistcoat – across the bow front – you know how they did, some of them – well, when he popped off, bless me if old Po-Face didn't turn up and say 'I'm having that'. Well, the old man kicking the bucket had upset me and I'd downed a few and before I'd quite taken in what was happening, Po-Face had nicked it.

FRAZER Never!

BARRY MAINWARING True as I'm standing on this station. So, I'll book in at The Red Lion and then I'll stroll round and pay him a call.

FRAZER I'll be seeing him as soon as I'm off the train. I'll tell him you're coming.

BARRY MAINWARING Will you do that for me?

FRAZER Of course. It'll be my pleasure.

CHURCH HALL, SAME EVENING

Frazer, Godfrey, Pike and Jones are sitting round with their kit. They are on duty.

FRAZER You should have seen Mainwaring's face when I told him I'd met his brother, drunk.

GODFREY It must have been a terrible shock to him.

FRAZER May be so – may be not. I've always said there was bad blood in that family and I was right. They're boozers the lot of them – boozers.

GODFREY My sister Dolly won't have drink in the house except for the parsnip wine she makes. I tried it once. I fell over.

PIKE My mum got ever so cross with Uncle Arthur last time he had one over the eight. He kept following her about, trying to tickle her to make her laugh, so she gave him a black eye and locked him in the coal house. That stopped him.

FRAZER And do you know something else? Yon Mainwaring's father was no more a master tailor than I am – he was a draper, just a common draper.

JONES Well, there's nothing to be ashamed of in coming from humble stock. I come from humble stock. My dad was a humble butcher. He didn't have a sign above his shop like I have to say 'High Class Butcher – Families waited on daily'. He couldn't wait on 'em daily because he didn't have a fridge. When the meat come in, he had to bung it out quick before it went off, and he couldn't afford good sawdust either. He had to cover his floor with mangy second-hand sawdust with old shavings and old tintacks in it. But he was a God-fearing man and he had a good life.

FRAZER I'll tell you another thing – according to the brother, our Captain Mainwaring's no better than a thief.

GODFREY I'm sorry – I can't believe that.

PIKE No – Mr Mainwaring is as honest as the day is long.

FRAZER Maybe, maybe, all the same I'd give a whole pound to be there when they meet.

THE OFFICE

Mainwaring and Wilson are sat at the desk.

WILSON He sounds a bit of a character.

MAINWARING He's that all right. Anyway – the sooner he leaves Walmington, the happier I'll be, I can tell you. Not that I'm ashamed of him, mind, but we both had the same start in life and he just threw away his talent.

WILSON While you 'got on', so to speak.

MAINWARING Wilson – I want you to picture two boys – one popular, good at games, hail-fellow-well-met – the other one shy – lonely – standing in the corner of the playground. Alone. What one was I?

WILSON Hail fellow, well met.

MAINWARING No – standing in the corner of the playground, alone. Later on, he was surrounded by girls and the laughing crowd – I just had my books – but while he was getting sozzled, I had a clear brain and a sharp eye. Do you know, Wilson, I used to take a cold bath every morning.

WILSON Did you indeed?

MAINWARING Oh, yes.

WILSON I imagine that would clear the brain.

MAINWARING Indeed it does – and that way of life has got me where I am today – trusted, respected and not afraid to look the whole world full in the face.

The phone rings, Wilson picks it up.

WILSON Hello? I think it's your brother, sir.

MAINWARING Tell him I'm not here.

WILSON Can I help you? **(He listens and then covers the mouthpiece)** He says he wants to speak to someone called Po-Face. **(He listens again)** He says if you're not here, he'll come round and see you at the bank in the morning. Shall I make an appointment for 10.30?

MAINWARING No – tell him I'm busy all day.

WILSON I'm afraid he's rather tied up all day.

We hear Barry's voice through mouthpiece.

BARRY MAINWARING **(Off)** All right then – I'll pop round to his house.

MAINWARING No – Elizabeth would have a fit.

BARRY MAINWARING **(Off)** Or, better still, I'll come over tomorrow evening and watch him playing soldiers.

WILSON Yes, why don't you do that?

MAINWARING No, Wilson you fool – it's the sherry party. Tell him I'll come round to see him tomorrow tea time – at The Red Lion.

WILSON **(Into phone)** Are you still there?

CORRIDOR OUTSIDE THE BEDROOMS OF SMALL HOTEL

Mainwaring is wearing his bank clothes, bowler, gloves. He has a rolled umbrella. He approaches, led by chambermaid.

MAID Mind the carpet there – it's a bit worn – it's the war you see. **(She arrives at the door of Barry Mainwaring's bedroom)** I'd better make sure he's in a fit state – he was a bit rough after lunch. **(She knocks)** What name is it?

MAINWARING Oh, just say a friend.

MAID A friend – I see. **(She goes in)**

Mainwaring waits as we hear the voices off.

MAID **(Voice off)** 'Ere, wake up – there's a person to see you.

BARRY MAINWARING **(Voice off) (Waking)** You what?

MAID **(Voice off)** A man – he's a friend – he's come to see you.

BARRY MAINWARING **(Voice off)** Tell him to go and boil his head.

MAID **(Voice off)** Ooh – let go – give over. **(She comes swiftly out of the bedroom, smoothes herself down)** He's awake – you can go in.

MAINWARING Thank you very much. Here's a shilling for you. **(Hands her coin)**

MAID Thank you, sir. **(She smoothes herself down)** He's a case, he is.

Mainwaring enters the bedroom. Barry is lying on the bed opposite the door.

BARRY MAINWARING Oh – it's you. I thought it was.

MAINWARING Hello, Barry – it's been a long time.

BARRY MAINWARING Fifteen years.

MAINWARING By the look of things, you haven't changed.

BARRY MAINWARING Neither have you – the same.

MAINWARING Don't start that. What are you here for? If you're after money, you're out of luck.

BARRY MAINWARING There's no need to get your rag up. **(He sits up on the side of his bed to pour a drink)** Have a drink.

MAINWARING No, thank you.

BARRY MAINWARING **(Pouring the remains out of a bottle of brown ale)** Please yourself.

MAINWARING I should have thought 5.30 was a bit early – even for you.

BARRY MAINWARING Po-Face, look at you – rolled umbrella, striped trousers, billy-cock hat – you've got on, haven't you?

MAINWARING I'm the branch manager.

BARRY MAINWARING Branch manager – ooh!

Mainwaring is uncomfortable.

BARRY MAINWARING That must be a bit of all right. Do you get your hand in the till whenever you're a bit short? **(Indicating watch)** That's what I've come for. I want that watch.

MAINWARING Well, you're not getting it.

BARRY MAINWARING You know perfectly well Dad wanted me to have it for looking after him.

MAINWARING Looking after him! All you did was pour whisky down his throat.

BARRY MAINWARING Well, I kept him happy, didn't I? A damned sight better than you – sitting on the end of his bed, looking miserable. I told him jokes – he loved a good joke, Dad did. You should have heard him laugh when I was telling him about you and that girl who worked in the sweet factory.

MAINWARING She was the assistant manageress.

BARRY MAINWARING Was she heck! She was a rock puller!

Mainwaring reacts.

BARRY MAINWARING She used to sling a great dollop of sticky rock over the hook and pull it and then sling it over the hook again and then pull it again. I told Dad that when you tried to pull her, she made you sling your hook. He laughed so much he choked on his bismuth and he was a goner. He died laughing, Dad did.

MAINWARING All that is beside the point. I have the watch and I'm sticking to it.

BARRY MAINWARING In that case we'll talk about it later. My train doesn't go till 9.30 – I've nothing much to do. I'll look in at the party.

MAINWARING You'll do nothing of the sort.

BARRY MAINWARING Who's going to stop me?

MAINWARING I'll have you thrown out.

BARRY MAINWARING That'll be a nice little scene won't it? You standing there all pompous, and me yelling at the top of my voice. 'Po-Face has nicked me watch!'

Mainwaring reacts.

BARRY MAINWARING 'Po-Face has nicked me watch!'

MAINWARING Be quiet. Somebody will hear you.

BARRY MAINWARING They'll hear me all right.

MAINWARING If I let you have it, will you give me your solemn oath that you'll be on that 9.30 train?

BARRY MAINWARING You have my word as a gentleman.

Mainwaring starts to take off the watch. The chain sticks and he tugs at it.

BARRY MAINWARING Don't pull the chain too hard – you might flush yourself.

Mainwaring throws the watch on the bed.

MAINWARING Just be on that 9.30 train. **(He crosses to the door)**

BARRY MAINWARING Ta-ta. Don't take any tin money.

MAINWARING **(At door)** To think – you've come to this – **(He goes out and closes the door)**

Barry gives the closed door the two-finger sign and blows a resounding raspberry.

CHURCH HALL

Pike, Frazer, Godfrey are in white coats. So too are Sponge, Hancock and Desmond Cullen-Jones. They are lined up for a 'clean hands' inspection by Wilson.

WILSON **(Going along line)** Good, good. Pike, what's this purple stain on your fingers?

PIKE You don't want to worry about that, Uncle Arthur. It's a gobstopper – look. **(Puts out a purple tongue)**

WILSON Do get rid of it before Captain Mainwaring sees you.

FRAZER When he came back from meeting that brother of his, he fair bit my head off – just because I asked him to tell me the time by his watch.

GODFREY Will we have the pleasure of meeting Captain Mainwaring's brother?

WILSON No, I don't think he's been invited.

FRAZER Have you lost your senses, Godfrey, man? That brother's the skeleton in the family cupboard. If he comes to the party, Mainwaring will be exposed to the world as the fraud that he is. Do you hear me – exposed to the world.

GODFREY Oh dear – I hope there's enough cucumber sandwiches.

Jones enters, dressed in his red jacket with medals.

JONES Left, right, left, right. Sorry I'm late, Mr Wilson. I've been killing the moths. This is my announcing suit.

WILSON You look very smart, Jonesey.

JONES Where's Captain Mainwaring?

• JO AUSTIN REMEMBERS •

'My main memory of this is Arthur's sheer delight in playing the role of his brother, Barry Mainwaring. It gave him the opportunity to show off his marvellous comedy talent to those of the audience who only knew him as the pompous Captain Mainwaring.

'It was a long time ago, but I think we pre-recorded all the "Barry" scenes to avoid the time loss of costume changes for both Arthur and John Laurie. The scene in the hotel room when the two brothers met was obviously not done live. Bill Pertwee rehearsed with Arthur and stood in for him during the first pass of the video recording – feeding the lines off the camera. This was the first time that studio video tricks had been used, and Arthur was very intrigued by the whole set-up. The camera crew – who were seeing all this for the first time – had great difficulty in restraining their laughter and keeping "po-faces" during the recording.'

WILSON He's gone to escort the general from the colonel's house. We'd better take up our positions. I'll go to the piano, and you get ready to announce the guests, Jonesey.

Warden, Vicar and Verger enter from church entrance.

WARDEN Cor blimey – what's going on here? Old folks' clinic?

JONES You're not supposed to come in that way. You're supposed to come through the front door, and I'm supposed to announce who you are.

WARDEN We know who we are. Where's the booze?

WILSON Oh really. We haven't started yet.

GODFREY Would you care for a cucumber sandwich?

WARDEN Ooh, lovely. (**He takes the plate from Godfrey who is standing by him. The plate contains small, dainty cucumber sandwiches. The Warden takes two sandwiches and stuffs them in his mouth**)

WARDEN They're nice. (**He passes the plate to the Verger and takes two more. The Verger takes one and passes the plate to the Vicar**)

VERGER They're tasty.

The Vicar takes one and hands the plate back to the Verger.

VICAR I say, how delicious. (**He takes one more as he hands the plate back. The Verger takes one and hands the plate to the Warden then takes one more. The Warden takes three more and hands the plate to Godfrey**)

WARDEN They're very good.

GODFREY There's only two left.

WARDEN Pity to waste them. Get some more.

Godfrey reacts.

CHURCH HALL

FRAZER (**Running from the window**) Sergeant Wilson, the brother's coming up the drive. I knew it, he'll be exposed, exposed.

Sound of crashes off.

BARRY MAINWARING That's a damn silly place to put a fire bucket. (**Falls against coats**) Who's drawn these curtains? Evening, all. Is this where the party is?

JONES Can I have your name, sir?

BARRY MAINWARING I'm Barry Mainwaring – jokes, carnival novelties.

JONES My lords, ladies and gentlemen, Mr Barry Mainwaring, jokes and carnival novelties.

BARRY MAINWARING Is it a fancy dress do, then?

VICAR You must be Captain Mainwaring's brother – how very nice to meet you.

BARRY MAINWARING It is fancy dress – he's come as a vicar. He's got his collar on the wrong way round. Never mind, have an exploding cigar.

PIKE Uncle Arthur, he's tiddly. You've got to do something.

WILSON What can I do, Frank?

PIKE Go talk to him.

WILSON Yes, yes, of course. (**He crosses to Barry**) How awfully nice to see you – we spoke on the phone. Do you remember? We weren't expecting you.

BARRY MAINWARING Well, I thought I was a bit rough on him this afternoon, so I popped round to apologise.

WARDEN Apologise? You don't want to apologise to Napoleon.

BARRY MAINWARING You call him Napoleon do you? That's a good one. Do you know what I used to call him? Po-Face.

WARDEN Po-Face? That's good.

VERGER If you ask me, that just about describes him.

VICAR That'll be quite enough of that, Mr Yeatman.

PIKE (**Pulling Wilson aside with Jones**) We can't have him here – he'll show Mr Mainwaring up.

FRAZER (**Joining them**) More guests are arriving – he'll be exposed. It'll be the ruin of him.

JONES More guests are arriving. We mustn't panic, whatever happens, we mustn't panic!

GODFREY Do you think he might like to go to the dressing room to wash his hands or something?

WILSON Good idea, Godfrey. Frank, take him in there and Jones, continue announcing the guests.

GODFREY Would you care for a cucumber sandwich?

Pike goes swiftly to Barry, who is standing with the warden.

BARRY MAINWARING No – they make me belch.

WARDEN There – I told you so.

BARRY MAINWARING Anyway, this chemist shop had a girl serving behind the counter, you see.

PIKE Excuse me – do you want to wash your hands? (**He grabs Barry by the arm and drags him to the dressing room, which is at the side of the stage**)

WARDEN That's a pity – he was just getting to the fruity bit.

VICAR Speaking for myself, I'm very glad he was stopped.

Cut to door by the dressing room. Pike shoves Barry through the door.

PIKE The basin's in the corner, I'll get you a towel. (**He closes the door and locks it**)

CHURCH HALL

Jones is announcing the guests.

JONES My lords, ladies and gentlemen, Captain Doubleday and Major Shoesmith.

FRAZER **(To Jones)** It's Major Doubleday and Captain Shoesmith.

JONES Oh. My lords, ladies and gentlemen, the other way around –

Barry knocks at the door.

BARRY MAINWARING **(Voice off)** Let me out. You've locked the damned door.

PIKE **(To Wilson)** Quick, Uncle Arthur, play the piano. I know how to keep him quiet.

Follow Wilson to piano, the Verger is beside it.

VERGER Can you play 'In the Mood'? That's always popular at parties.

GODFREY **(Approaching major)** I wonder if you'd care for a cucumber sandwich? They're very nice – my sister Dolly makes them.

SIDE OFFICE

Sponge is presiding over the sherry. Pike enters hurriedly.

PIKE Excuse me – **(Grabs bottle)** Emergency call – **(He passes the major and pauses)** Mr Godfrey there has got some lovely cucumber sandwiches – his sister Dolly makes them. **(He passes Wilson)** Come on, Uncle Arthur, play up. **(Pike crosses to door of dressing room. Unlocks it and pushes the bottle in)** You can have this, but you must promise to be as quiet as a little mouse.

HALL ENTRANCE

Mainwaring enters with general and a group of senior officers.

MAINWARING Ah, here we are then – Private Frazer will take your hat, sir.

JONES Can I enquire your name please, sir?

GENERAL Anstrutter-Stevens, Major General.

JONES **(To Mainwaring)** And can I enquire your name?

MAINWARING Captain Mainwaring – oh, get on with it, Jones.

JONES My lords, ladies and gentlemen, Major General Anstrutter-Stevens and Captain Mainwaring Esquire. And some other people.

MAINWARING Thank you, Jones.

WARDEN Hello, Napoleon.

MAINWARING Good evening.

WARDEN I've just met your brother.

MAINWARING You've done what?

WARDEN Yes, I thought that would wipe the smile off your face – your po-face.

Pike joins Mainwaring.

PIKE Excuse me – **(He takes Mainwaring aside)** Captain Mainwaring, there's nothing to worry about. I've locked him in the dressing room and he's promised to be as quiet as a little mouse.

MAINWARING What sort of state's he in?

PIKE Drunk.

MAINWARING Fat chance of him keeping that promise.

PIKE Oh, I think he will. I've bribed him. I've given him a bottle of sherry all to himself.

MAINWARING You stupid boy.

PIKE What was I supposed to do, then?

MAINWARING Don't use that tone to me. Jones, Frazer – go in there and bring him out.

FRAZER But all these people will see him – you'll be exposed.

MAINWARING Then shove him through the window.

JONES Right, sir, that's what we'll do. You can rely on us, sir. We'll shove him through the window.

GODFREY Would you care for a cucumber sandwich, sir?

MAINWARING Go away.

Wilson is playing the piano. Pike crosses with Frazer and Jones.

JONES Mr Wilson, could you play something while we push Mr Mainwaring's brother through the window.

WILSON What do you suggest?

FRAZER Something loud.

PIKE You go ahead – I've got a better idea. **(He moves towards the side office)**

DRESSING ROOM

Barry Mainwaring is swigging the bottle. Frazer and Jones burst in on him.

FRAZER **(Looking at the narrow window)** We'll never get him through there.

JONES He might just make it sideways. Excuse me, sir, I wonder if you'd mind if we pushed you through that window sideways?

BARRY MAINWARING **(By now, well away)** 'Ere, what's going on? Is the landlady after me?

They propel him towards the window.

SIDE OFFICE

Pike has up-ended a tall, large, thin cupboard and is manoeuvring it through the door, helped by Sponge.

PIKE That's it – gently does it.

CHURCH HALL

Mainwaring is talking to the general.

MAINWARING I was reading a most interesting pamphlet yesterday on field craft. I was particularly taken with a chapter on range detection, of infantry fire by means of crack and thump.

During this, Pike has crossed with the cupboard, assisted by Sponge.

PIKE Excuse me, Mr Mainwaring. Collecting the empties.

Mainwaring continues to talk to the general.

THE DRESSING ROOM

Frazer and Jones are trying to push Barry through the window.

FRAZER It's no good trying sideways – he's as broad as he is long.

BARRY MAINWARING Is this some sort of parlour game like sardines?

Pike enters with box.

PIKE Here, put him in this.

JONES That's a good idea. **(Goes to Barry)** We've finished with the window now. We wonder if you'd like to try the cupboard? **(He leads him to cupboard)**

BARRY MAINWARING Ah, it is sardines. **(Sees Frazer)** I'm not hiding with him, am I? He's an undertaker. You're not going to saw me in half, are you? **(They push him into the cupboard. The back comes off and he walks straight round)**

PIKE Lock it, Mr Jones.

JONES There we are.

PIKE And the bolt. Make sure he can't get out.

BARRY MAINWARING Ah, you spotted me. Who's turn is it to go in next?

FRAZER Hold on – give me that hammer.

MAIN HALL

Mainwaring is talking to the general.

MAINWARING Anyway, it appears that if you know the formula, you can tell the actual distance from yourself to the chap shooting at you, by the time between the crack and the thump.

During this there is loud hammering.

GENERAL What on earth's that noise?

MAINWARING It's my sergeant – he doesn't play very often. That'll be enough, Wilson.

Wilson reacts.

GENERAL No, I mean the hammering.

Hammering stops.

MAINWARING I don't hear any hammering. **(He crosses to Wilson)** Wilson, go and see what's happening. **(Wilson goes towards the door. Mainwaring goes back to the general)**

THE DRESSING ROOM

The back is now on the cupboard.

FRAZER There that's it. Get him in.

They shove Barry into the cupboard.

BARRY MAINWARING Ah, my turn again is it? Soon comes round, doesn't it?

They shut the door. Wilson enters.

JONES Come on, Sergeant Wilson, give a hand. Right, all together – lift.

They lift the cupboard. Barry's feet are revealed as the bottom comes off.

JONES He's not much of a weight is he?

PIKE It's always easier when you all pull together.

They move towards the door. Barry's feet walk with it.

FRAZER Look!

JONES **(Looking at Barry's dirty boots)** He doesn't look after his shoes nearly as well as Captain Mainwaring, does he?

MAIN HALL

The Vicar crosses to Mainwaring.

VICAR Captain Mainwaring, I hope your men are not doing any damage in the dressing room.

VERGER His Reverence has heard some very strange noises.

MAINWARING Oh, nothing to worry about. Just a little domestic matter.

WARDEN I think the Captain is putting a very brave face on it, Vicar.

MAINWARING Yes, well, if you'll excuse me – I'm discussing tactics with the general.

WARDEN **(Raising his voice)** It's nice to know Captain Mainwaring's got a brave face as well as another sort of face, isn't it?

The dressing room door opens. Frazer, Jones, Wilson, Sponge and Pike emerge, carrying the cupboard lengthwise.

MAINWARING Ah, well done, lads. **(To general)** My boys are doing a bit of clearing up.

GENERAL Ah yes, good show.

They pass him.

GENERAL Getting rid of the empty ones, eh?

FRAZER This one's a wee bit full.

Mainwaring reacts.

MAINWARING Everything all right, Wilson?

WILSON I think so, sir. Could I have a word with you in private?

MAINWARING Yes, of course. Would you excuse me, general?

SIDE OFFICE

Mainwaring and Wilson enter. Godfrey is there.

MAINWARING What's happening?

WILSON He passed out. Jonesey will take him in his van to the station.

MAINWARING Well done, Wilson.

WILSON **(Producing watch)** I took this back for you, sir. I know how much you value it.

MAINWARING Oh, thank you, Wilson. I appreciate that. **(He is about to put it in his pocket)** No, on second thoughts, he hasn't got much. See him on the train, Wilson – give it to him and wish him well. **(He gives the watch back to Wilson)**

WILSON Yes, I'll do that. **(Goes to door)** I hope he'll appreciate it. **(Goes)**

GODFREY **(Handing sandwiches)** There's only one left – would you like it, sir?

MAINWARING No, thank you, Godfrey. The general is waiting to talk to me.

Mainwaring goes into the hall. Godfrey, after hesitating, eats the sandwich himself.

GODFREY Delicious. Dolly has a wonderful way with cucumber sandwiches.

CHRISTMAS SPECIAL

Recorded: Friday 10/12/76

Original transmission: Sunday 26/12/76, 7.25–7.55pm

Original viewing figures = 13.7 million

ARTHUR LOWE .... CAPTAIN MAINWARING
JOHN LE MESURIER .... SERGEANT WILSON
CLIVE DUNN .... LANCE CORPORAL JONES
JOHN LAURIE .... PRIVATE FRAZER
ARNOLD RIDLEY .... PRIVATE GODFREY
IAN LAVENDER .... PRIVATE PIKE
BILL PERTWEE .... CHIEF WARDEN HODGES
FRANK WILLIAMS .... VICAR
EDWARD SINCLAIR .... VERGER
PAMELA CUNDELL .... MRS FOX
JANET DAVIES .... MRS PIKE
OLIVE MERCER .... MRS YEATMAN
JOAN COOPER .... DOLLY
ERIC LONGWORTH .... MR GORDON (TOWN CLERK)
COLIN BEAN .... PRIVATE SPONGE
PLATOON .... FREDDIE WILES, HUGH CECIL, ROGER BOURNE, MICHAEL MOORE, EVAN ROSS, GEORGE HANCOCK, FREDDIE WHITE, JIMMY MAC, VERNON DRAKE
LITTLE GIRL .... JAYNE TOFFMAN
OTHER EXTRAS .... 12 LADIES AND 3 MEN IN BAZAAR SCENE

THE LOVE OF THREE ORANGES

• ERIC LONGWORTH REMEMBERS •

'Little did I think in 1972, when I first appeared as Claude Gordon, town clerk of Walmington-on-Sea, that it was going to put a morsel of jam on my bread in old age, or that an appreciation society would be holding conventions up and down the country twenty-odd years later.

'One thing I didn't realise was the fact that *Dad's Army* appealed to young and old alike and this was brought home to me one sunny Sunday in 1975. The stage version had just opened at the Shaftesbury Theatre and all the Longworths had attended the first night, with the exception of my seven- and eight-year-old granddaughters, who'd been promised a visit to a Saturday matinee. This was fixed for the Saturday following that sunny Sunday when, with Mum and Dad, they had come over to Guildford for the day. There was I, up a very large Bramley apple tree picking apples, assisted by my youngest granddaughter, Amanda, down below. There had been no mention of *Dad's Army* since their arrival when suddenly, out of the blue, Amanda said: "Grandpa, can I meet Pike?" I nearly fell out of the tree – she was only seven!'

The Love of Three Oranges

INTERIOR. CHURCH HALL. DAY

The men are heard outside, marching.

WILSON **(Out of vision)** Platoon, halt. Left turn, stand at ease.

One step is heard late.

WILSON Try and get with the others, Jones. **(Wilson enters. He crosses to the office and knocks on the door)** Are you there, sir?

MAINWARING **(Out of vision)** Of course I'm here.

WILSON The men have fallen in and they really look awfully smart.

MAINWARING **(Out of vision)** Good, I'll come and see them.

Mainwaring enters. He is wearing white over-trousers, a white smock and a white, balaclava-shaped hood. Wilson reacts.

MAINWARING Wilson, why aren't you wearing your snow camouflage suit?

WILSON Well, sir, I came here via the High Street and I didn't want to look a fool in public.

MAINWARING I'm wearing it – I don't look a fool. **(He puts his uncamouflaged hat on)**

Wilson reacts.

MAINWARING Why haven't you brought the men inside?

WILSON It seemed rather a shame, the Verger spent all yesterday polishing the floor.

MAINWARING We can't worry about that, we've got a war to win. Bring 'em in.

WILSON Right. **(He moves to the door)** Would you mind coming in the hall, please.

JONES **(Out of vision)** Platoon, 'shun. In the hall, quick march.

They file into the hall. They are all in various versions of white. They are dressed as if the costumes have been improvised from whatever is available in their various homes. Jones has used sheets, Pike has done likewise. Frazer wears a slightly yellowing Victorian wedding dress. Godfrey sports a white pierrot costume with black bobbles and black edging round the ruffle at the neck.

JONES Halt. Left turn. **(He salutes Mainwaring)** Men halted and left turned, sir.

MAINWARING Thank you, Jones. Stand at ease. Well done, men, I'm proud of you. We can now follow the example of our Finnish allies and become completely invisible in the snow.

FRAZER There's just one thing, there's no snow.

MAINWARING Silence in the ranks. The point is, we're prepared. **(He moves to Jones)** Very good, Jones. What have you done to your spectacles?

Jones has white-washed his spectacles except for a very small hole in the centre.

JONES Camouflage, sir – camouflage. I have very colourful eyes, sir. People frequently remark comments in the shop. Well, I thought to myself, if they shows up in the shop, how much more so much will they show up in the snow?

MAINWARING I don't think it's necessary, Jones. **(He is about to pass on when he sees something else)** Your nose looks rather odd as well.

Jones has a plug of cotton wool in each nostril.

JONES Cotton wool, sir – cotton wool. When I'm in action I get very worked up and fractious and my nostrils flare and have an angry, red hue. Now, they don't show up in the shop 'cos I don't get worked up and fractious – well, nobody does over meat and sausages, but if I get worked up and fractious in the snow, they'd be like beacons.

MAINWARING I think you're getting into the realms of fantasy, Jones.

He passes to Pike. Pike pulls down a Klu Klux Klan-type face hood which has been rolled up under his helmet.

PIKE Booh –

MAINWARING Stop playing the fool, boy.

PIKE **(Pulling the hood up again)** I'm not playing the fool. Mum wouldn't let me put whitewash on my face, so Uncle Arthur suggested this.

MAINWARING Is this true, Wilson?

WILSON Well, he has very sensitive skin, it runs in the family.

MAINWARING Whose family?

WILSON His family.

MAINWARING I see. **(He passes to Frazer)** What's this, Frazer?

FRAZER It's all I could find.

MAINWARING It's a wedding dress.

FRAZER Aye – it was my mother's. Hold on a minute. There's a veil. **(He pulls down a veil)**

Mainwaring reacts.

FRAZER It was in the attic – and, do you know this, Captain Mainwaring, a poor wee mouse had passed away in the bustle.

MAINWARING What do you think, Wilson?

WILSON I suppose we should be grateful he hasn't brought the bouquet.

MAINWARING Find him something more suitable.

Mainwaring passes to Godfrey.

GODFREY Good afternoon.

MAINWARING Who put you up to this, Godfrey?

GODFREY It's my pierrot costume, sir. When I was at the Army and Navy Stores, we formed a little troupe and did one or two shows for charity and called ourselves the 'Gay Gondoliers'.

MAINWARING We can't have this, Wilson.

WILSON I thought it was rather good, sir, except for the pom poms.

GODFREY I'm quite prepared to cut them off, I just wondered if you'd mind me waiting until the bells ring and the snow's coming down.

MAINWARING No, I can't have that, Godfrey. You'll have to dress properly like everyone else. **(To the rest)** All the same, a good turn out. In the event of snow, we shall merge into the landscape.

PIKE Mr Mainwaring, what happens if it snows and we've left our disguise back home?

JONES Permission to speak, sir? I think we should have power to go up to a house and knock on the door and say 'I hereby requisition your sheets' – and I think you should give us a certificate of authority.

MAINWARING No, I don't think that would be a very good idea, Jones.

Jones reacts.

PIKE Here – Mr Frazer knows when it's going to snow, don't you, Mr Fraze? His joints creak, don't they?

FRAZER Aye – the bones creak and groan like old ships timbers.

PIKE Well, when he hears his bones, he could ring us up.

FRAZER Who's going to pay for the call?

Enter the Vicar and Verger.

VERGER Look at that floor – just look at it. Three hours I spent on that – backbreaking....

VICAR Never mind that, Mr Yeatman. Captain Mainwaring, can I have a word with you?

MAINWARING Can't you see I'm busy?

VICAR We're all busy in our different ways, Captain Mainwaring. I just wanted to give you plenty of notice that you can't have the hall Saturday fortnight.

MAINWARING What do you mean? I may need it for a vital military purpose.

VICAR Well, I need it for a church bazaar. We're going to raise money for comforts for the troops.

MAINWARING Comforts for the troops – ah, that's a horse of quite a different colour. Why haven't I heard about it before?

VERGER The parish council only decided half an hour ago, that's why.

VICAR That'll do, Mr Yeatman.

MAINWARING This is just the sort of project that will get our wholehearted support, isn't it, Wilson?

WILSON I shouldn't be at all surprised.

MAINWARING With the Home Guard behind you, we can give this whole affair a much broader scope. Now, time's short, so we'll need to act very quickly. You must get all the most important people in the town to a meeting. We'll form a small executive committee and, of course, we'll need a chairman.

FRAZER **(To himself)** A chairman, now I wonder who that will be?

INTERIOR. CHURCH HALL. DAY

A long table has been placed in the middle. Mainwaring is in the centre. Wilson is next to him on one side and the town clerk is on the other. Pike is nearby. The Warden, Vicar and Verger are at one end, Mrs Fox and Jones have not arrived. Frazer and Godfrey are at the other end. Also present are Mrs Yeatman, Private Sponge and Mrs Pike.

MAINWARING Right, as chairman of the Executive Committee may I call the meeting to order? First, I would like to welcome all...

HODGES **(Interrupting)** Hang on a minute. Why is it every time we have a meeting about anything, you're the chairman? Who elected you? That's what I want to know.

MAINWARING It was all perfectly legal and above board. The steering committee elected me.

HODGES Oh, yes – well, who picked the steering committee?

MAINWARING I did.

HODGES There you are, it's a fiddle.

MRS YEATMAN If you ask me, it's always a fiddle.

TOWN CLERK Speaking as town clerk, I'm sure we're all most happy to have Captain Mainwaring as chairman, and I've got a meeting of my General Purposes Committee at half-past four, so can we proceed?

MAINWARING Thank you. Now, it might be as well if we examine the offers of services that... **(He is interrupted by Jones and Mrs Fox entering)**

JONES Sorry I'm late, Captain Mainwaring – I've been coupon counting.

MAINWARING Yes well, sit down.

JONES It's always coupon counting the last Wednesday in

the month. I really dread it, you know, and that's the truth. If it wasn't for Mrs Fox, I don't think I could carry on. She's very good to me, you know, Mr Mainwaring.

MAINWARING I'm sure she is.

MRS FOX I do the odd hundred and make him a nice cup of tea and things. It's the least you can do, isn't it?

MRS YEATMAN Can we get on?

VICAR Here, here.

SPONGE Here, here.

VERGER I second that.

VICAR Be quiet, Mr Yeatman.

MAINWARING Yes, let's get on. Wilson, what offers of help do we have so far?

WILSON Well, Mrs Yeatman has very kindly said she'll do the tombola.

MRS PIKE She always does the tombola.

VERGER That's because she's very good at the tombola.

TOWN CLERK On the other hand, if this year Mrs Pike wants to do the tombola –

MRS PIKE I don't want to do the tombola.

WILSON Then why did you mention it, Mavis?

MRS PIKE Don't you start, you lay on the sofa in your muddy boots last night, didn't you?

WILSON Mavis, please –

MRS PIKE Wet the antimacassar and tried to wipe it off didn't you? Thought I wouldn't notice.

PIKE I told you not to rinse it in the rose bowl, Uncle Arthur.

WILSON Frank, do be quiet.

MRS YEATMAN Can we get on?

MAINWARING Yes, perhaps I'll deal with the other offers. Give me the list, Wilson. **(Aside to Wilson as he takes it)**

You're going to rue the day you ever met that woman, you know.

WILSON I'm doing quite a lot of ruing this very minute.

MAINWARING **(Reading from list)** Mr Godfrey is providing a stall for chutney.

GODFREY My sister Dolly is giving three small jars of honey and quite a lot of wine – elderberry. You've tried it, haven't you, Mr Frazer?

FRAZER Aye – once. I have to say I found it totally undrinkable. No doubt some fool will buy it in the name of charity.

MAINWARING Yes – good.

JONES I would like to say here and now that I will donate a monster brawn.

MAINWARING A monster brawn?

JONES That's right, Mr Mainwaring. You can either sell it a slice at a time on paper plates or you could have a monster brawn raffle.

PIKE What sort of a monster is it made from, Mr Jones?

MAINWARING Quiet, Pike.

JONES Oh – and Mrs Fox will do fortune telling and soothsaying in a gypsy tent.

FRAZER Fortune telling did you say?

MRS FOX That's right, cards or ball – whatever takes your fancy.

FRAZER It's the work of the devil on consecrated ground – bad will become of it.

MRS FOX I only charge sixpence, Mr Frazer.

FRAZER Aye – well, it's cheap.

MRS FOX And each person gets five minutes alone.

FRAZER Aye – well, it's in a good cause and you're a well built woman. I'll take my turn.

HODGES Mr Chairman – point of order – what's Mrs Mainwaring going to do?

MAINWARING That is not a point of order, Mr Hodges.

HODGES I see – that means she's not doing anything.

MAINWARING On the contrary, Mrs Mainwaring will be contributing some lampshades.

SEVERAL VOICES Lampshades?

MAINWARING It's a hobby she has. She makes them out of all sorts of odds and ends. It passes the time in the shelter.

PIKE **(To Hodges)** So sucks boo.

HODGES **(Stands)** Now, listen –

MAINWARING Pike – another outburst like that and you'll be sent home.

Pike reacts.

HODGES He's a young hooligan, that's what he is.

MRS PIKE **(To Hodges)** Never mind about him, what are you going to do?

TOWN CLERK Yes, do let's keep to the matter in hand.

VICAR As a matter of fact, Mr Hodges has a wonderful surprise for us – haven't you, Mr Hodges?

HODGES Yes – and it's better than a lot of old mouldy wine and lampshades. I am donating three oranges.

ALL Three oranges.

HODGES That's right, three oranges. I bet none of you have seen them for years. You can auction them off.

JONES Where did you get three oranges?

HODGES Never you mind. They'll raise a lot of money, that's all that matters.

MAINWARING Yes, well, I'm sure we're all very grateful.

VERGER I second that.

VICAR Be quiet, Mr Yeatman.

TOWN CLERK There was a function at Eastgate last week – they had sausage rolls. Couldn't we have sausage rolls?

VERGER On behalf of Mrs Yeatman, one thing's got to be clearly understood. If we're going to have sausage rolls, we've got to have sausages.

MAINWARING Thank you, Mr Yeatman.

JONES Well, I haven't got none and that's the truth.

TOWN CLERK I think they used some sort of vegetable concoction, but the trick was they had puff pastry. They were very nice.

MRS YEATMAN You can't have puff pastry without fat.

MRS PIKE Anybody knows that.

MRS YEATMAN Men don't know it, they think you wave a fairy wand. They don't have to queue for hours.

JONES Well, there's no good queuing at my shop 'cos I've got no fat neither.

MRS FOX You just take him for granted, all of you.

HODGES What are you talking about? I wouldn't go into his shop with wellington boots on.

JONES You couldn't 'cos you're not registered with me.

MAINWARING Please, please don't let our discussion become heated, after all, we are only trying to raise money to send comforts to the troops.

PIKE I've got an idea – why don't we club together and send 'em Mrs Fox?

There is a stunned silence and a gasp from Mrs Fox.

MAINWARING Pike – go into the office.

PIKE **(Going)** I'm sorry, Mr Mainwaring.

The rest of the dialogue follows and rises to a general hubbub. The participants converge on the office.

JONES There was no call for that. Don't you upset yourself, Mrs Fox.

Mrs Fox weeps into his hanky.

MAINWARING **(By door)** Wilson – come here.

INTERIOR. SIDE OFFICE

MAINWARING Pike, how dare you? **(To Wilson)** This is all your fault, Wilson, you're too lax with him.

MRS PIKE **(Who has followed)** Don't you blame the boy, it's all happened since he's been with you lot. **(She starts to hit Pike)** I'll box your ears, as big as you are.

PIKE No, don't, I was only joking.

VERGER Typical, typical – young folk are all the same.

VICAR Be quiet, Mr Yeatman, I'm sure the boy didn't mean any offence.

HODGES Hooligan – that's what he is, a hooligan.

MAINWARING You'll go in there, Pike, and you'll apologise to Mrs Fox.

MRS PIKE And you'll wash your mouth out with soapy water.

Fade on general chaos.

INTERIOR. MAIN HALL. DAY

A row of stalls against the back wall as follows:

Godfrey and Dolly are setting out jams and bottles. Notice reads 'Home made honey, jams, wines and chutney'.

Frazer's silhouette stall. There are several crude silhouettes hanging up. Frazer is busy setting out his black paper, scissors, paper, etc. Notice reads 'Expert silhouettes while you wait, sixpence'.

Mrs Pike is arranging her jumble stall with a lady helper. Notice reads 'Jumble sale'.

Jones has a stall with a huge brawn on it. Notice reads 'Raffle for monster brawn, tickets one penny'.

Mrs Yeatman is behind a tombola stall. Notice reads 'Tombola'.

There is an empty stall for Mrs Mainwaring's lampshades.

A striped tent, notice reads 'Madame Renard, fortunes told, sixpence and a shilling'.

Another stall with Hodges behind it, setting up his oranges.

The Vicar and Verger are fussing around a stall with two ladies behind it. Notice reads 'Afternoon teas'.

Everyone is in civilian clothes. Jones and Pike are gazing at the brawn.

JONES Look at that, Pikey, isn't it a picture?

PIKE I've never seen anything like it. It certainly is a monster brawn.

Mrs Fox pokes her head out from the tent. She is dressed in gypsy costume.

MRS FOX Oh, Mr Jones –

JONES **(Crossing to her)** Yes, Mrs Fox.

MRS FOX I seem to have lost one of my globes.

JONES Did you have them both when you came in?

MRS FOX Of course I did.

JONES Well, can't you just make do with one?

MRS FOX No, of course not. I've only got the small one for the sixpenny fortunes. People expect the larger one for the shilling fortunes.

JONES Well, haven't you got anything else you can look into?

PIKE **(Coming into picture)** I could run home and get my Mum's goldfish bowl.

JONES You can't expect Mrs Fox to tell fortunes looking into a goldfish bowl with fish swimming round going glub glub.

Frazer comes into the picture with the globe.

FRAZER Here, woman, is this yours?

MRS FOX Oh thank you, Mr Frazer.

FRAZER You left it amongst my things.

MRS FOX I'm sorry. **(She takes the globe)**

FRAZER Why do you call yourself Madame Renard?

MRS FOX It's French for Mrs Fox. **(She goes in)**

JONES There's no doubt about it, Mrs Fox is very good with the continental touch.

Mainwaring and Wilson come out of the office.

MAINWARING Everything all right, Godfrey?

GODFREY Yes, thank you, Mr Mainwaring. By the way, my sister Dolly and I thought it would be a good idea if we let people taste the wine first so that they would know what they were buying.

DOLLY Would you like to try some, Mr Mainwaring? It's my best elderberry. **(She pours out a glass)**

MAINWARING What, at two o'clock in the afternoon, oh no.

DOLLY Perhaps Mr Wilson would like to try some?

WILSON Oh how nice, thank you. **(He takes a mouthful, sucks in his breath between his teeth, rolls it round his mouth and swallows)**

MAINWARING What's all that palaver for?

WILSON That's the correct way to taste wine. Frenchmen always do it like that. One should, of course, spit it out.

MAINWARING We don't want any of those dirty foreign habits here, Wilson.

They pass on to the jumble stall.

MAINWARING You've got a lot of stuff there, Mrs Pike.

MRS PIKE Yes, Mr Mainwaring, people have been very generous.

Mainwaring points to a pink rowing cap.

MAINWARING Is that a man's cap?

MRS PIKE Yes, pretty isn't it? **(She picks it up)**

MAINWARING What on earth sort of man would wear a nancy thing like that?

MRS PIKE Arthur gave it to me.

MAINWARING Is that your cap, Wilson?

WILSON Yes, I won it for rowing.

MAINWARING They gave you a pink cap for a manly sport like rowing?

WILSON It's quite common in public schools to wear pink caps.

MAINWARING Extraordinary. **(He passes on to Frazer's stall)** Silhouettes, eh, that's quite a novelty, Frazer.

FRAZER Aye, would you like me to do you? Only sixpence.

MAINWARING Well, anything to help the war effort. **(He hands over the money)**

FRAZER Keep still then. **(He starts snipping at the black paper)**

Jones comes into shot.

JONES Captain Mainwaring, my monster's gone all shiny.

MAINWARING **(Turning)** What did you say, Jones?

FRAZER Keep still!

JONES It's too hot in here for it, it's starting to melt. What am I going to do?

MAINWARING It's perfectly simple, Jones, just take it outside in the yard and bring it in at intervals during the afternoon for people to see.

JONES Where would we all be without your organising ability, Captain Mainwaring? Come on, Pikey, give me a hand with the brawn.

PIKE Right, Mr Jones.

JONES Gangway for the brawn. Don't joggle it, Pikey, it's wobbly enough as it is. Gangway.

Frazer holds up the finish silhouette. It looks like a gingerbread man.

FRAZER There you are, it's you to a tee.

WILSON It's quite a good likeness, sir.

MAINWARING Rubbish, it's awful, it looks like a round lump.

FRAZER Well, you are a round lump.

MAINWARING I didn't pay sixpence to be insulted.

FRAZER I think you're getting a bargain.

MAINWARING If you were in uniform, Frazer, I should charge you with insulting behaviour. **(He moves on to the empty stall)** What's this stall doing empty, Wilson?

WILSON That's the stall for your wife's lampshades, sir.

MAINWARING Oh... yes... erm, will you come into the office a moment, Wilson.

They both cross to the office. Hodges has set his oranges on a plinth with green crepe paper.

HODGES How's that, Vicar? Don't they make your mouth water?

VICAR A rare sight indeed, Mr Hodges. Do you know, I haven't seen an orange for over two years.

VERGER If my memory serves me right, Your Reverence, that was just before the war in the scout's production of 'Good King Charles' – you played Nell Gwynn.

VICAR Ah, happy days.

INTERIOR. SIDE OFFICE. DAY

Mainwaring sits.

MAINWARING Sit down, Wilson. (**Wilson sits**) It's about my wife's lampshades.

WILSON Oh yes, sir.

MAINWARING You see, she's been making them for a year now, well, I didn't like to say anything to her – she's very sensitive to criticism, you know. Anyhow, the fact is, Wilson, they're rather unusual.

WILSON Unusual?

MAINWARING Not to put too fine a point on it, bizarre, but she was determined to bring them down here today to help out.

Wilson laughs.

MAINWARING What's the joke?

WILSON I was just thinking, sir, the bizarre for the bazaar.

Pause. Mainwaring stares hard.

WILSON You see, it's a play on... A play.

MAINWARING Yes, yes, I realised of course that her lampshades were bound to arouse a certain amount of ribald comment from the more plebeian factions in the town, but I thought, she's my wife and it's my duty to stand by her.

WILSON Very noble of you, sir.

MAINWARING Then came the incident of the bath.

WILSON The bath?

MAINWARING Yes, you see our bath at home is rather old, the enamel is chipped and there's a nasty brown stain underneath the taps. Well, I was in the ironmonger's yesterday and I saw this bath enamel, so I bought some. I thought I'd give Elizabeth a little surprise. Anyhow, this morning, while she was out shopping, I gave the bath a coat of the enamel.

WILSON Did it work?

MAINWARING Up to a point, yes, but it takes six hours to dry and unfortunately Elizabeth is very unpredictable – after all, how was I to know she'd take a bath in the middle of the day? Well, I was sitting in my study when it happened.

WILSON What happened?

MAINWARING I heard a scream coming from the bathroom. I dashed in and there she was, standing in the bath. The enamel paint had come away in a single sheet and was draped round her like a... like a....

WILSON Enamel skirt.

MAINWARING Quite, of course, there was hell to pay, we were in a bit of a quandary on how to get it off. We couldn't use chemicals, and pumice stone was quite of the question.

WILSON What about sandpaper?

MAINWARING No, no, no – very delicate skin, you know. So, I just pulled off all the bits there were hanging down and told her she'd have to let the rest wear off. Then she started to get hysterical, so to calm her down I said 'Don't worry, dear, no one's going to see you without any clothes on'.

WILSON Did it do any good?

MAINWARING Not really, she ran into the bedroom and locked the door. So she won't be coming down here this afternoon.

WILSON Oh, I am sorry, sir.

MAINWARING (**Getting up**) There is just a possibility that the situation can be retrieved. You see, if I can buy one of Hodges' oranges, it might calm her down. Elizabeth is very partial to oranges.

WILSON Well, let's hope it does the trick, sir.

MAINWARING (**Crosses to the door and turns**) There is one consolation, Wilson, at least I shall be spared the embarrassment of those damn lampshades.

INTERIOR. CHURCH HALL. DAY

Private Sponge is behind the lampshade stall. Pike is standing in front. Sponge is taking the shades out of a large box and is putting them on a table. They are wrapped in tissue paper. By now the hall is full of people.

SPONGE That's the lot, Pikey.

PIKE Good, Mr Mainwaring will be ever so pleased.

Mainwaring and Wilson come out of the office. Mainwaring crosses to the lampshades.

MAINWARING What are you doing, Pike?

PIKE I brought Mrs Mainwaring's lampshades.

MAINWARING (**Pulling Pike downstage and hissing at him**) How did you get hold of them?

PIKE Well, I was passing your house and I saw this big cardboard box on the doorstep, and as I was standing there, the front door opened and this lady's hand came round the edge of the door and a finger beckoned to me. So I went up the path and I noticed that the finger had white paint under the nail. Then the finger pointed to the box and I heard a mad laugh and the door slammed. Hey, it wouldn't be your daily woman gone potty, would it? Perhaps you ought to go home and find out.

SPONGE Hey, Pikey, here are two more I've unwrapped. **(He holds up two lampshades. Pike goes to him)**

PIKE Aren't they good? **(He takes them and holds them up)** Look everybody, look at these lampshades Mrs Mainwaring has made.

MAINWARING You stupid boy.

Cut to the Vicar and town clerk standing on the stage.

VICAR **(Clapping his hands)** Ladies and gentlemen, can I have your attention please? May I bid you all welcome to our winter bazaar, and here to perform the opening ceremony is our popular town clerk, Mr Gordon.

Applause.

JONES Pikey, go and bring the brawn in quick, we're opening.

PIKE Right-oh. Come on, Mr Sponge.

Pike and Sponge go.

TOWN CLERK Good afternoon, citizens of Walmington-on-Sea. As you know, the proceeds from this bazaar this afternoon are in aid of the town's comforts for the troops fund. Every penny you spend is another nail in Hitler's coffin, so go to it with a will. I now declare this bazaar well and truly open.

Applause.

MAINWARING Pompous idiot.

WILSON Well, at least he was brief.

HODGES **(Bawling through megaphone)** Ladies and gentlemen, walk up, walk up and have a look at my oranges. I shall auction them at half-past four. Walk up! Walk up!

WILSON **(At Mainwaring)** That man Hodges is making the whole thing sound like a fairground.

MAINWARING Dreadfully common, shouldn't be allowed.

Jones bawls into a megaphone right in Mainwaring's ear.

JONES Ladies and gentlemen, step this way and view my monster brawn. Tickets for the raffle one penny each. I have to tell you that, owing to circumstances beyond my control, the monster brawn will only be on view at certain periods during the afternoon, as it has to remain outside.

Pike and Sponge enter with the brawn.

PIKE/SPONGE Make way for the monster brawn.

PIKE **(To Mainwaring)** The monster brawn's here.

Cut to Frazer doing a silhouette.

FRAZER **(Shouting at man)** Will you keep still, I canna get your likeness if you fidget about.

Cut to Godfrey and Dolly. Godfrey is handing a pot of honey to a woman.

GODFREY There you are, one pot of honey. That will be a shilling.

DOLLY Perhaps you'd like to try some of my elderberry wine. **(She pours out a glass)**

MAINWARING I'm going to buy some tombola tickets, Wilson. They've got a bottle of whisky as one of the prizes. Elizabeth takes a drop now and then, purely for medicinal purposes, of course.

WILSON Yes, of course, sir.

INTERIOR. CHURCH HALL. DAY

JONES **(Into megaphone)** Ladies and gentlemen, it's three o'clock and the monster brawn will be on display for ten minutes.

Pike staggers in with the brawn.

PIKE Make way for the monster brawn. **(Bumps into Mainwaring)** It's here again.

Mainwaring moves to tombola stall.

MAINWARING I'll have another half a crown's worth of tickets, please.

MRS YEATMAN That's the third lot you've bought already, Mr Mainwaring. You are being generous.

MAINWARING Anything to help the war effort, you know. Besides, I'm rather keen to get hold of that bottle of whisky.

INTERIOR. CHURCH HALL. DAY

JONES **(Into megaphone)** Ladies and gentleman, it's a quarter to four, and the monster brawn will be on display once again.

PIKE Make away for the monster brawn. **(Bumps into Mainwaring)** Guess what?

MAINWARING **(To Wilson)** I think I'll buy some more tombola tickets, Wilson.

WILSON You've bought an awful lot, sir. Have you won anything?

MAINWARING **(Holding up a small doll with a ribbon round its waist)** Only a boat race favour, I'm afraid.

WILSON How nice, sir, it's Cambridge.

Mainwaring turns and bumps into the town clerk, who is swaying and mopping his brow.

MAINWARING Oh, I'm sorry, Mr Gordon.

The town clerk gives him a sickly grin and a wave and staggers

away. Mainwaring does a take and crosses to the tombola stall, followed by Wilson. Mrs Yeatman is handing the bottle of whisky to the Vicar.

VICAR **(To Mainwaring)** Look what I've wo,n Mr Mainwaring. Heaven has certainly smiled on me this afternoon.

MRS YEATMAN Do you want some more tickets, Mr Mainwaring?

MAINWARING I don't think I'll bother, thank you.

JONES **(To Pike)** Hey, Pikey, this brawn's starting to melt. Take it out in the yard, quick.

PIKE I'm fed up with lugging this thing in and out all the afternoon.

JONES/PIKE Make way for the monster brawn, make way for the monster brawn.

A girl, wearing lampshade on her head, passes Mainwaring and Wilson.

WILSON Look at that, sir.

MAINWARING What on earth…? **(He crosses quickly to the lampshade stall)** Sponge –

SPONGE Yes, Captain Mainwaring?

MAINWARING What's that child doing with one of my wife's lampshades on her head?

SPONGE Well, I can't sell them as lampshades, so I'm selling them as funny hats for kids.

MAINWARING How dare you sell…

The town clerk bumps into Mainwaring.

TOWN CLERK Ooops, sorry. **(He turns and bumps into Frazer, who has come into the picture)** Pardon me – **(He staggers off)**

MAINWARING What's the matter with him?

WILSON I hardly like to say it, sir, but I think he's tipsy.

MAINWARING How on earth could he be? What are those people doing over there?

Cut to three people sitting, swaying and laughing.

FRAZER **(Pushing in)** They're all drunk! Drunk!

MAINWARING Just a moment – **(He crosses to Godfrey)** How much wine have you sold, Godfrey?

GODFREY None I'm afraid, sir.

Mainwaring points to a row of empty bottles.

MAINWARING Then what are all those empty bottles?

GODFREY Nobody's buying it, but everybody's tasting it.

Pike comes into the picture and hands Mainwaring an envelope.

PIKE Mr Mainwaring, while I was taking the brawn out into the yard, a despatch rider drove up and asked me to give you this.

MAINWARING Where is he now?

PIKE Just getting on his motorbike.

MAINWARING Well, stop him, I want to talk to him.

Pike rushes out. Mainwaring and Wilson follow him. We hear the sound of a motorbike. Jones comes into the picture.

JONES I'm going to draw the raffle now, Mr Mainwaring. We can't keep lugging that brawn in and out all the time.

Pike returns.

PIKE I'm afraid he's gone. Er, Mr Jones, there's something out in the yard I think you ought to see. Come on.

JONES What is it?

PIKE Brace yourself for a shock.

Jones and Pike go out.

MAINWARING **(Looking at the envelope)** This is probably about the exercise tomorrow, Wilson. As soon as the auction's over, get all the men into the office.

Jones enters.

JONES Mr Mainwaring, that despatch rider has run over my brawn.

Pike staggers in with the brawn. It has a tyre mark through it.

MAINWARING How did this happen?

PIKE He sort of went – brmm, brmm…

Mainwaring reacts.

INTERIOR. CHURCH HALL. DAY

Hodges is on the platform with his oranges.

HODGES **(Through megaphone)** Walk up, walk up, it's half past four and I shall now auction my oranges.

The Verger is behind Mainwaring and Wilson.

MAINWARING I'm determined to get one of those oranges, Wilson.

The Verger reacts.

WILSON How high are you prepared to go?

MAINWARING Oh, where my wife's concerned, the sky's the limit.

The Verger hurries over to the platform.

VERGER **(Hissing to Hodges)** 'Ere – Mr Hodges –

Hodges leans over the edge of the platform.

VERGER I've just heard Captain Mainwaring say he's determined to get one of those oranges.

HODGES Well he's not going to, I'll see to that. **(He straightens up and crosses to the centre of the platform)** Right – lot one, the first orange. Who'll start the bidding?

MAINWARING Sixpence.

MRS YEATMAN A shilling.

HODGES Sold to the lady for one shilling.

MAINWARING Just a minute, I hadn't finished bidding.

HODGES That's your hard bun, mate, you should speak up a bit sharpish. You mumble, that's your trouble. Lot two, the second orange.

MAINWARING One shilling.

HODGES Any advance on one shilling. **(Ad lib)** . . . I'm withdrawing this orange from the sale.

MAINWARING Why?

HODGES It hasn't reached its reserve price.

MAINWARING What is its reserve price?

HODGES Mind your own business.

WILSON **(To Pike)** Frank, you buy the orange for Captain Mainwaring.

PIKE Right-oh, Uncle Arthur.

HODGES Next orange. **(Ad lib)**

MAINWARING **(Mime)** A shilling.

HODGES A shilling, I am bid. Two shillings anyone? **(Ad lib)**

Pike raises his hand, Mainwaring cannot see him.

HODGES **(Pointing at Pike)** Two shillings.

MAINWARING **(Mime)** Three shillings.

Pike raises his hand.

HODGES **(Pointing at Pike)** Four shillings. **(Ad lib)**

MAINWARING **(Mime)** Five shillings.

Hodges ad lib. Pike raises his hand.

HODGES **(Pointing)** Six!

MAINWARING **(Mime)** Seven!

Hodges ad lib. Pike raises his hand.

HODGES Eight!

Mainwaring mimes nine. Hodges ad lib. Pike raises hand.

HODGES Ten! Sold to Frank Pike for ten shillings.

Mainwaring turns on Pike.

WILSON Don't worry, sir, Pike bought it for you.

MAINWARING Then why didn't you tell me? I was bidding against myself.

WILSON I only had your interest at heart.

MAINWARING Get the men in the office, Wilson.

FRAZER Och, ten shillings for an orange, the boy's gone off his head.

INTERIOR. SIDE OFFICE. DAY

Mainwaring enters followed by Pike.

PIKE Here's your orange, Mr Mainwaring.

MAINWARING Thank you, Pike. **(The phone rings)** See who that is.

PIKE Right ho. **(He picks up the phone)** Hello, Mrs Mainwaring –

Mainwaring puts his hand over the mouthpiece.

MAINWARING Tell her I'm not here.

PIKE He says he's not here.

Mainwaring reacts.

PIKE Yes, I'll give him a message – I see – you're going to stay with your sister for a week.

MAINWARING **(Puts hand over mouthpiece)** Tell her I've got her an orange.

PIKE He's got you an orange... No, I don't think he'll do that.

Mainwaring reacts.

PIKE Oh, she's hung up.

Jones, Frazer, Godfrey and Wilson enter.

FRAZER You wanted to see us?

MAINWARING Yes.

WILSON I'll round up the others, sir.

MAINWARING Don't bother, come in and close the door, Wilson. **(He starts to peel the orange)** Gentlemen, I want to thank you for your work this afternoon. Once again, you have rallied round to help the war effort and the fact that I paid ten shillings for an orange will swell the coffers considerably.

PIKE You haven't paid me for it yet, Mr Mainwaring.

MAINWARING Quiet, boy. Yes, I paid ten shillings for an orange and I am going to share it with you.

FRAZER Man, you're generous to a fault.

GODFREY How kind.

JONES You're like father and mother to us, Mr Mainwaring.

Mainwaring divides the orange into sections and hands them round.

MAINWARING Here's to us, comrades in arms, to us.

ALL To us.

They pop the orange sections into their mouths. The door opens and Hodges enters.

HODGES 'Ere, Napoleon, I forgot to tell you – those oranges are for making marmalade!

Mainwaring reacts. Frazer reacts.

SERIES NINE **EPISODE ONE**

Recorded: Friday 8/7/77

Original transmission: Sunday 2/10/77, 8.10–8.40pm

Original viewing figures = 10.2 million

ARTHUR LOWE . . . . CAPTAIN MAINWARING
JOHN LE MESURIER . . . . SERGEANT WILSON
CLIVE DUNN . . . . LANCE CORPORAL JONES
JOHN LAURIE . . . . PRIVATE FRAZER
ARNOLD RIDLEY . . . . PRIVATE GODFREY
IAN LAVENDER . . . . PRIVATE PIKE
BILL PERTWEE . . . . CHIEF WARDEN HODGES
FRANK WILLIAMS . . . . VICAR
EDWARD SINCLAIR . . . . VERGER
GEOFFREY LUMSDEN . . . . CAPTAIN SQUARE
SAM KYDD . . . . YOKEL
HAROLD BENNETT . . . . MR BLUETT
ROBERT RAGLAN . . . . COLONEL
CHARLES HILL . . . . PERKINS, THE BUTLER
JEFFREY HOLLAND . . . . SOLDIER
BARRY LINEHAN . . . . VAN DRIVER
COLIN BEAN . . . . PRIVATE SPONGE
ALISTER WILLIAMSON . . . . BERT, A MAN AT THE PUB
MICHAEL STAINTON . . . . FRENCHY, A MAN AT THE PUB
PLATOON . . . . DESMOND CULLUM-JONES, FREDDIE WHITE, JIMMY MAC, MICHAEL MOORE, ROGER BOURNE, FREDDIE WILES, GEORGE HANCOCK, HUGH CECIL, EVAN ROSS, VERNON DRAKE
EXTRAS. . . . (FAT MAN) WILLIAM SULLY; (SECOND YOKEL) PERCY HAY-GREEN

WAKE-UP WALMINGTON

• JEFFREY HOLLAND REMEMBERS •

'Having been lucky enough to be picked for the supporting cast of the stage show of *Dad's Army*, in which I played a fireman and a mad German inventor, understudied Private Pike and eventually played Walker on the tour, I was delighted when David and Jimmy asked me to appear as an army truck driver in an episode of the last series to be made in 1977. It was not, however, without its problems!

'Although I had a driving licence, I was not the owner of a car and had little or no experience of driving one since passing my test four years previously. Imagine my consternation then on turning up for the shoot in Thetford to be faced with a 1940 army three-tonner with a crash gearbox! I only had to drive it two hundred yards and turn a corner, though, so I girded up my loins, climbed into the cab, went through a quick briefing on double-de-clutching with the owner and we were off.

"'Action!" shouted David and, grinding into first gear, I jolted away. I crept along at a snail's pace, which seems all right on the film, turned the corner rather gingerly and jerked to a halt, just managing to avoid running over Clive Dunn. We conducted our few lines of dialogue but, because of my inexperience, I was not able to pull away as expertly as they wanted and, as Captain Mainwaring had to be splashed with mud, they substituted the *real* driver for that bit. But I had made it into the TV episode, "Wake-Up, Walmington".'

Wake-up Walmington

EXTERIOR. FIRING RANGE. DAY

Large country house in far background. A few sandbags at the firing point, target a hundred yards away. Red flag flying. Pike is lying on the ground, firing. Jones is kneeling beside him. Frazer, Mainwaring and Wilson are standing behind. Godfrey and the rest of the platoon are sitting on the ground about twenty yards away.

JONES Don't jerk the trigger, Pikey, squeeze it like a lemon.

PIKE Like a lemon, yes, Mr Jones. **(He fires)**

WILSON **(Looking through field glasses)** That's rather good, Frank. **(To Mainwaring)** The men's shooting is certainly improving, sir. If it goes on like this, we shall have to call ourselves Mr Mainwaring's sharp-shooters.

Mainwaring gives him a look. Pike fires again. Cut to butler coming across the field from the house. Cut back to Pike getting up.

JONES Your turn, Captain Mainwaring.

MAINWARING What have I got to beat, Wilson?

WILSON Frazer has the best score so far. Two bulls, two inners and one outer.

MAINWARING **(Taking the rifle from Jones)** I think we can improve on that.

FRAZER Would you care to have a little wager, Captain Mainwaring?

MAINWARING I don't mind. Shall we say a shilling?

FRAZER Make it ten.

The butler approaches Sponge.

MAINWARING Ten shillings is rather a lot of money.

FRAZER You're backing out, are you?

MAINWARING Nothing of the sort.

PIKE I'll do the spotting.

He grabs the field glasses. The strap catches Mainwaring round the throat. Cut to the butler who stops and talks to Sponge. Mainwaring is firing.

MAINWARING Excuse me, can you tell me who's in charge here?

SPONGE **(Pointing)** Captain Mainwaring, he's the one shooting the gun.

BUTLER Thank you.

Cut to Mainwaring. He fires his third shot.

PIKE You're doing ever so well, Mr Mainwaring. That's two bulls and one inner.

Mainwaring gives Frazer a smug look and takes aim. The butler stands behind him and coughs just as he fires.

PIKE Missed!

Mainwaring takes aim. The butler coughs again as he fires.

PIKE Missed!

Mainwaring springs to his feet.

MAINWARING What do you think you're doing? Who are you?

BUTLER I'm Perkins, the butler from the big hall. I've got a message from his lordship. He says he's trying to take his afternoon rest, so will you stop shooting?

MAINWARING **(Going purple)** Afternoon rest! There's a war on and if his lordship doesn't like the noise, why does he have a firing range on his estate in the first place?

BUTLER This range is for real soldiers, not Home Guards, and you're only here on sufferance, so kindly jack it in, my good man. **(He turns on his heels and walks away)**

FRAZER I'll take my ten shillings now, Captain Mainwaring.

Mainwaring reacts.

INTERIOR. SIDE OFFICE. CHURCH HALL. DAY

WILSON **(Out of vision)** Platoon, dismiss.

The door opens. Mainwaring comes in and throws his hat on the desk. Wilson follows.

MAINWARING What a terrible day, Wilson. I've never been so humiliated in all my life.

WILSON You shouldn't take it too seriously, sir.

MAINWARING Not take it too seriously?

WILSON It's quite amusing, really. After all, it's true, we're not real soldiers.

MAINWARING We are wearing the King's uniform and fighting for our country. Trust you to stick up for that snooty butler.

WILSON He was only doing his job, sir, his lordship wanted an afternoon nap. I remember my uncle's butler was always…

MAINWARING I thought so, you all stick together, you privileged classes. Well, after the war, things are going to be very different. The common man will come into his own. This country will be run by professional people – lawyers, doctors, er, bank managers.

WILSON People like you?

MAINWARING Yes, people like me.

WILSON You mean common.

MAINWARING Watch it, Wilson.

WILSON I didn't know you were a socialist, sir.

MAINWARING How dare you? Take that back.

WILSON But you said, after the war, the country was going to be run by common men like you.

MAINWARING Not common men – 'the common man'. People who have got on by their own efforts and not because their fathers had a title – their days are over.

WILSON What will happen to them?

MAINWARING They'll have to work. This country will be a true democracy.

WILSON Supposing they don't want to work.

MAINWARING They won't have any say in the matter.

The door opens. Hodges comes in with a stirrup pump. He throws it in the corner.

HODGES I'm not having it. I am not having it.

MAINWARING What's the matter, Hodges?

HODGES I caught Mr Bluett using that stirrup pump to spray his greenfly.

Mr Bluett enters.

BLUETT 'Ere, give me my stirrup pump back.

HODGES You're not having it back, you abused it.

Mainwaring reacts.

BLUETT It's my pump, I'll do what I like with it.

HODGES It's not yours, it's on loan.

BLUETT I don't care, I'm having it back. **(Picks it up)**

HODGES **(Snatching it back)** Give it here.

BLUETT You wouldn't do that to me if I was 57 years younger.

WILSON Look, stop bullying poor old Mr Bluett.

BLUETT Yes, stop bullying me.

HODGES Soapy water corrodes the washer.

BLUETT I've been using soapy water for eighty years, it hasn't corroded me.

HODGES I don't care, I'm not having you abuse your pump and that's that.

BLUETT I hate you.

HODGES What!

BLUETT I said I hate you, and I'm not the only one. Do you know what the kids round here do when you turn your back? **(He presses his finger against his nose and sticks his tongue out)** Put that light out.

HODGES **(Aghast)** What?

BLUETT **(Repeats business)** Put that light out.

HODGES **(Sinks into the chair, almost in tears)** I can't believe it.

BLUETT See, he's got feet of clay.

MAINWARING I should go, Mr Bluett.

BLUETT I suppose that would be more tactful. He's not having my stirrup pump. **(He picks up the pump)** The bigger they are, the harder they fall. Put that light out. **(Business)**

HODGES Leave me alone.

Bluett goes.

HODGES **(Broken)** I can't stand any more. Do you know, Napoleon, I'm the most hated man in this town. People just aren't taking the war seriously.

MAINWARING I quite agree.

WILSON It's only human nature really, sir. After all, the Home Guard has been formed for two years now, and there hasn't been an invasion. People think we're wasting our time.

MAINWARING That's precisely what the Germans want, Wilson, to lull us into a sense of false security and catch us off our guard. Something has got to be done.

There is a knock on the door. Jones enters.

JONES Permission for you to receive a deputation, sir?

MAINWARING Yes, of course.

JONES Deputation, at the double, into the office, quick march.

Frazer, Pike, Godfrey and Sponge double into the office and line up in front of the desk.

JONES Deputation, halt.

MAINWARING Well?

JONES After our humiliating experience today, sir, the mens' morals are at rock bottom. What are we going to do, Captain Mainwaring, what are we going to do?

Mainwaring reacts.

FRAZER Do you know what they call us in the town? The geriatric fusiliers. **(Looking at Godfrey)** And, in some cases, it's true.

Godfrey reacts.

PIKE And my mum says that Home Guard training has turned Uncle Arthur from a mild-mannered man into a brute.

WILSON Frank, please.

PIKE Don't you remember, Uncle Arthur, when Mum made you do the washing up and you got cross and threw a cup in the sink and broke it.

WILSON That's not true, sir. What really happened was...

MAINWARING Please, Wilson, we don't want to hear about your sordid domestic life. The fact is, men, we've got to do something to make this town appreciate the value of the Home Guard.

JONES I look at it this way, sir, we are here to stop German paratroopers roaming the countryside and ravishing maidens, now...

PIKE Mr Mainwaring, you remember when we took part in that training film and we all dressed up as German soldiers, and the whole county was in an uproar, 'cos they thought we were the real thing?

WILSON And you had to report to the Area Commander the next morning. By the way, sir, you never told us what he said.

MAINWARING I don't wish to discuss it, Wilson, but we're certainly not going to wear German uniforms again, and that's that.

JONES I tell you what, Mr Mainwaring, we could disguise ourselves as a bunch of fifth columnists and roam the countryside. That would give the town a fright.

MAINWARING I think you're going into the realms of... Wait a minute, that might do the trick.

GODFREY I don't think I should care to roam the countryside ravishing maidens, sir.

MAINWARING Don't keep talking all the time, Godfrey. What do you think, Wilson?

WILSON It wouldn't work, sir. The alarm would be raised and the army would be on to us like a shot.

MAINWARING Not if G.H.Q. knew all about it.

HODGES Can I come in with you, Napoleon?

FRAZER We don't want him, sir.

MAINWARING Mr Hodges has had a similar experience. Like us, he's only doing his duty and he's been reviled for it. You can join us, Hodges – we'll shake this town out of its complacency.

HODGES **(Shaking Mainwaring's hand)** Put it there, Napoleon. You and me, together, will give 'em a shock they'll never forget.

INTERIOR. G.H.Q. OFFICE. DAY

The colonel is on the telephone to Mainwaring.

COLONEL I don't know what to say, Mainwaring. I'm not too happy about the idea at all.

INTERCUT: INTERIOR. SIDE OFFICE. DAY

MAINWARING But you must admit, sir, that something has got to be done to shake people out of their apathy.

COLONEL You may have a point there. I inspected the Dymchurch Home Guard platoon last week, and there were so many absentees it was like walking down a fish queue.

MAINWARING Well, there you are, sir.

COLONEL All right, but you must keep me informed of your every move.

MAINWARING Yes, of course. I'm leaving Godfrey in the office here, and I shall be in constant touch with him by phone. I'm going to call it 'Operation Wake-Up Walmington-on-Sea'.

COLONEL That's a bit long.

MAINWARING How about 'Operation Wake-Up Walmington', I'll leave out the 'on-Sea'.

COLONEL Just call it 'Operation Wake-Up'.

MAINWARING Will do.

COLONEL Where are you going to set up your H.Q.?

MAINWARING In the flour mill just outside the town. I've asked the men to rendezvous there on Saturday night after dark. I've instructed them not to shave and to look as suspicious as possible.

COLONEL What are they going to wear?

MAINWARING I've told them to dress like fifth columnists.

COLONEL What do fifth columnists wear? I've never seen one.

MAINWARING Well, sort of sinister clothes. I've told them to get themselves up like cut throats and desperados.

COLONEL I see. Well, good luck, Mainwaring.

MAINWARING Thank you.

COLONEL **(Hangs up)** Cut throats and desperados, eh.

INTERIOR. FLOUR MILL. NIGHT

The top floor. At the back, about eight feet up, is a gallery stacked with sacks of flour. Black-outs over windows. There is a telephone on the wall. A trapdoor on the floor opens, and Mainwaring comes through. He is dressed in rough trousers, jersey, donkey jacket and a peaked seaman's cap. He is wearing an eye patch and he has a revolver stuck in his belt.

MAINWARING Where's the light switch? **(He looks around, can't see, takes out his glasses, puts them on over his eye patch, crosses to the phone and takes it off the hook)**

OPERATOR **(Out of vision)** Number, please?

MAINWARING Walmington 382, please.

OPERATOR **(Out of vision))** And your number?

Mainwaring squints at phone, has trouble seeing, pulls up his eye patch.

MAINWARING 633.

OPERATOR **(Out of vision)** Hold the line, please.

Mainwaring puts his patch back on top of his glasses.

INTERCUT: INTERIOR. SIDE OFFICE. NIGHT

The Verger in office. The phone rings and he picks it up.

VERGER Hello.

MAINWARING Wake up, Roger.

VERGER Eh?

MAINWARING Wake up, Roger.

VERGER My name's not Roger and I haven't been asleep.

MAINWARING Who's that?

VERGER It's me, the Verger.

MAINWARING Where's Godfrey?

VERGER He's just popped out for a minute. He's asked me to mind the phone.

MAINWARING Well, he'd no business to. When he comes back, give him this message – Operation Wake-Up Roger, and tell him to ring 633. It's urgent. Got that?

VERGER Yes, I've got it. (**He writes**) 633.

Mainwaring hangs up.

INTERIOR. SIDE OFFICE. NIGHT

Godfrey enters.

VERGER Captain Mainwaring's just been on the phone for you. He left a message.

GODFREY What was it?

VERGER Er… oh yes, let me see, someone named Roger is having an operation… You've got to ring that number right away – it must be the hospital.

GODFREY (**Picking up phone**) Oh dear, I hope it's not serious. Hello – Walmington 633, please.

VERGER It could be appendicitis, it comes on very quick, you know.

GODFREY Did Captain Mainwaring say anything else?

VERGER Yes, he said you're not to go to sleep.

GODFREY I won't do that.

INTERCUT: INTERIOR. FLOUR MILL. NIGHT

The phone is ringing, Mainwaring picks it up.

GODFREY Hello, is that the hospital?

MAINWARING What? Is that you Godfrey?

GODFREY Yes, sir, how's Roger? Is he going to be all right?

MAINWARING What are you babbling about?

GODFREY I got a message that Roger had been taken ill with appendicitis and was having an operation.

MAINWARING (**Blows hard**) The message was that Operation Wake-Up has started.

GODFREY Oh… yes, of course. Operation Wake-Up, I'm so sorry, sir – but what's Roger got to do with it?

MAINWARING Godfrey, Roger means understand, now, pull yourself together and stay by that phone – and don't go to sleep.

GODFREY Don't worry, sir, I got that part of the message all right.

MAINWARING (**Puts phone down**) I shouldn't have left him in charge.

INTERIOR. FLOUR MILL. NIGHT

Frazer comes through the trap. He is dressed like Bill Sykes with a battered bowler. He is carrying his rifle and wearing an eye patch over his left eye.

MAINWARING Take that eye patch off, Frazer, I thought of it first.

FRAZER You canna wear an eye patch with glasses.

MAINWARING I'm not going to. When I want to look suspicious, I shall take them off.

FRAZER (**Taking off his patch**) Why don't you wear this one over your other eye, then you'll look even more suspicious.

MAINWARING Watch it, Frazer.

During this, two other members of the platoon come up through the trap. They are wearing rough clothes. Pike comes through. He is wearing a blue suit with stripes drawn on it in chalk, a black shirt, white tie and trilby hat. He has a cigarette dangling out of the corner of his mouth and he is carrying a Tommy gun.

MAINWARING What are you playing at, Pike?

PIKE Do you like it? I copied it from a photo of Edward G. Robinson in that film *Scarface*.

MAINWARING Brush that chalk off.

PIKE You said we were to dress like cut throats and desperados.

MAINWARING I didn't mean American gangsters.

PIKE Well, you should have said.

MAINWARING Brush it off at once.

Pike brushes clouds of chalk all over Mainwaring.

MAINWARING Not all over me.

Hodges comes through. He is dressed as a French apache,

beret and striped jersey. He is followed by Wilson who is wearing a Burlington Bertie outfit.

WILSON All right, sir? Do you think it fits the bill?

MAINWARING It looks absurd.

WILSON But I thought the whole idea was to look suspicious.

MAINWARING There's a difference between looking absurd and suspicious. Where did it come from anyhow?

WILSON I used to wear it every year for the tramp's ball at the Savoy.

MAINWARING I've never seen anything so stupid in all my life.

WILSON It's not half so stupid as wearing an eye patch with glasses.

MAINWARING Wilson, it doesn't surprise me that Pike is wearing something stupid. He's a young boy with a vivid imagination, who thinks everything is a game. But I presume the only reason you could have to get yourself up like that, would be to annoy me. So take off that hat and those spats and gloves.

WILSON If you insist, sir. **(He starts to pull fingers off gloves which come off one by one, whistles 'Jolly Brothers')**

Jones comes up. He is crudely dressed in nun's outfit.

MAINWARING Oh no.

JONES How's this, Mr Mainwaring? I bet you didn't know it was me.

MAINWARING I'm sorry, Jones, it won't do.

JONES Don't say that, Mr Mainwaring, it took me hours to think this up.

MAINWARING But you've got a moustache.

JONES Ah, that's the whole point, sir. A person strolling along nonchalant like, sees me and says – why has that nun got a moustache – and they will know that I am not a real nun but a man disguised as a nun, and I shall look suspicious.

MAINWARING But it's going too far, Jones.

JONES Let me be a nun, sir, let me be a nun. Everybody's dressing up as nuns these days, it's in all the papers.

MAINWARING Look, don't argue, Jones, just take it off.

JONES But if I take it off, I shall just have my ordinary clothes underneath and I won't look peculiar.

FRAZER I wouldn't say that, son.

JONES Now look, Jock.

MAINWARING That will do, Jones. Right, men, settle down, make yourselves comfortable, there's plenty of flour sacks. We move off as soon as it's light.

EXTERIOR. COUNTRY ROAD. DAY

Mainwaring and co. are marching along.

MAINWARING Platoon, halt. This is no good, Wilson, we don't look suspicious or furtive enough.

WILSON Perhaps if I turn my coat collar up, like this... **(He turns his collar up)** And make my eyes shifty, like this... **(Squints and rolls his eyes)** Is that better?

MAINWARING Not really. Jones –

JONES Yes, sir.

MAINWARING Tell the platoon to march like rabble in a shifty and furtive manner.

JONES Platoon, in a shifty and furtive manner like rabble, quick march.

They march along. An army truck appears in the distance.

MAINWARING Platoon, halt. Jones, stop that truck and ask the driver where the aerodrome is.

JONES Right, sir, I'll put on a German accent, that will sound suspicious.

MAINWARING Good idea.

Jones stands in front of the truck and waves his arms.

JONES Halt, halt.

SOLDIER You silly old fool, I nearly ran you over. What do you want?

JONES I vant to know vere de aerodrome is.

SOLDIER Eh?

JONES I vant to know vere de aerodrome is.

SOLDIER What aerodrome?

JONES Er... any aerodrome.

WILSON **(With bad German accent)** You heard what he said, vere is it?

SOLDIER Flippin' foreigners, you're all barmy.

MAINWARING Don't you take that tone with me, my man.

The van moves off. The back wheel goes through a puddle. Mainwaring gets wet.

PIKE Mr Mainwaring, you look even more suspicious now.

EXTERIOR. COUNTRY ROAD. DAY

Mainwaring and co. are standing in a group by the roadside.

MAINWARING We're getting nowhere at this rate, Wilson. We shall have to do something more drastic.

WILSON The next time somebody comes by, sir, why don't we grab Hodges and start hitting him, and make it look as if we're trying to get secret information out of him.

PIKE That's a good idea, Uncle Arthur, I'll hit him first.

HODGES You're not hitting me.

MAINWARING Don't worry, Hodges, we'll only pretend.

FRAZER That's right, son, we'll just pretend like this. **(He slaps Hodges' face)**

HODGES Ow, that hurt. I wish I hadn't come now.

MAINWARING Be quiet, and do as you're told.

JONES Captain Mainwaring, there's something coming.

A van comes up the road.

MAINWARING Frazer, Wilson, grab him – Jones, Pike – you interrogate him. Look frightened, Hodges.

PIKE **(In American)** So you won't talk, eh, buddy?

MAINWARING What are you talking in American for, you stupid boy, they're on our side.

PIKE Sorry, I forgot. So you von't talk, Herr?

MAINWARING Hit him.

Jones and Pike start hitting Hodges. The van stops, the driver leans out of the window.

DRIVER What's going on?

PIKE We are asking him questions.

JONES Jar, and we want the answers. Take that. **(Hits him)**

DRIVER **(Getting down)** Perhaps I can help, what do you want to know?

HODGES Don't tell 'em.

JONES Shut your mouth. **(Hits him)**

HODGES They're trying to get secrets out of me, they're fifth columnists.

DRIVER Don't talk rubbish. That's Mr Jones the butcher.

JONES **(In normal voice)** How did you know who I was?

DRIVER I live in Walmington, I know you all. **(To Hodges)** And I know you, mate. The last time I was in your shop, you short-changed me, I've been waiting for this. **(He hits him)**

EXTERIOR. SIX BELLS. DAY

Two yokels drinking beer. Three seamen finish their drinks, pick up their kit bags.

BERT Come on, lads, time to get back to the ship.

FIRST YOKEL Sailing tonight are you?

BERT You shouldn't ask that, old timer. Careless talk costs lives, remember?

FIRST YOKEL Sorry. If you walk down to the crossroads, you should be able to hitch a lift into Dover. It's only about twenty miles.

BERT Thanks, come on, Frenchy.

FRENCHY Au revoir, mes amis.

FIRST YOKEL **(To yokel)** French...

EXTERIOR. CROSSROADS. DAY

Mainwaring and co. are marching along. Hodges has a black eye.

HODGES **(To Wilson)** You did that deliberate, you held me while he hit me.

WILSON Oh, stop whining. It was your own fault.

JONES It serves you right. It's people like you who give us shopkeepers a bad name.

MAINWARING Halt. This is absurd, Wilson, nobody is taking any notice of us.

JONES Why don't we try those men over there, sir? **(He points to the three merchant seamen, who are sitting on the grass with their backs to them)**

MAINWARING This time I'll do the talking.

PIKE Are you going to speak with a German accent, Mr Mainwaring?

MAINWARING No, I am not.

Cut to front of seamen, sitting and smoking. Mainwaring, Wilson, Jones, Pike, Frazer and Hodges approach them from behind. The rest of the platoon sit on the verge and wait. Mainwaring taps the short, fat man on the shoulder.

MAINWARING Where's the aerodrome?

The man gets up and faces Mainwaring. They look each other up and down. Bert and Frenchy get up. Frenchy faces Hodges. They look each other up and down.

MAINWARING Just a minute. **(He motions his men away. They walk back in a tight group)** Those men look very suspicious Wilson.

WILSON They certainly do, sir.

PIKE Perhaps they're fifth columnists.

JONES They're dressed like us, they must be fifth columnists.

MAINWARING We can't be certain. After all, we're only dressed how we think fifth columnists would be dressed.

JONES Well, perhaps what we think fifth columnists are dressed like, is really what they are dressed like.

FRAZER We ought to ask to see their papers, Captain Mainwaring.

MAINWARING That's a very good idea.

They cross back to the seamen.

MAINWARING Who are you?

BERT Who are you?

MAINWARING Why are you dressed like that?

BERT Why are you dressed like that?

MAINWARING Stop repeating everything I say.

FRENCHY They look like spies to me, Bert.

WILSON Don't be absurd.

MAINWARING Show me your papers.

BERT Show me your papers.

MAINWARING I've had enough of this. (**He pulls out his revolver and points it at Bert**) In the name of the King, I demand to see your papers.

Bert takes the revolver, holding it by the barrel.

MAINWARING Give me my gun back.

BERT Not until you've shown us your papers.

MAINWARING You show us yours.

BERT We're not going to.

MAINWARING Oh yes you are.

BERT Oh no we're not.

Mix out as the two groups shout at each other.

EXTERIOR. SIX BELLS. DAY

Mainwaring and co. approach.

MAINWARING Halt. Gather round, men. (**They gather round Mainwaring**) Now, you all know what we're going to do. Come on.

HODGES Oy, you can leave me out of this, I've had enough.

MAINWARING All right, stay where you are, Hodges, and hold your tongue.

Wilson, Jones, Frazer and Pike follow Mainwaring to the table. They sit and stare at the yokels.

WILSON (**In accent**) Zat was a good morning's work, was it not?

PKE Yar, a good morning's work.

JONES Yar, yar, a very good morning's work.

FRAZER Aye, that's a fact. (**They all stare at him**) Yar, zat is a fact.

JONES Ve saw ze aerodrome.

PIKE (**To Wilson**) Did you write down how many planes there were, mein Herr?

WILSON I made many notes.

JONES And ve saw the ships in the harbour.

WILSON I also wrote down ze number of ships.

JONES But ve need more information.

FRAZER (**Pointing to Yokels**) Vi don't ve ask zem?

PIKE (**Narrows his eyes**) Zat is a good idea. Ve vill ask them some questions and ve will get ze answers, I promise you. (**He bangs the table**)

Mainwaring takes his revolver out and lays it on the table. The two yokels look at it, get up and run into the pub.

MAINWARING (**Getting up**) That's done the trick. Right, we'll get back to the mill and plan our next move. We'll cut across the fields.

INTERIOR. SIDE OFFICE. CHURCH HALL. DAY

Godfrey is at the desk. The Verger enters.

VERGER Hello, Mr Godfrey, are you still here?

GODFREY I've got to stay by the phone. Er, I wonder if you'd mind taking over for a minute.

VERGER Well, don't be long, it's nearly time for morning service.

GODFREY No, I won't. (**He goes to the door**)

The Vicar enters, wearing his surplice.

GODFREY Good morning, Vicar.

VICAR Good morning, Mr Godfrey.

Godfrey goes. We hear the sound of marching feet.

SQUARE (**Out of vision**) Platoon, halt.

VICAR If you don't mind, Mr Yeatman, I want to get my sermon out of the drawer.

VERGER (**Moving out of the way**) Upsy-daisy.

VICAR No it isn't.

Captain Square enters.

SQUARE Morning, padre, Mainwaring about?

VICAR No, he's not here.

SQUARE Sunday morning and he's not here, where the hell is he?

VICAR I've no idea.

The phone rings. The Vicar picks it up.

VICAR The Reverend Timothy Farthing. What? I'm afraid there's no one here. Oh dear.

SQUARE What's the matter?

VICAR It's the police over at Dymchurch. They want the Home Guard.

SQUARE That's typical of Mainwaring, not being here when he's wanted, lazy slacker. I'll take it. (**He grabs the**

phone) Hello, Captain Square, commander Eastgate Platoon Home Guard, don't you know... What! What! Good heavens! Are you sure? I'll come right away. **(He hangs up)** They say there's a bunch of fifth columnists over there. They're desperate characters, armed to the teeth and asking questions about aerodromes. They were last seen outside The Six Bells. I must get over there right away. **(To Verger)** Where is The Six Bells?

VERGER It's about five miles away, off the Dymchurch road.

SQUARE Blast, I haven't got any transport. We marched over here from Eastgate.

VICAR Captain Mainwaring's van is in the yard.

SQUARE Capital idea, padre.

VERGER Shouldn't you phone G.H.Q.?

SQUARE No, I can handle this. **(To Verger)** You come with me and show me the way.

VERGER Oh no, I don't want to get mixed up in any trouble. Besides, it's time for morning service and I've got to take the collection.

SQUARE Never mind about that, come on.

He pushes the Verger out of the door.

EXTERIOR. SIX BELLS. DAY

Van roars up. Square leans out.

SQUARE Which way did they go?

YOKEL They went that way, sir.

SQUARE Don't worry, we'll get 'em. Tally-ho.

The van roars off.

EXTERIOR. FLOUR MILL. DAY

Mainwaring and co. are approaching the mill.

EXTERIOR. ROAD. DAY

Van parked. Square on top, looking through field glasses.

VERGER Any sign of them, Captain Square?

SQUARE No, nothing.

View through field glasses as they pan round, stop. We see Mainwaring and co. going into mill.

SQUARE There they are! We've got 'em. Right, men, back in the van.

INTERIOR. FLOUR MILL. DAY

Mainwaring comes through the trap, followed by Wilson.

MAINWARING A good morning's work, Wilson.

WILSON Yes, sir, I think we gave them quite a fright.

FRAZER What are we going to do next, Captain Mainwaring?

MAINWARING We'll march on the gasworks.

JONES What for, sir?

MAINWARING At twelve o'clock, when everybody is cooking their Sunday dinner, we'll cut off the gas.

PIKE You can't spoil our Sunday dinner, my Mum will be furious.

MAINWARING I can't help that, boy. This is war.

EXTERIOR. FLOUR MILL. DAY

Square is standing by van. Platoon getting out.

SQUARE Right, men, surround the building. Not a sound.

INTERIOR. FLOUR MILL. DAY

WILSON What's all that noise outside?

Jones goes to the window.

JONES It's Captain Square, and he's got my van.

EXTERIOR. FLOUR MILL. DAY

Square is standing with Tommy gun.

SQUARE **(Shouts)** I'll give you one minute to come out with your hands up, otherwise I'll blast you out.

INTERIOR. FLOUR MILL. DAY

JONES Don't panic, he's going to blast us, he's going to blast us!

MAINWARING Quiet, Jones.

WILSON What are we going to do, sir?

MAINWARING Well, I'm certainly not going to surrender to that idiot, Square.

WILSON But you know what a trigger-happy maniac he is.

MAINWARING He won't shoot, even he's not as mad as that.

A stream of shots come through the window and hit the flour bags above. They all dive for the floor, a shower of flour falls on them.

EXTERIOR. FLOUR MILL. DAY

Square is holding a smoking Tommy gun.

SQUARE Charge! **(He runs into the mill, followed by his men)**

INTERIOR. FLOUR MILL. DAY

Mainwaring and co. get to their feet. They are covered in flour, coughing and spluttering. Square comes up through the trap.

SQUARE What the hell are you doing here, Mainwaring?

MAINWARING You madman, you nearly killed us.

SQUARE Ha ha, well, Mainwaring, you've been behaving like a clown for the past two years. Now you look like one.

WILSON He got you going – he took you in completely.

JONES Yes, we had you chasing all over the countryside.

SQUARE I knew it was him all the time.

MAINWARING Rubbish, you fell for it hook, line and sinker. You're a fool.

SQUARE You take that back, Mainwaring.

MAINWARING I'll do nothing of the sort. You've been a fool for years.

SQUARE Don't you call me a fool – you fool.

MAINWARING I shall report you to the colonel.

SQUARE Sneak – I'll have you blackballed at the golf club.

MAINWARING I'm not a member of the golf club.

SQUARE I'm not surprised, they don't have sneaks.

SERIES NINE **EPISODE TWO**

Recorded: Friday 1/7/77
Original transmission: Sunday 9/10/77, 8.10–8.40pm
Original viewing figures = 10.3 million

ARTHUR LOWE .... CAPTAIN MAINWARING
JOHN LE MESURIER .... SERGEANT WILSON
CLIVE DUNN .... LANCE CORPORAL JONES
JOHN LAURIE .... PRIVATE FRAZER
ARNOLD RIDLEY .... PRIVATE GODFREY
IAN LAVENDER .... PRIVATE PIKE
BILL PERTWEE .... CHIEF WARDEN HODGES
FRANK WILLIAMS .... VICAR
EDWARD SINCLAIR .... VERGER
JEAN GILPIN .... SYLVIA
ANTHONY SHARP .... COLONEL
JEFFREY SEGAL .... BRIGADIER
PAMELA CUNDELL .... MRS FOX
JANET DAVIES .... MRS PIKE
MELITA MANGER .... NORA
PLATOON .... MICHAEL MOORE, FREDDIE WHITE, FREDDIE WILES, EVAN ROSS, DESMOND CULLUM-JONES, VERNON DRAKE, JIMMY MAC, GEORGE HANCOCK, ROGER BOURNE

THE MAKING OF PRIVATE PIKE

• JEAN GILPIN REMEMBERS •

'At the time I was offered the part of Sylvia I couldn't drive, and of course the episode involves the character driving Pikey to the pictures at Eastgate. At the end of my interview with David Croft, he said: 'You're too intelligent for this role and you don't drive, but if I don't find anybody more suitable I'll cast you.' I went away thinking that was the end of that, but then I got a call from my agent saying I'd better learn how to drive quickly because he was offering me the role.

'I immediately took some lessons but didn't have time to take my test before we went off to film some of my scenes on location; private land was used for the driving scenes, which meant it didn't matter that I hadn't passed my test. Ian Lavender was extremely apprehensive about being driven by me and I was equally nervous about driving!

'The car was old-fashioned and you pressed a button for the ignition, not a key; when it came to the studio shots I couldn't get the car to start, so someone in the production crew told me not to worry, they'd pull the car off the the set to make it look like the two characters (Sylvia and Pikey) were driving off, and then put engine noises over the filming afterwards. Not being a driver, I thought: "Oh, that means I don't have to do anything." To my horror, I found we were being pulled right into the camera and afterwards people said: "You should have been steering." The poor cameraman was horrified when we were pulled straight towards him – but the audience loved it!'

The Making of Private Pike

PHONE BACKING. DAY

The colonel and head quarter brigadier are on the phone to each other.

COLONEL (**On the phone**) All in all, it sounds quite a party, sir.

INTERCUT: PHONE BACKING. DAY

BRIGADIER Oh yes. It's definitely the biggest exercise we've mounted so far. There'll be two brigades of infantry, a battery of 25-pounders, air support and we've even managed to rustle up a few tanks. Now, I'm relying on you to be one of the umpires.

COLONEL Ah. Well, I've hit a bit of a snag there. I've got the same old trouble with the leg – but I've managed to find a deputy, he runs the Walmington-on-Sea platoon. Mainwaring is his name, Captain Mainwaring.

BRIGADIER Is he up to it? He'll be pretty unpopular if he makes any wrong decisions.

COLONEL He's used to being unpopular, he's a bank manager.

BRIGADIER Well, I leave it to you. We need somebody who's neutral, unbiased and fair-minded.

COLONEL He's that all right.

INTERIOR. SIDE OFFICE. DAY

Mainwaring is at his desk. Wilson is opposite, going through the in-tray. Jones is pinning a notice on to the board.

MAINWARING Well, if I had my way, black marketeers would all be put up against a wall and shot.

WILSON Without a trial?

MAINWARING What's the point of trying them, waste of time and money. There's a war on, Wilson.

WILSON Have you heard any more about this umpiring business, sir?

MAINWARING Well, I've protested of course. I suppose it's an honour to be selected, but I've no time for umpiring – I'm a leader. I want to go in the forefront of the battle.

JONES You're quite right, Captain Mainwaring. You don't want to be an umpire, we never had no umpires when we was in the Sudan. General Kitchener didn't believe in them. All's fair in love and war he used to say – a very educated man, he was. He used to make us wait until the Fuzzie Wuzzies was about sixty yards away and then we used to mow 'em down. They was all dead, M r Mainwaring. They didn't need no umpires to tell them, they knew they was dead.

Mainwaring reacts.

WILSON Do you know something, sir? Talking of umpires reminds me of when I was at school. I caught a boy pinching tuck from the stodge.

MAINWARING Tuck from the stodge? Was this some foreign school?

WILSON No, no. Tuck was school slang for sweets, and the stodge was what we call the school sweet shop.

MAINWARING Extraordinary.

WILSON Anyway, the boy in question happened to be my fag.

MAINWARING Your fag?

WILSON A fag is a little boy who runs errands and cleans your study out. I didn't want to beat him.

MAINWARING Beat him!

WILSON Yes, sixth formers were supposed to sort of keep order.

MAINWARING If you ask me, the whole system reeks of depravity.

JONES You're right there, sir. But they turn out very brave officers, because they've been through all that depravity, you see.

Mainwaring reacts.

WILSON Anyway, I made him write out 100 times, 'The great umpire in the sky is always watching me'. I was rather proud of it, 'The great umpire in the sky is always watching me'. Then a few years ago I saw his name in the papers – he got three years for share-pushing. I should have made him write it out 500 times, shouldn't I? (**He laughs**)

The phone rings. Mainwaring picks it up.

MAINWARING Mainwaring – Walmington-on-Sea Home Guard.

INTERCUT: PHONE BACKING

COLONEL Ah, Mainwaring. I'm afraid it's no dice with the brigadier, you'll have to be an umpire.

MAINWARING I see – well, an order is an order, I suppose.

COLONEL I thought you'd see it that way. There is one compensation though, you'll get a staff car.

MAINWARING A staff car?

COLONEL That's right – what's more, it hasn't been

allocated, so you might be able to hang on to it. Anyway, it's yours for the time being. I'll get it along to you today.

INTERIOR. SIDE OFFICE. DAY

MAINWARING Thank you, sir. That's very good news. **(He puts the phone down)** I'm getting a staff car, Wilson.

WILSON How marvellous – why?

MAINWARING Well, obviously this umpiring thing is very highly important and, by doing it, I become something of a key figure.

WILSON What sort of a car will it be?

JONES They're usually Humber cars, sir – big powerful Humber cars with a glass wall in them, so the driver can't hear the secret plans.

MAINWARING Yes – well, I expect it will be a limousine of some sort.

Enter the Vicar, Verger and Hodges. Verger carries a Christmas pudding-size piece of putty on a tin plate.

VICAR This really is a beastly nuisance, Mr Hodges. Are you sure it's necessary?

HODGES What has to be, has to be, Vicar. You should know that, you say it often enough in those boring sermons.

VERGER The Vicar's sermons are not boring – there's several good bits in each one.

JONES What are you sticking your nose in for? No one asked you your opinion.

MAINWARING Jones, Jones – that'll do. What exactly is going on?

HODGES It's new black-out regulations – no smoking in the streets after dark, and all outside keyholes have got to be bunged up.

VERGER I've got enough putty here for every keyhole under His Reverence's jurisdiction, and it's fresh. Smell it, Your Reverence. **(He pushes the putty under the Vicar's nose)**

VICAR I have no desire to smell it, Mr Yeatman. I hate that horrid smell of linseed, it upsets my sinus.

MAINWARING Now, listen – half that keyhole is military property – and I'm not having putty put in it.

HODGES You've got to, Napoleon – it's regulations.

MAINWARING Who made them?

HODGES I did. It's been scientifically proved by experts that a thin shaft of light, no thicker than a pencil, shining through a keyhole can be seen by an enemy plane a thousand feet up.

Sylvia enters.

SYLVIA Hello, Mum said I'd find you here.

HODGES Oh, this is my niece Sylvia.

MAINWARING How do you do? **(Indicates Jones)** Corporal Jones.

JONES Yes, sir.

MAINWARING This is Sergeant Wilson.

JONES How do you do, Sergeant Wilson?

MAINWARING Not you, Jones.

WILSON **(Takes Sylvia's hand)** May I say how very pretty you look in uniform. Don't you think so, sir? You're so delightfully feminine, yet you still look efficient.

HODGES Just a minute, stop handling my niece.

WILSON I'm not handling her, as you put it.

HODGES Oh yes you are.

MAINWARING Mr Hodges, my men are not in the habit of handling young ladies. Sergeant Wilson is just being his usual polite self – aren't you, Wilson? Let go of her hand while I'm talking to you, Wilson.

There is a honking car horn off.

MAINWARING What on earth's that?

Pike rushes into the office.

PIKE Captain Mainwaring, sorry to interrupt, but the colonel has just driven into the yard.

JONES The colonel's just driven into the yard, Mr Mainwaring – turn out the guard. **(He goes to the main hall door)** Turn out the guard. There's nobody there, Mr Mainwaring.

WILSON They're outside, Jonesey.

JONES Oh, yes – fall in the guard – fall in the guard. **(He runs out)**

MAINWARING I'm afraid I've no more time to waste on this ridiculous business. My new staff car has just arrived. **(He rises and moves to the door)**

HODGES A staff car – how did you get a staff car?

MAINWARING My position entitles me to one.

HODGES Who are you kidding? Your position wouldn't entitle you to a pair of roller skates.

Mainwaring goes out, followed by Wilson.

THE CHURCH YARD. DAY

A small Austin 8 is parked there. The colonel is just getting out. Mainwaring salutes.

COLONEL Ah – here you are, Mainwaring. There's a box of thunderflashes in the back. You can use them to simulate mortar fire.

MAINWARING Thank you, sir.

COLONEL Sorry I can't stop, my car's waiting to pick me up outside.

JONES Squad. 'shun. Present arms.

All the remainder of the platoon do their best to present arms. Jones does likewise.

COLONEL **(Going towards gates)** You're pushing your luck a bit there, Corporal. Oh, there's not much juice in it – I'll send round four gallons, that should easily see the captain through the exercise. **(He goes)**

JONES Sloop arms.

Wilson and Mainwaring approach the car.

WILSON Is this it?

MAINWARING What do you mean, is this it?

WILSON It's rather small isn't it?

GODFREY I think it's rather sweet.

MAINWARING This sort of vehicle is absolutely first class for the sort of cut-and-thrust warfare that we're involved in. You can nip in, hit the enemy and nip out again.

FRAZER Aye – and you'd look a right Jessie sitting in anything bigger.

PIKE Is it bullet proof, Mr Mainwaring?

MAINWARING Of course it's not bullet proof.

Hodges enters.

HODGES Blimey, is that it? You don't call that a staff car, do you?

WILSON We happen to think it's rather charming.

HODGES I was right – I said you wasn't entitled to a pair of roller skates, they've sent you one. Come on, Vicar. Come on, Sylv.

MAINWARING **(To platoon)** Well, don't all stand there, staring at it. Send the men to the hall, Wilson, to maintain their rifles.

WILSON **(Goes to men)** Right, well you heard what the captain said.

They drift off to the hall except for Godfrey who sits and rolls bandages, and Frazer who hovers, and Jones who examines the car. Pike approaches Mainwaring.

PIKE Mr Mainwaring, please can I be your driver?

MAINWARING Don't be absurd, Pike.

PIKE I've got a provisional licence.

MAINWARING You don't even know how to drive.

PIKE Well, you could teach me – teach me to drive, Mr Mainwaring.

MAINWARING Quiet, Pike. Sergeant Wilson will be in charge of the driving.

Pike runs round the car.

PIKE Uncle Arthur – you'll teach me to drive.

WILSON Go away, Frank.

PIKE **(Whispers)** If you don't teach me, I'll tell Mum and you won't get your egg for breakfast on Sunday.

MAINWARING Right, as umpire I'll be taking my sergeant and my corporal, and possibly my runner – the rest of the platoon will go separately on foot. Get in the driving seat, Wilson. You're in the back, Jones.

PIKE Can I be the runner, Captain Mainwaring?

MAINWARING Not unless you behave. You go first, Jones.

JONES Yes, sir. **(Jones salutes and gets into the back of the car)**

Pike helps Mainwaring into the seat and shuts the door. Pike slams the door.

MAINWARING Good. That seems satisfactory.

JONES Permission to speak, Captain Mainwaring?

MAINWARING Yes, Jones.

JONES What we is doing is not proper army etiquette.

MAINWARING What are you talking about?

JONES It is not proper army etiquette for him, Sergeant Wilson, who is a sergeant, to be driving me, Corporal Jones, who is a corporal.

MAINWARING Yes. **(To Wilson)** Yes, well, I suppose Jones could drive, couldn't he?

WILSON I think it would be an excellent idea.

MAINWARING Change round.

Wilson gets out, Jones doesn't move.

MAINWARING I said change round, Jones.

JONES You'll have to get out, Captain Mainwaring, Mr Wilson's seat doesn't tip forward.

MAINWARING Oh, very well.

PIKE I'll help you, Captain Mainwaring.

MAINWARING **(Climbing out)** Out you get, Jones.

JONES **(Getting out)** Excuse me, sir. **(Jones climbs into the car)**

WILSON After you, sir.

MAINWARING Thank you. **(He sits down)**

WILSON Oh – I beg your pardon, sir, if I get in after you, I can't get in.

MAINWARING Do get yourself organised, Wilson.

PIKE I'll help you, Captain Mainwaring.

MAINWARING **(Climbing out)** Get out of the way, Pike. Get in, Wilson.

Wilson and Mainwaring get into their respective seats.

MAINWARING Yes, well that seems all right.

PIKE Captain Mainwaring – where's the runner go?

MAINWARING We're not concerned with that at the moment.

GODFREY Captain Mainwaring – how about the runner going on the running board?

MAINWARING Get on with whatever you're doing, Godfrey.

FRAZER There's just one thing, Captain Mainwaring, Sergeant Wilson looks more important than you.

MAINWARING How do you make that out, Frazer?

FRAZER Because he's sitting alone at the back.

MAINWARING **(Considers)** Yes – change places, Wilson.

Pike helps him out. Wilson gets out. Jones pips the horn.

MAINWARING What did you do that for, Jones?

JONES I just got an urge to test it.

MAINWARING Well, don't. You'll have the neighbours round.

WILSON After you, sir.

MAINWARING Don't start all that again, Wilson.

WILSON I'm sorry sir. **(Wilson sits)**

Mainwaring can't get in.

MAINWARING Wilson, I can't get in with your great bit fat body on that seat.

WILSON **(Getting out)** You're getting me very confused because you're shouting at me.

MAINWARING I am not shouting at you.

WILSON Well, you're speaking very, very loud.

Mainwaring gets into the car.

MAINWARING Just sit down.

They sit down. Mainwaring at the back, Wilson at the front.

MAINWARING Yes – that seems all right.

FRAZER Aye, that's fine. You can swank to your heart's content sitting there.

PIKE There's just one other thing, Captain Mainwaring – what about the runner?

MAINWARING Ah yes – stand on the run, er – that thing down there.

PIKE **(Trying it)** It's not safe, Mr Mainwaring, and I have to hang on with two hands, and I couldn't use my Tommy gun.

JONES Why don't we have him beside you, sir?

MAINWARING Oh no – I'm not having that.

WILSON No, if he sits there, he'll look just as important as Captain Mainwaring.

FRAZER He'll look more important, he's taller.

GODFREY You ought to face backwards, Captain Mainwaring, then he can cover your rear.

JONES That is quite correct, Captain Mainwaring, General Kitchener never advanced anywhere without covering his rear. **(To Mainwaring)** You see...

MAINWARING Yes, all right, all right – try that, Pike.

PIKE Don't bother to get up, Captain Mainwaring, I'll climb over. **(Pike tries to climb over Mainwaring to get to the spare seat)**

MAINWARING Pike, what are you doing? Where are you going?

PIKE I won't be a second – just have a bit of patience.

They achieve the desired positions.

MAINWARING Oh no – this won't do at all. We'll have to re-think the whole position. Get out, Wilson.

Fade on the chaos as they get out.

INTERIOR. SMALL MILK BAR

Behind the counter is a girl assistant. Pike is at the bar with Jones. He sucks up the last of the drink through a straw.

PIKE One more raspberryade please, Nora.

NORA You're going it a bit, aren't you?

PIKE Well, it's thirsty work – we've been going over our new staff car, haven't we, Mr Jones?

JONES Yeah – we've been going over our new staff car – sorting out the teething trouble problems.

Nora delivers new drink.

NORA That'll be threepence.

PIKE Threepence!

NORA Yeah – it's gone up. There's a war on, you know.

PIKE **(Paying)** Did you have staff cars in the Sudan, Mr Jones?

JONES No – nothing like that in those days. We had a staff camel once – it was very good in the desert, but it didn't have a horn and windscreen wipers, or anything like that.

The A.T.S. girl, Sylvia, enters. She sits at the bar.

SYLVIA Evening.

PIKE Hello.

SYLVIA Are you part of that Home Guard lot round at the church?

PIKE That's right. You were with the Warden, weren't you? You're Sylvia.

SYLVIA That's right. How did you know?

PIKE My Uncle Arthur told me – he's the sergeant.

SYLVIA Oh, I remember – randy old geezer, isn't he?

JONES You mustn't say that about Mr Wilson like that – he went to public school.

SYLVIA They're the worst. **(To Nora)** Lime crush please. Why aren't you a proper soldier?

PIKE What do you mean? I am a proper soldier.

JONES Yeah – we're all proper soldiers.

SYLVIA No, I mean why aren't you in the proper army.

JONES Well – I'm knocking on a bit, you know.

SYLVIA I wasn't meaning you.

PIKE I've got funny blood – there's not one in a million like me. If I crashed in my spitfire and got wounded, they couldn't transfuse me.

SYLVIA Ooh – fancy that.

PIKE I'm waiting to be called up for the secret service.

JONES I didn't know that.

PIKE Shut up.

SYLVIA What happens if you get wounded in the secret service?

PIKE I don't care – that's me all over.

Nora gives Sylvia the lime crush.

NORA Threepence please.

PIKE Have it on me.

SYLVIA Ooh, thanks. Won't your girlfriend get jealous if she sees us?

PIKE I don't have one – at least, not a special one. I play the field.

JONES Have you told Captain Mainwaring you're going in the secret service?

PIKE No, Mr Jones.

JONES You'll have to give him notice, you know. You can't just come in one evening and say, 'Goodbye, Mr Mainwaring, I'm off to the secret service' – and there's the bank to consider.

PIKE Mr Jones, I'm having a private conversation with this young lady, will you please not keep interrupting.

Jones is offended but not knowing how to deal with it.

JONES I see – I see. **(He goes to the door)** A friend in need, is a friend indeed. **(He goes out)**

SYLVIA **(Taking her drink)** Cheers.

PIKE Cheers.

SYLVIA You've got smashing eyebrows.

PIKE You what?

SYLVIA I said, you've got smashing eyebrows.

PIKE Have I? **(He looks upwards trying to see them)**

SYLVIA They're like Tyrone Power.

PIKE Are they? **(He pushes his eyebrows down with his hand trying to see them)**

SYLVIA **(Getting a mirror out of her bag)** Here, look.

PIKE **(He does so)** Ooh, yeah – I like Tyrone Power.

SYLVIA Do you got to the pictures a lot?

PIKE Yeah – we're going to the one at Eastgate tomorrow.

SYLVIA Cor – you don't half sweep a girl off her feet – what time shall I meet you?

PIKE I mean me and um – see you at the church hall at 6.30, after the parade?

SYLVIA **(Drinking)** Cheers.

PIKE **(Drinking)** Cheers.

THE CHURCH YARD. DAY

The platoon are drawn up. Mainwaring is addressing them.

MAINWARING Finally – to distinguish you from the opposing side, each of you will wear an arm band – are you ready, Jones?

JONES Yes, sir. The arm bands are present and correct.

MAINWARING Hand them out then.

JONES Yes, sir. **(He hands out the arm bands)**

MAINWARING Pike, will you stop looking at your watch.

PIKE I'm sorry, sir – are you going to be long?

MAINWARING I shall be as long as I need to be – there's a war on, you know. **(He turns to Wilson)** Why does that boy keep looking at his watch?

WILSON We're going to the pictures, sir.

MAINWARING He keeps looking at the gate as well.

WILSON That's the way to the pictures.

MAINWARING Tell him to stop fidgeting.

WILSON Yes, sir. Do stand still, Frank.

FRAZER **(Looking at his arm band)** Excuse me, Captain Mainwaring, my band doesn't say umpire – it just says UMP.

MAINWARING How do you account for that, Jones?

JONES Well, I look at it this wa,y sir. When you are wearing a band, all that will show will be UMP because the IRE will be under the arm. Therefore, to write it was superfluous – so I didn't.

MAINWARING I see.

WILSON I think he's got a point, sir.

FRAZER He was too mean to use the ink.

JONES Look who's talking.

MAINWARING Silence in the ranks. Well, there's no time to alter them – I shall wear this sash.

GODFREY Excuse me, Captain Mainwaring, sitting in your car with that sash, you'll look very important.

MAINWARING Godfrey, you must get out of this habit of talking in the ranks. Right then, parade here tomorrow morning – six o'clock sharp. Dismiss.

They dismiss. Pike grabs Wilson. Sylvia appears at the gate.

PIKE Uncle Arthur, you don't really want to go to the pictures tonight, do you?

WILSON Well, not all that much.

PIKE All right then, I'll go on my own.

WILSON Well, if you're going, I don't mind.

PIKE No – I wouldn't hear of it. You stop home and have a nice evening with Mum. Can I borrow seven and six?

WILSON Seven and six? The seats are only one and nine.

PIKE I might go in the two and threes.

WILSON Yes – but seven and six!

PIKE I might go with someone.

Wilson sees Sylvia in the gateway.

WILSON Oh – I see. Here – here's ten bob. Have a good time, Frank.

Mainwaring crosses.

MAINWARING Walk home with me, Wilson, there are one or two things to discuss.

WILSON Oh, all right, sir. Goodnight, Frank.

PIKE Goodnight, Uncle Arthur. Goodnight, Mr Mainwaring.

MAINWARING Goodnight, Frank.

Sylvia goes up to Pike.

PIKE Sorry it was so long.

SYLVIA Blimey – he does go on, doesn't he?

PIKE Oh, he's all right. We'd better hurry, we'll miss the Eastgate bus.

SYLVIA **(Indicating car)** Is this the staff car you were talking about?

PIKE Yeah – that's it. Let's go.

SYLVIA I drive one of those with the unit – are you in charge of it?

PIKE Well – sort of – yes.

SYLVIA Let's go in that then.

PIKE No we can't, that's Captain Mainwaring's.

She starts to get in.

SYLVIA I had 70 out of ours last week.

PIKE Hey – you're not allowed to get in, it's Captain Mainwaring's. **(He goes to the other door)**

SYLVIA You're in charge, there's no harm in sitting in it, is there?

PIKE No, there's no harm in sitting in it. **(Pike sits beside her)**

SYLVIA It's good, isn't it – oh look, he's left the keys in.

PIKE You'd better give them to me.

She starts the car.

SYLVIA Starts well, doesn't she.

PIKE Turn it off.

SYLVIA What's the matter, are you scared?

PIKE Go on – turn it off.

She turns it off.

SYLVIA Do you know something, I'm disappointed in you. I didn't think of you as a soppy boy.

PIKE I am not a soppy boy.

SYLVIA I thought you were a real man.

PIKE I am a real man.

SYLVIA I thought you could take snap decisions.

PIKE I can take snap decisions.

SYLVIA Good. You can tell me the way to get there. **(She starts the car and puts it into gear)**

PIKE Here – what are you doing?

SYLVIA Relax – we're going to the pictures.

PIKE You'll get into trouble – we'll both get into trouble.

She starts to turn the car in order to drive off.

EXTERIOR. ROAD. DAY

The car is driving along the road to Eastgate. We hear the voices.

SYLVIA What are you worried about? No one saw us.

PIKE No – but they might have done.

SYLVIA Pigs might fly.

PIKE You seem to forget, I've got a very responsible position in this town.

SYLVIA I think that's what first attracted me to you. Haven't you got thin knees?

PIKE They're not thinner than anybody else's.

SYLVIA They are, they're like sparrows.

PIKE Gerroff!

INTERIOR. THE CINEMA

Mix to two rows of the cinema. A barely intelligible, turgid love scene is in progress on the invisible screen, with

appropriate music. Pike sits with Sylvia in the back row but one. He sucks his thumb and is totally absorbed. There are two empty seats behind them. Sylvia is looking for the action.

SYLVIA Isn't it wonderful the way Robert Taylor puts his arm around her – so protective and romantic.

PIKE Yeah.

SYLVIA You look a bit like Robert Taylor – sideways on.

PIKE Yeah.

SYLVIA Do you think I look like her? **(There is no reply from Pike)** Do you think I need protecting?

PIKE Gerroff! **(Pike concentrates on the film. Suddenly there is a piercing scream from the screen and the music changes to high drama)**

SYLVIA Ooh – someone kicked me from behind. **(She turns)** Do you mind being more careful with your great big feet.

The close knit figures of Jones and Mrs Fox rise into view in the seats behind Pike.

PIKE Oh – hello, Mr Jones.

MRS FOX I'm ever so sorry – that awful scream gave me a real turn. Thank goodness you were with me, Mr Jones.

JONES This is Mrs Fox. We sometimes go to the cinema together, but there's nothing in it.

PIKE This is Sylvia – she thinks I'm like Robert Taylor – sideways on.

Customers shush them. They resume looking at the screen. Pike wishes to make an impression and decides to put his arm around Sylvia. Before completing the manoeuvre, he thinks better of it and returns to the thumb-in-the-mouth position. Sylvia feels his knee again.

PIKE Gerroff!

EXTERIOR. ROAD

Mix to car returning along the road, late evening. Note we were on double summer time so it didn't get dark until about eleven o'clock at midsummer. Voices are heard from the car.

PIKE Good picture, wasn't it?

SYLVIA Yeah.

PIKE I like Robert Taylor, don't you?

SYLVIA Yeah.

PIKE It's good having my car to drive in, isn't it?

SYLVIA It would be, if I wasn't hungry.

PIKE There wasn't time for a snack – my Mum will want to know where I've been.

SYLVIA **(Imitating)** My Mum will want to know where I've been.

PIKE That's not funny.

The car coughs and splutters.

PIKE What's that?

SYLVIA I expect the car's hungry and all.

The car coughs and comes to a halt. Cut to interior.

PIKE What's the matter?

SYLVIA It's stopped, hasn't it?

PIKE **(Slight panic)** Why has it stopped?

SYLVIA **(Impersonating an American)** I figure we've run out of gas, baby.

PIKE You've planned this, haven't you? You've done this deliberately.

SYLVIA Do you honestly think that I've nothing better to do than plan to run out of petrol, in the middle of a country road with you, you stupid-looking boy.

PIKE I'm not a stupid-looking boy – stop calling me a stupid-looking boy.

SYLVIA You're retarded, you are.

There is a short silence

SYLVIA What's the time?

PIKE Half-past ten. Any moment now, my mum will start worrying about me.

SYLVIA **(Imitating)** My mum will start worrying about me.

PIKE Shut up – what are we going to do?

SYLVIA Let's find a haystack and spend the night beneath the stars in each other's arms.

PIKE Gerroff!

SYLVIA All right then – get out and push.

PIKE Push! It's nine miles!

SYLVIA Have you got a better idea?

Pike gets out and starts to push.

PIKE Are you just going to sit there?

SYLVIA Yes.

PIKE You'll have to help up the hills.

SYLVIA We'll worry about that when the time comes.

THE CHURCH YARD. DAY

The platoon are standing around ready to move off. They are wearing their arm bands. Godfrey is checking his first aid kit. The car is absent.

FRAZER Yon Mainwaring – I've never seen him in such a state. If he goes on like this he'll burst a blood vessel.

GODFREY Oh dear – I don't think I've got anything for a broken blood vessel.

Jones enters and crosses to Wilson.

JONES Mr Wilson, sir, I've just seen my boy Raymond, and I've told him to scour the neighbourhood on his bicycle.

WILSON Thank you, Jonesey.

JONES Don't worry, Mr Wilson – the little car can't have gone far 'cos I never put the petrol in it.

Mainwaring returns from the side office.

MAINWARING I've just been on to the police, Wilson. Our vehicle hasn't been reported and they're sending out an all-car call.

WILSON They've only got one car.

MAINWARING Don't belittle the strength of the civil power, Wilson. Are all the men present?

JONES Yes, sir – all present and Bristol fashion – except Pike.

MAINWARING Except Pike – where's he got to?

WILSON Perhaps he slept late or something.

Mrs Pike enters

MRS PIKE Where is he then? What have you done with him? What have you done with Frank?

WILSON I haven't done anything with him, Mavis.

MRS PIKE You said he'd gone to bed early – his bed hasn't even been slept i. And where were you last night?

WILSON I wasn't anywhere.

Hodges enters.

HODGES **(Going to Wilson)** All right then – what have you done with her? Where are you hiding her, eh?

WILSON What on earth are you talking about?

HODGES You know perfectly well what I'm talking about. Where's my niece Sylvia?

WILSON How should I know?

HODGES She was last seen with a soldier, and she's not been heard of since. You were the said soldier, weren't you? I saw you ogling her in the office.

MRS PIKE What have you been up to, Arthur?

WILSON I really haven't been up to anything.

FRAZER It had to happen, the man's a sex maniac.

JONES Permission to speak, sir? I know nothing about it from personal experience, but I have a hunch that Private Pike has gone to the pictures at Eastgate.

MAINWARING What, at quarter to six in the morning?

GODFREY I fell asleep in the pictures once.

MAINWARING Don't keep interrupting, Godfrey, it's very irritating.

Godfrey reacts.

HODGES Look, I don't care what's happened to that soppy boy. What's he **(Indicating Wilson)** done with my niece?

MAINWARING What's far more important at the moment, is what's happened to my staff car?

An exhausted Pike pushes the car into the yard, helped by Sylvia.

MAINWARING Pike – where have you been with that car?

PIKE Nine miles up the road to Eastgate, and I've pushed it back every perishing foot.

HODGES **(To Sylvia)** And where have you been, Sylvia?

SYLVIA With him.

HODGES With him – with that soppy boy? **(He turns to Pike)** Do you mean to tell me that you've been out all night in that car with my niece? **(He turns to Mainwaring, Wilson and Mrs Pike)** He'll have to marry her.

Mainwaring reacts.

SYLVIA Are you out of your mind? I'm not marrying a soppy boy like him.

HODGES You spent the night with him, soppy boy or no soppy boy.

PIKE Stop calling me a soppy boy.

MAINWARING Pike, you're under arrest. Wilson, lock him in the office. Godfrey, you'll stay behind and guard him until the police arrive.

HODGES Don't you start bringing the police into it. I'm not having her dragged through the courts.

MRS PIKE Yes, you leave my boy alone. He was good as gold until he started going around with you lot. **(She turns to Pike)** I'll box your ears when I get you home. **(She starts to hit Pike with her handbag)**

MAINWARING Leave that man alone. I'm in charge here and justice will take its course.

HODGES Stop being pompous, Napoleon.

MAINWARING Keep out of this – escort him to the office, Wilson.

MRS PIKE Arthur, if you lay a finger on him, I'll make your life a misery for the rest of your days.

Wilson reacts.

FRAZER Captain Mainwaring, jut one small point. What are the police going to say when they find out the car wasn't immobilised?

JONES You're right, Mr Frazer – it's a criminal offence not to immobilise a car.

FRAZER Aye – and you're responsible – do you understand that? You're responsible.

MAINWARING I see. Well, none of these things will stop me from doing my duty, but it would be wrong for me not to take them into consideration.

JONES And, Captain Mainwaring, we're due at the rendezvous in seven minutes.

MAINWARING Yes – well, the army must come first. We'll take the whole matter up this evening. Private Sponge, fall the men in – get the petrol in the car.

EXTERIOR. ROAD. DAY

Mix to the staff car, which is stopped by the roadside. Mainwaring is just getting out. Jones is driving. Pike and Wilson are in the back. Pike has the thunderflashes on his knees.

MAINWARING Come with me, Jones. I'm just going to that rise to see if I can spot their positions.

JONES Yes, sir – coming, sir.

Mainwaring goes and Jones follows. Wilson starts to light a cigarette.

WILSON Do you want one, Frank?

PIKE No thanks, I don't. Yes, why not.

During this conversation, Wilson gives Pike a cigarette and lights it.

WILSON Frank – about last night.

PIKE I know we shouldn't have taken it, but we didn't do the car no harm.

WILSON No, no, I'm not talking about the car, it's about the girl. A lot of people know you spent the night with her and a lot of people are going to tell you what you both did was wrong.

PIKE I was pushing and she was steer...

Wilson interrupting because he is simply not listening.

WILSON Well, of course, you have offended against generally accepted conventions but, to my way of thinking, what you both did wasn't actually evil – do you follow me?

PIKE It was nine miles.

WILSON All the same, society – our sort of society – has a rather rigid framework and if we don't stay within it, people point the finger at us.

PIKE It took an hour to get up Grant Hill – twenty yards at a time.

WILSON But, just remember this, Frank. I understand. We haven't been all that close in the past, but now I feel somehow we're kindred spirits – sort of men of the world. Do you feel that too?

PIKE **(Deciding to go along with it)** Yeah – that's right – kindred spirits, we're men of the world.

WILSON Good lad. **(He sees Mainwaring returning)** Look out, he's coming back.

Wilson quickly extinguishes his cigarette. Pike bungles it and drops his into the thunderflash box. He scrabbles for it.

MAINWARING Right, drive on to the crossroads, Jones. **(He and Jones get into the car)**

PIKE Uncle Arthur – **(He mimes the cigarette is in the box. Wilson doesn't catch on)** Don't go yet, Mr Mainwaring.

MAINWARING Be quiet, Pike. I don't want to hear another murmur out of you all day.

PIKE You're going to hear more than a murmur in a minute.

They drive off. Pike frantically chucks the thunderflashes out one by one. They explode on either side of the car as they drive off.

SERIES NINE **EPISODE THREE**

Recorded: Friday 22/7/77

Original transmission: Sunday 16/10/77, 8.10–8.40pm

Original viewing figures = 19 million

ARTHUR LOWE .... CAPTAIN MAINWARING
JOHN LE MESURIER .... SERGEANT WILSON
CLIVE DUNN .... LANCE CORPORAL JONES
JOHN LAURIE .... PRIVATE FRAZER
ARNOLD RIDLEY .... PRIVATE GODFREY
IAN LAVENDER .... PRIVATE PIKE
BILL PERTWEE .... CHIEF WARDEN HODGES
FRANK WILLIAMS .... VICAR
EDWARD SINCLAIR .... VERGER
JANET DAVIES .... MRS PIKE
COLIN BEAN .... PRIVATE SPONGE
OLIVE MERCER .... MRS YEATMAN
ERIC LONGWORTH .... TOWN CLERK
FRED MCNAUGHTON .... MAYOR
PLATOON .... DESMOND CULLUM-JONES, GEORGE HANCOCK, FREDDIE WHITE, FREDDIE WILES, MICHAEL MOORE, JIMMY MAC, ROGER BOURNE, VERNON DRAKE, EVAN ROSS
NOTE: THE THETFORD ATC 1109 SQUADRON APPEARED AS THE SEA CADET BAND.
DOUBLES FOR ARTHUR LOWE .... DEREK WARE AND WILLIAM SULLY
DOUBLE FOR BILL PERTWEE .... JIMMY LODGE

Knights of Madness

• DEREK WARE REMEMBERS •

'Any seasoned stuntman will tell you that working with horses is tricky. Riding a horse in armour is hard work. In the first place, theatrical armour is like the real thing. Just like a good suit, armour is not tailored. The cost of a full compliment of gothic armour (circa 1485) was the equivalent of a Lear jet today. So, falling off a horse in a full suit of armour means whatever amount you're being paid, you're earning it.

'I was hired to double Arthur Lowe on this occasion and had negotiated a fee for two falls. One was whilst being lowered into the saddle on a rope and pulley. The horse had to move forward and I had to be dropped on to the ground. The other was as Mainwaring drew his sword and held it aloft in preparation for battle to commence, the weight of it had to cause him to topple sideways on to the ground.

'As usual, there was a joker in the pack. Due to the inclement weather, shooting overran and another stuntman, who had been hired only for the day, had to get back to London as he was "in continuity" on a film at one of the big studios. I therefore had to take over as Warden Hodges, whose horse had to rear, throwing him backwards. Getting a horse to rear on cue isn't easy. We'd hired a spirited horse especially but, try as I might I couldn't get him to throw his fore legs. He was a stallion and becoming so fractious I was having trouble holding him. Finally someone had the bright idea of shooting a stone from a catapult at his rear end. By that time, I didn't care, I just wanted to get the shot over with. As it happened, it worked quite spectacularly. As the stone hit him, my mount plunged forward, slithered, and brought himself to a halt by standing up. The fall was easy, though as usual I went home aching. Come to think of it, I never negotiated an extra fee for doubling Bill Pertwee, either.'

Knights of Madness

INTERIOR. SIDE OFFICE. DAY

Close up of notice on door: 'Wings for Victory' committee meeting. Silence.

A lot of noise is coming from the church hall.

INTERIOR. CHURCH HALL. DAY

TOWN CLERK Ladies and gentlemen, order, order.

MRS YEATMAN Can we get on please?

VERGER I quite agree – we've been here for two hours already.

TOWN CLERK Now, I think we're all agreed on the poster, which I think is very nice, tasteful and artistic. (**The town clerk holds up poster which reads: Walmington-on-Sea 'Wings for Victory' week**)

MRS YEATMAN It ought to have more colours.

TOWN CLERK You can't have a lot of colours in wartime, Mrs Yeatman. The climax of the 'Wings for Victory' week will be the grand march past on Saturday afternoon. Now the mayor, who will be on the podium, will take the salute, along with myself and other officers of the town council. First the sea scout's drum and bugle band, then a keep-fit display by the ladies' netball team led by Mrs Yeatman.

GODFREY A point of order, Mr Chairman, are they going to wear dresses or shorts?

MRS YEATMAN My girls will wear shorts of course, you can't do P.T. in dresses.

GODFREY Ladies' legs can lead to ribald remarks from the crowd. I don't want my sister Dolly upset.

HODGES What's wrong with a bit of leg – lovely.

FRAZER Aye, those thighs gleaming in the sunlight.

JONES You're right there, Jock, especially with little white ankle socks.

VICAR Can we raise the level of this discuss, please?

VERGER I quite agree, Your Reverence.

VICAR Be quiet, Mr Yeatman.

MRS YEATMAN Will you keep your dirty old men in order, Mr Mainwaring.

MAINWARING I'm completely indifferent to this whole discussion.

HODGES He's hardly said a word, he's sulking.

MAINWARING I am not sulking.

HODGES Oh yes you are, just because you haven't been made chairman.

MAINWARING If I had been chairman, we wouldn't have been here for two hours.

HODGES No, we would have been here for four hours.

Mainwaring reacts.

TOWN CLERK Well, we seem to be making progress. After that, we have the display of Morris dancing. Now, are there any more suggestions?

JONES Mr chairman, through the chair, can I take the floor?

TOWN CLERK Are we all in agreement that Mr Jones should take the floor? (**He looks round**) Right, carried. Mr Jones, the floor is yours.

JONES (**Getting up**) Thank you. Now, ladies and gentlemen, this is a litter bug. (**He holds up a poster with a large litter bug on it. Slogan reads 'Don't be a litter bug. Save waste paper'**)

JONES And this is a squander bug. (**He holds up a poster with a large squander bug on it. Slogan reads 'Don't be a squander bug'**)

JONES Why don't we have two people dressed up as these bugs? The litter bug could throw paper about and the squander bug could run around, throwing money all over the place.

FRAZER Hold on, hold on, who's going to supply the money?

JONES It will be imitation money.

TOWN CLERK I don't think we could have two bugs. We'll have to make do with one bug. After all, bug costumes cost money.

WILSON If we spend a lot on a squander bug costume, it does seem to rather defeat the object.

Mainwaring reacts.

MRS PIKE Frank's got a squander bug costume. I made it for him for the scout show last year.

PIKE I'm not going to wear that. It makes me look a fool.

VICAR I saw the show. I thought you looked rather sweet in it.

There is a pause. They all stare at the Vicar.

PIKE Please don't make me wear it, Mr Mainwaring, please.

MAINWARING You'll just have to sort it out amongst yourselves.

HODGES There you are, he's sulking again. Unless he can be in charge, telling everyone what to do, he sulks.

MRS YEATMAN Can we get on, please?

TOWN CLERK I quite agree, that's settled then. Frank Pike will be the squander bug. Now, the grand finale –

MAINWARING I've decided what it's going to be – my platoon will be doing it.

HODGES What do you mean? The Wardens are going to do the grand finale.

MAINWARING Look, the finale will be done by the Home Guard, and that's that.

TOWN CLERK Gentlemen, gentlemen, please. I suggest that the Wardens and the Home Guard share the finale.

VICAR I second that.

VERGER I third it.

VICAR Be quiet, Mr Yeatman.

TOWN CLERK All those in favour.

Vicar, Verger, Hodges, Mrs Yeatman and Mrs Pike raise their hands.

TOWN CLERK That's – **(Counts)** One – two – three – four – five – six – seven. Those against.

Mainwaring, Jones, Frazer and Pike raise their arms.

MAINWARING Lift your arm up, Wilson.

WILSON I can't be bothered, sir, the whole thing's such a crashing bore.

PIKE I'll do it. **(He lifts Wilson's arm)** There. Don't be cross with him, Mr Mainwaring, he gets too tired for anything at the end of the day.

MRS PIKE That's a fact.

Mainwaring and Wilson react.

TOWN CLERK One, two, three, four, five, six, seven – well, it seems I have the casting vote, so it's settled that the grand finale will be shared by Captain Mainwaring and Mr Hodges. **(Looking at Mainwaring)** What are the Home Guards going to do?

MAINWARING I'm not going to tell you in front of him. **(He nods towards Hodges)**

TOWN CLERK And what is your contribution going to be, Mr Hodges.

HODGES And I'm not going to tell you in front of him.

TOWN CLERK Oh dear, we seem to have reached an impasse. Well, whatever it is, I'm sure it'll be very nice.

INTERIOR. OFFICE AT BANK. DAY

Mainwaring is sitting at his desk. He is on the telephone. Wilson and Pike are filing some papers in the cabinet.

MAINWARING I got your estimate, Mr Jackson. I must say the price is rather high. No, I don't want the legs cut down.

PIKE Uncle Arthur, is Mr Mainwaring buying a table?

MAINWARING It must have 22 legs.

PIKE It's a big table.

MAINWARING And the tail must be 12 feet long.

PIKE Perhaps he's buying an aeroplane.

WILSON Don't talk rubbish. Get on with your filing, Frank.

MAINWARING And I want the smoke to come through the nose.

PIKE I know, it's an aeroplane that lays a smoke screen with legs.

MAINWARING I'm afraid it's too expensive. I'll have to cancel it. Good day. **(He puts the phone down)** We'll have to get someone else to make it, Wilson.

WILSON What about asking Frazer and Jones?

MAINWARING That's not a bad idea, there's plenty of room in Frazer's workshop.

PIKE Oh no, Mr Mainwaring – Mr Frazer and Mr Jones couldn't make an aeroplane.

MAINWARING Can't you ever make an intelligent remark, Pike? Haven't you told him, Wilson?

WILSON Not yet, sir.

MAINWARING I have decided, Pike, that as the Wings for Victory parade coincides with St George's Day, we will stage a fight between St George and the dragon. Good against evil, representing England's fight against Hitler.

PIKE Can I play St George?

MAINWARING No you can't.

Pike reacts.

WILSON Have you decided who is going to play St George, sir?

MAINWARING I should think that's pretty obvious, Wilson.

WILSON You, sir?

Mainwaring nods. Wilson reacts.

MAINWARING Well, I'm borrowing the armour from a friend of mine and I don't think he'll let anybody else wear it.

WILSON But a real suit of armour will be very heavy. Why don't you wear cardboard armour?

MAINWARING Oh no. A man in my position can't afford to be seen fighting a dragon in a suit of cardboard armour, Wilson.

WILSON But real armour is a bit dangerous, sir.

MAINWARING Oh, I shan't do anything strenuous. Just walk the horse round the dragon and shout, 'Cry God for Harry, England and St George!' Then I shall make a symbolic gesture at the dragon with my wooden sword, like this – **(Picks up ruler and makes gesture)**

WILSON What's the dragon going to do, sir?

PIKE Make a symbolic gesture back I should think.

MAINWARING Pike, leave the office.

INTERIOR. CHURCH HALL. DAY

A vaulting horse down right. Mainwaring and Wilson are standing by the office door.

MAINWARING Hurry up, Pike.

PIKE **(Out of vision)** I'm not ready yet. You can't come in.

MRS PIKE **(Out of vision)** He won't be a minute, Mr Mainwaring.

Jones enters.

JONES The dragon's outside, sir. The men are getting into it.

MAINWARING Well done, Jones.

The office doors opens. Mrs Pike enters.

MRS PIKE Come along, Frank.

Pike enters in his squander bug costume.

WILSON I must say you've made that awfully well, Mavis.

MRS PIKE Thank you, Arthur. The Vicar was right, he does look sweet in it, doesn't he? He's a dear little squander bug.

PIKE It's too short, Mum. **(He tries to pull it down)**

MRS PIKE Leave it alone. **(She slaps his hands)**

MAINWARING The question is, what should he do?

JONES He should say, er… 'Don't squander money like me, save for victory' – then he should throw money about.

MAINWARING Good. Try it, Pike.

PIKE Don't squander money like me, save for victory.

MAINWARING That's no good.

JONES He should skip around while he's saying it, sir. **(Jones exits)**

MAINWARING Good idea, skip around, Pike, and make gestures as though you were throwing money about.

Pike skips about, throwing money around.

PIKE Don't squander money like me, save for victory. **(He stops and stamps his foot)** I feel such a fool.

Frazer and Godfrey enter.

FRAZER The men are in the dragon, Captain Mainwaring. **(He sees Pike)** Heavens above, what is it?

WILSON A squander bug.

FRAZER He looks like a potato on two matchsticks.

MRS PIKE Have you finished with him now, Mr Mainwaring?

MAINWARING Yes, thank you, Mrs Pike.

MRS PIKE Come on, Frank. **(She pushes Pike towards the office. He is still trying to pull the bottom of the costume down)**

MRS PIKE And leave it alone, you'll put it out of shape.

FRAZER It's coming in now, sir.

MAINWARING Good.

JONES **(Out of vision)** Dragon, by the left, quick march.

The dragon enters with the platoon in it. The head is worn by Jones.

JONES Left, right, left, right, left, right. Dragon, right wheel.

The front half turns, the tail comes away and marches down level with the head.

JONES Dragon, mark time.

A shutter in head slides open. Jones pokes his head out.

JONES 'Ere, where do you think you're going?

SPONGE You said right wheel.

JONES I didn't say come apart. Get behind me.

MAINWARING Jones, get on the front. **(He grabs the tail and tries to join it to the body as it marches round. He gets mixed up in the body)**

The dragon circles. The dragon goes round in a tight circle. Its jaws open and shut. The tail gets caught in its mouth.

MAINWARING Stop, stop.

The dragon stops. The shutter opens and Jones pokes his head out.

JONES What's the matter, sir?

MAINWARING You've got your tail in your mouth, Jones.

JONES Sorry, sir, I'll take it out.

The jaws open and the tail drops out.

MAINWARING Right, men, get out of the skin and I'll explain what we're going to do. Help me on with the helmet, Wilson.

Wilson picks up the helmet and puts it on Mainwaring. It reaches his nose.

MAINWARING I can't put it on wearing my glasses.

WILSON I'll take them, sir. **(He takes the glasses and pushes the helmet on)**

MAINWARING Open the visor.

Wilson tugs at it.

WILSON It seems to be stuck, sir.

Pike comes out of the office. He is back in uniform. He crosses to Mainwaring with Jones, who has got out of the dragon's head.

FRAZER I think it's rusted. I'll get some oil. **(He goes)**

MAINWARING **(Shouting)** Open it, Wilson.

• GRAHAM BEDWELL REMEMBERS •

'Having some 200 people on location for "Knights of Madness" presented challenges to both technical crew and production, like making sure that the impoverished extras and the ever-hungry youngsters in the band didn't eat the location-caterers bare before the crew or cast got to their bacon rolls. And it was not only Private Godfrey who needed comfort stations, what with an everlasting supply of tea and coffee and a cold East Anglian wind blowing.

'The "sound stage" was complex too. We had to record ample wild tracks (sound effects used to cover cuts and edit points) to cover the interiors of the tents, exterior chatter, marching band and so on. We also had to make wild track recordings of Captain Mainwaring's voice in his armoured suit helmet, so that when the double was hauled up on to the horse for the actual shoot, we would have the genuine muffled sound quality. Arthur Lowe was not amused

'I wanted to get real Tannoy sound quality as the town clerk commentated on the two St Georges from the raised stage, rather than rely on post-production public address distortion added in the dubbing stage. With my assistant's help and a borrowed car battery, we got the ancient prop Tannoy sound system to work. The reserve Nagra tape recorder with a "gun" microphone situated at about a hundred feet from the loudspeakers was set up to give a realistic distant perspective for the wide shots. The foreground sound was recorded "close up" to match the camera shots on the stage. There were no dual track Nagra stereo recorders used in those simple monoral sound days. This gave the sound editor and the dubbing mixer the opportunity to select which perspective sound they required.

'During that week there was some foul weather and shooting was held up waiting for the cloud to lift. Most of the crew and cast sat in the production bus and I remember listening to John Le Mesurier talking about his days in the theatre and films. If only I had recorded such memories – what gems!'

PIKE I didn't know the dragon had arrived, Uncle Arthur, it's ever so good.

WILSON Oh, get out of the way, Frank. **(To Mainwaring)** It's rusted up, sir.

MAINWARING I can't hear.

JONES Wait a minute, there's a little door here. **(He opens a door in the side of the helmet and shouts)**

JONES Can you hear now, sir?

MAINWARING Aarrh – you nearly deafened me, Jones.

JONES Sorry, sir. **(Whispers)** Can you hear me?

MAINWARING I can hear, but I can't see.

JONES He can hear, but he can't see.

WILSON **(Looking at glasses)** I don't know, it's a bit difficult.

PIKE Let me have a go, Uncle Arthur. **(Pike takes the glasses and slips the arms through the slits in the visor)** How's that?

Mainwaring in helmet.

WILSON That's awfully clever, Frank. Can you see now, sir?

Mainwaring shakes his head. Frazer returns with an oil can and a screwdriver.

FRAZER We'll soon have it ope,n sir. **(He gets to work)**

Jones opens another door on the helmet.

JONES There's another little door this side, this helmet is full of little doors. **(Whispers)** Can you hear me, sir?

Frazer takes the glasses off and hands them to Pike. He lifts the visor.

FRAZER How's that, Captain Mainwaring?

WILSON You've gone very red, sir, are you all right?

MAINWARING Just put my glasses on.

Pike puts Mainwaring's glasses through the hole. The visor slips and catches his fingers.

PIKE Ow!

MAINWARING Stop playing the fool, boy! **(He lifts up the visor)** Help me on the horse, and we'll try the fight.

FRAZER Here's your sword, Captain Mainwaring.

JONES And here's your head bonker, sir. **(He hands him a flail mace)**

MAINWARING That's a vicious-looking weapon.

JONES It's quite harmless. I made it out of an old tennis ball.

PIKE It wouldn't hurt a fly. **(Snatches the flail mace away from Mainwaring)** See – **(He hits Mainwaring on the head. The visor snaps down. Mainwaring lifts it up)**

MAINWARING You stupid boy. Now, this is how we shall present the fight. Pay attention, men. (**They gather round**) I shall ride the horse into the middle of the village green, then the dragon will run round me. Have you got that, Jones?

JONES Run round you, yes, sir.

MAINWARING I will then raise my sword, like this, and shout 'Cry God for Harry, England and Saint George!' Then you paw the ground and charge, Jones.

JONES Paw the ground and charge, yes, sir.

MAINWARING I shall then touch you on the head with the sword, and the dragon falls down. Get into the skin.

JONES Yes, sir.

The platoon start putting the skin on.

MAINWARING Pike, Wilson, help me up.

Visor falls. They get Mainwaring on the hobby horse. Pike gets hand stuck.

WILSON I'm sure you'd be better off wearing a cardboard helmet, sir.

MAINWARING I am not wearing a cardboard helmet, Wilson, and that is that.

JONES We're all ready, sir.

MAINWARING Right.

FRAZER Your sword, sir. (**Hands Mainwaring the sword**)

The dragon circles Mainwaring, stops in front of him and paws the ground.

MAINWARING Cry God for Harry, England and Saint George!

The dragon charges.

FRAZER (**Stopping Jones**) Hold on, hold on, the smoke should come out of the nostrils, sir. Where's the smoke, Jonesey?

JONES I can't get it to work.

FRAZER Ach, you silly old fool. (**He dives underneath into the head**)

MAINWARING That smoke pouring out of its nostrils will frighten the wits out of the crowd, Wilson.

WILSON The whole thing frightens the wits out of me, sir.

FRAZER All ready, sir.

MAINWARING Cry God for Harry, England and Saint George! Paw the ground, Jones.

JONES Yes, sir, yes, sir.

The dragon paws the ground.

MAINWARING Let's have the smoke, Jones.

Nothing happens.

MAINWARING Where's the smoke?

The dragon starts to tremble. A loud coughing comes from the men inside. The dragon falls over on its side, and clouds of smoke billow out.

EXTERIOR. FIELD. DAY

A block and tackle is rigged up on the branch of a tree. The dragon skin is lying on the ground. A horse is tethered up. The platoon are gathered, with Wilson, Pike and Godfrey, round an object on the ground. Wilson has an old English sheepdog on a lead. Jones and Frazer are testing the block and tackle.

JONES That should do the trick, Jock. Let's hope it works.

FRAZER Yon Mainwaring must be mad wearing a real suit of armour, it's vanity, sheer vanity.

Jones crosses to the group.

JONES We're ready to hoist you, sir.

The group parts, and we see Mainwaring sitting on the ground in his armour. Pike is buckling on the last piece.

MAINWARING Right, help me up.

Jones and Pike help him to his feet with a lot of clanking.

MAINWARING What have you brought that stupid-looking dog for, Wilson?

WILSON Knights always had these, you know.

MAINWARING Why do you always have to give yourself airs. Why can't you act in a normal way, like me. Now, listen, men, on Saturday afternoon we shall assemble here, mount up, and march into town in procession, so we've only got today to sort out any problems that may arise. Get the horse, Pike.

PIKE Yes, Mr Mainwaring.

Mainwaring clanks towards the block and tackle. Wilson follows. He is holding the helmet.

WILSON This is ridiculous, sir. That armour's far too heavy for you.

MAINWARING Don't be a defeatist, Wilson. If our forefathers were able to wear this, so can I (**He stumbles**)

Jones fits the rope round Mainwaring.

JONES Private Sponge –

SPONGE Yes, Mr Jones.

JONES You'll be in charge of pulling Captain Mainwaring up, and don't let him dangle.

SPONGE Right, come on, boys. (**Sponge and three strong members of the platoon get hold of the rope**)

Cut to dog reaction.

JONES Right, heave.

Sponge and co. heave. Mainwaring goes up.

WILSON Just a minute, sir, you've forgotten your helmet.

JONES Lower him down, don't let him dangle.

They lower him down. Wilson takes off Mainwaring's glasses and puts the helmet on. He opens the visor and puts the glasses back on.

WILSON **(Closes the visor)** All right, sir?

JONES He can't hear you. I'll open the little door. **(He opens the door and whispers)** Can you hear me, sir?

MAINWARING Yes, of course I can. Get on with it.

JONES He's in a funny mood. Haul away.

Mainwaring goes up. Cut to Godfrey and Frazer.

GODFREY Oh dear, it would have been much better if Captain Mainwaring had let my sister Dolly knit him a suit of chain mail.

FRAZER Don't worr,y Godfrey, son. If anything goes wrong, we can always get him out with a tin opener.

Cut back to Mainwaring in air.

WILSON Bring the horse underneath, Frank.

Pike leads the horse under Mainwaring. They lower him slowly. Pike lets go of the horse and comes to look.

PIKE Cor, that's ever so good.

Mainwaring is a few inches off the saddle. The horse walks forwards and Mainwaring sinks to the ground with a clatter.

WILSON Why didn't you hold the horse, Frank?

PIKE You didn't say anything about holding it, Uncle Arthur. You just said bring it round.

JONES Pull him up, pull him up.

They haul Mainwaring up. Cut to dog reaction. Cut back. Pike has led the horse round and it is under Mainwaring.

JONES Lower, lower.

WILSON Hold the horse's head, Frank.

PIKE I am holding it.

JONES Lower, lower.

Mainwaring turns slowly and sits in the saddle, facing the tail.

MAINWARING Hand me the reins, Wilson, I can't see very well.

WILSON I'm afraid that's going to be a little difficult, sir.

JONES I told you not to let him dangle, lift him up.

They pull Mainwaring up, turn him round and lower him into the saddle.

PIKE All set, Mr Mainwaring. **(To horse)** Come on, gee up. **(Pike leads the horse forward)**

The rope is still attached to Mainwaring and pulls him back off the horse.

EXTERIOR. FIELD

Close up of Mainwaring. He lifts visor.

MAINWARING All ready, Jones.

Cut to dragon. Jones slides back the shutter and pokes his head out.

JONES All ready, sir.

Cut to Godfrey and Frazer.

GODFREY What a noble figure Captain Mainwaring makes.

FRAZER Aye, noble but stupid.

Mainwaring walks the horse forward and stops. The dragon paws the ground and walks towards Mainwaring.

MAINWARING **(Holding his sword aloft)** Cry God for Harry, England and – **(The horse sinks on its back legs and Mainwaring slips off)** Saint George!

WILSON Dragon one, Saint George nil.

They rush to Mainwaring who is lying on the ground.

MAINWARING **(To Wilson)** I think, after all, we'd better let Godfrey's sister knit me a suit of armour.

VILLAGE GREEN

Two marquees are pitched at either end of the green. At the edge, a stand decked in flags. With the mayor in the stand are the town clerk, mace bearer and several members of the town council. The sea scout's drum and bugle band finish and, led by the Verger, march off the green, past the mayor who takes the salute.

INTERIOR MARQUEE

Wilson is dressed as Lyon King at Arms. Mainwaring in chain mail, harlequin tights and pixie boots.

WILSON I don't know why you didn't go to the theatrical costumiers over at Eastgate like the rest of us, sir.

MAINWARING I didn't want to disappoint Godfrey's sister Dolly. She's been working day and night on this.

VILLAGE GREEN

TOWN CLERK Ladies and gentlemen, the Walmington-on-Sea ladies' netball team present a keep-fit display.

Mrs Yeatman leads her team on to the green.

TOWN CLERK Oh they're very nice, they are, Mr Mayor.

MAYOR If you like that sort of thing.

INTERIOR. MARQUEE

Frazer is looking through a crack in the tent.

FRAZER Will you look at those thighs.

MAINWARING Come away from there, Frazer.

Pike enters, dressed as a herald.

PIKE I feel such a fool, Mr Mainwaring.

MAINWARING Stop grumbling.

WILSON Oh really, Frank. We let you off doing the squander bug so that you could be a herald, and still you're not satisfied.

PIKE I don't like showing my legs.

WILSON **(To Mainwaring)** It's a pity we've got to go on before the Wardens, sir.

MAINWARING Well, Hodges won the toss and there's nothing we can do about it. It doesn't matter – after we've done Saint George and the dragon, anything he does will be an anticlimax.

WARDEN'S MARQUEE

Hodges dressed like Mainwaring. Wardens in dragon skin. Vicar in the head.

HODGES Now, I will tap you with my sword and you fall over, is that clear?

The dragon nods his head.

HODGES Cor, I can't wait to see Mainwaring's face when we get out there, he'll be green with envy.

The Vicar's head pops out.

VICAR I must say, Mr Hodges, I think Saint George and the dragon is a simply spiffing idea, so original.

The Verger enters.

VICAR Hurry up, Mr Yeatman, get changed into your herald costume. Oh, this is so exciting.

MAINWARING'S MARQUEE

Pike is holding his trumpet.

PIKE Uncle Arthur, this trumpet makes a smashing pea-shooter, look. **(He puts some peas in his mouth and hits Sponge, who is bending over dragon costume)**

SPONGE Ow, who did that?

MAINWARING Stop playing the fool, boy. I'd better try getting on the horse in this costume. Come on.

Mainwaring, Wilson, Jones, Frazer and Godfrey go out.

EXTERIOR. MARQUEE

The horse is tethered out of sight of the crowd.

MAINWARING Hold the horse, Frazer.

FRAZER You'll never get on wearing that, it's too long.

MAINWARING Just hold the horse. **(He puts his foot in the stirrup and tries to mount)** It's too long, Godfrey.

GODFREY Oh dear, I'm sorr,y sir.

MAINWARING It's no use being sorry. What am I going to do?

WILSON Pull your skirts up, sir.

Mainwaring pulls them up to his knees and tries to mount again.

MAINWARING It's no good.

WILSON Pull them up higher.

MAINWARING I'm not pulling them up any higher, Wilson.

JONES Couldn't you ride side-saddle, sir?

MAINWARING Don't be absurd, Jones. Whoever heard of Saint George riding side-saddle?

GODFREY I think I can make some adjustments, sir.

VILLAGE GREEN

Close up of Mrs Yeatman blowing whistle. Ladies march off. Applause from crowd.

TOWN CLERK Thank you, well done, ladies. Now, the next item on the agenda is a display by the Eastgate Morris dancers.

Music starts and dancers begin to dance on.

INTERIOR. MAINWARING'S MARQUEE

Godfrey is finishing slitting up the front and back of the chain mail with a pair of scissors.

GODFREY That should be all right, sir. When you get on the horse, you can drape it round you discreetly.

MAINWARING I suppose it will have to do, thank you, Godfrey.

FRAZER **(Looking through flap)** Bah, those Eastgate Morris dancers are rotten. Why aren't we doing our Morris dance, Captain Mainwaring?

MAINWARING Saint George and the dragon is much more spectacular. I bet the crowd have never seen anything like this before.

FRAZER **(Looking Mainwaring up and down)** Aye, that's a fact.

MAINWARING Get into the dragon skin, Jones.

JONES Yes, sir, yes, sir.

The platoon start to get into the skin.

MAINWARING Come and help me mount, Wilson.

Mainwaring and Wilson stroll out. Pike has his foot on the end of the string. Mainwaring's chain mail unravels. Mainwaring comes out of the tent, realises he doesn't have his helmet and walks back, chain mail unravelling.

MAINWARING Wilson, helmet please. (**He puts the helmet on. Stumbling business**)

EXTERIOR. VILLAGE GREEN

The Morris dancers finish.

TOWN CLERK And now we come to the grand finale, which is a surprise item and is shared by the Wardens and the Home Guard. First Captain Mainwaring's platoon will perform a – (**Reads**) Spectacular Medieval Extravaganza.

The crowd applaud. Pike comes on to the green. He tries to pull tabard down. Raises his trumpet and tabard rides up. Boy scout does bugle. Pike picks his trumpet up quickly and puts it to his lips. The crowd laugh.

INTERIOR. WARDEN'S MARQUEE

Hodges, Vicar and Verger are looking out. Verger is dressed as herald.

HODGES What's that stupid, soppy-looking boy doing?

VERGER He's dressed like me, Mr Hodges.

Mrs Yeatman hurries in.

MRS YEATMAN 'Ere, Morris –

VERGER What is it, Tracy?

MRS YEATMAN Mainwaring's lot are doing Saint George and the dragon as well. You'll be a real laughing stock.

HODGES What! I'll kill him. (**Pushing Verger**) Quick, get out there. (**Turns to Vicar**) And you get into the dragon skin.

VICAR Stop handling me, you know I don't like being handled.

HODGES Shut up and get on with it.

EXTERIOR. VILLAGE GREEN

Wilson leads Mainwaring on horse. The dragon follows. Crowd cheer.

TOWN CLERK Well, well, ladies and gentlemen, what a wonderful surprise. Captain Mainwaring is going to fight the dragon.

The Verger appears and blows trumpet.

MAINWARING What's that fool up to, Wilson?

WILSON I've no idea, sir.

Hodges rides on. He lifts visor. Mainwaring reacts.

MAINWARING Get off this field, Hodges.

Jones pokes his head out and shouts at dragon.

JONES 'Ere, what's your game? Clear off!

Vicar's head pokes out.

VICAR We'll do nothing of the sort. You clear off, you silly fellow.

JONES Look, Vicar, we thought of it first.

VICAR Oh no you didn't. Wel,l don't say you haven't been warned. (**His head pops back and he slams the shutter**)

TOWN CLERK Oh, it look as if Mr Hodges is going to fight the dragon.

The dragons paw the ground, smoke coming from nostrils.

TOWN CLERK No, I tell a lie. The dragon is going to fight the dragon.

The dragons start to fight and kick each other.

HODGES Right, Napoleon, you asked for it.

MAINWARING I'm not afraid of you, Hodges.

Hodges closes his visor, raises his sword and charges. Mainwaring does likewise.

TOWN CLERK Now the two Saint Georges are fighting each other. This is certainly giving history a new twist.

Mainwaring and Hodges are swiping at each other with their swords.

WILSON Be careful, sir. What are we going to do, Frank?

PIKE It's ever so good, Uncle Arthur – just like that film *Robin Hood.*

Mainwaring's sword breaks. The Wardens' dragon falls on its back. The crowd cheer. Mainwaring throws away his sword, gets his flail mace entangled in helmet.

WILSON We've got to do something, Frank.

PIKE Leave it to me, Uncle Arthur. (**He fills his mouth full of peas and aims his trumpet at Hodges. His horse rears, Hodges falls off**)

HODGES You flippin' hooligans.

Jones' dragon charges Hodges and chases him from the field. The crowd cheer. Mainwaring opens visor and acknowledges.

SERIES NINE **EPISODE FOUR**

Recorded: Friday 24/6/77

Original transmission: Sunday 23/10/77, 8.10–8.40pm

Original viewing figures = 11.1 million

ARTHUR LOWE	CAPTAIN MAINWARING
JOHN LE MESURIER	SERGEANT WILSON
CLIVE DUNN	LANCE CORPORAL JONES
JOHN LAURIE	PRIVATE FRAZER
ARNOLD RIDLEY	PRIVATE GODFREY
IAN LAVENDER	PRIVATE PIKE
FULTON MACKAY	DOCTOR MCCEAVEDY
BILL PERTWEE	CHIEF WARDEN HODGES
FRANK WILLIAMS	VICAR
EDWARD SINCLAIR	VERGER
COLIN BEAN	PRIVATE SPONGE
PLATOON	FREDDIE WILES, FREDDIE WHITE, EVAN ROSS, GEORGE HANCOCK, MICHAEL MOORE, DESMOND CULLUM-JONES, ROGER BOURNE, JIMMY MAC, VERNON DRAKE

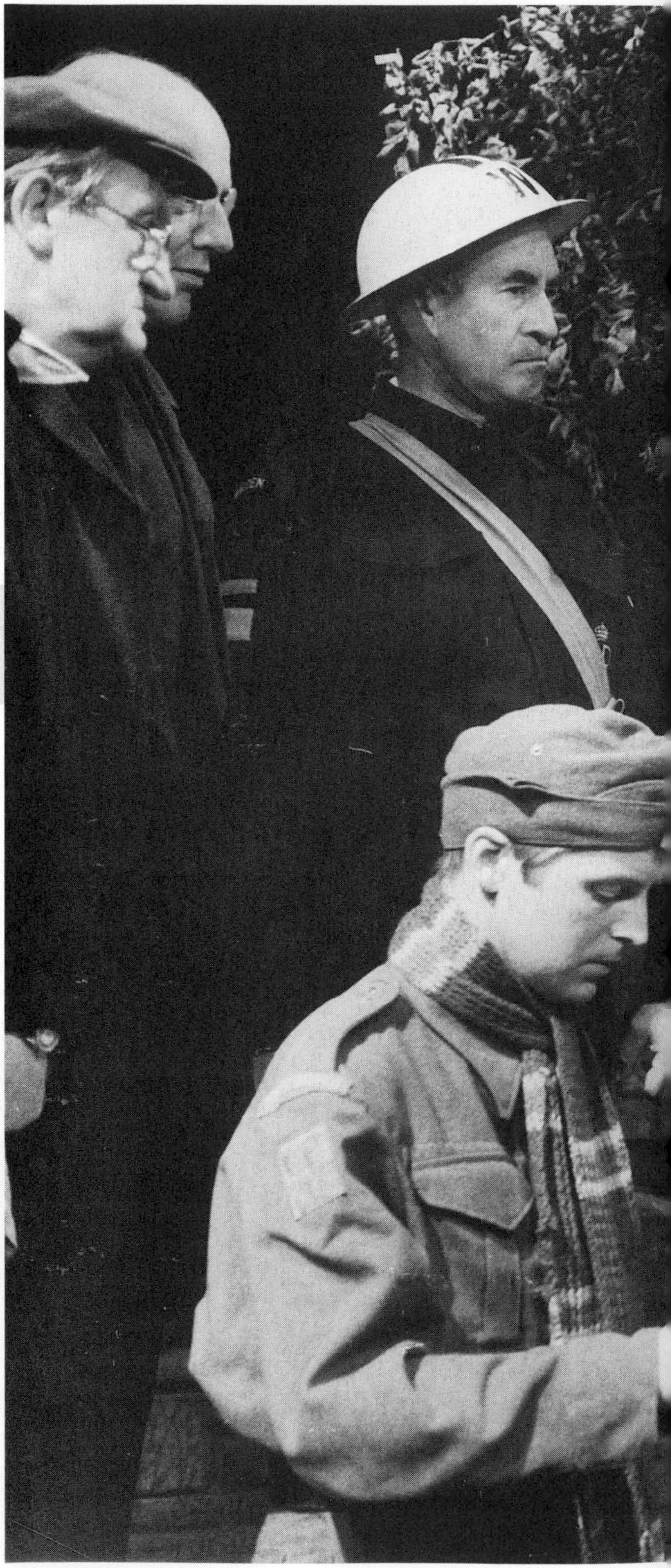

THE MISER'S HOARD

• VERONICA LAURIE REMEMBERS •

'I still enjoy settling down to see *Dad's Army*. Like millions of other people, I can appreciate why it remains so popular, even after all these years, although there may be moments when the antics of one or two of the characters in the Walmington platoon are a bit over the top. Jimmy Perry and David Croft cleverly caught some of the actors' idiosyncrasies and foibles for use in their scripts – no doubt with a bit of exaggeration – but I can't deny that you would find an echo of Frazer's irascibility in my father. He could be quick tempered and he certainly didn't suffer fools gladly, though he had a kindness and warmth that you seldom see in Frazer. However, you do catch a glimpse of it near the end of "Getting the Bird" when Frazer assures Sergeant Wilson that his secret will be safe with him, and you believe him – for once!'

IN ME

THE MISER'S HOARD

EXTERIOR. FUNERAL PARLOUR. NIGHT

Only the door and the swinging sign reading 'James Frazer, Undertaker' need be seen dimly.

INTERIOR. FUNERAL PARLOUR. NIGHT

It is old, eerie and candlelit. Frazer sits at his desk, working with his ledger. In front of him on the desk are several piles of sovereigns. Frazer is finishing a letter with a scratchy pen. He takes it up and reads.

FRAZER Dear Mrs Pickering, I hope you found the funeral arrangements for your late husband entirely satisfactory. May I say how sorry I was that the hearse ran out of petrol just outside the cemetery. I'm sure your dear departed husband would have been proud of the way you helped to push him to his final resting place. And what a fine strong woman your mother is. I hope you managed to get the mud off her skirt. I enclose my final account. **(He looks at separate paper and reads)** One solid oak coffin, £4 15s 3d. One set of brass handles 13s 6d. Transport £3 14s 2d – less 123 yards. Total £9 2s 11d. **(He turns to ledger)** Profit £3 6s 8 3/4d. Total for week £18 17s 2d – less 6s 1d housekeeping. **(He looks up)** Not bad, not bad at all. Maybe I'll have a small herring tomorrow as a wee treat and I'll be able to buy two more sovereigns. That'll make – **(He counts the piles)** 100 – 200 – 300 – 400 – 500 and 50 – 1 – 2 – 3 – 4. Present value £3,102 4s.

There is a knock on the front door.

FRAZER **(Alarmed)** Who's there? Who's there?

McCEAVEDY **(Out of vision)** It's me. Doctor McCeavedy.

Frazer sweeps the gold coins into an old box, which he replaces on the desk. He goes towards the door.

FRAZER I'm coming – I'm coming. **(He goes to the door and moves the blind to peer through the window. He recognises the doctor and throws open several bolts)** Come in, doctor – come in. I was just listening to I.T.M.A.

McCEAVEDY I'm here about old Mr Breuster.

FRAZER Has his time come?

McCEAVEDY Aye – God rest his soul.

FRAZER Dear oh dear – I'll be round to make the arrangements.

McCEAVEDY I came straight here – he went not twenty minutes since.

FRAZER In that case we've time for a wee dram. Sit ye doon. **(He takes two small glasses from a cupboard and a half bottle of whisky. He fills one half full. He then transfers half the amount in that glass to the other glass)**

FRAZER Long may our cup be full.

McCEAVEDY **(Looking at glass)** Hear, hear. **(They drink)** Doing the books are you?

FRAZER Aye. **(He points to a small pile of loose change)** Look at that – 9s, 4d – it's hardly worth my while. I'm a poor man, you know. I scarcely make enough to keep body and soul together.

McCEAVEDY Aye – it's a hard life. Well, I must be off. **(He puts his glass down and, taking his hand away, he knocks the box to the floor. The coins cascade out)**

Frazer reacts.

McCEAVEDY I'm sorry. **(He hurriedly gets down to pick them up)** Great Scott! They're sovereigns – hundreds of gold sovereigns.

FRAZER Is that a fact? Now I wonder how they got there?

MAINWARING'S OFFICE AT THE BANK. DAY

Doctor McCeavedy is sitting on the other side of Mainwaring's desk. Wilson stands beside Mainwaring.

MAINWARING I find what you are telling me almost beyond belief, Doctor McCeavedy.

McCEAVEDY I saw it with my own eyes. He's not my patient, you understand, so I'm breaching no confidence, but I formed the impression he's a touch unstable.

MAINWARING Yes – well, we have found him a little unpredictable – wouldn't you say so, Wilson?

WILSON Well, frankly no, sir. I find him very predictable. Every time you decide to do anything, he invariably says it'll be a sheer disaster. Mind you, he's very often right.

Mainwaring reacts.

McCEAVEDY The point is, if all that gold got stolen, I think it would turn his mind without a shadow of a doubt. **(He rises)** You need to persuade him to put it all in some place of safety.

MAINWARING **(Rising and shaking hands)** Well, thank you for giving me the gen. I'll do my best, you can count on that.

McCeavedy goes.

MAINWARING What do you make of that, Wilson?

WILSON To be perfectly honest, I don't think it's any of our business.

MAINWARING Of course it's our business. He's a comrade in arms and a client of the bank. As his commanding officer, his bank manager and his friend, it is my duty to advise him to sell those sovereigns and buy an annuity.

WILSON On which you would get commission.

MAINWARING On which I would get – that's nothing to do with it.

Pike enters with Frazer's account.

PIKE Here's Mr Frazer's account Mr Mainwaring. Just look, the poor old man's just got £15 6s 8d – we ought to have a collection for him. You could organise that, Mr Mainwaring, you're good at organising things.

MAINWARING Quiet, Pike. Just imagine, £15 6s 8d, and he's sitting on hundreds of them.

PIKE He's sitting on hundreds of what, Mr Mainwaring?

MAINWARING Mind your own business, Pike.

Pike puts his thumb in his mouth to think.

MAINWARING And take your thumb out of your mouth.

PIKE Sorry, Mr Mainwaring.

MAINWARING He hardly uses the account from one year's end to the next.

PIKE Is it coffins, Mr Mainwaring?

MAINWARING Is what coffins?

PIKE What Mr Frazer's sitting on?

MAINWARING Don't butt in. You know ,Wilson, I have it in the back of my mind that it's against the law to own more than five.

PIKE It doesn't sound like coffins.

MAINWARING They're supposed to be sold to help buy battleships and things.

PIKE It's not coffins – handles. Is it coffin handles, Uncle Arthur?

WILSON Oh do be quiet, Frank.

PIKE Well, am I getting warmer ? Go on, Uncle Arthur, tell me if I'm getting warmer.

WILSON Frank, will you stop?

MAINWARING Mind you – I never trusted him, his eyes are very close together, you know.

WILSON Are they ? I hadn't noticed.

MAINWARING In my position, one learns to read those sort of signs – it denotes a mean streak.

PIKE Begging your pardon, Mr Mainwaring, but it's not fair to say that about Mr Frazer, he's not always mean. He let me have three packets of crisps on Friday. He said they were very rare and valuable because they were proper pre-war ones.

MAINWARING He asked you to pay for them, I suppose?

PIKE Only the proper price – none of your black market.

MAINWARING How this boy ever got his school certificate, I shall never understand.

PIKE What have I done now?

MAINWARING I don't expect people who work for me to be bamboozled into buying second-hand crisps.

PIKE They weren't bad. They were a bit soggy, but the salt was dry as a bone.

MAINWARING Go away, Pike.

Pike chunters out of the office.

MAINWARING **(To Pike)** Get out. I shall have to have a word with Frazer.

WILSON Well, if Frank's fool enough to buy old, worn-out crisps, I don't see it's any of our business.

MAINWARING I'm not talking about crisps, Wilson. Try not to let your mind wander. I'm talking about sovereigns. He must be made to see that what he is doing is sheer folly.

WILSON He's very obstinate. If he thinks you're poking your nose into his private affairs, he'll send you away with your tail between your legs.

MAINWARING I don't often get sent away with my tail between my legs, Wilson.

WILSON Would you like me to drop a few hints?

MAINWARING Oh no. You beat about the bush far too much, I'll deal with it. I'll be very tactful, I'll bring the matter up tonight on parade.

Wilson reacts.

INTERIOR. MAIN HALL. NIGHT

Jones is lecturing to the platoon. They are sat around on chairs.

JONES Right – silence in the ranks and stop talking.

They chat on at the back.

JONES I said silence in the ranks.

Pike chats on.

JONES Private Pike, if you don't silence in the ranks, you'll find yourself on a fizzer for conduct to the prejudice, and not having silence in the ranks.

PIKE I was only finishing off my sentence.

JONES There won't be no time to finish off no sentences when the Bosche German is invading, young fellow me lad.

PIKE Well, he's not here now, is he?

FRAZER Whisht, man – let the old fool get on or we'll be here all night.

JONES Right – now, tonight we're going to practise doing things in our gas mask.

GODFREY Excuse me – respirator.

JONES What's that – who said that?

GODFREY I did – Captain Mainwaring likes us to call them respirators.

JONES Ah – well, that's as may be. The thing is this, we've got to train ourselves to such a high pitch that everything what we do in our everyday goings on, we can do in our gas mask.

FRAZER Respirator.

JONES That's right. I look at it this way – one day we'll be going about our business and suddenly Hitler will let it off. Are we down-hearted – no – we just put on our gas respirators, and carry on as usual, 'cos when you think about it, everything you do ordinary, you can do wearing this. I can serve in my shop, Pikey can carry on in the bank, Mr Frazer here can carry on furnish funerals and Mr Godfrey can go to the clinic, can't you, Mr Godfrey?

GODFREY I expect so – they won't be able to take my temperature.

JONES No – well, perhaps you'll be able to come back later and have your temperature took.

FRAZER We can't eat.

JONES Ah – no – you can't eat. That is true, but we can do everything else.

FRAZER We can't drink.

JONES No – no you're right, we can't drink, but except for eating and drinking, we can carry on just as if nothing's happened.

PIKE I won't be able to clean my teeth.

JONES Well, that don't matter, do it? I mean, who wants to clean their teeth when Hitler's gassing all over the place?

FRAZER You can't smoke.

PIKE Quite right, Mr Frazer. The cigarette would get shoved down your throat.

FRAZER He's talking a lot of nonsense – there's hundreds of things you can't do.

PIKE You can't play the trumpet for a start.

JONES Look, don't all jabber amongst yourselves, I'm the one who's giving the lecture.

FRAZER You're talking nonsense, man – sheer nonsense.

JONES Silence in the ranks. I'll have you on a fizzer for insubordination, Private Frazer – you're all behaving like a lot of rabble. Right, the next thing we're going to do is to practise doing things in our gas masks.

GODFREY Respirators.

JONES One more interruption from you, Private Godfrey, and I'll have you doubling round the church hall 50 times. First, I'm going to show you how to fix bayonets. On the command 'gas', I shall put on my respirator mask. Gas! **(He starts to put on his mask)** The important thing to do when you hear the command 'gas' is to hold your breath, and get this thing on as quick as possible. **(He gets it on. From now on he chunters inside his mask)** Then, you take your rifle in your left hand, and you get your bayonet in your right hand – **(He drops the bayonet and the rifle. He flounders around on the floor recovering them. He then kneels to put the bayonet on the rifle. Mainwaring enters during this and stands behind Jones)**

MAINWARING Jones – Jones – **(He taps him on the shoulder)** Jones – what are you doing?

JONES **(Still inside the mask)** I'm showing the men how to fix bayonets wearing their gas mask.

MAINWARING Take it off.

JONES **(Does so)** Sorry, sir. **(He salutes)** I'm showing the men how to fix bayonets wearing their gas masks.

MAINWARING Respirator.

PIKE We keep telling him.

MAINWARING Quiet, Pike. Fall the men in, Wilson.

WILSON Right – fall in in three ranks.

They fall in amongst the chairs.

MAINWARING Wilson – **(He beckons him)** do you notice anything strange?

Mainwaring nods towards the platoon. Wilson is a little mystified. Mainwaring nods again. Wilson smiles.

MAINWARING Do you notice anything strange, Wilson? **(He nods towards the platoon again)**

WILSON **(Looking at Mainwaring)** Your cap badge is just a trifle crooked and you keep nodding your head.

MAINWARING You have fallen the men in amongst the chairs, Wilson.

WILSON Oh, so I have – I'm awfully sorry. **(To men)** Would you clear the chairs to the back of the hall or somewhere, and then come back again.

MAINWARING Move.

The men stack the chairs during the following speeches.

MAINWARING **(To Wilson)** You're very dozy these days, Wilson. Are you getting enough sleep?

WILSON I think so, sir.

MAINWARING Well, you must try to notice things.

WILSON I noticed that your cap badge was crooked.

MAINWARING That's totally unimportant. **(More confidentially)** I'm going to talk to the men about money and security in broad terms.

WILSON Ah, how lovely.

MAINWARING We'll see if Frazer takes the hint. Be very careful not to give anything away by your expression – try to keep a blank face.

WILSON Certainly, sir.

MAINWARING Right – pay attention. Before you dismiss, I want to talk to you about savings. This war is costing us millions a day. Now, I expect most of you have worked hard all your lives.

JONES I've worked hard all right. When I was ten, I used to get up at five o'clock and follow the milkman round with his horse and every time he stopped, the milkman used to shout 'Hang on to that horse, you young shaver' and he wasn't a nice horse, Captain Mainwaring. In the winter, with the cold, he used to stamp his feet and tread on my toes, and in the summer, with his flies, he used to toss his head and throw me over his shoulder, and if I let go, the milkman used to clip me round the ear – and I only got tuppence a week. But they were good times.

MAINWARING Yes – well, there's a typical example of a man who has worked hard all his life. And I dare say, he has a few pounds tucked away. The point is, we must put our money to work – isn't that right, Wilson? (**He turns to Wilson who is looking away**)

WILSON Yes, sir.

MAINWARING What's the matter?

WILSON I was trying to keep a blank face.

MAINWARING (**Turning away**) As I was saying, we must put our money to work. Some people keep pound notes tucked in the mattress – this is foolhardy.

PIKE My Mum always keeps quite a lot concealed on her person. She says no one's likely to find it there – least of all Uncle Arthur.

WILSON Frank – be quiet.

GODFREY Captain Mainwaring, my sister Dolly keeps quite a bit in an old teapot – it has a broken spout.

MAINWARING You'll have to take a strong line about this, Godfrey – get her to put it in the bank.

FRAZER Captain Mainwaring, are you touting for business?

MAINWARING Certainly not – I'm just giving advice.

FRAZER It would sound just the same if you were touting for business.

MAINWARING Well, I'm not. Now, another point to consider is the risk. A bomb could drop or an incendiary or you could have a burglary. Burglars, of course, are particularly on the lookout for gold.

Frazer reacts to this.

MAINWARING Not that it's very likely that any of you have much gold. If you have, of course, the patriotic thing to do is to sell it to help the war effort.

FRAZER And put the money in your bank.

MAINWARING And put the money in – not necessarily. Right, that's all. Parade, 'shun. Officer on parade, dismiss.

The platoon do a right turn and salute. Mainwaring and Wilson start towards the office.

MAINWARING Come with me a moment, Wilson.

They go into the office.

INTERIOR. SIDE OFFICE. NIGHT

MAINWARING That seemed to go quite well, didn't it, Wilson?

WILSON Very well, sir.

MAINWARING I think I handled it quite subtly, didn't you?

WILSON Most diplomatically, sir.

MAINWARING I don't think Frazer suspected that I was referring particularly to him.

WILSON I don't think so. Mind you, when you said the word 'gold', I thought I did just notice him jump very slightly out of his skin.

MAINWARING A guilty conscience, I expect. But I am sure he has no inkling that I actually know.

WILSON Oh none at all.

There is a knock at the door.

MAINWARING Come in.

Frazer enters.

FRAZER Captain Mainwaring, I just want to say, if you think you're going to get your hands on my gold, you can think again. I don't trust banks, I don't trust bank managers, and I don't trust you. I just thought you'd like to know. That's all.

Mainwaring reacts.

INTERIOR. CORNER OF HODGES' THE GREENGROCER'S SHOP. DAY

Hodges is just finishing with a lady customer.

HODGES There you are, dear. Seven pounds King Edwards, sixpence. And the next?

The Verger moves in with the Vicar.

VERGER (**Confidentially**) I hear you've got onions?

HODGES Shush – do you want the whole world queuing out there? You can have half a pound – and that's only 'cos you're a regular. (**He hands a ready packed bag to the Verger**) Hello, Vicar – don't often see you here.

VICAR We don't often see onions here.

HODGES Shush – you can have half a pound, but only on condition you chop your sermon to eight minutes, including getting in and out of the pulpit. (**He hands the Vicar a ready packed paper bag**) There you are – shove 'em under your cassock and look holy. (**Conspiratorially**) Here – have you heard the scandal about old Frazer the undertaker?

VERGER Is there a woman involved?

VICAR Be quiet, Mr Yeatman. You shouldn't listen to gossip. What's he done?

HODGES He's hoarding thousands of gold coins in his shop. They say you can hardly move for them.

VICAR In that case, I shall ask him for a contribution to the Church Fabric Fund.

HODGES You'll be lucky. He's owed me 13s, 6d since last January. I've asked him for it until I'm tired. and if he doesn't pay up, I'll County Court him.

VERGER I always say this – parsimony can be a sin when it's taken to excess. Don't you agree, Vicar?

VICAR I've never really given it very much thought, Mr Yeatman.

VERGER Well, anyway – he can't take it with him, and that's a fact.

HODGES I don't know. I've heard he's going to have it put in his coffin, like them Vikings.

VICAR What a waste – I shall go and see him straight away.

HODGES (**To customer**) Hello, dear, what can I do for you?

INTERIOR. CHURCH HALL. SIDE OFFICE. NIGHT

Mainwaring is holding the phone.

MAINWARING Hello, operator – are you still getting no reply? I don't understand it. Thank you for trying.

Wilson and Pike enter as Mainwaring is putting the phone down.

MAINWARING I don't understand this, Wilson. Frazer's never missed a parade before. I do hope he's all right. Have you had any luck?

WILSON (**Rather tipsy**) Well, he wasn't at The Horse and Groom, and they hadn't seen him at The Fox since Christmas, because I've made enquiries.

PIKE And he made enquiries at The Red Lion, The Marquis of Granby, The Plough and The Goat and The William the Fourth. And what Mum's going to say if she sees you like this, doesn't bear thinking about.

MAINWARING Sit down, Wilson.

WILSON Thank you, you're most kind. He wasn't at Charlie's Café either.

PIKE No – we had a black coffee there – not that it's done much good.

WILSON Well, we are off duty.

MAINWARING It's a damned good job for you that you are. Sit there and keep quiet until you've sobered up a bit. We don't want the rest of the platoon to know their sergeant's a drunkard.

WILSON Frank – the gallant captain is cross with me.

Jones, Godfrey and Sponge enter.

JONES He's not down the library, Mr Mainwaring and he doesn't answer when you knock on his door – but he's took his milk in, so he's taking nourishment.

GODFREY I went to the Peabody Rooms, but he wasn't at the whist drive.

WILSON He's probably with a floozy in some gambling den in darkest Walmington. (**He laughs at his own joke**)

MAINWARING Wilson.

The phone rings. Mainwaring answers it.

MAINWARING Walmington-on-Sea Home Guard.

INTERCUT: INTERIOR. FUNERAL PARLOUR.

FRAZER Is that you, Captain Mainwaring?

MAINWARING Frazer – where are you? Why aren't you on parade?

FRAZER I'm not coming. It's all your fault – blabbering all over town about my gold. I can't move for people knocking at the door – even yon pilly wally Vicar. Well, you're not getting your hands on it – do you hear? I'm going to put it where no one will find it. (**He puts the phone down**)

MAINWARING Now, look here, Frazer... Hello – hello – He's put the phone down.

SPONGE Was he in a call box, Captain Mainwaring?

MAINWARING No – I didn't hear the tuppence go in.

SPONGE Then he was at home.

MAINWARING What's he going to do with it? That's the point.

JONES I look at it this way. If I was him, I would get all my gold and I would melt it down and when it was all hot and bubbly, I would pour it into a mould and make of it a large vessel, and when it was cool, I would paint it white and put it somewhere it didn't notice.

WILSON You mean you'd make a *vase de nuit*?

MAINWARING What was that, Wilson?

WILSON A *vase de nuit* – it's French.

MAINWARING I know – I've just forgotten the precise meaning.

WILSON It means literally a night vase.

MAINWARING A night vase?

WILSON A tiddly pot.

MAINWARING Be quiet, Wilson.

WILSON That's what we used to call them at school in the dorm – tiddly pots.

MAINWARING Wilson, I've told you to be quiet.

WILSON Tiddly pot.

PIKE I saw a film once called *The Miser's Gold* and this man buried all his ill-gotten golden nuggets in a field, and one day the farmer ploughed it, and when he came back all haggard, he couldn't find it and went and grovelled in the mud saying, 'Stones, stones, they've turned into stones. Where's my nuggets?'

MAINWARING Just a minute – I think you might have hit on something. He will bury it. The point is, where?

SPONGE In his garden.

JONES No, he wouldn't do it there – it's all concrete. You can't bury things in concrete. Not unless you have one of those rheumatic drills.

PIKE In Peabody Park.

MAINWARING Possible.

GODFREY In the sand dunes at night.

PIKE No – there's too many people in the sand dunes at night.

SPONGE The allotments – or the goods yard.

MAINWARING They're both possible. Let's face it, there are dozens of places.

JONES He'll probably do it tonight.

MAINWARING You're right, Jones. There's only one way to deal with this, we must shadow him.

PIKE Ooh – like George Raft.

MAINWARING We'll make out a roster. We'll keep him covered throughout the hours of darkness. Write down all the names, Sergeant Wilson.

Wilson is dozing.

MAINWARING Perhaps you'd better do it, Jones.

WILSON Tiddly pot.

INTERIOR. PHONE BOX. LATER THAT NIGHT

Jones is on the phone.

JONES Hello – hello. Is that you, Mr Mainwaring? Jones the butcher here.

INTERCUT: INTERIOR. SIDE OFFICE. NIGHT

MAINWARING What is it, Jones – any developments?

JONES Yes, sir – there's been some developments. He came out of his undertaker's shop with a box under his arm, not an undertaker's box, you understand, Mr Mainwaring.

MAINWARING No, of course not – go on.

JONES He look round, furtive, and then he went off and we followed him and we followed him and we followed him.

MAINWARING Yes – get on with it, Jones.

JONES Well, we followed him quite a long way, Mr Mainwaring, and then he went into the churchyard, so I said to Pike, 'You stop here and watch him'.

MAINWARING **(To the others)** Come on, come on, Wilson, he's in the churchyard.

Wilson hiccups.

JONES I must phone Mr Mainwaring at once, I thought. So I crept tippy toe, past all the stones, flitting from monument to monument like a wraith, so he wouldn't spot me, and I saw this phone box – that's hunky dory, I thought – and I got two pennies out – Hello – hello – he's hung up on me. I expect he's in one of his moods.

PHONE BACKING. NIGHT

The Verger is on the telephone.

VERGER Yes – hello – who is it?

INTERCUT: INTERIOR. PHONE BOX. NIGHT

HODGES It's me – Chief Warden Hodges. Guess what I saw on patrol just now?

VERGER Was it animal, vegetable or mineral?

HODGES Look, this isn't a game. I've just seen old Frazer sneaking into the churchyard with a box. I bet it's full of gold, and he's going to bury it.

VERGER But he says he hasn't got any gold.

HODGES What are you talking about? I tell you he's got a box and I heard it chink.

VERGER When the Vicar asked him for a donation, he

told him he was poor as a church mouse. I was there in person, he said it plain as a pikestaff – through his very own letterbox.

HODGES Well, I just thought the Vicar might like to find out what goes on in his churchyard at half-past one in the morning.

VERGER You're right – we'll be round in five minutes.

EXTERIOR. CHURCHYARD. NIGHT

Mainwaring's area, Frazer's area and Hodges' area, bounded by gravestones.

MAINWARING'S AREA

Pike is peeping over a stone, watching.

FRAZER'S AREA

Frazer is finishing a small excavation by a stone. He looks round, cackles. He digs again.

MAINWARING'S AREA

Mainwaring arrives. Pike starts. Jones, Wilson and Sponge join.

PIKE There he is, Mr Mainwaring. He keeps on digging a bit, then he looks round and cackles. (**Pike impersonates the cackle**) Then he digs again. He's been going on like that for ten minutes. Dig, dig, cackle, cackle, dig, dig. (**He mimes**) Dig, dig, cackle, cackle, dig, dig.

MAINWARING Quiet, Pike.

WILSON There's a new moon.

MAINWARING What's that got to do with it?

WILSON I sometimes cry when I see a new moon.

PIKE Well, now we're here, what are we going to do?

MAINWARING Just watch and let him make the first move.

JONES That's right, Mr Mainwaring, we did that once with the Fuzzie Wuzzies. We let them make the first move, we didn't have to wait long. The head man said one, two, three and they all chucked their spears at us, then we mowed them all down with machine guns. They was real battles in those days.

HODGES' AREA

Hodges, Vicar and Verger appear over a stone.

HODGES There he is.

VERGER Do you know what he's doing, Your Reverence – he's desecrating.

VICAR I don't think it's quite as bad as that, Mr Yeatman.

FRAZER'S AREA

Frazer puts the box into the hole.

FRAZER (**Cackling**) They'll never find it – they'll never find my gold. (**He cackles and covers up the hole**)

MAINWARING'S AREA

PIKE Uncle Arthur – I'm frightened.

MAINWARING Wilson, don't hold his hand.

WILSON Life is very cruel, Frank.

FRAZER'S AREA

Frazer finishes covering up the hole and moves away.

MAINWARING'S AREA

MAINWARING Wait till he reaches the gate, then we'll investigate.

HODGES' AREA

HODGES He's off – let's follow him.

VICAR Wait a minute – I can see some figures moving.

HODGES You're right.

FRAZER'S AREA

Mainwaring and party arrive.

MAINWARING That's the place. (**He indicates where Frazer has been digging**) Dig the earth away, Pike.

PIKE What with?

MAINWARING Your hands.

PIKE But there might be worms and slugs and crawly slithery things.

MAINWARING Get on with it. (**To Wilson**) You ought to have someone look at him, you know.

HODGES' AREA

HODGES They've got Army hats on. I do believe it's Mainwaring's lot.

VICAR What are they doing here? Come on, Mr Yeatman.

They leave.

FRAZER'S AREA

Pike is lifting out the box.

PIKE It's heavy – it must be chock full of gold.

MAINWARING Open it up.

PIKE It's locked.

JONES Here – prise it open with my bayonet.

SPONGE Do you think we should – after all, it's not ours.

MAINWARING Quite right, Sponge.

Hodges and party arrive.

HODGES Caught you red-handed. You were going to steal it, weren't you?

MAINWARING I was going to do no such thing.

VERGER What are you doing here then?

VICAR I'll deal with this, Mr Yeatman.

JONES Mr Mainwaring was going about his lawful practices.

HODGES What, in a churchyard at half-past one in the morning?

MAINWARING I am concerned for the welfare of one of my troops.

VERGER You were filching that box.

VICAR Will you be quiet, Mr Yeatman?

MAINWARING I'm taking this into custody. Tomorrow I shall try to convince Frazer that he should sell the gold and do something sensible with the money – such as buying an annuity.

VERGER On which you get commission.

MAINWARING On which I get – never mind that, it's got nothing to do with it.

VICAR Will you be quiet, Mr Yeatman?

INTERIOR. CHURCH HALL. DAY

The men are on parade. Mainwaring is addressing them. Vicar and Verger watch.

MAINWARING And so, Frazer, please believe me, we acted from the very best of motives, but surely the fact that we were able to get hold of your box so easily is ample proof of my point. The bank is the safest place for your valuables – be they in cash or in kind.

HODGES But not his bank.

MAINWARING Would you mind not interfering? Get the box, Wilson.

WILSON Yes. sir. (**He goes to the office**)

MAINWARING Now, Frazer, I want you to promise me that even if you don't sell the coins, you will put the contents of your box in the bank – any bank.

FRAZER Aye – that I will.

Wilson appears with the box.

WILSON Here it is, sir.

MAINWARING Have you the key, Frazer?

FRAZER Aye. (**He produces a purse and takes out a small key. He gives it to Pike**) Here you are, laddie – give it to the captain – he's a fine man.

Pike takes the key to Mainwaring. He takes it.

MAINWARING Thank you, Pike. Go back to your place.

PIKE Yes, Captain Mainwaring. (**Pike returns to his place. Mainwaring opens the lock**)

MAINWARING Rest assured, Frazer – my bank will take good care of it.

VICAR And a small donation towards the fabric of the church will be most gratefully received.

Mainwaring opens the box and takes out a brick.

MAINWARING It's a brick. It's a damned brick.

FRAZER Aye – Yon Vicar can have it for the fabric of the church. I'll look after my gold. (**He cackles again and runs off**) You'll not have my gold. (**Cackle, cackle**) You'll not have my gold.

Wilson and Mainwaring react.

SERIES NINE **EPISODE FIVE**

Recorded: Friday 15/7/77
Original transmission: Sunday 6/11/77, 8.10–8.40pm
Original viewing figures = 9.6 million

ARTHUR LOWE .... CAPTAIN MAINWARING
JOHN LE MESURIER .... SERGEANT WILSON
CLIVE DUNN................................ LANCE CORPORAL JONES
JOHN LAURIE .... PRIVATE FRAZER
ARNOLD RIDLEY .... PRIVATE GODFREY
IAN LAVENDER .... PRIVATE PIKE
BILL PERTWEE................................ CHIEF WARDEN HODGES
FRANK WILLIAMS .... VICAR
EDWARD SINCLAIR................................ VERGER
RONNIE BRODY................................ GPO MAN
ROBERT MILL .... ARMY CAPTAIN
KENNETH MACDONALD................................ ARMY SERGEANT
FELIX BOWNESS .... VAN DRIVER
COLIN BEAN .... PRIVATE SPONGE
STUART MCGUGAN .... SCOTTISH SERGEANT
BERNICE ADAMS................................ ATS GIRL
PLATOON.................. DESMOND CULLUM-JONES, VERNON DRAKE, MICHAEL MOORE, FREDDIE WHITE, FREDDIE WILES, GEORGE HANCOCK, ROGER BOURNE, JIMMY MAC, EVAN ROSS
EXTRAS .... (REGULAR ARMY SOLDIERS) MIKE HARRINGTON-SPIER AND LYNDON REDPATH
STUNTMEN .... JIM DOWDALL (FOR IAN LAVENDER) AND DEREK WARE (FOR CLIVE DUNN)

NUMBER ENGAGED

• JIM DOWDALL REMEMBERS •

'I was the person who had to climb the huge stack of furniture the platoon had assembled beneath the telephone wires. When I arrived at the location, a member of the production team explained the shot to me: the furniture lorry would arrive and Mainwaring's men would stop the vehicle and proceed to pile up the furniture, with Pike supposedly climbing up to retrieve the bomb. They wanted the stack to tip over on one side, depositing Pike in a midden.

'One of the special effects guys had got the furniture rigged so that a table at the bottom of the pile had two legs on hinges with small caster wheels fitted. Attached to the legs were pieces of wire which joined on to a central length of wire, running underneath the truck. The idea was that when I was on top of the stack, someone would pull the wire, collapsing the table in the process, and the stack would topple over in the required direction.

'I didn't think it would work because if the table legs were yanked too quickly, the height of the pile would cause it to smash in the middle, with me coming down with it. In 1977, when the episode was made, I was still quite green in terms of stunt work, perhaps not strong enough to voice my reservations too loudly. Boy, was that a lesson?

'Even though the pile of furniture was tied down, and there was a scaffolding tube through the centre for the first seven or eight feet, what I feared would happen, did. The guy yanked the legs from the table, the whole thing whiplashed in the middle and I tumbled off the top, landing on my feet to the right of the vehicle, just before a big chest of drawers landed on my head, knocking me out for several seconds.

'Despite the nasty accident, it was a great privilege to work on *Dad's Army*. The business I work in is very varied: one day you are a dead body floating in the Thames while the next you are setting yourself on fire at the end of Brighton Pier, but that episode was very memorable.'

Number Engaged

INTERIOR. SIDE OFFICE OF HALL. DAY

The platoon are packed into the office. Mainwaring is standing with Wilson in front of a blackboard, which is covered with a blanket.

MAINWARING Now, pay attention, men. Before we start, I want to apologise for the fact that we are all packed in here like sardines, but it's Warden Hodges turn to use the hall tonight and I'm afraid there's nothing I can do about it. Now, what I have to show you is very highly secret. Uncover the board, Wilson.

WILSON Right, sir. **(He reaches for the blanket)**

MAINWARING Just a minute, hold it. **(He crosses to the door and opens it, then crosses to the other door and looks out)** All clear, right, carry on, Sergeant.

Wilson takes the blanket off the blackboard. On it is drawn an aerial view of a line of telegraph poles.

WILSON There, isn't that nice?

MAINWARING All right, Wilson. Now, can anybody tell me what that is?

GODFREY Are you going to write a song, sir?

JONES That's a good idea, a platoon song. We had one out in the Sudan, you know.

MAINWARING All right, Jones.

JONES **(Singing)** Oh Lord Kitchener, he may look very odd but in spite of what they say, I don't think he really is a ...

MAINWARING Jones, please.

JONES Sorry, sir, I got carried away.

WILSON For goodness sake, tell them, sir.

MAINWARING Patience, Wilson, let them try and work it out for themselves. Anybody else?

PIKE I think I know, Mr Mainwaring.
Can I borrow the chalk, please? **(He takes the chalk, crosses to the board and starts to draw. He stands right in front)**

GODFREY I hope that boy's not drawing something questionable.

JONES Close your eyes, Mr Godfrey. I'll tell you if it's all right to look.

Pike steps back. He has drawn some cows looking over the wires with mountains in the background.

PIKE There you are, that's what I think it is , Mr Mainwaring.

WILSON That's rather good, Frank.

MAINWARING This isn't a game, boy. Go and sit down at once.

PIKE Well, I like that, you asked us to...

MAINWARING Another word out of you and I shall send you home. Now, this is an aerial view of a line of telegraph poles. You see the wires running along there. Now, these telephone wires are used for...

FRAZER Making telephone calls.

MAINWARING Making telephone... carrying highly important secret messages.

The door opens and Hodges and the Verger enter. They cross to a cupboard behind the desk.

HODGES Excuse me, Napoleon, I'm giving a lecture on gas attack and I want my rattles and whistles.

MAINWARING Quick, cover the board, Wilson.

Wilson does so. Hodges takes the rattles and whistles out of the cupboard.

HODGES Don't worry about me, just carry on.

MAINWARING What I'm telling my men is very highly secret.

HODGES Then why don't you take 'em on the roof? Right, we'll just get this lot sorted out.

MAINWARING **(Crossing to Hodges)** Now look here, Hodges...

Hodges tries one of the rattles in Mainwaring's face. Mainwaring reacts.

HODGES That's all right. **(He hands it to the Verger and tries another)** That's all right. **(He tries a third)** That's no good. **(He throws it back in the cupboard and tries the next one)** That's okay. Try the whistles.

VERGER Yes, Mr Hodges. **(He starts to blow the whistles)**

MAINWARING I'll give you exactly ten seconds to get out of this office.

HODGES I'm not going until I've tested all my rattles and whistles.

MAINWARING We'll see about that. Jones, clear them out.

JONES Yes, sir, yes, sir. **(He draws his bayonet)** Come on, out.

HODGES You flippin' hooligans.

VERGER His Reverence is going to hear about this.

The door closes behind them.

WILSON What a dreadful, common man he is, sir.

MAINWARING Unfortunately, in times of war, there are certain pompous men who just love to put on a uniform and strut about, giving orders. We've all met one.

FRAZER Aye, we have indeed.

MAINWARING Uncover the board, Wilson.

Wilson does so.

MAINWARING Now, the secret messages that are carried along these wires are…

HODGES **(Out of vision)** Gas! Gas! Gas!

Rattles noise.

MAINWARING These messages are…

HODGES **(Out of vision)** Gas! Gas! Gas!

Rattles noise.

MAINWARING Just a minute. **(He strides to the door and opens it)** Hodges! **(He goes through and closes it. Pause. The door opens. Mainwaring comes back, he crosses to the board)** That's the last we shall hear out of him. Now, as I was…

HODGES **(Out of vision)** All clear, all clear!

Mainwaring reacts. Whistles noise.

WILSON I'll go this time, sir. **(He crosses to the door, goes out. Pause. He returns)**

MAINWARING I hope you were diplomatic, Wilson.

WILSON Oh yes, I told him if he didn't shut up, I'd hit him.

PIKE **(To Jones)** Uncle Arthur's ever so good. Mum says when he's roused he's like a tiger.

MAINWARING This is it, men. Now, a highly secret, invasion-warning device has been set up on the coast not far from here. Its purpose is to detect enemy boats and landing craft long before they reach the shore, and so give us the vital time we need to prepare our defences. All the information is carried to G.H.Q. along these wires, which are patrolled day and night by regular troops. Now, next weekend, we shall take over the two mile stretch in our area for 24 hours. I don't have to stress the responsibility of this vital task. If anything should happen to those wires, it could alter the whole course of the war.

Vicar enters, followed by Hodges and Verger.

VICAR Sorry to bother you, Mr Mainwaring, I just want to finalise the arrangements for the church parade on Sunday.

MAINWARING I'm sorry, Vicar, we shall have to cancel it. Next Sunday we shall be on top-secret duties.

HODGES They're only guarding some old telephone wires.

MAINWARING That's classified information. How did you know that?

HODGES See this white hat, mate? Chief A.R.P. Warden, that's how I know, so put that in your pipe and smoke it.

WILSON **(Crosses to Hodges)** You know what I said to you outside the door just now? Well it still applies.

MAINWARING Believe me, Vicar, we're all very upset that we can't come to church.

VICAR Well, I'll come out to you, we'll have a simple service in the open air.

MAINWARING Oh.

VERGER But we haven't got any transport, Your Reverence.

VICAR Oh dear, I forgot that.

MAINWARING What a pity.

HODGES Don't worry, Vicar, I'll take you out.

MAINWARING Why don't you mind your own business?

EXTERIOR. COUNTRY ROAD. DAY

The telephone poles are running along the side of the road. There is large sandbag command post and a field kitchen. In the field behind is a huge pile of rotting straw and compost. A three-ton, covered army truck is waiting, with the engine running. Two soldiers are climbing aboard. A sergeant sees the last man up.

SERGEANT Everybody in, right? **(He crosses to the front of the truck where a captain is standing, looking at his watch. The sergeant salutes)**

SERGEANT All the men are aboard, sir. We're ready to move off.

CAPTAIN Thank you, Sergeant. Where the hell's that relief force got to? They're late.

EXTERIOR. COUNTRY CROSSROADS. DAY

Road-up signs, lamps, a crane with a large bucket on a hook, cement mixer, oil drums, etc. are littered around. Dozens of gas pipes are laid across the road. A large sign reads 'diversion'. Jones' van approaches. Jones is driving, with Mainwaring and Wilson sitting in the cab. The van stops.

WILSON Oh lord, the road's up. We'll have to take the diversion.

MAINWARING This is absurd. Look at the map, Wilson.

Sponge pokes his head through the hole. He holds up a thermos flask.

SPONGE Now we've stopped, would you like a cup of tea, sir?

MAINWARING Thank you, Sponge.

Sponge pours, and hands Mainwaring the cup.

WILSON According to the map, sir, our destination is only a mile straight down the road, but we can't go through, so we'll have to take the diversion.

MAINWARING That's miles out of our way. We're late enough as it is. Pike –

Pike pokes his head through.

PIKE Yes, Mr Mainwaring.

MAINWARING Remove that sign, we're going through.

PIKE Right.

WILSON Do you think that wise, sir?

MAINWARING Believe me, I know the British workman, Wilson. They've just put all that stuff up to spin the job out. That road's as sound as a bell.

WILSON But what about the pipes?

MAINWARING If we drive over them very fast, we won't feel a thing. You know your trouble, you just haven't got a scientific mind.

WILSON Can I get out and walk?

MAINWARING Please yourself.

Wilson gets out.

PIKE Ready, Mr Mainwaring.

MAINWARING Well done, Pike. **(Takes tea)** Thank you, Sponge. Right, Jones, back up and drive like hell.

JONES Back up and drive like hell, yes, sir, yes, sir.

Wilson and Pike stand by the roadside. Van backs up and goes over pipes very fast. It stops. Mainwaring gets out, glasses and hat askew. Tea stain on front of blouse. He turns cup, a few drops of tea trickle out.

EXTERIOR. COUNTRY ROAD. DAY

The captain and sergeant are standing by the truck. Jones' van approaches and stops.

CAPTAIN What has happened to that relief force? They're ten minutes late.

SERGEANT What's that dirty old butcher's van stopped for, sir?

CAPTAIN I've no idea. Tell them to move on.

SERGEANT **(Shouts)** Oi, you – clear off out of it. We're waiting for the relief force.

Mainwaring's face peers round the side of the cab.

MAINWARING We are the relief force.

EXTERIOR. COUNTRY ROAD. DAY

The platoon are unloading their kit from the back of the van. Cut to the army truck. The sergeant is sitting at the wheel, the captain is standing by the cab with Mainwaring.

CAPTAIN **(Handing over envelope)** Here are your orders. Now, captain, I can't stress too highly how important those telephone lines are. They must be guarded with your life, understand?

MAINWARING Yes, sir.

CAPTAIN By the way, why were you late?

MAINWARING We, er... had a bit of trouble with the van.

CAPTAIN Oh, you had to get out and push, did you? **(Points to tea stain)** Well, it's certainly made you sweat. Carry on. **(He gets in and the truck drives off)**

Wilson joins Mainwaring.

WILSON Nice young chap.

MAINWARING Jumped up little upstart. **(Shouts)** Right, men, get your kit into the command post. What's that terrible smell, Wilson?

WILSON **(Points to heap of rotting straw)** I think it's coming from that pile of rotting straw.

MAINWARING Why did they have to leave it there?

WILSON It's probably waiting for muck spreading. Still, it's a very healthy smell. Ah, I'm glad there's a field kitchen, we can have a brew up, I'm dying for a cup of tea, aren't you? Oh, I forgot, you've just had one, haven't you?

INTERIOR. COMMAND POST. DAY

The men are dumping their kit on the floor. There is a table, two chairs and a two-tier bunk in the corner. Mainwaring and Wilson enter.

MAINWARING Right, stand by for orders, men.

JONES You heard what the officer said, at the double, stand by for orders. The men are ready to receive orders now, sir.

MAINWARING Thank you, Jones. Now, first of all, Frazer, you're in charge of the cooking.

FRAZER There's just one thing, sir, the porridge for breakfast tomorrow will have to be put on soon so that it can simmer all night.

MAINWARING Go and do it then.

FRAZER If I'm going to catch some trout for supper, I won't be able to do it.

MAINWARING I don't follow you.

FRAZER There's a well stocked trout stream half a mile away. That's why I brought my rod.

WILSON That's poaching, sir. You can't allow it.

FRAZER Fish are all right, sir. It's only poaching if it's birds and beasts.

MAINWARING There you are, you see.

WILSON But that's absurd.

MAINWARING Look, Frazer knows what he's talking about, Wilson. He's a countryman born and bred, not a townie like you.

WILSON I only know that the gamekeeper on my uncle's estate always…

MAINWARING Wilson, I'm not interested in all that snobbish rubbish. There's a war on, we are on active service and we're entitled to live off the land.

WILSON We've got some corned beef.

MAINWARING I don't like corned beef. Off you go, Frazer. You cook the porridge, Pike.

PIKE Yes, Mr Mainwaring.

FRAZER Now, pay attention, laddie, we don't want watery porridge. One jug of water and one mug of oatmeal per person, is that clear?

PIKE Yes, Mr Frazer, one jug, one mug.

MAINWARING Now, sleeping arrangements.

The platoon all rush over to the bunks.

MAINWARING Control yourselves, men, we're not rabble.

WILSON Yes, stand back, stand back. I shall take the top bunk, Captain Mainwaring will take the bottom bunk.

MAINWARING Just a minute, Wilson. (**He takes him aside**) You're taking rather a lot on yourself, aren't you? Who gave you permission to tell people where to sleep?

WILSON Well, I –

MAINWARING This is a democratic unit and decisions will be made in a democratic way. Right.

WILSON Yes, sir.

MAINWARING I'll take the top bunk, you take the bottom.

Wilson reacts.

EXTERIOR. BOTTOM OF TELEGRAPH POLE. NIGHT

Jones is leaning against the pole. Pike is stirring the porridge in background. Both have rifles and tin hats.

JONES How's the porridge coming on, Pikey?

PIKE It's simmering away nicely. It's a bit thick though.

JONES That's all right. We don't want runny porridge. It's good stuff, porridge. I shall never forget when I was in the Sudan, we was marching through the desert for days, and we was all exhausted. Well, one of the Scottish soldiers fell on the ground, and we all halted. Then General Kitchener rode up on his horse and said, (**Puts hand on hip**) 'What's going on here?'

PIKE Mr Jones, why is it that when you're telling a story about General Kitchener, you always put your hand on your hip?

JONES That's the way he used to stand, all haughty like.

PIKE (**Putting his hand on his hip**) What, like that?

JONES (**Putting his hand on his hip**) Yes, like that.

PIKE Why?

JONES I can't go into all that now. Where was I? You've made me lose my thread.

PIKE The Scotch soldier was lying on the ground.

JONES 'Och aye, och aye, I canna go o,n sir, I canna go on,' he said. That's Scotch for 'I can't go on'. 'Stuff and nonsense, my good man,' said General Kitchener. 'Think of your great national hero, Robert the Bruce. He was lying in a cave and he was going to give up, when he saw a spider trying to climb up to the roof. Fifty times the spider tried until, finally, he made it, and Robert the Bruce was determined that, like that spider, he wouldn't give up, and neither should you.' Then the Scotch soldier leapt to his feet, gave a yell, and jumped up and down. 'That's better, my man,' said Lord Kitchener, 'that's lifted your morale'. Mind you, it wasn't the story that lifted his morale, a scorpion had crawled up his kilt.

PIKE What's that got to do with porridge?

JONES I dunno.

INTERIOR. COMMAND POST. NIGHT

The platoon are all asleep on the floor. Wilson is asleep in the bottom bunk, Mainwaring in the top.

EXTERIOR. BOTTOM OF TELEGRAPH POLE. NIGHT

PIKE Just think, Mr Jones, while we're standing here, those telephone lines up there are carrying all those secrets.

JONES Yes – all those secrets.

INTERCIT: PHONE BACKINGS. NIGHT

SERGEANT Coming to the pictures with me tomorrow night, Doreen?

GIRL No I'm not, you're all hands.

SERGEANT Oh come on, be a sport.

GIRL All right then, if you promise to behave yourself.

SERGEANT Where shall we go – Regal or the Odeon?

GIRL I don't know.

EXTERIOR. TELEGRAPH POLE

JONES You know what, Pikey, along that wire, decisions are probably being made at this very moment that could affect the whole course of the war.

PHONE BACKINGS

SERGEANT Well, make up your mind, Doreen.

GIRL I'm not fussy, you choose.

SERGEANT All right then, the Odeon.

INTERIOR. COMMAND POST. NIGHT

Mainwaring asleep in the bunk. He slowly starts to slip through a hole in the bunk. Cut to bottom bunk. Mainwaring above Wilson.

EXTERIOR. BOTTOM OF TELEGRAPH POLE. NIGHT

We hear distant sirens and ack ack fire.

JONES Here they come again, Pikey. Better go and wake Mr Mainwaring.

PIKE Right-oh.

JONES Don't rush in shouting and give him a start – wake him up quietly.

PIKE Quietly, yes, Mr Jones.

INTERIOR. COMMAND POST. NIGHT

Pike enters and creeps to Mainwaring, asleep in the bunk.

PIKE Mr Mainwaring, there's an air raid.

He holds the lamp above bunk. Looks at Mainwaring's figure.

PIKE Mr Mainwaring, you've shrunk. **(Yells)** Mr Mainwaring.

Loud sirens. Cut to bottom bunk. Wilson wakes, bangs his head on bulge. Mainwaring wakes and struggles.

MAINWARING Get me out! Get me out!

EXTERIOR. COUNTRY ROAD. DAY

The platoon are finishing breakfast.

MAINWARING Nothing like a good breakfast to start the day, Wilson.

WILSON The porridge was very thick.

MAINWARING I thought the boy did rather well, considering he's never cooked porridge before.

PIKE Mr Mainwaring –

MAINWARING Don't talk to an officer with your mouth full.

PIKE What do you want me to do with all the porridge that's left over, Mr Mainwaring?

MAINWARING What are you talking about, Pike?

PIKE Come and look.

Mainwaring, Wilson, Jones and Frazer follow Pike to field kitchen. Huge vat of porridge.

MAINWARING What on earth did you make all that porridge for? There's enough there for a hundred men.

PIKE I only did what Mr Frazer told me. One jug of porridge to one mug of water.

FRAZER Ach, son, I said one mug of porridge to one jug of water.

MAINWARING You stupid boy.

Hodges comes up the road on his motorbike. The Verger is on the pillion and the Vicar is in the sidecar.

WILSON The Vicar's here, sir.

MAINWARING I'd forgotten all about that. Let's get it over as quickly as we can. Get the men together for a service, Jones.

JONES Yes, sir. **(Shouts)** Right, gather round for a service, at the double.

The motorbike stops. The Vicar gets out of the sidecar and crosses to Mainwaring.

MAINWARING Good morning, Vicar.

VICAR Good morning, Mr Mainwaring, what a beautiful day. Hand the prayer books out, Mr Yeatman.

VERGER Yes, Your Reverence. **(He hands the books round)**

HODGES Well, I'll go and have a smoke, Vicar. I'll take you back when you've finished.

MAINWARING Don't you feel in the need of a little spiritual uplift, Mr Hodges?

HODGES Mind your own business, Napoleon.

VICAR Please stay, Mr Hodges, for my sake.

HODGES Very well, Vicar, if you put it like that.

VICAR **(Holding his arms out)** Come, join the flock. Brethren, we are gathered together in the true spirit of comradeship and brotherhood.

Hodges gives Mainwaring a glare. They all lower their heads.

VICAR Let us give thought to those things above, that control our destiny.

Cut to the top of the telegraph pole. A small bomb is jammed in the cross pieces amongst the wire.

VICAR Let us turn our faces to heaven and give thanks.

Mainwaring looks up and sees the bomb.

MAINWARING Good lord!

VICAR He is indeed, Captain Mainwaring.

VERGER **(Looking up)** Heavens above!

VICAR I'll do the praying, Mr Yeatman.

Jones looks up.

JONES Don't panic, there's a bomb on the wire, don't panic!

MAINWARING Take cover.

They all run and take cover behind the command post. The Vicar looks up.

VICAR Good heavens. **(He runs after the others. They all peer round the command post)**

JONES How did that get up there, Captain Mainwaring?

WILSON It must have been during that raid last night. It could blow up any minute.

MAINWARING No, it's perfectly safe where it is. It needs to hit the ground with considerable force to explode. But if it does slip, the explosion will bring that pole down and all the wires with it.

PIKE Shall I get on to G.H.Q., Mr Mainwaring?

FRAZER Aye, we ought to tell them, sir.

MAINWARING No, we must handle this ourselves. But I think we ought to inform the Post Office first.

GODFREY There's a phone box about a mile along the road. Shall I sprint down there and phone?

MAINWARING Stay where you are, Godfrey.

JONES Permission to speak, sir? Let me go in my van.

MAINWARING No, I want you here, Jones. Sponge –

SPONGE Yes, sir.

MAINWARING You go.

SPONGE Right, Captain Mainwaring.

JONES And you be careful with my van.

EXTERIOR. COUNTRY ROAD. DAY

Sponge runs into the picture.

MAINWARING Where have you been, Sponge? You've been gone over an hour.

SPONGE I'm sorry, Captain Mainwaring. After I made the phone call, I couldn't get the van started, so I had to run back.

JONES What did you do to my van?

SPONGE I didn't do anything to it.

MAINWARING Quiet, Jones, What did the telephone people say?

SPONGE They're sending a team of experts right away.

MAINWARING But that was over an hour ago.

A man appears on a bike. He is wearing a bowler hat, mackintosh and clips. There is a 5-foot ladder strapped to the crossbar.

WILSON Perhaps that's him now, sir.

MAINWARING Don't be absurd, Wilson, does he look like a team of experts from the G.P.O.?

MAN Morning, G.P.O., what's the trouble?

MAINWARING They said they were sending a team of experts.

MAN I may not be an expert but I know what I'm doing. **(He lays his bike in the road)**

MAINWARING **(Pointing to bomb)** Well, what are you going to do about that?

MAN **(Looking up)** Oh no, oh no, no, that's not in my territory at all, I'll have to report back.

MAINWARING So you refuse to go up.

MAN That's right.

MAINWARING In that case, I shall requisition your ladder. Jones, Pike – set it up.

JONES Yes, Mr Mainwaring.

They both get the ladder. Close up on Mainwaring.

MAINWARING Now, look here, my good man, I don't like your attitude. I shall report you to your superiors.

MAN You can report me to Winston Churchill as far as I'm concerned.

Cut to close up of Pike.

PIKE It's ready, Mr Mainwaring.

MAINWARING Good.

Mainwaring crosses to Pike and Jones at the pole. The 5-foot ladder is propped up.

MAINWARING You stupid boy.

PIKE It's not my fault if it's too short.

MAINWARING Come back out of the danger area.

Mainwaring, Jones and Pike cross back to the man.

MAINWARING Where's the rest of that ladder?

MAN There isn't any more.

MAINWARING Then how do you get up the pole?

MAN Use the leg irons.

MAINWARING Give them to me.

The man takes the irons off the back of his bike.

WILSON You'll never be able to get up there in those, sir.

MAINWARING I'll be the judge of that, Wilson. All we've got to do is to tie some rope round the bomb and lower it. Now, men, I'm not going to ask for volunteers. I shall go up the pole.

FRAZER Aye – like a monkey on a stick.

EXTERIOR. COUNTRY ROAD. DAY

Mainwaring is sitting on the ground. The man is strapping the leg irons on him.

JONES Let me go up that pole, Mr Mainwaring. You're too young to die, let me go.

MAINWARING Thank you, Jones, but I must go. (**He gets to his feet. Takes two paces and falls over**)

MAN I forgot to tell you – you can't walk in them, they're only for climbing.

MAINWARING Pike – you carry me.

PIKE What, on my own, sir?

MAINWARING Hodges, help Wilson to carry me.

HODGES I'll do no such thing. I'm a non-combatant, I'm keeping out of it.

MAINWARING I order you to carry me.

PIKE Why don't you shoot him, Mr Mainwaring? Go on, you're entitled to.

JONES You're yellow, that's what you are.

HODGES Oh, all right.

Hodges and Wilson pick Mainwaring up.

MAINWARING The rest of you, stand back. We don't want to risk too many lives. Forward. (**They carry him to the pole**) Right, Wilson, give me the rope. Now, I'll have that bomb down in two shakes of a lamb's tail. Up.

They push Mainwaring up.

WILSON Jam the irons in hard, sir.

HODGES Give him a hand up.

One of the irons catches in Hodges' trouser pocket and rips the seam.

HODGES Look what you've done. You! You!

MAINWARING Oh, you do make a fuss.

EXTERIOR. COUNTRY ROAD. DAY

Close up of Mainwaring.

MAINWARING This should do the trick.

Pull back. They are holding a blanket under the bomb.

MAINWARING Right, Frazer, stand by to cast.

Cut to Frazer, who is holding a fly rod.

FRAZER Aye, sir.

MAINWARING Wait a minute, better put our steel helmets on, men.

They put them on.

MAINWARING Right, Frazer.

Frazer casts the hook. It catches in the wires. He jerks it.

MAINWARING Left.

They move the blanket.

MAINWARING Right. Left. Left.

An open van comes along the road, piled with furniture. It stops.

WILSON It's jammed hard, sir, it won't come free.

MAINWARING Pull harder, Frazer.

DRIVER Want any help?

MAINWARING Tell him to get on about his business.

Wilson crosses to the van.

WILSON Would you mind moving on, please.

DRIVER I only asked if you wanted any help.

WILSON Well, we don't, so clear off.

DRIVER That's nice, ask a blasted civil question and all I get is a load of blasted cheek. (**The driver looks at Hodges, who is standing with his trousers flapping**)

DRIVER Do you want to borrow a safety pin, mate?

HODGES Get out of it.

DRIVER More blasted abuse. Don't worry, mate, I'm going. (**Tries to get the gear in**) Just as soon as I get these blasted gears sorted out. Get in, blasted thing, get blasted in.

JONES Permission to speak, sir? I've got an idea. Why don't we get that furniture on the van, pile it up and up and up, until it's high enough to reach the bomb.

MAINWARING Well done, Jones. (**Shouts**) Wilson, stop that man.

EXTERIOR. COUNTRY ROAD. DAY

The furniture is lashed in a tower on top of the van.

MAN There, that's the best I can blasted do.

MAINWARING Right, boy, up you get.

PIKE I'm not going up there, it's all wobbly.

JONES Let me go, sir, let me go up the wobbly tower of furniture.

• DEREK WARE REMEMBERS •

'My work on this episode required me, as a double for Corporal Jones, to be transported up in a large cast iron bucket attached to a small crane, climb on to the lip or edge of the contraption and to dislodge a prop bomb safely which had become tangled in overhead telephone wires. On the face of it, a pretty straightforward comedy stunt. The height was about 20 feet and once I had made the transfer, all the close stuff on the actor Clive Dunn would be shot on a specially constructed set of telephone wires about eight foot off the ground.

'Problems arose when I climbed on to the lip of the bucket, which was secured by two bolts on the sides. When my full weight was on the nearside edge to the wires, the rig kept tilting away from them and left me in danger of overbalancing and pitching earthward. What was required was for the base of the bucket to be additionally weighted to keep it upright. After several takes, I managed to climb into a suitable position literally to hurl myself at the wires. But, realistically speaking, as I was some years younger than the character Clive Dunn had created, my action was that of a much younger man and therefore I stepped out of character. However, such is the power of comedy action, the viewers didn't seem to notice.

'The really tough part came after the stunt was finished and I had to return to terra firma. No provision had been made – practical footholds on the telephone pole, for instance – and it was extremely difficult to climb back into the swaying bucket. I eventually hung full-length by my fingertips from the wires and dropped feet first 15 foot on to a rather old and well worn mattress someone had found nearby.'

GODFREY If it wasn't for my rheumatics I'd be shinning up there like greased lightning.

FRAZER Aye and if I had good eyesight I'd be up there like a shot.

MAINWARING Aren't you ashamed of yourself, Pike? These men are three times your age.

WILSON Come on, Frank, show us what you're made of.

PIKE You'll see what I'm made of, I'll be spread all over the road.

HODGES You're yeller.

PIKE All right, I'll go. **(He climbs up on the van and leans over to Wilson)** Mum's going to hear about this, Uncle Arthur.

WILSON Go on, Frank, get up there.

Close up of Vicar and Verger praying.

MAINWARING Oh, get on, boy.

PIKE It's not high enough, Mr Mainwaring, it's not high enough.

JONES Why don't we jack it up, sir?

MAINWARING We're not giving in yet, Jones.

JONES No, jack the lorry up, sir.

MAINWARING That's an idea. **(To driver)** Get a jack.

The driver goes to cab and gets jack.

DRIVER I hope you know what you're blasted doing, mate. **(He brings jack back)** Five blasted pounds this blasted furniture cost me.

Jones and Wilson put the jack in place.

MAINWARING **(Shouts)** Hold on tight, we're going to lift you up.

PIKE What?

Cut to Vicar and Verger. Jones pumps the jack up.

MAINWARING Higher, more, up, up, up.

The tower starts to topple, it goes over intact with Pike on top. Reaction close-ups. Pike drags himself out of the straw.

MAINWARING Can't you do anything right?

PIKE What's my Mum going to say when I go home smelling like this?

WILSON Are you all right, Frank?

PIKE You just wait, Uncle Arthur.

MAINWARING We'll have to think of something else, Wilson.

WILSON I think I may have the solution, sir. You remember yesterday, when we stopped where the road was up, remember, and you told me I hadn't got a scientific mind and you drover over the, er… you know, with the tea.

MAINWARING Get on with it, Wilson.

WILSON Well, there was a crane there. Why don't we use that?

MAINWARING Good idea. Frazer, Sponge, go and get the crane.

EXTERIOR. COUNTRY ROAD. DAY

The crane is parked beside the pole. Jones is in the bucket.

WILSON Good luck, Jonesey.

MAINWARING Yes, good luck, Jones.

JONES Thank you, sir.

Wilson shouts to Frazer, who is working the crane.

WILSON Take it away.

The bucket goes up. Cut to Jones in the bucket, level with the bomb. He tries to reach it.

JONES (**Shouts down**) I can't quite reach it, Mr Mainwaring, I'll have to climb on the pole.

Cut to Mainwaring.

MAINWARING Be very careful, Jones. That man's as brave as a lion, Wilson.

Cut back to Jones, who is holding the bomb.

JONES I've got it, I've got it, I've... whoa! (**He slips, so he is sitting on the crosspiece. He is gripping the bomb with his legs and holding on to the wires with his arms. Mainwaring and co. throw themselves on the ground**)

JONES Don't panic, I can't hold it!

The bomb falls into the porridge with a plop. Mainwaring and co. look up.

WILSON Lucky you made all that porridge, Frank.

PIKE I'm not such a stupid boy after all, am I, Captain Mainwaring?

MAINWARING (**Getting up**) No, I'm sorry, Pike.

WILSON What a good job we didn't have kippers for breakfast, sir.

Cut to Jones holding on to the wires.

JONES How am I going to get down, sir?

MAINWARING We'll think of something.

JONES What happens if I get a shock?

MAINWARING Don't worry – you won't get a shock unless someone makes a phone call.

JONES Permission to speak, sir? I think someone's on the line now.

Sparks start coming from the wires.

• GRAHAM BEDWELL REMEMBERS •

'I remember the filming of "Number Engaged" in particular. The Bedford flat bed furniture lorry was actually Hodges' greengrocery van with the body removed and a change of numberplates.

'When Corporal Jones was up the telegraph pole and dropped the bomb, it landed in a steaming cauldron of porridge. The property department had slightly over catered to allow for re-takes, so there was a surplus of Scott's porridge oats at the end of location shooting, which kept the Bedwell household well fed for the remainder of 1977!'

SERIES NINE **EPISODE SIX**

Recorded: Friday 29/7/77

Original transmission: Sunday 13/11/77, 8.10–8.45pm

Original viewing figures = 12.5 million

ARTHUR LOWE .... CAPTAIN MAINWARING
JOHN LE MESURIER .... SERGEANT WILSON
CLIVE DUNN................................ LANCE CORPORAL JONES
JOHN LAURIE .... PRIVATE FRAZER
ARNOLD RIDLEY .... PRIVATE GODFREY
IAN LAVENDER .... PRIVATE PIKE
BILL PERTWEE................................ CHIEF WARDEN HODGES
FRANK WILLIAMS .... VICAR
EDWARD SINCLAIR................................ VERGER
PAMELA CUNDELL................................ MRS FOX
JANET DAVIES .... MRS PIKE
COLIN BEAN .... PRIVATE SPONGE
JOAN COOPER................................ DOLLY
ROBERT RAGLAN .... COLONEL
PLATOON.................. ROGER BOURNE, DESMOND CULLUM-JONES,
.... FREDDIE WHITE, MICHAEL MOORE, FREDDIE WILES,
.... GEORGE HANCOCK, EVAN ROSS, JIMMY MAC, VERNON DRAKE

NEVER TOO OLD

• PAMELA CUNDELL REMEMBERS •

'This was my favourite episode. There is a scene where Mr Mainwaring, who's giving Mrs Fox away at her wedding, walks with her out of the church hall. When we practised the scene in rehearsals, we both tried walking through the door at the same time and got stuck. We laughed together, and then Arthur said: "Don't say anything, because nobody has seen it, and then when it comes to the actual recording we'll do it again and get a good laugh from the audience." And we did. That was a favourite moment of mine

'Being the last episode made for a very emotional time; it was also a special episode for me because my character, Mrs Fox, was getting married. She was a lovely character to play, someone who grew as the series progressed. I played her quite naturally in a way: I'm sort of bubby and a bit flirtatious, I suppose, which is how I tried to make Mrs Fox.

'I'll always be eternally grateful to David and Jimmy for giving me the chance to play her.'

INTERIOR. CHURCH HALL. EVENING

Godfrey is sweeping up or polishing the knob on Mainwaring's office door. Mrs Fox enters from the side office.

MRS FOX Oh – Mr Godfrey, you remember me, I'm Mrs Fox.

GODFREY Yes – can I help you?

MRS FOX I wanted a word with Mr Jones.

GODFREY They're marching round the town. He won't be free for quite a while.

MRS FOX I said I'd phone him at eight, but since I was passing I thought I'd put him out of his misery. Never mind, I'll phone as promised. Bye-ee.

GODFREY Goodbye.

She goes. The platoon is heard, off.

MAINWARING Left, right (etc.) Left wheel. (**They march into the hall**) Right wheel.

They assume the usual line-up positions. Godfrey joins them and Jones is missing.

MAINWARING Platoon, halt. Left turn. Order arms. Stand at ease. Where's Jones?

PIKE Excuse me, Mr Mainwaring.

MAINWARING What is it, Pike?

PIKE You know just as we came into the High Street, when you said right wheel?

MAINWARING Yes.

PIKE Mr Jones didn't.

FRAZER He walked straight on with a silly grin on his face.

MAINWARING Did you notice this, Wilson?

WILSON Yes, sir.

MAINWARING Why didn't you tell me?

WILSON Well – I didn't want to upset you.

MAINWARING Upset me?

WILSON Well, you were strutting out ahead of the men, making such a brave show, it seemed a pity to spoil it.

Mainwaring reacts. Jones marches in.

JONES Left, right, left, right. Right wheel. Halt. Left turn. Order arms. Stand at ease. Good evening.

MAINWARING Jones – where have you been?

JONES I saw a little throstle bird, sir. And I thought to myself, what a pretty throstle, isn't life wonderful – and when I looked round, you'd all gone and left me, Mr Mainwaring.

MAINWARING I'm surprised at you, Jones. Your mind is normally on war-like things, not birds. Right, fall out. Come with me into the office, Wilson.

WILSON Yes, sir.

They go into the office.

INTERIOR. SIDE OFFICE. EVENING

MAINWARING (**As he moves round to sit**) I'm very worried about Jones. He's getting very woolly in the head.

WILSON Yes, I had noticed.

MAINWARING If it goes on like this, I shall have to replace him. I can't be expected to face the Nazi invasion with a woolly-headed corporal.

There is a knock on the door.

MAINWARING Come in.

Jones enters.

MAINWARING Ah – Jones, I was just about to send for you.

JONES Permission to have a man-to-man, heart-to-heart talk with you, sir?

MAINWARING Of course. Sit down, Jones.

WILSON Here you are, Jonesey. (**He gives him his chair**)

JONES Can I start, sir?

MAINWARING Of course.

JONES Captain Mainwaring, have you noticed a spring in my step?

MAINWARING Well, I wouldn't have described it as that.

JONES What about you, Mr Wilson? Can you see a glint or gleam in my eye?

WILSON Well, now you come to mention it, Jonesey, you are a little different.

JONES I have fallen in love, Mr Mainwaring – with a woman.

MAINWARING I see.

JONES Sir, I have the honour to ask your permission to get married.

MAINWARING Well, it's really nothing to do with me, Jones.

JONES Don't say that, sir. You are my commanding officer and my very help in trouble.

WILSON You're not in trouble, are you, Jonesey?

JONES No, sir.

MAINWARING Well, you're technically a civilian, Jones. You're free to marry when and whom you wish.

JONES But do you give your permission, Captain Mainwaring?

MAINWARING Well – yes – all right.

JONES Bless you, Captain Mainwaring. I knew you wouldn't let me down. (To Wilson) He's a lovely man.

MAINWARING Who is the lady in question?

JONES Mrs Fox.

MAINWARING Ah – Mrs Fox. Well done. Are you sure you love her, Jones?

JONES I'm besotted with her.

MAINWARING That's not quite the same thing.

JONES I see her face everywhere I go. I see it in the trees and the hills. I even saw it yesterday on the gasworks. And every morning I see it on the pillow beside me. She's not really on the pillow, of course. You didn't think that, did you? And everywhere I glance, there she is – like a willow the wasp.

MAINWARING Yes, you're sure this is not just a passing fancy?

JONES No – definitely not a passing fancy – I've fancied her for 17 years.

Mainwaring reacts.

WILSON And you are absolutely sure you want to marry her?

JONES No, sir – I'm tortured by self-doubt – I'm only a humble butcher – is this true affection she feels, does she love me for myself, or does she love me for my meat?

MAINWARING When do you plan to get married?

JONES Well, there's the quandary, sir.

MAINWARING Why is that?

JONES I don't know if she'll have me.

WILSON You don't mean to say you haven't asked her?

JONES Oh yes, I've asked her – what's more, I've given her an ultimatum. She's going to ring me here at eight o'clock with the answer. Can I sit by the phone, Mr Mainwaring? Let me sit by the phone. Please let me sit by the telephone.

MAINWARING I'm sorry, Jones. I can't have you sitting by the phone.

WILSON I tell you what, Jones. You wait in the hall, and the second she calls, we'll let you know.

JONES Oh, Mr Wilson, what would I do without your compromising suggestions? I'll be waiting on tender hooks, Mr Mainwaring. (**He salutes in several different directions and goes**)

WILSON He's got it badly, hasn't he?

MAINWARING Yes… Wilson, I'm not very happy about those aiming marks in the yard – come and look at them.

They start to move to the outside door.

INTERIOR. MAIN HALL. EVENING

Frazer, Godfrey and Pike are in their not unusual position on the platform stairs.

FRAZER Here he comes.

PIKE What did he say, Mr Jones?

JONES He said yes. He's a lovely man – he really is a lovely man.

FRAZER You shouldn't have asked him. Mrs Fox is a fine, big, widow woman. You should take her, and damn the consequences.

JONES I don't think there'll be any consequences.

GODFREY Oh, by the way, she called round just before you got back.

JONES She called round. What did she say? What did she say?

GODFREY She said since she was passing, she'd put you out of your misery.

JONES Put me out of my misery? What does that mean?

FRAZER They do it to dumb animals when they're past hope.

Jones reacts.

GODFREY She said she'd ring as arranged. I think it's all going to be all right.

PIKE It's ever so exciting, isn't it? Can I come to the bachelor party the night before the wedding, Mr Jones?

JONES Course you can, Pikey – you can all come.

PIKE Here – there'll be a lot of bachelors at it, too. I'm, a bachelor, Mr Godfrey's a bachelor, Mr Frazer's a bachelor.

JONES Ah – but you haven't always been a bachelor, have you, Mr Frazer?

FRAZER Aye – that I have. Mind, I've never been short of the lassies. I've always had a strange power over women.

JONES Did you ever ask one of them and then she rang up later and said no?

FRAZER As a matter of fact, she said yes – after a while, you understand. She was a fine girl, she had long, sturdy legs and she loved to tread the path by the high cliffs, with the night wind blowing through her tresses. One dark night, she never came back. It seemed she'd been blown over the cliff and swept out to sea. Every night, I'd stand on that same cliff shouting, 'Jessie, Jessie – will ye no come back to me?'. But the wind just threw the words back in my face, mocking me – do you hear, mocking me. Years later I received a letter – I sensed it was news of her. (**He takes a letter from his wallet**) My fingers trembled as I opened it. I still keep it here, next to my heart.

PIKE Your heart's on the other side.

JONES Shut up, Pikey.

FRAZER **(Reads)** 'Dear Jock, I'll always love you. I still wear your ring. I'm in Singapore and I want to come home and be wed. Please send £40. Yours forever, Jessie.'

PIKE And did you send it?

FRAZER Come away, man. Do you think I'm made of money?

The phone rings in the office.

JONES It's the phone – it's the phone. Don't panic, don't panic – it's her – it's Mrs Fox. **(He dashes into the office)**

INTERIOR. SIDE OFFICE. EVENING

Mainwaring and Wilson are not present. Jones seizes the phone. As he talks, Mainwaring and Wilson re-enter.

JONES Hello, my darling. This is me. Now, you must give me your answer – and don't keep me in suspense any longer, because I love you and love you and love you and want to be with you forever and ever – oh. **(He hands over the receiver)** It's the colonel for you, sir.

Mainwaring takes the phone.

MAINWARING Hello, sir. Mainwaring here. Sorry about that.

Jones beats a hasty retreat.

INTERIOR. MAIN HALL. EVENING

The others are in the hall.

PIKE What happened?

FRAZER She turned you down. You're well out of it. There're lots of good fish in the sea.

JONES It wasn't her. But it'll be her any minute. I wish he'd get off that phone. **(He opens the door)** Are you going to be long, Mr Mainwaring?

MAINWARING Get out, Jones.

JONES Thank you very much, sir. **(He shuts the door)** He's still on the phone, and Mrs Fox will be trying to get through – and she'll get the engaged signal, brr brr – brr brr. I must think about something else. What shall I think about? **(To Pike)** You've got a young head on your shoulders, think of something else for me to think about.

PIKE Think about all those battles you've been in.

JONES That's it – battles We used to go in with the cold steel, you know. They did not like it up 'em, they did not like it up 'em.

The phone rings in the office.

JONES It's her, it's Mrs Fox, it's Mrs Fox. (He runs into the office)

INTERIOR. SIDE OFFICE. EVENING

Mainwaring is holding the receiver.

MAINWARING I see. I see. Yes, of course. **(To Jones)** Now, keep calm, Jones, it's for you.

JONES Thank you, Mr Mainwaring. **(Into phone)** Jones, the Butcher. **(He listens)** She wants me to sit down, Captain Mainwaring.

MAINWARING Oh dear – give him a chair, Wilson.

WILSON Here, Jonesey – sit down and try not to get too worked up.

JONES Thank you, Mr Wilson. **(To Mainwaring)** He's a lovely man – he really is a lovely man.

MAINWARING The phone, Jones.

JONES Oh, yes. I'm sitting down now. **(He listens calmly and answers flatly)** Yes – yes – yes. Thank you for letting me know. **(He puts the phone down. His lips start to tremble. He goes for his handkerchief and blows his nose)**

Mainwaring reacts.

JONES I'm trying to take it calmly – I really am trying to take it calmly.

WILSON Never mind, Jones – it's not the end of the world.

JONES She's a lovely woman, she really is a lovely woman. It's no good. I can't keep calm – I'm going to break. She said she loved me – she said yes – I'm going to marry Mrs Fox. **(He rises as he gets more excited)** I'm going to marry Mrs Fox, I'm going to marry Mrs Fox. **(He dashes into the hall)** I'm going to marry Mrs Fox... **(etc.)**

INTERIOR. SIDE OFFICE. EVENING. A WEEK LATER

Mainwaring is on the phone.

MAINWARING Yes, of course. Very well, Mrs Fox, I'll pop round this evening, and you can be sure that anything you say will be treated in the strictest of confidence. **(There is a knock on the door)** Come in. **(Wilson enters)** Very well – goodbye. **(He replaces the receiver)** Come in – sit down, Wilson. Have the men gone?

WILSON Yes – did you want them?

MAINWARING No – I wanted a word with you about, Jones.

WILSON He is excited about it all, isn't he? You'd think after a week he'd have calmed down a bit.

MAINWARING Yes – I suppose I'm doing the right thing by allowing him to go ahead.

WILSON You've no authority to stop him.

MAINWARING That's quite true, but I could advise him against it. On the other hand, it might work out. At least they're the same class.

WILSON Do you really think class matters?

MAINWARING Oh, there's no question of it. It's the families that stir up the trouble. I had to contend with all sorts of snobbish nonsense when I married Elizabeth.

WILSON Did you, as it were, marry beneath you?

MAINWARING Oh no – the family thought she did.

Wilson reacts.

MAINWARING Elizabeth was very well connected. Her father was the suffragan bishop of Clagthorpe, you know.

WILSON Was he really?

MAINWARING They had a large detached house in the Hedley Road – the best part, you understand.

WILSON Of course.

MAINWARING Elizabeth led a very sheltered life, I can tell you. She hadn't even tried tomato sauce until she met me. I soon changed all that.

WILSON Marrying you must have opened up a whole new world for her.

MAINWARING Oh, it did – undoubtedly. But I never felt at ease with her parents. I always had the feeling they were looking down their noses at me – even when I became assistant manager.

WILSON They weren't impressed by that?

MAINWARING Not a bit. It was a large branch, you know – I even had my own partitioned cubicle.

WILSON Just fancy that.

MAINWARING Anyway, Jones and Mrs Fox won't have all that to contend with. Between you and me, they've asked to see me. If it's advice they want, I shall be non-committal, 'Let no man put asunder' – eh, Wilson?

WILSON Quite right. Marriage seems to fall asunder pretty quickly anyway, doesn't it, sir?

MAINWARING Oh no – not in my case. My marriage has been very happy – very happy indeed. That'll be all, Wilson.

WILSON Of course, sir. Goodnight.

MAINWARING Goodnight, Wilson.

INTERIOR. MRS FOX'S FLAT. EVENING

The flat, probably Edwardian, over the hat shop in the main street of Walmington-on-Sea. It is busily furnished with chintzy covers, dolls, 1930s nick-nacks, chromium-plated lamp, chromium-plated table, etc. A door leads to the landing and another to the bedroom. The bell rings.

MRS FOX **(Out of vision)** Come in. Give it a push, it's open.

Mainwaring enters. He is in his bank suit and bowler, etc.

MAINWARING Mrs Fox – Mrs Fox –

She comes out of the bedroom, tying up her dressing gown.

MRS FOX Oh hello, Mr Mainwaring. My, it's not six already, is it?

MAINWARING Well, er... **(He looks at his watch)** Yes – six o-two, to be precise.

MRS FOX **(Looking at her cuckoo clock on the wall)** My clock's stopped again. I am sorry. Make yourself at home, I shan't be a second. I'll leave the bedroom door open, so we can go on talking while I'm getting dressed.

MAINWARING I'll come back in five minutes.

MRS FOX No, please don't go. I'm quite decent underneath.

MAINWARING I'm sure you are.

MRS FOX Sit yourself down.

MAINWARING Oh, very well.

Mrs Fox goes into the bedroom. Mainwaring sits on the sofa.

MRS FOX I hope you don't mind coming to my little nest. **(Mainwaring finds he is sitting on a bra)** It's humble – but it's all mine.

MAINWARING Yes, I'm sure. **(He shoves the bra on chair and places his hat over it)**

MRS FOX I wanted to have a few moments alone with you before the others arrive.

MAINWARING Others! What others?

She appears. She has a stocking in her hand and she is finding the toe.

MRS FOX Mr Wilson and Mrs Pike. **(She looks at the stocking)** Don't tell me I've got a catch. **(She shows him the stocking)** Do you think that'll run to a ladder?

MAINWARING I couldn't tell you, I'm sure.

MRS FOX Well, will you think it awful of me if I don't put them on?

MAINWARING Not in the least.

MRS FOX I don't like to see a lady with bare legs, but a ladder looks even more abandoned, don't you think so?

MAINWARING You're probably right.

Mrs Fox goes back into the bedroom.

MRS FOX Now, I expect you're wondering what's on my mind.

MAINWARING Yes, I am.

MRS FOX Well, the thing is this. I've always had what you might call a soft spot for you Mr Mainwaring – and a very high regard for you as well. **(She appears at the door, dressed, with her zip undone)** Oh dear, I'm not expressing myself very well. Mr Mainwaring, you don't want me to beat about the bush, do you?

MAINWARING I'm not entirely sure.

MRS FOX Well, I have no father, you see. In fact, no living relations at all. You wouldn't give me away, would you?

MAINWARING Give you away?

MRS FOX At the wedding.

MAINWARING Oh, I see. I suppose so, if you want me to.

MRS FOX Oh, Mr Mainwaring, you're a darling. **(She kisses him)** You've no idea what a weight that is off my mind. Would you zip me up?

MAINWARING Oh no – I couldn't really. Somebody might come in.

MRS FOX We'll lock the door.

MAINWARING That would be worse.

MRS FOX Anyway, you're practically a father to me now. It's not a very big one. **(She turns to show the zip)**

MAINWARING Oh – very well. **(He does it)** Now, I really must go. I'll come back when the rest are expected.

MRS PIKE Cooee – are you there?

MRS FOX Come in, Mrs Pike.

Mrs Pike enters.

MRS PIKE Come in, Arthur. Come in, Frank. Take your hat off, Frank. Where are your manners?

Pike and Wilson follow her into the room.

WILSON/PIKE Good evening, Mrs Fox.

PIKE You were here early, Mr Mainwaring.

MAINWARING No – I was merely punctual for my appointment.

MRS FOX Mr Mainwaring practically caught me in the bath.

MAINWARING Well, that's rather an exaggeration.

MRS FOX Anyway, he's been ever so kind to me. He's even zipped me up.

MRS PIKE I hope you don't mind me bringing Frank. We don't like leaving him on his own when there's a war on, do we, Arthur?

WILSON Well, I…

MRS PIKE There's so many funny people about. Take your scarf off, Frank.

PIKE What could funny people do to me, if they found me on my own in wartime?

MRS PIKE Never you mind.

JONES **(Out of vision)** Cooee – are you there, Mildred?

MAINWARING Mildred!

MRS FOX Come in, Jack.

JONES Hello, everybody.

MRS FOX Don't move. **(Jones freezes)** I want to remember you just standing there.

JONES Who, me?

MRS FOX Isn't he lovely?

JONES I'm sorry I'm late.

WILSON I think you're spot on time, Jonesey.

PIKE Mr Mainwaring was the first. He had to help Mrs Fox out of the bath and zip her up.

JONES What was that?

MRS FOX It was all very innocent, wasn't it, Mr Mainwaring?

MAINWARING Totally innocent.

MRS FOX Well, now Jack's here, we can start. Sit down, everybody.

MRS PIKE Sit down, Arthur. Sit down, Frank.

MAINWARING Oh, sit down, boy, sit down.

Mainwaring looks at bowler. Bra business. Mrs Fox takes out a list.

MRS FOX I'm happy to announce that Mr Mainwaring is going to give me away.

Pike applauds.

MRS PIKE Frank – give over.

MRS FOX Mrs Pike has very kindly consented to be matron of honour.

Wilson reacts.

JONES And Mr Wilson is going to be best man.

MAINWARING You're going to be best man?

WILSON Yes – that's right.

MAINWARING You'd better write down everything you have to do, otherwise you'll forget it.

Wilson reacts.

MRS FOX Now, clothing. Naturally, we're not going to have a white wedding.

PIKE Why not?

MRS PIKE Because there's a war on.

MRS FOX The bride and the matron of honour will be in turquoise. Now, what about the men?

JONES I shall wear my old regimental regalia, with medals.

MRS FOX That'll be nice – let's have all the men in uniform.

JONES With medals.

MAINWARING I don't think that's a good idea at all.

PIKE Mr Mainwaring and me haven't got any medals, have we, Mr Mainwaring?

MRS PIKE Arthur has.

Wilson smiles.

MAINWARING It's nothing to do with medals, I just think people are tired of uniform.

MRS FOX I don't agree at all. Let's vote. Hands up for uniform and medals.

Mrs Fox, Mrs Pike, Jones and Pike put their hands up.

MAINWARING Pike – put your hand down, this is nothing to do with you.

Bowler business. Mainwaring reacts.

WILSON We still seem to be outvoted, sir.

MRS FOX Uniform it is then. Now, flowers –

JONES **(To Mrs Fox)** Mildred, can't you get out of the bath on your own?

INTERIOR. MAIN HALL. DAY

Two or three trestle tables have been placed for simple wartime food, bridge rolls, meat paste, etc., English fruit, salad, a few sausage rolls and some simple cakes. The table by the stage contains a three-tier wedding cake. Mainwaring enters from the side office with the Vicar and the Verger. The Vicar is dressed ready for the service.

MAINWARING Everything is ready in the church, I checked it personally. It's Wilson's job, of course – but you can't rely on him.

Hodges enters.

HODGES Hello, Napoleon – I'm just off to the church. Everything under control, is it?

MAINWARING Yes, of course. I didn't know you'd been invited.

HODGES Of course I'm invited – I'm a friend of the bride. **(He winks)**

Mainwaring reacts.

PIKE **(Entering)** Most of the guests are sitting in church, Mr Mainwaring. Shouldn't Mr Jones be taking his place? It's five to.

MAINWARING Good lord – is it that late? **(He calls)** Jones –

Jones enters from the side office in red coat, etc.

JONES Captain Mainwaring, there's still no sign of Sergeant Wilson. I'm getting in such a state, Captain Mainwaring. Do you think it's bad luck when the best man doesn't turn up?

MAINWARING It's damned inconvenient. You'd better get over there.

PIKE He'll be here all right, Mr Jones. He was ready when I left but – **(Confidentially)** he said something a bit rude to my mum, and she had to put him in his place.

JONES It's a bad omen. Do you think I'm doing the right thing, Captain Mainwaring?

MAINWARING Of course you are . Take him over, Pike.

VICAR Yes – you go into the church. The bride will be here any second, and we don't want you meeting her before the ceremony, do we?

JONES No, we don't want that – that is a bad omen, that is a bad omen.

VERGER **(Calling after them)** Remember – I want it clearly understood – no confetti.

MAINWARING Yes, all right – we know all about that.

Enter Wilson. He is dressed in the uniform of an infantry captain World War One.

WILSON I really am most awfully sorry I'm late.

MAINWARING I should jolly well… What's all this?

WILSON I'm sorry, sir. Mavis, Mrs Pike, insisted. It's my uniform from the last war. She found it in an old trunk.

MAINWARING You look ridiculous.

WILSON I wouldn't have dreamt of putting it on, but she – well, she hid my trousers.

MAINWARING It's an officer's uniform.

WILSON Yes – I was an officer.

MAINWARING You never told me.

WILSON You never asked me. Besides, it wasn't important.

MAINWARING Those badges of rank belong to a captain.

WILSON I was a captain.

MAINWARING Well, I'm blessed. It doesn't count now, you know.

MRS FOX **(From side office)** Cooee. Are you there, Captain Mainwaring?

MAINWARING That's the bride. Get into the church at once, and try not to make a fool of yourself. I'm here, Mrs Fox.

Mrs Fox and Mrs Pike enter.

MAINWARING How charming you both look. You make a lovely bride, Mrs Fox.

MRS FOX It won't be Mrs Fox much longer.

MAINWARING No indeed. We're ready when you are, Vicar.

VICAR Off we go then.

VERGER Remember – I want a solemn undertaking – no confetti.

VICAR Come on, Mr Yeatman.

MAINWARING Will you take my arm, Mrs Fox?

MRS FOX Oh, Mr Mainwaring, I'm going to cry.

MAINWARING Do try not to.

INTERIOR. THE MAIN HALL. LATER

The Home Guard form a guard of honour with an arch of bayonets at the main door. The rest of the guests are spectators. Jones and Mrs Fox (Mrs Jones!) enter down the triumphant arch. The guests applaud.

VERGER No confetti – no confetti.

PIKE I'm going to throw confetti – so sucks, boo.

VERGER You young vandal, you.

HODGES Go on – stop being a spoilsport. **(He takes the Verger's cap off and puts a handful of confetti on his head. The Verger takes the confetti off his head and throws it at Hodges)**

VICAR Mr Yeatman, I thought you said no confetti.

Mainwaring and Wilson move to congratulate the pair. Dolly, Godfrey and Frazer are in a group.

DOLLY I did enjoy that.

GODFREY So did I.

FRAZER It's a pagan ceremony and, in this case, I should have thought, a complete waste of time. Where's the drink?

Sponge coming from the side office to Mainwaring and Wilson, who are together.

SPONGE Captain Mainwaring, the colonel's just been on the phone. He wants you to put the platoon on 30 minutes' standby.

MAINWARING Do you hear that, Wilson? Thirty minutes' standby. Something must be brewing up.

WILSON Well, we're all here.

MAINWARING Yes, we'll keep it under our hats for the time being, but we'd better speed things along. Start the speeches as soon as possible.

WILSON Yes, sir. Good idea.

MAINWARING And keep yours short.

WILSON Of course.

MAINWARING And don't get drunk.

Cut to Godfrey and Dolly. Pike joins them.

PIKE Here, have some of this Miss Godfrey. It's cider.

GODFREY Oh dear – I hope it won't make us tipsy.

PIKE Here's to the bride and groom. Perhaps you'll be next, Mr Godfrey?

DOLLY Charles nearly got married once, didn't you, Charles?

GODFREY Well, I wanted to.

DOLLY It would never have done – her parents lived in a bungalow.

GODFREY She married a farmer. I still see her from time to time.

DOLLY Do you?

GODFREY She's a widow now.

DOLLY **(Worried)** Is she?

PIKE **(Offering drinks)** Another one?

Wilson bangs the table.

WILSON May I have your attention, please?

JONES Pray silence for Captain Mainwaring who is acting as father of the bride.

Applause from the guests.

MAINWARING Ladies and gentlemen – Jack and Mildred. I'm not going to make a long speech.

HODGES Good.

MAINWARING I've known Jack for a number of years now. He's the salt of the earth. He's loyal, he's brave, he's kind. I say this without hesitation, Mildred, he is the first person you go to if you're in trouble.

JONES She's not in trouble, Mr Mainwaring.

MAINWARING I know. Good luck to you and I only hope that you'll be as happy as I have been with my dear wife, who unfortunately can't be with us today.

HODGES Where is she then?

MAINWARING She's staying with her sister. Ladies and gentlemen, I give you Jack and Mildred.

ALL Jack and Mildred. Speech.

JONES Speech – speech.

MRS FOX It's you – you've got to make a speech.

JONES Oh. Ladies and gentlemen, I would like to thank Captain Mainwaring for all the nice things he has said, and for being the father of the bride, which he isn't – and thank you all for coming. Good health.

The guests applaud.

MAINWARING Now you, Wilson, and hurry up and make it short.

WILSON I don't need to speak at all.

MAINWARING Yes you do. You propose the health of the bridesmaid. Quiet please, Sergeant Wilson is going to say a word or two.

Applause from the guests.

WILSON Ladies and gentlemen, it's my duty to propose the health of the bridesmaid – or in this case, the matron of honour. It so happens we've been friends for really quite a long time.

Mainwaring reacts.

WILSON Dear Mavis, you belong to that blessed band of women, who have so much affection, so much love to give and you give it freely, sometimes getting very little in return – and you look very pretty in that hat. Ladies and gentlemen, the matron of honour.

Mrs Pike is overcome. Pike's lip trembles.

ALL The matron of honour.

FRAZER Are we no going to have a slice of that cake?

MRS FOX We haven't cut the cake – whatever next?

JONES We'd forget our heads if they weren't screwed on – where's my bayonet?

SPONGE (**To Mainwaring**) Captain Mainwaring, the colonel's on the phone again. He wants to speak to you personally.

MAINWARING I'll come at once.

Jones and Mrs Fox start to take the cake to pieces. They get to the bottom section.

JONES (**Taking out bayonet**) Right – here we go.

MRS FOX Not that. It's cardboard. (**She lifts the bottom layer. Reveal s a plain sponge**) There's a war on, you know.

They start to cut the cake.

INTERIOR. SIDE OFFICE. DAY

Mainwaring is on the phone.

MAINWARING Hello – Mainwaring here.

INTERCUT: INTERIOR. COLONEL'S OFFICE

COLONEL Ah, Mainwaring. Things are a bit confused here, but all units are standing to, immediately.

MAINWARING Good lord – has the balloon gone up?

COLONEL Not exactly, but barges have been moving about the North Sea coast. The weather's right, so we can't take any chances.

MAINWARING Right – I'll get my men to action stations straight away.

COLONEL Good luck.

MAINWARING Thank you. (**He replaces the receiver and strides to the door**)

INTERIOR. MAIN HALL

MAINWARING Right – quiet everybody. May I have your attention? There's no cause for alarm, but I want all ranks of the Home Guard to parade outside in the yard, at once please. Pick up your rifles on the way.

Hodges approaches.

HODGES What's going on, Napoleon?

INTERIOR. SEA FRONT SHELTER. NIGHT

It is very dimly lit. Jones and Pike are on guard.

PIKE Mr Jones, I bet you didn't think you were going to spend your honeymoon with me.

JONES No, I didn't.

PIKE You were both going to the Esplanade Hotel in Eastgate, wasn't you?

JONES Never mind. Duty comes first. Do you think they'll give me the deposit back on the room?

A figure appears.

JONES Halt – who goes there?

Mrs Fox stands there in head scarf.

MRS FOX It's me – Mrs Jones.

JONES Mrs Jones? I don't know no Mrs Jones.

MRS FOX It's me, Jack.

JONES Oh, Mrs Jones – Mrs Jones the butcher's wife. I'll be forgetting me own name next.

MRS FOX Well, I just thought I'd come and sit with you awhile.

JONES Yes – good idea. (**Takes Pike aside**) Pikey – you keep a good look out, and me and Mrs Jones is going to sit down and have a bit of a chat.

PIKE And a bit of a cuddle, eh, Mr Jones?

JONES No, nothing like that. (**To Mrs Fox**) Come on, my precious.

Pike reacts. They go to the shelter and sit.

MRS FOX (**As they sit**) Jack – I've been thinking. When all this is over, can we live in a little cottage?

JONES Yea – with roses round the door.

MRS FOX That's right, and with a big fridge in the kitchen.

JONES What do you want a big fridge for?

MRS FOX To keep all the big joints of meat.

JONES After the war?

MRS FOX Yes – after the war. Not that we won't have a joint or two before that, of course.

Jones begins to look worried as the section enter.

PIKE Halt – who goes there?

MAINWARING All right, Pike, well done. Any sign of anything?

PIKE No, Mr Mainwaring, it's been ever so quiet.

MAINWARING Where's Jones?

PIKE **(Coyly)** Where he should be on his honeymoon night – with his bride.

MAINWARING You stupid boy.

Jones appears.

JONES I'm here, Mr Mainwaring. I was just having a little chat with my lady wife. But I was ever so alert, sir. I've sent her home now.

MAINWARING That's all right, Jones. Wilson found a bottle of champagne, so we thought we'd come round and drink your health. Hand out the glasses, Wilson.

WILSON I haven't brought any glasses.

MAINWARING Well – what's the good of champagne without glasses?

WILSON I thought you said you were bringing the glasses?

MAINWARING Where would I get glasses?

FRAZER I brought a couple of mugs for our cocoa – we can use them.

GODFREY And I've got a medicine glass.

MAINWARING They'll have to do, I suppose. Pour it out.

They start to pour.

MAINWARING Keep your eyes skinned out to sea, Pike – you're too young for champagne anyway.

Hodges appears.

HODGES What are you lot doing here?

MAINWARING In case you've forgotten, there's an invasion alert on.

HODGES Haven't you heard? It was a false alarm. We got the stand down half an hour ago.

WILSON So Hitler will not be coming tonight after all?

HODGES Just as well, with you lot guarding us.

There is a brief moment of silence.

MAINWARING What do you mean?

HODGES Well, look at you – what good would you lot be against real soldiers? They'd walk straight through you. Goodnight.

JONES Here, he'd no business…

MAINWARING Take no notice of him, men. **(Mainwaring raises his mess tin)** Here's to your future happiness, Jones.

ALL Here's to you, Jones.

PIKE Mr Mainwaring, the Warden wasn't right was he – saying the Nazis would walk right through us?

MAINWARING Of course he wasn't right.

JONES I'll tell you one thing. They won't walk straight through me.

FRAZER Nor me – I'll be beside you, Jonesey.

MAINWARING We'll all be beside you, Jones. We stand together, make no mistake about that. If anyone tries to take our home or our freedom away from us, they'll find out what we can do. We'll fight and we're not alone. There are thousands of us all over England.

FRAZER And Scotland.

MAINWARING And Scotland. All over the British Isles, in fact. Men who will stand together whenever Britain needs them.

WILSON Do you know, sir, I think it would be rather nice if we paid our own small tribute to them.

MAINWARING For once, I agree with you, Wilson – to Britain's Home Guard.

They all raise their mugs.

ALL To Britain's Home Guard.

HELP! HELP! HELP! HELP! HELP!

LOST DAD'S ARMY EPISODES

Your help would be very welcome in trying to find the three 'lost episodes' of *Dad's Army,* which were wiped and are no longer available in the BBC archive.

From series two, 'The Loneliness of the Long-Distance Walker', 'A Stripe for Frazer' and 'Under Fire' are missing.

I, like millions of other *Dad's Army* fans, have never had the chance to watch these episodes, something we might be able to remedy with your help.

Check your attics, your garden sheds, ask your relatives, perhaps somewhere, someone holds an old video recording of these black and white episodes.

If you need to know more, feel free to contact me direct on my email address: r.webber@virgin.net or write via my publisher at: Orion Publishing Group, Orion House, 5 Upper St Martin's Lane, London WC2H 9EA.

Many thanks.

RICHARD WEBBER

1792. Oct. Prussians evacuate. 319
Nov 6. Battle of Jemappes.
Nov 19. Decree of aid to all nations.
28 &c. enforced. & in Decr. 15, 18.
Dec. 13. Parlt. meets. Counter associations in England.
Penal laws in Ireland repealed.

1793. Jan 21. Execution of Louis: (Chauvelin dismd. order Jan. 24.)
Feb 1. Convention declares war.
Feb 12. Dumouriez ordd. to break off negottn.
April. Shock to credit. 5 mill. lent on Exchr. bills raised on goods.
May 6. Reform – Grey.
June 2. Brissotines delivered to the Club.
June 17. Address for peace 187 to 47.
June 24. Terrorist Constitution.
July & Aug. Condé & Valenciennes taken.
Siege of Dunkirk.
Siege of Toulon, to Decr.
Oct. Edinburgh Convention.
Execution of Marie Antoinette.
And of the Girondists.
Nov. And of the Duke of Orleans.
Scotch Bill opening the franchise &c.

1794. Jan 21. Meeting of Parlt.
Jan 31. Sardinian subsidy.
May 7. Robespierre's decree for free worship.
May 10. Couthon's decree.
May 12. Hardy, Horne Tooke &c. arrested.
May 16. Bill to suspend Habeas Corpus.
June 1. Naval Victory.
June Whigs take Office.
July 28. Robespierre &c. guillotined.
July. Austrn. Netherlands evacuated.
{ Condé &c. retaken.
{ D. of York driven out of Holland.
{ French masters to the Rhine.
{ Appointment of L. Fitzwilliam.
Oct 16. Law restricting political societies (Fr.)
Nov. 9. Jacobin Club forcibly dispersed.
Dec. 30. Meeting of Parliament.

1795. Holland allies off & def. with France.
Motions for peace.
Provision for Prince of Wales.
E. Fitzwilliam's vagaries in Ireland.
Ap – Sept. Prussians – & Russians – agst Poland. Dismemberment. Fr. refuse aid.
March. Vendean war ended by treaty.
(Exp. of Emigrés.)
June 9. Death of Louis XVII.

WILLIAM PITT THE YOUNGER

WILLIAM PITT THE YOUNGER

WILLIAM HAGUE

HarperCollins*Publishers*

HarperCollins*Publishers*
77–85 Fulham Palace Road,
Hammersmith, London W6 8JB
www.harpercollins.co.uk

Published by HarperCollins*Publishers* 2004

1

The author asserts the moral right to
be identified as the author of this work

A catalogue record for this book
is available from the British Library

ISBN 0 00 714719 8

Map research: Gregory Fremont-Barnes
Artwork: Leslie Robinson

The chronology of Pitt's life shown on the endpapers was written by W. E. Gladstone, who himself went on to serve four times as Prime Minister. He wrote these notes in 1838, as an ambitious but junior Member of Parliament.

Set in PostScript Linotype Minion with
Spectrum and Bauer Bodoni display by
Rowland Phototypesetting Ltd,
Bury St Edmunds, Suffolk

Printed and bound in Great Britain by
Clays Ltd, St Ives plc

For my mother and father,
who have passed on to me
their reverence for books

CONTENTS

PART THREE

PART FOUR

ILLUSTRATIONS

William Pitt the elder, First Earl of Chatham, by William Hoare. *(The Hall Bequest; on loan to the Stowe House Preservation Trust)*

Hester, Countess of Chatham, by Thomas Hudson. *(Private collection)*

Burton Pynsent, Somerset, which the elder Pitt inherited from Sir William Pynsent. *(Drawn and engraved by J. Bonnor. From* The History and Antiquities of the County of Somerset. . ., *Vol 1, 1791 by the Reverend John Collinson, F.A.S.)*

Pembroke College, Cambridge. *(Master and Fellows of Pembroke College, Cambridge)*

William Pitt as a boy of seventeen, by an unknown artist. *(Master and Fellows of Pembroke College, Cambridge)*

The collapse of the elder Pitt in the House of Lords, by John Copley (1779–81). *(© Tate, London 2004)*

Westminster in Pitt's day. *(By permission of the British Library. Shelfmark/man: 190.e.4. Page No/Folio: N 12)*

A sketch of Pitt around the time of his entry to Parliament at the age of twenty-one, by Thomas Lawrence (c.1780). *(Philip Mould, Historical Portraits Ltd)*

Lord Frederick North, by Nathaniel Dance (c.1775). *(National Portrait Gallery, London)*

The Second Marquis of Rockingham, with his private secretary Edmund Burke, by Joshua Reynolds (c.1766). *(Fitzwilliam Museum, University of Cambridge/Bridgeman Art Library)*

The Earl of Shelburne, after Reynolds. *(National Portrait Gallery, London)*

Charles James Fox, by Karl Anton Hickel (1793–94). *(National Portrait Gallery, London)*

'The Infant Hercules', by Thomas Rowlandson (1784). *(The British Museum – BM6402)*

'Master Billy's Procession to Grocer's Hall', by Rowlandson (1784). *(Guildhall Library, Corporation of London/Bridgeman Art Library)*

Downing Street in Pitt's time, from a watercolour drawing by J.C. Buckler. *(Hulton Archive/Getty Images)*

King George III, by Allan Ramsay. *(The Royal Collection © HM Queen Elizabeth II)*

'Deliver us from the Pitt of Destruction' (1788). *(The British Museum – BM7305)*

Pitt in his early years as Prime Minister, by Thomas Gainsborough (c.1787). *(Private collection, USA, courtesy of Historical Portraits Ltd)*

Holwood House, Pitt's favourite haunt for most of his first seventeen years as Prime Minister. *(Hulton Archive/Getty Images)*

The trial of Warren Hastings in Westminster Hall. *(British Library/HIP)*

William Wilberforce. *(Hulton Archive/Getty Images)*

William Wyndham Grenville, by an unknown artist (1807). *(Mary Evans Picture Library)*

Henry Dundas, by an unknown artist, after Lawrence. *(National Portrait Gallery, London)*

George Rose. Colour engraving by John Samuel Agar, after a portrait by Richard Cosway. *(National Portrait Gallery, London)*

George Pretyman Tomline, by Robert Cooper after Henry Edridge (1814). *(National Portrait Gallery, London)*

Pitt's elevation of Pretyman to the Bishopric of Lincoln in 1787 produced much ribaldry. By James Gillray. *(Corporation of London/HIP)*

Richard Brinsley Sheridan, by John Hoppner. *(Novosti/Bridgeman Art Library)*

Edmund Burke, by Reynolds. *(Scottish National Portrait Gallery)*

'An Excrescence', by Gillray (1791). *(Courtesy of the Warden and Scholars of New College, Oxford/Bridgeman Art Library)*

The execution of Louis XVI in 1793. Print by Faucher-Gudin. *(Mary Evans Picture Library)*

Pitt addressing the House of Commons on the outbreak of war, February 1793, by Hickel (1793–95). *(National Portrait Gallery, London)*

'Presages of the Millennium', by Gillray (1795). *(Fitzwilliam Museum, University of Cambridge/Bridgeman Art Library)*

'Promised Horrors of the French Invasion', by Gillray (1796). *(Musée de la Révolution Française, Vizille, France/Bridgeman Art Library)*

The Battle of the Nile, 1798, by Philip James de Loutherberg (1800). *(Tate Gallery. © Tate, London 2004)*

'The Nuptial Bower', by Gillray (1797). *(Library of Congress, Prints and Photographs Division. Reproduction number LC-USZC4–8793)*

Lady Eleanor Eden, by Hoppner. *(National Portrait Gallery, London)*

'Midas, Transmuting all into Paper', by Gillray (1797). *(Courtesy of the Warden and Scholars of New College, Oxford/Bridgeman Art Library)*

Henry Addington. *(Mary Evans Picture Library)*

Pitt as Lord Warden of the Cinque Ports. *(English Heritage Photo Library)*

Pitt's diagram showing how a wheeling company should turn. *(Acres Adams Papers. Lot 7 (53), reproduced courtesy of Giles Adams)*

Lady Hester Stanhope. *(Hulton Archive/Getty Images)*

'Britannia Between Death and the Doctor's', by Gillray (1804). *(Library of Congress, Prints and Photographs Division. Reproduction number LC-USZC4–8794)*

Pitt as Prime Minister once again at the age of forty-four, by Hoppner. *(Courtesy of the Honourable Society of Lincoln's Inn)*

'The Plum Pudding in Danger', by Gillray (1805). *(Musée de la Ville de Paris, Musée Carnavalet, Paris/Lauros/Giraudon/Bridgeman Art Library)*

Pitt's spirits were buoyed by news of Trafalgar, depicted here by William Stuart . . . *(Sotheby's Picture Library)*

. . . but shattered by the news of Austerlitz. Engraving by Beyer, after François Gérard. *(Mary Evans Picture Library)*

On the eve of his death, Pitt attempted to write his will, but could not summon the strength to do so. *(Private collection)*

Pitt's death mask, taken by Joseph Nollekens and drawn by George Scharf. *(National Portrait Gallery, London)*

Lawrence's posthumous portrait of Pitt. *(The Royal Collection © HM Queen Elizabeth II)*

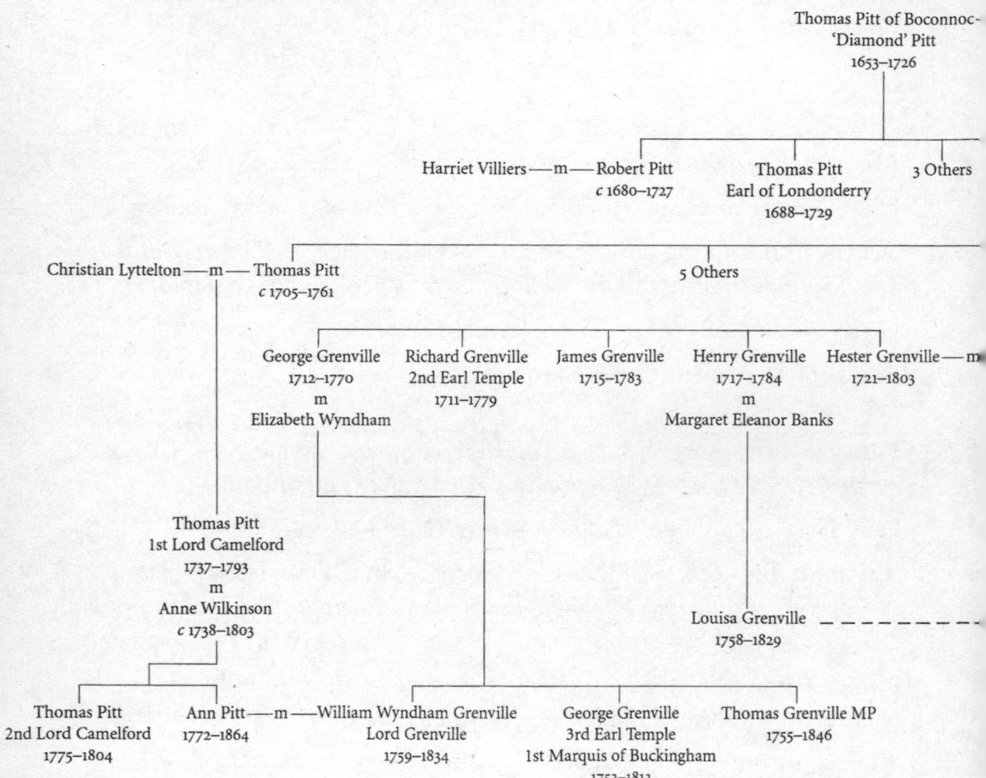
Thomas Pitt of Boconnoc
'Diamond' Pitt
1653–1726
Harriet Villiers — m — Robert Pitt
c 1680–1727
Thomas Pitt
Earl of Londonderry
1688–1729
3 Others
Christian Lyttelton — m — Thomas Pitt
c 1705–1761
5 Others
George Grenville
1712–1770
m
Elizabeth Wyndham
Richard Grenville
2nd Earl Temple
1711–1779
James Grenville
1715–1783
Henry Grenville
1717–1784
m
Margaret Eleanor Banks
Hester Grenville — m
1721–1803
Thomas Pitt
1st Lord Camelford
1737–1793
m
Anne Wilkinson
c 1738–1803
Louisa Grenville
1758–1829
Thomas Pitt
2nd Lord Camelford
1775–1804
Ann Pitt — m — William Wyndham Grenville
1772–1864
Lord Grenville
1759–1834
George Grenville
3rd Earl Temple
1st Marquis of Buckingham
1753–1813
Thomas Grenville MP
1755–1846

WILLIAM PITT'S FAMILY TREE

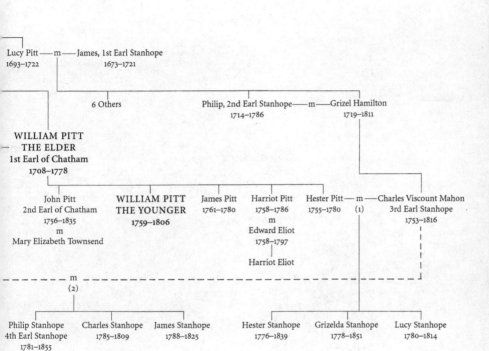

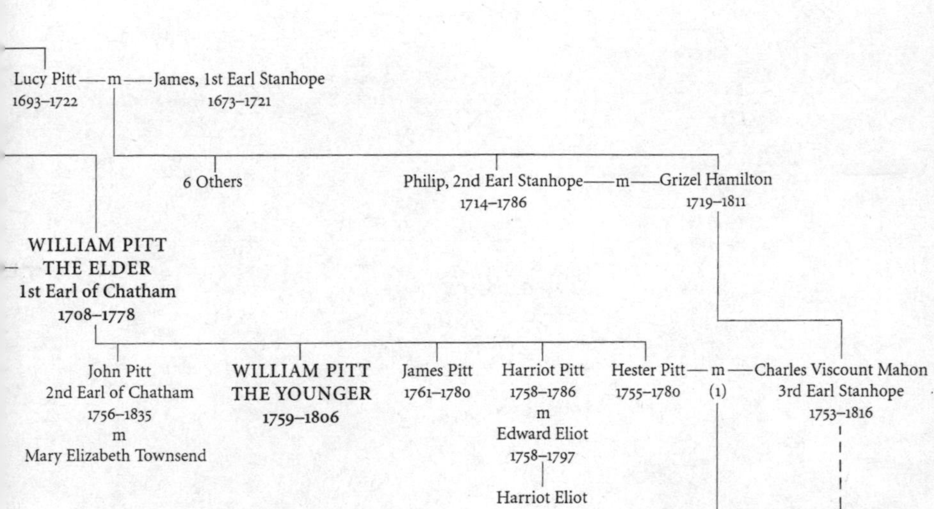

–m——Jane Innes
Lucy Pitt—m—James, 1st Earl Stanhope
1693–1722
1673–1721
6 Others
Philip, 2nd Earl Stanhope—m—Grizel Hamilton
1714–1786
1719–1811
WILLIAM PITT
THE ELDER
1st Earl of Chatham
1708–1778
John Pitt
2nd Earl of Chatham
1756–1835
m
Mary Elizabeth Townsend
WILLIAM PITT
THE YOUNGER
1759–1806
James Pitt
1761–1780
Harriot Pitt
1758–1786
m
Edward Eliot
1758–1797
Harriot Eliot
Hester Pitt—m—Charles Viscount Mahon
1755–1780
(1)
3rd Earl Stanhope
1753–1816
m
(2)
Philip Stanhope
4th Earl Stanhope
1781–1855
Charles Stanhope
1785–1809
James Stanhope
1788–1825
Hester Stanhope
1776–1839
Grizelda Stanhope
1778–1851
Lucy Stanhope
1780–1814

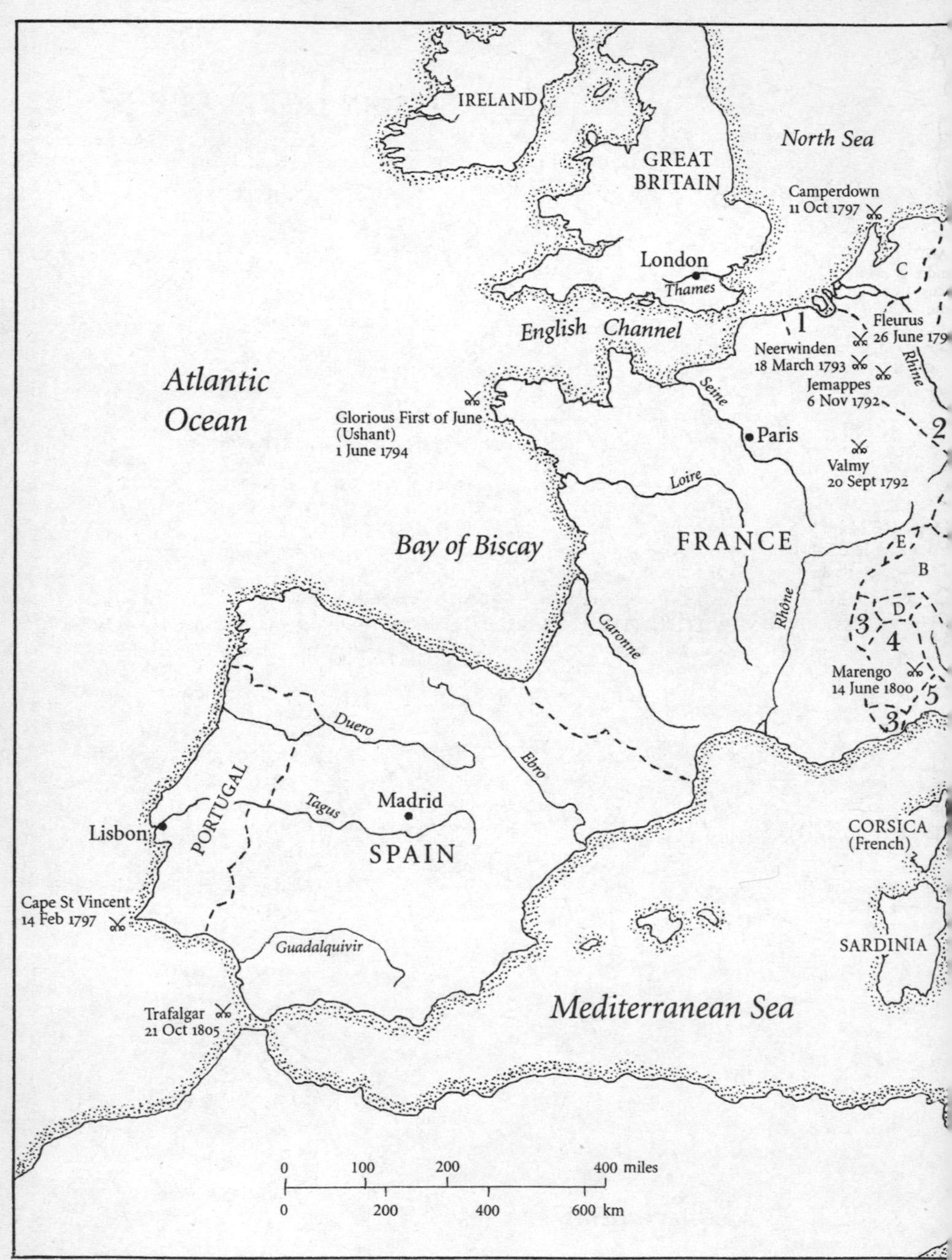
IRELAND
GREAT BRITAIN
North Sea
Camperdown
11 Oct 1797
London
Thames
C
English Channel
1
Fleurus
26 June 179
Neerwinden
18 March 1793
Jemappes
6 Nov 1792
Rhine
Seine
2
Atlantic Ocean
Glorious First of June
(Ushant)
1 June 1794
Paris
Valmy
20 Sept 1792
Loire
Bay of Biscay
FRANCE
E
B
D
3
4
Rhône
Garonne
Marengo
14 June 1800
5
3
Duero
Ebro
PORTUGAL
Tagus
Madrid
Lisbon
SPAIN
CORSICA
(French)
Cape St Vincent
14 Feb 1797
SARDINIA
Guadalquivir
Trafalgar
21 Oct 1805
Mediterranean Sea
0
100
200
400 miles
0
200
400
600 km

French Satellites
and French Conquests, 1792–1805

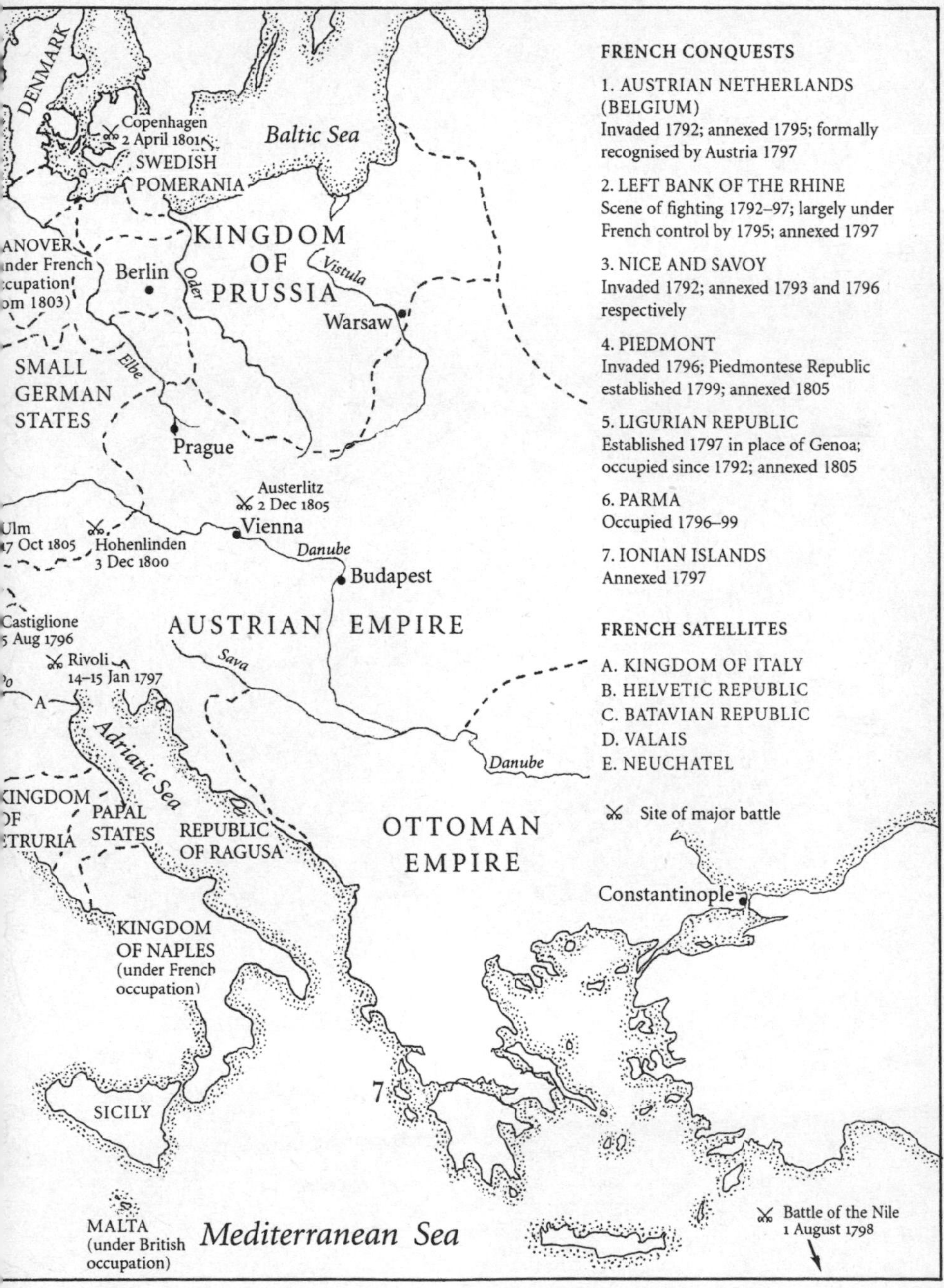
FRENCH CONQUESTS
1. AUSTRIAN NETHERLANDS (BELGIUM)
Invaded 1792; annexed 1795; formally recognised by Austria 1797
2. LEFT BANK OF THE RHINE
Scene of fighting 1792–97; largely under French control by 1795; annexed 1797
3. NICE AND SAVOY
Invaded 1792; annexed 1793 and 1796 respectively
4. PIEDMONT
Invaded 1796; Piedmontese Republic established 1799; annexed 1805
5. LIGURIAN REPUBLIC
Established 1797 in place of Genoa; occupied since 1792; annexed 1805
6. PARMA
Occupied 1796–99
7. IONIAN ISLANDS
Annexed 1797
FRENCH SATELLITES
A. KINGDOM OF ITALY
B. HELVETIC REPUBLIC
C. BATAVIAN REPUBLIC
D. VALAIS
E. NEUCHATEL
Site of major battle
DENMARK
Copenhagen 2 April 1801
Baltic Sea
SWEDISH POMERANIA
KINGDOM OF PRUSSIA
Berlin
Oder
Vistula
Warsaw
SMALL GERMAN STATES
Elbe
Prague
Austerlitz 2 Dec 1805
Vienna
Hohenlinden 3 Dec 1800
Danube
Budapest
AUSTRIAN EMPIRE
Castiglione
Rivoli 14–15 Jan 1797
Sava
A
Adriatic Sea
PAPAL STATES
REPUBLIC OF RAGUSA
OTTOMAN EMPIRE
Danube
Constantinople
KINGDOM OF NAPLES (under French occupation)
SICILY
7
MALTA (under British occupation)
Mediterranean Sea
Battle of the Nile 1 August 1798

Legend for map by Gregory Fremont-Barnes copyright © Osprey Publishing www.ospreypublishing.com

ACKNOWLEDGEMENTS

The writing of this book has been a hugely enjoyable process, and that is largely due to the many people who have been so ready to assist me with their time and knowledge.

I am particularly grateful to Christopher Wright and his staff at the British Library in the Manuscripts reading room, as well as their counterparts in the Rare Books reading room and the newspaper library, who have been so unfailingly efficient in finding any source I have wished to consult. I have benefited similarly from the work of the staff at Cambridge University Library, the House of Commons Library and the Public Record Office at Kew. Further afield, I particularly enjoyed the time I spent in the William L. Clements Library in Ann Arbor, Michigan, where John Dann, Brian Dunnigan and John Harriman made me especially welcome. Giles Adams, descendant of Pitt's last private secretary, William Dacres Adams, was extremely enthusiastic about my consultation of the many letters in his possession. He ensured that the time I spent at his home was enlivened by a flow of gastronomic and alcoholic refreshment of which Pitt would have heartily approved.

There were others who entered into the spirit of the research in similar vein. Simon Berry and his colleagues at Berry Brothers and Rudd held a convivial lunch for me at which Hugh Johnson's great knowledge of the history of wine was thoroughly tapped, and the capacity of eighteenth-century bottles closely examined. The late Roy Jenkins, Lord Jenkins of Hillhead, gave me valuable advice about the writing of such a book in the highly appropriate surroundings of Brooks's Club. It was thanks to his advice that I started writing when I did, in July 2002. It is sad that his death in 2003 means that his generous counsel is no longer available to others.

Everyone associated with the places at which Pitt had resided, in life or death, has been most welcoming. In particular I am grateful to Sir Roger Tomkys, the Master of Pembroke College Cambridge, Dr Tony Trowles at Westminster Abbey, Rowena Shepherd of English Heritage and Sally Mewton-Hynds, the Head Custodian at Walmer Castle. Stuart Macmillan, Head of Planning at Bromley Borough Council, explained the many layers of development which have taken place at or around Pitt's former house at Holwood. I am grateful to the developers of the site, Taylor Woodrow, for giving me access to the gardens.

Thanks are also due to John Black and Chris Russell, Council Members of the Royal College of Surgeons, who analysed for me the symptoms shown by Pitt during his many periods of illness, and produced fresh and clear advice on the likely cause of his death. Philip Mould's encyclopaedic knowledge of art has been of great assistance in assembling the illustrations and cover of the book. Among historians, I am grateful to Gregory Fremont-Barnes for reading and correcting the early manuscript, to Michael Duffy for his valuable comments on the text, and perhaps above all to John Ehrman, who encouraged this project from the outset but whose magnificent three-volume work *The Younger Pitt*, produced over a period of thirty years, will continue to stand as a definitive account of Pitt's life and times. Without the existence of John Ehrman's volumes, which guided me to so many fruitful sources, I could not have written my own book in such a relatively short time.

The enthusiasm of my agent, Michael Sissons, and my editors at HarperCollins, Richard Johnson and Robert Lacey, has been unflagging. So has the assistance of Sue Townsend, who typed much of the manuscript. I have received indispensable assistance from Susie Black and Mark Parsons, who despite being employed full-time in other duties on my behalf took on additional work in helping me to organise and check a multitude of sources and material. I owe further thanks for assistance or reading to Elana Cheah, George Osborne and Susi Ashcroft.

I pay tribute to my wife, Ffion, who has shown no trace of impatience at my immersion in the affairs of the eighteenth century so soon after being released from those of the present day. She has endured many meal times and weekends when I have been so preoccupied with events of the past that I must often have seemed to have been living in it, and yet has offered constant encouragement and insight, reading and commenting on each chapter as it emerged.

Many other people have written to me with suggestions or snippets of history. While I have not been able to incorporate into the book all of the material I have been sent, I am grateful to them for taking so much trouble. Finally, I should make clear that, even after receiving so much help, any errors, omissions or misconceptions are entirely my own responsibility.

William Hague
March 2004

PROLOGUE

On the morning of Tuesday, 9 June 1778 huge crowds gathered in the centre of London. People came in their tens of thousands, despite the pouring rain, to line the streets and windows around the old Palace of Westminster. 'The concourse of people assembled', wrote one of the following morning's newspapers, 'was beyond belief: the windows of all the houses, and even tops of some were crowded; as were the streets, though the spectators had been not only exposed to the rain for several hours, but to stand in dirt and wet nearly to the ankles . . .'[1]

From the entrance to Westminster Hall in New Palace Yard, through Parliament Street, Bridge Street, King Street and then the Broad Sanctuary outside the Great West Door of Westminster Abbey, they waited for hours; some noisily, regarding it as 'a scene only of festivity', some quietly, as they 'indulged a patriotic sigh to the memory of their country's protector'.[2]

At two o'clock in the afternoon those with a view of the North Door of Westminster Hall saw the procession emerge. First the High Constable of Westminster, then the messenger to the College of Arms in a mourning cloak, soon afterwards seventy poor men in cloaks with black staves in their hands, then a Standard, then a long line of servants. Eventually came a great banner and a coronet on a black velvet cushion and then the coffin, covered in a black velvet pall, adorned with the Arms of the deceased and borne by eight gentlemen.

The previous day an estimated hundred thousand people had filed through the black-draped Painted Chamber of the Palace to see the same coffin lying in state. For these were the remains of the Earl of Chatham, known to a previous generation before his ennoblement as 'the Great Commoner', and to a later generation accustomed to the fame of his son as the elder Pitt. He had ended his turbulent and unpredictable career with the most dramatic possible exit, collapsing in the House of Lords while denouncing the mismanagement of the war with America, and had died in May, a month later. He had been a dominating figure, the great political leader of his time. Whatever mixture of curiosity, gregariousness and reverence had brought vast numbers to line the route of his funeral procession, there is no doubt that every single one of them knew something of his life, achievements and opinions.

Among his contemporaries, the elder Pitt had excited every feeling from adoration to contempt. To the court of King George III, already in the nineteenth year of what would be a sixty-year reign, Chatham was impudent, unreliable and inconsistent. He had switched royal patrons in the 1740s out of opportunism, had been unable to work with the King's favourite Minister in the 1760s, and having schemed for years to return to office and regain his power, had retreated into hypochondria and depression once he was back. In the 1770s he had opposed the war with America, giving moral support to a colony in full rebellion, and had heaped scorn on the policies and Ministers of His Majesty. To the King he had been 'a snake in the grass',[3] and to other critics he was guilty of 'prevarication, self-contradiction, disregard of truth, mad ambition, mean popularity, pride, and the most intemperate passion'.[4] Few tears would be shed at Windsor, or among the supporters of the increasingly embattled administration of Lord North, that this powerfully persuasive voice was now forever silent.

Yet to many others this man who had so offended the King was the greatest figure in politics in their lifetimes, a man who had rescued an outnumbered nation from military defeat and vanquished her enemies, particularly the French, in the Seven Years' War, the greatest war they had ever known. To them he was 'that great and glorious Minister, who, to all succeeding ages, will be quoted as an illustrious example, how one great man, by his superior ability could raise his drooping country from the abyss of despair to the highest pinnacle of glory, and render her honoured, respected, revered, and dreaded by the whole universe'.[5] It was Chatham alone, they said, who had given direction, and a sense of purpose, and aggression to Britain's war effort; Chatham who produced the great 'year of victory' of 1759, when Horace Walpole had written 'our bells are worn threadbare with ringing of victories'.[6] Thus Chatham was revered as a brilliant maker of war, who had brought Canada and India under British dominion, yet he was also supported as a far-sighted man of peace by the opposition politicians, led by the great Whig magnate the Marquis of Rockingham, who now proceeded to the Abbey. For it was Chatham too who had pointed with wisdom and clarity to the folly of the war in America.

The bitter controversies of Chatham's lifetime had led to contrasting, and to simple observers confusing, approaches to his death. As the procession wound its way to Westminster Abbey the crowds must have wondered whether or not this was really meant to be a grand state occasion. The House of Commons had voted unanimously for a public funeral, a huge monument in the Abbey and the paying off of Chatham's substantial debts. The Corporation of London, ever devoted in its support for him, had unsuccessfully petitioned the King to permit his burial in St Paul's. Yet the House of Lords had voted against attending the funeral as a House, and there is no doubt that 'the greatest influence was made by the Court to prevent the members of either House attending the funeral'.[7] As a result the funeral arrangements were a compromise, a public procession without the pomp and pageantry which only the state was able to provide. Many onlookers would be disappointed, with the *Morning Post* commenting: 'The funeral procession was allowed, on all hands, to be a very pitiful pageant, considered as a national one; for instead of having a platform erected for it from Westminster Hall to the Abbey, as is usual in such cases, the attendants were obliged to wade through the mud, preceded by half a dozen *scavengers with their brooms*!' 'It is rather remarkable', the paper went on to point out, 'that St Martin's bells were ringing a merry peal during the interment of the late patriotic Earl.'[8]

The *London Evening Post* made a similar complaint: 'The most scandalous parsimony prevailed, and every mark of disrespect was shown to those members who did attend. Not half the quantity of cloaks, scarfs, or hatbands were provided – great complaints were made but the answer, was, "it would have been too expensive to have furnished more." Colonel Barré justly observed, "it is not a reign to complain in".'[9] Chatham had evidently complained too much.

Those who thought they would see the parliamentary leaders

assembled *en masse* found instead only about forty peers and twenty MPs among the many hundreds of people attending the ceremony. There was Rockingham, the foremost opposition politician; there Edmund Burke, his right-hand man; there General Burgoyne, the soldier turned opposition MP – but they were there 'more to vex the King's Ministers than to honour the memory of the Earl'.[10] Only one member of the government was present, Lord Amherst, who had commanded the army under Chatham, and only one member of the Royal Family, the Duke of Gloucester, the King's estranged younger brother. There were no Sheriffs, no Masters in Chancery in their gowns, no judges or Privy Councillors. The Lord Mayor was missing, as was the Speaker of the House of Commons, and there was not 'a sufficient number of Baronets to walk by themselves'.[11]

Still, the crowds had witnessed a solemn procession and a major event. Some of them might even have noticed the Chief Mourner, walking behind the coffin, the late Earl's second son, another William Pitt. On his left was his brother-in-law, Lord Mahon, and on his right his uncle, Thomas Pitt. With his mother choosing to stay at home rather than grieve in public and his elder brother at sea on the expedition to reinforce Gibraltar, the nineteen-year-old William performed his first public duty, walking behind the coffin of the father who had doted on him. That night he wrote to his mother:

> Harley Street
> June 9th, 1778
> My Dear Mother
>
> I cannot let the servants return without letting you know that the sad solemnity has been celebrated so as to answer every important wish we could form on the subject. The Court did not honour us with their countenance, nor did they suffer the procession to be as magnificent as it ought; but it had notwithstanding everything essential to the great object, the attendance being most respectable, and the crowd of interested spectators immense. The Duke of Gloucester was in the Abbey. Lord Rockingham, the Duke of Northumberland, and all the minority in town were present . . . All our relations made their appearance . . . I will not tell you what I felt on this occasion, to which no words are equal; but I

know that you will have a satisfaction in hearing that Lord Mahon as well as myself supported the trial perfectly well and have not at all suffered from the fatigue . . .

I hope the additional melancholy of the day will not have been too overcoming for you, and that I shall have the comfort of finding you pretty well tomorrow. I shall be able to give you an account of what is thought as to our going to Court.

And I am ever, my dear Mother, your most dutiful and affectionate son,

W Pitt[12]

Less than twenty-eight years would pass before William Pitt's own body would join that of his father beneath the same dark stone slab in the North Transept of Westminster Abbey. In that time, he would equal his father's fame and popularity while far exceeding his domination of politics and his endurance in office.

PART ONE

I

Elder and Younger

'There never was a father more partial to a son.'

William Wyndham Grenville[1]

'He went into the House of Commons as an heir enters his home; he breathed in it his native atmosphere, – he had, indeed, breathed no other; in the nursery, in the schoolroom, at the university, he lived in its temperature; it had been, so to speak, made over to him as a bequest by its unquestioned master. Throughout his life, from the cradle to the grave, he may be said to have known no wider existence. The objects and amusements, that other men seek in a thousand ways, were for him all concentrated there. It was his mistress, his stud, his dice box, his game-preserve; it was his ambition, his library, his creed. For it, and it alone, had the consummate Chatham trained him from his birth.'

Lord Rosebery[2]

It would scarcely be possible to imagine a more intensely political family than the one into which William Pitt was born on 28 May 1759. On his father's side, his great-grandfather, grandfather and uncle had all been Members of Parliament. His father, twenty-five years an MP, was now the leading Minister of the land. On his mother's side, that of the Grenville family, one uncle was in the House of Lords, and two others were in the Commons, one of them to be First Lord of the Treasury by the time the infant William was four years old. An understanding of Pitt's extraordinary political precocity requires us to appreciate the unusual circumstances of a family so wholeheartedly committed to political life.

It was in the year of William's birth that the career of his father, still also plain William Pitt, approached its zenith. Three years into what would later be known as the Seven Years' War, in which Britain stood as the only substantial ally of Prussia against the combined forces of France, Austria, Russia, Saxony and Sweden, the elder Pitt had become the effective Commander-in-Chief under King George II of the British prosecution of the war. In his view the war had arisen from 'a total subversion of the system of Europe, and more especially from the most pernicious extension of the influence of France'.[3] He was not nominally the head of the government, the position of First Lord of the Treasury being held by his old rival the Duke of Newcastle, but he was the senior Minister in the House of Commons. Through his powerful oratory he dominated both Parliament and the Ministry, and was acknowledged as the effective leader of the administration. As Newcastle himself said in October of that year: 'No one will have a majority at present against Mr. Pitt. No man will, in the present conjuncture, set his face against Mr. Pitt in the H. of Commons.'[4]

From taking office at the age of forty-eight in 1756 as Secretary of State for the Southern Department,* with a brief interruption of two months during the Cabinet crisis of 1757, Pitt had become the principal source of ministerial energy in both organising for war and in preparing a strategy for Britain to do well out of it. It was Pitt who gave detailed instructions on the raising and disposition of the troops and the navy, and Pitt who insisted on and executed the objective of destroying the empire of France. As the French envoy, François de Bussy, was to complain to the leading French Minister the Duc de Choiseul after meeting Pitt in 1761: 'This Minister is, as you know, the idol of the people, who regard him as the sole author of their success . . . He is very eloquent, specious, wheedling, and with all the chicanery of an experienced lawyer. He is courageous to the point of rashness, he supports his ideas in an impassioned fashion and with an invincible

* In the eighteenth century a British Cabinet contained two Secretaries of State (compared to fifteen today). The Secretary of State for the Southern Department dealt with matters relating to southern European countries, including France and Spain; the Secretary of State for the Northern Department dealt with northern European countries such as Russia. In 1782 this arrangement was revised into one Secretary of State for Foreign Affairs and one for Home and Colonial Affairs.

determination, seeking to subjugate all the world by the tyranny of his opinions, Pitt seems to have no other ambition than to elevate Britain to the highest point of glory and to abase France to the lowest degree of humiliation . . .'[5]

It was in 1759 that Pitt, previously dismissed as a rather unpredictable politician with a distinctly chequered career, came to be regarded as the saviour of the nation. His insistence on fighting a European war with offensives elsewhere – in America, the Caribbean, Africa and on the oceans of the world – was crowned with success within months of the birth of his second son, William. Instead of having to face the French invasion feared throughout much of the year, Britain celebrated a stream of military successes that summer and autumn: victory at Minden in Germany in August, the storming of Quebec which shattered French rule in Canada in September, the simultaneous news of victories which reinforced British dominance of India, and then the defeat and scattering of the French fleet at Quiberon Bay in November. These events brought about a change in the public perception of the elder Pitt, analogous to the regard in which Churchill was held after 1940 compared to the controversy which previously surrounded him. From then on there was a sense of reverence, sometimes of awe, towards him, both on parliamentary occasions and among the wider public. Tall, haughty, but always eloquent, he was the great orator and war leader who had placed himself beyond party gatherings and factions to be at the service of the nation. The young William, as he became conscious of the people and events around him, would know only a world in which his father was treated as a legend.

Such renown was a far cry from the frustrated ambitions of earlier generations of Pitts. Being a younger son, the elder Pitt had enjoyed little in the way of financial inheritance, but his ancestors and relatives had been well connected and often very wealthy for the previous century and a half. Pitt's forebears had included prominent and sometimes wealthy officials under Elizabeth I and James I, but it is Thomas Pitt of Bocconoc (1653–1726) who brings the family story to life. He was the buccaneering 'Diamond Pitt' who went to India and made a fortune in probably illegal competition with the East India Company, came back and purchased English property with it, including the medieval borough of Old Sarum,* and then returned to India on behalf of the Company as Governor of Madras. While there, he bought a 130-carat diamond for £25,000 which he hoped to sell to one of the European royal families for at least ten times as much. Returning to Britain during the War of the Spanish Succession (1702–1713), he discovered that European royalty was otherwise preoccupied, but eventually sold the diamond at a substantial but much smaller than expected profit to the Regent of France. With this and other earnings from his exploits in India, Thomas Pitt set about buying more estates, particularly in Cornwall. He was part of a new and often resented breed of rich men who came back from the East to buy property and parliamentary influence at home. He used his wealth to help all five of his children on their way in life, particularly the eldest son, another Thomas Pitt, who kept most of the family wealth and became Earl of Londonderry. A younger son, Robert Pitt, was put into Parliament for Old Sarum in 1705, for which he sometimes sat alongside his father. Robert Pitt was undistinguished, came close to disaster by being on the fringes of Jacobite attempts to overthrow the new Hanoverian dynasty, and died young, but not before fathering six children, the fifth of whom was William Pitt, the future Earl of Chatham. Once again the eldest son was a Thomas Pitt, who after much litigation and family dispute ended up with the lion's share of the family wealth.

The family lived at Stratford-sub-Castle near Salisbury, but at the age of ten William was sent with his eldest brother Thomas to Eton, an experience which proved decisive in his later determination to educate all of his own children at home. He remarked much later to the Earl of Shelburne that he 'scarce observed a boy who was not cowed for life at Eton; that a publick school might suit a boy of a turbulent forward disposition, but would not do where there was any gentleness'.[6]

It seems that Robert Pitt had intended William for the Church, but William himself had other ideas, joining the army at the lowest

* Old Sarum, near Salisbury, was to become the most famous of all rotten boroughs when early in the nineteenth century it continued to return two Members of Parliament while ceasing to have any voters at all. In 1728 Colonel Harrison, the Pitt nominee, defeated Henry Fox in a by-election by a four to one margin, literally four votes to one.

officer rank in the cavalry, as a Cornet of Dragoons. He never saw active service, since the long-serving Whig Minister Robert Walpole did an effective job of keeping Britain out of various international disputes at the time, but he took the opportunity to travel to the Continent on a modest version of the Grand Tour through France, Switzerland and Holland. This was the only time he left his native country; an eighteenth-century political career did not require extensive travel. Like his son, he was later to dispose of huge forces, alliances and treaties around the globe, while only once in his life leaving the shores of Britain. He was clearly determined to continue the emerging Pitt tradition of serving in Parliament, and was duly elected for the family borough of Old Sarum in the general election of 1734, but only after some acrimony when his brother Thomas suggested giving the seat to the sitting Member, with financial compensation for William instead.

Although Pitt seems to have been well disposed towards Walpole and the Whigs at the time he was elected, he soon fell in with key figures in the opposition, notably Lord Cobham, his ex-Colonel, and Prince Frederick, the Prince of Wales. The relationship between Prince Frederick and his father King George II was an early example of a noted Hanoverian tradition, being one of unmitigated hatred between monarch and heir. The Prince of Wales was truly loathed by both his father and mother. Queen Caroline once exclaimed when she saw the Prince pass her dressing-room window: 'Look, there he goes – that wretch! that villain! – I wish the ground would open this moment and sink the monster to the lowest hole in hell!'[7] Such loathing was exacerbated when the King's adoption of a Hanoverian mistress became public knowledge, so helping to make the Prince the more popular member of the Royal Family. Pitt, as a young MP and army officer, became part of the Prince's circle, with some of his early parliamentary speeches being unmistakably toadying towards the Prince. He became a regular opponent of Walpole, and was dismissed from his position in the army as a result.

A study of the rise to power of the elder Pitt over the subsequent twenty years provides four main conclusions which assist in appreciating the career of his son. First, elections in the eighteenth century were not contested by organised political parties with a programme or manifesto. Although in the mid-eighteenth century many politicians could still be roughly categorised as Whig or Tory, even this distinction was breaking down. The opposition to the long-running Whig administrations would generally include dissident Whigs as well as a rump of Tories. In any case, most Members of Parliament had no wish to pursue a political career as such and were not elected to pursue any particular policy, many seeing their duty as one of supporting the King's chosen Ministers unless they did something manifestly outrageous. As a result, politicians did not generally win power by campaigning at a general election and winning a majority for a specific programme, and nor did voters necessarily have the composition of the government foremost in their minds – no general election in the entire eighteenth century led directly to a change of government. There were really two routes into office: one was to be an ally of the Crown, or of someone who would inherit the crown in due course; the other was to make such a nuisance of oneself in Parliament that Ministers seeking a quiet life or a broad consensus would have to include the troublemaker in the government. The elder Pitt tried the first of these approaches for about ten years and then switched to the second, although by that time King George II was most reluctant to appoint him to anything. As Pelham, the leading Minister of the mid-1740s, wrote to Stephen Fox in 1746 on Pitt's appointment as Paymaster General: 'It is determined, since the King will not hear of Pitt's being Secretary att [sic] War, that he shall be Paymaster . . . I don't doubt but you will be surpris'd that Mr. Pitt should be thought on for so high and lucrative an employment; but he must be had, and kept.'[8] There was never any love lost between Pitt and the other leading politicians of the day or between him and either of the kings he served. Each time he was appointed to the government it was because his speeches were too effective or his support too great to keep him out.

Second, while the power of Parliament was still tempered by the authority and patronage of the Crown, it was the only forum in which the politicians of the time engaged with each other and staked out their positions. As a result, prowess in parliamentary debate was a most valuable political skill. The elder Pitt could never have advanced to high office without such skill since he lacked both money and the patronage of the King. The second Earl Waldegrave, chief confidant of George II, wrote in his memoirs:

> Mr. Pitt has the finest genius, improved by study and all the ornamental parts of classical learning . . . He has a peculiar clearness and facility of expression; and has an eye as significant as his words. He is not always a fair or conclusive reasoner, but commands the passions with sovereign authority; and to inflame or captivate a popular assembly is a consummate orator.[9]

Having finally thrown in his lot with King George II in 1746 in return for a place in the government, Pitt was happy to use his oratorical skills to advance arguments sometimes the exact opposite of those he had propagated in opposition, a phenomenon well known to this day. He had made his name in opposition denouncing the payment of subsidies for Hanoverian troops even to the point of saying he would agree to be branded on the forehead as a traitor if he ever supported the idea, but once in office he swiftly switched sides on the issue with 'unembarrassed countenance'.[10]

It is a tragedy for historians that parliamentary proceedings at the time of the elder Pitt were not officially recorded. Indeed, it was expressly forbidden to publish speeches delivered in Parliament, since it was thought that this would lead to popular pressure interfering with the judgements of an independent Parliament. By the time of the younger Pitt these matters were treated very differently, but this restriction illustrates the limited role of public opinion in the British constitution of the mid-eighteenth century.

Third, while his long career encompassed a fair amount of opportunism and inconsistency, the elder Pitt undoubtedly developed and held to a broad philosophy of how Britain should operate in military and foreign affairs. Although he would have called himself a Whig, the term Tory being largely pejorative and still heavily associated with suspected Jacobite sympathies, Pitt was usually distinct in his views from the great figures of the Whig aristocracy. He was, for instance, much more likely than them to quote popular support as a factor in favour of his views, something that they would have looked on as the folly of the mob. Pitt's views could be categorised as 'Patriot' or in 'the Country Interest', emphasising the views of a nation wider than the Whig oligarchy, and sometimes they were frankly Tory, such as opposing the existence of any significant standing army. Such opinions were associated with hostility to Continental entanglements and suspicion of the power of the Crown, two opinions woven together by the fact that the King was simultaneously but separately the ruler of Hanover.* Pitt believed in a maritime approach to foreign affairs, one which he brought to devastating fruition in the Seven Years' War and set out at its simplest in the Commons in the 1740s:

> I lay it down, Sir, as a certain maxim that we should never assist our allies upon the continent with any great number of troops. If we send our troops abroad, it should be rather with a view to improve them in the art of war, than to assist our allies . . . The only manner, therefore, in which we ought to support her [Austria] and our other allies upon the continent is with our money and our ships. My reason for laying this down as a maxim is, not only because the sea is our natural element, but because it is dangerous to our liberties and destructive to our trade to encourage great numbers of our people to depend for their livelihood upon the profession of arms . . . For this reason, we ought to maintain as few regular soldiers as possible, both at home and abroad. Another argument on this subject presents itself: our troops cost more to maintain them than those of any other country. Our money, therefore, will be of most service to our allies, because it will enable them to raise and support a greater number of troops than we can supply them with for the same sum.[11]

Throughout his career the elder Pitt emphasised the importance of overseas trade, an issue which regularly made him the darling of the City of London. To preserve and expand that trade, he believed in naval supremacy, the retention and expansion of the colonies, particularly in North America, and a firm stance against the Bourbon monarchies of France and Spain. Long after his death, elements of the same beliefs

* The Royal Family were Hanoverians by descent. In this period the King of England was also the hereditary ruler (Elector) of Hanover.

in trade and naval power would be discerned within the policies carried out by his son as Prime Minister.

Fourth, the elder Pitt cultivated a detachment from party as a healthy attribute in itself, along with a further detachment from the financial rewards and perquisites of office. Paymasters had traditionally made huge personal gains, usually by investing for their own account the balances of public money for which they were responsible, and taking a commission on foreign subsidies.* It was to the astonishment of other politicians and the delight of a wider public that on his appointment as Paymaster, Pitt lodged the balance of public money with the Bank of England and forwent his personal commission on a subsidy to Sardinia. It was as a result of such forbearance, as well as of his general political stance, that he was long regarded as different from other politicians, less corrupt and self-interested. Coupled with his apparent lack of interest in taking a title, this attribute led to him becoming known as 'the Great Commoner'. It was also as a result of these sacrifices that his income rarely kept up with his lavish domestic expenditure. The huge debts which this produced seldom seemed to trouble him, a trait faithfully reproduced in his famous son.

The elder Pitt spent a large proportion of his life visibly ill. He suffered from a wide range of ailments, all of which were then associated with gout; he was frequently lame and also suffered from 'gout in the bowels' and similar disorders. For him to give a speech in the Commons with a walking stick and a large part of his body wrapped in flannels was not uncommon. He would often retreat to his bed even at times of crisis, as this anecdote from the time of the Seven Years' War demonstrates:

> Mr. Pitt's plan, when he had the gout, was to have no fire in his room, but to load himself with bedclothes. At his house at Hayes he slept in a long room; at one end of which was his bed, and his lady's at the other. His way was, when he thought the Duke of Newcastle had fallen into any mistake to send for him and read him a lecture. The Duke was sent for once and came when Mr.

* Henry Fox, father of Charles James Fox, is thought to have made £400,000 as Paymaster, a vast sum in those days.

> Pitt was confined to bed by the gout. There was, as usual, no fire in the room; the day was very chilly and the Duke, as usual, afraid of catching cold. The Duke first sat down on Mrs Pitt's bed, as the warmest place; then drew up his legs into it, as he got colder. The lecture unluckily continuing a considerable time, the Duke at length fairly lodged himself under Mrs Pitt's bed clothes. A person, from whom I had the story, suddenly going in, saw the two ministers in bed, at the two ends of the room, while Pitt's long nose and black beard unshaved for some days, added to the grotesqueness of the scene.[12]

In 1760, the accession of George III, grandson of George II (and son of Prince Frederick, who after years of plotting for his accession with opposition figures, spoiled every calculation by dying before his father), set in motion a chain of events which led to Pitt's departure from government. Favouring a more hardline approach to Spain than his colleagues would accept, Pitt wished to continue in office only on the basis of assured control of the government, an ambition irreconcilable with the new King's advancement of his great favourite, the Earl of Bute.

Pitt left office at loggerheads with his colleagues but as a towering figure in public repute, which the King and Bute recognised by conferring on him and his descendants an annuity of £3,000 a year. Bute also tried to undermine Pitt's reputation by unusually making the details of the annuity public. Pitt complained that 'the cause and manner of my resigning' had been 'grossly misrepresented'. He had been 'infamously traduced as a bargain for my forsaking the public'.[13] As part of the same package a title was given to Pitt's wife, who became Baroness Chatham. For the moment, Pitt himself chose to stay in his arena of greatest influence, the Commons, rather than go to the Lords. Out of office he could now bestow more attention on his devoted wife and five children, including William, now two years old.

However many wise decisions were taken by the elder Pitt in the Seven Years' War, few compared in wisdom to his decision a few years earlier in 1754 to marry Lady Hester Grenville. Pitt was still unmarried at the age of forty-six. His most consistent and affectionate friendship had been with his sister Ann, although he reported falling in love with a French woman during his tour of the Continent. On the face of it, his decision to get married at that age, to someone he had known for years without apparently showing any previous romantic interest in her, seems sudden and strange. Pitt had one eye on posterity: it may simply be that he woke up one morning realising that if he did not find a wife and produce a family now he never would.

In any event, it was a marriage of great and enduring strength, supported by deep mutual affection. Hester proved utterly devoted to this difficult and often sick man, describing herself in early letters as 'ever unalterably your most passionately loving wife'. She was thirty-three at the time of their marriage and herself came from a powerful political family. Her uncle was the Lord Cobham with whom Pitt had intrigued twenty years before, and her brothers were highly active in politics, including both Richard, Earl Temple and George Grenville. The two families were already related because Pitt's elder brother Thomas had married Hester's cousin, but much has always been made of the strikingly different characters of the Pitts and the Grenvilles. Where the Pitts were demonstrative, emotional and argumentative, the Grenvilles were cool, methodical and loyal. Pitts had a spirit of adventure, Grenvilles an inclination to caution. And where Pitts enjoyed foreign and military matters in politics, Grenvilles were more at home with finance and administration. The seemingly better-balanced personality of the younger William Pitt is often ascribed to the fortuitous combination of these contrasting traits, although one of his biographers has commented: 'In the son – still more in the other children – was a full measure of the Grenville starchiness, which unhappily dulled the Pitt fire and brilliance.'[14] Most other commentators have concluded that alongside a brilliant and impetuous father, the younger Pitt was fortunate indeed to have a mother who had resilience, a calm temperament and an unfailing sense of duty.

In 1755 the elder Pitt purchased Hayes Place in what would now be south London, near the village of Bromley. Although in time he would regard it as only a modest residence it had twenty-four bedrooms, elegant gardens and several hundred acres of pasture and woodland. In 1765, with his fame and reputation at their height, he had the immense good fortune to inherit a large estate, Burton Pynsent in Somerset, from an admirer, Sir William Pynsent, whom he seems never to have met. Excited by the prospect of living on a far grander scale than was possible at Hayes, Pitt soon fought off the descendants of the deceased who tried to dispute the will, and set about vast alterations and landscaping. This included a 140-foot-high column in memory of Pynsent, raised as a token of humble thanks. The scale of these changes, in addition to the cost of selling Hayes and then repurchasing it at a higher price (he discovered he could not do without a large residence close to London), plunged Pitt into debts which remained with him for the rest of his life. One of the many inestimable services performed by Hester was to bring more careful management to the family's finances and to prevent further extravagances so that the debts did not become completely unsustainable.

The young William Pitt was born at Hayes in May 1759 'after a labour rather severe',[15] the fourth child in five years after Hester, John, and Harriot. The fifth and final child, James, was born two years later. These five children born within six years of each other made a great deal of noise: 'The young ones are so delightfully noisy that I hardly know what I write,'[16] wrote Pitt to his wife when she went to visit her own family. He seems to have taken the precaution of making alterations to the house at Hayes so that he could cut himself off, when he wished, from the sound and presence of his children.

It is clear that William soon emerged as a notably bright child and a particular favourite of both mother and father. Hester wrote within a few weeks of his birth: 'I cannot help believing that little William is to become a personage.'[17] Although there would have been many servants in the household, the children received a good deal of attention from their father after he left office in 1761. They grew up in a very comfortable home, decidedly rural in a well-ordered sort of way. The young children rode, bathed, went birdnesting and explored the countryside first around Hayes and then around Burton Pynsent. Some of these things stuck: the younger Pitt rode regularly for exercise throughout his life, and inherited from his father a love of landscape gardening for relaxation; but even in his earliest years he did not put outdoor pursuits at the top of his list. He showed early on a sharp intellect, highly advanced powers of speech and memory, and a clear interest in public affairs. All these attributes were cultivated constantly by his father.

Inevitably, there are plenty of stories in which visitors to the Pitt household claim prescience about the child's future greatness. Lady Holland, mother of Charles James Fox, is meant to have said, 'I have been this morning with Lady Hester Pitt, and there is little William Pitt, *not eight years old* and really the cleverest child I ever saw; and *brought up so strictly and so proper in his behaviour*, that, *mark my words*, that little boy will be a thorn in Charles's side as long as he lives.'[18] Other reports include the young William standing up on a mounting block and addressing the trees as if they were Members of the House of Commons. Such stories may be fanciful, but the essential point, that he was extraordinarily well versed in politics and philosophy at a remarkably early age, certainly stands up to examination. Family correspondence refers to him as 'the Philosopher', 'the Young Senator', 'Eager Mr. William' and 'Impetuous William'. In 1766, when he was seven, his tutor wrote of him and his sister:

> Lady Hester and Mr. Pitt still continue to surprise and astonish as much as ever; and I see no possibility of diminishing their ardour either by too much business or too much relaxation. When I am alone reading, Mr. Pitt, if it is any thing he may attend to, constantly places himself by me, where his steady attention and sage remarks are not only entertaining but useful; as they frequently throw a light upon the subject, and strongly impress it on my memory.[19]

The same tutor, Edward Wilson, who taught all the Pitt children at home because of their father's unforgiving recollections of public school, marvelled on another occasion that William 'seemed never to learn but merely to recollect'.[20] At the age of seven he was able to write letters in Latin to his father, and also did so in English in a rather pompous and wordy style. With his father delivering thundering orations against the Stamp Act in the Commons in early 1766, William showed an insatiable appetite for political news. 'I expect many sage reflections from William upon the public papers,' his father wrote to his mother, and later that year, with a peerage for the elder Pitt in prospect, William commented that he was glad he was not the eldest son, because 'he could serve his country in the House of Commons like his Papa'.[21]

A seven-year-old with such attitudes and interests in our own times would probably find them beaten out of him at school, and indeed that could as easily have happened in the 1760s. William had the advantage of mixing almost exclusively with his own siblings, his tutor and adult family members, most of whom encouraged his political interest. The poet William Hayley reported when William was a boy of fourteen that he 'eclipsed his brother in conversation'.[22] It is hard to think that he was not sometimes an irritation to his brothers and sisters; as the historian J. Holland Rose commented, 'the boy . . . narrowly escaped being a prodigy of priggishness'.[23] His narrow escape seems to have been made possible by an easygoing disposition and pleasant temperament, which made it easier for him to win friends in a small circle. He was also a rather sickly child, with frequently recurring problems in the nose and throat, and many coughs and colds. His fragility probably helped the other children to put up with his bookish ways.

Father and son showed a deep attachment to each other. 'If I should smoke,' the elder Pitt wrote, 'William would instantly call for a pipe.'[24] He would in later years describe William as 'the hope and comfort of my life'.[25] In 1772, when Hester took the three eldest children to Hayes and left William and his younger brother with their father at Burton Pynsent, the elder Pitt wrote:

> My dearest life will read with joy that the boys go on well. I believe William's *sequestration*, as he learnedly terms it, agrees better with his contemplative constitution than more talk and more romps. Airing, literature, the arts, tea-table, sober whist and lecturing Papa for staying out too late, together with the small amusement of devouring a joint of mutton, or so, before I can look about, make up our daily occupations.[26]

His wife replied: 'I do not in the least wonder that the style of William's present life agrees with him. It is certainly not better suited to the state of his constitution, than to the fineness of his mind, which makes him enjoy with the highest pleasure what would be above the reach of any other creature of his small age.'[27]

In 1772 William even wrote a play, performed by the Pitt children, which was wholly political in content and eerily foreshadowed the Regency crisis in which he would play the real lead role seventeen years later. It is obvious that he showed academic gifts and political interest from an exceptionally early age, encouraged and nurtured by the adults around him, and that he enjoyed a pleasant and sheltered upbringing in the midst of a loving family. In all these respects he was very fortunate, but he was not unique. There must have been something more to his formative years, even before he went to university at the age of fourteen, to equip him to carry out the functions of Prime Minister at the age of twenty-four.

There were at least three factors which, in the formation of the young William Pitt's personality and opinions, were not only fortunate but truly unique. The first was that a father who had himself dominated the House of Commons and presided over a government took an active, usually daily, role in his education. At no other time in British history has the head of one administration acted as the tutor of another. A home education seems to have been well suited in any case to a child of William's temperament and health, but Mr Wilson's tuition was frequently supplemented by the ministrations of the elder Pitt. Bishop Tomline, in his surprisingly uninformative biography of the younger Pitt written shortly after his death, reports that 'when his lordship's health would permit, he never suffered a day to pass without giving instruction of some sort to his children; and seldom without reading a chapter of the Bible with them'.[28] While the elder Pitt seems to have been attentive to all his children, he particularly enjoyed passing on to William examples of eloquence from contemporary or classical writers and speakers, and asking him to study them. He taught him to speak in a clear and melodious voice by making him recite each day passages from the best English poets, particularly Shakespeare and Milton. Another biographer of the younger Pitt, Lord Stanhope, wrote the following with the advantage of his father having spoken to Pitt himself:

> My father had the honour to be connected in relationship with that great man – and, as such, he had the privilege of being in the house with him sometimes for many weeks together. Presuming on that familiar intercourse, he told me, he ventured on one occasion to ask Mr. Pitt by what means – by what course of study – he had acquired that admirable readiness of speech – that aptness of finding the right word without pause or hesitation. Mr. Pitt replied that whatever readiness he might be thought to possess in that respect, he believed that he derived it very much from a practice his father – the great Lord Chatham – had recommended to him. Lord Chatham had bid him take up any book in some foreign language with which he was well acquainted, in Latin, Greek, or French, for example. Lord Chatham then enjoined him to read out of this work into English, stopping where he was not sure of the word to be used in English, until the right word came to his mind, and then proceed. Mr. Pitt states that he had assiduously followed this practice. At first he had often to stop for a while before he could recollect the proper word, but he found the difficulties gradually disappear, until what was a toil to him at first became at last an easy and familiar task.[29]

By the time he arrived at Cambridge in 1773, William could apparently read into English six or seven pages of Thucydides, without previous study of it and with barely a mistake. He may have been educated at home but he had in effect attended a master school in the use of language and its delivery. In addition he showed a strong early aptitude for mathematics. Uninhibited by peer pressure and required from the outset to meet adult standards, he developed early on a highly unusual ability to speak clearly, structure an argument, and think on his feet.

Secondly, he must have realised at a very early age that he belonged to a father and a family who stood apart from and were treated differently to everyone else. His father had become a national institution, and was greeted when he travelled with greater reverence than anyone else outside the Royal Family. When the Pitt family set off for their summer break by the sea in Weymouth or Brighthelmstone (modern-day Brighton) or Lyme Regis, bells were rung in their honour and flowers strewn before them. Travelling to Weymouth by coach in 1766, the family heard the bells of Yeovil ringing in their honour as they passed, and a deputation of Mohican chiefs, on their way to London with a petition, were waiting there to greet them. In an age when the inheritance of names and traits counted for more than it does today, the younger Pitt always knew that he was the son of a very great man, and that everyone else knew it too.

The third unique aspect of the younger Pitt's early life is more complex, more debatable, but no less compelling. In the years 1765 to 1768 the career of his father took a series of dramatic turns, briefly for the better and then decidedly for the worse. At this time the elder Pitt took a series of decisions, some of which would have seemed wise at the time, but many of which must have appeared almost immediately to have been risky or foolish. While a child between the ages of six and nine cannot normally be expected to appreciate the finer points of the political events of the day, it is hard to imagine that this boy, with his precocious interest in politics, did not absorb some deep and lasting lessons from what happened. His father was in this period not only his tutor but also a living daily example of the perils of politics.

Several times between 1763 and 1766 the elder Pitt was asked to return to head the King's government and refused to do so. By 1763, the King's mentor and friend, the Earl of Bute, had discovered he had neither the aptitude nor the appetite for day-to-day politics, and resigned. King George III thus learnt at an early stage of his reign that he had to work with at least some of the politicians already available in Parliament rather than invent new ones, and that an effective Minister whom he partly disliked could be a better bet than an ineffective one he doted on. Several years of political instability now followed. The government was at first headed by George Grenville, Hester's brother, who after a short time the King cordially hated and wanted rid of. Next came the Marquis of Rockingham, who did not have the parliamentary support to sustain an administration. Throughout this time, the elder Pitt reverted to his earlier behaviour of being a trenchant critic of Ministers, except that he now did so from a far more commanding position, that of a former head of the government. He broke off occasionally from his rural pursuits and the education of his children to go down to the House of Commons and thunder out his denunciation of the government, first attacking the Treaty of Paris, which brought an end to the Seven Years' War, for being too generous to the nation's enemies, then making no fewer than fifteen speeches attacking the handling of the case of John Wilkes, and then a determined campaign to overturn George Grenville's Stamp Act. The Stamp Act was a tax on legal documents in North America, introduced by Grenville as a means of raising revenue from the colonists, who enjoyed the protection of the British army but paid nothing towards it. It was deeply hated in America, and the elder Pitt was determined to overturn it, advocating conciliation of the colonies rather than aggravation of their discontent. Grenville having been forced from office, and the Stamp Act being overturned in early 1766, Pitt was once again acclaimed by the City and the crowds outside the Palace of Westminster. He was not in the least troubled that in pursuing this campaign he was also destroying the policies and administration of his brother-in-law.

The young William would certainly have heard of the devastating use his father had made of the power of speech on these occasions, and he is likely to have witnessed for himself his father's repeated decisions to refuse to take office unless given cast-iron authority over the government. The King could offer the leadership of an administration, but Pitt could refuse it. On one occasion in 1765 the Duke of Cumberland arrived at Hayes with an escort of guards, a Royal Duke sent personally by the King to invite the elder Pitt to form a government. We do not know if William was watching from the windows, but we do know that his father declined the offer, since 'nothing was conveyed that might have for object or end anything like my settling an administration upon my own plans'.[30] Being in office, his father knew, was not the same as being in power. Eventually, the only stumbling block to Pitt's return was the refusal of another brother-in-law, Richard, Earl Temple, to serve with him. But later in 1766 Pitt did indeed form a government and included in it most of the people he wanted. Protracted negotiation with the King was evidently worth it, a lesson not lost on his son, who was to be offered the premiership four times before accepting it.

It was at this stage that the elder Pitt made a major mistake. On becoming the King's First Minister he also accepted an earldom, 'Viscount Burton Pynsent and Earl of Chatham in the County of Kent'. In all probability, he wanted to set up his family as one of the great families of the land. He already had the estate. The next step was the title, and this was the great opportunity to acquire it. He was also tired and of course frequently ill, preferring to preside over an administration from the more genteel House of Lords without the endless knockabout of the Commons. The consequences were disastrous, according to the poet Thomas Gray the 'weakest thing ever done by so great a man'.[31] At a stroke, the Great Commoner was no more. The man whose reputation had partly rested on being apart from the landed aristocracy had joined it, and the man highly regarded for his independence from the King had accepted the generous patronage of the Crown. It did immense damage to his support around the country, which had always been his strongest card. Worse still, in practical terms it disabled his government from the outset in the House of Commons, where his oratorical skills were no longer available. One Minister resigned rather than face the additional workload and stress that would result. Chatham compounded all this by taking the title Lord Privy Seal rather than First Lord of the Treasury, again to lighten his burden but thereby omitting to control the central function of his government. It is unlikely that these mistakes were lost on his son. There is no evidence of what he thought about them, but throughout his career he steered well clear of repeating them.

The energy of Chatham's administration was spent within a few months, and so was his own. According to Admiral Keppel, later a celebrated naval and political figure: 'He [Chatham] *governs absolutely*, never deigns even to consult any of the Ministers, is now at Bath, and all business is at a stop.'[32] William watched his father retreat into illness, possibly into what would later be called manic depression. From the spring of 1767 he became an invalid, refusing to handle the business of government or to see more than a few chosen people, despite being supposed to be in charge of the country. This situation lasted for eighteen months until the King finally and reluctantly accepted that Chatham could not continue. Again there is no direct account of what young William thought of his father's illness or what effect it had on him. We do know of the patience, loyalty and sheer endurance displayed by his mother. Coping calmly with the dire illness of the man she loved, Hester also dealt personally with the incoming correspondence from Cabinet Ministers and even the King. It would be an exaggeration to say that she was running the government, which now lost its central direction, but she was highly effective at preventing the government from running her husband. It is unlikely that the sight of his mother dealing with all the great potentates of the nation did not make some lasting impression on William. Not only could his father be the master of other politicians, but his mother proved rather effective at it as well.

William Pitt lived through all these events, with enough knowledge to make some sense of them, before he was ten years old. They do not seem to have disturbed his studious mind or happy disposition, but they would certainly have demonstrated to him that there need be no limit to his ambition.

2

Cambridge and the World

'He is of a tender Age, and of a health not yet firm enough to be indulged, to the full, in the strong desire he has to acquire useful knowledge. An ingenious mind and docility of temper will, I know, render him conformable to your Discipline, in all points. Too young for the irregularities of a man, I trust, he will not, on the other hand, prove troublesome by the Puerile sallies of a Boy.'

THE EARL OF CHATHAM TO JOSEPH TURNER OF PEMBROKE COLLEGE[1]

'He was always the most lively person in company, abounding in playful wit and quick repartee; but never known to excite pain, or to give just ground of offence.'

BISHOP TOMLINE[2]

FOR A FOURTEEN-YEAR-OLD to be admitted as an undergraduate to Cambridge University was highly unusual in the eighteenth century, just as it would be today. A sample of undergraduate admissions to Pembroke Hall in the twenty years preceding Pitt's arrival there suggests that fewer than one in five of them were even under eighteen.[3] Yet Chatham and the assiduous tutor Edward Wilson had evidently decided that William could cope with a college environment in spite of his youth and continued illnesses. Since Wilson was a graduate of Pembroke Hall (later Pembroke College), Cambridge, and his brother was presently a Fellow there, it was decided that this would be the most suitable place for William to go. His name was entered into the college admissions book on 26 April 1773. Wilson was highly confident of the new student's prospects: 'He will go to Pembroke not a weak boy to be made a property of, but to be admir'd as a prodigy; not to hear lectures, but to spread light.'[4]

Wilson and Pitt travelled from Somerset to Cambridge together in October 1773, a journey which took them five days. When they arrived, Pitt immediately wrote an excited letter to his father:

> I have the pleasure of writing to my dear father, after having breakfasted upon College rolls, and made some acquaintance with my new quarters which seem, on the short examination I have given, neat and convenient . . .
>
> To make out our five days, we took the road by Binfield, and called in upon Mr. Wilson's curate there; who soon engaged with his rector in a most vehement controversy, and supported his opinions with Ciceronian action and flaming eyes . . . We slept last night at Barkway, where we learnt that Pembroke was a sober, staid college, and nothing but solid study there. I find, indeed, we are to be grave in apparel, as even a silver button is not allowed to sparkle along our quadrangles, &c.; so that my hat is soon to be stripped of its glories, in exchange for a plain loop and button.[5]

The 'neat and convenient quarters' were a set of rooms over the Senior Parlour where Thomas Gray had lived for many years. After that they had been occupied by Wilson's brother, who was now vacating them to travel abroad. These rooms were spacious and well inside the college, away from any noise or bustle in the road.*

Much as the fourteen-year-old was already fascinated by events around the globe, he was still living in a small world. At that time there were about fifty undergraduates at Pembroke, and a good deal fewer than a thousand in the whole university, which could be traversed on foot in less than fifteen minutes. The main subjects of study were Classical Literature, Moral Philosophy, Political Philosophy, Natural History, Medicine, Theology and Mathematics. For his first three years, Pitt played no part in the life of the university outside the Pembroke walls. He was one of eight Fellow Commoners in the college, sons of noblemen who paid higher fees and ate at the Fellows' table rather

* The main room of the set is now a function room, with portraits of Pitt and Gray on the walls.

than with others of the same age. The relationship between a tutor and a student was often far closer than is usual today, frequently with long continuity and daily tutorials in a far smaller community. Once again Pitt was to spend most of his time conversing with adults rather than with other teenagers.

Within a week of his arrival Pitt was writing to his father to report that he was already studying Quintilian and that the Master of the College, Dr Brown, had taken a special interest in him. He was conscious, as always, of being his father's son, expressing the hope 'that I may be, on some future day, worthy to follow, *in part*, the glorious example always before my eyes'.[6] Two weeks later he had fallen ill again and his father was urging him to work less hard: 'You have time to spare: consider there is but the *Encyclopaedia*; and when you have mastered all that, what will remain? You will want, like Alexander, another world to conquer.'[7] By then, however, the damage was already done, and his illness was sufficiently serious to cause alarm in the college and among his family, with the family nurse Mrs Sparry being sent to stay with him in his rooms. He was confined there for two months and then brought home until the summer of the following year. He was preceded home by a letter from the Master: 'notwithstanding his illness, I have myself seen, and have heard enough from his tutors, to be convinced both of his extraordinary genius and most amiable disposition . . . I hope he will return safe to his parents, and that we shall receive him again in a better and more confirmed state of health.'[8]

Pitt was so ill that it is said to have taken four days to transport him from Cambridge to Hayes, a journey which ought to have been possible in one day. Back in the bosom of his family, he was referred to the attentions of his father's physician, Dr Addington, the father of Henry Addington who was to become Pitt's friend and, in 1801, his successor as Prime Minister. It was at this point that Pitt received the famous piece of medical advice that may have influenced his social habits throughout the rest of his life and quite possibly contributed, three decades later, to his early death. Dr Addington recommended going to bed early, and ending the habit of studying classical literature into the night. He also recommended a specific diet, and regular daily exercise on horseback. His final recommendation was to drink a daily quantity of port wine, variously recollected down the generations as 'a bottle a day' or 'liberal potations', but at any rate a good deal of it. While this sounds surprising today, medical opinion of the time was that a regular infusion of alcohol could drive other less welcome toxins to disperse in the body and hopefully disappear. Pitt, methodical as ever, took all of this advice and continued to adhere to most of it throughout his life, particularly the requirement to ride and to drink port. He can be forgiven for thinking that this combination was healthy for him, since it was from this point in his adolescence that he enjoyed a substantial improvement in his health and finally shook off the debilitating complaints that had plagued him as a child.

Nevertheless, it was not until July 1774 that he returned to Cambridge, the devoted Edward Wilson still at his side. For the next two years his life fell into a pattern in which he spent the summer in Cambridge, when of course many other members of the college would be absent, and the winters with his family so that his health could be more closely attended to. In those winter months he was again under the close tutelage of his father. A letter of January 1775 from Chatham to his wife begins, 'William and I, being deep in work for the state', suggesting that political discussion continued apace between father and son.[9] In his Cambridge sojourns, Pitt now became more relaxed and at ease. He took trouble to assure his father that he was no longer working at night, and gave many accounts of riding, in accordance with the doctor's instructions, in the vicinity of Cambridge. In July 1774, on his return, he wrote, 'I have this morning, for the first time, mounted my horse, and was accompanied by Mr. Wilson, on his beautiful carthorse,' and 'Nutmeg performs admirably. Even the solid shoulders of Peacock are not without admirers; and they have jogged Mr. Wilson into tolerable health and spirits; though at first the salutary exercise had an effect that, for some time, prevented his pursuing it. The rides in the neighbourhood afford nothing striking, but, at the same time are not unpleasing, when one is a little used to a flat open country.'[10] By the end of August, the now much healthier fifteen-year-old seemed fully content and settled in. He wrote to his father, 'Mr. Turner, with whom I read the first part of the time I have been here, is now absent, and Mr. Pretyman supplies his place. During the interval of a day or two before the arrival of the latter, the Master read with me some part of Cicero De Senectute; of which he is a great admirer. He is in every respect as obliging as possible. Altogether, by the help of riding, reading, the newspapers, & c. time is past away very agreeably.'[11]

The arrival of Dr George Pretyman as Pitt's tutor presaged a lifelong friendship of deep mutual loyalty. Pretyman was the junior Fellow at Pembroke and he became Pitt's principal tutor and mentor. With him, Pitt continued the practice of contemporaneous translation of classical texts which he had started with his father. Pretyman (later known as Tomline after an inheritance) was only eight years older than Pitt himself, and it is clear they spent a great deal of time together. As we shall see, he went on to be an unofficial aide to Pitt in his early years as Prime Minister, always remained a close friend and adviser, and was with him when he died in 1806. Pitt would reward him in 1787 by making him Bishop of Lincoln, and was only thwarted by the determination of George III from making him Archbishop of Canterbury in 1805.

Pretyman's *Life of Pitt* has been excoriated for being of little literary or political merit and for tragically failing to give any private insights into Pitt's character, with which he must have been extremely familiar. But it is possible to glean from the book a little of what Pitt's life was like between the ages of fifteen and seventeen. 'While Mr. Pitt was under-graduate, he never omitted attending chapel morning and evening, or dining in the public hall, except when prevented by indisposition. Nor did he pass a single evening out of the college walls. Indeed, most of his time was spent with me.'[12] In the course of several years 'I never knew him spend an idle day; nor did he ever fail to attend me at the appointed hour.'[13] As Pitt's tutor, Pretyman was enormously impressed by the talents of his pupil who, having exhausted all the principal Greek and Latin texts, requested that they study the little-known rhapsody of Lycophron. This he read 'with an ease at first sight, which, if I had not witnessed it, I should have thought beyond the compass of human intellect'.[14]

Pretyman taught Pitt alternate sessions of Classics and Mathematics. The eager pupil excelled in both fields, and continued to give particular attention to speaking styles. 'When alone, he dwelt for hours upon striking passages of an orator or historian, in noticing their turn of expression, in marking their manner of arranging a narrative . . . A few pages sometimes occupied a whole morning . . . He was also in the habit of copying any eloquent sentence, or any beautiful or forcible expression, which occurred in his reading.'[15] The focus of Pitt's learning was therefore narrow, but always practical and invariably intense. He showed very little interest in contemporary literature, European languages (although he developed a working knowledge of French) or the wave of French philosophical writing pouring forth at the time. There is no evidence that he spent a single day reflecting on theology, despite the fact that a very large proportion of his fellow students would have been preparing for a career in the Church, a path to which his close friend and tutor was also inclined. His intellectual diversions from Classics and Mathematics extended at a later stage to attending lectures in Civil Law, with the Bar in his mind as a stopgap or supplement to politics. He always had a thirst for information about public affairs in the wider world. Even in 1773, before his arrival in Cambridge, we find him writing to a Mr Johnson, 'Can you tell whether Governor Hutchinson's speech to the General assembly at Boston together with their answer and his reply again have been yet published together? If they have will you send them down.'[16]

Pitt had a very clear sense of what facts he wanted to know and which subjects he wanted to study, and was happy to leave aside fields of theoretical discussion which preoccupied many of his contemporaries. It is impossible to escape the very simple conclusion that throughout his teens he was consciously preparing for a career at the forefront of politics, and, certain of what was required from the close observation of his father, directed his studies to that end.

It may be thought from all of this that Pitt must have been dry and dull from a social point of view, but all who knew him are adamant that this was not the case. It was at this stage, at the age of seventeen in 1776, that his daily life began to broaden out and for the first time he developed his own circle of friends. He took his Master of Arts degree without an examination, as he was entitled to do as the son of a nobleman. He had intended to sit the examinations for a Bachelor of Arts degree but was prevented by his failure to attend for sufficient terms to qualify. This did not mean, however, that he would now leave Cambridge. He had at last been able to find friends approximating to his own age, and was freer to go about to other colleges and, increasingly, on short trips to London. Possibly conscious of how little he had experienced the life of the university in his first three years, and still being too young to do anything else, he decided to stay in residence at Pembroke for the time being, albeit moving rooms in 1777 when the previous occupant of his original set returned.

He was not slow in making friends, and now laid the foundations of many lifelong relationships. His close friends included Edward Eliot, who later became his brother-in-law, lived with him in Downing Street and was a member of the Board of the Treasury; Lord Westmorland, later Lord Lieutenant of Ireland and Lord Privy Seal; William Meeke, later Clerk of the Parliament in Dublin and an MP; Lord Granby, later Duke of Rutland, Lord Lieutenant of Ireland in Pitt's first administration, and instrumental in getting him into Parliament; J.C. Villiers, later a member of the Board of Trade; Henry Bankes, later a supportive MP for many years; John Pratt, later Lord Camden and a member of Pitt's governments; and Lord Euston, who became MP for Cambridge University alongside Pitt. It is easy to imagine a brilliant young man such as Pitt, holder of a famous political name, exploding into the company of such a talented and politically motivated group. Pretyman tells us: 'He was always the most lively person in company, abounding in playful wit and quick repartee; but never known to excite pain, or to give just ground of offence . . . Though his society was universally sought, and from the age of seventeen or eighteen he constantly passed his evenings in company, he steadily avoided every species of irregularity.'[17] Whether by inclination, calculation, or awareness of so many eyes being upon the son of Chatham, Pitt was careful as a teenager to do nothing which would disgrace his family or return to haunt him. In any case, he had no need of excesses to make him popular with his peers. William Wilberforce, part of a more dissolute set at Cambridge at the time but later to become another lifelong friend, referred to his 'distinctive peculiarity that he was not carried away by his own wit, though he could at any time command its exercise, and no man, perhaps, at proper seasons ever indulged more freely or happily in that playful facetiousness which gratifies all without wounding any'.[18]

Pitt's Cambridge friends, then, provided lively company and intellectual stimulation, and while not subject to many vices undoubtedly drank a good deal of port together. They were, however, all of a type, generally the sons of noblemen, and all familiar with politics and classics. Pitt was friendly and charming in their company, but he gained no experience in dealing with other types of people in other situations. The latitudinarian and Newtonian influences on Cambridge at the time emphasised the power of reason, and Pitt would have met far fewer people who were impervious to rational persuasion than would have been the case elsewhere.

He would have encountered very few women indeed, and certainly none at all on equal terms or in any intellectual environment. Nor did he have to cope with the company of people not of his choosing. It may have been because of his Grenville starchiness or it may partly have been the result of his education in the cloistered atmosphere of his home and college that Pitt was to be known throughout his life as aloof, difficult and sometimes haughty towards most people he met. The pattern of his character was now set: a brilliant and tireless interest in practical questions, a tremendously relaxed and talkative enjoyment of chosen company, and a stern face presented to the outer world.

Outside the college dining rooms inhabited by Pitt and his friends, life in the city of Cambridge would have looked and sounded very much as it had done for many decades. The first paved street in the city appeared in 1788, some years after Pitt left Pembroke, and gas lighting did not follow until 1823, well after his death. Yet as the 1770s drew to a close the Britain beyond the walls of Oxbridge colleges was on the brink of a social and economic transformation which even the brilliant Cambridge graduates gathering to discuss public affairs could not possibly have foreseen. In the coming years they would have to respond to it, and their lives and careers would be increasingly shaped and buffeted by it.

War has always been a spur to invention, and the Seven Years' War was no exception. The invention of the spinning jenny in 1764 and improvements upon it in the following years brought about a revolution in the cotton industry and British manufacturing. That revolution gathered pace as Pitt studied his books at Cambridge, and was to become a mighty engine of economic growth throughout his political career. Cotton exports from Britain were £200,000 in 1764, and had risen to £355,000 by 1780, but had rocketed to £9,753,000 by the time of Pitt's death in 1806, going on to form nearly half of total British exports.[19]

The use of coal and coke in iron production was also getting under way, further transformed by the use of steam engines and blast furnaces from 1790. This was the dawn of the Industrial Revolution, and it would bring huge changes in the demography of Britain. By 1800, the great cities of manufacturing and trade such as Manchester, Liverpool, Birmingham, Leeds and Bristol would dwarf the previously largest cities (other than London) such as Norwich, Exeter and York. London was, and would remain, the largest city in the British Isles, but at the end of the eighteenth century many of what are today its central districts were still villages surrounded by fields. A German visitor, Carl Moritz, wrote of the view from the top of St Paul's Cathedral in 1782: 'beneath me lay a packed mass of towers, houses and palaces, with the London squares – their green lawns in their midst – adding pleasant splashes of colour in between. At one end of the Thames stood the Tower of London, like a city with a forest of masts behind it; at the other lay Westminster Abbey lifting up its towers. The green hills skirting the Paddington and Islington districts smiled at me from afar while nearer by lay Southwark on the opposite bank of the Thames.'[20] At this stage St James's Park was 'nothing more than a semi-circular avenue of trees enclosing a large area of greensward in the midst of which is a swampy pond. Cows feed on the turf and you may buy their milk quite freshly drawn from the animal.'[21]*

We do not know whether the future politicians gathered around the young Pitt discussed the first stirrings of the Industrial Revolution,

* In his wonderful book recounting his travels in England, Moritz also remarks on the 'incomparable' English habit of 'roasting slices of buttered bread before the fire . . . this is called "toast"'.

but the ingredients were present all around them. Agricultural productivity was rising much faster than in neighbouring France, as farm sizes increased and the population began to move to the cities. Coal output in 1775 was already nearly three times what it had been in 1700. The growth of the cotton industry and trade with the expanding Empire provided new employment on a huge scale. Population growth, facilitated by the availability of food and work, started to accelerate, with the population of England growing from five and a half million to seven million between 1751 and 1781. By 1841 it would reach fifteen million.[22] The transport system was beginning to improve, with the canals undergoing expansion to link manufacturing centres and ports, and turnpike roads growing rapidly from 1750 onwards.

The huge expansion and movements of population would create immense political and social strains, but at the time of Pitt's Cambridge education these trends had yet to gather their full momentum. It would undoubtedly have seemed in the 1770s that such changes as were happening could be safely accommodated within the existing political and economic order. The real explosion of agricultural and manufacturing production and export growth took place after 1780, just as Pitt entered Parliament, when in a twenty-year period the proportion of national output exported rose from 9 per cent to 16 per cent even while a war of unprecedented intensity was raging. Pitt and his colleagues in government would face the challenge of coping with economic change on a scale never witnessed before, and at a time when that change was unpredictable and uneven. They would also be the last generation to conduct the business of the nation without the advantage of the dramatic advances in travel and communications which were also on the way.

Although Pitt, on his increasing forays to the capital, would find it possible in the late 1770s to eat breakfast in London and dinner (generally taken in the late afternoon) in Cambridge, road travel was still an arduous business. It was not practical at this time, nor would it be for some decades, to make a tour even of a country as small as England without spending weeks or months doing so and being incommunicado for part of the time. As a result, Pitt in office would rarely stray north of Northampton or west of Weymouth. When

William Wilberforce rushed to a crisis public meeting in York in 1795, taking less than forty-eight hours to make the journey from Westminster, it was regarded as an extraordinary achievement, made possible only by extra teams of horses as well as outriders to clear people from the last twenty miles of the route. Within fifty years, he could have done it in nine hours on the train. The fact that advances in communications came later than a great deal of other economic change would limit the ability of politicians to understand what was happening and to respond to it quickly.

Throughout the whole of this period all orders and correspondence dealing with a burgeoning national economy and war on a global scale would have to be conveyed by letter carried by a despatch rider on a horse, or on board ship. The complications this entailed for international diplomacy would be unimaginable today. Wars could be declared while peace proposals were still on their way from a foreign capital. A message sent by sea did not necessarily travel faster than a fleet. In 1762, when the Seven Years' War widened into conflict between Britain and Spain, the enterprising British Admiralty sent a message to British forces in India to set off immediately to attack the Spanish colony in Manila in the Philippines. Arriving seven months after the original message had been sent from London, the British achieved the ultimate surprise attack, since word had still not arrived from Madrid that war had been declared at all. Their ships sailed under the Spanish defenders' guns unchallenged before launching their successful assault. In the Nootka Sound crisis of 1790, the interval between events on the ground on the west coast of North America and a response from London could be anything up to a full year. It is therefore vital to remember that governments of this period, including Pitt's administrations, were often groping in the dark when dealing with war or disorder, guessing at events, and trying to remember to err on the side of caution. This would not help them to cope with the convulsions which would shake the world in their lifetimes.

The first of these convulsions, and one which ranked high in the conversations of Pitt and his friends, was already taking place in the

1770s. In 1775 the diverging interests of Britain and the thirteen American colonies exploded into war, and Pitt's letters of the time are peppered with requests for news, information and documents relating to it. The repeal of the Stamp Act in 1766 had made Chatham a hero across the Atlantic, with statues of him erected in American towns, but ironically it was Chatham's own victories that paved the way for this further and disastrous conflict. With the French cleared from Canada, the colonies had much less need of Britain to protect them. Instead, they found British commitments to Indian tribes getting in the way of the territorial expansion to the west which a rapidly growing American population now sought. And the emerging British Empire was now so vast and varied that the interests of one colony could be entirely different from the interests of the whole. When the British government reduced the duties on the export of tea to North America, it was meant to be excellent news for the troubled finances of the East India Company, but it was disastrous for the lucrative smuggling trade in Massachusetts. The result was the Boston Tea Party and, several years later, open conflict.

British political opinion was deeply divided over the developing war in America, but few in London would have doubted the capacity of Britain to bring the recalcitrant colonies to heel. The 350 ships and 25,000 soldiers assembled in America by the early summer of 1776 in the name of the King constituted an awesome display of military power. Yet they were to find, like the Americans themselves two centuries later in Vietnam, that regular troops fighting by conventional methods in vast, impenetrable terrain could win most of the battles but still not win the war.

Chatham, in his dying years, and after some time in which he took no part in politics, made three celebrated visits to the House of Lords to thunder against the folly of British policy. As Macaulay put it in his brilliant essay on Pitt, 'Chatham was only the ruin of [the elder] Pitt, but an awful and majestic ruin, not to be contemplated by any man of sense and feeling without emotions resembling those which are excited by the remains of the Parthenon and of the Colosseum.'[23] In 1775 he called for conciliation of the colonies: 'We shall be forced ultimately to retract; let us retract while we can not when we must.'

His son sat transfixed in the Gallery of the Lords, and his letter to his mother shows how he was now applying his judgement of classical speeches to contemporary debaters:

> Nothing prevented his [Chatham's] speech from being the most forcible that can be imagined . . . The matter and manner both were striking; far beyond what I can express . . . Lord Suffolk, I cannot say answered him . . . He was a contemptible orator indeed, with paltry matter and a whining delivery. Lord Shelburne spoke well . . . Lord Camden was *supreme* . . . Lord Rockingham spoke shortly but sensibly; and the Duke of Richmond well . . . Upon the whole, it was a noble debate.[24]

On the second occasion, Chatham presciently warned that the war would soon widen into conflict with France and Spain, insisting on the need to make immediate peace with America. Once again, an excited son was in the Gallery:

> I cannot help expressing to you how happy beyond description I feel in reflecting that my father was able to exert, in their full vigour, the sentiments and eloquence which have always distinguished him. His first speech took up half an hour, and was full of all his usual force and vivacity . . . He spoke a second time . . . This he did in a flow of eloquence, and with a beauty of expression, animated and striking beyond conception.[25]

Chatham's warnings went unheeded; strategic mistakes contributed to a serious British defeat at Saratoga, followed by rejoicing in Paris and the entry of France and later Spain and Holland into the war. The tired and dispirited head of the government, Lord North, asked George III for permission to resign and to sound out Chatham on the terms on which he would form a government. Not only did the King refuse, referring to Chatham as that 'perfidious man', but Chatham was now on his last legs. Against the advice of his doctors, he went to the House of Lords on 17 April 1778, entering the Chamber supported on the shoulders of William and his son-in-law, Lord Mahon. Dramatically, the entire House of Lords rose to greet him. It is hard to imagine that William Pitt ever forgot the poignancy of this moment and its illustration of the greatness of his father. Chatham's voice was weak, and he was almost unable to stand; at times his speech wandered, but his message was clear: now the war had been widened it was too late to sue for peace. 'Shall this great kingdom . . . fall prostrate before the House of Bourbon? . . . Shall a people that fifteen years ago was the terror of the world now stoop so low as to tell its ancient inveterate enemy, "Take all we have, only give us peace". In God's name . . . Let us at least make one effort; and if we must fall, let us fall like men!'[26] He sat down exhausted, and trying to rise to speak for a second time, fell backwards unable to do any more, a moment immortalised in Copley's famous painting, as his sons John and William rushed to his aid. He was taken to Downing Street, then two days later to Hayes, and died on 11 May. The role of chief mourner at his father's funeral the following month became Pitt's first public duty.

The following month left Britain facing the growing prospect of defeat abroad and deeper divisions at home. The war with the colonies had been bluntly opposed not only by Chatham but by the main body of the Whig opposition under the Marquis of Rockingham. Many British officers, John Pitt among them, had refused to serve in the American campaigns. They were, however, happy to fight the Bourbons, and John Pitt was now despatched on the expedition to Gibraltar. By 1779 the French and Spanish fleets were cruising unmolested in the English Channel, the Royal Navy too weak and dispersed to fight them, and their waste washed ashore on the south-coast beaches of a humiliated Britain. When efforts to clear the Channel of the enemy failed, the government brought to court martial the naval commander Admiral Keppel, a leading Whig: this move backfired badly on them when Keppel was acquitted and the government was shown to have been seriously incompetent in equipping the navy for war. The opposition, the young Pitt among them, rejoiced. As crowds broke the windows of senior Ministers, Pitt wrote to Edward Eliot a letter which reveals his partisanship and his dry humour with friends:

> I am just come from beyond the Throne in the House of Lords . . . The short Interval between the duties of a Statesman and a Beau, allows me just Time to perform that of a good Correspondent . . . I rejoice to hear that the good People of England have

> so universally exerted their natural Right of Breaking Windows, Picking Pockets etc. etc., and that these Constitutional demonstrations of Joy, are not confined to the Metropolis . . . The Conquering Hero himself has this evening made his Entry and every Window in London (a Metaphor I learnt in the House of Lords) is by this time acquainted with his Arrival . . . I begin to fear that the Clamour may subside, and the King still be Blest with his present faithful Servants. Most sincerely and illegibly Yours W. Pitt.[27]

As Pitt prepared to leave Cambridge that year, opposition to the government of Lord North and to the King's policies was in full cry, along with a widespread feeling that the political system was failing. Chatham had been followed by two weak Prime Ministers, the Duke of Grafton and Lord North, who had easily been dominated by the King. People beyond the ranks of the normal opposition began to accept that there was too much power vested in the Crown, too many placemen in key offices, too little competence in government, too little attention to the efficiency and effectiveness of the navy, too much waste of government money, and too little representation of large parts of the population. Early in 1780 there was uproar in the Commons as the opposition succeeded in carrying a motion that 'the influence of the Crown has increased, is increasing, and ought to be diminished'.

The efforts of John Wilkes in the 1760s had helped to ignite radical and irreverent opinion. After Chatham's departure from government in 1761 Wilkes had brought out a regular publication, the *North Briton*, which heaped insults on the Earl of Bute and the Royal Family. Outlawed, he eventually stood for Parliament in Middlesex, which had a wide franchise, and was repeatedly re-elected and repeatedly expelled by the Commons. The cry of 'Wilkes and liberty' had become a popular chant.

Spurred on by Edmund Burke, who coupled his passionate belief in tradition and monarchy with relentless criticism of the excesses of governments, opposition figures responded to this discontent by calling for 'economical reform' and 'parliamentary reform', and Pitt was to become an early devotee of both. Economical reform was directed at the patronage and alleged corruption of the system of offices surrounding the Crown. The objectives of its proponents were to reduce the number of sinecures and Crown offices, and to disqualify various placemen and contractors from being elected to the House of Commons while they were dependent on the patronage of the King. This programme was put forward by the Rockingham Whigs as a means of reversing the growth of the Crown's power under Grafton and North. Parliamentary reform was supported more enthusiastically outside Parliament, largely by the growing middle class in the newly expanding cities who sought in various ways to redistribute the parliamentary seats, which were now completely adrift from the distribution of the population. Cornwall, for instance, had forty-four Members of Parliament, while the far greater population of London had ten.

The politicians of the time who put forward these reforms did not envisage that they were embarking on a long-term programme of political change. Their intention was to restore balance to what they regarded as a near-perfect constitutional settlement, arrived at in the Glorious Revolution of 1688 when William III and Mary replaced the fleeing James II. That settlement involved the ultimate supremacy of Parliament, a guaranteed Protestant succession to the Crown, and religious tolerance for all Protestants, even though Dissenters were still barred from political office. It was credited with maintaining a stability within Britain unheard of in previous centuries, and it had been achieved without bloodshed, unlike the overthrow of the monarchy in the English Civil War. It kept both the Crown and a wider democracy in check. To the Whigs of the late eighteenth century the need was to correct its balance rather than to rebuild it. Parliamentary reform received the backing of Chatham in his final years, and Pitt would start his career holding to these views, calling for both economical and parliamentary reform, a position true to the views of his father and the fashions of the time.

No student of history should underestimate the influence of the Glorious Revolution on the politicians of a century later. It was the basis of the country's political framework, and many MPs would continue to vote against any alteration of constituency boundaries right up to 1832 in the belief that such a perfect settlement should not be violated in any respect. But it was also the basis of the country's religious framework, and it is impossible to understand the politics of the eighteenth century without an appreciation of the role of religion in national life.

The Cambridge University attended by Pitt was not open to Roman Catholics, and served as a seminary for the Anglican clergy. We have seen how Pitt attended chapel twice a day in his early years at Pembroke. This was not because he was religious in feeling, but because religion was deeply interwoven with politics, custom and national outlook. Indeed, it was commonplace in society, as the debauched lives of many politicians demonstrated, to be irreligious in private while adhering unfailingly to the religious settlement inherent in 1688. The reason people felt strongly about religious questions was not in the main because they cared about the niceties of theological debates – any more than Henry VIII left the Church for theological rather than personal and political reasons – but because religion had come to symbolise the constitution of the country and its foreign policy.

Britain had fought endless wars by the end of the eighteenth century against His Most Christian Majesty the King of France, with the Stuart Kings of the seventeenth century having been suspiciously close, through the Catholic Church, to England's historic foe. James II, whose behaviour precipitated the 1688 Revolution, even privately apologised to Louis XIV for summoning a Parliament without his permission.[28] Protestant Huguenots had fled to England from Catholic persecution in France, and it was Charles I's attempts to plan a comeback with Catholics in Scotland and Ireland that had led to the second stage of the Civil War in the 1640s and to Cromwell's merciless destruction of Catholic power in Ireland. In more recent memory, in both 1715 and 1745–46, Jacobite attempts to restore the Stuarts to the throne in place of the Hanoverians had been assisted by Catholic powers, specifically France and Spain. To the great majority of people in England it was therefore unthinkable to allow Catholics to hold office. Far beyond the Church and Parliament, Catholicism meant to most people treachery and invasion, bloodshed and persecution. Any acceptance that

Catholics could have the rights and privileges of other Englishmen was therefore pandering to foreigners – in particular the French – returning to Jacobite sympathies and destroying a fundamental attribute of Englishness.

Just as the collapse of the Soviet Union two centuries later led to changes in political attitudes in the countries that had stood guard against it, so the collapse of the Jacobite threat after 1745 led to a steady breaking down of the political and religious battle lines in the late eighteenth century. Fear of the Jacobites had kept the suspect Tories out of office for a generation, and the Whigs, who prided themselves on the 1688 settlement, were permanently in power from 1714 to the 1760s. Now that party system had broken down, with parliamentary factions forming and re-forming, able to hold office in many combinations and putting leading Whigs out of office in the 1770s. To politicians the religious prohibitions were breaking down too, and many saw a need to amend the absolutism of the constitutional hostility to Roman Catholics. The conquest of Canada had brought vast numbers of Catholics of French descent into the British Empire. The Quebec Act of 1774 officially recognised the toleration of their religion. Added to that, the war in America made it essential to recruit soldiers who were Catholics, leading Parliament in 1778 to end the practice of requiring recruits to take an oath denying the supremacy of the Pope.

Beyond Westminster, many people who did not appreciate the need for such changes were suspicious of the motives behind them. Such suspicion was political dynamite, and it was accidentally detonated in the summer of 1780 by Lord George Gordon, leader of the Protestant Association. His attempt to take a petition to Parliament calling for the repeal of the 1778 Act resulted in a crowd of 60,000 forming across the river from the Palace of Westminster, siege being laid to Members of Parliament, and then five days and nights of perhaps the worst rioting London had ever experienced. Order was only restored after resolute action by the King, and the calling in of 15,000 troops and militia. Many hundreds of people were killed and scores of London's most prized residences destroyed in untold scenes of savagery and destruction. Pitt, in his rooms at Lincoln's Inn, was in the centre of it, apparently free from danger but witnessing London in flames in all directions. With the relaxed humour that was becoming his trademark he wrote to his mother: 'Several very respectable lawyers have appeared with musquets on their shoulders, to the no small diversion of all spectators. Unluckily the Appearance of Danger ended just as we embodied, and our military Ardour has been thrown away.'[29] He could not have failed to notice, however, the huge power of religious issues, and the dangers of letting popular feelings run out of control. As he contemplated the end of what he called the 'placid uniformity' of Cambridge life, and the start of a political career, he was learning that great issues were at stake – of war and peace, of monarchical or parliamentary power, of the rights of religious minorities, and of how to administer and control a society changing unpredictably at home and suffering military humiliation abroad. It was a dramatic and exciting time to enter politics. If he was to have any influence on it, he needed a career, he needed money, and he needed a seat in Parliament.

3

Ambition on Schedule

'Appelby is the Place I am to Represent.'

WILLIAM PITT

'A dead minister, the most respectable that ever existed, weighs very light in the scale against any living one.'

EARL TEMPLE

'CHATHAM', STANHOPE REMARKED in his 1860s biography of Pitt, 'had been a little unthrifty.'[1] This was putting it mildly. On the death of Chatham in 1778, Parliament voted £20,000 – the equivalent of something approaching £2 million today* – to rescue his family and his memory from financial embarrassment. They also voted an annuity of £4,000 in perpetuity to the Earldom of Chatham, now inherited by William's elder brother John. Theoretically, William Pitt was left £3,500 by his father. In practice, there was no money to honour this legacy, since the whole of the generous grant by Parliament would be taken up by his father's debts. William had also been left a share of the mortgaged properties at Burton Pynsent and Hayes, but none of this came his way until Hayes was sold, by which time he was already Prime Minister. His total income as he prepared to move from Cambridge into the wider world was £600 a year, in the form of a

* Assessments of inflation over such long periods are at best approximate. In this book any illustrations of the present-day value of money in Pitt's time are based on the index agreed in 2003 by the House of Commons Library, the Bank of England and the Office of National Statistics.

grant from his elder brother. This was to prove insufficient for the needs of a young gentleman laying the foundations of his career and travelling about in the south-east of England a good deal. When he needed more he submitted a request to his mother. 'My finances', he tells her in November 1778, 'are in no urgent Want of Repair; but if I should happen to buy a Horse they will be soon, and therefore, if it is not inconvenient to you, I shall be much obliged to you for a draught of 50£.'[2] Or in December 1779: 'The approach of Christmas, and the expense of moving, oblige me to beg you to supply me with a draft of 60£.'[3]

He was particularly assiduous in assuring his mother that he would not drink too much or work too hard, as in this letter from Cambridge in January 1780:

> The Charge of looking slender and thin when the doctor saw me, I do not entirely deny; but if it was in a greater degree than usual, it may fairly be attributed to the hurry of London, and an accidental cold at the Time . . . The use of the horse I assure you I do not neglect, in the properest medium; and a sufficient number of idle avocations secure me quite enough from the danger of too much study . . . Among the Principal Occupations of Cambridge at this Season of Christmas are perpetual College Feasts, a species of Exercise in which, above all others, I shall not forget your rule of moderation.[4]

His mother helped him financially whenever she could, but since the annuity settled upon Chatham by the King in 1761 and now due to her was frequently in arrears she was not always able to do so. Soon Pitt had borrowed £1,000 at 5 per cent from the friendly banker Mr Thomas Coutts, in return for his signing over the paternal legacy which would never be paid. In order to pursue a career at the Bar, however, he needed a residence at Lincoln's Inn, which required still more substantial resources. He wrote hopefully to his mother:

> It will very soon be necessary for me to have rooms at Lincoln's Inn . . . The whole expense of these will be Eleven Hundred Pounds, which sounds to me a frightful sum . . . The rooms are in an exceeding good situation in the new Buildings, and will be perfectly fit for Habitation in about two months. Soon after that

> time it will be right for me to begin attending Westminster Hall during the term, and then chambers will be more convenient than any other residence . . . I have done no more than to secure that they may not be engaged to any other person till I have returned an Answer, and I shall be glad to know your opinion as soon as possible. You will be so good as to consider how far you approve of the idea, if it be practicable, and whether there are any means of advancing the money out of my fortune before I am of Age.[5]

Desperate to help him, his mother was no doubt behind the surprise suggestion by his uncle Earl Temple that he would advance Pitt the necessary sum. Having paid the first instalment, Earl Temple disobligingly died, and Pitt secured the chambers on the promise of his late uncle's obligation, while mortgaging them the following year to obtain more cash. Already, at the age of twenty-one, he had dipped a toe into the vicious whirlpool that his personal finances would become.

From his late teens Pitt enjoyed the busy life of a young man who could move about freely, flitting between the family homes, attendance at Lincoln's Inn and the Galleries of the Lords and Commons in London, and the reassuring intellectual security of Pembroke College. He was often in London with his brothers and sisters, frequently staying in Harley Street at the house of his older sister Hester, who in 1775 had married Lord Mahon, son of Earl Stanhope, and by early 1780 had three children. Pitt seems to have attended the opera occasionally, having developed a taste for music at Cambridge even though Pretyman subsequently insisted that he had 'no ear',[6] and reported attending masquerades and evenings at the Pantheon,* but he was not keen on the wilder social events:

> Nerot's Hotel, Wednesday Night [1779]
> James is gone with my sisters to the ball as a professed dancer,

* The Pantheon, on Oxford Street to the east of Oxford Circus, was a prominent venue for concerts and dances and was described by Horace Walpole as 'the most beautiful edifice in England'. Today the site is occupied by a store of Marks & Spencer.

> which stands in the place of an invitation; a character which I do not assume, and have therefore stayed away.

He continued to prefer more intellectual evenings. It was at a dinner in Lincoln's Inn during the Gordon Riots that the celebrated encounter took place between the twenty-one-year-old Pitt and the already famous historian Edward Gibbon, who was publishing the second and third volumes of his momentous *Decline and Fall of the Roman Empire*. Another young lawyer, James Bland Burges, described how Gibbon had just concluded a series of 'brilliant and pleasant' anecdotes 'with his customary tap on the lid of his snuff box', when 'a deep toned but clear voice was heard from the bottom of the table, very calmly and firmly impugning the correctness of the narrative, and the propriety of the doctrine of which it had been made the vehicle'. Gibbon saw

> a tall, thin, and rather ungainly looking young man, who now sat quietly and silently eating some fruit. There was nothing very prepossessing or very formidable in his exterior, but, as the few words he had uttered appeared to have made a considerable impression on the company, Mr. Gibbon, I suppose, thought himself bound to maintain his honour by suppressing such an attempt to dispute his supremacy. He accordingly undertook the defence of the propositions in question, and a very animated debate took place between him and his youthful antagonist, Mr. Pitt, and for some time was conducted with great talent and brilliancy on both sides. At length the genius of the young man prevailed over that of his senior, who, finding himself driven into a corner from which there was no escape, made some excuse arising from the table and walked out of the room.

Gibbon stalked out 'in high dudgeon', and 'when we returned into the dining-room we found Mr. Pitt proceeding very tranquilly with the illustration of the subject from which his opponent had fled, and which he discussed with such ability, strength of argument, and eloquence, that his hearers were filled with profound admiration'.[7]

It had been clear for some years that a career as a lawyer would be a fallback for Pitt, and the proximity to the House of Commons of the law courts, literally yards away in and around Westminster Hall, provided an additional incentive for him. As it turned out, his legal career was not long, but during it he again showed his usual mixture of easy ability and high popularity in private company. Another lawyer of the time recalled: 'Among lively men of his own time of life, Mr. Pitt was always the most lively and convivial in the many hours of leisure which occur to young unoccupied men on a Circuit, and joined all the little excursions to Southampton, Weymouth, and such parties of amusement as were habitually formed. He was extremely popular. His name and reputation of high acquirements at the university commanded the attention of his seniors. His wit, his good humour, and joyous manners endeared him to the younger part of the Bar.'[8]

He was called to the Bar in the summer of 1780, but it is clear throughout all his correspondence that his overriding fascination remained with politics. In the summer of 1779 it was thought by some that Parliament might be dissolved two years ahead of its maximum seven-year term. The war was going badly, Lord North and his colleagues appeared dejected and the King was even forced to preside at a Cabinet meeting to try to deter North's enemies from attacking his First Minister. Pitt turned his thoughts to how and where he could enter Parliament.

Pitt wanted to be in Parliament from the earliest possible date, but it did not accord with his concept of himself simply to represent any constituency which was available. He had a very clear idea of where he wished to represent, and from the summer of 1779 expressed an explicit interest in being one of the two Members for Cambridge University.* This was not simply because he spent a good deal of time there and was familiar with the place, since there was little need in this period for most Members of Parliament to know or to spend time in their constituencies. Rather it was because from the outset he wanted to be a particular type of politician, and that would require a particular type of constituency.

* Cambridge and Oxford Universities had two Members each. The University Members were finally abolished in 1948.

From the perspective of the twenty-first century, accustomed as we are to universal suffrage and the periodic redrawing of constituency boundaries to keep up with the changing distribution of population, the electoral basis of the House of Commons in the eighteenth century seems extraordinary and chaotic. It was not democratic in any modern sense of the term, and was not intended to be; but it was intended to ensure that the *interests* of every part of the country were represented, and that an element of competition took place among the aristocracy and country gentry as to who would have access to power and the spoils of office.

The House of Commons in 1780 had 558 Members, around a hundred fewer than today, with 489 from England, forty-five from Scotland and twenty-four from Wales. Ireland had a separate Parliament which was to be given increased powers in 1782, so there were no Irish seats in the House of Commons at this stage. Only the English constituencies were of interest to Pitt as he sought his first election to Parliament. Of these the generally most prestigious were the forty counties, each of which elected two Members. For two reasons, however, these were of little appeal to a politician who aspired to high office. First, they had a relatively wide franchise, embracing all males who owned the freehold of land with a rental value of more than forty shillings a year, and could have electorates running into many thousands. A contested election in Yorkshire, for instance, could easily produce 20,000 voters at the poll. As a result they were extremely expensive to contest (William Wilberforce's two opponents in Yorkshire in 1807 reportedly spent over £100,000 each – the equivalent of more than £5 million), and the funds had to be found by the candidate, or a rich patron, or his supporters. Often huge sums were spent on a 'canvass' of county seats to see whether it was worth putting a particular candidate forward before embarking on the immense expense and trouble of actually contesting the election. In the 1780 election, only two counties would actually go to the lengths of having a contest.

As an additional obstacle it had been agreed in 1707, as part of an earlier attempt to rein in the patronage of the Crown, that an MP accepting an office of profit from the Crown such as a ministerial position would resign his seat and fight a by-election. This practice continued into the early twentieth century, sometimes leading to the defeat of freshly appointed Ministers such as Winston Churchill in 1908. In the eighteenth century the expense of fighting a county seat over and over again would have prohibited a ministerial career. On the whole, the counties were represented by 'independent country gentlemen' from long-established local families, but occasionally a contested county could give great authority to a popular campaign, such as the repeated re-election of John Wilkes for Middlesex in the 1760s.

By far the most numerous constituencies were the 203 cities and boroughs which elected 405 Members between them. These were heavily weighted to the south-west of the country and to seaports, and were still based on the wealth and prominence of towns in mediaeval times. The entitlement to vote in these constituencies varied hugely, sometimes being relatively wide as in the counties (the City of Westminster itself being an example), sometimes limited to the few dozen members of the corporation of the town, and sometimes limited to the owners of certain properties or 'burgages'. It was thus variously possible to control a borough by instructing the voters, by bribing the corporation, or simply by owning sufficient burgages. Landowners would commonly instruct their tenants how to vote, and since the voting itself was openly recorded this rarely left the voters with much of a choice. In other circumstances voters could sell themselves to the highest bidder. As Thomas Pitt wrote in 1740: 'There are few [Cornish] boroughs where the common sort of people do not think they have as much right to sell themselves and their votes, as they have to sell their corn and their cattle.'[9] The provision of meals and alcohol was a standard part of such bribery; alcohol could be useful in other ways too, as George Selwyn, MP for Gloucester, complained in 1761. 'Two of my voters were murdered yesterday by an experiment which we call shopping, that is, locking them up and keeping them dead drunk to the day of election. Mr. Snell's agents forced two single Selwyns into a post chaise, where, being suffocated with the brandy that was given them and a very fat man that had the custody of them, they were taken out stone dead.'[10]

Over half of the boroughs could be purchased in one way or another, an average price in the late eighteenth century being around

£3,000 to £4,000. They would be bought by the major political families, who might control half a dozen such seats; or by 'Nabobs' returning with money from India and seeking to use their wealth to purchase influence; or, amazingly by the standards of later centuries, by the Treasury itself, which would often use several tens of thousands of pounds of the King's money, and some of the taxpayer's, to procure the election of government candidates in a general election.

Pitt set his face against contesting most of these constituencies. He could not afford the expense of fighting one of the truly open boroughs, nor was he well enough known in any of them to have a chance of success. He did not want to be instructed how to vote in Parliament by a patron who had purchased his election, and he was not a supporter of the government. He received tentative offers from his cousins of the old family borough of Old Sarum, which Thomas Pitt had pawned to the Treasury in 1761 as he fled bankruptcy, and of Buckingham, which was in the pocket of Earl Temple. Not only were these offers vague, but he told his mother he was worried that taking them up could not 'be done on a *liberal, Independent* Footing'.[11] For Pitt was even now pursuing the ideal of being different from other politicians. He already combined a radiant intellectual self-confidence with his deep sense of being Chatham's son, and Chatham had cultivated at the high points of his career the notion of detachment and independence from party and patronage (although he had been happy to represent the pocket boroughs of the Duke of Newcastle for many years). Pitt, who was carried along by the demands for economical and parliamentary reform as the answer to the corruption and waste so evident under Lord North, aspired to succeed in politics through 'character' rather than through 'influence'. Steeped in the classical texts which praised the 'virtue' of outstanding figures, he could be forgiven for envisaging his own heroic role as an answer to the corruption of the times and a reinforcement of the traditions of his father. He already knew enough not to be naïve about political methods, and would be happy to let 'influence' be used on his behalf, but throughout his entire career he would seek to maintain the independence and incorruptibility of his own character, and at all costs the appearance of it.

Thus it was idealism as well as familiarity which led him to seek election for Cambridge University. 'It is a seat of all others', he wrote to his mother in July 1779, 'the most desirable, as being free from expense, perfectly independent, and I think in every respect extremely honourable . . . You will perhaps think the idea hastily taken up, when I tell you that six Candidates have declared already; but I assure you that I shall not flatter myself with any vain hopes.'[12]

It is not clear who had encouraged Pitt to have such hopes, for vain they appeared to be for a twenty-year-old up against the long-established candidates of the main political groupings. Writing for support to opposition figures, he received a rather dusty reply from the Marquis of Rockingham: 'I am so circumstanced from the knowledge I have of several persons who may be candidates, and who indeed are expected to be so, that it makes it impossible for me in this instance to show the attention to your wishes which your own as well as the great merits of your family entitle you to.'[13] He also received a rather patronising putdown from the normally helpful Earl Temple: 'As to your prospect of success, I cannot form any opinion . . . How far it may be advisable for you before you have more ripened in your profession to launch out into the great ocean of politicks . . . is a matter of great doubt . . . The memory of your father & the great character you have attained speak forcibly in your favour; but a dead minister, the most respectable that ever existed, weighs very light in the scale against any living one.'[14]

Pitt the young idealist was not put off by this lofty discouragement, and commenced his canvassing.* He busied himself writing to acquaintances around the university, 'I rely on the support of my own College and my musical friends, both which characters, I hope prejudice you in my favour.'[15] But in the event there was to be no election in 1779. In early 1780 Pitt was still sitting in the Gallery of the Commons watching the debates of the same Parliament, the North administration still battling on. His letters exulted in seeing the government defeated several times: 'What the consequence will be, cannot be guessed, but

* The franchise in the universities was based on membership of the University Senate, and was thus possessed only by academics. These constituencies were also unusual in having a secret ballot. The electorate of Cambridge University was a little over seven hundred strong in the early 1780s.

I have no ideas of Ministry being able to stand.'[16] He watched excitedly as Edmund Burke – 'I had no Idea till now of his Excellence'[17] – brought in his sweeping proposals for economical reform, seeking to abolish the special royal jurisdictions in Wales, Cheshire, Lancaster and Cornwall, to reduce the Civil List through which money was provided to the King, and to abolish the offices of Master of the Household, Treasurer, Comptroller, Cofferer, the Board of the Green-Cloth, the Wardrobe Office, the Jewel Office, the Keepers of Stag Hounds, Buck Hounds, Fox Hounds, and many other Crown offices. A Bill was introduced to exclude government contractors from being Members of Parliament, along with the presentation of damning evidence of their greed and inefficiency. At last major reform seemed in the offing.

Yet Pitt also watched as one by one Burke's proposals were watered down and then abandoned, and as the much-vaunted Contractors Bill was crushed in the House of Lords. He watched Lord North take on the chin the famous motion condemning the influence of the Crown, and then render it meaningless by defeating a motion asking the King not to dissolve Parliament until the influence of the Crown at elections had been diminished. Pitt learnt the lesson, one he would not forget as he led a government facing a hostile House of Commons only four years later, that even a government assailed on all sides can tough it out for a time if it sticks together and has the solid support of the King. And he soon learnt a second lesson: a government working with the King could spring a nasty surprise.

Parliament rose in mid-August after a long and exhausting session. No sooner had opposition politicians relaxed into their summer watering holes than, on 1 September, George III agreed to North's request that Parliament be dissolved and an immediate general election announced. With the opposition surprised and disorganised, opinion backing the government against the recent Gordon Riots, and the Treasury's money doing its work in marginal cases, the North administration was confident of broadly maintaining its majority. By now Pitt had secured the support of the Earl of Shelburne, who led a small band of parliamentarians still loyal to the memory of Chatham. He wrote an effusive letter of thanks, saying he was 'truly sensible of this fresh instance of that friendly assistance which our family has eminently experienced from your Lordship'.[18] When the election was called, Pitt rushed to Cambridge, but his contest was hopeless. On 16 September it was announced that he had come bottom of the poll of five candidates, the two seats for Cambridge University being won by a sitting Member who supported the government and a previous runner-up who was a strong follower of Rockingham. Pitt had been squeezed out. He wrote philosophically to his mother:

> Pemb. Hall, Sept. 16 [1780],
> My dear Mother,
> Mansfield and Townshend have run away with the Prize, but my struggle has not been dishonourable.
> I am just going to Cheveley [the seat of the Duke of Rutland] for a day or two, and shall soon return to you for as long as the *law* will permit, which will now be probably the sole object with me. I hope you are all well.
> Your ever dutiful and affectionate
> W. Pitt[19]

It was not an easy autumn for the family. Pitt's sister Hester had never fully recovered from the birth of her third child in February. She died in July. Over the next few years Pitt and his bereaved brother-in-law Lord Mahon would become close friends, but this was a sad time made even worse by the news the following year that the youngest brother, James, had died on naval service in the West Indies at the end of 1780. Pitt wrote to Pretyman: 'I have to regret the loss of a brother who had every thing that was most amiable and promising, every thing that I could love and admire; and I feel the favourite hope of my mind extinguished by this untimely blow. Let me however, assure you, that I am too much tried in affliction not to be able to support myself under it; and that my poor mother and sister, to whom I brought the sad account yesterday, have not suffered in their health, from so severe a shock.'[20]

With the death of Earl Temple the previous year, Pitt's mother had now lost in rapid succession her husband, elder brother, eldest daughter and youngest son. After Hester's death William spent time at Hayes or Burton Pynsent with his mother, and at other times kept up his flow of excited and informative letters. By November 1780 he could report at last that he would be a Member of Parliament. His Cambridge friend Lord Granby had now succeeded his grandfather as Duke of Rutland. Wanting to see Pitt in Parliament as soon as possible, he approached his friend Sir James Lowther, who controlled a number of boroughs in the north of England. As Lowther's cousin William had been returned in the election for both Appleby and Carlisle and chose to sit for the latter, Lowther needed a new Member for Appleby. Such rearrangements in the few months after a general election were entirely customary in the eighteenth century. Lowther had a reputation as a rather dominating patron, but he was prepared to lift any normal conditions for the son of Chatham. Pitt wrote to his mother:

> Lincoln's Inn, Thursday night [November 1780]
>
> My dear Mother,
>
> I can now inform you that I have seen Sir J. Lowther, who has repeated to me the offer He had before made, and in the handsomest manner. Judging from my Father's Principles, He concludes that mine would be agreeable to his own, and on that Ground, to me of all others the most agreeable desires to bring me in. No Kind of Condition was mentioned, but that if ever our Lines of Conduct should become opposite, I should give Him an opportunity of choosing another Person. On such Liberal Terms I could certainly not hesitate to accept the proposal, than which Nothing could be in any respect more agreeable. Appleby is the Place I am to represent, and the Election will be made (probably in a week or Ten days) without my having any trouble, or even visiting my constituents.[21]

The offer from Lowther was liberal enough to provide Pitt with freedom of action unless he completely reversed his political stance. William Pitt, aged twenty-one, was now a Member of Parliament.

4

Brilliant Beginnings

> 'He was the wittiest man I ever knew, and what was quite peculiar to himself, had at all times his wit under entire control.'
>
> WILLIAM WILBERFORCE ON WILLIAM PITT

> 'It is a most accursed, wicked, barbarous, cruel, unnatural, unjust and diabolical war ... Where is the Englishman who on reading the narrative of those bloody and well-fought contests can refrain lamenting the loss of so much British blood shed in such a cause, or from weeping on whatever side victory might be declared?'
>
> WILLIAM PITT, 12 JUNE 1781

WILLIAM PITT WALKED onto the floor of the House of Commons as a Member of Parliament for the first time on 23 January 1781. For around 230 years the Commons had met in St Stephen's Chapel in the Palace of Westminster, with the Speaker's chair placed on the altar steps, and the Members sitting on either side in the tiered choir stalls.* In more recent times the Chapel had been altered to make it more suitable for parliamentary gatherings: a Strangers' Gallery had been added on both sides, supported by columns reaching down among the Members, wooden panelling added throughout, and the lighting improved by enlarging the windows at the end nearest the River Thames and the hanging of large brass chandeliers from a lowered ceiling. There were nowhere near enough places for all the Members

* This is the origin of the layout of the House of Commons to this day, although the current Chamber was built on a different location within the new Palace of Westminster after the fire of 1834, and rebuilt after being bombed in 1941.

to sit, and the result, then as now, was that on major occasions the Chamber had a crowded and intimate atmosphere, easily roused to boisterousness and ribaldry.

The day on which Pitt took his seat was the first time the House had sat since breaking for Christmas in early December 1780. The floor of the House would have been busy, as it was around the end of January each year that Members were required to answer the 'call of the House', an actual rollcall of the Members who could in theory suffer a penalty for failure to attend. Looking around him Pitt would have seen an all-male legislature, younger in its average age than we would expect to see today, with around a hundred Members, more than one in six, being aged under thirty (compared to four Members out of 659 under thirty after the 2001 general election). He would have recognised among the Members a large slice of the youthful aristocracy – sixty-seven sons of peers, often the younger sons, were elected to the Commons in the election of 1780; his father had been right to call the Commons a 'parcel of younger brothers'.[1] Scattered among them he would have seen several dozen senior officers of the army and navy, including General Burgoyne, who had surrendered at Saratoga in the American War of Independence, and the celebrated Admiral Keppel, who had lost his seat but immediately been given another one. He would have seen the legal profession in force, with around eighty trained lawyers on the benches on both sides of the House. It being winter, the country gentlemen would also be in town and taking their seats in large numbers, although most of them would take a great deal of persuading to stay any later than Easter. Some of them would have worked for their financial and political independence by climbing the ladder of government offices and Crown appointments, accepting the advice of Hans Stanley, Ambassador to St Petersburg: 'Get into Parliament, make tiresome speeches, you will have great offers; do not accept them at first; then do; then make great provision for yourself and family, and then call yourself an independent country gentleman.'[2]

As commerce and industry expanded, so did the number of merchants and other businessmen sitting in the House. In this Parliament seventy-two Members were actively engaged in business, many more than twenty years before. A higher proportion than in the past were there as the culmination of their business efforts rather than in order to actually procure trade in Parliament, although about a quarter of them were engaged in government contracts and Treasury loans. Nevertheless, this was primarily an assembly of gentlemen and noblemen. They would not have embraced among their number many representatives of the emerging middle class, and even years later Pitt's great friend George Canning would be sneered at in the Commons for his humble background. But the aristocratic origins of the Members certainly did not mean that the atmosphere in the small debating Chamber was reserved or formal. The German visitor Carl Moritz was 'much shocked by the open abuse which Members of Parliament flung at each other', and complained that 'they enter the House in greatcoats, boots and spurs! It is not unusual to see a Member stretched out on one of the benches while the rest are in debate. One Member may be cracking nuts, another eating an orange or whatever fruit may be in season; they are constantly going in and out .... Whenever one of them speaks badly or the matter of his speech lacks interest for the majority, the noise and laughter are such that the Member can hardly hear his own words.'[3]

The one exception to this disorderly appearance might have been the Treasury bench, the front bench on the Speaker's right. For here sat the Members of His Majesty's Government in court dress, symbolising their proximity to the King and their employment in his service. Pitt took his seat somewhere on the back benches opposite them, sitting naturally enough with the opponents of a government his father had denounced. Most of those seated around him would call themselves Whigs, but Pitt recognised that the party labels of the early eighteenth century now had little meaning. 'I do not wish', he had written two years earlier, 'to call myself any Thing but an Independent Whig which in words is hardly a distinction, as every one alike pretends to it.'[4]

The success of the Whigs in the early eighteenth century had itself contributed to the term losing much of its meaning. The Jacobite cause was dead, and Tories who had the ability or the desire to seek office had called themselves Whigs, much as a Republican in the post-Civil War southern United States would need to call himself a Democrat. George III had said to Pitt's father in 1765: 'You can name no Whig familys that shall not have my Countenance; but where Torys come to me on Whig principles let us take them.'[5] Domestic political divisions had further broken down with the disappearance of the most burning political issue of the mid-eighteenth century, the entanglement of British affairs with those of Hanover. Unlike his grandfather, George III was an utterly English King, who was much less preoccupied with his ancestral country, and only occasionally did he let it complicate his politics.

Most of the MPs had not in any case entered politics in order to pursue a political agenda, quite apart from the fact that it was still frowned upon to come into Parliament or even government with a preconceived notion of what should be done. As Sir Lewis Namier put it in his comprehensive study of eighteenth-century politicians *The Structure of Politics at the Accession of George III*: 'Men went there [the House of Commons] "to make a figure", and no more dreamt of a seat in the House in order to benefit humanity than a child dreams of a birthday cake that others may eat it . . . The seat in the House was not their ultimate goal but a means to ulterior aims.'[6]

Soame Jenyns, the author and Cambridgeshire MP, writing in 1784, said: 'Men . . . get into Parliament, in pursuit of power, honours, and preferments, and till they obtain them, determine to obstruct all business, and distress government. But happily for their Country, they are no sooner gratified, than they are equally zealous to promote the one, and support the other.'[7] Apart from the few such as Pitt who really did go into Parliament in order to be politicians, Namier identified the following as making up the majority of MPs: the 'inevitable Parliament men' who were part of the completely political families such as the Townshends, Cornwallises and Cavendishes; the 'country gentlemen' who sought primacy in their own county; the 'social climbers' who sought peerages; the 'placemen and purveyors of favours' who sought commissionerships and various offices and sinecures; those seeking 'professional advancement' in the army, the navy, the Civil Service or the law; the 'merchants and bankers' who sought government contracts and arranged public loans, particularly in wartime; and occasionally a small number seeking immunity from prosecution or arrest.

We should not be surprised that this was the nature of Parliament in an age when there were no salaries or pensions for MPs, and little concept of meritocratic preferment in the services of the state. The network of patronage which spread out from the Crown and the Ministers on the Treasury bench extended far into positions in every county, regiment and even church. Indeed, the bishops and peers in the House of Lords were generally even more craven than MPs in their susceptibility to such 'influence', since they often hoped for a more lucrative diocese or a step up in the ranks of the peerage.

Any eighteenth-century government could therefore usually rely on a large majority in the House of Lords. The combination of large-scale patronage and a general predisposition among the 'country gentlemen' that the King should be able to get his way, provided he did not directly assault the role and power of the aristocracy, meant that governments usually held the upper hand in the Commons as well. At any one time, about a quarter of the Commons might hold some government office, sinecure or pension. More than a third would regard themselves as entirely independent of any factional party, although some would certainly be open to 'influence' at its most persuasive. On top of that, there would be about twenty MPs whose seats had been directly purchased for them by the Treasury. These various groups tended to coalesce around the leading members of one of the factions chosen by the King to head his ministry. And so it was that Pitt would have looked across the Chamber at the 'King's friends' and the 'country gentlemen' massed behind the complacent-looking figure of Lord North, First Lord of the Treasury for more than a decade.*

Lord North is generally remembered in British history without much respect or affection. Overweight and perhaps overpromoted, he is thought of as an uninspiring figure who carelessly lost the American colonies. He did indeed lack the administrative drive required from the centre of government at a time of war, but he was nevertheless an astute politician and a formidable parliamentarian. Despite his corpulence and tendency to doze off in debates, he could still command the House of Commons by means of powerful speeches and a noted

* Lords could be Members of the House of Commons if they held Irish or Scottish peerages or a courtesy title. Lord North, for instance, was heir to the Earldom of Guilford, and went on to the House of Lords when he succeeded to this title in due course.

sense of humour. During one long speech by George Grenville which reviewed the history of government revenues, North went into a sound sleep, having asked his neighbour to wake him when the speaker reached modern times. When he duly received a nudge, he listened for a moment and then exclaimed, 'Zounds! You have waked me a hundred years too soon.'[8]

North is often thought of as a 'Tory Prime Minister', but he himself would have rejected both labels. True, there were Tories among the 'country gentlemen' who backed him, but these were the remnants of a now meaningless term. As for 'Prime Minister', he had explicitly denied being such a thing, lest he be held even more accountable for the failings of the government of which he was undoubtedly the senior member. Desperate to give up office for at least the last two years, but bound to the King by a mixture of duty and gratitude (George III had paid off his debts of £18,000), he had soldiered on with a war he no longer believed in. Despite experiencing some kind of nervous breakdown, he had maintained his outward good humour and amiability: 'Constant threats of impeachment, fierce attacks upon himself and all his connexions, mingled execration of his measures and scorn of his capacity, bitter hatred of his person . . . seemed to have no effect on his habitually placid deportment, nor to consume his endless patience.'[9]

Lord North governed with the support of a small band of his own followers, along with the factions commanded by Lord Sandwich and Lord Gower, as well as the ever-helpful friends of the King. Alongside him on the front bench in the Commons Pitt would have seen Lord George Germain, Secretary of State for the Colonies, who had borne the brunt of directing the war and was even now hoping that the thrust into the southern colonies by Lord Cornwallis and his troops would finally defeat George Washington. Elsewhere on the Treasury bench would be Henry Dundas, the Lord Advocate for Scotland, who had begun developing an iron grip on the forty-five Scottish seats and was now a leading spokesman of the government in the Commons, albeit one who doubted that the government's remaining life would be very long. Altogether, North could rely on around eighty MPs from his own and allied factions along with 140 'King's friends', so he needed the support of about fifty of the more than two hundred independents in order to win a majority in a full House.[10]

Facing North's Ministers and sitting on the front bench of the opposition side of the House was Charles James Fox. Fox, thirty-two years old the next day and son of the politician Henry Fox, who had become Lord Holland, was considered the most eloquent debater in Parliament. Brilliant, generous, impulsive, emotional and hugely persuasive, he was an unceasing opponent of North and the war. The King hated and mistrusted him, and the feeling was mutual. Fox was inconsistent, unpredictable, a chronic gambler and a relentless womaniser, but his friends adored him and his hold over his followers was powerful. His colourful private life – he would shortly commence an affair with Georgiana, Duchess of Devonshire – would undoubtedly damage his political prospects. One critical MP noted that it was not possible to 'trace in any one action of his life anything that had not for its object his own gratification'.[11] He and his brother were said to have lost £32,000 in a single night of gambling, and when he was not betting at Brooks's he was doing so at the races. Horace Walpole, son of the longest-serving Prime Minister Robert Walpole, and writer of extensive but biased political memoirs, recalled him as 'the hero in Parliament, at the gaming table, at Newmarket. Last week he passed four-and-twenty hours without interruption at all three, or on the road from one to the other; and ill the whole time.'[12] In a life which from this point on would be increasingly intertwined with that of Pitt, Fox would stand out as his opposite in almost every personal respect: a rounded figure who enjoyed social gatherings, cultivated a party following, revelled in all the pleasures of the senses and in no way regarded political success as the sole object of his life. He would become Pitt's arch-rival, and would eventually consider that he had only one thing in common with him: 'The only thing like good about him is his inattention to money.'[13] But for the moment he would attempt to draw Pitt into his circle, and he would do so as a dominant figure in the opposition, enjoying the devoted support of a wide circle of friends who considered that, in the words of Gibbon, 'perhaps no human being was ever more perfectly exempt from the taint of malevolence, vanity or falsehood'.[14]

Fox was the spokesman and inspiration of the Rockingham Whigs. Near him would have been Edmund Burke, secretary to Lord Rockingham, another figure of immense eloquence and persecutor of the King's Ministers. Self-righteous and impassioned, he was driven on by his belief that the power and habits of George III were destroying the balance of the settlement of 1688. Around and behind Fox and Burke sat much the largest opposition grouping, comprising seventy to eighty Members.

Elsewhere on the opposition benches were the leaders of another but much smaller opposition faction, less than ten in number: John Dunning, who the previous year had successfully proposed the motion calling for a reduction in the powers of the Crown, and Colonel Barré, famed for accompanying General Wolfe in the storming of the cliffs at Quebec. The leaders of their grouping were the Earl of Shelburne and Lord Camden, who, like Rockingham, sat in the House of Lords. This grouping were the heirs of Chatham – Shelburne and Camden having served in his last government – and they were now joined in the new Parliament by Lord Mahon, John Pratt and, inevitably, William Pitt. As a new MP Pitt therefore looked to the Earl of Shelburne as his nominal leader. Shelburne was, after all, one of the few people who had encouraged Pitt in his bid for election at Cambridge the previous year. Intellectually brilliant, well informed about the full range of political and economic issues, and an enthusiastic exponent of the mix of economic liberalism and administrative improvements which Pitt would strongly support, Shelburne was nevertheless handicapped by what others saw as deficiencies of character. He could not resist displaying his brilliance and allowing others to see that he was manipulating them: 'He flattered people in order to gain them, and he let it appear by his actions that his smooth words were sheer hypocrisy.'[15] For the moment, however, he headed the small group of Chathamite loyalists.

These factions in Parliament manoeuvred for position and waited on events, but the politician who still mattered the most in the kingdom was George III himself. The King was a man of simple and straightforward views. The constitution must be upheld, which meant the rights of the Crown must be asserted. His coronation oath was inviolate. No politician should be trusted. No colonies could be surrendered in case others, including Ireland, rebelled. A good life required a regular diet, a huge amount of exercise, and marital fidelity. The Royal Family should set an example. His son, the Prince of Wales, was incapable of setting an example and had become a total disgrace. Disappointed by Bute, who had failed him, by George Grenville, who had lectured him, and by Chatham, who had let him down, George III had at last found in Lord North a politician with the pleasing combination of political staying power and a propensity to be bullied by his monarch. There was no question but that the policies carried out by North and his colleagues were the King's policies, and that detailed decisions about political and military appointments and the approach to the war had been made by the King himself. When the opposition in Parliament attacked the policies of North, they were in fact attacking the actions of the King; the assaults of Burke on Crown appointments and the Civil List were another proxy for doing so.

The King was desperately worried that the war would end in defeat, and even spoke privately of abdicating rather than bearing the humiliation of himself and his kingdom. Not least among his concerns was that defeat in the war would mean the fall of North. The only other group of leaders in Parliament with widespread support were the Rockingham Whigs, to whom he could be forced to turn. That could mean being forced to accept Ministers he disliked intensely, and measures he would hate to see carried out in his name. Such Ministers would impose peace with America, abolish much of his patronage, and insist on having as junior Ministers some of his strongest opponents whom they would wish to reward. In contemplating these questions, George III was having to face up to some of the problems left unresolved by the 'perfect' constitutional arrangements resulting from 1688. The King had the right to choose a government, and the Commons the right to hold that government to account and even overturn it, requiring the King to nominate another. But what happened if a majority of the Commons decided to force a particular government upon the King? Rockingham and Fox intended to do so. George III would hate it. There was no answer written down in the settlement of 1688. The King still controlled many appointments and sinecures throughout the country, including Army appointments. What happened if the Commons insisted on taking all of those powers of appointment for itself? The King normally retained the right to choose particular Ministers and to continue some from one government to the next, even when the leading Minister changed. What happened if a new leading Minister came to him with a list of Ministers already decided and a majority of the House of Commons behind him?

George III was a wily political operator, and was determined not to show the weakness of his grandfather George II. The Duke of Newcastle had once forced George II into a corner in 1746 by presenting the collective resignation of all senior Ministers; when George III heard that he might try the same thing in 1762 he had fired him before he could open his mouth.

As 1781 opened, these political and constitutional questions hung in the balance. The war had gone a little better over the previous year, and the election had been satisfactorily concluded. The opposition seemed to have run out of steam and now, according to one of its members, was 'if not dead at least asleep'.[16] This was the political scene as William Pitt considered how to make his maiden speech.

A maiden speech in the House of Commons, then as now, was usually a rather humble affair. A Member would prepare for it for days, or even weeks, and would then rise nervously to advance a not too controversial proposition and accompany it with many thanks and pleasantries. Pitt's maiden speech, delivered on 26 February 1781, was the exact opposite: delivered apparently on the spur of the moment and certainly without a note, radiating confidence despite taking place in a packed House debating a crucial motion, advancing a strong argument against the policies of the government and the Crown, and incidentally demolishing a key point of the previous speaker's argument. The effect was to make him a major figure in the House of Commons from the very beginning of his career in it.

The occasion of Pitt's speech was a major debate on Edmund Burke's renewed attempt to introduce economical reform. Uncertain of the government's majority, North had not prevented Burke from reintroducing his proposed legislation, but with the government's confidence growing by late February Ministers determined upon voting the Bill down at its second reading on 26 February. In the fierce debate which ensued, Lord Nugent had just finished speaking against the Bill and in defence of the government when opposition Members cried out 'Mr. Pitt! Mr. Pitt!', trying to get him to speak. Some historians have taken the view that this was merely spontaneous impatience from some Members who thought that Pitt had been in the House for more than a month and ought now to take a speaking role. Stanhope's account, in which the Middlesex MP George Byng asks Pitt during Nugent's speech whether he will reply to it, receives an uncertain reply, and then spreads the word to other Members that Pitt is about to rise even though he has now resolved not to, seems a more likely explanation.[17] Since this was a subject dear to Pitt's heart and he had been sitting through the debate for some time, it is fair to assume that he had a good idea about what he would say in a speech, even if he had not committed himself to making one. Members who thought they were listening to an entirely unplanned performance were therefore probably under a misapprehension, but it was one that added to the awesome impression that this new parliamentary orator now made on them.

Pitt's speech was clear, logical and consistent with his known views. The government, he said, should have come forward itself with reductions in the Civil List, rather than the opposition have to bring the matter up:

> They ought to have consulted the glory of their Royal Master, and have seated him in the hearts of his people, by abating from magnificence what was due to necessity. Instead of waiting for the slow request of a burdened people, they should have courted popularity by a voluntary surrender of useless revenue . . . It would be no diminution of true grandeur to yield to the respectful petitions of the people . . . magnificence and grandeur were not consistent with entrenchment and economy, but, on the contrary, in a time of necessity and of common exertion, solid grandeur was dependent on the reduction of expense.

The House was riveted. Pitt then pointed out that Lord Nugent had said he would have been happy to support the Bill if the reduction in Crown expenditure it called for was to be given to the 'public service' instead, in which case he would have become one of its warmest advocates. Nugent had told the House there was no such provision in the Bill, and therefore he opposed it. He was now to be briskly swatted in a manner that became entirely familiar to Members of Parliament over the next twenty-five years. Pitt said that the only merit he could claim in a competition with the noble Lord was that his eyes were somewhat younger than his. He could therefore read the clause in the Bill which demonstrated the exact opposite of what Lord Nugent had suggested. Pitt read out the whole of the relevant clause, and went on to read out another which had caused Nugent's confusion. Having fitted this unanswerable point into his general argument, he then argued that the Bill should be supported because it would reduce the influence of the Crown. He attacked the idea that the £200,000 that would be saved was too insignificant a sum to bother with. 'This was surely the most singular and unaccountable species of reasoning that was ever attempted in any assembly. The calamities of the crisis were too great to be benefited by economy! Our expenses were so enormous, that it was ridiculous to attend to little matters of account! We have spent so many millions, that thousands are beneath our consideration! We were obliged to spend so much, that it was foolish to think of saving any!' Finally, he said that 'it ought to be remembered, that the Civil List revenue was granted by Parliament to His Majesty for other purposes than those of personal gratification. It was granted to support the power and the interests of the Empire, to maintain its grandeur, to pay the judges and the foreign ministers, to maintain justice and to support respect; to pay the great offices that were necessary to the lustre of the Crown; and it was proportioned to the dignity and the opulence of the people.' He said he considered the Bill essential to the being and the independence of his country, and he would give it the most determined support.

Pitt's speech did not win the debate. Sufficient of the independents and country gentlemen rallied to Lord North to allow him to defeat Burke's Bill by 233 votes to 190. But there is no doubt that the speech catapulted Pitt into the front rank of parliamentary orators. It was the evidence that, although still only twenty-one years old, he had entered the Commons fully formed as a politician and debater, able to marshal an argument and engage in a debate on equal terms with Members two and three times his age. It was the first exposure of other politicians to the speaking style which had resulted from the years of rehearsing and reciting with Chatham and Pretyman: structured, logical and controlled. In recent years Fox had been idolised as the greatest of parliamentary orators, with Pitt himself later referring to him wielding 'the wand of the magician',[18] but Pitt's style was in complete contrast to that of Fox. Fox's style was to embrace his hearers with emotions, his speeches charging back and forth repeatedly but returning again and again to the point on which he hoped to stir his hearers to action. Pitt's style was to encircle his listeners with logic, building up his argument piece by piece in a structure always clear in his mind, and forsaking emotion for the objective of leaving his audience with no intellectual option but to agree with his final unifying conclusion. One observer recalled: 'Mr. Fox had a captivating earnestness of tone and manner; Mr. Pitt was more dignified than earnest . . . It was an observation of the reporters in the gallery that it required great exertion to follow Mr. Fox while he was speaking, none to remember what he had said; that it was easy and delightful to follow Mr. Pitt, not so easy to recollect what had delighted them.'[19]

Pitt's compelling power of argument was one reason his maiden speech made such an impression. Perhaps a still greater reason was his manner, confidence and voice. The great parliamentary diarist Sir Nathaniel Wraxall commented:

> Sanguine as might be the opinions entertained of his ability, he far exceeded them; seeming to obtain at his outset that object which other candidates for public fame or favour slowly and laboriously effect by length of time and regular gradation . . . It was in reply to Lord Nugent that Pitt first broke silence from under the gallery on the Opposition side of the House. The same composure, self possession, and imposing dignity of manner which afterwards so eminently characterised him when seated on the Treasury Bench distinguished him in this first essay

> of his powers, though he then wanted three months to have completed his twenty second year. The same nervous, correct, and polished diction, free from any inaccuracy of language or embarrassment of deportment, which, as First Minister, he subsequently displayed, were equally manifested by him on this occasion. Formed for a popular assembly, he seemed made to guide its deliberations from the first moment that he addressed the Members composing it.

Pitt's speech, he said, 'impressed more from the judgement, the diction, and the solemnity that pervaded and characterised it, than from the brilliancy or superiority of the matter . . . He seemed to possess himself as much as though he had pronounced the speech in his own closet; but there was no display of studied or classic images in any part of it; nothing gaudy, superfluous, or unnecessary.'[20]

Ministers and opposition leaders were unanimous and generous in their praise. Lord North declared it 'the best *first* speech he ever heard'.[21] Burke exclaimed that Pitt 'was not merely a chip off the old "block", but the old block itself'.[22] Above all, Charles James Fox appeared to be ecstatic at the emergence of such an eloquent figure on the opposition side of the House. Horace Walpole reported:

> Mr. Pitt's first speech, brilliant and wonderful as it was, was scarcely more remarkable than the warmth and generosity with which Mr. Fox greeted the appearance and extolled the performance of his future rival. Incapable of jealousy, and delighted at the sudden display of talents nearly equal to his own, he hurried up to the young Member to compliment and encourage him. As he was doing so, an old Member of the House (I think a General Grant) passed by them and said, 'Aye, Mr. Fox, you are praising young Pitt for his speech. You may well do so; for, excepting yourself, there's no man in the House can make such another; and, old as I am, I expect and hope to hear you both battling it within these walls as I have done your fathers before you.' Mr. Fox, disconcerted at the awkward turn of the compliment, was silent and looked foolish; but young Pitt, with great delicacy, readiness, and felicity of expression, answered, 'I have no doubt, General, you would like to attain the age of Methusaleh [sic].'[23]

Pitt knew that his maiden speech had been a success, and when he wrote to his mother the next day his pleasure in it was only just under the control of his usual modesty:

> I know you will have learnt that I heard my own Voice yesterday; and the Account you have had would be in all respects better than any I can give if it had not come from too partial a Friend. All I can say is that I was able to execute in some measure what I intended, and that I have at least every reason to be happy beyond measure in the reception I met with. You will, I dare say, wish to know more particulars than I fear I shall be able to tell you, but in the meantime you will, I am sure, feel somewhat the same Pleasure that I do in the encouragement, however unmerited, which has attended this first Attempt.[24]

Fortunately the younger Pitt's parliamentary speeches are more extensively recorded than those of his father. The reporting of parliamentary proceedings was forbidden earlier in the eighteenth century, but in 1771 this rule had been shown to be unenforceable after the City of London magistrates proposed only nominal fines on several writers who had been in the Public Gallery and written accounts in the newspapers. By the time of Pitt's entry to Parliament the reporting of speeches was therefore in effect allowed, but no provision was made for the reporters, who had to compete with everyone else to get into the Gallery and then strain to hear above the noise. Unless the account was supported by a text issued by the speaker, something only furnished by Pitt three times in twenty-five years, the reports were often unreliable, incomplete, or biased. Nevertheless we know most of the content of Pitt's speeches, including the two interventions he made in debates before the House rose for the 1781 summer recess. His speeches of 31 May and 12 June followed up the success of his maiden speech and confirmed, albeit in a thinner House, the impression he had already made. On the first occasion, the debate was about a government Bill to appoint Commissioners of Public Accounts. Fox and Pitt rose to speak simultaneously when Lord North sat down, and Fox, who at this stage was going to any lengths to draw Pitt into his circle of friends, gave way for Pitt to speak. Once again he made a forceful argument, telling the Commons that it alone had the right to hold the strings of the national purse, and 'to delegate this right . . . is a violation of what gives them their chief consequence in the legislature, and what, above all other privileges, they cannot surrender or delegate without a violent breach of the constitution'. And once again he showed a mastery of detail, as Horace Walpole recounted: 'the Young William Pitt has again displayed paternal oratory. The other day, on the commission of accounts, he answered Lord North, and tore him limb from limb. If Charles Fox could feel, one should think such a rival, with an unspotted character, would rouse him. What if a Pitt and Fox should again be rivals . . .'[25] William Wilberforce thought the same, as he wrote to a friend in Hull: 'The papers will have informed you how Mr. William Pitt, second son of the late Lord Chatham, has distinguished himself. He comes out as his father did, a ready made orator, and I doubt not but I shall one day or other see him the first man in the country. His famous speech, however, delivered the other night did not convince me, and I stayed in with the old fat fellow [Lord North].'

Pitt's other speech of the summer does genuinely seem to have been unpremeditated. Fox had moved a motion for the conclusion of immediate peace with the Americans, and in the ensuing debate two Members claimed that Chatham had really been in sympathy with the war. Pitt was provoked to intervene with a speech of his own, and Wraxall recorded what happened:

> Pitt attempted to justify and explain that line of opinion attributed to his noble relation . . . he denied that his father had ever approved of the war commenced with America which, on the contrary, he had condemned, reprobated, and opposed in every stage. After thus throwing a shield over the memory of his illustrious parent, and rescuing him from the imputation of having countenanced or supported coercive measures for the subjugation of the colonies beyond the Atlantic, he then diverged with equal vehemence and majesty of expression to the topic immediately before the assembly. Referring to the epithet of *holy* which Lord Westcote had given to the contest, he declared that he considered it as unnatural, accursed, and unjust, its traces marked with persecution and devastation, depravity and turpitude constituting its

> essence, while its effects would be destructive in the extreme. The English language seemed inadequate fully to express his feelings of indignation and abhorrence, while stigmatising the authors of so ruinous a system. As a specimen of parliamentary eloquence, it unquestionably excelled his two preceding speeches, leaving on his audience a deep impression, or rather conviction, that he must eventually, and probably at no remote distance of time, occupy a high situation in the councils of the Crown, as well as in the universal estimation of his countrymen.
>
> Dundas, who rose as soon as Pitt sat down, seemed to be thoroughly penetrated with that truth, and by a sort of a political second sight appeared to anticipate the period when this new candidate for office would occupy the place on the Treasury bench then filled by his noble friend in the blue ribband [Lord North].[26]

Dundas indeed, while as usual that night defending both his colleagues and the war, was coming to have great respect for the eloquent young figure on the opposition benches. He wound up the debate without creating any animosity between himself and Pitt, and went out of his way to compliment him on 'so happy an union of first-rate abilities, high integrity, bold and honest independence of conduct, and the most persuasive eloquence'.[27] The foundations of a formidable alliance were being laid.

At the end of the debate the government won the vote by 172 to ninety-nine. It was indicative of how the political atmosphere had improved for the North administration as the year had gone on. Government optimism about the war was high, with Lord George Germain writing on 7 March: 'So very contemptible is the rebel force now in all parts, and so vast is our superiority everywhere, that no resistance on their part is to be apprehended that can materially obstruct the progress of the King's arms in the speedy suppression of the rebellion.'[28] North was back in control of the Commons, with his majorities increasing through the spring and summer as the independents went home and the opposition was able to rely only on its most partisan supporters.

Pitt's attacks had not brought down the government – far from it – but they had impressively launched his own career. As well as enjoying himself in the Commons at this time, his social life was busy and fun. He became a member of Brooks's Club in February 1781 after being proposed by an eager Charles James Fox, but he kept his distance and characteristically preferred the company of a small circle of intimate friends. He became a member of Goostree's, a small club on Pall Mall which in 1780 was effectively taken over by Pitt and some of his friends. The old friends from Cambridge were there, Pratt, Bankes, Euston and Edward Eliot, along with Pitt's elder brother and his cousin William Grenville. But there were also new friends: Richard Pepper Arden, who would later serve in Pitt's governments; Robert Smith, whom he would send to the Lords as the first Lord Carrington; Thomas Steele; and William Wilberforce, the wealthy son of a banker who owned an estate in Yorkshire and had just spent a small fortune ensuring his own election for Hull. Wilberforce adored Pitt's company:

> He was the wittiest man I ever knew, and what was quite peculiar to himself, had at all times his wit under entire control. Others appeared struck by the unwonted association of brilliant images; but every possible combination of ideas seemed present to his mind, and he could at once produce whatever he desired. I was one of those who met to spend an evening in memory of Shakespeare at the Boar's Head, East Cheap. Many professed wits were present, but Pitt was the most amusing of the party, and the readiest and most apt in the required allusions.[29]

At Goostree's the young friends drank and discussed politics, in effect moving the familiar dining atmosphere of Cambridge into Pall Mall. This was already Pitt's favourite way of spending an evening, and it would remain so throughout his life, but, as ever, he had a clear sense of what he must not get drawn into. Gambling was highly fashionable, and Wilberforce was wealthy enough to indulge in it with gusto. Pitt lacked wealth, but not self-discipline. Wilberforce noted: 'We played a good deal at Goostree's, and I well remember the intense earnestness which Pitt displayed when joining in those games of chance. He perceived their increasing fascination, and soon after suddenly abandoned them forever.'

When Parliament rose for the summer Pitt returned to his legal practice on the Western Circuit to earn a little money. At the end of August he wrote to William Meeke: 'I have this circuit amassed the immense sum of thirty guineas without the least expense either of sense or knowledge . . . I shall return to town with the fullest intention of devoting myself to Westminster Hall and getting as much money as I can, notwithstanding such avocations as the House of Commons, and (which is a much more dangerous one) Goostree's itself. Adieu.' It is not surprising that he expected for some time to be practising as a lawyer while occasionally speaking in the House of Commons against a government that had once again recovered its poise and seemed destined to continue in office. Yet even as he wrote, more than three thousand miles away in the marshes and woodlands of Virginia, George Washington's troops were closing in on a trapped British army. The outcome would shatter the hopes of the King and his Ministers and begin more than two years of political convulsions. It would be a time of crisis which would only be ended by the rise to power of Pitt himself.

5

Death of Two Governments

'The enemy carried two advanced redoubts by storm . . . my situation now becomes very critical; we dare not show a gun to their old batteries, and I expect that their new ones will open tomorrow morning . . . the safety of the place is therefore so precarious that I cannot recommend that the fleet and army should run great risque in endeavouring to save us.'

LORD CORNWALLIS, 15 OCTOBER 1781

'Those persons who have for some time conducted the public affairs are no longer His Majesty's Ministers.'

LORD NORTH, 20 MARCH 1782

MUCH OF THE FIGHTING between British troops and American colonists had been concentrated in and around the northern American states, but at the end of 1779 the British Commander-in-Chief, Sir Henry Clinton, had embarked on a new strategy. By launching a sudden offensive in the Deep South, the British would take the Americans by surprise, encourage what was believed to be a large number of colonists in that area still loyal to the Crown, and do so before further French reinforcements could arrive in the course of 1780. Landing in the Carolinas with 7,600 men early in the new year, Clinton accomplished his initial objectives. With the capture of Charleston after a protracted siege in May, he dealt a heavy blow to the rebels. In the summer he returned to his principal base in New York, leaving four thousand British troops in the south under the command of Lord Cornwallis, a rival general with whom Clinton's relations were severely strained.

For much of the next year, the American war seemed to have sunk into stalemate. Where fighting took place, the British were generally the technical victors, but this rarely improved their ability to hold on to territory, since lines of communication were so difficult; neither did it bring the war any nearer to a conclusion, as most of the population remained hostile. The operations conducted by Cornwallis in the south were a good example of this. A full year of manoeuvring and skirmishes culminated in the Battle of Guilford Courthouse in North Carolina in March 1781, where Cornwallis inflicted severe losses on the Americans but his own army was left too weak to follow up the advantage. The American General he defeated, Nathanael Greene, commented, 'We fight, get beat, rise, and fight again.'

Complacency and confusion brought the ruin of British strategy in the summer of 1781. Clinton was afraid that the Americans under George Washington and the French forces under Lafayette would combine against him in New York. As a result he was unwilling to send any reinforcements to Cornwallis, and sometimes asked for troops to be sent back. In addition, Clinton believed, on the basis of intelligence reports, that 1781 would be the last year in which France would make any serious effort to help the Americans, and that consequently there was a good deal to be said for simply sitting tight. The summer passed with confusing and bad-tempered messages being sent back and forth between Clinton and Cornwallis: the confusion was compounded not only by Clinton's uncertain instructions to his subordinate, but also by his messages sometimes arriving in the wrong order.

Clinton's caution was to lead to catastrophe. Washington and Lafayette were not combining against him in the north-east, but against Cornwallis as he marched north through Virginia, and their decision to do so would bring them final victory in the war. At the beginning of October 1781, as he fortified the town of Yorktown on Chesapeake Bay, Cornwallis had fewer than nine thousand troops to face at least 16,000 French and Americans. Within days his position was desperate, and on 15 October he wrote to Clinton: 'the safety of the place is therefore so precarious that I cannot recommend that the fleet and army should run great risque in endeavouring to save us'.[1] Clinton now realised the gravity of the position: 'I see this in so serious a light that I dare not look at it'.

On 17 October Clinton belatedly set sail from New York with a fleet and a small army to relieve the siege of Yorktown. Five days later they arrived at the approaches to Chesapeake Bay, where they came across a small boat carrying three people who told them that the battle was already over. On the very day that the relieving force had left New York, Cornwallis had surrendered. The ships turned round and headed back to New York. The war was lost.[2]

Across the Atlantic, Members of Parliament had no inkling that the war was approaching its climax. After spending the summer on the Western Circuit Pitt passed some weeks with his mother at Burton Pynsent, where the visitors included Pretyman. A letter to his mother written from Dorset gives us some insight into his life at the time, and a reminder of his dislike of society parties:

> Kingston Hall, Oct. 7, 1781.
> My Dear Mother
> I have delayed writing to you longer than I intended, which I hope is of little Consequence, as Harriot will have brought you all the News I could have sent – an account of that stupid Fête at Fonthill,* which, take it all together, was, I think, as ill imagined, and as indifferently conducted, as anything of the sort need be . . . By meeting Lord Shelburne and Lord Camden, We were pressed to make a second Visit to Bowood, which, from the addition of Colonel Barré and Mr. Dunning, was a very pleasant party. – Since that Time I have been waging war, with increasing success, on Pheasants and Partridges – I shall continue Hostilities, I believe, about a week longer, and then prepare for the opening of another sort of campaign in Westminster Hall. Parliament, I am very glad to hear, is not to meet till the 27th of Novr, which will allow me a good deal more leisure than I expected.[3]

* The seat of William Beckford, the rich, eccentric and flamboyant son of the late William Beckford, who had been Lord Mayor of London and an ally of Chatham.

Pitt's reference to a 'campaign' in Westminster Hall meant that he was intending to do further legal work in the courts there that autumn. The visit to Bowood was for a meeting of the small Chathamite party, which continued to maintain a separate identity from the main opposition grouping of Rockingham and Fox, and was now planning for the session ahead. They were not exactly in high spirits about it, as Lord Camden's letter of 8 November to Thomas Walpole shows: 'You may be anxious to know whether I shall take any part in the House. I protest I do not know. Our opposition is scattered and runs wild in both houses under no leader. God knows how all this will end.'[4] Although Cornwallis had surrendered three weeks earlier, news of this had not yet arrived in London. The government circulated its supporters with a routine request to attend the autumn session, and the opposition made little effort to mobilise its supporters, being unaware of any new opportunity.

It was on the morning of Sunday, 25 November 1781, only two days before the opening of Parliament, that the first news of the defeat at Yorktown arrived in London, by means of a messenger sent from Falmouth to Lord George Germain's house in Pall Mall. Lord George got into a hackney coach, collected two other Ministers, and proceeded to take the news to Lord North at 10 Downing Street. North was said to have reacted 'as he would have taken a ball in his breast . . . he opened his arms, exclaiming wildly, as he paced up and down the apartment during a few minutes, "O God! it is all over!" Words which he repeated many times under emotions of the deepest consternation and distress.'[5]

Sure enough, Yorktown would bring the fall of the North government, but it did not do so immediately. The King's reaction to the news was characteristically unyielding: 'I trust that neither Lord George Germain nor any member of the Cabinet will suppose that it makes the smallest alteration in those principles of my conduct which have directed me in past time and which will always continue to animate me under every event in the prosecution of the present contest.'[6]

Ministers were more despondent, but played for time by announcing that the war would go on, although offensive operations would no longer be conducted. The opposition, unprepared for the calamity, lacked the numbers to turn out the Ministers, but mobilised its supporters as quickly as it could. The administration beat off the initial opposition onslaught on 12 December by forty-one votes (220 to 179), but with increasing signs of divisions among Ministers about the future of the war.

Pitt was at the forefront of the efforts to expose ministerial disunity and uncertainty, and in these weeks proved himself a formidable parliamentary operator. He rose to speak on the second day of the session, and Wraxall described the scene:

> In a speech of extraordinary energy (throughout the course of which he contrived with great ability to blend professions of devoted attachment to the person of the King with the severest accusation of his Ministers), he fully confirmed the high opinion of his judgement and parliamentary talents already entertained throughout the country . . . He concluded by calling on Ministers to state without circumlocution or deception what were their intentions as to the further prosecution of the American war, and to give some general idea of the manner in which it was henceforward to be pursued. A sort of pause took place when he resumed his seat, while the eyes of all present were directed towards the Treasury bench . . .[7]

With North and Germain declining to answer Pitt directly, Dundas took to his feet. He insisted that the war would not necessarily be continued, and implied disagreement in the Cabinet, all of which gave Pitt a great debating victory.

On 14 December Pitt was again on his feet denouncing the incapacity of Ministers when he spotted a three-way conversation taking place on the government benches between Lord George Germain, who remained what would now be called a hawk on continuing the war, Lord North, who had become decidedly dovish, and a third Minister, Welbore Ellis. Pitt paused in his speech and, drawing a parallel with the Greek characters of the Trojan War, said: 'I shall wait till the unanimity is better settled, and until the sage Nestor of the Treasury Bench has brought to an agreement the Agamemnon and the Achilles of the American War.' In the light of all we know about Pitt's education, it may be no surprise that he could easily make a spontaneous classical allusion, but it came as an impressive revelation to the House of Commons. In Wraxall's words once again, 'its effect was electric, not only on the individuals to whom it was personally directed, but on the whole audience. The two Ministers and the Treasurer of the Navy in some confusion resumed their former attitudes. We cannot sufficiently appreciate or admire the perfect self-possession which, while addressing a crowded House of Commons, could dictate to a youth of little more than two-and-twenty so masterly an allusion. The conclusion of his speech breathed not a little of the spirit of his deceased father, while he seemed to launch the vengeance or the indignation of a suffering and exhausted nation on the heads of Ministers.'[8]

Pitt's parliamentary reputation was now reaching the stratosphere. Horace Walpole wrote of the same speech: 'Another remarkable day; the army was to be voted. William Pitt took to pieces Lord North's pretended declarations and exposed them with the most amazing logical abilities, exceeding all the abilities he had already shown and making men doubt whether he would not prove superior even to Charles Fox.'[9] Fox nonetheless remained a generous colleague on the opposition benches, referring to Pitt as his 'Honourable Friend' and saying, as the MP Sir Samuel Romilly recorded in his memoirs, 'in an exaggerated strain of panegyric . . . he could no longer lament the loss of Lord Chatham, for he was again living in his son, with all his virtues and all his talents . . . He is likely soon to take precedence of all our orators.'[10]

By now North had come to the conclusion that peace must be made irrespective of the consequences, and Germain was increasingly isolated in the Cabinet. Even so, the view of the majority of Ministers was not put into effect because they were unwilling to impose their views on an intransigent King. Dundas pressed for the removal of Germain from the Cabinet, along with Lord Sandwich, First Lord of the Admiralty, in order to reunite the government and remove the opposition's most attractive targets. As ever, North prevaricated. Eventually, when the House returned from its Christmas recess on 21 January 1782, his hand was forced by Dundas and the Paymaster General, Richard Rigby. They declared that they would not attend the

House of Commons so long as Germain remained in office, a threat sufficiently potent, given the influence of Dundas over the Scottish seats, to bring down the government.[11] By the end of January it was announced that Germain would be leaving the government and going to the Lords as Lord Sackville.

The departure of Germain was not accompanied by any change or clarification of policy, and the opposition, predictably, was now beginning to throw everything in its armoury at Sandwich. North had only staved off the collapse of his administration rather than rescued it. The government was tottering to its doom. The Commons was thronged with Members ready for the annual 'call of the House' and the opposition was fully mobilised. Most important of all, those independents and county Members who had supported North began to peel away. Pitt enjoyed himself to the full, speaking regularly against the government, performing the role for which he had been trained in the environment to which he was most suited. Yet even in the thick of these battles he took great care to mark himself out as a different type of politician, free of any base or corruptible motives, and always at a safe distance from the main party groupings.

While joining in the opposition onslaught on Lord Sandwich on 24 January, Pitt said, according to Pretyman, that he 'supported the motion from motives of a public nature, and from those motives only. He was too young to be supposed capable of entertaining any personal enmity against the earl of Sandwich; and he trusted that when he should be less young it would appear that he had early determined, in the most solemn manner, never to suffer any private or personal consideration whatever to influence his public conduct at any one moment of his life.'[12] Such a statement by a young Member, carrying as it does the implication of a long future career, would in today's House of Commons be regarded as unbelievably pompous and pretentious. Coming as it did from Pitt, the son of Chatham and already one of the foremost debaters of the House, Members seem to have taken it in their stride. It marks a major difference in attitude between Pitt and his future rival Fox. Pitt's statement of 24 January is something that Fox, who was often motivated by personal friendships above political consistency, is most unlikely ever to have said. While the two men applied themselves energetically to bringing the government to its knees in the early weeks of 1782, it would have been apparent to a shrewd observer that not only the style but also the content of their speeches was subtly different. Wraxall noted that 'no man who attentively considered the different spirit which animated their speeches whenever the sovereign became indirectly the subject of their animadversion could fail to remark their widely dissimilar line of conduct'.[13] Fox, who the previous year had privately described the King as a 'blockhead',[14] 'designated or characterised him [the King], in fact, as under the dominion of resentment, unfeeling, implacable, and only satiated by the continuance of war against his former subjects . . . more as a tyrant and an oppressor than as . . . the guardian of a limited constitution'.[15] Pitt, by contrast, 'repressed any intemperate expressions and personally spared the Sovereign. He separated the King from his weak or evil counsellors; admitted the purity of intention by which he was ever impelled; professed ardent attachment to the person as well as to the family of the reigning Monarch and declared that it would be best manifested by exposing the delusion that had been practised on him.' In this respect, of course, it was Fox rather than Pitt who was unusual. For an opposition politician to burn his boats so completely with the monarch was clearly foolhardy, but Fox was given to impulses and had decided that in any case he would soon be able to force himself into office. Pitt, still at the start of his career, was playing a longer game, and the content of these speeches was the first sign that he was both more calculating and more consistently ambitious than his future rival. In addition, while Pitt had learnt from his father to be suspicious and wary of the King, he had also acquired at his father's knee a healthy contempt for the great Whig magnates such as Rockingham, with whom Fox was in close alliance. While Pitt believed that the corrupting influence of the Crown had grown too extensive, he also knew that it would not be consistent with maintaining a balanced constitution to put the King's most essential powers into the hands of the Whig aristocracy.

These fundamental differences in temperament and outlook would do much to account for the total breach between Pitt and Fox which was now not far away, but for the moment they joined in pouring their verbal firepower into the stricken vessel which the North administration had become. On 27 February, with the county Members voting overwhelmingly against North, the government was defeated by nineteen votes (234 to 215) in a packed House on a motion which called for the end of the war in America. Desperate consideration was given to recruiting opposition figures to the government, including an idea put forward by Dundas of bringing in Lowther, Rutland and Pitt and their friends with offers of honours and junior ministerial posts. It is unlikely that such attempts would have succeeded even had they been made, and in any case the opposition benches were now massing to deliver the final blow. On 8 March a motion of no confidence in the government was defeated by only ten votes, with Pitt acting as a teller for the opposition.* In excitement he wrote to his mother the following day: 'I came to town yesterday in time for a very good debate; and a division which, though not victorious, is as encouraging as possible – 216 against 226, on a question leading directly to removal, is a force that can hardly fail.'

Pitt was right. Both sides strove to bring their maximum numbers to bear in the next debate on 15 March. This followed weeks of 'the most violent exertions on both sides'.[16] Now 'every artifice of party was used by the Opposition to encourage their friends and to terrify or hold out to popular odium the adherents of Administration. Lists were published and disseminated through the kingdom, containing the names of the members who voted on each question . . . it produced . . . a powerful effect on weak or timid individuals.'[17] This time the government clung on by only nine votes (236 to 227). No eighteenth-century government could remain in office if its majority on a question of confidence was in single figures and declining. With a further debate set for 20 March, North prepared to resign. He advised the King to send for Rockingham and Shelburne, to which the King replied: 'My sentiments of honour will not permit me to send for any of the Leaders of Opposition and personally treat with them.'[18]

Despite the King's protestations, North knew his support was

* In the House of Commons, then as now, the votes are counted by two Members from each side who act as 'tellers' and who are not themselves included in the voting figures.

sliding further and that he had no option. On the afternoon of 20 March he arrived at the House of Commons and attempted to speak, but was drowned out by a furious opposition who thought he was trying to prevent the debate from taking place, and insisted that the opposition spokesman Lord Surrey should have the floor. After extensive points of order, in which Pitt once again took part, North was eventually given the floor, assuring the House that 'those persons who had for some time conducted the public affairs, were no longer His Majesty's Ministers. They were no longer to be considered as men holding the reins of government and transacting measures of state, but merely remaining to do their official duty, till other Ministers were appointed to take their places.'[19]

As ever, North retained his sense of humour. Members had anticipated a long sitting, and huddled around the entrance of the House of Commons waiting for their carriages to be brought as the snow fell around them. Lord North had his carriage waiting. 'Good night, gentlemen,' he said to them cheerily, 'you see what it is to be in the secret.' At last he had been able to give up the burden he had wanted to shed for so long. For George III, however, the worst of his nightmares had come true.

Defeat at the hands of the American colonists was to have a massive impact on the politics, society and trade of Great Britain. The prime focus of Britain's empire would now move to the Caribbean, and India would play an ever larger role in its affairs. Relations with the new United States of America would centre on trade, despite the contribution of trading disagreements to the outbreak of war in the first place, with a vast expansion of commerce between Britain and its former colonies which would be crucial to British success in almost all subsequent major wars. In the immediate aftermath of the war, a wounded Britain would pursue a relatively cautious and risk-averse foreign policy. And in those same short years, the seeds of British hostility to slavery, planted by promises of freedom made to slaves during the fighting in America, would grow rapidly into British leadership of the efforts to abolish the slave trade.

In domestic politics, dissatisfaction with the pursuit and handling of the war would bring to a high pitch the demand for constitutional change by means of parliamentary reform, although it would not be many years before a conservative reaction set in. Pitt would make the campaign for such reform his personal crusade for some three years after the North government fell. Equally important, the war had revealed that the British state was ill-equipped to deal with the growing military, political and financial complexity of major conflict. A Cabinet system which relied on the separate relationships of individual Ministers with the King, and had no member who would actually admit to the title of Prime Minister and freely interfere with other departments, was no way to produce a consistent or effective strategy in times of crisis. A figure such as Chatham could dominate his colleagues and give aggressive direction to warmaking at the height of the Seven Years' War, but a more diffident figure such as Lord North provided no central point of coordination or control.

Beneath Cabinet level, the finance and administration of government departments were certainly inefficient and corrupt, moving even Lord North himself in 1780 to set up a statutory commission to examine the public accounts. The stage was set for far-reaching reform of the practices of British government by any future set of Ministers who had the confidence and the power systematically to set about it.

The fall of Lord North was not to produce such a government. It was, of course, abundantly clear that the King would now have to accept into ministerial posts the politicians who had hitherto made up the opposition and who for years had denounced the war, the North administration, and often by implication the King himself. George III's repugnance at promoting such people was extreme, and he had rejected all previous attempts to recruit the Rockingham Whigs to office because of the demands they presented. Unsurprisingly, these demands had included recognition of American independence, the appointment of large numbers of opposition politicians to positions in the government and the Royal Household, and serious economical reform. The King had no regard for Rockingham, along with the deepest possible dislike of Fox, and felt utterly humiliated by the prospect of having to treat with them. He churlishly accused Lord North of deserting him, privately threatened to abdicate, and drew up a message to Parliament which referred to his leaving the country 'for ever'.[20]

Evidently reflecting that there were worse things than being King of England even without its American colonies, George in the end allowed the intransigent side of his character to be tempered by the manipulative abilities he also possessed. While the Rockingham Whigs exulted in Westminster about the spoils of office which would now be coming their way, and Fox openly and regularly referred to the King as 'Satan',[21] George resolved to make their arrival in government as uncomfortable as possible. First, he refused to have any direct negotiations with the Rockinghams, and instead conducted negotiations through the smaller of the opposition groupings led by Shelburne. Secondly, he denied the Rockinghams any general ability to create new peerages and honours, while showering honours upon the Shelburnites: John Dunning, who conducted the initial negotiations, became Lord Ashburton with a pension of £4,000 a year for life; Colonel Barré became Treasurer of the Navy with a life pension of £3,200 a year – to give only the two most obvious examples. As a result 'inextinguishable jealousies arose, and mutual distrust manifested itself on every occasion'.[22] Thirdly, he insisted on retaining the Lord Chancellor, Lord Thurlow, from the previous administration when the new Cabinet was formed. Dundas also continued in office as Lord Advocate.

It seems that initially the King even asked Shelburne rather than Rockingham to head the new government, but with Rockingham having far greater numbers in the Commons, Shelburne declined to do so. The Cabinet that was thus formed included Rockingham as First Lord of the Treasury, Shelburne and Charles James Fox as Secretaries of State (Fox responsible for foreign affairs and Shelburne for home and colonial affairs), Pitt's friend Lord Camden as President of the Council, and Lord John Cavendish as Chancellor of the Exchequer. While the King had to accept a complete reversal of policy, in that all these Ministers sought peace with America, he had succeeded in creating a divided administration. As Lord John Russell later observed: 'Two parties were made in the Ministry, one of which looked to the favour of the Court, not to the support of the country . . . The composition of the Rockingham Ministry was a masterpiece of royal skill.'[23]

When the House of Commons met again on 8 April 1782, the leading figures sat on the side opposite that to which they had grown accustomed for many years. In the eighteenth century this meant not only a change of position but a change of costume – since Ministers wore court dress – and Wraxall speaks of astonishment at them 'emerging from their obscure lodgings, or coming down from Brooks's . . . now ornamented with the appendages of full dress, or returning from Court decorated with swords, lace, and hair powder . . . some degree of ridicule attached to this sudden metamorphosis, which afforded subject for conversation, no less than food for mirth'.

Pitt would now sit on the government, rather than the opposition, side of the House, but he was not included among the Ministers who took their place on the front bench in court dress. In early March he had made in the Commons what seemed to many a rash and presumptuous declaration: 'For myself, I could not expect to form part of a new administration; but were my doing so more within my reach, I feel myself bound to declare that I never would accept a subordinate situation.'[24] At the age of twenty-two he was declaring, in other words, that he would serve as a senior Minister in the Cabinet or not serve in a new government at all. Many commentators found this too much to take, even from the son of Chatham who had become an accomplished debater. Horace Walpole described it as 'so arrogant a declaration from a boy who had gained no experience from, nor ever enjoyed even the lowest post in any office, and who for half a dozen orations, extraordinary indeed, but no evidence of capacity for business, presumed himself fit for command, proved that he was a boy, and a very ambitious and a very vain one. The moment he sat down he was aware of his folly, and said he could bite his tongue out for what he had uttered.'[25]

It has indeed been claimed that as soon as Pitt made this statement he thought he had gone too far, and consulted Admiral Keppel, who was sitting near him, for advice about making a clarification. On the other hand, it would have been wholly uncharacteristic of him to make a major statement of his own ambitions without thinking about it carefully in advance, and we have the assurance of Pretyman that he had decided to make this statement some days before. We cannot know for sure who was right, or whether Pitt was responding to rumours or negotiations and trying to elevate himself in the pecking order of a new administration. We can judge, however, that his statement is wholly consistent with his view of himself and his approach to politics. He already had immense confidence in his own abilities, but even more important he was determined to succeed on the basis of those abilities and not through attachment to a large party or a more senior political figure. He could only preserve the independence and incorruptibility for which he wished to be known by either being in an office so senior that he had freedom of action, or being out of office where he could say what he wished. Office in a more junior position would have turned him into the sort of politician he did not want to be, dependent on the patronage of others and having to accept a party line which he would have no role in determining. It seems likely, therefore, that his statement of March 1782, however grating on many of his listeners, was absolutely deliberate. Certainly his resolve in sticking to it was to be put to an immediate test. Shelburne put to Rockingham the case for giving Pitt a senior position, but it does not seem to have been high among his priorities, and he had already secured a disproportionate share of other positions. Instead, Pitt was offered the Vice-Treasurership of Ireland, outside the Cabinet but the position his father had first held in government, and one which carried a very generous salary of £5,000 a year, probably nine or ten times his income at the time. He refused it. When the elder Pitt had accepted this office he was frustrated from more than a decade in opposition; the younger Pitt was prepared to wait.

Pitt was not a Minister in the new government, but he now had the opportunity to pursue an objective dear to the hearts of many who had opposed the former government: parliamentary reform. The movement of population over the centuries meant that by the late eighteenth century some large towns had no representation in Parliament of their own, while other places with almost no people at all were represented by two Members. The war in America had provided fertile ground for the belief that reform was essential to the good governing of the country, since it was assumed that MPs in closer touch with a wider range of people would have been less inclined to tolerate its continuation. Associations were formed around the country to campaign for the redistribution of parliamentary representation, and variously calling for the abolition of the most rotten boroughs, an increase in the number of county Members, and triennial rather than septennial Parliaments. The most prominent of these were the Westminster Association, with which Fox had associated himself as he adopted a more populist position on these issues in 1780; the Kent Association, of which Pitt's brother-in-law Lord Mahon was a leading light; and the Yorkshire Association, led by the Reverend Christopher Wyvill of Constable Burton in North Yorkshire. Wyvill and his Yorkshire colleagues were to prove formidable campaigners, all the more so since they resisted more radical demands such as a wide extension of the franchise, were prepared to compromise on the issue of shorter Parliaments, and included the solid body of the country gentry of one of the major county seats of the land. Pitt's many attempts to introduce parliamentary reform from 1782 onwards were heavily influenced by Wyvill, although nominally he was more closely attached to the Kent Association, to whose committee he had been elected in October 1780.

With the formation of a government more friendly to reform, the Duke of Richmond, now a member of the Cabinet as Master General of the Ordnance, hosted a meeting of the leading reformers in late April to consider how to seek parliamentary approval for reform as rapidly as possible. It was decided that Pitt had the necessary ability and respect in the Commons to lead the case for reform. He gave notice in the House that on Tuesday, 7 May he would 'move for a Select Committee to take into consideration the present state of the representation of the Commons of England'.[26]

It was necessary caution on behalf of Pitt and the reformers to call for a Select Committee inquiry rather than to present a specific programme of reform. For all the fact that the new administration was sympathetic to the idea in principle, it would still be a tall order to get Members of Parliament to vote for changes which would do many of them out of their seats, and even Ministers themselves were divided. With the exception of Fox, the prime interest of the Rockingham Whigs had always been in economical reform, with the objective of diminishing the influence of the Crown at the expense of the Whig aristocracy, not in parliamentary reform, which had the objective of providing a fairer basis for the system of power which the aristocracy operated. Rockingham himself was not an enthusiast, and Burke was frankly opposed, although Fox appears to have persuaded him to absent himself on the occasion of Pitt's speech.

The House was crowded on 7 May, not so much with Members as with a huge crowd attempting to enter the Public Gallery, which had to be locked after an hour. Pitt set out the case for reform in a speech lasting an hour and a half. First, he praised the new government: 'the ministers had declared their virtuous resolution of supporting the king's government by means more honourable, as well as more permanent, than corruption; and the nation had confidence in the declarations of men who had so invariably proved themselves the friends of freedom, and the animated supporters of an equal and fair system of representation'.[27] He went on to lament what had happened to the British constitution:

> That beautiful frame of government, which had made us the envy and admiration of mankind, in which the people were entitled to hold so distinguished a share, was so far dwindled and departed from its original purity, as that the representatives ceased, in a great degree, to be connected with the people. It was the essence of the constitution, that the people had a share in the government by the means of representation; and its excellence and permanency was calculated to consist in this representation, having been designed to be equal, easy, practicable, and complete. When it ceased to be so; when the representative ceased to have connection with the constituent, and was either dependent on the crown or the aristocracy, there was a defect in the frame of representation, and it was not innovation, but recovery of constitution, to repair it.[28]

This was very much the spirit in which Pitt, Wyvill and the moderate reformers campaigned. They were not seeking a radical change to bring in a wider measure of what we now regard as a genuine democracy, nor were they consciously starting down any road which would lead 150 years later to universal suffrage and more or less equal representation. They simply wished to rectify the imbalances which had arisen over time so that parliamentary representation recovered some of its respectability, authority and independence. There were boroughs, Pitt claimed,

> which had now in fact no actual existence, but in the return of members to the house. They had no existence in property, in population, in trade, in weight . . . Another set of boroughs and towns, in the lofty possession of English freedom, claimed to themselves the right of bringing their votes to market. They had no other market, no other property, and no other stake in the country, than the property and price which they procured for their votes. Such boroughs were the most dangerous of all others. So far from consulting the interests of their country in the choice which they made, they held out their borough to the best purchaser, and in fact, they belonged more to the Nabob of Arcot than they did to the people of Great-Britain . . . Such boroughs . . . were sources of corruption; they gave rise to an inundation of corrupt wealth, and corrupt members, who had no regard nor connection, either for or with the people of this kingdom.[29]

Pitt attacked the argument that the constitution could not be changed, saying he was afraid 'that the reverence and the enthusiasm which Englishmen entertained for the constitution, would, if not suddenly prevented, be the means of destroying it; for such was their enthusiasm, that they would not even remove its defects, for fear of touching its beauty'.[30]

Pitt's motion was supported by the veteran Alderman Sawbridge and by Richard Brinsley Sheridan, the famous Covent Garden playwright who was also a new MP, but opposed by his own cousin Thomas Pitt of Bocconoc. Appropriately enough for someone who elected himself as Member of Old Sarum, Thomas pointed out that equality of representation never was nor could have been the basis on which their ancestors meant to erect the liberties of England, or they would never have allowed 'the little county of Rutland to send as many members to that assembly as Yorkshire or Devon'.[31]

This was to be the majority view. When the 'orders of the day' were moved to cut short further debate on Pitt's motion, 161 voted aye, and Pitt and Fox led 141 in voting no. Pitt was disappointed, writing to his mother: 'The failure of my motion was rather unexpected, and might perhaps have been prevented if so strong an Opposition had been foreseen. I believe it is a very small party that is heartily for it,'[32] but other reformers took heart from the narrow defeat, certainly not suspecting that this was the closest they would come to parliamentary reform for half a century. A further meeting of reformers was held at the Thatched House Tavern in St James's Street on 18 May, calling for a new wave of petitions from across the country, and Pitt and Wyvill resolved to continue to work closely together.

Even as this meeting took place the obstacles to meaningful reform were becoming ever clearer. On 17 May Alderman Sawbridge moved a motion for shortening the duration of parliaments, still set at seven years. He was supported by both Pitt and Fox, but Burke could no longer restrain himself. As Sheridan later described it to a friend: 'On Friday last Burke acquitted himself with the most magnanimous indiscretion, attacked W. Pitt in a scream of passion, and swore Parliament was and always had been precisely what it ought to be, and that all people who thought of reforming it wanted to overturn the Constitution.'[33] If Pitt needed any further reminding that the Rockingham Whigs did not share his attachment to genuine reform, he certainly received it the following month when a further plank of reform was opposed by Fox himself. On 19 June Lord Mahon introduced a Bill for combating bribery at elections, only to find that Fox opposed it and succeeded in removing many of the proposed penalties in it as being too severe. Mahon withdrew the Bill in disgust. 'This was,' Pretyman tells us, 'I believe, the first question upon which they [Pitt and Fox] happened to differ before any separation took place between them. I must, however, remark that although they had hitherto acted together in Parliament, there had been no intimacy or confidential intercourse between them.'

Fox had always been courteous and generous to Pitt. But by the end of June 1782, with Fox and the new government approaching a major crisis, Pitt owed them nothing.

Dundas was always a perceptive observer of events. 'Unless they change their idea of government, and personal behaviour to the King,' he said of the new government, in which he continued as Lord Advocate, 'I do not believe they will remain three months.'[34] He would turn out to be exactly correct, and however arrogant Pitt's refusal to hold a junior office may have seemed, he would lose nothing from standing apart from the intense feuding and personal enmities which characterised the short-lived Rockingham administration.

Rockingham himself had two great strengths: he was consistent and principled in his Whig views, and among the Whigs he was foremost in wealth and connections. From his vast mansion of Wentworth Woodhouse* his influence upon the rest of the landed Whig aristocracy radiated across the land. These strengths had helped him to maintain the Whigs as a forceful opposition party through the 1770s and to hold them in readiness as an alternative government. But once he was in office as First Lord of the Treasury they were more than outweighed by his weaknesses: inexperience in government, timidity in arbitrating between fractious Ministers, and a bodily constitution which was not up to the strain. He was indecisive and forgetful, better known for his interests in racing, farming and horse-breeding than for having strong opinions about most political issues. George III thought that he 'never appeared to him to have a decided opinion about things'.[35] This was a government held together by its leader rather than driven forward by him.

The single most important change in British politics brought about under the Rockingham government was the legislative independence granted to the Irish Parliament in May 1782, but this was in no way a premeditated act. Irish opinion was united behind the fiery politician Henry Grattan, who seized the chance to demand home rule provided

* Wentworth Woodhouse, near Rotherham, remains to this day the largest private house in Britain.

by the coincidence of a new government in London, military defeat overseas, and the existence of 100,000 armed Irish Volunteers who had been set up to defend the country in the absence of British troops. While the new Lord Lieutenant of Ireland, the Duke of Portland, pleaded in vain for time, Grattan made the most of his advantage, backed by the threat of force, and the Ministers gave in. For the moment the issue was settled, but time would show that the discontents of Ireland had been appeased but not resolved.

The change of government meant peace negotiations to end the war with America, and separately with France, Spain and Holland, would now begin. Major operations on the American mainland may have been over, but Britain and the Continental powers continued to battle for a stronger negotiating position. The Spanish were determined to retake Gibraltar, ceded to Britain in 1713, and in the West Indies the British and French fleets manoeuvred among their colonies. From there in late May came news of a devastating British victory. On 12 April, only three weeks after Lord North had left office in the shadow of military humiliation, Admiral Rodney decisively defeated the French fleet near Dominica, and in doing so restored Britain's naval superiority and saved the West Indian colonies. A nation that had begun to despair of recovering its domination of the oceans now rejoiced: 'The capital and the country were thrown into a delirium of joy.'[36]

While Rodney's great victory elated the country, it only served to exacerbate the differences over the peace negotiations between the two Secretaries of State, Fox and Shelburne. The conflict between these two men was at the heart of the intense rivalries which would pull the government apart. Shelburne had been flattered by George III, who had clearly wanted him to be the head of the government if only Fox and the other Rockingham Whigs would allow it. Fox, for his part, had no shortage of reasons for distrusting Shelburne, both personal and political. For one thing they were cousins, and 'an old prejudice' between the two branches of the family had remained active for decades.[37] Probably still more offensive to Fox was that after all the work he had done and the speeches he had given to turn out the North ministry, it was Shelburne who had acquired the lion's share of the spoils and could often outvote him in the Cabinet. Added to this poisonous mixture was an issue of real substance between them: Fox believed that the independence of America should be granted unconditionally, while Shelburne felt that it should be contingent on the satisfactory conclusion of a treaty with America's European allies. Since Shelburne, as Home and Colonial Secretary, had responsibility for the negotiations with America, while Fox, as Foreign Secretary, had responsibility for the negotiations with European enemies, there were two Ministers with two different policies responsible for the same interrelated set of negotiations. The composition of the Rockingham ministry thus provided the perfect recipe for mistrust, bitterness and eventual chaos.

The Cabinet had agreed to the unconditional independence of America, but Shelburne, possibly emboldened by Rodney's victory, continued to pursue his own plans and sent his own representative, Richard Oswald, to the negotiations in Paris behind Fox's back. Fox was enraged by 'this duplicity of conduct',[38] believing that Shelburne was deliberately undermining the negotiations or seeking to bring down the government in concert with the King. By the end of June Fox was trying to bring matters to a head in the Cabinet and to have the policy decided one way or the other, even if it meant the 'absolute rupture'[39] of the government. The feud had reached its peak, but the climactic meetings of the Rockingham Cabinet were to take place without Rockingham himself. At the beginning of June, according to Wraxall, 'when he rose to address the House [of Lords], he declared that he felt himself so severely indisposed as to be almost incapable of uttering a word . . . "The disorder universally prevalent afflicts me so violently, that at times I am not completely in possession of myself."'[40] It is hard to imagine a modern Prime Minister making such a disarmingly honest admission. In any event, he took to his bed and was still there as his Ministers squared up to each other at the end of June.

Pitt, in the meantime, occasionally busied himself on the back benches while planning a summer on the Western Circuit to improve his finances. He was also anxious that his mother's annuity, long since in arrears, should be paid by the government. On 27 June he wrote from Lincoln's Inn to his mother:

> My brother tells me he has mentioned to you that Ld Rockingham is ill, wch is unfortunately in the way of any thing more at present; but Ld S[helburne]. told me yesterday that Ld R. had expressed himself as wishing to do something that might give you a security for the future. You are very good in thinking of communicating any share of what I am sure your own occasions may demand entire; mine are not so pressing but that they will wait very tolerably at present; and I shall expect that Westminster Hall will in good time supply all that is wanting.
>
> The Circuit begins on Tuesday sen'night.* I hope to call in my way westward, if not certainly in my return; and I shall undoubtedly be able to make some stay after it is over, tho' my plan for the remainder of the summer is not quite settled . . . Lord Rockingham's very precarious state occasions a great deal of suspense, and if it ends ill, may, I am afraid, produce a great deal of confusion . . .[41]

The plans Pitt was making to visit his mother and join the Western Circuit would be abandoned only a few days after he wrote this letter. At a Cabinet meeting on 30 June to discuss the peace negotiations Fox was outvoted. If he had resigned as Secretary of State that day it would have been seen as a resignation on a matter of principle. By delaying in order to consult his friends it was to become seen as a matter of pique. For at 11.30 in the morning of 1 July 1782 Charles Watson-Wentworth, second Marquis of Rockingham and First Lord of the Treasury, breathed his last. The one man who had held the government together was gone, and his body was scarcely cold before the battle over his successor was joined in earnest.

* The term 'se'nnight', meaning one week, was still in common usage at this time.

6

The Youngest Chancellor

> 'Our new Board of Treasury has just begun to enter on business; and tho' I do not know that it is of the most entertaining sort, it does not seem likely to be very fatiguing . . . Lord North will, I hope, in a very little while make room for me in Downing Street, which is the best summer Town House possible.'
>
> William Pitt, Chancellor of the Exchequer, 16 July 1782

> 'W. Pitt Secretary of State! and Lord Shelburne Premier! Surely the first cannot be qualified for such an office, and the last is, in my opinion, little to be depended upon.'
>
> Lord Mornington, 12 July 1782[1]

The uneasy coalition which had surrounded Rockingham was rent asunder within hours of his death. Fox had been on the brink of resigning, but seeing a chance to acquire genuine control of the government, nominated the Duke of Portland as First Lord of the Treasury. Portland was another traditional Whig aristocrat, now forty-four years old, but more suited to ministerial office and more dedicated to politics than Rockingham had been. He was known for 'integrity, ability, and firmness',[2] but certainly not for oratory or inspiration. Fox's intention in putting Portland forward was that one less than totally effectual Whig magnate would succeed another, and Fox, while disqualified from being First Lord of the Treasury himself because of the intense animosity between him and the King, would be in charge. George III, however, was no laggard when he saw an opportunity for which he had been waiting. Having failed even to enquire about the health of the dying Rockingham in the preceding weeks, the King wrote to Shelburne immediately on receiving news of his death, offering him the leadership of the government 'with the fullest political confidence'.[3] Oddly enough, the Rockingham Whigs were the grouping most caught by surprise by the death of their leader, probably because physicians had forecast his recovery, while their rivals were immediately ready for action. One of them wrote: 'All is confusion at present, for as his friends from the declaration of his physicians did not think him in immediate danger the blow is the severer. Nobody at present can say who will be the successor . . . C. Fox's idea at five o'clock this afternoon was in case His Majesty would not put the Duke of Richmond at the head of the Treasury to put the Duke of Portland there . . . they will not hear at this present moment of Shelburne . . .'[4]

Hear of it or not, the Whigs were presented with a *fait accompli*. Shelburne was to be First Lord of the Treasury, provided he could assemble a government around him. With Parliament about to break for the summer recess he would then have several months in which to fortify his parliamentary position. A new stage of confusion now reigned over who would serve under Shelburne. Fox consulted his friends about resigning, while the King took the unusual step on 3 July of speaking to each Cabinet Minister individually to explain that Shelburne would head the administration. According to Shelburne, 'Mr. Fox, spoke to the K. rather in a strong way & seemed surprised to find that His M. dare have any opinion of his own.'[5] The newspapers of the time demonstrate the bewilderingly rapid changes in the situation. The *Morning Chronicle* of 2 July printed a leaked list of the potential new government, with William Pitt as Treasurer of the Navy (a position outside the Cabinet and one he would have been unlikely to accept); by 6 July Fox is reported to have resigned and Pitt to be on his way to being a Secretary of State; and on 9 July it was said that Fox would be in the government after all, as Chancellor. In fact, on 4 July Fox had handed in his seals of office to the King and had 'an angry Conversation' with Shelburne. He could not bear to serve under the ministerial rival who he believed had spent the last three months undermining him.

While controversy raged around Fox, the undaunted Shelburne set about bringing Pitt into the government. Without Fox in the Cabinet, a powerful House of Commons debater would be needed in the front rank of the administration, and Pitt was one of the few men answering to that description. In addition, Shelburne regarded Pitt as one of his supporters and someone with very similar views to himself. He had tried to include him in the government at a more junior level only three months before. Now the need, and the opening, were clear. Fox himself, in one of his last friendly conversations with Pitt, said to him after Rockingham's death: 'They look to you; without you they cannot succeed; with you I know not whether they will or no.' 'If', replied Pitt, 'they reckon upon me, they may find themselves mistaken.' In recounting this to others, Fox is said to have added presciently: 'I believe they do reckon on Pitt, and I believe they will not be mistaken.'[6]

It may be that Pitt had not fully absorbed the possible consequences of Rockingham's death on the day it happened. Perhaps more likely is that he was still rather in awe of Fox, and was keeping all his options open. Overnight reflection and the possibility of high office soon led him to be tempted. He wrote to his mother on 2 July: 'With regard to myself, I believe the arrangement may be of a sort in which I may, and probably ought to take a part.'[7] By 5 July he was writing: 'Fox has chosen to resign, on no Ground that I can learn but Lord Shelburne being placed at the Treasury . . . My lot will be either at the Treasury as Chancellor of the Exchequer, or in the Home department as Secretary of State. The arrangement cannot be finally settled till tomorrow or next day; but every thing promises as well as possible in such circumstances. Mr. Townshend certainly makes part of this fresh arrangement, and probably in a more forward post, which is to me an infinite satisfaction.'[8]

This was a reference to Thomas Townshend, the only other Member of the House of Commons likely to occupy one of the top positions in the government. While the negotiations continued about who would occupy exactly which post, all attention remained on Fox, who now began to realise that he had gravely damaged his political career.

As a Secretary of State, Fox had felt seriously undermined by Shelburne, and had differed with him on a major aspect of policy. While he therefore had good grounds for resignation upon Shelburne becoming First Lord, these points were not widely appreciated even by other members of the government. Thus while Burke joined Fox in resigning, the senior members of the government saw no reason not to stay put in the Cabinet. The differences of opinion over the peace negotiations were not public knowledge, and for a politician openly to attack the backstairs influence of the King would have been going too far in the eighteenth century, at least until the great crisis which was still a year and a half away. The fact that Fox negotiated about the possibility of staying in the government for two or three days in the belief that Shelburne might accept his American policy (which he subsequently did) strengthened the perception that there was no good reason why he should not have carried on in the government. His uncle the Duke of Richmond remained in the Cabinet, saying he could 'see no reason at present for suspecting that the Measures on which we came in will not be pursued, and under this persuasion I think it would be very wrong not to support this Ministry merely because Lord Shelburne is at the Treasury'.[9]

Seeing that he was losing the argument and was believed to have resigned out of personal animosity, Fox sought to explain himself in the Commons on 9 July, but probably made matters worse by the vituperative nature of his attack on Shelburne. He said of the new First Lord and his colleagues that 'they would abandon fifty principles for the sake of power, and forget fifty promises when they were no longer requisite to their ends . . . and he expected to see that, in a very short time they would be joined by those men whom that House had precipitated from their seats'.[10]

The prediction he was making was that Shelburne would now form an alliance with Lord North. This was particularly unfortunate, since it was exactly what Fox himself would proceed to do the following year. Among those who took exception to the intemperate nature of Fox's attacks on Shelburne was Pitt. Seated on the government front bench for the first time, although not yet officially in office as Chancellor of the Exchequer, Pitt now had a stake in the success of Shelburne and the isolation of Fox. For all the ostensibly friendly relations between them over the previous years, he seems to have had no hesitation in adding to Fox's wounds with a thrust of his own rapier:

> The Right Honourable Secretary assures us, that it was with the sole view of preventing dissensions in the Cabinet he retired from office. I believe him, because he solemnly declares it; otherwise I should have attributed his resignation to a baulk in struggling for power. If, however, he so much disliked Lord Shelburne's political principles or opinions, why did he ever consent to act with that nobleman as a colleague? And if he only suspected Lord Shelburne of feeling averse to the measures which he thought necessary to be adopted, it was his duty to have called a Cabinet Council, and there to have ascertained the fact before he took the hasty resolution of throwing up his employment.[11]

In vain did Fox protest that he had indeed called a meeting of the Cabinet to try to settle differences. The death of Rockingham and the evident anger of Fox at the elevation of Shelburne had obscured the original point of his resignation. By 10 July, as a new writ was moved for an election in Appleby to confirm Pitt's position in the Commons as Chancellor of the Exchequer, the dust settled on a remarkable ten days in the politics of the eighteenth century. The events of early July 1782 amplified the appearance of Fox as a politician whose brilliance was flawed by rashness and personal enmity. The King could now say that his experience of Fox had 'finally determined me never to employ him again'.[12] The same events led to Pitt becoming Chancellor of the Exchequer and one of the most senior members of the British government at the age of twenty-three. Above all, the fact that Pitt had accepted office in the same circumstances as those in which Fox had rejected it would have lasting consequences for themselves and the country for the rest of their lives. The two most eloquent Members of the House of Commons had hitherto spoken from the same side of the House. Now they would never do so again.

Pitt's re-election for Appleby was, of course, a formality. Given Lowther's influence, he once again had no opponents. Not having to trouble himself with the election, and the House of Commons entering on its recess, he was able to contemplate his new situation with some leisure. The position of Chancellor of the Exchequer was a senior one in the government, but not as powerful as would normally be the case today. Its origins go back to the beginning of the twelfth century, when a chequered table was used for calculating expenditure and receipts. In the thirteenth century, the official responsible for making such calculations became known as the Chancellor of the Exchequer. By Pitt's time, the Chancellor ranked second in the Treasury after the First Lord, an arrangement still nominally intact in the twenty-first century. Since the position of Prime Minister was far less well developed than today, however (and was not yet an official title), the First Lord was likely to concentrate much more heavily than now on Treasury business, and the Chancellor was not regarded as the Treasury's departmental head.

Although he was in the Cabinet, Pitt had therefore not acquired extensive administrative power. He had ended up as Chancellor because at least three other people had turned it down in the game of Cabinet musical chairs between 1 and 10 July, and it was clear that the position he had been given had had to fit in with the demands of others. As Chancellor he would have a seat on the Treasury Board, with another seat given to his friend Edward Eliot, but Shelburne intended to be an activist First Lord with a firm grip on Treasury matters. Pitt's role and power within the government would expand in due course, but only because he was indispensable to it in the House of Commons. Other than Townshend, nominally senior to him as a Secretary of State but a less effective speaker, General Conway and Dundas, who survived yet another change of government as Lord Advocate but remained outside the Cabinet, Pitt was the only spokesman in the House of Commons of a government which did not enjoy a majority. The other members of the Cabinet were all in the Lords: Shelburne himself as First Lord, Lord Grantham as a Secretary of State, Lord Thurlow yet again as Lord Chancellor, Lord Keppel as First Lord of the Admiralty, Lord Camden as President of the Council, the Duke of Grafton as Lord Privy Seal and the Duke of Richmond as Master General of the Ordnance.

These grand figures of eighteenth-century politics – great landowners, political veterans or military experts – seemed happy to accept among their number in the Cabinet a young man who, for all his antecedents and abilities, was nevertheless a penniless twenty-three-year-old with no previous experience of office. More than two hundred years later, British Cabinets are no longer dominated by the aristocracy, but it would be impossible in practice for any twenty-three-year-old to achieve Cabinet rank, and would in any case be universally regarded as inappropriate. Sure enough, Pitt would receive some criticism on grounds of his youth, and a great deal more on becoming First Lord of the Treasury only eighteen months later. Yet at this point in history, for such a young person to enjoy such a high rank was regarded as unusual rather than ludicrous.

How was it that opinion in the eighteenth century could accept youthful seniority to an extent inconceivable two centuries later? Part of the explanation for Pitt's rapid rise lies, of course, in the unusual circumstances of 1782. One group of politicians had left office because of defeat in the war; now another group had left because of arguments over the peace: the system was literally running out of talented material. But more generally, politics in the eighteenth century was more of a younger man's game. We have already seen that fully a hundred MPs in the early 1780s were under the age of thirty. Ability, family connections, and the sometimes early retirement or death of senior colleagues allowed some of them to rise more rapidly than could be the case in modern politics. Pitt was not alone in reaching senior office in his twenties. Charles James Fox was an MP at the age of nineteen and a Lord of the Admiralty at twenty-four. At the time of his dramatic resignation as a Secretary of State in 1782 he was still only thirty-three. Another leading Whig of the coming years, Charles Grey, became an MP at twenty-two and was a leading opposition spokesman throughout his twenties. On Pitt's own death in 1806, the new government would include Lord Henry Petty as Chancellor of the Exchequer at the age of twenty-six. For a politician to hold Cabinet rank or its equivalent in his twenties during the late eighteenth or early nineteenth century was therefore uncommon, but not unknown.

Attitudes to age and power were bound to be different from today in a period when immense and absolute power was wielded throughout Europe by monarchs who were themselves very young. Maria Theresa had assumed the throne of Austria and precipitated the War of the

Austrian Succession at the age of twenty-three in 1740. Her successor Joseph II, on the throne in the 1780s, had been co-Regent at the age of twenty-four. Of the other great monarchs of Europe at the time Pitt took office as Chancellor, Louis XVI of France had become King at the age of twenty, Frederick the Great King of Prussia at twenty-eight, Catherine the Great Empress of Russia at thirty-three, and Gustavus III King of Sweden at twenty-five. George III himself, albeit without the absolute power of his fellow monarchs, had ascended to the throne at twenty-two. At a time when inheritance was more widely prized, it was easier to believe that the offspring of great leaders could themselves take on the burdens of leadership at an early age. There seems no doubt that Pitt was a beneficiary of that belief, and his early oratorical performances had strengthened its applicability to him.

A final consideration in the eighteenth-century acceptance of youthful success is that the number of young prodigies in many disparate fields was far greater than it is today. Perhaps the greater risk of early death produced an impulse to young brilliance, and certainly the intensive use of private tutors added to it: Alexander Pope wrote his first verses aged twelve, and was famous at twenty-three; Henry Fielding's plays were being performed in London when he was twenty-one; Adam Smith was a Professor of Logic at twenty-eight; the evangelist George Whitfield was preaching to crowds of tens of thousands in London when aged twenty-five; Isaac Newton had commenced his revolutionary advances in science in the previous century at the age of twenty-five; and Mozart had composed symphonies when eight years old and completed tours of Europe at the ripe old age of fifteen. If a young man seemed brilliant enough he would be accepted, indulged and given patronage, and so it was with William Pitt.

Pitt had never had a spacious residence in London, having become accustomed to staying in his rooms at Lincoln's Inn or at his brother's house in Grafton Street. Since Shelburne preferred to stay in his house in Berkeley Square rather than move into the Downing Street house given by King George II in the 1730s to the incumbent First Lord of the Treasury, Pitt was able to look forward to moving in there instead.

Lord North had lived there for many years as First Lord of the Treasury, and had been in no hurry to move out upon losing his job. Pitt wrote to his mother on 16 July:

> Our new Board of Treasury has just begun to enter on business; and tho' I do not know that it is of the most entertaining sort, it does not seem likely to be very fatiguing. In all other respects my situation most perfectly satisfies, and more than satisfies me, and I think promises every thing that is agreeable . . . Lord North will, I hope, in a very little while make room for me in Downing Street, which is the best summer Town House possible.[8]

The residence in question was one of fifteen terraced houses erected in the 1680s along the northern side of Downing Street. They were of poor quality, with inadequate foundations, but one of them was linked in the 1730s with the impressive house behind it, overlooking Horseguards Parade and originally built for the Countess of Lichfield, daughter of Charles II. The house was originally No. 5 Downing Street, and it was only three years before Pitt moved in that it was renumbered No. 10. Little did those who carried out the renumbering suspect that they were changing the vocabulary and symbolism of power in Britain for centuries to come. In August 1782 Pitt moved in. Although his initial occupation of No. 10 would last only eight months, he would go on to live there for by far the greater part of his adult life, and for longer than any other person since. It is not surprising that to begin with he found it a huge place: 'I expect to be comfortably settled in the course of this week,' he wrote on 30 July, 'in a part of my vast, awkward house.'[9]

He benefited from the construction of a new vaulted kitchen and from a series of major repairs in 1766 which resulted in many of the characteristic features recognisable today: the lamp above the door, the lion's-head doorknocker, and the black-and-white chequerboard floor in the entrance hall. Other alterations, such as the creation of the modern Cabinet Room, would take place later in his tenure, in 1796. Externally, Downing Street at that time still had terraced houses along the other side from No. 10, as the new Foreign Office building was not constructed until the 1860s. It would have looked and seemed much more like a normal street, albeit a well-to-do one, and for Pitt it provided the great advantage of a short walk or ride to the Houses of Parliament.

In the summer of 1782 Britain was still at war, and Ministers found it difficult to get away from London despite the parliamentary recess. Pitt managed to go shooting briefly in September, and described his lifestyle in a letter to his mother:

> My dear Mother,
>
> I am much obliged to you for your letter, which I received yesterday on my return from Cheveley, where I had been for two days. A short visit for such a distance; but as my brother was going there, I thought it worth the exertion, and it was very well repaid by a great deal of Air and Exercise in shooting, and the finest weather in the world. The finest part of all indeed is a fine east wind, which, as the fleet is just sailed for Gibraltar, is worth every thing. I assure you I do not forget the lessons I have so long followed, of riding in spite of Business; tho' I indeed want it less than ever, as I was never so perfectly well. All I have to do now is to be done quite at my own Hours, being merely to prepare for the busy season; which is very necessary to be done, but which at the same time is not a close Confinement. We are labouring at all sorts of official Reform, for which there is a very ample Field, and in which I believe we shall have some success.
>
> Downing Street, Thursday Sept. 12 [1782][15]

Incredibly by today's standards, Pitt as Chancellor of the Exchequer did not need any dedicated officials of his own. He explained to his mother that his secretary was an army friend of his brother, but since the job had no duties but that of receiving about £400 a year, 'no profession is unfit for it'. Otherwise, 'I have not yet any private secretary, nor do I perceive, at least as yet, any occasion for it.'[16]

The standards of ministerial conduct were also rather different from those expected today: Pitt's sister Harriot was soon expecting him to find a job for a friend, and his mother evidently looked to him to rectify the arrears in the payment of her annuity. Pitt showed early on the characteristics which would be with him throughout his ministerial life and would mark him out from other politicians of the time: his sense of propriety, which in this instance made him reluctant to push his mother's case while Lord Shelburne was dealing with it, and a lack of interest in the lesser forms of patronage which led him to tell his sister that he would do what he could for her friend, but 'of all the secrets of my office I have in this short time learnt the least about Patronage'.[17] He was always embarrassed when pressed to deal with minor issues by acquaintances or relatives, sending on one such to Shelburne with the note: 'Mr. Pitt cannot help forwarding this trifling request.'[18]

Pitt attended the Treasury Board conscientiously, and worked on two specific schemes of reform which would be put to Parliament the following year. One was to streamline and clean up the operation of the Customs, abolishing sinecure positions granted for life and discontinuing fees on business done. The other measure was intended to regulate public offices, stopping the sale of positions and the abuse of perquisites, which resulted, for example, in the large-scale theft of government stationery. But although Pitt appears to have worked diligently, he did not become an intimate colleague or confidant of the First Lord, Lord Shelburne.

By all accounts, Shelburne was a difficult person to get to know or like. He was clever and hardworking, and intellectually attracted to much the same causes as Pitt, favouring economical and parliamentary reform, peace treaties which emphasised the enhancement of free trade, a liberal commercial settlement with Ireland, and the creation of a new Sinking Fund to repay the national debt. Like Pitt he was a disciple of Adam Smith, who had recently provided the intellectual framework for advocates of free trade. Yet for all his qualities, Shelburne was never generally trusted. He had a sound grasp of diplomacy, trade and finance, but did not understand the psychology of his individual colleagues, who found that he was too remote, too critical, or at other times too given to flattery for his sincerity to be accepted. George Rose, who became Secretary to the Treasury that summer and who would subsequently be one of Pitt's closest colleagues, described Shelburne in his diaries as 'sometimes passionate or unreasonable, occasionally betraying suspicions of others entirely groundless, and at other times offensively flattering. I have frequently been puzzled to decide which part of his conduct was least to be tolerated.'[19] Shelburne, he said, had 'a suspicion of almost anyone he had intercourse with, a want of sincerity, and a habit of listening to every tale-bearer who would give him intelligence or news of any sort'.[20] Even worse for the new government, Shelburne's public character bore out this private assessment. Before the Lords had risen for the summer, Shelburne had claimed that Fox had never raised his differences over policy towards America in the Cabinet. Fox demanded a retraction, and Lord Derby the following day accused Shelburne in the Lords of 'a direct deviation from the truth'. Shelburne's pathetic reply was that 'he made no such assertion; but he had certainly said, that "in his opinion" that was the cause, and the exclusive cause; but he had not asserted it as a fact'.[21] In August, Christopher Wyvill was very pleased to receive a letter from Shelburne saying that he would 'deal nobly' with the reform ideas of the Yorkshire Association, but soon afterwards when Shelburne realised that many Ministers were opposed to parliamentary reform he had to tell Wyvill that his letter was meant 'as a communication to you personally',[22] and not as a statement of government policy. The impression spread that this First Minister could not be trusted.

Far and away the most important task of the Shelburne government was to conduct the peace negotiations in Paris. Within weeks of taking charge, Shelburne was forced to concede the point on which Fox had tried to insist: the unequivocal acknowledgement of American independence. Previously he had pursued his ideal of the American colonies remaining in some form of association with Great Britain while being granted extensive territory towards the Mississippi and the Great Lakes, some of it provided from Canada. Finally dropping the idea of any such association, he now concluded with the colonies by the end of November the preliminary articles of peace which gave them both the territory they desired and the acknowledgement of their complete independence. The settlement with America allowed Britain to drive a far harder bargain with France and Spain, including on the vital issue of the Spanish claim to Gibraltar. In September the Spaniards had attacked Gibraltar but met with a crushing defeat. Shelburne and the King were inclined to exchange Gibraltar for Puerto Rico or West Florida, but too much blood had now been spilled in the defence of the Rock for British opinion willingly to give it up. This was a view shared by many senior Ministers, probably including Pitt, and Shelburne was only able to maintain unity in the Cabinet by the unusual device of not calling it together for a meeting.

It was in the middle of these disagreements and negotiations, with the preliminaries of peace with America signed on 30 November but the negotiations with the European powers still underway, that Parliament assembled in early December. With both Fox and North, along with their followers, on the opposition benches, the government's position was precarious, and much would ride on Pitt's ability to put its case in the Commons. Observers had expected Shelburne to use the recess to bring some of the opposition forces into the government's ranks and thereby secure a majority. But 'on the opening of the session, it soon . . . became evident that no such Ministerial approximation had taken place, and the Administration relied for support upon its own proper strength or ability'.[23] Historians have estimated the strength of the parliamentary factions that Christmas at 140 MPs behind Shelburne (including the 'King's friends'), 120 followers of North, and ninety supporters of Fox.[24] The government was thus heavily outnumbered unless all the independents came to its aid.

There were several reasons why Shelburne had done nothing to strengthen his government when he had the opportunity. The first was that he did not understand the House of Commons, and had taken some highly speculative and wildly over-optimistic assessments of the numbers from the normally reliable government official John Robinson as facts. He wrote to one colleague that he would have the support of 'almost all the property of the Country, and that he did not believe his opponents in the H. of Commons would exceed 60'.[25] The second reason was that although Shelburne himself could not countenance negotiating once again with Fox, Pitt would under no circumstances serve alongside Lord North, and any alliance with an opposition grouping would therefore make the existing government difficult to hold together. At least, Shelburne assured himself, Fox and North were such long-standing opponents that they could not join forces against him.

The government that met in Parliament that winter was therefore hamstrung, overconfident, and preoccupied with its own differences over the peace negotiations. Within days it was under pressure. On the opening day, Shelburne was asked whether the peace terms with America would stand whatever happened in the European negotiations, to which he replied: 'This offer is not irrevocable; if France does not agree to peace, the offer ceases.'[26] On the following day, when Fox raised this in the Commons, all the Ministers present gave an answer diametrically opposite to that of their leader, with Pitt twice insisting that the agreement with America was unconditional. Shelburne was now in difficulties, with the King asking him to persuade Pitt to recant his 'mistake', but with Pitt sticking to his honest reply, declaring that 'on mature consideration, and he persisted in it . . . recognition could not be revoked, even if the present treaty should go off'.[27]

Shelburne was on the brink of a successful negotiation in Paris, but he had embarrassed his government and alienated more of his colleagues. Ministers found that they were shut out of the peace negotiations, and by the end of January 1783 both Keppel and Richmond resigned. The government was thus in grave difficulties as it prepared to present the final outcome of the negotiations to Parliament on 27 January, with a debate arranged for 17 February. In the final articles of peace, the French gained Tobago and St Lucia, but had to hand back all their other conquests. Britain recognised Spanish control of Minorca and the Floridas, but kept Gibraltar. The Dutch recovered Trincomalee in Ceylon, but had to accept free navigation by British ships in the East Indies. Given all the circumstances it was not a dishonourable settlement, and Shelburne was proud of the fact that it laid the foundations for the expansion of trade with both America and the Continent. Sadly for him, the parliamentary position of his government was now so perilous that the merits of his peace proposals were lost amidst the scramble for power of February 1783.

The morale of government supporters was low as both Houses gathered on 17 February to debate the preliminaries of peace. Ministers tabled a modest motion expressing 'satisfaction' at a settlement which offered 'perfect reconciliation and friendship', but try as he might Pitt could not persuade William Grenville, his cousin and future Foreign Secretary, to second the motion; William Wilberforce agreed to do so instead. Even as Parliament met, the government's disintegration gathered pace. The Duke of Grafton, upon hearing that Richmond's seat in the Cabinet would be taken by Pitt's friend the young Duke of Rutland, without prior consultation with himself, resigned on the spot. Rutland was to have the unusual distinction of turning up to his first Cabinet meeting on the same day that the government resigned. A senior resignation on the day of a vital debate was bad enough, but as government Members entered the Commons they witnessed a spectacle far more ominous: Charles James Fox and Lord North were sitting together on the opposition front bench.

In the preceding days two of the most dedicated enemies in eighteenth-century politics had buried their differences and come together. Fox had actually opened contact with North the previous July, only days after denouncing Shelburne on the grounds that he might do the same. On 14 February North and Fox had met, agreeing to differ on parliamentary reform, with Fox promising to make no further attacks on the influence of the Crown. It seems that he was prepared to pay any price in order to ditch Shelburne and defeat the machinations of the King. If necessary he would denounce the results of the peace negotiations, on which he had himself been working the previous year with no prospect of achieving a better result.

The Ministers had realised in early February that their situation was desperate. Pitt had persuaded Shelburne to let him approach Fox with a view to bringing him back within the government. On 11 February he had called on Fox at his house off St James's Street. Fox asked whether Shelburne would remain First Lord of the Treasury. Pitt said he would. Fox said that 'It was impossible for him to belong to any administration of which lord Shelburne was the head.' Pitt responded that 'if that was his determination, it would be useless for him to enter into any farther discussion', as 'he did not come to betray lord Shelburne', and left.[28] Pretyman observed: 'This was, I believe, the last time Mr. Pitt was in a private room with Mr. Fox; and from this period may be dated that political hostility, which continued through the remainder of their lives.'[29]

The only hope now of saving the government was the recruitment of Lord North. But Pitt 'inflexibly refused' to sit in the Cabinet with the man who 'had precipitated Great Britain into disgrace as well as debt'.[30] In desperation Dundas approached North anyway at least for support, implying that North might be subject to impeachment if he did not support the government on the peace treaty. Dundas told North's friend William Adam, 'If Lord Shelburne resigns, Fox and Pitt may yet come together and dissolve Parliament, and there will be an end of Lord North. I see no means of preventing this but Lord North's support of the Address.'[31] This threat may have finally pushed North into doing the exact opposite, teaming up with Fox in order to get back into power. Whatever the underlying motives, Fox and North now joined forces. With the Lords approving the peace proposals by the alarmingly narrow majority of seventy-two to fifty-nine, North and Fox joined to savage them in the Commons. Fox attacked 'the sacrifice of our chief possessions in America, Asia and Africa', saying, 'If ever the situation of a country required a coalition of parties . . . it is that of the present.'[32] In response to incredulous attacks on his 'unnatural junction' with Lord North, he said, 'It is neither wise nor noble to keep up animosities forever . . . My friendships are perpetual, my enmities are not so.'[33]

Pitt had to reply to the debate. It was four o'clock in the morning, and he was tired. In one of his less effective speeches he argued that 'the clamours excited against the peace were loud in proportion to their injustice; and it was generally the case, that where men complained without cause, they complained without temper'.[34] He attacked the 'unnatural alliance' of Fox and North, saying it was 'undoubtedly to be reckoned among the wonders of the age',[35] but made a mistake by also attacking Sheridan, telling him to reserve his talents for the stage. Sheridan rose immediately afterwards to say that 'If ever I again engage in the composition he alludes to, I may be tempted . . . to attempt an improvement on one of Ben Jonson's best characters, the character of the Angry Boy in the Alchymist.'[36]

Wounded by this devastating retort, Pitt and his colleagues were in any case on the way to defeat. The Commons divided 224 to 208 against them. Pitt wrote from Downing Street to his mother at a quarter to seven in the morning: 'You are, I hope, enough used to such things in the political world as changes, not to be much surprised at the result of our business at the House of Commons . . . The two standards of Lord North and Fox produced 224 against us, 208 for us. This I think decisive . . . we should at least leave the field with honour. I am just going to bed, and I am perfectly well in spite of fatigue.'

The government had received a mortal blow, and before Shelburne could attempt any recovery Fox and North prepared the *coup de grâce*, tabling a fresh motion for 21 February saying that the concessions to Britain's enemies were 'greater than they were entitled to'. This second debate covered much the same ground as the first, but after his lacklustre speech on the Monday, Pitt turned up on the Friday to give a two-and-three-quarter-hour speech that ranks as one of the finest he ever delivered. This was in spite of being taken ill, and 'actually holding Solomon's porch door [the door between the Chamber of the Commons and the Members' Lobby] open with one hand, while vomiting during Fox's speech to whom he was to reply'.[37]* Knowing that the government was doomed and his own reputation rather dimmed from his previous performance, he gathered himself up to denounce the Fox–North coalition and to set out his own attitude to politics and office. After a long justification of the peace proposals he defended Shelburne, saying the debate originated 'rather in an inclination to force the Earl of Shelburne from the treasury, than in any real conviction that ministers deserve censure for the concessions they have made'.[38] He tore into Lord North: 'Whatever appears dishonourable or inadequate in the peace . . . is strictly chargeable to the noble lord in the blue ribbon [North], whose profusion of the public's money, whose notorious temerity and obstinacy in prosecuting the war which originated in his pernicious and oppressive policy, and whose utter incapacity to fill the station he occupied, rendered peace of any description indispensable to the preservation of the state.'[39]

* It is possible that this incident occurred on the Monday, in which case it would help to explain Pitt's inferior speech on that occasion.

Pitt raged against the Fox–North alliance: 'It is the Earl of Shelburne alone whom the movers of this question are desired to wound. This is the object which had raised this storm of faction; this is the aim of the unnatural coalition to which I have alluded. If, however, the baneful alliance is not already formed, if this ill-omened marriage is not already solemnised, I know a just and lawful impediment, and, in the name of the public safety, I here forbid the banns!'

With an eye on the future, Pitt set out his own approach to office, saying that if the government was voted out he would

> confidently repair, as to an adequate asylum from all the clamour which interested faction can raise. I was not very eager to come in, and shall have no great reluctance to go out, whenever the public are disposed to dismiss me from their service. It has been the great object of my short official existence to do the duties of my station with all the ability and address in my power, and with a fidelity and honour which should bear me up, and give me confidence, under every possible contingency or disappointment . . . High situation, and great influence, are desirable objects to most men, and objects which I am not ashamed to pursue, which I am even solicitous to possess, whenever they can be acquired with honour, and retained with dignity. On these respectable conditions, I am not less ambitious to be great and powerful than it is natural for a young man, with such brilliant examples before him [his father], to be. But even these objects I am not beneath relinquishing, the moment my duty to my country, my character, and my friends, renders such a sacrifice indispensable. Then I hope to retire, not disappointed, but triumphant; triumphant in the conviction that my talents, humble as they are, have been earnestly, zealously, and strenuously employed . . .[40]

When in opposition in the future, he said, he would behave entirely differently from the opposition of that day: 'I will not mimic the parade of the honourable gentleman [Fox] in avowing an indiscriminate opposition to whoever may be appointed to succeed. I will march out with no warlike, no hostile, no menacing protestations; but hoping the new administration will have no other object in view than the real and substantial welfare of the community at large.'[41] And calling on the memory of his father, he said: 'My earliest impressions were in favour of the noblest and most disinterested modes of serving the public: these impressions are still dear, and will, I hope, remain for ever dear to my heart: I will cherish them as a legacy infinitely more valuable than the greatest inheritance.'[42]

Wraxall commented: 'those who heard Mr. Pitt address the House . . . cannot easily forget the impression made upon his audience by a speech that might be said to unite all the powers of argument, eloquence, and impassioned declamation'. The speech did much for Pitt's reputation, and according to one opposition MP, Thomas Pelham, it was 'unanimously acknowledged . . . to be the finest speech that ever was made in Parliament'.[43] Against the united opposition, however, it could not win the vote. The government again went down to defeat, this time by 207 to 190, and the Shelburne ministry was finished. On 23 February Shelburne announced his resignation, and on the twenty-fourth he delivered it to George III. He asked the King to raise Thomas Townshend to the peerage, to which the King agreed, and Townshend subsequently became Lord Sydney.* This left William Pitt as the most senior member of the administration in the House of Commons. As the King and the supporters of the government looked in desperation for some final means of preventing the Fox–North coalition from coming to power, Pitt was suddenly the obvious and only person with a chance of leading any alternative government. Shelburne would now suggest to the King that a twenty-three-year-old Member of Parliament be invited to become Prime Minister, and Dundas would work furiously to bring it about. It is testimony to the extraordinary nature of both the situation and the individual that the King would agree to do so, and that the twenty-three-year-old would have the presence of mind to say no.

* Townshend earlier toyed with the title of Lord Sydenham, and his decision not to adopt that name was to be of lasting importance to the people of Australia, since a few years later Sydney was to be named after him.

7

Brief Exuberance

'I am clear Mr. Pitt means to play false.'

KING GEORGE III, MARCH 1783

'I had thought, from the first formation of the coalition, that Mr. Pitt was extinguished nearly for life as a politician, and wished to see him at the Bar again, under a conviction that his transcendent abilities would soon raise him to great eminence in his profession.'

GEORGE ROSE, SECRETARY TO THE TREASURY, IN 1783

THE DEFEAT OF SHELBURNE, and the happy translation of Townshend to the Upper House as Lord Sydney, meant that there was only one person left who could both hold his own in Parliament and did not belong to the Fox–North alliance. Twenty-three he might be, but after his speech on that Friday night, 21 February 1783, his reputation for ability and integrity stood high. It did not take long for those who had burnt their boats with Fox and North to alight on Pitt as the only available life-raft. Shelburne raised the idea on the Sunday, and on the Monday morning, 24 February, Dundas wrote to Shelburne:

> My Dear Lord,
>
> I cannot refrain from troubling your Lordship with a few lines upon a subject of the most serious importance; and the particular ground of my addressing you arises from the words which dropped from you yesterday morning relative to Mr. Pitt. I did not pay much attention to them when you uttered them, but I have revolved them seriously and candidly in the course of the

> day yesterday, and I completely satisfied my own mind that, young as he is, the appointment of him to the Government of the country is the only step that can be taken in the present moment attended with the most distant chance of rearing up the Government of this country . . . He is perfectly new ground, against whom no opposition can arise except what may be expected from the desperation of that lately allied faction, which I am satisfied will likewise gradually decline till at last it will consist only of that insolent aristocratical band who assume to themselves the prerogative of appointing the rulers of the kingdom. I repeat it again that I am certain the experiment will succeed if His Majesty will try it.[1]

From Pitt's first arrival in Parliament Henry Dundas had admired his abilities. In declaring himself an enthusiast for Pitt to lead the government, Dundas was opening a quarter of a century of close friendship and steadfast allegiance. Forty-one years old, Dundas had been trained to drink and to argue at the Scottish Bar. Many of Westminster's aristocrats would have found him coarse or dogmatic, but he always showed courage, a readiness for rough debate, fierce loyalty, and a gift for building a political machine based on patronage and rewards. His objective was the exercise of power rather than to take the leading role for himself. It would turn out that he and Pitt could find in each other precisely the qualities each of them needed in their ally: Pitt could supply oratory, intellect and integrity, while Dundas could bring cunning, solid votes and the arts of the political fixer.

The leading members of the defeated government looked around at each other and came to the same conclusion as Dundas. The only chance of frustrating the opposition was to present as head of the government someone relatively new, completely untainted, and possessed of an ability to win over the House of Commons. Extraordinary though it might be on grounds of age, they could muster no alternative. Both Shelburne and the Lord Chancellor, Lord Thurlow, concurred with the advice of Dundas and put it to the King. George III, who had determined with regard to Fox that he 'would never employ him again', was ready for anything provided it meant that Fox would not be returning to power. On the afternoon of Monday, 24 February 1783

William Pitt was summoned to the King and, three months before his twenty-fourth birthday, became by far the youngest person before or since to be invited to accept the office of First Lord of the Treasury and, in effect, Prime Minister.

The temptation must have been great. He was young, but he had known no other life, and had prepared from infancy to lead the political life of the nation. Even if he tried and failed, he would have held the highest office in the land, acquired its status, and could for the rest of his life be an alternative to whoever held it. As Horace Walpole put it: 'The offer was no doubt dazzling, and so far worth accepting, as to *obtain the chariot for a day*, was glorious at his age, and to one so ambitious. It was placing him at the head of a party, – a rank which he must always preserve, in or out of place.'[2]

Pitt also knew that the government had been defeated by only seventeen votes three nights before, and that opposition MPs had been fired up with the objective of removing Lord Shelburne rather than himself. He was no doubt still savouring the adrenalin of his triumphant speech of defiance. All the indications are that his first thought was that he could do it.

At 6.30 p.m. George III wrote to Thurlow that he had made the offer to Pitt, who had 'received it with a spirit and inclination that makes me think he will not decline though he has very properly desired time to weigh so momentous a step'.[3] The King was optimistic that he would be rescued from disaster; Pitt had clearly given him cause to think that was likely. But tempted though he was, Pitt was not dazzled. Several times he had seen his father reject the invitation of the King to lead a government, and once he had watched him accept it and then regret it. It appears that over the following hours he weighed the options coolly. On the one hand, his Sovereign and ministerial colleagues wished him to accept the challenge. Many Members of Parliament concurred, despairing of the whole previous generation of political leaders – 'Of all the public characters of this devoted country (Mr. Pitt alone excepted) there is not a man who has, or who deserves, the nation's confidence,' wrote Sir Samuel Romilly the following month.[4] The object on offer was also unmistakably his principal ambition. Yet on the other hand, he had watched the King forsake his father, and owed him little; and many of the colleagues urging him on were entering the evening of their political careers, while his was at its dawn. It would do nothing for his future to please his fellow Ministers but look ridiculous by being First Lord of the Treasury for a week. In the uneasy constitutional balance of the eighteenth century, the King could nominate whom he wished to lead a government, but the House of Commons could reject his choice.

Pitt's decision therefore came down to a matter of arithmetic, meticulously analysed and coldly assessed. Long into the night he sat with Dundas, going down the list of Members of Parliament and assessing their attitudes. It is not known how much port might have assisted the initial calculations, but it seems they were not wholly unfavourable. The following morning Dundas wrote to his brother in Edinburgh, telling him of the secret while urging him to keep it:

> I was with him [Pitt] all last night, and Mr. Rigby and I have been with him all this morning, going through the state of the House of Commons. I have little doubt that he will announce himself Minister to-morrow, and I have as little doubt that the effects of it upon the House of Commons will be instantly felt. Not a human being has a suspicion of the plan, except those in the immediate confidence of it. It will create an universal consternation in the allied camp the moment it is known. Still, secrecy![5]

At 9.30 that morning Pitt wrote to his mother, evidently wishing she was there to assist him.

> My Dear Mother,
>
> I wished more than I can express to see you yesterday. I will, if possible, find a moment today to tell you the state of things and learn your opinion. In the meantime the substance is, that our friends, almost universally, are eager for our going on, only without Lord Shelburne, and are sanguine in the expectation of success – Lord Shelburne himself most warmly so. The King, when I went in yesterday, pressed me in the strongest manner to take Lord Shelburne's place, and insisted on my not declining it till I had taken time to consider. You see the importance of

> the decision I must speedily make. I feel all the difficulties of the undertaking and am by no means in love with the object. On the other hand, I think myself bound not to desert a system in which I am engaged, if probable means can be shown of carrying it on with credit. On this general state of it I should wish anxiously to know what is the inclination of your mind. I must endeavour to estimate more particularly the probable issue by talking with those who know most of the opinions of men in detail. The great article to decide by seems that of numbers.
>
> Your ever dutiful and affectionate W Pitt

The secret did not last long, and by the evening of the twenty-fifth rumours of Pitt accepting office were sweeping Westminster. For two more days he weighed the matter, perhaps waiting for parliamentary support to be manifested once the news was well known. In the absence of that 'he seemed averse, thinking he will not be supported in the House of Commons'.[6] By the evening of the twenty-sixth, Pitt was telling the King that only the 'moral certainty' of a majority in the Commons would satisfy him that he could become First Lord. Dundas made a last effort to persuade him, assuring him that Lord North could be persuaded to desist from active opposition, thus tipping the balance. He believed Pitt was now persuaded. But just as the entreaties of the unfortunate Dundas had inadvertently helped push North into his pact with Fox, so his pleading with Pitt helped to highlight the crux of the decision, with the opposite effect to that intended. On the afternoon of Thursday, 27 February Pitt wrote to Dundas that what he had told him that morning 'seemed to remove all doubt of my finding a majority in Parliament, and on the first view of it, joined to my sincere desire not to decline the call of my friends, removed at the same time my objections to accepting the Treasury'. But he said he had now reconsidered matters and his final decision was 'directly contrary', for this reason: 'I see that the main and almost only ground of reliance would be this, that Lord North and his friends would not continue in a combination to oppose . . . Such a reliance is too precarious to act on. But above all, in point of honour to my own feelings, I cannot form an administration trusting to the hope that it will be supported, or even will not be opposed, by Lord North, whatever the influence may be that determines his conduct.' For all Pitt's earlier insistence that personal factors would never sway him, at no time could he bring himself to make any concession to cooperation with Lord North. This, he said, had '*unalterably* determined' him to decline the King's invitation. 'I have to beg', he finished by writing to a distraught Dundas, 'a thousand pardons for being the occasion of your having so much trouble in vain.'[7]

In Dundas, Pitt had acquired a valuable ally who would stand by him for the rest of his life, but his decision that afternoon left his new lieutenant exasperated and demoralised, all the more so because he was assembling a dinner for leading peers and MPs that night for 'hailing the new Minister'.[8] Dundas told his brother, 'How it will all end, God only knows. I don't think I shall give myself any more trouble in the matter.'[9] While Dundas explained the adverse turn of events to his disappointed dinner guests, Pitt proceeded to a long and difficult audience with the King. George III must have remembered the truculent refusal of Chatham to accept office on many occasions as he came up against the trenchant refusal of another Pitt. 'Nothing', the King wrote to Shelburne, 'could get him to depart from the ground he took, that nothing less than a moral certainty of a majority in the House of Commons could make him undertake the task; for that it would be dishonourable not to succeed, if attempted.'[10]

For the third time in twelve months Westminster was enveloped by complete confusion as to who would next form the government of the country. When the Commons reassembled to hear details of the new government, they found no such government was in the making, although Pitt was still in office as Chancellor of the Exchequer. He would devote himself in the coming days to presenting and arguing for a Bill to provide for freer trade with America, leaving the King to renew his struggle to find a government that he thought he could live with. George sent first for Lord Gower, who could not muster enough support in the House of Commons, and then for Lord North, in an attempt to divide him from Fox. North refused the Treasury for himself, said he could support Pitt from the sidelines (the very thing Pitt would not rely on), and otherwise favoured his coalition with Fox. A struggle now commenced between George III and Fox which both saw, correctly, as being of major constitutional importance. The King decided he could only have North back in office with Fox alongside him if they would agree to serve under an independent figure, 'a peer not connected with any of the strong parties that distract this kingdom'.[11] This would greatly reduce the power of the Fox–North coalition, and would preserve the King's prerogative of nominating his own First Minister. Fox, by contrast, wished to impose the Duke of Portland as First Lord of the Treasury, just as he had tried to do the previous July. This would put effective power into Fox's own hands, and demonstrate that the ultimate decision on the composition and leadership of the government lay in the House of Commons. In the political parlance of the day, this was 'storming the closet'.*

Given that North could not or would not serve without Fox, and that between them they commanded majority support in the Commons, there now arose a serious constitutional crisis. The wishes of the King and the opinions of a firm majority in Parliament were in direct conflict. For the King this was a far graver situation than the governmental crises of the previous year. When giving office to Rockingham, he had managed to sow division in the government at the outset and to maintain a loyal faction within it. This time he was presented with a previously agreed coalition which insisted on having its way and would not so easily be fooled again.

As the month of March wore on the King thrashed about for a way to avoid the inevitable, and the country had no effective government. Gower now bizarrely suggested turning to Thomas Pitt, Pitt's cousin and veteran Member for Old Sarum, to form an administration. The King was prepared to try even this, asking for 'Mr. Thomas Pitt or Mr. Thomas anybody'.[12] Disappointingly for the embattled monarch, yet another Pitt showed sound self-knowledge, pronouncing himself 'totaly [sic] unequal to public business, but most certainly unequal to a task like this'. Instead he recommended allowing the coalition to take office but withholding all royal favours from it, and warned the King that things were now getting dangerous, that this could be the most

* This expression arose from the King's use of a small room, 'the closet', for meetings with Ministers.

important decision of his reign, and that 'every symptom of a distempered state seemed to prognosticate the danger of some convulsions if the temper of the times was not managed with prudence'.[13]

The King was not yet ready for prudence. He again talked of abdicating, and once more turned to Lord Gower to form a government, a project which, as before, turned out to be hopeless. By 12 March George was in his last ditch, sending for North and agreeing that Portland could be First Lord of the Treasury, and then trying to play the two of them off against each other while being as uncooperative as possible. The next ten days were taken up with highly complex negotiations, during which the King exasperated Portland by refusing to discuss the provisional appointment of Ministers until he could see the whole list, and the Fox and North parties fell out with each other over who was to have which jobs.

Even greater confusion would now commence. On 20 March Portland informed the King that the coalition could not after all agree on the composition of a government, largely because of the King's insistence on trying to insert Lords Stormont and Thurlow into the Cabinet. Facing disaster, the Fox–North parties decided that night to swallow the pill and accept the appointment of Stormont, and the following day Portland was finally able to present an agreed list of the Cabinet to the King. George, however, had already seen a chance of rescue, and after Portland's previous visit had written a one-line letter to Pitt:

> Queen's House, March 20 1783.
> Mr. Pitt, I desire you will come here immediately.
> G.R.[14]

Incredibly, the whole negotiation with Pitt now began again. Pitt saw the King and then met Dundas and Rutland. They agreed that if the coalition really could not sort itself out 'he would accept of the Government, and make an administration . . . But he insisted to have the secret kept, because he was determined to have it distinctly ascertained before going again to the King, that North and Fox . . . had quarrelled among themselves about the division of the spoils.' Since the coalition had, however, now 'yielded the point in dispute' to the King, it assumed that the Portland–Fox–North government would now take office. Despite this, George III continued to implore Pitt to take office and rescue him. Pitt wavered. Historians have found it difficult to explain his actions over the subsequent few days. The Commons was due to meet again on 24 March, and Fox and North looked forward to the House being resolute in their support. In the meantime, however, Pitt maintained his negotiations with the King, who therefore continued to defy the coalition and the Commons. At two o'clock in the morning on the day the Commons was to meet, Pitt summoned Dundas from his bed for urgent discussions. Dundas wrote to his presumably bewildered brother, 'I flatter myself Mr. Pitt will kiss hands as First Lord of the Treasury on Wednesday next.'[15] It was now Monday: Pitt and the King clearly had evolved a plan between them. The King wrote to Thurlow that 'after every sort of chicanery from the Coalition' he had broken off further negotiations 'with the consent of Mr. Pitt',[16] and that he now expected him to take office. But whatever Pitt expected to happen in the House that afternoon to cement the arrangement did not come to pass. He seems to have been waiting for significant numbers in the Commons to ask him to take on the government. Unfortunately, while he waited for a lead from them, they awaited a lead from him. Most of the partisan Members of the House were in any case firmly committed to Fox and North, and the remainder were now confused by Pitt's own speech.

He attacked the Fox–North coalition effectively: 'there may be a seeming harmony while their interests point the same road, but only a similarity of ideas can render political friendships permanent',[17] and 'Gentlemen talked of forgiving animosities and altering their political opinions with as much ease as they could change their gloves,'[18] but the substance of his speech only fed the uncertainty. He did not directly oppose a motion for an address to the King demanding the formation of an administration, while some of his possible allies did oppose it, and although he stated that he knew of no arrangement for a new administration, he later said 'he had some reason to imagine an administration would be formed, if not in one, at least, in two or three days'.[19] Some Members thought that 'the whole of Mr. Pitt's conduct was inexplicable'.[20] Walpole called it 'a long, guarded, and fluctuating speech'.[21]

In fact, Pitt was waiting for a great expression of support from the benches of the Commons. The King hoped that if Pitt said 'that every man attached to this Constitution must stand forth . . . that He will meet with an applause that cannot fail to give him every encouragement'.[22] Pitt himself later explained to Carmarthen that 'he had in the debate on Monday . . . purposely endeavoured to collect the real wishes of thc independent part of the House', but had not found 'any reason to expect a substantial support from thence'.[23] He had thus been on a public fishing expedition in the House of Commons that day, but had found no one biting on the line. As a result he wrote to the King the next day 'with infinite pain', explaining that 'it is utterly impossible for Him, after the fullest consideration of the actual situation of what passed yesterday in the House of Commons, to think of undertaking, under such circumstances, the Situation which Your Majesty has had the condescension and Goodness to propose to him'.[24] It was the first demonstration of an enduring trait in Pitt's character: his need to show his disinterestedness and dignity meant that he sought power by acclamation rather than being seen to grasp for it.

Pitt's reputation does not appear to have been damaged by this fiasco, and it must be remembered that the details of his negotiations with the King were not widely known. Furthermore, while his speech of 24 March failed to produce a wave of enthusiasm for him to lead the government, it added to his reputation for integrity and independence, since he could easily have thrown in his lot with the Fox–North coalition instead. He was pressed by them to continue in office as Chancellor of the Exchequer in a new government, and Wraxall observed that 'it rested with him to have composed one of the new triumvirate . . . aided by a judgement far beyond his years', he rejected 'the seductive proposition'.[25] More generally, of Pitt's refusal to lead a government the Duke of Grafton commented: 'The good judgement of so young a man, who, not void of ambition, on this trying occasion, could refuse this splendid offer, adds much to the lustre of the character he had acquired, for it was a temptation sufficient to have over-set the resolution of most men.'[26]

Still more important for the future, the fact that so much had turned on Pitt's actions underlined the point that he was the only alternative to the men about to take office. Of course this was no consolation to the now utterly despairing King. He sent Pitt the following letter:

> Windsor
> March 25th 4.35 p.m.
> Mr. Pitt,
> I am much hurt to find you are determined to decline at an hour when those who have any regard for the Constitution as established by law ought to stand forth against the most daring and most unprincipled faction that the annals of this Kingdom ever produced.
> GR[27]

He now drafted his speech of abdication, ending: 'May I to the latest hour of my Life, though now resolved for ever to quit this Island, have the Comfort of hearing that the Endeavours of My Son, though they cannot be more sincere than Mine have been for the Prosperity of Great Britain, may be crowned with better success.'[28] Once again, he did not carry out this threat. Thurlow reminded him that Kings could find it very easy to leave their country but very difficult ever to come back, James II being a case in point. On 31 March Pitt gave a valedictory speech to the Commons as Chancellor of the Exchequer, declaring that he was 'unconnected with any party whatever; that he should keep himself reserved, and act with which ever side he thought did right'.[29] On 2 April, Fox, North and their colleagues arrived to take office and kiss the King's hand. As Fox did so, Lord John Townshend noticed the King 'turn back his ears and eyes just like the horse at Astley's [riding school] when the tailor he had determined to throw was getting on him'.[30]

The closet had been stormed. Fox was now triumphant, back in office as Secretary of State for Foreign Affairs, with an acquiescent Whig grandee, the Duke of Portland, as First Lord of the Treasury and Lord North as Secretary of State for the Home Department. Lord John

Cavendish, who had been Chancellor of the Exchequer before Pitt, resumed his former position. The coalition had succeeded in refusing to accept Lord Thurlow as Lord Chancellor, but as George III would not accept anyone else the position was simply left vacant.

The relations of this government with the King were not good, and never would be. Fox cheerfully observed that the King 'will dye soon & that will be best of all'.[31] George adopted a royal version of working to rule, and simply refused to grant any peerages or other honours at the request of his new Ministers, making it impossible for them to send Lord North to the Upper House as they wished. As they took office, the King wrote to Pitt's cousin Earl Temple:

> I shall most certainly refuse any honours that may be asked by them; I trust the eyes of the Nation will soon be opened as my sorrow may prove fatal to my health if I remain long in this thraldom; I trust You will be steady in Your attachment to Me and ready to join other honest Men in watching the conduct of this unnatural Combination, and I hope many months will not elapse before the Grenvilles, the Pitts and other men of abilities and character will relieve Me from a Situation that nothing but the supposition that no other means remained of preventing the public finances from being materially affected would have compelled me to submit to.[32]

Rarely in history has a monarch been so utterly determined to overthrow the government acting in his name. In achieving that objective, the King and his fellow conspirators, the Lords Temple and Thurlow, knew that Pitt was a vital instrument. They could well have interpreted the events of March 1783 as showing that Pitt could not be relied upon. But more importantly, the same events had shown that no alternative government to the Fox–North coalition could hold its own in the House of Commons without Pitt at its head. No one else had even come close to rescuing the King. These events had therefore strengthened Pitt's position should any 'accident' befall the administration. So while some, such as George Rose, believed that 'Mr. Pitt was extinguished nearly for life as a politician',[33] others thought the outlook for him was distinctly promising. By June bets were being laid at Brooks's

Club that Pitt or Temple would be Prime Minister by Christmas, with odds of four to one against.[34]

Pitt himself moved quickly out of Downing Street, and developed the habit of staying with his friends in Wimbledon. He seemed genuinely relaxed about leaving office. One of the puzzles about Pitt is whether his protestations of caring little whether or not he was in government – 'I had no great desire to come in and shall have no great reluctance to go out' – represented his genuine feelings or were an affectation to enhance the impression of an independent character. Honest though he had often proved himself to be, we know from his assertion on 24 March that he knew of 'no arrangement' for a new administration, when he was in full negotiation with the King, that he was not always truthful when trying to demonstrate his independence of action. A far more glaring example of this would become apparent when the stakes were even higher. It is also obvious that he was prepared to fight hard to retain office or to acquire it. He must have known, looking around him in the House of Commons, that he merited high office, and that he was one of the very few people actually capable of governing the country.

Three factors would seem to have combined to make Pitt at this stage in his career both ambitious for office and yet relaxed about the gaining or losing of it. The first was this very sense of meritocratic superiority. Shortly after Pitt became Prime Minister, Wraxall wrote his famous account of his personal style:

> in his manners, Pitt, if not repulsive, was cold, stiff, and without suavity or amenity. He seemed never to invite approach or to encourage acquaintance, though when addressed he could be polite, communicative, and occasionally gracious ... From the instant that Pitt entered the doorway of the House of Commons, he advanced up the floor with a quick and firm step, his head erect and thrown back, looking neither to the right nor to the left, nor favouring with a nod or a glance any of the individuals seated on either side, among whom many who possessed five thousand pounds a year would have been gratified even by so slight a mark of attention. It was not thus that Lord North or Fox treated Parliament, nor from them would Parliament have so

> patiently endured it; but Pitt seemed made to guide and to command, even more than to persuade or to convince, the assembly that he addressed.[35]

His immense intellectual self-confidence was combined with a second factor: the expectation that his hour would come. In part this was the natural feeling of a young man who had advanced far in politics at an early age. Old politicians have the advantage of seeing events in the perspective of the past, but young ones have the satisfaction of accepting events in the perspective of the future. The elder Pitt had lived for seventy years. As an ex-Chancellor of the Exchequer at the age of twenty-three the younger Pitt could look forward to decades of pre-eminence in politics among colleagues still unborn. More immediately, he would undoubtedly have known from his cousin Temple and his own dealings with the King of the iron determination of George III to change the government when he could. Perhaps this explains one of Wraxall's other observations, that Pitt 'even while seated on the Opposition bench, appeared to anticipate his speedy return to power as certain, and only to wait for the occasion presenting itself to resume his former functions'.[36]

Such calculations would have reinforced Pitt's confidence even in defeat, but there is a third factor which is also of great significance. His achievements to date helped to put him at the centre of a small circle of talented or loyal friends whose friendship sustained him when in office, but all the more so when out of it. Wilberforce recalled that after Pitt's defiant speech of 21 February, 'I remember our all going to Mr. Pitt's from the House of Commons after our defeat about eight in the morning, where a dinner had been waiting for us from eleven or twelve the preceding night, and where we all laughed heartily.'[37] On the day of his resignation as Chancellor of the Exchequer, Pitt joined Wilberforce for supper at Goostree's and they stayed up much of the night. Pitt and his friends then descended on the house Wilberforce had inherited in Wimbledon, then a village in rural Surrey and a seven-mile ride from Westminster. Wilberforce's diary recorded: 'Delicious day, – lounged morning at Wimbledon with friends, *foining**

* Fencing with a weapon designed for thrusting or lunging – but in this context meaning verbal fencing.

at night, and run about the garden for an hour or two.'[38] Wilberforce's house had eight or nine bedrooms* and a large garden. He explained that 'Mr. Pitt, who was remarkably fond of sleeping in the country, and would often go out of town for that purpose as late as eleven or twelve o'clock at night, slept at Wimbolton for two or three months together.'[39]

Notwithstanding the fact that he had recently held one of the highest offices in the land, Pitt briefly found that spring and summer the exuberance of youth. Thomas Orde, MP for Aylesbury and one of Pitt's circle, soon to become Chief Secretary of Ireland, was expected by Lord Shelburne to report to him on what Pitt was up to, and wrote: 'He passes, as usual, most of his time with his young Friends in a Society sometimes very lively – Some little excess happen'd lately at Wimbledon . . . In the Evening some of the Neighbours were alarmed with noises at their doors, but Nobody, I believe, has made any reflection upon a mere frolic – it has only been pleasantly remarked, that the Rioters were headed by Master P. – late Chancellor of the Ex –, and Master Arden, late Sollicitor Genl.'[40] Wilberforce's diary that summer reads: 'Sunday July 6th, Wimbledon. Persuaded Pitt and Pepper [Arden] to church. July 11th. Fine hot day. Went on water with Pitt and Eliot fishing. Came back, dined, walked evening. Eliot went home. Pitt stayed.'

Pitt's behaviour among friends was the polar opposite of the icy coldness which Wraxall had observed. The explanation given by Wilberforce for this contrast is that Pitt was the 'shyest man' he ever knew: 'great natural shyness . . . and even awkwardness . . . often produced effects for which pride was falsely charged on him.'[41] Pitt is himself meant to have said to Wilberforce, 'I am the shyest man alive.'[42] Yet with these friends he threw off his restraints, writing to Wilberforce one afternoon from the Commons: 'Eliot, Arden and I will be with you before curfew and expect an early meal of peas and strawberries.'[43] One of the friends, Dudley Ryder, the future Earl of Harrowby, found one morning that the expensive hat he had worn to the opera the

* One of these rooms was known as 'Pitt's room' until the demolition of the house in 1958.

previous night had been cut up by Pitt and scattered over the flowerbeds.

The same spirit infected their proceedings everywhere. Harriot Pitt wrote one evening that she could hardly write for the noise of their laughter, and the MP George Selwyn noted one night in 1782: 'When I left the House, I left in one room a party of young men, who made me, from their life and spirit, wish for one night to be twenty. There was a table full of them drinking – young Pitt, Lord Euston, Berkley, North &c. &c. singing and laughing *à gorge déployée*.'[44]

Pitt's friends revered him. Wilberforce said of his humour: 'Mr. Pitt was systematically witty . . . the others were often run away with by their wit. Mr. Pitt was always master of his. He could turn it to any end or object he desired.'[45] Later in his career they would come to regard him as 'something between God and Man'.[46] This was in spite of his unprepossessing appearance. Pitt's niece, Lady Hester Stanhope, would write many years later that 'Mr. Pitt's was not a face that gave one the idea of a clever man. As he walked through the park, you would have taken him for a poet, or some such person, thin, tall, and rather awkward; looking upwards as if his ideas were *en air* and not remarking what was passing around him.'[47] All agreed that only his eyes gave force to his appearance: they 'lent animation to his other features . . . they lighted up and became strongly intelligent',[48] and 'lighted up in a manner quite surprising. It was something that seemed to dart from within his head, and you might see sparks coming from them,'[49] even though he often 'had a sort of slovenly or negligent look'. Outside the House of Commons he seemed to lack presence, being ungainly and with little in the way of elegance or polished manners. Yet in the House of Commons, this strange-looking young man was the principal opposition to what His Majesty reluctantly called his government.

Pitt now had a political following as well as a circle of friends. Dundas had become a permanent lieutenant, and the Marquis of Carmarthen wrote that 'I am proud to own my conduct should be regulated by yours.' Thomas Pitt observed of the King that 'it was to him alone that we must look up . . . when the moment should be ripe for it'.[50] Pitt's chosen style of opposition was judicious, displaying 'neither an illiberal, a vindictive, nor an undistinguishing resistance to Ministerial measures'.[51] Riding to and fro from Wimbledon, he was regularly on his feet in the Commons. In April he exchanged sharp words with Ministers over the disadvantageous terms on which they had raised a loan – the Ministers argued that Pitt's delay in leaving office had left them in a difficult situation. Later in the session he brought forward the Bills on which he had worked as Chancellor, principally directed at removing waste from government departments. One of these was defeated in the Commons, and the other in the Lords. Pitt was not impressed by successors who did not have the political will or the concern for public money to carry his measures through.

It was once again to parliamentary reform that he directed his greatest efforts in the spring of 1783, and on which he suffered his most severe disappointment. On 7 May, the anniversary of his narrowly defeated motion to set up a Select Committee on parliamentary reform, he brought to the Commons a more specific plan to prevent bribery at elections, to disenfranchise boroughs guilty of corruption, and to add a hundred new Members for London and the counties. He had agreed with Wyvill a moderate approach to reform, rejecting in his speech any idea of universal suffrage and stressing that he only wished to correct 'a deviation from the principles of that happy constitution under which the people of England had so long flourished'. He had real hopes for success, and the added bonus of advancing a course on which Fox and North were clearly divided. But Wyvill had hoped that Pitt would be proposing reform as a senior Minister; now this was not to be, and powerful forces were stacked against them. MPs turned out to be more hostile to a specific plan of reform than they were reassured by it; public apathy seemed more apparent than enthusiasm as the petitions and addresses failed to flow in the numbers needed; and while Fox gave nominal support to Pitt's motion, North opposed it in a brilliant speech which maximised the vote against it. The vote went 293 to 149 against reform. Pitt wrote to his mother: 'My defeat was much more complete than I expected.'

Fox had been civil to Pitt in the early weeks of the new government, no doubt with a possible view to recruiting him to it and disabling the opposition. There can be little doubt, however, that as Pitt watched Fox participate in a government which failed to argue for parliamentary reform, failed to deliver further economical reform, and failed to improve upon the peace terms which it had formerly denounced, he felt his breach with Fox was complete. And very soon the King would again put temptation in his way.

On 12 August 1783 George, Prince of Wales would come of age, requiring the creation of his own establishment and household. The attempt to settle his financial affairs would come within an ace of destroying the Fox–North administration within three months of it taking office. True to Hanoverian tradition, the Prince of Wales was developing a personality the precise opposite of that of his father, the King. In his late teens he had become a notorious philanderer, beginning at the age of sixteen by seducing one of the Queen's Maids of Honour and going on to have a string of mistresses, at least two of whom he passed on to Charles James Fox. At Brooks's Club and elsewhere he socialised with the very politicians whom his father detested. As the King put it: 'The Prince of Wales on the smallest reflection must feel that I have little reason to approve of any part of his conduct for the last three years; his neglect of every religious duty is notorious; his want of common civility to the Queen and me, not less so; besides his total disobedience of every injunction.'[52]

Fox succeeded in persuading the other Ministers that his friend the Prince should be granted an income of £100,000 per annum, a proposition the Duke of Portland then had to put to the King, along with the information that the Prince had already run up debts of £29,000. George III responded: 'It is impossible for me to find words expressive enough of my utter indignation and astonishment at the letter I have just received from the Duke of Portland.' Continuing the explosions for several days, the King proposed £50,000 per annum instead. The government was paralysed, and when the Commons assembled to hear Fox make a statement on the matter he was not able to say anything at all. Not knowing what to do, Portland was surprised to find a little later, on 18 June, that the King had apparently mellowed in his attitude, and the Prince was induced to accept a compromise: £50,000 a year and the paying off of debts of £60,000, along with a dutiful exchange of letters between father and son.

The King had not actually mellowed; he had merely calculated the political odds. In the interim he had consulted Temple, telling him that he had 'decided to resist this attempt [the £100,000 proposal], and to push the consequences to their full extent, and to try the spirit of the Parliament and of the people upon it';[53] but Temple advised him that it would be difficult to form a new administration if Ministers were dismissed on such a pretext. The King decided to bide his time but to take further soundings, possibly in order to be readier for the next such occasion. Thurlow was sent to sound out Pitt on the strength of his commitment to parliamentary reform, which the King opposed, and his readiness to make a bid for power with the support of the Crown. Pitt responded that he would take office, but on his own terms, as he made clear to Temple: 'I stated in general that if the King's feelings did not point strongly to a change, it was not what we sought. But that if they did, and we could form a permanent system, consistent with our principles, and on public ground, we should not decline it. I reminded him how much I was personally pledged to Parliamentary reform on the principles I had publicly explained, which I should support on every seasonable occasion.'[54]

Pitt was not ready to abandon the ideals of independence and integrity on which he had set his heart. He did want office, but knew he did not need to trade his opinions in order to get it, also telling Temple, 'I think . . . what has passed will not tend to delay our having the offer whenever things are ripe for it.'[55]

Since it was now July, and Parliament was rising for the summer, there was no prospect of matters 'ripening' in the next few months. On 22 July Pitt wrote to his mother from his brother's house in Savile Street: 'I resume at last my pen, tho' with no other Reason than ought to have made me do so every day for this month past. I can indeed hardly make out how that period has slid away, in which I have done little else but ride backwards and forwards between Wimbledon and London, and meditate plans for the summer, till I find the summer half over before I have begun to put any in execution.'[56] In early August he was writing from newly fashionable Brighthelmstone, to which he had gone to take 'some dips'. 'By all I learnt before I left London, I now think things may possibly go thro' the rest of the summer as they are, tho' much longer there is every reason to believe, they will not.'[57] In early September he was in Dorset at the house of Henry Bankes, meeting up with Eliot and Wilberforce. The short-sighted Wilberforce was teased for nearly shooting Pitt while aiming at some partridges, but we do not know how close he came to disabling the next Prime Minister.

Wilberforce, Eliot and Pitt had decided to visit France for the early autumn. Before doing so Pitt attended the King's levée at St James's. Ever in close touch with Temple, Pitt reported to him: 'I am still inclined to believe . . . that the King does not like to hazard dismissing the present Ministry till he has found some ostensible ground of complaint, or till he sees the disposition of Parliament next Session . . . I am just returned from St. James's . . . The King was gracious as usual, and he inquired as to the time of my stay [in France] in a manner which I rather thought significant.'[58]

Pitt thus departed for France knowing that he might once again be called upon to form a government at any time when he got back. Proximity to political power, however, did anything but bring efficiency to his travelling arrangements. When the three friends met at Sittingbourne ready to cross the Channel they found that each had expected the others to provide the letters of introduction necessary to travel comfortably in a foreign country. Upon receiving a last-minute letter introducing them to a Monsieur Coustier, they headed for his house at Rheims, only to find that he was a grocer with a small shop and one room behind it. 'For a few days we lived very comfortably together,' wrote Wilberforce, 'but no French was learned except from the grammar, we not having a single French acquaintance. At length we desired our friend the *épicier* to mention us to the Lieutenant of the Police.'[59] The policeman thought they were spies, seeing that they were in 'wretched lodgings' and had no attendants, but told the local Abbé that these three young men claimed to be '*grands seigneurs*', and one of them the son of the great Earl of Chatham. Soon Pitt was writing to Harriot: 'Tomorrow we are to dine at a magnificent Palace of the Archbishop's . . . and as a French Abbé is not proverbial for silence, we have an opportunity of hearing something of the language.'[60] Pitt learned French quickly, his ear being 'quick for every sound but music'. He enjoyed the political discussions, telling the Abbé that the first part of the British constitution to decline would be 'the prerogative of the King and the authority of the House of Peers'. But in a week of staying with the Archbishop, politics was far from their sole concern. Wilberforce noted: 'N.B. Archbishops in England are not like Archevêques in France; these last are jolly fellows of about forty years of age, who play at billiards, &c. like other people.'[61]

With news of their presence in France now spreading before them, the three friends went on to Paris, and then on to the vicinity of the French court assembled in Fontainebleau. They were presented to Louis XVI, 'a clumsy strange figure in immense boots'. Wilberforce describes being 'every evening at the parties of one or other of the French Ministers, in whose apartments we also dined – the Queen being always among the company present in the evening, and mixing in conversation with the greatest affability'.[62] Pitt had a lively time with the Queen, Marie Antoinette, who made fun of the manner of his arrival in France and repeatedly teased him about whether he had heard lately from the grocer. 'Mr. Pitt,' Wilberforce reported, 'though his imperfect knowledge of French prevented his doing justice to his sentiments, was yet able to give some impression of his superior powers.' Pitt's ability to learn quickly and to charm people of every kind in private company was thoroughly on display on the visit to France. He behaved throughout with relaxed good humour, even when the French 'crowded around Pitt in shoals . . . he behaved with great spirit although he was sometimes a little bored when they talked to him about the parliamentary reform'.

A second Pitt trait visible on this visit was his lack of interest in proposals of marriage. He was offered the hand of the seventeen-year-old daughter of the fabulously wealthy Jacques Necker, a highly ambitious French politician who would play a significant role in the events of the Revolution. According to Wilberforce: 'It was suggested to the late Lord Camden by Mr. Walpole, a particular friend of M.

Necker's, that if Mr. Pitt should be disposed to offer his hand to Mademoiselle N . . . such was the respect entertained for him by M. and Madame Necker, that he had no doubt the proposal would be accepted.'[63] It is said that Pitt responded, 'I am already married to my country,' but, perhaps fortunately, no definite record of this remains.*

Even on this journey Pitt was more interested in making alliances of another kind: it was another attribute of his that he was a shrewd political talent-spotter. George Rose, the highly able former Secretary to the Treasury, was also travelling in France at the time:

> I received a letter from Mr. Pitt at Rheims, desiring I would stay at Paris till he could get to me, which he said he would do as soon as possible. On our meeting, the conversation was quite confidential. In the course of it I found he was as little disposed to future connexion with Lord Shelburne as myself, and he manifested an earnest desire for a permanent and close intimacy with me . . . Having hesitated only from a consciousness of my own insignificance as to any essential service I could render him . . . I gave him my hand with a warm and consenting heart. From that moment I considered myself as inalienable from Mr. Pitt, and on that feeling I acted most sacredly to the last hour of his invaluable life.[64]

Pitt's thoughts were on planning for a government. With Parliament due to resume on 11 November, he had intended to return to England in late October. On 22 October a special messenger arrived from London, asking him to return immediately. Who sent the messenger is not known, but between George III, Temple and Thurlow the cogs of a conspiracy against the government were turning once again. Pitt had enjoyed his summer of youthful play, from the garden at Wimbledon to the forest of Fontainebleau. He had experienced for six months a relatively carefree existence. On 22 October 1783, the clatter of hooves in a French courtyard brought it forever to an end.

* Instead she married the Swedish Ambassador in Paris, becoming Madame de Staël. She became a powerful intellectual force in European politics, a friend of Goethe and an antagonist of Napoleon. If Pitt had married her it would have made a formidable combination.

8

From Plotter to Prime Minister

'We are in the midst of a contest, and I think, approaching to a crisis.'

WILLIAM PITT, NOVEMBER 1783

'The deliberations of this evening must decide whether we are to be henceforward free men or slaves; whether this House is the palladium of liberty or the engine of despotism.'

CHARLES JAMES FOX, 17 DECEMBER 1783

PITT AND HIS COMPANIONS returned to Dover from their sojourn in France on 24 October 1783. Within weeks they would be embroiled in one of the great constitutional crises of British history, and within months Pitt himself would exercise a domination of British politics which would span more than two decades and end only with his death. Yet few observers could have charted the course which would bring the ungainly and no doubt weary-looking young man making his way across Kent to London to such pre-eminence in so short a time, for no one could foresee with confidence the results of a head of state mounting a political *coup d'état* against his own government.

Pretyman tells us that Pitt returned to England 'with an intention of resuming his profession of the law, if there should appear a fair probability of the administration being permanent'.[1] In fact, he was feverishly busy with political meetings immediately on his return to London, knowing that something dramatic could happen in the coming session. By 3 November he was writing to Lord Mahon that he had hoped to visit him at his country house, Chevening, 'but I have had so much to do ever since I have been in town that I have found it impossible . . . Time is every day more precious . . . I trust you will be in town in *a very few days,* for there are several things in which I am quite at a loss without you.'[2] While Pitt prepared for the meeting of Parliament in London, Temple called other opponents of the government together at his own country residence, Stowe, mindful of the King's request to be ready to rescue him from his 'thraldom'. Nothing in the summer had changed George III's attitude. Fox had hoped that 'if we last the Summer, the Public will think that the King has made up his mind to *bear* us, and this opinion alone will destroy the only real cause of weakness that belongs to us'.[3] But as Wraxall observed, George allowed his Ministers to 'dictate measures; gave them audiences, signed papers, and complied with their advice; but he neither admitted them to his confidence nor ceased to consider them as objects of his individual aversion'.[4]

George III opened the new session of Parliament on 11 November, dutifully reading from the throne the speech written for him by the Ministers he hated. Opposition spokesmen found little to criticise in this broad statement of government intention: in the Lords Temple criticised the state of government finances, and in the Commons Pitt pointed out that the definitive peace treaties were almost identical to the much-criticised provisional articles of peace which he and Shelburne had defended. There was nothing at this stage to vote against or object to, and Pitt wrote to his mother that night: 'We have to-day heard the King's Speech, and voted the Address without any opposition. Both were so *general* that they prove nothing of what may be expected during the Session. The East India business and the funds promise to make the two principal objects.'[5]

The 'East India business' would indeed provide the spark to ignite the coming conflagration. All were agreed that the methods by which Britain governed its Indian dominions must be reformed, but the disagreement about how to do so would be spectacular. In the days when 'Diamond Pitt' had made his fortune in Madras British affairs in India were controlled exclusively by the East India Company. Even then, the huge sums to be made from holding positions of influence in India made the Company's affairs increasingly important in domestic

British politics. By the middle of the eighteenth century, the designs of the French on developing an Indian empire made Indian affairs even more directly a matter of governmental concern. From 1751, when Robert Clive wrecked the plans of the French and succeeded in holding Arcot against an enemy army which outnumbered his by forty to one, British power and responsibilities in India grew rapidly. By 1754 Britain was sending regular troops to India rather than relying solely on those employed by the Company, and three years later Clive routed the French and their allies at the Battle of Plassey. In 1764 a hostile coalition of Indian Princes was similarly annihilated at the Battle of Buxar. Backed by conquering troops, the East India Company had acquired the power to nominate Indian rulers, depose local governments and expel foreign invasions. Originally established to conduct trade, the Company was now ruling an empire.

By the early 1770s the individuals within the East India Company controlled vast patronage and wealth, while the Company itself was virtually bankrupt as a result of taking on so many responsibilities at the same time as paying out huge dividends. In 1773 the government of Lord North introduced a Regulating Act to put the governing of British possessions in India more nearly within political control, creating a Governor General, a Council and a Supreme Court, and regulating the conduct of the Company's business and behaviour. This system did not work, largely because the Council was usually at bitter loggerheads with the Governor General, Warren Hastings. In 1779, beset by internal divisions, Hastings had to face a wave of Indian revolts and the arrival of a new French fleet in the East at a time when no British reinforcements were available because of the war in America. He resolved the crisis with immense skill and ruthlessness, using, as one historian put it, 'diplomacy, bribery, threats, force, audacity, and resolution',[6] demolishing every enemy and extending British power still further. In the process, and perhaps inevitably, he committed acts of retribution against enemies and paid vast sums of money to allies. Such tactics produced the desired result, but, when written down on paper in the House of Commons and examined by high-minded people who had never set foot in India, they seemed to have a doubtful ethical basis, to say the least.

In 1781 a Select Committee of the Commons was set up to investigate the judicial system of Bengal, numbering among its members Edmund Burke. Burke had become obsessed with Indian affairs, and would years later bring about the impeachment and trial of Warren Hastings. Now, as a member of the Fox–North government, he was able to frame a Bill which would bring true political control and accountability to Indian affairs. It was this Bill, the East India Bill, which an excited Charles James Fox presented to the House of Commons on 18 November 1783, a week after the opening of Parliament. And it was this Bill which, within a month, would bring down his government.

Ostensibly, the Bill was designed to separate the political and commercial functions of the Company. The key proposal was to create a Board of seven Commissioners, with great powers over the Company's officers in India, and eight Assistants who would manage the Company's commercial affairs. The Commissioners would be answerable to Parliament for their decisions, thereby creating the accountability hitherto missing. Crucially, they would also be appointed by Parliament. The Crown would neither appoint them, nor have the right to dismiss them. For Fox and Burke this proposal was perfectly natural: they had long criticised the extent of Crown patronage, and were clearly in favour of making the Company's political actions accountable to Parliament. Surely, then, the Board must be appointed by Parliament. The storm of controversy this proposal would arouse lay in its practical effect: while Fox controlled the majority in Parliament these extremely powerful Commissioners would be nominated by him. Even if he left office thereafter, his appointees would still be in place, and because in practice their power would reach into commercial matters, they would control patronage and wealth on a scale which could rival that of the rest of the Kingdom combined.

We do not know whether this side-effect of the Bill was one of the principal objectives Fox and Burke had in mind, but we do know that they were alert to the controversy it would create. Fox said that the debates on the Bill would be 'vigorous and hazardous' and 'of a very delicate nature'. Their strategy for getting it through was to take the moral high ground on Indian affairs, and to rush it through its parliamentary stages before concerted opposition to it could be mounted. In the opening debates on 18 and 27 November Fox argued that this business had forced itself upon him and upon the nation, since the 'rapacity' of the Company's servants had produced 'anarchy and confusion'. The government was called upon to save the Company from imminent bankruptcy. In the first debate Pitt responded that '*Necessity* was the plea for every infringement of human freedom. It was the argument of tyrants: it was the creed of slaves.'[7] He called for more time to debate the Bill, and also for a 'call of the House' to take place two weeks later as, seeing his opportunity, he attempted to bring the country gentry to Parliament as soon as possible. Four days later he wrote to Rutland:

> We are in the midst of a contest, and I think approaching *to a crisis*. The Bill which Fox has brought in relative to India will be, one way or other, decisive for or against the coalition. It is, I really think, the boldest and most unconstitutional measure ever attempted, transferring at one stroke, in spite of all charters and compacts, the immense patronage and influence of the East to *Charles Fox, in or out of office*. I think it will with difficulty, if at all, find its way through our House, and can never succeed in yours. Ministry trust all on this one die, and will probably fail . . . If you have any member within fifty or a hundred miles of you who cares for the Constitution or the country, pray send him to the House of Commons as quick as you can.[8]

Pitt was perceptive in his letter about the course events would now take, except in relation to the House of Commons, where he was far too optimistic: Fox was able to steamroller all before him. In the decisive Second Reading debate of 27 November, Pitt sought to whip up opposition with extreme language in denouncing the Bill – 'One of the boldest, most unprecedented, most desperate and alarming attempts at the exercise of tyranny that ever disgraced the annals of this or any other country'[9] – but found himself defeated at the end of the day by 229 votes to 120. A triumphant Fox had won the votes and the arguments. As the Bill passed rapidly through its remaining stages in the Commons, Burke delivered his great tribute to the leadership of

Fox: 'He is traduced and abused for his supposed motives. He will remember that obloquy is a necessary ingredient in the composition of all true glory; he will remember that it was not only in the Roman customs, but it is in the nature and constitution of things, that calumny and abuse are essential parts of triumph ... He is now on a great eminence, where the eyes of mankind are turned to him. He may live long, he may do much; but here is the summit, – he never can exceed what he does this day.'[10] This was classic Burke, emotional, grandiloquent, and completely carried away with the feelings of the moment, but it demonstrated the exultation now arising in the ranks of the government's supporters. With three-figure majorities behind them in the Commons, and the knowledge that any eighteenth-century government was seldom defeated in the Lords, they thought they were home and dry. On 3 December Fox was even emboldened to announce the names of the prospective Commissioners. Needless to say, these were all supporters of the Fox–North coalition, including Lord North's eldest son. The Chairman was to be Earl Fitzwilliam, nephew of the deceased Rockingham and another grandee of the Whigs. It was said with some justice that all the nominees were better known at Brooks's than in India. Despite this confirmation that the personal patronage of Fox and his allies would be vastly extended, the opposition in the Commons had been vanquished, and Pitt did not even attend the final debates. On 9 December Fox himself carried the Bill to the House of Lords, accompanied by excited supporters and telling his friends that his majority in the Lords would be at least two to one.

In any normal parliamentary situation, Fox would indeed now have been assured of success. He had a large majority, his most controversial piece of legislation was nearly through, his power would shortly be greatly extended, and there was no sign of any dispute with the King. But this was not a normal situation. Beyond the debating chambers of Westminster, powerful forces began to stir. Initially taken by surprise, the Court of Proprietors of the East India Company now pulled themselves together, censured their Chairman for supporting Fox and petitioned Parliament to say that the Company was in a better financial position than the government had declared, and that the Bill amounted to a 'total confiscation' of its property. Newspapers began to attack the Bill, saying that if it passed Fox would be 'the most dangerous subject in Europe'. Caricatures were published depicting a rampaging Fox taking the spoils to himself. Such opposition Fox knew about, and could live with, but he did not know of Temple's memorandum to the King, delivered by Lord Thurlow on 1 December. In it, Temple warned George that the India Bill was 'a plan to take more than half of the Royal power, and by that means to disable His Majesty for the rest of the reign'. He went on to consider how the passage of the Bill could be prevented, ruling out the long-disused royal prerogative of simply refusing assent to it: 'The refusing the Bill, if it passes the Houses, is a violent means . . . An easier way of changing his Government would be by taking some opportunity of doing it, when, in the progress of it, it shall have received more discountenance than hitherto. This must be expected to happen in the Lords in a greater degree than can be hoped for in the Commons. But a sufficient degree of it may not occur in the Lords if those whose duty to His Majesty would excite them to appear are not acquainted with his wishes, and that in a manner which would make it impossible to pretend a doubt of it, in case they were so disposed.'[11] Stated much more bluntly, the King carried sufficient weight in the House of Lords to have the Bill defeated there, and then use that defeat as a reason for throwing out the government. He could only achieve this, however, if he made it absolutely clear to those Lords susceptible to his influence that this was his wish.

In league with Thurlow and Temple was John Robinson, the former government official who had managed a succession of elections for the Treasury, but whose opposition to the India Bill now led him to assist the opposition. He calculated that if the opposition was suddenly to be placed in government it would have 149 definite supporters in the Commons and 231 certain opponents, with 178 'hopeful' or 'doubtful'. These numbers were not encouraging, and were consistent with the large majorities Fox had enjoyed. Nevertheless, it was thought that a significant number of Members could be induced to change sides once the government itself had changed hands, and that if, additionally, an election were held, the new government could secure 253 supporters against 123 opponents. Such figures were highly speculative, and this was after all the same House of Commons in which it had not been possible to form an alternative government earlier in the year. Nevertheless, more was now at stake, and the opportunity to ditch the Fox–North coalition might not recur.

Whatever the calculations, Temple and Thurlow knew they could not succeed without the cooperation of Pitt, and that so far he had repeatedly refused to take office. On 9 December they approached him, using the ageing Lord Clarendon, a long-serving but middle-ranking Minister under North, as a go-between, since any meeting between the principal conspirators would have aroused suspicions. Clarendon recorded that he had been sent to find out 'the sentiments of him, who must from the superiority of his talents and the purity of his character be a leader in this important business. He was found well disposed to the work and not deterred from the situation of things and the temper of men. He concurred in the opinion that there should be no dismission till a strong succession was secured, that the future plan should be well formed before the present was dissolved. He prudently asked if this overture proceeded from authority, and could be carried on through a proper and safe channel to the fountain head. Those judicious questions being answered in the affirmative, he said he would consider and consult on the matter, and that there should be no delay in speaking more positively on it.'[12]

By the eleventh Pitt was sending, through Clarendon, his advice on tactics to the King: 'His opinion is to see by a division the force on each side in the House of Lords . . . The great Patriot's sentiments should be known and enforced to all who, from their situation, affection or regard for his honour and for the constitution, ought to be attentive to them, no one who can be directly or indirectly influenced to do right should be left unreminded of the necessity to appear in numbers whenever the bill now depending is agitated. The passing it may change the nature of government, the rejecting it may lessen even to dissolution the power of those who formed it.'[13]

Pitt's willing involvement confirmed the advice that George III had been given that 'certain persons' were ready 'to receive the burthen'. On the same day the King gave Temple a card which stated:

> His Majesty allowed Earl Temple to say, that whoever voted for the India Bill was not only not his friend, but would be considered by him as an enemy; and if these words were not strong enough, Earl Temple might use whatever words he might deem stronger and more to the purpose.[14]

The die was cast.

The King now summoned the Archbishop of Canterbury and told him to vote the opposite way on the India Bill to his previous disposition, an instruction to which the Archbishop dutifully adhered. Meanwhile, Temple made widespread and effective use of the royal card residing in his pocket. Confusion mounted rapidly: some of the King's friends took Temple's word on the King's opinions, others refused to believe it. Ministers were caught completely unprepared. Portland, the nominal head of the government, 'did not believe this report for some time as His Majesty had never expressed to him the slightest disinclination to give the Bill his full support, & even on the Friday when the Duke was with him did not give him the least hint of what had passed with Lord Temple'.[15] News of the King's views continued to spread, while both sides avoided discussing it publicly – the opposition because it would be accused of complicity in an unconstitutional manoeuvre, and the government because it did not want the rumour to be confirmed.

As the Lords debated the Bill on 15 December, and Fox and Pitt watched from the Bar of the House, Fox still expected a majority of twenty-five. George Rose even overheard one government supporter saying to another, 'I wish I were as sure of the kingdom of heaven as I am of our carrying the Bill this evening.'[16] In fact, the King's intervention had caused at least twenty-seven members of the Lords to change sides, and late that night they inflicted their first defeat on the Bill, by eighty-seven votes to seventy-nine. Fox was outraged, writing to his mistress Mrs Armistead: 'We are beat in the H. of Lds by such treachery on the part of the King & such meanness on the part of his *friends* in the H. of Lds as one could not expect even from him or them.'[17] Two days later, on 17 December, both Houses met for the climactic debates. In the House of Lords the India Bill was formally and finally thrown out by an increased opposition majority of nineteen. Down the corridor in the House of Commons, government supporters raged against the actions of the opposition, arguing that if people other than Ministers influenced the actions of the King, then Ministers were placed in an impossible position. They passed a resolution that to report any opinion of the King in order to influence debates was 'a high crime and misdemeanour', and another launching an inquiry to begin the following week. Fox thundered forth his denunciation of what had happened: 'The deliberations of this evening must decide whether we are to be henceforward free men or slaves; whether this House is the palladium of liberty or the engine of despotism; whether we are prospectively to exercise any functions of our own, or to become the mere echo of secret influence.' The Lords, he said, had 'forfeited by their conduct every claim to the character of gentlemen, and degraded the characteristic independence of the peerage as well as vilified the British Legislature in the eyes of all Europe'.[18]

While it was clear to all involved that the King's intervention in the House of Lords had been decisive, it was of huge importance to Pitt and his colleagues that they were not implicated in a conspiracy to use 'secret influence' and to encourage arguably unconstitutional action. Temple had become trapped in verbal contortions in the Lords when questioned on his role, and had ended by owning up to a meeting with the King, while not confirming what was said. Pitt, the prize now within his grasp, took an approach that was far simpler, as well as ruthlessly dishonest. The rumour, he said, was simply 'the lie of the day', and he could not believe that such importance had been 'ever before imparted to mere rumour and hearsay'. Throughout the controversies of the coming months he would maintain that he knew of no plan to unseat the previous government, an assertion believed by many of his contemporaries and all of his earliest biographers for many decades after his death.

On 18 December Pitt and Temple had audiences with the King. Pitt indicated his readiness to take office at the head of a new government, and at midnight that night Portland, Fox and North were meeting together when messengers arrived from the King asking them to surrender their seals of office. 'I choose this method,' the King wrote to North, 'as Audiences on such occasions must be unpleasant.'[19] On Friday, 19 December 1783 a packed House of Commons watched as Pitt's friend Pepper Arden rose and moved a new writ for an election in the Borough of Appleby: 'In the room of the Rt Hon William Pitt, who, since his election, has accepted the office of First Lord of the Treasury and Chancellor of the Exchequer.'* The massed ranks of the supporters of the Fox–North coalition, now gathering on the opposition benches, burst into laughter. For one thing, they were laughing at Arden's high-pitched voice, and for another at the appointment of a twenty-four-year-old to be the First Minister of the Kingdom. More ominously, they were laughing with confidence. As Fox put it: 'We are so strong . . . I think we shall destroy them almost as soon as they are formed.' Pitt would become Prime Minister with a large majority of the House of Commons determined to force his immediate removal.

Why did Pitt decide to take office in December 1783, having refused to do so earlier in the year? He had previously ruled it out on the grounds that he could not be sure of a majority in the House of Commons, and that was as true now as it had been before. What had changed?

There were two major differences between this situation and his previous opportunities to lead a government. The first was that the likely balance of power between Pitt as Prime Minister on the one hand and George III on the other had changed. Had Pitt taken office in March 1783, he would have done so at the whim of the King, and to a large extent as a creature of the King's making. Having made him, the King could have unmade him, by trying to dictate policy, control appointments, or at some stage dismissing him and turning back to Lord North, or even Shelburne, or some other figure who could cobble together an administration. The circumstances of December 1783 were quite different. The King had declared political war on a majority of the House of Commons and on almost all its senior figures, including

* Pitt's re-election for Appleby, although a formality, was once again required by his acceptance of ministerial office.

the entire parties of Charles James Fox and Lord North. The abuse of royal power he had perpetrated was now under ferocious attack in that assembly. In this situation, it was not merely desirable to George III that Pitt should lead the government; it was indispensable to him. He literally could not do without the one man who could take on all comers in the House of Commons and at the very least hold his own. And such was the enmity now created between the King and the new opposition that he would not be able to let them back into office for a very long time, thus securing Pitt's position for the future, if only he could get through the first few months. Pitt knew all this, and he also knew that if he could succeed in outwitting the hostile majority in the Commons and somehow entrench himself in office, his achievement would have been so great that his political following would be strong and his authority hard to challenge.

It was because of these realities that Pitt was able to take office on his own terms in a manner he could not have insisted upon earlier that year. He had made clear in the summer that he would only serve as First Lord of the Treasury if he could pursue his cherished goal of parliamentary reform, a project to which George III was unremittingly hostile. Now indeed he took office with the apparent understanding that although he could not expect the King and other diehard traditionalists such as Thurlow actually to support parliamentary reform, they would not actively prevent him from bringing it forward. Hence Pitt could take charge in Downing Street knowing that he had a large measure of freedom of action, and that the King's need to keep him in office would allow him to maintain that freedom.

The second major difference between March and December 1783 was that matters had truly come to a head. Pitt's attack on the India Bill as 'the exercise of tyranny' had been wild exaggeration, but there is no doubt that the successful passage of the Bill would have helped to cement the Fox–North coalition into power, and brought a great deal of valuable patronage under their control. If the government was not thrown out now, it might be much harder to do so later. A ready pretext might not easily recur, and the combination of powerful conspirators who brought about the coup in the House of Lords that December might have disintegrated if it was not put to use. Since Pitt was only twenty-four it would be an exaggeration to say that this was 'now or never', but he must have recognised that it might be 'now or not for a very long time'. The stakes were high enough for the risk to be worth taking.

And risk it was. Given the constitutional precedents and conventions prevailing at the time, no substantive defence of the King's action was possible. From 1688 onwards it had been understood that the King would operate only through his Ministers, who could then be held accountable in Parliament and who needed a majority in the House of Commons to support them. Now the King had acted through other politicians in order to depose his Ministers, and had proceeded to appoint a new government to which a majority of the House of Commons was clearly opposed. It is no wonder that Fox and the Whigs railed against this outrage: not only had they been deprived of office, but the constitutional settlement they had been brought up to believe was sacrosanct had been comprehensively violated. Wraxall admitted that the King's action 'appears at first sight subversive of every principle of political freedom', but went on to make the one real defence, albeit in exaggerated language, of what the King had done: 'We must, however, candidly allow that he was not bound to observe any measures of scrupulous delicacy with men who had entered his Cabinet by violence, who held him in bondage, and who meditated to render that bondage perpetual.'[20] In other words, the constitution was breaking down, and the Ministers were themselves violating it by proposing greatly to extend their own power, an action against which the King had to defend himself.

It would turn out that a great majority of opinion in the country would agree with this latter defence of the King, and would give strong support to his actions and his new Prime Minister, notwithstanding the fact that he had broken all the rules. George III would join a long line of political rulers, which now stretches from Julius Caesar to Charles de Gaulle, in succeeding in taking unconstitutional action because he enjoyed great popular support for it. But this was far from apparent to the King's friends as Pitt's appointment was announced on 19 December, and the opposition benches rocked with laughter. Those who contemplated joining Pitt in office had to reckon with the likelihood that when the Commons met again in January it would vote them straight out of office with endless motions of no confidence and a refusal to authorise taxes. It would not take many weeks for a Commons majority to make the governing of the country impossible, which was the whole reason governments required a majority in the House of Commons in the first place. Worse still, the talk of 'high crimes and misdemeanours' raised the possibility of the impeachment of those who took office in these circumstances, and trials conducted by Parliament.

Veterans of politics blanched when faced with such prospects. It was the hope of many, evidently including Temple, that Pitt would ask the King to dissolve Parliament and call an immediate general election, in which all the advantages of incumbency and Treasury money would rest with Pitt and the King's friends. Certainly this is what Fox and North expected him to do. He did not do so. There were several reasons for this. First, an eighteenth-century general election needed 'preparation', with careful arrangement of candidates and money. There had been no time to do this. Second, a Land Tax Bill had to be enacted by early January for the public finances to be secure. Third, the Parliament had four years yet to run, and early dissolutions were deeply unpopular with many independent and county Members who would face the huge expense of an early election. Pitt needed their support, and an election could have pushed them into hostility without depriving them of their seats. Fourth, a general election in the middle of a session, let alone in the middle of a Parliament, was without precedent since 1688 other than on the death of a monarch, and would add further to the doubtful constitutional basis of all that had gone before.

The most effective way, albeit an extremely difficult and hazardous one, to show that the new government was legitimate, was to win over a majority in the existing House of Commons. If that proved impossible, and the opposition succeeded in rendering government inoperable, then at least there would be a more convincing pretext for a general election, and opinion would be more likely to rally to the new government. Pitt's strategy was therefore to construct a government from among the few people willing to serve, to attempt to win over a majority of the Commons by taking on the opposition, to tempt the opposition into intemperate measures if it continued in the majority, and then to call an election if really necessary, by which time opinion in the country would be more solidly on his side.

Fox's strategy was also to avoid a dissolution, since that would bring the full weight of government influence on to Pitt's side in an election. He would not immediately supply the pretext for an election by 'stopping the supplies', but he would take every other measure to humiliate Pitt and vote down whatever policies the new government attempted.

The stage was set for one of the great political confrontations of British history.

The early days of the battle were not auspicious for Pitt. He first attempted to cut through all the problems by sending a mutual friend, Lord Spencer, to ask Fox to join the government, but without Lord North and without the India Bill as proposed. A confident Fox turned this down flat. Two days after taking office Pitt received a body blow when Temple, who had taken office on 19 December as a Secretary of State, resigned on the twenty-first. Historians have never been able to agree on why he did so. Wraxall and other contemporary commentators thought it was because Pitt would not dissolve Parliament. Stanhope thought it was because the King had not recognised Temple's previous service as Lord Lieutenant of Ireland or his recent services by elevating him to a dukedom. The explanation given by his brother, William Grenville, in the House of Commons at the time was that he wished to be 'ready to meet any charge that shall be brought against him', and would be able to 'answer for his conduct whenever he shall hear the charge'.[21] This has a ring of truth. Ministerial resignations usually take place for more than one reason, and it is likely that Temple simply took fright at the difficulty of the whole situation, with the added fear that he might be impeached. Dundas, eagerly taking office as Treasurer of the Navy, thought Temple was a 'dammed dolter-headed coward', and the King was still referring to 'his base conduct' six years later. Whatever the reason for it, this resignation left Pitt terribly exposed, deprived of his leading colleague and senior spokesman in the Lords. Pretyman recalled that: 'This was the only event, of a public nature, which I ever knew disturb Mr. Pitt's rest, while he continued in good health. Lord Temple's resignation was determined upon at a late hour in the evening of the 21st; and when I went into Mr. Pitt's bedroom the next morning he told me, that he had not had a moment's sleep. He expressed great uneasiness at the state of public affairs; at the same time declaring his fixed resolution not to abandon the situation he had undertaken, but to make the best stand in his power, though very doubtful of the result.'[22]

By the morning of Tuesday, 23 December, Wilberforce was writing in his journal: 'Morning Pitt's . . . Pitt nobly firm . . . Cabinet formed.'[23] It was indeed formed, but it was not very distinguished. Senior figures who had held high office in the past such as Lord Camden and the Duke of Grafton declined to take part in this risky enterprise. Pitt was able to form a small Cabinet of seven members, including himself: the conspirator Lord Thurlow back as Lord Chancellor, the trusty Gower as President of the Council, Pitt's young friend the Duke of Rutland as Lord Privy Seal, Admiral Lord Howe as First Lord of the Admiralty and, as Home Secretary and Foreign Secretary, Lord Sydney and the Marquis of Carmarthen. The latter two held the two highest offices after Pitt and Thurlow, but were considered by William Grenville, who would one day succeed each of them, as 'unequal to the most ordinary business of their own offices'.[24] Hardly any of the others could make an effective speech, and all of them except Pitt were in the House of Lords: the huge burden of debating in the House of Commons would fall almost entirely on Pitt himself.

At the more junior levels of the government Pitt relied on bringing in his young friends, with George Rose and Tom Steele as Secretaries to the Treasury, Henry Dundas as Treasurer of the Navy, William Grenville and Lord Mulgrave as Paymasters of the Forces and Richard Pepper Arden as Solicitor General. The list was completed by the Duke of Richmond as Master General of the Ordnance (he would later agree to join the Cabinet in the same role), Lloyd Kenyon as Attorney General and Sir George Yonge as Secretary at War.

This list of undistinguished peers and youthful companions was not immediately impressive. One commentator noted that the main attribute of the new government was its collective capacity for drink. Sir Gilbert Elliot dismissed the Ministers as 'a set of children playing at ministers [who] must be sent back to school, and in a few days all will have returned to its former course'.[25] Of the many commentaries writing off the chances of the new government the most famous came from Fox's friend Mrs Crewe, who said to Wilberforce: 'Well, he [Pitt] may do what he likes during the holidays, but it will be only a mince-pie administration, depend on it.'[26] William Eden, at that stage still a political opponent, wrote that 'They are in desperate straits even for Old men and Boys to accept situations.'[27] Pitt's youth was again derided, with his opponents composing a jingle called 'Billy's Too Young to Drive Us', and even Robinson, now advising him on the parliamentary numbers, describing him as 'a delicate high spirited mind, beset by Boys, Theoreticks and prejudiced persons'.[28] Pitt's position was seen as weak by most observers, and hopeless by some. As the Commons rose for the Christmas recess, Fox allowed the Land Tax Bill to pass, but in return extracted a promise that Parliament was not about to be dissolved. It would convene again on 12 January 1784. The battle for supremacy would then commence on the floor of the House of Commons.

9

The Struggle for Supremacy

'The country calls aloud to me that I should defend this castle; and I am determined therefore that I WILL defend it.'

WILLIAM PITT, FEBRUARY 1784

'It was a struggle between George the Third's sceptre and Mr. Fox's tongue.'

SAMUEL JOHNSON

PITT HAD NO CHANCE to savour being First Lord of the Treasury at the age of twenty-four. He worked without pause through the Christmas of 1783 to bolster his precarious position. He knew that in two weeks' time he would be facing a House of Commons in which he at present had no majority, and that all the other great parliamentary speakers of the age – Fox, Burke, North, Sheridan – would be arrayed against him. The burden of defeating them would rest entirely with him, and if he failed, so would the blame.

Pitt employed all the tools at his command. From his earliest hours as Prime Minister he showed the cool ruthlessness which characterises those politicians who are capable of seizing power and keeping it. For all his difficulty in finding credible Ministers he had no compunction in shirking those who might have brought seniority, but whom he considered liabilities. One of these was Charles Jenkinson, who was so close to the King that his inclusion would have cast doubt on Pitt's denial that he had been part of a plot. More significantly, he excluded Shelburne, his former patron and leader, who had brought him into his last government as Chancellor of the Exchequer. Shelburne, as a former First Lord of the Treasury, had great seniority and acknowledged abilities, but he was unpopular and Pitt had not enjoyed working with him. He found himself excluded. The absence of any previous head of an administration in his government helped to underline the fact that Pitt alone was in charge. As Dundas observed: 'This young man does not choose to suffer it to be doubtfull who is the effectual Minister.'[1]

Next, with the ready cooperation of George III, Pitt opened the floodgates of government patronage which had been locked tightly shut during the Fox–North administration. Thomas Pitt received a peerage, and Sir James Lowther was promised an earldom. Several other borough patrons received peerages. The promise of a peerage to the second son of the Duke of Northumberland was followed by six of the seven MPs under his control switching sides to support the new government. Lord Weymouth switched sides when his brother received a peerage. One MP who was in acute financial difficulty was granted a royal pension for his wife, and promptly became a Pitt supporter. Others who held minor offices at the disposal of the King or his Ministers were careful to change their allegiance, and those who declined to do so found themselves dismissed. The father of Pitt's friend Edward Eliot suddenly became Lord Eliot. He controlled six seats in Cornwall which would now vote differently in any general election. One MP received a letter from Lord Sydney saying that Pitt 'would be happy to know if there are any wishes of yours that he can meet or promote'.[2] 'They are crying peerages about the streets in barrows,' said Horace Walpole, and the Duke of Portland noted that the powers of the Crown had been 'let loose without reserve'.[3] Throughout his career Pitt would be bored by endless requests for minor preferment, but when he needed to use patronage to obtain serious support in a crisis he did not believe in half measures.

The King himself joined in the effort, bringing the full weight of the throne to bear on peers who controlled seats in the House of Commons but had not voted the right way in December. He caused the Duke of Newcastle to change sides, leading three of his six MPs to support Pitt and the others to abstain or resign. By the turn of the year Pitt could feel a little more optimistic. He had not written to his mother for seven weeks (and does not seem to have done so again for another eleven), but she had evidently been encouraging him that he was doing the right thing. On 30 December he wrote: 'You will easily believe it is not from inclination I have been silent so long . . . Things are in general more promising than they have been, but in the uncertainty of effect the Persuasion of not being wrong is, as you say, the best Circumstance and Enough; tho' there is satisfaction in the Hopes at least of something more.'[4] He wrote from his brother's house in Berkeley Square, having had no time to move back into Downing Street.

Each day Robinson would calculate the level of support in the Commons as the flow of patronage took effect; he would himself later be rewarded by the elevation of his son-in-law, Lord Abergavenny, to an earldom. His initially pessimistic assessment was transformed in the early days of January to showing a small majority for Pitt, and by 10 January he even reckoned that Pitt might have 240 supporters against 196 opponents, with thirty-six of the remaining ninety-six classed as 'very hopeful'.[5]

We do not know whether Pitt believed what were becoming wildly inflated figures, but it seems that Fox did believe similarly optimistic ones on the other side, and was betting at Brooks's on a three-figure majority against Pitt. Lord North spent the recess giving generous dinner parties to keep the opposition's troops in line, and Fox remained confident, having talked before Christmas of 'the weakness of young men in accepting offices under the present circumstances of affairs, and he mentioned their youth as the only possible excuse for their rashness'.[6]

There was no doubting that Pitt had made progress during the Christmas break, but if he had the impression that he would now have command of the House of Commons he was rapidly disabused of it when he arrived to be sworn in once again as the Member for Appleby on 12 January 1784. The House was packed, with the Public Gallery 'holding as many persons as ever were wedged together'.[7] Fox had already been on his feet demanding a Committee to inquire into the State of the Nation, and was able to deny Pitt the floor when he sought to read a message from the King. He denounced the 'secret influence' by which the India Bill had been wrecked, and demanded to know whether the House could debate in freedom or was under threat of dissolution in a manner reminiscent of the Stuart Kings before the Civil War.

When Pitt was finally allowed to respond to the furious attack he adopted the tactics which would become characteristic of his approach to the long debates of the next two months. His method was simple: he offered no defence of the means by which the government had been changed, since he denied knowledge of them; he was as uninformative as possible about the likelihood of an election; and he bluntly refused to leave office. At all times he kept calm, Wraxall describing him as 'The Minister, who in sullen majesty or in contumelious silence heard unmoved their clamorous denunciations seated calmly on the Treasury bench . . . Always preserving the command of himself, he was never led into deviations from caution and prudence.'[8] He rebutted the charge of relying on 'secret influence' in a manner of high contempt for the accusation:

> I came up no back stairs. When I was sent for by my Sovereign to know whether I would accept of office, I necessarily went to the Royal Closet. I know of no secret influence, and I hope that my own integrity would be my guardian against that danger . . . Little did I think to be ever charged in this House with being the tool and abettor of secret influence. The novelty of the imputation only renders it so much the more contemptible. This is the only answer I shall ever deign to make on the subject, and I wish the House to bear it in their mind, and judge of my future conduct by my present declaration: the integrity of my own heart, and the probity of all my public, as well as my private principles, shall always be my sources of action.[9]

In claiming that he would act with integrity and in accordance with his principles, Pitt was telling the truth as well as contrasting himself with the sacrificing of principles when the Fox–North coalition was created. He was building up the image of himself as an independent figure who had come to the aid of the King and the nation, an image which would soon operate dramatically to his advantage. But in claiming no knowledge of secret influence or of the 'back stairs' he was once again not telling the whole truth. He was not an innocent bystander who happened to be in touch with the King on the day the government fell. To have admitted the full truth would have been cataclysmic: instead he turned his denial to advantage. As John Cannon noted in his book *The Fox–North Coalition* (1969): 'It was the lie of a master, perfect of its kind, superb in its insolence, and totally successful; its very unctuousness carried the war into the enemy's camp, smearing them as the purveyors of shabby slanders and cheap rumours.'[10]

The simplicity and audaciousness of Pitt's tactics would bring success. But as MPs voted on the night of 12 January, he found that he still faced a solid, even though reduced, opposition majority. He was defeated by thirty-nine votes (232 to 193) on a Committee on the State of the Nation, by fifty-four votes on a motion attacking the 'unconstitutional abuse of the name of the King', and had to let through a whole string of motions designed to make a dissolution more difficult by postponing the consideration of vital Bills and forbidding the government to spend money once Parliament was dissolved. On his first day facing the House of Commons, the twenty-four-year-old Prime Minister had taken a battering.

The following day found Ministers demoralised. A government defeat by thirty-nine votes was, one of them thought, 'sufficient to have made prudent men despair of their undertaking'. Carmarthen noted that the Cabinet meeting that day found that it would be difficult to surmount the obstacles being created to a dissolution, and 'at the same time it appeared impossible to go on with the public business with the H. of Commons against us . . . Mr. Pitt even hinted at giving the thing up; this however was represented to him by us all as betraying both the Crown and people, as well as highly disgraceful to ourselves personally.'[11] They resolved to go on. The King came to London from Windsor to express directly to Pitt his own firm resolve, the Duke of Richmond offered to join the Cabinet, and Pitt gave notice that he would introduce his own India Bill.

The opposition kept up the pace in response, passing a motion on 16 January by twenty-one votes stating that the continuation of the

Ministers in office was 'contrary to Constitutional principles'. While unsuccessfully resisting this motion, Dundas expanded further on Pitt's insistence that the new Ministers were entirely innocent of plotting any intervention by the King in the House of Lords: 'I defy any man even to insinuate that any one of His Majesty's Cabinet has ever had the least share of that secret influence upon which this motion is founded . . . The throwing out of the India Bill was a matter previous to their appointment, a matter in which they had no concern, and for which they can share no blame, even if I allow, for argument's sake, that blame is due anywhere.'[12]

While continuing to display outrage at the very idea that they had consciously overturned the former government, Pitt and his colleagues turned to the language of sweet reason in trying to get their own India Bill up and running in the Commons. The Second Reading of this Bill, set for 23 January after Fox had used his majority to delay it by two days to show who was boss, would be a crucial test of strength. If Pitt could get such a major piece of legislation through the Commons he would have every right to argue that his government enjoyed legitimacy; if he could not, he would obviously be hamstrung.

Pitt's India Bill was simpler than that of Fox, and it enjoyed the support of the East India Company itself. His plan was to create a political Board of Control, appointed by the government, which would govern India along with the Directors of the Company, but leave the patronage unaffected. He put everything into winning over the independent MPs, delivering an eloquent speech which stressed that the Bill could be amended once it passed its Second Reading and entered Committee. When the debate ended that Friday night, Fox succeeded in defeating the Bill by eight votes (222 to 214).

The margin was narrow, but Pitt's only immediate hope of winning over a majority in the House of Commons as it stood was dashed. With no majority in the House, he did not even have the power to adjourn it. He sat in silence – 'sulky silence', as one opposition MP called it[13] – as Fox and other Members demanded to know what would happen now. Pitt simply sat there as the questions were flung at him, knowing that he might have to call an election but not wishing to say so, until Fox adjourned the House at 2 a.m. on the Saturday morning and called it back again for noon. That afternoon Pitt was finally induced by one of his own supporters, who broke down in tears in the course of his question, to concede that the House would still be in session the following Monday, without giving any assurances after that.

As the Cabinet met throughout most of that weekend, Ministers pressed Pitt to call an immediate election. This course was also strongly favoured by the King. They were conscious that if an election was not called at this point it could not be called for another two months, since the Mutiny Bill, a Bill which had to be passed every year to renew the government's powers in an emergency, needed to be approved by 25 March. Any election called in February or early March would make this impossible. It seems that Pitt and his colleagues were in favour of an election by the time they concluded their dinner on the Saturday, but against one some five hours later when they had finished their port.

Despite the beseeching voices of many of his colleagues, Pitt decided against dissolution for much the same reason as before: he was not yet ready for it. If an election were called and the result was not markedly different from the current composition of the Commons – and that is how most eighteenth-century elections turned out – then the game really would be up. Pretyman tells us: 'He still feared, that he should not gain sufficient strength, in a new parliament, to give stability to his administration; and therefore he chose to submit for some time longer, to all the inconveniences and difficulties of struggling against a majority of the house of commons; and to encounter all the violence with which he was threatened . . . He had, indeed, the satisfaction of perceiving, that the favorable disposition of the public towards himself, was gradually increasing, and that his opponents were growing every day more unpopular.'[14]

With the House of Commons now locked in a stalemate, Fox argued that the refusal of Pitt to leave office in defiance of the votes of the Commons would lead to 'universal anarchy'. Pitt's response was that 'He considered himself as performing an act of necessary duty to his King and country, and so long as that continued to be the case he should persevere.' That Pitt would simply stay in office despite all the

defeats heaped upon his head never seems to have occurred to his opponents until this point. There was no precedent for this situation. For six weeks now the country had had a government with no power to govern, and a House of Commons which did not seem to have the power to turn it out. Fearing that his Ministers might lose their nerve, George III now summoned them all to him as a body and 'declared a fix'd and unalterable resolution on no account to be put bound hand and foot into the hands of Mr. Fox, that rather than submit to that he would quit the Kingdom for ever'.[15] The King was determined that, whatever happened, Pitt would have to soldier on. To do so, Pitt needed new weapons and new support. And now, beneath the raging debates and deadlocked procedures of the House of Commons, the very ground of politics began to move.

It started on 16 January, in the City of London, when the Corporation sent an address to George III congratulating him on his 'salutary and constitutional' exercise of his prerogative. Each day thereafter similar addresses trickled in, until soon some fifteen a week were arriving from towns, cities and counties throughout the country. Eventually more than two hundred such addresses would arrive, many times more than could be remembered on any previous occasion by any politician alive, and many of them signed by thousand upon thousand of people. Even small towns produced dozens of signatures on their addresses; those from Devon, Leicestershire, Wolverhampton, Staffordshire, Buckinghamshire, Oxfordshire, Coventry, Berkshire, Dorset and Newcastle upon Tyne each carried over a thousand; the second address from Glasgow more than four thousand; that from Bristol more than five thousand; and the City of Westminster, the constituency of Fox himself, produced eight thousand signatures supporting the actions of the King. At meetings across the land attempts by supporters of Fox and North to produce a counter-movement were voted out or howled down.[16]

In two years there had now been five governments. Ministries had come and gone, alliances had been formed and broken, plots had been hatched and insults hurled with seemingly very little reference to the people outside the walls of Westminster. Many of those people had now had enough, and they were finally moved to do something about it. As the representatives of the Corporation of Wakefield proceeded to London with their address, they carried a large blue flag which read 'THE KING! THE CONSTITUTION! THE PEOPLE! AND PITT FOREVER!'[17]

Three factors came together to bring about a surge in peacefully expressed popular opinion of a kind hitherto unknown in eighteenth-century Britain. The first was that the advent of the Industrial Revolution brought an increasing awareness of what was happening in day-to-day politics. An emerging middle class wanted to read news, an improving transport system was able to carry it, and an eager newspaper industry was able to supply it. In the thirty years before Pitt took office, newspaper circulation in Britain doubled. Small country newspapers which had previously sold a few hundred copies were now able to sell several thousand. Many of them carried bluntly expressed political opinion, and would increasingly be purchased by proprietors who wished to dictate it. They also carried extensive reports of parliamentary debates, which had barely been reported at all until the decade before this crisis. It was a novelty, and sometimes a shock, to read what was going on in Parliament. By the early 1780s an interested and educated citizen could find out more fully and immediately what was being said and done in his name than ever before (and certainly more fully than his counterpart in the twenty-first century could manage from the newspapers of today).

The second factor was the prevailing popular view that the country which had held its head high in the world and vanquished its enemies in the Seven Years' War had now been brought low by the mismanagement and machinations of manoeuvring politicians. Exports had declined during the war with America, and what might later have been called a 'feel-good factor' was far from present. There had been a long war against Britain's American cousins which had ended in total defeat, not only at their hands, but at those of the French. A mighty Royal Navy had at one stage yielded to Continental countries the control of the English Channel. The Dublin Parliament had been given independence simply because it demanded it, and large parts of London had been ransacked by the greatest mob violence anyone could recall. In the aftermath of these disasters it seemed that little had been done to restore the standing of the country, or to rectify the parlous state of its finances. The national debt had mounted to the point where the interest paid on it was taking up most of the country's taxes. The political leaders in Parliament seemed to be mainly interested in throwing each other out of office, and people simply wanted this to stop. Moreover, many of them regarded the unprincipled alliance between Fox and North as the ultimate demonstration of the political machinations they despised, and thus had little sympathy with complaints from these quarters that the normal rules had been broken.

The third and crowning factor in the weight suddenly developed by public opinion was that Pitt recognised it and knew how to harness it. Although he had never had much personal contact with the wider populace, he had learnt as a child of his father's high public reputation in his days as 'the Great Commoner', and he had not forgotten it. He knew it was important to 'have the Impression and Effect of Numbers on our Side', and was arguably to become the first leader of a government to take some account of public opinion as a matter of course. What is more, Pitt had always known how he wanted to present himself: as a man of independence and integrity, detached from any faction and free of any outside influence, and therefore different from the generality of politicians. Since the impression he wished to convey of himself had always been clear in his mind, he had done nothing as a young MP or private individual which would conflict with it. The image he had crafted for himself seemed the perfect answer to the corruption and venal motives which were thought to have brought the country low, and his disassociation from parties or factions seemed the ideal alternative to the Fox–North coalition.

However convenient or well-calculated Pitt's attributes may have been, they would have been little-known beyond Westminster when he became the First Minister in December 1783. As luck would have it, however, even as Fox marshalled his forces for the furious debates of January 1784, an opportunity arose for Pitt to impress indelibly on the minds of a far wider audience the exact image he wished to present. On 11 January Sir Edward Walpole died, leaving vacant the Clerkship of Pells. This position was a classic sinecure, involving no work but paid £3,000 a year for life. Appointment to it was in the gift of the First Lord of the Treasury, now Pitt himself. As he was a young man with negligible means, it was widely assumed that he would appoint himself to it. As Stanhope noted, 'Such a course would have been in complete conformity with the feelings and the practice of his age,'[18] guaranteeing his financial independence in or out of office. Yet instead of taking it, he offered it to Colonel Barré, an MP and a hero of the capturing of Quebec, who had controversially been granted a pension of £3,200 a year under Rockingham and Shelburne, on condition that he give the pension up. At a stroke Pitt maintained the Colonel's income while reversing an unpopular action of a previous administration and saving the taxpayer £3,000 a year, giving nothing to himself. This decision was widely reported, and made a hugely positive impression. As a display of disinterestedness it was more dramatic and became more widely known than his father's refusal of the normal perquisites of the office of Paymaster, although it was to contribute to personal debts of similar proportions. People who remembered that Chatham had rescued the country from disaster now began to look to his son, 'honest Billy', to do the same.

By early February, as Pitt prepared for fresh opposition attacks, the emerging trend in opinion in the country was becoming clear, and the House of Lords chipped in by passing a resolution attacking the 'unconstitutional' actions of the House of Commons by one hundred votes to fifty-three. This was of little practical import, except to demonstrate that while Fox maintained a majority in the Commons, Pitt had all the other elements of the British constitution, Crown, Lords and public, rallying behind him. He entered the debates of February with confidence, even drawing attention on 2 February to his own calm temperament, another part of his developing public image, by saying in the Commons that he had 'endeavoured to avoid being caught by the violence of their proceedings, and had preserved as calm and governed a temper as the nature of the case would admit'.[19]

In addition to the continued postponement of Commons business by Fox, Pitt now had to deal with the pressure from independent Members who wanted everything to be settled by him and Fox creating a new government together. On 2 February they put forward a motion calling for 'a firm, efficient, extended, united Administration' following a meeting at the St Alban's Tavern in Westminster. Neither Pitt nor Fox could object to this, since, however ridiculous they now believed it to be, they did not wish to offend the independents. Over the following months there were two serious bouts of negotiations. From Pitt's point of view the second of these, in late February, came perilously close to success. Lord North had offered to step aside to make things simpler, the Duke of Portland as the opposition's negotiator was happy to make concessions, and conditions set down by George III for the creation of a new coalition in the hope that they would be impossible to satisfy were very nearly agreed to. In the end the talks broke down over the meaning of the word 'equal', which Pitt evasively refused to define. As Wraxall put it, 'with whatever complacency and ostensible alacrity Pitt invariably received the propositions for such a junction, it is difficult to persuade ourselves that he could cordially desire their accomplishment. He beheld the prize for which they were contending nearly attained and secured. His insatiable ambition impelled him to govern alone.'[20]

This seems like an accurate assessment. Pitt could now see the light at the end of the tunnel, and had no wish to come to terms with his opponents. The opposition's majorities in February were generally lower than in January, and in two debates in which Fox seemed to be moving towards 'refusing the supplies' his majorities fell to twelve and nine. Pitt noted that 'the enemy rather flinches' at postponing the supplies, as it became apparent that Fox could not necessarily carry his supporters with him in cutting off the essential revenue or expenditure of the state. Increasingly, Pitt referred to his own popular support, describing Fox as 'the champion of a small majority of this House against the loud and decided voice of the people'.[21] From now on he even seemed to goad the opposition into attempting to do its worst, calmly and provocatively telling the House on 18 February that 'the King, notwithstanding their recommendations, had not thought proper to dismiss his Ministers, and that they had not resigned'.[22] On 20 February the opposition achieved its last great success by carrying, by a majority of twenty, a motion calling on the King to 'give effect' to the wishes of the House. Pitt's response was utterly defiant:

'Dreadful therefore as the conflict is, my conscience, my duty, my fixed regard for the Constitution of our ancestors, maintain me still in this arduous post . . . The situation of the times requires of me, and, I will add, the country calls aloud to me, that I should defend this castle, and I am determined therefore that I will defend it!'[23] Five days later the King gave a similar answer, claiming that 'There is no charge or complaint suggested against my present ministers, nor is any one or more of them specifically objected to; and numbers of my subjects have expressed to me, in the warmest manner, their satisfaction of the late changes I have made in my Councils.'[24]

The swelling support for Pitt and the utter frustration of the supporters of Fox finally boiled over in the streets on 28 February. On that day, a Saturday, Pitt was due to receive the Freedom of the City of London from the strongly supportive Corporation. Early in the morning a huge crowd gathered in Berkeley Square, where Pitt was still living with his brother, and formed an excited procession to the City, where Pitt received the Freedom in the Grocers' Hall, and a speech of praise from none other than the celebrated radical John Wilkes, who spoke of Pitt's 'youth, capacity, and firmness' and his 'noble act of disinterestedness in favor of the public'.[25] Pitt was then accompanied back through London by 'a great concourse of people', some of whom took over pulling the carriage in which he sat with his brother and Lord Mahon. Matters now began to get out of hand, as his brother later recalled:

> A Mob is never very discreet, and unfortunately they stopped outside Carlton House [residence of the Prince of Wales] and began hissing, and it was with some difficulty we forced them to go on. As we proceeded up St. James's Street, there was a great Cry, and an attempt made to turn the Carriage up St. James Place to Mr. Fox's house . . . in order to break his windows . . . which we at last succeeded in preventing their doing . . . This attempt brought us rather nearer in contact with Brooks, and the moment we got opposite . . . a sudden and desperate attack was made upon the Carriage . . . by a body of Chairmen armed with bludgeons, broken Chair Poles – (many of the waiters, and several of the Gentlemen among them) – They succeeded in making their

> way to the Carriage, and forced open the door. Several desperate blows were aimed at Mr. Pitt, and I recollect endeavouring to cover him . . .[26]

In the ensuing struggle Pitt was finally taken to the safety of White's, a far more supportive club, whilst his carriage was practically demolished. Lord Chatham mildly concluded his account by saying 'I never went to Brooks any more,' but the political consequences were more far-reaching. As news of the events spread across the country, it reinforced the impression that Pitt had become the hero of the people and that the opposition were now resorting to desperate measures to try to unseat him.

It did not help the public standing of Fox that the alibi with which he demonstrated that he could not have personally been involved in the affray was that he was in bed with his mistress at the time. The contrast between the extremely liberal approach to love affairs and gambling of Fox on the one hand, and the apparently spotless probity of Pitt and indeed George III on the other, added further momentum to the popular tide running in favour of the new government. Fox and North were running out of options, and the resolve of some of their supporters in the Commons was beginning to buckle. Facing hostility from their electors as the loyal addresses poured in, some MPs who had regularly voted against Pitt now switched to abstaining. By the first week of March Fox was still defeating Pitt on the floor of the House, but his majorities were down to single figures.

Pitt and Robinson continued to chip away at the diminishing majority: they had made a net gain of six in by-elections since the contest began, and the honours were still flowing – one opposition supporter who surprised his colleagues by voting with Pitt in the crucial division of 8 March became a peer two months later. On that day Fox moved a remonstrance to the King arguing that 'No administration . . . can serve His Majesty and the public with effect, which does not enjoy the confidence of this House.'[27] When the votes were counted he had defeated the government by only one vote (191 to 190). It was all but over. At the beginning of the crisis, Gibbon had predicted: 'Billy's painted Galley will soon sink under Charles's black

William Pitt the elder, First Earl of Chatham, by William Hoare. The only head of an administration in British history to father one of his successors.

Hester, Countess of Chatham, by Thomas Hudson. Her resilience, calm temperament and sense of duty did much to forge the character of her second son.

Below Burton Pynsent, Somerset. Despite the protests of the Pynsent family, the elder Pitt happily accepted the house and estate as an inheritance from Sir William Pynsent. The column on the left was erected to mark his gratitude.

Above left Pembroke College, Cambridge. The rooms occupied by Pitt, and earlier by Thomas Gray, are on the first floor on the left of the picture.

Left William Pitt as a boy of seventeen, by an unknown artist. 'He was always the most lively person in company, abounding in quick wit and repartee.'

Above right 'Let us fall like men!' The collapse of the elder Pitt in the House of Lords, by John Copley (1779–81). William Pitt and his brother rush to the aid of their father, while his enemy the Earl of Mansfield looks stonily the other way.

Right Westminster in Pitt's day. The Abbey dominated the horizon; the Palace of Westminster consisted of lower-lying buildings by the river with only Westminster Hall, in the top centre of the picture, standing out above the skyline.

A sketch of Pitt around the time of his entry to Parliament at the age of twenty-one, by Thomas Lawrence (*c.*1780).
'The Election will be made without my having any trouble, or even visiting my constituents.'

Right Lord Frederick North, First Lord of the Treasury 1770–82, by Nathaniel Dance (1780). An astute politician, he nevertheless led Britain to defeat in the American War of Independence.

Below The Second Marquis of Rockingham, with his private secretary Edmund Burke, by Joshua Reynolds (*c.*1766). Foremost amongst the Whigs in wealth and connections, his sudden death in 1782 intensified the political crisis.

Left The Earl of Shelburne, after Reynolds. His short-lived ministry suffered from his 'want of sincerity, and a habit of listening to every tale-bearer'.

Below Charles James Fox, by Karl Anton Hickel (1793–94). Pitt's arch-rival for a quarter of a century, he inspired the intense affection of his followers and the hatred of the King.

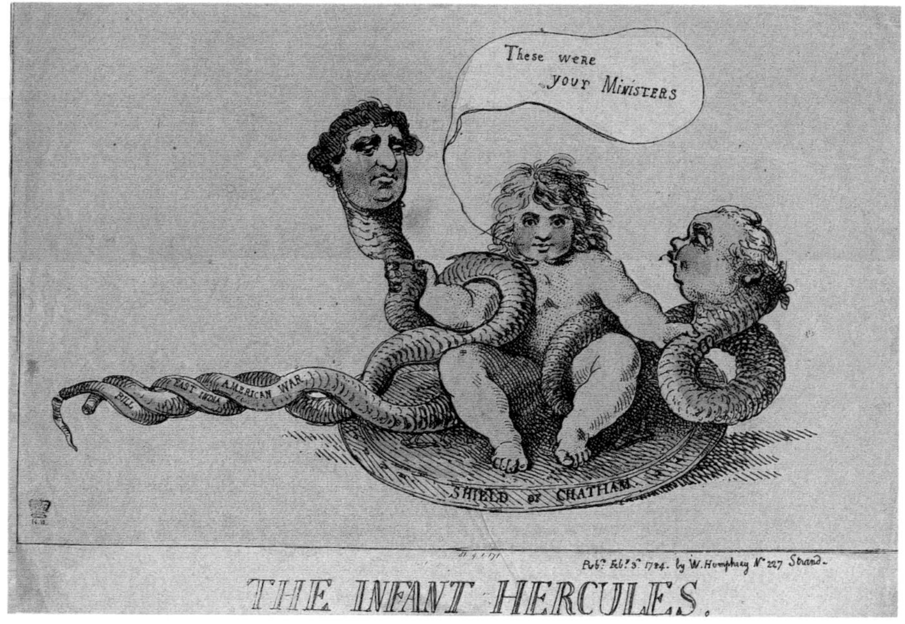

'The Infant Hercules', by Thomas Rowlandson (1784). Cartoons published during the constitutional crisis of early 1784, such as this one, emphasise Pitt's youth, purity and ancestry.

'Master Billy's Procession to Grocer's Hall', by Rowlandson (1784). Pitt proceeded through cheering crowds to accept the Freedom of the City of London. That night there was a riot from which he had to be hauled to safety.

Above Downing Street in Pitt's time. William Pitt resided in No. 10, on the right, for longer than any other politician in history.

King George III, by Allan Ramsay. He coupled a powerful sense of duty and rectitude with a loathing for most politicians.
His apparent madness in 1788 presented Pitt with a severe political crisis.

collier.' In fact it was Fox's vessel which was now holed beyond repair.

The next day, Fox had to let the crucial Mutiny Bill pass through the Commons, lacking the votes to obstruct it. By 10 March Pitt was writing excitedly to the Duke of Rutland, whom he had sent to Ireland as Lord Lieutenant:

> We yesterday were beat only by one, on the concluding measure of opposition . . . To-day, the mutiny bill has gone through the committee without any opposition (after all the threats) to the duration for a twelvemonth. The enemy seem indeed to be on their backs . . . but their object is certainly to lie in wait, or at least catch us in some scrape, that may make our ground worse with the public before any appeal is made there. The sooner that can be done I think the better, and I hope the difficulties in the way are vanishing . . . I write now in great haste, and tired to death, even with victory, for I think our present state is entitled to that name. Adieu, my dear Duke.[28]

Tired he must have been after three months of continuous parliamentary struggle, and crisis meetings through every weekend and holiday. Now he could take the time to move back into Downing Street, from where he wrote to his mother on 16 March, possibly for the first time that year.

> Tuesday night, March 16
>
> My Dear Mother,
>
> 'Tho it is in literal truth, but a single moment I have, I cannot help employing it to thank you a thousand and a thousand times for the pleasure of your letter. I certainly feel our present situation a triumph, at least compared with what it was. – The joy of it is indeed doubled by the reflection of its extending and contributing to your satisfaction among other benefits. I begin to expect every day a little more leisure, and to have some time for reading and writing pleasanter papers than those of Business.
>
> Ever, my dear Mother, your dutiful & affectionate,
>
> W. Pitt[29]

The obstacles to an election were indeed now vanishing: candidates were largely in place, the Mutiny Bill would soon be enacted, and opinion out in the country could hardly be more favourable. On 23 March Pitt wrote to Rutland: 'Our calculations for the new elections are very favourable, and the spirit of the people seems still progressive in our favour.'[30] Meanwhile George III had written to the banker Henry Drummond to borrow £24,000 at 5 per cent. The 'spirit of the people' would not be the only factor working in Pitt's favour.

It was decided that the King would announce the Dissolution of Parliament in a short speech from the throne in the House of Lords on 24 March. That morning Pitt received an unexpected visit from an anxious-looking Lord Chancellor, Lord Thurlow. He reported that in the early hours the Great Seal of England had been stolen from his house. This was of some significance, since the Great Seal was required to authenticate royal commands in Parliament, and an election could not be called without it. To this day no one knows what happened to the Great Seal, and it is very probably lying on the bed of the Thames. James II had dropped an earlier Great Seal into the river as he fled in 1688, in order to inconvenience William III. In any event, Pitt, describing the theft as 'a curious manoever [sic]' and refusing to be ruffled, summoned a special meeting of the Privy Council, which issued an order for the minting of a new Great Seal. Craftsmen worked all through the night to complete it so that the Royal Proclamation dissolving Parliament could be issued the following day. The King proceeded to the Lords on schedule, saying: 'I feel it a duty which I owe to the constitution and to the country, in such a situation, to recur as speedily as possible to the sense of my people by calling a new parliament . . . I trust that . . . the various important objects which will require consideration may be afterwards proceeded upon with less interruption and with happier effect.'[31] Across the country, the extraordinary mixture of democracy, bribery and skulduggery which came together to form an eighteenth-century general election began in earnest.

'Tear the enemy to pieces,' Pitt wrote to Wilberforce in Yorkshire on 24 March. This was not an election in which any quarter would be given. The feelings of candidates and voters alike ran particularly high, fuelled by the dramatic events of the preceding months and the record number of caricatures, pamphlets and newspapers which had carried the arguments to the country. Pitt had certainly won the war of the caricatures, appearing as 'Master Billy' or 'The Infant Hercules', whilst Fox was variously depicted as Guy Fawkes, Satan or Cromwell.[32]

While the mood of the nation was clearly for Pitt, it remained to be seen how that would be translated into parliamentary seats, given the usual importance of local factors in an eighteenth-century election, and the control of so many boroughs by individuals or tiny electorates. It was not normally possible in a general election in this period to ascertain any trend in national opinion at all; nor did any coherent national view about the parties and factions necessarily exist. Even when a government lost support in the open constituencies where general public opinion did hold some sway, it was often able to counteract it through the judicious use of patronage and money in the more closed constituencies. The general election of 1784 is unusual in that large numbers of people were prepared to vote for or against local candidates on the basis of their national loyalties. Pitt enjoyed the upper hand in that battle of loyalties, as well as all the powers of incumbency, and the combination of these two forces would be crushingly decisive.

That Pitt was gaining strongly was apparent within days of the Dissolution of Parliament. Modern politicians are used to the idea that an election campaign runs for four or five weeks, and is followed by a single day of polling and results. An eighteenth-century election was almost exactly the other way round, with only a few days' interval after the Dissolution before polling took place, and results flowing in over a five-week period. The poll would be open in some constituencies for a few hours, while in the City of Westminster in this election it would be open for forty days. Voting was often brought to a halt by the withdrawal of a candidate who lost heart, since the open voting (the ballot was not secret) allowed running totals to be continually assessed, or it might last until everyone who could vote or was likely to vote had cast his ballot. There was no national campaign in the sense of politicians travelling around the country: for a Member of Parliament who was unopposed or who enjoyed a safe majority, elections were therefore a time of extended leisure.

Pitt, of course, had previously enjoyed the certainty of unopposed return in Appleby – even though, after over three years as its MP, he had still never visited the place. Yet as a teenager he had set his heart on being one of the Members for Cambridge University, and it was thence that he set out as soon as Parliament was dissolved. Embarrassingly, the *Morning Herald* revealed that he had written to a Cambridge voter announcing himself as a candidate for Cambridge and saying Parliament had been dissolved, in a letter dated 24 March but postmarked 23 March – before this event had taken place. But Pitt was now so popular that such trivia need not have troubled him. He refused a nomination for the City of London and, keeping the possibility of election at Bath in his back pocket, travelled with evident confidence to Cambridge. He told Wilberforce: 'I set out this evening for Cambridge, where I expect, notwithstanding your boding, to find everything favourable. I am sure, however, to find a retreat at Bath.'[33] He spent a week canvassing in Cambridge alongside his friend Lord Euston, amidst the scribbling of hurried notes to candidates across the country, and when the poll was held on 3 April Pitt received 359 votes and Euston 309, unseating the two sitting members, Townshend and Mansfield, who received 281 and 185 respectively. Both of them had opposed Pitt in the Commons in the preceding months. It was a sweet victory for Pitt, only four years after he had received 147 votes in the same constituency and come bottom of the poll. He had achieved another of his life's ambitions, and would represent Cambridge University until the day he died.

Pitt sat down to write a polite letter declining nomination for Bath – 'nothing but the particular circumstances of my connection with this place could have prevented my embracing an offer so flattering to my feelings'[34] – then returned to Downing Street to rest and await other results. After four days of voting any majority for Fox and North in the Commons had disappeared. The early boroughs gave Pitt thirteen net gains, but it was when the counties began their elections on 6 April that the scale of his triumph became evident. Shows of hands at county meetings left veteran MPs who had backed Fox unwilling even to contest the election: Thomas Coke of Norfolk found that his 'bringing forward one of Fox's desperate resolutions has ruined him with all thinking men'.[35] Those who did contest the election in counties such as Gloucestershire or Suffolk were overwhelmingly defeated. In Yorkshire, where the Rockingham connection should have guaranteed one of the two seats for Fox, the canvass was so overwhelmingly for Pitt that William Wilberforce and an ally were returned unopposed. Lord Fitzwilliam complained that they had been 'beat by the ragamuffins'.[36] The four most prestigious county seats in England were those of Yorkshire and Middlesex, and all of these were now in the hands of Pitt supporters. The many established MPs ejected from the Commons became known as 'Fox's Martyrs'.

From the City of Westminster came the news that Fox himself was struggling to hold his seat, despite the Prince of Wales parading through the streets in his colours, and the energetic campaigning of Georgiana, Duchess of Devonshire. Twenty-three days of voting elapsed before Fox moved narrowly into second place, which would have given him one of the two seats, but the voting and the campaigning continued, in perhaps the most hotly contested constituency election of the entire century. Tens of thousands of pounds were spent on each side, vast quantities of alcohol were disbursed, dinners were held for hundreds of voters at a time, street fights between supporters of the candidates became common, 'miscreants' who attempted to vote twice were put on the ducking stool, and an unknown number of votes were cast by people who were not really voters at all.

Fox's supporters concentrated on defeating Sir Cecil Wray, who was considered the weaker of the two government candidates. In particular they attacked him for switching sides to join Pitt, and alleged that he wished to close Chelsea Hospital. The election literature gives a flavour of the intensity of the campaign:

To be Sold by Auction
By JUDAS ISCARIOT
At the Prerogative Arms, Westminster
CHELSEA HOSPITAL
With all the Live and Dead Stock
JUDAS ISCARIOT is extremely sorry he cannot put up for sale
PUBLIC INGRATITUDE
Having reserved that Article for Himself

Another Foxite advertisement for the election ran:

At Covent Garden
FREE ELECTION: A FARCE
Old Obstinate, by Mr. King
Admiral Broadside (first Court Candidate) Lord Hood
Judas (second Court Candidate) Sir Cecil Wray
Champion of Liberty, Mr. Fox[37]

The Hood and Wray campaign retaliated with advertisements for Fox in the name of Oliver Cromwell, and circulated a list of mock reasons to vote for Fox which included:

> – Because Mr. Fox has never acted according to the wishes of his constituents, but treated them with every mark of contempt.
>
> – Because Mr. Fox's family have never robbed the public of Three Hundred and Seventy Thousand Pounds, as is maliciously asserted.[38]

They reacted to the involvement of the Duchess of Devonshire with a leaflet which read:

Hired for the day
SEVERAL PAIR OF RUBY POUTING LIPS
OF THE FIRST QUALITY
To be kissed by rum Dukes, queer Dukes, Butchers, Dray-men,
Dustmen and Chimney Sweepers[39]

and songs such as:

I had rather kiss my Moll than she;
With all her paint and finery;
What's a Duchess more than woman?
We've sounder flesh on Portsmouth Common![40]

With the beautiful Duchess steadily strengthening Fox's position as she planted kisses on the cheeks of shopkeepers and labourers, the King went so far as to suggest to Pitt that all tactics, legal or not, should be employed: 'Though the advance made by Mr. Fox this day can only have been by bad votes, yet similar measures must be adopted rather than let him get Returned for Westminster.'[41] Strong language was employed in the pamphlets which were circulated in abundance, Fox being described in one of them as 'the high priest of drunkenness, gaming, and every species of debauchery'.[42] Fox had taken the sensible precaution of having himself returned for Kirkwall and neighbouring boroughs in Orkney (where there were a total of twelve far less troublesome voters), but he fought desperately to retain the Westminster constituency, since his defeat there would be the icing on the cake of Pitt's victory.

By 7 May all the results were in, except for the City of Westminster, where the voting continued. It was clear that Pitt had won a huge victory, approximating to some seventy net gains, which would give him a comfortable three-figure majority in the Commons. This far exceeded the expectations of the opposition, and was probably better than Robinson's own estimates, although the final versions of these have not survived. There had been the predictable swing to the incumbent government in closed boroughs where Treasury and royal money, along with the effects of patronage, had had their effect. Even so, less money was spent on behalf of the Crown in this election than in those of 1774 or 1780. The victory drew its size as well as its quality from larger than expected gains in the open seats where public opinion could make itself felt. In the counties, only one supporter of Fox or North was successful in an actual poll, out of the eighty seats available, although others were elected by arrangement or without a contest. The emphatic verdict wherever large numbers of voters had participated added great moral authority to the obvious statistical weight of Pitt's victory.

The new House of Commons was due to meet on 18 May. On the morning of the seventeenth the voting in the City of Westminster was still going on after forty days. Pitt described it as 'forty days poll, forty days riot, and forty days confusion'. In the midst of great disputes about the validity of some of the votes and with the Commons about to meet, the High Bailiff announced a result in Westminster, but granted a 'scrutiny' of the count to the Pittite candidate Sir Cecil Wray, whom Fox had now defeated. The figures stood at Lord Hood (who was also for Pitt) 6,694, Fox 6,234 and Wray 5,998. No Members were declared returned for the City of Westminster until the scrutiny, which would involve an investigation of every vote, had taken place.

It was thus as the Member for Orkney that an enraged Fox returned to the House of Commons on 18 May. He took his seat on the opposition front bench with literally scores of the Members who had supported the Fox–North coalition now missing. Across from him, firmly seated on the Treasury bench, and with a great majority arrayed behind him, was William Pitt. Still ten days short of his twenty-fifth birthday, he was now indisputably at the helm of a nation and an empire.

PART TWO

10

Power and its Limits

'No one who had not been an eye-witness could conceive the ascendancy which Mr. Pitt then possessed over the House of Commons.'

WILLIAM WILBERFORCE

'He is not a great Minister. He is a great young Minister.'

THE EARL OF MANSFIELD

'ON THE FIRST MEETING of the House of Commons, the most careless observer who had sat in the preceding Parliament could not fail to perceive, on surveying the opposition benches, how vast a diminution had taken place in that ardent, numerous, and devoted phalanx which lately surrounded Fox,'[1] is how Wraxall described the scene in the Commons immediately after the 1784 election. 'But Fox did not lose the occasion of commenting with indignant severity on the conduct of the high bailiff of Westminster; observing, not without reason, that the House, which ought to have consisted of 558 members, was incomplete, none being returned for the city which had elected him as one of its representatives.'[2]

The new Parliament thus began with a continuation of the election. The controversy over whether Fox should have been returned for Westminster was to rage for many months. The initial attempt of Fox and his supporters to overturn the declaration of a scrutiny was defeated by ninety-seven votes (233 to 136), while their attempt to amend the address to the King on the opening of Parliament was defeated by 168 votes (282 to 114). Lord North tried to deflate the triumphant atmosphere on the government benches by warning Pitt of 'the mutability of ministerial greatness', and pointing out that the number of votes cast in the House with the opposition was similar to the number so cast at the beginning of the previous Parliament – in which he was voted out as First Lord of the Treasury. In reality, the new government was far more secure in the Commons than any of its recent predecessors, but the voting figures in the first two divisions revealed an important fact for those who paused to reflect on it: Pitt's majority was very large, but very variable. Members of Parliament who would loyally support him on a matter of government policy would not necessarily do so on other matters not central to the ability to govern, of which the Westminster scrutiny was an early example.

Pitt's insistence that the challenge to Fox's election at Westminster should go ahead, even though the government already enjoyed a huge majority, was later to bring him his first defeat in the new Parliament. It has been much criticised by historians as an uncharacteristic and immature act of vindictiveness based on poor judgement, but that is an armchair analysis, too distant from the intense political feelings of the spring of 1784, and asks us to expect too much of Pitt, or of almost any newly victorious leader. In order to imagine the atmosphere of the time it is necessary to remember the immense importance attached to the City of Westminster result: the government side had spent perhaps a quarter of its total national resources in that one constituency, the Prince of Wales had just held a lavish party at Carlton House to celebrate Fox's victory, and the narrow result was widely believed to have been accompanied by major fraud. It is also the first instinct of a politician who has knocked his opponent to the ground to find some means of preventing him from getting up again.

Added to this, it must be borne in mind that relations between Pitt and Fox were now extremely poor. Pitt knew that Fox would have had him impeached if he could have mustered the votes to do so in the previous Parliament. In the opening debates, he now took pleasure in 'sarcastically congratulating' Fox on 'the extent of his fame, which, spreading to the remotest corner of Great Britain, had procured his election for the Orkney and Shetland Islands'.[3] With more feeling in the next session he was to describe Fox's position as 'a situation, in which, to the torments of baffled hope, of wounded pride, and disappointed ambition, was added the mortifying reflection, that to the improvident and intemperate use he had made of his power and influence, while they lasted, he could alone attribute the cause of all those misfortunes to which he was used, so constantly, so pathetically, but so unsuccessfully, to solicit the compassion of the house'.[4] It was now a relationship of 'great mutual asperity',[5] and Fox was to say that summer, of his own increasing absences from the House: 'To be present at the daily or rather hourly equivocations of a young hypocrite, is at once so disgusting to observe and so infamous to tolerate, that the person who listens to them with forebearance [sic], becomes almost an accomplice in them.'[6]

As things turned out, it would have benefited Pitt to have ended the Westminster scrutiny forthwith. Yet to expect him to have done so would be to ask him to except himself from the general rule of politicians – that magnanimity is to be shown only when it is either inconsequential or positively hurtful to the enemy. Moreover, he did not know at this stage that the scrutiny, being so legalistic, would take many months to examine even a small proportion of the votes. In beating off another opposition challenge to the scrutiny on 8 June by seventy-eight votes, Pitt carried a motion for it to be conducted with 'all despatch'.

In the meantime, the King had delivered his speech at the opening of Parliament, written for him by Pitt for the first time, paving the way for higher taxes 'after a long and expensive war' and a final resolution of Indian affairs. These two subjects would, indeed, be all that there was time to address in the short session before the August recess. In tackling them Pitt would show abilities, energy and strength of purpose which would win him much admiration. He would begin to develop and reveal the working habits which would characterise the long years in power to come. Yet the success he would enjoy and the support he would receive would perhaps lead him to think that similar success and support for a wider range of objectives was more assured than it really was.

* * *

The budget which Pitt presented in the House of Commons on 30 June 1784 was the first of at least twenty-two that he would ultimately deliver as First Lord of the Treasury and Chancellor of the Exchequer. His aptitude for learning rapidly and his prodigious attention to mathematics as a boy led naturally on to a mastery of financial detail which many onlookers found dazzling. Wraxall noted that 'he performed this arduous task in a manner at once so voluminous, accurate, and masterly, as to excite universal admiration . . . Pitt may, indeed, be regarded as a political phenomenon not likely to recur in the lapse of many ages.'[7] The following year Lady Gower would remark on 'so perfect a knowledge of the Commerce, Funds, and Government of the Country that one must imagine, to hear him on these subjects, that he had the experience of fifty years . . . The Opposition even cannot help expressing Astonishment.'[8]

Any idea that a twenty-five-year-old could not run the country was now firmly laid to rest, all the more so because Pitt managed to combine in his budget a certain degree of boldness with a display of integrity which, together, brought a good deal of popularity. The financial position he inherited was dire. A country with annual tax revenues of about £13 million was paying £8 million a year interest on a national debt which now amounted to £234 million. The last four years of the American War had added some £80 million to that debt, and it had been further inflated by the habits of Pitt's predecessors, who sold government stock at a nominally low interest rate but at a large discount. This kept the interest rates low, but eventually gave the lenders a very healthy return by hugely inflating the capital which would one day have to be repaid. Pitt had longer-term designs on addressing these problems, through the establishment of a Sinking Fund to repay the debt and the sale of stock at higher rates of interest. At this stage he had neither the time nor the financial resources to put these in place, but he did create a new system by the sale of a £6 million loan necessary that year by distributing it according to the best terms offered among sealed bids, which were opened in the presence of the Deputy Governor of the Bank of England. Previous governments had often channelled the sale of government stock to their friends and supporters as a form of patronage; Pitt's new system brought the raising of government loans up to the standards of modern times. 'Honest Billy' had struck again.

Even with this loan, Pitt needed to raise taxes. 'Irksome as is my task this day,' he told the Commons, 'the necessities of the country call upon me not to shrink from it; and I confide in the good sense and patriotism of the people of England.'[9] Rather than create controversy by a sharp increase in one tax, he chose to spread the burden over a wide range of items – hats, ribbons, paper, hackney coaches, bricks, candles, linens, calicoes, coal, gold and silver plate, imported silk, exported lead, postage rates, and shooting certificates. With the exception of the coal tax, which he withdrew within a week on finding the reaction so strongly against it, Pitt had judged matters well. The money raised allowed him to fund the new loan while concentrating on a bold reform elsewhere: to assist government revenues by tackling the thorny issue of smuggling.

Smuggling had become a way of life in many coastal areas of Britain, and it is estimated that some 40,000 people were engaged in it. At the heart of this huge trade was the smuggling of tea, which had become a household staple in the Britain of the eighteenth century, but attracted import duties averaging 119 per cent. Pitt now announced that he would 'lower the duty on tea to such a degree as to take away from the smuggler all temptation to his illicit trade'.[10] He reduced the average duty to 25 per cent, making up the immediate shortfall of revenue by increasing the window tax (not introducing it, as is sometimes thought) on a graduated scale for people with more than four windows. In time, the huge reduction in smuggling which followed would in any case bring an increase in revenue. This was not achieved without a difficult tussle with the smugglers, who responded to the budget by trying to starve the market of tea and to bid up its price to impossible levels. Pitt's response was methodical and effective, extending the distance from the coast within which smugglers' ships could be seized and, with the close advice of the leading tea merchant Richard Twining, bringing in emergency stocks, pledging government support for the purchase of extra tea in Europe and encouraging responsible dealers into the market at a crucial juncture. The whole manoeuvre was extremely successful, and would pave the way for a similar attack on the smuggling of spirits at a later stage. While Fox tried in vain to oppose the move, on the thin basis that people would have to pay more tax on other things to make up for the tea-drinkers, it was generally popular, and was well received by the less well-off, who now enjoyed cheaper tea while still not having to pay tax on their windows.

Notwithstanding the intense pressures on taxes and debt, Pitt went out of his way at this time to provide for major expenditure on the navy. The war with America had not only wrecked the state's finances, it had also exposed the inability of the navy to control the seas and protect British trade, along with appalling maladministration and corruption in the dockyards. Pitt allocated more than £2 million for the building of new warships, and instituted a Parliamentary Inquiry into the state of the fleet and dockyards. The importance he placed on the expansion of trade, and his attachment to the attitudes and successes of his father, made maritime power a natural interest and one he would maintain throughout his life.

On 6 July 1784, fresh from the successful presentation of his budget, Pitt brought his India Bill before the House of Commons. This was essentially the same measure as the one narrowly rejected earlier that year: it set up a Board of Control appointed by the King and consisting of Ministers responsible for 'the superintendence and control over all the British territorial possessions in the East Indies and over the affairs of the Company'. The key question of the appointment of the officials of the Company was left in the hands of its Directors. The dramatic consequences of the 1784 election were demonstrated by the fact that in January, Fox had been able to defeat this bill; now Pitt was able to carry it by a majority of 211 (271 to sixty). Pitt was himself appointed to the Board of Control, along with the relevant Secretary of State Lord Sydney, and Pitt's two most rapidly rising stars, Dundas and William Grenville. In the years to come Dundas, in Pitt's absence, would preside at most of the meetings and become the real power in the government on Indian matters. The India Bill had been put together as a compromise amidst the urgent need to present an alternative to Fox's plans, yet it was to stand the test of time. While Indian affairs, in the shape of the record as Governor General of Warren Hastings, would consume a vast amount of parliamentary time in the coming decade, the form of government for India, save for an occasional amending Act, was now settled for the next three quarters of a century.

The ease of Pitt's mastery of finance and victory on India impressed even seasoned observers. Edward Gibbon, who was scarcely predisposed in Pitt's favour, wrote from Lausanne that autumn that people on the Continent were 'biassed by the splendour of young Pitt, and it is a fair and honourable prejudice. A youth of five-and-twenty, who raises himself to the government of an empire by the power of genius and the reputation of virtue, is a circumstance unparalleled in history, and, in a general view, is not less glorious to the country than to himself.'[11]

Pitt's first budget had displayed an approach to problem-solving which was unusual among the politicians of the time. He clearly enjoyed finance, administration and the business of government as such, in contrast to Lord North, who was reliable but lazy, or Fox, who saved his greatest energies for more exciting or sensuous pleasures. Pitt loved to gather experts and bright younger people around him, with whom he could then get to the heart of the matter and come up with a solution. He had been eager to draw on the talents of the most enterprising tea merchants as he attacked smuggling, and even went himself down to Leadenhall Street to confer with them. As Ireland began to preoccupy him that autumn he would draw to him another talented expert, John Beresford, who would spend many hours with him, and write out for him a good deal of his correspondence and instructions. Pitt's ready mastery of detail led officials and outsiders to enjoy working with him, one of them noting his 'extraordinary memory', which was 'so tenacious that he never forgot anything he had once learned'.[12]

This is the Pitt familiar to us, whether in Cambridge tutorials or at his father's knee. He liked to pick up ideas from other people and then apply his own mind to improving them – Lord Mahon, for instance, had produced proposals on tackling smuggling through a sharp reduction in duty – and Dudley Ryder, a friend and later Cabinet colleague, would refer to his 'peculiar talent of making persons with whom he conversed pleased with themselves by taking up their ideas

– and enlarging upon them and improving them'.[13] As a result Pitt preferred to do his thinking informally, with work and companionship blending into one.

Such an approach often led to powerful ideas, but it was not easily suited to Cabinet government. A list of the bright young men with whom Pitt liked to surround himself would not have included a single member of his Cabinet. Furthermore, he had only served in government for eight months prior to becoming First Lord of the Treasury himself, and that had been under Shelburne, who was anything but a model of consultation and collective decision-making. Pitt had thus received no education in Cabinet government. The effect of this would be compounded by all of the early decisions of his government being concerned with matters on which he could act without the detailed involvement of his Cabinet colleagues: the budget, which fell entirely within his own sphere; India, on which policy had already been decided before the election; and Ireland, on which he needed the advice of the Duke of Rutland and Thomas Orde, as Lord Lieutenant and Chief Secretary of Ireland respectively, rather than that of Cabinet Ministers. Consequently he did not need to get into the habit early on of informing and involving his senior colleagues. The style of discussion evolved in Cambridge common rooms made no provision for colleagues to be kept informed of decisions.

It is not surprising, therefore, that Pitt would always have colleagues, from senior Ministers to the less expert or intelligent MPs, who felt excluded from his circle. He would usually overcome the problems this caused by sheer ability, but sometimes he would be caught unawares by objections or opposition. Having arrived at a chosen policy through rational deliberation, he could be vulnerable to over-optimism when not all the people he had to deal with were susceptible to reason. He would also find that Ministers or MPs who had not been involved in arriving at a particular view felt free to express a different one. Such realities were probably not apparent to him as the Commons rose for its recess in August 1784. The coming year would reveal them.

* * *

When Parliament was sitting, Pitt was now fully back in residence at 10 Downing Street, with Wilberforce and Eliot as regular house-guests. Once the session was over he hankered as usual for more rural air, and from the summer of 1784 to the autumn of 1785 he rented a house on Putney Heath, a short distance from the noise and smells of eighteenth-century London. He wrote to his mother on 28 August: 'The end of the Session has hardly yet given me any thing like leisure; as the Continual Hurry of some months leaves of course no small Arrear of Business now to be despatched. I hope, however, in about Ten days, or possibly a week, to be able to get as far as Brighthelmstone . . . I am already in a great measure a country gentleman, because, tho full of Business, it is of a nature which I can do as well at Putney . . . I look forward with impatience to being enough released to be with you at Burton, and work the more cheerfully in Hopes of it.'[14]

A few weeks later he wrote to his mother that his excursion to the south coast had taught him that he could not afford to be more than a day's distance from London. 'The principal cause of my being detained at present is the Expectation of materials from Ireland, and persons to consult with from that country . . . The scene there is the most important and delicate we now have to attend to, but even there I think things wear a more favourable Aspect.'[15] Pitt was now bringing his powers of analysis and sense of optimism to Irish affairs. It was to be a serious trial for both these attributes.

The economic condition of the people of Ireland throughout the eighteenth century was characterised by deep and enduring poverty. Attempts to develop successful industries were repeatedly frustrated by laws passed at Westminster: any study of Irish history in this period provides some understanding of how a lasting sense of grievance against the English was developed. Central to trading arrangements at this time were the Navigation Acts, which provided that exports from Britain to the colonies must be carried in British ships. Amendments to these laws in the 1660s removed the right of Irish ships to carry exports from either Britain or Ireland to the rest of the Empire. The English response to the development of a successful cattle trade in Ireland was to forbid the import of Irish cattle into England, thus destroying the Irish trade. The Irish also had the prospect of developing a strong trade in wool and woollen goods, but this was destroyed by an Act of 1699 that prohibited the export from Ireland of all goods made up or mixed with wool – except to England and Wales, where they were subject to a level of duties which made them completely unsaleable. The devastation of such a principal industry caused immense economic hardship.

Rebellion in Ireland had sometimes taken the form of a boycotting of trade with England, which of course only made the economic situation worse, but there is no doubt that the legal framework under which the Catholic majority in Ireland were forced to live was deeply oppressive. Catholics were excluded from Parliament and from property rights, and even the poorest had to pay tithes to the established Church, notwithstanding their different religion. The needs of war and the intensity of Irish discontent had led to some relaxation of the economic restrictions on Ireland in 1780. Irish ships were permitted to sail as British, the right to export wool and glass was restored, and Catholics were allowed to inherit property. Nevertheless, a myriad of restrictive laws and prohibitive duties remained, and the war had contributed to a recession in the Irish linen trade, one of the few industries which had established itself successfully. The Duke of Rutland, on taking office as Lord Lieutenant, found Ireland in a state of political and economic disorder, writing to Pitt from Dublin on 15 August 1784: 'This city is in a great measure under the dominion and tyranny of the mob. Persons are daily marked out for the operation of tarring and feathering; the magistrates neglect their duty . . . the state of Dublin calls loudly for an immediate and vigorous interposition of Government.'[16]

With the budget and India now out of the way, Pitt brought the searchlight of his enquiring mind to bear on the Irish situation through the autumn of 1784. He exchanged long letters with Rutland and Thomas Orde, the Chief Secretary whom he had sent over with him. In addition, he drew heavily on the expertise of John Beresford, the Chief Commissioner of the Revenue in Ireland, requesting that he come to London for several months. Beresford was to spend many hours on an almost daily basis with Pitt as he developed his thinking. For Pitt believed that the economic condition of Ireland was the root cause of its discontents, and began to think of a radical liberalisation of English–Irish trade as the answer. While meant to be on holiday at Brighton in September 1784, he was not only sending so many notes to Sydney that he added to one, 'I am afraid I shall completely tire you with seeing my hand,'[17] but also writing at considerable length to Orde, saying that the great question was 'what is it that in truth will give satisfaction and restore permanent tranquillity to Ireland? Much has been given already, and the effect has been very little in proportion . . . I believe what you have stated to be perfectly just – that the internal poverty and distress of the country is the radical cause of all the discontent that prevails. Of that the cure must be gradual and probably slow . . . If we remove some things that are perhaps not barely pretexts but real additional causes of discontent, that one great cause will still remain. In such a situation we . . . must trust to the progressive operation of a prudent system to extinguish at length the seeds of this disorder.'[18]

Orde had pressed Pitt to respond to Irish problems with the 'utmost liberality', and Pitt was inclined to do so, writing to Rutland in October: 'I own to you that the line to which my mind at present inclines . . . is to give Ireland an almost unlimited communication of commercial advantages, if we can receive in return some security that her strength and riches will be our benefit, and that she will contribute from time to time in their increasing proportions to the common exigencies of the empire.'[19] Such a solution was not only supported by Pitt and Beresford's conclusion that small measures of amelioration would make little difference to the problem; it was also in line with beliefs dear to Pitt's heart and which would influence his policies throughout his lifetime. The first of these, strongly influenced by Adam Smith's recent publication of *The Wealth of Nations*, was that the growth of trade would bring benefits to all the countries involved, even if temporarily painful adjustments had to be made in industries hitherto shielded from competition. The second belief was that a lasting solution to the Irish hostility towards England could only be achieved by somehow unifying first the economic and then the political interests of the two countries. The solution which therefore naturally presented itself to him was a major opening up of trade between England and Ireland, accompanied by a modest contribution from Ireland to the defence needs of the whole kingdom. Over time this would alleviate poverty in Ireland, while giving people on both sides of the Irish Sea a greater economic and political stake in each other's success.

In the longer term, Pitt may have already been thinking of a more radical and permanent solution. Rutland suggested to him that 'without an union Ireland will not be connected with Great Britain in twenty years longer'.[20] The amalgamation of the two Parliaments would indeed represent the culmination of Pitt's policy, and sixteen years later, in the midst of another great crisis, he would bring it about. For the moment he framed his proposals as ten resolutions, reducing the duties on all manufactures and produce levied in Britain and Ireland on each other's goods to the lowest rate levied by either, and giving Ireland the freedom to import from and export to Britain the goods of other countries without them being subject to increased duties. He accompanied this with an eleventh ingenious formula requiring the Irish to contribute a varying amount to defence expenditure when their total revenue was above a certain level.

In early February Orde presented the proposals to the Irish Parliament. The carefully balanced package was seriously undermined, and in retrospect fatally so, by a concession made by Orde in order to get it through in Ireland: the contribution to defence would only be made when the overall Irish budget was in surplus. Pitt was not pleased, telling Orde that he wished 'any consequence had been risked rather than such a concession'. He asked Rutland and Orde to try to restore the original proposal, but in the meantime decided to go ahead in putting the resolutions to the House of Commons in London.

The new session of Parliament at Westminster had been opened by the King on 25 January 1785, with Pitt in an apparently strong political position. His plan was to carry his Irish proposals through Parliament, present a budget that would build on the success of his first one the previous year, and finally to succeed in winning a majority in Parliament for parliamentary reform, on which he had been working hard with Wyvill since December. Naturally optimistic, and confident in the force of his arguments, everything seemed to go well when Pitt presented the Irish resolutions to the Commons on 22 February. It was a classic Pitt speech, answering all possible objections one by one while providing a seemingly unanswerable argument for change. He condemned the treatment of Ireland over the previous century, describing it as a 'system of cruel and abominable restraint'.[21] He said 'the system had been that of debarring Ireland from the enjoyment and use of her own resources; to make the kingdom completely subservient to the interests and opulence of this country, without suffering her to share in the bounties of nature, in the industry of her citizens, or making them contribute to the general interests and strength of the empire'.[22] He called for 'a system of equality and fairness' which would create a 'community of benefits' and a 'community of burdens', describing a system of trade with Ireland that would not 'aggrandize the one or depress the other' but 'should seek the aggregate interests of the empire'.[23] And in a peroration of great power he told the Commons: 'Surely, after the heavy loss which our country has sustained from the recent severance of her dominions, there ought to be no object more impressed on the feelings of the House than to endeavour to preserve from further dismemberment and diminution – to unite and to connect – what yet remains of our reduced and shattered empire . . . Of all the objects of my political life, this is in my opinion the most important that I ever have engaged in; nor do I imagine I shall ever meet another that shall rouse every emotion of my heart in so strong a degree as does the present.'[24]

Pitt was optimistic that the strength of opposition in the Commons would now be 'less than threatened'. He was wrong. Fox took the opportunity to denounce the proposals for freer trade, seeing a chance to create hostility to Pitt. Two opposition politicians with strong business connections, Lord Sheffield and William Eden, began to mobilise opposition to the resolutions. With the assistance of Josiah Wedgwood and his powerful interests in the pottery industry they argued that equality of trade between Britain and Ireland would seriously disadvantage their domestic industries. The Irish had cheaper labour and lower taxes, and English manufacturers would therefore be undermined. By early March demands from businesses for the extensive amendment of the resolutions were beginning to make themselves felt in Parliament. Pitt was forced to start thinking of concessions, and it was at this very point that a so-far compliant House of Commons began to rebel.

While Pitt's mind was absorbed in the intricacies of Irish trade, the much-disputed Westminster scrutiny had dragged on. It was indeed being discovered that many votes had been fraudulently cast – in the parishes of St Margaret and St John '400 persons had voted, as inhabitants of those parishes, not one of whom could be found to exist'[25] – but the fraud was fairly evenly spread among the candidates, and had so far made no difference to the result. The heavy employment of lawyers meant the whole process was costing many thousands of pounds, with protracted examination of every vote. It was thought that if it continued at this pace, the process would not be completed for a good two years. Furthermore, for most observers and even participants the passions of the previous year's election had now cooled. Politics was moving on to other issues, and Fox was in any case able to sit in Parliament. Even Pitt's supporters were finding the continuation of the scrutiny embarrassing, Wraxall describing it in his memoirs as 'one of the strongest acts of Ministerial oppression and persecution which I have witnessed',[26] despite having voted for it himself.

By late February the government was able to win a division authorising the scrutiny to carry on by only nine votes. Fox knew how to pull the heartstrings even of his enemies, saying of Pitt, 'I was always prepared to find in him a formidable rival, who in the race of glory would leave me far behind; but I believed him incapable of descending to be my persecutor.'[27] The scrutiny, he said, was 'obviously intended to weary out my friends by expense. A sum of £30,000 a year will be swallowed up on the two sides. My own last shilling may soon be got at, for I am poor. Yet in such a cause I will lay down my last shilling.'[28] Pitt's normally supportive back benchers could stand it no longer. On 3 March, when Fox's supporters again moved that 'an immediate return' should be made for the City of Westminster, many of Pitt's habitual supporters abstained, allowing Fox to win by thirty-eight votes (162 to 124). The following day he and Lord Hood were declared elected for the City of Westminster.

For Pitt this was a nasty shock. The House of Commons might be happy to sustain him in government, but that did not mean it would always do his bidding. With his attention focused elsewhere, he had not been sufficiently in touch with parliamentary opinion to know that a defeat was heading his way. Now he had not only appeared vindictive, he had been defeated as well. The defeat in no way imperilled his government, and when Fox tried to follow up his success by moving that the records of the proceedings against him be expunged from the journals of the House he was heavily defeated by 105 votes (242 to 137). The MPs knew what they were doing: 'They wished to control and to restrain, but had no desire to overturn the Administration.'[29]

This sudden defeat intensified the pressure on Pitt as he tried to defend his Irish proposals, and delayed his plans to bring parliamentary reform before the House. Nevertheless, he now proceeded with his attempt to enact the cherished dream of his earlier years: a reform of elections to the House of Commons which would make them more representative of the shifting population of the country. He had been keeping his cards close to his chest on this subject all through 1784, but in early December he summoned Wyvill to Downing Street, causing him to abandon his plans for a long foreign tour in favour of working on a new plan for reform. Wyvill thought the prospects of success were 'improved beyond our utmost expectations'.[30] Pitt too was suffering from his natural over-optimism, writing to Rutland on 12 January: 'I really think that I see more than ever the chance of effecting a safe and temperate plan, and I think its success as essential to the credit, if not the stability, of the present administration, as it is to the good government of the country hereafter.'[31]

The plan evolved by Pitt and Wyvill was indeed 'temperate', involving a small extension of the right to vote and the disenfranchising of thirty-six rotten boroughs, with their seventy-two seats being reallocated to the largest counties and the Cities of London and Westminster. £1 million was to be used to sugar the pill, by actually buying out those who had interests in the boroughs concerned. By keeping his proposals modest, Pitt thought he had a chance of finally bringing about some change to a centuries-old system which many people still regarded as inviolable. He also prepared the ground carefully with the most senior of those people, George III himself. Conscious that the King was implacably opposed to such reform, and mindful of the process by which he had himself come to power, Pitt was careful to ensure that there would be no royal intervention to obstruct his legislation. In a letter to the King on 19 March he raised 'the possibility of the Measure being rejected by the weight of those who are supposed to be connected with Government'. He implied that such a thing would bring about his resignation, saying that it 'might weaken and dissolve the Public confidence, and in doing so would render every future effort in Your Majesty's service but too probably fruitless and ineffectual'.[32] The King replied that: 'Though I have ever thought it unfortunate that He had early engaged himself in this measure . . . out of personal regard to Him I would avoid giving any opinion to any one on the opening of the door to Parliamentary Reform except to Him.'[33]

With that key flank secure, Pitt did everything he could to muster support among his friends. Dundas, who had always opposed reform until his close alliance with Pitt, was once again implored to support it – and would be much taunted for agreeing to do so. Pitt wrote to Wilberforce in Nice asking him to come back to Westminster to assist him and speak in the debate. But MPs knew that the King disliked reform, and that senior members of the Cabinet such as Thurlow were opposed to it. Some of them thought Pitt was bringing it forward for the sake of consistency rather than out of conviction. And, not knowing where a process of reform might ultimately lead, many of them decided to stay safely with the existing system, and, in saving themselves, for a second time in two months to see themselves as saving Pitt from himself.

It was thus to a sceptical House that Pitt outlined his plans on 18 April 1785. He said that no one 'reverenced the venerable fabric' of the constitution more than he did, 'but all mankind knew that the best institutions, like human bodies, carried in themselves the seeds of decay and corruption; and therefore he thought himself justifiable in proposing remedies against this corruption, which the frame of the Constitution must necessarily experience in the lapse of years'. The whole force of the argument as he presented it was that reform was in keeping with British history rather than in conflict with it: 'If we looked back to our history, we should find that the brightest periods of its glory and triumph were those in which the House of Commons had the most complete confidence in their Ministers, and the people of England the most complete confidence in the House of Commons. The purity of representation was the only true and permanent source of such confidence.' Now he wanted to 're-establish such a relation', and Members should not be alarmed by 'unnecessary' fears. 'Nothing was so hurtful to improvement as the fear of being carried farther than the principle upon which a person set out.'[34]

The House listened in respectful but ominous silence. One observer wrote: 'He was heard indeed, with great attention, but with that sort of civil attention which people give to a person who has a good claim to be heard, but with whom the hearers are determined to disagree, and though there were nearer 500 than 450 in the House, I never saw them behave so quiet, and yet so apparently determined.'[35] In the lobbies, MPs who often supported Pitt muttered that they wished he would 'keep clear of this absurd business'. Fox gave nominal support to the idea of reform, while criticising the details and leaving his friends to vote against Pitt for the sake of opposition. Once again, it was Lord North who gave a highly effective Commons performance in response to Pitt's speech. He drew attention to a glaring weakness, which was that despite all the efforts to arouse popular support for the reform proposals, very few petitions had been received. 'What are we to infer from this circumstance? Is it apathy in the people? We were taught to believe that all England would with one voice support the plan for amending the national representation. Well may I exclaim with the man in the "Rehearsal",* "What horrid sound of silence doth assail mine ear!"'[36]

With the controversies of the war receding and national prosperity on the increase, Wyvill had indeed found it difficult to drum up the expressions of popular support that Pitt had needed. One hundred and seventy-four MPs supported Pitt in the vote that night, but 248, including most of the opposition and some of his own close allies such as Rose and Grenville, voted against him. Parliamentary reform was just not going to happen in that generation. To Pitt it was deeply

* A well-known satirical play of the time.

discouraging. Wilberforce captured the mood in Downing Street in his diary: 'Terribly disappointed and beat. Extremely fatigued. – spoke extremely ill, but commended. Called at Pitt's – met poor Wyvill.'[37] Pitt was learning that being in office was not always the same as being in power.

Why could such a generally popular Minister with a large majority in the Commons not carry a proposal so dear to his heart? The reality was that an eighteenth-century Prime Minister did not possess the tools of party discipline available to his more recent counterparts. Pitt's supporters did not constitute a 'party' in any sense we would recognise, except that they generally supported the idea of Pitt being the head of government. They were not elected on any manifesto or programme, and were made up of a disparate mixture of 'Pittites', 'King's friends' and fairly independent country gentlemen. Moreover, in the eighteenth century the passing of legislation was not regarded as part of the fundamental business of government. Just because an MP supported a particular set of Ministers in carrying on His Majesty's Government did not mean that he would necessarily support them in changing the law. Thus a matter such as parliamentary reform was regarded as a question of individual opinion and conscience, rather as twenty-first-century MPs would regard a vote on capital punishment or abortion, and not remotely as a question affecting confidence in the government. Pitt was therefore no more able to insist on parliamentary approval of his reform proposals than Margaret Thatcher would be able two hundred years later to insist on the return of the death penalty. He was almost alone in seeing it as a question fundamental to what he wanted to achieve.

Pitt was deeply disappointed both by this setback and by his defeat in the Westminster scrutiny. In both cases over-optimism and a degree of obstinacy had led him to defeat. In neither case had he foreseen it. Whether or not he was unnerved by this experience, he certainly made a large number of concessions on other subjects in the weeks that followed. In his second budget, on 9 May 1785, he could point to increasing revenues and vastly reduced smuggling as a result of his measures of the year before, and to come still nearer to balancing the books he proposed some further tax increases on such items as servants, shops, gloves and pawnbrokers' licences. The proposal to impose for the first time a tax on the employment of female servants caused much ribaldry at Pitt's expense, along with aspersions directed at his own lack of knowledge of women (the subject of a later chapter). More seriously, the tax on the rents of retail shops caused riots outside 10 Downing Street, where Pitt was burnt in effigy, and the newly formed General Chamber of Manufacturers, which was already campaigning against his Irish proposals, forced the repeal in April of the tax on linens and calicoes which he had imposed the previous year. For all the success of his general approach to finance, and the compelling logic of his Irish propositions, Pitt now found himself seriously on the defensive, with the string of defeats already undermining his authority.

By the time he came to put the Irish resolutions to the Commons in detail in May, he had found it necessary to make so many exceptions and modifications that instead of eleven resolutions there were now twenty. Special provisions were to be made concerning fishing, the copyright of books, patents, and trade in various parts of the world: Irish ships would not be able to trade beyond the Cape of Good Hope, nor import goods from the West Indies, unless they were the produce of the colonies. The original simple solution was scarcely recognisable, with Wedgwood writing happily: 'He has now brought into the house a system so much altered, and with so many additions, that it may be called a new one . . . and in every one of these, new alterations and amendments are made before it passes.'[38]

The task of getting the same set of proposals through two Parliaments, one sitting in Dublin and the other in London, was proving extremely difficult. The original concession on the Irish contribution to defence inserted in Dublin had now been struck out in Westminster. With the multitude of amendments and qualifications attached to them, the resolutions passed comfortably through the Commons at the end of May, with Pitt putting a brave face on all the changes, saying that they were 'perfectly consistent' with the general plan. But Fox and the other opponents of both his government and his Irish policy were cleverly concentrating on his most vulnerable point: that the resolutions as amended in Westminster still had to be carried through the Parliament in Dublin. Fox, who was enjoying his sudden popularity with Manchester manufacturers, also argued that the requirements being set in Westminster were taking away from the Irish the legislative independence they had been granted in 1782: 'I will not barter English commerce for Irish slavery.'[39] The opposition of Irish politicians to the proposals designed to benefit their country grew sharply.

Once again, Pitt seemed to underestimate the danger, telling Rutland when the resolutions passed the Lords in July that the session had been 'in all respects triumphant'. But on 13 August Orde's motion to begin consideration of the resolutions in the Dublin Parliament was carried by the Irish House of Commons by only nineteen votes, revealing that any detailed examination of them would be hopeless. The whole laudable and idealistic project, which had occupied so much of Pitt's thoughts and time for a full year, now had to be abandoned. There was no way of getting the two Parliaments to vote for the same policy. Pitt was stoical in defeat, writing to Rutland: 'We have the satisfaction of having proposed a system which I believe will not be discredited even by its failure, and we must wait times and seasons for carrying it into effect . . . I believe the time will yet come when we shall see all our views realized in both countries, and for the advantage of both.'[40] However brave a face he might put on it, a policy he regarded as of central importance had been totally frustrated, with no hope of reviving it in the near future.

The end of the parliamentary session in the summer of 1785 must have come as a relief to Pitt. As he travelled to Burton Pynsent that August to visit his mother he would have known that he was still highly regarded and secure in office, but that his inexperience had shown. The Earl of Mansfield had commented with some force, 'He is not a great Minister. He is a great young Minister.'[41] It was now more than a year since Pitt's sweeping victory in the 1784 election, and the policies he proposed in his first year of office reveal much about his political views. Although some of his proposals had been radical in nature, his intention in every field, from finance to the constitution to Irish trade, was to bring about practical rather than revolutionary change. Not only was his mind naturally attuned to searching for workable remedies to complex problems, it was also his political instinct to seek improvements to the established order of things rather than to overturn that order.

It would be easy, in the terminology of today's political ideas, to think of Pitt's reduction in tea duties in favour of the window tax as a deliberate move to what would now be called more 'progressive' taxation, or to see his proposals for parliamentary reform as the starting point from which to advance to equal representation and universal suffrage, but he would not have thought of his policies in these terms. The view has often been expressed that Pitt was more 'liberal' or 'progressive' in his early years in office, and more 'conservative' or 'reactionary' in later years in a time of war. The alternative explanation, that he sought throughout the maintenance of a balanced constitution and a general increase in prosperity, and later changed his approach in dramatically changed circumstances, is much more likely to be the one that he himself would recognise. The terms 'left wing' or 'right wing' had not yet come into existence, and Pitt would not have seen himself as moving along a spectrum of political positions. The changes he made to taxation were designed to bring the budget nearer to balance, rather than to redistribute income as an end in itself. Similarly, his proposals for parliamentary reform were designed to permit the main features of the electoral system to continue more credibly, not to initiate a movement towards what is now referred to as democracy.

An understanding of this is crucial to appreciating why Pitt could persist in calling himself an 'independent Whig' while being regarded for the two hundred years after his death as the founder of what became the nineteenth-century Tory Party. When he called himself a Whig he meant he was a defender of the constitutional balance between King and Parliament arrived at in 1688. History knows him as a Tory because of his emphasis on evolutionary change, his belief in the maintenance of the principal institutions of the country and the policies pursued by his allies after his death.

Pitt's behaviour throughout the rest of his time in office would be affected by the setbacks and disappointments of 1785. Although he would still search for simple and elegant solutions to complex problems, he would in future take even greater care to prepare the ground, and would rarely risk defeat. He had not enjoyed the experience of finding himself in a minority in a Parliament where he was meant to be dominant, and, with the exception of one policy already set in motion, he would never again in the eighteenth century suffer such direct parliamentary reverses on matters central to the government. From now on he would temper his idealism with more wariness of the entrenched opinions of others.

11

Private by Nature

'He was indeed endowed, beyond any man of his time, with a gay heart and a social spirit.'

LORD MORNINGTON[1]

'Pitt does not make friends.'

WILLIAM WILBERFORCE[2]

AFTER THE SETBACKS of the summer of 1785, Pitt's friends were anxious for him. Wilberforce wrote from Lausanne in early August: 'I cannot help being extremely anxious; your own character, as well as the welfare of the country are at stake . . . You may reckon yourself most fortunate in that cheerfulness of mind which enables you every now and then to throw off your load for a few hours & rest yourself. I fancy it must have been this which when I am with you, prevents my considering you as an object of compassion, tho' Prime Minister of England; for now, when I am at a distance, out of hearing of your foyning, and your [illegible] other proofs of a light heart, I cannot help representing you to myself as oppressed with cares and troubles.'[3]

Wilberforce saw Pitt in one light when thinking of him as Prime Minister, but in quite another when thinking of him as a carefree friend. The difference is not surprising. Pitt's manner outside his immediate circle was aloof and austere – 'I know the coldness of the climate you go into,' Shelburne told a colleague about to visit Pitt. He 'never partook of the common amusements of London life' once war had begun in the 1790s, and very rarely once in office in the 1780s.[4] In more familiar company his shyness evaporated, along with any need to compensate for his youthfulness by appearing stern: it was said by Lord Mornington (later Marquess Wellesley, and the future Duke of Wellington's brother, who became a close friend) that in 'society' 'he shone with a degree of calm and steady lustre, which often astonished me more than his most splendid efforts in Parliament. His manners were perfectly plain . . . his wit was . . . quick and ready.'[5] Pitt had no social ambitions, and it was rare for him deliberately to set out to make a friend, although George Rose, and later George Canning, were exceptions to this. The talented collaborators of his first eighteen months in office – Beresford, Wyvill and Twining – passed in and out of his mind along with their areas of expertise.

Pitt was at his happiest in the company of his Cambridge companions or his family, and in the summer recess of 1785 he was instrumental in bringing family and friends closer together. His sister Harriot had by this stage moved into Downing Street with him, and sometimes acted as his hostess. Pretyman's wife observed ' 'twas pity She was his Sister, for no other woman in the World was suited to be his wife'.[6] Edward Eliot, still one of Pitt's closest friends, often stayed there too, and the result was a strong attachment between sister and friend. When Eliot's father suggested their marriage be delayed until an expected inheritance had come to his son, Pitt intervened with a letter from Downing Street, saying that a delay could not 'be reconciled to the happiness of either of them',[7] and they were married less than a fortnight later.

By late September Pitt was at Brighton with his intimate friends, going on to Salisbury to meet the happy couple and then to Burton Pynsent to see his mother. Three weeks later he had returned to Downing Street, once again via Brighton, writing to his mother on 20 October: 'Your letter found me exceedingly safe at Brighthelmstone, not-withstanding all the perils of thunder and lightning, which overtook me at Mr. Bankes's at the end of a long day's shooting, and were attended with no more consequences than a complete wetting. My conscience has reproached me a good deal for not having sent this certificate of myself sooner.'

Pitt was now twenty-six, but the delicacy of his childhood meant that his mother never lost her fear of him catching a cold. Her letters of this time to Edward Wilson convey a mother's mixture of pride and anxiety. In November 1784 she writes, 'I have lived a long time upon the pleasure of expecting him, and if he comes I shall live a long time after upon the pleasure of having seen him.'[8] Four months later, Pitt had still not made it to Burton Pynsent: 'What infinite happiness that my young great man should have stood this most rigorous season without suffering more from it than a common cold . . . I cou'd not help a thousand tears about it, tho' Harriot was very attentive in giving me continual accounts of him . . . His not making me his intended visit alter'd extremely the whole cast of the winter to me, for it would have secured me a foundation of pleasure that wou'd have carried me more agre'ably through it.'[9]

She need not have worried about his physical well-being. Throughout his twenties Pitt enjoyed robust good health: it was only in his mid-thirties that pressure of war and quantity of alcohol began to take their toll. His weight was stable, being recorded in the Weighing Books at 3 St James's Street in 1783 as eleven stone 11.5 pounds in shoes and frock coat, and twelve stone exactly three years later. The weighing scales can still be seen at the same location, now the headquarters of Berry Brothers and Rudd. At this stage the only intrusion on his health was the growth of a cyst on his cheek early in 1786. There were no anaesthetics in the eighteenth century, but the doctors said the cyst had to be cut out, and John Hunter, Surgeon Extraordinary to George III, was appointed to do it. Pitt refused to have his hands tied, as would have been normal during a painful operation, and sat motionless with his eyes fixed on the Horseguards clock, having been told the operation would take six minutes. Hunter is said to have observed that he had never seen 'so much fortitude & courage in all his practice',[10] while the only comment of his patient was: 'You have exceeded your time half a minute.'

With Wilberforce in Europe and Eliot honeymooning with Harriot, Pitt spent his Brighton retreat in the early autumn of 1785 with his other closest Cambridge friends, Bob Smith, John Pratt and Tom Steele. In itself, this should not have been regarded as surprising: many twenty-six-year-olds continue with their circle of teenage friends until circumstances force them to change, and to Pitt's mind becoming Prime Minister was not such a circumstance. Nevertheless, the habits and friendships of such a pre-eminent twenty-six-year-old occasioned a great deal of comment. Pitt's lack of interest in enlarging his social circle meant that it did not grow to encompass any women outside his own family, a fact that produced a good deal of rumour. From late 1784, satirical verses about Pitt and his friends and colleagues appeared under the title 'Criticisms of the Rolliad' in the *Morning Herald*. The writers were witty gentlemen ensconced in Brooks's Club, and the title was based on the Pittite MP John Rolle, to whose partisanship they had taken a particular dislike. Deprived of power, they enjoyed themselves hugely penning couplets which would annoy the government. Sometimes they were simply sarcastic about Pitt's age, as in this famous extract:

A sight to make surrounding nations stare,
A Kingdom trusted to a school boy's care.

Other verses were directed at the physical appearance of Pitt's Ministers. Lord Sydney, for example, had a prominent chin:

O, had by nature but proportion'd been,
His strength of genius to his length of chin,
His mighty mind in some prodigious plan,
At once with ease had reach'd Hindostan!

For Grenville, who would later become a prominent ally of Pitt, comment was reserved for a different part of his anatomy:

What plenteous stores of knowledge may contain,
The spacious tenement of Grenville's Brain;
Nature, in all her dispensations wise,
Who form'd his headpiece of so vast a size,
Hath not, 't is true, neglected to bestow
Its due proportion to the part below;
And hence we reason, that to serve the state
His top and bottom may have equal weight.

Other verses attacked Pitt's Downing Street circle:

The Lyars

In Downing Street, the breakfast duly set,
As Bankes and Pretyman one morn were met,
A strife arising who could best supply,
In urgent cases, a convenient lie . . .

There were many verses drawing attention to Pitt's lack of knowledge of women, such as these 'On the Immaculate Boy':

'Tis true, indeed, we oft abuse him,
Because he bends to no man;
But slander's self dares not accuse him
Of stiffness to a woman

and:

The virulent fair
Protest and declare
This Ministry's not to their hearts;
For say what they will,
To them Master Bill,
Has never discovered his parts.

A particular prominence was reserved in the 'Rolliad' for Pitt's friendship with Steele, highlighted by the visits to Brighton. George Rose and Tom Steele were both Secretaries to the Treasury, and the 'Rolliad' implied that the hardworking Rose was jealous of the fresh-faced Steele:

But vain his hope to shine in Billy's eyes,
Vain all his votes, his speeches, and his lies.
Steele's happier claims the boy's regard engaged,
Alike their studies, nor unlike their age:
With Steele, companion of his vacant hours,
Oft would he seek Brighthelmstone's sea-girt towers;
For Steele relinquish Beauty's trifling talk,
With Steele each morning ride, each evening walk;
Or in full tea-cups drowning cares of state
On gentler topics urge the mock debate.

There were many references in the 'Rolliad' to Steele making or drinking tea, considered at that time to be a feminine preoccupation:

> Where beauteous Brighton overlooks the sea,
> These be his joys: and STEELE shall make the Tea.

Such rumours and writings were always more of a tease than an accusation, but those who read them or wrote them must have had their suspicions. We have no sure evidence that Pitt was homosexual: no surviving letter or diary of any of his friends gives any hint of it, no enemy directly alleged it even after his death. Nevertheless there was a good deal of innuendo and gossip. At the height of the constitutional crisis in 1784, Sheridan had compared Pitt to James I's favourite the Duke of Buckingham, a clear reference to homosexuality. Socially, Pitt preferred the company of young men, and would continue to do so as he advanced into his thirties and forties. But in other respects his behaviour did not offer any clue to homosexual inclinations. It also seems unlikely that a man with such an overpowering sense of ambition and duty, who easily commanded the willpower to avoid misdemeanours at Cambridge and to stop gambling at Goostree's, whose whereabouts were always known and who, according to Pretyman, never locked his bedroom door at night, would take any sexual risk that would threaten his political career.

This may, of course, be the answer to the mystery: that Pitt had homosexual leanings but suppressed any urge to act on them for the sake of his ambitions. Social attitudes were more hostile to such tendencies in the late eighteenth century than they are today, or had been only a few decades before. It is possible that the suppression of private feelings added to Pitt's apparent aloofness and his dedication to work. He could be charming to women, but it seems certain that he rejected intimacy whenever it was proffered – and would do so publicly at a later date. In practical terms it appears that Pitt was essentially asexual throughout his life, perhaps one example of how his rapid development as a politician stunted his growth as a man.

Pitt may have lacked the appetite for new social relationships, but he would also have discovered that a politician who comes to high office inevitably faces formidable difficulties in making new friends. Colleagues at the top of a government are generally thrown together by some mixture of duty, conviction and circumstances; hardly ever by friendship, as usually becomes apparent whenever one of them runs into trouble. Those outside high office seeking to become friends of such a powerful Minister as Pitt will usually have been seeking advancement or promotion, and Pitt even more than most Ministers found such matters distasteful. Add to that his natural shyness and bookish, problem-solving mind, and it is not surprising that he clung to the familiar. His lack of experience of a world beyond Cambridge and Westminster sometimes put him at a disadvantage, as the setbacks of 1785 had demonstrated. Wilberforce, while testifying to Pitt's 'extraordinary precision of understanding', also observed: 'You always saw *where* you differed from him and *why*. The difference arose commonly from his sanguine temper leading him to give credit to information which others might distrust, and to expect that doubtful contingencies would have a more favourable issue than others might venture to anticipate.'[11] Another MP commented that Pitt's mind 'was confined to the details of business, before He had sufficiently acquainted himself either with Politicks or men', and a later ministerial colleague, William Windham, said that Pitt had not had 'the opportunities of seeing men and manners, except as a minister, not the most favourable way of seeing men'.[12] As a result, the air of innocence which continued to characterise Pitt's personal friendships affected his political decision-taking, and led naturally to disappointments.

What lay behind the contrasting sides of Pitt's personality – the testimony of Mornington and others to his delightful company, and yet of Wilberforce that he 'did not make friends'? How was it that he had so much to discuss with some people, but to others had nothing to say? He is not alone among politicians in dividing the people around him, probably unconsciously, into three groups. One very small group consisted of his absolutely nearest and dearest. This included his mother, for whom he would make any financial sacrifice, and his surviving sister, to whom he was obviously deeply attached. Later in life his niece, Lady Hester Stanhope, would fulfil a similar role. He evidently loved being near to them, but had no interest in their political opinions. Many politicians seek in their families a release from politics, and find family members less well informed about politics than their other friends: once in office Pitt would write to his mother with news of political successes coupled with reports of his health, but he no longer sought her opinion about national affairs.

The second group comprised those people with whom Pitt needed regular contact because of their rank or position, but whose company he would never have sought for its own sake. Foremost among this group is King George III himself. Pitt and the King had stood together and triumphed in the crisis of 1783–84: each needed the cooperation of the other, and there is no doubt that a mutual respect and a working relationship had developed. Yet even the long years to come, working in harness, would not give rise to personal warmth between them. Not surprisingly, Pitt seemed to find long audiences with the King tiresome. George III was given to intransigent declarations and flitting from one subject to another, neither of which would have appealed to Pitt's rational and focused mind. Rather than seeing the King personally, he developed the habit of writing to him at length on serious issues, setting out the arguments in a logical way and awaiting a written reply. The temperaments of the two men were very different; so too would be their perceptions of the period before they formed their alliance. Pitt probably never forgot the slight to his father's memory when the court boycotted his funeral, and certainly would not have forgotten the hostility he felt to the apparent abuse of royal power during the war in America. For his part, the King evidently never forgot the earlier refusal of Pitt to form a government, and when delirious in 1789 he 'abused Mr. Pitt much . . . & called him a Boy; said that He had wanted him to step forward at the close of Lord Lansdowne's [Shelburne's] Administration, but that He was afraid'.[13] For all the fact that they would work closely together for many years, and that the King would subsequently pour much praise on Pitt's head, a personal distance would always remain.

The same pattern of necessity of alliance but absence of intimacy characterised Pitt's relations with most other political figures, including his entire Cabinet until it was later joined by his brother, his cousin Grenville, and Dundas. Pitt observed the forms of social interchange with his Cabinet colleagues, hosting Cabinet dinners from time to time and occasionally dining alone with Sydney or Carmarthen. But these people were pieces on his political chessboard rather than contributors to his ideas or his enjoyment of life. All of the senior Ministers with whom he started out would at some stage complain vehemently of being unaware of major decisions. The deeply conservative Thurlow was almost always opposed to Pitt's ideas of reform, remained personally close to the King and was a rival centre of power within the administration. Pitt had a weary respect for him, but often left him out of decisions. When the Bill to restore to the original owners Scottish estates confiscated in the 1745 rebellion was presented in the House of Lords (having been pressed on Pitt by Dundas), Thurlow said that he welcomed it but, despite being a member of the Cabinet, had no previous knowledge of the Bill's existence. Sydney fumed that control of Indian affairs passed steadily into the hands of Dundas, and Carmarthen would find that Pitt would take over many of his functions as soon as a foreign-policy crisis erupted. Pitt needed Cabinet colleagues, but he felt no need to keep them fully involved.

Similarly, he needed support in Parliament, but while he was highly attentive to young Members who showed promise he did little to cultivate the support of MPs in general. He had no inclination to entertain Members of Parliament on any systematic basis, and only called in at supportive clubs, such as White's, if he had a specific purpose. Even Goostree's closed down, probably in part because he never went there. His family tried to remind him of the need to be more sociable, and for a while Harriot's presence in Downing Street made a big difference. She wrote to her mother on 28 February 1786 that there were to be 'three or four more Assemblies to *take in every Body* . . . And ye Young World are *very* desirous of it . . . I hope you will like this Plan, and indeed I believe your having said so much about ye *tristesse* of our Administration made my Brother think of it.'[14] This was Pitt's answer: hold a few big parties to get the whole business of being sociable with a wider circle over and done with. We should not exaggerate Pitt's isolation: he attended a large number of official functions, was almost always at the King's levées, where the court and Ministers congregated, and met many deputations. Much as he did these things, however, he did not seek the continued company or closer friendship of those he met. He preferred to present his face to the world in the one public forum where he naturally cast off all shyness and reserve: the House of Commons. It was only through his eloquence there that he gave public vent to the full range of his personality.

Pitt's third grouping of associates was the one which every politician needs: a small group of friends, usually acquired before taking office, who overlap the boundary between personal and political life. Such friends provide the opportunity for confidential and disinterested political discussion, and at the same time social companionship. These were the familiar friends from Cambridge and Goostree's: Wilberforce, Eliot, Bankes, Pratt, Steele and Pretyman. Pitt was not starry-eyed about his friends, and did not usually promote them to high office if he did not think they were up to it. Although he made Steele a Secretary of the Treasury, he would reserve the big leaps in seniority for colleagues who showed the greatest ability, such as Dundas and Grenville. While he successfully secured the Bishopric of Lincoln for Pretyman in 1787, this removed him from the far more influential situation of being Pitt's *de facto* private secretary.

In general, however, while Pitt was happy for patronage to be employed in order to bolster his government's authority and numbers in Parliament, he was less likely than other politicians of his day to seek preferment for his friends. His attempts to promote Pretyman within the Church right up to being Archbishop of Canterbury are something of an exception to this, as is his making his elder brother First Lord of the Admiralty, although he expected the latter to do a job and moved him when he was not sufficiently good at it. Whenever the subject of Pretyman's preferment came up, Pitt became irrational. As early as January 1783, during his brief first tenure as Chancellor of the Exchequer, he had sought to persuade Shelburne to make Pretyman Dean of Worcester even though he did not qualify on age grounds. It was a matter on which he was 'firmly anxious to be of all the service in my power to my friend', and it would 'oblige me in a point I have extremely at heart'.[15] Beyond that, he did not shower his friends with the titles or decorations which he was happy to distribute to others to make his government secure, and it would not have accorded with his treasured concept of incorruptibility to do so. His friends' understanding of this had a reciprocal side: if they felt strongly about an issue, they were able to differ with him publicly. Many of his close associates, including Wilberforce, Bankes and Rose, voted against him on at least one important occasion. It is a measure of his open mind, pleasant temper and genuine friendship that he did not seem to hold it against them, but the fact that his friends did not receive unfair rewards and were not subject to strict political control probably contributed to the rather weak sense of discipline and loyalty among his wider following. If the Prime Minister's own closer associates could rebel from time to time, then why on earth couldn't everyone else?

Nevertheless, these friends were Pitt's mainstay. Whenever they met in some combination in Downing Street, or Brighton, or Wilberforce's villa in Wimbledon, Pitt was able to mix ministerial responsibility with social frivolity as he pleased. While his preoccupations and duties had moved on enormously since he had met them, he seemed entirely content with the friends he had. This happy situation could not last. He was to discover in 1786 that even a Prime Minister cannot command his friends never to change, or not to die.

No Prime Minister, then or now, has enjoyed such a thing as a 'typical' working day. When he could, Pitt breakfasted in Downing Street at 9 a.m., often with a visitor or a member of the government, but he evidently abandoned this if the pressure of urgent business was too great. He would spend most of the day in committees or other meetings, perhaps taking a ride in St James's Park, with Rose or Steele or Dundas, around midday. He would eat dinner, as was usual in the eighteenth century, at about five o'clock, often taking some hours over eating and drinking with his close companions, and 'laying aside all care enjoy their conversation till the evening hour of business arrived'.[16] He would return to work, with papers or officials, at about 9 p.m. until late at night. Even when he was staying in Wimbledon with Wilberforce or Dundas, or in his rented house in Putney, Mrs Pretyman Tomline says that 'the Evenings were *usually* spent in *business*. Such for many years was the constant tenor of Mr. Pitt's life.'[17] In practice, given Pitt's preference for informality and decision-taking in small groups, the boundaries between pleasure and business were less strict than this timetable suggests. The summer recesses in particular provided an opportunity for exactly the type of thinking Pitt liked to do. Dundas recalled that 'in transacting the business of the State, in forming our plans &c. we never retired to Office for that purpose. All these matters we discussed & settled either in our morning rides at Wimbledon, or in our even'g walks at that place. We were accustomed to walk in the evening from 8 oClock to sometimes 10 or Eleven in the Summer Season.'[18] When Parliament was sitting the opposite would apply, as Pitt was often required to be in attendance at the House of Commons throughout the late afternoon and evenings, frequently long into the night.

Every head of government brings his or her own habits and working methods to the job, but for a Prime Minister coming to office in a more modern age there are also certain established ways of conducting and recording business. A new Prime Minister in the twenty-first century inherits a small army of private secretaries and officials who continually take minutes and issue instructions, a Secretary to the Cabinet through whom commands can be given to the entire Civil Service, and an established pattern of meetings through which the heads of all government departments can be commanded or consulted. In Pitt's day none of these things existed. It was up to a new First Lord of the Treasury to decide for himself what staff he might require, what they would do, and the extent to which he would try to interfere in departments beyond the Treasury.

In the absence of any established system for placing decisions in front of him, Pitt's continued habit of concentrating on one subject at a time in order to get to the bottom of it led on other subjects to 'dilatoriness and procrastination, his great vices', according to Wilberforce. There was no system for dealing with correspondence, but Ministers who were so minded, such as Dundas, Rose and later Grenville, could be very efficient and prompt at getting through it. Not so Pitt, who would simply put letters aside if they were not relevant to the matter at hand or otherwise of interest to him. By today's standards, of course, he wrote huge numbers of letters, of which thousands still survive, but he did not create a support system able to cope with the vast amount of correspondence received by a head of government in an age when letters were the principal means of communication. He knew this was a fault, writing to Eliot even before he came to power: 'You have had too much of my Correspondence ever to wonder at its want of Punctuality,'[19] but simply lived with the problem throughout his life. He once wrote to Wilberforce: 'By the simple operation of putting off only from one day to the next, I have now been some months without writing to you.'[20] A Russian envoy who gave Grenville some papers to show to Pitt asked him not to leave them with him, 'for he will not be able to find them again a day later among the immense mass of papers which reach him from all sides and encumber all his tables and desks'.[21] Requests for honours were particularly likely to sit at the bottom of a pile for many months, often causing great offence to MPs, Ambassadors, and aristocratic families. Undoubtedly Pitt felt he would catch up with everything whenever there was a break in the pressure of business, but since no break ever came he never did catch up. George III 'observed that Mr. Pitt was apt to put off laborious or disagreeable business to the last', and would eventually go through it 'with extraordinary rapidity' in an 'irregular mixture of delay and hurry'.[22]

It may be wondered how someone who so neglected important correspondence and showed no interest in courting social connections could possibly survive as head of the government in the eighteenth century, let alone become the second-longest-serving holder of that position in the whole of British history.* The answer lay in his thorough and comprehensive grasp of each subject which did grab his attention, the impressive way in which he conducted the business of government in meetings, the energy which he brought to pursuing his main objectives, and his ability – most of the time – to dominate and dazzle the House of Commons. His friends and supporters ended up forgiving him his faults because of the strength of his compensating qualities,

* The longest-serving was Sir Robert Walpole, First Lord of the Treasury and Chancellor of the Exchequer 1721–42.

but they sometimes found it a sore trial. As Sir James Harris would complain after Pitt had appointed him Ambassador to The Hague: 'is it impossible to move him who *speaks* so well to write one poor line . . . ?'[23] The result of this inattention to correspondence was that Pitt often had to dash off letters of apology, such as one assuring his banker Thomas Coutts that he had not intended 'any mark of neglect or disregard towards you', and that his complete failure to reply to letters was the result of 'pressure of business and from no other motive'.[24]

In office Pitt found it steadily harder to travel. He rarely went further than Somerset, a journey he would make once or twice a year to visit his mother, but often his planned expeditions in that or other directions were postponed or cancelled through the pressure of events. He occasionally went to Cambridge, although the university made few demands on him as a constituency, and he would become High Steward of the University, an honorary and ceremonial role, in 1790. He liked to go shooting, which he could do at Rutland's estate, Cheveley, in conjunction with a visit to Cambridge, or at Bankes's property in Dorset on the way to or from Somerset. He made such journeys by carriage, although he occasionally rode on horseback to and from Cambridge. For the greater part of the time his duties kept him in or near to London, and it was therefore near London that he looked for a more permanent and substantial rural retreat than the house he had rented on Putney Heath.

While licking his political wounds in August 1785 Pitt had the chance to buy Holwood House near Bromley in Kent, a former hunting lodge, not far from his birthplace and about fifteen miles from Westminster. He bought it along with the neighbouring two-hundred-acre farm for a little under £7,000 (£675,000 would be the equivalent in 2004), taking on a £4,000 mortgage. This was a lot of money for Pitt, although it brought him what was only a modest residence by the standards of the politicians of the day, with six bedrooms in total; Harriot thought it was ideal for her unsociable brother in being 'a small House which will not allow of many Visitors'. He added a single-storey dining room, but would later abandon plans for more ambitious expansion of the building as his debts mounted. From November 1785 he went there, Pretyman recalled, 'upon every opportunity, but rarely without a friend or two, and in general some person in office joined him there, that business and recreation might be mixed'.[25]

Pitt had fixed ideas about the nature of his recreation. According to Pretyman he not only had no ear for music, 'nor had he much taste for Drawings or Paintings. He was more attentive to Architecture and used sometimes, in the early part of his life, to amuse himself with drawing a plan of the best possible House.'[26] Like his father, he enjoyed rearranging the landscape and creating new vistas, levelling and planting an iron-age camp, creating new walks, digging out a pond, and employing large numbers of labourers without regard to the cost. 'After toiling in his room over revenue details or foreign dispatches . . . he would walk out, and taking his spade in his hand grub up a thistle or a weed, or give directions about the removal of a shrub, or the turning of a walk, with as much earnestness and interest as if he had nothing else to occupy his thoughts.'[27] This process of 'improvement' went on for many years, with Pitt and any unlucky visitors occasionally joining in the effort. Mornington recalled him 'working in his woods and gardens with his labourers, for whole days together, undergoing considerable bodily fatigue, and with so much eagerness and assiduity, that you would suppose the cultivation of his villa to be the principal occupation of his life'.[28] For Pitt it was vital to maintain some sort of contact with rural activity – he had over two hundred sheep on the farm – and to have a ready retreat from Westminster. With its commanding views over the Kent countryside, Holwood became his favourite haunt throughout his first seventeen years as Prime Minister.*

Initially, Pitt does not seem to have expected the purchase and development of Holwood to have caused him any financial difficulty, and at the same time he did not hesitate to send large sums of money to the aid of his mother. By the mid-1780s the annuity conferred on her by the King had fallen seriously into arrears. As First Lord of the Treasury Pitt was eventually able to set that right, but putting the appropriate fund onto a sustainable basis took some time, and in the

* Pitt's house has not survived, but his pond and walled garden are intact. The view over the Vale of Keston is still splendid, although some pylons have intruded on it. 'Pitt's Oak', a tree under which he apparently sat to read, lives on.

meantime he personally sent whatever was necessary to relieve his mother's anxiety. 'As to the £2000 you mentioned,' he says in a letter of December 1785, 'I have only to entreat you not to suffer a moment's uneasiness on that account. I can arrange that with Mr. Coutts without difficulty, and without its coming across any convenience or Pleasure of my own; tho none I could have would be so great as to be able to spare you a moment of trouble or anxiety. If Mr. Coutts wishes any further security for the 700£ which you mention as due to Him, it will also be very easy to settle that to his satisfaction.'[29] Such things, he said, in another letter, would be no difficulty to him: 'The income of the Lord of the Treasury and Chancellor of the Exchequer together will really furnish more than my Expenses can require.'[30]

Pitt's combined salaries totalled nearly £7,000 a year (and would increase to nearly £10,000 in 1792, when the King insisted he take the office of Lord Warden of the Cinque Ports). This was a handsome sum for those days, and should have allowed him to live reasonably comfortably, but not extravagantly, while permitting a fair amount of entertainment, maintenance of horses, and travel. For three reasons, however, Pitt's income never remotely kept up with his expenses. First, he had no capital, and in 1786 he ensured he never would have any by transferring to his mother the sum of £5,800 which he was meant to one day receive out of his inheritance from his father. He was able to give her this sum by raising a loan on his share of Burton Pynsent and then paying the interest on her behalf. Secondly, he had been borrowing from 1780 onwards, since completing the purchase of his chambers in Lincoln's Inn, and had repeatedly taken on new loans in order to repay old ones. John Ehrman has calculated that by 1787 Pitt was paying interest on a total of nearly £16,000, including the mortgage of Holwood.

Thirdly, despite balancing the nation's books with great precision, creativity and care, Pitt had not the slightest interest in monitoring his own finances while he was in office. This is a common fault among politicians, many of whom to this day barely trouble to look at their bank balance until they are out of power. Personal finances can easily seem a matter of petty detail to someone who holds the whole nation's affairs in his hands. Additionally, Pitt had never witnessed his father being troubled for a second by any thought of where money might come from.

In Pitt's defence, he was still only in his mid-twenties, and many people of that age are happy to borrow large amounts, confident that they can repay it in the infinity of life which stretches before them. He knew he had a substantial salary as Prime Minister, and that if he lost office his services would be much sought after at the Bar. He might also have thought that the delays in receiving his salary from the Treasury, often amounting to about twelve months, were contributing to his growing debts. Yet by the autumn of 1785 he could see that his financial affairs were running out of control, and, lacking the time or the patience to sort them out himself, he asked his friend Bob Smith, a banker and now MP for Nottingham, to work out where his money was going.

The results were horrifying. Smith soon found forgotten and unpaid bills amounting to £7,914, more than Pitt's annual income. Smith told Wilberforce that the bills for provisions 'exceed anything I could have imagined', and generally increased when Pitt was away from home, suggesting that his servants were regularly robbing him. The meat bill for January 1785 was £96, which in the prices of the day represented approximately 1.7 tonnes of meat. Pitt was also spending £1,000 or £2,000 a year on wine, but this paled into insignificance in comparison to the expense of running his stables, which for the three years from July 1783 to July 1786 had cost £37,930. This was a vast sum, probably sufficient to run a sizeable racing stable, which Pitt certainly did not possess. Ehrman has concluded that Pitt was being 'grossly cheated'.

After Smith's investigation many of these costs were brought down, but not sufficiently to create a surplus: the combined effect of generosity to friends, property purchases, feverish landscaping, and aid to his mother, meant that Pitt would continue to go more deeply into debt. For the subsequent fifteen years until he left office in 1801 there is no evidence that Pitt gave any greater attention to his finances than hitherto. Until then, matters would not come to a crunch, since it seems that traders and bankers owed money by the Prime Minister did not pursue the debt too aggressively. However great his personal financial problems, he would not change his nature. He would not seek or for some time accept any sinecure, even though his mother though it right 'that he should in some proper way secure to himself such an Establishment as is necessary to him in these expensive times and fit for him according to the rank he holds in the world'.[31] In 1789, when a group of merchants in the City of London offered him £100,000 to pay off his debts and have a good deal left over besides, he refused it point blank, saying 'no consideration on earth could induce me to accept it'. Lack of interest in money was an integral part of his vision of integrity and incorruptibility, even if it meant that he always owed a good deal of it.

The happy and unchanging circle that surrounded Pitt socially could not last. In the autumn of 1785 William Wilberforce entered a deep depression, and emerged as a convert to evangelical Christianity. He began to consider that the way he had lived and the things he had fought for were relatively worthless, and wrote in his diary: 'It was not so much the fear of punishment by which I was affected, as a sense of my great sinfulness in having so long neglected the unspeakable mercies of my God and Saviour; and such was the effect which this thought produced, that for months I was in a state of the deepest depression, from strong convictions of my guilt.'[32] On 27 November he noted: 'I must awake to my dangerous state, and never be at rest till I have made my peace with God. My heart is so hard, my blindness so great, that I cannot get a due hatred of sin, though I see I am all corrupt, and blinded to the perception of spiritual things.'[33]

Wilberforce wrote to his friends explaining his new beliefs and saying that he would now live in a stricter, less social and less partisan way. He told Pitt that 'though I should ever feel a strong affection for him, and had every reason to believe that I should be in general able to support him, yet I could no more be so much a party man as I had been before'.[34] Pitt may have neglected the letters of people who bored him, but his reply to Wilberforce is worth quoting in full for the rare insight it gives into his mind.

Downing St.,
December 2, 1785.
My Dear Wilberforce,

Bob Smith mentioned to me on Wednesday the letters he had received from you, which prepared me for that I received from you yesterday. I am indeed too deeply interested in whatever concerns you not to be very sensibly affected by what has the appearance of a new æra in your life, and so important in its consequences for yourself and your friends. As to any public conduct which your opinions may ever lead you to, I will not disguise to you that few things could go nearer my heart than to find myself differing from you essentially on any great principle.

I trust and believe that it is a circumstance which can hardly occur. But if it ever should, and even if I should experience as much pain in such an event, as I have found hitherto encouragement and pleasure in the reverse, believe me it is impossible that it should shake the sentiments of affection and friendship which I bear towards you, and which I must be forgetful and insensible indeed if I ever could part with. They are sentiments engraved in my heart, and will never be effaced or weakened. If I knew how to state all I feel, and could hope that you are open to consider it, I should say a great deal more on the subject of the resolution you seem to have formed. You will not suspect me of thinking lightly of any moral or religious motives which guide you. As little will you believe that I think your understanding or judgement easily misled. But forgive me if I cannot help expressing my fear that you are nevertheless deluding yourself into principles which have but too much tendency to counteract your own object, and to render your virtues and your talents useless both to yourself and mankind. I am not, however, without hopes that my anxiety paints this too strongly. For you confess that the character of religion is not a gloomy one, and that it is not that of an enthusiast. But why then this preparation of solitude, which can hardly avoid tincturing the mind either with melancholy or superstition? If a Christian may act in the several relations of life, must he seclude himself from them all to become so? Surely the principles as well as the practice of Christianity are simple, and lead not to meditation only but to action.

I will not, however, enlarge upon these subjects now. What I would ask of you, as a mark both of your friendship and of the candour which belongs to your mind, is to open yourself fully and without reserve to one, who, believe me, does not know how to separate your happiness from his own. You do not explain either the degree or the duration of the retirement which you have prescribed to yourself; you do not tell me how the future course of your life is to be directed, when you think the same privacy no longer necessary: nor, in short, what idea you have formed of the duties which you are from this time to practise. I am sure you will not wonder if I am inquisitive on such a subject. The only way in which you can satisfy me is by conversation. There ought to be no awkwardness or embarrassment to either of us, tho' there may be some anxiety: and if you will open to me fairly the whole state of your mind on these subjects, tho' I shall venture to state to you fairly the points where I fear we may differ, and to desire you to re-examine your own ideas where I think you are mistaken, I will not importune you with fruitless discussion on any opinion which you have deliberately formed. You will, I am sure, do justice to the motives and feelings which induce me to urge this so strongly to you. I think you will not refuse it; if you do not, name any hour at which I can call upon you to-morrow. I am going into Kent, and can take Wimbledon in my way. Reflect, I beg of you, that no principles are the worse for being discussed, and believe me that at all events the full knowledge of the nature and extent of your opinions and intentions will be to me a lasting satisfaction.

Believe me, affectionately and unalterably yours,

W. Pitt.

They duly met, and Wilberforce recorded that 'He tried to reason me out of my convictions, but soon found himself unable to combat their correctness, if Christianity were true. The fact is, he was so absorbed in politics, that he had never given himself time for due reflection on religion.'[35] Perhaps this was another instance of how Pitt ceased to develop outside political matters. Wilberforce now became a different kind of Member of Parliament, more independently minded, mounting determined attempts to prevent any kind of official activity or entertainment on a Sunday. Pitt continued for many years to indulge his friend and happily to discuss his chosen subjects. In trying to ensure that Wilberforce's strong religious beliefs would find practical outlets he encouraged him, as we shall see, to take up the cause which students of history will never separate from the name of Wilberforce: abolition of the slave trade. But the friendship between them would never be the same now that their social habits and philosophical outlook differed, and from now on when Pitt stayed at Wimbledon it was generally at Dundas's villa rather than that of Wilberforce, which was in any case sold in late 1786.

Pitt had rejoiced at the marriage of Harriot to his great friend Edward Eliot. Soon she was pregnant, and on 20 September 1786 the baby was born in Downing Street. Pitt wrote to his mother: 'I have infinite joy in being able to tell you that my sister has just made us a present of a girl, and that both she and our new guest are as well as possible.'[36] Harriot was not well for long. Within two days she had a fever, and within five days she was dying. Hours before she died Pitt wrote anxiously to his mother's assistant and companion Mrs Stapleton: 'I cannot help very much fearing the worst . . . In this distressful situation I scarce know what is best for my mother – whether to rely for the present on the faint chance there is of amendment, or to break the circumstances to her now, to diminish if possible the shock which we apprehend.'[37]

On 25 September Harriot died. Pretyman recorded: 'It was my melancholy office to attend this very superior and truly excellent woman in her last moments; and afterwards to soothe, as far as I was able, the sufferings of her afflicted husband and brother – sufferings which I shall not attempt to describe. It was long before Mr. Pitt could see any one but myself, or transact any business except through me . . . From this moment Mr. Eliot took up his residence in Mr. Pitt's house, and they continued to live like brothers. But Mr. Eliot never recovered his former cheerfulness and spirits, nor could he bring himself again to mix in general society.'[38] Pitt told his distraught mother that he would have come straight to her, 'but I am sure you will approve of my not leaving poor Eliot at this time'. The baby girl, christened Harriot, was brought up at Burton Pynsent, and Hester

Chatham thought her 'the most enchanting little thing'. But Pitt's mother had now lost three of her five children; only Pitt and his elder brother remained. Pitt had lost not only his sister, but the motivator and organiser of any hospitality for people beyond his immediate circle. The burdens of office were mounting on him; and now, along with Harriot, his happy private household had died.

The rupturing of the old circle brought new friendships and habits. Dundas had already become Pitt's right-hand man in many ways, an able and loyal deputy in House of Commons debates and an efficient political fixer who increasingly had Scottish and Indian affairs well under his control. He worked hard and drank hard, two attributes which endeared him to Pitt. Already there were 'hints of jealousy respecting Dundas, who is said to take possession of the Minister and to conduct him as he pleases'.[39] With Dundas, Pitt could sit after dinner ranging over every issue and even taking executive decisions, consuming a fair quantity of claret or port in the process. Pitt would become known as a 'three bottle man', a reference to his heavy consumption of port wine. The possibility that he drank up to three bottles of port at a single sitting on a fairly regular basis has always seemed to modern observers to be either rather unlikely or highly eccentric.

Several facts must be borne in mind. First, attitudes to alcohol were far more liberal than today. Indeed, the difficulty of obtaining clean drinking water meant that alcohol, often watered down, was often considered safer and healthier. Secondly, port represented a very large part of British consumption of wine. One surviving cellar book of the 1760s shows the stock of port to be twice that of all other wines combined. It was at least as common to drink port as claret, and more so at times of war with France. Third, a typical bottle contained only three quarters of a pint of liquid, little more than half the amount of a standard seventy-five-centilitre bottle of today. While the shapes of the bottles had changed during the eighteenth century to resemble those we would recognise now, they were hand-blown, with a larger punt (the indentation at the base of the bottle) and thicker glass.

The space inside was therefore substantially smaller. Fourth, port wine in this period was fortified with brandy, but not as heavily as in later periods, and was therefore somewhat weaker than its namesake today – around 14 to 15 per cent alcohol by volume. Taken together, these facts imply that three bottles of port in Pitt's day would be roughly equivalent to one and two thirds of a bottle of strong wine today. This is still a large amount of alcohol to consume, but not an unimaginable one.

Pitt and Dundas evidently enjoyed outlining their future speeches and those of the opposition once the wine had been flowing. On one occasion Dundas made such a good effort as an opposition Whig that Pitt stood aside from the debate the following day and made him make the actual speech in response, to the mystification of the Commons. It was also alleged that when Pitt and Dundas had been dining and drinking liberally with Charles Jenkinson in Croydon, they drunkenly rode through an open toll-bar gate between Streatham and Tooting, and were fired at by the toll keeper. The writers of the 'Rolliad' enjoyed this story to the full:

> Ah, think what danger on debauch attends!
> Let Pitt o'er wine preach temperance to his friends,
> How, as he wandered darkly o'er the plain,
> His reason drowned in Jenkinson's Champagne,
> Rustic's hand, but righteous fate withstood,
> Had shed a premier's for a robber's blood.

In addition to the greater prominence of Dundas and drink, a further addition to Pitt's circle in the late 1780s was Jane, Duchess of Gordon. She stepped in as a hostess for the bachelor Prime Minister, entertaining government supporters at her house in Pall Mall in competition to the Whig gatherings on Piccadilly hosted by the Duchess of Devonshire. In her late thirties at the time she became associated with Pitt, she seems to have been a rather dominating character who was intelligent but also coarse and unconventional. She may have intended Pitt for her eldest daughter Charlotte, but in any event after a few years of generous hospitality at Pall Mall and at Downing Street (which she called 'Bachelor Hall'), the friendship between them withered. Years later she is meant to have said to him: 'Well, Mr. Pitt, do you talk as much nonsense now as you used to when you lived with me?', to which he immediately replied, 'I do not know, madam, whether I talk so much nonsense, I certainly do not *hear* so much.'[40]

The Duchess of Gordon brought herself fairly briefly into Pitt's life. It was not his style to go out and seek such company. He had been happy with the friends he already had, and if they fell away he became closer to those indispensable to his work and power. This is not surprising. Friendships most often prosper when they start on fairly equal terms, and no one in the nation was now on equal terms with Pitt. He needed relaxation and convivial company, which he clearly enjoyed immensely, but he did not sit thinking about how to find it. As he put the defeats of 1785 behind him, his thoughts were once again on the nation's finances, and increasingly on international affairs. The period of his great ascendancy was about to begin.

12

Spreading His Wings

'Eloquence, transcendent eloquence, formed the foundation and the key-stone of Pitt's Ministerial greatness. Every other quality in him was accessory.'

Sir Nathaniel Wraxall[1]

'You know that I am not partial to Pitt, and yet I must own that he is infinitely superior to anything I ever saw in that House, and I declare that Fox and Sheridan and all of them put together, are nothing to him; he, without support or assistance, answers them all with ease to himself, and they are just chaff before the wind to him.'

Richard Rigby[2]

The restoration to health of the nation's finances was at the heart of Pitt's approach to government, and his success would be fundamental to his growing reputation. A country too weakened by war to make useful alliances among its neighbours could at least conclude, in the words of one envoy writing to Pitt, 'a permanent Alliance with that most formidable of all Powers, the Power of Surplus'.[3] For Pitt, management of the budget had the great advantage of being within his direct control as First Lord of the Treasury, and was a matter to which he was perfectly suited in temperament and intellect. As the parliamentary session opened in January 1786 he prepared to crown his previous measures with a new plan for the repayment of the national debt. In both economic and foreign affairs, his natural skill would now combine with a good deal of luck to bring him great renown.

Both skill and luck still seemed in short supply in the first weeks of the session of 1786. At the opening of Parliament, Fox had dwelt on the possibility of a renewed attempt by Pitt to carry through his Irish policy, a measure, he said, 'detestable in the eyes of the manufacturers of Great Britain and Ireland'.[4] Pitt had no such intentions, but was in any case in immediate trouble over his intention to fortify Plymouth and Portsmouth against attack from the sea at a cost of £760,000. The argument over these fortifications was a classic of eighteenth-century politics: it involved open disagreement between two members of the Cabinet, the Duke of Richmond as Master General of the Ordnance in favour of them, and Admiral Lord Howe as First Lord of the Admiralty against them; and it pitched the desire for strong defences into direct conflict with a deep-seated British suspicion of fortresses which might one day buttress the abuse of royal power. Mistrust of permanent forts was a hangover from the Civil War of the 1640s (following which every defensible castle had been deliberately ruined), but 140 years later it still packed a potent political punch.

Pitt in his later years would not have allowed two senior Ministers to oppose each other so obviously. At this stage, however, his political control of the Cabinet was incomplete; Richmond was a grand old man of politics and Howe was a non-partisan Admiral, and Pitt was grateful to both of them for joining his government. But Richmond was widely regarded among MPs as high-handed, and Howe actively canvassed the support of some of them, leaving Pitt to try in vain to overcome the gut instinct of opposition among the most independently-minded members. He reached back in history to demonstrate that this was no dangerous innovation: 'During the reign of Queen Anne, at the time when the victories of the British arms were forming an era in the history of Europe, at which England looked back with pride, and other nations with amazement, did our ancestors think it incompatible with their fame, with their liberty or their constitution, to fortify the most vulnerable parts of their coasts, as it was now proposed to do?'[5] He found himself up against one of Sheridan's most brilliant speeches, in which the proposals were comprehensively denounced as 'fallacious, dangerous, expensive, and unconstitutional',[6] and as dawn broke on 28 February 1786 the Commons divided exactly equally: 169 votes for the fortresses and 169 against them. When the Speaker cast his vote against the proposal, Pitt was yet again defeated.

Pretyman tells us that 'Mr. Pitt greatly lamented this failure,'[7] but as Harriot wrote: 'The Opposition brought up all their forces, but they are not very considerable; and the question was lost by the disinclination of the country gentlemen particularly of all the western gentlemen.'[8] The defeat was taken as a further sign that this was 'a very loose Parliament'[9] rather than as a vote of no confidence in Pitt.

Pitt's education in the uncertainties of parliamentary support and the dangers of Cabinet division was now complete, and his recovery from it would be spectacular. He had been working for months on finding a way of steadily repaying the national debt, telling Wilberforce that he was 'half mad with a project which will give our supplies the effect almost of magic in the reduction of debt'.[10] The proposals were developed in typical Pitt fashion. Drawing on the ideas of the celebrated economist Dr Price and the conclusions of a commission set up by Lord North, he hammered out the actual proposals with Rose, William Grenville and a small group of talented experts. Grenville, Pitt's cousin and an increasingly useful aide and confidant, simultaneously chaired a Commons Committee to examine in detail the government's income and expenditure.

The manner of Pitt's preparation for the unveiling of his master plan in a flawless three-hour speech to the Commons on 29 March 1786 tells us a great deal about his intellectual confidence and verbal facility. Pretyman remembered:

> Mr. Pitt passed the morning of this day in providing the calculations which he had to state, and in examining the Resolutions which he had to move; and at last he said that he would go and take a short walk by himself, that he might arrange in his mind what he had to say in the House. He returned in a quarter of an hour, and told me he believed he was prepared. After dressing himself he ordered dinner to be sent up; and learning at that moment that his sister (who was then living in the house with him) and a lady with her were going to dine at the same early hour, he desired that their dinner might be sent up with his, and that they might dine together. He passed nearly an hour with

> these ladies, and several friends who called in their way to the House, talking with his usual liveliness and gaiety, as if having nothing upon his mind. He then went immediately to the House of Commons, and made this 'elaborate and far-extended speech,' as Mr. Fox called it, without one omission or error.[11]

Observers of Pitt's speeches always found that 'every word seemed to be the best which the most diligent study could have selected'.[12]

It is hard to imagine in a later age the extent of the preoccupation of late-eighteenth-century politicians and commentators with the national debt. We are accustomed to the debt inflating in bad times and being reduced in good ones, and have often seen it greatly diminished as a problem by either inflation or economic growth. But the policy-makers of the 1780s did not know that they were on the brink of an Industrial Revolution which would multiply the size of their economy many times over; their experience of recent decades was of the inexorable growth of the nation's debt until it was now some sixteen times greater than the annual income of the state. Pitt was therefore responding to what was seen as a national problem of immense importance, and he and his proposals were acclaimed because he not only announced a policy, but also the method and resources by which it could be put into effect.

Pitt was able to announce that government revenues were now rising strongly, partly due to 'the happy æra of the restoration of the peace' and partly 'owing to the regulations that have been taken to crush clandestine trade'.[13] As a result, his revenues were now £15.4 million a year against expenditure of £14.5 million, even allowing for the largest peacetime navy Britain had ever maintained. The creation of a £900,000 surplus after so many years of deficit was in itself regarded as a huge achievement; Pitt now went on to propose additional taxes on spirits and hair powder* to round the surplus up to £1 million, and to commence immediately an annual payment of £1 million into a Sinking Fund. Furthermore, he proposed to add to the fund the interest on the debt redeemed so that it would grow at

* Gentlemen customarily wore powdered wigs in the eighteenth century. Pitt's legacy of taxes on powder would lead to a change in fashion in favour of natural hair.

a compound rate, and to entrench it by an Act of Parliament with independent Commissioners set up to supervise it. Parliament would only be able to go back on it by passing a new Act. The 'magic' of compound interest meant that within twenty-eight years, Pitt claimed, each £1 million set aside would provide £4 million for repayment of debt.

He spoke without a note, telling the House that 'we have nothing indeed to fear. We may lay despondent thoughts aside.'[14] Wraxall described the huge attendance in the Commons and said that 'Pitt seemed on that evening to put into action all his powers of captivating, convincing, and subduing his hearers. The rapidity with which he laid open the state of the finances could only be equalled by the luminous manner of conveying his ideas, and the facility, as well as perspicuity, that accompanied all his calculations. The meanest intellect might follow and comprehend his positions: they were apparently simple and level to every capacity ... The universal attention which had been concentrated upon Pitt while he spoke became liberated when he closed his oration, the floor soon presenting a scene of disorder, noise, and confusion.'[15] The proposal for the Sinking Fund and the manner of presenting it seemed to crown the pervading sense of Pitt's honesty and ability in financial affairs. It also widened a growing separation between him and his kinsman Lord Mahon, now Earl Stanhope, who had worked on a different scheme and tried in vain to insist on it, but in general the effect was to confirm Pitt's popularity and to leave the opposition with little to say. Pretyman noted: 'Never was the admiration of any public measure more warm and general ... Mr. Fox ... pledged himself to produce a plan on a future day, which should have a preferable claim to the concurrence of the house: this was probably said without much consideration, as he never mentioned the subject again.'[16]

In part, Pitt was the beneficiary of a general improvement in trade which followed the end of the American War, and he recognised as much. Nevertheless, his measures cemented his reputation and meant that financial recovery and the name William Pitt were clearly linked in people's minds. Throughout 1786 he focused not only on sound finance, but on the expansion of trade: frustrated on the Irish policy with which he sought greater trade within the British Isles, he turned his attention to treaties with other European powers. To help him do this, he recruited 'men of business' with an ability to handle matters of trade and international negotiation which the initial membership of the government could not muster.

As the years went by, Pitt would show himself increasingly happy to recruit able men whatever their previous political inclination, and particularly happy to enlist them from the ranks of the Whig opposition, whose strength was thereby eroded. Already in 1784 he had sent one prominent Whig, Sir James Harris (later Earl of Malmesbury), to The Hague as Ambassador; now in 1786 he recruited William Eden from the ranks of the opponents of his Irish propositions. John Beresford was the mutual friend who brought Eden over to Pitt. Rose commented caustically that it was 'a remarkable confirmation of Walpole's satirical axiom, that every man in the British Legislature had his price; for Pitt thought him worth purchasing. And, though he had previously been engaged in active opposition to him up to the session of 1785 . . . he evinced so much insight into matters of finance and trade, that no pains were spared to secure his cooperation.'[17] The Whigs were not amused, and probably even less so when Pitt brought into the government another able man, Charles Jenkinson, soon to be Lord Hawkesbury, as President of the Board of Trade. Jenkinson had been so closely associated with George III that Pitt had not dared to include him in his initial administration: he was the archetypal 'King's friend'. Pitt was now emboldened to bring him in, for 'the cry of secret influence, which during Lord North's administration made Jenkinson unpopular, had become almost extinct, while his talents rose every day in the public estimation'.[18] Pitt wrote to his mother in July 1786, saying of Jenkinson's promotion: 'This, I think, will sound a little strange at a distance, and with a reference to former ideas; But he has really *fairly* earned it and attained it at my hands.'[19]

With William Grenville in place as Jenkinson's deputy, Pitt had assembled a strong team to secure commercial treaties for the Empire. In pursuing such treaties he was once again giving energy to the fashion and opportunity of the time, rather than inventing an original idea: many Continental countries were seeking commercial treaties with each other – France had already concluded a treaty with Portugal and would later do so with Russia and Spain. As a disciple of Adam Smith, Pitt needed no encouragement to seek freer trade, but in the late eighteenth century commercial treaties did not constitute free trade as we would know it today. Rather they were reciprocal agreements which reduced certain duties or gave access to otherwise highly protected shipping. The conclusion of a commercial treaty with France was in any case required by the terms of the peace treaty of 1783. Pitt carefully supervised the intensive negotiations between Eden and the French which resulted in the signing of a treaty at Versailles on 26 September, the day after Harriot's death. The terms were generally advantageous to Britain, because they made it easier to trade manufactured goods in France; and where they helped the French, such as in the reduction of duty on French brandy, they suited Pitt's approach to finance. Four million gallons of French brandy were being smuggled into Britain every year, while the duty was paid on only 600,000. As with tea, the smuggling of brandy could now be made a futile exercise.

Two centuries on, in an age of much freer trade, the conclusion of such a treaty may seem of obvious merit. Yet at the time, a commercial treaty with France was fraught with political risks for Pitt. The debate on the Irish propositions had shown how easily manufacturers could be roused against a reduction in import duties, and France was widely regarded, for obvious reasons, as a basically hostile country. It has been rightly argued that the negotiation of the treaty is another example of 'Pitt's idealism and optimism leading him into a potentially dangerous political situation'.[20] Yet in this instance he was successful, partly because he had learned his lessons from Ireland and kept the negotiations under his own strict control with a constant view to domestic opinion, and partly because Eden managed to negotiate a remarkably advantageous treaty, benefiting British manufacturers of products as varied as hardware, cutlery, cottons, woollens, porcelain and glass. The French concessions were the first outward sign of the weakness of the French state and economy, which was now only three years away from revolution. Despite the risk of embarrassing the French, Pitt had no scruple about arguing in the Commons that the terms massively favoured Britain: 'France could not gain the accession of £100,000 to her revenue by the treaty; but England must necessarily gain a million.'[21] He was determined not to be defeated again.

Ironically in the light of later events, it was Fox who argued that a treaty with France was dangerous to national security, stating that 'France is the natural political enemy of Great Britain . . . and that she wishes, by entering into a commercial treaty with us, to tie our hands and prevent us from engaging in any alliance with other Powers.'[22] Responding to such sentiments from Fox and also from Burke, Pitt argued that 'I shall not hesitate to contend against the too frequently advanced doctrine that France is, and must be, unalterably the enemy of Britain. My mind revolts from this position, as monstrous and impossible. To suppose that any nation can be unalterably the enemy of another is weak and childish.'[23] As the treaty passed the Commons in February 1787 by 134 votes (252 to 118), Pitt may indeed have believed he was strengthening the peace. He did not know that he would spend half the remainder of his life leading his country in the greatest war with France Britain would ever know.

However much the autumn of 1786 was marred by personal sorrow over Harriot's death, the reception accorded to the Sinking Fund and the French treaty had greatly bolstered Pitt's position. Additionally that summer, he had confounded the opposition and manoeuvred himself away from a potentially serious embarrassment by surprising all observers with his attitude to the impeachment of Warren Hastings.

Hastings' achievements in India had been immense but controversial, and when Pitt and Dundas declined to create a single supreme authority in India, he decided he had had enough of the infighting and sailed for home at the beginning of 1785. Pitt replaced him as Governor General with Lord Cornwallis, who had surrendered to the American forces at Yorktown, to whom he soon granted the very powers which Hastings had desired. Pitt's doubts about Hastings were therefore evident from the beginning; Dundas had himself moved the vote of censure against Hastings in 1782. Nevertheless, when Hastings arrived home in June 1785 with a far from immense fortune of £74,000, he seems to have expected honours rather than trouble. He hastened to see Pitt, who was courteous towards him while making no mention of an honour, but only days later Burke was giving notice of his intention to move resolutions in the Commons regarding 'a gentleman just returned from India'.

These developments were ominous for Hastings, who, although admired by Thurlow and George III, lacked effective allies in the House of Commons. Ranged against him were formidable parliamentary operators in Burke, Fox, and Sheridan, constantly abetted by Philip Francis, an implacable enemy of Hastings who had fought a duel with him in India and was now an MP himself. In April 1786 Burke began to put before the Commons twenty-two charges of tyrannical or arbitrary conduct on the part of Hastings. Pitt argued in response that Hastings should be able to make a statement of his own in his defence at the Bar of the House, and suggested that while Hastings' administration of India had certainly had faults, 'Those faults were highly compensated and fully counterbalanced by the general tenor of his conduct.' With characteristic care, he also said: 'For my part I am neither a determined friend nor foe to Mr. Hastings ... his innocence or guilt must be proved by incontestable evidence.'[24]

Pitt had given Hastings his chance. The result, from Hastings' point of view, was catastrophic. To this day, the two easiest ways to lose the sympathy of the House of Commons are to talk down to it or to bore it. Hastings managed to do both. Failing to take his cue from Pitt and to argue in a short statement that his alleged crimes were more than counterbalanced by his achievements, he mounted a lengthy rebuttal which lasted well over a full day, and the latter part of which had to be read out by the clerks. The effect of this 'on a popular assembly accustomed to splendid displays of eloquence was tame and tedious after the lapse of the first hour'.[25] 'I left Bengal', Hastings informed the Commons, 'followed by the loudest proofs of universal gratitude and since I landed in England I have had the unanimous thanks of the Court of Directors for my services of five-and-thirty years ... It did not occur to my mind that any other person could urge an accusation against me.'[26] This dismissive attitude won him no friends in the Commons.

Hastings had thrown away a good deal of parliamentary sympathy.

Even so, the government was still prepared to defend him. On 1 June Burke brought forward the first charge, the so-called 'Rohilla charge', dealing with Hastings' war on the Rohillas (an Afghan tribe who had ruled an area north of the Ganges) in 1781, the very point on which Dundas had led the original censure. The opposition hugely enjoyed the fact that Dundas now defended Hastings, partly on the grounds that the slate had since been wiped clean by Hastings' reappointment under Lord North. Ministers and government supporters joined Dundas in defeating the charge by 119 to sixty-seven.

All seemed set for this process to be repeated on other charges. To increase the discomfiture of the government, Fox himself brought forward on 13 June the 'Benares charge', alleging tyrannical conduct towards the Indian Prince Cheit Sing. Fox was not particularly interested in India, but he enjoyed turning the event into a major parliamentary occasion, with queues forming at six in the morning to hear him speak. By forcing Pitt himself to defend Hastings, Fox would gain a new stick with which to beat the government, and Pitt would offend many of a liberal conscience, including some of his own friends such as Wilberforce.

What followed was a political bombshell. The Benares charge dealt with Hastings' conduct in a desperate situation during the Mahratta War in 1781 when he had responded to Cheit Sing's failure to pay a levy by increasing it ten times over and deposing him. Typically, Pitt had immersed himself in the subject shortly before the debate. During it he beckoned to Wilberforce to speak to him behind the Speaker's Chair, where he asked: 'Does not this look very ill to you?' 'Very bad indeed,' Wilberforce replied.[27] Pitt then rose, saying that 'by a most laborious investigation' he had now 'been able to form . . . a final and settled opinion'.[28] He then 'laid open the whole system of feudal tenures, together with the nature of military and civil subordination as recognised throughout Hindostan',[29] and proceeded to demolish the arguments of Fox and Burke as being based on a misunderstanding of Indian circumstances. Nevertheless, he went on to say that he regarded the level of the fine imposed by Hastings as 'beyond all proportion exorbitant, unjust, and tyrannical',[30] and without committing himself to a final vote of impeachment added that it was his opinion that 'this act of oppression was such as ought to be made one of the articles of that impeachment, being in his judgement a very high crime and misdemeanour . . . This proceeding destroyed all relation and connection between the degrees of guilt and punishment; it was grinding; it was overbearing.'[31]

Suddenly the whole position was reversed. With Pitt voting aye, 'full fifty individuals followed Pitt without hesitation. Dundas never opened his lips during the whole evening, but he took care to vote with his principal.'[32] The Benares charge was carried by 119 votes to seventy-nine. From that moment the impeachment of Warren Hastings for his conduct as Governor General of India moved from being an improbability to a near certainty. Months later Pitt would vote for further charges against Hastings, and he and Dundas would actively cooperate with the opposition in the final framing of the impeachment. Instead of retirement and a seat in the Lords, Hastings would face trial in Westminster Hall, possible imprisonment and certain financial ruin. Indeed, the trial was to drag on for seven years, from a splendid and hugely well attended opening in 1788 to Hastings' ultimate acquittal in 1795, by which time about one third of the peers who were to have passed judgement on him had died. Burke and the other opposition MPs who managed the impeachment were regularly preoccupied with it, as was a good part of the House of Lords. Hastings spent £71,000 in his defence. By that stage, the whole business reflected little credit on anybody.

Historians have argued for two hundred years about Pitt's apparent change of mind. Why did he throw Hastings to the wolves? Hastings and others blamed Dundas for converting him over breakfast on the day of the debate. It was argued that Dundas was seeking to thwart the King and to destroy Hastings' influence at the same time. Pitt was thought by others to be destroying Hastings as a possible rival, or, in a particularly Machiavellian move, to be deliberately letting the opposition tie itself up with the impeachment for years to come. None of these theories holds much water. Hastings was not conceivably a rival to Pitt in British politics, and Pitt could not have known that the trial would take so long. Another theory, that he did not realise how influential his own vote would be, is even less convincing: after all his recent defeats he would not knowingly have supported a lost cause.

The truth seems to be that Pitt was acting in line with his own vision of himself as a figure of independence and integrity, particularly when it came to financial matters, with the added incentive of political calculation thrown in. Wilberforce himself had no doubt of Pitt's motives, saying many years after Pitt's death: 'Oh how little justice was done to Pitt on Warren Hastings business! People were asking, what could make Pitt support him on this point and on that, as if he was acting from political motives; whereas he was always weighing in every particular whether Hastings had exceeded the discretionary power lodged in him . . . He paid as much impartial attention as if he were a jury-man.'[33] From what we know of Pitt this is believable. He always hated financial misconduct, and had cut his political teeth condemning abuses of power. He cannot have failed to notice, however, that on this matter there was a particular political advantage to displaying the independent judgement in which he in any case believed. Fox had tried to push him into a trap; Pitt's vote against Hastings made the trap fall uselessly to one side. The opposition could not now lay the blame for every arbitrary act recently committed in India at Pitt's door.

Pitt had also discovered that at least one major plank of his original reforming agenda, parliamentary reform, could not proceed, and that this was hugely satisfactory to the King, Thurlow and others of the old guard. His actions on Hastings asserted his political independence from this group, and meant he could not be attacked as their creature. The neatness of Pitt's apparently inexplicable *volte face* lay in the fact that he neither expressed the view that the opposition was right, nor left them any ground on which to attack him. Pitt the shining model of integrity was utterly intact, but Pitt the Prime Minister had also asserted his power. Happy is the politician who can serve both his main objectives with a single act, however mysterious it may appear to others.

At the end of 1786 Pitt was still trying to coax Edward Eliot out of the seclusion into which Harriot's death had sunk him. He wrote to his mother:

> Downing Street, Nov. 13, 1786.
>
> My Dear Mother,
>
> Having been all the morning in the Court of Exchequer, I have not yet seen my Brother; but Eliot and I are both going to dine there; which I am very glad to do on many accounts, and I reckon it is a step gained for Eliot. I flatter myself he has even made some progress in these two days, and I dare say will, in a little while, more and more. To-morrow I hope to get to Holwood, where I am impatient to look at my works. I must carry there however only my passion for planting, and leave that of cutting entirely to Burton.[34]

Pitt's confidence was boosted by his experience of 1786 as a hugely successful year. At the beginning of it Orde had written that 'this will be a Session of Tryal for Mr. Pitt, and that He will now be shaken, or his Stability confirmed'.[35] Yet by early 1787 Wraxall could write: 'Pitt had attained at this time to an almost unexampled height of Ministerial favour and popularity.'[36] In 1787 he was soon following up his advantage with further financial reforms. Once again taking up an idea first examined in the early 1780s, he decided on a massive simplification of government accounting. As successive governments had sanctioned expenditure or loans for different purposes, the Treasury had by now accumulated 103 separate accounts, each of which had to be kept separate from the rest. This was not just an internal inconvenience: traders found that goods subject to Customs and Excise duties were liable for payments into dozens of different accounts, creating work for the officials and major potential for fraud. In February 1787 Pitt produced yet another dazzling *tour de force* on financial matters which, it was said, 'might challenge the annals of Parliament to produce a finer specimen of financial eloquence'.[37] He proposed to base the Treasury on a single Consolidated Fund, abolishing a myriad of existing duties and substituting for them a completely new schedule. To effect this, he introduced no fewer than 2,537 separate resolutions into the House of Commons, appearing in complete command of the smallest detail. This time even the opposition was awestruck. Burke rose and expressed the thanks of the country, saying he would not 'content myself with a sullen acquiescence, but will bear testimony to the masterly and perspicuous manner in which a plan has been developed which promises accommodation to the merchant combined with augmentation and advantage to the revenue'.[38]

Pitt was somewhat less successful when he tried serious reform of the administrative machinery of government, bedevilled as it was with sinecures and other appointments which were regarded as 'freehold' and therefore held for life. Having failed in his attempt to bring about the outright abolition of some sinecures after his first term as Chancellor of the Exchequer in 1783, he now opted for the simpler approach of leaving positions vacant as they arose, thereby reducing expenditure. He strengthened the Excise at the expense of the Customs, ended the abuse of franking of letters by MPs (which was costing £40,000 a year),* but got into a drawn-out battle with Post Office officials over his insistence on introducing mail coaches and higher postal rates as the basis of a more efficient postal service. His system eventually proved successful, but the recriminations and bitterness partly sparked by Pitt's rather high-handed intervention carried on for a good ten years.

A far more popular interest was the finances of the Royal Family, and in particular those of the Prince of Wales, which were again reaching crisis point in 1787. The previous year Pitt had asked Parliament to write off arrears on the Civil List of £210,000, and in return, ever keen to control major items of expenditure, had insisted on statements of royal expenditure in future. By 1787, however, the Prince of Wales alone had run up debts totalling £370,000. The King refused to contemplate paying them unless given an itemised list of how they were incurred, which the Prince refused to provide. With King and heir once again at daggers drawn, the credibility of the monarchy required Pitt and Dundas to negotiate between them. Pitt himself had to go to Carlton House to see the Prince, a political intimate and drinking companion of his opponents, in order to suggest a solution. This was eventually agreed: the Prince provided details of his finances, Pitt asked the Commons for an additional £221,000, and the King agreed to provide a further £10,000 a year to his son from the Civil

* MPs were allowed to post letters without paying for them. They often abused the system by posting letters for other people.

List. The Prince was, of course, literally a heartbeat from becoming King George IV (although as it turned out he had a further thirty-three years to wait), and Pitt may have been mindful of the need to improve relations with the future King. If so he would be disappointed, but in any event he acted correctly and with the reputation of the monarchy in mind.

Parliamentary discussion of the payments to the Prince brought serious embarrassment to the opposition when the rumour that he had secretly married his mistress Mrs Fitzherbert surfaced on the floor of the House. The couple had indeed secretly married in December 1785, and done so illegally, since they did not have the King's consent. The Prince had assured Fox at the time that there was not 'any ground for these reports' of such a marriage. Remembering this, Fox now stood up in the Commons to say that the marriage 'never did happen in any way whatsoever; and was from the beginning a base and malicious falsehood',[39] adding that he spoke 'from direct authority'. When Mrs Fitzherbert read these remarks in her morning newspaper at Carlton House she was outraged. Caught between a lie and a furious wife, the Prince decided to keep the wife and abandon the lie, telling Sheridan to go down to the Commons and admit as much.

The incident created major strains among the opposition, the Prince's secretary saying in 1788 that 'the Prince was afraid of Fox, and that his opinion of Mr. Pitt was much altered since the negotiation on the subject of his debts . . . and that this coolness to Fox was much increased by Mrs FitzHerbert, who never would forgive his public declaration on her subject in the House of Commons, and had taken every opportunity of alienating the Prince's mind from him'.[40] As it turned out, when the Regency crisis erupted later that year, Fox and the Prince would still prove to be keen allies. But before then, Pitt had to deal with the first major foreign-policy crisis of his career, and another delicate issue at home.

It is clear that Wilberforce considered Pitt to have given little reflection to religious matters. On one occasion he prevailed on Pitt to join him in listening to a sermon by a noted evangelical preacher, Richard Cecil, evidently hoping that it would stir Pitt into a stronger commitment to religion. He was disappointed when Pitt turned to him on the way out of the church and said, 'You know, Wilberforce, I have not the slightest idea what that man has been talking about.'[41] When a delegation of Dissenting Protestants, who were not part of the established Church, came to see him in January 1787 to put their case for repeal of the Test and Corporation Acts which debarred them from a wide range of public offices, he gave them a polite hearing but no sign of enthusiastic support. The champion of parliamentary, financial and administrative reform was not about to add the extension of religious toleration to his favourite causes.

On the face of it, Pitt would have been a natural supporter of the Dissenters' cause, and he had received strong support from them in the 1784 general election on the basis of his enthusiasm for parliamentary reform. Their grievance was a powerful one. The Corporation Act of 1661 required members of municipal corporations to have taken the sacrament in the Church of England, and the Test Act of 1672 placed a similar requirement on those holding any civil office or a commission in the army or navy: these Acts were designed to keep Catholics out of office at a time, as Pretyman put it, 'when the conduct of the king upon the throne justified a strong suspicion that he was inclined to popery'.[42] Although the effects of the Acts had been partly mitigated since 1727 by annual Indemnity Acts, as well as by irregular enforcement, a sense of grievance at the anomalous and inconsistent results was powerfully felt. It was possible, for instance, for a Dissenter to sit in Parliament for a borough in which he could not be a member of the corporation. While some corporations seemed to draw most of their membership from Dissenters, others had used the test acts vindictively: in the 1740s the City of London had introduced heavy fines for refusing to take public office, and then nominated for office Dissenters who could not accept it.

To reform such laws would have been in tune with the more rationalist and tolerant attitudes of the late eighteenth century, but Pitt drew back from doing so. The Anglican Church was powerful, and not likely to be in ready agreement with the removal of its privileges; many people, and they would have included Pretyman and Wilberforce with their abundant opportunities to influence Pitt, were opposed to any weakening of the connection between Church and state. Others suspected the motives of more radical non-conformist opinion, particularly in the aftermath of the American War, and feared this could open the door to the advancement of more secular and revolutionary views. Pitt consulted the Archbishop of Canterbury, John Moore, who found that only two of the sixteen Bishops who attended a meeting on this subject favoured reform.

Pitt must have known what answer he would receive from the Bishops, but it was as well to seek their opinion, since he would have had little chance of carrying reform against the combined opposition of the Church, the King and the more conservative Members of Parliament. He was not prepared to risk another defeat over a matter which failed to stir his own conscience and which seemed to make little practical difference to most people's lives. As a result, when the repeal of the Acts was moved on 28 March 1787, Pitt followed the now ageing and blind Lord North, to whom he paid his first noticeable tribute, in asking the Commons to preserve the status quo. 'Were we', he argued, 'to yield on this occasion, the fears of the members of the Church of England would be roused, and their apprehensions are not to be treated lightly. It must, as I contend, be conceded to me that an Established Church is necessary . . . no means can be devised of admitting the moderate part of the dissenters and excluding the violent; the bulwark must be kept up against all.'[43] Pitt found that opposition to reforms was safer ground than proposing them: the pleas of the Dissenters were rejected by 176 votes to ninety-eight. Pitt would lead the Commons in delivering a similar verdict in future years; moderately so in 1789, and impatiently and emphatically so as the French Revolution gathered pace in 1790.

With an unwanted confrontation thus avoided, and financial reforms successfully carried through, Pitt was in the fortunate position of being able to bring the parliamentary session of 1787 to an unusually early end on 30 May. By then he was being forced to bring his mind to bear on events overseas more urgently than at any time in his experience. It would mark his transition from a youthful financial expert to a serious player in the power struggles of Continental Europe.

* * *

The ignominious end of the American War had left Britain friendless and isolated in European affairs. France, Spain and Holland had all fought against her in the later stages of the war; defeat meant she was despised in the rest of Europe's most powerful courts. The Emperor Joseph II of Austria considered Britain 'fallen entirely and forever . . . descended to the status of a second-rank power, like Sweden or Denmark'.[44] British leaders found their isolation entirely appropriate, with George III writing to Carmarthen in July 1784: 'Till I see this Country in a situation more respectable as to Army, Navy, and Finances, I cannot think anything that may draw us into troubled waters either safe or rational.'[45]

At that stage, Pitt's views were similar to those of the King. While maintaining and rebuilding the navy, his policy was to concentrate on economic recovery and to stay clear of foreign entanglements. In August 1785 he had written to Rutland: 'let peace continue for five years, and we shall again look any Power in Europe in the face'.[46] His concentration on the nation's finances was bearing fruit, and by the end of 1785 he could not only contemplate a budget surplus but a sharp rise in the price of government securities, or consols as they were then known. Britain was becoming dramatically more creditworthy. Pitt was not uninterested in foreign affairs, but in the first three years of his leadership of the government they were not his prime focus. In a British Cabinet of this time, a First Lord of the Treasury could involve himself in foreign affairs if he so wished, but the vast majority of overseas business would have been handled by the Foreign Secretary, in this case the Marquis of Carmarthen, who conducted his own correspondence with the King without necessarily involving the First Lord in the day-to-day details.

As Foreign Secretary, Carmarthen was far more concerned than either Pitt or George III about Britain's lack of powerful allies, writing to Pitt on 9 June 1784: 'Were it possible for England to be permitted to remain perfectly quiet and undisturbed . . . no one could hesitate a moment to adopt that system of tranquillity . . . I cannot however by any means flatter myself with the hopes of our being permitted to pursue so salutary a plan.'[47] Some kind of alliance was necessary to 'secure to this country a prospect of remaining unmolested by France'.[48]

In particular, he sought to restore the British alliance with Habsburg Austria, still one of the great military and political powers of Europe, with vast lands and population in the east as well as strategically important territory in northern Italy and present-day Belgium. This consideration induced Britain in 1784 to hover on the Austrian side of their furious argument with the Dutch over fortresses in the Netherlands and the navigation of the Scheldt, which the Dutch had been able to close to shipping in order to ruin Antwerp as a major port while Amsterdam prospered. Carmarthen's hopes of an Austrian alliance were to be frustrated in 1785: Pitt and George III were cautious about making any worthwhile commitment to an ally. The Austrians presumably saw little to be gained from it, and George III in any case antagonised Joseph II by completely separate action in his capacity as Elector of Hanover.

British Ministers took no part in George III's actions as head of state of Hanover, but to other Continental powers it was impossible to separate his actions as head of state of one country from the behaviour of the other. By signing the *Fürstenbund* pact between Hanover, Prussia and Saxony to oppose the Austrian ambition of quite literally swapping the Austrian Netherlands for Bavaria, George III fired the final torpedo into the sinking hopes of an Anglo–Austrian alliance. Carmarthen complained bitterly that Britain had now become unknowingly 'involved in a German quarrel', upsetting the Russians as well as the Austrians and thus depriving Britain of any ally big enough to counterbalance France, but the general weakness and poor reputation of Britain at the time were also major factors in the failure of his diplomacy. Sir Robert Murray Keith, the British envoy to Vienna, said at the end of 1785 that 'England seems to be almost entirely out of the question . . . and matters . . . must take a new and more favourable turn, before she can again resume her place and weight amongst the nations of Europe.'[49]

It was to be events in the ever troublesome Netherlands that would now push a deeply cautious Pitt into exerting his weight in foreign affairs, and to do so in a way which would take Britain back to a far stronger position in Europe. The signing in late 1785 of a Franco-Dutch defensive alliance formalised the rapid growth of French influence in the United Provinces (corresponding approximately to the Netherlands of today), despite their head of state being the anglophile Stadtholder William V, grandson of George II. Several factors came together to boost French influence among the Dutch: Britain had gone to war with Holland in the later stages of the American War of Independence, France had just helped the Dutch to see off the ambitions of Joseph II, and an emerging middle class was increasingly dissatisfied with the weak William V, preferring to support 'patriot' activists whose leanings were pro-French. Sir James Harris, Ambassador to The Hague, told Carmarthen that 'the game is entirely lost here'.

Such a development could not be ignored in London. The Dutch United Provinces were of crucial strategic significance to eighteenth-century Britain for two reasons. First, French domination of Antwerp, Amsterdam and the other ports of the Low Countries would put the entire eastern coastline of the English Channel into hostile hands during any confrontation between Britain and France. The implications for both trade and military operations were obvious. Second, Franco-Dutch cooperation could become a severe threat to British interests in India. One British diplomat had written in February 1784: 'the great object of the French Ministry is to ruin us in the East-Indies, which they hope to accomplish by the means of the Dutch traducing Great Britain'.[50] Whether or not this was true, it was a fear strongly felt.

In early 1786, Pitt agreed to the first active steps to counteract French influence, sending some £9,000 in secret-service money* to Harris, who was the only effective coordinating agent of anti-patriot and pro-Stadtholder opinion. The desperately worried Harris said he needed more, warning Carmarthen in October 1786 that 'Holland is to be Mistress of the Republic, and France is to govern Holland.'[51] But Pitt felt that matters had not yet come to a crisis, and he was, of course, negotiating the commercial treaty with France at the same time. He told Carmarthen that Harris should '*redouble every possible effort*', but was not prepared to commit himself further. The situation continued to deteriorate, and the ever frustrated Carmarthen, claiming illness, now asked Harris to correspond directly with Pitt rather than

* This money was drawn from a Foreign Office fund not subject to parliamentary scrutiny.

observe the official form of going through the Foreign Secretary. The long-term effect of this precedent was to enhance the ease with which Pitt intervened in foreign affairs, but the short-term result was the one desired: to make Pitt clearer in his mind that the Dutch crisis must be faced up to. His level of interest was changed, although not at the moment his policy. Pitt wrote to Harris on 5 December 1786: 'I conceive it impossible to think of taking any step that can commit this country to the risk of extremities . . . The great object now seems to be that to which I conceive you point, *to endeavour to keep together a party which may act with advantage, both for their own country and for us, on some future day, if it should arrive*.'[52]

Early 1787 saw Pitt send a further £12,000 of secret-service money to Harris, while the position continued to deteriorate. By February Harris was reporting that Amsterdam was in a 'state of great fermentation' and that the 'patriotic association . . . has actually signed a *formal convention with France*'.[53] He insisted that there was sufficient latent support among the population for the House of Orange, and opposed to French influence, for the French to be faced down if only Britain would be strong. On 1 May he wrote: 'If we lose this country, France will acquire what she has always considered as the climax of her power . . . There is *good stuff* enough here to vanquish twice the strength of our opponents; and, if we will be *bold* enough to assume the style and tone which belong to us, *I will pledge my head on the event*.'[54] At his request he came to brief the whole Cabinet at the end of May. In the Cabinet, Thurlow and Richmond argued against all 'half measures' and said Britain should prepare for full-scale war. Soon there would be newspaper reports of the Cabinet being 'warmly and earnestly divided upon the subject of Dutch affairs', as Pitt remained extremely cautious, acknowledging 'the *immense* consequence of Holland being preserved as an Independent State' but saying the government must 'weigh maturely whether anything could repay the disturbing that state of growing affluence and prosperity', which would make the country stronger to face France in the future.

The upshot was that Pitt provided Harris with a further £70,000 of what he assured the King was 'only pecuniary assistance'. He steered his own course between a more hawkish Cabinet on the one hand,

and on the other a King who was still suspicious of getting involved in anything at all. Harris thought that if Britain threatened action, 'France would shrink from the challenge'. Pitt did not trust such assertions: he was prepared to support a strong anti-French party among the Dutch, but not to threaten war.

In the summer of 1787 the Dutch crisis reached its climax. Pitt had hoped during the parliamentary recess to see more of Britain than he had ever seen before by visiting Scotland via a house Wilberforce had taken in the Lake District, and also staying at Castle Howard in Yorkshire. Such a trip was not to happen, then or indeed ever. For at the end of June the Princess of Orange, who was made of sterner stuff than her husband William V, announced that she would go to The Hague, repossess the capital and impose a settlement on the rival factions. As she had thought likely, she was stopped by pro-French patriot troops, briefly placed under arrest and then sent packing. These events brought a new player into the game, for the Princess was the sister of Frederick William II, the new King of Prussia. He demanded an apology and assembled 20,000 troops on the frontier. The French, Prussian and British governments negotiated and hesitated, while Holland moved closer to a patriot revolution. Pitt, remaining in London for the summer, took day-to-day charge of all despatches and decisions, and sent William Grenville to The Hague in July to assess the accuracy of Harris's reports, and then to Paris in August to try to settle matters with the French without war. These missions marked another step forward for Grenville in Pitt's confidence, and he would increasingly emerge as a possible Foreign Secretary.

On 13 September 1787 the die was cast: the Prussian army invaded the United Provinces. Patriot forces in Holland asked France to come to their defence. All of Europe expected the French to respond. On 19 September Pitt chaired a Cabinet meeting which resolved to fit out an additional twenty-three ships of the line and to 'augment' the army in case of war with France. Pitt told Wilberforce: 'things have at last come to a crisis – the French have notified their determination to give assistance to Holland which we *cannot* acquiesce in'.[55] Now that the Prussians had brought matters to a head, Britain could be bolder and ready to fight. Within days it became clear that war would not be necessary. The patriot army fled before the Prussian advance, and by 20 September William V was back in The Hague. Amsterdam, the main site of patriot feeling, surrendered on 10 October. The pro-French activists who had planned for revolution were left with the stunned realisation that France, the most powerful nation in Europe, had not lifted a finger to come to their aid.

Such a result left Pitt triumphant. Some of his colleagues would have triggered war without an ally, at an earlier stage, while the purer isolationism of the King could have abandoned Britain's friends in the United Provinces to French domination. Pitt had been lucky in how events turned out, but had managed events in such a way as to take advantage of his luck when it came along. He wrote to Harris at the end of September: 'There seems but one opinion in this country on the propriety of our efforts; and if the struggle had become necessary, I believe, we should have had nothing to regret or to fear from it.'[56] The threat of French military intervention had induced him to arm the fleet: the absence of such intervention said much about the growing weakness of France. While British policy had been directed from 10 Downing Street in the final months of the crisis, French policy was subject to competing factions at their court, resulting in commitments on which they could not deliver. France was now humiliated, and for Britain the way was open to the next year's Triple Alliance with Holland and Prussia. The years of isolation were over. Count Vorontsov, the Russian Ambassador in London, was to write: 'The part played by England in these affairs has been brilliant and courageous, and the conduct of Mr. Pitt on this occasion is very like that which his late father pursued . . . How would the father have rejoiced in them had he lived on till now!'[57]

13

Insanity and Crisis

'November 24, 1788: His Majesty passed the whole day in a perfectly maniacal state.'

MEDICAL BULLETIN, QUEEN'S LODGE, WINDSOR

'If this lasts beyond a certain Time, it will produce the most difficult and delicate crisis imaginable in making Provision for the Government to go on.'

WILLIAM PITT, NOVEMBER 1788

WHEN PITT FINALLY had a chance to visit his mother at Burton Pynsent in December 1787 he could celebrate four years as First Lord of the Treasury and the King's First Minister. The economic and diplomatic successes of 1786–87 had confirmed his domination of the political scene, and he could look forward to the 1788 session of Parliament with equanimity. The main events of the spring and summer of 1788 would reinforce his earlier successes: the Triple Alliance of Britain, Holland and Prussia seduced Prussia away from any new *entente* with France. Pitt therefore presented his fifth budget in May in triumphant mood. Announcing that he had by now repaid £2½ million of the national debt and spent £7 million on the improvement of the navy and yet still had a budget surplus without any additional taxes, he contrasted this with the ballooning budget deficit of France: 'Our rival, therefore, who engaged in a war for the emancipation of our late colonies, which object she accomplished, and from which she projected to draw immense advantages, has failed in her ambitious calculations.'[1]

Pitt's principal difficulties in the 1788 session arose once again over Indian affairs. The trial of Warren Hastings had begun in February, and it soon became clear that it would be a very long business. Having thrown Hastings overboard, Pitt declined to do the same to the former Chief Justice of India, Sir Elijah Impey, who was accused of similar crimes but whose impeachment was narrowly defeated in the Commons after he had spoken skilfully in his own defence. It was soon becoming clear to the opposition leaders that much of their time could now be consumed in the prosecution of Hastings, a course on which Burke had insisted on taking them. Sheridan was telling the Duchess of Devonshire that he wished Hastings would 'run away, and Burke after him'.[2]

Pitt must have viewed these developments with satisfaction, but he himself ran into trouble over the need to pass fresh legislation concerning the responsibilities of the East India Company, always a thorny issue, since it was the one which had brought him to power in such controversial circumstances in 1783. The Directors of the Company had decided, now that fears of imminent war had receded, that it was no longer their responsibility to pay for the transport or maintenance of troops sent to protect India unless they had requested them. Pitt and Dundas insisted that such costs had always been intended to be met from the Company's revenues. At the end of February they brought forward the India Declaratory Bill to make this clear, but thereby opened themselves to the obvious attack that, having come to power by opposing the extension of ministerial power over the East India Company, they were now extending it themselves. With some of his own supporters alarmed by this apparent about-turn, Pitt made matters worse in the debates of early March by giving one uncharacteristically poor speech and then failing to speak at all after a particularly effective attack on him by Fox. His majority fell to fifty-seven (182 to 125), which represented a moral defeat. Grenville wrote: 'What hurt us, I believe materially, last night, was that Pitt, who had reserved himself to answer Fox, was just at the close of a very able speech of Fox's taken so ill as not to be able to speak at all.'[3] It seems he had been drinking heavily the night before with Dundas and the Duchess of Gordon: this was one of the very rare occasions when alcohol visibly affected his parliamentary abilities.

Pitt knew by now when to beat a retreat. Defeat on a matter so central to the very creation of the government would have been fatal. Within two days he was back in the Commons on his usual form, making a conciliatory speech and moving amendments to the Bill which explicitly restricted ministerial patronage over the Company. The Bill was passed, but the episode was a sharp reminder after two years of triumphs that no government could take Parliament for granted.

In the summer of 1788 Pitt began to tighten his grip on the government itself. The Cabinet he had cobbled together in desperate straits in December 1783 had been filled with grandees he needed at the time but who had often neither performed well nor become close to him personally. Steadily over the next four years he would replace them with men who were closer to him, or who had greater ability – or ideally both. In doing so, Pitt did not have the complete freedom of action, subject only to the constraints of party management, of a modern Prime Minister. He was very much the first among equals rather than the unchallenged master of the entire administration. Care had to be taken to avoid the sympathetic resignations of other Ministers if one of them were dismissed, and any new appointments needed to command at least the acquiescence of the King. Pitt's most powerful Cabinet rival, the Lord Chancellor Lord Thurlow, was able to feel secure in office despite frequent public disagreements with Pitt because he was a particular friend of the King and had unlimited access to the Royal Closet. For Pitt to dismiss him would be extremely difficult.

Nevertheless, Pitt began from June 1788 to take opportunities as they presented themselves to create the Cabinet he really wanted. Lord Howe, the First Lord of the Admiralty, had frequently upset both his Cabinet colleagues and the government's supporters in Parliament, most recently over navy promotions. As Parliament rose for the summer, Pitt was now able to ease him out, making a highly unusual appointment in his stead. He wrote to his mother from Downing Street on 19 June:

> The Session ends most satisfactorily, and its close will be accompanied by some Events which add not a little to that satisfaction

> . . . It is no other than this, that a new arrangement in the Admiralty is, from various Circumstances, become unavoidable, that Lord Howe must be succeeded by a Landsman, and that Landsman is my Brother. I have had some doubts whether the public may not think this too much like monopoly, but that doubt is not sufficient to counterbalance the Personal Comfort which will result from it and the general advantage to the whole of our system. – You will, I am sure, be happy to hear that Lord Howe does not quit without a public mark of Honour by a fresh step in the Peerage . . .[4]

Pitt's appointment of his elder brother, the second Earl of Chatham, to the Cabinet may seem hard to square with his general disdain for patronage and strong sense of probity. But in the eighteenth century the involvement of whole families in politics – Grenvilles, Cavendishes, Townshends – was common, and there would be due deference to the status of Chatham as the eldest son of his great father. There seems to have been very little criticism or resentment of the appointment voiced at the time. Pitt's motives were no doubt mixed: it gave him an ally in the Cabinet and much greater control of a wayward Admiralty; it must also have assuaged any feelings of guilt he may have had towards an elder brother he had always outshone. While Pitt generally prized ability as the main factor in making promotions, he had a weakness for making exceptions for some of his nearest and dearest, Pretyman being another case in point. The result in this case would not be a happy one. His brother suffered from the 'two vices [of] insuperable indolence and total want of economy',[5] and was so disorganised that he would become widely known as 'the late Lord Chatham' long before he died. While Pitt had the satisfaction of appointing his brother to such a senior role in 1788, it meant that years later he would face the painful task of removing him.

At the same time Pitt sought to promote his old but much-derided friend Pepper Arden, then Attorney General, to the higher legal position of Master of the Rolls. This opened up a fierce turf war with Thurlow, who as head of the judiciary considered this appointment to be within his own gift. Thurlow's threats to resign carried little weight with Pitt, who by this stage would have been glad to see the back of him. Pitt got his way. Inch by inch, he was asserting control of his administration.

Once again Pitt hoped to visit the Lake District that summer, and once again he was prevented from doing so by events overseas. Sweden had rashly attacked Russia, and he stayed in London through August to keep in touch with events. He explained to his mother the endless delays in visiting her:

> Downing Street, August 29, 1788.
>
> My Dear Mother,
>
> I have been every day, for I know not how long, hoping to be able to tell you the day when I should have the happiness of seeing you at Burton; but, as too often has happened, every day has brought some fresh incident to put it off. – This week would, I believe have pretty nearly enabled me to speak positively, but an accidental cold (which has no other inconvenience than a swelled face and the impossibility of going to St. James's) will oblige me to defer till next week the conclusion of business which I hoped to have got rid of this. – The exact time, and the interval for which I can be at liberty, must at all events depend upon News from abroad, where so many things are going on, that although we have every reason to be certain that no consequences can arise otherwise than favourable to us, a good deal of watching is necessary. – My hope was to have been able to make a pretty long stay at once whenever I reach Burton; but even if that should not be the case, I can do it at twice, and I am pretty sure of a good deal of leisure in the course of the interval before Parliament meets . . .[6]

He made it to Somerset in September, but later in the autumn the leisure he had hoped for would be cut brutally short. By now, Pitt had mastered Parliament, transformed the national finances and outfaced mighty France – with all the popularity and reputation these achievements had brought; yet within weeks he would be fighting for his political life amidst one of the most dramatic crises in the history of Britain. For in October the King fell ill, and by 5 November it seemed that George III, King of England, Scotland, Wales and

Ireland, Elector of Hanover and ruler of an empire, had gone quite mad.

George III, now aged fifty, was obsessed with maintaining his health, driving his servants to exhaustion or exasperation with the incessant regularity and restless energy of his exercise regime. He rose early in the mornings, rode before breakfast, ate simple meals without an excess of wine and dealt assiduously with his correspondence. A simple stroll could cover twelve miles, and if the Queen journeyed in her coach, he would often prefer to ride alongside it. Such physical discipline was probably encouraged by the serious illnesses he had suffered in the early 1760s shortly after ascending the throne. There had been sufficient concern at the time to warrant the passing of the Regency Act of 1765, which provided for a Council of Members of the Royal Family in the event of the King dying while his children were still young. Since that time, either because of his disciplined lifestyle or in spite of it, he had escaped serious illness. He had been lucky enough too to escape assassination in 1786 when a middle-aged woman tried to stab him as he stepped out of his carriage. The thin knife failed to penetrate his waistcoat: the King went on to his levée 'with the most perfect composure', and the woman went on to a mental hospital for the rest of her life.

In the summer of 1788, as Pitt waited in London for news from the Baltic, the King and Queen went to the spa waters of Cheltenham to assist George's recovery from a 'bilious fever' he had suffered in June. He celebrated his apparent return to health with a tour of western England, visiting farms, houses and churches. At times his behaviour seemed a little over-excited and eccentric, such as when he beat time to Handel's *Messiah* in Worcester Cathedral as if conducting an orchestra, and woke up the Dean before dawn to insist on looking round the cathedral, but at the time this did not cause undue alarm. It was only when he was back at Windsor in October that he fell visibly ill again. To his great distress he found he could not do his work, writing to Pitt: 'I am afraid Mr. Pitt will perceive I am not quite in a situation to write at present, but I thought it better even to write as loosely as

I have here than to lett [sic] the box return without an answer to his letter.'[7]

On 22 October the King became enraged with his doctor, who noted: 'I wrote a note to Mr. Pitt immediately on my return to London, and informed him that I had just left the King in an agitation of spirits nearly bordering on delirium.'[8] The King's efforts to carry on as usual with his levée on 24 October had the effect of adding to the growing sense of alarm rather than dampening it. He knew there was something wrong with him, saying to the Duke of York in the days that followed, 'I wish to God I may die, for I am going to be mad.' By 5 November he had become violent and deranged, seizing the Prince of Wales by the collar and hurling him against a wall during dinner at Windsor. Rumours of his condition spread rapidly, with government stock falling on the markets amidst a widespread belief that he was dying.

Suddenly Pitt had to face a political crisis of the first order. Not only did he have the responsibility of giving calm leadership to the country while such rumours were rampant, but he also faced the imminent prospect of political doom. If the King died, the Prince of Wales would immediately become King George IV, and there was little doubt that he would dismiss Pitt, install Fox, and call a general election with all the powers of patronage and the Treasury deployed on the side of the Whigs. The independents and country gentlemen would then desert Pitt in droves, and even his great personal popularity would not be sufficient to keep him in power. On the other hand, if the King was insane and stayed insane, a Regent would have to be appointed. The Regent would inevitably be the heir to the throne, so the Prince of Wales would enjoy the power to turf out the government anyway. Small wonder that Pitt wrote to Pretyman: 'If this lasts beyond a certain Time, it will produce the most difficult and delicate crisis imaginable in making Provision for the Government to go on.'[9]

As the days passed, it became clear that the King was not dying, but neither was he getting better. While the Archbishop of Canterbury prepared special prayers for the King's health to be said in every church, the medical bulletin sent to Pitt by a team of physicians headed by Dr Warren offered little hope:

> Nov. 6 . . . The King's delirium has continued through the whole day. Nov. 10 . . . H.M. . . . is very incoherent . . . Nov. 12 . . . H.M. talked in a quiet but incoherent way the whole night . . . Nov. 15 . . . H.M. has been deranged the whole day, in a quiet and apparently happy way to himself. Nov. 18 . . . H.M. had a good night, but the disorder remains unabated . . . Nov. 22 . . . H.M. is entirely deranged this morning in a quiet good humoured way . . . Nov. 24 . . . His Majesty passed the whole day in a perfectly maniacal state . . .[10]

The nation's leaders and royalty united in expressing their grief and concern for the King. Yet in the political world such public sentiments are inevitably accompanied by private but rapid calculations on the consequences for everyone else. An unexpected crisis of great magnitude invariably throws a powerful searchlight onto human personalities, and the events of the weeks that followed would leave us with defining memories of the key players. Among them would be the 'rats': MPs and peers whose loyalty to Pitt evaporated as his loss of power seemed imminent. Their behaviour would threaten his control of Parliament at a critical time, and they would include among their number his most senior colleague, Thurlow himself. Then there would be the presumptuous, who believed that power would now fall into their hands like an apple from a tree, and whose overconfidence would lead them into error, the Prince of Wales and Charles James Fox among them. There would also be the disorganised, who worked on the division of the spoils rather than presenting a coherent argument in the meantime, namely the Whig opposition. Perhaps most of all the searchlight falls on Pitt himself, who emerged at his most brilliant, with every ounce of debating prowess and political skill he possessed being much required and well displayed. His triumph against all expectation would bring, in the words of the great historian Macaulay, 'the moment at which his fame and fortune may be said to have reached the zenith'.[11]

Pitt's most pressing need was for time, since only time offered any hope of the King recovering before a Regency could be declared. He was able to obtain the first instalment of this by adjourning Parliament for two weeks as soon as it met on 20 November, assisted by the continued absence of Fox, who was frantically returning across Europe from an extended sojourn in Italy with Mrs Armistead. His other need was to get the best possible medical attention for the King. Pitt's first step in this respect was to bring in Dr Anthony Addington, the very man who had prescribed plenty of port for him fifteen years before, and who had the added merit of having once maintained a lunatic asylum. In contrast to the gloomy prognostications of Dr Warren, Addington thought that the King could recover, and this view was further strengthened after the arrival on the scene in early December of Dr Francis Willis, who was brought in by the Queen because of his long experience in treating mental disorders. In the coming weeks the diverging medical opinions of Warren and Willis would assume huge political importance: the greater the chances of the King recovering, the easier it would be for Pitt to advance the argument that strict limitations should be imposed on the power of a Regent. If the limitations were sufficiently tight, Pitt could hamstring the Prince and the Whigs even while they held power, and thus both protect the King's position and maximise the chances of a political comeback for himself.

The idea of such limitations would not go down well with the Prince of Wales himself, who had now taken over the management of the Royal Household despite bitter arguments with the Queen. At first the Prince showed every sign of deep concern about his father. He called Pitt to see him on 8 November, but made no mention of the political situation. According to Grenville, Pitt was treated 'with civility, but nothing more'. Having received no indication from the Prince that he would wish them to continue in office as they were, the Cabinet discussed during November whether they would be prepared to form a coalition government with the Whigs if asked to do so. George Rose described the scene:

> Mr. Pitt desired to ascertain the opinions of the members of the Cabinet respecting the propriety or expediency of joining the opposition, if it should be in their choice, under any circumstances whatever. He put the question directly to the Chancellor [Thurlow], who said he considered it an abstract question, and could not answer it distinctly. Mr. Pitt said it was a plain question,

> – Would his Lordship join with the opposite party under any circumstances? to which he would give no answer. Other members, by their silence, more than anything else, left an impression on Mr. Pitt's mind that they were impressed with an idea that a junction of some sort might be expedient for the country, but his own determination was fixed beyond all possibility of being shaken – not to entertain the idea of a junction at all.[12]

Pitt had decided to stand as he was or to fall. He was now a proud man, who had not ascended to the pinnacle of power and popularity in order to negotiate for a job in a government he did not control. He may also have had a genuine concern, referred to by Rose, about what the King would feel if he recovered his sanity only to find that his allies were now in cahoots with his enemies. Pitt's direct questioning of Thurlow suggests that he already knew his Lord Chancellor was playing a double game. Once the King's insanity was plain, Thurlow was attentive to the Prince of Wales and entered into negotiations with the opposition, which in the absence of Fox were masterminded by Sheridan. The gist of the deal they constructed seems to have been that Thurlow would help from within the government to minimise any restrictions on the Regency, and in return would be retained as Lord Chancellor when the opposition duly came to power. This negotiation hit a snag, since it involved the ditching of the obvious Whig candidate for Lord Chancellor, Lord Loughborough. The prospect of this horrified a confused and ill-informed Fox when he finally returned to London in late November, but the discussions between Thurlow and the opposition continued. Thurlow even innocently asked the Cabinet 'if anybody knew the colour of Mr. Fox's chaise, in order to form a guess from them whether it had been seen on the road to Windsor', while in reality he was actively engaged in negotiating with Fox's colleagues.[13] Pitt did not confront him directly, but carefully excluded him from the making of any arrangements for the Regency.

In the meantime, the Whigs were becoming impatient and very confident. As the Prince of Wales was telling his brother that their father was now 'a compleat lunatick',[14] Fox was telling him that 'Your Royal Highness would be . . . sure of enjoying the situation that belongs to you in a few weeks.'[15] They preoccupied themselves with discussion of a new Cabinet: should Grey or Cavendish be Chancellor of the Exchequer? Would the Duke of Portland return as nominal head of the government, assuming that Fox would be a Secretary of State? It did not help their cause that these discussions became so advanced that on 28 November the *Morning Post* was able to print a list of those who would hold office in the new administration. Much as one Whig, Sir Gilbert Elliot, might warn them against 'this triumphant sort of conversation, especially before the battle is won, or even fought', the impatience and frustration of the Whigs after five years in opposition were boiling over by the time the King's condition had lasted a month. Lord Loughborough was even asserting that the Prince of Wales could simply take over the government by going to Parliament and announcing that he had done so. Another argued that it was 'just as if the King were dead'.[16] While the Whigs ached for Parliament to meet, the Prince himself returned from Windsor to London and spent his evenings drinking and gambling in Brooks's, a fact which soon became widely known.

The Whigs suffered additionally from a serious lack of cohesion. Key grandees such as Portland and Devonshire were away from London when the King fell ill, Fox missed the start of the crisis and was repeatedly ill himself throughout the course of it, Sheridan was busy ingratiating himself with the Prince, and Burke was steadily losing patience with the rest of them for failing to do their homework on the historical precedents and the nature of the King's illness. In Downing Street, by contrast, one man was bending every fibre of his mind to out-manoeuvring them all. Pitt had visited the King himself several times in November, and had evidently been distressed by what he saw. He was instrumental in getting the King moved to the more restful atmosphere of Kew, where the doctors thought there would be a better chance of recovery than at Windsor. On 3 December Pitt joined the other members of the Privy Council to examine the physicians on oath about the King's ability to conduct business and the prospects for his recovery. They were unanimous that he could not carry out any business, but all except Warren thought that he might one day recover. As it happened, the King now had a better spell, and the arrival of Dr

Willis gave further hope. While Willis came armed with a straitjacket and three strong assistants, he was also prepared to let the King do certain things prohibited by the other physicians, such as use a razor, in return for good behaviour. The King could sometimes converse perfectly well, as when he remarked on Willis having moved from the Church to the medical profession: 'You have quitted a profession I have always loved, & you have Embraced one I most heartily detest.'[17] Most of the time, however, he remained erratic, as when he shook hands with a tree believing it to be the King of Prussia. Overall, Pitt could have taken some comfort from the medical reports as Parliament gathered in early December, but he still faced a formidable challenge. Behind the scenes, Thurlow was assuring Sheridan that he was a man of no party – 'and to a man of your discernment that is saying enough'.[18]

Pitt now took every step possible to use up time. On 4 December he set up a Commons Committee to question the doctors, and five days passed before the meeting could be held. Once again the doctors were divided, Warren now being seen as the 'opposition' doctor and Willis as the 'government' doctor. Willis asserted that he had seen ten patients with a similar condition, and nine of them had gone on to recover. The King was actually suffering from what twentieth-century doctors would diagnose as acute intermittent porphyria. As its name suggests, this condition can come and go, but it was not remotely understood or identified at the time. The presumption of an imminent Regency therefore remained. When the Commons met for the first full debate on the matter on 10 December, lists of the prospective Whig government were circulating widely.

In the history of the long rivalry between Pitt and Fox, covering twenty-three years of debates on the floor of the House of Commons, the debate of 10 December 1788 stands out as a classic. In many ways the circumstances mirrored those of early 1784, when Pitt first entered office and clung to it: Pitt showing calm patience and playing for time in the face of adversity, while Fox and his colleagues commenced with huge advantages and steadily threw them away.

Pitt rose on 10 December to deliver a speech typically methodical and reasonable, no doubt irritatingly so in the minds of his opponents. There were 'steps to be taken as preliminaries' to the discussion of what to do about the King's illness, and they were 'such as he could not conceive likely to create any difference of opinion'. Pitt wished the House to have 'the advantage of the wisdom of their ancestors to guide their proceedings', and therefore moved for the appointment of another Committee to examine the relevant precedents. This course of action had two advantages: it would take up more time, and it would reveal that in previous cases, such as the madness of Henry VI in 1454, restrictions had been imposed on the power of Regents.

Such a motion did nothing but goad an opposition keen to get on with the actual handover of power. To them, the examination of precedents the most recent of which was more than three hundred years old was nothing other than deliberate time-wasting. The confidence and sweeping assertiveness of Fox's reply was as characteristic of him as the minute attention to the power of detail was of Pitt. Fox had spent most of the time since his belated return from the Continent feeling seriously ill and trying to reassert his authority in his own party. He was bored by technical details at the best of times, and would have wanted in any case to find some all-purpose argument which would frustrate Pitt's attempts to impose restrictions on a Regency. A convenient argument was indeed to hand: that the complete incapacity of the King was equivalent to his death, at least for the time being, and the powers and majesty of the throne should therefore pass to his heir. Fox 'had no hesitation', he therefore announced, 'in declaring it as his decided opinion, that His royal highness the Prince of Wales had as clear, as express a right to assume the reins of government, and exercise the powers of sovereignty during the continuance of the illness and incapacity with which it had pleased God to afflict his Majesty, as in the case of his Majesty's having undergone a natural and perfect demise'.[19]

He would have been better advised to have said nothing. Pitt is reported to have slapped his thigh in an unusually public display of relish, and said to his companions, 'I'll unwhig him for the rest of his life.' For, convenient as it may have been for Fox to put this argument at this particular moment, it sat ill with the Whig attachment to the constitution of 1688, which he had always pledged himself to defend. The supremacy of Parliament was fundamental to the Whig view of

Britain's history and constitution, and the implication that anyone had the right to assume the powers of the monarchy in defiance of deliberations in Parliament was a blatant contradiction of Whig orthodoxy.

Pitt responded 'with the rapidity of lightning'.[20] He seems to have seen at once that Fox's speech had given him both strategic and tactical opportunities. Strategically, he could now be the defender of the constitution as well as of the King, and tactically a whole new argument had been opened up which would take yet more time to be considered. Thus every statement of Fox was immediately turned back on him, with Pitt arguing that 'the doctrine advanced by the right honourable gentlemen was itself . . . the strongest and most unanswerable for appointing the committee he had moved for'.[21] Furthermore, 'To assert such a right in the Prince of Wales, or any one else, independent of the decision of the two houses of parliament, was little less than treason to the constitution of the country.' He told the Commons that as a result 'A new question presented itself, and that of greater magnitude even than the question which was originally before them . . . The question now was, the question of their own rights.' Attacked by Burke as 'one of the Prince's competitors', Pitt repeated the charge of treason against the opposition benches. He achieved his objective: the debate on the Regency was now enlarged from one on practical implementation to one on fundamental principles. While the Committee on precedents met the next day, predictably coming up with nothing new, Fox's speech caused disquiet in the opposition and sarcasm in the press. The *Morning Chronicle* noted: 'An old Whig wishes a reduction of prerogative, a new Whig wishes to extend it, if it will serve his faction.'[22]

On 12 December, when the Commons met to receive the report on precedents, Sheridan made matters worse for the opposition by reminding Pitt of 'the danger of provoking that claim to be asserted which had not yet been preferred', in other words the threat that the Prince of Wales would simply assume the throne. Pitt replied that the Commons should 'do their duty in spite of any threat, however high the authority from which it might proceed',[23] and liberally embellished his case that the question of 'right' must now be fully debated since 'it was a question that shook the foundation of the constitution'.[24] By focusing debate on this question, Pitt was able to postpone further the consideration of the practical implementation of a Regency, even though the King's condition had now been well known and persistent for some six weeks. He prepared to move resolutions on 16 December asserting 'the right and duty' of Parliament to determine what should now happen, throwing in for good measure that it was still necessary to determine how to give Royal Assent to an Act of Parliament needed to create a Regency when the King himself was unable to signify it.

The question of Parliament's rights would provide the climactic debate, and would reveal the strength of support in these changed circumstances for both Pitt and Fox. Some thirty MPs and twenty peers had already formed the 'Armed Neutrality' group, and had in effect defected to the opposition in expectation of its victory. Such a large-scale defection made it possible for the Whigs to run Pitt very close. Yet the night before the debate the biggest of the 'rats' threw himself back into the government's ship. Faced with uncertain offers of employment from the Whigs, the confidence of Dr Willis about the King's eventual recovery and the strength of Pitt's constitutional arguments, Thurlow joined battle with Lord Loughborough in the House of Lords very much on Pitt's side. For even greater effect, he made an emotional declaration of loyalty to the King, clutching his heart and declaring, 'When I forget my King, may God forget me!' These dramatic words flew around the country in newspapers and pamphlets, the readers no doubt little suspecting the background of treachery behind Thurlow's protestations. MPs, on the other hand, watched from the Bar of the House with incredulity. Pitt's reported comment was 'Oh, what a rascal!'

When the Commons met for the key debate on 16 December, the betting at Brooks's on the outcome was even. Both main protagonists were ill, Fox apparently with dysentery and other ailments (at times in this period he thought he was dying), while Pitt was developing a severe cold and a sore throat. Yet for both everything was at stake. Grenville thought Fox gave one of the best speeches he had ever delivered. He asked whether the practice in their enlightened times should be 'grounded on precedents drawn from so dark and barbarous a period of our history as the reign of Henry VI',[25] and poured scorn on Pitt's arguments: 'When the King of England is in good health the monarchy is hereditary; but when he is ill, and incapable of exercising the sovereign authority it is elective.'

Once again, however, Pitt turned every argument of Fox against him. Fox had said that Pitt had been 'so long in the possession of power, that he cannot endure to part with it from his grasp'.[26] Pitt responded that this was 'unfounded, arrogant, and presumptuous'.[27] Fox had 'thought proper' to announce himself as the new administration. This, Pitt argued, made it all the more necessary to examine the precise restrictions to be imposed on a Regency, since it was now clear that a particular party intended to install itself in government in that event, with consequences for 'his Majesty's being able to resume the exercise of his own authority'.

With MPs wavering and the 'Armed Neutrality' group at large, these points mattered. Pitt won the arguments in a House in which he had in any case a natural advantage, and at the end of the debate won the vote by 268 votes to 204. It was a triumph, and it revealed that he was still in control of Parliament. The days before Christmas were spent in further debates on Pitt's resolutions, but for all his success in taking up time, he could not avoid setting to work on the terms of the Regency. Despite his parliamentary victories, the triumph he really needed was the recovery of the King.

Throughout December the King was quieter, but showed little sign of recovering his senses. Warren and Willis continued to disagree about the prospects for recovery. Despite continued majorities in the debates of later December of approximately the same size as in the key decision of 16 December – majorities sufficiently convincing that on Christmas Day Thurlow told Fox that their negotiation was at an end – Pitt now had to set out exactly how a Regency would operate. He first did so in a private letter to the Prince of Wales on 30 December, containing proposals which, according to the Prince himself, imposed 'such restrictions as no Dictator could possibly . . . ever have been barefaced enough to have brought forward'.[28]

Pitt's proposals specifically vested control of the Royal Household in the Queen, laid down that the Prince as Regent would have no power to grant peerages except to his brothers, and that he would not be able to dispose of any property of the King nor grant permanent offices or pensions except in specified circumstances. The Prince worked with Fox, Loughborough and Burke to produce his reply of 2 January 1789. He argued that such tight restrictions would be 'injurious' both to the monarchy and the public interest: 'It is with deep regret the Prince makes the observation, that he sees . . . a project for producing weakness, disorder and insecurity in every branch of the administration of affairs. – A project for dividing the Royal Family from each other – for separating the court from the state.'[29] This was not far wide of the mark. Pitt intended the Prince and the Whigs to be almost paralysed while in office, and to be denied the opportunity to win support by using patronage. By imposing such tight limitations, he would protect the King's interests in the event of his recovery and ease his own return to power.

Three days later Pitt wrote again to the Prince, courteously but firmly, and this time on behalf of the whole government. 'The King's servants . . . beg leave respectfully to assure your Royal Highness that if the plan which they took the liberty of submitting to your Royal Highness had appeared to them in the light in which they have the mortification to observe that it is considered by your Royal Highness, it would never have occurred to them to propose it,' but nevertheless, 'They still feel themselves bound to adhere to these principles in the propositions to be offered to the consideration of Parliament.'[30]

A Regency Bill was now due to be prepared, it having been agreed that Parliament could be opened and Royal Assent to Acts signified by means of the Great Seal during the incapacity of the King and before the appointment of a Regent. Yet further delay ensued, for as with so many events in the preceding years Pitt was not only skilful but also lucky. The death of Charles Cornwall, the Speaker of the House of Commons, on 2 January necessitated an election, and it did not help the supporters of Dr Warren's views that Cornwall had been in his care. The process of election not only took up time, it enabled Pitt to install a loyal acolyte in the Speaker's chair to deal favourably with any procedural disagreements: William Grenville was duly put forward and elected by 215 to 144, against the protests of the opposition. The opposition then added to its own difficulties by proposing a new Committee of Inquiry to examine the King's physicians, in the apparent belief that this would show the King's illness to be sufficiently serious that the proposed restrictions on the Regency would be harder to sustain. Consequently another ten days were taken up without Pitt having to produce his Bill, and the result was in any case the opposite of that which the Whigs desired: the optimism of Dr Willis and most of the physicians was becoming greater. Pitt had agreed to this new inquiry with a show of reluctance, but no doubt with private satisfaction. He was being delivered from disaster by the errors of his opponents, who in retrospect would have done far better to say very little until government was within their grasp.

Pitt was also being increasingly encouraged and sustained by popular opinion. In the crisis of 1784 the weight of public addresses in his support had been one of the decisive factors in his favour. The lesson had not been lost on him, and it is probably no coincidence that the first address on this occasion came from his own city of Cambridge. The ever loyal merchants and bankers of the City of London voted their thanks to Pitt at a meeting on 7 January, and took advertisements in newspapers to say so. Other addresses came in from as far afield as Perth, Aberdeen, Stirling, Glasgow, Gateshead, Southampton, Maidstone and Leicester. Well might the opposition *Morning Herald* attack such addresses: Gateshead was 'A borough which probably most of our readers have not heard of before . . . where shopkeepers of the *lowest* order, *keelmen*, and *pitmen* reside,'[31] but the trend in public opinion was undeniable. Lord Fitzwilliam was told that in Yorkshire 'the neighbourhood hereabouts seem so horridly infatuated in their opinions of the rectitude of Mr. Pitt's conduct'.[32] The fact was that George III was very popular, widely respected for his diligence and personal morality. In the opinion of some Pitt was even more popular, and the Whig Sir Gilbert Elliot complained: 'Mr. Pitt is the only object the nation can perceive, and the only thing they think valuable in the world; and I rather think they would be content and pleased to set aside the whole Royal Family, with the Crown and both Houses of

Parliament, if they could keep him by it.'[33] In pamphlets, the opposition tried to turn Pitt's pre-eminence to its advantage:

> PRINCE PITT! or the Minister of the Crown. Greater than the HEIR APPARENT! who, having already destroyed the People's Rights by an undue Exertion of the Prerogative of the Crown, is now willing to raise himself above the Prerogative by *seizing on the Sovereignty of these Kingdoms.*[34]

Its efforts were to no avail. Both the Whigs and the Prince were thoroughly unpopular, on grounds of presumption, disunity, licentiousness and the grave disadvantage of not being Pitt.

As Pitt presented five resolutions to the Commons on 16 January embodying his unaltered restrictions on the powers of a Regent, he could therefore count on solid parliamentary and public support. Sheridan attacked his prohibition on the Prince's creation of peerages, pointing out that Pitt himself had created forty-eight peerages up to this time, but this key proposal was carried by fifty-seven votes, and the other restrictions by larger majorities. By the end of January, Fox's health was giving way, and while the Whigs continued protracted negotiations about the formation of their new government they were despondent and divided. Pitt had run rings round them.

Even so, Pitt's situation at the end of January 1789 was, in Wraxall's words, 'peculiarly arduous and critical. From the summit of power, he beheld himself suddenly about to be precipitated by an event of the most unexpected nature, against which he neither had taken, or could take, any measure of precaution. Three months had already elapsed since the King's seizure, and no indications of restoration to intellect were as yet perceptible . . . Pitt possessed no landed estate, no funded property, nor even life annuity.'

We do not know for certain what Pitt intended for himself if he were to be ejected from office in the subsequent few weeks. It is said that he intended to return to the Bar, and certainly his fame and ability would have guaranteed him a good living from it. What we can be sure about is that he was taking every possible measure, down to the smallest detail, to maximise his chances of survival in office on his own terms. He had now dragged matters out for a good twelve weeks, and his principal objective was to continue the debate until the King recovered. His fallback plan was to create such tight restrictions on the Regency that the Whigs would be unable to entrench themselves in power unless the King's madness continued for years. It may also have occurred to him that such restrictions, combined with his own successful assertion of his parliamentary dominance, might make a Whig administration so difficult to operate that the Prince would have to keep him on for the moment, with all the further opportunities that would bring. There could only be a remote chance of such an outcome, but Pitt had made the chances of one of these things happening as high as it was possible to make them. His mind remained, as it always had been, utterly focused on power.

On 5 February Pitt introduced a Regency Bill into the House of Commons, to give effect to the resolutions he had already moved. Once it passed the Commons and the Lords, and Royal Assent was signified by means of the Great Seal, the Prince would be the lawful Regent and Pitt's job would be at his disposal. The Bill passed the Commons on 12 February, the debates having been distinguished only by Pitt's acceptance of a three-year time limit on the restriction on the creation of peerages – a period so long as to be academic – and Burke's intemperate explosions against Pitt and the King. Burke was deeply dissatisfied with Fox and his other colleagues for their ineffective handling of the crisis, and had all along urged a more forensic approach. Now in frustration he exclaimed, 'Have we forgotten that we are debating relative to a monarch smitten by the hand of Omnipotence? Do we recollect that the Almighty has hurled him from his throne, and plunged him into a condition that may justly excite the pity of the meanest peasant in his dominions!'[35] This did little for the opposition's case, and Pitt maintained his majorities.

On 16 February the Bill was introduced into the House of Lords. Within days Pitt's five-year-old administration could be dismissed. In the Irish Parliament the government had been defeated, and a Loyal Address to the Prince was being prepared. From Bath, Fox was telling his supporters to ignore reports that the King's condition was improving: 'I hope by this time all ideas of the Prince or any of us taking any measure in consequence of the good reports of the King, are at an end; if they are not, pray do all you can to crush them . . . let me know by the return of the post on what day the Regency is like to commence.'[36] But on the very day on which Fox wrote these words, 17 February, the public bulletin issued by the King's physicians referred to 'a state of convalescence'. George III had recovered. Thurlow, who the King called to Windsor that day, was able to confirm it. After a Cabinet meeting on the nineteenth, Thurlow went to the Lords to move the postponement of consideration of the Regency Bill, while Pitt dashed off an excited note to his mother: 'The public account this morning is that the King continues advancing in Recovery. The private one is that he is to all appearance perfectly well, and if it were the Case of a Private man, would be immediately declared so . . . This intelligence will be welcome enough to excuse a short letter, and I could not resist the pleasure of communicating it.'[37] Four days later the King wrote to Pitt:

> Kew, Feb. 23d, 1789.
>
> It is with infinite satisfaction I renew my correspondence with Mr. Pitt by acquainting him with my having seen the Prince of Wales and my second son; care was taken that the conversation should be general and cordial . . . I am anxious to see Mr. Pitt any hour that may suit him to-morrow morning, as his constant attachment to my interest and that of the public which are inseparable must ever place him in the most advantageous light.
>
> G.R.[38]

Pitt's triumph was complete. The King's recovery had saved him with only days to spare, but if it had not been for his own skill in extending the debate and exploiting the blunders of the opposition, George III would have recovered to find his enemies in power. London rose up in a tumult of rejoicing, displaying 'a blaze of light from one extremity to the other'. From late March onwards, formal festivities celebrated the King's recovery. On 1 April, two thousand people attended a Victory Ball organised by White's at the Pantheon: Pitt attended it after a celebratory dinner with his brother, Dundas, the Duchess of Gordon and the now renowned Dr Willis. On the following night the King gave a concert and dinner at Windsor. The table setting in front of

Pitt included 'the number 268, the first majority in the House of Commons, written in sugar-plums or sweetmeats'.[39] On 23 April, St George's Day, a Service of Thanksgiving was held at St Paul's Cathedral amidst all the splendour of the British state and the unrestrained enthusiasm of the crowds. Six thousand children sang for the King, but the Prince of Wales and the Duke of York were widely criticised for laughing and giggling during the service, and Fox was greeted with 'an universal hiss which continued with very little intermission' throughout his journey to the cathedral. Pitt's reception was reminiscent of 1784, the cheering crowds insisting that the horses of his carriage be removed so that they could pull him back to Downing Street themselves.

In his budget that spring Pitt had money to spare to revoke the ever more unpopular shop tax while reforming the taxation of tobacco to destroy yet another part of the smugglers' trade. By the summer of 1789 his career and his popularity had reached their apogee. On 14 July he wrote to his mother from Downing Street confessing to a little gout but insisting that he was otherwise well, and hoping to visit her soon. The recess promised, he thought, 'a good share of holidays'. Although events in France were 'coming to actual extremes', this made that country 'an object of compassion, even to a rival'.[40] Pitt could not foresee the volcanic consequences for himself and his world of what was happening even as he wrote. It was the very day that the *sans culottes* of Paris took the Bastille by storm.

14

Trials of Strength

'Great Britain, is now incontestably in possession of the balance of Europe, for the first time perhaps since the days of K. Henry the 8th.'

ALLEYNE FITZHERBERT, BRITISH ENVOY TO THE HAGUE, 1790[1]

'I feel that we have nothing for it, but to go on with vigour and to hope for the best.'

WILLIAM PITT, MARCH 1791[2]

PITT MAY HAVE CONSIDERED France in 1789 to be 'an object of compassion', but not so much as to agree actually to send compassionate assistance. Jacques Necker had come to power in France the previous year, as Director General of Finances and Minister of State, with the mission of rescuing his country and King Louis XVI. He had met Pitt on the famous trip to France six years before, and now, facing food riots after the failure of the 1788 harvest, he wrote to him to ask for emergency consignments of flour. On 3 July Pitt responded to the French Ambassador:

> Mr. Pitt . . . has felt the strongest desire to be able to recommend sending the supply of flour desir'd by Monsr Necker and had hopes from the information at first given him . . . that it would be practicable . . . Mr. Pitt has now the mortification to find that, according to the accounts of the persons most conversant with the corn trade, the present supply in this country compar'd with the demand, and the precarious prospect of the harvest render it impossible to propose to Parliament to authorize any exportation.[3]

The British Corn Laws prohibited the export of wheat or flour when the price of wheat reached forty-four shillings a quarter,* and it was now a good deal higher. Reserves of flour, however, were relatively plentiful, and Pitt could have supplied the 20,000 sacks the French asked for if he had thought it politically essential and gained parliamentary approval. His refusal to do so was unfortunate in at least one sense: having insisted for years that it was possible for Britain and France to enjoy friendly relations, he would henceforth be regarded by the French as deeply unsympathetic. A genuine friend to France, he would now never be seen as one. He has sometimes been criticised for failing to send crucial supplies which might have helped avert the Revolution,[4] but it is probably a mistake to think that last-minute supplies from Britain could have tipped the balance in the days that followed, and his decision must be seen in the context of the domestic situation. The English harvest of 1788 had also been poor, and that of 1789 was looking little better due to the wet weather. Shortages of food could easily produce public disorder, as France had now discovered, and Pitt decided that caution was to be preferred to generosity.

Across the Channel in early July 1789, the circumstances required for a total breakdown of civil order now coincided – summer heat, food shortages, financial collapse and ministerial weakness. The significance of the events of 14 July, when the hated state prison, the Bastille, was stormed by the Paris crowds, was not immediately understood; in retrospect it was the day on which Louis XVI lost control of events. Soldiers joined the rioters, a revolutionary militia patrolled the streets, 32,000 muskets fell into their hands, and the King was forced to take back Necker as his Minister even though he had just dismissed him.

Although the flames of the Revolution burst forth that summer, the tinderbox of social and economic frustrations which fuelled it had been accumulating for decades. Britain had experienced its own convulsions in the civil wars of the seventeenth century, but had emerged from them with a general acceptance of a 'balanced' constitution. The settlement of 1688 implied a contract between monarchy and aristocracy, whose mutual dependence united them in defending

* A quarter was eight bushels, approximately a quarter of a ton of grain.

each other, while the House of Commons provided for the interests of the wider nation to be forcefully, if patchily, represented. Governments might come and go, but the national consensus behind a constitutional monarchy and a powerful parliament endured.

Eighteenth-century France had made no such adjustment in preceding generations. The writ of absolutist monarchy still ran. From the advent of Louis XIV in the mid-seventeenth century, France had seemed to provide the very definition of royal power and 'enlightened despotism', represented in physical form by the unimaginable splendour of Versailles. France had been the superpower of western Europe, with a population four times that of England and a military capability no European power could ignore: Spanish, Austrian, Dutch and British Ministers could spend their lives responding to the initiatives and intrigues of the King of France and his powerful court. Yet as the eighteenth century wore on, this splendid edifice became rotten and hollow. The French nobility enjoyed no automatic role in the governing of the nation, no contract or understanding with the monarchy – nor was there any outlet through which an emerging middle class could wield even a modicum of influence. When the true crisis came, the French King would lack allies, and the frustrations accumulated over decades would be immense. The lack of provincial representation in the capital and the centralisation of the French state meant that events within Paris were decisive for the whole nation: convenient when the monarchy was strong, but catastrophic if it became weak. The result was that Louis XVI's power was still absolute but it was brittle, and the state's response to the crisis 'oscillated between despotism and capitulation'.[5] The culture of a strong state restrained by popular protest had already developed in France, and is arguably still recognisable in political events as recent as the 1990s, when strikes and demonstrations brought the abandonment of reforms favoured by a newly elected government.

In the 1780s the crisis came. France had been humiliated in the Seven Years' War at the hands of Frederick the Great and the elder Pitt, and while technically victorious in the American War of Independence she had accumulated vast debts in the process, which now tipped the state into bankruptcy. In London, Pitt could raise taxes and design a Sinking Fund to address Britain's indebtedness, but in France there was no equivalent leader to do so, and no Parliament able to sanction it on behalf of the people. In the meantime, the 'diamond necklace affair' of Marie Antoinette helped to ruin the image of the Royal Family,* and the privileged position of the unreformed Catholic Church was deeply resented. Such factors combined with the nature of a country whose philosophers were particularly attracted by the new age of reason and the appeal of science to make the coming Revolution far more intensely anti-monarchical and anti-clerical than anything experienced in Britain.

The French failure in the Dutch crisis of 1787 only made matters worse – Napoleon would later identify it as a key element in the onset of revolution. Now, as the harvest failed and bread became scarce, the French state was in retreat. The calling of an Assembly of Notables in 1787 had led to the summoning of the Estates-General in 1789, a body not called upon since 1614. There, in the Third Estate, a previously disenfranchised but ambitious middle class asserted its power, turning itself in the summer of 1789 into a National Assembly with the power to override all previous laws and conventions. The King and Queen were brought back from Versailles by hostile crowds and required to remain in the Tuileries. The French monarchy was on its knees.

In 1789, and for a good two years thereafter, most British politicians greeted the dramatic developments across the Channel with varying degrees of cheerfulness. 'How much the greatest Event it is that ever happened in the World! & how much the best!'[6] wrote Fox that July. Grenville noted that 'they will not for many years be in a situation to molest the invaluable peace which we now enjoy'.[7] The British Ambassador in Paris, the Duke of Dorset, considered the Revolution 'actually concluded', although he had to return to Britain for good at the end of July after a letter he had written to the Comte d'Artois

* Marie Antoinette was believed to have schemed to obtain a diamond necklace of enormous value from Cardinal de Rohan, and then refused to pay for it. In fact both she and the Cardinal were victims of a fraud perpetrated by the Comtesse de La Motte, who tricked the Cardinal into thinking that he would win the Queen's regard by providing the necklace, obtained it from him and then sold it.

congratulating him on his escape was intercepted and read out in the National Assembly. French suspicion of Britain was further heightened, but in general the view from Westminster was that France was now out of action and might well develop a constitutional monarchy. With Parliament in recess, Pitt was able to avoid any statement on the matter until February 1790, when he gave this positive assessment:

> The present convulsions of France, must, sooner or later, terminate in general harmony and regular order; and though the fortunate arrangements of such a situation might make her more formidable, it might also render her less obnoxious as a neighbour . . . Whenever the situation of France should become restored, it would prove freedom rightly understood; freedom resulting from good order and good government; and thus circumstanced France would stand forward as one of the most brilliant Powers in Europe; she would enjoy just that kind of liberty which I venerate.[8]

Only Burke railed against the Revolution, warning of its wider consequences: 'Whenever a separation is made between liberty and justice, neither is in my opinion safe.'[9] At that stage he was a lone voice: it would be some time before the Revolution ran out of the control of its progenitors.

In its early stages, therefore, the French Revolution did not become an issue in British domestic politics. Instead, in the summer and autumn of 1789 Pitt was engaged in a further strengthening of his position in the Cabinet. Sydney had now spent five and a half years as the Secretary of State overseeing home and colonial matters. The prospect of legislation against the slave trade (the subject of the next chapter) was sufficiently unattractive to him to finally push him into leaving the government, a step which a grateful Pitt rewarded by advancing him in the peerage to the rank of Viscount. The opening gave Pitt his biggest opportunity to strengthen the Cabinet since its formation, and he now brought Grenville down from the Speaker's Chair after only one session in it to take Sydney's place.*

* This would be unheard of today, when the Speakership of the Commons is regarded as a disqualification from subsequent partisan activity, but in those days it could be a stepping stone to higher office.

William Grenville was the third son of the former Prime Minister George Grenville, and was therefore Pitt's cousin. His intelligence and reserve made him a typical scion of the Grenville family. In many ways he was similar to his cousin: born in the same year, he had excelled at Oxford in mathematics and classics, was elected to Parliament at the age of twenty-two and had a mind suited to administration and finance. Like Pitt, he had a rather forbidding bearing, but those who got to know him found him 'uncommonly good-humoured' and 'easy in his manner'.[10] He differed from Pitt in being financially as well as politically ambitious, and in sometimes displaying a rigid obstinacy. By comparison to his cousin he would in future years show more unyielding determination to advance certain liberal causes such as slave-trade abolition and Catholic relief, but also be more hardline and unforgiving in questions of peace or war. His promotion to Secretary of State in 1789 marked his advance into the front rank of British politicians. It also opened him up to ceaseless caricature: much fun was made of his unusually large head and posterior, and he would be depicted in a Gillray cartoon in 1795 holding his bottom towards a fire with the caption 'A keen-sighted politician warming his imagination'.

Grenville had done his job seeing Pitt through a difficult period in the Commons during the Regency crisis; he in turn was replaced as Speaker by Henry Addington, another young MP and supporter of Pitt, and son of the Pitt family doctor. Twelve years later Pitt would nominate him as Prime Minister. At the same time William Eden was rewarded for his efforts on the French commercial treaty by being made a peer as Lord Auckland: Pitt was making clear that defecting members of the opposition could do very well in his employment. Later in the year, Pitt also needed a new Lord Lieutenant of Ireland. His great friend the young Duke of Rutland had died in that post in 1787, and he had persuaded his cousin Temple (the one who had resigned from the government after three days in 1783), now advanced to the rank of Marquis of Buckingham, to take the post. The petulant Buckingham resigned through ill-health in 1789, and threatened further to resign the Lord Lieutenancy of his county if the King did not make him a duke. For all Pitt's efforts, this proved impossible: George III would not create dukedoms outside his own family, and had in any case not forgotten Buckingham's desertion of him six years before. The patient Pitt went to Stowe, Buckingham's family seat, to smooth ruffled feathers, writing to his mother from Holwood on 21 November: 'My excursions all proved extremely pleasant. The last has been to Stowe, where I went last Sunday, and found Lord Buckingham getting much better.'[11] He now sent the young Earl of Westmorland to Ireland, launching him on a political career that would span almost four decades.

Despite the pleasant 'excursions', Pitt had continued to expand his workload. In addition to his command of the Treasury and leadership of the Commons, he had kept up the close supervision of foreign policy to which the Dutch crisis of 1787 had introduced him. As international events were no respecters of parliamentary sittings, the result was that he worked still harder when Parliament was sitting, and was still less able to leave London when it was not. He did not seem to mind this, except when it distressed his mother. Having twice planned a trip to the north of England and had to cancel it he ceased to think of it again. There is every sign that he enjoyed the need to work hard, the respect it brought from others, the despatches from overseas mingled with Treasury business, the complexity of events and the messengers and horses waiting outside in Downing Street to carry his next command.

In the summer and autumn of 1788 he had stayed on hand to manage the consequences of the crisis in the Baltic. After Catherine II of Russia and Joseph II of Austria had jointly made war on the Ottoman Empire, Gustavus III of Sweden had taken the opportunity to attack Russia in the north. The result was that the Russians crushed the Swedes while temporarily leaving the Austrians to be mauled by the Turks. With the Danes preparing to join the attack on desperate Sweden, Britain and Prussia threatened intervention to preserve Sweden as a viable power. This was an age of enterprising diplomacy: at a time of slow-moving communication Ambassadors sometimes had to take matters into their own hands, rarely more so than the British Ambassador in Copenhagen, Hugh Elliot, on this occasion. He went over to Sweden, found an exhausted Gustavus III preparing for the Danish attack, said to him, 'Sire, give me your Crown; I will return it to you with added lustre,' emboldened the Swedes and then returned to bully the Danes into an armistice. Throughout this he was backed by the idea floated in Berlin that a British fleet would support Prussian armed intervention, a threat never actually approved in London. Elliot's behaviour obviously annoyed Pitt and Carmarthen, but it had the desired effect: the Danes refrained from war and the Swedes were saved from annihilation. Once again, the timely threat of British intervention, albeit unauthorised on this occasion, had brought success. The diplomatic isolation in which Pitt had come to power now seemed very distant.

In the autumn of 1789 the war in the East came closer to home. The demands made on his territories by Joseph II in pursuit of the war with Turkey created rebellions across his Empire, including in the Austrian Netherlands. As Austria threatened to send troops to enforce the imposition of imperial rule, Holland and Prussia proposed to recognise Belgian independence to break Austria's involvement in the Low Countries. Prussia was in any case contemplating war against the Austrians while they were preoccupied with Turkey, and Pitt had found them increasingly troublesome and wayward allies. Belgic independence was not favoured in London, where Austrian influence over this buffer between Holland and France was regarded as preferable to French influence. Britain, unwanted as an ally by anyone a few years before, was now courted by Austria as well as by its established allies Holland and Prussia. While the Belgians were declaring a republic, British influence ensured that the Triple Alliance would not intervene without Austrian consent. As it happened, the situation was saved by the sudden death in February 1790 of Joseph II, who was succeeded by his brother Leopold II. Leopold wanted peace on all fronts, and asked Britain to mediate.

These events illustrated to Pitt both the need and the opportunity for Britain to play a decisive role in European affairs. Even a war focused on the Baltic and Black Seas had soon touched Britain's vital national interest in the Low Countries. With the Triple Alliance in place, France out of action for the moment, Austria friendly and smaller powers such as Sweden looking to Britain to defend their interests, Pitt was suddenly in a position to promote a general European settlement and bring peace to the Continent. It really did look as though Britain was, as Alleyne Fitzherbert, British Envoy to The Hague, put it, 'incontestably in possession of the balance of Europe'. Pitt now promoted a solution that was typical of him: the man who had found an elegant answer to problems such as rising national debt and over-complex taxes could see the solution to the whole European crisis. He sought nothing less than a huge collective agreement on European peace on the basis of the pre-war frontiers – the *status quo ante bellum*. British mediation brought agreement between the Austrians and the Prussians at Reichenbach in July 1790 on exactly this basis. The Austrians ended their war with Turkey and promised to respect the constitutional rights of the Netherlands, under Austrian sovereignty. In return, the Triple Alliance would seek the end of the war between Russia and Turkey, and encourage Belgian respect for Austrian sovereignty. The agreement was also intended to give added security to Poland, always at risk from Prussia, Austria and Russia, and to guarantee peace in the Baltic. The last piece in the jigsaw would be the isolated Russians, who it was thought would be left with little option but to end the war.

Pitt's concept for European peace was thus both brilliant and ambitious. His purpose, as he once wrote in his notes, was 'to prevent (if it can be done without too great effort or risk) any material Change in the relative situation of other Powers – particularly Naval Powers – and to diminish the temptation to wars of ambition'.[12] It was a noble purpose and manifestly in the interests of his country. In pursuing it he had the good fortune to be supported by outstanding diplomatic brains, such as Joseph Ewart, the British envoy in Berlin, and Auckland, now heading for The Hague. In their turn, they respected Pitt and knew that it was now he who pulled their strings. As Ewart wrote to Auckland in November 1790: 'I trust Mr. Pitt will write to your Lordship himself in a satisfactory manner; and you know better than I do of what consequence the opinions of others are.'[13] In other words, the Duke of Leeds, the Foreign Secretary, did not call the shots.* Yet Pitt's all-embracing jigsaw still lacked one very big piece: the cooperation of Russia. Tens of thousands of Russian soldiers had died to gain

* The Marquis of Carmarthen had succeeded to the title fifth Duke of Leeds in 1789.

territory in the Crimea and wider access to the Black Sea, as Prince Potemkin flung them against the walls of Turkish forts. The Empress Catherine II had no intention whatever of returning to her pre-war frontiers.

The overconfidence which would lead Pitt into confrontation with the mighty Catherine the Great was fed by the outcome of yet another international crisis in the course of 1790. Ostensibly, it was about the right to trade and settle on an island off the north-west coast of America. In reality, it determined whether it would be Britain or Spain who held the upper hand in the future development of North America and the Pacific.

The western coastline of the Americas had been colonised by the Spanish at various points in South America and all the way up to their settlement of San Francisco. In the early 1780s, however, Captain James Cook had explored the north-west coast on the same voyage which led to his eventual death in Hawaii. Small British expeditions returned there later in the decade, creating a trading depot at Nootka Sound, on Vancouver Island in present-day Canada. At the same time, the Russians had established themselves on Kodiak Island to the south of Alaska, and were mounting expeditions further south. The Spanish sent a warship to the north, which anchored at Nootka Sound in May 1789. In July they arrested the British sailors there, impounded several British ships, pulled down the British flag and proclaimed their rights to the whole west coast of the Americas up to the Gulf of Alaska, beyond which was to be left to the Russians.

In the twenty-first century, an equivalent event would cause a diplomatic crisis within minutes. It is perhaps the ultimate illustration of the slowness of communication in the pre-telegraph age that news of this incident did not reach London until the following year. The first confused report of it in January 1790 was followed by a note from Madrid insisting that Britain punish any further trespassers and complaining of the infringement of Spanish territorial rights. The Spanish claim rested on a Papal Bull of 1493 which had granted to Spain all overseas territories not yet occupied, but it was a claim Britain had never accepted. Leeds sent an equally peremptory note to the Spanish, insisting on the British right to trade or settle in the area, a right which would be 'asserted and maintained with a proper degree of vigour'.[14] He demanded the return of the ships allegedly seized, the payment of compensation, and refused to discuss any other questions until these points had been satisfied.

Not for the first time, Pitt was not happy with the actions of his Foreign Secretary, who he felt was taking too hard a line without knowing all the facts, and inflaming the situation unnecessarily. Once again he decided to take the matter in hand himself, sending a more conciliatory note at the end of February whilst still demanding compensation and the return of seized property. For some weeks the issues simply lay on the diplomatic table, as both governments waited for more definite news of what had actually happened on the other side of the world. The British prepared a small naval expedition to be sent to the disputed area (knowing it would take a year to get there), while the Spanish explained the situation to the French in case they needed an active ally, and began small-scale military preparation.

It was in April 1790 that matters escalated rapidly. A retired British naval Lieutenant, John Meares, returned from Nootka with an account of several British ships being seized there and British prisoners being ill-treated in Spanish prisons in Mexico. He also confirmed that the Spanish were now claiming as their own some territories which he, Meares, had already claimed for Britain in the name of George III. Shortly afterwards, news arrived from Anthony Merry, the British envoy at Madrid, that Spanish naval preparations now included the fitting out of fourteen ships of the line. Pitt and the Cabinet acted swiftly, demanding immediate satisfaction 'for the outrages committed' while authorising the navy to fit out forty ships of the line and to recruit the necessary sailors by press gang if necessary. The news took the country by surprise, with government stock falling on the markets. Pitt told the Commons that the Spanish claim was 'the most absurd and exorbitant which could well be imagined; a claim which they had never heard of before, which was indefinite in its extent, and which originated in no treaty ... If that claim were given way to, it must deprive this country of the means of extending its navigation and fishery in the Southern Ocean, and would go towards excluding His Majesty's subjects from an infant trade, the future extension of which could not but prove essentially beneficial to the commercial interests of Great Britain.'[15]

Both countries now considered a great deal to be at stake. For Britain, a whaling industry in the Pacific could prove hugely lucrative, British exploration and settlement in the Pacific had only just begun (the first British penal colony in Australia had been founded two years before, by ships which sailed into Botany Bay only six days ahead of the French), and the right to trade in furs and other products from the American mainland was of obvious importance. In any case, a claim to a huge extension of territory from a country Britain had fought three times in wars in the previous fifty years could not be accepted. For Spain, an increase in British activity in the Pacific would threaten her own trade and whaling industry in South and Central America, and ultimately her control of the Philippines. The dispute would decide which country would have the advantage in the settlement and development of the principal remaining inhabitable and uncolonised region of the globe.

Pitt's approach to the continuing negotiations with Spain was firm but imaginative: he wanted compensation and the withdrawal of the Spanish claim, but he also sought a comprehensive agreement to allow free settlement by Europeans along the north-west coast of America and the freedom for settlements to trade with each other in a new and more positive relationship. This was typical of Pitt – seeking a permanent and beneficial long-term solution out of today's short-term crisis. That approach did not suit Leeds, who seemed to think the only choice was between war and 'disgrace'. For the second time in three years the belligerence of the Foreign Secretary had to be restrained. Nevertheless, Pitt was clear about preparing for war. He himself had a meeting with a Spanish American leader passing through London who sought support for independence from Spain for parts of South America. Plans were made to attack Spanish colonies in the Caribbean and to defend British outposts against attack by Americans. The rapid naval mobilisation benefited from the unstinting support Pitt had given for many years to the Royal Navy. If fully mobilised, the battle fleet would now consist of almost a hundred ships of the line. Even aside from this crisis, 'It was no uncommon thing', wrote the son of the Comptroller of the Navy, 'for Mr. Pitt to visit the Navy Office to discuss naval matters with the Comptroller, and to see the returns made from the yards of the progress in building and repairing the ships of the line; he also desired to have a periodical statement from the Comptroller of the state of the fleet, wisely holding that officer responsible, personally to him, without any regard to the Board.'[16] In the meantime, the Spanish continued their own preparations, but suffered the disappointment that the partial French naval mobilisation ordered by Louis XVI in order to give them support precipitated a debate in the National Assembly, the result of which was a decree that the King no longer had the power to make war without its permission.

This was how matters stood in June 1790 when Pitt asked George III to dissolve Parliament and declare a general election. The Parliament elected in 1784 had now run for more than six years of its seven-year limit. Pitt had probably hoped to call an election in 1789, but after the Regency crisis time was needed for those whom Grenville termed '*Messieurs les Rats*' to return to the government's side. As described in Chapter Nine, the 1784 election had taken on something of the character of a national contest; in contrast the 1790 election reverted to the eighteenth-century type, with local and personal factors blurring any national trend. The opposition found it worthwhile to contest more seats than before, and the Treasury spent more money, but there was no expectation of any significant change. Both sides decided not to repeat the expensive experience of pitched battle for the two seats of the City of Westminster, and they were divided between them by agreement. On 24 June Pitt wrote to his mother from Downing Street: 'I cannot yet say that I am arrived at a Period of much leisure, tho it is comparatively something like it, and the occupation arising from the Elections is diminishing fast every day . . . upon the whole I have no doubt of our being considerably stronger than in the last Parliament . . . Our foreign business remains still in suspense, and I hardly know what to conjecture of the probability of Peace or War.'[17] To the extent that national factors played a role in the election, the general prosperity of the country, the personal popularity of Pitt, and a natural rallying to the government at the thought of war probably all helped a little. Opposition attempts to revive debates on parliamentary reform and the Test Acts in the run-up to the elections were dismissed by Pitt. The overall result gave him a small but definite increase in his Commons majority, estimated by historians at twenty-five net gains.[18]

In July Pitt sent a fresh demand to Madrid demanding 'an Admission, that the Court of Spain was not in Possession' of Nootka Sound but making clear that 'any other Grounds of Claim . . . will still be open to Discussion'. The Spanish Minister, Count Floridablanca, was now on the ropes. He had no definite commitment of support from France, while Britain was mobilising a formidable naval force, the addition of ten Dutch warships showing that her allies were behind her. On 24 July he caved in to Pitt's immediate demand, although this left the larger issues unsettled and his call for mutual naval disarmament was rejected in London. Negotiations about the wider rights of Britain and Spain in the Pacific continued, but the threat of war remained, the Spanish being emboldened by a belated decision by the French National Assembly to fit out forty-five ships of the line to help them. Tension rose between London and Paris, the French being warned on no account to move their navy into conjunction with that of Spain. Thirty-seven British warships were now at sea.

The detailed British proposals being considered in Madrid involved regulated British trade and fishing rights in the Pacific, the restoration of the Nootka settlement, and the dropping of all Spanish claims over the North American coast north of 31° North, in other words anywhere north of the southern reaches of California. In return, British ships would keep out of Spanish territory and settlements. To the horror of Floridablanca, these terms were categorically rejected in late October by the Spanish Cabinet, who declared for war. At the very last minute, once again abandoned by France and facing an ultimatum from Britain, he managed to devise a new draft agreement with the British envoy in Madrid, abandoning the strict latitude in limits but permitting free settlement to the north of the 'coast already occupied by Spain'. When the Spanish King Charles IV gave his hasty approval, his Cabinet was outmanoeuvred and the agreement made. Spain had saved a minimum of face, but the substance of all the main British points had been conceded. The warships returned to port as Pitt savoured another international victory.

Once again Pitt had steered a judicious course to an unqualified success. He had held back from presenting the final ultimatum until British military preparations were complete and the Spanish were not sure of their allies. When that moment had arisen he had seized his chance, and the result was victory without war. Auckland wrote to him: 'I am convinced that if less firmness, energy, and activity had been shown on our part, or even that if our fleet had not been found in the readiest and most perfect state that has been known in the annals of Great Britain, the reparation made to us would have been incomplete . . . In short, there never was a business better conducted or better concluded, and there never was a moment in which our country held such pre-eminency among nations.'[19]

From being a novice in foreign affairs three years before, Pitt was now a confident statesman on the international stage. He had bent Spain, France and Denmark to his will and secured alliance or friendship with Holland, Prussia, Sweden, Poland and Austria. Now he would turn his attention to Russia.

During the crises over Holland in 1787 and Nootka Sound in 1790, Pitt had been fortunate in that Parliament was not in session at the climactic moments. It had therefore not been necessary for each manoeuvre or development to be explained or questioned. It was in the rather different circumstances of the first session of the new Parliament in November 1790 that he prepared the series of diplomatic moves intended to force Russia to relinquish her recent conquests and to make the peace in Europe universal. The impact of international events on domestic politics was immediately felt. The convention with Spain was approved by a large majority, but Pitt needed to present a supplementary budget in December 1790, only eight months after his previous one. The naval mobilisation and the stand-off with Spain had cost no less than £3,133,000 – a sum he proposed to pay off within four years through additional and temporary taxes.

There were also lengthy debates on whether the trial of Warren

Hastings could be carried over into the new Parliament or had expired with the last one. Pitt came down decisively in favour of continuation, delivering a speech which showed such complete mastery of all precedents and arguments that Wilberforce wrote that it was one Pitt 'never could have made if he had not been a mathematician. He put things by as he proceeded, and then returned to the very point from which he had started, with the most astonishing clearness.'[20]

Most important of all for his future direction of the government, he asked the King to give Grenville a peerage and thereby transferred him to the House of Lords. For nearly seven years Pitt had had to cope with Thurlow as the senior representative of the Cabinet in the Lords; Grenville's arrival there as a Secretary of State made him a clear rival and the principal government spokesman there in place of Leeds. The King's acceptance of the idea in the hope that it would smooth relations between Pitt and Thurlow suggests a political innocence he had not exhibited before his bout of madness. The move meant that Pitt would all the more have to shoulder the burden of debates in the Commons, with only Dundas at his side as a capable speaker, but he had never minded that. It certainly did not please Thurlow, or indeed other members of the Cabinet who, as usual, were not informed by Pitt in advance. Richmond, a wise but sometimes ineffective operator who had been loyal to Pitt through seven difficult years, wrote a pained letter of complaint. He protested that he had not been consulted, that Grenville would not now be easily available to lead a government (a point which Pitt had presumably already quietly noted), and that 'of all things this is a measure the least calculated to conciliate the Chancellor . . . But perhaps Mr. Grenville and Mr. Dundas, who know that the Chancellor does not like either of them, may not be sorry to force him out. I wish this may not end in breaking up that administration on which they both depend.'[21] Pitt knew what he was doing. Having patiently built up his naval forces in readiness for a conflict with Spain, he was even more patiently building up his Cabinet forces ready for a final showdown with Thurlow. Now he would wait for the opportunity to strike.

It was thus amidst Cabinet rivalry, the presentation of a fresh budget and arcane debates on the Hastings trial that Pitt oversaw his next major foreign initiative. The Russians had made peace with the Swedes, but were still at war with Turkey, from whom they had made substantial territorial gains on the Black Sea coast. Unless they could be persuaded to give back a large proportion of this territory much of the earlier British diplomatic success could unravel: Austria would be unwilling to implement the Reichenbach agreement giving up its own conquests, the Prussians would be unhappy with that, and Poland gravely concerned about the expansion of Russian territory. Ewart urged Pitt to recognise that Russia's gains would destabilise the balance of power in Europe: 'Should Russia be extricated from her present difficulties . . . without restoring everything to the Porte, she would probably very soon recover her influence at Warsaw, at Copenhagen, at Stockholm, & even at Constantinople . . . while the influence of the Allies would sink at all those places, in the same proportion; and that unbounded confidence in the naval power of Great Britain, by which Prussia has been & may continue to be directed, would be destroyed.'[22]

British diplomats were particularly concerned about the position of Poland, which had the potential to be a major trading partner for Britain and which needed international support if it was to be a bulwark against Russia. It was envisaged that both Poland and Turkey could join the Triple Alliance, possibly followed by Sweden and Denmark, thus creating an impressive force for stability in Europe.

The logic of requiring Russia to give up some of its gains, in particular the fortress of Ochakov at the mouth of the Dnieper on the Black Sea coast, therefore seemed sound. It was a final and crucial piece of an intricate jigsaw. In early January 1791 a series of complex and interrelated despatches was sent from London to other European capitals seeking varying degrees of support and cooperation to bring this about. This was ambitious, Leeds speaking of a 'permanent System of Good understanding and friendship' for the Continent,[23] but most diplomats were confident; one thought the appearance of a British fleet in the Baltic 'will probably suffice to frighten the Russians into almost any terms that may accompany it'.[24] It also seems to have been assumed that the policy would be readily accepted in Britain. Auckland, who was unsure about the true importance of Ochakov, nevertheless thought that 'nothing can be more brilliant than our position in England'.[25]

In fact, all the assumptions on which confidence in this policy were based turned out to be wrong. The military importance of Ochakov was disputed even by those who had been there, other countries were not motivated by the same vision of permanent friendship and peace to the same extent, Catherine II was not frightened of anyone, and British domestic opinion would prove hard to persuade that seeking the return to Turkey of a fortress in the Black Sea merited the risk of war with Russia. Difficulties began to emerge in February, when the flat rejection of the proposals by Russia was accompanied by uncertain sounds from other capitals. While Prussia joined in pressing the British demands, the Dutch were unwilling to risk a war, the Swedes demanded a subsidy, the Spanish were not prepared to help and the Austrians became markedly less cooperative and were actually playing a double game with the Russians. Berlin and London now looked to each other for assurances of continued support. On 11 March Frederick William II of Prussia sent a message to London insisting that it was necessary either to climb down or to force the Russians to acceptable terms. In London, the Cabinet held lengthy meetings on 21 and 22 March, and did not easily find agreement. Grenville was now doubtful about the policy and Richmond frankly opposed to it, but Pitt and Leeds were for going on. The result was that the Cabinet ordered thirty-nine ships of the line to be made ready for the Baltic and ten for the Black Sea, offered a subsidy to Sweden and ordered an ultimatum to be sent to Russia.

Unlike in previous crises, the approach to war was immediately subject to parliamentary debate. In the Lords, Grenville's defence of the government was accompanied by a most unhelpful contribution from Thurlow, who warned of the lack of allies and the strength of Russia. In the Commons, Pitt was less effective than usual: he was constrained from mentioning British ambitions for extended alliances with other states, and his argument that Turkey was important to Prussia and therefore to Britain was not convincing. Although MPs gave him a majority of ninety-three, the debate was not a comfortable experience for the government and his majority should really have been higher. Neither MPs nor the press could see how the war was going to be fought, or indeed why it should be fought for a faraway fortress of which they had never before heard. The Russian envoy Vorontsov was particularly adept at mobilising public discontent with the situation through the press. Pitt himself was becoming dispirited. Some intelligence suggested that even the Prussians could not be relied upon to join Britain in a war with Russia. He was reduced to saying to Stafford, 'I feel that we have nothing for it, but to go on with vigour and to hope for the best.'

Pitt was now in serious trouble. At Cabinet meetings on 30 and 31 March the split in the government itself became more serious: Richmond, Thurlow, Grenville, Stafford and Camden were all unhappy with the policy to some degree. It was clear Pitt would have to retreat. Facing humiliation, he took the opportunity afforded by Danish compromise proposals to send a message to Berlin requesting that the final ultimatum not be delivered to Russia. Leeds, who had always favoured a hardline approach, would not sign the capitulatory message, and Grenville had to do so instead. Fresh Commons debates on 12 and 15 April gave Pitt majorities of eighty and ninety-two, but afforded much sport to the opposition. Fox, who had his own source of information in St Petersburg, advocated alliance with Russia rather than war against her: 'We had no alliance with Turkey, and were only called upon to gratify the pride of our ministers, and to second the ill judged policy of Prussia.'

Pitt's grand design for European peace had collapsed. He was distressed and, unusually for him, even emotional. Ewart wrote an account of a conversation he had with him at about this time, in which Pitt complained:

> 'All my efforts to make a majority of the House of Commons understand the subject have been fruitless; and I know for certain that, tho' they may support me at present, I should not be able to carry the vote of credit . . . They can be embarked in a war from motives of passion, but they cannot be made to comprehend a case in which the most valuable interests of the country are at stake. What, then, remains to be done? Certainly, to risk my own situation, which my feelings and inclination would induce me to do without any hesitation; but there are unfortunately circum-

> stances in the present state of this country which make it certain that confusion and the worst of consequences might be expected, and it would be abandoning the King.'
>
> After . . . repeating, even with the tears in his eyes, that it was the greatest mortification he had ever experienced, he said he was determined not to knock under but to keep up a good countenance . . . in the meantime he hoped means might be found to manage matters so as not to have the appearance of giving up the point.[26]

Pitt was facing international humiliation and the ruin of his grand design for Europe. Ewart was sent to Berlin to explain that Britain now sought a peaceful compromise with Russia – the Prussians were actually rather relieved. On the following day, 21 April, Leeds resigned. He had not been happy in the Cabinet for some time, and the abandonment of his policy was the last straw. Clearly, Pitt thought of resigning too, but perhaps only momentarily. The defeat he had suffered was analogous to the loss of his Irish propositions in 1785: he had not been able to win sufficient support for a comprehensive and elegant solution to a seemingly intractable problem. This defeat, however, was very much bigger for being on the international stage. Yet he had maintained a decent majority in Parliament, and there was no general call in the country for his resignation. No one else in the Commons could hold a government together against Fox and the Whigs, and George III would certainly not want him to go. In any case, he probably reflected that after so many victories and achievements he was not going to bow out of politics for good in his thirty-second year.

In St Petersburg, the Empress displayed a bust of Fox and acidly observed that 'dogs that bark do not always bite'. She made her own peace with Turkey, keeping Ochakov and a large slice of territory beyond it. The European powers would continue to jostle for advantage in Central and Eastern Europe, leading in only a few years to the destruction of Poland and the continual disruption of alliances against France. A heavy price would be paid for the defeat of Pitt's grand design.

* * *

In June, Pitt moved Grenville sideways to replace Leeds as Secretary of State for Foreign Affairs. As the other Secretary of State he appointed Dundas, temporarily at first in anticipation of Cornwallis returning from India; but Cornwallis had no appetite for a parliamentary role and was in any case engaged in fresh warfare in India. At last Pitt had his two closest and most able acolytes by his side officially as well as unofficially, and he emerged from the crisis with a more united – and talented – Cabinet team. Divided the Cabinet may have been over Ochakov, but it was in the ranks of the opposition that a true schism was now taking place. The French Revolution had continued unabated, with the abolition of titles and the resignation of Necker. Soon, in June 1791, Louis XVI would make his ill-fated attempt to escape, the 'flight to Varennes', and would be brought back to Paris and suspended from his duties as King. In November 1790 Burke had published his denunciation of the Revolution, *Reflections on the Revolution in France*. Events in Paris would soon redefine political debate and allegiance in Britain.

The views of Fox and Burke on the merits of the Revolution had diverged from the beginning. In April 1791, Fox said in the Commons that he 'admired the new constitution of France, considered altogether, as the most stupendous and glorious edifice of liberty which had been erected on the foundation of human integrity in any time or country!'[27] By contrast, Burke argued that the French 'had completely pulled down to the ground; their monarchy; their church; their nobility; their law; their revenue; their army; their navy; their commerce; their arts; and their manufactures', and had shown themselves 'the ablest architects of ruin that had hitherto existed in the world'.[28]

Relations between the two men had deteriorated during the Regency crisis, and Fox had taken little trouble to try to repair them since. In the spring of 1791 a Bill to reconstitute the government of Canada – setting up a lower and an upper province to give English- and French-speakers some measure of independence from each other – was proceeding through the Commons. Fox used some of the debates on the Bill to lavish praise on the French Revolution, and his friends tried to shout Burke down when he rose to answer. As a result, Burke wound himself up to a fury. On 6 May he used a further debate on the Canada Bill to reply to Fox's view of the Revolution, calling him a 'Right Honourable Gentleman' rather than a 'Right Honourable Friend', and saying: 'It is indiscreet at any period, but especially at my time of life, to provoke enemies, or to give my friends occasion to desert me; Yet, if my firm and steady adherence to the British Constitution placed me in such a dilemma, I would risk all . . .' When Fox whispered that there was no loss of friends, Burke continued: 'Yes, there *is* a loss of friends. I know the price of my conduct. I have done my duty at the price of my friend. Our friendship is at an end.'[29] Fox rose to reply, but the tears rolled down his face. Horace Walpole recorded: 'He, though still applauding the French, burst into tears, and lamentations on the loss of Burke's friendship, and endeavoured to make atonement; but in vain, though Burke wept too.'[30]

In the short term this traumatic separation, which Pitt happily aggravated by congratulating Burke on his speech and offering cooperation in the defence of the constitution, did not threaten the cohesion of the rest of the Whigs. Many of those who shared Burke's hostility to the Revolution, such as the Duke of Portland, were still prepared to keep quiet about it and accept Fox's leadership. But a fault line had been opened which would widen as the Revolution intensified.

Pitt and Grenville were determined to stand apart from the troubles in France, but both domestically and internationally the consequences of the Revolution were intruding more and more. In July 1791 five days of riots took place in Birmingham after Joseph Priestley, clergyman, scientist and discoverer of oxygen, held a dinner to celebrate the fall of the Bastille. The following month Leopold II of Austria and Frederick William II of Prussia published the Declaration of Pillnitz, appealing to other European countries for concerted action to restore the French monarchy. This initiative was not welcomed in London: war on the Continent would spell fresh trouble in the Low Countries. Grenville explained that 'His Majesty has observed the most exact and scrupulous neutrality . . . With respect to the concert which has been proposed to His Majesty and to other powers . . . the King has determined not to take any part either in supporting or in opposing them.'[31] Pitt and his Ministers were united in seeking to avoid intervention in French affairs, and comforted by the knowledge that the imperial powers were not planning to take action without the Royal Navy to support them. He was confident that Britain could remain at peace. At a dinner in October 1791, when Burke told him that the French Revolution posed a danger to the other monarchies of Europe, he answered, 'Never fear, Mr. Burke: depend on it we shall go on as we are, until the Day of Judgement.' Burke replied: 'Very likely, Sir, it is the day of no judgement that I am afraid of.'[32] Within a year the slide to war would have begun.

15

The Cautious Crusader

> 'As soon as I had arrived thus far in my investigation of the Slave Trade, I confess to you, so enormous, so dreadful, so irremediable did its wickedness appear that my own mind was completely made up for Abolition.'
>
> William Wilberforce, 1789

> 'If we listen to the voice of reason and duty, and pursue this night the line of conduct which they prescribe, some of us may live to see a reverse of that picture, from which we now turn our eyes with shame and regret. We may live to behold the natives of Africa engaged in the calm occupations of industry, in the pursuits of a just and legitimate commerce. We may behold the beams of science and philosophy breaking in upon their land, which, at some happy period in still later times, may blaze with full lustre.'
>
> William Pitt, 1792

In the grounds of Holwood, where Pitt used to love to cut and plant, a celebrated oak tree lived on into the twentieth century. Only a small stump remains today.* One day in 1787, Pitt sat beneath this tree with one of his closest friends, discussing a subject which was moving rapidly from being an accepted part of the economy to a burning moral outrage: the Atlantic slave trade. The friend was William Wilberforce, who later wrote: 'When I had acquired so much information, I began to talk the matter over with Pitt and Grenville. Pitt recommended me to undertake its conduct, as a subject suited to my character and talents. At length, I well remember, after a conversation

* The spot is commemorated by a stone bench erected by Earl Stanhope in 1862.

in the open air at the root of an old tree at Holwood, just above the steep descent into the Vale of Keston, I resolved to give notice on a fit occasion in the House of Commons of my intention to bring the subject forward.'[1] Pitt enjoined Wilberforce to take up the cause of abolishing the slave trade without delay: 'Do not lose time or the ground may be occupied by another.'[2] He would have been happy, after his tortured conversations with his old friend about the purpose of his life and his role in politics, that Wilberforce had found an intensely political subject with which to occupy his time. Wilberforce the zealous campaigner would provide far more agreeable company and support for Pitt than Wilberforce the agonised doubter.

Finding a purpose for his friend was not, however, Pitt's only motive. Wilberforce would be an eloquent and indefatigable campaigner, and Pitt had already come to believe in the justice of this cause. In the first place, people educated in the late eighteenth century were influenced by Enlightenment values to find slavery morally unacceptable, and Pitt would have known that the two writers he most respected had pronounced strongly against it. Pitt's commitment to freer trade and reformed taxes owed much to Adam Smith; in *The Wealth of Nations* Smith had argued that slavery was an inefficient system of production, for slaves had no prospect of owning property and possessed no incentive to work. In addition, William Paley, whom Pitt described as 'the best writer in the English language', had published in 1785 his *Principles of Moral and Political Philosophy*, including a rejection of slavery. Pitt was highly influenced by such thinking, making it impossible to group him politically with more trenchant or instructive conservative opinion. For two and a half centuries ship-owners had plied their trade in human cargoes across the Atlantic, and for all Elizabeth I's view that such activities would 'call down the vengeance of Heaven',[3] there had been no interference from governmental authority. Now, in the late eighteenth century, the combination of Enlightenment values, the confidence of Christian evangelism, the maturing of the West Indian sugar trade, the growth of European interest in Africa and the rise of a literate middle class in Britain would come together to bring the slave trade under sustained and impassioned challenge.

Wilberforce was motivated, above all, by Christian evangelical values: if the Christian gospel was indeed intended to be made available to all men, then Negroes could receive the Holy Spirit and be saved just as readily as others. While tactical arguments inevitably became important to him, he always saw it as a matter of pure principle. Whatever the practical and economic arguments for it, he could not accept that Providence had intended a trade 'so enormous, so dreadful, so irremediable'[4] to be carried on. Therefore, 'Let the consequences be what they would, I from this time determined that I would never rest till I had effected its abolition.'[5]

The force of passionately held principle was now about to collide with the rock of immense vested interests. More than half the slave trade of the late eighteenth century was carried on in British ships (the rest being mainly French and Portuguese), and in ports such as London, Liverpool and Bristol a huge amount of capital was committed to it. A Parliamentary Commission would find that in 1775 alone, 74,000 Negroes were taken from Africa to the Americas, although the real number may have been significantly higher. The cumulative numbers being enslaved were therefore immense. Economically this traffic reinforced Britain's colonial system in two ways: providing slave labour for the sugar plantations of the British West Indies as well as for other destinations such as the southern United States, and providing a valuable cargo for the hundreds of ships which took manufactured goods to Africa from Britain and could then go on to make large profits on an Atlantic crossing. The human consequences of the trade were unspeakable. The methods by which slaves were captured by traders or rival tribes were bad enough, but that was only the beginning: they were then flogged into the ships and chained in tiny spaces for a three-month voyage. Slave ships were famous for their unbearable stench, with many of the slaves dying in epidemics or driven mad. Whips were used without limit, those who became unfit for work were often killed, with many deaths soon after arrival, and those who survived spent the rest of their lives without property, freedom or hope.

Despite the prevalence of British shipping in the slave trade, slavery had always sat uneasily with British law. An Act of 1750 forbidding the abduction of blacks was not enforced, but a key legal judgement of the Lord Chief Justice Lord Mansfield in 1772 made clear that a claim to a slave as property was not acknowledged by the law of England, and that 'the claim of slavery never can be supported'.[6] Any slave held on English soil was thereby set free, but this did nothing to stop British ship-owners from continuing the trade overseas. It was non-conformist groups in Britain and America who developed the crusade against slavery throughout the eighteenth century. Quakers were particularly at the forefront, starting from 1727 when the London Meeting of the Society of Friends passed a resolution condemning the slave trade and the owning of slaves. By the 1750s the Quakers of Philadelphia had joined in, refusing for instance to transcribe wills for those who intended to bequeath slave property. By this stage Montesquieu's *The Spirit of Laws* had been published in London, arguing that 'The state of slavery is bad of its own nature: it is neither useful to the master nor to the slave; not to the slave, because he can do nothing thro' a motive of virtue; not to the master, because he contracts all manner of bad habits with his slaves.' Yet it was the Christian evangelists who kept the debate alive, including the American theologian Jonathan Edwards and the English founder of Methodism, John Wesley. Their arguments in turn would motivate a new generation, Granville Sharp, James Ramsey and Thomas Clarkson, who together would take active political steps to attack the trade through pamphlets and in Parliament.

1783 was an important year for this work. The Quakers began the first petition to Parliament calling for the total abolition of the slave trade, and a survivor of the terrible events aboard the slave ship *Zong* brought his story to Granville Sharp. Two years earlier, the *Zong* had suffered an epidemic and run low on water while crammed with slaves. The captain, Luke Collingwood, could either sell the sick survivors at low prices in Jamaica, taking the loss himself, or he could make the underwriters pay if the slaves had been lost while the safety of the ship was being secured. For financial gain he decided to throw the slaves alive into the sea, far out in the Atlantic, many of the last batch having to be shackled because they knew what was about to happen.

The story of the *Zong* caused an outcry in Britain among a public who knew little or nothing of the evils of the slave trade. The burgeoning newspaper industry which had enabled Pitt to draw on popu-

Above 'Deliver us from the Pitt of Destruction' (1788). Pitt is shown forcing his way into the offices of the East India Company as he pushed his India Declaratory Bill through the Commons. Britannia is depicted weighed down by his taxes.

Right Pitt in his early years as Prime Minister, by Thomas Gainsborough (*c.*1787). Ungainly in appearance and austere in manner to all except close friends, his exceptional abilities allowed him to dominate the political scene in his twenties.

Holwood House, Pitt's favourite haunt for most of his first seventeen years as Prime Minister. Ambitious plans for expansion were abandoned as his debts mounted.

The trial of Warren Hastings, the result of an unexpected manoeuvre by Pitt, initially attracted huge crowds to Westminster Hall. By the time Hastings was acquitted seven years later, about one third of the Lords sitting in judgement had died.

William Wilberforce, tireless campaigner for the abolition of the slave trade, thought Pitt the wittiest man he ever knew.

William Wyndham Grenville, by an unknown artist (1807). 'That proud man' was Pitt's cousin and Foreign Secretary, but refused to serve in his final administration.

Henry Dundas, Pitt's drinking companion, political fixer and War Minister whose closeness to the Prime Minister aroused much resentment, after Lawrence.

George Rose, one of Pitt's diehard loyalists, who served him assiduously as Secretary to the Treasury.

Hic jacet
The MINISTER endeavouring to eke out Dr. PR.TY...N's Bisho-prick.

Above George Pretyman Tomline, Pitt's tutor, whom he promoted within the Church at every opportunity and attempted to install as Archbishop of Canterbury, by Robert Cooper after Henry Edridge (1814).

Left Pitt's elevation of Pretyman to the Bishopric of Lincoln in 1787 produced much ribaldry. Pretyman had been Dean of St Paul's Cathedral, the dome of which Pitt is shown placing over the central tower of Lincoln Cathedral, by James Gillray.

Above Richard Brinsley Sheridan, the playwright who became one of Pitt's most effective opponents in the Commons, by John Hoppner.

Left Edmund Burke, whose emotional breach with Fox over the French Revolution foreshadowed Pitt's wartime supremacy in domestic politics, by Reynolds.

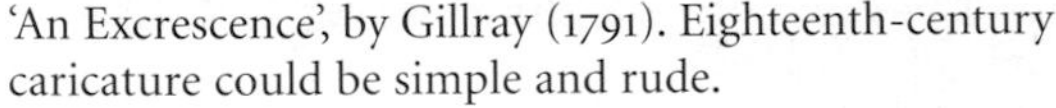

'An Excrescence', by Gillray (1791). Eighteenth-century caricature could be simple and rude.

Below The execution of Louis XVI in 1793 was denounced by Pitt as 'the foulest and most atrocious deed'; war between Britain and France was already inevitable. Print by Faucher-Gudin.

Above Pitt addressing the House of Commons on the outbreak of war, February 1793, by Hickel (1793–95). Fox sits opposite him, and Addington is in the Speaker's Chair.

Left 'Presages of the Millennium', by Gillray (1795). Pitt is depicted as Death, scattering Fox, Wilberforce and Sheridan behind the hooves of his Hanoverian horse, while the Prince of Wales, who was seeking settlement of his debts at this time, kisses his bony backside.

'Promised Horrors of the French Invasion' (1796). Gillray's vivid portrayal of the possible consequences of defeat: Pitt is whipped in St James's Street, the Cabinet and Royal Family are massacred, French troops occupy White's, while a guillotine is set up at Brooks's.

The Battle of the Nile, 1798, by Philip James de Loutherberg (1800). The destruction of the French flagship *L'Orient*, 'by which near a thousand souls were hastened into eternity', came amidst the annihilation of the French Mediterranean fleet.

lar support in his great confrontation with Fox in 1783–84 allowed such reports of the slave trade and the vocal opposition to it to be carried across the country. The following year, James Ramsey wrote two powerful pamphlets denouncing the trade, and the year after that Thomas Clarkson, another brilliant Cambridge graduate, joined the cause. He had won a prize for his essay on slavery and, like Wilberforce, he determined on his life's work in what we imagine as the rural idyll of eighteenth-century England: 'Coming in sight of Wades Mill in Hertfordshire, I sat down disconsolate on the turf by the roadside and held my horse. Here a thought came into my mind, that if the contents of the Essay were true, it was time some person should see these calamities to their end.'[7] It was this combination of brilliant young men with deep religious faith who would form the nucleus of the Committee for the Abolition of the Slave Trade set up in May 1787, which Wilberforce was asked to help. They decided to focus on abolishing the trade in slaves rather than slavery itself, since it provided a far more easily attainable target and threatened neither an immediate attack on property nor a revolution in the West Indies.

By 1787, therefore, the abolitionist cause was well organised, and Wilberforce was moving to its forefront. His opposition to slavery was not new – at the age of fourteen he had written a letter on the subject to his local newspaper – but his utter dedication to the cause now gave him a new focus and responsibility. His first move would be to persuade the Commons to establish a Committee of Inquiry the following year; to that end he and his colleagues began in advance to assemble all the information they could about the economics, practicalities and inhumanities of the trade. Pitt's support meant that information held by the Customs was made available, even though, as George Rose commented, 'It is quite unprecedented to allow anyone to rummage the Custom House Papers for information who have no Employment in the Revenue.'[8] Clarkson began his great journeys across Britain, which would eventually entail interviewing 20,000 sailors and obtaining examples of the equipment used on the slave ships such as branding irons, leg shackles, thumbscrews and instruments for forcing open the jaws of the slaves.

Pitt approached the subject with his usual optimism, encouraging

Wilberforce and trying to follow up the Anglo–French Commercial Treaty by getting Eden to persuade the French government 'to discontinue the villainous traffic now carried on in Africa'.[9] He seems to have had in mind a quick agreement with France to act against the slave trade together, which would reduce domestic opposition to its abolition in Britain and remove the argument that if Britain ended the trade the French would take it up.

On 7 December 1787, Pitt wrote to Eden from Downing Street: 'The more I reflect upon it, the more anxious, and impatient I am that the business should be brought as speedily as possible to a point; that, if the real difficulties of it can be overcome, it may not suffer from the Prejudices and interested objections which will multiply during the discussion . . . If you see any chance of success in France, I hope you will lay your Ground as soon as possible with a View to Spain also. I am considering what to do in Holland.'[10] But Pitt's hopes of speedy international agreement to knock the slave trade on the head were far wide of the mark: opinion was turning against slavery in other countries, but they lacked the popular and parliamentary channels through which opinion could be brought to bear; they also had no equivalent of the Quakers and Britain's Abolitionist Committee. In January 1788 the French government sent a sympathetic but discouraging reply. No international agreement, even in principle, was available. The long grind of the efforts to persuade the British Parliament to act unilaterally would now begin.

In February 1788 Pitt set up a Committee of the Privy Council to inquire into the slave trade. Wilberforce was due to move for a Parliamentary Inquiry in May. As it happened he fell seriously ill, probably with what we now know as ulcerative colitis, and in March doctors feared for his life. Still convalescing in May, he asked Pitt to move his motion for him, giving notice of a motion for Abolition of the Slave Trade to be moved the following year. Wilberforce would never forget his delight at Pitt's undertaking to do so 'with a warmth of principle and friendship that have made me love him better than I ever did before'.[11] And so it was Pitt himself who on 9 May 1788 moved for an Inquiry into the Slave Trade. He did so with great caution, deliberately avoiding giving his own views: a tactic which brought some mockery from Fox and Burke but succeeded in securing the passage of the motion without dissent.

Why was Pitt proceeding so cautiously when he knew his own mind and the case was so strong? The answer is that he faced a situation analogous to his experience on parliamentary reform three years before, and on that subject he had been badly beaten. While he and the leading members of the opposition favoured change, many of his senior colleagues in the government and a likely majority of the country gentlemen of the House of Commons were unpersuaded. They feared the economic and international consequences of renouncing the slave trade. The proponents of the trade were now mobilising their forces and marshalling their arguments: the evidence they presented to the Privy Council Inquiry emphasised the barbarities practised on each other by African tribes, and claimed that slaves were now thankfully saved and transported from situations in which they were previously killed. Pitt faced opposition to any serious move against the slave trade from members of the Royal Family and much of his own Cabinet, including Sydney, who was responsible for the colonies, and, inevitably, Thurlow. Even Pitt's closest confidant in the government, Dundas, was opposed to abolition because of the tens of millions of pounds of assets involved in the West Indies and his view that a ban would be an encroachment on the legislative rights of the colonies. Exactly as in the case of parliamentary reform, Pitt could put forward the case, but he could not insist that the government be collectively committed to it without destroying the government altogether. While he was criticised at the time for not being 'zealous enough in the cause of the Negroes, to contend for them as decisively as he ought',[12] in fact at this stage he was doing as much as he could without actually bringing down his ministry, an action which would not in any case have produced success.

Pitt's commitment to the cause and the difficulties it would have to surmount were vividly illustrated by the events of that summer. A senior MP, Sir William Dolben, one of the Members for Oxford University, had inspected for himself a slave ship lying in the Thames. Horrified by the narrow spaces and shackles he saw, he immediately brought in a Bill to limit the number of slaves who could be conveyed in any one ship to one for each ton of the vessel. The Bill passed easily through the Commons, supported by Pitt, but then hit very rough water in the House of Lords. With wartime heroes attacking the measure and Cabinet Ministers opposing it or sitting on their hands, Thurlow abandoned all restraint and attacked the Bill as the result of a 'five days fit of philanthropy'. Pitt was outraged, so much so that he was indeed prepared to risk the government. He told Grenville that if the measure was defeated in the Lords, 'the opposers of it and myself cannot continue members of the same Government'.[13]

It duly went through, but only narrowly and with many amendments. With Pitt's help, a replacement Bill was rammed through the Commons in a single day (and then again in another day because they had made a mistake); fresh amendments moved by Thurlow were narrowly defeated in the Lords, Pitt apparently refusing to let Parliament rise for the summer recess until the measure was passed. He had got his way, but it had been a pyrrhic victory. If so much political capital was required to get such a minor measure through Parliament, what hope could there be of outright abolition?

The hope lay in eloquence and inquiry. The inquiries of the Privy Council and the Commons' Committee on Trade produced evidence which Pitt thought 'irresistible'. For all the disappointments of the last few years, he still harboured a belief in the power of reason. As for eloquence, it was bestowed in great measure on the principal supporters of abolition: each of three great debates, in 1789, 1791 and 1792, would produce from one of them a specimen of parliamentary eloquence rarely matched through the ages. In the debate of 12 May 1789, postponed by the Regency crisis, Wilberforce delivered his most celebrated speech against the trade. According to Burke, it was 'not excelled by any thing to be met with in Demosthenes'.[14] He brought before the Commons the compelling evidence presented to the inquiries, argued that an end to the trade would make West Indian slave-owners treat the existing slaves better, maintained that the growth of other trade would come to the aid of Liverpool and other ports, and appealed, perhaps naively, to a sense of right and wrong:

> Sir, the nature and all the circumstances of this Trade are now laid open to us. We can no longer plead ignorance, we cannot evade it, it is now an object placed before us, we cannot pass it. We may spurn it, we may kick it out of our way, but we cannot turn aside so as to avoid seeing it. For it is brought now so directly before our eyes that this House must decide, and must justify to all the world, and to their own consciences, the rectitudes of their grounds and of the principles of their decision.[15]

Pitt gave strong support to his friend, but the suspicion that the French would take away British trade if Parliament abolished it remained very strong. Wilberforce had sufficient support for evidence to be heard in the next session at the Bar of the House, but by no means enough to push the matter to an immediate vote. It was tragically unfortunate for the tens of thousands of slaves being shackled in irons each year on the west coast of Africa that the crime against humanity which their treatment represented was brought to the attention of the British Parliament just at the moment that events crowded in on the political world. As we have seen, 1789 brought the outbreak of revolution in France; 1790 brought a general election in Britain and unrest in the French West Indian colony of Saint Domingue, which created fears for the safety of European planters if the much larger slave populations broke free.

The public debate in Britain had continued, with much popular hostility to the trade. William Cowper had published his poem 'The Negro's Complaint',* and Josiah Wedgwood had produced his medallion showing a slave in chains with the inscription 'Am I not a Man and a Brother?' Grenville had replaced Sydney as the Secretary of State responsible for the colonies, and he was a staunch ally of Pitt on slavery. Yet no progress was made in securing commitments from other

* Forced from home and all its pleasures
Afric's coast I left forlorn,
To increase a stranger's treasures
O'er the raging billows borne.
Men from England bought and sold me,
Paid my price in paltry gold;
But, though slave they have enrolled me,
Minds are never to be sold . . .

countries, and when Wilberforce rose again nearly two years later, on 18 April 1791, with a motion 'To prevent the further importation of slaves into the British Colonies in the West Indies', MPs were not yet convinced. Once again, Pitt backed Wilberforce unequivocally: of all the subjects he had had to consider in Parliament, 'There never had been one in which his heart was so deeply interested as the present . . . The slave-trade was founded in injustice; and it is therefore, such a trade, as it is impossible for me to support, unless gentlemen will, in the first place, prove to me, that there are no laws of morality binding upon nations.'[16] But it was Fox's turn to reach the greatest heights of eloquence. He spoke of rape, robbery and murder, detailing shocking instances of the ill-treatment of slaves, challenging the House to 'sanction enormities, the bare recital of which is sufficient to make them shudder'. He summed up: 'Humanity . . . does not consist in a squeamish ear. It belongs to the mind as well as the nerves, and leads a man to take measures for the prevention of cruelty which the hypocritical cant of humanity contents itself in deploring.'[17]

Fox's speech was much admired, but it is a characteristic of the House of Commons down to the present that it can be full of admiration for a particular speech without the slightest intention of agreeing to the recommendations contained in it. Those speakers ranged against the oratory of Wilberforce, Pitt and Fox were far less striking parliamentary performers, but they spoke for a sullen majority. One said he declined to 'gratify his humanity at the expense of the interests of his country, and . . . thought we should not too curiously inquire into the unpleasant circumstances with which it was perhaps attended'.[18] Others once again argued that France, Spain and Holland would step in to take any trade from which Britain desisted. This issue remained the great problem for the abolitionists; Pitt had been right to seek to resolve it at the very beginning, but wrong as it turned out to think it could be done. At the end of the debate eighty-eight Members voted for Wilberforce's motion, and 163 against it.

The abolitionists were not deterred, and determined on a huge effort for the following year. Their campaign would see half a million signatures delivered to Parliament in 519 petitions from all over Britain. Events, however, were not moving their way. The violence and radicalism of the French Revolution were exploding, and the presence of radical elements among the abolitionists made their case more suspect in the eyes of many. Worse still, the slaves of Saint Domingue, encouraged by the ideals of freedom proclaimed in the French Revolution, rose up in revolt and took pitiless vengeance on their former masters, precipitating a war which would continue for twelve years. None of these events reduced in any way the powerful logic of the arguments for abolition of the slave trade, but in practice they made the atmosphere deeply unpromising. Pitt advised Wilberforce to postpone putting a further motion before the House. Wilberforce wrote of people being 'panic-struck with the transactions of St. Domingo, and the apprehension or pretended apprehension of the like in Jamaica, and other of our islands. I am pressed . . . to defer my motion till next year.'[19] Nevertheless, he pushed ahead: on 2 April 1792 the Commons would again debate the abolition of the slave trade.

In spite of Pitt's doubts, he remained true to his friend, and the honours of eloquence that night would rest with him when he delivered 'one of the richest specimens of his own uncommon powers'.[20] Yet before he spoke, Dundas, acknowledged as a defender of the slave trade over many years, rose to propose that the word 'gradual' be inserted into Wilberforce's motion for abolition. His doing so has often been seen by commentators and historians as at loggerheads with Pitt, who later that night would give full-hearted and passionate support to outright abolition. Yet Dundas was Pitt's greatest ally, in conference with him over port almost every working evening. It is surely unlikely that the 'gradual' option had not been discussed or even agreed between them. By speaking for total abolition, Pitt demonstrated his sincerity (which had been much questioned in recent months), maintained his integrity, stood by his friend, and maximised whatever slight chance there might have been of the motion being passed. But by allowing Dundas to propose the compromise, if that is what he did, he allowed the abolitionist cause to escape another direct defeat. The compromise provided a home for the majority of MPs who could no longer defend the slave trade in their hearts but remained fearful of the consequences of immediate abolition. There is no documentary evidence that Pitt and Dundas colluded on this point, nor has there been previous speculation about it, but it would have been neither surprising nor irregular for them to have done so. Such a tactic would have been classic Pitt: maintaining his own 'character' while finding some means of getting his way. The insertion of the word 'gradually' was approved by 193 votes to 125, while outright abolition was heavily defeated by 230 to 85. In subsequent weeks, Dundas would move resolutions naming 1800 as the date for abolition, which after debate became 1796. If Pitt did indeed put Dundas up to his manoeuvre, he could briefly consider himself well satisfied with the outcome. The British slave trade would be abolished, albeit in four years' time, provided the House of Lords or war did not get in the way.

Pitt's own commitment to abolition is hard to question when one reads his speech, delivered at the end of a long debate as the sun rose on 3 April 1792. It was considered by contemporaries to be one of his greatest ever. Without doubt, it brings together the characteristics of his finest efforts: the building up at great length of arguments of overwhelming logic combined with brilliant spontaneity, the delivery of a peroration which could have been months in the writing but was actually on a theme suggested to him by Wilberforce the previous morning, and the enduring tragedy that some of his greatest feats of oratory could not be matched by accompanying executive action.

'Do you think nothing', he asked the Commons, 'of the ruin and the miseries in which so many other individuals, still remaining in Africa, are involved in consequence of carrying off so many myriads of people? Do you think nothing of their families which are left behind? Of the connections which are broken? Of the friendships, attachments, and relationships that are burst asunder? Do you think nothing of the miseries in consequence, that are felt from generation to generation?'[21] He sought to turn the argument about other countries on its head:

> How is this enormous evil ever to be eradicated, if every nation is thus prudentially to wait till the concurrence of all the world shall have been obtained? . . . There is no nation in Europe that has, on the one hand, plunged so deeply into this guilt as Britain; or that is so likely, on the other, to be looked up to as an example, if she should have the manliness to be the first in decidedly

> renouncing it . . . How much more justly may *other* nations point to *us*, and say, 'Why should we abolish the slave-trade, when Great Britain has not abolished?' . . . This is the argument with which we furnish the other nations of Europe, if we again refuse to put an end to the slave-trade. Instead therefore of imagining, that by choosing to presume on their continuing it, we shall have exempted ourselves from guilt, and have transferred the whole criminality to them; let us rather reflect that on the very principle urged against us, we shall henceforth have to answer for their crimes, as well as our own.[22]

He attacked the idea of 'gradual' abolition (which does not mean that he did not suggest it to Dundas as a fallback): 'By waiting for some contingency, or by refusing to proceed till a thousand favourable circumstances unite together . . . year after year escapes, and the most enormous evils go unredressed.'[23] But it was on the future of Africa that he brought his speech to its brilliant close:

> Why might not some Roman Senator, reasoning on the principles of some honourable gentlemen, and pointing to *British barbarians*, have predicted with equal boldness, '*There* is a people that will never rise to civilization – *there* is a people destined never to be free – a people without the understanding necessary for the attainment of useful arts; depressed by the hand of nature below the level of the human species; and created to form a supply of slaves for the rest of the world.' Might not this have been said . . . as truly of Britain herself . . . as it can now be said by us of the inhabitants of Africa?[24]

He concluded:

> We may live to behold the natives of Africa engaged in the calm occupations of industry, in the pursuits of a just and legitimate commerce. We may behold the beams of science and philosophy breaking in upon their land, which, at some happy period in still later times, may blaze with full lustre; and joining their influence to that of pure religion, may illuminate and invigorate the most distant extremities of that immense continent. Then may we hope that even Africa, though last of all the quarters of the globe, shall enjoy at length, in the evening of her days, those blessings which

> have descended so plentifully upon us in a much earlier period of the world.[25]

As dawn broke and the first rays of sunlight shone through the windows above him, he chose two lines from Virgil's *Aeneid* to illustrate the coming of dawn in Africa:

> Nosque ubi primus equis Oriens adflavit anhelis;
> Illic sera rubens accendit lumina Vesper.
>
> And when the rising sun has first breathed on us with his panting horses,
> Over there the red evening star is lighting his late lamps.

Such spontaneity was nothing to the boy who had practised unrehearsed classical allusions with his father every night, but to other parliamentarians it was breathtaking. A few hours later Wilberforce wrote: 'Windham, who has no love for Pitt, tells me, that Fox and Grey, with whom he walked home after the debate, agreed with him in thinking Pitt's speech one of the most extraordinary displays of eloquence they had ever heard. For the last twenty minutes he really seemed to be inspired . . . He was dilating upon the future prospects of civilizing Africa, a topic which I had suggested to him in the morning.'[26]

That morning, Pitt had scaled one of the highest peaks of his eloquence. With such persuasiveness in its aid, how could this cause fail? Yet Pitt would not live to see the slave trade abolished by the British Parliament: 'gradually' would come to mean very slowly indeed. By the time he got another chance to act against the trade, war and illness had taken his mind and his will elsewhere.

16

The View from the Precipice

'Peace and economy are our best resources; and with them I flatter myself we have not . . . much to fear.'

WILLIAM GRENVILLE, AUGUST 1791[1]

'It is indeed mortifying to be exposed to so many interruptions of a career the most promising that was ever offered to any Country.'

WILLIAM PITT, NOVEMBER 1792[2]

WHEN WILLIAM PITT ROSE in the House of Commons on 17 February 1792 to deliver his ninth annual budget, he gave his most expansive, optimistic and confident assessment of the nation's finances. It must have been a proud moment, for this speech represented the culmination of eight years' careful stewardship of the Treasury and a celebration of increasing prosperity: in it were contained his greatest achievements and his dearest hopes. His earlier tax rises had boosted revenues, as had the war on smuggling, but above all a general increase in trade and business was bringing the money flowing in. As the cotton mills boomed, exports of British manufactures had increased by 65 per cent in ten years, a growth that was still accelerating. Duties levied on a wide range of goods – spirits, wine, soap, tobacco, bricks, tiles, starch, paper and printed goods for example – were pouring into Pitt's coffers. This buoyancy he attributed to 'the invention and application of machinery', 'the extension of our navigation and our fisheries', the commercial treaty with France and, above all, the 'constant accumulation of capital', a power identified by Adam Smith which would now act 'with a velocity continually accelerated, with a force continually increased'.[3]

With a budget substantially in surplus, Pitt could make a speech which many of his successors might envy, repaying more of the national debt and reducing taxes at the same time. The taxes to be repealed were astutely chosen: first the tax on female servants, about which Pitt had always been taunted, was abolished; with it went the tax on carts and wagons and the tax on candles. Houses with fewer than seven windows were exempted from the window tax. With the international crisis involving Spain and Russia now over, Pitt lopped £200,000 off the budget of the army and navy, and devoted that sum and more to his cherished project of debt reduction. To entrench it for the future, government loans would henceforward require a corresponding increase in the payments made into the Sinking Fund. It would be only fifteen years, Pitt claimed, before the fund would reach its target and the saved interest payments would be available for expenditure rather than debt redemption. It was this fifteen-year horizon which led Pitt into the statement widely regarded as the most ill-judged he ever made:

> I am not, indeed, presumptuous enough to suppose, that when I name fifteen years, I am not naming a period in which events may arise, which human foresight cannot reach, and which may baffle all our conjectures. We must not count with certainty on a continuance of our present prosperity during such an interval; but unquestionably there never was a time in the history of this country, when, from the situation of Europe, we might more reasonably expect fifteen years of peace, than we may at the present moment.[4]

We now know, of course, that in fact Europe was on the brink of the greatest war it had ever known, and that the first hostilities between Austria and France were only weeks away. Yet at the time it was delivered that February afternoon, Pitt's confident assertion of a peaceful outlook would have raised few eyebrows in Britain. The arch-rival France was paralysed by revolution and seemed incapable of mounting an aggressive war. The rulers of Austria and Prussia appeared to be afraid to act on their hostility to the Revolution without British and Dutch support, neither of which was forthcoming. The Russians might well be preparing the dismemberment of Poland, but Pitt and his colleagues had burnt their fingers trying to settle eastern affairs, and were no longer involved in them. Pitt and Grenville had adopted a new isolationism: in the words of one envoy, 'peace and plenty is the sum of our politics'.[5] At home there had been the first signs of disorder fomented by events in France, and the added worry of a bad harvest in 1791, but the government was clear that an emphasis on peace and prosperity was the best defence against popular discontent. Britain would only enter a war if its vital national interests were threatened directly, and at that moment no country seemed likely to threaten them.

Such was the assessment of Pitt and his Ministers, and by any conventional assessment their analysis was correct. They could not yet appreciate the extent to which conventional notions of power and diplomacy were breaking down. Industrial progress meant that ideas as well as news could now be communicated, and the 'Age of Reason' was generating ideas whose associated fears, emotions and conflicts were not constrained by any balance of power.

Although Pitt had now led the government for more than eight years, he was still only thirty-two years old. He was lively and witty company when he chose to relax, 'a most affectionate, indulgent and benevolent friend, and so easy of access', according to Lord Mornington.[6] Even so, the pressure of events and the rupturing of his original social circle six years before had led him steadily to assume a heavier workload. In the late summer and early autumn of 1791 he was able to escape from London for some time and pay two visits to Somerset while also visiting the King in Weymouth, but for several years the need to deal with foreign crises had kept him in Downing Street or Holwood with few breaks. He was still in good health, although outbreaks of gout had become a little more common: these and occasional colds often led him to write embarrassed letters to his mother insisting any ailment was minor. For instance, he wrote to her from Downing Street on

4 October 1791: 'I am very sorry the newspapers have done so much honour to my Gout. I had in fact just enough for a few days to furnish materials for a paragraph but it was very little inconvenience while it lasted, and has left none behind it.'[7] He continued his enjoyment of alcohol, particularly in the company of Dundas. According to one account, the two of them came into the Commons noticeably under the influence shortly after the eventual outbreak of war in February 1793, leading to the memorable lines in an opposition newspaper:

> I cannot see the Speaker, Hal, can you?
> What! Cannot see the Speaker, I see two![8]

There is no suggestion, however, that such consumption affected his capacity for work. Whether or not Pitt was an alcoholic at this stage, he was certainly a workaholic whose entire life was devoted one way or another to the business of government. This was largely the result of taking upon himself the overall direction of foreign affairs in addition to holding both the senior positions at the Treasury, but it was made complete by the absence from his life at this period of any intimate companion outside the government. Harriot was dead, Wilberforce changed, and Eliot often away. The Duchess of Gordon had receded in her role as a hostess, and Lady Hester Stanhope was still some years from assuming that position. Even Pretyman was now a more distant friend, having become Bishop of Lincoln. Pitt spent his time with the ever-present Dundas, and worked hard alongside Grenville, who in addition to being Pitt's cousin married Ann Pitt, daughter of Lord Camelford, in 1792. In early 1791 Pitt had promoted within the government other close friends who had always been part of his circle: Thomas Steele became Joint Paymaster General alongside Dudley Ryder, and was replaced as a Secretary to the Treasury by Charles Long, another Cambridge friend. The indispensable George Rose remained the other Secretary to the Treasury, but Pitt resolved to make him Clerk of the Parliaments as well, occasioning another angry confrontation with Thurlow.

Among the members of this group Pitt could relax as well as allow his mind to wander over the political scene. Politics and play had been enmeshed ever since he was a child, and were all the more so now.

There is every indication that he was happy for this to be so, but it is also clear that he understood the group's political importance and saw the need to add fresh talent to it. While he was not socially approachable in Parliament, he spent a great deal of time listening to the speeches made in the House or in its Committees, showing a capacity for talent-spotting which few leaders of governments have ever matched. One historian has pointed out that the young Members chosen each year by Pitt for the privilege of seconding the Loyal Address to the King included two future Prime Ministers and five future Cabinet Ministers.[9] It is even more striking that later in the 1790s Pitt's ministry would include four of the five Prime Ministers who would govern Britain for the twenty-two years after his death – and the fifth would also serve with him at a later stage.

A study of 1792 yields two outstanding examples of Pitt's approach. In March, he complimented the young MP Robert Jenkinson, son of Lord Hawkesbury, on a speech which was 'a specimen of clear eloquence, strong sense, justness of reasoning, and extensive knowledge'.[10] As second Earl of Liverpool, Jenkinson was to be Prime Minister for fourteen and a half years in the next century. Later that year Pitt met the young George Canning, who was thought of as a future Whig politician. He invited him to Downing Street, and Canning explained that it was 'personally with Yourself that I am ambitious of being connected'.[11] Within ten months he was an MP, and his attachment to Pitt eventually bordered on the fanatical. Decades later he would be Foreign Secretary and, briefly, Prime Minister.

Pitt's attitude to patronage was selective and certainly selfless. Offered the great honour of becoming a Knight of the Garter by the King in 1791, he suggested that it be given to his elder brother instead. It was only on the King's insistence in August 1792 – 'I am so bent on this that I shall seriously be offended at any attempt to decline'[12] – that Pitt accepted the sinecure of Warden of the Cinque Ports vacated by the death of the Earl of Guilford (formerly Lord North). This carried £3,000 a year and the residence of Walmer Castle on the Kent coast, a place of which Pitt would eventually become very fond. Pitt was full of good intentions about the use to be made of his additional income. He wrote to Eliot, who had suggested that some of the money could help with the further redevelopment of Holwood: 'Your proposed distribution allows me much more latitude than I mean to allow myself, as in this instance I am inclined to apply the whole as a Sinking Fund for some time, and postpone any participation for Holwood until a good deal of debt is paid off.'[13] In spite of this attempt to apply his national budgetary rules to his own finances, the money would in fact soon be swallowed up by his customary uncontrolled personal expenditure.

Holding the wardenship of the Cinque Ports was an obvious pleasure to Pitt, but what was important to him was that he had never asked for such a favour. He was bored by the requests of the aspiring nobility and ambitious clergy whose pleading letters resided for many months on his desk. On the other hand, he never hesitated to use the power of patronage over ministerial appointments and peerages for clear political ends. Officeholders who had gone against him in the Regency crisis were ruthlessly removed at its conclusion, and his generous creation of peerages granted for political loyalty was criticised for inflating the size of the House of Lords. He had already created forty-three new English peerages and would eventually create eighty-nine of them, increasing the size of the Lords by around 40 per cent.[14]

Taken together, the tightened grip on appointments, the rewards for loyalty, and the scouting for new ability are the actions of a man who intended to remain in power for a long time to come. After eight years in office, most Ministers throughout history are nearing the end of their political or physical capabilities. The extraordinary precocity of Pitt's arrival at the Treasury at the age of twenty-four meant that his outlook was entirely abnormal; he was thirty-two years old, and only now seeing the fruits of long-nurtured policies. While he had faced the prospect of dismissal in 1789 and possibly entertained the idea of resignation in 1791 after the Ochakov fiasco, his ambition even at this stage should not be underestimated. His constant awareness of his 'character' would not permit him to hold office in dishonourable or humiliating circumstances, but it was very much his purpose to ensure that such circumstances did not come about.

It is in this light that we should consider his persistent approaches to leading figures among the opposition Whigs from 1791 onwards. He tried to bring in the Duke of Grafton, a grand old man of the Whigs, albeit one who had supported his father, in February 1791. Acting through Grenville, whose cousin Tom adhered to the opposition, he offered three Cabinet posts to the Whigs the following month. These approaches, intended to bring senior Whigs into the Cabinet and thereby to create a powerful new alignment in British politics, are generally associated with the prospect and outbreak of war, but they began early in 1791 when no major conflict was contemplated. They are also easy to link with the growing public disorder of May 1792, since that is when Pitt himself made a determined effort to recruit the 'Portland Whigs' or even the whole Whig Party into the government, but the care with which this was done suggests it was part of a plan. Indeed, Pitt was so persistent over a period of some three years in trying to recruit senior Whigs individually, split them as a party, or annex them collectively, and returned to this course so repeatedly despite several rebuffs, that it must have been a regular preoccupation for him throughout this time.

Pitt's determination to recruit Whigs into the government may shed some light on his otherwise mysterious reaction to the affair of Robert Adair and his visit to St Petersburg in 1791. Adair was a friend and supporter of Fox who arrived in St Petersburg shortly after Pitt's humiliating climbdown in the Ochakov crisis. The Russians evidently showed him key parts of their correspondence with the British government during the crisis. Adair also gave the Russians advice, not necessarily in accordance with the policy of the British government, and passed on to the Austrian Ambassador in St Petersburg a letter from the Russian Ambassador in London, discussing with him the possibility of Austria keeping Belgrade in the peace settlement. This was very much at odds with the position of the Foreign Office. Adair sent reports of all this to Fox, using a code which Fox had given him. These letters were intercepted by the Foreign Office, although it never managed to decode the enciphered sections.*

Ministers had in any case been riled that Fox had a representative

* These sections are written in a 'book code', often used in the eighteenth century. Without longer samples or knowledge of the relevant book, they are almost impossible to decipher.

in a foreign court cutting across the official British representatives. Pitt observed in the Commons that 'better terms might have been obtained at Petersburg, had it not been for certain circumstances of notoriety hostile to the political interests of England'.[15] Grenville had already observed that the idea of opposition representatives attending the courts of Europe 'would go very near to an impeachable misdemeanour'.[16] Not surprisingly, the existence of Adair's letters to Fox containing secret codes was considered within the government to have the potential to be seriously damaging to Fox, whose actions could be depicted as little short of treason. The Foreign Office Under Secretary, James Bland Burges, discussed the matter with Pitt only days before the final Commons debates on Ochakov in February 1792, and believed that Pitt was about to reveal the letters publicly: 'If I mistake not, on Monday the fate of the Opposite Parties in this country will finally be settled, and Mr. Fox and his Adherents for ever ruined and undone.'[17]

Yet Pitt made no public mention of the matter in that debate, nor ever again in his life. Five years later Bland Burges explained to Grenville that Pitt had made him promise not to mention it to anyone but the two of them, and had himself kept the copies of the letters: 'After the meeting of Parliament, Mr. Pitt desired me to give them to him. I accordingly did so, and he locked them up in one of his own boxes; since which time I have not seen them.'[18]

Why did Pitt lock away the evidence that might have ruined his greatest rival? This question has tantalised his biographers, and was not resolved by Pretyman's accusations against Adair in his *Life of Pitt* in 1821 or by Adair's subsequent publication of the correspondence and his assertion that his name was not cleared only because Pitt did not bring the matter up. The most thorough analysis of the subject has been conducted by John Ehrman, who concluded that in all probability it was an act of generosity on the part of Pitt, bearing in mind the sharp reverse he had suffered when pursuing a personal matter against Fox over the Westminster Scrutiny in 1785. This must be admitted to be a possibility, although not surprisingly a politician's mind is more cynical. Certainly there was a risk that the use of the documents might backfire for some reason, making Pitt look vindictive or stupid.

He will have weighed that risk, but he may also have concluded that a successful hounding of Fox would not serve his purposes. For one thing, there had been rumours in 1791 that George III was tiring of Pitt and looking to replace him. For Pitt, Fox was one of the principal keys to the door of Downing Street: as long as Fox was a power in the House of Commons, Pitt was indispensable to the King. Often as he might wish to wound Fox, while George III lived it would be foolish to destroy him. And with or without the King, wounding or destroying Fox made no sense if Pitt wished to bring about a realignment of political loyalties. The intention to bring the conservative Whigs into government was already in Pitt's mind: an all-out attack on Fox's reputation was more likely to turn Fox in their eyes into a friend to be defended or a martyr to be respected than a colleague with diverging views who could be abandoned. Furthermore, Tom Grenville's discussions with Whig leaders embraced the possibility of Fox joining Pitt in government; they foundered on Fox's refusal to serve under Pitt and Pitt's refusal to leave the Treasury. It would have been the ultimate realisation of Pitt's ambitions for Fox to serve under him in government, and for the Prince of Wales to be able to accept a Pitt-led government when the throne was finally his some time in the future. Such thoughts might seem fanciful in the light of the acrimonious years which had just passed, but to write them off would be to underestimate the ambition of a man who became Prime Minister at twenty-four. Nor were these hopes so unrealistic: many of the Whigs finally threw in their lot with Pitt two years later, and nearly two decades later, when the Prince finally received the powers of Regency, he maintained the heirs of Pitt in office rather than turn to the heirs of Fox.

Pitt's suppression of the evidence which could have damaged Fox makes sense against the backdrop of his ambitions. It may be further evidence of the importance he attached to a political realignment. He intended to be in office for a long time if circumstances permitted, and it was in his nature to try to shape those circumstances by looking far ahead. The inclusion of parts of the opposition in the government would not only strengthen his personal position, but would make it more likely that he could enact many of the measures dear to his heart in the years to come. The existing government and opposition sides of politics had been thrown together by the circumstances of 1782–84, and were now an out-of-date mixture of attitudes to a long-concluded war, a distant royal coup, and party leaders at least one of whom was now dead. From Pitt's point of view, a government shorn of Thurlow but including some of the Whigs would be more likely to make progress on issues like parliamentary reform and abolition of the slave trade, and much more likely to persuade George III to accept such things. Such a grouping would combine a belief in the continuity of British constitutional principles with a readiness to make sensible reforms in tune with the times. Coupled with the advantages of sustained peace and expanding prosperity, this would be a tantalising vision, the hope and dream of a still-young Prime Minister.

Pitt's hopes for a political realignment and longevity in office would be realised, but in circumstances which would be the ruin of every other hope he cherished. For within days of his triumphant budget speech of February 1792, Europe began its agonising slide into the abyss.

In March a series of calamities hit European politics. Leopold II of Austria died after an illness of only a few hours, to be succeeded by his more hardline son Francis II. Austria and Prussia published their treaty of alliance and invited Russia, Saxony, Holland and Britain to join a counter-revolutionary war. The latest stage of upheaval in Paris – France would have five Foreign Ministers that year – saw the hawkish Girondin Ministers come to power. It only added to the confusion and tension that Gustavus III of Sweden was assassinated while attending a masked ball. Austria and France were in sharp disagreement over the rights of German Princes to shelter French *émigrés* outside France's eastern frontier.

With the new French leaders believing that war would unite their people behind the Revolution, conflict was now inevitable: France declared war on Austria on 20 April. This raised the prospect of a French invasion of the Austrian Netherlands, but even so Pitt and Grenville were determined to stay out of the conflict. They resisted the friendly approaches of both sides and decided that war in the

Austrian Netherlands would not require British involvement provided the neutrality of the Dutch United Provinces was respected.

Indeed, Pitt's eyes that April were on domestic matters. It was the month of his oration on the slave trade, and a time of growing domestic agitation. Over the winter, radical and pro-reform societies had expanded greatly in membership and had begun to circulate their publications widely. The Society for Constitutional Information (SCI) sympathised with the French Revolution and included Earl Stanhope (formerly Lord Mahon) as one of its leading lights; more ominously, the London Corresponding Society (LCS) and its Sheffield equivalent were claiming many hundreds of members from industries and trades. In February Thomas Paine had published the second part of his *Rights of Man*, calling for revolution and the end of all hereditary government. Within weeks up to 200,000 copies were in circulation, available at sixpence each. In London, radical Whigs such as the young MP Charles Grey formed an association called the Friends of the People to push for immediate parliamentary reform. They secured a debate in the Commons for 30 April.

The debate of 30 April was a watershed for the Whig party and in the life of Pitt. The conservative Whigs declined to support Grey's motion; Fox held his party together for the moment by supporting Grey but saying that 'he should have hesitated' about the timing. It was apparent to Fox that agitation for reform at this moment would spread alarm and stood no chance of success in Parliament. For the same reasons, Pitt now emphatically opposed some of the notions he had himself advocated in more settled times. Pushing for reform now, he told the Commons, could bring 'anarchy and confusion'. He said he 'retained his opinion of the propriety of a reform in parliament . . . but he confessed he was afraid, at this moment, that if agreed on by that house, the security of all the blessings we enjoyed would be shaken to the foundation'. The constitution could not be tampered with at such a time and with unforeseeable consequences, since it was 'a monument of human wisdom, which had been hitherto the exclusive blessing of the English nation'.[19] And so Pitt slammed the door on reform, not knowing he would never open it again.

Against the background of Whig division and concern about

domestic stability, Pitt saw an opportunity to reconstruct the Cabinet. As it happened, the long-simmering feud with Thurlow now boiled over. The Lord Chancellor's behaviour towards Grenville in the Lords had been increasingly rude and dismissive – he had even tried to adjourn a debate while Grenville was on his feet speaking – and he resented Pitt's intrusion into legal appointments. For his part, Pitt had never forgotten Thurlow's perfidy during the Regency crisis.

On 8 May, Thurlow spoke in opposition to Pitt's views on the slave trade, not a new development in itself. It was a week later that he finally overdid it, attacking Pitt's budget proposal for the repayment of new loans, saying that 'the scheme is nugatory and impracticable – the inaptness of the project is equal to the vanity of the attempt'.[20] As a result the proposal was very nearly defeated. For Pitt, this was the last straw. It was also the ideal opportunity to strike – George III could not possibly afford to lose Pitt on an issue affecting the financial stability and credibility of the government. Pitt's letter to Thurlow was to the point:

> Downing Street, Wednesday,
> May 16, 1792.
> My Lord,
> I think it right to take the earliest opportunity of acquainting your Lordship that being convinced of the impossibility of His Majesty's service being any longer carried on to advantage while Your Lordship and myself both remain in our present situations, I have felt it my duty to submit that opinion to His Majesty, humbly requesting His Majesty's determination thereupon.
> I have the honour &c.,
> W. Pitt[21]

Thurlow had always assumed the King would protect him but George III now bowed to the inevitable, writing to Dundas that evening: 'The Chancellor's own penetration must convince him that however strong my personal regard, nay affection, is for him, that I must feel the removal of Mr. Pitt impossible with the good of my service. I wish therefore that the Great Seal may be delivered to me at the time most agreeable to the Lord Chancellor.'[22]

Thurlow was sacked, and formally left office a few weeks later. Now Pitt had the coveted post of Lord Chancellor to add to the tempting fruits he could dangle before certain of the Whigs. He was framing a Royal Proclamation which warned against 'wicked and seditious writings' and asked magistrates to prosecute the authors, printers and distributors of such material while preserving order and 'due submission to the laws'. The proclamation was motivated by genuine alarm among Ministers about the entirely new situation they faced: revolutionary ideas were being circulated in a country suffering from the effects of a poor harvest while war was erupting across the Channel. It also produced, however, the happy side effect of driving a still deeper wedge into the ranks of the Whigs, some of whom thought it an unnecessary overreaction, while others thought it essential. Pitt took care throughout May to consult conservatively inclined Whig leaders such as Portland and Loughborough. He first suggested a Privy Council meeting which they could all attend together, but they saw the trap and suggested they could 'act in concert though not in conjunction'.[23] Once Thurlow had gone, Pitt offered the Lord Chancellorship to Loughborough, along with three Cabinet places and the Lord Lieutenancy of Ireland for other Whigs.

For the moment Pitt had overestimated the severity of Whig divisions. To all of them he was still the unprincipled power-seeker of 1783 who had colluded with George III in removing them from their rightful place in government. While the Portland Whigs would not now oppose Pitt's new measures, they were not yet ready for a breach with Fox, who in consequence was drawn into the discussions. As long as the Whigs continued to function as a party, Pitt's hopes of seducing them into government were up against two powerful obstacles: Fox would not serve under Pitt, and George III would not want him anyway.

Portland tried to edge the Whigs into coalition, arguing that 'the security of the country required it . . . That Pitt was of such consequence in the country, and the Prince of Wales so little respected, that we considered it as impossible . . . to form an administration of which Pitt was not to be a part.'[24] Fox said he was prepared to join in a coalition, but not with Pitt as the nominal head of it. For Pitt this would always be a sticking point. Neither now nor in any later negotiation throughout the whole of his life would he countenance holding any government position other than First Lord of the Treasury. He probably did not imagine that Fox could be brought into the government at this point in any case, but he was so determined to impress his sincerity on Loughborough that he told him that Fox could come in later: 'He was a little apprehensive of Fox's opinions relative to the French Revolution, and hinted that he was afraid he had gone *too far.* That this was an objection to his coming *at once into the Foreign Department.*'[25] This implied that Fox could become Foreign Secretary a little later if some of the Whigs would now take the plunge. Fox, however, was adamant that Pitt would have to give up the Treasury, and insisted on knowing whether the King had been informed of the talks, which of course he had not. Faced with no response from Pitt on these issues, the Whigs concluded, probably rightly, that his main intention was to divide them, and the negotiations broke down. Pitt decided to bide his time. He expressed his disappointment to Dundas that the Whigs would only provide 'half support',[26] but was content for the moment to have sown fresh seeds of division among them.

This initial bout of negotiations had an interesting postscript. Portland continued to entertain the idea of a coalition with some neutral figure at the head of it, and encouraged the Duke of Leeds, Pitt's former Foreign Secretary, to imagine himself in that role. Leeds was bold enough to visit the King on 14 August to put the idea before him, only to find to his shock and embarrassment that George III had no idea such specific talks had taken place, and was horrified by the idea of the return of the Whigs: '*Anything Complimentary to them, but no Power!!!*'[27] Leeds then found himself summoned to see a frosty Pitt, who said, according to Leeds' own account, 'that *there had been no thoughts of any alteration in the government, that circumstances did not call for it, nor did the people wish it, and that no new arrangement, either by a change or coalition, had ever been in contemplation!!!*'[28]

Pitt would have been intensely irritated by the involvement of a former Minister he had been quite pleased to see the back of. His denial that any 'new arrangement' had been in contemplation was, however, stretching the truth a long way. True enough, no agreement had got to any formal stage, but the discussions had been fairly specific. In any event, Leeds was now put off the scent for good.

Throughout the party manoeuvring at Westminster, the government deliberately stood rock-still in foreign affairs, insisting that Britain would remain neutral provided its treaty obligations were respected – in other words, the territorial integrity of Prussia and Holland. In May, Catherine II sent a huge Russian army into Poland. When the Poles mounted a brave resistance they found themselves invaded at the beginning of 1793 by the Prussians from the west. Poland would again be partitioned in a tragedy analogous to that of 1939. Britain had sought her as an ally little more than a year before. Now she was abandoned to her fate, since there was nothing practical any other nation could do to help.

Neutrality was one leg of Pitt's design for continued peace for Britain; the other leg was the effective maintenance of order within the British Isles. The Royal Proclamation of May had produced, as it was intended to, a vast number of loyal addresses from throughout the kingdom expressing support for the government. New army barracks were built near the main manufacturing towns, such as Sheffield, Manchester and Birmingham, to ensure that troops could be more rapidly on the scene in the event of violent disorder. Troop dispositions in and around London were also strengthened. As it happened, the immediate threat diminished. Across the Channel, French forces had fared badly in their attempted invasion of the Austrian Netherlands. Ministers could be reasonably confident that their peace policy would hold. George III closed the parliamentary session on 15 June, expressing the government's priority to secure the 'uninterrupted blessings of peace'.

In fact, the largest spark of all was about to fly into the Continental tinderbox. Prussia declared war on France, and prepared an invasion force to be commanded by the Duke of Brunswick. His manifesto of 25 July was uncompromising and inflammatory: the authority of Louis XVI would be restored, those who defended French territory would face reprisals, and the revolutionary National Guards would not be given the respect of the normal rules of war. The near-universal belief across Europe was that the Revolution would now be crushed by the Prussian and Austrian armies who would sweep into a divided and defenceless France. Ministers in London even worried about the result of such a French defeat, and the possibility that a grateful Louis XVI would join the other imperial powers of Europe in a formidable alliance.

The reality was to be very different. The imminent threat of invasion, combined with Louis XVI's earlier dismissal of the Girondin Ministers, radicalised the French Revolution. On 10 August the Tuileries was stormed, the Swiss guards defending it slaughtered, Louis XVI taken into custody and the monarchy suspended. The elected representatives had now lost control to the direct democracy of the crowds. Liberty was replaced by fear, as Parisians watched the first slicing of the guillotine. The demand was for all traitors to be killed. In the first week of September the prisons were invaded and several thousand of their occupants grotesquely butchered, those from aristocratic families or the Catholic Church meeting particularly terrible deaths. Fired by revolutionary zeal, 50,000 French soldiers blocked the invading army's route to Paris.

Brunswick had evidently expected a relatively easy march to the capital, with a minimum of organised resistance. Having easily mopped up the frontier fortresses such as Verdun, he was in for a shock. At Valmy, east of Reims, the Prussians found themselves outnumbered by the French and at the wrong end of a formidable cannonade. They withdrew from the field, and facing extended supply lines and an epidemic of sickness, Brunswick decided to pull out of France entirely for that year. The invasion had started too late in the year for a conventional military campaign to succeed.

Whatever the military merits of withdrawal may have been from the Prussian point of view, it was a political catastrophe for the imperial powers and the French monarchy. Auckland commented, 'I never recollect any event which occasioned so great and so general an astonishment,'[29] and the confidence of the revolutionaries in Paris rose dramatically. Militarily and politically, the French now went onto the offensive. They invaded the Austrian Netherlands afresh, and sent an army into Savoy (which belonged to the King of Sardinia, who had also joined the war against them). They swept all before them. By 14 November Brussels was in their hands. On 16 November the French issued a decree asserting their right to pursue Austrian troops wherever they fled, a direct threat to Dutch territory. On the nineteenth they promulgated a fresh decree offering fraternity and assistance to all other nations which wished to recover their 'freedom' and ordered it to be translated and distributed abroad. On 27 November they declared the permanent annexation of Savoy, and a week later put Louis XVI on trial for his life.

At the same time, signs of serious discontent became apparent in Britain and Ireland. The wet weather of 1792 had produced another poor harvest. Now the popular Societies were mushrooming in numbers and were talking of forming a national Convention. Some of them sent congratulatory addresses to France on the military victories and the overthrow of the monarchy. Scotland in particular was in ferment, with riots in the major cities and a General Convention of scores of bodies and Societies called for December. Ireland saw food riots, and urban areas of England were said to be 'ripe for revolt'.[30] Rumours abounded of the activities of French agents and secret shipments of arms.

Oddly enough, Pitt had passed most of that autumn relatively at ease by comparison with much of the previous five years. He had spent seven weeks out of London, taking in visits to his mother in Somerset and to his new residence of Walmer Castle. At the beginning of November Grenville too had been away from the capital, a sign that the dramatic escalation of events at home and abroad was not expected by Ministers. In October the French had still been looking for an alliance with Britain, although formal diplomatic relations had been ruptured by the overthrow of the monarchy. In early November Grenville was still insisting that Britain would be able to remain neutral. By the thirteenth, however, Pitt and his colleagues were alarmed. Pitt wrote to Cabinet colleagues summoning them back to London, saying to the Marquis of Stafford:

> The strange and unfortunate events which have followed one another so rapidly on the Continent are in many views matter of serious and anxious consideration . . . However unfortunate it would be to find this country in any shape committed, it seems absolutely impossible to hesitate as to supporting our ally [Holland] in case of necessity, and the explicit declaration of our sentiments is the most likely way to prevent the case occurring . . .
>
> Perhaps some opening may arise which may enable us to contribute to the termination of the war between different powers in Europe, leaving France (which I believe is the best way) to arrange its own internal affairs as it can. The whole situation, however, becomes so delicate and critical, that I have thought it right to request the presence of all the members of the Cabinet . . .[31]

On the same day Grenville asked Auckland in The Hague to make clear that there would be 'no hesitation as to the propriety of his assisting the Dutch Republic, as circumstances might require against any attempt made on the part of any other power to invade its dominions or to disturb its government'.[32] As in 1787, Britain was prepared to fight for Dutch independence.

Historians can only speculate about whether the French would have gone ahead with their aggressive decree of 16 November if they had known of Grenville's instructions of the thirteenth.[33] The slowness of eighteenth-century communication meant that by the time the French knew that Britain had drawn a line in the sand, they had already decided to cross it. Shortly afterwards, French warships entered the Scheldt, and the attitude of British Ministers changed sharply. Grenville summoned the Marquis de Chauvelin, the French Ambassador in London (who was no longer officially accredited but was still present), to make clear the importance Britain attached to her obligations to the Dutch. Naval mobilisation was begun. The policy of 'peace and plenty' was about to run aground.

War was now a likely, although not a certain, prospect. What Ministers knew for certain was that they must suppress and reverse the apparent tide of popular agitation. Disturbed by the radicalism of the press, Ministers ensured that a loyal and supportive new newspaper, the *Sun*, was established in October. In November loyal Associations opposed to the pro-revolutionary Societies were springing up all over the country, the Association for Preserving Liberty and Property against Republicans and Levellers being the most prominent. At the beginning of December Pitt recalled Parliament, necessitated by a fresh Royal Proclamation which called out the militia in many counties. Thomas Paine was tried and found guilty of seditious libel in his absence in France, and an Aliens Bill was announced to regulate the movement of foreigners in Britain. Pitt drew back from other measures such as suspending Habeas Corpus, and by mid-December the atmosphere had become calmer amidst every sign that the weight of popular opinion was loyal to the King and the government.

The social and political condition of Britain in the late eighteenth century was radically different from that of revolutionary France, and Pitt has always been criticised for an overreaction to discontent, but he and his colleagues would have felt themselves to be in entirely uncharted territory, and were without the benefit of a leisurely socio-economic analysis to reassure them. There had been riots before, sometimes at the same time as the approach of hostilities overseas, but never before accompanied by the rapid spread throughout the nation of radical political ideas inspired by the example of revolution in a neighbouring country.

In early December a shaken Dundas was returning from Scotland when a letter from Pitt found him at Northallerton in Yorkshire. Pitt wrote:

> The impression here from calling out the Militia is as favourable as we could wish, and people who a few days ago were inclined to despond begin to tell us that we shall only be attacked for having made so great an exertion when there was so little real danger. I believe myself that the chief danger at home is over for the present, but I am sure there is still mischief enough afloat not to relax any of our preparations, and things abroad still wear such an aspect that nothing but our being ready for war can preserve peace.

Pitt's hardline approach did nothing for the unity of the Whigs. Fox had outraged conservative opinion on 1 December by proposing a toast at the Whig Club to 'equal liberty to all mankind'. He saw the actions of the government as a further step in the destruction of civil and political liberties, adding to the constitutional outrage of 1784. He told the Commons that the danger of popular insurrection did not exist, and that 'we are come to the moment, when the question is, whether we shall give to the king, that is, to the executive government, complete power over our thoughts'.[34] This was too much for the Whig grandees, many of whom supported Pitt's measures. Not for nothing would George III regard Portland in particular as a 'true lover of order'.[35] They refused to vote with Fox in the December debates, with the result that he went down to defeat in the Commons by the crushing margin of 290 to fifty. The break-up of the Whigs now seemed inevitable. Over Christmas the indecisive Portland was pressed by his friends to announce a formal division in the party. He hesitated, but Pitt thoughtfully stuck a knife into the wound on 4 January 1793 by again offering Loughborough the Great Seal as Lord Chancellor. This time he accepted. Pitt's determination to split the Whigs was at last bearing fruit. His determination to keep the country out of the war, however, was proving of little avail.

There can be no doubting the sincerity with which Pitt and Grenville sought in December 1792 to avoid war. For a long time their hopes and plans had rested on it. They held meetings that month with a variety of French intermediaries, particularly de Chauvelin and a senior French diplomat, Hugues Bernard Maret, some of which offered hope of reassurance and conciliation. The authority of the French representatives was, however, often unclear, and their assurances of French intentions towards Holland were belied by the apparent build-up of French troops on the Dutch frontier. Certain sticking points could not be overcome: the British wanted clear guarantees of Dutch territory; the French could not give them convincingly, and insisted on recognition of the revolutionary government.

To make matters worse, a further French decree of 15 December stated that occupied territories would be incorporated into France, that all rivers should be declared open to all nations, and that any country hostile to the French principles of republican government would be regarded as an enemy. The British response was clear: 'England never will consent that France shall arrogate the power of annulling at her pleasure, and under the pretence of a . . . natural right, of which she makes herself the only judge, the political system of Europe, established by solemn treaties, and guaranteed by the consent of all the powers.'[36] The communication of this at the end of December was accompanied by British messages to capitals around Europe, proposing that France be asked to return to her pre-war frontiers and pledge not to foment trouble in other countries; in return the French Republic would be recognised and left in peace.

These proposals came too late to make a difference, and they were not in any case put directly to the French by the British government, partly because formal diplomatic relations had ceased and partly because Pitt needed the cooperation of the other powers in order to make them credible. He was to be criticised later for not communicating this initiative more clearly to the French, but had already discovered over Ochakov the hazards of pressing a concerted policy before it had been agreed. Indeed, the initiative was an echo of the *status quo ante bellum* proposals of 1790–91. It was too late, but it is at least clear that British Ministers genuinely wanted peace. It has been observed that the striking feature of British policy at the end of 1792 is the reluctance to take advantage of an unprecedented opportunity to join with all the other powers of Europe in attacking France and her interests. Until the last moment, British policy remained pacific.[37]

There was probably little more that Pitt and Grenville could have done to stop the slide into war. Negotiations with diplomats lacked credibility when any commitments entered into could be overturned by dramatic and all-encompassing decrees issued to popular acclaim in Paris. The revolutionaries were fired up by their successes and in the business of making sweeping political statements, without necessarily understanding or even noticing the diplomatic consequences of their actions. To the extent that French policy towards Britain was calculated at all, it was almost certainly based on a misreading of British opinion: French agents were greatly encouraged by signs of unrest without understanding the solidity and responsiveness of the British state. The crucial and historical importance of Dutch territory to British strategic interests was also not appreciated in the heady atmosphere prevailing in Paris.

For their part, British leaders were similarly to misread the situation and the capabilities of the French. It was thought that if war came it would be short, and that the hopeless financial situation of the French government would soon limit its ability to wage war. In fact, both the countries now contemplating hostilities against their traditional foe possessed a capacity for warmaking they had never before known: Britain because of an emerging Industrial Revolution which provided factories and finance, and France because of a quickening political revolution which mobilised its huge population and placed the vast resources of state, Church and aristocracy at the disposal of revolutionaries. Both sides were capable of sustaining war for many years to come. Neither understood that this was so.

In early January 1793, Grenville's peace proposals were rejected in the French Convention amidst passionate speeches. The war Pitt had hoped so desperately to avoid now seemed certain.

PART THREE

17

A Tutorial in War

'The more monstrous and terrible the system has become, the greater is the probability that it will be speedily overthrown. From the nature of the mind of man, and the necessary progress of human affairs, it is impossible that such a system can be of long duration; and surely no event can be looked for more desirable than a destruction of that system, which at present exists to the misery of France, and the terror of Europe.'

William Pitt, 21 January 1794[1]

'I particularly represented to Mr. Pitt that . . . by undertaking too much He would do nothing well.'

The Duke of Richmond[2]

The event which took place in France on 21 January 1793 was almost beyond the imagination of those who had known the power of French Kings, the splendour of their courts, and the absolutism of their rule. On that day, shortly after ten o'clock in the morning, Louis XVI laid his head on the block beneath the guillotine. Moments later the exultant crowds cheered the execution of their King. This was the unequivocal answer of the French Revolution to the enmity of the imperial powers of Europe. A reprieve had been rejected in the ruling Convention by 380 votes to 310, Danton later declaiming: 'Let us fling down to the Kings the head of a King.'[3] The rulers of the other nations of Europe were aghast. For them, this act, 'the foulest and most atrocious deed',[4] in Pitt's words, represented the overthrow of all law and authority. The execution of Louis XVI symbolised the confidence and zeal of the revolutionaries: it defied the monarchies of Europe to do their worst.

Pitt's horror at Louis XVI's death was no doubt genuine, but that was not what was causing him to prepare for war that January. For Pitt, the coming conflict was not about monarchists against republicans or the internal affairs of France, but was necessitated by the French assault on the balance of power in Europe in general and on the security of the Low Countries in particular. Of course these factors were intimately connected: the Revolution had created foreign hostility which in turn fuelled both the paranoia and the determination of the revolutionaries – France must take the war to its enemies and ensure that those who would impose a monarchy in Paris would find their own monarchies overthrown. This in turn directly challenged the strategic interests of countries which otherwise preferred to stay aloof, particularly Holland and Britain.

Yet Pitt in early 1793 did his utmost to keep these factors distinct. He was not seeking to overturn the Revolution, but to safeguard the British national interest. As war loomed, he called on France to renounce 'all ideas of aggrandizement' and to 'confine herself within her own territories'.[5] Months after it broke out he was happy to confirm that 'if sufficient security and reparation could be had for this country', he could 'allow their government to remain even upon its present footing'.[6] To Pitt, it was important to be clear that the reason for war was British security and not French royalty. He was no doubt conscious that it was necessary to motivate the British public, and he hoped for a short war in which France would be taught not to cause trouble, even with its changed government. His position was also a reflection of his own honest opinion that the war was not justified unless British interests were directly threatened. He believed, too, that the clear limitation of the objectives should eventually make it easier to find a solution. Pitt's careful, practical and problem-solving mind was at work again, but so was the misunderstanding which would plague him in the years to come: an underestimation of how much Britain's powerful neighbour had changed. It would turn out that the Revolution was an animal that could not be caged. The new political beast now at large would react to prodding and restraint by bursting forth with ever greater fury.

If Pitt underestimated France in the longer term, he was nevertheless clear in his mind after the events of November and December 1792 that war was unlikely to be avoided. He would be criticised by nineteenth-century Whig historians for making war too readily, an accusation levelled by Fox and the Whig minority at the time. Fox acknowledged that Louis XVI's execution 'stained the noblest cause that ever was in the hands of Men',[7] but saw the war against France as the reinforcement of despotic monarchies. He thought Pitt was failing to settle matters by negotiation because 'Pitt in these businesses is a great Bungler.'[8] True enough, there were several conciliatory approaches from the French to Pitt and Grenville in January 1793. Some of the French leaders saw where events were heading, and understood the danger of war with Britain even as opinion in the British government was hardening. But the overtures from Paris were always hampered by their decree of 15 December 1792, which stated that revolution would be instituted in all conquered territories. Pitt's speech of 1 February shows the importance he attached to this:

> They have explained what that liberty is which they wish to give to every nation; and if they will not accept of it voluntarily, they compel them. They take every opportunity to destroy every institution that is most sacred and most valuable in every nation where their armies have made their appearance; and under the name of liberty, they have resolved to make every country in substance, if not in form, a province dependent on themselves, through the despotism of jacobin societies . . . We see, therefore, that France has trampled under foot all laws, human and divine. She has at last avowed the most insatiable ambition, and greatest contempt for the law of nations, which all independent states have hitherto professed most religiously to observe; and unless she is stopped in her career, all Europe must soon learn their ideas of justice – law of nations – models of government – and principles of liberty from the mouth of French cannon.[9]

Concessions were offered to British sensitivities in letters from the French Foreign Minister Pierre Lebrun and Napoleon's future Foreign Minister, Maret, in mid-January. Maret's letter was conveyed to Pitt by an acquaintance of his called William Miles who, somewhat to Pitt's annoyance, had set himself up as a channel of communication. When Miles passed on the letter, which offered to remove 'the offensive matter' in the November and December decrees in return for British recognition of the Republic, he was disappointed by Pitt's reaction outside the Cabinet Room:

> Pitt received Maret's letter with great good humour from me, with all the marginal notes exactly as I had scribbled them, went into the Cabinet with it, and in half an hour came out furious, frighted with the whole of its bile, with the addition of Mr. Burke, who attended tho' not of the Cabinet; and returning me the paper, prohibited me from corresponding with the French Executive Council on the subject of Peace or War. I went away chagrined.[10]

The Cabinet may have known at this time of the extensive French preparations for a further campaign in the Low Countries. Amidst the nuances and concessions of different approaches, they probably decided that they had to be guided by actual events and what was really happening on the ground. A final French diplomatic mission was despatched to London in late January, but was overtaken by events. The execution of Louis XVI was followed by the expulsion from Britain of the former French Ambassador, Chauvelin, under the new Alien Act. His return to Paris precipitated the French into rescinding the commercial treaty with Britain and ordering the invasion of Holland. On 1 February the Convention declared war on Britain and Holland. There was not a single dissenting vote.

The news arrived in London six days later. On 12 February Pitt led the Commons debate on the King's message announcing the beginning of the war. Britain had, he said, 'pushed, to its utmost extent, the system of temperance and moderation', but had 'been slighted and abused'. He concluded:

> Such is the conduct which they have pursued; such is the situation in which we stand. It now remains to be seen whether, under Providence, the efforts of a free, brave, loyal and happy people, aided by their allies, will not be successful in checking the progress of a system, the principles of which, if not opposed, threaten the most fatal consequences to the tranquillity of this country, the

security of its allies, the good order of every European government, and the happiness of the whole of the human race.[11]

Pitt's brilliant reputation had been made in peace. Now it would be tested in war.

Pitt was not by instinct a military man. He had always been an enthusiast for the navy: it was partly due to him that Britain at the outset of war possessed by far the most formidable navy in the world. He had not, however, ever seen a battlefield and had little knowledge of the army, disarmingly admitting in 1794 that 'I distrust extremely any Ideas of my own on Military Subjects.'[12] Nevertheless, he soon busied himself in his typically methodical and purposeful way in preparing for the coming conflict, no doubt hoping that it would be a temporary interruption of his peacetime objectives.

On the outbreak of war in February 1793 he faced three major challenges. The first was the need to deal with the deteriorating economic situation whilst simultaneously meeting the anticipated expenses of the conflict. Government stocks lost over 20 per cent of their value that winter, partly because of international tensions but also because the rapid accumulation of capital which Pitt had lauded the year before had hit a cyclical contraction. There was a sharp rise in bankruptcies, accompanied by a run on the small banks and 'Deputations from every Class of the mercantile World' beating on Pitt's door.[13] He responded in April by deliberately increasing the money supply: issuing new exchequer bills and for the first time permitting the Bank of England to issue £5 notes (£10 had been the previous minimum). These measures helped to stop the contraction of credit and the withdrawal of gold and silver from the banks.

The economic situation stabilised in subsequent months. Presenting his first wartime budget on 11 March, Pitt made permanent the temporary taxes designed to finance the naval mobilisation of 1790, provided for a sharp increase in military spending but, even faced with war, resolved to continue the payments into his cherished Sinking Fund: 'Whatever degree of exertion may be made in the present contest, which involves the dearest and most sacred objects, still we must not allow ourselves to neglect what likewise involves in it the permanent interests of ourselves and our posterity.'[14] Not only would £1 million go into the Fund, but also the extra £200,000 he had allocated the previous year. Pitt's determination to continue the increased payments into the Sinking Fund is a poignant reminder that he and his contemporaries could not have imagined the scale and duration of the conflict then beginning. In time his Sinking Fund project would become discredited, since it relied for its success on the existence of a surplus. If the government had to borrow at high rates of interest in order to repay past borrowings financed at a lower rate, then a Sinking Fund became self-defeating; and it would not be long before these conditions would prevail.

The second challenge that spring was to put into meaningful form the *de facto* alliance of countries now at war with France. In March the French merrily added to the growing list by declaring war on Spain, but the allied powers possessed no unified statement of war aims or mechanism for coordinating their military activities. The task of creating some broad agreement on objectives fell principally to Grenville, and it was not an easy one. Russia and Prussia were busy suppressing the brave revolts of the Poles, and the Austrians were still pursuing their cherished goal of obtaining Bavaria in exchange for relinquishing the Austrian Netherlands. It was thus a fundamental flaw from the outset in what became known as the First Coalition against France that Britain's major Continental allies, Prussia and Austria, were fighting from different motives than those of Britain and Holland. For them, Holland mattered little to their security but Poland mattered a great deal. An independent Poland could become the next centre of revolution after France, or by dynastic merger with Saxony could become a greater power in the region. Alternatively, if it was to be partitioned, then an agreed distribution of the spoils was important to maintaining a balance of power. This preoccupation with Poland was perhaps underestimated in London, and would certainly prove deeply destructive to the war effort in the west. To Pitt, who had to avert his gaze from what he called the 'odious' second partition of Poland in 1793, events in western Europe had to be separated from those in the east. For his allies, however, they were intimately connected.

For the meantime at least, the First Coalition was constructed around a series of bilateral conventions. France was now at war simultaneously with Britain, Holland, Spain, Portugal, Prussia, Austria, Sardinia, the Kingdom of the Two Sicilies, many northern Italian states and many small German states of the Holy Roman Empire. A bankrupt and divided nation was about to take on the combined might of almost the whole of the rest of Europe. The French navy was heavily outnumbered, and French military operations were plagued by workers' strikes and administrative collapse. In theory the army could command 270,000 men, but already they faced 350,000 allied soldiers preparing to attack them on four fronts. It is little wonder that Ministers in London thought the war would be over in one or two campaigning seasons.

The conduct of finance and the construction of alliances were nothing new to Pitt, but the third major challenge he faced that spring required something new of him. This was the choice of how to deploy the available British forces in Europe and around the world. At full strength, the navy could put more than six hundred vessels to sea, manned by more than 100,000 men. The army, however, was very small – fewer than 14,000 men in the British Isles with perhaps twice as many again deployed to India and the West Indies. Its leadership and professionalism were at a low ebb and it possessed neither the size nor the capability to make a major contribution to a land war. The quickest and traditional way for eighteenth-century Britain to fight in Europe was to hire German mercenaries; this tradition was now continued, with the employment of 14,000 troops from Hanover and eight thousand from Hesse. Financial muscle and naval might were what Britain could bring to the war: not surprisingly Pitt, Dundas and Grenville considered they could emulate the great Chatham by blockading France, taking away her colonies such as those in the West Indies whose economic value could be transferred from France to Britain, while leaving most of the Continental fighting to others who were happy to be paid for it.

If this was indeed the strategy it contained one major defect in its conception: it would not of itself deliver any knockout blow against

France. The Duke of Richmond seems to have been alone in arguing for all forces to be concentrated on a thrust into north-west France to support the royalists in that region and face the French with yet another front. It also contained a defect in its execution: Ministers were easily diverted from it when unexpected pressures arose elsewhere. For the French now took the initiative, invading Holland in late February and presenting the Dutch with an immediate crisis. Pitt and Dundas decided to send across the Channel what little reserves they had, 1500 men from the Brigade of Guards. As it turned out, the French were heavily defeated by the Austrians twice in the course of March, removing the immediate threat to Holland. But Britain had now begun a commitment to the campaign in the Low Countries from which it would not be possible to withdraw. Furthermore, the British troops on the Continent had been hurriedly put under the command of the Duke of York, George III's twenty-eight-year-old second son, who had been in place to command the Hanoverians, who were not yet ready. As a result, he would come to command a steadily larger force, despite lacking the authority and the military experience to do so successfully.

It is therefore evident that in the opening weeks of the war the seeds of future military and diplomatic failure were being liberally sown. For the moment such problems were masked by the success of allied armies. The French were expelled from Belgium and were soon besieged by the Austrians and Prussians in Valenciennes, Condé and Mainz. More British troops were sent over to enlarge the Duke of York's army and permit him to begin an advance into French territory with the objective of taking Dunkirk on the Channel coast. In the Pyrenees too, the French were coming under pressure. Rebellion brewed in many provinces of France. Pitt seemed to have every ground for his usual optimism. Domestic opposition to the war was limited to Fox and a diminishing group of friends. The latest motion for parliamentary reform was massively defeated in the Commons. It must have seemed a picture of steady progress in the war and relative tranquillity at home.

Yet the allies were fighting a new type of war in an old-fashioned way. The sieges on France's borders were further inflaming the Revolution without killing it, and while many governments might have sued for peace when surrounded by a formidable coalition advancing on several fronts, the new revolutionaries were neither willing nor even able to do so. In the British Cabinet, Richmond chafed at the absence of any decisive blow. He thought that if everything was thrown into north-west France Britain 'might be able at once to terminate this War'.[15] He pressed for a withdrawal of British troops from Flanders, telling Pitt he was trying to do too much by dividing the forces between Flanders, the Mediterranean, the West Indies and plans for coastal raids on France: 'I stated to Mr. Pitt that I thought He was going on much too fast in His Calculations. That men just raised upon paper were not soldiers . . . I particularly represented to Mr. Pitt that very proper [as] His schemes & Ideas were they were much too vast to be executed within any Thing like the Time He talked of. That . . . by undertaking too much He would do nothing well.'[16] The truth was that, in common with that of other nations, British policy was partly being directed with post-war ends in mind. Seizing the rest of the West Indies would cement Britain's maritime and financial power, while fighting in Flanders would help to entrench the Austrians in Belgium and diminish the chances of a Bavarian exchange.

The allied success on the frontiers, coupled with low French morale (their highly respected commander in Flanders, Dumouriez, defected to the Austrians), now turned up yet another notch the violence of the ever-escalating Revolution. Suspicion of treachery reached boiling point amidst rumours of the workings of 'Pitt's gold' – a term applied both to British subsidies to Continental powers and to suspected bribery of French officials. All who had advocated moderation in the course of the Revolution fell under suspicion. On 2 June 1793 the Girondin Deputies found their exit from the Convention barred by 150 cannon, and handed many of their colleagues into custody. Robespierre and the Jacobins took power and began the reign of terror. In the coming months, Parisians would witness the ceaseless descent of the guillotine ending the lives of political prisoners, the Girondin leaders, failed Generals and Louis XVI's Queen Marie Antoinette alike. Wealth was confiscated, Christianity abolished and all normal social and economic rules swept away. In the middle of it all a resolution was passed declaring William Pitt an enemy of the human race.

The triumph of the Jacobins sparked an upsurge of rebellion, some of it royalist in nature, not only in the Vendée but also in Marseilles, Lyons and Toulon. Yet the destruction of all traditional institutions and responsibilities also provided the chance for France to be the first nation in the modern world to wage total war. On 23 August 1793 the Convention declared that:

> From this moment until that in which our enemies shall have been driven from the territory of the Republic, all Frenchmen are permanently requisitioned for service in the armies. The young men shall fight; the married men shall forge weapons and transport supplies; the women will make tents and clothes and will serve in the hospitals; the children will make up old linen into lint; the old men will have themselves carried into the public squares to rouse the courage of fighting men, to preach the unity of the Republic and hatred of Kings . . .[17]

This was the beginning of the *levée en masse* which through the 1790s would see France call up for military service at least one and a half million men, the greatest such number the world had ever seen. In the spring and summer of 1793 alone, half a million men became available for service, ruthlessly organised from the centre by Lazare Carnot, wielding the dictatorial powers of the Committee of Public Safety. In the words of one historian, 'The people had appropriated the absolutist heritage and taken the place of the King.'[18] Western Europe's most populous nation became wholly mobilised for civil and external war.

From this moment on, the two sides in the war fought with an entirely different level of intensity and commitment. On the one side were imperial powers seeking to contain France, maintain or adjust a balance of power, and keep one hand free for Poland or the West Indies. On the other was a huge population fighting for national survival and ideological objectives, and driven by all-pervading fear. When the fortress cities on the borders duly fell to the Austrians and Prussians, fully 25,000 French troops were allowed to march out of them with the traditional honours of war, on condition they no longer fought against the allied powers. But the French were not playing by these old-fashioned rules. The troops in question were marched to the Vendée and elsewhere to crush peasant uprisings with the utmost ruthlessness.

Once more the forces of the Revolution were about to go violently onto the offensive, this time with the Duke of York's advance on Dunkirk in their path. York cannot be fully blamed for what happened after he laid siege to Dunkirk in August: some British forces intended for his army had been diverted to the Mediterranean as Pitt sought to stretch his small forces still further, the siege train of heavy guns was late in arriving due to confusion at the Admiralty, and the Prussians called off an offensive which would have drawn French forces away from Dunkirk because they resented the Austrian advance into Alsace. Thus the problems which characterised the allied war effort were all present, as was the renewed vigour of the French. The British heavy guns arrived just in time to be abandoned in early September, as the Duke of York's 14,500 men fell back before 45,000 French under General Jean Houchard. Days later, Houchard defeated another allied force under the Prince of Orange. By the end of that year northern France would again be free of the enemy. The most salutary illustration of the contrasting cultures of the two sides is that while the beaten allied commanders retained their posts, Houchard was guillotined for failing to pursue the enemy with sufficient aggression. The power of numbers and terror was beginning to tell.

Pitt reacted to the defeat at Dunkirk with his customary optimism and resilience: 'It is certainly a severe check,' he wrote to Rose, 'but I trust only a temporary one; and it ought only to have the effect of increasing, if possible, our exertions.'[19] He had certainly learnt one or two lessons himself, since his way of doing business through personal intervention and failure to take minutes had probably contributed to the failure to provide timely naval assistance at Dunkirk, because a promise to the army Chief of Staff to investigate what could be done was not followed up;[20] from then on, as another biographer has pointed out, 'He saw commanders before they embarked, but ceased to correspond with them in the field.'[21] His innate optimism, which had probably been strengthened by his many peacetime successes against the odds, was reinforced by the surprise news shortly after the retreat from Dunkirk that British forces had taken possession of the Mediterranean port of Toulon after being invited to do so by the local population. Ministers were delighted by the news, dining the next night 'in the highest spirits' on a good deal of turtle and claret, with Pitt considering this blow to the French 'in every view the most important which could be struck towards the final success of the war'.[22]

He and Dundas were determined to use Toulon as a base for expanded operations in the south of France. With the expedition for the West Indies about to sail, however, York embattled in Flanders, and other forces being assembled to assist royalists in Brittany, the troops required simply did not exist. Nevertheless, Pitt set out to find them, almost as if he was inventing a new tax or fund with which to balance the budget. On 16 September he drew up a list showing how 34,000 troops could be found for Toulon, including items such as five thousand Hessians from Flanders, six thousand Neapolitans, three thousand Spanish and so on. His memo concluded: 'It seems not unreasonable to expect that, by the Beginning of next year, there may be an army in the south of France of near 60,000 men.'[23]

What followed revealed four common problems with the allied campaign. First, the numbers set down on paper never existed in reality. The effective forces engaged in the defence of Toulon would never exceed 12,000 (not 34,000), with around two thousand British among them (not 6,200). Secondly, allied commitments could not be relied on – the Austrian contingent only set off after the battle was over. Third, distant Ministers did not always appreciate whether a particular town or city was militarily defensible. Toulon is a port at the mercy of the hills and peninsula around it, and could not be held against a large army. Fourth, cooperation with French royalists raised a delicate question of whether Britain shared their objectives. Pitt and Grenville were soon differing over the emphasis to be placed on this, with Grenville resisting any public commitment towards the restoration of monarchy as an objective, while Pitt was prepared to say when sending Sir Gilbert Elliot as Commissioner to Toulon that Britain was not precluded from dealing with other forms of 'regular Government', but that monarchy was 'the only one from which we expect any good, and in favour of which we are disposed to enter into concert'.[24]

It is hard to escape the conclusion that the British war effort in 1793 suffered from the lack of a consistent strategic thrust. Furthermore, the mismatch between chosen objectives and the materials available to deliver them was itself a failure of strategy. Pitt ran the war through Dundas, who as Secretary of State for Home Affairs and the Colonies had direct responsibility for it, and through Grenville as Foreign Secretary. Their efforts in these early stages suffered from inexperience and a tendency to interfere in operational matters, which combined with Pitt's naturally optimistic nature to produce unrealistic assumptions. On the other hand, Pitt brought to the leadership of the war effort his usual diligence and capacity for controlling government departments. Through his two Secretaries of State he oversaw the whole effort of the British state in a way Lord North in the American War of Independence would never have contemplated. He even deputised for them if they were away, writing to Grenville, who had borrowed Walmer Castle for a holiday in October 1793: 'You need have no scruple in sending me as much business as you please, as . . . I have at present nothing to do.'[25]

As usual, when the burden of work increased, Pitt's controlling nature led him to take more of it upon himself. Wilberforce's diary depicts him racing back and forth between Holwood and Downing Street: 'June 22. To Holwood with Pitt in his phaeton – early dinner, and back to town,' and a little later, 'To town, 14th of September, to see Pitt – a great map spread out before him.'[26] But Pitt's mind was not as easily adapted to warfare as had been that of his father, who thrived on it, or as would be that of Winston Churchill, who had concerned much of his life with it. Grenville would later complain that in military matters 'he has very little knowledge of that detail, and still less habit of applying his mind to it, and his sanguine temper is very apt to make him think a thing *done* in that line when it has been shown that it *may be done* whereas unfortunately the difference is infinite'.[27]

In Pitt's defence, his strategy was evidently to employ Britain's naval and financial strengths while using the army wherever possible to discomfort the French and give encouragement to allies. Since the defeat of France on land could only be accomplished through the success of Continental armies, this approach was by no means irrational. It was designed to produce minimum risk during a short war and maximum leverage at the end of it, and if the French had duly collapsed before the weight of Austrian and Prussian columns in 1793, the British strategy would no doubt have been thought entirely appropriate and successful. It may have been a mistake that the government allowed British forces to be drawn ever more deeply into the Low Countries, and it was certainly a major failure that the assault on Dunkirk was seriously delayed. No doubt too, Pitt and his colleagues would have been wiser to think twice before investing their resources and credibility in Toulon. In each case, however, they faced agonising decisions: inaction on the Low Countries would have been strange for a country which went to war specifically to defend them, and a refusal to try to make the most of the uprising in Toulon would have sent a signal to all potential rebels against Paris that Britain could not help them even when it had a large fleet outside the harbour. The alternative strategy advanced by the Duke of Richmond, throwing everything into an invasion of the Vendée in the north-west, could only have succeeded in ending the war if accompanied by successful allied advances into eastern France. As these did not happen, it is probable that no conceivable British strategy in 1793 would on its own have brought France to her knees.

In being the first head of the Treasury directly to coordinate the conduct of a war, Pitt was accelerating the constitutional development of a true Prime Minister. He was now thirty-four years old, and had been at the nation's helm for nearly ten years. The pressures of 1793 intensified his worst habits and occasional ailments: a harbinger of far worse to come in the years ahead. Even more letters than usual went unanswered, Rose recording in his diaries that with so much going on, 'It is no wonder that the trivial impertinences of some of his correspondents, and the importunities of others, did not meet sometimes with that attention which in their self-complacency they thought their due. But as most people resent the appearance of being slighted or neglected, this was the source of much dissatisfaction and unpopularity.'[28] Pitt's reliance on alcohol was also becoming a little more noticeable. He himself was worried that his liberal imbibing on a visit to the Corporation of Canterbury with Addington in September 1793 would produce adverse comment in the papers. As it was, Addington recalled that the *Morning Chronicle* 'only stated that the Chancellor of the Exchequer was observed, in walking to his carriage, to oscillate like his own bills'.[29] His young protégés noticed the change, Canning saying after a dinner a few months later that Pitt drank 'I know not how much madeira',[30] and Jenkinson commenting that 'The first visible effect of Public Affairs upon his Health was in the Autumn of 1793 after the retreat of the British army before Dunkirk.'

The principal manifestation of the effect on his health was the more frequent recurrence of gout from the summer of 1793 onwards. As usual, Pitt was always anxious to reassure his mother whenever he was ill that he was actually fine. He wrote from Holwood in June: 'The Gout, after having made a visit in due form, and staid [sic] a reasonable time, is now taking its Leave. I was able without any inconvenience to come here yesterday Evening, and your Letter found me enjoying a fine day from my window.'[31] A month later he writes: 'I have Holidays enough for a good deal of Country air, and have the advantage of having parted with my Gouty shoe, and found the full use of my legs.'[32] Two weeks later, he is hoping to visit his mother at Burton Pynsent: 'I think I may be at liberty in about a Fortnight, but I should wish to regulate my motions a little by Eliot's and Lord Stanhope's, tho not exactly in the same Way by each of them.'[33] In other words, he wanted to be with his mother at the same time as his friend Edward Eliot, but definitely not at the same time as his cousin Stanhope who had supported the French Revolution. Pitt hated the idea of his mother being anxious, either about his health or her own finances. Later that year he again sent her money, blithely assuring her in spite of his mounting debts that it was no problem: 'I can furnish without difficulty three hundred Pounds, and will immediately desire Mr. Coutts to place that sum to your account . . . I trust you will never scruple to tell me when you have the slightest occasion for any aid I can supply.'[34]

The late summer provided something of a lull in the administrative bustle of 1793. Pitt managed a visit to Burton Pynsent in August, and spent some time at Walmer in September, taking the sea air and shooting partridges while the despatches went back and forth. He had not forgotten domestic politics, and had once again that summer attempted to pick off some of the ablest and most conservative Whigs by inviting them to join the government. Windham was offered the Home Office to spread some of Dundas's burden, and Earl Spencer was offered the Lord Lieutenancy of Ireland. Pitt needed more ability in his government, and he had not forgotten his longer-term aspirations. For now he was once again rebuffed, but once again he would bide his time. In the meantime, plans were being made for the military campaigns of 1794: Pitt must have dearly hoped that autumn that the next news from Belgium or Toulon would be of victories, and that within a year he could go back to presiding over 'peace and plenty'.

It was not to be. By November not only were the Austrians being cleared from French territory in the north, but the situation in Toulon was becoming critical. The reinforcements Pitt had sketched out on paper had failed to materialise, and the 12,000 allied soldiers fit for duty were soon facing 30,000 French who had moved on from suppressing the rebellions in Lyons and Marseilles with pitiless harshness. Pitt's perennial optimism – he wrote on Christmas Day 'there is still a very good chance of all proving right in that quarter'[35] – was misplaced. He did not know that eight days earlier, after weeks of bitter internal arguments and mounting losses, Admiral Lord Hood, who had tried to organise the defence of Toulon, ordered its evacuation. It was a sickening scene, soldiers, civilians and children screaming and scrambling for the boats, the navy trying to destroy some of the twenty-two French ships of the line which had been captured in port while taking on board 15,000 royalist refugees who knew what fate awaited them if left behind. Many drowned, thousands were indeed left behind and executed. By Christmas Toulon was back in the hands of a vengeful French army. The cost of its four-month defence, in human life, military hardware and political credibility, had been high. Meanwhile, troops held back from Toulon in order to make a landing in the Channel and join French rebels in Brittany failed to link up with the rebel force, and by mid-January 1794 were heading back home while the rebels were defeated.

As the New Year began, the forces of the French Revolution had held or expelled the armies of the First Coalition on every front, while simultaneously suppressing major revolts and hugely increasing their own strength. The French had successfully exploited the advantages of superior numbers and interior lines of communication and supply, giving them an ability to move large forces to the right point which could not be matched by their disparate and far-flung enemies. They had succeeded in creating a culture of total war, with an army in which failure was drastically penalised and merit rewarded: 275 French Generals were dismissed in the course of 1793. By contrast, the allies often appeared to focus more on the post-war world than on the war itself: Prussia and Austria seemed to fear that too great an effort would leave them vulnerable to the other at a later stage. Above all, the Continental allied powers were preoccupied by Poland, Austria looking over its shoulder while huge Prussian and Russian forces were committed there. To British observers this was a squalid land-grab; to the imperial courts it was a battleground as vital for their future stability and security as the frontiers of France. Whatever the justification, the effect was undeniable: revolutionary France was stronger at the end of 1793 than it had been at the beginning. Richmond had feared earlier that year 'that the moment is so critical and pressing, that if time is given, France, with her Resources, may recover'.[36] The opportunity for a quick victory had passed.

Pitt could have been forgiven if he had wept. Yet in fact his belief that a rapid victory could be achieved was still strong. He knew the importance of finance, and he considered the French to be unable to escape the consequences of bankruptcy. Wilberforce recalled: 'How well do I remember his employing in private, with still greater freedom and confidence, the language which in a more moderate tone he used in the House of Commons, that the French were in a gulf of bankruptcy, and that he could almost calculate the time by which their resources would be consumed!'[37]

Furthermore, Pitt's experience of Britain left him unable to believe that a government based on expropriation and arbitrary murder could endure. The French were only 'compelled into the field by the terror of the guillotine', and as a result would not maintain their exertions.

'On this ground, the more monstrous and terrible the system has become, the greater is the probability that it will be speedily overthrown. From the nature of the mind of man, and the necessary progress of human affairs, it is impossible that such a system can be of long duration; and surely no event can be looked for more desirable than a destruction of that system, which at present exists to the misery of France, and the terror of Europe.'[38]

Pitt spoke these words in the House of Commons in January 1794. That same month the government received intelligence reports of growing unrest around Britain and a plan by radicals to call a national convention. Much as he might predict the speedy collapse of France, it was at home that Pitt now had to contemplate the danger of insurrection.

18

Frustrations of Supremacy

> 'I mean to submit to the house, that at the present moment, perseverance in the contest is more wise and prudent, and more likely in the end to effect a safe, lasting, and honourable peace, than any attempt at negotiation.'
>
> WILLIAM PITT, 27 MAY 1795[1]

THE FAILURE TO GAIN a decisive advantage over France in 1793 was arguably the single most calamitous occurrence in the life of Pitt, for from it so much of the pain and tragedy of later years unfolded. On the surface, as we have seen, he retained his sanguine disposition. Jenkinson noted that 'I never saw any Public Man who appeared so little desponding or who bore up so firmly against misfortunes. He had particularly the faculty of laying his cares aside, of amusing himself with an idle book, or a comparatively trivial conversation, at the time he was engaged in the most important business, & I have heard him say that no anxiety nor calamity had ever seriously affected his sleep.'[2] But as the war progressed Pitt would find it harder to sleep soundly, and from 1794 onwards the opportunities for enjoying trivia and idle books would become rarer: 'I am however fully persuaded that the public misfortunes which he was doomed to witness had the most sensible effect in undermining his Constitution.'[3] The mental pressures would now become intense, and would begin to take a physical toll.

1794 opened with a dramatic multiplication of the threats which Pitt had to face: the military situation was more daunting, the unity of the anti-French coalition was faltering, the possibility of an invasion of the British Isles growing, the appearance of domestic rebellion mushrooming, and the carefully calibrated budgetary plans of previous years were broken beyond repair. Such a situation was no longer a mere interruption of routine, but required an entirely new level of effort and concentration. To a mind which was apt to concentrate on one subject at a time it would mean strain, and to a man who felt he must control the whole of the essential business of government it would mean a workload of crushing weight.

Pitt's declaration that a government based on terror would be overthrown was the centrepiece of his speech at the opening of Parliament on 21 January 1794. It is perhaps revealing that his confidence in victory was predicated on the internal collapse of the enemy rather than the military success of the allies. His new emphasis on the criminal nature of the French regime not only enabled him to avoid the hazarding of military predictions, but helped to unite what was becoming a domestic coalition under his leadership. Fox that day had moved an amendment to the King's Speech calling for 'peace with France . . . without any reference to the nature or form of the government that might exist in that country'.[4] The continued opposition of Fox to the 'madness' of the war, which he claimed had been started 'by artifice'[5] and ought to result in French success as 'the least Evil of any that can happen',[6] was finally driving the conservative Whigs into Pitt's long-since opened arms. Fox's amendment mustered only fifty-nine votes in the Commons, after Portland the previous night had chaired a meeting at Burlington House which had decided to give 'a full, firm, unequivocal support, both of the war and of its conductors'.[7] A formal coalition, involving the political realignment Pitt had sought for three years, would have to await the end of the parliamentary session, when ministerial responsibilities could more readily be changed, but from now on such a coalition was highly likely. The formal break-up of the Whigs who had followed Rockingham and Fox had begun.

Pitt thus enjoyed a supremacy in British politics which the eighteenth century had never before witnessed. The opposition in the Commons was reduced to a rump, and many of those would later cease to attend on a regular basis, while in the Lords it was literally down to a handful. In the years after 1784 Pitt had struggled with an unreliable parliamentary majority, but the affairs of the nation nevertheless prospered. The years after 1794 brought the reverse: his majority on almost every question was stable and massive, while the state of the nation moved from difficult to dire.

The army was being hugely expanded, although it remained very small on its own compared to that of France. The 1794 Estimates provided for 175,000 regular troops, 34,000 German mercenaries and nearly 100,000 militia and Fencibles (essentially mounted militia). Such expansion, combined with the full mobilisation of a navy with well over a hundred ships of the line, blew Pitt's previous budgetary projections to pieces. His new budget required the raising of an £11 million loan along with additional taxes on items such as rum, spirits, bricks, tiles and plate glass.

But the central question was not so much how the forces were to be paid for, as how they should be employed. An expedition had sailed for the West Indies the previous November, and by May had taken possession of the French colonies of Martinique, St Lucia and Guadeloupe in addition to Tobago, captured the previous year. In the Mediterranean Hood's fleet was overseeing a British attack on Corsica, where despite the rivalry between the army and the navy, May saw a major victory with the fall of Bastia. In addition, much time was spent by the Cabinet in February and March considering home defence, as a response to many rumours of an imminent French invasion. Troops and militia in the south-east of England were reinforced, and gunboats and floating batteries positioned along the coast. Other troops were held ready for renewed attempts to link up with royalist rebels in north-west France, and many others were being trained and equipped.

In the light of so many far-flung deployments, the British contribution to the war on the Continent in 1794 could be substantial but by no means immense. Forty thousand troops, many of them Germans in British pay, were envisaged for an allied army of over 300,000 which would provide the main thrust through Flanders into the heart of France. This time a huge knockout blow was envisaged, without the permanent siege warfare of 1793. The Austrian Emperor, Francis II, would himself arrive at the front in April and be on hand to mastermind this climax to the war. Coordinating conferences were held between British and Austrian Generals, with the preference of the latter for continuing to deal with the Duke of York persuading Pitt and Dundas to leave him in charge of the British forces for another campaign, rather against their better judgement.

Apart from questions of leadership, the planned campaign suffered from two disadvantages. The first was that the allies were heavily outnumbered by the French, whose forces on all fronts were possibly double those committed by the allies that year. The second was that once again soldiers who existed on paper took time to appear in human form. The British contingent would not reach full strength until the summer, by which time the decisive battles had been fought. More seriously, the Prussians had become distinctly half-hearted about the whole exercise. The Earl of Malmesbury (formerly James Harris, who had so distinguished himself in Holland in 1787) had been sent as a special envoy to Berlin at the end of 1793, and found the Prussians mainly concerned with Poland and desperately short of money. A long history of British finance keeping reluctant allies in play was about to commence. The Prussians initially sought £2 million for their expected contribution of 100,000 troops, a request that put the British government 'under great difficulties from the enormity of the sum in question'.[8] Protracted negotiations produced a compromise finally signed in April: 62,400 troops in return for £50,000 a month and £400,000 of 'preparation money'. The Dutch would provide some of the money and the British most of it, and these two countries were to control the fate of any territory gained as a result. Such heavy payments led to an opposition attack in Parliament, but the government was happy that a great allied force could now thrust into France.

It would soon be disappointed. Superior French numbers and generalship halted the allied advance in early May after some initial successes. At the Battle of Turcoing on 18 May the French regained the initiative, with the British and Austrians retreating in some disorder. The effect of this not necessarily disastrous reverse was magnified by events in Poland, where the great Polish patriot Thaddeus Kosciuszko was leading the uprising which regained control first of Warsaw and then of most of what was left of Polish territory. Frederick William II of Prussia left Berlin for the East, and soon Francis II of

Austria departed the French campaign. The truth was that the allies lacked the will, the focus and the manpower to overcome the armies of the Revolution.

In the same depressing month Malmesbury was recalled to London to discuss how to make best use of the subsidised Prussian forces. He found that Pitt and the other senior Ministers actually had their minds on domestic matters: 'so fully employed in their discoveries and examinations of seditious and treasonable practices, that I had very short and very few conversations with them'.[9] Pitt had refrained from any general clampdown on radical opinion in the course of 1793, which on the whole had been a period of domestic tranquillity. His most recent speeches against parliamentary reform had been aimed at driving a wedge between moderate reformers and radical agitators, and he would certainly have hoped that a policy of restraint might avert the danger of domestic discontent becoming united with radical causes.

By late 1793, however, trouble was brewing. The combination of the spread of revolutionary ideas, the recent creation of urban populations, and opposition to the war, all perhaps exacerbated by the short-lived economic downturn of 1792–93, did produce an apparent threat of serious unrest. As ever, Scotland gave particular cause for concern. There the senior judge, the Lord Justice Clerk, Robert McQueen of Braxfield, presided in the courts. His maxim was 'Let them bring me prisoners and I will find them law.' He had already become notorious for imposing disproportionate penalties – up to fourteen years' transportation to Australia – on two men convicted of seditious activities under the new restrictions imposed in 1792. The end of the year saw a 'British Convention' held in Edinburgh, which ominously modelled its proceedings on those used in Paris, and provoked the authorities into a number of further arrests.

The government knew by January 1794 that the radical Societies, the LCS and SCI, were making plans for a 'General Convention of the People' later that year. Spies reported a sharp increase in radical activity, reporting that 'violence will be used very soon'.[10] There were many rumours of caches of pikes and spears. Sheffield magistrates talked of 'a most horrid conspiracy against State and Church under the pretence of Reform',[11] and many thousands of people attended a meeting at Chalk Farm, just north of London, to demand an end to threats to liberty such as the Scottish trials.

Since rumours of French invasion plans were rife at the same time, it is not surprising that the government was concerned. It is no doubt true, as most historians have concluded, that many of the reports of spies and magistrates were embellished for effect, but it must nevertheless have felt to Ministers like a perilous moment. There were no opinion polls to guide them on where public sentiment might be heading, and no comprehensive intelligence or instant transmission of it to give them early warning of a serious revolt. They all lived with the memory of the Gordon Riots of 1780 and the more recent disturbances in Birmingham, when many days of havoc had erupted with very little warning. Now, however much matters might be exaggerated, a plan hatched by sympathisers with the French Revolution to call a National Convention of radical activists indisputably existed. Pitt decided that tolerance had been stretched beyond the limit.

The authorities struck on 12 May, beginning with the arrest in the early hours of the Piccadilly shoemaker Thomas Hardy, Secretary of the LCS. Further arrests and the seizure of the books and papers of the radical Societies followed. These documents were brought to the House of Commons, where Pitt moved for a Select Committee to examine them. They reported on the sixteenth, whereupon Pitt proposed the suspension of Habeas Corpus, in effect the introduction of imprisonment without trial. He moved for leave 'to bring in a bill to empower his Majesty to secure and detain all such persons as should be suspected of conspiring against his person and government'.[12] He told the House of clear evidence that the Societies had been in correspondence with the Jacobins in France, and less convincing evidence 'that arms had been actually procured and distributed by these societies'.[13] While he did not believe that an uprising would be successful, he argued it was right 'to prevent, by timely interference, the small misery which a short struggle might necessarily produce'.[14]

For Fox, these measures were evidence of a royal plot and tantamount to the destruction of liberty. He and his diminished band caused the Commons to divide fourteen times over the legislation, but he could muster only twenty-eight votes. As far as Parliament was concerned, Pitt now had a free hand. On the same day, four more leading activists were arrested, including the noted radical Horne Tooke, who had been imprisoned in 1778 for his attempts to raise funds for the Americans when they were at war with Britain. Others hid or escaped the country, while a small cache of arms was discovered in Edinburgh. Some of those arrested were questioned by members of the Privy Council, including Pitt. One of them, John Thelwall, wrote an account of his questioning which portrays Pitt as irritable and strained:

> Pitt. What does he say? (Darting round, very fiercely, from the other side of the room, and seating himself by the side of the Chancellor.)
> Lord Chancellor (with silver softness, almost melting to a whisper). He does not mean to answer any questions.
> Pitt. What is it? – What is it? – What? (fiercely) . . .[15]

The arrests and accompanying legislation of May 1794 marked a major change in the way Pitt was viewed by contemporaries and has been regarded by historians. The champion of enlightened reform had now become the chief agent of repression. Some of the trials for high treason which followed later in the year would prove embarrassing to the government, in some cases because of the draconian nature of the penalties imposed, but mostly because convictions were not secured. Macaulay summed up the critical verdict of historians:

> Men of cultivated minds and polished manners were, for offences which at Westminster would have been treated as mere misdemeanours, sent to herd with felons at Botany Bay. Some reformers, whose opinions were extravagant, and whose language was intemperate, but who had never dreamed of subverting the government by physical force, were indicted for high treason, and were saved from the gallows only by the righteous verdicts of juries.[16]

Yet at a time when the terror in France was reaching its height and the military situation was grave, it is not surprising that Ministers felt they had to respond to actual plans for domestic disturbance with a heavy hand. Whatever the embarrassments they were later to suffer, there is no doubt that they achieved their prime objective: the General Convention of the People never took place, and the radical Societies were deterred from becoming too headstrong. Deterrence, not punishment, seems to have been Pitt's goal at this and later stages of popular discontent: if so, he must be judged largely successful.

The Ministry now needed some good news, and mercifully there was some to hand. From the beginning of May Admiral Howe had been at sea with the Channel Fleet searching for a huge grain convoy sailing from America to France. For nine anxious days from 19 May it was also known that a French fleet had put to sea from Brest although its whereabouts were undetected. Howe found it well out in the Atlantic on the twenty-eighth, was hampered by fog, but on the day known ever after as 'the Glorious First of June' inflicted what was seen in Britain as a major defeat on the French navy. The French had to run for harbour while Howe triumphantly towed six captured ships of the line into Portsmouth. Britain exploded with rejoicing, some of it carefully orchestrated – the King, Queen, Pitt, Dundas and Chatham all joined in the tumultuous welcome at Portsmouth – and some of it spontaneous – London was again ablaze with light and the audience at the opera broke into 'Rule Britannia' and the National Anthem.

The victory reduced the fears of invasion and increased the hopes of victory. But the disturbing truth was that the French had achieved their main object of bringing the grain convoy safely home, albeit at a heavy price for their navy. On the main front they were still advancing against the Duke of York and the Austrians, and once again had the conquest of Belgium in their sights. Pitt could stamp out rebellion in Britain and bask in the prowess of the navy, but France was no nearer to being beaten.

Pitt had now been trying for three years to bring leading Whigs into his ministry, but had so far only succeeded with Lord Loughborough in January 1793. The events of early 1794, during which the Portland

Whigs had given robust support to the government while the Foxite Whigs had maintained an implacable opposition, presented the best opportunity yet. After the suspension of Habeas Corpus, Pitt asked Portland to come to see him to discuss 'the probability of our forming a ministerial arrangement'.[17] They met on 23 May. The negotiations took place over several weeks, during which the news rolled in from the battlefronts: first the elation of the Glorious First of June, but then mounting concern for Belgium after the decisive French victory at Fleurus on 26 June separated the allied armies and sent York retreating northwards. Late June saw Pitt desperately sending reinforcements to Ostend, but it was to no avail. By the end of July Belgium would be back in French hands, and Holland directly threatened once again.

The mounting problems at home and on the Continent brought only one benefit: they encouraged Portland and his colleagues to join Pitt in a united government. Indeed, it is likely that only a crisis of these dimensions enabled Pitt to overcome the deep enmity and mistrust felt for him by his former opponents. They had never forgiven him for his behaviour in 1784. As Lord John Cavendish put it: 'With the temper & disposition of Pitt & the Systems & Schemes of the K[ing] & his friends, it is not possible for any man who has the feelings of a Gentleman to continue for any time to act with them.'[18] But by now the Portland Whigs had been emphatically at odds with Fox for nearly two years, and their hostility to Pitt was at last outweighed by the threats posed by domestic disorder and external revolution to the aristocratic order in which they believed. Pitt's comments to Pretyman in 1793 suggest he had got the measure of them: 'They see that their titles & possessions are in danger, & they think their best chance for preserving them is by supporting Government & joining me.'[19] By early July Pitt and Portland had agreed on a new Cabinet – or thought they had.

Pitt was prepared to pay a high price to achieve the objective he had held so long in view. In a Cabinet enlarged from ten to thirteen members, he was prepared to give no fewer than five places to his former opponents, in addition to the one already given to Loughborough. A startled Addington suggested to Pitt that he might now be outvoted in his own Cabinet, but he replied happily that he was 'under no anxiety on that account, since he placed much dependence on his new colleagues, and still more on himself'.[20] Many of his own supporters thought far too much was being conceded: Canning said they 'either grumble pretty audibly at the distribution of so great a part of the powers among new comers, or at best, shake their head',[21] and Rose complained that this was not so much the recruiting of some men of talents 'but a junction of parties on a footing of mutual interest'. He thought Pitt's long-standing followers would resent the titles and positions they had hoped to obtain going to their old opponents instead: 'Numbers of Mr. Pitt's friends, who would have liked marks of favour or of honour, remained perfectly contented and satisfied without them, aware of the difficulties in the way of their obtaining them; almost every one of whom will feel mortification and grow uneasy when they see the Duke of Portland's adherents carrying their point.'[22]

But Pitt was following a strategy to which his followers had not been party: his objective was a junction of parties if it could be attained. For him, this was not only about winning the war but also about securing his flanks in the longer term, giving him a dominance which would add to his power and security in any future Regency crisis or comparable instance. He intended the coalition to be permanent, and to that end was happy to give the newcomers a liberal helping of honours as well as responsibilities: there were peerages for some of Portland's faction, a Lord Lieutenancy for his son, and a Knighthood of the Garter for Portland himself. The King, who would have preferred to bestow this most prestigious of knighthoods on the victorious Howe, grumbled, 'I cannot see why on the D. of Portland's head favours are to be heaped without measure.'[23] But Pitt could certainly see why. He wanted his new allies to be bound tightly to him.

Cabinet reshuffles are sensitive moments among politicians, often determining for years to come the course of careers or the concentration of power. In the eighteenth century such events were usually more important than elections, and this was the most radical shuffle on which Pitt had ever embarked. In fashioning the new Cabinet, he produced a political masterpiece – provided it could hold together. Two vacancies in the existing Cabinet were created by the death of

Lord Camden and the amicable retirement of the Marquis of Stafford. The addition of three new places therefore meant he had five to give away. Grenville would be unaffected as Foreign Secretary, but the overworked Dundas would retain responsibility for War and Colonies while shedding Home Affairs. The Home Department would become the preserve of Portland, for whose benefit a third office of Secretary of State would be revived. Pitt would thus be able to retain direct control of the war through Dundas and Grenville while Portland would be in charge of domestic order, pitting him into the most direct possible confrontation with his erstwhile colleagues. Windham, the one opposition Member of the Commons to join the Cabinet, and then considered the most able of the recruits, would become Secretary at War, in the Cabinet but working under Dundas. Three great Earls of the Whig aristocracy were the others to be included: Mansfield for his experience, Spencer for his ability, and Fitzwilliam for his connections as the new master of Wentworth Woodhouse, the nephew and heir of Rockingham.

This was a neat construction, but not surprisingly it suffered from two common hazards of radical ministerial reconstruction: the presence of ambiguously phrased understandings which helped the reaching of initial agreement but would cause disputes later on, and the shock of individual Ministers not privy to the negotiations when the full picture became apparent to them. Each of these defects came close to blowing apart Pitt's new creation over the next four months. First came the shocks to the individuals. Windham was disappointed not to be a Secretary of State, and believed that as a junior to Dundas he would be shut out of any real control over the war. This caused the Whigs to demand a larger role for Portland, who now wanted the Home Office with its power over the colonies intact. On 5 July the negotiations were deadlocked, having already lasted six weeks and with less than a week to go before Parliament would rise for the summer recess and some of the key players would disperse. Pitt then proposed swapping Grenville with Portland, which Grenville, who had already shown some signs of exasperation with Foreign Affairs, assented to but Portland did not. A compromise of leaving the West Indies with the Home Office while India went with the War Office evidently satisfied

Portland, but it was now the turn of Dundas to be unhappy. Rather than give up the great powers and patronage of the Home Office, he decided to resign altogether. He was probably exhausted, and very likely angry with Pitt for excluding him from the negotiations.

On 9 July Pitt had to drop everything to try to keep his most reliable colleague and drinking companion by his side. At a quarter to noon he wrote to Dundas:

> I shall give up all hope of carrying on the business with comfort, and be really completely heart-broken, if you adhere to your resolution. Had I had the smallest idea that it would be the consequence, no consideration would have tempted me to agree to the measure which has led to it; and yet, after all that has now passed, it seems impossible for me to recede. Under these circumstances you must allow me to make it a personal request in the strongest manner I can, that you will consent to continue Secretary of State in the way proposed. On public grounds, and for your own credit, I feel most sincerely convinced that you ought to do so; but I wish to ask it of you as the strongest proof you can give of friendship to myself; and of that you have given me so many proofs already that I do flatter myself you cannot refuse this, when you know how anxiously I have it at heart.[24]

He asked for an immediate answer and a meeting. Dundas wrote back from Wimbledon expressing his 'most poignant concern' for his friend but showing no sign of backing down or coming into London where Pitt could persuade him. For Pitt this was a true crisis: to gain the Whigs but to lose Dundas would leave him personally bereft and politically defeated. He hastened to St James's Palace, and persuaded George III himself to write a note to Dundas. As the King put it: 'Though I do not quite approve of the West Indies being added to the Home Department, I will reluctantly acquiesce in the arrangement; but I at the same time, in the strongest manner, call on Mr. Secretary Dundas to continue Secretary of State for the War.'[25] Pitt then proceeded to Wimbledon carrying this letter himself, and interrupted Dundas at dinner with his family. Dundas relented. The new Cabinet was complete.

Fresh from this close shave, a triumphant Pitt was able to announce the new government on 11 July, the day Parliament rose for the summer. It was a sad day for Fox, for over half his party had now gone over to Pitt. He wrote to his nephew: 'I cannot forget how long I have lived in friendship with them, nor can I avoid feeling the most severe mortification, when I recollect the certainty I used to entertain that they would never disgrace themselves as I think they have done . . . I feel nothing but contempt.'[26] He and his remaining followers were marginalised for the duration of the war.

But the birth pangs of the new ministry were not finished yet. Pitt and Portland had left one large area of ambiguity in their agreement, and it would soon catch up with them. Earl Fitzwilliam had joined the Cabinet on the express understanding that he would become Lord Lieutenant of Ireland as soon as Pitt's friend the Earl of Westmorland could be removed from that position; Pitt was in any case happy for the Whigs to take on the responsibility of keeping peace and order across the Irish Sea. The ambiguity lay in the speed and scale of the Whig expectations, for while Pitt was in no hurry to make this change and expected other Irish officeholders to be unaffected, Fitzwilliam was soon letting it be known that his arrival in Dublin was imminent, and was envisaging a whole new administration. The opposition in Ireland, urged on by the brilliant oratory of Henry Grattan, became excited at the prospect of Fitzwilliam's arrival, partly because of an anticipated shift in the control of patronage, and partly because of Fitzwilliam's liberal attitude to Catholic emancipation. All parties had agreed on the previous year's Catholic Relief Act of 1793, which had admitted Catholics to the holding of various civil and military posts and given them voting rights akin to those of Protestants based on property ownership (which in practice gave the vote only to a small minority). Fitzwilliam and other Whigs favoured building on this by giving Catholics the right to sit in the Irish Parliament – not that very many of them would be elected on the existing franchise. Pitt himself had always taken a liberal view of Irish affairs and sought to accommodate Catholic concerns. His line on further Catholic relief was 'not to bring it forward as a government measure; but if Government were pressed, to yield it'.[27]

By October disagreements over Ireland and Fitzwilliam's appointment were threatening to break up the new Cabinet. Fitzwilliam threatening to resign from the Cabinet if he was not formally appointed, and it was clear that the other Whigs would go with him if he went. On the other hand, if he took office, it was clear that he intended to make a 'clean sweep' of many offices, including that of the Irish Chancellor, Lord Fitzgibbon. Dundas was disgusted with the new members of the Cabinet – 'I would rather give them the government altogether than to be so swindled'[28] – while Pitt searched for a solution while thinking, 'I have nothing to reproach myself with, in what has led to this misunderstanding; and I must struggle as well as I can.'[29]

The result was a meeting of the key Cabinet members at which Pitt succeeded in making common ground with his new colleagues and in giving Fitzwilliam clear instructions while agreeing to appoint him before the end of the year. It seems extraordinary today that no minutes were kept of such a meeting, and the only authoritative account of what was decided is contained in a memorandum written by Grenville the following year, after Fitzwilliam's Lord Lieutenancy had exploded in a new burst of misunderstanding. The memorandum itself shows how sorely Pitt needed a private secretary at his meetings, including as it does such items as: 'It appears that Lord Fitzwilliam conceives himself to have stated to Mr. Pitt, in their first conversations on the subject of Ireland, that he was apprehensive Mr. Beresford [whom Pitt had regarded as a highly effective head of the Revenue in Ireland since working with him so closely in 1785] should be removed, and that Mr. Pitt made no objection in reply to this. Mr. Pitt has no recollections of anything having been said to him which conveyed to his mind the impression that Mr. Beresford's removal from his office was intended.'

According to the memorandum, it was made clear at the meeting that Fitzwilliam's wish to strengthen the government in Ireland did not extend to creating an entirely 'new system', and that on important policy issues 'Lord Fitzwilliam should transmit all the information he could collect, with his opinion, to the King's servants here, and that he should do nothing to commit the King's government in such cases without fresh instructions from hence.' On Catholic relief, no firm view was expressed except that 'A strong opinion was stated that Lord Fitzwilliam should, if possible, prevent the agitation of the question at all during the present Session.'[30]

As far as Pitt was concerned, the matter was now resolved. Fitzwilliam wrote that 'I go to Ireland – though not exactly upon the terms I had originally thought of,'[31] but the Cabinet had remained united and misunderstandings had apparently been cleared up. Once a sinecure was found for Westmorland, Fitzwilliam set out for Ireland in December 1794. Pitt would not have expected that in January the whole issue of Fitzwilliam and Ireland would be back on his desk with a vengeance. But it would be a crowded desk, for by the end of 1794 the whole political and military sky had darkened.

Pitt had always been well known for his ability to bear a cheerful countenance during adversity. Sir Gilbert Elliot had noted after Dunkirk in 1793 that 'Pitt seemed to carry it off better than the rest, treating it as a misfortune, but as an occurrence to be looked for in all wars.'[32] From the summer of 1794 that *sang froid* would be sorely tested, and by the following year he would be experiencing bouts of strain, illness and depression, to which he was not accustomed.

On 10 July, the day before the new Cabinet was announced, Pitt made a spirited defence of the war in the Commons. It would be 'the most shameful weakness and timidity' and 'the meanest dereliction of their duty' to lose heart now because of 'some towns in Flanders, the possession of which had in all wars been the fluctuating and unstable consequence of every temporary advantage'.[33] He continued to rail against the Terror underway in Paris: 'It was impossible to put an end to this most furious tyranny, without destroying the present government of France.'[34] As it happened, that very government was about to fall. In the coup of 9 Thermidor (the French Republican equivalent of 27 July) the members of the French Convention, many of whom knew they would be Robespierre's next victims, indicted the dictator and took control of the National Guard. That night, Robespierre shot himself in the jaw but failed to kill himself, and the next day he followed his many victims to the guillotine. His death marked an end to the Terror and the return of greater social and political freedom in Paris, but in no way did it bring any diminution in French determination vigorously to prosecute the war. Ironically, it was the easing of some of the military and financial pressures on France which gave the Convention the confidence to bring the Terror to an end. By autumn 1794, the French had not only retaken Belgium, but had driven the Austrians completely from the west bank of the Rhine, secured the way into northern Italy, and pushed the Spanish across the eastern Pyrenees. Even in the West Indies, British progress had petered out as sickness began to take a heavy toll on the expedition despatched by Pitt; an attack on Saint Domingue had been unsuccessful and the French had managed to regain half of Guadeloupe.

The French success on all fronts created major challenges for the British government in matters of strategy, diplomacy, finance and personnel. The basic strategic question was whether to make a renewed attempt to attack France on the Continental fronts, subsidising allied armies where necessary, and by these means try to prevent the fall of Holland while hoping to exhaust the French; or to do as Auckland now urged and withdraw from 'all continental exertions and interference',[35] concentrating almost exclusively on naval power to blockade France and sweep the West Indies in order to force a negotiated end to the war.

The outcome was that for the moment the Continental strategy remained in place, with the addition of much stronger plans than hitherto, favoured by Windham, to assist an invasion of France by *émigrés* and counter-revolutionaries. There was no sign, however, of effective and coordinated action by Britain's allies: Pitt and Grenville were soon deeply frustrated with Prussian inactivity, Dutch apathy about their defences, and Austrian demands for money. Pitt evidently spoke sharply to the Prussian Ambassador at the end of September about Berlin's failure to deliver any results in return for more than £1 million so far sent to it. The subsidy was cancelled, and it was in any case soon known in London that the Prussians had begun talks with the French. Britain's Triple Alliance with Holland and Prussia was reaching its end. Meanwhile the Austrians were demanding a £6 million loan, guaranteed by the British government, in return for 200,000 soldiers in the field. Pitt was already raising a loan of £18 million that year, in a country whose total government revenues in the year before the war were less than £16 million, but he found a way of going ahead and the Austrian commitment to a 1795 campaign was kept alive.

It was clear by now that the British war effort had not been as well run as it should have been. Pitt had to steel himself for some delicate decisions on senior personnel, starting with the Duke of York. The King's second son no longer commanded the respect of the troops in the field. As Pitt put it to his brother at the end of September, 'There is more and more reason to fear that his general management is what the army has no confidence in, and while that is the case there is little chance of setting things right.'[36] In November he wrote a 'very honest and firm' letter to the King, requesting the recall of the Duke of York. George III replied that he was 'very much hurt' and maintained that the defeats were not the fault of his son but of 'the conduct of Austria, the faithlessness of Prussia, and the cowardice of the Dutch'.[37] Nevertheless, he agreed to his son's removal from the field.

Some days later Pitt embarked on a yet more distasteful task, beginning a letter, 'My Dear Brother, I do not write to you till after a very painful struggle in my own mind . . .' Chatham had not distinguished himself as First Lord of the Admiralty. While he never opposed his younger brother on a matter of policy, he lacked the drive and intellectual grasp to run the navy at the height of a global war. It had evidently become increasingly embarrassing and irritating to Pitt that this was obvious to all concerned, and he referred to an earlier meeting which he had hoped would clear the air: 'After the full explanation passed between us some time since, I had really flattered myself that there was an end of the distressing embarrassment which we had experienced . . . But I cannot disguise from you that from various circumstances (which I see no good in dwelling upon), and especially from what passed at the Cabinet yesterday, I foresee too evidently the renewal of that embarrassment and the utter impossibility that business should permanently go on between you and those with whom in your present department you must have continual intercourse without that cordiality and complete mutual confidence which at the present moment is indispensable.' Coming to the crunch, the letter stated 'fairly though reluctantly' that Pitt believed 'the time is come when it will be the best for us both, as well as for the public service, if you will exchange your present situation for one of a different description'.[38]

Pitt had taken a risk six years earlier in making his brother First Lord of the Admiralty. Now he knew he had to remove him, but offered him either of two Cabinet positions without portfolio (President of the Council or Privy Seal) instead. He cannot have enjoyed his brother's immediate reply, asking for a meeting, asserting that he had not failed in his duty and fearing that his removal would be 'subjected to great misconstruction'.[39] But Pitt was unyielding, replying the next day that whether his brother thought him right or wrong he hoped he would give him credit for the sincerity of his opinion, and entreating him to make the matter 'as little painful as possible by reconciling your mind to what I have proposed'. He did not agree to a meeting: 'I hoped I had said enough in my former letter to show you that my opinion was formed (however reluctantly) on grounds which will not admit of its being changed.'[40]

Eventually Pitt yielded to his brother's entreaties for a meeting, but only on the basis that 'I trust your decision will have been such as to relieve me from the most anxious of all situations. My own opinion remains and must remain the same.' His feelings, however motivated, had led him to great generosity towards his brother – a seat in the Cabinet, the rank of Knight of the Garter, and possibly also sending him money he could ill afford. Ultimately, however, his head ruled his heart, and his family was subordinate to the needs of the state. Chatham duly surrendered his portfolio but remained in the Cabinet. The brothers exchanged dutiful letters of devotion, but their relationship was seriously affected.

Events were crowding in on Pitt. Just before these dismissals he had suffered the embarrassment of being called to court as a defence witness in the trial of Horne Tooke for high treason. He was called upon to confirm that he had himself campaigned for parliamentary reform at extraparliamentary meetings in 1782, one of the very things for which the defendant was now on trial. The discomfort of this experience was not alleviated by the verdict of not guilty delivered soon afterwards: all the main London trials under the new legislation failed in similar fashion and further prosecutions were abandoned, while the Edinburgh courts did achieve one hanging. On top of all this, Holland was on its last legs by the end of the year, and when the new session of Parliament was opened on 30 December 1794 it was none other than William Wilberforce who moved an amendment to the King's Speech 'advising his Majesty to order a negociation [sic] for peace on such terms as should be deemed just and reasonable'.[41]

Wilberforce had announced at the time of his religious conversion that he would 'not be so much a Party man', and now he showed it. What is more, he was supported by another of Pitt's old friends, Sir Henry Bankes from Dorset. Pitt gave a spirited response, arguing that a peace made with the expansionist French government would be meaningless. 'Do the gentlemen who now desert the war . . . hope for a free and useful commerce? Do they expect that the armies on both sides will be disbanded, and the fleets be called home?'[42] He said he was still confident of success: 'All wars depend now on the finances of the nations engaged in them,'[43] and the objective was to 'oblige France to make efforts to which she is now unequal'.[44] Wilberforce's amendment mustered seventy-three votes, against 246 for the government, but the debate was personally wounding to Pitt – Portland thought him 'pretty seriously hurt by it'.[45] At the very least it showed that a stronger body of opinion was now swinging towards peace.

Within days, still worse was to follow. The severe winter froze the rivers of Holland, allowing French troops to launch an unexpected invasion across the ice. Amsterdam fell on 20 January: at the end of the month the icebound Dutch fleet became the first ships in the history of warfare to surrender to a force of cavalry. Holland was knocked out of the war, and her resources could soon be expected to be deployed on the French side.

With so many misfortunes accumulating so rapidly it is not surprising that there was some discontent with the government, even among Pitt's regular supporters. Disillusionment with the war fed dissatisfaction with government departments and a feeling amongst Pitt's long-standing friends that he was surrounded by the wrong people.

John Mitford, the Solicitor General, wrote to Pitt with a blunt analysis on two occasions in early 1795: 'The present situation of publick affairs . . . sours the minds of the best friends of government; & they are particularly affected by observing, as they conceive, a languor in every department . . . That you have called to your assistance those who only bring you weakness, who want every moment your protection, & daily consume your good fame.'[46] A few weeks later he wrote: 'You must be aware that almost all your friends feel something of the same uneasiness. Many of them apprehend that what they long ago foretold has at length happened; that you are completely surrounded, that you stand in effect alone, that you are no longer your own master, & that if you can extricate yourself from the chains prepared for you, you have not a moment to lose. What has happened in Ireland seems to be generally considered as a death blow.'[47]

Once again Ireland, and in particular Fitzwilliam's conduct and policy, was exploding onto the political scene. Pitt had been preoccupied throughout January: Holland was falling, the army in retreat towards northern Germany, reinforcements being found for the West Indies, and major Commons debates on the army estimates and a renewed opposition motion for peace with France demanded his time. Fitzwilliam would subsequently complain that a despatch he sent to London on 15 January, which took twelve days to arrive, was not even considered for another eleven days, thus greatly extending the confusion which arose in this period. Pitt and his senior colleagues were simply too busy to turn their minds back to Ireland in late January – by the time they did so in mid-February, a major political storm had erupted.

Fitzwilliam's conduct on his arrival in Dublin at the beginning of January suggests that either he had a different understanding of the ministerial discussions of the previous November, or that he believed that the Cabinet in London would not stand in his way once he had assumed office as Lord Lieutenant. It is possible that Pitt's formula of not proposing further Catholic relief but being prepared to 'yield if necessary' emboldened Fitzwilliam to depart from the agreed line. It seems likely too that in character and beliefs he was not suited to a position requiring delicate management of men and strict adherence to negotiated positions: he very strongly believed that the problems of Ireland could only be solved by putting the Catholics on an equal footing to the Protestants, and then 'both descriptions should forget all their former differences'.[48] Within days of arrival he dismissed John Beresford, Pitt's long-standing adviser, as First Commissioner of the Revenue in Ireland. Other immediate dismissals and appointments were soon creating a new administration in Dublin, and one that would be much more in accordance with Fitzwilliam's own views. He had only been in Ireland ten days when his despatch of 15 January suggested that he would soon wish to pass a Bill to allow Catholics to sit in the Irish Parliament, and that not to do so would be 'exceedingly impolitik'.[49] Fitzwilliam was now being borne along by the tide of Catholic sentiment which his own airing of opinions in the months before his appointment had helped to initiate.

These events caused alarm among Irish Protestants, intensely annoyed Pitt who regarded the dismissal of Beresford as 'an open breach of a most solemn promise',[50] and forfeited Fitzwilliam's support among his Whig friends in the Cabinet. The government's softly-softly approach to Catholic emancipation was blown apart: on the one hand the Irish Parliament was under pressure from a petition with half a million signatures demanding passage of a Bill to secure the admission of Catholics, and on the other George III was telling Pitt that such a policy would be 'overturning the fabrick' of the 1688 Revolution, and was 'beyond the decision of any Cabinet of Ministers'.[51] In any case, Ministers were absolutely clear that the Bill should be resolutely opposed, and by late February were unanimous that Fitzwilliam should be brought home. Fitzwilliam then made matters worse by not departing until 25 March, while public disorder and excitement worsened.

He was replaced by Pitt's long-standing friend, the new Lord Camden (formerly John Pratt), whose swearing in was accompanied by a huge riot but who managed to secure the defeat of the Bill in the Irish House of Commons in May. Fitzwilliam never forgave the rest of the government for the way he had been treated during his extremely brief ministerial career, but he had created a genuine crisis for the administration when it was beset by difficulties elsewhere. In one sense, however, he also helped the new ministry to pull together, for Pitt found that his new Whig colleagues gave him unstinting support when they realised that Fitzwilliam had overplayed his hand. Portland in particular had reacted as a loyal lieutenant rather than the leader of a rival faction.

Taken all round, Pitt's Cabinet from early 1795 was stronger than in earlier years. The highly able Earl Spencer had replaced Chatham at the Admiralty, and while the Irish crisis was erupting Pitt finally sacked Richmond as Master of the Ordnance. Disillusioned with the conduct of the war after his advice had been rejected, Richmond had absented himself from Cabinet meetings. It was typical of Pitt that he allowed this situation to drift for some months rather than confront a man who had once provided much-needed ballast in his Cabinet, but also typical that when forced to address the situation by Richmond's written complaints he did so with elegant bluntness. The letter of dismissal makes clear that 'your Grace's ceasing to attend the Cabinet, and your breaking off the habits of familiar and friendly intercourse between us, proceeded entirely from yourself . . . I see that your resuming a seat in the Cabinet must prove equally unpleasant and embarrassing to public business – this consideration must decide my opinion.'[52] In Richmond's place, Pitt brought in the hugely experienced Lord Cornwallis. While true power still lay with the key triumvirate of Pitt, Dundas and Grenville, departments which were vital to an effective war effort were now in more capable hands.

Efforts in London to energise the coalition against France produced another Cabinet crisis in March 1795, with Pitt and Grenville in sharp disagreement for the first time. Pitt was desperate to keep the coalition in being: in early March he and Grenville were still negotiating with Austria over the terms of the proposed loan, and were offering up to £1 million to Russia in return for an army of 55,000 men in action against France. Despite rumours of peace talks between Berlin and Paris, Pitt succeeded in overruling a deeply sceptical Grenville in the Cabinet (initially by six votes to five) to make a further offer of aid to Prussia if that would keep her in the war. The opinion of the Cabinet was, in George III's words: 'There is no Force sufficient without the co-operation of the Prussians to prevent the French seizing every port in the North Sea.'[53] When Grenville threatened to resign, Pitt played for time. Grenville eventually settled for refusing to sign the despatch and having his dissent noted in the Cabinet Minutes on 8 April – within days he was vindicated by the news that a Franco–Prussian treaty had been signed at Basle.

Pitt had kept his Cabinet together through a series of crises, but his international coalition was now disintegrating. Tuscany had made peace with France in February, and soon Prussia's treaty with France, acknowledging French possession of the whole left bank of the Rhine, was additionally signed by Sweden. In May, Holland concluded a humiliating treaty with Paris, giving up several cities, a vast fine and a commitment to support a French army. The Spanish, also beaten on the battlefield, were working towards a treaty with France which would be signed in July, restoring the previous frontier. Russia was not yet ready for active participation, still digesting the territory of Poland. It was now only Britain and Austria, along with Piedmont and the two Sicilies, fighting against the might of a rampaging France. What was left of the British army on the Continent was no longer operating alongside the Austrians, and embarked from Bremen for England in early April. Meanwhile, in the West Indies, Guadeloupe and St Lucia had been lost to French forces and local insurrection.

Pitt affected to be undismayed by this series of disasters. In late April he wrote one of his cheerful 'please don't worry' letters to his mother, describing his latest sufferings from gout as 'very moderate and regular', and referring to 'the Weakness & distraction of France, which seems likely to lead to the best solution of all our difficulties'.[54] In May he responded to a renewed motion for peace from Wilberforce by calling for perseverance not negotiation. He contrasted the ability of Britain to finance the war with the French only maintaining their efforts 'by requisitions, by robbery, and plunder'. He concluded: 'By a vigorous prosecution of the war for a short time longer, we have every reasonable prospect that we shall be able to procure for ourselves a solid, permanent, and honourable peace.'[55]

While the Austrians geared up for an autumn offensive, Windham persuaded Pitt, against the better judgement of Dundas, to support a landing by French *émigrés* on the coast of Brittany. Accordingly, on

6 June four thousand were put ashore at Quiberon Bay, achieving initial success and surprise as well as adding to their forces from the local peasantry. But the *émigrés* were too timid and their force too small to exploit their success with sufficient speed, and in July they faced a strong French counterattack which drove them back to the sea. The survivors were taken prisoner. Later they were slaughtered on the orders of the Convention in Paris. The human cost of mistakes in a revolutionary war was very high.

For all his professed optimism, it cannot have been anything but an unhappy time for Pitt. What would be wholly successful expeditions had been sent to seize the Dutch colonies in Ceylon and Cape Town in the light of Holland's defeat, but every other initiative of 1795 had ended in diplomatic failure or military defeat. While overall the economy had continued to expand after the brief downturn of 1793, there was a serious shortage of wheat after a series of poor harvests, which brought sharp price rises in the summer of 1795. Pitt had refused grain exports to France in 1789 because the price was over forty shillings a quarter, but in the summer of 1795 prices reached seventy-eight shillings, and in August briefly touched 108 shillings. There were riots in Downing Street, with Pitt's windows being broken, and serious disturbances in many cities. Huge but orderly meetings were held, such as one alleged to have mustered a hundred thousand people at St George's Fields in London at the end of June to demand peace, reform and cheaper food.

Reports of the riots in Downing Street brought a typically concerned letter to Pitt from his mother. Pitt's reply reflects his constant wish to assure her that all was well even in the most troubled times: 'I take shame to myself for not reflecting how much a mob is magnified by Report; but that which visited my Window with a single Pebble was really so young and so little versed in its Business, that it hardly merited the Notice of a News Paper. The Ceremony has not been repeated since.'[56]

Further embarrassment was caused that summer for the government, and indeed for the entire political establishment, by the vast debts of the Prince of Wales. As the Prince sulkily prepared for his marriage to Caroline, daughter of the Duke of Brunswick, it had become apparent that his debts were of the order of £600,000, despite the large sums given to him over the previous twelve years. Pitt's plans to raise the Prince's allowance, with a proportion of it set aside for creditors, ran into trouble from all sides in Parliament, where demands were made for larger sums to be reserved for debt repayments – all of which took up a good deal of Pitt's time at the height of a war and during a serious food shortage.

The paying off of his debts was the only reason the Prince had agreed to what would be a catastrophic marriage, solemnised on 8 April 1795 in St James's Chapel Royal. He sent his mistress, Lady Jersey, to greet his bride at Greenwich, asked for brandy as soon as he saw her, was drunk at the wedding, and slept with her once only – although thereby producing Princess Charlotte nine months later. For her part, Princess Caroline was soon embarking on her own life of political mischief and sexual adventure: the Queen had warned before the marriage that the Princess's 'passions are so strong' that in Brunswick 'she was not to be allowed even to go from one room to another without her Governess'.[57] The rivalry and hatred which characterised the marriage would culminate in Caroline banging on the doors of Westminster Abbey in 1821 while the Prince was being crowned George IV without her.

The military failures and domestic disturbances of the summer of 1795 led Pitt quietly to reappraise his aspirations for the war. The idea of a humiliated France coming to terms under pressure of revolt and invasion was now only a dream. Pitt was being forced back on the naval and colonial strategy advocated by Auckland the previous year, writing to his brother in early August after news of Quiberon Bay and the Spanish treaty: 'I incline to think that our plan must now be changed, and that the only great part must be in the West Indies, where I trust enough may yet be gained to counterbalance the French successes in Europe.'[58] This is what Dundas had long since wanted.

In September the two of them travelled to Southampton to wave off a huge expedition to the West Indies under Sir Ralph Abercromby which eventually totalled 32,000 men. They believed that British success in the West Indies would combine with the internal state of France, also suffering serious food shortages, to create the circumstances for an honourable negotiated peace. With that in mind, Pitt was hopeful too of the results of the latest round of political change in Paris, where a government of five ruling Directors entrenched itself in August. Previous French governments during the Revolution had collapsed under attack from revolutionary crowds: this one dealt with rebellion by firing cannon loaded with grapeshot at point-blank range into the hostile protesters, and was highly pleased with the skill and ruthlessness of the rising young artillery officer who was prepared to order this, one Napoleon Bonaparte – who had earlier distinguished himself by being instrumental in driving the allied fleet out of the harbour at Toulon. In September Pitt described the more stable constitution emerging in France as 'a very fortunate event'.[59]

Whether it was to be peace or continued war, the new British strategy was the only effective one which could be mounted in late 1795. But as Parliament met on 29 October it was easy to see which outcome Pitt and his colleagues preferred. The King's Speech referred to 'a general sense . . . throughout France, that the only relief from the increasing pressure of these difficulties must arise from the restoration of peace, and the establishment of some settled system of government'.[60] The reference to France wishing for peace was political code for Britain being prepared to contemplate it. On the way to deliver the speech, the window of the King's carriage was shattered by a bullet or other projectile. The crowds outside chanted 'No war! No Pitt! Peace, Peace, Bread, Bread!'

Pitt told his friend Pepper Arden that summer that he had experienced more sleepless nights that year 'than during the rest of his administration put together'.[61] According to Pretyman, he had become 'so wholly engrossed by the State of Public Affairs that he had no leisure, and lost all relish, except for the company of his intimate friends'.[62] The emotional pain of dismissing his brother from the Admiralty seems to have affected him considerably, and the accumulating strain of so many near resignations and terrible disappointments, along with unfamiliar unpopularity, must have been enormous. While always known among his friends for his ability to 'put his cares aside', those cares were now too great to be forgotten in the dead of night. From 1795 onwards, the mental pressures on Pitt had a pronounced physical effect. The physician Sir Walter Farquhar, who would attend him for the rest of his life, first saw him in 1795. He later wrote:

> I found him in a state of general debility – the functions of the stomach greatly impaired & the Bowels very irregular – much of which I attributed to the excess of public business and the unremitting attention upon subjects of anxiety and interest. I thought myself called upon to urge the necessity of some relaxation from the arduous Duties of Office, in order to regain strength & afford the natural functions time & opportunity to rally. This Mr. Pitt stated to be impossible. There appeared at this time to be little or no constitutional mischief done, but the symptoms of debility with a gouty tendency, which Dr. Addington (as Mr. Pitt mentioned to me) had always remarked from his infancy, were likely to become formidable if neglected.[63]

Pitt wrote to Henry Addington, Speaker of the Commons, that October: 'I am going next Thursday for a week or ten days to Walmer, and hope to return with my Budget prepared to be opened before Christmas; and if that goes off tolerably well, it will give us peace before Easter.'[64] He would show that he and Britain were still prepared to fight. But he also said to Lord Mornington and Wilberforce around the same time: 'My head would be off in six months were I to resign.' His sense of duty and superiority would in any case have made it hard for him to give up the burdens he had now carried for nearly twelve years. In the midst of war and disorder, he felt absolutely bound to carry on as Prime Minister. His career was reaching a point familiar in the lives of politicians with a long tenure of office, where it ceases to be fulfilling and instead becomes consuming. It marks the transition in his life story from the fable of brilliant youth to the legend of grinding endurance.

19

Insurmountable Obstacles

'My sentiments are only those of disappointment. But I have the satisfaction of knowing that this feeling of disappointment is unaccompanied with any reflection, unmingled with regret, unembittered with despondency.'

WILLIAM PITT, 30 DECEMBER 1796[1]

'What I have done so far is nothing. I am only at the beginning of the career that lies before me. Do you suppose that I have triumphed in Italy for the mere aggrandizement of the Directory lawyers, the Carnots, the Barras of this world? What an idea! A republic of thirty million men! With our habits, our vices! How can it be possible? It is a wild dream, with which the French are infatuated, but it will pass like so many before it. They must have glory, the satisfactions of vanity. But as for liberty, they understand nothing about it.'

NAPOLEON BONAPARTE, MAY 1796[2]

IN PRIVATE, in the autumn of 1795 many of Pitt's senior colleagues in the government were opposed to making overtures for peace. Some of the new Ministers adopted the hardest line: it was, after all, the intensity of their opposition to the French Revolution that had pushed them into Pitt's Cabinet in the first place. Portland and Windham were appalled at talk of peace without a comprehensive victory. Dundas and Grenville were also sceptical, although the latter was certainly concerned about growing domestic hostility to the war, and thought that peace negotiations would help the government's case by demonstrating the intractability of the French.

George III himself was deeply suspicious of any negotiations. At

Pitt's behest he sent a message to Parliament on 9 December 1795 indicating that Britain would 'meet any disposition to negociation on the part of the enemy with an earnest desire to give it the fullest and speediest effect, and to conclude a treaty of general peace',[3] but his private views were much less pacific. In a memorandum to Pitt he argued that time should be given for the West Indies expedition to succeed. Pitt's reply argued that this would take too long (particularly as a large part of the expedition had been forced back to port in Britain by the weather), and that if the government waited any longer, parliamentary opinion might force it to seek peace from a correspondingly weaker position.

It is hard to know how seriously to take Pitt's concern that MPs could break ranks – only eighty-six had so far voted against the war, including Wilberforce, who was now returning to the fold in the belief that an honourable peace was not available – but it certainly suggests that he thought his huge majority was shaky. George III, never one to be impressed by parliamentary opinion of any kind, was not impressed: 'My mind is not of a nature to be guided by the obtaining a little applause or staving off some abuse; rectitude of conduct is my sole aim. I trust the rulers in France will reject any proposition from hence short of a total giving up any advantage we may have gained, and therefore that the measure proposed will meet with a refusal.'[4]

The King's confidence that negotiations would fail almost certainly made him happier to agree to them. On the other hand, Pitt was influenced to try for peace by some of his closest advisers: Auckland wrote a pamphlet advocating negotiations, and George Rose had written to Pretyman: 'It is heart-breaking that they should go on without a rational Hope in the Mind of a human Being of the smallest possible Advantage to the Country in the Cause it is embarked in.'[5]

To Pitt, the arguments for negotiation were stacked high: the French appeared to be ruined financially, exhausted militarily and divided politically, and the Revolution seemed at last to have run its course; the prospect of the major British effort heading to the West Indies would be a further inducement for them to make peace on terms which ended their aggression; a continuation of the war presented the risk of Austria making peace and leaving Britain facing France more or less alone; domestic distress and discontent had reached a new peak with the violence directed at the King and 150,000 people gathering to protest before the opening of Parliament; and the French would in any case be shown up as the aggressors if a reasonable attempt at negotiation was rebuffed. The importance of negotiations in allowing Pitt to get back on top of the domestic political situation would have been a powerful factor in his mind, and much more so than in the calculations of other Ministers and the King.

Perhaps equally telling in Pitt's head was his understanding that the approach he had taken to financing the war could not be sustained for much longer. In his budget of 7 December he announced another loan of £18 million, and a new tax on legacies, part of which he would not succeed in getting through Parliament. This continued his policy of making the most of the immense creditworthiness of Britain to finance the war through loans, while only raising taxes to cover the interest. Since the beginning of the war he had so far raised taxes by a little over £1 million, while expenditure had increased by over £20 million a year. By the following year, some £70 million would have been added to the national debt, almost equal after three years of war to the entire expense of the eight-year American War of Independence. He could continue this for another year, and no Minister available at the time could have matched Pitt's resourcefulness in financing a war or the confidence he enjoyed throughout the financial system. Nevertheless, he knew this could not go on much longer without paying exorbitant rates of interest or seeking huge increases in domestic taxation. The prospect of presenting such measures to a Parliament which he already feared might turn in greater measure against the war was not an attractive one.

Pitt therefore decided in late 1795 that notwithstanding royal and ministerial misgivings, he would seek peace if it could be obtained on honourable and durable terms. In February 1796, instructions would be given to the British envoy in Berne to make an approach to his French counterpart. But in the meantime Pitt had also been clear in his mind that it would not be possible to achieve a worthwhile peace or win the war without the restoration of domestic order.

The new and highly dangerous factor in the riots and protests of the second half of 1795 had been the shortage of bread. Such a difficulty was well suited to being resolved by Pitt's problem-solving brain. The government had already started buying grain from overseas on its own account, rather than relying on traders. In November 1795, within days of the opening of Parliament, Pitt established a Parliamentary Inquiry into the high price of corn, resulting in government intervention being replaced by bounties on particular types of imports. In early 1796 government stocks of grain were released judiciously into the market, accelerating a sharp fall in prices which was by then underway. Pitt also instigated a new Act permitting bread to be made with a mixture of inferior grains and substitutes, the loaves concerned to be marked with the letter 'M' (signifying a mixture). This did not prove to be acceptable even to hungry eighteenth-century consumers, but a variety of other expedients provided some marginal help and showed he was taking the problem seriously: the use of wheat was prohibited in distilleries, and in the manufacture of starch and hair powder. (Whatever Pitt had against hair powder, the combination of this measure with the taxes he had already imposed on it soon drove it out of general use.)

These measures did something to reduce the political temperature out on the streets, which in any event dropped sharply in the opening months of 1796. But Ministers were also conscious that previous unruly episodes had ceased when the government showed its toughness and strength. There seems to have been no doubt in the minds of Pitt, Portland and the others directly concerned that the violence directed at the King's person and the atmosphere which accompanied it required a parallel response from the authorities. Pitt told the Commons on 10 November that 'the public had seen with becoming indignation, that a virtuous and beloved sovereign had been attacked in the most criminal and outrageous manner . . . if, instead of stating grievances, the people were excited to rebellion; if, instead of favouring the principles of freedom, the very foundation of it was to be destroyed, and with it the happiness of the people, it was high time for the legislature to interpose with its authority'.[6]

The LCS had effectively invited this response by calling at huge meetings and demonstrations in the previous weeks not only for parliamentary reform but for opposition to the war and the government's policies across the board. Literature had apparently been distributed showing 'prints of guillotining the King and others'.[7] The 'others' no doubt included the First Lord of the Treasury. Pitt responded with two new Bills: the Seditious Meetings Bill, which he introduced into the Commons, and the Treasonable Practices Bill, which Grenville introduced in the Lords. These were to become known as Pitt's 'gagging Bills', and they represented a significant ratcheting-up of his repressive response to discontent. Meetings of more than fifty people were to be banned unless they had the permission of the magistrates, any meeting could be dispersed and the speakers arrested on magistrates' orders, and severe penalties were to be imposed on those who attacked the constitution or gave support to the nation's enemies.

For Fox, these measures were an outrageous attack on liberty, intended to 'prohibit all public discussion, whether in writing or in speaking, of political subjects'. He told the Commons that 'if you silence remonstrance and stifle complaint, you then leave no other alternative but force and violence'.[8] He called a huge public meeting in mid-November, and maintained an eloquent parliamentary attack:

> Say at once, that a free constitution is no longer suitable to us; say at once, in a manly manner, that upon an ample review of the state of the world, a free Constitution is not fit for you . . . But do not mock the understandings and the feelings of mankind by telling the world that you are free – by telling me that if out of the House, for the purpose of expressing my sense of the public administration of this country, of the calamities which this war has occasioned, I state a grievance by petition, or make any declaration of my sentiments which I always had a right to do; but which if I now do, in a manner that may appear to a magistrate to be seditious, I am to be subjected to penalties which hitherto were unknown to the laws of England.[9]

For Pitt, by contrast, what was at stake was the primacy of Parliament over the mob: 'The sole object of the bill was, that the people should look to parliament, and to parliament alone, for the redress of such grievances as they might have to complain of, with a confident reliance of relief being afforded them, if their complaints should be well founded and practically remediable.'[10] Alarmed by the turn of events, the massed ranks of his supporters did not waver. A second reading of the Seditious Meetings Bill was carried in the Commons by 213 to forty-three.

Pitt was conscious that the argument had to be won out in the country as well as in Parliament, but was convinced that the great majority of people were on his side. He was worried when he heard at the end of November that his old ally in fighting for parliamentary reform, the Reverend Christopher Wyvill, who had grown disillusioned with him during the war, had called at short notice a county meeting in Yorkshire to oppose the gagging Bills. Yorkshire still carried immense weight among the English counties: Pitt considered it vital that the government's view should prevail there.

He was now to benefit from the complete absence of bitterness in his personality, as his friendly and forgiving behaviour towards Wilberforce since their disagreement over the war at the beginning of the year had helped to bring Wilberforce back to his side. Wilberforce was the leading politician of Yorkshire, and his presence at the meeting in York called for Tuesday, 1 December would provide a chance of defusing it. As he discussed the matter with Pitt in Downing Street on Sunday, 29 November, it seemed impossible for him to get to York in time. But Pitt immediately lent him one of his own coaches and four horses (Wilberforce was told by a Minister: 'If they find out whose carriage you have got, you will run the risk of being murdered'[11]) to enable him to perform an amazing feat for the eighteenth century. Hurtling up the Great North Road, he covered sixty-seven miles to Alconbury by Sunday night, and another 106 miles to Ferrybridge, north of Doncaster, by Monday night. Outriders cleared the way for him on the last twenty miles into York, where he arrived in the nick of time, utterly unexpected, and delivered one of the best speeches of his life to a crowd of thousands in the castle yard. The result was a loyal address to the King rather than a statement of opposition. A horseman was sent to London to take the news to Pitt. The episode illustrated that once again the nation was prepared to rally to him.

The mood in early 1796 showed that the immediate domestic crisis had passed. Even so, the previous year had revealed the narrow margin of subsistence by which many people lived, and it gave rise to further parliamentary discussion of how to alleviate their situation. Pitt responded sympathetically in February 1796 to the introduction by the opposition MP Samuel Whitbread of a bill to regulate agricultural wages. He produced ideas of his own, and committed himself to further examination of the issue: 'The present situation of the labouring poor in this country, was certainly not such as could be wished, upon any principle, either of humanity, or policy.'[12] He did indeed apply himself to this issue in the course of 1796, and introduced a Bill at the end of the year 'for the better support and maintenance of the poor'. In the circumstances which followed it did not receive his continuous attention, nor parliamentary time and support, joining the list of other reforming measures which Pitt abandoned during the exigencies of war. He was always liable to put off certain things while concentrating on a simple objective, intending to return to them at a later stage. This was as true with policy initiatives as with letters seeking his patronage. In 1796 he evidently felt that, above all, the country needed a secure peace, and that everything else would have to wait.

Pitt's efforts to reclaim his mastery of domestic opinion were largely successful. Cheaper bread, French aggression and the government's firm response produced a collapse in support for the radical Societies during 1796. By the end of the year the LCS was in debt and no longer a political threat. The new and parallel policy of seeking peace abroad, however, was sharply rebuffed. On 22 March 1796 the French responded to the British approaches in Berne by demanding the retention of all their conquests (including Belgium, the left bank of the Rhine, and Savoy), while the British must surrender all of theirs (in Corsica and the West Indies). Peace was clearly not on the table, although the government's tactic of putting the French in a worse light had certainly succeeded. According to Grenville they had 'in fact played our Game better for us than we could have hoped'.[13]

Yet the peremptory French rejection of peace feelers also showed their confidence: since the allies were once again at loggerheads over subsidies while the French were preparing a sweep into northern Italy under Bonaparte, such confidence was not misplaced. Pitt cannot have been happy when he responded to a full-scale onslaught by Fox on the whole conduct of the war and the failed attempt to negotiate, on 10 May 1796. His defence of the latter was that 'the terms proposed by the enemy cut short all further treaty; and as to the communication of the result, it will have, at least, the important consequence of dividing the opinions of France, and uniting those of England'.[14]

His majority was unaffected by events, and was confirmed in the country after his decision to hold a general election that summer. As in 1790, he had let the Parliament run for six years of its seven-year maximum. There now seemed to be a window between the domestic unrest of the previous winter and the further trials soon expected in the war. The election produced neither excitement nor any discernible shift of opinion. With the advantage of adding the Portland Whigs to what was already a large majority, the government could claim 424 seats against ninety-five for the opposition and thirty-nine independents or waverers.[15]

Thirteen years before, Pitt could only have dreamt of such parliamentary and electoral dominance. Yet by all accounts his mood that summer was bleak, and in private his usual air of confidence and optimism often deserted him. Rumours abounded that the Austrians were making peace. Pitt wrote to Grenville of his anxiety to negotiate: 'In this situation it would be inexcusable not to try any chance that can be tried, honourably and safely, to set on foot some decent plan of pacification . . . either now or a few months hence, we shall be left to sustain alone the conflict with France and Holland, probably joined by Spain, and perhaps favored more or less openly by the Northern powers. But with proper exertion we can make our party good against them all.'[16] He was described by friends as 'not in his usual spirits'.[17] Wilberforce would later comment that the mounting stress meant 'his temper was not so entirely free from those occasional approaches to fretfulness'.[18]

One description of Pitt's working habits is contained in the diary of Charles Abbot, later Speaker of the House of Commons.

> March 17, 1796. – Dined at Butt's with the Solicitor-General and Lord Muncaster. Lord Muncaster was an early political friend of Mr. Pitt, and our conversation turned much upon his habits of life. Pitt transacts the business of all departments except Lord Grenville's and Dundas's. He requires eight or ten hours' sleep. He dines slightly at five o'clock upon days of business, and on other days after the House is up; but if thrown out of his regular dinner of one sort or the other, he becomes completely ill and unfit for business for a day or two. This has happened to him in the present Session. He will not suffer anybody to arrange his papers, and extract the important points for him. In his reception of the merchants, when they wait upon him, he is particularly desirous of satisfying them that his measures are right. Lord Hawkesbury, on the contrary, entertains them with telling them what he knows of their business, instead of hearing what they have to tell him.[19]

It is not surprising that Pitt was depressed and irritable that summer. From April onwards, Bonaparte had rampaged across Italy, repeatedly defeating the Austrians and knocking Piedmont out of the war. It was a campaign of brilliant manoeuvres, forced marches and stirring rhetoric. Bonaparte told his troops: 'Soldiers, in fifteen days you have gained six victories, taken twenty-one flags, fifty-five cannon and several strongholds . . . You have won battles without cannons, crossed rivers without bridges, you have made forced marches without shoes, bivouacked without brandy and often without bread. Only soldiers of liberty were capable of undergoing all that you have undergone.'[20]

The French had discovered one of the greatest military commanders of all time. Bonaparte's victories totally distracted the Austrians from their intended efforts on the Rhine, and further encouraged Spain to join with France in assuming control of the Mediterranean while invading Portugal. Madrid signed an offensive alliance with Paris in August, and declared war on Britain on 5 October 1796.

Nevertheless, the morale of Pitt and his Ministers picked up towards the end of the summer. He went to Weymouth in early September to visit the King, and from there wrote to his brother to tell him that Lord Mansfield's death meant he could now be President of the Council, a rather meaningless promotion intended to assuage the humiliation of the previous year. He also mentioned that a mission to Berlin to try to stir the renewed involvement of the Prussians had come to nothing. 'We therefore see nothing left (in order to bring the question of peace and war to a point) but to send directly to Paris. The step of applying for a passport will be taken immediately . . . Our great apparent difficulty is finance, which can only be removed by bringing people to a temper for very unusual exertions.'[21] Pitt stressed again in this letter that it was important to 'satisfy the country that we have done enough towards general peace',[22] particularly in view of an imminent war with Spain. Much of his greater predilection for negotiations than that shown by his colleagues stemmed from his sensitivity to public opinion.

Against this background, and with the additional encouragement of fresh internal troubles in France, with large numbers of royalists being elected to popular assemblies, Pitt decided to mount another peace initiative. He wrote to his mother from Downing Street on 6 September, explaining that he would not make it to Burton Pynsent until the end of the year at the earliest, referring to the state of France as 'of itself very encouraging'.[23] Military developments had also taken a turn for the better. The Austrians, under the Archduke Charles, were making progress against the French in western Germany, moving back across the Rhine on 20 September. Britain was again on top of the seesaw of conquest in the West Indies, with Abercromby's expedition retaking St Vincent, St Lucia and Grenada along with some smaller Dutch colonies. Further encouragement came from St Petersburg. Catherine the Great, having annihilated Poland, was now more interested in waging war against the French Revolution. October brought news that the Russians were prepared to send 60,000 men to join the war in return for a subsidy, and it was decided to offer them about £1½ million. Corsica was also to be offered to the Empress, although by November the entry of Spain into the war was forcing the evacuation of all British troops and ships in the Mediterranean.

Overall, these developments seemed to strengthen the British government's hand in October 1796 as the first substantive peace talks got underway in Paris. Initial approaches through Denmark for a passport had been rejected by the French, but accepted when applied for directly. The Earl of Malmesbury, one of Britain's most experienced diplomats and hero of the 1787 triumph in Holland, was sent to France. His going did not please the hawks in the Cabinet such as Dundas, or the suspicious Austrians, or hardline opponents of the French Revolution such as Burke, who said Malmesbury's journey to Paris was slow because 'he went the whole way on his knees'.[24]

Malmesbury would spend nearly two months there gauging the atmosphere, negotiating with the French, hoping to be joined by an Austrian representative and awaiting final instructions from London. When the possible terms for peace were sent to him from London in December, Pitt had stiffened them from an earlier draft made in the relative despair of the summer. The British demands involved the Austrian Netherlands either being returned to Austria or made independent, a French withdrawal from most of northern Italy, a restoration of much of the territory formerly belonging to German states, no French control of St Domingo, and British retention of most of the colonies seized from the Dutch, including Ceylon and the Cape of Good Hope. This was compatible with France keeping the territories which she had, since 1793, occupied on her eastern and south-eastern borders, together with the return of her West Indian colonies.

Ministers do not seem to have had high hopes of this negotiation succeeding, although they thought they would at least once again put the French in a difficult position. In the meantime it was necessary to prepare for another year of war, and in particular to guard against the renewed danger of invasion. On 18 October Pitt proposed to the Commons a further expansion of the army and the militia: 15,000 men to be selected by ballot to join the armed services, 60,000 to be added to the militia and the addition of 20,000 horsemen for home defence raised by requiring every person who kept ten horses to provide one horseman and a horse. Facing the need for another loan of £18 million in the run-up to the budget, Pitt hit upon a new way of raising this amount on advantageous terms. He called it the 'loyalty loan' and invited the public to subscribe to it, thereby avoiding having to go back to the financial markets. The result was extraordinary: £5 million was subscribed on the first day, and the entire amount was raised by

5 December, after the books had been opened for only four days. The Dukes of Bedford and Bridgwater each subscribed £100,000, Pitt's friend Bob Smith (who was now the first Lord Carrington) £40,000. Pitt himself went in for £10,000 (which he then had to borrow), and Dundas and Grenville felt they should do the same. The loyalty loan was a triumph, but the mounting costs of war still required increasingly serious hikes in taxation. In the budget statement of 7 December 1796, Pitt proposed £2 million of additional taxes, levied on spirits, sugar, stage coaches, postage, auctions, fine tea and many other items. He also revealed that in the recess he had approved a loan of £1.2 million to Austria without parliamentary approval, an announcement that brought a stormy debate but a large government majority the following day.

December 1796 was also the month in which the hopes for peace were dashed. Late one Sunday night Pitt wrote to Dundas: 'A new scene is opened on the Continent by an event of which the account is just come – the death of the Empress of Russia on the 17th of last month . . . I am afraid much good is not in any case to be expected from the new Emperor. It is difficult to say whether one ought to regret the most that she had not died sooner or lived longer.'[25]

The new Tsar, Paul I, rejected any active participation in the war. This emboldened the French, who were indeed about to send an invasion force across the Channel from Brest. Their fleet, consisting of seventeen ships of the line and twenty-six other vessels carrying 15,000 troops, sailed just as Malmesbury was presenting the new British proposals in Paris. A message was sent to stop them sailing, but it did not arrive in time. Making the best of the situation, the French then rejected what they described as a British 'ultimatum'. Malmesbury was given forty-eight hours to leave Paris: the following week he was back in Downing Street dining with Pitt.

Not only was peace not available, but the French invasion force was now at sea. Their chosen destination was Bantry Bay, on the reckoning that an invasion of Ireland would meet with a partly sympathetic population and create immense difficulties in London. The expedition turned out to be a fiasco, meeting December gales, driving snow and the intrepid attacks of a single British frigate, the *Indefati-*

gable. When they gathered off Bantry Bay on 21 December they were missing eight ships, one of which was carrying the Admiral and the General who were meant to be in charge. A fresh storm then drove them back out to sea on Christmas Day. By mid-January they were back in Brest, apart from one ship of the line which British vessels drove aground on the coast of Brittany. Not for the first time, the British Isles were saved by the weather. A French force on this scale would have outnumbered the Irish militia if it had been able to disembark, and would quite probably have triggered civil war in Ireland.

There could be no doubt in Westminster now that the war would go on, and that it had to be won. Pitt addressed the Commons on 30 December, saying his sentiments were 'only those of disappointment'. He defended the proposed peace terms as 'fair, just, and reasonable', and asked: 'Are we to persevere in the war with a spirit and energy worthy of the British name and of the British character?'[26] He used his speech to show his own spirit and resolve. But he also knew the situation was grave: after four years of war Britain was left with one exhausted ally and a powerful alliance against her. The war had already driven him to impose burdens and restrictions on the people which he could not have imagined in 1792. They were not enough. Now he would have to find fresh reserves of energy within himself and the nation for a war without end.

Pitt had not managed to visit his mother that autumn, but he had found some recreation closer to home. The endless discussion of Foreign Office business frequently threw him together with his twenty-six-year-old protégé George Canning, whom he had made a Foreign Office Under Secretary. Canning's rapid elevation to the front bench was a recognition of his obvious ability, but may also have been partly the result of a wish by Pitt to keep a closer eye on Grenville in the light of the recent differences between them. Canning had made it his business to get to know Pitt well; well enough to press his claims for promotion on an indulgent Prime Minister. There had already been grumbles around Parliament that he was too close to Pitt, and much too familiar. He had once even been seen to touch Pitt on the shoulder, an action unthinkable to the majority of MPs. Canning wrote his own explanation of this in his journal:

> The complaint was that my manner with Pitt in the House of Commons is too familiar – But whereas other persons, Country gentlemen and others, some of great consequence, and who have known and supported Mr. Pitt for years – treat him with the utmost respect and distance, and if they venture to address him at all, do it in a manner, the most humble and deferent, I, it seems, stand in no awe whatsoever – but talk to him without reserve or hesitation at all times and laugh and make jokes – and *once* was seen, when I wanted to speak to him, and he was looking another way, to put my hand on his shoulder. How can you conceive a more silly thing to trouble people's heads than this? . . . I know indeed that I have, with people whom I like, old or young, great or small, something of a *caressing* manner (I think I must call it so, for I do not recollect any other word to express it) and so have a great many other people – a great many have it *not* – and with *that* class it is not right to make use of it . . . They consider Mr. Pitt, naturally enough, as one of the latter class, the *non-shakers* – whereas he is in fact a very hearty, *salutation-giving, shake hands* sort of person – and one therefore whom I feel it is natural to take by the arm, or *to touch upon the shoulder even* (which is the great offence) . . . But if it be wrong it must be altered.[27]

Canning then learnt to ride, and found the advantages of this included being able to call on Pitt at Holwood. He sometimes found his hero alone, and would spend hours talking and riding with him. He told a friend: 'I think I have never left him without liking him better than before. I could not admire or love him more, even if I had no obligations to him; though in that case, I should give a freer, because less suspicious testimony of the claims which, I think, he has to be both loved and admired.'[28] We cannot know for sure that this hero–protégé relationship had no physical aspect; some may have suspected it at the time: Pitt behaved in a strange, trancelike way at Canning's wedding in 1800, and in 1804 Lady Hester Stanhope told Canning that Pitt 'is attached to you in a way unlike what he feels about anybody else'.[29]

But, as other biographers have pointed out, there is no evidence that the friendship was possessive.[30] Pitt seemed actually to encourage Canning's marriage, and was in general happy to take or leave the friends who wandered into his life, enjoying the company of those who managed to provide companionship and political ability at the same time.

As it happened, Canning witnessed a rare development in Pitt's life – an apparently close friendship with a woman. If he was alone at Holwood Pitt would travel to nearby Beckenham, to the home of Lord Auckland. There he mixed with Auckland's family, including his attractive daughter Lady Eleanor Eden. Canning reported of one occasion: 'it was a whole holiday – spent entirely in the country – in riding, and rambling about with Lord Auckland, the Chancellor and Pitt all the morning – and in playing all sorts of tricks, frolics and fooleries, with the same persons and with the addition and assistance of all the Edens from dinner-time to bed-time'.[31] It was not long before rumours about the relationship between Pitt and Eleanor Eden were spreading widely, reflected in Auckland's letter to John Beresford on 22 December 1796:

> We are all well here, and I will take the occasion to add a few words of a private and confidential kind. You may probably have seen or heard by letters a report of an intended marriage between Mr. Pitt and my eldest daughter. You know me too well to suppose that if it were so I should have remained silent. The truth is she is handsome, and possessed of sense far superior to the ordinary proportion of the world; they see much of each other, they converse much together, and I really believe they have sentiments of mutual esteem; but I have no reason to think that it goes further on the part of either, nor do I suppose it is ever likely to go further.

Beresford replied:

> December 27, 1796
>
> I certainly heard of the report which you mention, and saw it in the newspapers. Lord Camden has more than once asked me if I knew anything about it. I answered, as I shall continue to do, that I knew nothing about it.

Pitt seems to have realised early in 1797 that the matter was getting out of hand. On 20 January he wrote to Auckland from Downing Street:

> My dear Lord, – Altho' the anxious expectation of public business would at all events have made it difficult for me to leave town during the last ten days, you may perhaps have begun to think that it cannot have been the only reason which has kept me so long from Beckenham. The truth is, that I have felt it impossible to allow myself to yield to the temptation of returning thither without having (as far as might depend upon me) formed a decision on a point which I am sensible has remained in suspension too long already. Having at length done so, I should feel myself inexcusable if (painful as the task is) any consideration prevented me from opening myself to you without reserve. It can hardly, I think, be necessary to say that the time I have passed among your family has led to my forming sentiments of very real attachment towards them all, and of much more than attachment towards one whom I need not name. Nor should I do justice to my own feelings, or explain myself as firmly as I think I ought to do, if I did not own that every hour of my acquaintance with the person to whom you will easily conceive I refer has served to augment and confirm that impression; in short, has convinced me that whoever may have the good fortune ever to be united to her is destined to more than his share of human happiness.
>
> Whether, at any rate, I could have had any ground to hope that such might have been my lot, I am in no degree entitled to guess. I have to reproach myself for ever having indulged the idea on my own part as far as I have done without asking myself carefully and early enough what were the difficulties in the way of its being realised. I have suffered myself to overlook them too long, but having now at length reflected as fully and as calmly as I am able on every circumstance that ought to come under my consideration (at least as much for her sake as for my own), I am compelled to say that I find the obstacles to it decisive and insurmountable. In thus conveying to you, my dear Lord, what has been passing in my mind, and its painful and unavoidable result, I have felt it impossible to say less. And yet it would be almost a consolation to me to know that even what I have said is superfluous, and that the idea I have entertained has been

> confined solely to myself. If this should be the case, I am sure this communication will be buried in silence and oblivion. On any other supposition I know that I but consult the feelings of those who must be most in my thoughts by confiding it to your discretion. And in doing so I have every reason to rely on your prudence, kindness, and on those sentiments of mutual friendship which I hope will not be affected by any change which may at the present moment be unavoidable in what has lately been the habits of our intercourse. For myself, allow me only to add that, separated as I must be for a time from those among whom I have passed many of my happiest moments, the recollection of that period will be long present to my mind. The greatest pleasure and best consolation I can receive will be if I am enabled to prove how deep an interest I must always take in whatever may concern them.
>
> They will not, I am sure, be less dear to me thro' life than they would have had a right to expect from the nearest and closest connection.
>
> Believe me, my dear Lord, under all circumstances,
> Ever sincerely and faithfully yours,
> W. PITT.

Auckland's reply described the shock and disappointment of his wife and daughter. He said 'it has been impossible for Ly. Ad. & for me not to remark that you entertained the partiality which you describe; and it has been for several weeks the happiest subject of conversation that we have had thro' the course of a very happy life, to consider it in every point of view. We had from an early period every reason to believe that the sentiments formed were *most cordially* mutual: and we saw with delight that they were ripening into an attachment which might lay the foundation of a system of most perfect happiness, for the two persons for whom we were so much concerned.'[32] He went on to probe for the nature of the 'insurmountable obstacle' protested by Pitt:

> We presume that the obstacles alluded to are those of circumstances. (If there are any others we hope you will confide them to us.) I do not mean circumstances of Office & of the Public;

they might create a temporary suspension, but could create no permanent difficulty. As to circumstances of fortune, I may be imprudent in the idea, but I cannot think that they ought in such a case to create an hour's interruption in an intercourse essentially sought & loved by us all; still less that they ought to affect the ultimate result, tho' they may impede it. I am sure that the person alluded to has steadiness of mind to wait any indefinite period of Time for that difficulty if possible to be got over. I am sure also that it would be happiness to her, as it has often been to her mother, to share such difficulties, & to endeavour also to lessen them. I only regret that my own position puts it out of my power to remove those difficulties. I have about 2000£ belonging to her from a legacy, & what I owe to the others will not allow me to add much to it.

He finished by inviting Pitt to come back and 'talk about the whole at leisure & again & again'. Pitt's reply was immediate:

Downing Street: January 22nd, 1797, 2 P.M.

My dear Lord, – If I felt much more than I could express in writing to you yesterday you will guess that these feelings are all, if possible, heightened by the nature of your answer. I will not attempt to describe the sense I have of your kindness and Lady Auckland's, much less how much my mind is affected by what you tell me of the sentiments of another person, unhappily too nearly interested in the subject in question. I can only say, but it is saying everything, that that consideration now adds to my unavailing regret as much as under different circumstances it might have contributed to the glory and happiness of life.

Indeed, my dear Lord, I did not bring myself to the step I have taken without having, as far as I am able, again and again considered every point which must finally govern my conduct. I should deceive you and everyone concerned, as well as myself, if I flattered myself with the hope that such an interval as you suggest would move the obstacles I have felt, or vary the ground of my opinion.

It is impossible for me, and would be useless, to state them at large. The circumstances of every man's private and personal situation can often on various accounts be fully known and fairly

> judged of by no one but himself, even where, as in the present case, others may be equally interested in the result. On the present occasion I have had too many temptations in the opposite scales to distrust my own decision. I certainly had to contend with sentiments in my own mind such as must naturally be produced by a near observation of the qualities and endowments you have described, with those of affectionate attachment, of real admiration, and of cordial esteem and confidence.
>
> If anything collateral could add strength to these sentiments, they would have derived it (as you know from what I have said already) from every circumstance, with respect to all parts of your family, which could tend to render such a connection dear and valuable to my mind. Believe me, I have not lightly or easily sacrificed my best hopes and earnest wishes to my conviction and judgment. Believe me, also, further explanation or discussion can answer no good purpose. And let me entreat you to spare me and yourself the pain of urging it further. It could only lead to prolonged suspense and increased anxiety, without the possibility of producing any ultimate advantage.
>
> Feeling this impression thus strongly and unalterably in my mind, I have felt it a trying but indispensable duty, for the sake of all who are concerned, to state it (whatever it may cost me to do so) as distinctly and explicitly as I have done. Having done so, I have only to hope that reading this letter will nowhere be attended with half the pain I have felt in writing it.
>
> I remain, my dear Lord,
> Ever sincerely and affectionately yours,
> W. PITT.

Auckland had to concede defeat, as Pitt described in a letter to Addington:

> The first answer indeed which I received on Saturday, tho' thoroughly kind, was the most embarrassing possible, as it stated the sentiments entertained to be mutual and pressed for explanation and discussion, proposing at the same time any interval of delay in order to take the chance of overcoming the difficulties and desiring me to continue coming in the interval as if nothing had happened. I had then nothing left but to convey in my answer

> quite explicitly tho' with as much tenderness as I could, that the decision I had felt myself obliged to take was final and that further discussion could only produce increased anxiety and could lead to no good. This was understood and received as I meant it should; and the answer I received last night, considers the thing as over, and proposes to contradict the reports gradually.

Did Pitt really fall in love with Eleanor Eden? The words he addressed to Auckland certainly suggest that he was happy for this to be thought to be the case – the use of the word 'attachment' in the eighteenth century conveyed the impression of strong affection, and usually of sexual desire. Pitt would have known what he was saying. Yet the profession of such an attachment, coupled with the countervailing 'decisive and insurmountable obstacle', must also have seemed to him to be a neat formula which dishonoured no one and avoided the potentially greater embarrassment of saying it was all a mistake. To simply admit that he had no desire to marry the good-looking Eleanor would have been to invite a new round of ribaldry and innuendo at his own expense.

In later years, Pitt was happy for others to continue to believe that had he been a private citizen he would have married Eleanor Eden. Lady Hester Stanhope formed the impression that it 'almost broke his heart when he gave her up'. Interestingly, however, his explanation – some six or seven years later – of why he had not proceeded was varied, and might be considered less than convincing. He had, he said, thought 'she was not a woman to be left at will when business might require it, and he sacrificed his feelings to his sense of public duty'. In addition, 'there is her mother, such a chatterer! – and then the family intrigues. I can't keep them out of my house; and, for my King's and country's sake, I must remain a single man.'[33] These sound like the arguments of a man making excuses rather than one reluctantly abandoning a passionate love.

It seems unlikely then that Pitt set out with an intention to marry Eleanor Eden and later changed his mind. Far more probable is that he did not initially realise what other people would make of his friendship with Auckland's family, and that he simply liked Eleanor's company without wishing to take it further. There are many candidates to be considered for the role of 'insurmountable obstacle' if his opening letter is to be taken at face value. Auckland raised the issue of finance, and Pitt's debts were certainly heavy after continued years of neglect, along with the added burden of the loyalty loan he invented. Another possibility is shortage of time; but hard-working as he was, it is clear that Pitt had sufficient time to enjoy friendships and recreations if he wanted to. A third possibility is the state of his health, but his complaints were erratic rather than chronic, and did not prevent him from doing anything else. The fourth possibility is simply sexual. Dundas is said to have wagered £500 that Pitt never touched a woman. At thirty-seven years old he had no experience of intimacy with the opposite sex. It is likely therefore that he lacked either inclination or confidence, and had never even thought about Eleanor Eden in a sexual sense, while enjoying her company. The latter possibility must be the most likely decisive obstacle in Pitt's mind, although it may also have been a mixture of any or all of these things. Given the need to be categoric in his letters to Auckland, he probably chose to express a general unwillingness to marry in the form of a single, albeit mysterious, problem. The episode has often been described as 'Pitt's one love story'. It seems unlikely that he would have given it that title himself.

However Pitt reflected on this unfortunate incident, it is unlikely to have dominated his thoughts for many days. On the last day of January 1797, the Spanish grand fleet put to sea with the apparent intention of a junction with the French. The British Mediterranean fleet in their path was outnumbered two to one.

20

Breaking Point

'No crisis so alarming, or nearly so alarming, has ever been known in England since the Revolution of 1688. One night the Ministers were roused from their slumbers by the booming of the distant cannon.'

LORD STANHOPE[1]

'There is one great resource, which I trust will never abandon us, and which has shone forth in the English character, by which we have preserved our existence and fame, as a nation, which I trust we shall be determined never to abandon under any extremity . . . that we know great exertions are wanting, that we are prepared to make them, and at all events determine to stand or fall by the laws, liberties, and religion of our country.'

WILLIAM PITT, 10 NOVEMBER 1797[2]

THE TWENTY-SEVEN SHIPS of the line that headed west through the Straits of Gibraltar in February 1797 represented the pride and might of Spain. Between them they mounted more than 2,300 guns, including 136 aboard a single ship, the *Santissima Trinidad,* then the largest warship in the world. But what happened to them when they entered the Atlantic would reaffirm with devastating clarity that, however desperate the situation on the Continent, Britain could assert her command of the seas. The Spanish ships were intercepted off Cape St Vincent by a far smaller force of British warships under Sir John Jervis, joined from the Mediterranean by the audacious and frequently disobedient Commodore Horatio Nelson. The Spanish, many of whose sailors had never been to sea before, let alone experienced the point-blank violence of a sea battle, soon found their ships divided into two forces and raked by superior British gunnery. Faced with the potentially massive firepower of the Spanish vessels, Nelson performed one of his legendary feats of daring. Directly confronting the *Santissima Trinidad* with a ship scarcely half her size, he was able to board and capture the *San Nicolas* and then use her as a bridge to capture the huge *San Josef* as well. The loss of this and other enormous three-deckers tore the heart from the Spanish navy in a matter of hours. The survivors limped to Cadiz, and while the Spanish Admiral was court-martialled, Jervis and Nelson returned to Britain to an earldom and a knighthood respectively.

The Battle of Cape St Vincent removed for years to come the threat of Franco-Spanish domination of the English Channel in the manner of 1779, and for Pitt it provided immediate and much-needed political relief when news of it arrived in London in early March. It followed by only four weeks reports of a fresh disaster for the Austrians in Italy: at the Battle of Rivoli in mid-January Napoleon had won yet another decisive victory. He could now dictate his terms to the Pope, consolidate French power in northern Italy and take the war towards Austria's own heartland. It would only be a few weeks before the French were marching through Carinthia and were reported to be within sight of the spires of Vienna.

The news of St Vincent therefore coincided with the realisation in London that Britain's only remaining major ally might face imminent collapse. It was a moment which illuminated the pattern of warfare for years to come: French domination of the landmass of western Europe, and British dominion of the seas. While an invasion force could still slip past the Royal Navy, as the aborted expedition to Bantry Bay had shown, it ran the risk of disaster if caught on the high seas. For the evidence was emerging after the Glorious First of June and the Battle of Cape St Vincent that British victories at sea were not the result of random factors or good luck, but were the product of a clear superiority in naval warfare. The shock of the loss of control of the Channel during the American War of Independence had induced Pitt and Parliament to devote unprecedented peacetime resources to rebuilding the navy in the 1780s: the administrative reforms pursued by Sir Charles Middleton and overseen by Pitt also had a telling effect.

Such efforts were all the more productive because they were built on the foundation of an unrivalled seafaring tradition and experience: most of the nearly 280,000 men serving in the navy and the merchant marine as recorded in the census of 1801 were willing recruits. The large peacetime navy had fostered the emergence of several brilliant commanders. Once war broke out the British advantage at sea was consolidated by the early successes: French sailors could not be trained effectively when they could not safely leave port, and only Britain could easily import suitable timber for warship building from the Baltic. The loss of experienced French sailors in these early engagements was hard to make up – in the Glorious First of June and at Cape St Vincent the numbers of French and Spanish sailors killed in action were six times that of British. British ships tended to be more durable even though they were smaller, and they enjoyed a technological advantage in gun design which permitted them to fire heavier broadsides with greater frequency. Thus by 1797, while no army could stand against Napoleon on the Continent, no navy could overcome the British at sea. Faced with an increasingly hostile Continent, the navy represented for Britain her longest arm and most vital shield.

The news of Cape St Vincent helped Pitt to promote the recovery of national sentiment in the wake of the first of the many crises of 1797. In late February there had been a run on the Bank of England caused by fears for the financial system and the possibility of invasion. Ludicrously but understandably, such fears were exacerbated when 1,400 French ruffians or '*banditti*' managed to set foot on the British coast, first anchoring off Ilfracombe and then coming ashore in Pembrokeshire. This, the last landing of enemy forces on the British mainland up to the present day, did not have the remotest hope of any military success. Surrounded by local militia and volunteers (and according to some accounts believing that the scarlet cloaks of women peasants represented an elite force of Guards), the forlorn 1,400 soon capitulated.

Strategically irrelevant as it may have been, this incident fed the febrile atmosphere of that winter, with stocks falling to a record low and £100,000 a day being withdrawn from the Bank of England at the end of February. The Bank's stocks of bullion were down to

£1.2 million: if they were exhausted in the next few days the nation would be bankrupt and the entire system of finance and credit which had provided the tens of millions of pounds to sustain the war would collapse.

Pitt was well suited to such a crisis. His response was to promote the wider circulation of notes while suspending the obligation of the Bank to meet its commitments with bullion. It was a tense weekend as the Cabinet met on Saturday, 25 February, and the King agreed to Pitt's exceptional request to hold a Privy Council at Buckingham House on the Sunday. There an Order in Council was agreed suspending cash payments 'until the sense of Parliament can be taken'.[3] On the Monday, the authorities issued calming statements while the Lord Mayor of London led the City merchants in undertaking to accept notes, rather than gold, as legal tender for any amount. From 2 March, after Pitt secured the passage of the necessary legislation within two days, the Bank was able to issue £1 and £2 notes without regard to the previous £5 minimum. Such measures maintained the circulation of money and helped narrowly to avert a financial crash. Pitt had been forced by an emergency to create the paper money supply which would become a permanent feature of the economy. Successful as this was, it must have been an agonising step for a man who understood the risks of inflation and had recently witnessed the French currency spiral into worthlessness after the excessive issuing of *assignats* – paper currency secured on confiscated land. Years later Grenville would say that it caused Pitt the most painful day of his political life.[4]

Pitt would have felt a good deal of pain as he outlined the circumstances and the measures to the House of Commons on 28 February. Notwithstanding his effective response to the crisis, he was the financial wizard who now had to explain how he had so nearly presided over national bankruptcy. Fox and Sheridan denounced the mismanagement which they alleged had produced the crisis; many attacked the huge subsidies paid to the Austrians in gold bullion, which had never been popular and had undoubtedly depleted the Bank's reserves. Pitt won the day by 244 to eighty-six, but he had taken another knock, which his wittiest critics were happy to record in verse:

Of Augustus and Rome
The poets still warble,
How he found it of brick
And left it of marble.
So of Pitt and of England
Men may say without vapour,
How he found it of gold
And left it of paper.[5]

For all the criticism, Pitt's experience and decisiveness in financial matters must have helped the restoration of confidence in the markets. Certainly his measures were vindicated: within a short time credit was expanding once again, the government was able to raise fresh loans, a Commons Committee of Inquiry found the Bank's finances to be in rather better shape than suspected, and the convertibility of notes into specie was eventually restored. A new copper coinage was introduced later that year, and long-term reforms of the Royal Mint and the eventual (but well into the next century) introduction of silver coins were set in train. Britain's two great advantages in its contest with France were the prowess of its navy and the vast capacity and creditworthiness of its financial system. Whatever Pitt's failings as a war leader, he was adept at leveraging both of these assets.

Indeed, throughout March he was once again working on a new loan to Austria as part of the effort to keep her in the war. Having witnessed the French subjugate most of western Europe over the previous four years, Pitt and his colleagues were extremely apprehensive about Britain facing France alone. On 4 April he resisted (by 266 votes to eighty-seven) an attack on his latest proposal to provide a subsidy of £3.5 million to Austria: 'It cannot be a measure of economy to abandon the plan of availing ourselves of the co-operation of his imperial majesty by contributing money to his assistance. When we consider the amount of the expense, and the magnitude of the service, there is no ground of comparison between them!'[6]

Over the next few days Pitt explained to George III that it was once again necessary to seek a negotiated peace, given 'the *extreme* difficulty of providing even now for the pressing and indispensable exigencies of the public service', and that a unilateral peace between

France and Austria 'would produce a pressure on this country which ought by all possible means to be avoided'.[7] The King was reluctant to contemplate yet another attempt at treating with the French, but the Cabinet was unanimous. Grenville doubted that Britain had the will to fight alone, and Pitt worried that such a war could not be sustained financially. There were rumours that the Dutch, now allies of France, were preparing an invasion force, and all prospect of successful land operations against the French had disappeared. In the West Indies, British forces had done well in capturing Trinidad from the Spanish in February, but were racked by massive casualties from disease – from which at least 50,000 British soldiers would die in the West Indies between 1793 and 1802, many times more than were killed by enemy action.

In these circumstances, it is not surprising that Pitt and his colleagues decided on a renewed bid for peace, with the coordinated involvement of Austria and the mediation of Russia. Accordingly, a Foreign Office official, George Hammond, was despatched to Vienna in early April. As so often with the slow-moving communication of the eighteenth century, it was already too late. Hammond arrived in Vienna on 30 April: on 18 April the Austrians had signed a peace agreement with Napoleon at Leoben. This would lead later in the year to the Treaty of Campo Formio, which represented a huge strategic victory for France but a sop for Austria: the map of northern Italy was redrawn around the Cisalpine republic dominated by France; the Austrian Netherlands and many Mediterranean islands were ceded to the French; in addition the Venetian republic was destroyed and Venice awarded to the Austrians. Austria was out of the war. As the Dutch prepared a hostile fleet, and Napoleon returned to France to head the 'Army of England', Britain stood alone.

By any standards the circumstances of April 1797 constituted a major crisis in the life of the British nation and the career of William Pitt. But between the middle of April and the beginning of June a new and previously unsuspected circumstance would arise which would compound the crisis to make it the most alarming then imaginable.

The one remaining guarantor of Britain's territorial integrity and independence was the navy. On 15 April the Channel Fleet at Spithead in Hampshire, the main assembling point for vessels based at Portsmouth, was ordered to sea. On 16 April, Easter Sunday, it refused. The Royal Navy had mutinied.

The trouble had been brewing for some weeks. In March, Lord Howe, who was still the sailors' favourite Admiral, received some letters of complaint from within the navy while he was taking the waters at Bath. These pointed out that the army and militia had recently received an increase in their allowances; navy seamen by contrast had received no pay rise since the reign of Charles II, over a hundred years before. Furthermore, their pay was often in arrears, and merchant seamen were paid many times more. No doubt those who had fought in the only major victories Britain had experienced during the war to that date felt their efforts were not being recognised.

The letters to Howe disappeared into the bureaucracy of the Admiralty, while the widespread resentment simmered across the fleet. When Lord Bridport, who had succeeded Howe at Spithead, hoisted the signal to sail, the seamen on the latter's former flagship the *Queen Charlotte* gave three cheers of defiance, an example followed by the rest of the fleet. The mutiny which now developed was, at least in its initial stages, a wonderfully British affair. The men made clear that they would sail if the French put to sea, but not otherwise until their demands were met. These demands, communicated to the First Lord of the Admiralty, Earl Spencer, when he hastened to Portsmouth after consultation with Pitt, were not unreasonable. The seamen wanted improved pay, better rations, improved care for the sick and wounded, fairer distribution of prize money, and less frequent confinement on board when in harbour. Thirty-two delegates were elected from the sixteen ships in question to present these demands; while some officers were held hostage they were not harmed, and in the meantime the orderliness and readiness of the fleet were maintained. It was probably the best-behaved mutiny in history.

Nevertheless, a mutiny it was, and given the situation it did not take the government long to conclude that it should make concessions to it. There was one dangerous moment during the negotiations when

Admiral Gardner lost his temper with one of the delegates, seized him by the collar and threatened to have all the delegates hanged. Instead it was the Admiral who was sent ashore, while Pitt accepted Spencer's requests to grant much of what the seamen demanded. A pay rise would be recommended to Parliament, rations properly made up, and George III agreed to pardon the men for their mutiny.

Viewed from London, it seemed that the mutiny had been settled. Preparations were begun to pass the necessary regulations and vote the extra money (totalling £536,000 in a full year) necessary to meet the agreement. With matters apparently under control, Pitt got on with presenting his budget on 26 April. After the success of the loyalty loan in December and the restoration of confidence in the financial system in March, he was able once again to raise a large loan. As had become usual in the years of war, he accompanied this with a miscellany of tax increases in order to pay the interest and maintain payments into the Sinking Fund. He expressed his sorrow at the financial situation, saying it was 'impossible for me not to feel considerable regret, and great personal disappointment in being compelled, however reluctantly, to propose an addition to the ample and large provision already made, towards defraying the expenses of the country in a wide and calamitous war, and increase the present burthens which are borne with unexampled patience by all ranks of the community'.[8] He went on to announce an increase in stamp duty and in the tax on newspapers. Some of the other increases illustrate how he was attempting to keep the war going by scrabbling around for an accumulation of tiny amounts: a change in the tax on advertisements was to bring in an extra £20,000, the regulation of stamps on attorney's certificates would bring in £15,000, and a new tax on ornamental plate would bring in £30,000. It was to be the last time that Pitt could finance the conflict without a massive and widespread rise in taxation; his fear that this would make the war politically unsustainable was a major factor in maintaining his determination to try once again for peace.

Pitt made clear at the time of the budget that seamen's pay would be increased, but there was a short delay before the money was officially voted and other aspects of the agreement ratified. George III was critical of the delay: 'it would be idle to lament that the measures for increasing . . . pay have been delayed for two weeks coming forward in Parliament'.[9] To Ministers, the implementation of the agreement within a couple of weeks probably seemed like acting with lightning speed, but to the seamen themselves, who had risked their necks in confronting their officers and government, the delay was inexplicable – however much else the House of Commons might have to do. Rumours began to spread in the fleet that the government was going back on the deal and that the ringleaders would be arrested. Opposition MPs were happy to stir the pot in Parliament, giving notice of a vote of censure because of the delay.

On 9 May Pitt duly brought in a Bill to increase seamen's allowances, which was passed through the Commons in a single day. The vote of censure was the next day defeated by 237 to sixty-three. On 7 May, however, the mutiny had started all over again. This time the Channel Fleet put their officers ashore and sailed off to St Helens, an anchorage off the Isle of Wight. Within days there was also trouble in ships based at Plymouth and Weymouth, and in the North Sea Fleet based at Yarmouth and the Nore (an anchorage in the Thames Estuary near the mouth of the river Medway, and a holding area for the vast number of vessels entering and leaving the Thames). Once again, Admiral Lord Howe was sent to the rescue. Pitt despatched him to Portsmouth from London despite him suffering agonies of gout, and he was then rowed around the fleet to assure them that all was well and the agreement was indeed being implemented. Indeed, a further concession was made: officers would not return to ships whose crews had made written complaints of being mistreated by them. By mid-May Howe had brought the Channel Fleet once again under control. The crews expressed their regret (again), all concerned were pardoned (again), Howe and the crews' delegates enjoyed sumptuous dinners together and 'Rule Britannia' was sung around the fleet. On this occasion no time was wasted in getting the crews out of port and into action: on 17 May the Channel Fleet obeyed its orders to put to sea.

The fleet at the Nore received the same assurances on the seventeenth as had been given to the fleet at St Helens, but a different combination of personalities and circumstances was at work there. Howe could not be sent to two places at once, and the seamen at the

Nore were led by a well-educated rabble-rouser by the name of Richard Parker who had joined the navy after emerging from a debtors' prison. Parker's motives were more political than the straightforward grievances of the men of the Channel Fleet, as he evidently sympathised with revolutionary ideas. He also set up more of an alternative command, insisting that he be called 'President' or sometimes 'Rear Admiral', while holding meetings in the state cabin of the *Sandwich*, the flagship of Vice Admiral Buckner. Parker's mutineers demanded additional concessions, including an end to punishments for recaptured deserters and the removal of a much wider swathe of officers; they also positioned their vessels to make ready for a blockade of London, and drew to their cause the majority of ships at Yarmouth, which were essential to prevent a Dutch invasion.

The scale, motives and strategic location of the mutiny at the Nore presented Pitt with the gravest crisis he had ever confronted. In the last week of May, almost every possible misfortune seemed to join together in a confluence of disaster. It was known definitively that the Austrians had made peace with France, the fleet at the Nore was exchanging artillery fire with the army at Tilbury, disorder was breaking out in the army itself among the artillery stationed at Woolwich, the ships meant to guard against the Dutch invasion were refusing to do so, the opposition were mounting a renewed push for parliamentary reform on the floor of the Commons, and the Cabinet was racked with division over the next effort to make peace.

The events of a single day, 26 May, illustrate the pressure Pitt was under. Having spent the previous day deciding how to deal with the latest mutiny, he woke to hear artillery fire in the distance: Wilberforce's journal records: 'Pitt awaked by Woolwich artillery riot, and went out to Cabinet.'[10] It was at that Cabinet meeting that Ministers decided to proceed on the assumption that the Austrians had abandoned them. At the same time, government stocks had fallen to their lowest ever level, and there were reports of 'the soldiery rising'.[11] News was being received of Dutch troops preparing for an invasion, and the naval mutiny continued out of control. Yet Pitt had to spend the whole of the late afternoon and evening of that day in the House of Commons, fighting off a renewed opposition motion to bring in parliamentary reform. As it turned out, this was the last throw of an utterly disillusioned opposition, who felt their arguments were ignored by the vast majority of MPs. Fox indicated that he would soon withdraw from parliamentary debate: 'I certainly think that I need not devote much of it [time] to fruitless exertions and to idle talk in this House.'[12]

Despite the parlous situation on every front, Pitt gave a lengthy speech of trenchant opposition to the reform he had once championed. The House must 'consider the danger of introducing an evil of a much greater magnitude than that we are now desirous to repair'; it would not be prudent 'to give an opening for those principles which aim at nothing less than the total annihilation of the constitution'.[13] He defended himself against the charge of having changed his mind: 'Whatever may have been my former opinion, am I to be told that I am inconsistent, if I feel that it is expedient to forgo the advantage which any alteration may be calculated to produce, rather than afford an inlet to principles with which no compromise can be made,'[14] and he ridiculed Fox for having claimed public opinion was on his side but having made no progress in the previous year's general election: 'The right honourable gentleman, the house will recollect, was accustomed to assert last session of parliament, with equal boldness and vehemence as now, that the sense of the country was against the system of Ministers. Good God! Where can the honourable gentlemen have lived? In what remote corner of the country can he have passed his time?'[15] Canning thought the speech 'flat', but Pitt's ability to engage in detailed and effective debate at such a moment suggests he kept calm even in this extreme crisis. Whatever he felt inside, he would have known that the slightest indication of a loss of nerve on his part could have brought the collapse of all financial, political and military confidence.

A story of this period was often told by Earl Spencer to illustrate Pitt's cool nature. As Lord Stanhope described it: 'On a subsequent night there had come from the fleet tidings of especial urgency. Lord Spencer thought it requisite to go at once to Downing Street and consult the Prime Minister. Pitt being roused from his slumbers, sat up in bed, heard the case, and gave his instructions. Lord Spencer took leave and withdrew. But no sooner had he reached the end of the street than he remembered one more point which he omitted to state. Accordingly he returned to Pitt's house, and desired to be shown up a second time to Pitt's chamber. There after so brief an interval he found Pitt as before, buried in profound repose.'[16]

Whether or not such sound sleep was the product of a calm nature or complete exhaustion we do not know, but Pitt's response to the continuing mutiny was certainly decisive and effective. He regarded the time for concessions as over. Pay rises were given to the army, supplies to the rebellious fleet were cut off and gun batteries assembled to confront them, and the navigational buoys and beacons at the mouth of the Thames were removed. He introduced two Emergency Bills specifying severe penalties on anyone exciting sedition in the services or communicating with mutineers. The death penalty was to be imposed on anyone assisting them. Meanwhile, the heroic Admiral Duncan sailed off to maintain his blockade of the entire Dutch navy with only his flagship and one other vessel. By regularly signalling to his non-existent fleet he maintained the fiction that the rest of the British ships were just over the horizon.

By early June the ships involved in the mutiny were beginning to slip away quietly and return to their official stations. Faced with a powerful show of force, and possibly realising they had overstated their demands and made a mistake in following Parker, the seamen steadily chose to call it a day. When Parker finally decided to take the *Sandwich* and any other remaining ships over to the enemy, the crews decided to surrender both the ships and the ringleaders to the authorities. This time there was to be no pardon. Twenty-three of them were executed: on 30 June Parker was hanged from the yardarm of the *Sandwich*.

The mutiny was truly over, but it had been a close-run thing in which initially poor intelligence and the neglect of legitimate grievances had brought the nation to the brink of catastrophe. Once faced with the crisis Pitt had reacted with great wisdom, making concessions to reasonable complaints but acting to crush a revolt which was taken too far. Even so, he and the Cabinet had experienced a scare sufficient to convince them that matters could not go on like this. Pitt would declare in private that it was 'his duty as an English Minister and a Christian to use every effort to stop so bloody and wasting a war'.[17]

He believed Britain needed peace. The only alternative was to ask the country to make the financial and political commitment to an intensified war.

The multiple crises of the first half of 1797 seriously affected Pitt's domestic political standing. Since he had now been leading the government for over thirteen years there were few misfortunes which could not one way or another be attributed to him. By this time, if discontent arose in the parliamentary ranks, there was no shortage of offended grandees ready to feed on it: Leeds, Thurlow and the Marquis of Lansdowne (formerly the Earl of Shelburne) had all been pushed out into the cold by Pitt but had not left the political scene. In mid-May some combination of these dormant but not extinct figures and unhappy MPs promoted a plot to replace Pitt with the Earl of Moira; a veteran of the American War who had also led the expedition to Quiberon, he had become a key adviser of the Prince of Wales, but commanded wide respect. Their prime objective was peace, to which they believed Pitt now posed an obstacle. The plot fizzled out in early June: there was insufficient support for it from the established political groupings, George III took no notice of a letter from Moira proposing a change, and the restoration of internal order and external peace feelers at the beginning of June may have caused the discontent to recede. Yet Moira certainly claimed to have found a great deal of unhappiness with Pitt's leadership, writing to the Duke of Northumberland after meetings with MPs: 'they are violent against Pitt, though they vote with him, but they will not bear the Opposition as a party. Their object is to make some effort to save the country from the evident ruin into which it is most rapidly running.'[18]

Pitt's leadership was therefore being seriously questioned in 1797, and it is not surprising, given his sensitivity to opinion, that he questioned it himself. There is some evidence that at the height of the naval crisis he lost his customary optimism: the following year Auckland would write to Mornington: 'You know that (excepting perhaps during the naval mutiny) he never has inclined to despondency or even to serious discouragement: At present he entertains strong Hopes that all will, somehow, end well.'[19] Pitt himself believed that peace was essential, and there is a strong suggestion that in early 1797 he was prepared to step aside as Prime Minister if doing so would allow peace to be negotiated. According to Pretyman, in the unpublished part of his life of Pitt:

> It was imagined, though probably without foundation, that the French Government would be more disposed to make peace with a new Minister than with Mr. Pitt; & Mr. Pitt, therefore, entertained some idea of resigning. He mentioned this circumstance to the King & had several conferences with his Majesty upon the subject. After much deliberation the plan was abandoned, on the ground that a new, strong Administration, consisting of persons of true constitutional principles, could not then be formed, & Mr. Pitt remained in office; but the consideration of this business had gone so far that it was settled, in case of Mr. Pitt's resignation that he should be succeeded by Mr. Addington, Speaker of the House of Commons, & this was known at the time to Mr. Addington himself & scarcely to any other person.[20]

It was indeed known to Addington, who decades later told his biographer that 'Pitt told me, as early as 1797, that I must make up my mind to take the government.'[21] Pitt had become steadily closer to Addington since the latter had succeeded Grenville as Speaker in 1789. Addington was the son of the elder Pitt's friend and physician; he was also a highly able man who might have gained additional merit in Pitt's eyes from being an ally, but one whose position excluded him from policy disagreements with the Prime Minister. It was to Addington that Pitt had written his frank letter about Eleanor Eden, and it seemed to be only Addington who could tell Pitt to stop drinking. Three years later the diarist Joseph Farington noted: 'Mr. Addington . . . lives abt. a mile from Holm Park – Mr. Pitt is now with him & has been 10 days for the benefit of his health. Sir Walter Farquhar has been down to see him & allows him & the Speaker to drink a bottle between them after dinner (port wine) but none after supper. – Mr. Pitt one night pressed for some, but the Speaker was rigid.'[22]

Addington was in a strong position to be a candid friend to Pitt, since they had known each other for over thirty years. They were the same age, and had been friends since they were seven years old. Addington had an uncomplicated nature: loyal to his friends, of whom Pitt was the longest-standing, strictly supportive of the established Church, and utterly devoted to his family of seven children. Such qualities and long acquaintanceship encouraged Pitt to treat him as a confidant and steadily to promote his career. Addington was initially reluctant to make speeches in Parliament, but Pitt pushed him into seconding the Address at the opening of Parliament in 1786, and then into succeeding Grenville as the Speaker in 1789, in which position his obvious even-handedness and integrity made him a popular figure within the House of Commons. As a politician, however, Addington had weaknesses. In particular his strong desire to be liked and his discomfort when faced with personal acrimony would make it much harder for him to be a Minister than to be the generally respected presiding officer of the House of Commons.

When Eliot explained the possible transfer of the premiership Mrs Pretyman is reported to have exclaimed: 'Addington! . . . are you all mad?' and Eliot apparently replied, 'Addington would do very well *under the direction of Mr. Pitt, – for a time – It would not do for ever*, but it would do Mr. Pitt good to be out of Office for a little while.'[23] This statement is important, coming as it does from one of Pitt's closest friends, since it is so revealing about how Pitt thought of resignation both in 1797 and later. He was thirty-eight years old, and even though he had been in office for thirteen and a half years he regarded resignation as a respite rather than retirement. That he could employ his abilities as anything other than a dominant figure in politics, in or out of office, did not occur to him.

In any event, the succession of crises in 1797 almost certainly made it harder rather than easier for Pitt to contemplate going ahead with the mooted resignation, and there was no real evidence at the time that any alternative Prime Minister would have found it easier to make peace – except perhaps Fox, which Pitt, George III and a majority in Parliament would have found unthinkable. However Pitt wrestled with this problem, some combination of duty, ambition and conceit about his own abilities relative to those of others persuaded him that it was better to continue. For all the political damage he had sustained, he still towered above his contemporaries, and it would not have been difficult to reason that he was the only man with the strength and experience either to insist on peace or to lead a still more difficult war.

Pitt's decision to continue meant that from then on he was psychologically prepared for both war and peace. Once a new round of peace negotiations was underway, the point at which he could consider voluntarily surrendering office had passed. For while he could cope with the idea of temporarily stepping aside to ease the path to peace, he had no intention at all of resigning if his own renewed push for peace ended in failure. If that were to happen, he would have to take on the responsibility of rousing himself and the nation to an even greater effort in war.

Should that prove necessary, so be it, but he was convinced in June 1797 that it was right to try once again to make peace on honourable terms. A settlement in which Britain retained some of its colonial gains, albeit while recognising the enhancement of French power on the Continent, would at least give a pause from conflict while only accepting what was now an accomplished fact: French forces were not going to be defeated on land in the foreseeable future. While peace would therefore require Britain to cut its losses on the Continent, it would also allow her to consolidate her maritime strength and recover her financial position. Pitt continued to be far more sensitive than his colleagues to the problems of raising finance and maintaining public support: he could not be sure of holding the nation together, particularly in the light of the mutinies and the growing problems in Ireland, while implementing the necessary levels of taxation and military recruitment for Britain to fight France alone. With Austria out of the war, it would take years for the exertion of naval and financial strength to bring France to her knees. To Pitt, the logic of the case for attempting a settlement was therefore compelling.

Others, however, were more reluctant to find compromises with the French after so much blood had been shed and French power had grown too extensive for her neighbours to live comfortably. George III in particular thought that: 'If both Houses of Parliament are in as tame a state of mind as it is pretended, I do not see the hopes that either war can be continued with effect or peace obtained but of the most disgraceful and unsolid tenure.'[24] Within the Cabinet, Grenville complained of 'dejection, cowardice and disaffection'.[25] When the French responded to the British request for further talks with the stipulation that they should be held in Lille, with Britain represented by an emissary empowered to conclude 'a definitive and separate treaty of peace' (that is, without reference to any former allies), Grenville opposed the talks.

Stormy Cabinet meetings took place in the closing stages of the Nore mutiny, reaching a climax on 15 June. The Whigs – Spencer, Portland and Windham – supported Grenville, Windham noting: 'Lord Grenville observed truly, that we were at a period at which nothing but firmness could save us; that if we were to continue these concessions there was no reason why the government should exist at the end of a twelvemonth.'[26] But Pitt, who by now had differed from his cousin so frequently that the old trust between them was evaporating, was supported by Loughborough, Cornwallis, Chatham, Liverpool and Dundas. The Cabinet therefore agreed to send an emissary, once again to be the Earl of Malmesbury, to Lille, with Grenville's dissent noted in the minutes. As Malmesbury set off, the greatest of all the opponents of the French Revolution, Edmund Burke, died at Beaconsfield, 'rather irritated than flattered by the supposition of his recovery being possible'.[27] The foremost advocate of war had passed away just as talk of peace was once again revived.

Malmesbury journeyed to Lille unsure whether the large crowds which gathered round his carriage were the result of novelty value in that region, or the curiosity of the Flemish, or 'from the desire of peace being much stronger in the people of France than it was eight months ago'.[28] Certainly, the initial outlook was not without promise: the French negotiators were affable personally, and made demands – such as the renunciation of the long-held English claim to the throne of France, and compensation for the ships destroyed at Toulon in 1793 – which were awkward but not insoluble. Britain was willing to acknowledge French sovereignty in Belgium, Luxembourg, Avignon, Savoy and Nice and to restore her colonial possessions, while keeping Trinidad, Ceylon and the Cape of Good Hope, all taken by British forces from French allies.

In private, Pitt was prepared to go even further for peace. He had told Malmesbury as he set out that 'he would stifle every feeling of pride to the utmost to produce the desired result'.[29] He was even prepared to accept Grenville's resignation if it meant a treaty could be arrived at, afterwards telling Malmesbury that '*rather than break off this treaty, we should have given way either on the Cape or Ceylon*. That Lord Grenville, who from the beginning had declared he would *never consent* to any concession on *either of these points* . . . but had the negotiation gone on, and depended on this particular point, he, or Lord Grenville, *must* have gone out; and he added, *it would have been Lord Grenville*.'[30] Pitt used Canning as a separate line of communication to Malmesbury, leaving the latter complaining that 'the instructions and opinions I get from the Minister, under *whose orders I am bound to act*, accord so little with the sentiments and intentions I heard expressed by the Minister *with whom I wish to act*, that I am placed in a very disagreeable dilemma'.[31]

Malmesbury agreed with Pitt that Britain should bend over backwards for peace, particularly since he thought that in the absence of war all the tensions and disagreements ignited within France by the Revolution would turn inwards and '*peace will palsy this country* most completely . . . all the violent means they have employed for war will return upon them like a humour driven in'.[32] The majority of the French people did indeed appear ready for peace, having themselves suffered food shortages, severe inflation, civil war and huge losses at the front. Difficulties over the separate French negotiations with the Portuguese threatened the talks but did not appear insurmountable. Pitt rather than Grenville held sway, vindicating Canning's sycophantic judgement in June that Pitt 'has exerted himself, and is really master now'.[33] With the mutiny and the immediate financial crisis behind him, Pitt gave way to his inherent optimism, writing to Malmesbury on 14 September that he would stand fast for peace, and that it could be attained: 'My ultimate determination will be what I think you know.

I believe, however, all will end in what I shall reckon more than well.'[34]

It was tragically symbolic of Pitt's life that this renewed moment of confidence was followed by one of the worst weeks he would ever experience; already in Paris there had been another *coup d'état*, in which the three hardline members of the five-man Directory used the army to oust the moderates: 'Between the hours of 5 and 7 A.M. on Monday morning, the greatest number of them were taken into custody without the smallest resistance, and, in the course of that day, sentence of banishment pronounced upon them.'[35] Malmesbury reported to Pitt that this 'violent revolution' was 'the *most unlucky event that could have happened*', particularly given that he was 'very near obtaining the great object of our wishes'.[36] He was given twenty-four hours by new French negotiators to agree to impossible terms, under which Britain would surrender all her conquests without exception. Once again, all hopes for peace were dashed; Britain could not possibly contemplate such terms unless, in Canning's words, she was prepared to be 'trampled on'.[37]

Pitt was already feeling unwell when Malmesbury returned on 20 September. On the same day, he received the news that his lifelong friend and brother-in-law Edward Eliot was dead. Eliot had been one of his closest companions, joining his family, and often in the past residing at 10 Downing Street. His death left Pitt more grief-stricken than at any time since Harriot's death eleven years before. Wilberforce wrote that: 'The effect produced on Mr. Pitt by the news, which came in a letter from Lord Eliot by the common post with his others, exceeded conception. Rose says he never saw and never expects to see anything like it.'[38] The blow was all the harder because, as Pitt explained to Addington, it came 'at a moment when I was quite unprepared for the event'.[39]

Pitt had already been complaining of headaches which he had 'not been able to get rid of for several days'.[40] Now, following such catastrophic personal and political news, he had severe abdominal pains. The relationship between his declining health and his struggle to control events in the world around him was becoming sharper. He was now sick, disappointed and distraught; it cannot be known how close he came to despair.

* * *

Whatever his emotional and physical wounds, in Pitt's mind the time for giving up had passed. He did not enjoy that quality of resilience which belongs to politicians who have families, money or other careers to fall back on; but he did command the even greater stamina and persistence of the politician who has nothing else to live for. In late September 1797 he either looked deep into his soul and found a new reserve of strength, or else simply shut the disasters from his always practical mind and gave his usual 'unremitting Attention to the ... Business'.[41]

He toyed with one remaining and intriguing possibility for finding peace: an apparent offer from the highest levels of the French Directory to come to acceptable peace terms in return for a personal bribe of £2 million. Under this extraordinary scenario, Britain could retain the Cape of Good Hope for £800,000, and Ceylon for £1.2 million. Pitt went so far as to contemplate a payment of '450,000*l.* if the conditions are satisfactory',[42] but the project collapsed in October.

With it went the truly final chance of peace. Pitt was never one to let his private troubles be visible to more than a handful of those close to him, and Malmesbury reported him as being 'in spirits', with 'supplies for two more campaigns'.[43] Pitt's friend Lord Mornington, whom he was now despatching to India as Governor General, went to Walmer and found 'Mr. Pitt in the highest spirits, entertaining officers & country Gentlemen with his usual hospitality.'[44] His spirits would be lifted still higher in October by a new and crushing naval victory. The Dutch fleet had at last put to sea and on 11 October was intercepted by Admiral Duncan at the head of the very ships involved in the outright mutiny only four months before. In the bloody and numerically evenly-matched Battle of Camperdown, off the coast of Holland, British seamanship and weight of metal again proved decisive. As Duncan towed seven captured ships of the line towards the Nore, leaving the Dutch navy devastated, Pitt rose from his sickbed to begin the celebrations, writing to his mother from Walmer: 'Lord Duncan joined us very opportunely on Friday at Dover Castle, where We had gone the day before to be present at a *Feu de Joie* in honour of his Victory ... We shall probably ... visit the Fleet in our Way back tomorrow sennight, when the King intends to go on Board. Such a ceremony will be no bad Prelude for the opening of the Session.'[45]

It did indeed set the scene for a new spirit in the country and its Prime Minister. Since peace was not available on any but the most abject terms, war must now be fought without restraint. Pitt had gone much further than many of his colleagues or the King found comfortable in trying to make peace; now he would unambiguously become the embodiment of national determination to win the war. On 10 November 1797 he attacked 'the duplicity, the arrogance and violence' of the French Directory in a speech in the Commons.[46] In a rousing peroration he declared:

> there is not a man, whose stake is so great in the country, that he ought to hesitate a moment in sacrificing any portion of it to oppose the violence of the enemy; nor is there, I trust, a man in this happy and free nation, whose stake is so small, that would not be ready to sacrifice his life in the same cause . . . There may be danger, but on the one side there is danger accompanied with honour; on the other side, there is danger with indelible shame and disgrace; upon such an alternative, Englishmen will not hesitate . . . There is one great resource, which I trust will never abandon us, and which has shone forth in the English character, by which we have preserved our existence and fame, as a nation, which I trust we shall be determined never to abandon under any extremity, but shall join hand and heart in the solemn pledge that is proposed to us, and declare to his Majesty, that we know great exertions are wanting, that we are prepared to make them, and at all events determined to stand or fall by the laws, liberties, and religion of our country.[47]

When he sat down, the Commons rose as a body and sang the chorus of 'Britons Strike Home':

> Britons Strike Home! Avenge your Country's Cause!
> Protect your King! Your Liberty, and Laws!

For Pitt, the rallying of the House of Commons meant the political authority to raise much heavier taxes and more troops. The man who had done everything he could for peace was now destined to be Britain's longest-serving leader in war.

21

Caution to the Winds

> 'The House will decide whether they will . . . make a great and unusual exertion to resist the enemy, or . . . leave the country open to the ruinous projects of an insolent and overbearing enemy.'
>
> William Pitt, 4 January 1798[1]

> 'Victory is not a name strong enough for such a scene.'
>
> Nelson, after the Battle of the Nile, August 1798[2]

By November 1797, Pitt had been to the edge of despair and sprung back from it. Finding peace unattainable and facing the possibility of abject failure in war, an outcome highly likely to have brought his career to a premature close, he rallied both himself and the nation. Hitherto he had aimed to achieve the containment of France in a war of short duration with the lightest possible burdens falling on the people of Britain. His successive but unsuccessful attempts to negotiate with the French Directory had been aimed at bringing peace before the time at which military requirements and rising taxation would change the nature of everyday life. French military prowess, and the absence of cohesion among his allies, had meant that this balanced and sometimes hesitant strategy had ended in failure.

The return of Malmesbury after the coup of September 1797 did not end the need to make strategic choices – whether to seek fresh Continental alliances, mount colonial offences or concentrate on home defence – but it simplified the political imperatives of Pitt's situation. There was no choice now but to abandon the search for negotiation and the early resumption of normality. The nation must make 'a great and unusual exertion to resist the enemy', as Pitt told the Commons on 4 January 1798, or 'suspend all defensive precautions, and leave the country open to the ruinous projects of an insolent and overbearing enemy'.[3] There was no escape now from losing many lives, spending vast sums and taking great risks. It would turn out that militarily, financially and personally, Pitt was of a mind and temperament to take them.

The first illustration of this changed approach was the budget which Pitt presented to the Commons on 24 November 1797. The national debt had grown by nearly £120 million in five years of war (an increase of nearly 50 per cent). Such an increase could not continue without ruining the financial prospects of future generations, a matter always dear to Pitt's heart. As he explained: 'We ought to consider how far the efforts we shall exert to preserve the blessings we enjoy will enable us to transmit the inheritance to posterity unencumbered with those burdens which would cripple their vigour and prevent them from asserting that rank in the scale of nations which their ancestors so long and so gloriously maintained.'[4] In any case, loans were becoming much harder to raise, and the interest rates required were rising sharply. It was therefore necessary to collect far more in tax, but the policy of innumerable taxes on small items such as hair powder and plate glass had been pushed very near its limits. From September onwards, Pitt set to work on a fundamental change in the nature of taxation. In his customary fashion he spent many hours closeted with Rose at Holwood and then circulated draft papers to colleagues whose financial advice he respected, such as Addington and Lord Hawkesbury (formerly Robert Jenkinson).

The resulting proposal was enough of a bombshell to bring Fox scuttling back to the Commons under pressure from his distressed constituents. For Pitt now proposed to take the 'assessed taxes', those levied on windows, houses, servants, carriages and horses, and treble them. What is more, he suggested a graduated scale, which involved particularly huge increases for the better-off. Requiring as it did the state to know more of an individual's circumstances and an acceptance that tax need not be levied at a flat rate, this so-called 'Triple

Assessment' – a forerunner of income tax – was bound to be controversial. Pitt thought it affected about 800,000 people and would supply him with £8 million a year. It was a major change in both the level and the principles of taxation.

The debates raged back and forth that Christmas, with Fox attacking a measure which 'tends to the immediate destruction of their [taxpayers'] trade, the annihilation of their fortunes, and possibly to the loss of liberty of their persons'.[5] Pitt had to make certain concessions and exemptions which reduced the eventual yield of the tax to less than £5 million, but on the principle he got his way. He would come back the following April with a further budget and yet more taxes, but in the meantime Addington suggested the idea of a Voluntary Contribution to supplement the assessed taxes, which, rather like the loyalty loan of the previous year, was an unexpected success and raised over £2 million. Pitt himself subscribed £2,000 he did not have.

The success of the Voluntary Contribution was another indicator of national sentiment, which was becoming more resolute as Britain stood alone in the war. Ministers now sought to whip up anti-revolutionary feeling: one vehicle by which they did so was a new weekly publication, the *Anti-Jacobin*. Inspired and coordinated by Canning, the *Anti-Jacobin* printed anonymous contributions, some of which were written by Pitt in the form of poems. This example gives the flavour of the publication:

> I am a hearty Jacobin,
> Who own no God, and dread no sin,
> Ready to dash through thick and thin
> For Freedom:
> Whatever is in France, is right;
> Terror and blood are my delight;
> Parties with us do not excite
> Enough Rage.
> Out boasted Laws I hate and curse,
> Bad from the first, by age grown worse,
> I pant and sigh for Univers-
> al suffrage

Such propaganda was necessary in a situation in which Pitt's popularity was by no means universal. On 19 December a Thanksgiving ceremony was held at St Paul's in honour of the succession of naval victories, attended by the entire body politic – Royal Family, Cabinet and Houses of Parliament, as well as the naval commanders. Pitt had Pretyman deliver the sermon, and told him to make clear 'that God, who governs the world by His providence, never interposes for the preservation of men or nations without their own exertions'.[6]

On the way to the cathedral Pitt was heckled and hooted at by members of the crowds who were evidently not happy with the latest exertions they had been called upon to make. When he went home that night it was thought prudent to give him an escort of cavalry. Even so, he retained his faith in the good sense and patriotism of the majority, embarking on an arming of the civilian population on a scale never known, or risked, before. Years later he would assert that 'From an army to consist of the round bulk of the people, no man who knows the British character could have the least fear.'[7] When he and Dundas appealed for more volunteers to take 'an active part in the defence of the country',[8] and accompanied it with fresh legislation requiring the listing of all males between the ages of sixteen and sixty not involved in military activity, the number of volunteers mushroomed. By the summer of 1798 more than 100,000 armed volunteers were enrolled in hundreds of companies and associations. The British people, it seemed, were ready to make their exertions.

It was to the British people that Charles James Fox rose to make a toast on 24 January 1798 as two thousand people thronged the Crown and Anchor tavern in London in honour of his forty-ninth birthday. When the Duke of Norfolk proposed a toast to Fox's health, he additionally coupled it with a toast to 'Our Sovereign's health: The Majesty of the People!'[9] In the climate of the times, this was a highly controversial thing to do. A Whig toast to 'the people' was meant to express their attachment to the principles of 1688, but after 1789 'the people' implied far more radical and egalitarian ideas, along with a sympathy with the French Revolution. Norfolk was therefore dismissed as Lord Lieutenant of the West Riding of Yorkshire, and sacked from his command of a militia regiment.

In evident defiance of this, Fox repeated the toast at another dinner in May, creating a new storm of controversy. Government supporters sought his prosecution or reprimand, but Pitt, learning from his experience of the Westminster scrutiny in 1784, thought that such action would give Fox 'too much consequence'.[10] Nevertheless he sought the advice of Dundas on whether Fox should be reprimanded by the Speaker, and 'If after a reprimand he offers a new insult (as he probably would at the next meeting of the Club), he might be sent to the Tower for the remainder of the Session.'[11] In the end, wise counsels prevailed and it was decided merely to remove him from the Privy Council, an act performed by a delighted George III, who personally struck Fox's name from the list. Fox had now seceded from the political system; refusing to attend the House of Commons, he sold his house in London and went into temporary retirement, leaving Pitt's domination of the domestic landscape even stronger.

For Pitt, who had battled through Christmas without a break to ensure the passage of his budget, the spring of 1798 became an uninterrupted ferment of activity. The search for new allies was in full swing, and was already looking promising, since the Austrians were unhappy with the Treaty of Campo Formio within weeks of signing, the Tsar was becoming interested in confronting the French, and there was a new King of Prussia, Frederick William III. The incentive to create a new coalition against France was much enhanced by the fact that the French were rampaging well beyond any previous notion of their frontiers. Rome was occupied and Switzerland invaded, with the expansionist Directory aiming 'to unite Holland, France, Switzerland, the Cisalpine and Ligurian Republics by an uninterrupted continuity of territory'.[12]

From the beginning of the year, Grenville was proposing a four-power alliance of Britain, Russia, Prussia and Austria to take on the expansionist ambitions of the French. Pitt and Grenville were determined that any new international coalition would be more carefully coordinated and more united on its objectives than the First Coalition had been, with the explicit aims of confining France to her pre-war boundaries, and the creation of strong buffer states such as Belgium and Piedmont, guaranteed by a Quadruple Alliance. Pitt never lost his taste for seeking a permanent and all-embracing solution to the temporary problems of the day; in building a new alliance he was seeking not only to win the war but to create a sustainable system for the enforcement of peace in the future. In the years to come he would keep this objective in mind, but the negotiations in the spring of 1798 were not easy: Austro–Prussian rivalry, the future status of Belgium, and the failure of Austria to ratify the terms of her previous loan agreement with Britain were all serious obstacles. Subsidies were offered to the Prussians to no immediate avail, and for some time the Cabinet agonised over whether to make a renewed alliance with Austria alone or to hold out for the objective of a quadruple agreement. This diplomatic morass had still not been disentangled as renewed threats of internal rebellion and external attack were once again coming to a climax.

Within Britain, patriotism and repression had combined to reduce the danger posed by the radical Societies such as the LCS, and a new wave of arrests in April 1798 helped to keep them at bay. But across the Irish Sea the risk of the authorities losing control and even facing an armed and coordinated rebellion was gathering pace on a vastly greater scale. From his arrival in Dublin in 1795 after the Fitzwilliam fiasco, Camden had struggled to maintain order in the face of economic discontent, revolutionary sympathies and sectarian outrages. There was a recession in the linen trade at the same time as radical ideas spread amongst the Protestants of Ulster, while the mutual hostility of Catholics and Protestants became more explicit and more highly organised. Orange Lodges were formed, which took advantage of attempts by the authorities to suppress revolt and confiscate arms by destroying Catholic property in Ulster and driving the Catholic population to the south. Catholic reaction produced an organisation called the Defenders, along with the non-sectarian United Irishmen, which soon formed its own secret Directory and made contact with Paris. Plans were being made in early 1798 for a coordinated nationwide rebellion in conjunction with a French invasion, expected at any time. For despite the victory at Camperdown, the possibility of a major French invasion fleet evading the Royal Navy to attack the British Isles in general and Ireland in particular remained. Ships and troops were known to be massing in Brest, Dunkirk and Toulon.

Against this background, Pitt was once again forced to give much attention to internal order: the arrests in England were accompanied by attempts by the Irish authorities to smash the embryonic rebellion – many of the ringleaders were arrested at a single house in Dublin on 12 March. Pitt had always taken a liberal view of Irish affairs, but in this atmosphere of emergency his response to those in the Commons who urged 'conciliation' of Irish grievances was a strong one. Conciliation, he said, meant

> That we should make every concession and every sacrifice to traitors and rebels, to men who are industriously propagating the most dangerous principles, engrafting upon the minds of the people the most destructive doctrines, wantonly seducing and deluding the ignorant multitude, encouraging the most criminal correspondence with the enemy, exciting the commission of treason in Ireland, under the specious pretence of parliamentary reform, and forming, in conjunction and co-operation with the professed enemy of all liberty, morality and social happiness, plans for separating that country from Great Britain, and for converting Ireland into a jacobinical republic under the wing and protection of republican France.[13]

On 20 April he moved once again for the suspension of Habeas Corpus, denouncing those 'who are going on with the daring purpose of corresponding with the French'.[14] To critics, this was the high-water mark of 'Pitt's Terror', but to Pitt himself and the majority in Parliament it seemed that only unfailing strength could now save the country.

It was in this fevered climate that Pitt was faced in April 1798 with an agonising strategic choice. He was receiving entreaties from Baron Franz Thugut, the Austrian Chancellor, and from the Kingdom of Naples to once again send a British fleet into the Mediterranean. Since he wished to draw Austria back into the war, and to raise the morale of the Neapolitans in the face of the proximity of the French army, the logic for doing so was obvious. On the other hand, the danger of an attempted French invasion of the British Isles was high, and the removal of any naval forces to the Mediterranean would reduce the chances of intercepting it at sea.

Spencer advised him on 6 April that sufficient ships were not available to send a permanent squadron to the Mediterranean, although Lord St Vincent, currently blockading Cadiz, could 'take a sweep round the Mediterranean and do all the mischief he can to the French navy'.[15] There were clearly great risks to operating in the Mediterranean at all, which was why the navy had withdrawn from there two years before: not only could home defence be jeopardised, the force deployed there could find itself cut off if the Spanish broke out of Cadiz. But Pitt's caution of previous years had now evaporated; for some months he had been ready to raise the stakes in his struggle. By the end of April he had decided to override the Admiralty advice, sending a fleet through the Straits of Gibraltar and necessarily removing others from the defence of Ireland. This decision has been compared to that of Winston Churchill in 1940, when tanks desperately needed for the defence of Britain in the event of a German invasion were sent instead to North Africa.[16] It was indeed a comparable gamble, and it was to be even more rapidly vindicated.

Pitt focused in late April on introducing yet another budget, paying tribute to the 'true patriotism, and distinguished zeal'[17] of the many people who had made voluntary contributions, but also introducing new taxes on salt, tea and armorial bearings. Even in the sixth year of war, he retained the entire ministerial responsibility for financing the war effort as well as the overall responsibility for its strategic direction. No modern Minister could conceive of carrying such burdens simultaneously, even for a short time, and the strain on any man's physical, creative and intellectual energies of dealing with both the minutiae of finance and the operations of war on a daily basis must have been immense.

As Pitt took his budget proposals through the Commons in May, it was clear that the military storms which had been gathering that spring were about to break. On 19 May Napoleon set sail from Toulon in the company of both a fleet and an army, his destination unknown.

On the same day, the authorities in Dublin succeeded in apprehending the principal remaining ringleader of the planned rebellion, Lord Edward Fitzgerald, a former army officer and a cousin of Charles James Fox, who had been turned against Britain by the excesses of coercion in Ireland and had been negotiating with the French. Fitzgerald was mortally wounded in the struggle to arrest him. The authorities found among his papers detailed plans for an all-out rebellion, scheduled for four days later. A widespread rebellion did indeed now break out, but it had already been decapitated with the arrest of Fitzgerald and his co-conspirators. Without them, Dublin remained secure, and the main centres of rebellion were in Wicklow and Wexford.

Even so, the situation seemed dire, and Camden was almost in despair for want of reinforcements from the mainland. In early June Pitt finally sent several thousand troops, to be followed by English militia. He also decided to replace Camden with Cornwallis, who would go to Dublin as both Lord Lieutenant and Commander-in-Chief. Cornwallis arrived in Dublin on 20 June; by then, however, the rebellion had spent its force. Tens of thousands of peasants led into battle by priests had fought valiantly but were too disorganised to overcome relatively small units of troops and militia armed with cannon. As the rebellion was crushed, loyalist militia took a pitiless revenge. It was a shattering blow to the United Irishmen, utterly defeated by treachery, coercion and the continued absence of the much-vaunted French invasion.

Ireland had forced its way back into Pitt's brain, and the conclusions he would draw would be radical and historic. For the moment, however, tension was high, he was once again unwell, and his patience was wearing thin. On 25 May he was engaged in presenting an Emergency Bill to the Commons to increase the supply of manpower for the navy by lifting the exemption from naval service hitherto enjoyed by men working in sea and river trades. This was opposed by George Tierney, a Foxite MP who had taken it upon himself to harass the government and lead a handful of parliamentary malcontents in the absence of Fox and other Whigs. Pitt became angry with Tierney's call for longer consideration of the Bill: 'He acknowledges that, were it not passed in a day, those whom it might concern might elude its effect, thus assigning himself the reason for its immediate adoption. But if the measure be necessary, and that a notice of it would enable its effect to be eluded, how can the honourable gentleman's opposition to it be accounted for, but from a desire to obstruct the defence of the country?'[18]

Tierney immediately appealed to the Speaker to rule as unparliamentary the accusation that he was deliberately 'obstructing the defence of the country'. Addington failed to intervene decisively, and while the Pitt of former years might have made a deft semi-withdrawal of the insult while leaving it on the record, the Pitt of 1798 simply repeated the accusation. He insisted that Tierney was seeking 'to obstruct the measures employed for the defence of the country. He knew very well that it was unparliamentary to state the motives that actuated the opinions of gentlemen, but it was impossible to go into arguments in favour of a question, without sometimes hinting at the motives that induced an opposition to it. He submitted to the judgement of the house the propriety and necessity of the arguments he had urged, and he would not depart from any thing he had there advanced, by either retracting or explaining them.'[19]

What followed seems incredible from the vantage point of more than two hundred years later, but at the time was wholly predictable and in conformity with the manners of the age. The next day, Pitt received from Tierney a challenge to a duel, which he immediately accepted.

In the eighteenth century, a duel was still the standard way in the upper reaches of society to obtain 'satisfaction' when insulted. Honour demanded that such a challenge should be met. The usual format involved each man appointing a 'second', usually a close friend, who together ensured that moral support was given, fair play observed, and the matter ended as soon as appropriate. The great majority of duels did not involve fatalities, sometimes because the participants deliberately fired wild, but often because it was not easy for an untrained man to hit an opponent with a pistol shot at a reasonable distance. Only two shots from each participant were normally allowed. Nevertheless, fatalities and serious injuries did occur. Fox had been injured in a duel in 1779. In the United States, six years after Pitt's duel, Alexander

Hamilton, the leader of the Federalists, was mortally wounded in a duel with Vice-President Aaron Burr.

Pitt prepared for the contest with his usual sense of both thoroughness and integrity. Addington recalled: 'I was dining with Lord Grosvenor, when a note was brought me from Mr. Pitt, stating that he had received a hostile message from Mr. Tierney, and wished me to go to him, which I did as soon as the party at Lord Grosvenor's broke up. Mr. Pitt had just made his will when I arrived. He had sent in the first instance to Mr. Steele to be his second; but finding that he was absent, he sent next to Mr. Ryder. On the following day I went with Pitt and Ryder down the Birdcage Walk, up the steps into Queen Street, where their chaise waited to take them to Wimbledon Common.'[20]

Thus it was that on the afternoon of Sunday, 27 May 1798, the British Prime Minister walked out onto Putney Heath and duly took twelve paces before turning and firing at his opponent. Mercifully, both of them missed; Pitt apparently fired his second shot into the air, and the seconds then intervened to give 'their decided opinion that sufficient satisfaction had been given, and that the business was ended with perfect honour to both parties'.[21] A small crowd had watched the affair, which took place near the gibbet of a recently hanged criminal. Back in Downing Street, Pitt sat down to explain the matter to Dundas, telling him that 'I had occasion to visit your neighbourhood this morning, in order to meet Mr. Tierney,'[22] and from Holwood next day he wrote a classic among the many letters of reassurance to his mother: 'I have nothing to tell that is not perfectly agreeable. The newspapers of to day contain a short but correct Account of a meeting which I found it necessary to have with Mr. Tierney . . . The business terminated without any thing unpleasant to either Party . . .'[23]

For all Pitt's insouciance, there was nevertheless a good deal of shock at what had transpired. Duels among politicians were by no means unknown, and would continue to take place for some decades: Canning and Castlereagh fought a celebrated duel in 1809, and the Duke of Wellington would repeat the feat of duelling while Prime Minister in 1829. Nevertheless, Pitt had risked his life just as the dangers from invasion and rebellion neared their peak. George III wrote: 'I trust what has happened will never be repeated . . . Public characters have no right to weigh alone what they owe to themselves; they must consider also what is due to their country.'[24] He evidently did not share the humour of those who laughed at the idea of Pitt's lanky frame duelling with the rotund figure of Tierney: they suggested that an outline of Pitt should have been chalked on Tierney, and no shots outside it should have been allowed to count.

Most incensed of all, however, was Wilberforce, who combined concern for Pitt with hostility to duelling and outrage that such a thing should have happened on a Sunday. He was 'more shocked than almost ever',[25] and gave notice of a Commons motion 'Against the Principle of Duels'. In response, Pitt made clear that he would regard such a motion as one of censure: 'If any step on the subject is proposed in Parliament and agreed to, I shall feel from that moment that I can be of more use out of office than in it; for in it, according to the feelings I entertain, I could be of none. I state to you as I think I ought distinctly and explicitly what I feel.'[26] The agonised Wilberforce, under intense pressure from other MPs to withdraw his motion, duly did so, and was heartily thanked by Pitt for his 'cordial friendship and kindness'.

We do not know whether Pitt's duel affected him psychologically, or whether its aftermath opened the floodgates of the strain and stress of the previous months. Whatever the cause, within days of discharging his pistol on Putney Heath he was back in his sickbed, and would not be seen in the Commons for some weeks. This was part of an increasingly familiar pattern, in which he would sustain for months on end his ability to deal with multiple crises and controversies, but would collapse after his many tasks had reached some kind of climax. In June 1798, Wilberforce and Auckland described him as 'seriously' or 'very' ill.[27] Pitt himself confessed to Pretyman that he had been 'making Exertions beyond my real Strength'.[28] Even when he was meant to be well, his daily habits had steadily changed, and either exhaustion or alcohol was regularly keeping him in bed until eleven o'clock in the morning.

When ill, Pitt outwardly retained his famed equanimity, complaining about newspaper coverage of his illness 'that he cannot be ill quietly'.[29] Soon he was insisting to his mother, as usual, that he was absolutely fine: 'I am growing stronger and stronger every day, and am as well as ever I was.'[30] This, of course, was nonsense. Two months later, in early August, Auckland wrote: 'He is greatly recovered, but is much shaken in his constitution, and must be very attentive as to diet, exercise, and hours. His spirits are as good and his mind as active as ever.'[31]

Pitt went to Walmer to take a couple of weeks' sea air, and then to visit his mother at Burton Pynsent in late August, but was back in Downing Street at the end of the month. His sense of duty and his need to control events meant that he could not rest for long, and this in turn meant that he did not give himself the chance to stage a full recovery. His physician Sir Walter Farquhar later wrote of this period: 'I invariably and more urgently pressed the necessity of some relaxation from business, as I uniformly found a considerable accession of unpleasant symptoms in the Constitution from mental anxiety upon public affairs. All that I could do under such circumstances was to direct my attention to the stomach and bowels, and to strengthen and aid them by gentle bitters and mild medicines. For some years the health of Mr. Pitt was variable, & much affected by the change of seasons & of situation, but by great management & rigid attention to diet, he was generally relieved.'[32]

Farquhar prescribed certain changes which involved a reduction in wine consumption (to some extent replaced with ale instead), the drinking of mineral waters, more exercise and more regular, smaller meals. Pitt seems to have stuck to this regimen at least for a time, when the House was not sitting in the summer and early autumn of 1798, but both physician and patient recognised that the origins of his illness lay in the incessant activity of his mind. Added to this was the pressure caused to one of such an optimistic disposition by seemingly endless disappointments and setbacks. Pitt told Pretyman at the end of October that 'Farquhar's Regimen (aided probably by our Victories and the State of the Revenue) has succeeded so well that . . . I have great hopes of being equal to the Busy Scene that is approaching.'[33] Opposition newspapers circulated reports that summer, assisted by the striking combination of news of the duel and Pitt's illness, that he was going insane, an allegation emphatically denied by his friends. The rumour-mongers were certainly wide of the mark, but no doubt enjoying their mischief. What is clear, however, is that the impact of military victory or defeat was ultimately felt in Pitt's digestion, an effect which, when combined with other attributes of his lifestyle, would eventually kill him.

Pitt was not the only one who would feel the tension that summer, for after Napoleon sailed from Toulon on 19 May, Nelson, now a Rear Admiral, simply could not find him. For ten weeks Nelson would criss-cross the Mediterranean in an increasingly frantic search for an entire army at sea. It may seem incredible that it was not possible to locate a force totalling 335 ships travelling at an average speed of only one knot, and indeed it was thought to be so at the time. Rose commented in September, before definitive news of Napoleon's whereabouts had reached London, that it was 'the most extraordinary Instance of the kind I believe in the Naval History of the World'.[34] On 9 June the French arrived unmolested at Malta, which was quickly wrested from the centuries-old control of the Knights of St John. When news of this reached Nelson, he still could not be sure that Napoleon would not turn west and head out into the Atlantic, eventually launching a direct attack on Britain, but he guessed that he was heading for Egypt. He sailed so quickly to Alexandria that he had been and gone by the time Napoleon and his army actually arrived and stormed the city. The British Mediterranean Fleet had headed north to Turkey as the French army secured its position in Egypt and dealt a heavy defeat to the Mamelukes at the Battle of the Pyramids on 21 July.

A mixture of motives seems to have drawn Napoleon to Egypt. British naval prowess made it too dangerous to hazard a large-scale invasion of the British Isles, while the defeat of all Continental enemies had left the great military commander, like Alexander in India two thousand years before, with 'no more worlds to conquer'. In order to prosecute a war directly against British interests, and accelerate the rise of his own reputation and power, Napoleon chose to strike at 'the key to the commerce of the East'. The seizure of Egypt could be a major blow to the British Empire, which was why Dundas feared 'the calamitous consequences'[35] when he heard the news. The Suez route to India would fall under French control, and British dominion over India could ultimately be threatened. Being utterly unexpected, Napoleon's strategy also had the great merits for which he always looked: shock and surprise. It had the potential to be a strategic masterstroke.

Napoleon, however, was not omniscient. He would not have known at the time he decided to sail for Egypt that Pitt had decided to send a British fleet, now numbering fourteen ships of the line, back into the Mediterranean. A huge amount now depended on how that fleet would perform. For on the afternoon of 1 August the lookout of the British line-of-battle ship *Zealous* spotted on the horizon a forest of masts which could only be the French Mediterranean Fleet. They were at anchor in Aboukir Bay, at the mouth of the Nile, in line of battle. One of the most decisive naval encounters of history was about to begin.

In Aboukir Bay, the French Admiral Brueys had taken up a classic and formidable defensive position. He had placed his thirteen ships of the line close to the coast, with the additional cover of shore batteries and a fort. But Nelson viewed these 'with the eye of a seaman determined on attack', and was determined 'to conquer, or perish in the attempt'.[36] Nelson, already known for improvisation and daring, took three decisions at the outset which Brueys had not expected. First, he decided to attack immediately, with the first British ship rounding the point into the bay as the sun set. Second, he concentrated his attack on the opposite end of the French line from the one which the weather conditions would have suggested was more liable to be attacked, thus putting the greatest pressure on the weakest French ships. Third, he sent some of his ships actually around the French vanguard to position themselves in the narrow space between the enemy and the shore, an action fraught with navigational and military risks but exposing the French to broadsides from both sides simultaneously.

It was as a result of these decisions that the Battle of the Nile produced an outcome far more complete than the British naval victories at Camperdown or Cape St Vincent the previous year, when a badly mauled enemy had eventually limped away. The confined space of the waters of Aboukir Bay and the brilliance of Nelson's tactics meant that the Battle of the Nile was a battle of annihilation. The murderous cannonades of the Royal Navy, coming from both port and starboard, soon turned the vanguard and centre of the French line into an avenue of utter carnage. No navy on earth could withstand such a bombardment, much of it delivered at almost point-blank range. Although the French defended themselves gallantly, and Brueys himself fought on for some hours until dying of his wounds, the initial disposition of their force meant there was virtually nothing they could do. By late evening the flagship *L'Orient* was ablaze, with results recorded by Midshipman John Lee: 'The din of war raged with such incontrollable violence – till at last an awful and terrific glare of light blinding the very sight showed *L'Orient* blowing up, with an astounding crash, paralysing all around her, by which near a thousand souls were hastened into eternity.'[37] Fully eleven of the thirteen French ships of the line were destroyed or captured that night. The remaining two escaped from the battle, to be captured at a later date.

Reports of the devastating victory took three months to reach Britain, partly because the frigate initially carrying the news was captured on the way back. Even weeks after the battle, therefore, the mood in London was jittery and strained. In late August the French had landed 1,100 men in north-west Ireland at Killala and routed the local militia while recruiting some locals to their side. If this expedition had been meant to trigger a successful rebellion it was too late, and shortly afterwards the small force was crushed by Cornwallis with 11,000 men.

Throughout this episode, Pitt had waited anxiously for news of Nelson, writing on 30 August: 'The reports of Nelson's success are again revived from various quarters, and will, I really believe, some how or other, prove true at last.'[38] This time, his optimism was vindicated. When the full extent of the victory at the Nile became known, the rejoicing in Britain knew no bounds. The Royal Navy had destroyed an entire French fleet, and inflicted ten times as many casualties as it had suffered. Napoleon and his army were stranded in Egypt. Pitt returned to Downing Street from Holwood 'in the highest possible spirits', according to Pretyman. 'Mr. Pitt is confident that Buonaparte *must be destroyed*. Oh my Love what joy!'[39]

In fact, Napoleon was not destroyed, but he had made a mistake he would regret for the rest of his life, ruminating after Waterloo: 'If, instead of the expedition to Egypt, I had undertaken that against Ireland, what could England have done now?'[40] He had indeed made an error with multiple consequences: his army was cut off in Egypt, Turkey reacted to French aggression in the Mediterranean by joining the war against France, and the seizure of Malta had deeply upset Tsar Paul I of Russia, who held a quixotic and romantic attachment to the chivalrous ideas of the Knights of St John. A new coalition against France was in the making. The possible threat to India gave renewed force to British expansion there: the following year Mornington would go to war against Tipu Sultan, who had sought help from the French, and secure large tracts of territory for the East India Company. Above all, the French virtually gave up hope of challenging Britain at sea. In the words of one French historian: 'Aboukir changed everything, as the navy lethargically resigned itself to its fate and left it to the army to ensure the survival of the Revolution . . . Aboukir marked the end of France as a naval power.'[41]

Pitt's happy mind raced that autumn, seizing the opportunity of victory on the Nile and the suppression of the Irish rebellion to find comprehensive solutions to the problems he had encountered that year. He sought a new coalition with clearly defined aims, a more sustainable and productive method of raising finance, and a settlement in Ireland which would end once and for all its propensity to rebellion and openness to invasion.

The British government would put a great deal of energy in the autumn of 1798 into assembling a new international coalition, but it would not bear fruit that year. Indeed, the protracted negotiations, interminable jealousies and constant demand for subsidies from the possible allies did not augur well, and were from the outset reminiscent of the First Coalition. Both Russia and Austria sought subsidies from Britain in return for troops at war: by late October the seeming impossibility of coming to agreement had left Pitt writing that he was sanguine only of 'continuing to fight well our own battle; and Europe must probably be left for some time longer to its fate'.[42] The Prussians did at least make a definitive proposal, that their army would invade Holland with the support of a British fleet, but as the winter of 1798 set in no progress on this had been made.

Grenville's cousin, Tom Grenville, was sent as an emissary to Prussia: it is a reminder of the hazards of travel in the eighteenth century that his journey from London to Berlin was initially aborted by contrary winds; on the second attempt his ship became stuck in ice off the German coast, obliging him to wade ashore without his possessions. Having set out in November 1798, he finally arrived in March 1799. The construction of a new coalition was therefore full of the ups and downs, disappointments and false hopes which wore away at Pitt's health, but he and Grenville continued to work for a structured alliance with 'one complete & digested system',[43] with objectives agreed in advance.

Diplomacy was one of the three preoccupations of Pitt that autumn as he enjoyed a respite from illness. The second was finance: he wanted to find a way of maintaining the principle he had established in tripling the assessed taxes the previous year – that people with higher incomes should pay proportionately more – but he wanted to find a new way of requiring it. The triple assessment had proved to be too much subject to evasions, alternative interpretations and exemptions. He sought a more reliable and acceptable method of raising about £10 million a year.

His solution was revolutionary, and was set out in his budget speech of 3 December 1798: income tax. In this two-and-a-half-hour speech he explained that in order 'to repress those evasions so disgraceful to the country', it was necessary to obtain 'a more specific statement of income'.[44] Going back to first principles, he listed what he thought was the total annual income of each part of the economy (£20 million of land rental, £3 million from mines and canal navigation, £12 million from profits on the capital employed in foreign commerce, etc.), which was largely guesswork at the time. He estimated the total at £102 million, and proposed to levy a tax of 10 per cent on the whole amount. This new, and temporary, form of tax was, he said, justified by 'justice and expediency . . . It looks anxiously to the alleviation of the burdens of the country, by a great temporary exertion; it looks to the equality of the tax, and the general efficacy of the measure, conscious that on them depends our success in the great cause in which we are engaged – That is to furnish the means of providing for the debt created in two years, within the same period we formerly provided for the debt created in one.'[45] Income tax would thus be fair, collectable, and would provide for the more rapid repayment of the greater debts now being incurred. It would be applied on a sliding scale, zero on incomes below £60 a year, and then one twentieth on those over £60, rising to one tenth on incomes over £200.

In explicitly shifting tax from expenditure to income, doing so through one principal tax, and giving the tax authorities the power to require an itemised schedule of income, Pitt was launching a revolution in the financing of government. It would indeed be temporary, and would be abolished after the end of the war, only to return in a permanent form from the middle of the nineteenth century under Sir Robert Peel. The resentment at the powers given to a government department to intrude into private matters was deeply felt. Nevertheless, the entire complex measure had passed through the Commons by January 1799, always by commanding majorities, due to the obvious realities that the financial need was urgent, the previous scheme had not worked, the principle had been discussed for some time, and no alternative ideas were available.

Pitt's third preoccupation was with Ireland. If income tax was the solution to the financial situation, and a comprehensive alliance was the solution to war on the Continent, then the solution to rebellion in Ireland was one which had been much longer in his thoughts: the complete Union of the Westminster and Dublin Parliaments. To Pitt, the repeated failures and risks of Irish policy throughout his entire career pointed to one conclusion. The failure of his Irish propositions in 1785, which had been his first serious political rebuff, seemed to demonstrate that it was impossible to carry out policies to the mutual economic benefit of Britain and Ireland when they could be unpicked by two separate Parliaments, each voting in accordance with its own self-interest. In the Regency crisis four years later, the Irish Parliament had been prepared to throw in its lot with the Prince of Wales and prepare for a Regency at a different time and under different conditions from those being set by the House of Commons. Every Irish crisis in the nine years since then had been fed, in Pitt's view, by demands for Catholic emancipation on the one hand and by Protestant intransigence on the other. In 1792 he had written to the then Lord Lieutenant, the Earl of Westmorland:

> The idea of the present fermentation gradually bringing both parties to think of an Union with this country has long been in my mind. I hardly dare flatter myself with the hope of its taking place; but I believe it, though itself not easy to be accomplished, to be the only solution for other and greater difficulties.
>
> The admission of the Catholics to the . . . suffrage could not then be dangerous. The Protestant interest – in point of power, property, and Church establishment – would be secure, because the decided majority of the supreme Legislature would necessarily be Protestant; and the great ground of argument on the part of the Catholics would be done away, as, compared with the rest of the Empire, they would become a minority.[46]

This was Pitt's vision: an Ireland in which Catholics could be given full rights of citizenship, including the right to sit in Parliament, because Protestants need not fear a local Catholic majority if the Irish representatives were seated at Westminster, and the Catholics need not fear Protestant oppression if the affairs of Ireland were subject to the vote of all MPs. The rebellion of 1798 gave Pitt the opportunity to implement this long-cherished policy, and an added justification for doing so: 'Will any man tell me, when we come to treat of peace, for instance, or to consider any subject of alliance with any foreign power, or upon any question of trade or commerce, that then the local prejudices, I say prejudices, for they have great influence, may not occasion a difference between the legislatures upon points that may be essential to the welfare of the British Empire?'[47] This would be part of Pitt's case, eloquently developed in the Commons through 1799, for Union.

To Pitt it was entirely logical as well as safe for such a Union to be accompanied by Catholic emancipation. Indeed, it would be in the expectation of such relief that Catholics in general would support it.

Pitt's key lieutenants in Dublin, Cornwallis and Castlereagh, thought such a policy essential. As Cornwallis put it: 'Until the Catholics are admitted into a general participation of rights (which when incorporated with the British government they cannot abuse) there will be no peace or safety in Ireland.'[48]

The problem was that Catholic emancipation would not be acceptable to a wide range of other people, including senior members of the Irish administration, many Members of the Irish House of Commons, and George III himself. The result was a fudge, in which Union was to be brought about with Catholic emancipation both implied and expected, but with no actual commitment on it pronounced. The Irish Lord Chancellor, Lord Clare, was instrumental in influencing Pitt towards this compromise, meeting him twice in October at Holwood and writing to Castlereagh on 16 October: 'I have seen Mr. Pitt, the Chancellor, and the Duke of Portland, who seem to feel very sensibly the critical situation of our damnable country, and that the Union alone can save it. I should have hoped that what has passed would have opened the eyes of every man in England to the insanity of their past conduct, with respect to the Papists of Ireland; but I can very plainly perceive that they were as full of their popish projects as ever. I trust, and I hope I am not deceived, that they are fairly inclined to give them up, and to bring the measure forward unencumbered with the doctrine of Emancipation. Lord Cornwallis has intimated his acquiescence in this point; Mr. Pitt is decided upon it, and I think he will keep his colleagues steady.'[49]

His budget behind him, Pitt brought the matter to a decision in the Cabinet on 21 December 1798. The Cabinet announced that 'His Majesty's government has decided to press the measure of an Union as essential to the well-being of both countries . . . and will even in the case (if it should happen) of any present failure, be renewed on every occasion till it succeed, and that the conduct of individuals on this subject will be considered as the test of the disposition to support the King's government.'[50]

The determined tone of this announcement was meant to make the Union seem inevitable as well as to make it a matter of confidence in the government. The difficulties the project would face became evident on 22 January 1799, when the Irish House of Commons approved the principle by only one vote, 106 to 105. But in Westminster Pitt showed that he would brook no opposition. In his speech of 23 January he attacked 'the blind zeal and phrenzy of religious prejudices' and 'old and furious family feuds', which 'combine to make a country wretched'.[51] Three days later he wrote to Cornwallis instructing him to dismiss all officeholders who had opposed the government in the Irish House of Commons. He went ahead and introduced resolutions on the principles of a Union into the Commons on 31 January, in what was widely hailed as one of his greatest speeches. According to Auckland it 'surpassed even the most sanguine expectations of friends, and perhaps even any former exhibition of Parliamentary eloquence'.[52] It was one of only three speeches in his life which Pitt had specially revised and circulated as a text. He called for generosity to be coupled with certainty:

> I know that the inhabitants of Great Britain wish well to the prosperity of Ireland; that, if the Kingdoms are really and solidly united, they feel that to increase the commercial wealth of one country is not to diminish that of the other, but to increase the strength and power of both. But to justify that sentiment, we must be satisfied that the wealth we are pouring into the lap of Ireland is not every day liable to be snatched from us, and thrown into the scale of the enemy. If, therefore, Ireland is to continue, as I trust it will for ever, an essential part of the integral strength of the British empire; if her strength is to be permanently ours, and our strength to be hers, neither I nor any English minister can ever be deterred, by the fear of creating jealousy in the hearts of Englishmen, from stating the advantages of a closer connection, or from giving any assistance to the commercial prosperity of that kingdom.[53]

Ireland needed capital; Britain needed security. Each could provide it to the other. This was how Pitt, much motivated by the failures of the past, set out a vision of what could be achieved in the future.

This was Pitt at the beginning of 1799, confident, determined and eloquent. Wilberforce noted two weeks before Christmas: 'Supped with Pitt *tête-à-tête*. Much talk about Europe, Ireland, income-tax, Lord

Cornwallis, Union. He is, of course, in high spirits, and, what is better, his health, which had seemed to be again declining a few weeks ago, is now, I am assured, more radically improved than one could almost have hoped.'[54] His friends concurred on this, Hester Chatham writing to George Rose to thank him for 'the perfectly happy account of my dear son's health, after so long an exertion of his strength'.[55] Pitt was in his fortieth year, and had now led the government for fifteen years. From the days of military tension, incapacitating illness and rumours of insanity only months before, he had once again emerged as the incomparable master of the House of Commons and indispensable leader of the government.

Yet the grand design of Union with Ireland contained a serious flaw. Pitt would find a way to ram through its enactment, aided by differing understandings of the likelihood of Catholic emancipation. But those who held differing views on this subject would one day come into collision, and Pitt's liberal views on the matter were the very opposite of those of King George III. His categoric opinion had been stated in a letter to Pitt of 13 June 1798: 'No further indulgences must be granted to the Roman Catholics, as no country can be governed where there is more than one established religion; the others may be tolerated, but that cannot extend further [than] to leave to perform their religious duties according to the tenets of their Church, for which indulgence they cannot have any share in the government of the State.'[56]

Pitt would have known that this difference would be a major difficulty, but for years he had succeeded in manoeuvring George III into agreement with projects he found unpalatable, numerous peace initiatives among them. He was probably confident that he could get his way without precipitating a crisis, and in any case the risks he had run since the darkest days of September 1797 had paid off. Militarily, personally and politically he had sailed closer to the wind than ever in his life, and was now the stronger for it. Surely he could do the same again.

22

The Dashing of Hope

'I do, indeed, consider the French revolution as the severest trial which the visitation of Providence has ever yet inflicted upon the nations of the earth; but I cannot help reflecting, with satisfaction, that this country, even under such trial, has not only been exempted from those calamities which have covered almost every other part of Europe, but appears to have been reserved as a refuge and asylum to those who fled from its persecution, as a barrier to oppose its progress, and, perhaps, ultimately as an instrument to deliver the world from the crimes and miseries which have attended it.'

William Pitt, 3 February 1800[1]

'In what sort of state did I leave France, and in what sort of state do I find it again? I left you peace and I find war! I left you conquests, and the enemy is crossing our frontiers. I left our arsenals full, and I find not a single weapon! I left you the millions of Italy, and I find spoliatory laws and poverty everywhere!'

Napoleon Bonaparte, November 1799[2]

Having pulled himself and the nation together at the end of 1798, Pitt was once again confident and decisive as he entered upon the seventh consecutive year of war and his sixteenth year of leading the government. There is no doubt that he was tired, each bout of illness leaving him less able to sustain the schedule he had once maintained from breakfast time until late in the evening. Now his colleagues increasingly noticed, and grumbled, that he remained asleep in the mornings; Grenville commented that it was possible to do a morning's work 'before the day breaks in Downing Street'.[3] Pitt had less time for side issues, and became more dependent still on Dundas and Grenville as his senior colleagues. In the 1780s a zealous, hardworking and inquisitive Pitt had wrested control of foreign policy from Leeds, a Foreign Secretary in whom he never had much confidence. In 1799, by contrast, British foreign policy at the crucial moment of the formation of the Second Coalition against France was increasingly dictated by Grenville as Pitt relaxed his hold on detail. When the Continental powers resumed hostilities with France, Grenville could even say to Pitt that it brought 'credit and reputation to myself'[4] rather than to the government as a whole.

Pitt's physical resilience may have been waning, but it is testimony to his sanguine nature that his optimism about the war and his determination to succeed still shone. Against the endless setbacks on the Continent could be set a string of British naval victories and colonial conquests. At the same time, Britain was enjoying remarkable economic success despite the burdens of war. Control of the seas and the ever-quickening Industrial Revolution meant British trade was expanding rapidly: Pitt would proudly tell the Commons in June 1799 that exports the previous year neared £34 million, representing an increase of more than 20 per cent in a single year, and a huge surplus over imports. Such prosperity helped the government to maintain domestic order, and now it was hoped that the Union with Ireland would make that good order more durable. In Europe, the French military position was vulnerable and exposed, with their brilliant General trapped in the Middle East while the great imperial powers of Austria, Prussia and Russia gathered themselves for a further war against France.

It was a promising outlook, and Pitt must have felt that one more heave would do it. His work for the last six years had been like the labour of Sisyphus, using ever greater reserves of strength and ingenuity to roll the boulder up the hill. On each occasion, his hopes had been destroyed – he was cheated of victory in 1793 and 1794 largely by the ineffectiveness of allies, and of peace in 1796 and 1797 by the hardening demands of radical French leaders. Now there was a new, and perhaps greater than ever, opportunity to defeat France and secure a lasting peace. One more time he could bend body and mind to gain victory, vindication, and an end to the financial and human waste he had never sought or relished.

In early 1799, Pitt did not want for decisiveness: the government took whatever measures necessary to secure financial revenues, public order and Irish Union. Notwithstanding the almost even division in the Irish House of Commons, Pitt was determined that the measure would ultimately be passed in Dublin as well as London. He was prepared to give it time, but more significantly he was prepared to give the money, titles and rewards necessary to turn a truculent Irish Parliament into a cooperative one.

Pitt's transcendence over normal politics was partly due to his incorruptibility – 'Honest Billy' never sought rewards for himself, as his bankers well knew. But his concept of incorruptibility was applied strictly to himself, and did not prohibit dealing with others on the only terms they understood. In 1784 he had not hesitated to deploy the patronage of the Crown in his great confrontation with Fox. If the Irish House of Commons now required an even greater flow of favours in order to vote itself out of existence, then so be it. Thus Cornwallis was authorised by Pitt to carry out 'a little *quiet* coercion if it should be necessary'.[5] By May, Cornwallis was so deeply into this 'coercion' that it repelled him: 'It has been the wish of my life to avoid all this dirty business, and I am now involved in it beyond all bearing . . . How I long to kick those whom my public duty obliges me to court!'[6] He and Castlereagh embarked on a programme of public persuasion which would eventually be accompanied by every known device of influence: pensions and appointments were handed out in order to create a parliamentary vacancy or win over a vote; £1.5 million was eventually put on the table to purchase Irish seats from those who controlled them. Peerages were touted on an unprecedented scale, with Cornwallis sending a regular stream of requests for them to Pitt. By August, Cornwallis could report 'cordial approbation of the measure of Union'.[7]

Pitt was equally determined to screw down the lid of anti-sedition laws on the boxed-in activities of the radical Societies. He had become adept in financial matters at setting up a House of Commons Committee to inquire into a certain subject in order to buttress his eventual actions with the findings of a cross-section of MPs. 1799 provided a good example of the broader use of this technique: a Commons Committee on sedition reported in March, and Pitt responded in April with a new Bill to suppress new radical organisations such as United Scotsmen and United Englishmen. It contained tighter regulations on lecturing and printing; Pitt argued that the liberty of the press was 'the most invaluable bulwark of liberty', but that provisions to enable the tracing of all publications to their publishers were necessary because 'we have seen the liberty of the press abused in a way most calculated to pervert and mislead the lower orders'.[8]

This is a typical illustration of the arguments Pitt deployed for each aspect of his 'terror' – the restrictions were necessary in order to preserve the essence of traditional liberties. To opponents, of course, the measures themselves represented the removal of important freedoms. Pitt gave no trace of agonising over such measures: 'We must feel ourselves bound to accommodate our precautions to the evil which we have discovered.'[9] He has been criticised over the years for taking such harsh measures, and sometimes seen as changing his philosophy markedly over the years, but the truth seems to be that his liberal disposition was always subject to practical considerations. In his mind, progressive instincts were subject to the need to preserve the constitutional framework he cherished.

Pitt continued to treat the House of Commons with great respect. Although the remnant of the Whigs could provide only token opposition, he had not forgotten that the Commons was the source of his power. Lord Holland's analysis, that Pitt missed the absent Fox because he needed an enemy against which to rally his supporters, certainly rings true: 'Mr. Pitt earnestly laboured to draw his opponents back to Parliament, and that, with that view, he sometimes taunted and attempted to exasperate the absent members, and at others studiously magnified the talents and importance of those who were left behind ... he is also said to have found, that the want of opponents in Parliament deprived him of the readiest weapon which he could hold up in terrorem to the King, to force his compliance with any unpalatable measure, or to deter him from insisting on unreasonable objects.'[10]

Once again, on 7 June 1799, Pitt set out a budget at great length and in intricate detail. While he celebrated the flourishing of British trade, he already had to admit that the much-vaunted income tax was not going to produce the sums envisaged, principally because of evasion. He was thus obliged to borrow more than he intended, and even so had to stretch his financial ingenuity still further with fresh taxes on sugar, coffee and, remarkably, a small tax on banknotes.

Such problems seemed manageable when compared to the apparently parlous state of the French Republic. Quite apart from the economic consequences of high taxes, confiscations, soaring inflation and interruption of trade, France now faced a military situation which was the most adverse since her experience of invasion and revolt in 1793. The French had at first dealt successfully with the renewed outbreak of hostilities in Italy, when the Neapolitans jumped the gun and marched on Rome in November 1798. This had led to a spat between London and Vienna, since the Austrians believed the presence in Naples of Nelson and Lord and Lady Hamilton had contributed to their ally going to war without consulting them. Within weeks the French had routed the Neapolitan forces, Nelson was evacuating the Royal Family and the Hamiltons, and yet another republic was declared. But from then on military events turned sour for the overstretched French forces: a counter-revolution had swept them from southern Italy by June; Napoleon's advance against the Turks had been stopped at Acre (partly by a small British force led by Sydney Smith) and he was forced to retreat towards Cairo; revolts were brewing in Belgium, Luxembourg and formerly royalist regions of France such as the Vendée and Brittany; fighting broke out between the French and Austrian armies on the Rhine in March; and both Russia and Prussia seemed to be readying themselves for war. Austria formally declared war on France on 11 March.

The Second Coalition against France was therefore coming together, but doing so in a shambolic and accidental manner analogous to the First. Negotiations had been fraught for many months: Austrian refusal to honour the terms of an earlier loan agreement with Britain led Grenville to concentrate on Prussia rather than Austria, and also led to the collapse of a draft convention with Russia at the end of 1798. By February 1799 an Anglo–Russian agreement had been reached, extending subsidies to the Russians of well over £1 million a year in return for 45,000 troops. So far so good, but the presence for months in Berlin of Tom Grenville failed to arrest the continual seesawing of the attitudes of Frederick William III, who varied at one extreme from asking for a subsidy for fully 230,000 troops, to the other extreme of not fighting at all. By May it was clear that the Prussians could not be counted on – Tom Grenville thought them 'past the help of man'.[11] The Second Coalition was thus to be very far from the Quadruple Alliance with prior agreement on war aims which Pitt and Grenville had set out to form: the absence of Prussia and the difficulties the Austrian and Russian armies experienced in working together made it flawed from the outset.

Nevertheless, there was still hope that the coalition could be completed and could deliver a crushing blow to a momentarily stricken France. By late March the Austrian Archduke Charles was advancing across the Rhine. In early April the French were also defeated in Italy at Austrian hands, and by the end of the month the Russian General Suvorov was triumphantly entering Milan. Great swathes of Italian territory were passing into allied hands, including the capture of Turin at the end of May. Except in Switzerland, the French army was now in desperate straits, with Pitt and Grenville additionally contemplating a massive £3 million subsidy to entice the Prussians into the war. There was the real prospect that France could be defeated. From the disparate elements of the Second Coalition, an overall plan was indeed created: the Prussians and Austrians would invade eastern France, Suvorov would take on the French in Switzerland, the Austrians would maintain the pressure in northern Italy, and Britain, with additional Russian support, would mount an invasion of Holland, encouraging a Dutch revolt against the French as they did so.

For Pitt and Grenville this was a return to a Continental strategy with a vengeance. While more risky than a naval and colonial strategy, it offered the prospect of actually ending the war. For years Dundas had warned, always correctly, about the danger of putting British forces ashore on the Continent. Now he cast doubt on the likelihood of 'the Dutch coming forward to aid the progress of our arms'.[12] But for Grenville, a British intervention on the Continent was fundamental to providing vigour and even some coordination to the allies, and Pitt was happy at this point to be guided by Grenville and to sanction a strategy which at least provided some hope of final success.

The summer of 1799 saw French difficulties deepen. Zürich fell to the Austrians in early June, and Mantua to Suvorov in July. Counter-offensives failed, and by August all of the Italian territory conquered by Napoleon had been lost. The French army was desperately short of clothing and ammunition. Meanwhile the Prussians continued to waver. Against this background of diplomatic need and military opportunity a rather unpromising British invasion force was assembled for Holland. It was to be commanded by the experienced Ralph Abercromby, albeit with the Duke of York nominally in charge as Commander-in-Chief, and Pitt's elder brother, Chatham, would accompany it. As in previous phases of the war, it was difficult to make forces set down on paper appear in reality: the Russians could not supply the 20,000 troops intended, nor could 12,000 British troops go ashore in the first wave as had been planned because they lacked the necessary numbers of transports.

Pitt was in Kent with Dundas at the end of July when the final decisions about the expedition had to be made. By then it was clear that the Austrians under Archduke Charles were not supporting the Russian flank north of Switzerland as intended, but were instead proceeding to Mainz, motivated partly by uncertainty about British intentions in the Netherlands. News of a more dramatic shock arrived on 1 August – the Prussians categorically refused to join the war, and proposed to negotiate with France for a peaceful withdrawal of French troops from Holland. A Swedish contingent intended to join the British invasion of Holland was withdrawn at the same time. Should the invasion now go ahead, without a Prussian army engaging the French in the same region and without many of the forces originally envisaged? The military advice was that it should be postponed. Pitt, more accustomed to taking risks after the previous year's success in the Mediterranean, overruled the doubters. Once the decision was made, he told

Grenville, 'we shall now hear no more of difficulties'.[13] He decamped to Walmer, and sailed through the invasion convoy on the morning of 14 August to see it off.

Pitt was in good spirits that summer. The many frustrations seemed surmountable. Even without Prussia, the combined forces of Austria, Russia and Britain could defeat a weakened France. In Parliament, his budgetary measures had been approved, although renewed attempts to abolish or mitigate the slave trade had been defeated. Early in July he had thrown his weight behind the Slave Trade Limitation Bill, intended to restrict the area of the West African coast open to the trade, but while it passed the House of Commons it got nowhere in the Lords. The old enemy, Thurlow, teamed up with a younger son of George III, the Duke of Clarence, to defeat the measure outright. It remained the case that the one reforming liberal measure to which Pitt was still committed could not yet be carried through Parliament. Wilberforce never doubted Pitt's determination to abolish the slave trade; the failure to make progress after so many years meant that many others did.

It was far more important to Pitt that the war was at last going his way. The news of French defeats amidst new fighting on the Continent had buoyed his spirits, Grenville reporting that 'Pitt's health and spirits are revived by this tide of success in every quarter.'[14] In the spring and summer of 1799 he even relaxed a little and showed his old social sparkle, becoming friendly with Princess Caroline – although not as friendly as Canning, who was seen too often with the Princess in the light of her voracious sexual appetite: he was described by Lady Minto as 'charming' and 'captivating' to the ladies at her house. At another dinner party, 'Lady Charlotte [North] was to present the Queen of Prussia's bust to Mr. Pitt, and make him kiss it, which, after some difficulty, he performed.'[15] Wilberforce described a more conventional social scene that May: 'To Holwood by half-past four. Pitt riding out . . . Pitt, Canning, and Pepper Arden came in late to dinner . . . Evening: Canning and Pitt reading classics.'[16]

The pressure of war had lifted a little from Pitt's shoulders, and the prospect of clear-cut victory was greater than at any time in perhaps five years. He had once again rolled the boulder to the top of the hill.

But once again, it would soon come crashing down, bringing with it most of what remained of his health and his hopes.

Four events would combine to turn the sunny optimism of the summer of 1799 into the bleak events of 1800. The first was the rain, which fell heavily on much of England in August 1799, damaging the harvest and beginning a cycle of bad weather which would culminate in serious shortages of corn and record prices over the following two years. Before long, inflation and an uncertain food supply would undermine the economic growth and political order of which Pitt was understandably proud.

The second adverse development was the failure of the allied advance on France at the very point it was meant to be strongest: Switzerland. This was very largely due to lack of coordination and understanding among the allies. Suvorov, whom the Austrians despised in spite of his victories, was still in northern Italy with most of the Russian forces when the Archduke Charles set off north from Switzerland with the Austrians, partly motivated by concern over the British move on Holland, which the decidedly anti-Austrian Grenville had declined to explain fully to Vienna. The result was that in August an inviting gap had opened up between the allied armies: Suvorov conducted an epic march into the mountains in an effort to fill it, while Austrian attempts to repair the damage were belated or delayed, Grenville commenting on the Austrian Chancellor Thugut: 'If he were paid to thwart all our measures and to favour those of France, he could not do it more effectually.'[17] Suvorov stormed his way into Switzerland to find an allied force had already been defeated in a fresh battle at Zürich; short of troops and bereft of any of the Swiss volunteers he had been promised, he was pulling out of Switzerland by October, retreating with great honour but with the frontiers of France intact.

The third major setback was the state of Britain's own invasion of Holland. This started promisingly enough in the second half of August, with the capture of key forts and the surrender on 30 August of the entire Dutch navy, or at least what was left of it after Camperdown. Celebrations were held in London, and Pitt's mind raced on, envisaging a sympathetic Dutch insurrection and the speedy withdrawal of British forces, to using the same troops to attack Brest and destroy the main French fleet. At the same time he was complaining of 'the blind and perverse selfishness of Austria's counsels',[18] but hopes still ran high. By 10 September the Duke of York had joined Abercromby in Holland with 20,000 British and Russian troops, making up an allied force of around 30,000 in all.

This was all well and good, but the invasion of Holland had been originally conceived as one prong of intense military pressure being applied to the French on many fronts. Without the participation of the Prussians, and in the absence of further progress by other allies, the French were under no immediate pressure to withdraw from Holland, and the Dutch did not have the confidence to rise against them. Poor intelligence about French strength and movements discouraged Abercromby from taking risks with the only land strike-force Britain possessed. The result was a bogged-down conflict not far from the coast. A series of pitched battles in late September and early October produced mixed success, but casualties were far too high for a relatively small army to sustain. By mid-October the Duke of York was negotiating with the French to withdraw his army peacefully in return for the release of thousands of French prisoners held in England.

Pitt had been assiduous in writing to his mother and sister-in-law throughout the Dutch campaign to assure them of the safety of his brother. His letter to Lady Chatham from Holwood on 21 October illustrates his ability to maintain a cheerful countenance in abject circumstances:

> We have just received accounts from Holland, by which I find my brother is perfectly well, and all further suspense and anxiety is happily removed, as an agreement is being concluded, by which our army is to evacuate Holland within a limited time, and is ensured from all molestation in doing so. It is certainly no small disappointment to be coming away by compromise instead of driving the enemy completely before us, as we once had reason to hope; but under all the difficulties which the season and circumstances have produced, it ought to be a great satisfaction to us to know that our valuable army will be restored to us safe and

> entire. The private relief it will be to your mind as well as to my own is of itself no small additional consolation.[19]

True enough, the army had been preserved, and indeed the Dutch fleet captured. But overall, the Dutch expedition had only added to the chapter of humiliation which the record of British incursions on the Continent now formed. Of course, there were recriminations. Chatham told Pitt that the failure could 'fairly be attributed to the misconduct of the Russian General and the Russian troops'.[20] On the other hand, Abercromby considered the Duke of York 'the most ungracious weak prince in Europe . . . he knows as little of the country as if [he] had been bred in Sweden'.[21] In reality, the responsibility went all the way to the top: Pitt and Grenville had overridden Dundas and military advice to send an under-equipped expedition across the Channel with uncertain objectives. Grenville's faith in a Dutch uprising and a Prussian alliance had been too strong, and Pitt's readiness to take risks in the hope of victory had become too prevalent.

The fourth dangerous event was yet another dramatic change in the Paris power structure, the consummating upheaval of the French Revolution as it began to turn back towards monarchy. For Napoleon now executed a daring personal escape from Egypt, having won a sufficiently devastating victory over the Turks at the end of July to return to France with honour. His westward voyage across the Mediterranean took forty-five days and required the evasion of many Royal Navy patrols, but culminated in mid-October in his return to France and the adulation of a beleaguered population. The speech in which he thundered: 'In what sort of state did I leave France, and in what sort of state do I find it again?'[22] set the stage for the coup of 18 and 19 Brumaire (9 and 10 November), in which the Directory was abolished and power vested in three Consuls: the Abbé Sieyès, Roger Ducos and Napoleon. There was little doubt which individual was in charge: beset by enemies and shortages, the French had tired of revolutionary ideals and sought a strong leader. In the words of François Furet: 'In 1789, the French had created a Republic, under the name of a monarchy. Ten years later, they created a monarchy, under the name of a Republic.'[23]

The course of the war was still in the balance that autumn. For the moment the French had recovered their position but still faced numerically superior opponents as well as suffering from exhaustion with war. On Christmas Day, 1799, Napoleon wrote personal letters to the Emperor Francis II of Austria and to George III, proposing an end to the war. He did not put forward specific proposals, but his letters were full of enlightened arguments for peace and, ironically in the light of his subsequent career, rejected 'ideas of vain greatness'.

It was a measure of French weakness that Napoleon made such an overture, and it was largely seen as such in allied capitals. While Tsar Paul I would have nothing more to do with the Austrians, both St Petersburg and Vienna seemed to remain committed to the war. In London, the Cabinet had been clear after the setback in Holland that the war must go on. Dundas, who made clear his wish to resign when Pitt would let him from November 1799, was all the more adamant that British forces should stay clear of the Continent, but he remained isolated in the Cabinet. All through the autumn of 1799 options for the invasion of France in 1800 were discussed in London, while British messengers fanned out across Europe in vain attempts to create Austro–Russian cooperation.

It was against this background of uncertain strategy, political resolve, and confidence that the condition of France was weak and her government in a state of flux, that the overture from Napoleon was judged. In hindsight, it may seem strange that a Prime Minister who was so determined on peace in the failed negotiations of 1796 and 1797 was so ready to reject a peace feeler at the end of 1799, but Pitt was quite clear, as he noted for a parliamentary debate a few weeks later, that there was a 'difference from state when We Negotiated'.[24] This included matters such as 'Diminution of French Armies and Want of military Supplies' and 'State of Finances – Bankruptcies'. The advantage therefore lay with the allies. In addition, Pitt considered on the basis of past experience and the seeming fragility of Napoleon's power that 'Perfidy' and 'Want of Stability' meant that any peace agreement could swiftly be revoked. Given the rise of royalist sentiment in parts of France and the creation of a consular dictatorship, there was a trend towards monarchy which Britain should encourage in setting out the conditions for peace, while not excluding peace with the current French government if it proved to be stable and reliable.

This was Pitt's consistent view through the winter of 1799–1800, and it enjoyed fairly solid political support with the exception of the Foxites, even in the end among waverers such as Wilberforce. Pitt had set out his views to Canning in November, saying that Britain could fight '*One* or *Two* Campaigns more', or, if the coalition collapsed, a 'defensive War by ourselves'.[25] He could not make peace with a 'Revolutionary Jacobin government'. On New Year's Eve, 1799, he wrote from Downing Street to Dundas in Scotland on receipt of the French overture:

> I think we can have nothing to do but to decline all negotiation at the present moment, on the ground that the actual situation of France does not as yet hold out any solid security to be derived from negotiation, taking care, at the same time, to express strongly the eagerness with which we should embrace any opening for general peace whenever such solid security shall appear attainable. This may, I think, be so expressed as to convey to the people of France that the shortest road to peace is by effecting the restoration of Royalty, and thereby to increase the chance of that most desirable of all issues to the war; but at the same time so as in no degree to preclude us from treating even with the present Government, if it should prevail and be able to establish itself firmly.[26]

The Cabinet met in the first week of January 1800, and approved a response which was probably too haughty to win friends in France: it was sent from Grenville to the French Foreign Minister Talleyrand as a calculated snub to Napoleon. A further attempt by Talleyrand to open negotiations later that month was also rebuffed.

The government's rejection of the peace overtures occasioned a fierce parliamentary debate on 3 February 1800, Fox reappearing in the Commons for that day only to ask why the government had not put Bonaparte's statement of peaceful intentions to the test. Pitt responded with an extremely lengthy speech, describing the French Revolution as 'the severest trial which the visitation of Providence has ever yet inflicted upon the nations of the earth',[27] and cataloguing its outrages: 'The all-searching eye of the French revolution looks to every part of Europe, and every quarter of the world, in which can be found an object either of acquisition or plunder. Nothing is too great for the temerity of its ambition, nothing too small or insignificant for the grasp of its rapacity.'[28] He attacked the personal character and conduct of Napoleon, saying that no reliance could be placed on his disposition or principles. Peace could only be made with a stable government, and 'is then military despotism that which we are accustomed to consider as a stable form of government?'[29] He said he had wished for peace, and laboured for it, but the circumstances had now changed because the enemy was unreliable and the war could be won: 'When we consider the resources and the spirit of the country, can any man doubt that if adequate security is not now to be obtained by treaty, we have the means of prosecuting the contest without material difficulty or danger, and with a reasonable prospect of completely attaining our object?'[30]

Fox, by contrast, thought Napoleon sincere: 'Peace & Peace upon good terms might be had nobody now doubts.'[31] Within months he would regard Napoleon as having 'surpassed . . . Alexander & Caesar, not to mention the great advantage he has over them in the Cause he fights in'.[32]

Two weeks later Pitt had another fierce clash with Tierney, who challenged him to state the object of the war in one word, without any 'ifs and buts'. Pitt responded: 'I can tell him that it is security: security against a danger, the greatest that ever threatened the world. It is Security against a danger which never existed in any past period of society.'[33] He then went on to turn the 'ifs and buts' against his opponent in a legendary demonstration of his debating ability.

> He says that any attempt at explanation upon this subject is the mere ambiguous unintelligible language of *ifs* and *buts*, and of special pleading. Now, Sir, I never had much liking to special pleading; and if ever I had any, it is by this time almost entirely gone. He has besides so abridged me of the use of particles, that though I am not particularly attached to the sound of an *if* or a

> *but*, I would be much obliged to the honourable gentleman if he would give me some others to supply their places. Is this, however, a light matter, that it should be treated in so light a manner? The restoration of the French monarchy, I will still tell the honourable gentleman, I consider as a most desirable object, because I think that it would afford the strongest and best security to this country and to Europe. *But* this object may not be attainable; and *if* it be not attainable, we must be satisfied with the best security which we can find independent of it. Peace is most desirable to this country; *but* negociation may be attended with greater evils than could be counterbalanced by any benefits which would result from it. And *if* this be found to be the case; *if* it afford no prospect of security; *if* it threaten all the evils which we have been struggling to avert; *if* the prosecution of the war afford the prospect of attaining complete security; and *if* it may be prosecuted with increasing commerce, with increasing means, and with increasing prosperity, except what may result from the visitations of the seasons; then I say, that it is prudent in us not to negociate at the present moment. These are my *buts* and my *ifs*. This is my plea, and on no other do I wish to be tried, by God and my country.[34]

Pitt's analysis that Napoleon could not be trusted was certainly correct; he was also correct in thinking that France was moving back to monarchy, although he would have been astounded at this point to learn that it would be through the person of Napoleon himself. On the information available to him, his judgement in carrying on the war when the enemy seemed to be weakening and attempting a manoeuvre to find a breathing space or divide the allies was sound. Yet if he could only have seen a few months ahead, he might very well have reverted to his more pacific stance of 1797. For the Second Coalition was on its way to the most calamitous dissension and defeat.

Alongside the affirmation of the war's objectives and consideration of how to pursue them, the project of ramming the Union through the Dublin Parliament was gathering pace. The specific plan involved adding one hundred seats to the 558 in the British House of Commons, paying £7,500 per seat to the proprietors and patrons of the abolished Irish boroughs. This and every other form of eighteenth-century persuasion was applied to the final debates of the Irish House of Commons. Votes were said to change hands at four thousand guineas apiece, while later that year twenty-one new peerages or elevations in the peerage involving those who had voted on the measure revealed the liberal deployment of patronage. Recently published evidence suggests that some £30,000 of secret-service money was deployed to promote the Union in 1799 and 1800, and that part of it was used to provide secret annuities for Irish MPs.[35] While the Protestant legislators were bribed to support the Union, Catholic opposition was neutralised by the implication (but not specific commitment) that their emancipation would inevitably result. How this was to be accomplished, given the intensity of the opposition to it, was not clear: George III had minuted Cornwallis on 31 January 1800: 'though a strong friend to the Union of the two Kingdoms, I should become an Enemy to the movement if I thought a change of the Situation of the Roman Catholics would attend this measure'.[36]

Catholic emancipation remained the unspoken companion of the Union. By July George III was hailing 'the happiest event of my reign'[37] as the session in Westminster closed with the Act of Union passed in both Dublin and Westminster. Once the Irish Parliament had been dealt with, Pitt had taken the lead in pushing the necessary Bill through the Commons from April onwards. His speech of 21 April included a section on the importance of maintaining the British constituencies untouched while the hundred Irish seats were added to them. His open admission of an alteration in his previous views on the merits of parliamentary reform suggests that the years of war had indeed changed his political outlook: 'I have not forgotten what I have myself formerly said and sincerely felt upon this subject; but I know that all opinions must necessarily be subservient to times and circumstances; and that man who talks of his consistency merely because he holds the same opinion for ten or fifteen years, when the circumstances under which that opinion was originally formed are totally changed, is a slave to the most idle vanity.' Seeing now the consequences of changes to other constitutions and the strength of the British one in the face of all its challenges, Pitt felt the form of representation should not 'be idly and wantonly disturbed from any love of experiment, or any predilection for theory . . . I think it right to declare my most decided opinion, that, even if the times were proper for experiments, any, even the slightest change in such a constitution must be considered as an evil.'[38]

Experience had indeed hardened him against the ideals of his youth. And the experiences of the next few months were to be some of the hardest of all. The price of wheat continued to rise steeply. Poor spring weather and torrential rain in mid-summer raised the prospect of the second bad harvest in a row. The link between food prices and public disorder would be reaffirmed by riots that autumn; in the meantime the returning atmosphere of domestic insecurity was added to when the King was shot at in the Drury Lane Theatre (the culprit then spent forty years in the mental asylum of Bedlam). At the same time, Pitt's financial calculations were going awry. Income tax had produced less than £2 million in 1799 instead of the expected £6.5 million. The Commons baulked at a measure presented by Pitt in April obliging taxpayers to itemise their income in an attempt to prevent evasion. He had to abandon the measure and substitute a far more moderate alternative.

Even so, he was raising far larger sums in tax than had ever been known before, yet still needed a loan of £18.5 million for 1800. The creation of income tax had been intended to pay for more of the war's costs while it was actually in progress, rather than using taxes simply to fund the accumulating debt. But in effect, by 1800 Pitt was back to raising ever larger loans. His parliamentary workload that summer was heavy: the Union and financial issues coincided with the need to defend the government's renunciation of the Convention of El Arish, in which Sydney Smith, after his heroic defence at Acre, had overseen a Franco–Turkish agreement that the French army would be taken home from Egypt in British ships.

All these issues added to the pressures on Pitt that summer, but none was so great as the difficulty of contending with the strains of the coalition and sharp disagreements between his two long-standing lieutenants over the course of the war. By March 1800 the unpredictable

Tsar Paul I had tired of criticism of his troops and the lack of Austrian support for his army the previous year, and communicated to London his withdrawal from the coalition, despite the offer of a massive £3.5 million subsidy. This development threw a reluctant Grenville back into the arms of Austria and diminished the military resources available to attack France, further complicating British decision-making.

In a memorandum at the end of March Dundas argued cogently that it was time to switch wholeheartedly to a naval strategy which would clear the Spanish from a good deal of their empire and open up the South American market for British trade. He wished to capture New Orleans, Tenerife, Concepción in Chile and sites on the Rivers Plate and Orinoco. This was in sharp conflict with the Cabinet's already decided intention of sending the army into the Mediterranean to strike at France from the south. Other plans, variously abandoned and resurrected through the early months of 1800, included the occupation of Belleisle off the coast of northern France or Walcheren off the coast of Holland. With Dundas preferring this option to a Mediterranean expedition, and Grenville preferring to attack the Bordeaux region, sharp notes were exchanged between them, Grenville telling Dundas: 'Do this, or anything else that you prefer, but for God's sake, for your own honour, and for the cause in which we are engaged, do not let us, after having by immense exertions collected a fine army, leave it unemployed, gaping after messengers from Genoa, Augsburg, and Vienna, till the moment for acting is irrecoverably past by. For this can lead to nothing but disgrace.'[39]

For any party leader or Prime Minister, sustained disagreement with or between senior colleagues is the most wearying and time-consuming of difficulties. Not only were Pitt's principal Secretaries of State at loggerheads, but Dundas, the one closest to him, was begging to leave office. His nights had become sleepless, his health was deteriorating and his wife was pressing him to retire from the front line of politics. But Pitt was adamant, and may well have suggested that he himself could not go on without his right-hand man. He lectured Dundas about his duty: 'It is impossible for any consideration to reconcile my mind to the measure you propose . . . Let me therefore entreat you for all our sakes, to abandon wholly this idea, and to reconcile yourself to a duty which however difficult and painful, you are really at the moment not at liberty to relinquish.'[40] In the end, Dundas bowed to Pitt's will and even promised he would not leave before the end of the war.

Still more serious was the consequence of Cabinet indecision and disagreement, which led to the British army being put to no effective use throughout a crucial year of war. An expedition did eventually sail to the Mediterranean, but arrived in Minorca too late to affect the fighting on the Continent between the Austrians and the French. Storms and the strength of the French defences prevented any landing being made at Belleisle. Other small landings got nowhere, and an eventual attempt to seize the Spanish naval port of Cadiz was cancelled in bad weather. Cornwallis wrote of 'twenty-two thousand men floating round the greater part of Europe, the scorn and laughing stock of friends and foes'.[41]

It is hard to escape the conclusion that the pressure of parliamentary, ministerial and international events in the summer of 1800 was too much for Pitt's weakened constitution. He still did an enormous amount: he held his government together, secured the passage of the Act of Union, obtained funding for the war and maintained the wider political resolve to see it through. But he could no longer do everything. Disagreements among colleagues, and the lack of any obvious course of action for what might be the last throw of the war, left him uncertain, exercising too little grip, and prone to his long-standing vices of procrastination and the readiness to grasp at the latest encouraging news. In early June he changed his mind on military plans on two consecutive days. Nearly seventeen years into his premiership, and perhaps for the first time in his life, William Pitt did not know what to do.

And then the hammer-blow fell. On 6 May Napoleon had left Paris and moved an army with his customary rapid speed through Switzerland to Milan. South-west of Milan on the morning of 14 June he divided his forces to prevent the Austrians escaping, but soon found himself under full-scale Austrian attack. The battle, known to history as Marengo, was, as Wellington would later say of Waterloo, 'a damned close run thing'. By the time Napoleon managed to recall the forces he had sent away the French were almost done for, but General Desaix is said to have commented on arrival, 'The battle is completely lost; but it is only two o'clock, and we still have enough time to win another battle before the day is done.'[42] He did not survive the day, joining some 6,500 French and seven thousand Austrian casualties. But at the end of the day the French held the field and Napoleon, albeit narrowly, had cemented his personal power in Paris and decisively repulsed the Austrian army. It was 'the baptism of Napoleon's personal power'.[43]

Had the battle gone the other way that day, the history of the next fifteen years would have been dramatically different. There were already many plots behind Napoleon's back, and his power would probably not have survived a clear defeat. Instead he became the unrivalled champion of France, and the military prospects of the Second Coalition were shattered.

News of Marengo arrived in London on 24 June. Once again, Pitt's health was about to snap under the weight of so many pressures and disasters. He seemed to behave bizarrely at Canning's wedding on 8 July, although he should have found it a joyous occasion, having encouraged the match, bringing Canning and his bride Joan Scott together at Walmer, and giving Canning promotion so that he was better provided for. Pitt travelled to the wedding in a carriage with the officiating clergyman, Mr Leigh, and the best man, John Frere, who recounted that a man 'recognised Pitt and saw Mr. Leigh, who was in full canonicals, sitting opposite to him. The fellow exclaimed, "What, Billy Pitt! and with a parson too!" I said, "He thinks you are going to Tyburn to be hanged privately"; which was rather impudent of me; but Pitt was too much absorbed, I believe in thinking of the marriage, to be angry.'[44] At the ceremony Pitt seemed too nervous to sign the register, suggesting that he was either distressed, ill, or much influenced by alcohol.

By the end of July George Rose was telling Pretyman that Pitt was again unwell. He was to get little rest that summer, staying at Downing Street much of the time to deal with an increasingly difficult international situation and an alarming domestic one. The Austrians had now been forced to a truce, and in late August the French proposed a similar truce with Britain, in effect the cessation of naval operations. This was not quick enough to save the French garrison on Malta from capitulating to a British blockade on 4 September. But Pitt found the issue 'delicate'. On the one hand a naval armistice would favour the French, and on the other Britain's refusal to agree to it would bring new French assaults on the beleaguered Austrians. Satisfactory terms could not be agreed, but Cabinet disagreements over the prospect of a truce absorbed much of Pitt's time, with Dundas, Canning and Windham fearing that he might be too prone to concede an unsatisfactory peace agreement now that the coalition was disintegrating.

At home the price of wheat was reaching 120 shillings a quarter, and Pitt was writing to Addington on 8 October that 'the question of peace or war is not in itself half so formidable as that of the scarcity with which it is necessarily combined, and for the evils and growing dangers of which I see no adequate remedy'.[45] The following day he was again writing to Addington canvassing ideas for intervention in the corn markets and the punishment of unscrupulous dealers; by the next day he was more seriously ill, suffering from his 'old Complaint in the Bowels, Loss of Appetite, & is a good deal shook; he cannot carry a Glass of Beer to his Mouth without the aid of his second Hand'.[46]

It was becoming a familiar pattern: Farquhar had tried to get him to a spa in Cheltenham or Bath, but he refused. Instead, he agreed to go to Addington's house at Woodley in Berkshire. Addington noted that Pitt needed 'rest and *consolation*'.[47] After a week he thought 'he is certainly better, but I am still very far from being at ease about him',[48] and then after three weeks at Woodley: 'Mr. Pitt's health . . . is so well established as to render him fully equal to any exertions that may be required of him.'[49]

Pitt had once again pulled himself together, although his close colleagues must have begun to wonder how long this could go on. When he returned to Downing Street the weight of business was unforgiving. Food riots were taking place all over the country. Pitt had followed the price of corn anxiously throughout his illness, and he disagreed sharply with the free-market-orientated Grenville about the merits of government intervention. In a classic example of his practical approach to policy-making, Pitt rejected in a Commons speech of 11 November both the idea of pure free trade and of a whole new system of regulation, in favour of improved bounties on imports and other measures to encourage economy in the use of grain:

> To go beyond the remedy which is plain, practical, sanctioned by the soundest principles, and confirmed by the surest experience, must ever be a dangerous course: – it is unsafe in the attempt, it is unworthy of a statesman in the design, to abandon the system which practice has explained and experience has confirmed, for the visionary advantages of a crude, untried theory. It is no less unsafe, no less unworthy of the active politician, to adhere to any theory, however just in its general principle, which excludes from its view those particular details, those unexpected situations, which must render the scheme of the philosophic politician in the closet inapplicable to the actual circumstances of human affairs. But, if it be unwise to be guided solely by speculative systems of political economy, surely it is something worse to draw theories of regulation from clamour and alarm.[50]

Having done what it could to alleviate food shortages, the Cabinet also showed improved decisiveness on military matters, resolving to send 15,000 men to Egypt to clear out the stranded French army. On 27 November Pitt gave the Commons a spirited defence of the war: 'Is it nothing that, having had to struggle . . . for our very existence as a free state, with our commerce marked out as an object of destruction, our constitution threatened, we have preserved the one unimpaired, and most materially augmented the other; and, in many particulars, increased our national wealth, as well as its glory?'[51]

But the matters which had gone from bad to worse now lurched to the catastrophic. The truce between France and Austria had ended in November without a peace agreement. On 3 December the Austrians were again decisively defeated by the French at Hohenlinden, leaving Vienna exposed. By Christmas Day Austria had again sued for peace. At the same time Britain's other major erstwhile ally, Russia, was moving into open hostility. Apparently incensed by the British occupation of Malta without provision for the restoration of the Knights of St John, Tsar Paul I gave a lead to neutral Baltic countries which had long complained of being stopped and searched by Royal Navy ships enforcing the blockade of France. To Britain, the war could not be waged without the right to search neutral shipping: Russia, Denmark and Sweden now formed the League of Armed Neutrality 'to oblige England to allow neutral ships to pass without search'.[52]

Admiral Sir Hyde Parker was told to prepare a fleet for the Baltic to assert British naval power, with Nelson to assist him. Yet again the fortunes of war had turned full circle. Britain was again alone, save for distant Turkey and the minor forces of Naples and Portugal. Napoleon was supreme in Paris and dominated western Europe, while in London Cabinet unity and prime ministerial stamina had been stretched as far as they would go.

23

Resignation with Hesitation

'A discussion has naturally taken place, in consequence of the Union, on the question of the Catholics, and it has very lately been brought to a point which will very soon render it impossible for me to remain in my present situation.'

WILLIAM PITT TO BISHOP TOMLINE, 6 FEBRUARY 1801[1]

'When the crew of a vessel was preparing for action, it was usual to clear the decks by throwing overboard the lumber, but he never heard of such a manoeuvre as that of throwing their great guns overboard.'

RICHARD BRINSLEY SHERIDAN, 16 FEBRUARY 1801[2]

ON 2 FEBRUARY 1801 William Pitt gave the House of Commons his customary display of debating prowess. Ill and overworked he may have been, but it had been noted eighteen years before when he vomited through the Commons doorway and went on to give a brilliant oration that he possessed 'amazing powers of mind which bodily infirmity seemed never to obscure'.[3] His unscripted rebuttals of criticism had never lost their architecture of neatly arranged arguments supporting a crushingly logical conclusion. Responding that day to Grey's opposition attack on the reasons for conflict with the League of Armed Neutrality, questioning the nature and importance of British maritime rights, Pitt said he 'must begin with his doubts, and end with his certainties; and I cannot avoid observing that the honourable gentleman was singularly unfortunate upon this subject, for he entertained doubts where there was not the slightest ground for hesitation, and he contrives to make up his mind to absolute certainty upon points in which both arguments and fact are decidedly against him'.[4] After examining every argument of necessity and legal right, Pitt hectored the opposition: 'The question is, whether we are to permit the navy of our enemy to be supplied and recruited – whether we are to suffer blockaded forts to be furnished with warlike stores and provisions – whether we are to suffer neutral nations, by hoisting a flag upon a sloop, or a fishing boat, to convey the treasures of South America to the harbours of Spain, or the naval stores of the Baltic to Brest or Toulon? Are these the propositions which gentlemen mean to contend for?'[5] The House supported him by its usually emphatic 245 votes to sixty-three.

It seemed like business as usual. The war continued, expeditions were underway, the budget was in an advanced state of preparation and Pitt was dominating the floor of the Commons. Although rumours were beginning to spread, many of the MPs who cheered his words that evening would have been astonished to know that two days earlier he had placed his likely resignation before the King, and that three days later it would be accepted.

They would eventually be even more perplexed to discover that this resignation of a Prime Minister of seventeen years' standing was over an issue not then at the forefront of parliamentary debate, and on which Pitt was not known to have trenchant views: giving Catholics the right to sit in Parliament. Dundas considered that historians would never believe that the Pitt ministry resigned on this question, and certainly many contemporaries refused to do so. Pitt's apparently sudden departure from office has always been regarded as one of the most mysterious episodes in his entire career. It came at an unexpected time – even to himself – over a disagreement with George III which nevertheless had for some months and even years been wholly predictable, and was swiftly followed by Pitt's disavowal of the very principle on which he had surrendered the job he loved, along with the near rescinding of his resignation a month after the event. There has been much disagreement about his motives, shrouded by the conflicting signals given off by his overworked and probably exhausted brain. Why did William Pitt, at the age of forty-one and with no alternative career or pursuits in mind, precipitately resign from the only office he ever wished to hold?

Catholic emancipation had been the spectre at the feast of the celebrations of the Union with Ireland. Pitt had long envisaged that a further extension of the rights of Catholics, to include the right to hold public office, would be a logical corollary of the Union: it was part of binding the whole Irish population into the newly united nation, with Protestants safe from any fear of a Catholic majority in Dublin. To Pitt, it was a matter of practical politics rather than religious faith. Wilberforce had lamented many years before that Pitt had little interest in religious questions as such. He had opposed the repeal of the Test Acts in 1787, and decided in 1798 to postpone Catholic emancipation until after the Act of Union – in both cases simply because of the strength of the likely opposition from monarch, Church and conservative politicians to his liberal inclinations.

A comprehensive and very Pitt-like solution to all of these problems was quietly put forward within the government in the summer of 1800. Both Catholics and Protestant Dissenters would be admitted to public office by the repeal of the Test Acts. At the same time the bitterly hated tithe payments to the Irish Church would be commuted into rents, while the Church of England would benefit from better pay for some of the clergy. A new oath for officeholders would recognise that revolutionary Jacobinism rather than Catholicism was now Britain's enemy, and would require a specific rejection of revolutionary doctrine. It was a package designed to create Cabinet unity and political saleability to the wider political nation.

In particular, Cabinet unanimity would be vital to secure the acquiescence of George III. Throughout the 1790s, Pitt had been used to getting his way when his political needs clashed with the entrenched opinions of the King: he had forced George III to dismiss Thurlow, had conducted peace negotiations with France in 1796 in spite of royal hostility, and had most recently employed Cabinet unity to overcome the King's objections to the Egyptian expedition. He evidently assumed that, if necessary, the same trick could be performed again. If the

Union was going to be a success, then religious grievances including Catholic emancipation ought to be addressed in 1801, and he accordingly summoned Cabinet Ministers together for a discussion in September 1800 before Castlereagh, the Irish Secretary, was due to return to Dublin.

It was unfortunate for Pitt that the Lord Chancellor, Lord Loughborough, was staying with the King in Weymouth when this meeting was called. Pitt's letter to Loughborough of 25 September apologised for proposing to shorten his holiday, but explained the necessity of discussing 'the great question on the general state of the Catholics' as well as the policy on the tithes and clergy.[6] Since this communication enabled Loughborough to ingratiate himself with the King and sound him out on the Catholic question before attending the Cabinet meeting, it can appear in retrospect to be the action of a political innocent. But Pitt, who was of course weighed down at this point by reversals in the war and an imminent personal collapse, could not conceivably leave the Lord Chancellor out of such a meeting or conceal from him the reason for it. He had to trust in confidential communication within the Cabinet.

Pitt thus started out on this delicate issue handicapped by a serious misjudgement of two very powerful figures. He seems to have underestimated the extent to which George III – whom he did not intend to be aware of the Cabinet discussions at this stage – would regard Catholic emancipation as an issue of an entirely different order even to the huge issues of war, peace and Cabinet appointments on which he had previously given way. To the King this was not only a political matter, but a religious and personal one, 'beyond the decision of any Cabinet of Ministers', as he had ominously warned years before. In his opinion, the admission of Catholics to public office would be a direct violation of his Coronation Oath to uphold the established Church. His beliefs in religion, faithfulness, duty and clarity came together to make him, on this one issue, utterly unyielding – a fact no doubt discovered in short order by Loughborough when he raised the matter before departing Weymouth for London.

Pitt was also misjudging Loughborough himself. They had enjoyed good relations since Loughborough had been the first of the Whigs to jump ship and join Pitt upon the outbreak of war. Pitt had forgotten that a politician capable of ratting on one set of colleagues can very easily rat on another. George III was shrewder, saying on hearing the news of Loughborough's death in 1805, 'Then, he has not left a greater knave behind him in my dominions.'[7] Loughborough later admitted telling the King of the proposed Cabinet discussion, and possibly showed him related memoranda. There can be little doubt that the two egged each other on. George III had been advised by Loughborough six years before that Catholic emancipation would indeed violate the Coronation Oath, in conflict with all other legal opinion including that of the Lord Chief Justice.

Loughborough no doubt felt under an even greater obligation to oppose the measure having once again heard the King's views, and he proceeded to do just that at the Cabinet meeting on 1 October. He opposed the section of the proposals dealing with Catholics, and partly as a result the meeting was indecisive. Mention having been made of the hostility of the King, Pitt undertook to speak to him 'the moment He returned'.[8] He now compounded his earlier misjudgement of George III by neglecting to do this. The rapidly deteriorating situation overseas, the continuing crisis over corn prices, his serious illness in October, and his reluctance to create a premature crisis all encouraged his habitual procrastination. It was shortly after this episode that George III commented that Pitt was 'apt to put off laborious or disagreeable business to the last, but then, when forced to it, got through it with extraordinary rapidity'.[9]

During the autumn Cabinet opposition grew to include Portland, Westmorland, Liverpool and Chatham, with Westmorland additionally warning the King that the matter would soon come to the fore.[10] Loughborough, to be fair, continued to warn Pitt of the danger, asking him, according to Rose, 'whether he thought it would be judicious to propose a measure of this sort, to which the King was notoriously so averse, and on which the whole bench of bishops would be against him; probably many lords from opinion, others from an inclination to follow the King; most likely, Lord Chatham, as well as others of the Cabinet, with many of his most confidential friends, such as the Speaker, the Master of the Rolls, &c'.[11] The matter was still unresolved in January 1801 as Parliament, complete with a hundred Irish Members brought in by the Act of Union, prepared to meet (the Chamber of the Commons was modified to accommodate them). No specific proposals being agreed, Pitt drafted an anodyne King's Speech which referred to 'the great object of improving the benefits of that happy Union, which, by the blessing of Providence, has now been effected',[12] while concentrating on the need to confront the League of Armed Neutrality.

With Parliament about to resume, Pitt called a meeting on 25 January to ascertain once again the views of the Cabinet. The meeting was called at short notice, and Chatham, Liverpool and Loughborough were all absent. This appears to have been a classic use by Pitt of prime ministerial power to control Cabinet meetings, timings, and agendas with a view to obtaining the right result. Those who attended were under the impression that it was a preliminary meeting in advance of another the next day, but given the general agreement in the absence of opponents, Pitt decided a further meeting was unnecessary. The detailed proposals, put together by Castlereagh, were generally supported, although Camden observed that 'Mr. Pitt should proceed with the utmost caution', given everything he had heard 'of the King's Opinion being so decided'.[13]

It cannot be known for certain why Pitt was so determined to get his way on a matter which might be considered as of secondary importance to a government heavily embroiled in one war and about to embark on another, simultaneously facing serious shortages of food, yet of primary importance to powerful figures who were trenchantly opposed to any change. He had generally observed the rule which has since become an axiom of politics, that battles should be 'big enough to matter but small enough to win', but it is questionable whether this issue possessed either of those attributes.

That Pitt was persuaded of the merits of Catholic emancipation is not a sufficient explanation of his action, since he had been forced to abandon many a cherished project over the years because of the strength of political opposition. The probable truth is that he felt under an obligation to some of his closest colleagues who were very strongly in favour of the measure, most notably his Irish team of Cornwallis and Castlereagh, who had always understood that this policy would eventually go ahead, and his most senior lieutenants Dundas and Grenville, with whom he had encountered serious difficulties in the preceding year. He would not want to let these Ministers down, and some of them believed the King would buckle, Cornwallis writing that 'if Mr. Pitt is firm, he will meet with no difficulty'.[14] Pitt may have believed this, but in any event would not have felt he was walking on the thinnest of ice since, even having put the matter to the King from a united Cabinet, he could still retreat if absolutely necessary. Rose, who often worked with Pitt on an hourly basis, wrote that 'I am very strongly inclined to believe that Mr. Pitt had not, in the first instance, an intention of pressing the Catholic question on the King immediately.'[15] Pitt may therefore have been trying to satisfy his colleagues that the matter was being attended to, avoiding a split, while keeping his mind on other things and working out how to get round the King at a later stage.

Whatever his intentions, Pitt's misplaced faith in Cabinet confidentiality was to prove fatal, since the discussions of 25 January were almost immediately leaked to George III. At the King's levée on 28 January, in Pitt's absence, he exploded within earshot of many observers at the unfortunate Dundas: 'What is the Question which you are all about to force upon me? what is this Catholic Emancipation which this young lord, this Irish Secretary has brought over, that you are going to throw at my Head? . . . I will tell you, that I shall look on every Man as my personal Enemy, who proposes that Question to me . . . I hope All my Friends will not desert me.'[16]

The force of this eruption shattered the ice beneath Pitt's feet in an instant. No such event had occurred in the entire seventeen years of his ministry. Whether it had been parliamentary reform, abolition of the slave trade, the dismissal of the Duke of York from Flanders or the peace negotiations with France, George III had always kept his private feelings to himself, except in discussion with Pitt or other members of the Cabinet. On this issue he was prepared to proclaim his most emphatic opposition to the views of the Cabinet, and he did not mind who heard him. What is more, his language was chillingly reminiscent of the words he employed in 1783 which presaged the downfall of the Fox–North coalition and the appointment of Pitt.

Nor did the King let matters rest there. While the Cabinet convened to consider what was now a crisis – with a majority in favour of Catholic emancipation but a powerful minority still against – George III was lobbying Loughborough, Auckland, the Archbishop of Canterbury and Addington. To the last-named he wrote that 'the most mischievous measure is in contemplation . . . This is no less than the placing the Roman Catholics of the kingdom in an equal state of right to sit in both houses of parliament . . . I know we think alike on this great subject. I wish he would . . . open Mr. Pitt's eyes on the danger arising from the agitating this improper question, which may prevent his ever speaking to me on a subject on which I can scarcely keep my temper.'[17]

Addington, a trusted confidant of both George III and Pitt, now became a go-between. Both men knew, after the aborted discussions of 1797, that if Pitt were to resign Addington would be his likely successor. On the night of Saturday, 31 January, on the basis of Addington's discussions but without further reference to the Cabinet, Pitt wrote to the King with a powerful summary of the case for Catholic emancipation. He explained that he was 'on full consideration convinced that the measure would be attended with no danger to the established church . . . But the grounds on which the laws of exclusion now remaining were founded, have long been narrowed, and are since the Union removed: – that those principles, formerly held by Catholics, which made them considered as politically dangerous, have been for a course of time gradually declining and, among the higher orders particularly, have ceased to prevail.' He argued that the days of foreign pretenders supported by Catholic powers overseas were over and that 'modern Jacobinism' was now the threat, that Catholic clergy could be made more dependent on the government and therefore more easily controlled, and that a new oath administered by the preachers and teachers of all Christian faiths would allow 'the security of the Constitution and Government' to be 'effectually strengthened'.[18]

Having stated his case, Pitt went on to explain how he proposed to act:

> It would afford him indeed a great relief and satisfaction, if he may be allowed to hope that your Majesty will deign maturely to weigh what he has now humbly submitted, and to call for any explanation which any part may appear to require. In the interval which Your Majesty may wish for consideration, he will not on his part importune Your Majesty with any unnecessary reference to the subject and will feel it his duty to abstain himself from all agitation of this subject in Parliament, and to prevent it, as far as depends on him, on the part of others. If on the result of such consideration Your Majesty's objection to the measure proposed should not be removed, or sufficiently diminished to admit of its being brought forward with Your Majesty's full concurrence, and with the whole weight of your Government, it must be personally Mr. Pitt's first wish to be released from a situation which he is conscious that, under such circumstances, he could not continue to fill, but with the greatest disadvantage.

This threat, however, came with a simultaneous olive branch:

> At the same time, after the gracious intimation which has been recently conveyed to him of Your Majesty's sentiments on this point, he will be acquitted of presumption in adding, that if the chief difficulties of the present crisis should not then be surmounted, or very materially diminished, and if Your Majesty should continue to think that his humble exertions could in any degree contribute to conducting them to a favourable issue, there is no personal difficulty to which he will not rather submit than withdraw himself at such a moment from Your Majesty's service. He would even, in such case, continue for such a short further interval as might be necessary to oppose the agitation or discussion of the question, as far as he can consistently with the line, to which he feels bound uniformly to adhere, of reserving himself a full latitude on the principle itself, and objecting only to the time, and to the temper and circumstances of the moment. But he must entreat that, on this supposition it may be distinctly understood that he can remain in Office no longer than till the issue (which he trusts on every account will be a speedy one) of the crisis now depending shall admit of Your Majesty's more easily forming a new arrangement, and that he will receive your

'To the Nuptial-Bower he led her Blushing like the Morn.' The NUPTIAL-BOWER; — with the Evil-One, peeping at the Charms of Eden. from Milton.

Above In 'The Nuptial Bower' (1797) Gillray shows Pitt's courting of Lady Eleanor Eden, while Fox is depicted as a demon gnashing his teeth. The implication is that marriage would have enhanced Pitt's popularity, but such notions were insufficient to move him.

Right Lady Eleanor Eden, by Hoppner. When rumours of Pitt's attachment to her began to spread, he ended the friendship, citing 'an insurmountable obstacle'.

Power of securing Public Credit
Key of Public Property
BANK OF ENGLAND
MIDAS, Transmuting all, into GOLD PAPER.
History of Midas, — The great Midas having dedicated himself to Bacchus, obtained from that Deity, the Power of changing all he Touched.
Apollo fixed Asses Ears upon his head, for his Ignorance — & although he tried to hide his disgrace with a Regal Cap, yet the very Sedges which grew
from the Mud of the Pactolus, whisper'd out his Infamy, whenever they were agitated by the Wind from the opposite Shore. —

Above 'Midas, Transmuting all into Paper' (1797). Gillray's portrayal of Pitt's decision to permit the issuing of small-denomination notes to end the run on the Bank of England: 'the most painful day of his political life'.

Right Henry Addington, Pitt's long-standing friend and chosen successor. Once Addington became Prime Minister, Pitt's regard for him turned steadily to contempt.

As Lord Warden of the Cinque Ports, Pitt threw himself into the preparations to resist a French invasion of the Kent coast. Walmer Castle is shown in the background.

It was typical of Pitt to apply his mathematical skills to the drilling of his volunteers. In these notes he drew up diagrams and algebra to show how a wheeling company should turn.

Right Lady Hester Stanhope, Pitt's niece, who became 'a light in his dwelling' in his final years.

Below 'Britannia Between Death and the Doctor's', Gillray (1804). As Pitt returns to office he boots Addington out of the door whilst trampling on the ambitions of Fox. Meanwhile, Napoleon threatens the nation.

Constitutional Restorative
BRITANNIA between DEATH and the DOCTOR'S. ___ " Death may decide, when Doctor's disagree." ___

Left Prime Minister once again at the age of forty-four, Pitt had to face immense military, diplomatic and parliamentary difficulties with his reserves of energy and health near their end. By Hoppner.

Below 'The Plum Pudding in Danger' (1805). Gillray's classic representation of Pitt's struggle with Napoleon. The French dominate Europe while Britain is invincible at sea.

Pitt's spirits were buoyed by news of Trafalgar, depicted here by William Stuart, 'the most decisive and complete victory that ever was gained over a powerful enemy'. . .

. . .but shattered by the news of Austerlitz, where the Austrian and Russian armies were crushed by Napoleon. Engraving by Beyer, after François Gérard.

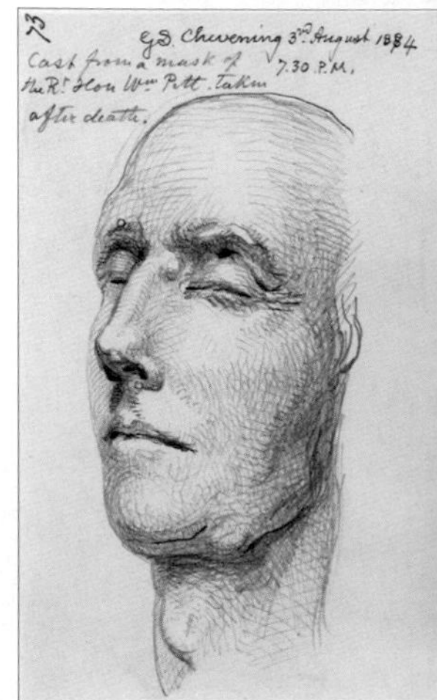

Above On the eve of his death, Pitt attempted to write his will, but despite several attempts to begin a line could not summon the strength to do so.

Above right Pitt's death mask, taken by Joseph Nollekens and drawn here by George Scharf. His physician said he 'died of old age at forty-six as much as if he had been ninety.'

Right Lawrence's posthumous portrait of Pitt commemorated his intense dedication to the national finances.

> Majesty's position to carry with him into a private situation that affectionate and grateful attachment which your Majesty's goodness for a long course of years has impressed on his mind.[19]

Finally he added a rebuke:

> He has only to entreat Your Majesty's pardon for troubling you on one other point, and taking the liberty of most respectfully, but explicitly, submitting to your Majesty the indispensable necessity of effectually discountenancing, in the whole of the interval, all attempts to make use of your Majesty's name, or to influence the opinion of any individual or descriptions of men, on any part of this subject.[20]

George III replied the next day, expressing his 'cordial affection' for Pitt and his 'high opinion of his talents and integrity', but explained that his 'sense of religious as well as political duty' prevented him 'from discussing any proposition tending to destroy this groundwork of our happy Constitution, and much more so that now mentioned by Mr. Pitt, which is no less than the complete overthrow of the whole fabric'. In response to Pitt's entreaties that he refrain from influencing opinion in the meantime, the King countered with the proposal that he would 'abstain from talking on this subject' if Pitt would 'stave off' the whole matter, although he added 'I cannot help if others pretend to guess at my opinions, which I have never disguised.' Finally he said he hoped that Pitt's sense of duty 'will prevent his retiring from his present situation to the end of my life; for I can with great truth assert that I shall, from public and private considerations, feel great regret if I shall ever find myself obliged at any time, from a sense of religious and political duty to yield to his entreaties of retiring from his seat at the Board of Treasury'.[21]

The opening of Parliament and the debate on the Address now intervened, and in the meantime Addington was being pressed by George III to form a government if necessary: 'Lay your hand upon your heart,' the King said to him, 'and ask yourself where I am to turn for support if you do not stand by me.'[22]

The day after the debate on the Address, Pitt wrote a further letter to the King, expressing disappointment at his refusal even to consider the proposals or to undertake to disassociate himself from public opposition to them:

> . . . he must frankly confess to your Majesty that the difficulty even of his temporary continuance must necessarily be increased, and may very shortly become insuperable, from what he conceives to be the import of one passage in your Majesty's note, which hardly leaves him room to hope that Your Majesty thinks those steps can be taken for effectually discountenancing all attempts to make use of your Majesty's name, or to influence opinions on this subject, which he has ventured to represent as indispensably necessary during any interval in which he might remain in office.[23]

As a result, on 5 February 1801 George III accepted Pitt's resignation. In reply, he said he had hoped that the matter would have been resolved by 'the strong assurance I gave Mr. Pitt of keeping perfectly silent on the subject whereon we entirely differ, provided on his part he kept off from disquisition on it for the present'. Instead: 'I must come to the unpleasant decision, as it will deprive me of his political service, of acquainting him that, rather than forego what I look on as my duty, I will without unnecessary delay attempt to make the most creditable arrangement, and such as Mr. Pitt will think most to the advantage of my service, as well as to the security of the public.'[24]

Addington agreed the same day to form a ministry, Pitt having assured him of his support and said to him, 'I see nothing but ruin, Addington, if you hesitate.'[25] From Pitt's point of view, Addington was the perfect successor. He was respected on all sides of the House of Commons and George III found him congenial. In addition, and very significantly, he owed his political career wholly to Pitt, and on most subjects was likely to be highly susceptible to his opinions. There is some evidence that Pitt already had his eye on a more substantial long-term successor, the junior MP Spencer Perceval, who was about to become Solicitor General, but at this stage had only been a Member of Parliament for five years. Perceval would indeed become Prime Minister in due course, and would develop a command of the House of Commons comparable to that of Pitt at his most formidable, but it was too early in 1801 to place him or any other newcomer into the front rank. In any case, at the age of forty-one Pitt was not looking for a replacement for himself; Addington fitted the bill because he could credibly fill Pitt's place for now, without necessarily wanting or deserving to keep it for good.

Pitt's letters to his closest associates in the hours after he received the King's definitive response have a matter-of-fact and almost contented tone. To his brother he admitted: 'I did not foresee the extent of the consequences to which within this week the question has led,' but said that what he had done had been 'right towards the King, the public and my own character . . . I am most happy to find that the Speaker feels it is his duty, in which I have most strongly and decidedly encouraged him, not to decline the task.'[26] On a letter to Pretyman he wrote a postscript saying: 'Rose, I believe, will write to you, and very likely in a tone of despondency which I am sure the case does not call for.'[27] In resignation, as in office, Pitt's tone was straightforward, correct and self-sacrificing.

Political resignations, though, are rarely so simple. However much a single event or issue may dictate the timing of a major resignation, there are usually, except in the case of misdemeanour or retirement, accompanying grievances or calculations which cause it to be submitted or accepted. There is no doubt that without the sudden eruption of the Catholic issue, Pitt's resignation would not have taken place when it did. The fact that the King and the Prime Minister differed so markedly on an issue which they both regarded as important, and one of them considered to be of the highest possible importance, was obviously a major problem. Nevertheless, Pitt and George III had, for over seventeen years, found a way of maintaining their partnership despite strong disagreements on a range of subjects. On this occasion, they were both prepared to countenance mutual abstinence from the subject in some form, and Pitt's initial letter expressing his 'personal wish to be released' but also his readiness to submit to any 'personal difficulty rather than withdraw himself at such a moment' is well short of an adamant insistence on resignation. Given these indications of flexibility, some further explanation is required as to why two men who had worked together productively for so long parted company within the space of a few days, and without any meeting taking place between them.

Why did George III not try harder to keep the man he had once begged to come into office, by stressing Pitt's duty in a dire international situation and at least briefly considering his proposals, if only to reject them and then have everyone stay silent? No doubt the answer is in part the intense annoyance he felt at being placed in such a difficult position by Ministers whom he knew had been scheming behind his back, albeit incompetently, for months. Significantly, however, the affront the King felt on this score came on top of a mounting sense of grievance against Pitt and his fellow Ministers which had developed in his mind in the course of 1800. He had been unhappy with the government's conduct of the war that summer, not without good reason, and was frustrated that the Cabinet had ignored his views. In addition, Pitt's many distractions, ill-health and consequent shorter working hours made him neglectful of keeping regular contact with the King, sometimes going for weeks even in London without seeing him. Pitt himself admitted that 'other Business and want of Health often made him postpone both written and personal communication with the King'.[28]

George III was therefore becoming distinctly fed up with what he could have seen as rather high-handed treatment from his senior Ministers. Even so, throughout most of the previous seventeen years he would have known that he had to keep Pitt at all costs for fear of the likely alternatives, in particular Charles James Fox. But in the late 1790s Pitt's very domination of the political scene had removed any such danger in the foreseeable future. Fox had absented himself from Parliament, and even if he resumed his attendance (which he was about to do), no conceivable coalition could any longer be constructed with him at the head of it. The old Whig party had been broken, and the views of the conservative Whigs such as Portland, Windham and Spencer who had joined the government in 1794 had become indistinguishable from those of Pitt. A change of Prime Minister would therefore no longer mean a change of the government's political complexion. All that was needed was a new man capable of leading such a government, and since George III had formed an increasingly high opinion of Addington, and Pitt himself had floated him as a replacement when contemplating resignation in 1797, the solution was obvious. If George so wished it, he could now have a government supported by Pitt and many of the current Ministers but no longer headed by Pitt. This is not to say that he was being untruthful in expressing the hope that Pitt could have remained his Prime Minister until the end of his life, but it did mean that if a serious dispute arose between them he no longer had to sacrifice his trenchantly held views.

Pitt's motives in that crucial first week of February were more complex, but all the evidence is that to him it was not such a straightforward matter as simply resigning rather than being unable to implement a policy he regarded as crucial. He would in any case have been distracted by the need to make multiple decisions on other matters, including a major parliamentary debate and preparation for the budget which was to be delivered two weeks later. The impression that a number of factors were playing on his mind when he contemplated resignation is reinforced by the way in which his letter to the King of 31 January left so many options open, and by the fact that his assessment to colleagues of whether he would be resigning changed thereafter from day to day – although this would partly reflect uncertainty over the King's final response. But Pitt cannot have thought he was resigning solely over the principle of Catholic emancipation, since he was happy to support as his successor a man who was specifically against it. What else was going on in his head?

Pitt's main quarrel with the King was not over the merits of Catholic emancipation, but rather over the manner in which he was now being opposed by the Crown. He found both the King's public explosion on the matter and his refusal even to consider the advice of Ministers to be unacceptable, apparently telling Canning that 'He went out, not on the Catholic Question simply as a measure in which he was opposed, but from the manner in which he had been opposed, and to which, if he had assented, he would, as a Minister, have been on a footing totally different from what he had ever before been in the Cabinet.'[29] In his letter to his brother on the day his resignation was accepted, Pitt complained of 'the imprudent degree to which the King's name was committed on a question not yet even regularly submitted to him. Under these circumstances, with the opinion I had formed and after all that had passed, I had no option, and had nothing left but to consider how I could execute the resolution which became unavoidable'.[30]

From the very beginning of his political career, Pitt had been interested in holding power rather than being in office for its own sake. He had gone to great lengths in 1783 to show that he was not a creature of the King, and had been careful to come into office only when he could dictate most of the terms. To be publicly contradicted by the monarch offended his pride, damaged his authority, and contradicted his view of how government should be conducted.

The importance of the immediate events should not therefore be understated, but there were additional factors at work. Pitt's health, which had totally disintegrated only four months before, was again failing. He was suffering from gout at the time of his resignation, and he was to show unusual emotion over the next few weeks, being 'very unwell . . . – gouty and nervous'[31] at the end of February. Pretyman thought that this was one of 'several collateral circumstances', and that 'release from Office' had become an important consideration.[32]

Pretyman also believed that the need once again to consider peace was 'the principal' of the other factors involved.[33] With the collapse of the Second Coalition, British strategy was now essentially to do well enough in the war over the next few months to be able to make a reasonable peace with Napoleon. The circumstances therefore closely paralleled those of early 1797, when Pitt had felt that an alternative Prime Minister might find it easier to conclude a satisfactory peace. He could not have contemplated resigning if the alternative to him had been Fox, but a government led by Addington would be likely to be true to his achievements and susceptible to his influence while he stepped back from the front line.

In addition, the differences between George III and his Ministers over military strategy in the summer of 1800 had been deeply frustrating to Pitt as well as to the King. As the summer had worn on with the army left unused, Pitt and Dundas had become exasperated when the King for a time withheld agreement to an expedition to attack the Spanish port of Ferrol. Pitt had reminded Dundas of the importance of 'striking some blow' or they would see 'the spirit of the country let down, the government quickly censured, and the impatience and clamour for peace on any terms increasing every hour'. If the King did not agree, their only remaining option would be 'begging His Majesty to find servants whose judgement he can trust more than ours'.[34] Such feelings, however fleeting, must have added to Pitt's readiness to leave office when confronted with even greater intransigence.

Decisions made for more than one reason are more difficult than those which rest on a single point. Pitt would have had to weigh this accumulation of reasons for giving up against his long-standing confidence that he was the natural Prime Minister, when the King's behaviour pushed him to the brink. According to Pretyman, the impression Pitt gave to colleagues on 2 February was that 'he did not propose to resign'. He spent the next day 'weighing the arguments', with the result that 'those for immediate resignation were found to preponderate', and drafted his final letter that afternoon 'without however absolutely resolving to send it'.[35] Addington believed that Catholic emancipation was the 'sole cause of Pitt's resignation', partly, no doubt, because Pitt would only have discussed it with him or any wider audience in these terms. To resign over a clear issue was true to his concept of integrity and 'character'. Yet the difficult balance of his decision was reflected in his uncertainty, and was to be further demonstrated by the bizarre events which were to follow.

Pitt's resignation had been accepted, but a new administration had still to be formed and no immediate announcement was made. As a result, the political world was not only stunned by the steadily expanding rumours that the seventeen-year premiership of Pitt was at an end, but for the time being was left to guess at the reasons why. Assertions that Pitt had gone mad soon resurfaced, while some believed it was a clever manoeuvre which would allow him to return to office with a fresh team of Ministers. Fox considered that it was all 'a mere juggle', and could not imagine 'that Pitt goes out merely because he can not carry an honest & wise measure'.[36] There was some alarm in the City, which was calmed when it became clear that Pitt was not leaving office immediately and there would be an orderly transition to an Addington administration.

Addington himself was immediately on the receiving end of much derision, since friends and foes alike considered Pitt's abilities to far exceed those of his replacement. Dundas wrote to Pitt on 7 February that Addington was 'totally incapable' of carrying on a government: 'It is impossible for me not to whisper into your ear my conviction that no arrangement can be formed under him as its head that will not crumble to pieces almost as soon as formed.'[37] Lady Malmesbury thought 'It is impossible that Pitt's friend and creature should be his real successor, or more than a stop-gap,'[38] and Pretyman regarded Addington as 'no more equal to what he has undertaken than a Child'.[39] While Pitt assured Canning that Addington had not grasped at office, but that 'it was impossible to have behaved with more confidence, more openness, more sincerity than Addington had done',[40] and told the Commons on 16 February that he 'had already filled one situation of great importance with the most distinguished ability and this is the surest augur of his services, in another exalted situation',[41] the opposition was scornful.

By this stage it was clear that all of the most senior Ministers responsible for directing the war – Dundas, Grenville and Spencer – would leave office with Pitt and were not prepared to serve under Addington. This brought forth Sheridan's withering attack:

> When the crew of a vessel was preparing for action, it was usual to clear the decks by throwing overboard the lumber, but he never heard of such a manoeuvre as that of throwing their great guns overboard. When an Election Committee was formed, the watchword was to shorten the business by knocking out the brains of the Committee. This was done by striking from the list the names of the lawyers and other gentlemen who might happen to know a little too much of the subject. In this sense the right hon. gentlemen had literally knocked out the brains of the administration and then, clapping a mask on the skeleton, cried, 'Here is as fine vigour and talent for you as any body may wish to see'. This empty skull, this skeleton administration, was the phantom

> that was to overawe our enemies, and to command the confidence of the House and the people.[42]

In the same debate, Pitt finally explained to the Commons what had happened:

> I have no wish to disguise from the House, that we did feel it an incumbent duty upon us to propose a measure on the part of government, which, under the circumstances of the union so happily effected between the two countries, we thought of great public importance and necessary to complete the benefits likely to result from that measure: we felt this opinion so strongly, that when we met with circumstances which rendered it impossible for us to propose it as a measure of government, we equally felt it inconsistent with our duty and our honour any longer to remain a part of that government.[43]

As Addington scrambled to form an administration from whatever talent was available, the presumption was that Pitt would leave office after the budget on 18 February. He had resigned in businesslike fashion, but the process of temporarily carrying on the business of government, with obviously undiminished ability and support, became increasingly distressing to him and his supporters.* Pretyman found initially that 'I never saw Mr. Pitt in more uniformly cheerful spirits, although everyone about him was dejected and melancholy. He talked of his quitting office with the utmost composure.'[44]

But at the royal levée on 11 February Pitt seems to have been taken aback by the King's kindness towards him. George III knew, of course, that he needed Pitt's support for the new administration, and as others have observed, he was probably grateful for being allowed to win.[45] He told Pitt in front of onlookers: 'You have behaved like yourself throughout this business. Nothing could possibly be more honourable . . . I do not care who hears me.'[46] He then took Pitt for half an hour into his closet for a further conversation, in which Pitt apparently became tearful more than once.

Seven days later Pitt presented his budget to the Commons, which,

* Those who recall Margaret Thatcher's resignation in 1990, followed by a commanding Commons performance and supporters in tears, will readily imagine the atmosphere.

even though it involved a loan of £25.5 million and swingeing tax increases encompassing tea, paper, sugar, timber, pepper, horses, insurance and postage, was greeted without dissent. Such unanimity had never been known in the previous seventeen years. George III wrote to him: 'My Dear Pitt [a term of address he had never used before], as you are closing, much to my sorrow your political career, I cannot help expressing the joy I feel that the Ways and Means for the present year have been this day agreed . . .'[47]

That evening, Rose recalled: 'I went to him at his desire, and we were alone more than three hours . . . in the course of which he was, beyond all comparison, more affected than I had seen him since the change first burst upon me.'[48] When Rose suggested that Addington had taken advantage of the situation, 'there was . . . no actual admission on the part of Mr. Pitt that he thought with me on the subject, but there were evident demonstrations of it, and there were painful workings in his mind, plainly discernible; most of the time tears in his eyes, and much agitated'.[49]

Rose was joining Charles Long and Canning as trusted acolytes of Pitt who would not serve Addington. Cornwallis, Castlereagh, Camden and Windham were further adding to the list of those leaving the government. All the senior figures who had supported Pitt on the Catholic issue were resigning with him. Addington found a new Foreign Secretary in Hawkesbury, and was able to keep the Duke of Portland. With poetic justice, Loughborough was to be replaced as Lord Chancellor by Lord Eldon, a deeply conservative member of Pitt's governments who would hold his new office for twenty-five of the next twenty-six years. Loughborough was utterly astonished at his dismissal amidst the wreckage of the government he had helped to destroy, and even turned up at the first meetings of Addington's Cabinet – where he had to be told that he was no longer wanted.

The stage was set for Pitt's imminent departure from office when on 19 February, with the dramatic timing that always distinguished George III's bouts of madness, Pitt told Rose that 'His Majesty's mind was not in a proper state'.[50] Within days the King had taken leave of his senses as completely as in 1788, making it impossible for Pitt and the other resigning Ministers to surrender the seals of office. The change of government was caught in suspended animation, and the renewed prospects of Regency brought the complicating presence of the Prince of Wales onto the scene.

An awkward meeting took place between Pitt and the Prince at Carlton House to discuss the old and vexatious subject of the terms of a Regency. While Pitt was apparently happy to hand over the government to Addington, he was as determined as he had been twelve years before to ensure that any attempt by the Prince to bring in Fox and his followers would be hamstrung. Pitt was therefore at his most reserved and correct, which means extremely so, and according to Pelham was 'more stiff and less accommodating than he should have been'.[51] He said he would give advice to the Prince on condition that competing advice was not sought from the ranks of the opposition, and explained that the highly restrictive terms of the possible Regency laid down by Parliament under his direction in 1789 should once again apply, pointing out for good measure that this approach was now backed by many of the Whigs who had previously opposed it, leaving the Prince with no hope of any amendment. Inevitably, rumours flew that the accession of the Prince as Regent might result in a different administration to the one then being formed by Addington, either by the inclusion of the opposition – Fox reluctantly agreed to resume his seat in Parliament – or by reverting to Pitt with a fresh understanding on Catholic emancipation. Given, however, the long history of poor relations between the Prince and Pitt, there was probably little substance to this idea.

As the crisis over the King's health continued through the end of February, Pitt's public presence remained as commanding as it had been since his resignation became known. When he spoke in the Commons on 27 February, Wilberforce referred to his 'extreme eloquence'.[52] He decided to introduce a Regency Bill on 14 March, if the King had not by then recovered. As it turned out, George III yet again managed to stage a rapid return to health in the nick of time before his son could obtain even a temporary grip on any levers of power. After seeming in danger of his life on 2 March, he went to sleep and then 'awoke much refreshed, and from that time steadily mended'.[53]

As the King recovered his senses, he left no doubt as to who and what he attributed this latest bout of insanity. Even during the course of it he had muttered, 'I am better now, but I will remain true to the Church,'[54] suggesting that it was the prospect of Catholic emancipation that had sent his mind into a spin. Once restored to health, he asked Dr Willis to tell Pitt that 'I am now quite well, quite recovered from my illness; but what has he not to answer for, who is the cause of my having been ill at all?'[55]

According to Malmesbury, Pitt had already been feeling 'a great deal' uneasy about the possible cause of the King's illness, though he had been 'too haughty to confess it'.[56] Now, said Pretyman, he was 'struck extremely' by the news from Willis.[57] He very quickly sent an assurance to the King, later put in writing by Rose in the following terms: 'It affords me great satisfaction to be able to say to Your Majesty that I am authorized by Mr. Pitt to assure your Majesty that (in whatsoever situation, public or private, he may happen to be) he will not bring forward the question respecting the Catholics of Ireland: and that if it should be agitated by others he will supply a proposition for deferring the consideration of it.'[58]

What was Pitt doing? If he had been prepared to give in February the undertaking he now gave in March, the entire crisis and his resignation would have been unnecessary. Having resigned ostensibly over Catholic emancipation, he was now prepared to forgo the policy for the foreseeable future. To his supporters at the time, this seemed to be a strong argument for not giving up office after all, and to later commentators the inconsistency has appeared baffling.

The truth seems to be that Pitt had no remaining expectation that he or anyone else could pursue Catholic emancipation during the lifetime of George III, and the concession he was making therefore cost nothing. He had not resigned in order to pursue the policy at a later date, but over the manner of the King's opposition to him, and possibly for other unrelated reasons already discussed. Honour and character mattered more to Pitt than the pursuit of a particular policy: by his being prepared to resign, honour was now satisfied on the Catholic question, just as honour had been satisfied in his duel with Tierney even though no one had been hit. The question could now be put aside – although Pitt left the door open to returning to it in another reign.

The pledge to the King must also have done something to assuage Pitt's guilt about the return of George III's malady, but it may also have been part of an immediate political calculation. For on the same day that the King was blaming Pitt for his illness, George Rose was recording that 'Mr. Pitt seems to admit more than he has at all heretofore done, during the last four weeks, the possibility of its being right that he should remain in, or rather return to, his situation; in which possible case it would become necessary to dispose honourably and advantageously of Mr. Addington.'[59] The arch-loyalists of Pitt – Rose, Canning, Pretyman – now seized the moment to urge him to rescind his resignation. Senior Cabinet members led by Dundas joined in, even including Portland, who had already agreed to serve under Addington. Canning wrote to Pitt on 8 March that the 'public interest' required him to stay in office; against that was 'nothing but miserable, petty, personal considerations'.[60]

Pitt hesitated. Against all the factors which had caused him to resign, he now had to weigh the fact that honour on the immediate issue had been satisfied, and that the respect paid to him over the preceding month had reminded him how much he enjoyed being First Lord of the Treasury. Yet while his sentiments reversed themselves, the same self-sacrificing nature which had led him to be so heedless of his own health and finances while in office now prevented him from making any overt attempt to stay in it once he had said he would leave. It was not in his nature to give any public indication of discomfort or desire. His combination of shyness, pride and sense of honour meant that he could be kept in power by the actions of others, but not now by his own hand. In March 1783 he had hesitated to accept the premiership while waiting for the House of Commons to call on him to do so, which, without a lead, they failed to do. Exactly eighteen years later, he hesitated and waited again, and left his situation to the goodwill of others. 'Pitt will not stir unless Addington begins,'[61] Canning reported to Malmesbury.

The result was not surprising. Overtures were made to Addington, possibly through Portland, to see whether even at this stage he would stand aside. They met with a frosty response: he had already given up the post of Speaker, a job he had loved doing, and had only done so on the understanding he was to be Prime Minister. He would not retreat without a fight. When Pitt heard this he immediately drew back. He made it clear to Dundas that he could only carry on if it was 'a spontaneous desire' of Addington that he should do so, 'much beyond a bare acquiescence'.[62] Even such acquiescence was not forthcoming. It was too late. Some time later, Pitt explained to a dejected Canning: 'I make no scruple of owning that I am ambitious – but my ambition is character not office. I may have engaged myself inconsiderately, but I am irrecoverably engaged.'[63]

It is impossible to know what mixture of remorse and relief filled Pitt's mind as he handed over the seals of office to George III on the afternoon of Saturday, 14 March 1801. He had been First Lord of the Treasury for seventeen years and eighty-five days. He must have known as much as ever that he loved being in power. It seems he was as certain as he always had been that he was not prepared to beg for it.

PART FOUR

24

The Limits of Magnanimity

'One of the noblest instances of true magnanimity that was ever exhibited to the admiration and imitation of mankind.'

WILLIAM WILBERFORCE ON PITT, 1801[1]

'Pitt is to Addington as London is to Paddington.'

GEORGE CANNING, 1801

PITT HAD BEEN ENGAGED in full-time politics from within a few months of his twenty-first birthday, and probably had little memory of what life was like before he became Prime Minister. When he left office in March 1801, at the age of forty-one, he had been First Lord of the Treasury and Chancellor of the Exchequer for almost the whole of his adult life. He had lived in 10 Downing Street for a longer continuous period than any politician before or since, and for almost half his entire existence. To be suddenly bereft of the endless flow of despatches, correspondence, messengers and official business which had given shape to his days for as long as he could remember must have been a mental shock, however welcome a respite it might provide from the mounting strain.

The psychological impact of surrendering office after a long period at the top is heightened in the case of a politician who retires when relatively advanced in years, because it is so obviously a conclusion to his or her life in government. Pitt, by contrast, was still younger at this time, after having completed the second-longest continuous term as First Lord of the Treasury in the whole of British history, than any subsequent holder of that office even at the time they entered it. It was entirely possible that decades of active political life still stretched before him. Whatever his distress over resigning in the course of February and March 1801, any depression was no doubt mitigated by the absence of any sense of having retired. Only George III appeared to think that Pitt's political career was over, but even he was attentive in courting his support for the Addington ministry: 'If we three do but keep together, all will go well,' he told Pitt and Addington in the course of a levée.[2]

In the opening stages of the Addington government, Pitt was closely consulted by his successor, and was intimately involved in advising on and then supporting the proposed terms of peace with France. He therefore remained privy to the most important of all government business. That he would not simply disappear was evidenced by his rising to speak in the House of Commons within ten days of his resignation to defend the conduct of the war and to respond to opposition charges that he had abandoned his responsibilities, explaining that 'He had lived to very little purpose for the last seventeen years of his life, if it was necessary for him to say that he had not quitted his situation in order to shrink from its difficulties.'[3]

Pitt would not in any case have allowed private unhappiness to break the surface of his public character. While he may have permitted himself to speak to Rose or Pretyman with tears in his eyes, he could never betray such weakness to a wider circle, or even to his mother. Whatever he felt inside, he gave no appearance of regrets or bitterness, insisting that he had no complaints about the conduct of Addington or George III, and appearing, according to Canning, 'really as full of spirits in his new idleness as a boy just come home for the holidays'.[4] Wilberforce thought his behaviour towards Addington set a new standard in magnanimity. Pitt had assured Addington of his support, indeed persuaded him to take office on that basis, and this pledge he regarded as 'solemnly binding, not redeemable by any lapse of time, nor ever to be cancelled without the *express consent* of Mr. Addington'.[5]

Pitt maintained this outward contentment in spite of the fact that, for a man with no capital or private income, loss of office necessitated a dramatic and adverse change in his domestic circumstances. Moving out of Downing Street was one thing – he managed to secure for a year and a half or so the remainder of a short lease on an apartment in Park Place off St James's Street. Far more serious was the loss of his income as First Lord and Chancellor (which represented around £7,000 of his £10,000 annual income), and that the end of his status as Prime Minister punctured the ever-inflating balloon of credit which his personal finances now constituted. Investigations by George Rose the previous year had revealed 'a History of Debts and Distresses as actually sickened me'.[6] It is possible that concern about debts contributed to Pitt's distraction and illness in 1800, but it would also be entirely consistent with his normal practice if he were not concerned about such matters at all. Even now, as creditors became 'extremely importunate'[7] and a comprehensive survey revealed debts totalling £46,000 (the equivalent of around £2.75 million today), Pitt was reluctant to accept help. He was aware, however, that with his income now down to £3,000 a year as Lord Warden of the Cinque Ports, remedial action was urgent and necessary. In particular, his beloved Holwood would have to be sold, but since it was heavily mortgaged the money raised would be unlikely to cover more than a very small part of his total debts. Rose, Pretyman and other close friends realised that somehow other sources of income would have to be found, a course made much more difficult by Pitt's unyielding rejection of almost all possible sources of help.

Indifference to personal finances is not uncommon among people who consider their whole life to be devoted to public purposes. Mental denial of the extent of the problem is also commonplace among people who become heavily indebted. Added to these possible tendencies was Pitt's generosity of spirit, which led him to give money to his mother and to lend it to his brother when he was already running a large overdraft. On top of that was his unfailing optimism, which even now led him to make more optimistic assumptions about his debts than those made by Rose. In Pitt's case these psychological traits were reinforced by an overriding determination never to place himself under an obligation to anyone who could make use of it – although he presumably did not think of his creditors in that light. Faced with the prospect of the loss of office in 1789 in the Regency crisis, he had turned down a mooted gift of £100,000 from his backers in the City without a moment's hesitation. His friends now raised the prospect of a vote of public money from Parliament, a means used to clear Pitt's father's debts after his death, but Pitt told Rose of 'his fixed resolve on no consideration whatever to accept anything from the public . . . Rather than do which he would struggle with any difficulties; that if he had had the good fortune to carry the country safe through all its dangers, and to have seen it in a state of prosperity, he should have had a pride in accepting such a grant; but under all the present circumstances of the situation of the country, and of himself, it was utterly inconsistent with his feelings to receive anything.'[8]

Fresh offers from the City were similarly turned down. George III himself, who had paid off the debts of Lord North in the 1770s, offered £30,000 and was happy for Rose to arrange matters so that the source of the money would not be known to Pitt. As Rose later recounted: 'The scheme was found to be impracticable without a communication with Mr. Pitt. On the mention of it to him he was actually more affected than I recollect to have seen him on any occasion; but he declined it, though with the deepest sense of gratitude possible.'[9] At a later stage he would also turn down Addington's offer of the Clerkship of the Pells, the very sinecure he was praised for refusing in his opening days as Prime Minister, but one that would have given him another £3,000 a year. Rose canvassed the idea of Pitt's friends buying Holwood at auction at a greatly inflated price, but concluded that this 'would immediately excite suspicion in Mr. Pitt's mind, and wholly defeat the scheme'.[10]

Eventually, Pitt was prevailed upon to accept assistance from his closest friends: people to whom he was already obliged by years of friendship. Those who subscribed £1,000 each included Pretyman, Rose, Dundas and Lords Camden, Bathurst and Carrington. Wilberforce, Long and a private secretary, Joseph Smith, contributed £500 each. This exercise raised £11,700. Combined with the sale of Holwood for £15,000 and a drastic reduction in Pitt's household, horses and carriages – he now had to travel in 'a common chaise' – this was sufficient to rescue the immediate situation. When the lease on the desirable Park Place expired, Pitt had to move to more distant York Place, now part of Baker Street.*

There can be little doubt that if Pitt had been married, or had intended to leave politics, his attitude to money at this stage of his life would have been different. He could have accepted one of the large sums on offer and have earned a generous income in the Law Courts if he had chosen to step back from politics and live comfortably. In February 1801, his long-suffering banker Thomas Coutts wrote to him with a reminder that he had not 'paid a due attention to your Private affairs', and advocating a new career in the law which would bring 'both Fame & Fortune'. As he put it: 'Who is there with a Brief that would not fly to put it into such Hands?' It would 'elevate your character beyond every point you have yet attained' and also bring in 'at least £3,000 a year'.[11]

While Pitt did speak to Rose of returning to the Bar rather than be dependent on others, there is no sign that he ever really envisaged developing a life away from public affairs. His pastimes remained limited to reading and admiring classical texts, and the purchase of books was the only item among his vast expenses which constituted the acquisition of material possessions. Pitt had dedicated his life to politics from infancy. Relatively young as he still was, he was not going to change. His attitude to money reveals that he intended his life to remain as it was: single, devoted to public affairs, and free from any questionable obligation. As a result he would tolerate his new circumstances without any trace of complaint.

Deprived as he was of executive power and supporting staff, Pitt would nevertheless have had no reason to feel lonely. Those who had worked closely with him in office revered his abilities; coupled with his charm and companionship in private, this made his loyal friends very loyal indeed. Despite Pretyman's responsibilities as Bishop of Lincoln, he spent a good deal of time in 1801 working with George Rose to attend to Pitt's needs. Long and Canning remained ardent friends, while senior political allies such as Dundas and Camden would

* At the time of writing Pitt's former residence is a branch of Pret-à-Manger, a chain of sandwich shops.

take no line in public which contradicted any statement by Pitt. Pitt's company was widely sought – 'when he was in town he was engaged every day to dinner'.[12] In December he attended 'a great feast in Trinity College Hall' in Cambridge and then stayed with Pretyman, whose wife found his mastery of classics still so strong that it was 'as if he had been doing nothing at all in his life but studying Greek and Latin'.[13]

Although Holwood was sold in 1802, Pitt still had Walmer Castle to fall back on: before long he had rented an adjoining forty acres which allowed him to indulge his love of planting trees and creating walks, in this case to the sea. As at Holwood, he set out to change the property to suit his needs, ordering the construction of a bridging section between the central section of the castle and the 'Gunners' Lodgings' in one of the turrets, thus creating additional bedrooms. Possessing small but attractive dining and reception rooms alongside a terrace, Walmer was soon host to an ever-growing procession of guests, including, in the course of 1802, Canning with his family and Pitt's niece, Lady Hester Stanhope, who would return on a more permanent basis the following year.

Taken together, Pitt's loyal friends, good nature, lack of materialism and confidence about his future prospects meant that he slid more easily into his new circumstances than many might have expected. His optimism about the possibility of returning to office is understandable, since his successor had essentially been nominated by him, installed in accordance with his wishes, and would have great difficulty surviving without his support. He did not consider Addington to be remotely his equal, but was furious with Canning for pointing out Addington's inferiority in a series of abusive and widely circulated rhymes, including the well known 'Pitt is to Addington as London is to Paddington'. He even forced Canning to send an apology to Addington – 'fulsome in expression, but manifestly written under constraint'[14] – and tried to persuade him to accept office in Addington's government. Canning was too devoted to Pitt to accept, ending his letter of explanation to him: 'I shall be always in whatever situation, however separated, or however brought together, unalterably and most affectionately, Yours, G.C.'[15] Other key allies of Pitt shared Canning's dismissive view of the new Prime Minister but, in the manner of more experienced politicians, waited to see how he would perform. Grenville kept a surly and sceptical eye on the peace negotiations, while Dundas, although also sceptical, lent Addington his villa at Wimbledon and kept in touch with the new administration.

Few outside the Whig opposition made open attacks on Pitt; one exception was Auckland, who had never got over Pitt's refusal to marry his daughter and subsequent refusal to promote him to the Cabinet. He was suspected of playing a role in stirring the King's passion on the Catholic question, and in a Lords debate after the change of government alleged that 'there is in this business a mystery',[16] and that Pitt must have had hidden motives for resigning. Pitt did not trouble himself to become embroiled with those he considered small fry: he simply froze Auckland out of his life from that moment on.

Addington was nicknamed 'the Doctor' by his detractors, but within a few months his unassuming style and apparent competence were winning supporters. MPs who had not liked Pitt's haughty manner found Addington 'easy, frank, jovial',[17] and some observers enjoyed the 'plain story' instead of 'fine speeches'.[18] As Sydney Smith had once said of Pitt: 'At the close of every brilliant display an expedition failed or a kingdom fell. God send us a stammerer!'[19] George III was certainly delighted with the new Prime Minister, bestowing on him the splendid White Lodge in Richmond Park and referring with pride to '*His own Chancellor of the Exchequer*' as if he were a newborn baby.[20]

Luck played its part in giving the new government a political honeymoon. There was a good corn harvest for the first time in some years, and, above all, British forces won two spectacular military successes. The most spectacular of these was at Copenhagen on 2 April 1801, where it was the turn of the Danish fleet to be at the wrong end of Nelson's devastating mixture of audacity and disobedience. Having commenced a violent exchange with the entire Danish navy and its shore batteries, Nelson was ordered to withdraw by Admiral Sir Hyde Parker. This was the famous occasion on which he paced the deck furiously before announcing to his captain: 'You know, Foley, I have only one eye – I have a right to be blind sometimes . . . I really do not see the signal.'[21] Instead he ordered his own signal to keep fighting to be nailed to the mast, and by the next day he was on shore accepting the capitulation of what little remained of the Danish fleet. With this, and the coincident assassination of Tsar Paul on 23 March, the League of Armed Neutrality was destroyed and the British right to search neutral shipping boldly reasserted.

It was not long before news arrived that the expedition to Egypt had also triumphed. Although Sir Ralph Abercromby had been killed, the French army left behind by Napoleon had been decisively defeated, and the surrender of its remnants was only a matter of time. Both of these victories were the product of decisions taken during Pitt's administration, but they came as a tremendous bonus to his successor, and were seen as strengthening the hand of the government in peace negotiations.

With the Austrians having concluded a new peace treaty with the French at Lunéville in January, and Britain facing unrest and exhaustion after more than eight years of war, Addington and his colleagues were clear that peace must be concluded. The war had been fought to an impasse, with the French more dominant on the Continent but Britain emphatically the mistress of the seas. Rather than continuing with the war in such circumstances, Addington was prepared to give up a good deal of Britain's overseas conquests. As Hawkesbury, the new Foreign Secretary, talked to the French negotiator Monsieur Otto throughout the summer, Pitt was closely consulted on all the principal points. His approach, which closely guided and influenced that of Addington, was consistent with his attempts to negotiate peace in 1796 and 1797. Free of the ideological fervour of Windham or the diplomatic stubbornness of Grenville, and believing that economic expansion was preferable to colonial acquisition, Pitt was always prepared to support major sacrifices of territory in return for the chance of a stable peace.

The preliminary articles of peace were signed on 1 October 1801, and later embodied in the Treaty of Amiens in March 1802. The French were to withdraw from Naples, the Roman states and Egypt, already a *fait accompli*. Taken together, however, the Treaties of Amiens and Lunéville left them with the greater part of what they had fought for: domination of the Netherlands and northern Italy, and a major extension of French territory on the left bank of the Rhine. Britain, by contrast, was to restore to France, Spain and Holland all of the colonies and islands conquered during the war, with the exception of Trinidad and Ceylon. Highly controversially, British forces were to withdraw from the Cape of Good Hope and to return Malta to the Order of St John.

Many of Pitt's former Cabinet colleagues were appalled by the peace terms. Windham described them as 'the death-warrant of their country'.[22] Grenville was trenchantly opposed, bemoaning 'the sacrifice of those points on which our security in a new contest may principally depend'.[23] Dundas would not cause trouble out of loyalty to Pitt, but privately complained that the surrender of Martinique, Malta, Minorca, the Cape and the Dutch settlements in the East and West Indies, 'and to have obtained nothing in return but the name of peace, is such an act of weakness and humiliation as nothing in my opinion can justify'.[24]

Most ex-Prime Ministers would have removed themselves a good distance from such tricky and controversial negotiations, yet Pitt, according to Malmesbury, 'counselled, and, of course, directed, the whole'.[25] His readiness to do so is deeply revealing of his attitude to politics: whatever the merits of the agreement it is clear that his sense of public duty, goodwill to his successor and responsibility for the nation's affairs whether in or out of office all had genuine substance. Grenville complained that Pitt had 'by some strange infatuation so implicated himself in the present system of folly & weakness'.[26] But Pitt was being entirely consistent with his previous stance and his conception of himself. On 3 November he gave a strong endorsement of the proposals in a Commons debate, making a classic Pitt analysis: 'If we had retained all our conquests, it would not have made any difference to us in point of security . . . They would only give us a little more wealth; but a little more wealth would be badly purchased by a little more war.' What mattered was the nation's 'pecuniary resources', which Britain still had 'in abundance'; but they should not be 'lavished away in continuing a contest with the certainty of enormous expense' when the nation 'could not now think of balancing the powers on the continent'.[27] In peace Britons could look to the 'immense wealth of this country, and the natural and legitimate growth of that wealth, so much superior to the produce of rapacity and plunder' which the

French had relied on.[28] This was what Pitt had always believed: national success would be built on finance, not war.

In any event, the signing of peace proved hugely popular across the nation. Towns and cities were illuminated, crowds celebrated in London, and the terms were endorsed by naval and military leaders such as Nelson and Cornwallis. Parliamentary approval was overwhelming. By April 1802 Addington was able to introduce the first peacetime budget for ten years, repealing Pitt's income tax and greatly reducing the armed forces. Once again Pitt was consulted in detail and gave his approval, although he sounded a cautionary note in closing yet another Commons speech on 5 April 1802 with a warning to Addington that his proposals must not cut across his cherished Sinking Fund.

Addington had enjoyed a successful first year in office. His confidence had grown, and he was beginning to like the job. Pitt had given him more robust support and involvement than any Prime Minister has ever given to his successor. Now, however, the work in which Pitt had been engaged at the time of his resignation had been rounded off, and Addington was more firmly established; a situation which led naturally to less frequent consultation and less easy agreement. Pitt's friends believed he was being used, and his detractors were jealous of his seemingly undiminished stature. Exceptional as their long friendship and recent cooperation may have been, nothing could prevent Pitt and Addington from becoming a threat to each other.

Those close to Addington, such as his brother Hiley, made the most of the early successes of his administration as they spread the word for the government in the coffee houses of Westminster. It was Addington, not Pitt, who was presiding over peace, tax reductions, plentiful food and a supportive Parliament, and there was a general election in the offing. Newspapers such as *The Times*, which had withdrawn its support from Pitt's government when he stopped financing it,*

* It had been common in the late eighteenth century for governments and political factions to pay small subsidies to friendly newspapers, but by this stage newspaper sales had grown so strongly that such payments were ceasing to carry much influence.

had swung behind the Addington ministry. The need to influence both press and backbench opinion meant that the age of 'spin' had already arrived. But it was natural that attempts to cast the new Prime Minister in a more favourable light than his predecessor would cause tensions behind the scenes of their steadfast alliance. As is common in politics, the groups around two powerful men became locked in rivalry even while the principals were perfectly content with each other.

Canning in particular was frustrated by Pitt's position, writing to John Frere: 'I do love him, and reverence him as I should a Father – but a father should not sacrifice me, with my good will. Most heartily I forgive him. But he has to answer to himself, and to the country for much mischief that he has done.'[29] Rose remained contemptuous of Addington's ability in financial matters, telling Pretyman that Pitt had prepared 'a grand Plan of Finance which he has given to Mr. A but I fear the latter will hardly be made to understand it'.[30] Pretyman himself took the opportunity of a walk with Pitt in December 1801 to tell him that unquestioning support for Addington would be 'a betrayal of the interests of his country. I mentioned the pains which had been taken, and which were still continued, to lower him in the estimation of the public, and I ventured to say that his present conduct was precisely what his enemies wished and his friends could not approve.'[31]

For the moment, Pitt held firm, telling Canning that 'Addington's power is established for this reign at least and that the safety of the country would be hazarded by any attempt to shake him.'[32] Canning would complain of Pitt's 'blind obedience and self-abasement . . . yet this is the mind that governed the world'.[33] But the seeds of suspicion had been planted, and Pitt's sensitivity was heightened. In February 1802, when Tierney attacked Pitt's financial stewardship while complimenting Addington, and Addington made only the briefest defence of his predecessor, Pitt was furious. On 10 February a stinging letter hurtled from Walmer Castle to Downing Street:

> My Dear Sir,
> You will not wonder if the account which has reached me this morning, of Monday's debate, has engaged not a little of my

> attention. I know how little newspapers can be trusted for the exactness of their reports . . . But if the substance of what passed is anything like what is represented, I should not deal honestly if I did not take the first moment to own to you that I think I have much to wonder at, and to complain of, and that what is due to my own character will not suffer me to leave the matter without further explanation . . .[34]

Addington was suitably stung, describing Pitt's letter as 'a severe addition to the trials which it has been my lot to undergo'.[35] He assured Pitt of his friendship and sent Thomas Steele, Pitt's old friend who now served under him, to explain in detail what had happened and how Tierney had been answered earlier in the debate. Pitt was content, but he was now on the alert.

Although Pitt was on his guard to defend his reputation, he did not take active steps to promote it. It was not his style to court MPs, and the age of the well-placed interview or carefully-staged speech outside Parliament had not yet arrived. Nevertheless, attempts to denigrate his achievements in office produced a counter-reaction from his admirers, who decided positively to celebrate his policies, his character and in particular his wartime endurance. In May 1802, when opposition MPs moved for a Committee of Inquiry into Pitt's administration, Pitt loyalists led by Lord Belgrave responded by not only defeating the opposition move, but passing a motion 'That the Right Hon. William Pitt has rendered great and important services to his country, and especially deserves the gratitude of this House.'[36]

Such a motion was highly unusual, but it was carried by a large majority, and capped on 28 May by a huge celebration of Pitt's forty-third birthday organised by Canning and held in the Merchant Taylors Hall. Pitt himself did not attend, and Canning would not have intended him to, since he would have been embarrassed by the proceedings. Nearly a thousand people attended the dinner, and many more could not obtain tickets. The culmination of the evening was a song written by Canning called 'The Pilot that Weathered the Storm'. A sample of its eight verses gives its flavour:

At the footstool of Power let Flattery fawn;
Let Faction her idols extol to the skies;
To Virtue in humble retirement withdrawn,
Unblamed may the accents of gratitude rise!

And shall not *his* memory to Britain be dear,
Whose example with envy all nations behold?
A statesman unbiased by int'rest or fear,
By power uncorrupted, untainted by gold!

It ended with an explicit call for Pitt's return in the event of the resumption of war:

And O! if again the rude whirlwind should rise,
The dawning of peace should fresh darkness deform,
The regrets of the good and the fears of the wise
Shall turn to the pilot that weathered the storm.

This notion of Pitt, brilliantly put into words by Canning, would live on for decades. Commemorative medals printed after his death would show on their obverse a rock against which waves pounded to no effect. Pitt's qualities of phlegmatic self-sacrifice and resilience under intense pressures gave rise, now that he was out of office, to a legend of endurance and integrity. He remained by far the best-known and most recognised politician in the country: when he unexpectedly visited Shepton Mallet that December the crowds removed the horses from his carriage and pulled him to the inn. New Members of the Parliament about to be elected were awed when they saw him for the first time. He could be forgiven for thinking that his time would come again.

For the moment, Pitt's refusal to be drawn into open controversy with Addington was trenchant. In the same week as the Merchant Taylors dinner, Canning, who wanted to 'worry the doctor like a pole-cat',[37] precipitated a Commons debate on the slave trade with the deliberate intention of publicly dividing Pitt and Addington. Canning, however, was still a novice compared to the two Prime Ministers; Pitt stayed silent, and Addington simply granted Canning's wish that grants of land in Trinidad would not be made without further consideration of 'the gradual abolition' of the slave trade. At the end of June Addington was careful to consult Pitt on the text of the King's Speech closing the session of Parliament. Pitt thought the speech 'excellent', but suggested alterations to 'heighten a little the principal tirade' and the insertion of two or three additional topics.[38]

On 29 June Addington called a general election. Pitt proceeded to Pembroke Hall to commune with his Cambridge constituents, who once again returned him unopposed. Overall, the elections were uneventful, and certainly satisfactory from Addington's point of view. The opportunity to 'make' his own Parliament strengthened his position, which with the support of Pitt and the acquiescence of much of the 'old opposition' of the Foxite Whigs (as opposed to the 'new opposition' collecting around Grenville) seemed on paper to be very strong indeed. Harmony was maintained: Pitt visited Addington after the election, Addington generously but unsuccessfully offered Pitt the Clerkship of the Pells, and Pitt persuaded Castlereagh to join the government.

On Addington's horizon, however, was appearing the blackest of clouds. Only months after the signing of the Treaty of Amiens, mutual suspicion between London and Paris was again raising the prospect of war. Steadily through the autumn the situation would deteriorate: Britain objected to the French occupation of Switzerland and annexations in northern Italy, while noting that Napoleon had now been declared First Consul for Life; the French were furious at attacks on Napoleon in the English press and the British refusal to evacuate Malta in the light of French activities and the absence of international guarantees. No one had regarded Addington as a war leader, probably even including himself. The pressure from Pitt's friends now became intense, and he began to concede in private that Addington would not be up to the job. By August, Canning thought Pitt 'disgusted with the Doctor and his system as much as one could wish . . . but – as to *acting*, no hopes of that yet'.[39]

As it happened, talk of returning to power had to be put to one side when Pitt fell seriously ill. After leaving office the previous year he had experienced a fresh bout of stomach pains and vomiting. Now, in September 1802 he wrote to Farquhar, who recorded that Pitt 'complained of severe morning sickness, & absolute dislike to all food, with all the unpleasant Symptoms of aggravated debility. In consequence of this Letter I went down to Walmer, & remained there for a Week. I found the Stomach rejecting everything, & the bowels obstinately refusing their office – the nerves seriously affected – the habit wasted – & the whole system deranged. These distressing and discouraging Symptoms continuing for some days unabated in spite of the most powerful remedies, Mr. Pitt expressed himself with his usual good humour, that he believed he had at last baffled the art of Medicine, and that the Expedients to rescue him were at an end.'[40] Eventually, a tepid bath and a strong 'night draught' appeared to produce a 'sudden & surprising' recovery. As ever, Pitt's first instinct was to write to his mother in case she heard 'an exaggerated account of my having been unwell'. He reassured her that he was well recovered from an attack 'brought on partly by a sudden change of weather, and partly by a little over-exercise in shooting'.[41] By contrast, Pretyman's account refers to 'a most violent illness of a bilious nature, and his life was for some hours in imminent danger'.[42]

Pitt had now suffered serious gastro-intestinal problems for at least four out of five consecutive years, usually in the late summer and autumn after a busy period of travel or work. Yet his illness in 1802, which took the most alarming form so far, could not have been brought on by the strains of office, and followed a period in which he was thought to have been drinking less heavily than in previous – or later – years. Medical opinion of the time tended to think of Pitt's problem as a diffused form of gout, but whatever type of inflammation or ulcering was crippling his digestion, it was chronic, and each bout was more severe. He at last acceded to Farquhar's advice to pay an extended visit to the spa waters at Bath. He would not, however, obey any injunction to remove his mind from public business.

When Grenville visited Pitt at Walmer in October for a rapprochement, he found him 'very thin', his complexion and looks 'by no means . . . those of a man in health',[43] but considering renewed war as inevitable and contemplating returning to office. Pitt's stipulation, wholly in character and in line with his conduct for the previous twenty years, was that it must be 'manifest that the thing was not of his seeking', and that he would undertake it 'only . . . *if His Majesty should think it useful to His services to lay these commands upon him*'.[44] By early November he was in Bath, pronouncing himself much better already and asking Rose to visit him. Rose prevailed on him to remain absent from the opening sittings of the new Parliament and, eventually, to cease advising Addington and his colleagues: 'By giving his unqualified support to the present Ministry he would lose the confidence of the country.'[45]

Pitt stayed at Bath for some weeks through November and December 1802 and took the opportunity to visit his mother, whom he would never see again. While reflecting and receiving news, he became increasingly incensed at the conduct of the Addington ministry. He was 'beyond measure surprised'[46] that Dundas was ennobled as Lord Melville without any prior consultation with himself – Dundas had helped to keep Scotland safe for the ministry in the general election – and seemed to take this as an attempt to nobble his closest ally. Then he was furious when former Ministers were attacked in *The Times* for 'deserting their post in the hour of danger upon some frivolous pretext, or for some mysterious intrigue'.[47] To cap it all, he found the presentation of Addington's budget on 8 December to be offensive and its content appalling. Addington's policy of raising extra finance for current expenses through unfunded debt went against the principles which had guided Pitt throughout his budgets, and violated his most cherished views and achievements.

By the time Pitt left Bath on Christmas Eve to spend Christmas with George Rose, he was fuming. Even so, he had become recalcitrant again about taking office unless war broke out, and intervened to prevent Canning rounding up the signatures of senior figures to call for changes in the government. He told Malmesbury at the end of December that he would wait. He would judge Ministers by their actions. Not to do so would be 'a dereliction of character, and . . . a breach of faith'.[48] He prevented Rose from mounting an open attack on the budget even though he was 'perfectly persuaded that the whole of these statements were founded on gross errors'.[49] In the meantime, debate on his possible return to power had surfaced in the House of Commons. While Sheridan argued that if the nation depended on only one man it would not deserve to be saved, Canning produced the over-excited rejoinder in reference to Pitt: 'He cannot withdraw himself from the following of a nation; he must endure the attachment of a people whom he has saved.'[50]

As he contemplated his battered health, the approach of war, and the incompetence of Addington's financial management, Pitt clung to the vision of 'character' he had pursued throughout his whole career. But that vision no longer provided the answer. While 'character' impelled him to keep his word and to avoid any grasping for office, it also required him to serve the country and to take charge when others could not cope. His friends chafed while he waited on events. In Malmesbury's perceptive phrase that Christmas, 'He did not know very well how to separate himself from himself.'[51]

However high Addington may have been riding in the summer of 1802, he knew by the end of the year that the threat of war and the ominous silence of Pitt spelt trouble of the most serious nature. He persuaded Pitt, whose friends were trying to keep him away from Addington, to visit him at Richmond early in the new year. Rather alarmingly for Addington, Pitt's acceptance was written from Dropmore, the home of Grenville. Then and on other occasions in January the two men made an effort to get on, despite Pitt's private criticisms of the budget. Pitt told Rose that Addington would need to withdraw some of his budget or he, Pitt, would expose the errors in it 'both for the sake of my own character and the deep public interests involved'.[52] Pitt and Addington spent many hours together without any discussion of a reshuffle, apparently until the final minutes of their conversation, and then, Pitt told Rose, 'In the chaise, coming into town, when they had reached Hyde Park, Mr. A., in a very embarrassed manner, entered on the subject by saying that if Lord Grenville had not stated the indispensable necessity of Mr. Pitt coming into office to carry on the government, he should have been disposed himself to propose his return to administration.'[53] The offer seems to have been vague and unspecific, and the response was not surprisingly non-committal. Addington would later maintain that at some stage that January Pitt had expressed a willingness to take a Cabinet post, a claim which Pitt would always deny. The result was inconclusive, with Pitt still absenting himself from Parliament.

On 9 February while at Walmer he 'suffered severely from a bilious attack, which however had yielded to the Prescriptions of Mr. Hulke the Apothecary at Deal',[54] but which was accompanied by gout in one of his feet. Sick as he was, his mind would not be still; he wrote to his brother, who remained in the Cabinet, of the need for 'a firm determination' to raise taxes and prepare for war. Fox commented that 'half the world' thought Pitt's illness a 'sham',[55] and it certainly did not check an increasing demand for his return, Wilberforce noting on 8 March: 'Pitt's return talked of and wished.'[56] On 19 March none other than Henry Dundas, now First Viscount Melville, arrived at Pitt's door. Pitt's staunchest ally and drinking companion now came as a messenger from Addington. He brought a specific proposal: neither Addington nor Pitt would be Prime Minister – they would both serve as senior members of the government while Pitt's brother, Chatham, would be First Lord of the Treasury.

Addington's proposal was his attempt at a compromise, and harked back to arrangements often made in the eighteenth century, such as in the Fox–North coalition, in which a neutral but respected figure became the nominal head of a government and the genuinely powerful Ministers became Secretaries of State. Melville no doubt thought he was being helpful, but it seems surprising that anyone so familiar with Pitt's personality could entertain any hope of this proposal being successful. To his brother, Pitt had been generous to a fault, raising him to the Cabinet and persuading him to stay there, lending him money and arranging the Knighthood of the Garter. But the idea that Pitt would serve beneath him in government was ludicrous in the extreme. Moreover, Pitt had himself changed the nature of Cabinet government so that a powerful Treasury stood at its centre. He would have considered a power-sharing arrangement in government as old-fashioned and utterly inappropriate in war.

Pitt's response, as recounted by Melville to Addington, constitutes one of the clearest and earliest definitions of prime ministerial power in the British system of government:

> Besides this consideration, he stated, not less pointedly and decidedly, his sentiments with regard to the absolute necessity there is, in the conduct of the affairs of this country, that there should be an avowed and real minister possessing the chief weight in council and the principal place in the confidence of the King. In that respect there can be no rivality or division of power. That power must rest in the person generally called the First Minister; and that minister ought, he thinks, to be the person at the head of the finances . . . If it should come . . . to a radical difference of opinion . . . the sentiments of the Minister must be allowed and understood to prevail, leaving the other members of administration to act as they may conceive themselves conscientiously called upon to act under such circumstances.[57]

True to himself, and no doubt mindful of his experience as Chancellor of the Exchequer in 1782–83 as well as of his father's final administration, Pitt was not interested in office if it was divorced from genuine power and authority. Neither his reason nor his pride would suffer it.

If political calculation also entered into Pitt's rejection of Addington's first proposal, it did not take long to produce the desired effect. Ten days after Melville's visit to Walmer, another of his old friends, Charles Long, arrived as a further messenger from Addington. He brought with him an offer unique in the annals of British politics: a proposal from the incumbent Prime Minister voluntarily to surrender his office to a leading rival who was not then a member of the government. Addington had decided to settle for a more junior position in the government he had constructed, with the intention that most of his colleagues would continue in post under Pitt's leadership. Ministers such as Hawkesbury and Castlereagh were in any case clear that Pitt should be in charge. Addington was even happy to see Pitt's acolytes such as Canning and Rose join the administration, while keeping out Grenville, who had provided the lead for the 'new opposition'.

On 3 April 1803, as Pitt considered this new situation, his mother died at Burton Pynsent. There is little record of his reaction, other than of his talking to Rose 'a good deal . . . respecting the death of his mother, and of feelings awakened by that event'.[58] It must be likely that a man who had always been so conscious of his mother's feelings experienced deep emotions on her death, but it did not affect Pitt's sense of political purpose. His visit to London would now take in a meeting with Addington on 10 April and his mother's funeral in Westminster Abbey on the sixteenth. Whatever the distress of the moment, Addington must have been reasonably confident that his offer would be accepted by Pitt, with resulting harmony all round. He had committed himself to an act of rare political generosity, albeit out of realism, and few politicians in history would have turned him down.

Yet William Pitt was different. Some mixture of pride, experience, contempt or correctness made him question even now the value of the proffered chalice. As Charles Long departed Walmer he noticed Lord Grenville arriving. Grenville told Pitt that he should only return to office at the invitation of the King, not through negotiation with Addington. What is more, Pitt as Prime Minister should have the freedom to dispose of other offices as he wished, with Addington out of the senior ranks of the ministry, members of the opposition brought in, and Ministers free to air their views on the Catholic question even if they did not pursue it as a policy. It is easy to imagine the case he would have put: Addington had betrayed his weakness, and Pitt could hold out for accepting office on his own terms. He should be free to employ the best talents available in a national life-or-death struggle with Napoleon. How could he enter a government committed to maintain much of its mediocrity?

Grenville knew his man. His arguments were in line with Pitt's long-standing approach. Melville had warned Pitt that 'no step could be more injudicious on your part than an attempt to form an administration mixing in it Lord Grenville with the leading parts of His Majesty's present Government. None of them, in my opinion, could sit down in council with him without depreciating their character in the eye of the public,'[59] but Pitt decided he would rather have the support of the Grenvillites, who had once been his colleagues, than that of the Addingtonians, whom he was coming to despise. He met Addington at Long's house in Bromley on 10 April. There he told him that he would return as Prime Minister at the invitation of the King and on the recommendation of the present Ministers, but that any members of his previous administration as well as the current one could be included in his new government. He envisaged Addington leaving the government altogether, and taking a peerage along with a newly created position as Speaker of the House of Lords.

Pitt was clear: he would only hold office on his own terms. For that, he was prepared to gamble that a sitting Prime Minister and Cabinet with a large majority in Parliament would recommend not only his leadership, but in large measure their own dissolution.

25

The Old Addiction

'Is it upon the wisdom, the vigilance, and the energy of these ministers that we can rely, when we have seen that no one measure for the public defence can they be truly said to have originated, when several they have retarded or enfeebled?'

WILLIAM PITT, 23 APRIL 1804[1]

'I admire my uncle most particularly when surrounded with a tribe of military attendants.'

LADY HESTER STANHOPE, 1803[2]

NO STUDENT OF POLITICS would be surprised at what happened when Addington took to his Cabinet Pitt's demand that they themselves should support giving him unfettered freedom to replace them. It is a sign of how cowed Addington was by Pitt, how nervous he was of his disapproval, and how uncertain he was about the waging of war, that he was prepared to put this proposition to his colleagues at all. Even though he had now been Prime Minister for two years, he could not escape from a feeling of inferiority towards his old friend who had now become a rival. His long friendship with Pitt, and the many years of observing his talents as Prime Minister from the Speaker's chair in the 1790s, meant that Addington could not in his own heart believe that he should be Prime Minister if Pitt wished to return – a relationship between a Prime Minister and his predecessor probably unique in British history. In April 1803, Addington was caught between this deference to Pitt on the one hand, and his wish to preserve some measure of dignity for himself, his policies and his colleagues on the other. It would take several days for the second of these influences marginally to outweigh the first, a process which, in Pitt's eyes, produced a degree of dissembling and confusion that further lowered Addington in his esteem.

According to Rose, on 10 April 'Mr. A. cheerfully consented to' the various stipulations which Pitt had made.[3] But on the twelfth, no doubt after some reflection and discussion with Cabinet colleagues, Addington wrote to Pitt to say that he 'continued to think the arrangement, as proposed by Mr. Pitt, would not be considered admissible by his colleagues; trusting, therefore, he would not tenaciously adhere to it',[4] and asking for further discussions following a meeting of the Cabinet the next day. Pitt, who was 'much struck with Mr. A. saying that he *continued* to be of an opinion, the contrary of which he had distinctly expressed in conversation',[5] sent the categoric response that 'the arrangement as proposed by him was indispensable'.[6]

It seems that the Cabinet, which duly met on the thirteenth at the home of Pitt's brother, would have happily acquiesced in the return of Pitt at their head: many of them, after all, had served under him only two years before and, like Addington, did not wish to be opposed to him. Understandably, however, they could not stomach the idea of Pitt being free to bring in such figures as Grenville and Windham, who had so vociferously attacked the Treaty of Amiens and gone into outright opposition. They could not therefore agree 'to new-model, reconstruct and in part to change the government, instead of strengthening it'.[7]

Given that it was Addington who had proposed that Pitt should return as Prime Minister and gone on to agree to his conditions, even under some protest, Pitt was highly unamused by this subsequent response. He resolved that 'He would in future receive no overtures but such as may be made by the express command of His Majesty',[8] and sent Addington an extremely curt response:

> My dear sir,
> I need only acknowledge the receipt of your letter, and am yours sincerely
> W. Pitt

Addington had been hamfisted; Pitt rather unrealistic. Addington's muddled attempts to do something highly unusual had come up against Pitt's experience of the need for genuine power. The result of this botched negotiation between two long-standing friends and allies left both of them in a weaker political position as well as mutually estranged. Addington had revealed his weakness as Prime Minister just as war was breaking out, and now risked Pitt's public wrath and opposition. From Pitt's point of view, his chances of forming a strong government in the future were diminished by the bad blood that now duly flowed: his followers and those of Addington became more hostile to each other, and some of his friends such as Melville and Malmesbury held Grenville to blame for ruining the negotiations, pushing the latter further into becoming a separate political force. Pitt's attempt to dissolve the Addington administration brought some scorching criticism from former colleagues whom he had earlier persuaded to become members of it. Lord Redesdale, the Lord Chancellor of Ireland, addressed him in no uncertain terms. He recalled that Pitt had asked him to serve under Addington 'for his sake', so that government did not fall into the hands of the opposition: 'how then could those who consented to assist in different ways towards the forming of that administration, conceive that they were acting in a manner disagreeable to you; & particularly how could they conceive that they were acting so as to warrant your sacrificing them at a future period to men who apparently were acting in contradiction to your wishes'[9] – a reference to Grenville and others who left the government in 1801. Pitt was also weakened in the eyes of George III, who when Addington belatedly told him of the negotiations considered it 'a foolish business from one end to the other', and that Pitt might have wished to carry 'his plan of *removals* so extremely far and so high that it might reach *him*'.[10]

The recriminations were such that both principals tried to set on record what they thought they had been doing, with Addington referring back to the discussion in January in which he had understood Pitt to be ready to take office without such sweeping conditions. Pitt set out his own position in four letters to Addington over nine days between 15 and 24 April, with the obvious objective of protecting his position with the King. He made clear that all he had asked for was 'full authority to form, for *his Majesty's consideration*, a plan of arrangement in *any* manner I thought best for his service, as *well out of those who were in the former, as those who are in his present government*.'[11] Nevertheless, he was further from power at the end of the negotiation than at the beginning of it. The Speaker of the Commons recorded: 'Mr. Pitt left town to go to Walmer. His conduct in the whole transaction is very much disapproved by Lord Melville, Lord Chatham, Lord Castlereagh, Lord Hawkesbury, Steele, &c.'[12] It must have been still more vexing for Pitt that Addington now turned to the Whigs to help strengthen his ministry: in May, Tierney, Pitt's long-standing critic and duelling opponent, was appointed Treasurer of the Navy. Addington was burning his bridges.

On 18 May 1803 Britain declared war on France. The Treaty of Amiens, greeted with such acclamation by the British public, had lasted less than fourteen months. The final British ultimatum had not been one that was likely to be accepted: it required French withdrawal from Holland and Switzerland, and continued British occupation of Malta. The British decision to bring matters to a head caused anger and surprise in Paris – Napoleon reacted harshly by imprisoning all British subjects who happened to be travelling in France at the time – but it reflected tacit recognition in London that a trusting and generous peace settlement with Napoleon was not going to work, and that the further passage of time would strengthen the power of France vis-à-vis Britain. Russian mediation, accepted in principle by the government after Pitt's intervention in its favour, came to nothing. After the briefest of interruptions, the long war would be resumed.

Neither country was prepared for immediate hostilities. Although the French army remained huge, neither their navy nor the British forces in general was manned for all-out conflict. The early moves would involve a British blockade of Continental ports and the assembly by the French of an invasion force across the Channel. While Ministers inexperienced in warfare struggled to mobilise the armed forces, Pitt's mind was alive with proposals. Wilberforce had recorded at the end of April: 'To Long's, Bromley Hill. There found Pitt . . . Heard the complete story of the late negociation with Addington – his plan of defending the country, if war. His mind of the same superior cast. Did not get to dinner till almost eight o'clock. William Long, Lord Camden, Pitt, and I, chatted till bed-time, half-past twelve. Tuesday, After breakfast long discussion with Pitt. Talked about navy's state, as day before . . .'[13] As the Commons met to debate the war on 23 May, Pitt was ready to burst forth with plans of action. Whatever the failings of the government, he would explain how war should be conducted. He would do so in a House of Commons many of whose Members had not encountered him before – he had not attended since the general election of the previous year – using all the powers of oratory which had matured during twenty-two years of debates.

Even Pitt's arrival in the House of Commons that day was sufficient to cause excitement. While some 150 new Members buzzed with anticipation of him speaking, older hands noted the change in his appearance from previous years. The repeated bouts of ill-health had taken a visible toll, and one politically unsympathetic diarist, Thomas Creevey, recorded: 'I really think Pitt is done: his face is no longer red, but yellow; his looks are dejected; his countenance I think much changed and fallen, and every now and then he gives a hollow cough. Upon my soul, hating him as I do, I am almost moved to pity to see his fallen greatness.'[14] Pitt himself admitted to Pretyman that he 'came to Town a good deal unwell'.[15] But as the Members called 'Mr. Pitt! Mr. Pitt!' for him to speak, the adrenalin would have run strongly in his veins. He loved the House of Commons, and his greatest moments had been addressing it; now in a moment of great crisis he was being called on to use his abilities to the full.

He did not disappoint. Keyed up with a genuine desire both to advise the nation and to display his spellbinding techniques to a new generation, Pitt delivered a speech which, in the generous words of Fox, 'Demosthenes might have envied'.[16] It has always been deeply unfortunate for historians that a change in the procedures for admission to the Public Gallery that day left reporters unable to hear Pitt's speech. Consequently it was not widely reported in the press, but there can be no doubting its impact on the Commons. Perhaps the best account of the occasion was written by a new Member, John Ward.

He recounted that Pitt was 'cheered before he had uttered a syllable', and sat down to 'the longest, most eager, and most enthusiastic bursts of applause I ever heard in any place on any occasion'. It was 'The greatest, of his harangues . . . "Bonaparte absorbing the whole power of France;" "Egypt consecrated by the heroic blood that had been shed upon it;" "the *liquid fire* of Jacobinical principles desolating the world;" . . . an electrifying peroration on the necessity and magnitude of our future exertions; all this was as fine as anything he ever uttered.'[17] The hostile Creevey agreed: 'Then came the great fiend himself – Pitt – who, in the elevation of his tone of mind and composition, in the infinite energy of his style, the miraculous perspicuity and fluency of his periods outdid (as it was thought) all former performances of his. Never, to be sure, was there such an exhibition: its effect was dreadful.'[18]

The evidence of the decline in Pitt's physical powers was clear. Ward said that 'he exhibits strong marks of bad health. Though his voice has not lost any of its depth and harmony, his lungs seem to labour in those prodigious sentences which he once thundered forth without effort.'[19] Yet overall, the inspiring call to arms, the denunciation of France and the characteristic call for a financial plan for the waging of war left many Members in little doubt as to who would be best placed to fight it. The contrast with Addington, who rather risibly turned up in the House in the uniform of an officer of the Woodley Yeomanry, and delivered an uninspiring effort, could not have been greater.

In delivering this epic oration, Pitt was doing much more than putting on a memorable performance. He was consciously adopting a new strategy which was intended to take him back to power while remaining true to his stated commitments and self-defined character. Despite the progressive decline in his health, he simply could not bear to be away from the action when so much was at stake. Both duty and ambition impelled him towards his comeback. Yet he still felt the pull of his initial commitments to Addington, even after the rupture of the recent negotiations, and was reluctant to indulge in all-out opposition which would offend his many friends within the government and make it harder for him subsequently to form an administration. He therefore embarked on a 'middle course' in which he would not immediately attempt to overthrow the government, much to the frustration of Canning and Grenville, but would assiduously attend the House of Commons and begin to dominate affairs through sheer merit. He would speak against 'weak or pernicious half measures'.[20] He would, quite simply, show activity, knowledge and purpose which would make him indispensable.

It is hard to fault Pitt's judgement in taking this approach. The alternatives to it were all unpalatable: to go into sudden outright opposition to Addington so soon after the April negotiations would have seemed opportunistic and would have involved going back on his word; to continue to give unstinting support to Addington would have been intellectually dishonest; and to resume a lofty absence from Parliament at a time of war would have been so far from Pitt's nature as to be intolerable to him. Nevertheless, his strategy of 'constructive engagement' had the one serious drawback of being a potentially lonely one. Out of office, even more than when he was in it, Pitt neglected to cultivate a following or to create any sense of 'party' around him. The flattering of less-talented MPs was neither in his nature nor in accordance with his view of how politics should work; he thought that ability and character should always count for more than partisan manoeuvres by which politicians tried to foist themselves upon the King. Such an attitude was, of course, an integral component of the status and respect he enjoyed, but its drawback was that when out of office he could not presume on the automatic support of any massed ranks of MPs. Since most MPs were aligned in one way or another with government or one of the opposition factions (there was an Old Opposition led by Fox and a New Opposition clustered around Grenville), the number of votes for a 'middle course' would not be large.

This much became very clear on 3 June, less than two weeks after Pitt's electrifying speech. When the opposition tabled a motion of censure against the government, Pitt did not wish to support it, but nor did he wish to see it heavily defeated. Instead, he suggested to the government that it move 'the Orders of the Day' to shelve the debate. An indignant Addington, discovering more backbone now that he was up against the wall, refused to countenance a tactic which would have implied that the government feared defeat. Caught between the two sides, Pitt decided to move 'the Orders of the Day' himself, but could muster only fifty-eight votes in the division, while the followers of Addington, Fox and Grenville amassed 335 votes together to make sure they could go on to fight each other. Pitt and those who had voted with him thereupon left the House, and the government easily defeated the censure, sponsored by Grenville's faction, by 275 to thirty-four.

These divisions were a reminder of what Pitt should have known, that a government was very difficult to overthrow if it retained the confidence both of the King and of the country gentlemen in Parliament. Many MPs might have been happy to see Pitt at the helm again, but that did not mean that they would vote to turn out the King's government within days of the outbreak of war. While the King expressed 'much pleasure'[21] to Addington on the result, Canning reflected on Pitt that 'to have a hearty following, he must take an intelligible line of conduct',[22] and Pitt privately admitted that he had not shown 'good *generalship*'.[23] This setback may have contributed to Pitt's disillusionment that month with the idea of returning to government at all. He wrote to Dundas on 19 June: 'The more I reflect on the whole state of things and parties, the more convinced I am that all idea of my returning to office (especially in the precarious state of my health) ought from the present (to say *the least*) to be considered as wholly out of the question; and I ought to look only to remaining a private man, making use of the few occasions which may offer in which, by any opinion in Parliament I can contribute to do any good or prevent any mischief.'[24]

It would take many months and rising uncertainty about Addington's conduct of the war before Addington would have to face the prospect of Commons defeats. His position was stronger than Pitt had expected. Yet Pitt seems to have been confident that his own depth of experience gave him more influence than the voting totals of 3 June suggested. He persisted in his overall approach, often supporting the government but picking a quarrel with it when he thought it was wrong. Addington's budget on 13 June involved reinventing income tax, which had been abolished only the preceding year. It was proposed that income would now be taxed at source, getting round the massive scale of evasion which had plagued Pitt's earlier efforts. Pitt objected to income from property and government debt being treated differently. He pressed his point tenaciously, exchanging some sharp words with Addington. Once again he forced a vote against the government, and although he was again defeated (150 to fifty), the government caved in the following day.

Not surprisingly in these circumstances, the relationship between Pitt and Addington steadily deteriorated. While an anxious Addington still referred to Pitt in the House as his 'Right Honourable Friend', Pitt had ceased to use this mark of alliance when referring to Addington. When he found the government dilatory in pursuing the necessary scale of military conscription, he declared that he would move a motion on it in the Commons himself. Once again, Ministers caved in to his demands. The war had only just begun, but the government was finding that Pitt was a very big thorn to have regularly in its side. As the parliamentary session came to an end in August, and Pitt made for Walmer Castle, it was decided within Addington's circle that moves should be set in hand to diminish Pitt's reputation. A pamphlet entitled 'A few cursory Remarks upon the State of Parties during the Administration of Mr. Addington' appeared under the authorship of a 'Near Observer', attacking Pitt for his conduct towards Addington and his apparent arrogance in the April negotiations. It went on to praise Addington, maintaining that his only fault was his deference towards Pitt. The amount of inside information suggested that sources extremely close to Addington had assembled the material, although Addington himself would always deny that he had been in any way involved.

In publishing this pamphlet Addington's supporters were making a serious mistake, for they were needling a proud man who was highly conscious of his reputation and who could still do far more damage to the government than he had thus far attempted. By early October, Pitt was telling Rose that the pamphlet was 'one of the most malignant, false and artful statements he ever saw'.[25] He was sufficiently incensed to initiate the publication of a counter-pamphlet, and 'to superintend the work, to throw in fresh materials, and to suggest new arguments'.[26] The work of the 'Near Observer' was thereupon answered by a 'More

Accurate Observer' giving a 'Plain answer to the Misrepresentations and Calumnies' previously circulated. This in turn opened a general 'pamphlet war', bringing forth a further rejoinder and a raft of other publications flying back and forth. For politics to be conducted in this way was something of an innovation, made possible by advances in printing and distribution. While not reaching the wider public, it created intense feelings among the participants, Malmesbury considering that it 'produced no other effect than creating a degree of personal enmity between them they till now never had, nor ever would have entertained, if these officious scribblers had not come forward'.[27] Pitt's own direct involvement showed, however, that it was not just 'scribblers' who were at work, as the remnants of goodwill which he felt for Addington were being destroyed. But although Pitt was put out by the growing animosity, it seems unlikely that he was consumed by it. For, that autumn at Walmer, he found additional company and new activities which would unexpectedly provide a most fulfilling period of his life.

The return to active participation at Westminster had produced an immediate impact on Pitt's health, but the inventive attentions of Farquhar seemed to have brought things under control. As Farquhar remembered it:

> Upon his return to Town . . . political Events again involved him in care, fatigue, & anxiety, which brought on a renewal of the former unpleasant Symptoms. He could retain nothing on his Stomach, nor could he sit down to dinner without being sick. It was evident to me that these debilitating Feelings were considerably encreased [sic] by the long & constant attendance in the House of Commons & still more aggravated by the lateness & irregularity of the hour of dinner. I therefore suggested the indispensable necessity of guarding against such fasting, by having every day at 2 o'clock a hot Luncheon with 1 or 2 glasses of good brisk Ale. Mr. Pitt first objected strongly to this, but particularly to the Ale, as his old & valued Friend Dr Addington had constantly forbidden his taking it, – however with his usual good nature he

> consented to make the trial. This Plan which was adopted and adhered to with great regularity produced the most beneficial effect, & enabled him to go through his Parliamentary Duties with comparative ease & comfort to himself.[28]

Returning to Walmer in August 1803 in this fragile but tolerable state, Pitt astonished his friends by doing something which, while characteristically kind, was most uncharacteristically accommodating to a woman. The death of his mother a few months earlier had left his niece, Lady Hester Stanhope, adrift. Her mother, Pitt's sister Hester, had died when she was four years old, and Lady Hester had long since been unable to live with her eccentric and intolerant father (Lord Mahon, by now third Earl Stanhope), from whom Pitt was also now estranged. Having toured the Continent for a few months, this vivacious and attractive twenty-seven-year-old returned to England homeless.

Pitt's initial reaction when this problem was first foreseen had been unsurprising: 'Under no circumstances could I offer her a home in my own house.'[29] But faced with the reality of her situation, he relented. Her nephew and Pitt's biographer the fifth Earl Stanhope later wrote: 'He welcomed his niece to his house as her permanent abode. Henceforth she sat at the head of his table, and assisted him in doing the honours to his guests . . . Lady Hester quickly formed for him a strong and devoted attachment, which she extended to his memory so long as her own life endured. On his part he came to regard her with almost a father's affection . . . On the whole her young presence proved to be, as it were, a light in his dwelling.'[30] She was indeed overjoyed to be given a home which was the centre of so much activity and attention, writing in November:

> To express the kindness with which Mr. Pitt welcomed my return, and proposed my living with him would be impossible; one would really suppose that all obligation was on his side. Here, then, am I, happy to a degree; exactly in the sort of society I most like. There are generally three or four men staying in the house, and we dine eight or ten almost every other day. Military and naval characters are constantly *welcome* here; women are not, I *suppose*,

> because they do not form any part of our society. You may guess, then, what a pretty fuss they make with me.[31]

Tall and 'handsome' rather than beautiful, Lady Hester evidently abounded in wit and mimicry, which entertained the indulgent Pitt and must have markedly enlivened the long-established bachelor atmosphere of his home. Lord Mulgrave commented that Pitt was 'as good as he is great' to take compassion on her 'in a way which must break in upon his habits of life'.[32] He, like many other visitors, would later be at the sharp end of her wit. After unexpectedly becoming Pitt's Foreign Secretary in 1805 he arrived at the Pitt household for breakfast and remarked that he had been given a broken spoon, receiving the retort: 'Have you not yet discovered that Mr. Pitt sometimes uses very slight and weak instruments to effect his ends?'[33] Lady Hester was withering about politicians she found pompous or boring, referring to Castlereagh as his 'monotonous Lordship'.[34] When Lord Abercorn received the Knighthood of the Garter from Addington and wore it conspicuously, 'she humiliated him in public by alluding to his infirmity, asking if he used the order to tie up his broken leg',[35] and she was rude about the Prince of Wales and the 'broad bottom' Grenville. Such behaviour must have rankled with many, but it never seemed to disturb Pitt's tolerant good humour. It was typical of him to make the very best of a friendship brought about by circumstance and necessity, but for which he would never have gone looking.

Coincident with this uplift in Pitt's domestic circumstances, necessity on a larger scale brought about a second change in his lifestyle which might have surprised those who thought they knew him. Bookish, intellectual and unhealthy as he was, he now took on a voluntary but active military role as Colonel of a corps of volunteers. With Napoleon massing a huge army and constructing thousands of barges across the Channel, the government embarked in the summer of 1803 on the raising of a great number of armed volunteers. So many hundreds of thousands came forward for enrolment that Addington's Ministers were caught unprepared: there were insufficient weapons to arm them, and administrative chaos was common. By the end of the year there were 340,000 volunteers enrolled, none of them in a more crucial situation than those on the south coast in the vicinity of the Cinque Ports, where Pitt now applied himself with great enthusiasm to their raising and training. He rode regularly along the Kent coast, preparing plans for the 'driving of the country' so that the invaders would be bereft of livestock and transport, and was soon 'an excellent soldier', according to Mulgrave.[36] Lady Hester Stanhope wrote to a friend that:

> Mr. Pitt absolutely goes through the fatigue of a *drill-sergeant*. It is parade after parade, at fifteen or twenty miles distant from each other . . . If Mr. Pitt does not overdo it and injure his health every other consideration becomes trifling. You know me too well not to be aware of the anxiety I am under upon this account; and the extreme care I take, or rather endeavour to take, of this blessing (so essential to him in pursuing his active line of conduct, therefore *invaluable* to his country), is rewarded by his *minding* me more than any other person, and allowing me to speak to him upon the subject of his health, which is always an unpleasant one, and one he particularly dislikes . . . He had a cough when I first came to England but it has nearly or quite left him. He is thin but certainly strong, and his spirits are excellent.[37]

Pitt's new martial habits were happily coupled with his studious instincts. His surviving notes from this period contain a long series of algebraic formulae and diagrams illustrating the angle and pace at which a wheeling company should turn, and including such discoveries as: 'if the Front of the Company consists of a greater number of Files than Eight, the distance of this Point of Intersection from the wheeling Flank will increase in the same Proportions'.[38]

It had not been envisaged for many years that the holder of the sinecure of Lord Warden of the Cinque Ports and Constable of Dover Castle would take his responsibilities so literally. Yet Pitt, who had admitted to doubting his own military judgement while Prime Minister, clearly relished applying himself to a task made urgent by extreme national danger. By October he was organising the fitting-out of 170 gunboats stationed between Margate and Hastings, and was disgusted at the lack of cooperation and support such efforts received from the government. As the expectation of invasion neared its peak, Pitt wrote to Rose on 18 October: 'I am much more inclined than I have ever been hitherto to believe that some attempt will be made soon.'[39] By November he thought that his men could give 'a very good account' of themselves in the event of invasion, but that if the enemy broke through the initial defences they would soon be in the approaches to London. His experience in what was potentially the front line persuaded him that the Addington ministry was genuinely not up to the job, with the overall preparedness for defence 'very far short of what it ought to have been, and what it easily might have been'.[40]

Invasion fears were still high in early December. Pitt postponed going to Westminster for the session which had opened at the end of November because 'I shall be so constantly occupied all next week in going round to my different battalions.'[41] But for all the scares, the French were not going to make a serious attempt to invade England that year. Their ships of the line were scattered and bottled up in their ports by the Royal Navy's blockade. While Napoleon was already famous for his forced marches and surprise manoeuvres on land, he could not take the risk of sending an entire army into what might easily have been a massacre at sea. In the words of the rather complacent First Lord of the Admiralty, Earl St Vincent, 'I do not say the French cannot come. I only say they cannot come by water.'[42]

Pitt returned to the Commons on 9 December, his ability to pursue his strategy of pushing and outshining the government strengthened by the first-hand experience he had now acquired. Rose had urged him not to 'pass over in silence the disgraceful misconduct of ministers, which he felt on various points at least as strongly as myself',[43] while not entering into '*systematic* opposition'.[44] As the government came under strong attack from Windham in the debate on the ninth for its handling of the volunteer regiments, Pitt gave Addington succour by rebutting the criticisms, but then went on to suggest a number of improvements to the organisation, distribution and officering of the volunteers. Some of his points were so well founded that the government brought in a Bill the following day in order to accommodate them. Pitt returned to Walmer for Christmas, enjoying the immersion in politics and military affairs sufficiently to cancel a planned restorative visit to Bath. It was the start of an intensified pattern of behaviour, to which he had always been susceptible, of considering his duties to be much more important than his health.

Pitt had reason enough that New Year to think his health a low priority. Hester Stanhope wrote on 14 January: 'We are in almost daily expectation of the coming of the French, and Mr. Pitt's regiment is now nearly *perfect* enough to receive them . . . His most intimate friends say they do not remember him so well since the year *ninety-seven*.'[45] In addition, opposition factions were beginning to manoeuvre as the Addington ministry faltered. On New Year's Eve 1803, Grenville wrote to Pitt to urge him to lead the opposition against Addington – 'An understanding between the considerable persons in the country, forgetting past differences, and uniting to rescue us.'[46]

Pitt agreed to meet his cousin and old ally. In the course of three meetings in London in early January a deeply frustrated Grenville, who was fed up with 'middle lines, and managements and delicacies',[47] failed to persuade Pitt to change his stance. Just as Pitt's negotiations with Addington had failed because he had wanted to retain the possibility of working with Grenville, so he would not form an opposition with Grenville because he wished to retain the goodwill of many members of the government when it came to forming his own administration – and the government did currently enjoy a sizeable majority in Parliament. Strident opposition would therefore make it ultimately harder to form an alternative administration and, he told Grenville, 'have very little chance of accomplishing its object of changing the administration, and certainly none of doing so in time to afford the country the benefit of abler counsels'.[48] Pitt's line of thinking had not changed: while he was willing to return to office, the call to do so must come from within the existing government and with the ready agreement of the Crown.

Grenville was bitterly disappointed. Determined to seek a change of government by frontal attack, he now took the step which would separate his career from that of Pitt, irrevocably as it turned out. On 31 January 1804 he wrote to Pitt to explain that he had agreed with other opponents of Addington 'that the government which now exists is manifestly incapable of carrying on the public business', and that 'an administration comprehending as large a proportion as possible of the weight, talents and character to be found in public men of all descriptions' should be formed.[49] He had come to this agreement with none other than their prime enemy of the last twenty years, Charles James Fox. The message to Pitt was clear: if he wanted to stick to his 'middle course', he would have to do it on his own.

It would be easy to think, particularly in the light of later events, that Pitt made an error of judgement in rebuffing Grenville and sending him into the arms of a rival. After all, he did not disagree with Grenville's central objective of forming an alternative and broadly based government, making clear to him in March that he would seek to include him, and even Fox, in any administration he might form. The argument that old rivalries should be set aside at a time of national extremity in no way offended Pitt, yet he was almost certainly right in believing that the Addington government was less likely to break up if faced by a united but minority coalition in Parliament. The best chance of effecting a change of government was for Pitt to be available as a figure above parties. Furthermore, Pitt had never believed in 'storming the closet' with a government unwelcome to the King. His power had been born through repulsing a similar assault on George III when Fox had made an earlier alliance of convenience with Lord North. The fact that the King was once again seriously unwell that February made this consideration all the more important. And since Addington would shortly contemplate resigning only on the condition that Grenville and Fox would not come in with Pitt, Pitt's refusal of Grenville's offer seems to have been based not only on integrity but also on sound tactics.

The risk, of course, was that the widening difference with Grenville and his followers would become unbridgeable, and that even a new government would face a united Grenville–Fox coalition against it. But in the uncertain atmosphere of early 1804 it would have seemed a risk worth taking. The government's difficulties were mounting, and there was talk once again of a Regency, in discussion of which Lord Moira advised the Prince of Wales 'that the Prince's only chance for governing the country without Mr. Pitt, with any degree of comfort, was at least to satisfy the public that the refusal came from Mr. Pitt'.[50]

Since, however, the Prince would be unlikely to offer Pitt the leadership of the government, he would end up giving just such a refusal. Pitt confirmed this to Dundas when he wrote of receiving intelligence that Fox would advise the Prince, in the event of a Regency, to ask Pitt to join 'a strong and comprehensive Government'. Pitt had not changed his long-standing position – 'I do not see how under any circumstances I can creditably or usefully consent to take part in any Government without being at the Head of it.'[51] He needed the government to fall soon and to be invited back by George III himself, unencumbered by commitments and alliances.

So would Addington fall? The truth was that nearly a year of renewed war had produced no dramatic successes, but no great disasters either. The French had moved into northern Germany and taken over George III's Electorate of Hanover. On the other hand, the British were recovering territories in the East and West Indies which they had evacuated at the beginning of the short-lived peace; the French army had proved so far unable to cross the Channel; and Nelson was in position in the Mediterranean to protect Malta and Naples. The situation was somewhat analogous to that of early 1940. A government with an ostensibly secure parliamentary majority had so far survived a rather 'phoney' war with one or two administrative foul-ups but no obvious catastrophe. Yet, also as in 1940 under Neville Chamberlain, there was an expectation that the greatest trial of strength still lay ahead, and that a worthy Prime Minister who had been appointed in peacetime did not possess the panache and authority required during all-out war. Addington simply could not win the respect of his opponents. Fox dismissed his performance with the words: 'It is no excuse that he is a fool,'[52] and Canning was still fashioning his verses into rapiers:

> If *blocks* can from danger deliver,
> Two places are safe from the French:
> The one is the mouth of the river,
> The other the Treasury bench.[53]

This atmosphere, possibly along with the risk of Fox and Grenville actually succeeding in making themselves the alternative government, propelled Pitt from late February 1804 to accentuate the critical side of his middle course rather than the supportive one. On 27 February he made what Canning described as a 'Most *magnificent* speech, of *details*'[54] attacking the government's preparedness for invasion. Canning exulted, 'Yesterday was a *nice* day. They cannot stand many such, and many such they will have.'[55] Relations between Pitt and Addington fell to a new low, Addington visibly annoyed and Pitt miffed that many of his criticisms were rejected. On 15 March in a debate on the navy he went further, and Ministers who had been alternately stroked and prodded by his oratory now felt its lash. France, he said, had 'attained new and extraordinary energies . . . We ought to meet them with at least equal, not inferior, activity and energies.'[56] Yet the navy 'is at the present moment much inferior, and less adequate to the exigency of the danger, than at any period in former times'.[57] He attacked the competence of Lord St Vincent – 'between his Lordship as a Commander on the Sea, and his Lordship as First Lord of the Admiralty, there is a very wide difference' – and contrasted 'the terrible activity of the enemy with the alarming supineness of our Government'. At the end of the debate, Addington could still muster a majority of seventy-one (201 to 130), and Pitt was disappointed that there were 'no *converts*, no *convinced* country gentlemen, no honest good sort of people quitting the Ministry'.[58]

But the injuries he was inflicting were internal ones, and the blood began to flow within the Cabinet. On 20 March 1804 the Lord Chancellor, Lord Eldon, asked Pitt to meet him a few days later, and Pitt accepted.[59] Eldon had never been much attached to Addington, regarding himself as 'the King's Chancellor'. He offered to act as an intermediary between Pitt and the King, for the moment keeping Addington in the dark. This seemed to provide the spur for Pitt to finally come off the fence and bring Addington down by frontal attack. He was additionally emboldened by information that the Ministers who 'feel the insufficiency of the present Government, and wish my return to office' included Portland; Eldon; Chatham; Castlereagh; Charles Yorke, the Secretary at War; Lord Hobart, the Secretary for War and the Colonies; and Hawkesbury.[60] He informed Melville on 29 March that he intended to write to the King as soon as the latter's health improved, 'explaining the dangers which I think threaten his Crown and his people from the continuance of his present Government, and representing to him the urgent necessity of a speedy change'.[61]

From this point on, the Addington administration looked increasingly hapless as it came under merciless fire from both Pitt and Fox in the Commons and Grenville in the Lords. By 17 April Pitt was telling Dundas that 'Government has taken very serious alarm . . . I am much inclined to think that in a few days they must capitulate.'[62] Pitt had not joined the alliance of Fox and Grenville, but he certainly joined in the destruction of the ministry. He gave Eldon a letter for the King on 22 April, and tore into the government on the floor of the Commons on the twenty-third. This was 'the most important and the most critical period that ever existed in [Britain's] history',[63] fortifications had been neglected while Ministers had given only a 'pompous enumeration of the force of the country',[64] and since this was his true opinion it would be 'treason to the best interests of my country, if . . . I did not openly declare it'.[65] The government majority fell to fifty-two. Two days later Pitt was on his feet again, attacking the government for maintaining the wrong proportions of militia and reserves. Its majority went down to thirty-seven (240 to 203). In the Lords, Grenville was running Ministers even closer, and sometimes inflicting actual defeats.

Addington could not take any more. A Prime Minister could live with a majority of thirty-seven, but not when it should have been hundreds. The sense of Parliament was moving against him. Even before the culminating debates at the end of April, he had sent an indirect message to Pitt that he would be 'inclined to resign his situation' if he could be assured that Pitt was not 'connected' with Grenville and Fox.[66] He advised the King to commission Eldon to speak to Pitt, not knowing that such conversations had been underway for a month. On 29 April he told the Cabinet that he would be resigning as soon as possible after he had delivered the budget the following day. Eldon wrote to Pitt on the thirtieth requesting his plan of a new government to submit to the King.

* * *

Pitt had got what he wanted: he had brought down Addington and done so faster than Fox and Grenville had anticipated, or even desired. Foxites grumbled, 'We are the pioneers, digging the foundation; but Mr. Pitt will be the architect to build the House, and to inhabit it.'[67] Nevertheless, it was by no means clear as yet that he could form a strong administration. He had already told Grenville that he would do everything he could to persuade the King to permit him to form a government including both Grenville and Fox, but that 'He was not prepared to make it a *sine qua non*.'[68] He believed that the country needed a great coalition, but for whatever reason, perhaps because of the King's fragile condition or perhaps because the King could still turn back to Addington, he would not refuse to serve if George III would not agree to it. Melville, with prophetic wisdom, counselled against forming a narrower government, asking 'whether the government formed on the narrow scale would be much better than the present; and in the meantime all the jealousies and heartburnings of party spirit would be lurking, and ready to burst out the first favourable moment'.[69] Yet Pitt's confidence in himself was such that he believed that, if necessary, he could once again shoulder the immense burdens of a wartime government without the support of a broader coalition.

In any case, Pitt believed he might well get his way with the King. On 2 May he submitted a forcible letter through Eldon making the case for including not only Grenville but Fox in the new Cabinet. He cited the need to raise taxes, the impression that would be made abroad, and even the advantage that Fox could not stir the Catholic issue from within the government. In the background, Rose was calculating that Pitt could command only a narrow majority in the Commons if Fox, Grenville and Addington were all in opposition.

The King's reply was not encouraging. As Rose put it, 'from the style of the letter, his Majesty must have been in a state of some irritation at the time of writing it'.[70] It contained disparaging remarks about Grenville and Melville, and a point-blank refusal to admit Fox to the government. The King referred with irritation to Pitt's resignation in 1801, 'when the most ill-digested and dangerous proposition was brought forward', and said that Grenville had become a 'Follower of . . . wild ideas'. As for Fox, he expressed 'his astonishment that Mr.

Pitt should one moment harbour the thought of bringing such a name before His Royal notice'.[71] He did not even agree to see Pitt to discuss the matter. On 6 May Pitt responded with a 'temperate and respectful answer',[72] saying that he was 'ready to acquiesce in that decision, and submit myself to Your Majesty's commands', but insisting on a meeting so that he could put the case directly for a broader government: 'Unless your Majesty should so far honour me with your confidence as to admit me into your presence for this purpose, I am grieved to say that I cannot retain any hope that my feeble services can be employed in any manner advantageous to your Majesty's affairs, or satisfactory to my own mind.'[73]

This letter did the trick. George III was no fool when it came to recognising political reality. He agreed to see Pitt the next day, becoming the very personification of charm and reason. When Pitt remarked that he was looking better now than at the time he resigned in 1801, George replied that 'that was not to be wondered at as he was then on the point of *parting* with an old friend; as he was now about to *regain* one'.[74] In the three-hour meeting the King even went so far as to agree to Grenville and his supporters returning to government. He could not agree to the admission of Fox, but accepted Pitt's suggestion that Fox could be appointed an Ambassador or serve on a foreign mission. All in all, he performed a considerable climbdown. Pitt commented: 'Never in any conversation I have had with him in my life has he so baffled me.'[75] Canning was sent to tell Grenville the good news, and Pitt then went to him personally.

Pitt was on the brink of coming back into power with the best of all worlds – at the invitation of the King, by recommendation of the previous government, and in coalition with a good deal of the opposition. With Grenville in the Cabinet and Fox neutralised, he could use his easy dominance of the Commons to lead a strong government against Napoleon. The day after the meeting with the King, Rose found Pitt 'in the highest spirits possible', under the impression that 'so fair an opening presented itself for Fox, as to afford a reasonable certainty that he would not allow it to escape him'.[76] Even after a quarter of a century in politics Pitt could still let his natural optimism run away with him. In reality, his strong government was already stillborn. The previous night, even though Fox had generously made clear that the King's veto on him need not prevent his allies from joining the government, neither his own party nor that of Grenville would agree to do so on such a condition. On principle, since they had advocated a government based on the inclusion of all the most talented people, they could not join one on the basis of 'exclusion'.

This was bad news. Pitt would return to office as Prime Minister devoid not only of much of the health and vigour he had once possessed, but also of a broadly based Cabinet and a secure parliamentary majority. Rose even questioned whether he should take up office at all in such circumstances, and thought 'this argument affected him a little at first, but he soon roused himself, said he was committed, and would go on, certain that all would do well; that he should go through the remainder of the session . . . without great embarrassment; and that in the summer he should undoubtedly be able to strengthen the administration in some way or another'.[77] Apparently incensed by the behaviour of Grenville, whose impatience earlier in the year had led to the alliance with Fox while it was his own route to power that had proved successful, Pitt declared, according to Eldon, that 'He would teach that proud man, that, in the service and with the confidence of the King, he could do without him, though he thought his health such, that it might cost him his life.'[78]

In that spirit, and with that knowledge, Pitt once again received from George III the seals of office as First Lord of the Treasury and Chancellor of the Exchequer, on 18 May 1804. Just short of his forty-fifth birthday, he returned to office as by far the most experienced Minister in the land. On the same day in Paris, the thirty-five-year-old Napoleon was proclaimed hereditary Emperor of the French. From a position of political weakness and personal frailty, Pitt now had to take on the greatest military genius in the world as he approached the peak of his power.

26

Back, But Never the Same

> 'I have received a broad hint to retire after this recent experiment. I beg leave to say, broad as the hint may be, it is not broad enough for me to take it.'
>
> William Pitt, House of Commons, 18 June 1804[1]

> 'I felt it my duty frequently to urge the necessity of his retiring from public business altogether, but Mr. Pitt's memorable reply was, that his Country needed his Services, & he would rather prefer to die at his Post, than desert it.'
>
> Sir Walter Farquhar[2]

Pitt seemed confident in May 1804 that he could once again overcome a good deal of initial hostility and consolidate his position at the head of government. He was no doubt mindful that on the previous occasion he had taken office as Prime Minister, over twenty years before, he had turned scepticism into adulation and defeat into a triumph. He could reflect, too, that this time he was free of many of the great obstacles he had faced on the former occasion. Then he had been an untried twenty-four-year-old with no majority in the Commons who had been assisted into office by means considered by many to be a constitutional outrage. Now he was a statesman of international standing, with immense experience of peace and war, and with at least a small, if untested, parliamentary majority.

Yet the reality was that not only Pitt's personal resilience but also his political position was fundamentally weaker in several respects than the one he had enjoyed in 1783. For one thing, there had been no doubt at the beginning of his first premiership that he enjoyed the resolute backing of a wily monarch whose reign could still last for decades. The position now was starkly different. George III was sixty-five years old, and was suffering from increasingly frequent bouts of insanity. Always strong-willed, after forty-three years on the throne his patience had become thin and his attention span erratic. Even when he was meant to be sane, his behaviour was often strange – in late May 1804 he responded to a cheering crowd of Eton boys by saying that 'in future he should be an Anti-Westminster',[3] insulting a rival school in a manner not normally befitting a King. At the prorogation of Parliament that July he missed out a page of the speech Pitt had prepared for him, shortening it by about a quarter, while his audience affected not to have noticed.

Amidst these small but abundant signs of decay, it is not surprising that politicians gathered ever more earnestly at Carlton House around the Prince of Wales, with even Grenville now joining Fox, Grey, Fitzwilliam and Moira among his key advisers. The real power of politicians always depends not on the station they presently hold, but on the general expectation of their future influence. Pitt could not command a majority in the Commons on the basis of an assured future, nor through a personal following he had never cultivated: opposed by the parties of Fox, Grenville and Addington, he depended on those MPs who automatically adhered to the King's ministry. As a result the King's condition had a tangible effect on the true power Pitt exercised, encouraging opposition, discouraging younger Members from hitching their star to his, and even affecting the readiness of foreign governments to make diplomatic commitments.

Pitt's dependence on a royal power which was losing its force was that much greater because there were conceivable alternatives to him, whereas George III had been left with nowhere else at all to turn in 1783. To Fox, he had 'surrendered himself up entirely into the hands of the Court',[4] while Pitt considered himself to have properly come to office at the request of the King. The truth was that George III had been very reluctant to part with Addington, and felt neither the need nor the wish to deploy his powers of patronage as unswervingly in

Pitt's favour as had been the case in the crisis of 1783–84. Determined to have his way on matters affecting his own household, he made some changes to positions such as those of Lords of the Bedchamber* (including dismissing Lord Amherst for not voting with Addington), which Pitt had to struggle to counteract in order to avoid embarrassment. It always made Pitt 'bilious' to spend hours on appointments to sinecures in which he was not personally interested, but it was a small sign of things to come that much time in the opening weeks of his new administration had to be devoted to keeping such matters in order.

The weaknesses of Pitt's position extended beyond matters of monarchy. In 1783 he had faced a hostile Commons with an ace in his pocket – the threat of a general election which would unseat many of his opponents. In 1804 this card was both of lower value and harder to play: a general election would probably not produce much change in the parliamentary balance, given the absence of such clear-cut issues as those prevailing in 1784, and the dissolution of a Parliament only two years old would have been difficult to justify. Pitt's power was greater when he faced a hostile majority which could be reversed than it would be now, dependent on a small majority in a House he could not change.

As in 1783, Pitt was to lead a government in which he carried a disproportionate burden of the work on his own shoulders. His undistinguished Cabinet of 1783 had sat in the House of Lords while he handled the Commons himself with only Dundas to give material assistance (and Dundas was not initially in the Cabinet). In 1804, Castlereagh was the only Cabinet Minister by Pitt's side in the Commons. Pitt would therefore once again take upon himself the management of a fractious assembly, but at a time when he was two decades older, with far less stamina and with a war to conduct at the same time. Canning bemoaned the 'narrow, shabby government' – partly because he was not put in the Cabinet himself – and told his wife that the Cabinet were widely laughed at.

In fact, the Cabinet of 1804 should be judged stronger than that

* Ceremonial positions in the King's household.

of 1783. Six of the Addington Cabinet remained in office, including two future First Lords of the Treasury, Hawkesbury as Home Secretary and Portland as Lord President. Eldon remained Lord Chancellor, while Westmorland, Chatham and Castlereagh continued as Lord Privy Seal, Master General of the Ordnance and President of the Board of Control respectively. Melville and Camden were the old warhorses who returned with Pitt, the former as First Lord of the Admiralty and the latter as Secretary of State for War. Mulgrave became Chancellor of the Duchy of Lancaster, and Pitt made his old friend Dudley Ryder, now Lord Harrowby, Foreign Secretary, a position which he took on with great misgivings, 'but his friendship for Pitt made him not hesitate in accepting it'.[5] The Cabinet was thus not undistinguished or incompetent, but it was a far cry from the combination of Fox, Spencer, Grenville, Windham and Fitzwilliam along with the best of his loyalists that Pitt had originally envisaged.

A further weakening factor from the very outset was that Pitt's final attacks on the Addington administration and calls for a more vigorous prosecution of the war had created high expectations of the actions he would now take. In 1783, merely staying in office and managing the nation's recovery from war constituted success; in 1804 Pitt was expected to surpass his predecessor in waging war, defending the country against imminent invasion, constructing new alliances and obtaining all the necessary finance on top of the vast amount spent since 1793. It is no wonder that there were some reports of him wearing a miserable countenance. Wilberforce noted 'Pitt not in spirits'[6] in July, and the admittedly partisan Grey wrote that 'He looked very miserable . . . I would rather be any man in England than him.'[7] John Ehrman has drawn attention to the consistent accounts of Pitt's distraction and unhappiness on 31 August 1804 – one official apparently finding him 'completely under the influence of anxiety & dejection', and another observer finding him wandering alone early in the morning in St James's Park 'looking like death with his eyes staring out of his head and steadfastly fixed on the ground'.[8] Lady Hester Stanhope's account of Pitt's day is suggestive only of the normal business of government, but on a sick man it would have taken a heavy toll:

> In town, during the sitting of parliament, what a life was his! Roused from his sleep (for he was a good sleeper) with a despatch from Lord Melville; – then down to Windsor; then, if he had half an hour to spare, trying to swallow something: – Mr. Adams with a paper, Mr. Long with another; then Mr. Rose: then, with a little bottle of cordial confection in his pocket, off to the House until three or four in the morning; then home to a hot supper for two or three hours more, to talk over what was to be done next day: – and wine, and wine! – Scarcely up next morning, when rat tat-tat – twenty or thirty people one after another, and the horses walking before the door from two 'til sunset, waiting for him. It was enough to kill a man – it was murder![9]

Yet equally, there are clear accounts of Pitt retaining his qualities of good humour and playfulness in private even through these times – perhaps justifying Dundas's analysis that he was 'either in a garret or a cellar'. Since he was now unable to escape London for Walmer Castle very often, Pitt rented a house on the familiar territory of Putney Heath, where he could obtain at least a little of the rural atmosphere which was so essential to him. There he was visited by an initially awestruck William Napier (later General Sir William Napier), a friend of the Stanhopes. Napier was struck by Pitt's 'gentle good nature',[10] and left an enduring portrait of the two sides of his personality:

> Mr. Pitt liked practical fun, and used to riot in it with Lady Hester, Charles and James Stanhope, and myself; and one instance is worth noticing. We were resolved to blacken his face with burnt cork, which he most strenuously resisted, but at the beginning of the fray a servant announced that Lords Castlereagh and Liverpool desired to see him on business. 'Let them wait in the other room,' was the answer; and the great Minister instantly turned to the battle, catching up a cushion and belabouring us with it in glorious fun. We were, however, too many and strong for him, and, after at least a ten minutes' fight, got him down and were actually daubing his face, when, with a look of pretended confidence in his prowess, he said, 'Stop, this will do; I could easily beat you all, but we must not keep those grandees waiting any longer.' His defeat was, however, palpable, and we were obliged to get a towel

> and basin of water to wash him clean before he could receive the grandees. Being thus put in order, the basin was hid behind the sofa, and the two lords were ushered in. Then a new phase of Mr. Pitt's manner appeared, to my great surprise and admiration. Lord Liverpool's look and manner are well known – melancholy, bending, nervous. Lord Castlereagh I had known from my childhood, had often been engaged with him in athletic sports, pitching the stone or bar, and looked upon him as what indeed he was, a model of quiet grace and strength combined. What was my surprise to see both him and Lord Liverpool bending like spaniels on approaching the man we had just been maltreating with such successful insolence of fun! but instantly Mr. Pitt's change of manner and look entirely fixed my attention. His tall, ungainly, bony figure seemed to grow to the ceiling, his head was thrown back, his eyes fixed immovably in one position, as if reading the heavens, and totally regardless of the bending figures near him. For some time they spoke; he made now and then some short observation, and finally, with an abrupt stiff inclination of the body, but without casting his eyes down, dismissed them. Then, turning to us with a laugh, caught up his cushions and renewed our fight.[11]

Pitt maintained throughout his life a rigid distinction between his public bearing and his private entertainment: when Napier saw him in the distance on Horseguards Parade he received a look which 'emphatically spoke . . . "pass on, this is no place for fooling."'[12] But in both spheres the strain was visible. In public people noticed his regular coughs and yellowing complexion. In private, Napier noted: 'Mr. Pitt used to come home to dinner rather exhausted, and seemed to require wine, port, of which he generally drank a bottle, or nearly so, in a rapid succession of glasses; but when he recovered his strength from this stimulant he ceased to drink.'[13] The signs of alcoholism were all too plain.

As soon as Pitt was back in Downing Street the pressures were unrelenting. On 5 June Fox himself visited Pitt in the company of Robert Livingston, the American envoy in Paris. Livingston, a well-known republican, claimed to bring a peace proposal from France, but Pitt, sceptical about further agreements with Napoleon, concluded that if the French were serious they 'would have found some less exceptionable channel of communication'.[14]

Parliamentary time was initially taken up by a further attempt by Wilberforce to achieve the gradual abolition of the slave trade theoretically agreed on by the Commons twelve years before. Once again, Pitt spoke strongly in favour of 'abolishing that inhuman traffic',[15] but the effort, endorsed by the Commons, yet again ran aground in the Lords. As ever, in the coming months Pitt considered lack of Cabinet unity and the extent of royal hostility on the question of slave-trade abolition to be too great to overcome. By the following February he was imploring Wilberforce not to make a further attempt; Wilberforce disregarded him and was defeated. To the end of his life Pitt would remain hamstrung on this issue because the people he depended on for wider support did not share his abolitionist instincts. There must have been a strong chance, however, that he could have forced the issue had he mustered the energy and time to do so.

The principal early initiative of Pitt's new ministry was the Additional Force Bill, outlined to the Commons by Pitt on the same day he met Fox to discuss peace. The Bill represented Pitt's attempt to implement the better distribution of the armed forces he had so recently and vociferously demanded from the back benches. The size of the regular army would be permanently increased and that of the militia reduced, enabling him to create a fairer system of recruiting and ultimately have greater forces available for service overseas. Since it was the only major piece of legislation the government would present in 1804 before Parliament rose for the summer, and all the opposition groupings of Fox, Grenville and Addington managed to find fault with it, the debates on the Bill became the key test of the strength of the new government. When the second reading of the Bill was carried on 5 June by only forty votes (221 to 181) it was clear that Pitt's control of Parliament would require great and regular effort. Rose's forebodings were well founded: the opposition groupings were strong in number and ruthless in behaviour, all of them harbouring their own jealousies and resentments about Pitt's return.

The record of the third reading debate on 18 June is instructive for three reasons. First, the maximum effort of the government's side and a huge turnout of MPs still produced a broadly similar result, with a majority of forty-two (265 to 223). Second, much of Pitt's own speech was defensive in the wake of incessant attacks. He not only spent considerable time defending his proposals, but felt it necessary to justify his right to be in office and to underline his determination to remain there. In complete consistency with his long-held view, he defended 'the principle, that it is the prerogative of his Majesty to choose his ministers',[16] and in a mood of defiance which echoed early 1784 he made clear that he would not take the 'broad hint' to retire. If the Bill was defeated he would 'merely treat it as the decision of this house on the dry merits of the bill'.[17] Third, his new Cabinet was too fragile for the unguarded and inflammatory language of Canning, who also spoke in that day's debate. He attacked the record of the previous administration with no regard to the fact that many of its members had been appointed to the new one. The Home Secretary, Hawkesbury, handed in his resignation, and Pitt had to turn his time and his charm to getting him to withdraw it.

Much of this was, of course, nothing more than politics as usual, but it underscored the difficulty for Pitt of meeting high expectations of a vigorous war effort when he had to spend a large amount of his time dealing with a divided Parliament and a jittery Cabinet. The Additional Force Bill would prove to be little more successful in producing the right numbers and balance of soldiers than the efforts by Addington which Pitt had so scathingly assaulted. Yet there is no doubt that Pitt's arrival in Downing Street gave a new tempo to some much-needed preparations: Melville and the Admiralty rapidly improved the navy's fighting condition, while Pitt himself oversaw improvements to the defences of south-east England.

Invasion fears once again reached fever pitch in late July when Napoleon sited himself at Boulogne. His plans for an attack on England were sufficiently advanced for the commemorative medal for the troops to be struck. Nevertheless, British skill in blockading French warships in their ports and the sudden death of a key French Admiral denied Napoleon even the briefest opportunity to cross the Channel. As he himself had put it, 'Let us be masters of the Channel for six hours, and we are masters of the world.'[18] But the Channel remained unsubdued.

As the autumn of 1804 advanced, Pitt divided his time between Downing Street and Putney Heath. The extended stays in the sea air at Walmer, which had done much to improve his health the previous year, had gone forever. His greatest preoccupation was one familiar to him from the 1790s: British forces were distinguishing themselves in the West Indies and India, but the absence of deployments and allies on the Continent of Europe meant that France could not be defeated. Pitt's notes of the time reveal his now entrenched mistrust of Napoleon's character – 'The arrogance, the presumption, the self-will of unlimited and idolized power . . . the restless and incessant activity of guilty but unsated ambition'[19] – and show his thoughts turning to the creation of a new alliance with Austria and, in particular, Russia. Britain and Russia, he thought, were 'the only Powers that for many years can have no jealousy or opposite interests'.[20]

Napoleon's proclamation of himself as hereditary Emperor, and the French kidnap and murder of the young Duc d'Enghien,* had brought Tsar Alexander to consider renewing the war against France. Throughout 1804 talks between London and St Petersburg centred on possible joint operations to expel the French from southern Italy and on the potential size of British subsidies to Russia. Given their previous experiences at the hands of Napoleon, Britain's potential allies were initially unimpressed with the £5 million Pitt set aside for all of them – Austria, Prussia and Sweden included. The importance Pitt attached to securing a Russian alliance was demonstrated that autumn when he sent Lord Granville Leveson Gower, a personal friend and the son of the Marquis of Stafford, to St Petersburg as the new ambassador. This had the additional merit of removing Leveson Gower from the clutches of an infatuated Lady Hester Stanhope, but there is no suggestion that Pitt's motives for the appointment were anything other than political.

While diplomacy moved ponderously forward – Leveson Gower

* The Bourbon Prince the Duc d'Enghien was kidnapped in neutral Baden, taken to France, tried by military court and shot. Napoleon believed, with some justification, that the Prince had been plotting a royalist insurrection. His arrest on foreign soil, and his swift execution, outraged the royal courts of Europe.

would finally secure a preliminary treaty with the Tsar in April 1805 – the war was widening closer to home. Since Napoleon looked to Spain for finance and naval assistance, British spies kept a careful watch on Spanish shipping movements. Amidst rising tension, the Cabinet decided in September to intercept a Spanish convoy in the Atlantic carrying a huge quantity of gold bullion and detain it until satisfactory assurances were received from Madrid. Such a plan was difficult to execute in practice: the Spanish ships defended themselves, unsuccessfully and with heavy loss of life, and in December Spain declared war on Britain. Pitt was unapologetic, and in Parliament the following February would adamantly defend the pre-emptive British action: 'Suppose we had suffered these two millions of treasure to go into Cadiz, and from thence, as of course it would, to the coffers of France; suppose the two fleets of France and Spain had joined ... Suppose we had come to parliament to be excused for having relaxed our efforts ... What would have been the language ... [of the opposition] if we were to throw ourselves on the lenity of the House?'[21]

War with Spain had almost certainly been inevitable, and Pitt's actions matched the aggressive spirit with which he wanted to wage the contest (as well as being true to the legacy of his father, who had left the Cabinet in 1761 over its refusal to make a pre-emptive attack on Spain). Yet they underlined the need for allies as Pitt struggled for the third time in twelve years to create a coalition against France. At the same time, he knew it was vital to strengthen the government by bringing at least one element of the opposition on board. With Portland ill, Melville past his prime and Camden sometimes timid, Pitt needed no reminding that it was important to bolster his Cabinet as well as to add to his majority. As in the early 1790s, his plan to do so did not lack ambition. From July to November 1804 he made concerted efforts to bring the Fox and Grenville parties into government either in part or in their entirety, and to achieve a parallel reconciliation of George III with the Prince of Wales. If successful, it would have amounted to nothing less than a coalition of all the bitterest enemies of the previous quarter of a century, and a coming together of almost the whole political establishment.

It was typical of Pitt to pursue such a sweeping solution, but also not unusual that his brilliant conception was frustrated by the simple inadequacies of human nature. It took all the efforts of Pitt and Eldon on the one side, and Moira and Tierney on the other, to get the King and his son to observe the barest civilities towards each other. The Prince pulled out at the last minute from a carefully arranged meeting of reconciliation in August, and withdrew from an arrangement painstakingly concocted by Pitt and Moira for the King to oversee the education of the eight-year-old Princess Charlotte, heir presumptive to the throne. It was late November before George III and the Prince actually met and were polite to each other, but the progress in their relationship had been far too slight for them to get onto the subject of bringing together their favourite politicians in some enduring rapprochement. In the absence of that, the King's veto on Fox was maintained, thereby ensuring the continued exclusion of Grenville and such figures as Spencer and Windham as well. The King, who explained that 'what he did not forget he could not forgive',[22] told Rose at the end of September that he could not 'admit Mr. Fox into his councils, even at the hazard of a civil war'.[23] Pitt attempted that autumn to pick off some of the opposition individually, as he had done with some success in 1793, offering jobs to Moira and Tierney, but in the absence of broader harmony the bait was not taken.

The failure of this renewed effort to create a broader government must have been a great disappointment to Pitt, since it maintained his precarious dependence on the health of George III and threw him back on the only other option available for the strengthening of his ministry in the short term. The King had secretly hoped that Pitt and Addington would patch up their differences: Pitt now needed the support of Addington and the roughly sixty MPs who took their lead from him. Even this was a delicate operation, requiring the revitalisation of a severed friendship and the placating of existing members of the government who would be disgusted by Addington's return to the Cabinet. Pitt steeled himself to this task in early December 1804, having put off the opening of the next session of Parliament until January. The Foreign Secretary, Harrowby, had been injured in a fall, and while Canning eagerly volunteered to take on his duties, Pitt for the moment refrained from filling the position so that he had a spare place in the Cabinet for the forthcoming negotiations.

With Hawkesbury as go-between, Pitt and Addington were brought together on 24 December, and apparently resumed their friendship with charming but suspicious ease. For all his contempt for Addington, Pitt could always respond to political necessity, and entered the room with the words 'I rejoice to take you by the hand again.'[24] In any case, Pitt probably felt little dislike of Addington as a person, but had rather been affronted by Addington becoming Prime Minister, even at his own behest. Now Pitt was careful to build a ceiling on Addington's career into the framework of their new relationship: the offer to him to join the Cabinet as President of the Council was coupled with an insistence that he go to the House of Lords. Whatever happened thereafter, Pitt would at least have removed one rival from the Commons. Addington, a less calculating and always good-natured man, eventually accepted this stipulation in return for a Cabinet post for his ally the Earl of Buckinghamshire, and promises of lesser positions for his key supporters. He was reluctant to leave the Commons, but on 14 January 1805 it was announced that, ennobled as Lord Sidmouth, he would take over from Portland as President of the Council, with Buckinghamshire becoming Chancellor of the Duchy of Lancaster in place of Mulgrave, who moved up into the vacant position of Foreign Secretary.

For the moment, Pitt's government was strengthened. Both he and Addington earnestly professed to the rest of the world the genuine nature of the reconciliation. Addington, who had probably never shaken from his psychological make-up the need for Pitt's approval, wrote that Pitt's conduct had 'convinced me that it is his ardent wish, as God knows it is mine, that past differences should be forgotten and that our future conduct may manifest perfect coincidence of opinion, and the re-establishment of former intimacy'.[25] Wilberforce found Pitt bridling at the idea that the friendship was not real, saying as they walked in St James's Park, 'I think they are a little hard upon us in finding fault with our making it up again, when we have been friends from our childhood, and our fathers were so before us, while they say nothing to Grenville for uniting with Fox, though they have been fighting all their lives.'[26]

There was no doubt something genuine in these protestations, but it would also have been impossible for either man to forget entirely the harsh words of the previous years. Pitt had only turned to Addington as a last resort, and Addington had been known to comment on Pitt's 'ungovernable passion for power and pre-eminence'.[27] Hawkesbury's warning that 'the Devil will be at work to separate you, as he was before'[28] was well founded: tension between their respective acolytes would soon resurface. Canning was deeply offended by the deal done without his knowledge, and some long-standing Pitt supporters, such as the Marquis of Stafford, who controlled half a dozen parliamentary seats, took serious umbrage. As usual it fell to Sheridan to highlight Pitt's predicament with wicked humour: 'Lest the government should become too full of vigour from his support, he thought proper to beckon back some of the weakness of the former administration . . . the administration would be too brilliant and dazzle the House, unless he called back a certain part of the mist and fog of the last administration to render it tolerable to the eye.'[29]

Pitt had done the only thing he could to give temporary strength to his government while simultaneously striving for the much-sought Russian alliance. Having set aside for the second year running the intention of going to Bath for the restoration of his health, he spent the new year constructing a response to a fresh peace overture from Napoleon. The British response stated that negotiation could only take place in consultation with other Continental powers – meaning in particular the Russians. It was followed by the despatch to Leveson Gower on 21 January 1805 of a state paper which became a cornerstone of British foreign policy, much of which was drafted in Pitt's own hand. In advocating 'At the Restoration of Peace, a general agreement and Guarantee for the mutual protection and security of the different Powers, and for reestablishing a general System of Public Law in Europe',[30] the paper built on Pitt and Grenville's ideas from the 1790s for a comprehensive solution to European wars, and was the basis, long after Pitt's death, for the British negotiating position at the end of the Napoleonic Wars. There would be a new system of 'Solidarity and Permanence' under which the main powers would protect each other against aggression; Britain and Russia would 'take an active Part' in maintaining the peace; France would be reduced to her original frontiers while the ability of the small states on her borders to resist aggression would be enhanced – Sardinia, Austria, Prussia and Holland would all gain territory in place of helpless smaller states, with Dutch independence fully re-established.

Pitt's 'Memorandum on the Deliverance and Security of Europe' has become a famous illustration of the idea of 'balance of power'. In proposing considerable territorial rearrangement he showed 'no special tenderness to nationality',[31] but typically sought a lasting and all-embracing solution to the problems which had plagued him. Once again he was demonstrating his extraordinary staying power. Beleaguered as he might be, his strengthened majority and mastery of foreign policy shows him in January 1805 to be purposeful, successful, dignified and in control. It is the last moment at which we glimpse Pitt as he wanted us to know him.

In late January 1805 a visitor to Windsor was shocked to hear the sound of loud and angry voices in the Royal Closet. Inside, Pitt and George III, who had always cloaked their many disagreements in charming and felicitous language, were engaged in a furious row. The cause was the death on 18 January of John Moore, the Archbishop of Canterbury, and the resulting need to appoint a new head of the Anglican Church. The King had long intended that Manners Sutton, the Bishop of Norwich, would be elevated to this role, and it is possible that Pitt had even agreed to this at an earlier stage. But more recently Pitt had decided to put forward his oldest friend, George Pretyman, Bishop Tomline of Lincoln and Dean of St Paul's, partly at the behest of Pretyman himself. It is hard to think that Pitt was anything other than at fault in pressing this appointment: two hundred years later such a move would certainly be denounced as 'cronyism'. Pretyman was not without his qualifications, but no one could seriously believe that Pitt would have so strongly advanced his cause had he not been a close friend.

How was it then that Pitt was so determined, and was driven to the point of fury in the King's presence, to get his way on behalf of his friend? The answer lies partly in his personal loyalty to one or two exceptional friends or relatives whom he would favour irrespective of their merits – Pretyman and Chatham being the outstanding examples. But it lies too in his attitude to patronage, in which he was careful to distinguish between political appointments such as Ministers, where a job he regarded as important needed doing, and elevations within the Church or the peerage, in which he had little interest other than as an occasional means of reinforcing his political position. Part of the power of a First Lord of the Treasury lay in his control of such patronage. He did not therefore care so much who was appointed – although in Pretyman's case he obviously did – as who dictated the appointment, for on that the credibility and standing of his administration partly depended. Pitt was therefore doubly angered that he could not only not fulfil his promise to his friend, but would also suffer a demonstration of political weakness. The King's refusal to accept his nomination defied precedent, and, Pitt complained, 'will certainly not be understood by the public, in any other light than as a decisive mark of your Majesty's not honouring him with that degree of weight and confidence which his predecessors have enjoyed'.[32] He even suggested the possibility of his resignation, but George III was no fool. Pitt could not credibly resign as Prime Minister just because he was not allowed to make his best friend the Archbishop of Canterbury. Manners Sutton became the Archbishop, and Pitt had to calm down.

There is an amusing exchange of letters among Pitt's papers which illustrates the eagerness with which Church of England Bishops sought the patronage of the First Lord of the Treasury. A new Bishop of Norwich was now required, and Pitt received the following letter from the Bishop of Bristol:

> Sir,
>
> I have heard from so many quarters that you have been kind enough to think of recommending me to His Majesty to succeed to the vacant See of Norwich that I can no longer refrain expressing my gratitude to you, if such is your intention & of informing you that by so doing, you will be conferring a lasting obligation upon me, which I shall ever have a pride in acknowledging.

Pitt replied the same day with:

> My Lord,
>
> In answer to the letter which I have just had the honour of receiving from your Lordship, I am sorry to be under the necessity of acquainting your Lordship that the Report which has reached you respecting the See of Norwich has arisen without my knowledge, and that I can not have the satisfaction of promoting your wishes.[33]

In February 1805 Pitt could at least reap some dividends from bringing the Addingtonians onto his side. Assailed by the opposition that month over the Spanish war and continued difficulties in military recruitment, he was able to beat off its attacks by far larger majorities than those of the previous summer. On 18 February he presented what would be the last of his many budgets to the Commons: another loan of £20 million and further tax increases on salt, horses, legacies, postal charges and property. Disturbingly, however, some of the more minor tax measures did not get through the House, and Pitt was sometimes tetchy in debates, at least once coming off worst to the formidable Sheridan, who launched a devastating attack on his conduct towards Addington:

> If I had come down to the house and described the noble lord as the fittest man in the country to fill the office of chancellor of the exchequer because it was a convenient step to my own safety, in retiring from a situation which I had grossly abused and which I could no longer fill with honour and security;– . . . If, when I saw an opening to my own return to power, I had entered into a combination with others, whom I meant also to betray, from the sole lust of power and office, in order to remove him;– and if . . . I had then treated with ridicule and contempt the very man whom I had before held up to the choice of my Sovereign . . . then, indeed, I should have merited the contempt and execration of all good men.[34]

Such an attack demonstrates the unremitting hostility which faced Pitt on the opposition benches. Even though the country was at war, he could expect no quarter or benefit of the doubt from them. Furthermore, their opportunity to strike him hard was at last arriving. On 18 March Wilberforce was with Pitt when he received an envelope he had been anxiously awaiting. 'I shall never forget', recorded Wilberforce 'the way in which he seized it, and how eagerly he looked into the leaves without waiting even to cut them open.'[35]

The document in question was the Tenth Report of the Commission of Naval Inquiry. This wide-ranging inquiry into the management of the navy had been set up by Earl St Vincent in 1802, and had so far published a series of worthy but fairly innocuous reports. The Tenth Report, however, contained direct and serious criticism of the conduct of Dundas, now Lord Melville, as Treasurer of the Navy in the 1790s in Pitt's earlier administration. It transpired that Alexander Trotter, the Admiralty Paymaster, had used funds intended for the navy in his private transactions, albeit without any eventual loss to the public purse. Melville, it seemed, had turned a blind eye to these practices and might sometimes, albeit unwittingly, have been in possession of some of the money in question himself.

Speculation by Ministers with public money had been commonplace in the mid-eighteenth century, as noted in earlier chapters. Rules were enacted against this in the 1780s, and by 1805 the Treasury's more effective management of funds had rendered it extremely difficult. Trotter, and Melville by implication, had been caught between the corrupt standards of one generation and the particular rules of the next, rather like Italian politicians arraigned in the late twentieth century for misdemeanours which had only just ceased to be widespread. For all the fact that Melville had been burdened with far weightier responsibilities at the time, and had almost certainly not knowingly or actually defrauded anyone, opposition politicians sensed a chance to do great damage to the ministry. The motion tabled for debate on 8 April 1805 by the radical MP Samuel Whitbread attacked Melville for acting 'in a manner inconsistent with his duty, and incompatible with those securities which the legislature has provided for the proper application of the public money'.[36]

Melville had many enemies, among them not only the entire opposition but many of the Addingtonians who were now technically supporters of Pitt's government, for he had made no secret in the later stages of Addington's ministry of his view that its removal was essential. Nor could he rely on the support of independently-minded MPs who would weigh the matter on its merits. For Pitt, the affair must have had echoes of the row over the Archbishop of Canterbury only weeks before: if Melville were driven from office he would lose a Minister who had been a close friend and an almost indispensable member of his previous government, but it would also be a savage blow to the standing of the government he now led.

An utterly ruthless man would have thrown Melville to the wolves, shielding the rest of the government by forcing his resignation. Pitt could certainly be ruthless, and he abhorred financial irregularity, but he was also loyal to friends and too proud to give the opposition a victory. He decided to tough it out, taking the debate himself and defending his friend. Pitt may also have acted from a feeling of guilt, if a letter he had written twenty years earlier had lodged in his memory. As it happened, the services of Alexander Trotter had been recommended to Dundas by Pitt himself, at the instigation of Thomas Coutts. Pitt had written to Coutts in December 1785: 'I have taken an opportunity of mentioning Mr. Trotter's name to Mr. Dundas, as a person of whose character I had heard a very respectable testimony.'[37] No one else may have known it, but the person who had landed Dundas with the problem was Pitt himself.

It is not surprising that the defence of financial irregularities did not come easily to Pitt. In place of the vote of censure, he proposed that the matter be referred to a Select Committee, as the Commission of Inquiry had not been able to conduct anything like a fair trial. He pointed to clear errors in the Report as evidence of the need for further investigation, and argued that 'no defalcation, any mischief, any evil whatever' had resulted from the admittedly improper use of money. It was a manful effort, but a far cry from his ringing speeches on Irish Union or slavery, or declarations of war. Some observers thought it 'miserable – his powers of language even seemed to fail him in this worst of causes'.[38] Towards the end of the debate, Wilberforce rose and Pitt turned to face him. 'It required no little effort', Wilberforce recalled, 'to resist the fascination of that penetrating eye,'[39] but resist it he did, placing, as ever, his conscience ahead of his friends in declaring his support for Whitbread's motion. The outcome was now impossible to predict.

The vote took place in the early hours of 9 April, when the Speaker announced that there were 216 Ayes and 216 Noes. Ten minutes later a highly agitated Speaker gave his casting vote against Pitt, censuring Melville and defeating the government. Melville would have to resign.

For Pitt this was a moment of despair. For all politicians, longevity in office requires ever more energy to be consumed in defending the errors of the past, and in keeping at bay the ever-expanding ranks of the jealous, the offended and the impatient. Pitt was beginning to pay the price of his long career, and of loyalty to close friends, while neglecting to cultivate a wider circle of followers. One of his supporters, Lord Fitzharris, noted:

> I sat wedged close to Pitt himself the night when we were 216 to 216; and the Speaker, Abbott (after looking as white as a sheet, and pausing for ten minutes), gave the casting vote against us. Pitt immediately put on the little cocked hat that he was in the habit of wearing when dressed for the evening, and jammed it deeply over his forehead, and I distinctly saw the tears trickling down his cheeks. We had overheard one or two, such as Colonel Wardle (of notorious memory) say they would see 'how Billy looked after it.' A few young ardent followers of Pitt, with myself, locked their arms together, and formed a circle, in which he moved, I believe unconsciously, out of the House; and neither the Colonel nor his friends could approach him.[40]

It was a time of intense pressure. Pitt would now face fresh motions for Melville's name to be struck from the Privy Council and criminal prosecutions to be commenced. Addington (now Sidmouth), enraged by Pitt's defence of Melville and continued closeness to him, was contemplating resignation from the Cabinet. And in the meantime a war was going on: while Pitt waited anxiously for news from St Petersburg, a group of French warships managed to get out of Toulon and enter the Atlantic. Pitt's health was crumbling. Once again that Easter plans to visit Bath had to be abandoned. 'Every public event of importance which crowded on Mr. Pitt's mind', said Farquhar, 'produced a corresponding effect upon the body, and I felt it my duty frequently to urge the necessity of his retiring from public business altogether, but Mr. Pitt's memorable reply was, that his Country needed his Services, and he would rather prefer to die at his Post, than desert it.'[41]

27
Too Many Enemies

'England has saved herself by her exertions and will, as I trust, save Europe by her example.'

WILLIAM PITT, NOVEMBER 1805

EVEN THOUGH Britain was at war and the Armée d'Angleterre remained threateningly encamped at Boulogne, the spring of 1805 was a time of intense partisanship in British politics. In Malmesbury's view: 'The transactions relative to Lord Melville exceeded in party spirit and savage feeling all that I ever recollect in this country.'[1] Almost alone among the opposition, Grenville stayed aloof from a controversy which would 'add to the distractions of the country when the very foundations of its safety are shaken both within and without'.[2] The strong feelings were manifested not only between government and opposition, but within the ranks of the government itself, since the evident relish with which some of the Addingtonians attacked Melville, and Pitt's continuing warmth towards him, once again placed Pitt and Sidmouth on a course of conflict.

Sidmouth resented Pitt's friendship with 'a certain person [Canning] who is more imprudent and obnoxious than ever . . . and allowed to appear in the House of Commons more and more as the prochain ami',[3] and tried to urge Pitt – who showed little sign of wishing to discuss the matter with him – to fulfil earlier commitments to him by bringing Buckinghamshire into the Admiralty in Melville's place. Pitt, however, was now in no mood to reward Sidmouth's faction, and besides placed such importance on the Admiralty that he was determined to appoint a naval expert in whom he had confidence. His choice fell on the ageing Sir Charles Middleton, who as Comptroller of the Navy had been instrumental in introducing many improvements to its efficiency during Pitt's first administration. Elevated to the peerage as Lord Barham he now duly joined the Cabinet, to Sidmouth's distress and fury. After only three months back in government, Sidmouth considered this 'decisive proof that my continuance in office could neither be useful to the public, nor honourable to myself'.[4]

Pitt's patience with Sidmouth was probably already wearing thin, but, needing his support for the government at least for the moment, he embarked on damage limitation. He assured Sidmouth of his continued friendship, promised that Middleton's appointment would only be temporary, and, in Sidmouth's words, 'that every allowance would be made for the peculiar situation of my friends on many questions that might arise, and every consideration shown to their just and admitted pretensions'.[5] In other words, places in the government would eventually be found for Sidmouth's key supporters, and in the meantime they would be given some leeway on controversial issues. Since the use of that leeway, by Hiley Addington and others, to continue to attack Melville's conduct would make Pitt even more reluctant to admit any of them into the government, this was a compromise agreement which had self-destruction written into its terms.

Pitt's troubles and embarrassment over Melville were not over with the Commons defeat and Melville's consequent resignation. When the House returned from its Easter recess, opposition MPs were in full cry for the impeachment or prosecution of Melville, for his removal from the Privy Council, and for a Select Committee to examine those parts of the report not relevant to a prosecution. Pitt had to handle the tortuous business of determining the terms of reference and the membership of the Committee – matters on which he managed to restore respectable government majorities. But on substantive issues concerning Melville he was in trouble, unable to rely on the Addingtonians or independents such as Wilberforce. He faced possible defeat on 6 May on the question of striking Melville's name from the Privy Council, and finally, putting the survival of his government ahead of loyalty to his friend (who himself advised Pitt to give way), announced that he had already, 'however reluctantly from private feeling, deemed it incumbent on me to propose the erasure of the noble lord's name from the list of privy councillors'. He went on to confess that he 'certainly felt a deep and bitter pang in being compelled to be the instrument of rendering still more severe the punishment of the noble lord. This is a feeling of which I am not ashamed. It is a feeling which I will not, which I cannot erase from my bosom. It is a feeling that nothing but my conviction of the opinion of parliament, and my sense of public duty could possibly have overcome.'[6]

Pitt regarded Melville not only as a long-standing friend but as one of the greatest servants of the nation. The action he had to take against him, and the knowledge that there would be more to come, seems to have distressed him deeply. Yet the way in which he bit his tongue with Sidmouth and deferred to the Commons demonstrates his instinct for political survival. Furthermore, he went on to deal patiently and courteously, for days at a time even at the height of a war, with accusations in a further Commission Report that he had himself been party to illegal transactions. He was questioned by the Commissioners of Inquiry on six occasions in May, and briefly the opposition had some hopes of following up its destruction of Melville with the ensnaring of Pitt himself. For a man whose reputation was built on integrity and financial probity, a great deal was at stake. The most difficult matter to explain was the issuing in 1796 of 'navy bills', a form of government debt raised by the Admiralty, without parliamentary approval and for the securing of money which was then put to secret purposes. Pitt had actually used the money as part of a complex transaction to maintain the ability of a key banker to provide government debt at a time when the Bank of England was coming under strain. By setting out the facts of the case, setting up a further Select Committee to examine the handling of such situations and arguing strongly to the Commons that the 'violation of law' was 'justifiable by the particular circumstances of the case',[7] he extricated himself from the controversy. Even Fox thought it only 'a slight delinquency'.[8] Pitt's integrity was intact, but his time, energy and health were being consumed.

Beset as he was by these difficulties, and living all the more an unhealthy life of irregular eating, inadequate sleep, constant meetings and an all too adequate supply of alcohol, Pitt retained his mental acuity and tactical good sense. Several illustrations of this were provided by the decision of Fox and Grenville to seek to embarrass the embattled Pitt by moving for Catholic emancipation, the very issue on which he had resigned four years earlier. Their motion, which went down to a heavy defeat on 13 May, caused Pitt little difficulty although it certainly took up more of his time. His conduct when he met a delegation of Irish Catholics to discuss the matter was impeccable and impressive. Although one of his visitors recalled him to be wearing 'dirty boots, and old fashioned lank leather breaches', he was 'otherwise well dressed & cleanly, his hair powdered etc.' His eyes were still 'very busy and speaking' although now 'bad and ill-coloured', and his speech 'very direct and distinct'. He was civil but straightforward, and explained politely that the proper time for emancipation had not arrived. After telling them candidly that he would have to oppose the measure if it were brought up, he saw them to the hall 'bowing and smiling all the way'.[9] When it came to the debate, he did not attempt any contorted logic to explain why he was now opposed to something he had previously resigned over favouring, simply making it clear that 'I remain this day of that opinion,'[10] but that he had discovered the issue to be so controversial that if brought forward now 'it would only tend to revive those animosities which I wished to extinguish'.[11] The Fox–Grenville attack made no headway.

Recollections of the Catholic debate furnished a further illustration of how the teenage orator and memoriser of the 1770s was still living on in the battered Prime Minister of 1805. The debate marked the Commons debut of the fiery Irish leader Henry Grattan, who exhibited a speaking style highly demonstrative and unusual in the Commons. Fitzharris recalled that at supper afterwards, Pitt 'gave us some specimens of passages in Grattan's speech, in which the correctness of Pitt's powers of imitation, both as regarded the tone and action of the speaker, was very striking, but almost less so than the display that it afforded us of the capability of his retentive memory. Whole sentences to our ears appeared to be repeated verbatim, and to have been conveyed without the loss of even an article from St. Stephen's to Downing

Street.'[12] In company at least, Pitt retained his good humour and his dominance over colleagues. A few months later Malmesbury would find his explanation of the intricacies of European diplomacy 'most minute and clear',[13] and the painter Thomas Lawrence, who saw Pitt at a gathering of Cabinet colleagues, noticed that 'all seemed to be impressed with an awe of him. At times it appeared like Boys with their Master.'[14]

While these essential attributes of Pitt's leadership remained intact, there is no doubt that the intense demands made on his weakened constitution exacerbated his long-standing vices. Wilberforce, who struggled for months to get Pitt to make an Order in Council ending the traffic in slaves to conquered Guiana – this was eventually done in September 1805, along with a prohibition on the importation of slaves to all conquered territories – considered that Pitt's 'procrastination . . . has increased to such a degree as to have become absolutely predominant'.[15] His correspondence was seriously neglected, lying around in Downing Street or Walmer unattended to or even unopened. Pitt could not find the time to attend to his friends: one letter from Pretyman begins 'we have been all greatly mortified and surprised at not hearing from you', and another from Wellesley in India 'I have some reason to complain of your silence'; Camden complained to Malmesbury of 'Pitt's want of little attentions'.[16] When his private secretary William Dacres Adams asked Hester Stanhope to send some papers up from Walmer Castle she found them 'in great confusion', and added, 'I wish you would ask him some day if he would like me to bring any more to town when I come, for at this moment perhaps it is difficult to say what are there he may want.'[17] Pitt was simply too busy and now too tired to deal with anything he regarded as trifling, and he was more and more often in bed all morning – although frequently after sitting up all night in the Commons – and unwilling to do paperwork in the evenings. Stamina, adrenalin and willpower had always carried him through the spring and summer, the season of parliamentary sittings, while he held office. By the summer of 1805 he was managing to keep going, but he no longer had the energy or the time to oversee the work of the Cabinet in the manner of his earlier years.

The pressures of both parliamentary politics and international events early in the summer of 1805 were immense, and Pitt's popularity in the country had declined. William Dacres Adams managed to save one letter from an infuriated member of the public which adopts a tone familiar to politicians of the present day, expressed in the language of that time:

> I say Billy,
>
> You infernal Blackguardly Son of a Thief . . . You Bottle Nosed . . . Rascal Prime Minister egad my Old Buck you'll be getting alongside of the Devil soon but he'll shave your Timbers for you and give you a Broadside and send you – but he will not send you to Windsor to drink 3 bottles of Wine after Dinner . . . while many a Poor thing cannot get Bread and all through you . . . and all because you suppose if there is any Riot you can call upon the Volunteers to aid and abet you . . . you meagre looking hound . . .[18]

As further difficult debates about Melville loomed and relations with some of the Addingtonians worsened, Pitt had to focus his mind on a tense military and diplomatic scene. In June, the French squadron which had escaped into the Mediterranean had still not been detected: Nelson had taken twelve ships of the line to the Caribbean in the search for it. The question of where the French warships would reappear or attempt to congregate was a vital one, since any loss or interruption of British command of the Channel would give Napoleon the opportunity to invade England after two years of waiting.

At the same time, Pitt maintained his tireless effort to create a new coalition against France, obstructed by the long delays in communicating across the length of Europe as well as by a good deal of military caution and mercenary haggling on the part of prospective allies. Leveson Gower agreed a preliminary treaty with Russia on 11 April, but it took over a month for news of it to reach Downing Street and it was dependent on the involvement of Austria and Prussia, contained outstanding differences over Malta, and would come into operation only after a Russian effort to achieve peaceful agreement with France. Austria was wavering and demanding heavy subsidies, Sweden likewise, and Prussia was interested in acquiring from the French possession of

George III's Electorate of Hanover – something which Pitt thought it neither right nor possible to concede.

It was Napoleon himself who was to startle the Austrian and Russian courts out of lumbering negotiations and into wholehearted alliance with Britain. His annexation of Genoa in early June along with the granting of Lucca as a fiefdom to his sister, and his assumption of the title of King of Italy, all spoke more powerfully of the need for a new alliance than any entreaties by Pitt. Yet it would be September before signatures were in place and armies beginning to move, and even then Prussia remained tantalisingly indecisive. Pitt therefore had nothing concrete to tell the Commons before they rose for the summer in July, although he did take the precaution of asking for authority to pay out £3.5 million in foreign subsidies.

Necessarily kept in the dark about foreign affairs, the Commons busied itself with domestic acrimony. Melville gave a two-hour defence of his conduct at the Bar of the House of Commons, insisting that the money in question had never been used to provide him with a personal profit. As with Warren Hastings nearly twenty years before, the Commons was unimpressed by a defiant defence, in this case of something it had already censured. In some confusion, MPs voted against impeaching Melville but in favour of his prosecution, a verdict overturned two weeks later in favour of impeachment. Pitt was relieved that Melville would be tried by his peers rather than in the courts, but the process of arriving at this conclusion had ruptured once and for all his political association with Sidmouth. Sidmouth had favoured the harder line of prosecution, and his brother Hiley and other acolytes had spoken for it publicly in vengeful terms. To Pitt, this made it impossible to reward Sidmouth's supporters with the promised places in the government, and to Sidmouth in turn this meant that it was impossible to remain in the Cabinet.

By this stage, the parliamentary session had only days to run, and Pitt could afford to lose Sidmouth and his followers if he could broaden his government in other ways during the recess. His mind had turned back to what he had wanted in the first place: the incorporation of the Grenville and Fox parties into the ministry. Canning told his wife that he had urged, and Pitt had promised, 'expedition in making overtures'.[19] Having made use of Sidmouth for six months, Pitt was happy to discard him, as Sidmouth himself ascertained perfectly easily after a fruitless meeting with Pitt instigated by the King: 'It is evident to me that he has a connection with opposition in his view, and that he is desirous of maintaining that sort of relation with me and my friends, which without hampering him in any way, may be very convenient for the purpose of negotiation.'[20]

Pitt knew he was prepared to lose Sidmouth, but he could not know for sure that he could construct an alternative coalition, however meticulously he prepared for it. In both military affairs and domestic politics he would increasingly be operating throughout the rest of 1805 on a wing and a prayer, despatching forces to Europe in the expectation of an alliance with Prussia but without its confirmation, and failing to take any steps to win the continued support of Sidmouth even though there was far from any certainty that Grenville and Fox could be recruited. In his ambition and optimism he remained the man he had been when he first became Prime Minister, when he had incurred serious defeats on parliamentary reform and the Irish propositions because he could envisage and design his eventual objective but not be sure of winning sufficient support to get there. What is more, the fulfilment of one hope became dependent on the other, since Pitt believed that the creation of a European alliance which included Prussia would be so much in accordance with Grenville's views that it would be possible to bring at least his part of the opposition into the government.

With Pitt unwilling to promote any of Sidmouth's adherents, and additionally and provocatively unwilling to express any regrets about that position, Sidmouth resigned from the government after a further conversation with Pitt on 4 July 1805. Sidmouth left office offended by Pitt's haughty and distant attitude and mystified by his parting remarks. He recorded that when he asked Pitt if his conduct had been in any way improper, 'the latter holding out his hand, replied, with tears in his eyes: "Never: I have nothing to acknowledge from you but the most generous and honourable conduct, and I grieve that we are to part!"'[21] Such a remark probably reflected a mixture of sincerity and calculation: Pitt's real anger was directed at Sidmouth's friends, and additionally he did not want him to go out into automatic opposition.

Fox thought it was typically incompetent of Sidmouth to resign too late in the session to make any immediate difference in Parliament, but hoped that the resignation 'may do great good, as furnishing evidence of the impossibility of Pitt's going on with any set of Ministers who are not his own mere creatures and tools'.[22]

Pitt made up for the resignations of Sidmouth and Buckinghamshire by shuffling the chairs in his existing Cabinet in order to have sufficient placemen available for dismissal in the event of his being able to recruit the more talented Ministers he had in mind. Camden became President of the Council, Castlereagh took on the War Department as well as the Board of Control, and Harrowby came back from his illness to be Chancellor of the Duchy of Lancaster. Pitt was prepared to offer six places in the Cabinet to the opposition, and Canning found him in July to be fully intent on creating a broader government, and that 'nothing ever was more cordial & comfortable than P. He really seems to have shaken a weight off his mind, & to have a pleasure in opening himself fully on all subjects.'[23]

Events would prove, however, that Pitt had let Sidmouth go too easily, and that the broader government he sought would come up against precisely the same obstacles against which it had foundered in May of the previous year. Grenville now felt bound to Fox, and to the principle of all the most talented figures in the country being invited to join the government, and on this point rebuffed Pitt's initial approaches through their mutual friend Bathurst. While Fox renewed his disclaimer of office if the rest of the opposition wished to go in without him, his colleagues did not find this acceptable, and he was not prepared to serve in a government with Pitt at the head of it. The positions of Fox and Pitt in 1805 were therefore identical to the ones they had adopted in 1784: Pitt would only have Fox in a subsidiary capacity, and Fox could only serve with Pitt on an equal basis. What really made the project a hopeless one was that George III also held to his position of 1784: on no account did he want Fox in the government at all, and he was now happy to extend this veto to Grenville.

It was late September when George III finally dashed any hopes Pitt might have had of creating a broad coalition. Pitt had waited until he had the opportunity to talk to the King at length and in person, visiting him at his summer residence in Weymouth. He had no doubt hoped to have some more constructive signals from the opposition by this point, and he was conscious of the need to tread carefully with a King who was not only mentally fragile but also failing physically, steadily going blind and already without the use of one eye. When Rose arrived in Weymouth and spoke to the King on 22 September, it was clear that Pitt would not get his way:

> His Majesty then told me that Mr. Pitt had made very strong representations to him of the necessity of strengthening his government by the accession of persons from the parties of Lord Grenville and Mr. Fox, but that he was persuaded there existed no necessity whatever for such a junction; that we did very well in the last session, and he was confident we should not be worse in the ensuing one; that affairs on the Continent wore a good appearance, and that, at least, it was desirable to see how they would turn out . . . I observed to his Majesty that there would be an unavoidable necessity in the next session of Parliament to resort to new and extraordinary measures of taxation, which would put our force in the House of Commons to a very different test from anything that had passed in the last session . . . I was perfectly convinced, if Mr. Pitt should be confined by the gout, or any other complaint, for only two or three weeks, there would be an end of us . . . I had not the good fortune, however, to make any impression whatever on His Majesty.[24]

All in all, George III had formed a 'positive determination . . . against admitting a single man from the Opposition into Government'.[25] Pitt was very disappointed, notwithstanding the immense difficulties of creating a coalition even had the King been agreeable. In despair for the prospects of the government a few months later he would say to Melville: 'I wish the King may not live to repent, and sooner than he thinks, the rejection of the advice which I pressed on him at Weymouth.'[26] Yet, as ever, he was prepared to carry on if necessary, despite the lack of allies and his failing health. He had evidently had a 'violent cold and rheumatism'[27] in early July, and when he generously called on Sidmouth on 29 September to sympathise over the severe illness of his young son Henry, Sidmouth wrote that 'Pitt looked tolerably well, but had been otherwise.'[28] Whatever his physical state, Pitt was left placing his hopes for parliamentary survival on showing clear progress in the war. In a letter to Harrowby he said that the government simply had to 'prepare to fight the Battle as well as We can'.[29] And as it happened, some of the most decisive battles of history were now only weeks away.

In the summer of 1805, the naval war became fast-moving and dangerous. Nelson's anxious search for the French fleet which had entered the Atlantic in April took him to the West Indies and back on a journey of over 6,600 miles in a little over two months. The French ships, reinforced by the Spanish, eventually ended up back in port at Ferrol, but the anxiety of the British at this pattern of events was nothing compared to the coming rage of Napoleon. The French plan had been for a much larger force, including the French warships blockaded in Brest, to congregate in the West Indies, draw in that direction as many British forces as possible, and then descend on the English Channel to cover the full-scale French invasion of England. But by the time the French Admiral Villeneuve arrived at Ferrol, Nelson was on his way back from the West Indies, and the ships at Brest had never got out at all. Ordered by Napoleon to nonetheless make for Brest and create a powerful combined fleet, Villeneuve found a British squadron in the way and sailed back to Ferrol and then to Cadiz. This move wrecked all prospect of threatening British command of the Channel that summer and left Napoleon in a fury. Pacing up and down at Boulogne on 13 August, he denounced 'that bloody fool Villeneuve' and tore into the apparently useless condition of his navy.

Abandoning the invasion plan he had cherished for over two years, Napoleon prepared instead to turn the full force of his military power and strategic ability against the Austrians who were now mobilising in the east. It was not, of course, immediately apparent in Britain that the French army at Boulogne was marching away, and in any case it was necessary to neutralise the large force of French and Spanish warships now concentrated at Cadiz. Nelson, who had returned briefly to Britain, was instructed to resume the Mediterranean command, with the objective of seeking battle with the French and Spanish fleet. During his brief stay in London he made arrangements for his name to be engraved on his coffin lid (made from the timbers of *L'Orient*, the French flagship destroyed at the Nile), and also called on Pitt at Downing Street. Six weeks before the Battle of Trafalgar, and both nearing the end of their lives, the long-serving Prime Minister and the renowned Admiral sat together and discussed how to defeat the enemy force at Cadiz. Nelson promised Pitt a victory not merely 'honourable to the parties concerned', but one that would 'bring Buonaparte to his marrow bones'.[30] Afterwards he told his family that 'Mr. Pitt paid me a compliment which, I believe, he would not have paid to a Prince of the Blood. When I rose to go, he left the room with me and attended me to the carriage.'[31]

Nelson left Portsmouth on HMS *Victory* on 16 September, by which time Napoleon, conducting one of the most dramatic of his legendary forced marches, was about to cross the Rhine with almost 200,000 men. His objective was simple: to shatter the Third Coalition almost the moment it was formed.

If the forces were set down on paper, the French, as so often in the 1790s, were at a serious disadvantage. French aggression and 'Pitt's gold' had brought Russia, Austria and Sweden into alliance with Britain, with Prussia still open to offers. Some 400,000 allied troops were stirring into action from the Adriatic to the Baltic. The French would be, Pitt noted, 'attacked in all Quarters from Italy to the Elbe'.[32] There would be a major Austrian offensive in northern Italy, and on their right an Austro-Russian army would proceed down the Danube, through southern Germany and into France. Additional Russian forces would advance further north, link up with Swedish forces in Pomerania and also unite with a small British force in Corfu to secure southern Italy. With the exception of this small Mediterranean expedition, and an army of six thousand men sent to recapture the Cape of Good Hope, Pitt and the Cabinet decided to concentrate all other available British forces on a landing in north Germany of up to 65,000 men. Pitt was no doubt conscious that the many British colonial conquests in the 1790s had failed to bring France to her knees; he would now concentrate as much of a land force as Britain could muster on joining in a series of decisive blows against France itself. A large British army in Germany would have the added benefits of encouraging Prussian participation in the war, and directly helping to free Hanover and Holland from French control, both of which were prime British objectives. In October, Harrowby would be despatched by Pitt to Berlin with an offer of £2.5 million in return for active Prussian participation in the war, without which there would be a big hole in the plan. But by the end of October a Prussian declaration of war against France was regarded as 'almost inevitable'.[33]

Pitt's strategy has been criticised for faults similar to those which hamstrung his previous efforts to defeat the French. The British army was still undermanned for what was being asked of it, since Pitt's recruiting measures initiated the previous summer had been no more successful than those of the Addington ministry, and it was in any case more difficult to transport such a large force to north Germany than the plans assumed it to be. More seriously, some historians have considered the small size of the force sent to the Mediterranean as evidence of Pitt's 'incurable fault of frittering away his military force in small detachments'.[34] It is true that, once again, Pitt was to some extent disposing of his forces in order to bring allies into play. Yet it is also true that those allies were essential, and that the strategy adopted in 1805 envisaged a far stronger concentration of force than Pitt had employed before. It is highly doubtful that a much larger army operating in the Mediterranean would have had any decisive effect, and it would of course have been exposed to attack en route by the powerful enemy naval force with which Nelson was hoping to deal. A fair conclusion must be that Pitt showed in 1805 that he had learnt some important strategic lessons; the weak points in the Third Coalition were the continued indecision in Berlin and the perennial difficulty of coordinating disparate forces spread around Europe against an enemy who could move between them at remarkable speed.

The collision of immense forces was now inevitable. The Emperor Francis of Austria and Tsar Alexander of Russia were themselves taking the field at the head of huge armies to fight Napoleon. In late October,

Pitt was 'in great spirits' as he continued to hope for Prussian involvement. Having set all the wheels of war in motion, and with Parliament in recess, he was able to make short visits to Walmer and to Lord Bathurst's house in Gloucestershire.

Since these were the last occasions on which he was observed at ease, many of those who spent time with him subsequently recorded their impressions. Almost incredibly, he seems to have retained the sanguine temper and pleasant disposition of his youth. Sir Arthur Wellesley, the future Duke of Wellington, saw Pitt twice that autumn and remarked that he was 'extremely lively, and in good spirits', riding up to twenty miles a day, 'but it was at that time the fashion to sup, and he . . . took a great deal of port-wine and water'.[35] Lord Fitzharris, who was with Pitt in Gloucestershire, remembered that 'nothing could be more playful, and, at the same time, more instructive, than Pitt's conversation on a variety of subjects while sitting in the library at Cirencester. You never would have guessed that the man before you was Prime Minister of the country, and one of the greatest that ever filled that situation. His style and manner were quite those of an accomplished idler.'[36] William Dacres Adams remarked that even with 'almost the whole weight of the government on his own Shoulders – so delightful was his temper, that . . . no hard word or look ever escaped him, but all towards me was kindness and indulgence',[37] and Lord Eldon, who asked Pitt whether he thought men in general were honourable or corrupt, received the answer 'that he had a favourable opinion of mankind upon the whole, and that he believed that the majority was really actuated by fair meaning and intention'.[38]

Such freedom from bitterness would now be put to its final test.

When Malmesbury dined with Pitt on 2 November 1805 he found him unwilling to give credit to reports of the surrender of an entire Austrian army to Napoleon. As Malmesbury put it: 'I clearly perceived he disbelieved it more from the dread of its being true, than from any well grounded cause. He . . . almost peevishly said, "don't believe a word of it, it is all a fiction,"' and 'in so loud a voice as to be heard by all who were near us'.[39] But the following day Mulgrave and Pitt came to

Malmesbury with a Dutch newspaper of which, it being a Sunday, they could not obtain a translation. It was therefore Malmesbury who broke the terrible news: Napoleon's rapid advance had surprised and isolated the army of General Mack, who had not only suffered heavy losses but also surrendered at Ulm with 30,000 troops. The road to Vienna was now open to the French. To Malmesbury, Pitt's reaction 'left an indelible impression on my mind, as his manner and look were not his own, and gave me, in spite of myself, a foreboding of the loss with which we were threatened'.[40]

It was a sharp setback, and by mid-November Napoleon was residing in the Habsburg Palace at Schönbrunn. Yet Napoleon had taken a strategic risk, trespassing on Prussian territory in order to accelerate his march to the east, and leaving extended lines of communication at the mercy of massive allied armies if Prussia were to join the war. In the meantime, the Tsar had arrived in Berlin to an enthusiastic welcome, with Russia and Prussia signing an agreement which would bring Prussia into the war against France by the middle of December if mediation did not succeed. For Britain, the vexing problem of Hanover remained, since its acquisition by Prussia was part and parcel of the deal with the Tsar, but Napoleon nevertheless faced the prospect of an encircling ring of enemies with 180,000 Prussian troops about to join the opposing camp.

The week which began with the news of Ulm on Sunday, 3 November would come to encapsulate the story of Pitt's struggle against France. The news of Ulm was all too representative of Napoleon's ability to outmarch and outfight any other force on the Continent of Europe, but the rest of the week would bring reports of Britain developing an unchallenged dominion of the seas, and would culminate in Pitt's single most famous speech of defiance and inspiration. For in the early hours of Thursday, 7 November, news reached London of a huge naval battle fought on 21 October off Cape Trafalgar in south-west Spain.

The combined fleet of French and Spanish warships had left Cadiz bound for the Mediterranean, but had been intercepted by Nelson and attacked by his fleet in a daring and unconventional formation. In the ensuing action the largest fleet at Napoleon's disposal had been destroyed. The despatch of Admiral Collingwood reported 'twenty sail of the line captured . . . The most decisive and complete victory that ever was gained over a powerful enemy.'[41] It was the Nile all over again, but this time on twice the scale, and it would open more than a century of British naval supremacy. Nelson, who had sent to his fleet perhaps the most famous signal in the annals of the Royal Navy – 'England expects that every man will do his duty' – had given Pitt the crushing victory he had promised him in Downing Street, but had lost his own life in the process. Pitt was wakened with the news, and later that month Fitzharris noted his reflections:

> I shall never forget the eloquent manner in which he described his conflicting feelings when roused in the night to read Collingwood's despatches. Pitt observed, that he had been called up at various hours in his eventful life by the arrival of news of various hues; but that whether good or bad he could always lay his head on his pillow and sink into sound sleep again. On this occasion, however, the great event announced brought with it so much to weep over as well as to rejoice at, that he could not calm his thoughts; but at length got up, though it was three in the morning.[42]

In Britain, naval victories have always brought forth tumultuous rejoicing, and Trafalgar, the greatest of them all, was no exception. The scenes as Pitt travelled to the annual Lord Mayor's Banquet at the Guildhall on the Saturday night, 9 November, were reminiscent of those at the peaks of his popularity in 1784 and 1789. His carriage was hauled along by exultant crowds, and once inside he was toasted by the Lord Mayor as 'the Saviour of Europe'. Arthur Wellesley considered that 'he returned thanks in one of the best and neatest speeches I ever heard in my life'.[43] It must have been one of Pitt's shortest speeches, and it has certainly become the most famous:

> I return you many thanks for the honour you have done me; but Europe is not to be saved by any single man. England has saved herself by her exertions, and will, as I trust, save Europe by her example.

This simple, dignified but uplifting speech was the culmination of an entire lifetime of speech-making. It was to be the last time his voice would be heard in public.

According to Wellesley, Pitt did not seem ill that evening, and indeed bullied the opposition MP Thomas Erskine out of making a partisan speech during the course of the meal; but all was not well behind the scenes. According to Farquhar: 'In the months of October and November 1805 he suffered much from an Increase of his usual pains in the Stomach and in the Head – the loss of Appetite, with the addition of flying pains in his feet and limbs.' Farquhar urged him to go to Bath, 'but he would not leave Town where anxious business detained him. At this period indeed, with the encreasing Symptoms of disease, an accumulation of public business appeared to overpower him.'[44]

Pitt was waiting anxiously for news from Harrowby in Berlin, himself about to suffer some kind of breakdown under the extreme stress and difficulty of the negotiations. On the face of it, the prospects were still good, and the Prussians were actively discussing military dispositions and the coordination of their plans with the British, even as the issue of Hanover remained unresolved. Pitt was still optimistic: he wrote to Canning the day of the news of Trafalgar that Europe could still be saved by the end of the year. The continuing absence of a decision by Frederick William III, however, began to wear on the nerves of Ministers as November progressed: the Cabinet was evidently very troubled by the continuing lack of an agreement with Berlin at its meeting on 23 November. The uncertainty bore heavily on Pitt, for both the prospects for military victory and the recruitment of additional domestic support for the government depended a great deal on a Prussian alliance. In the absence of the latter, he was being pestered by Canning for promotion to the Cabinet, and at the end of November he decided to bring both Canning and Charles Yorke into the Cabinet to strengthen its ability in the House of Commons.

Canning had also joined Farquhar in urging Pitt to take the waters at Bath – after Farquhar had prescribed 'gentle bitters with Rhubarb and Magnesia' Pitt had 'again rallied but only for a short time'. Once again suffering from gout, he agreed to go to Bath to try to recover his health before the opening of the next session of Parliament in January. A suitable house was found for him at 2 Johnson Street, and he left London on 7 December. As is inevitable when a Prime Minister moves location for some weeks during a major crisis, many others followed. Pitt had numerous visitors – Canning, Melville, Mulgrave and Hawkesbury – who came to him to transact official business but also to provide company and humour. While he was still 'counting moments'[45] for news from Berlin, Mulgrave and Canning tried to occupy him with correcting their verses celebrating the Battle of Trafalgar. Canning recorded that it was 'a great comfort to have happened to contribute so much to his amusement, and his criticisms have really helped me a great deal in amending & perfecting the Poem'.[46] For much of December the efforts to restore Pitt's health appeared to go to plan. He had to be careful about the times at which he visited the Pump Room, because a large crowd would form in expectation of his appearance, but he started drinking the waters soon after his arrival, then stopped when the gout returned, and resumed around Christmas Day. He wrote to Farquhar on 15 December that 'I do not at present see the smallest occasion to accept your kind and friendly offer of coming here,' and reported that his pulse had been found to have been weaker than it should be and 'beating near an hundred', but the treatment he had been prescribed seemed 'already to have had a very good effect'.[47] He apparently remained in good humour throughout, although Canning wrote on 20 December: 'I think he is weak beyond what he ought to be & business quite overpowers him.'[48]

As he strove to recover his health, Pitt knew that the fate of Europe hung in the balance. He could not have been aware that before he had set out for Bath that fate had already been decided. Even without the involvement of the Prussians, Napoleon faced the prospects of a junction of two large Russian and Austrian armies. By mid-December rumours were reaching London of a great engagement, and it was thought to have been a successful one. A Treasury Minister, William Huskisson, writing to Pitt on 19 December, expressed the hope that 'the news received to-day is sufficiently authentic to justify my congratulating you on the favourable prospect it opens'.[49]

In fact, Tsar Alexander and the Emperor Francis had advanced towards Napoleon as innocents to the slaughter. Knowing he was outnumbered and desperate to bring on a battle before his opponents could come together, Napoleon had used every trick in his extensive book to lull them into thinking he was retreating. As a result they placed their armies in an exposed position: a combination of French tactical retreats, forced marches and sudden counterattacks onto high ground left the Austrian and Russian armies on 2 December in a shockingly inferior position. What would be known to history as the Battle of Austerlitz lasted little more than ten hours. At the end of it the Austrian and Russian armies had been destroyed as effective fighting forces: one third of their numbers were killed, wounded or captured, and the rest were in headlong retreat. Within four days Austria had capitulated; its surrender involved the ceding of large territories to Napoleon: Venetia, Dalmatia and Istria. The German Princes who had supported Napoleon were recognised as Kings. The Russians withdrew into Poland and the Prussians abandoned all immediate thoughts of entering the war. As a result, the British expedition building up its strength in north Germany would be left exposed. Pitt had laboured for eighteen months to assemble the Third Coalition. At Austerlitz Napoleon destroyed it in a single day. Reports of the catastrophe began to appear in London newspapers on 29 December. As Pitt began to worry about a fresh deterioration in his health on 1 January 1806, the despatches winging their way towards him would confirm the ruin of all his hopes.

28

'How I Leave My Country'

'... I have done too much. When in conversation with persons upon important business, I felt suddenly as if I had been cut in two.'

WILLIAM PITT, 13 JANUARY 1806[1]

'There was something missing in the world – a chasm, a blank that cannot be supplied.'

CHARLES JAMES FOX, ON HEARING OF THE DEATH OF PITT, JANUARY 1806[2]

WE CANNOT KNOW FOR SURE whether the news of the Battle of Austerlitz and the collapse of the Third Coalition accelerated the death of William Pitt. Many who knew him well certainly thought that it did. According to George Rose, 'on receiving the account of the armistice after Austerlitz the gout quitted the extremities, and he fell into a debility which continually increased'.[3] Wilberforce considered that the news broke Pitt's heart, 'and the accounts from the armies struck a death blow within'.[4]

To a man who was already as sick as he had ever been, and who was prone to 'every public event of importance' producing a 'corresponding effect upon the body', no news could have been worse, for most of the things Pitt cared about – country, government, and indeed his own position and power – were suddenly and simultaneously placed in danger. The disappointment was all the greater for coming about by such a narrow margin. According to Harrowby, the Prussian army had been 'so far engaged' that without 'the unfortunate Battle of Austerlitz' it would 'have advanced rapidly and all might have been saved'.[5] It was the tragic culmination of thirteen years in which each resurgence of hope for the war on the Continent had been followed by comprehensive defeat. Pitt's great misfortune was that strategies which would have been highly likely to succeed in earlier wars did not work against French armies which had been fired up by revolution and were now led by Napoleon. This defeat, even though it did not involve a single British soldier, was the most serious of all.

Castlereagh arrived in Bath on 3 January 1806 with the bleak and authoritative official accounts of events on the Continent. Although at this stage there was still room to hope that Prussia and Russia could act together, news would soon follow that the Prussian Minister, Count Haugwitz, had signed an agreement with Napoleon on 15 December which secured Hanover for the Prussian Crown. There was nothing left to cushion the blow. Canning's letter to Pitt on New Year's Eve ended disconsolately with: 'I hate to walk the streets in such ill news.'[6]

To even the most robust of Ministers such news would have come as a crushing disappointment. It would have been impossible to contemplate with anything other than dread the opening of Parliament set for only three weeks later – and already once postponed – when opposition forces which almost equalled those of the government would inevitably try to overturn Pitt's administration. What is more, they would have five or six exhausting months in which to do it, during which failure must once again be courageously defended, and evidence of hope once again scraped from an almost empty barrel. The country was not in danger of invasion – Trafalgar had seen to that – but it was hard to see any means by which French domination of Europe could be resisted. Any success at all would require still greater raising of manpower and levying of taxes. For Pitt, there was therefore nothing to look forward to.

Austerlitz may well have broken Pitt's spirit. Yet it is also clear that he had not been getting better as he should have done, and as he was accustomed to, for some time before the dreadful news. There had been no consistent improvement in his health in the days before he heard of Austerlitz, and the deterioration over the two weeks afterwards was only gradual. Years later, Wellington denied that the bad news from the Continent caused Pitt's death, and asserted that his health was in any case 'destroyed by long and previous exertions in the House of Commons, and by deluging his stomach with port wine and water, which he drank to excess, in order to give a false and artificial stimulus to his nervous system'.[7]

For a time, he continued neither better nor worse, although steadily weaker and thinner from eating so little for some weeks. Farquhar joined him at Bath on 4 January and 'was very much shocked at his appearance'. Pitt 'was much emaciated, very weak, feeble, and low . . . He attempted to join the Dinner Table, which at length he did with great difficulty. He eat [sic] very little, but drank some Madeira & Water as had been his usual custom.'[8] That Pitt was depressed is clear from his letter to Melville of 3 January, in which he expressed his frustration about the Austrian armistice and the Russian retreat: 'It is the more provoking, because subsequent to the action the allied army is stated to have been still 85,000 strong.'[9] Three days later he wrote a characteristically methodical and businesslike letter to Castlereagh on the difficult question of what should now be done with the British troops in Germany: 'I certainly feel a strong desire to see so valuable a body of troops at home; but . . . By bringing them away now, I fear we should hardly give a fair chance to the good disposition of Prussia.'[10] At the same time he had to acknowledge that he was genuinely sick, and unlikely to be well for the opening of Parliament: 'I am sorry to say that I have more ground to gain, before I am fit for anything, that I can almost hope to accomplish within a fortnight. Bath is no longer thought of use, and I shall move as soon as I can.'[11]

Pitt was determined at least to be near London, the better to manage the parliamentary situation. While Farquhar and the other doctors debated whether he should be moved, the patient seems to have been fairly insistent, and they decided that 'his own anxiety for the measure would have rendered it absolutely expedient'.[12] Farquhar noted that Pitt was now 'a man much worn out. One day his eyes were almost lifeless, & another his voice hollow & weak, while his pulse was remarkably weak, & generally from 100 to 120.'[13] If Pitt was to survive at all, it is probable that his only hope of sustained recovery was complete rest, mental as well as physical; but that he would not obtain. He insisted on speeding what was meant to have been a slow journey to London, heading for his house at Putney and not taking up the many offers of accommodation which flowed from Canning, Camden and Hawkesbury.

Leaving Bath on 9 January, where a silent crowd watched him leave Johnson Street, Pitt refused to make the planned overnight stop at Chippenham and decided to carry on to Marlborough. Accompanied by Farquhar and Charles Stanhope, he managed to eat a little, and the next day disregarded the possibility of stopping at Newbury in order to carry on to Reading. After one further stop on the afternoon of Saturday, 11 January at Salt Hill, a few miles north of Windsor, a further two hours' travelling saw him back at home in Putney Heath. On arrival there, he is said to have made the melancholy remark, upon seeing a map of Europe, 'Roll up that map, it will not be needed these next ten years,' although whether he did so cannot be established reliably. Pitt seems to have regarded himself at this point as being in an extended state of convalescence. On the twelfth he would write to his long-standing friend Marquis Wellesley (formerly Lord Mornington, who had just returned from the governing of India, and brother of the future Duke of Wellington) that he was 'recovering rather slowly from a series of stomach complaints', but believed he was 'now in the way of real amendment'.[14]

By contrast, Farquhar was becoming extremely anxious. Dining with Malmesbury on the night of the tenth while Pitt slept at Reading, he said that 'Pitt was emaciated so as not to be known, and nothing could save him but complete and entire rest; that any exertion, mental or bodily, would infallibly kill him.'[15] Farquhar would later write in his own defence that he 'most earnestly entreated' Pitt not to proceed to Putney Heath 'from the apprehension of the business in which he might be involved by his proximity to London'. He repeated his 'conviction of the indispensable necessity there was of Mr. Pitt's retiring from Public Life, at least for a time'. Pitt, however, 'declared his resolution of proceeding & submitting to the consequences, whatever they might be'.[16]

Trying to keep Pitt away from work as much as possible, Farquhar arranged for Pretyman to take up residence in Pitt's house and act once again as his private secretary. He prevailed on Pitt 'to give me a pledge that he would open no Letters, and attend to no business', and would let Pretyman manage his correspondence. Thus Pitt was installed in his own house with Pretyman to hand, along with Lady Hester Stanhope and her half-brothers Charles and, later, James. Medical treatment was supervised by Farquhar with the assistance of two of the leading doctors of the time, Henry Reynolds and Mathew Baillie.

Pitt had now lost a great deal of weight. Lady Hester Stanhope was shocked by his appearance: 'I said to myself, "It is all over with him." He was supported by the arms of two people, and had a stick, or two sticks, in his hands, and as he came up, panting for breath . . . I retreated, little by little, not to put him to the pain of making a bow to me, or of speaking.'[17] Pretyman recalled that 'his countenance was totally changed, his eyes were lifeless and his voice was hollow'.[18] Even so, Pitt felt well enough to be taken out for 'an airing' in his carriage on the Sunday, and 'expressed himself much satisfied with his amendment'.[19] In spite of everything, he seemed determined to bear up, and William Dacres Adams had been hugely impressed in the preceding days by the 'wonderful fortitude with which he bore such a mental and bodily pull upon his nearly exhausted powers'.[20]

On Monday the thirteenth, things seemed to be going sufficiently well for Pitt to take another drive in his carriage and for Farquhar to leave him for twenty-four hours. It turned out to be a great mistake. Whether through Pretyman's weakness – he later wrote that Pitt 'had felt himself so much better'[21] – or the insistence of the Ministers concerned, both Hawkesbury and Castlereagh were admitted to see Pitt in order to discuss the situation of the British troops in Germany. Their anxiety to discuss matters with him was understandable, since the situation was critical and they did not like to decide on a complete withdrawal from the Continent without consulting him. It was not possible to be Prime Minister and be shielded from urgent business without appointing a deputy. Pitt's mind had to focus on the fate of an expedition in which over six hundred lives had been lost at sea, and which would probably now have to come home with nothing to show for its efforts. The meeting of Parliament was eight days away. Treasury Ministers were also admitted to see him that Monday, as yet more business could not wait any longer for attention. Pitt was simply not up to it. Canning also saw him that night, and thought 'the change since Bath dreadful! And his appearance such as I shall never forget.'[22] He wrote to his wife that Pitt's illness was 'nothing specific but weakness, total exhaustion, inability to eat any thing, and an extinction of voice after a quarter of an hour's attempt at conversation . . . Poor, poor P.'[23]

That evening, it seems that Pitt could feel his condition deteriorating. He told Pretyman, 'I feel something here', putting his hands on his stomach, 'that reminds me I never shall recover; not cold, but a general giving way.'[24] Next day he confessed to an anxious Farquhar that he had disobeyed his injunctions and done too much: 'When in conversation with persons upon important business, I felt suddenly as if I had been cut in two.'[25] It was from this point on, 14 January 1806, that all who saw Pitt were appalled by his condition and believed he could not survive. Only two days earlier the doctors had thought that he might be back at work within a month. Now Farquhar summoned Reynolds and Baillie to join him in permanent residence at Putney Heath. Wellesley visited Pitt that day and later recalled, 'notwithstanding Mr. Pitt's kindness and cheerfulness, I saw that the hand of death was fixed upon him'.[26] Farquhar considered Pitt's symptoms now to be 'truly & immediately alarming'.[27] Rose was admitted to see him for a few minutes the following day, and found him 'lying on a sofa, emaciated to a degree I could not have conceived . . . I felt it of importance not to touch on any topic that could agitate his mind . . . His countenance was changed extremely, his voice weak, and his body almost wasted, and so indeed were his limbs.'[28]

Rose feared that the government faced defeat in Parliament if Pitt could not attend, and wanted to raise the possibility of a 'dignified resignation', given that there was little hope of Ministers being able to survive for several months without being able to consult Pitt at all. No one, however, wanted to put this forward while any hope of recovery could be entertained, and in any case it was impossible to discuss such a matter with Pitt himself. Ministers, with Hawkesbury in nominal command, decided to tough it out for the moment. They were in no doubt, as Canning put it, that 'if he fails, all is up, to be sure',[29] but the traditional dinners were held at Downing Street for the Queen's birthday and the eve of the opening of Parliament on 18 and 20 January. Parliament was duly opened on the twenty-first, with the opposition forbearing to press for an immediate division but announcing that it would commence doing so the following week.

In the meantime, Pitt lay in his room at Putney, coughing and retching and unable to keep down even small cups of broth. Cabinet Ministers told Rose on Sunday the nineteenth that they had heard Pitt's health was improving, but he had seen enough to know better. James and Hester Stanhope found Rose in tears in the road a few hundred yards from Pitt's house in Putney, unable to say more than 'I fear there is danger.'[30] That night, Pitt managed to eat two eggs and keep them on his stomach, which gave the doctors a flicker of hope. It was the last such positive sign, since his condition was again worsening on the twentieth, exacerbated by a 'low Fever' which persuaded his doctors that 'the case was beyond the reach of medical Skill'.[31] By now Pitt was finding it painful to speak, and had fainted more than once. Although he again managed to eat two eggs on the twenty-first, the pessimism of his doctors was not relieved.

From this point on the large number of Ministers and others who called at the house were not admitted to see him. Even his brother, who the previous week had apparently breezed in and addressed him as if they were in a Cabinet meeting, was not allowed into Pitt's room. Only Pretyman, the doctors and the Stanhope siblings kept watch over him and tried to ease his pain. James Stanhope's account records that on the Wednesday morning, 22 January, Pitt's pulse was reaching 130: 'He was very faint, and could not retain any nourishment he took. It was then considered necessary to acquaint Mr. Pitt with his danger, which the Bishop of Lincoln did at about eight on Wednesday morning.'[32]

It cannot have been a surprise to Pitt to hear that he was thought to be dying. He apparently 'received the intelligence of his own danger with an unexampled firmness',[33] and simply asked Farquhar 'how long he thought he might hold out?'[34] Farquhar's assertion in response that it was still possible to recover he greeted with a 'half smile' which 'showed that he entertained no such hope'.[35] Farquhar's hopes in any case sat uneasily with Pretyman preparing to administer the Sacrament.

Pitt, never a religious man, refused this on grounds of his weakness, but agreed to pray with Pretyman, nevertheless saying that he had 'neglected prayer too much to allow him to hope it could be very efficacious now'.[36] After that he attempted to write a will, but was unable to do so. Dictating it instead to Pretyman, he managed a signature. Accepting that he had few assets, he expressed the hope that 'the Public may be kind enough to think of me. I have not earned it – I do not mean that – but perhaps in their generosity they may do something.'[37] He asked for Sir Walter Farquhar to be paid a thousand guineas in payment of his fees, for £12,000 to be given to the friends who had provided him with money in 1801 (although Rose was appalled that Pitt accidentally omitted him from the list of those who had raised the money), asked for pensions to be granted to his nieces and nephews, and assigned his papers to his brother and Pretyman.

Farquhar's surviving note of that day is very clear: 'Not a ray of hope left.'[38] He later told Malmesbury that Pitt 'preserved his faculties till within twelve or fourteen hours of his death, which came on rapidly, and that Pitt died of old age at forty-six as much as if he had been ninety'.[39] Certainly Pitt was exhausted through work and worry, and had refused to rest for some years while his health was clearly deteriorating. On top of this, he had drunk far too much for far too long, and was undoubtedly an alcoholic for whom 'the early habit of the too free use of Wine operated unquestionably to weaken the Powers of the Stomach'.[40] In addition, he had for many years suffered recurring attacks of gout, vulnerability to which he had presumably inherited from his father. Over time, the medicines he was given may also have weakened him, since he continued to take regular prescriptions which were intended only for immediate relief; as Farquhar put it, 'debility was perpetually calling for new aids & new props, which gave only temporary relief, & at last lost their efficacy'.

Any or all of these factors may have weakened Pitt, but it seems unlikely that they would have killed him. Most historians have assumed that his death was related in some way to gout, which may have 'crystallised in the kidneys, leading to renal failure'.[41] The modern term for this is hyperuricaemia, in which uric acid accumulates in the blood, crystallises in the joints, causing gout, and then in the kidneys, producing exquisite pain, obstruction and ultimately failure. Yet this explanation is unconvincing: renal pain is so intense that Pitt would not have been able to work at all when he was ill; he would not have had the periods of remission between illnesses; and it would have caused pain in a different area of his body to that which was reported. Alternative explanations have included cancer, which is unlikely on grounds of age and which, like hyperuricaemia, would not have come and gone at intervals over the years, or even cirrhosis of the liver.

It is, of course, impossible to know for sure what killed Pitt. Much the most likely explanation, however, is that he suffered from peptic ulceration of his stomach or duodenum. The advanced complications of such ulceration are virtually unknown two hundred years later, but they fit reasonably well with the symptoms reported by Farquhar for the last eleven years of Pitt's life. Periodicity is a classic sign of such an illness, and Pitt's reported symptoms of morning sickness, retching at the sight of dinner, and inability to eat without vomiting are all consistent with it. Repeated vomiting would also produce dehydration, which in turn would cause the headaches and weak pulse which are clearly documented. The lack of adequate nutrition would also lead to the evident impairment of bowel function, and a feeling that some sustenance could be obtained through alcohol – since alcohol is partly absorbed through the lining of the stomach itself. The fact that Pitt reported pain in and around the upper abdomen provides further support for this theory. While an outside possibility is chronic pancreatitis, in all probability Pitt was dying of gastric or duodenal ulceration. Two hundred years later he would have been cured in a few days by therapy with antibiotic and acid-reducing drugs. In 1806, there was nothing that could be done for him.

As night came on Wednesday, 22 January 1806, Pitt's mind began to wander. He said an affectionate goodbye to Hester Stanhope, but was anxious when she left, repeating, 'Where is Hester? Is Hester gone?'[42] Farquhar then gave him some champagne and asked him not to 'take it unkind' when it turned out he had pain from swallowing it. Pitt replied, 'I never take anything unkind that is meant for my good.' He became incoherent as the night wore on, his comments focused exclusively on international events and the condition of England. The boy who had wanted to 'serve his country in the House of Commons' was still thinking about it in the final hours of his life. He occasionally cried out 'Hear Hear!' as if sitting in the Commons, and at other times seemed to speak to a messenger. Still somehow conscious of the need for good news from the Continent, he asked about a letter from Harrowby, and 'frequently inquired the direction of the wind'; then said, answering himself, 'East; ah; that will do; that will bring him quick.'[43] In the early hours a wellwisher arrived with a phial of 'hartshorn oil', which he claimed had previously rescued people from imminent death. Farquhar duly poured it down Pitt's throat, but the response was only 'a little convulsive cough'.[44]

At about half past two, Pitt's moaning and verbal wanderings ceased. Then, according to James Stanhope, 'in a tone I never shall forget, he exclaimed, "Oh, my country! how I leave my country!" From that time he never spoke or moved, and at half-past four expired without a groan or struggle. His strength being quite exhausted, his life departed like a candle burning out.'[45]

For the second time in the memory of many of those watching, the doors of Westminster Hall opened to the funeral procession of a national leader named William Pitt. Once again, it was led by the High Constable of Westminster dressed in a black silk scarf, hatband and gloves with his silver staff in hand, but this time leading a far longer and grander procession than in 1778, with drums, fifes and trumpets preceding the seemingly endless ranks of Members of Parliament and peers, along with three Royal Dukes. Chatham, who had missed the funeral of his father, walked behind the coffin of his younger brother as the slow-moving procession took fully half an hour to cover the few hundred yards from Westminster Hall to the Abbey. The procession of 1778 had tramped through the mud, but this one crunched on the huge quantity of gravel which workmen had been busy spreading since four o'clock that February morning.

It was Saturday, 22 February 1806. Pitt's body had lain in state in the Painted Chamber of the Palace of Westminster for the previous two days, during which time tens of thousands of mourners paid their respects to the body. They passed through the chamber, draped in black and hung with 132 banners of the Chatham arms, at the rate of up to seventy-five a minute. The funeral itself brought out the distress of Pitt's friends: Wilberforce was said to be in tears throughout the ceremony; Mulgrave so affected 'as scarcely to be able to support himself';[46] Canning felt 'a feeling of loneliness & dismay which I have never felt half so strongly before';[47] and Rose was 'in danger of being completely overcome' from the loss of 'one of the purest-minded and best men to whom God . . . ever gave existence'.[48] After Pitt's body had been lowered into the vault already containing his father, mother and sister Harriot, Wellesley speculated as to 'what sepulchre embosoms the remains of so much human excellence and glory?'[49]

There was undoubtedly a sense of national loss. The invitations to the funeral and the medallions struck at the time showed Britannia weeping and carried the inscription 'NON SIBI SED PATRIAE VIXIT': 'He lived not for himself but for his country'. Newspapers printed long obituaries reminding their readers that 'every faculty of his mind was devoted to the Public Service'.[50] Their tributes rested in particular on Pitt's maintenance of British independence and security in the preceding years, extending the legend of 'the pilot who weathered the storm': 'By his unabating zeal and provident counsels we have been guarded from the baneful contagion of revolutionary doctrines, and though ruin and misery have fallen on many States, and seems to impend over others, this Country is free, formidable, and we trust, secure . . . in him we have lost the great prop of our security . . .'[51] Less supportive newspapers described him as a 'great man, for such he has been considered even by the parties who opposed him', but pointed out that 'his second administration was attended with circumstances which lessened the splendour of his distinguished name; and the nation has to regret that his sun should have set amid clouds and storms, instead of descending temperately to a serene and brilliant horizon'.[52] Opposition politicians joined in the avalanche of tributes. Fox said he was 'very sorry, very, very sorry', and went on to add that 'one feels as if there was something missing in the world – a chasm, a blank that cannot be supplied'.[53] Grenville had received the news of his cousin's impending death with 'an agony of tears'.[54] Sidmouth referred to an 'affection that has never been extinguished'.[55]

Yet the death of a Prime Minister at a time of political and international crisis cannot be without controversy and difficulty. When, on 27 January, the Yorkshire MP Henry Lascelles brought forward a motion for a public funeral for an 'excellent statesman', and 'an inscription expressive of the public sense of so great and irreparable a loss',[56] some of those who had opposed Pitt in his final years felt obliged to argue against it. Windham incensed Pitt's friends by opposing the motion even though he had been a member of his earlier administration. He argued that the cause of defeating the French Revolution 'had not been well conducted in his hands', the war had not been won and 'we should never have heard of honours and titles given to Lord Nelson for the glory of a defeat'.[57] More predictably, Fox argued that he could not agree to a motion describing Pitt as an 'excellent statesman': 'It cannot be expected that I should so far forget the principles I have uniformly professed, as to subscribe to the condemnation of those principles by agreeing to the motion now before the House.'

The majority view was generous and overwhelming, and the motion was carried by 258 votes to eighty-nine. When it came to the subject of Pitt's debts, the generosity became unanimous. Even Fox declared he had never given a vote with more satisfaction as the House of Commons voted £40,000 'towards' Pitt's debts – the present-day equivalent would be over £2 million. In addition, his dying wishes were respected, with a pension of £1,200 a year being granted to Lady Hester Stanhope, and a further £600 a year to each of her two sisters.

It was not at all clear that the great sum of £40,000 would be sufficient to clear debts that had piled up at an even greater rate than usual towards the end of Pitt's life. Attempts to calculate the addition to his debts in the last year alone reached a figure of £24,000. Pitt had simply never mustered the time and energy to master his own finances: 'How could a man so circumstanced, find time to look into his affairs?' protested Lady Hester Stanhope. In his later years she had 'fixed on some glaring overcharge' now and again 'just to put a check upon them', but 'what with great dinners, and one thing and another, it was impossible to do any good. As for your talking about English servants being more honest than those of other countries, I don't know what to say about it.'[58] Spendthrift and defrauded to the end of his life, Pitt left to his executors a morass of obligations which took fifteen years to sort out before probate was granted in 1821. His dying wish for the repayment of the friends who had assisted him with almost £12,000 was disregarded, partly on the insistence of Wilberforce, who had envisaged that all of Pitt's debts would be paid by private subscription, and did not wish to see the taxpayer pay even more. With that set aside, the parliamentary grant used to the full and his assets sold (almost £5,000 for his furniture and over £2,600 for his stocks of wine), there was a sufficient surplus for his surviving servants to be paid as he had wished and for a small amount to be divided between Chatham and Pitt's nieces. It was perhaps surprising that any such inheritance became available at all.

Funeral arrangements and private affairs were one thing, but the most pressing and monumental question which arose immediately on Pitt's death was who was to govern the country and prosecute the war. His Cabinet colleagues showed sufficient self-awareness to decide on the day after his death that it was hopeless for them to continue. As a result, George III, who had been 'deeply affected' by news of Pitt's impending demise,[59] was driven to the extremity against which he had struggled for so long: he sent for Grenville to be First Lord of the Treasury, knowing full well that it would mean Fox entering a senior position in government. The King bowed quietly to the inevitable, and what was to be known as 'the Ministry of All the Talents' took office in early February with Grenville as Prime Minister, Fox as Foreign Secretary and Sidmouth as Lord Privy Seal. This proved to be a most uneasy coalition, whose initial hopes for negotiating peace were soon disappointed. It did, however, succeed in finally winning parliamentary approval for the complete and immediate abolition of the slave trade, which was enacted in law early in 1807.

'Pitt's friends' went into opposition, but they would not be there for long. Having pursued a parallel career to that of Pitt, Fox now followed him swiftly to the grave, and died of dropsy in September. Although Grenville strengthened his position with a general election in 1806, his attempts to pursue an extension of the toleration of

Catholics in the armed forces came up against the predictably rigid intransigence of George III, precipitating his removal from office and a fresh and divisive general election in 1807.

Pitt's friends were soon back in government, this time to stay. They governed Britain for many years in the spirit and amid circumstances he would have recognised – slowly inching towards victory over Napoleon while struggling to maintain domestic order in the face of regular shortages and a quickening Industrial Revolution. Their government would be led initially by Portland, then by Spencer Perceval until his assassination in 1812, then for almost fifteen years by Liverpool (formerly Hawkesbury), then briefly by Canning and finally by the Duke of Wellington. Taken together, Pitt's friends and admirers would be in government for twenty-three consecutive years, more than even their hero had managed. Their power was uninhibited by the accession of the Prince of Wales as Regent in 1811, and as George IV in 1820.

The final defeat of France in 1815 opened the way for Castlereagh to construct a European settlement of which Pitt would have heartily approved, the Royal Navy remained mistress of the seas, and the economy and population grew rapidly. Catholic emancipation would not be conceded until 1829, and Pitt's successors would succeed in obstructing parliamentary reform until the triumphant Whigs secured the Great Reform Act of 1832. In a broadened political system, the party of Liverpool, Canning and Wellington would develop into that of Peel, Derby and Disraeli. William Pitt, the man who saw himself as above considerations of party, and once described himself as 'an independent Whig', would have had no idea that he had left behind him an enduring political force – the Conservative Party.

In purely statistical terms, the unique status of William Pitt in British history is beyond challenge. The extraordinary event of a twenty-four-year-old becoming Prime Minister had never happened before, and it is a safe assumption that it will never happen again. Pitt's youth sets him completely apart from all other British leaders: even when he lay dying he was still younger than almost any other holder of his office. Of the thirty-seven British Prime Ministers who have succeeded him, only two, the second Earl of Liverpool and Tony Blair, have served at an age younger than that of Pitt at the time he died – and even they were respectively eighteen and nineteen years older than Pitt when he first took office. Pitt served at the head of government for a total of eighteen years and eleven months, second only to Walpole in length of service, and far longer than any subsequent Prime Minister: almost half as long again as Gladstone and Salisbury, eight years longer than Margaret Thatcher, and more than twice as long as Asquith, Wilson, Churchill or Baldwin. To hold such high office for so long is in itself an extraordinary feat, made possible only by a combination of unusual circumstances and exceptional abilities.

That Pitt's oratorical and intellectual abilities were indeed exceptional is not in doubt. From the beginning to the end of his twenty-five years in the House of Commons his 'transcendent eloquence' was the indispensable foundation of his power. In an age when the art of parliamentary debate stood at one of the highest levels in its history, with the benches of the Commons resonating to the voices of Fox, North, Sheridan and Burke, Pitt stood at the peak, always the equal and sometimes the master of the greatest orators Westminster has ever known. The incomplete records and expansive speaking style of the eighteenth century mean that his phrases have not flowed easily into the language of later centuries, but it is clear that even in an age of eloquence his contemporaries regarded some of his efforts – on the slave trade in 1792, on union with Ireland in 1799, and on the resumption of war in 1803 – as among the greatest and most sustained displays of declamation they had ever witnessed. With rarely an error, never a word out of place, and never a speech without a clear and logical architecture, Pitt exercised to its full range the natural speaking ability which his father's tuition had extended until it was extraordinary. It was in the House of Commons, and only there, that he was wholly comfortable in a public arena, where all stiffness and reserve fell away, and where he could confidently display his true personality knowing he could not be matched.

Pitt's passions and preoccupations became clear very early in his life: the mathematics, classical texts, political issues and humorous repartee which made up almost his entire existence at Cambridge remained his favourite pastimes until the day he died. Concentration on each of them fortified the quickness of a versatile mind, so that if Fox blundered on the floor on the Commons, as he did in December 1788, it was not many seconds before Pitt was ready with his counterthrust. The same quickness of mind and enjoyment of solving problems gave him the earnest enthusiasms of the early years in office – the freeing of Irish trade, the commercial treaty with France, the budgetary measures to defeat smuggling, the creation of the Sinking Fund – projects which drove him 'half mad' with excitement and concentration.

Allied to his youthful alignment with the emerging intellectual influences of his time – the economist Adam Smith, the philosopher John Locke, the novelist William Paley – these intellectual abilities produced in Pitt an aptitude for financial reform and enlightened politics which was on full display in the 1780s. He was lucky to preside over a period of natural economic expansion as the Industrial Revolution took shape, and his reforms were often based on the thinking of commentators or Commissions who had gone before him, but even so his achievements in creating a simpler and more sustainable basis for the nation's finances and cutting through many of the complexities of regulation and administration were great. His confident exposition of the benefits of freer trade helped to create the climate in which later governments could go further, his struggle to produce a fair and productive method of taxation proved to be the basis of income tax, and his reforms of the financial system helped to keep Britain creditworthy through a war which lasted long after his death. At the same time he ended much of the corruption with which that system had previously been associated.

Such advances must always be immensely to his credit, for although they seem in retrospect necessary things to have done, no Lord North would have bothered to tackle such a wide range of issues, and no Fox would have done so in such intricate detail. Pitt's dedication to driving the processes of government from the centre, and, in his early years at least, with a minute attention to its intricacies, allowed him not only to enact much-needed reforms but also to enhance the pre-eminence of the Treasury in British government, and greatly to strengthen the coordination of government departments. By doing so, he fortified the British state for a lengthy war and against the buffetings of social discontent through the Industrial Revolution, while helping to prepare it for the management of an Empire which would encompass a quarter of the globe. As the first First Lord of the Treasury systematically to intervene in the work of other departments and happily to take over their functions at times of crisis, Pitt was arguably the first modern Prime Minister. By defending at all costs his own reputation for integrity and ending a good deal of the 'jobbing' and jostling for sinecures, he helped to restore faith in the British state after a period in which it had been much discredited among its own people.

These achievements are unambiguous. On the basis of them and his unusual longevity in office, Pitt cannot be denied a place among the major figures of British history. Yet there is room for dispute about the rest of his legacy, which calls for finer judgements, as well as a paradox about his personality which has made him hard to know. Often professing his dedication to peace, Pitt nevertheless became Britain's longest-serving war leader. Despite his tireless efforts, no decisive advantage was gained in war during his lifetime. A champion of domestic reform, he undoubtedly became the author of repression, and despite his trenchant stands in favour of parliamentary reform, Catholic emancipation and the abolition of the slave trade, he was unable to bring any of them to enactment. How do we explain these apparent failures or changes of view? Was Pitt, as Fox always maintained, too interested in power to advance the cause of any principle? Was he ineffective as a war leader? And were those political failings, if that is what they were, somehow bound up with his complex personality? It is, after all, undeniable that he exhibited an unusual mixture of personal traits: a man who won ardent friends but to others was distant and aloof; a brilliant debater who could be profoundly shy; the undisputed master of the nation's finances whose neglect of his own pocket left him with vast personal debts.

Even admirers of Pitt must concede that he did not become a fully rounded personality. Not only was he apparently uninterested in sexual relationships, but without any interest in music, art, society or modern literature and languages he was cut off from many of the interests of the vast majority of his social and political peer groups. There can be no doubt that the spectacular speed of his political ascent contributed to this personal isolation. Even single-minded politicians often develop a wide range of other interests when they are out of office or waiting at length for a parliamentary seat or ministerial promotion. Yet even the most rounded politician finds the pursuit of new interests while holding ministerial office to be almost impossible. Pitt was in such a situation, with only two intervals in his entire life, from the age of twenty-three onwards. As a result he was, in his forties, very much the same person as in his twenties. This left him with certain weaknesses, such as his lifelong tendency to be too sanguine about people and too optimistic about impending events, in addition to his narrowness of personal enjoyments and tastes. On the other hand, an unchanging personality had its good side. It is to his credit that after a lifetime of political batterings Pitt still possessed the endearing personal attributes which appealed so much to his closest friends: a ready wit, an enjoyment of simple fun, an ability to put his troubles to one side, and a freedom from rancour, bitterness, or any tendency to blame others for his misfortunes.

There is no doubt that, had he chosen to, Pitt could have used his position as Prime Minister to widen his circle of interests and friends. He chose not to. He had set his course when very young, and had mentally committed himself exclusively to public life. To him, relaxing among his established friends was appealing, but adding other pursuits or friendships for the sake of being sociable would have been pointless. His lack of wider interests can even be seen as a necessary part of the selflessness on which he prided himself and which he always exhibited.

It is impossible to understand Pitt without appreciating the importance in his personality of that sense of self-sacrifice. Many politicians feel a conflict between public ambition and their private needs. For Grenville it was always important to acquire money and land at the same time as pursuing a political career; for Fox the temptations of social, sensual and intellectual pursuits outside Parliament generally competed with it. Many of the MPs around Pitt were ambitious for titles, money or social standing. Pitt reached beyond them all to a point where selflessness and political purpose joined together; where the sacrificing of such objects was indistinguishable from his own sense of unsurpassable ambition. His disdain for wider society, indifference to money and refusal of honours were not in conflict with his desire to run the country but were a direct result of it. The shunning of such attractions allowed him to hold in his own mind to a concept of virtue, but also marked him out as extraordinary and incorruptible in the perception of others. It is the extent of Pitt's self-sacrifice that illustrates his devotion to seeking power – his refusal of the permanent income of the Clerkship of the Pells in 1784 and his resistance to generous offers of assistance or ideas of employment after his resignation in 1801 both confirmed that his mind was only ever fixed on holding office for the long term. Whereas to others it may have seemed bizarre to pursue a public career while being heedless of money or society or titles, to Pitt, eyes always focused on leading the nation, such abstinence went along with devotion to country. Wilberforce maintained that 'love of country' was Pitt's dominant attribute, and there is no reason to doubt it. It is clear, too, that his love could only be consummated in power. Service and ambition formed a single identity in his mind.

This unchanging conception of himself gave Pitt the qualities he would be remembered for: endurance, self-sacrifice, concentration, and a carelessness for personal consequences. It also impelled him to take the highest office in the land when it was made available to him, provided it came with its powers unimpeded. His careful refusal of office in 1783 and 1803 occurred because on both occasions he felt he might be hamstrung, and because he wanted to respond only to a more powerful and wider call for him to step forward; similarly, in 1801 he resigned because his power was being impaired. When offered real power he took it, whatever the risks: in 1783 despite the risk of impeachment, in 1804 despite the risk of political isolation, and he battled on in 1806 despite the risk of his own physical demise. His view of the purpose of his life was so overpowering that on each occasion he felt he had to serve, despite all the dangers. His painful death, trying to work on as Prime Minister in a desperate crisis, was the logical culmination of his approach to life.

That Pitt's mind was focused on winning and holding power is clear from the way he bent his abilities to all the necessities of practical politics. While he always demonstrated his own purity and applied a rigorous standard of independence to himself, he knew he could achieve nothing without pulling the various political levers which caused others to move as he wished. He was happy to see the liberal distribution of peerages to secure his government in place in 1784, and again to persuade the doubtful of the merits of Irish Union in 1800. He was even happy to bribe his way to success if it was truly necessary for overriding national purposes, as Irish MPs and French Ministers knew. On at least one occasion he told a direct and crucial lie. Idealism did not cloud his practical thinking. 'Honest Billy' marked himself out as different, with great success, while treating others in accordance with the established habits of the time.

One of the charges against Pitt is that he was too interested in power at the expense of his principles. To Fox, Pitt was the man who sold out to George III and his court in both 1783 and 1804. In the Whig view, Pitt corrupted the constitution by coming to the rescue of George III on the former occasion, and prevented the formation of a broadly based ministry by taking office without Fox and Grenville on the latter one. It can be argued that by being prepared to take office and rescue the King, Pitt actually stood in the way of some of the more liberal policies he purported to support. But there is, of course, an argument of at least equal power the other way, and one which Pitt would have felt very strongly. If the King was to retain the power to nominate Ministers, then it was important that capable people were ready to serve. What Fox really sought in both 1783 and 1804 was to leave the King with no choice at all. Catholic relief and parliamentary reform were not in any case enacted until a quarter of a century after Pitt's death, and it may have been unrealistic to have expected him to carry them through. Pitt's one resignation and various refusals of office show that he was not prepared to be the King's puppet. He believed in a balanced constitution in which a clearly identified and powerful Prime Minister served under a King who nevertheless retained a good deal of his prerogative, the alternative to which was chaos and constitutional deadlock.

In his political outlook, Pitt was an improver rather than a radical.

His attachment to planting and cutting in the gardens of Holwood and Burton Pynsent, and to toying with architectural improvements to wherever he lived, mirrored his approach to politics. His financial measures and changes to the machinery of government were sometimes far-reaching, as his attempts at parliamentary reform were intended to be, but the purpose of all of them was to make the existing order work more effectively, rather than to replace it altogether. He enjoyed redesigning the structures of government, but would on no account risk their collapse. This is what would define him as a Tory in the eyes of later generations, and at a time of international instability there was much to be said for a leader of such a disposition. The drawback was that it sometimes limited his vision and adaptability, leaving it to others to make the first responses to the social and economic problems thrown up by low agricultural wages and the rise of factories. In his analysis of trade and finance, he showed little evidence of knowledge or thought about social consequences.

This preference for redesign rather than revolution also explains what many have considered to be his political about-turns. Parliamentary reform was dear to his heart in peacetime, but he saw it as unthinkable when revolution arose across the Channel. Catholic emancipation he would press for, but not to political destruction – he saw it as one thing to persuade the King of the merits of a measure, but quite another to force on him something to which he was diametrically opposed. Such pragmatism and concern with stability allowed Pitt's memory to be traduced in later years, and was quoted in aid of those who flatly opposed Catholic emancipation or parliamentary reform.

Less forgivable is Pitt's greatest failure: the inability to secure final abolition of the slave trade. The sincerity of his opposition to this dreadful trade was all too plain, but so is the fact that he lost the energy, focus and will to pursue the matter to a successful conclusion in the early 1800s. The fact that abolition was so speedily secured by Grenville and Fox soon after Pitt's death suggests that he too could have secured it if he had marshalled his forces to do so. The truth was that by 1805, weighed down by the conduct of the war and deeply troubled by domestic controversies, Pitt was a spent force as a reformer. It is a lesson that the energy and force of a political career are finite

– Pitt tested the natural limits of how long it is possible to be at the top. From 1783 to 1792 he faced each fresh challenge with brilliance; from 1793 he showed determination but sometimes faltered; and from 1804 he was worn down by the simultaneous combination of a narrow parliamentary majority and a war on a knife-edge, all to be faced with his own strength much reduced.

It was reported by Lord Stanhope that when Pitt's mother was asked whether father or son was the more brilliant statesman, she came down in favour of the father. In truth, while both the elder and the younger Pitt possessed the ability to dominate the House of Commons, their skills in government were very different. Pitt's analytical mind and attention to detail performed wonders in the peacetime years after 1783 on matters on which Chatham could never have focused. But once war came, 'the guidance of Chatham would have been worth an army'.[60] While each wartime decision by Pitt can be justified on its merits, it is impossible to escape the sense that if his father had been there all energies would have been galvanised towards some single aggressive stroke which would have ended the war.

Such criticism of Pitt, however, has often been excessive. He had to work with troublesome and often selfish allies, and was frequently let down. At the same time he inherited a British army which was a weak and inefficient instrument for waging war in Europe – it would take some years after his death for Wellington and the experience of the Peninsular War to mould it into the force which would finally shatter the dreams of Napoleon at Waterloo. In naval matters, Pitt was both more fortunate and more far-sighted. The political attention and financial priority he gave to naval armament even in peacetime were vindicated by events, as were some of his extremely delicate and risky strategic decisions on naval deployment during the war. The naval pre-eminence he helped to engineer was vital to British security.

So while it is possible that a better strategist might indeed have come nearer to winning the war, a worse one could have lost it outright. As the years of conflict went by, Pitt's unending creative ability to finance the war, produce resources, return to the fray and simply persist made his own person into a symbol of endurance and national resilience. No alternative leader could provide such a combination:

Addington was not warlike, Grenville would have been more inflexible, Fox for peace at any price, and Portland uninspiring. Thus while Pitt can easily be criticised by historians, it is little wonder that he had so many adherents in his own time.

The final and perhaps gravest charge made against Pitt is that in his desire for power and his partnership with George III he made war on France unnecessarily, and accompanied it with an unwarranted degree of domestic repression. Yet it is hard to see how Britain in 1793 could have avoided going to war with France either then or shortly thereafter. Pitt himself had been determined on peace, but Britain could not accept French domination of the Low Countries without putting herself through national humiliation and at permanent strategic risk. Given that the national consensus for war was sufficiently powerful to split the Whig party asunder, it is difficult to maintain that any viable British government could have remained at peace. As for repression, it is true that Pitt erred on the side of safety rather than liberty, but it is vital to understand the uncertainties and fears of the times. The collapse of France, the most populous and powerful nation of Europe, from absolutist monarchy into untrammelled revolution, brought the sweeping away of a long-established and dominant system. Authorities in other countries experienced a huge shock. Of course, British society was different from that of France. Its history, social structure and economic condition made it less prone to revolution. But Pitt had no academic papers to assure him of this at the time, and no reliable means of forecasting how opinion might develop in an age when ideas could be transmitted far faster than ever before. His erring on the side of safety, and therefore of 'repression', was absolutely in line with his own attachment to the continuity of the nation's institutions and with the instincts of most of his countrymen. He should therefore be absolved of the severest criticisms made of him. He had long desired to split the Whigs, but he did not declare war in the interests of doing so. Nor did he use repressive policies to do so, although he did seize on the conjunction of circumstances to impose domestic order and simultaneously split the opposition in the manner of any skilled politician worth his salt.

Pitt's motivation was to manage and preserve the state rather than drastically to change it. As a result, he did not come into office to carry out a fixed programme and then retire. In his mind the endurance of the British constitution and the tenure of his own role had no limit. It is not surprising therefore that he was attacked for conservatism. Equally, it is unsurprising that in the eyes of many he provided a bulwark of stability and a reassuring sense of protection. Such is the spirit of the tributes made to him, which emphasise a sense of loss rather than of lasting achievement. His monument in Westminster Abbey laments 'the irreparable loss of that great and disinterested Minister', whereas that to his father salutes the man under whom 'divine providence exalted Great Britain to an height of prosperity and glory unknown to any former age'.

Pitt himself would have greeted all such verdicts with a philosophical air. One of his most appealing characteristics was that however stern the appearance he felt it necessary to present to the world, he did not take himself too seriously in private. He did, however, give himself an extremely serious purpose in life. He chose for himself a vast but simple role. He would use the abilities which nature and education had given him to lead, improve and maintain the country he genuinely loved, admitting into his life nothing which would deflect him. Once Pitt is understood in this light, the paradoxes of his personality fall away. His concept of himself was breathtaking in its ambition but also in its simplicity; his drive to power and leadership so great that all other considerations, including his own health and lifestyle, were subordinate to it. Therein lies his true rarity, just as much as it lies in his youth and longevity in office, for the result was a dedication to public service so intense as to be rare even in the annals of Prime Ministers. He was Prime Minister of Britain in a turbulent period of history, and faced some of the greatest crises which peace or war in their turn could bring. He was by far the youngest person ever to hold such office. Yet above all, he is a source of fascination because from his early childhood to the hour of death, he so aligned his life with the fate of his country that at no moment of his existence could he separate himself from it.

NOTES

BIBLIOGRAPHY

INDEX

NOTES

Prologue

1 *Gazette and New Daily Advertiser*, 10 June 1778
2 *Morning Post*, 10 June 1778
3 Ayling, *The Elder Pitt*, p.275
4 Black, *Pitt the Elder*, p.43
5 Ibid., p.308
6 Ayling, *The Elder Pitt*, p.262
7 *London Evening Post*, 9–11 June 1778
8 *Morning Post*, 10 June 1778
9 *London Evening Post*, 9–11 June 1778
10 *Morning Post*, 10 June 1778
11 *London Evening Post*, 9–11 June 1778
12 PRO, Pitt Papers

ONE : Elder and Younger

1 Rogers, *Recollections by Samuel Rogers*, p.187
2 Rosebery, *Pitt*, p.6
3 Chatham to Benjamin Keene, 23 August 1757, Pitt Mss, William L. Clements Library, Michigan
4 Newcastle to Hardwicke, 25 October 1759, BL Add Mss 35419, fol.36
5 Bussy to Choiseul, 30 August 1761, quoted in Black, *Pitt the Elder*, p.215
6 Fitzmaurice, *Life of Shelburne. 1st Marquis of Lansdowne*, Vol. I, p.72
7 Hibbert, *George III*, p.3
8 Pelham to Lord Ilchester, 1 May 1746, Ilchester (ed.), *Letters to Henry Fox, Lord Holland*, pp.12–13
9 Waldegrave, *Memoirs from 1754–1758*
10 Ayling, *The Elder Pitt*, p.99
11 Speech assigned to Pitt under the character of Julius Florus, in the *London Magazine* of the year 1744, Thackeray, *A History of the Right Hon. William Pitt, Earl of Chatham*, Vol. I, pp.126–7
12 Undated anecdote, quoted in Black, *Pitt the Elder*, p.198
13 Chatham to Sir James Eyre, 14 October 1761, Pitt Mss, William L. Clements Library, Michigan
14 Rose, *A Short Life of William Pitt*, p.2
15 Chatham to Sister Ann, 28 May 1759, Rosebery, *Chatham: His Early Life and Connections*, p.111
16 Chatham to Lady Chatham, Williams, *The Life of William Pitt, Earl of Chatham*, Vol. II, p.128
17 Ayling, *The Elder Pitt*, p.248
18 Lady Holland to Lord Holland, Russell, *Memorials and Correspondence of Charles James Fox*, Vol. I, p.25
19 Reverend Wilson to Lady Chatham, 13 September 1766, Taylor and Pringle (eds), *Correspondence of William Pitt, Earl of Chatham*, Vol. III, p.65
20 Rose, *William Pitt and National Revival*, p.49
21 Reverend Wilson to Lady Chatham, 2 August 1766, Taylor and Pringle (eds), *Correspondence of William Pitt, Earl of Chatham*, Vol. III, p.27
22 Hayley, *Memoirs of the Life and Writings of William Hayley*, Vol. I, p.127
23 Rose, *A Short Life of William Pitt*, p.3
24 Taylor and Pringle (eds), *Correspondence of William Pitt, Earl of Chatham*, Vol. IV, p.184n
25 Earl of Chatham to Pitt, 22 September 1777, ibid., p.440
26 Earl of Chatham to Lady Chatham, 3 April 1772, ibid., pp.207–8
27 Lady Chatham to Earl of Chatham, undated, ibid., p.207n
28 Tomline, *Memoirs of the Life of the Right*

Honourable William Pitt, Vol. I, p.4

29 Stanhope, *Address delivered by Earl Stanhope at the ceremony of his installation as the Lord Rector of Marischal College and University, Aberdeen*, 25 March 1858, p.20

30 Williams, *The Life of William Pitt, Earl of Chatham*, Vol. II, p.173

31 Gray to Wharton, 26 April 1766, Ayling, *The Elder Pitt*, p.355

32 Keppel to Lord Rochford, 23 January 1767, Pitt Mss, William L. Clements Library, Michigan

TWO : **Cambridge and the World**

1 Lord Chatham to Joseph Turner, 3 October 1773, Pembroke College Archives

2 Tomline, *Memoirs of the Life of the Right Honourable William Pitt*, Vol. I, p.6

3 Pembroke College Cambridge Society, *Annual Gazette*, No.8, June 1934, p.18

4 Ibid., p.19

5 Pitt to Chatham, 8 October 1773, Taylor and Pringle (eds), *Correspondence of William Pitt, Earl of Chatham*, Vol. IV, pp.288–9

6 Pitt to Chatham, 15 October 1773, ibid., p.294

7 Chatham to Pitt, 30 October 1773, ibid., p.310

8 Ibid., pp.311–12

9 Chatham to Lady Chatham, 18 January 1775, ibid., p.370

10 Pitt to Chatham, 15 and 27 July 1774, ibid., pp.355, 358

11 Pitt to Chatham, 31 August 1774, ibid., p.362

12 Tomline, *Memoirs of the Life of the Right Honourable William Pitt*, Vol. I, p.5

13 Ibid., p.6

14 Ibid., p.8

15 Ibid., p.7

16 Pitt to Mr William Johnson, 1 May 1773, Pembroke College Archives

17 Tomline, *Memoirs of the Life of the Right Honourable William Pitt*, Vol. I, p.6

18 Wilberforce, *Sketch of Mr Pitt*, quoted in Rosebery, *Pitt and Wilberforce*, p.15

19 Rose, *William Pitt and National Revival*, p.30

20 Moritz, *Journey of a German in England in 1782*, p.76

21 Ibid., p.29

22 Wrigley and Schofield, *The Population History of England 1541–1871*, pp.208–9

23 Macaulay, essay in *Encyclopaedia Britannica*, eleventh edition, p.667

24 Pitt to Lady Chatham, 21 January 1775, Taylor and Pringle (eds), *Correspondence of William Pitt, Earl of Chatham*, pp.376–7

25 Pitt to Lady Chatham, 31 May 1777, ibid., pp.437–8

26 Ibid., pp.519–20n

27 Pretyman Mss HA 119/108/39/112

28 See Phillips, *The Cousins' Wars*, p.64

29 Pitt to Lady Chatham, June 1780, Chatham Papers, PRO 30/8/12, fol.182

THREE : **Ambition on Schedule**

1 Stanhope, *Life of the Right Honourable William Pitt*, Vol. I, pp.23–4

2 Pitt to Lady Chatham, 30 November 1778, Chatham Papers, PRO 30/8/12, fol.32

3 Pitt to Lady Chatham, 18 December 1779, Chatham Papers, PRO 30/8/12, fol.127

4 Pitt to Lady Chatham, 3 January 1780, Chatham Papers, PRO 30/8/12, fol.132

5 Pitt to Lady Chatham, 30 November 1778, Chatham Papers, PRO 30/8/12, fol.32–3

6 Tomline, unpublished Chapter XXVII of his *Life of Pitt*, Rosebery, *Bishop Tomline's Estimate of Pitt*, p.34

7 Burges, *Selections from the Letters and Correspondence of Sir James Bland Burges*, p.61

8 Mr Jekyll, quoted in Stanhope, *Life of the Right Honourable William Pitt*, Vol. I, pp.63–4

9 'The Present State of the Boroughs in the County of Cornwall', Chatham Papers, PRO, quoted in Namier, *The Structure of Politics at the Accession of George III*, p.299

10 Namier, *The Structure of Politics at the Accession of George III*, p.78
11 Pitt to Lady Chatham, 27 March 1780, Chatham Papers, PRO 30/8/12, fol.155
12 Pitt to Lady Chatham, 3 July 1779, Chatham Papers, PRO 30/8/12, fol.93
13 Marquis of Rockingham to Pitt, 7 August 1779, Stanhope, *Life of the Right Honourable William Pitt*, Vol. I, pp.31–2
14 Temple to Pitt, 18 July 1779, Chatham Papers, PRO 30/8/182, fol.95
15 Pitt to Robert Wharton, 16 July 1779, Pembroke College Archives
16 Pitt to Lady Chatham, 14 March 1780, Chatham Papers, PRO 30/8/12, fol.149
17 Pitt to Edward Eliot, 14 March 1780, Pretyman Mss HA 119/T108/39/250
18 Pitt to Shelburne, c.June 1780, Pitt Mss, William L. Clements Library, Michigan
19 Pitt to Lady Chatham, 16 September 1780, Chatham Papers, PRO 30/8/12, fol.191
20 Pitt to Pretyman, 1780, Tomline, *Memoirs of the Life of the Right Honourable William Pitt*, Vol. I, p.20
21 Pitt to Lady Chatham, November 1780, Chatham Papers, PRO 30/8/12, fol.201–2

FOUR : **Brilliant Beginnings**

1 Duke of Newcastle to Lord Chancellor, 3 September 1755, Yorke, *The Life and Correspondence of Philip Yorke, Earl of Hardwicke*, Vol. II, p.238
2 Walpole (ed. Jarrett), *Memoirs of the Reign of King George III*, Vol. III, p.107
3 Moritz, *Journeys of a German in England in 1782*, pp.50–3
4 Pitt to Westmorland, 26 July 1779, Duke Mss, quoted in Ehrman, *The Younger Pitt*, Vol. I, p.58
5 Heads of my Conversation with Mr. Pitt [in the King's handwriting]; Fortescue, *The Correspondence of King George III . . .*, Vol. I, no. 100, p.124
6 Namier, *The Structure of Politics at the Accession of George III*, p.2
7 Jenyns, *Thoughts on a Parliamentary Reform*, pp.29–30
8 Bickley, *The Diaries of Sylvester Douglas, Lord Glenbervie*, Vol. I, p.238, quoted in Valentine, *Lord North*, p.174
9 Brougham, *Historical Sketches of Statesmen who Flourished in the Time of George III*, pp.55–6
10 For more information on Lord North's support see Christie, *The End of North's Ministry 1780–1782*, pp.208–10
11 Selwyn to Carlisle, 12 March 1782, Historical Manuscripts Commission, *The Manuscripts of the Earl of Carlisle Preserved at Castle Howard*, p.591
12 Walpole to Mann, 17 May 1781, Walpole, *The Letters of Horace Walpole*, Vol. VIII, p.41
13 Fox to O'Bryen, 19 February 1801, BL Add Mss 47566, fol.75
14 Gibbon, *Miscellaneous Works of Edward Gibbon*, Vol. I, p.168
15 Rae, *Wilkes, Sheridan, Fox: The Opposition under George III*, p.314
16 Lord Hillsborough to William Eden, 21 March 1801, BL Add Mss 34417, fol.325
17 Stanhope, *Life of the Right Honourable William Pitt*, Vol. I, pp.54–5
18 Ibid., p.133
19 Butler, *Reminiscences of Charles Butler*, Vol. I, p.161
20 Wraxall, *The Historical and the Posthumous Memoirs of Sir Nathaniel William Wraxall 1772–1784*, Vol. II, p.77
21 Russell, *Memorials and Correspondence of Charles James Fox*, Vol. I, p.261
22 Wraxall, *The Historical and the Posthumous Memoirs . . .*, Vol. II, p.78
23 Russell, *Memorials and Correspondence of Charles James Fox*, Vol. I, p.262
24 Pitt to Lady Chatham, 27 February 1781, Chatham Papers, PRO 30/8/12, fol.205–6
25 Horace Walpole on Pitt, quoted in Rose, *William Pitt and National Revival*, p.88
26 Wraxall, *The Historical and the Posthumous Memoirs . . .*, Vol. II, p.122
27 Dundas, 12 June 1781, quoted in Stanhope, *Life of the Right Honourable William Pitt*, Vol. I, p.62
28 Germain to Clinton, 7 March 1781, quoted in Christie, *The End of North's Ministry 1780–1782*, p.262

29 R.I. and S.W. Wilberforce, *The Life of William Wilberforce*, Vol. I, p.18

FIVE : Death of Two Governments

1 *London Gazette*, 24–27 November 1781
2 For a fuller account of these events see Hibbert, *Redcoats and Rebels*, pp.314–31
3 Pitt to Lady Chatham, 7 October 1781, Chatham Papers, PRO 30/8/12, fol.268–9
4 Camden to Walpole, 8 November 1781, Lullings Mss, quoted in Christie, *The End of North's Ministry 1780–1782*, p.268
5 Wraxall, *The Historical and the Posthumous Memoirs*..., Vol. II, p.139
6 Ibid., p.142
7 Ibid., p.47
8 Ibid., p.162
9 Walpole's journal, 14 December 1781, Walpole, *Journal of the Reign of King George III, From the Year 1771 to 1783*, Vol. II, pp.485–6
10 Romilly (ed.), *Memoirs of the Life of Sir Samuel Romilly*, Vol. I, p.192
11 For a full account of these events see Christie, *The End of North's Ministry 1780–1782*, pp.267–8
12 Tomline, *Memoirs of the Life of the Right Honourable William Pitt*, Vol. I, p.39
13 Wraxall, *The Historical and the Posthumous Memoirs*..., Vol. II, pp.150–1
14 Russell, *The Life of Charles James Fox*, Vol. I, p.267
15 Wraxall, *The Historical and the Posthumous Memoirs*..., Vol. II, p.151
16 Ibid., p.188
17 Ibid., p.237
18 George III to Lord North, 19 March 1782, quoted in Fortescue, *The Correspondence of King George III*..., Vol. V, p.397
19 Christie, *The End of North's Ministry 1780–1782*, pp.368–9
20 George III, March 1782, Draft Message to Parliament, Fortescue, *The Manuscripts of J.B. Fortescue, Esq., Preserved at Dropmore*, n3601, p.425
21 Selwyn to Carlisle, 19 March 1782, *The Manuscripts of the Earl of Carlisle Preserved at Castle Howard, Historical Manuscripts Commission, XV Report*, p.599
22 Wraxall, *The Historical and the Posthumous Memoirs*..., Vol. II, p.257
23 Russell, *The Life of Charles James Fox*, Vol. I, pp.284–5
24 24 March 1783, Stanhope, *Life of the Right Honourable William Pitt*, Vol. I, p.70
25 Steuart (ed.), *The Last Journals of Horace Walpole*, Vol. II, p.416
26 William Pitt, 7 May 1782, *Parliamentary Register 1792*, Vol. VII, p.105
27 7 May 1782, Hathaway, *The Speeches of the Right Honourable William Pitt in the House of Commons*, Vol. I, p.27
28 Ibid., pp.27–8
29 Ibid., p.29
30 Ibid., p.30
31 Wraxall, *The Historical and the Posthumous Memoirs*..., Vol. II, p.307
32 Pitt to Lady Chatham, c.May 1782, Chatham Papers, PRO 30/8/12, fol.224–5
33 Sheridan to Fitzpatrick, 20 May 1782, Russell, *Memorials and Correspondence of Charles James Fox*, Vol. I, p.338
34 Henry to Robert Dundas, 25 March 1782, Matheson, *The Life of Henry Dundas, First Viscount Melville*, quoted in Ehrman, *The Younger Pitt*, Vol. I, p.79
35 Fitzmaurice, *Life of Shelburne. 1st Marquis of Lansdowne*, p.373
36 Wraxall, *The Historical and the Posthumous Memoirs*..., Vol. II, p.319
37 Caroline Fox to Lord Holland, 5 February 1795, BL Add Mss 51732, fol.170
38 C.J. Fox to T. Grenville, 10 June 1782, Buckingham, *Memoirs of the Court and Cabinet of George III*, Vol. I, p.41
39 Ibid.
40 Wraxall, *The Historical and the Posthumous Memoirs*..., Vol. II, p.347
41 Pitt to Lady Chatham, 27 June 1782, Chatham Papers, PRO 30/8/12, fol.303–4

SIX : The Youngest Chancellor

1 Earl of Mornington to Grenville, 12 July 1782, Fortescue, *The Manuscripts of J.B. Fortescue, Esq., Preserved at Dropmore*, Vol. I, p.162
2 Earl of Shelburne, 5 May 1783, *Parliamentary Register*, Vol. XI, p.167
3 George III to Lord Shelburne, 1 July 1782, quoted in Fortescue, *The Correspondence of King George III . . .*, no. 3827
4 Cannon, *The Fox–North Coalition*, p.20
5 Duke of Leeds, Political Memorandums 5, 20 March 1782–28 February 1783, BL Add Mss 27918, fol.79
6 Russell, *Memorials and Correspondence of Charles James Fox*, Vol. I, p.447
7 Pitt to Lady Chatham, 2 July 1782, Chatham Papers, PRO 30/8/12, fol.233–4
8 Pitt to Lady Chatham, 5 July 1782, ibid., fol.237–8
9 Gilbert, 'Political Correspondence of Charles Lennox, Third Duke of Richmond', D.Phil, 1956, quoted in Mitchell, *Charles James Fox*, p.53
10 9 July 1782, *Parliamentary History*, Vol. XXIII, March 1782–December 1783, p.163
11 Wraxall, *The Historical and the Posthumous Memoirs . . .*, Vol. II, p.368
12 George III to Lord North, 7 August 1782, quoted in Fortescue, *The Correspondence of King George III . . .*, Vol. VI, p.97
13 Pitt to Lady Chatham,16 July 1782, Chatham Papers, PRO 30/8/12, fol.237–8
14 Pitt to Lady Chatham, 30 July 1782, ibid., fol.243
15 Pitt to Lady Chatham 12 September 1782, ibid., fol.264
16 Pitt to Lady Chatham, 10 August 1782, ibid., fol.258
17 Pitt to Lady Chatham, 30 July 1782, ibid., fol.242
18 Pitt to Shelburne, 3 August 1782, Pitt Mss, William L. Clements Library, Michigan
19 Harcourt, *The Diaries and Correspondence of the Right Hon. George Rose*, Vol. I, p.25
20 Ibid., p.28
21 *Parliamentary Register*, Vol. VIII, 1781–82, pp.369–70
22 Shelburne to Wyvill, 3 October 1782, Wyvill, *Political Papers*, Vol. III, pp.337, 341
23 Wraxall, *The Historical and the Posthumous Memoirs . . .*, Vol. II, p.392
24 Ehrman, *The Younger Pitt*, Vol. I, p.85
25 Browning (ed.), *Memoranda of Francis, Fifth Duke of Leeds*, p.76
26 *Parliamentary Register*, Vol. XI, 1782–83, p.15
27 Cannon, *The Fox–North Coalition*, p.42
28 Tomline, *Memoirs of the Life of the Right Honourable William Pitt*, Vol. I, pp.67–8
29 Ibid., p.68
30 Wraxall, *The Historical and the Posthumous Memoirs . . .*, Vol. II, p.415
31 Stanhope, *Life of the Right Honourable William Pitt*, Vol. I, pp.93–4
32 21 February 1783, Wright (ed.), *Speeches of Charles James Fox in the House of Commons*, Vol. II, p.130
33 *Parliamentary Register*, Vol. IX, 1782–83, p.283
34 Hathaway, *The Speeches of the Right Honourable William Pitt . . .*, Vol. I, p.48
35 Ibid., p.49
36 Ibid., p.50
37 R.I. and S.W. Wilberforce, *The Life of William Wilberforce*, Vol. I, p.26
38 Hathaway, *The Speeches of the Right Honourable William Pitt . . .*, Vol. I, p.59
39 Ibid., p.63
40 Ibid., pp.61–2
41 Ibid., p.62
42 Ibid., p.63.
43 Pelham Correspondence, Vol. III, 1779–1789, BL Add Mss 33128, fol.254

SEVEN : Brief Exuberance

1 Dundas to Shelburne, 24 February 1783, Chevening Mss U150/C404/2
2 Russell, *Memorials and Correspondence of Charles James Fox*, Vol. II, p.43
3 George III to Lord Chancellor, 24 February 1783, Fortescue, *The Correspondence of King George III . . .*, Vol. VI, no. 4133, p.249
4 21 March 1783, Romilly (ed.), *Memoirs of the Life of Sir Samuel Romilly*, Vol. I, quoted in Rose, *William Pitt and National Revival*, p.124
5 The Lord Advocate (Dundas) to his brother, 25 February 1783, Stanhope, *Life of the Right Honourable William Pitt*, Vol. I, p.105
6 Kenyon's diary, February 1783, Kenyon Mss, quoted in Cannon, *The Fox–North Coalition*, p.66
7 Pitt to the Lord Advocate (Dundas), 27 February 1783, Stanhope, *Life of the Right Honourable William Pitt*, Vol. I, p.107
8 The Lord Advocate (Dundas) to his brother, 27 February 1783, ibid., p.108
9 Ibid.
10 George III to Shelburne, 27 February 1783, Fitzmaurice, *Life of Shelburne. 1st Marquis of Lansdowne*, Vol. III, p.370
11 George III to Thurlow, 2 March 1783, Fortescue, *The Correspondence of King George the Third . . .*, Vol. VI, no. 4150
12 Fitzmaurice, *Life of Shelburne. 1st Marquis of Lansdowne*, Vol. III, p.375
13 Memorandum by Mr Thomas Pitt [in the King's handwriting], Minutes of the meeting of 7 March 1783, Fortescue, *The Correspondence of King George III . . .*, Vol. VI, no. 4169, p.268
14 George III to Pitt, 20 March 1783, Chatham Papers, PRO 30/8/103, part 1
15 Lord Advocate (Dundas) to his brother, 24 March 1783, Stanhope, *Life of the Right Honourable William Pitt*, Vol. I, p.112
16 George III to Lord Chancellor, 24 March 1783, Fortescue, *The Correspondence of King George III . . .*, Vol. VI, no. 4242, p.307
17 Wraxall, *The Historical and the Posthumous Memoirs . . .*, Vol. III, p.43
18 *Parliamentary Register*, Vol. IX, 1782–83, p.536
19 Hathaway, *The Speeches of the Right Honourable William Pitt . . .*, Vol. I, p.67
20 Charles Jenkinson to Robinson, 24 March 1783, quoted in Cannon, *The Fox–North Coalition*, p.78
21 Russell, *Memorials and Correspondence of Charles James Fox*, Vol. II, p.79
22 George III to Pitt, 24 March 1783, Chatham Papers, PRO 30/8/103, part 1
23 Jenkinson to Robinson, 24 March 1783, Atkinson to Robinson, 25 March 1783, Abergevenny Mss, quoted in Cannon, *The Fox–North Coalition*, p.78
24 Pitt to George III, 25 March 1783, Fortescue, *The Correspondence of King George III . . .*, Vol. VI, no. 4249, p.311
25 Wraxall, *The Historical and the Posthumous Memoirs . . .*, Vol. III, pp.41–2
26 Duke of Grafton's diary, February 1783, Anson (ed.), *Autobiography and Political Correspondence of Augustus Henry, Third Duke of Grafton*, p.369
27 George III to Pitt, 25 March 1783, Chatham Papers, PRO 30/8/103, part 1
28 Draft of Message from King to Parliament, c.28 March 1783, Fortescue, *The Correspondence of King George III . . .*, Vol. VI, no. 4260, p.317
29 Hathaway, *The Speeches of the Right Honourable William Pitt . . .*, Vol. I, p.71
30 Russell, *Memorials and Correspondence of Charles James Fox*, Vol. II, p.28
31 Memorandum of the Duke of Leeds, 26 March 1783, BL Add Mss 27918, fol.67
32 George III to Lord Temple, 1 April 1783, quoted in Fortescue, *The Correspondence of King George III . . .*, Vol. VI, no. 4272, p.330
33 Harcourt, *The Diaries and Correspondence of the Right Hon. George Rose*, Vol. I, p.45
34 *Morning Herald*, 24 May 1783, quoted in Mitchell, *Charles James Fox*, p.61
35 Wraxall, *The Historical and the Posthumous Memoirs . . .*, Vol. III, p.217

36 Ibid., p.73
37 Wilberforce, *Sketch of Mr. Pitt*, quoted in Rosebery, *Pitt and Wilberforce*, p.8
38 Wilberforce's diary, 4 April 1783, R.I. and S.W. Wilberforce, *Life of William Wilberforce*, Vol. I, p.28
39 Wilberforce, *Sketch of Mr. Pitt*, quoted in Rosebery, *Pitt and Wilberforce*, p.4
40 Thomas Orde to Shelburne, 17 July 1783, Lansdowne Mss, Bowood, quoted in Ehrman, *The Younger Pitt*, Vol. I, p.108
41 Wilberforce, *Sketch of Mr. Pitt*, quoted in Rosebery, *Pitt and Wilberforce*, p.16
42 Furneaux, *William Wilberforce*, p.13
43 Pitt to Wilberforce, undated, Duke Mss, quoted in Pollock, *Wilberforce*, p.19
44 Diary, 21 March 1782, George Selwyn, *His Letters and Life*, p.217
45 Bodleian Library Wilberforce Mss e.11, fol.31–3
46 Lord Muncaster, quoted by Sir J. Legard, 10 December 1806, Bodleian Library Wilberforce Mss d.13, fol.361
47 Meryon (ed.), *Memoirs of the Lady Hester Stanhope, as related by herself in conversations with her Physician*, p.187
48 Wraxall, *The Historical and the Posthumous Memoirs . . .*, Vol. III, p.217
49 Meryon (ed.), *Memoirs of the Lady Hester Stanhope . . .*, p.69
50 Minute made by Thomas Pitt of his conversation at the Queens House, 28 March 1791, BL Add Mss 69143, fol.21
51 Wraxall, *The Historical and the Posthumous Memoirs . . .*, Vol. III, p.111
52 George III to Colonel Hotham, quoted in Hibbert, *George III*, p.241
53 Buckingham, *Memoirs of the Court and Cabinet of George III*, Vol. I, p.304
54 Pitt to Earl Temple, 22 July 1783, Fortescue, *The Manuscripts of J.B. Fortescue, Esq., Preserved at Dropmore*, Vol. I, p.216
55 Pitt to Earl Temple, 10 July 1783, Stanhope, *Miscellanies*, p.26
56 Pitt to Lady Chatham, 22 July 1783, Chatham Papers, PRO 30/8/12, fol.305
57 Pitt to Lady Chatham, 8 August 1783, ibid., fol.307
58 Pitt to Temple, 10 September 1783, Stanhope, *Miscellanies*, pp.34–5
59 Wilberforce, *Sketch of Mr. Pitt*, quoted in Rosebery, *Pitt and Wilberforce*, p.9
60 Pitt to Lady Harriot Pitt, 1 October 1783, Chatham Papers, PRO 30/8/12, fol.314
61 R.I. and S.W. Wilberforce, *The Life of William Wilberforce*, Vol. I, p.36
62 Wilberforce, *Sketch of Mr. Pitt*, quoted in Rosebery, *Pitt and Wilberforce*, p.10
63 Ibid., p.11
64 Harcourt, *The Diaries and Correspondence of the Right Hon. George Rose*, Vol. I, pp.31–2

EIGHT : **From Plotter to Prime Minister**

1 Tomline, *Memoirs of the Life of the Right Honourable William Pitt*, Vol. I, p.132
2 Pitt to Lord Mahon, 3 November 1783, Stanhope, *Life of the Right Honourable William Pitt*, Vol. I, p.135
3 Fox to Lord Northington, 17 July 1783, BL Add Mss 47567, fol.13
4 Wraxall, *The Historical and the Posthumous Memoirs . . .*, Vol. III, pp.117–18
5 Pitt to Lady Chatham, 11 November 1783, Chatham Papers, PRO 30/8/12, fol.370
6 Reilly, *Pitt the Younger*, p.91
7 Hathaway, *The Speeches of the Right Honourable William Pitt . . .*, Vol. I, p.91
8 Pitt to Rutland, 22 November 1783, Rutland, *Correspondence Between the Right Hon. William Pitt and Charles Duke of Rutland*, pp.3–4
9 Hathaway, *The Speeches of the Right Honourable William Pitt . . .*, Vol. I, p.93
10 Stanhope, *Life of the Right Honourable William Pitt*, Vol. I, p.143
11 Buckingham, *Memoirs of the Court and Cabinet of George III*, Vol. I, pp.288–9
12 A report to B. Alvensleben, 9 December 1783, Bodleian Library Clarendon Mss Dep. c.347, fol.604
13 Second report to the same, 17 December 1783, ibid., fol.605

14 Buckingham, *Memoirs of the Court and Cabinet of George III*, Vol. I, p.285
15 George North to Thomas Pelham, 16 December 1783, BL Add Mss 33100, fol.472
16 Harcourt, *The Diaries and Correspondence of the Right Hon. George Rose*, Vol. I, p.48
17 Fox to Armistead, BL Add Mss 47570, fol.156
18 Wraxall, *The Historical and the Posthumous Memoirs . . .*, Vol. III, pp.195–6
19 George III to Lord North, 18 December 1783, Fortescue, *The Correspondence of King George III . . .*, Vol. VI, no. 4546, p.476
20 Wraxall, *The Historical and the Posthumous Memoirs . . .*, Vol. III, p.191
21 22 December 1783, Stanhope, *Life of the Right Honourable William Pitt*, Vol. I, p.159
22 Tomline, *Memoirs of the Life of the Right Honourable William Pitt*, Vol. I, pp.173–4
23 Wilberforce's diary, 23 December 1783, R.I. and S.W. Wilberforce, *The Life of William Wilberforce*, Vol. I, p.48
24 Grenville, BL Fortescue Mss 'commentaries', Chapter III, pp.4–6, quoted in Jupp, *Lord Grenville*, p.45
25 Minto, *Life and Letters of Sir Gilbert Elliot*, Vol. I, p.91
26 Wilberforce's diary, 22 December 1783, R.I. and S.W. Wilberforce, *The Life of William Wilberforce*, Vol. I, p.48
27 William Eden to John Baker-Holroyd, 4 January 1784, Supplementary Auckland Papers, BL Add Mss 45728, fol.12
28 John Robinson to Jenkinson, 22 December 1783, BL Loan 72/29, fol.164

NINE : **The Struggle for Supremacy**

1 Orde to Shelburne, 18 December 1783, Landsdowne Mss, Bowood, quoted in Ehrman, *The Younger Pitt*, Vol. I, p.133
2 Lord Sydney, 31 December 1783, Egerton Mss 2136, fol.237, quoted in Cannon, *The Fox–North Coalition*, pp.159–60
3 Portland to Sandwich, 30 December 1783, Sandwich Mss, quoted in ibid., p.156
4 Pitt to Lady Chatham, 30 December 1783, Chatham Papers, PRO 30/8/12, fol.322
5 Cannon, *The Fox–North Coalition*, p.162
6 Wright (ed.), *Speeches of Charles James Fox in the House of Commons*, Vol. II, p.313
7 *Morning Chronicle*, 13 January 1784, quoted in Ehrman, *The Younger Pitt*, Vol. I, p.138
8 Wraxall, *The Historical and the Posthumous Memoirs . . .*, Vol. III, p.276
9 12 January 1784, Stanhope, *Life of the Right Honourable William Pitt*, Vol. I, p.171
10 See Cannon, *The Fox–North Coalition*, p.165
11 Browning, *Memoranda of Francis, Fifth Duke of Leeds*, p.94
12 Cannon, *The Fox–North Coalition*, p.170
13 Stanhope, *Life of the Right Honourable William Pitt*, Vol. I, p.176
14 Tomline, *Memoirs of the Life of the Right Honourable William Pitt*, Vol. I, p.225
15 Browning (ed.), *Memoranda of Francis, Fifth Duke of Leeds*, p.97
16 Cannon, *The Fox–North Coalition*, pp.187–8
17 Ibid., p.188
18 Stanhope, *Life of the Right Honourable William Pitt*, Vol. I, p.178
19 Hathaway, *The Speeches of the Right Honourable William Pitt . . .*, Vol. I, p.140
20 Wraxall, *The Historical and the Posthumous Memoirs . . .*, Vol. III, p.281
21 Ibid., p.307
22 Ibid., p.292
23 Stanhope, *Life of the Right Honourable William Pitt*, Vol. I, p.190
24 *Parliamentary Register*, Vol. XIII, pp.220–1
25 Tomline, *Memoirs of the Life of the Right Honourable William Pitt*, Vol. I, p.303
26 Lord Chatham to Tomline, 4 February

1821, Pretyman Mss 562:1821, quoted in Ehrman, *The Younger Pitt*, Vol. I, pp.140–1
27 *Parliamentary History*, quoted in Cannon, *The Fox–North Coalition*, p.201
28 Pitt to Rutland, 10 March 1784, Rutland, *Correspondence Between the Right Hon. William Pitt and Charles Duke of Rutland*, pp.7–8
29 Pitt to Lady Chatham, 16 March 1784, Chatham Papers, PRO 30/8/12, fol.324
30 Pitt to Rutland, 23 March 1784, Rutland, *Correspondence Between the Right Hon. William Pitt and Charles Duke of Rutland*, p.9
31 24 March 1784, *Parliamentary History*, Vol. XXIV, p.774
32 Cannon, *The Fox–North Coalition*, p.222
33 Pitt to Wilberforce, 24 March 1784, Stanhope, *Life of the Right Honourable William Pitt*, Vol. I, p.202
34 Pitt to Corporation of Bath, 6 April 1784, printed in *London Chronicle*, 10 April 1784
35 J. Freeman to Lord Sydney, 11 April 1784, Brotherton Mss, quoted in Cannon, *The Fox–North Coalition*, p.214
36 Furneaux, *William Wilberforce*, p.31
37 Debrett, *History of the Westminster Election*, p.158
38 Ibid., p.96
39 Ibid., p.99
40 Ibid.
41 George III to William Pitt, 13 April 1784, Chatham Papers, PRO 30/8/103, part 1
42 Debrett, *History of the Westminster Election*, p.99

TEN : Power and its Limits

1 Wraxall, *The Historical and the Posthumous Memoirs . . .*, Vol. III, p.360
2 Ibid., p.387
3 Ibid., p.395
4 Hathaway, *The Speeches of the Right Honourable William Pitt . . .*, Vol. I, p.240
5 Wraxall, *The Historical and the Posthumous Memoirs . . .*, Vol. IV, p.121
6 *Morning Herald*, 30 July 1784, quoted in Mitchell, *Charles James Fox*, p.73
7 Wraxall, *The Historical and the Posthumous Memoirs . . .*, Vol. III, p.428
8 Lady Gower to Lord Granville Leveson Gower, 19 February 1785, Granville (ed.), *Lord Granville Leveson Gower, First Earl Granville: Private Correspondence. 1781–1821*, Vol. I, pp.5–6
9 Stanhope, *Life of the Right Honourable William Pitt*, Vol. I, p.221
10 Ibid., pp.216–17
11 Mr. Gibbon to Lord Eliot, 27 October 1784, quoted in ibid., p.237
12 Wilberforce, *Sketch of Mr. Pitt*, quoted in Rosebery, *Pitt and Wilberforce*, p.14
13 Dudley Ryder, Lord Harrowby, quoted in Thorne (ed.), *The House of Commons 1790–1820*, Vol. IV, p.815
14 Pitt to Lady Chatham, 28 August 1784, Chatham Papers, PRO 30/8/12, fol.335–6
15 Pitt to Lady Chatham, 7 October 1784, ibid., fol.337–8
16 The Lord Lieutenant to William Pitt, 15 August 1784, quoted in Stanhope, *Life of the Right Honourable William Pitt*, Vol. I, p.263
17 Pitt to Sydney, 10 September 1784, William J. Clements Library, Michigan
18 Ashbourne, *Pitt: Some Chapters of His Life and Times*, p.87
19 Pitt to Rutland, 7 October 1784, Rutland, *Correspondence Between the Right Hon. William Pitt and Charles Duke of Rutland*, p.34
20 Pitt to Rutland, 16 June 1784, ibid., p.19
21 Hathaway, *The Speeches of the Right Honourable William Pitt . . .*, Vol. I, p.197
22 Ibid.
23 22 February 1785, ibid., p.199
24 Ibid., p.209
25 Tomline, *Memoirs of the Life of the Right Honourable William Pitt*, Vol. I, p.438
26 Wraxall, *The Historical and the Posthumous Memoirs . . .*, Vol. IV, p.95

27 Ibid., p.75
28 Ibid., p.76
29 Ibid., p.98
30 Rev. Wyvill to Rev. Wilkinson, 9 December 1784, Wyvill, *Political Papers*, Vol. IV, p.119
31 Pitt to Rutland, 12 January 1785, Rutland, *Correspondence Between the Right Hon. William Pitt and Charles Duke of Rutland*, p.77
32 Pitt to George III, 19 March 1785, Clements Transcripts I, 326, quoted in Barnes, *George III and William Pitt*, pp.125–6
33 George III to Pitt, 20 March 1785, Chatham Papers, PRO 30/8/103, part 1
34 Hathaway, *The Speeches of the Right Honourable William Pitt . . .*, Vol. I, p.238
35 Daniel Pulteney to Duke of Rutland, 19 April 1785, Manners, *The Manuscripts of His Grace the Duke of Rutland, G.C.B., Preserved at Belvoir Castle*, p.202
36 Wraxall, *The Historical and the Posthumous Memoirs . . .*, Vol. IV, p.114
37 Wilberforce's diary, 18, 19 April 1785, R.I. and S.W. Wilberforce, *The Life of William Wilberforce*, Vol. I, p.78
38 Savage and Finer (eds), *The Selected Letters of Josiah Wedgwood*, pp.282–3
39 30 May 1785, *Parliamentary History*, Vol. XXV, Feb. 1785–May 1786, p.778
40 Pitt to Rutland, 17 August 1785, Rutland, *Correspondence Between the Right Hon. William Pitt and Charles Duke of Rutland*, pp.107–9
41 Wraxall, *The Historical and the Posthumous Memoirs . . .*, Vol. IV, p.166

ELEVEN : **Private by Nature**

1 Earl Mornington, 'Recollections of Mr. Pitt's Character', 22 November 1836, BL Add Mss 37416, fol.379
2 Wilberforce's diary, 10 March 1785, R.I. and S.W. Wilberforce, *The Life of William Wilberforce*, Vol. I, p.78
3 Wilberforce to Pitt, c.2 August 1785, Chatham Papers, PRO 30/8/189, part 2
4 Pretyman, Draft Life of Pitt, Chapter XXVII, BL Add Mss 45107, fol.24
5 Earl Mornington, 'Recollections of Mr. Pitt's Character', 22 November 1836, BL Add Mss 37416, fol.378–9
6 Notes by Mrs Tomline, October and November 1801, Stanhope Mss U1590/S5/C41
7 Pitt to Lord Eliot, 8 September 1785, quoted in Reilly, *Pitt the Younger*, p.134
8 Lady Chatham to Mr Wilson, 2 November 1784, quoted in Ashbourne, *Pitt: Some Chapters of His Life and Times*, p.153
9 Lady Chatham to Mr Wilson, 19 March 1785, quoted in ibid., p.154
10 Ehrman, *The Younger Pitt*, Vol. I, p.594
11 Wilberforce, *Sketch of Mr. Pitt*, quoted in Rosebery, *Pitt and Wilberforce*, p.14
12 Horner, *Memoirs of Francis Horner*, Vol. I, p.315
13 Bladon (ed.), *The Diaries of Colonel the Hon. Robert Fulke Greville*, p.187
14 Headlam (ed.), *The Letters of Lady Harriot Eliot, 1766–1786*, p.135
15 Pitt to Shelburne, 13 January 1783, Pitt Mss, William L. Clements Library, Michigan
16 Tomline, unpublished Chapter XXVII of his *Life of Pitt*, Rosebery, *Bishop Tomline's Estimate of Pitt*, p.34
17 Notes by Mrs Tomline, October and November 1801, Stanhope Mss U1590/S5/C41
18 17 May 1809, Farington, *The Diary of Joseph Farington*, Vol. V, p.162
19 Pitt to Elliot, 22 August 1786, Pretyman Mss HA 119/T108/39/228
20 Wilberforce to Pitt, 30 September 1785, R.I. and S.W. Wilberforce, *Correspondence of William Wilberforce*, Vol. I, p.7
21 Count Woronzow to Lord Grenville, 2 July 1800 [in French], quoted in Fortescue, *The Manuscripts of J. B. Fortescue, Esq., Preserved at Dropmore*, Vol. VI, p.259
22 Bickley (ed.), *The Diaries of Sylvester Douglas, Lord Glenbervie*, Vol. I, p.149
23 Sir James Harris to Lord Carmarthen, 18 July 1796, Cobban, *Ambassadors and Secret Agents: The Diplomacy of the First Earl of Malmesbury at the Hague*, p.80

24 Pitt to Thomas Coutts, 30 June 1787, Pitt Mss, William L. Clements Library, Michigan
25 Tomline, unpublished Chapter XXVII of his *Life of Pitt*, BL Add Mss 45107(J), fol.36
26 Ibid., fol.35
27 Ibid., fol.36
28 Harcourt, *The Diaries and Correspondence of the Right Hon. George Rose*, Vol. I, p.293
29 Pitt to Lady Chatham, 1 December 1785, Chatham Papers, PRO 30/8/12, fol.347–8
30 Pitt to Lady Chatham, 29 May 1784, ibid., fol.333
31 Hester Chatham to Thomas Coutts, 17 March 1786, Pitt Mss, William L. Clements Library, Michigan
32 R.I. and S.W. Wilberforce, *The Life of William Wilberforce*, Vol. I, p.89
33 Ibid., p.91
34 Ibid., p.94
35 Ibid., p.95
36 Stanhope, *Life of the Right Honourable William Pitt*, Vol. I, p.313
37 Pitt to Mrs Stapleton, 25 September 1786, quoted in ibid., pp.313–14
38 Tomline, *Memoirs of the Life of the Right Honourable William Pitt*, Vol. II, pp.3–4
39 Thomas Orde to Duke of Rutland, 30 November 1784, Manners, *The Manuscripts of His Grace the Duke of Rutland, G.C.B., Preserved at Belvoir Castle*, p.152
40 Tomline, unpublished Chapter XXVII of his *Life of Pitt*, BL Add Mss 45107(J), fol.33

TWELVE : Spreading His Wings

1 Wraxall, *The Historical and the Posthumous Memoirs*. . ., Vol. IV, p.284
2 Richard Rigby, quoted in a letter from Lieutenant General James Grant to Earl Cornwallis, 16 April 1787, quoted in Ross (ed.), *Correspondence of Charles, First Marquis Cornwallis*, Vol. I, p.291
3 Elliot to Pitt, August 1788, Chatham Papers, PRO 30/8/132, part 2
4 Tomline, *Memoirs of the Life of the Right Honourable William Pitt*, Vol. I, p.504
5 Hathaway, *The Speeches of the Right Honourable William Pitt*. . ., Vol. I, pp.291–2
6 Wraxall, *The Historical and the Posthumous Memoirs*. . ., Vol. IV, p.266
7 Tomline, *Memoirs of the Life of the Right Honourable William Pitt*, Vol. I, p.520
8 Harriet Pitt to Lady Chatham, 28 February 1786, Eng. Mss 1272, no. 54, John Rylands Library, quoted in Black, *British Foreign Policy*. . ., p.27
9 Eden to Beresford, 28 February 1786, *The Correspondence of the Right Hon. John Beresford*, Vol. I, p.302
10 Pitt to Wilberforce, 30 September 1785, quoted in R.I. and S.W. Wilberforce, *The Correspondence of William Wilberforce*, Vol. I, p.9
11 Stanhope, *Life of the Right Honourable William Pitt*, Vol. I, pp.290–2
12 Tomline, unpublished Chapter XXVII of his *Life of Pitt*, BL Add Mss 45107(J)
13 Hathaway, *The Speeches of the Right Honourable William Pitt*. . ., Vol. I, p.306
14 Ibid., p.305
15 Wraxall, *The Historical and the Posthumous Memoirs*. . ., Vol. IV, pp.289–92
16 Tomline, *Memoirs of the Life of the Right Honourable William Pitt*, Vol. I, p.542
17 Harcourt, *The Diaries and Correspondence of the Right Hon. George Rose*, Vol. I, pp.69–70
18 Wraxall, *The Historical and the Posthumous Memoirs*. . ., Vol. IV, p.307
19 Pitt to Lady Chatham, 13 November 1786, Chatham Papers, PRO 30/8/12, fol.355
20 Black, *British Foreign Policy*. . ., p.105
21 12 February 1787, Hathaway, *The Speeches of the Right Honourable William Pitt*. . ., Vol. I, p.359
22 12 February 1787, *Parliamentary History*, Vol. XXVI, pp.397–8
23 Ibid., p.392

24 Stanhope, *Life of the Right Honourable William Pitt*, Vol. I, p.298
25 Wraxall, *The Historical and the Posthumous Memoirs . . .*, Vol. IV, p.317
26 Ibid., p.318
27 R.I. and S.W. Wilberforce, *The Life of William Wilberforce*, Vol. V, p.341
28 Hathaway, *The Speeches of the Right Honourable William Pitt . . .*, Vol. I, p.320
29 Wraxall, *The Historical and the Posthumous Memoirs . . .*, Vol. IV, p.337
30 Hathaway, *The Speeches of the Right Honourable William Pitt . . .*, Vol. I, p.331
31 Ibid.
32 Wraxall, *The Historical and the Posthumous Memoirs . . .*, Vol. IV, p.341
33 R.I. and S.W. Wilberforce, *The Life of William Wilberforce*, Vol. I, p.341
34 Pitt to Lady Chatham, 13 November 1786, Chatham Papers, PRO 30/8/12, fol.377–8
35 Orde to Lansdowne, 24 January 1786, Bowood Mss, quoted in Mitchell, *Charles James Fox and the Disintegration of the Whig Party 1782–1794*, p.102
36 Wraxall, *The Historical and the Posthumous Memoirs . . .*, Vol. V, p.47
37 Ibid., p.401
38 Ibid., p.402
39 Stanhope, *Life of the Right Honourable William Pitt*, Vol. I, p.334
40 Lord Buckingham to Grenville, 11 November 1788, quoted in Fortescue, *The Manuscripts of J. B. Fortescue, Esq., Preserved at Dropmore*, Vol. I, p.362
41 Lloyd Jones, *Darkness and Light, Ephesians 4.17–5.17*, p.50
42 Tomline, *Memoirs of the Life of the Right Honourable William Pitt*, Vol. II, p.28
43 Stanhope, *Life of the Right Honourable William Pitt*, Vol. I, p.337
44 Duffy, *The Younger Pitt*, p.166
45 George III to Carmarthen, 6 July 1784, BL Add Mss 27914
46 Pitt to Rutland, 8 August 1785, quoted in Rutland, *Correspondence Between the Right Hon. William Pitt and Charles Duke of Rutland*, p.102
47 Black, *British Foreign Policy . . .*, p.73
48 Ibid.
49 Keith to Hailes, 12 December 1785, Kent Archive Office U269/C191
50 Black, *British Foreign Policy . . .*, p.41
51 Sir James Harris to the Marquis of Carmarthen, 10 October 1786, quoted in Malmesbury, *Diaries and Correspondence of James Harris, First Earl of Malmesbury*, Vol. II, p.197
52 William Pitt to Sir James Harris, 5 December 1786, quoted in ibid., p.211
53 Sir James Harris to the Marquis of Carmarthen, 23 February 1787, quoted in ibid., p.237
54 Sir James Harris to the Marquis of Carmarthen, 1 May 1787, quoted in ibid., p.256
55 Pitt to Wilberforce, 22 September 1787, Pitt Mss, William L. Clements Library, Michigan
56 William Pitt to Sir James Harris, 28 September 1787, quoted in Malmesbury, *Diaries and Correspondence of James Harris, First Earl of Malmesbury*, Vol. II, p.347
57 Count Woronzow to his brother, quoted in Stanhope, *Life of the Right Honourable William Pitt*, Vol. I, p.350

THIRTEEN : Insanity and Crisis

1 Wraxall, *The Historical and the Posthumous Memoirs . . .*, Vol. V, p.98
2 Duchess of Devonshire's diary, 20 November 1788, Sichel, *Sheridan*, Vol. II, p.404
3 Stanhope, *Life of the Right Honourable William Pitt*, Vol. I, p.361
4 Pitt to Lady Chatham, 19 June 1788, Chatham Papers, PRO 30/8/12, fol.408–9
5 Wraxall, *The Historical and the Posthumous Memoirs . . .*, Vol. V, p.152
6 Pitt to Lady Chatham, 29 August 1788, Chatham Papers, PRO 30/8/12, fol.410
7 George III to Pitt, 20 October 1788, Chatham Papers, PRO 30/8/103, part 2
8 George Baker's diary, 17 October–7 November 1788, quoted in MacAlpine and Hunter, *George III and the Mad Business*

9 Pretyman Mss HA 119/T108/42
10 Reports of Sir George Baker, on behalf of Dr Warren, quoted in Rose, *William Pitt and National Revival*, pp.410–11
11 Macaulay, essay contained in *Encyclopaedia Britannica*, eleventh edition, p.672
12 Harcourt, *The Diaries and Correspondence of the Right Hon. George Rose*, Vol. I, p.90
13 Ibid.
14 Duke of York and Prince of Wales to Prince Augustus, 3 December 1788, Aspinall, *The Correspondence of George, Prince of Wales*, Vol. I, no. 339, p.405
15 Fox to Prince of Wales, c.25 November 1788, ibid., p.384
16 Unaddressed letter of Windham, 26 November 1788, Windham, *The Windham Papers*, Vol. I, pp.88–9
17 George III, 5 December 1788, Bladon (ed.), *The Diaries of Colonel the Hon. Robert Fulke Greville*, p.119
18 Duchess of Devonshire's diary, Sichel, *Sheridan*, Vol. II, p.413
19 Hathaway, *The Speeches of the Right Honourable William Pitt*..., Vol. I, p.374
20 Wraxall, *The Historical and the Posthumous Memoirs*..., Vol. V, p.210
21 Hathaway, *The Speeches of the Right Honourable William Pitt*..., Vol. I, pp.375–7
22 *Morning Chronicle*, 10 December 1788
23 12 December 1788, *Parliamentary History*, Vol. XXVII, p.731
24 Hathaway, *The Speeches of the Right Honourable William Pitt*..., Vol. II, p.381
25 Fox, 1 December 1788, *Parliamentary History*, Vol. XXVII, p.757
26 Wraxall, *The Historical and the Posthumous Memoirs*..., Vol. V, p.228
27 Hathaway, *The Speeches of the Right Honourable William Pitt*..., Vol. I, pp.400–1
28 Stanhope, *Life of the Right Honourable William Pitt*, Vol. II, p.18
29 Hathaway, *The Speeches of the Right Honourable William Pitt*..., Vol. I, p.407
30 Stanhope, *Life of the Right Honourable William Pitt*, Vol. II, pp.19–20
31 *Morning Herald*, 20 January 1789, quoted in Derry, *The Regency Crisis and the Whigs 1788–9*, p.130
32 John Dixon to Fitzwilliam, 24 December 1788, Wentworth Woodhouse Mss, fol.34(h), quoted in ibid., p.117
33 Elliot to Lady Elliot, 18 December 1788, Minto, *Life and Letters of Sir Gilbert Elliot*, Vol. I, p.248
34 Reilly, *Pitt the Younger*, p.164
35 Wraxall, *The Historical and the Posthumous Memoirs*..., Vol. V, p.301
36 Russell, *Memorials and Correspondence of Charles James Fox*, Vol. II, p.302
37 Pitt to Lady Chatham, 19 February 1789, Chatham Papers, PRO 30/8/12, fol.418
38 George III to Pitt, 23 February 1789, Chatham Papers, PRO 30/8/103, part 2
39 Minto, *Life and Letters of Sir Gilbert Elliot*, Vol. I, p.300
40 Pitt to Lady Chatham, 14 July 1789, Chatham Papers, PRO 30/8/12, fol.421

FOURTEEN : **Trials of Strength**

1 Fitzherbert to Leeds, 1 January 1790, BL Add Mss 28065, fol.1
2 Black, *British Foreign Policy*..., p.305
3 Rose, *William Pitt and National Revival*, p.543
4 See ibid.
5 Furet, *The French Revolution 1770–1814*, p.13
6 C.J. Fox to R. Fitzpatrick, 30 July 1789, BL Add Mss 47580, fol.139
7 William Grenville to Marquis of Buckingham, 13 June 1789, Buckingham, *Memoirs of the Court and Cabinet of George III*, Vol. II, p.47
8 5 February 1790, *Parliamentary History*, Vol. XXVIII, p.351
9 Burke to Depont, November 1789, quoted in Copeland (ed.), *The Correspondence of Edmund Burke*, Vol. VI, p.40
10 Burges to Ewart, 7 July 1791, Burges, *Selections from the Letters and Correspondence of Sir James Bland Burges*, p.175

11 Pitt to Lady Chatham, 21 November 1789, Chatham Papers, PRO 30/8/12, fol.422
12 Pitt's notes dated 1791, Chatham Papers, PRO 30/8/195, fol.49
13 Ewart to Auckland, November 1790, quoted in Rose, *William Pitt and National Revival*, p.590
14 Leeds to Merry, 2 February 1790, PRO FO 72/16, fol.87–8
15 *Parliamentary Register 1790*, Vol. XXVII, p.565
16 Hamilton (ed.), *Letters and Papers of Admiral of the Fleet Sir Thos. Byam Martin, G.C.B*, Vol. III, p.381
17 Pitt to Lady Chatham, 24 June 1790, Chatham Papers, PRO 30/8/12, fol.424
18 See Duffy, *The Younger Pitt*, p.112
19 Stanhope, *Life of the Right Honourable William Pitt*, Vol. II, p.63
20 R.I. and S.W. Wilberforce, *The Life of William Wilberforce*, Vol. I, p.286
21 Duke of Richmond to Pitt, 24 November 1790, quoted in Stanhope, *Life of the Right Honourable William Pitt*, Vol. II, p.80
22 Ewart to Pitt, 13 December 1790, Chatham Papers, PRO 30/8/133, part 2
23 Leeds to Elgin, 4 February 1791, PRO FO 7/23, fol.71–2
24 Jackson to Burges, 4 August 1790, Bodleian Library Dep. Bland–Burges Mss 36, fol.60
25 Auckland to Keith, 19 February 1791, quoted in *Memoirs and Correspondence of Sir Robert Murray Keith*, Vol. II, p.377
26 Rose, *William Pitt and National Revival*, p.617
27 Speech of April 1791, Wright (ed.), *Speeches of Charles James Fox in the House of Commons*, Vol. IV, p.199
28 9 February 1790, Burke (ed. Clark), *Reflections on the Revolution in France*, p.66
29 Stanhope, *Life of the Right Honourable William Pitt*, Vol. II, p.94; see account in Moore, *Sheridan*, pp.470–1
30 Horace Walpole to M. Berry, 12 May 1791, quoted in Lewis, *Horace Walpole's Miscellaneous Correspondence*, Vol. XI, p.263
31 Grenville to Keith, 19 September 1791 [originally in cipher], PRO FO 7/28
32 Pellew, *The Life and Correspondence of the Right Hon. Henry Addington*, Vol. I, p.72

FIFTEEN : The Cautious Crusader

1 R.I. and S.W. Wilberforce, *The Life of William Wilberforce*, Vol. I, pp.50–1
2 Furneaux, *William Wilberforce*, p.72
3 See footnote in Reilly, *Pitt the Younger*, p.196
4 Wilberforce, 12 May 1789, *Parliamentary History*, Vol. XXVIII, p.48
5 Ibid.
6 Reilly, *Pitt the Younger*, p.196
7 Clarkson, *The History of the Rise, Progress, and Accomplishment of the Abolition of the African Slave-Trade by the British Parliament*, Vol. I, p.210
8 Rose to Wilberforce, 27 September 1787, Bodleian Library Wilberforce Mss d.17, fol.8
9 Pitt to Auckland, 2 November 1787, Auckland, *Journal and Correspondence. William Eden Auckland*, Vol. I, p.267
10 Pitt to Eden, 7 December 1782, Chatham Papers, PRO 30/8/102, fol.113
11 Reilly, *Pitt the Younger*, p.197
12 James Stephen to Wilberforce, R.I. and S.W. Wilberforce, *The Life of William Wilberforce*, Vol. II, p.225
13 Pitt to Grenville, 29 June 1788, in Fortescue, *The Manuscripts of J.B. Fortescue, Esq., Preserved at Dropmore*, Vol. I, p.342
14 Edmund Burke, *Parliamentary Register*, Vol. XXVI, p.155
15 Pollock, *Wilberforce*, p.90
16 Hathaway, *The Speeches of the Right Honourable William Pitt . . .*, Vol. II, pp.14–15
17 Pollock, *Wilberforce*, p.108
18 18 April 1791, *Parliamentary History*, Vol. XXIX, p.282
19 Reilly, *Pitt the Younger*, p.199
20 *Diary and Woodfall's Register*, no. 946, 3 April 1792
21 Hathaway, *The Speeches of the Right Honourable William Pitt . . .*, Vol. II, p.71

22 Ibid., pp.74–5
23 Ibid., p.75
24 Ibid., p.80
25 Ibid., p.82
26 R.I. and S.W. Wilberforce, *The Life of William Wilberforce*, Vol. I, pp.345–6

SIXTEEN : The View from the Precipice

1 Grenville to Auckland, 23 August 1791, quoted in Fortescue, *The Manuscripts of J.B. Fortescue, Esq., Preserved at Dropmore*, Vol. II, p.172
2 Pitt to Dundas, 27 November 1792, William L. Clements Library, Michigan
3 Hathaway, *The Speeches of the Right Honourable William Pitt . . .*, Vol. II, pp.43–5
4 Ibid., p.36
5 Elgin to Straton, 16 March 1792, Ipswich HA 239/2/ 274, quoted in Black, *British Foreign Policy . . .*, p.388
6 Earl Mornington, 'Recollections of Mr. Pitt's Character', 22 November 1836, BL Add Mss 37416, fol.380
7 Pitt to Lady Chatham, 4 October 1791, Chatham Papers, PRO 30/8/12, fol.442
8 Rose, *William Pitt and National Revival*, p.279
9 See Duffy, *The Younger Pitt*
10 1 March 1792, *Parliamentary History*, Vol. XXIX, p.995
11 Canning to Pitt, 26–28 July 1792, quoted in Ehrman, *The Younger Pitt*, Vol. II, p.184
12 George III to Pitt, 6 August 1792, Chatham Papers, PRO 30/8/103, part 3
13 Pitt to Eliot, 21 August 1792, author's collection
14 See Reilly, *Pitt the Younger*, p.203
15 Stanhope, *Life of the Right Honourable William Pitt*, Vol. II, p.119
16 Grenville to Auckland, 29 July 1791, BL Add Mss 34438, fol.378
17 Burges to A. Burges, 24 February 1792, Bodleian Library Dep. Bland–Burgess Mss 47, fol.409
18 Burges to Grenville, 18 February 1797, Chatham Papers, PRO 30/8/337, part 1
19 Hathaway, *The Speeches of the Right Honourable William Pitt . . .*, Vol. II, pp.88–93
20 Tomline, *Memoirs of the Life of the Right Honourable William Pitt*, Vol. II, p.440
21 Stanhope, *Life of the Right Honourable William Pitt*, Vol. II, p.149
22 George III to Dundas, 16 May 1792, quoted in ibid., p.150
23 Duke of Portland, 13 May 1792, Chatham Papers, PRO 30/8/168, fol.73
24 10 June 1792, Malmesbury, *Diaries and Correspondence of James Harris, First Earl of Malmesbury*, Vol. II, p.420
25 17 June 1792, ibid., p.430
26 Pitt to Dundas, 25 November 1792, William L. Clements Library, Michigan
27 Browning (ed.), *Memoranda of Francis, Fifth Duke of Leeds*, p.188
28 Ibid., p.194.
29 Auckland to Straton, 9 October 1792, Ipswich HA 239/2/283, quoted in Black, *British Foreign Policy . . .*, p.405
30 Ehrman, *The Younger Pitt*, Vol. II, p.216
31 Stanhope, *Life of the Right Honourable William Pitt*, Vol. II, p.173
32 Grenville to Auckland, 13 November 1792, no. 20, Most Secret, PRO FO 37/41
33 See Ehrman, *The Younger Pitt*, Vol. II, p.208
34 Wright (ed.), *Speeches of Charles James Fox in the House of Commons*, Vol. IV, p.451
35 George III to Portland, 16 August 1795, Aspinall, *The Later Correspondence of George III*, Vol. II, no. 1283, p.379
36 Ehrman, *The Younger Pitt*, Vol. II, p.239
37 See Black, *British Foreign Policy . . .*

SEVENTEEN : A Tutorial in War

1 Hathaway, *The Speeches of the Right Honourable William Pitt . . .*, Vol. II, p.174
2 Richmond, in PRO WO 30/81, quoted in Ehrman, *The Younger Pitt*, Vol. II, pp.267–8
3 Rose, *William Pitt and the Great War*, p.112
4 1 February 1793, *Parliamentary History*, Vol. XXX, p.271

5 Hathaway, *The Speeches of the Right Honourable William Pitt . . .*, Vol. II, p.100
6 *Parliamentary Register*, Vol. XXXV, 1793, p.675
7 C.J. Fox to D. O'Bryen, 23 January 1793, BL Add Mss 51467, fol.29
8 C.J. Fox to Lord Holland, 23 November 1792, BL Add Mss 47571, fol.23
9 Hathaway, *The Speeches of the Right Honourable William Pitt . . .*, Vol. II, p.103
10 Evans, *Correspondence of Miles*, 13 January 1793, dated retrospectively 1 March 1804, p.204, quoted in Ehrman, *The Younger Pitt*, Vol. II, p.251
11 Hathaway, *The Speeches of the Right Honourable William Pitt . . .*, Vol. II, p.130
12 Pitt to Windham, 21 September 1794, Windham, *The Windham Papers*, Vol. I, p.246
13 William Huskisson to William Haley, 15 April 1793, BL Add Mss 38734
14 Hathaway, *The Speeches of the Right Honourable William Pitt . . .*, Vol. II, p.133
15 Richmond to Dundas, 1 July 1793, Melville Mss, BL Loan Mss 57/107, 719d
16 Richmond, in PRO WO 30/81, quoted in Ehrman, *The Younger Pitt*, Vol. II, p.267
17 *Archives Parliamentaires* LXXII, p.674, quoted in Blanning, *The French Revolutionary Wars 1787–1802*, p.100
18 Furet, *The French Revolution 1770–1814*, p.140
19 Pitt to Rose, 13 September 1793, quoted in Harcourt, *The Diaries and Correspondence of the Right Hon. George Rose*, Vol. I, p.128
20 Duffy, *The Younger Pitt*, p.186
21 Ibid.
22 Pitt to Westmorland, 15 September 1793, Cambridge University Library Add Mss 6958/7, quoted in Ehrman, *The Younger Pitt*, Vol. II, p.303
23 Pitt's notes, 16 September 1793, Chatham Papers, PRO 30/8/196, fol.51–2
24 Pitt to Lord Grenville, 5 October 1793, quoted in Fortescue, *The Manuscripts of J.B. Fortescue, Esq., Preserved at Dropmore*, Vol. II, p.438
25 Ibid., p.436
26 Wilberforce's diary, 22 June and 14 September 1783, R.I. and S.W. Wilberforce, *The Life of William Wilberforce*, Vol. II, pp.29, 45
27 Grenville to Thomas Grenville, 3 August 1801, quoted in P. Macksey, *Statesmen at War: The Strategy of Overthrow*, p.5
28 Harcourt, *The Diaries and Correspondence of the Right Hon. George Rose*, Vol. I, p.130
29 Pellew, *The Life and Correspondence of the Right Hon. Henry Addington*, Vol. I, p.91
30 Canning's journal, Canning Mss, quoted in Hinde, *George Canning*, p.35
31 Pitt to Lady Chatham, 7 June 1793, Chatham Papers, PRO 30/8/12, fol.452
32 Pitt to Lady Chatham, 2 July 1793, ibid., fol.454
33 Pitt to Lady Chatham, 15 July 1793, ibid., fol.457
34 Pitt to Lady Chatham, 11 November 1793, ibid., fol.460
35 Pitt to Rose, 25 December 1793, quoted in Harcourt, *The Diaries and Correspondence of the Right Hon. George Rose*, Vol. I, p.132
36 Richmond to Pitt, 3 April 1793 (U1590 s501/14), quoted in Mori, *William Pitt and the French Revolution 1785–1795*, p.168
37 R.I. and S.W. Wilberforce, *The Life of William Wilberforce*, Vol. II, p.92
38 Hathaway, *The Speeches of the Right Honourable William Pitt . . .*, Vol. II, p.174

EIGHTEEN : **Frustrations of Supremacy**

1 Hathaway, *The Speeches of the Right Honourable William Pitt . . .*, Vol. II, pp.297–8
2 Jenkinson, quoted in Rosebery, *Letters Relating to the Love Episode of William Pitt*, p.49

3 Ibid.
4 Hathaway, *The Speeches of the Right Honourable William Pitt . . .*, Vol. II, p.166
5 C.J. Fox to Lord Holland, 25 April 1794, BL Add Mss 47571, fol.120; 21 June 1974, Wright (ed.), *Speeches of Charles James Fox in the House of Commons*, Vol. V, p.319
6 Russell, *Memorials and Correspondence of Charles James Fox*, Vol. III, p.47
7 William Windham to Edmund Burke, 18 January 1794, quoted in Copeland (ed.), *The Correspondence of Edmund Burke*, Vol. VII, p.526
8 Duffy, *British War Policy: The Austrian Alliance*, pp.39–44, quoted in Mori, *William Pitt and the French Revolution 1785–1795*, p.164
9 6 May 1794, Malmesbury, *Diaries and Correspondence of James Harris, First Earl of Malmesbury*, Vol. III, p.93
10 23 January 1794, Report from Spy Lynam, Thale (ed.), *Selections from the Papers of the London Corresponding Society*, p.109
11 Rose, *William Pitt and the Great War*, p.185
12 Hathaway, *The Speeches of the Right Honourable William Pitt . . .*, Vol. II, p.202
13 Ibid., p.201
14 Ibid.
15 Thompson, *The Making of the English Working Class*, pp.18–19, quoted in Ehrman, *The Younger Pitt*, Vol. II, p.396
16 Macaulay, essay in *Encyclopaedia Britannica*, eleventh edition, p.674
17 Reilly, *Pitt the Younger*, p.233
18 Lord J. Cavendish to Lady Ponsonby, 4 April 1793, Grey Mss, Durham University Library, quoted in Mitchell, *Charles James Fox*, p.133
19 Tomline, draft of his *Life of Pitt*, BL Add Mss 45107(C) (see notes on the reverse of p.15)
20 Pellew, *The Life and Correspondence of the Right Hon. Henry Addington*, Vol. I, p.121
21 Marshall, *The Rise of Canning*, p.75, quoted in Ehrman, *The Younger Pitt*, Vol. II, p.414
22 Harcourt, *The Diaries and Correspondence of the Right Hon. George Rose*, Vol. I, p.194
23 George III to Pitt, 13 July 1794, Chatham Papers, PRO 30/8/103, part 2
24 Pitt to Dundas, 9 July 1794, quoted in Stanhope, *Life of the Right Honourable William Pitt*, Vol. II, p.253
25 George III to Dundas, 9 July 1794, quoted in ibid., p.254
26 Fox to Lord Holland, BL Add Mss 47571, fol.143–6
27 Stanhope, *Life of the Right Honourable William Pitt*, Vol. II, pp.285–6
28 Ashbourne, *Pitt: Some Chapters of His Life and Times*, p.184
29 Pitt to Windham, BL Add Mss 37844, fol.80
30 Ashbourne, *Pitt: Some Chapters of His Life and Times*, pp.189–90
31 Earl Fitzwilliam to Edmund Burke, 18 November 1794, Copeland (ed.), *The Correspondence of Edmund Burke*, Vol. VIII, p.78
32 Kelly, *Strategy and Counter Revolution*, pp.341–2, quoted in Duffy, *The Younger Pitt*, p.187
33 Hathaway, *The Speeches of the Right Honourable William Pitt . . .*, Vol. II, p.229
34 Ibid., p.228
35 Auckland to Pitt, 1 December 1794, Auckland, *Journal and Correspondence. William Eden Auckland*, Vol. III, p.273
36 Pitt to Lord Chatham, 22 September 1794, quoted in Stanhope, *Life of the Right Honourable William Pitt*, Vol. II, p.259
37 George III to Pitt, 24 November 1794, Chatham Papers, PRO 30/8/103, part 3
38 Pitt to Lord Chatham, 1 December 1794, quoted in Ashbourne, *Pitt: Some Chapters of His Life and Times*, p.174
39 Lord Chatham to Pitt, 1 December 1794, quoted in ibid., p.175
40 Pitt to Lord Chatham, 2 December 1794, quoted in ibid., pp.175–6
41 Hathaway, *The Speeches of the Right Honourable William Pitt . . .*, Vol. II, p.236

42 Ibid., p.241
43 Ibid., p.246
44 Ibid., p.250
45 Portland to Fitzwilliam, 7 January 1795, Fitzwilliam Mss F.31.36, quoted in Pollock, *Wilberforce*, p.129
46 Sir John Mitford to William Pitt, 25 January 1795, Chatham Papers, PRO 30/8/170, fol.163
47 Sir John Mitford to William Pitt, 14 February 1795, ibid., fol.167–8
48 Earl Fitzwilliam to George III, 22 April 1795, Aspinall, *The Later Correspondence of George III*, Vol. II, p.338
49 Fitzwilliam to Portland, 15 January 1795, quoted in Ehrman, *The Younger Pitt*, Vol. II, p.431
50 Stanhope, *Life of the Right Honourable William Pitt*, Vol. II, p.301
51 George III to Pitt, 6 February 1795, Chatham Papers, PRO 30/8/103, part 2
52 Pitt to Duke of Richmond, draft, 27 January 1795, author's collection
53 George III to Pitt, 29 March 1795, quoted in Aspinall, *The Later Correspondence of George III*, Vol. II, p.324
54 Pitt to Lady Chatham, 20 April 1795, Chatham Papers, PRO 30/8/12, fol.464–5
55 Hathaway, *The Speeches of the Right Honourable William Pitt . . .*, Vol. II, p.305
56 Pitt to Lady Chatham, 18 July 1795, Chatham Papers, PRO 30/8/12, fol.468
57 Queen Caroline to Duke of Mecklenburg Strelitz, August 1794, Aspinall, *The Correspondence of George, Prince of Wales*, Vol. III, p.9
58 Pitt to Lord Chatham, 3 August 1795, quoted in Stanhope, *Life of the Right Honourable William Pitt*, Vol. II, p.349
59 Pitt to Rose, 11 September 1795, quoted in Harcourt, *The Diaries and Correspondence of the Right Hon. George Rose*, Vol. I, p.202
60 Hathaway, *The Speeches of the Right Honourable William Pitt . . .*, Vol. II, p.307
61 Arden to Camden, 14 August 1795, Camden Mss C 224/1, quoted in Ehrman, *The Younger Pitt*, Vol. II, p.463
62 Tomline, unpublished Chapter XXVII of his *Life of Pitt*, BL Add Mss 45107(J), fol.34
63 Rosebery, *Letters Relating to the Love Episode of William Pitt*, pp.31–2
64 Pitt to Addington, 4 October 1795, quoted in Stanhope, *Life of the Right Honourable William Pitt*, Vol. II, p.328

NINETEEN : **Insurmountable Obstacles**

1 Hathaway, *The Speeches of the Right Honourable William Pitt . . .*, Vol. III, p.35
2 Furet, *The French Revolution 1770–1814*, p.189
3 Hathaway, *The Speeches of the Right Honourable William Pitt . . .*, Vol. II, p.342
4 George III, 31 January 1796, Stanhope, *Life of the Right Honourable William Pitt*, Vol. II, pp.xxxi–xxxii
5 Pretyman Mss T108/44, quoted in Reilly, *Pitt the Younger*, p.242
6 Hathaway, *The Speeches of the Right Honourable William Pitt . . .*, Vol. II, pp.324, 327
7 Wilberforce's diary, 18 November 1795, quoted in R.I. and S.W. Wilberforce, *The Life of William Wilberforce*, Vol. II, p.112
8 10 November 1795, Wright (ed.), *Speeches of Charles James Fox in the House of Commons*, Vol. VI, p.8
9 10 November 1795, *Parliamentary History*, Vol. XXXII, p.279
10 Hathaway, *The Speeches of the Right Honourable William Pitt . . .*, Vol. II, p.338
11 Pollock, *Wilberforce*, p.134
12 Hathaway, *The Speeches of the Right Honourable William Pitt . . .*, Vol. III, p.365
13 Lord Grenville to Wickham, 15 April 1796, *Wickham Correspondence*, Vol. I, p.343
14 Hathaway, *The Speeches of the Right Honourable William Pitt . . .*, Vol. III, pp.418–19

15 See Duffy, *The Younger Pitt*, p.112
16 Pitt to Grenville, 23 June 1796, quoted in Fortescue, *The Manuscripts of J.B. Fortescue, Esq., Preserved at Dropmore*, Vol. III, pp.214–15
17 Ehrman, *The Younger Pitt*, Vol. II, p.630
18 Wilberforce, *Sketch of Mr. Pitt*, quoted in Rosebery, *Pitt and Wilberforce*, p.18
19 Stanhope, *Life of the Right Honourable William Pitt*, Vol. III, pp.4–5
20 Fremont-Barnes, *The French Revolutionary Wars*, p.39
21 Pitt to his brother Lord Chatham, 4 September 1796, quoted in Stanhope, *Life of the Right Honourable William Pitt*, Vol. II, pp.381–2
22 Ibid., p.382
23 Pitt to Lady Chatham, 6 September 1796, Chatham Papers, PRO 30/8/12, fol.474
24 Ehrman, *The Younger Pitt*, Vol. II, p.645
25 Pitt to Dundas, December 1796, quoted in Stanhope, *Life of the Right Honourable William Pitt*, Vol. II, p.405
26 Hathaway, *The Speeches of the Right Honourable William Pitt . . .*, Vol. III, pp.35, 46, 58
27 Canning's journal, 1793–95, Canning Mss
28 21 August 1796, Stapleton, *George Canning and His Times*, p.38
29 Lady Hester Stanhope to Canning, 1804, quoted in Ehrman, *The Younger Pitt*, Vol. III, p.94
30 See ibid., pp.94–7
31 Canning to Rev. William Leigh, 4 October 1796, Canning Mss 14
32 Rosebery, *Letters Relating to the Love Episode of William Pitt*, pp.6–7
33 Meryon (ed.), *Memoirs of the Lady Hester Stanhope . . .*, pp.17–19

TWENTY : **Breaking Point**

1 Stanhope, *Life of the Right Honourable William Pitt*, Vol. III, p.38n
2 Hathaway, *The Speeches of the Right Honourable William Pitt . . .*, Vol. III, p.174
3 Order in Council, 26 February 1797, *Parliamentary Register*, Vol. I, p.642
4 Grenville, 2 July 1811, *Parliamentary Debates*, Vol. XX, May–July 1811, p.824
5 Stanhope, *Life of the Right Honourable William Pitt*, Vol. III, p.20
6 Hathaway, *The Speeches of the Right Honourable William Pitt . . .*, Vol. III, p.101
7 Pitt to George III, 8 April 1797, quoted in Aspinall, *The Later Correspondence of George III*, Vol. II, no. 1526, p.560
8 Hathaway, *The Speeches of the Right Honourable William Pitt . . .*, Vol. III, p.108
9 George III to Spencer, 9 May 1797, *Private Papers of Spencer*, Vol. II, p.124, quoted in Ehrman, *The Younger Pitt*, Vol. III, p.25n
10 Wilberforce's diary, 26 May 1797, R.I. and S.W. Wilberforce, *The Life of William Wilberforce*, Vol. II, p.219
11 Wilberforce's diary, 28 May 1797, ibid., p.220
12 30 May 1797, *Parliamentary History*, Vol. XXIII, p.732
13 Hathaway, *The Speeches of the Right Honourable William Pitt . . .*, Vol. III, p.129
14 Ibid., p.131
15 Ibid., pp.134–5
16 Stanhope, *Life of the Right Honourable William Pitt*, Vol. III, p.39
17 Malmesbury, *Diaries and Correspondence of James Harris, First Earl of Malmesbury*, Vol. III, p.355
18 Moira to Northumberland, 15 May 1797, Aspinall, *Later Correspondence of George III*, Vol. II, p.xxv
19 Auckland to Mornington, 22 April 1798, BL Add Mss 37308, fol.135
20 Tomline, draft account for his *Life of Pitt*, BL Add Mss 45107(H), fol.14 (notes on reverse side) and fol.15
21 Pellew, *The Life and Correspondence of the Right Hon. Henry Addington*, Vol. I, p.183
22 30 October 1800, Farington, *The Diary of Joseph Farington*, Vol. I, p.293
23 Notes by Mrs Tomline, October and November 1801, Stanhope Mss U1590/S5/C41
24 George III to Lord Grenville, 1 June

1797, quoted in Fortescue, *The Manuscripts of J.B. Fortescue, Esq., Preserved at Dropmore*, Vol. I, p.327

25 Grenville to Buckingham, 3 May 1797, Buckingham, *Memoirs of the Court and Cabinet of George III*, Vol. II, p.377

26 Windham's diary, 15 June 1797, p.368

27 Sir Gilbert to Lady Elliot, 3 June 1797, Minto, *Life and Letters of Sir Gilbert Elliot*, Vol. II, p.405

28 Lord Malmesbury to Lord Grenville, 6 July 1797, Malmesbury, *Diaries and Correspondence of James Harris, First Earl of Malmesbury*, Vol. III, p.366

29 Ibid., p.355

30 Ibid., p.132

31 Ibid., p.496

32 Ibid., p.498

33 Canning to Leigh, 30 June 1797

34 Pitt to Malmesbury, 14 September 1797, Malmesbury, *Diaries and Correspondence of James Harris, First Earl of Malmesbury*, Vol. III, p.538

35 Lord Malmesbury to Lord Grenville, 9 September 1797, ibid., p.513

36 Lord Malmesbury to Pitt, 9 September 1797, ibid., p.520

37 Canning to Rev. William Leigh, 27 September 1797, Canning Mss 13

38 Wilberforce to Lord Muncaster, 20 September 1797, Stanhope, *Life of the Right Honourable William Pitt*, Vol. III, p.63

39 Pitt to Addington, 27 September 1797, ibid.

40 Pitt to Dundas, 6 September 1797, ibid., p.64

41 Rose to Pretyman, 26 September 1797, Pretyman Mss 435/44, quoted in Ehrman, *The Younger Pitt*, Vol. III, p.98

42 Pitt to Secret Agent, 23 September 1797, Stanhope, *Life of the Right Honourable William Pitt*, Vol. III, p.62

43 Malmesbury's diary, 27 September 1797, Malmesbury, *Diaries and Correspondence of James Harris, First Earl of Malmesbury*, Vol. III, p.568

44 Earl of Mornington, 22 November 1836, 'Recollections of Mr. Pitt's Character', BL Add Mss 37416, fol.381

45 Pitt to Lady Chatham, 22 October 1797, Chatham Papers, PRO 30/8/12, fol.478–9

46 Hathaway, *The Speeches of the Right Honourable William Pitt . . .*, Vol. III, p.172

47 Ibid., pp.173–4

TWENTY-ONE : **Caution to the Winds**

1 Hathaway, *The Speeches of the Right Honourable William Pitt . . .*, Vol. III, p.254

2 Blanning, *The French Revolutionary Wars 1787–1802*, p.195

3 Hathaway, *The Speeches of the Right Honourable William Pitt . . .*, Vol. III, p.254

4 Copeland, *War Speeches of Pitt*, pp.228–9, quoted in Reilly, *Pitt the Younger*, p.277

5 Fox, 14 December 1797, *Parliamentary History*, Vol. XXXIII, pp.1112–13, quoted in Stanhope, *Life of the Right Honourable William Pitt*, Vol. III, p.77

6 Pretyman to Mrs Pretyman, 1797, quoted in Ashbourne, *Pitt: Some Chapters of His Life and Times*, pp.346–7

7 Hathaway, *The Speeches of the Right Honourable William Pitt . . .*, Vol. III, p.247

8 Gee, 'The British Volunteer Movement 1797–1807', D. Phil 1981, quoted in Duffy, *The Younger Pitt*, p.158

9 24 January 1798, *Annual Register, 1798*, part II, p.6

10 Malmesbury's diary, 8 May 1804, Malmesbury, *Diaries and Correspondence of James Harris, First Earl of Malmesbury*, Vol. IV, p.310

11 Pitt to Dundas, 5 May 1798, quoted in Stanhope, *Life of the Right Honourable William Pitt*, Vol. III, p.128

12 Sorel, *L'Europe et la révolution française*, p.286, quoted in Blanning, *The French Revolutionary Wars 1787–1802*, p.228

13 Hathaway, *The Speeches of the Right Honourable William Pitt . . .*, Vol. III, p.257

14 Ibid., p.277

15 Rose, *William Pitt and the Great War*, p.366
16 See Ehrman, *The Younger Pitt*, Vol. III, p.140
17 Hathaway, *The Speeches of the Right Honourable William Pitt . . .*, Vol. III, p.287
18 Ibid., p.299
19 Ibid., p.300
20 Pellew, *The Life and Correspondence of the Right Hon. Henry Addington*, Vol. I, p.205
21 Stanhope, *Life of the Right Honourable William Pitt*, Vol. III, p.131
22 Pitt to Dundas, 27 May 1798, quoted in ibid.
23 Pitt to Lady Chatham, 28 May 1798, Chatham Papers, PRO 30/8/12, fol.482
24 George III, 30 May 1798, Stanhope, *Life of the Right Honourable William Pitt*, Vol. III, Appendix, p.xiv
25 Wilberforce's diary, 28 May 1798, R.I. and S.W. Wilberforce, *The Life of William Wilberforce*, Vol. II, p.280
26 Pitt to Wilberforce, 30 May 1798, quoted in Stanhope, *Life of the Right Honourable William Pitt*, Vol. III, p.133
27 Auckland, *Journal and Correspondence. William Eden Auckland*, Vol. IV, p.11
28 Pitt to Pretyman, 19 June 1798, Pretyman Mss HA 119/T108/42/100
29 Pitt to Mrs Pretyman, July 1798, Pretyman Mss T108/42, quoted in Reilly, *Pitt the Younger*, p.284
30 Pitt to Lady Chatham, 9 July 1798, Chatham Papers, PRO 30/8/12, fol.484
31 Pitt to Lord Auckland, 1 August 1798, quoted in Stanhope, *Life of the Right Honourable William Pitt*, Vol. III, p.138
32 Rosebery, *Letters Relating to the Love Episode of William Pitt*, pp.49, 32
33 Pitt to Pretyman, 24 October 1798, Pretyman Mss HA 119/T108/42/110
34 Pretyman Mss T108/44, quoted in Reilly, *Pitt the Younger*, p.283
35 Dundas to Huskisson, 17 September 1798, BL Add Mss 38735, fol.132
36 Hewitt (ed.), *Eyewitnesses to Nelson's Battles*, p.74
37 Ibid., p.84
38 Pitt to Lady Chatham, 30 August 1798, Chatham Papers, PRO 30/8/12, fol.494–5
39 Pretyman to Mrs Pretyman, undated 435/45, quoted in Ehrman, *The Younger Pitt*, Vol. III, p.149
40 Napoleon to Las Casas, Rose, *William Pitt and the Great War*, p.364
41 Accera and Meyer, *Marines et révolution*, quoted in Blanning, *The French Revolutionary Wars 1787–1802*, p.196
42 Pitt to Grenville, 29 October 1798, Dropmore IV, 355, quoted in Ehrman, *The Younger Pitt*, Vol. III, p.201
43 Grenville to Whitworth, no. 36, Most Secret, 16 November 1798, PRO FO 65/41
44 Hathaway, *The Speeches of the Right Honourable William Pitt . . .*, Vol. III, p.307
45 Ibid., p.324
46 Ashbourne, *Pitt: Some Chapters of His Life and Times*, p.281
47 Hathaway, *The Speeches of the Right Honourable William Pitt . . .*, Vol. III, p.359
48 Cornwallis, quoted in Watson, *The Reign of George III*, p.399
49 Clare to Castlereagh, 16 October 1798, quoted in Barnes, *George III and William Pitt*, p.358
50 21 December 1798, Pretyman Mss, quoted in Ashbourne, *Pitt: Some Chapters of His Life and Times*, p.285
51 Hathaway, *The Speeches of the Right Honourable William Pitt . . .*, Vol. III, p.354
52 Auckland to Beresford, 2 February 1799, quoted in Stanhope, *Life of the Right Honourable William Pitt*, Vol. III, p.172
53 Hathaway, *The Speeches of the Right Honourable William Pitt . . .*, Vol. III, p.387
54 Wilberforce's diary, 14 December 1798, quoted in Stanhope, *Life of the Right Honourable William Pitt*, Vol. III, pp.166–7
55 Lady Chatham to Rose, 8 December 1798, quoted in Harcourt, *The Diaries and Correspondence of the Right Hon. George Rose*, Vol. I, p.208

56 George III to Pitt, 13 June 1798, quoted in Rose, *Pitt and Napoleon*, pp.243–4

TWENTY-TWO : **The Dashing of Hope**

1 Hathaway, *The Speeches of the Right Honourable William Pitt* . . ., Vol. IV, p.2
2 Furet, *The French Revolution 1770–1814*, p.209
3 Grenville to Canning, January 1800, Canning Mss 63
4 Grenville to Pitt, 2 August 1799, Dacres Adams Mss, formerly PRO 30/58/2.58
5 Pitt to Cornwallis, 17 November 1798, quoted in Ehrman, *The Younger Pitt*, Vol. III, p.186
6 Cornwallis to Major General Ross, 20 May 1799, *Correspondence of Charles, First Marquis Cornwallis*, Vol. III, pp.100–1
7 Cornwallis to Portland, 13 August 1799, ibid., p.121
8 Hathaway, *The Speeches of the Right Honourable William Pitt* . . ., Vol. III, p.410
9 Ibid., p.405
10 Holland, *Memoirs of the Whig Party*, Vol. I, p.92
11 Thomas Grenville to Lord Spencer, 12–13 May 1799, BL Add Mss 75961
12 Dundas to Grenville, 29 July 1799, Fortescue, *The Manuscripts of J.B. Fortescue, Esq., Preserved at Dropmore*, Vol. V, p.206
13 Pitt to Grenville, 2 August 1799, ibid., p.224
14 Grenville to Mornington, 27 September 1799, BL Add Mss 70927, fol.34
15 Minto, *Life and Letters of Sir Gilbert Elliot*, Vol. III, p.61
16 Wilberforce's diary, 18 May 1799, quoted in Stanhope, *Life of the Right Honourable William Pitt*, Vol. III, p.183
17 Grenville to Thomas Grenville, 16 July 1799, Fortescue, *The Manuscripts of J.B. Fortescue, Esq., Preserved at Dropmore*, Vol. V, p.147
18 Pitt to Windham, 30 August 1799, BL Add Mss 37844, fol.200
19 Pitt to sister-in-law Lady Chatham, 21 October 1799, Stanhope, *Life of the Right Honourable William Pitt*, Vol. III, p.200
20 Chatham to Pitt, 25 September 1799, Dacres Adams Mss, formerly PRO 30/58/2, n65
21 Dundas Papers, Scottish Record Office, Melville Castle Muniments GD 51/1/703/11, quoted in Reilly, *Pitt the Younger*, p.291
22 Furet, *The French Revolution 1770–1814*, p.209
23 Ibid., p.215
24 Pitt's notes, Chatham Papers, PRO 30/8/197, fol.318
25 Ehrman, *The Younger Pitt*, Vol. III, p.334
26 Pitt to Dundas, 31 December 1799, Stanhope, *Life of the Right Honourable William Pitt*, Vol. III, p.207
27 Hathaway, *The Speeches of the Right Honourable William Pitt* . . ., Vol. IV, p.2
28 Ibid., p.26
29 Ibid., p.45
30 Ibid., p.54
31 Lord Holland to Caroline Fox, 21 January 1800, BL Add Mss 51735, fol.165
32 Fox to O'Bryen, 16 July 1800, BL Add Mss 47566, fol.47
33 Hathaway, *The Speeches of the Right Honourable William Pitt* . . ., Vol. IV, p.61
34 Ibid., pp.64–5
35 See Wilkinson, *The Duke of Portland*, p.152
36 Minute by George III dated 31 January 1799, Clements Transcripts IX, 021, quoted in Barnes, *George III and William Pitt*, p.362
37 29 July 1800, *Parliamentary History*, Vol. XXV, p.494
38 Hathaway, *The Speeches of the Right Honourable William Pitt* . . ., Vol. IV, pp.77–8
39 Grenville to Dundas, 10 April 1800, quoted in Rose, *Pitt and Napoleon*, pp.267–8
40 Pitt to Dundas, 4 November 1799, Melville Mss, William L. Clements Library, Michigan
41 Reilly, *Pitt the Younger*, p.294
42 *Mémoires de M. de Bourienne, Ministre d'état sur Napoléon, le Directoire, le Consulat, l'Empire et la Restauration*, Vol. IV, p.122, quoted in Blanning, *The*

French Revolutionary Wars 1787–1802, p.223
43 Furet, *The French Revolution 1770–1814*, p.218
44 Festing, *John Hookham Frere and His Friends*, p.31
45 Pitt to Addington, 8 October 1800, quoted in Stanhope, *Life of the Right Honourable William Pitt*, Vol. III, p.244
46 Pretyman Mss T108/44, quoted in Reilly, *Pitt the Younger*, p.298
47 Henry Addington to Hiley Addington, 19 October 1800, Sidmouth Mss 152M/C1800/OZ54
48 Pellew, *The Life and Correspondence of the Right Hon. Henry Addington*, Vol. I, p.266
49 Ziegler, *Addington*, p.89
50 Hathaway, *The Speeches of the Right Honourable William Pitt . . .*, Vol. IV, p.101
51 Ibid., p.121
52 Drummond to Grenville, 4 October 1800, PRO FO 22/38

TWENTY-THREE : **Resignation with Hesitation**

1 Ashbourne, *Pitt: Some Chapters of His Life and Times*, p.311
2 16 February 1801, *Parliamentary History*, Vol. XXXV, p.969
3 R.I. and S.W. Wilberforce, *The Life of William Wilberforce*, Vol. I, p.26
4 Hathaway, *The Speeches of the Right Honourable William Pitt . . .*, Vol. IV, p.139
5 Ibid., p.145
6 Pitt to Lord Loughborough, 25 September 1800, Stanhope, *Life of the Right Honourable William Pitt*, Vol. III, p.268
7 Rose, *William Pitt and the Great War*, p.451
8 Earl Camden, Memorandum on Pitt's Retirement, 1803–4, quoted in Willis, *Bulletin of the Institute of Historical Research* XLIV, no. 110, p.250
9 George III's diary, 29 January 1801, quoted in Bickley (ed.), *The Diaries of Sylvester Douglas, Lord Glenbervie*, Vol. I, p.149
10 Harcourt, *The Diaries and Correspondence of the Right Hon. George Rose*, Vol. I, p.301
11 Ibid., pp.302–3
12 Hathaway, *The Speeches of the Right Honourable William Pitt . . .*, Vol. IV, p.136
13 Earl Camden, Memorandum on Pitt's Retirement, 1803–4, quoted in Willis, *Bulletin of the Institute of Historical Research* XLIV, no. 110, p.252
14 *Cornwallis Correspondence*, Vol III, p.331, quoted in Stanhope, *Life of the Right Honourable William Pitt*, Vol. III, p.273
15 Harcourt, *The Diaries and Correspondence of the Right Hon. George Rose*, Vol. I, p.305
16 Earl Camden, Memorandum on Pitt's Retirement, 1803–4, Willis, *Bulletin of the Institute of Historical Research* XLIV, no. 110, p.252
17 George III to Henry Addington, 29 January 1801, Sidmouth Mss 152M/C1801/OR39
18 Barnes, *George III and William Pitt*, p.373
19 Ibid., pp.374–5
20 Pitt to George III, 31 January 1801, quoted in Stanhope, *Life of the Right Honourable William Pitt*, Vol. III, p.xxviii
21 Barnes, *George III and William Pitt*, pp.377–9
22 Pellew, *The Life and Correspondence of the Right Hon. Henry Addington*, Vol. I, p.287
23 Barnes, *George III and William Pitt*, p.380
24 Ibid.
25 Pellew, *The Life and Correspondence of the Right Hon. Henry Addington*, Vol. I, p.288
26 Pitt to Chatham, 5 February 1801, quoted in Ashbourne, *Pitt: Some Chapters of His Life and Times*, pp.310–11
27 Pitt to Tomline, 6 February 1801, quoted in ibid., p.311
28 Earl Camden, Memorandum on Pitt's Retirement, 1803–4, Willis, *Bulletin of the Institute of Historical Research*

XLIV, no. 110, p.255
29 Malmesbury, *Diaries and Correspondence of James Harris, First Earl of Malmesbury*, Vol. IV, p.78
30 Ashbourne, *Pitt: Some Chapters of His Life and Times*, p.310
31 Malmesbury's diary, 26 February 1801, quoted in Malmesbury, *Diaries and Correspondence of James Harris, First Earl of Malmesbury*, Vol. IV, p.18
32 Tomline, draft account for his *Life of Pitt*, BL Add Mss 45108(F), fol.20–1
33 Ibid., fol.20
34 Pitt to Dundas, 25 July 1800, Melville Mss, William L. Clements Library, Michigan
35 Tomline, draft account for his *Life of Pitt*, BL Add Mss 45107(H), fol.16
36 Fox to O'Bryen, 16 February 1801, BL Add Mss 47566, fol.72
37 Stanhope, *Life of the Right Honourable William Pitt*, Vol. III, p.280
38 Lady Malmesbury to Lady Minto, 8 February 1801, Minto, *Life and Letters of Sir Gilbert Elliot*, Vol. III, p.198
39 Pretyman Mss T108/44, quoted in Reilly, *Pitt the Younger*, p.301
40 Malmesbury's diary, 14 March 1801, quoted in Ziegler, *Addington*, p.96
41 16 February 1801, *Parliamentary History*, Vol. XXXV, pp.962–3
42 Ibid., p.969
43 Ibid., p.970
44 Pretyman Mss, quoted in Rose, *William Pitt and the Great War*, pp.442–3
45 See Ehrman, *The Younger Pitt*, Vol. III, p.525
46 Rose, *William Pitt and the Great War*, p.444
47 George III to Pitt, 18 February 1801, quoted in Stanhope, *Life of the Right Honourable William Pitt*, Vol. III, p.xxxii; see also note on p.xxiii: 'The note of Feb. 18, 1801, beginning "My dear Pitt," is the only one of the whole series which thus commences, and seems to have been both intended and accepted as a token of especial regard.'
48 Harcourt, *The Diaries and Correspondence of the Right Hon. George Rose*, Vol. I, p.308
49 Ibid., p.309
50 Reilly, *Pitt the Younger*, p.303
51 Pelham to Malmesbury, quoted in Stanhope, *Life of the Right Honourable William Pitt*, Vol. III, p.296
52 Wilberforce's diary, quoted in ibid., p.298
53 Ibid., p.299
54 Ibid., p.294
55 Malmesbury, *Diaries and Correspondence of James Harris, First Earl of Malmesbury*, Vol. IV, p.34
56 Stanhope, *Life of the Right Honourable William Pitt*, Vol. III, p.303
57 Ehrman, *The Younger Pitt*, Vol. III, p.528
58 Rose to George III, quoted in Harcourt, *The Diaries and Correspondence of the Right Hon. George Rose*, Vol. I, p.360
59 Ibid., p.329
60 Canning to Pitt, 8 March 1801, quoted in Ashbourne, *Pitt: Some Chapters of His Life and Times*, p.319
61 Malmesbury's diary, 8 March 1801, Malmesbury, *Diaries and Correspondence of James Harris, First Earl of Malmesbury*, Vol. IV, p.36
62 Dundas to Pelham, 11 March 1801, quoted in Ashbourne, *Pitt: Some Chapters of His Life and Times*, p.322
63 Malmesbury, *Diaries and Correspondence of James Harris, First Earl of Malmesbury*, Vol. IV, p.81

TWENTY-FOUR : The Limits of Magnanimity

1 R.I. and S.W. Wilberforce, *The Life of William Wilberforce*, Vol. III, p.21
2 Pellew, *The Life and Correspondence of the Right Hon. Henry Addington*, Vol. I, p.331
3 Hathaway, *The Speeches of the Right Honourable William Pitt . . .*, Vol. IV, p.184
4 Aspinall, *The Later Correspondence of George III*, Vol. III, p.xix
5 Malmesbury, *Diaries and Correspondence of James Harris, First Earl of Malmesbury*, Vol. IV, p.78
6 Rose to Pretyman, 18 October 1801, Pretyman Mss 435/44, quoted in

Ehrman, *The Younger Pitt*, Vol. III, p.534

7 Pretyman to Rose, 27 August 1801, quoted in Harcourt, *The Diaries and Correspondence of the Right Hon. George Rose*, Vol. I, p.424

8 Diary, 19 March 1801, ibid., p.338

9 Ibid., p.215

10 Ibid., p.406

11 Coutts to Pitt, 22 February 1800, Dacres Adams Mss, formerly PRO 30/58/4, n18

12 Stanhope, *Life of the Right Honourable William Pitt*, Vol. III, p.363

13 Ehrman, *The Younger Pitt*, Vol. III, p.540n

14 Holland, *Memoir of the Whig Party*, Vol. I, p.175

15 Canning to Pitt, 28 August 1801, Rose, *Pitt and Napoleon*, pp.325–6, quoted in Marshall, *The Rise of Canning*, p.225

16 Auckland, *Journal and Correspondence. William Eden Auckland*, Vol. IV, p.132

17 Dean Milman to Lewis, 27 January 1858, in Lewis, *Essays on the Administrations of Great Britain from 1783 to 1830*, p.272

18 Southey, *Letters from England*, April 1802, no. 12, p.75

19 Ziegler, *Addington*, p.111

20 Stanhope, *Life of the Right Honourable William Pitt*, Vol. III, p.321

21 Fremont-Barnes, *The French Revolutionary Wars*, p.84

22 Stanhope, *Life of the Right Honourable William Pitt*, Vol. III, p.360

23 Barnes, *George III and William Pitt*, p.398

24 Fremont-Barnes, *The French Revolutionary Wars*, p.88

25 Malmesbury's diary, 3 October 1801, Malmesbury, *Diaries and Correspondence of James Harris, First Earl of Malmesbury*, Vol. IV, p.62

26 Grenville to Tom Grenville, 25 February 1802, Grenville Papers, Vol. II, Add Mss 41852, fol.99, 100

27 Hathaway, *The Speeches of the Right Honourable William Pitt . . .*, Vol. IV, p.208

28 Ibid., p.212

29 Festing, *John Hookham Frere and His Friends*, p.58

30 Pretyman Mss 108/44, 45, quoted in Reilly, *Pitt the Younger*, p.311

31 Pretyman to Rose, 23 December 1801, quoted in Harcourt, *The Diaries and Correspondence of the Right Hon. George Rose*, Vol. I, p.442

32 Pitt to Canning, c.September 1801, Canning Mss, William L. Clements Library, Michigan

33 Canning to Leveson Gower, 3 January 1802, Granville (ed.), *Lord Granville Leveson Gower, First Earl Granville: Private Correspondence. 1781–1821*, Vol. III, p.315

34 Pitt to Addington, 10 February 1802, quoted in Stanhope, *Life of the Right Honourable William Pitt*, Vol. III, p.369

35 Addington to Pitt, 11 February 1802, quoted in ibid., p.370

36 Ibid., p.379

37 Canning to Sneyd, 10 February 1802, Bagot, *George Canning and His Friends*, Vol. I, p.188

38 Pitt to Addington, 26 June 1802, quoted in Pellew, *The Life and Correspondence of the Right Hon. Henry Addington*, Vol. II, p.71

39 Canning to Frere, 27 August and 7 September 1802, quoted in Festing, *John Hookham Frere and His Friends*, p.86

40 Rosebery, *Letters Relating to the Love Episode of William Pitt*, p.33

41 Stanhope, *Life of the Right Honourable William Pitt*, Vol. III, p.393

42 Tomline, draft account for his *Life of Pitt*, BL Add Mss 45107

43 Grenville to Thomas Grenville, 19 October 1802, BL Add Mss 41852, fol.126

44 Ibid., fol.131

45 Pretyman to Rose, 11 November 1802, quoted in Stanhope, *Life of the Right Honourable William Pitt*, Vol. III, p.406

46 Ibid., p.426

47 Ibid., p.424

48 Malmesbury, *Diaries and Correspondence of James Harris, First Earl of Malmesbury*, Vol. IV, p.159

49 Stanhope, *Life of the Right Honourable William Pitt*, Vol. III, p.429

50 Ibid., p.421
51 Malmesbury, *Diaries and Correspondence of James Harris, First Earl of Malmesbury*, Vol. IV, p.119
52 Pitt to Rose, 28 January 1803, quoted in Stanhope, *Life of the Right Honourable William Pitt*, Vol. III, p.434
53 Ibid., pp.431–2
54 Rosebery, *Letters Relating to the Love Episode of William Pitt*, p.35
55 Fox Mss, BL Add Mss 47575, fol.23
56 Stanhope, *Life of the Right Honourable William Pitt*, Vol. IV, p.20
57 Mellville (Dundas) to Addington, 22 March 1803, quoted in Pellew, *The Life and Correspondence of the Right Hon. Henry Addington*, Vol. II, p.116
58 Harcourt, *Diaries and Correspondence of the Right Hon. George Rose*, Vol. II, p.30
59 Melville (Dundas) to Pitt, Dacres Adams Mss, 16 June 1803, quoted in Ziegler, *Addington*, p.179

TWENTY-FIVE : The Old Addiction

1 Hathaway, *The Speeches of the Right Honourable William Pitt . . .*, Vol. IV, p.309
2 Cleveland, *Life and Letters of Lady Hester Stanhope*, p.52
3 Harcourt, *The Diaries and Correspondence of the Right Hon. George Rose*, Vol. II, p.38
4 Ibid., p.39
5 Ibid.
6 Ibid., p.40
7 Ziegler, *Addington*, p.178
8 Harcourt, *The Diaries and Correspondence of the Right Hon. George Rose*, Vol. II, p.40
9 Redesdale to Pitt, 16 April 1803, Chatham Papers, PRO 30/8/170, fol.200–1
10 George III, quoted in Malmesbury, *Diaries and Correspondence of James Harris, First Earl of Malmesbury*, Vol. IV, pp.90, 92
11 Pitt to Addington, 15 April 1803, quoted in Pellew, *The Life and Correspondence of the Right Hon. Henry Addington*, Vol. II, p.123
12 Colchester's diary, 19 April 1803, Colchester (ed.), *The Diary and Correspondence of Charles Abbot, Lord Colchester*, Vol. I, p.416
13 Wilberforce's diary, 26 April 1803, quoted in R.I. and S.W. Wilberforce, *The Life of William Wilberforce*, Vol. III, pp.95–6
14 Creevey to Currie, 21 May 1803, Maxwell, *The Creevey Papers*, p.15
15 Pretyman Mss T108/42, quoted in Reilly, *Pitt the Younger*, p.321
16 Stanhope, *Life of the Right Honourable William Pitt*, Vol. IV, p.47
17 Rt Hon. J.W. Ward to the Rev. E. Copleston, 30 May 1803, quoted in ibid., pp.48–9
18 Creevey to Currie, 24 May 1803, Maxwell, *The Creevey Papers*, p.15
19 Rt Hon. J.W. Ward to the Rev. E. Copleston, 30 May 1803, quoted in Stanhope, *Life of the Right Honourable William Pitt*, Vol. IV, p.50
20 Malmesbury's diary, 8 June 1803, Malmesbury, *Diaries and Correspondence of James Harris, First Earl of Malmesbury*, Vol. IV, p.270
21 George III to Addington, 4 June 1803, quoted in Stanhope, *Life of the Right Honourable William Pitt*, Vol. IV, p.56
22 Canning to Leigh, 8 June 1803, Canning Mss 15, quoted in Hinde, *George Canning*, p.118
23 Malmesbury's diary, 8 June 1803, Malmesbury, *Diaries and Correspondence of James Harris, First Earl of Malmesbury*, Vol. IV, p.270
24 Pitt to Dundas, 19 June 1803, Melville Mss, William L. Clements Library, Michigan
25 Harcourt, *The Diaries and Correspondence of the Right Hon. George Rose*, Vol. II, p.52
26 Ibid., p.63
27 Ziegler, *Addington*, p.196
28 Rosebery, *Letters Relating to the Love Episode of William Pitt*, pp.35–6
29 Cleveland, *Life and Letters of Lady Hester Stanhope*, p.47
30 Stanhope, *Life of the Right Honourable William Pitt*, Vol. IV, pp.85–7

31 Cleveland, *Life and Letters of Lady Hester Stanhope*, pp.52–3
32 Mulgrave to Phipps, 3 September 1803, quoted in Phipps, *Memoirs of the Political and Literary Life of Robert Plumer Ward*, Vol. I, p.143
33 Cleveland, *Life and Letters of Lady Hester Stanhope*, p.87
34 Haslip, *Lady Hester Stanhope*, p.44
35 Ibid.
36 Lord Mulgrave to Major General Phipps, Curzon, *The Personal History of Walmer Castle and its Lords Warden*, p.106
37 Cleveland, *Life and Letters of Lady Hester Stanhope*, p.54
38 Undated, Dacres Adams Mss, formerly PRO 30/58/7, n53
39 Harcourt, *The Diaries and Correspondence of the Right Hon. George Rose*, Vol. II, p.70
40 Ibid., p.71
41 Pitt to Rose, 2 December 1803, quoted in Stanhope, *Life of the Right Honourable William Pitt*, Vol. IV, p.102
42 Bryant, *Years of Victory 1802–1812*, p.77
43 Harcourt, *The Diaries and Correspondence of the Right Hon. George Rose*, Vol. II, p.65
44 Ibid., p.64
45 Cleveland, *Life and Letters of Lady Hester Stanhope*, pp.56–7
46 Grenville to Pitt, 31 December 1803, Dacres Adams Mss, formerly PRO 30/58/4, n117
47 Grenville to Buckingham, Buckingham, *Memoirs of the Court and Cabinet of George III*, Vol. III, p.342, quoted in Jupp, *Lord Grenville*, p.328
48 Pitt to Grenville, 4 February 1804, quoted in Fortescue, *The Manuscripts of J.B. Fortescue, Esq., Preserved at Dropmore*, Vol. V, p.213
49 Grenville to Pitt, 31 January 1804, quoted in Stanhope, *Life of the Right Honourable William Pitt*, Vol. IV, p.116
50 Ibid., p.138
51 Pitt to Dundas, 29 March 1804, Melville Mss, William L. Clements Library, Michigan
52 Fox to Lauderdale, BL Add Mss 47564, fol.184
53 Stanhope, *Life of the Right Honourable William Pitt*, Vol. IV, p.59
54 Marshall, *The Rise of Canning*, p.260
55 Ibid.
56 15 March 1804, *Parliamentary Debates*, 1st Series, Vol. I, p.926
57 Hathaway, *The Speeches of the Right Honourable William Pitt . . .*, Vol. IV, p.288
58 Marshall, *The Rise of Canning*, p.261
59 For the letter of acceptance see Pitt to Eldon, 20 March 1804, quoted in Twiss, *The Private and Public Life of Lord Chancellor Eldon*, Vol. I, p.438
60 Pitt to Dundas, 11 April 1804, Melville Mss, William L. Clements Library, Michigan
61 Pitt to Melville, 29 March 1804, quoted in Stanhope, *Life of the Right Honourable William Pitt*, Vol. IV, p.142
62 Pitt to Dundas, 17 April 1804, Melville Mss, William L. Clements Library, Michigan
63 Hathaway, *The Speeches of the Right Honourable William Pitt . . .*, Vol. IV, p.305
64 Ibid., p.310
65 Ibid., p.326
66 Earl Bathurst, 'Negotiations between Pitt, Fox, Grenville and the King', *Report on the Manuscripts of Earl Bathurst, Preserved at Cirencester Park*, p.34
67 23 April 1804, Colchester, *The Diary and Correspondence of Charles Abbot, Lord Colchester*, pp.496–7
68 Ehrman, *The Younger Pitt*, Vol. III, p.648
69 Melville to Pitt, 3 April 1804, Stanhope, *Secret Correspondence connected with Mr Pitt's return to Office in 1804*, pp.20–1
70 Harcourt, *The Diaries and Correspondence of the Right Hon. George Rose*, Vol. II, p.116
71 George III, Dacres Adams Mss, formerly PRO 30/58/5, n16a
72 Harcourt, *The Diaries and Correspondence of the Right Hon. George Rose*, Vol. II, p.118
73 Pitt to George III, 6 May 1804, quoted

in Stanhope, *Life of the Right Honourable William Pitt*, Vol. IV, p.xii

74 Harcourt, *The Diaries and Correspondence of the Right Hon. George Rose*, Vol. II, p.122

75 Stanhope, *Life of the Right Honourable William Pitt*, Vol. IV, p.171

76 Harcourt, *The Diaries and Correspondence of the Right Hon. George Rose*, Vol. II, p.125

77 Ibid., pp.127–8

78 Lord Eldon to Perceval, undated, Twiss, *The Private and Public Life of Lord Chancellor Eldon*, Vol. I, p.449

TWENTY-SIX : **Back, But Never the Same**

1 Hathaway, *The Speeches of the Right Honourable William Pitt . . .*, Vol. IV, p.361

2 Rosebery, *Letters Relating to the Love Episode of William Pitt*, pp.36–7

3 Harcourt, *The Diaries and Correspondence of the Right Hon. George Rose*, Vol. II, p.147

4 C.J. Fox to T. Coutts, 31 December 1805, Bodleian Library Mss North c.12, fol.8

5 20 May 1804, Malmesbury, *Diaries and Correspondence of James Harris, First Earl of Malmesbury*, Vol. IV, p.318

6 Wilberforce's diary, 6 July 1804, quoted in R.I. and S.W. Wilberforce, *The Life of William Wilberforce*, Vol. III, p.187

7 Grey to Lady Grey, 8 May 1804, Trevelyan, *Lord Grey of the Reform Bill*, p.137

8 Ehrman, *The Younger Pitt*, Vol. III, p.753n

9 Meryon (ed.), *Memoirs of the Lady Hester Stanhope . . .*, p.65, quoted in Duffy, *The Younger Pitt*, p.220

10 Bruce, *Life of General Sir William Napier*, p.28

11 Ibid., pp.31–2

12 Ibid., p.32

13 Cleveland, *Life and Letters of Lady Hester Stanhope*, p.62

14 Harcourt, *The Diaries and Correspondence of the Right Hon. George Rose*, Vol. II, p.151

15 30 May 1804, *Parliamentary Debates*, 1st series, Vol. II, p.472

16 Hathaway, *The Speeches of the Right Honourable William Pitt . . .*, Vol. IV, p.360

17 Ibid., p.361

18 Thiers, Vol. V, p.189, quoted in Stanhope, *Life of the Right Honourable William Pitt*, Vol. IV, p.215

19 Ibid., p.225

20 Ibid.

21 Hathaway, *The Speeches of the Right Honourable William Pitt . . .*, Vol. IV, pp.401–2

22 Harcourt, *The Diaries and Correspondence of the Right Hon. George Rose*, Vol. II, p.176

23 Ibid., p.156

24 24 December 1804, Colchester, *The Diary and Correspondence of Charles Abbot, Lord Colchester*, p.538

25 Addington to his brother, Lord Ellenborough, the Speaker, and Mr Yorke, 24 December 1804, quoted in Pellew, *The Life and Correspondence of the Right Hon. Henry Addington*, Vol. II, p.331

26 Wilberforce's diary, 1 February 1805, quoted in R.I. and S.W. Wilberforce, *The Life of William Wilberforce*, Vol. III

27 Addington to Hiley Addington, 6 October 1804, Sidmouth Mss, quoted in Ziegler, *Addington*, p.228

28 Hawkesbury to Addington, 19 December 1804, Sidmouth Mss, quoted in ibid., p.232

29 Moore, *Sheridan*, Vol. II, p.330

30 State Paper FO 65/60, fol.6–7 (originals are in Pitt's hand and are in the Dacres Adams Mss, formerly PRO 30/58/8)

31 Temperley, *Foundations of British Foreign Policy, from Pitt–1792 to Salisbury–1902*, p.9

32 Pitt to George III, quoted in Aspinall, *The Later Correspondence of George III*, Vol. II, no. 3014, p.283

33 Bishop of Bristol to Pitt, 8 February 1805; Pitt to Bishop of Bristol, 8 February 1805, Dacres Adams Manuscripts, formerly PRO 30/58/6, nos 24 and 25

34 Barnes, *George III and William Pitt*, p.455
35 Wilberforce's diary, 18 March 1804, quoted in R.I. and S.W. Wilberforce, *The Life of William Wilberforce*, Vol. III, p.218
36 Hathaway, *The Speeches of the Right Honourable William Pitt . . .*, Vol. IV, p.423
37 Pitt to Coutts, 29 December 1785, Pitt Papers, William L. Clements Library, Michigan
38 J.W. Ward to Ivy, 9 April 1805, quoted in Romilly, *Letters to Ivy from the First Earl of Dudley*, p.27
39 Stanhope, *Life of the Right Honourable William Pitt*, Vol. IV, p.281
40 Notebook of Lord Fitzharris, 1806, Malmesbury, *Diaries and Correspondence of James Harris, First Earl of Malmesbury*, Vol. IV, p.355n
41 Rosebery, *Letters Relating to the Love Episode of William Pitt*, pp.36–7

TWENTY-SEVEN : Too Many Enemies

1 Malmesbury, *Diaries and Correspondence of James Harris, First Earl of Malmesbury*, Vol. IV, p.346
2 Grenville to Buckingham, 27 May 1805, Buckingham, *Memoirs of the Court and Cabinet of George III*, Vol. III, p.422
3 Henry Addington to Hiley Addington, 16 April 1805, Sidmouth Mss 152M/C1805/OZ75
4 Sidmouth to Pitt, 22 April 1805, Pellew, *The Life and Correspondence of the Right Hon. Henry Addington*, Vol. II, p.358
5 Henry Addington to Hiley Addington, 28 April 1805, Sidmouth Mss 152M/C1805/OZ63
6 Hathaway, *The Speeches of the Right Honourable William Pitt . . .*, Vol. IV, p.435
7 Ibid., p.461
8 *Parliamentary Debates* V, pp.418–19, quoted in Ehrman, *The Younger Pitt*, Vol. III, p.762
9 12 March 1805, quoted in MacDermot (ed.), *The Diary of Denys Scully*, pp.81, 86
10 Hathaway, *The Speeches of the Right Honourable William Pitt . . .*, Vol. IV, p.438
11 Ibid., p.441
12 Malmesbury, *Diaries and Correspondence of James Harris, First Earl of Malmesbury*, Vol. IV, p.355
13 Ibid., p.347
14 7 November 1804, Farington, *The Farington Diary*, Vol. III, p.14
15 R.I. and S.W. Wilberforce, *The Life of William Wilberforce*, Vol. III, pp.232–3
16 Pretyman to Pitt, 4 July 1801, Dacres Adams Mss, formerly PRO 30/58/4, n40; Wellesley to Pitt, 1 January 1804, Dacres Adams Mss, formerly PRO 30/58/5, n1; Malmesbury, *Diaries and Correspondence of James Harris, First Earl of Malmesbury*, Vol. IV, p.321
17 Lady Hester Stanhope to W.D. Adams, 1805, quoted in Cleveland, *Life and Letters of Lady Hester Stanhope*, p.65
18 Dacres Adams Mss, formerly PRO 30/58/7.56
19 Canning to Joan Canning, 9 July 1805, Canning Mss 20
20 Henry Addington to Hiley Addington, 1 July 1805, Sidmouth Mss 152M/C1805/OZ59
21 Sidmouth Mss, Mary Anne's Notebook
22 Fox to O'Bryen, 7 July 1805, Russell, *Memorials and Correspondence of Charles James Fox*, p.89
23 Marshall, *The Rise of Canning*, p.287
24 Harcourt, *The Diaries and Correspondence of the Right Hon. George Rose*, Vol. II, pp.199–200
25 Ibid., p.201
26 Stanhope, *Life of the Right Honourable William Pitt*, Vol. IV, p.369
27 Pellew, *The Life and Correspondence of the Right Hon. Henry Addington*, Vol. I, p.371
28 Sidmouth to Hiley Addington, 29 September 1805, quoted in Stanhope, *Life of the Right Honourable William Pitt*, Vol. IV, p.337
29 Pitt to Harrowby, 27 September 1805, Harrowby Mss XII, quoted in Ehrman, *The Younger Pitt*, Vol. III, p.805
30 Coleman, *Nelson*, p.314
31 Stanhope, *Life of the Right Honourable*

William Pitt, Vol. IV, p.330

32 Notes by Pitt in 1805, Dacres Adams Mss 30/58/8, quoted in Ehrman, *The Younger Pitt*, Vol. III, p.797

33 25 October 1805, *Diaries and Letters of Sir George Jackson*, Vol. I, p.348

34 Fortescue, *British Statesmen of the Great War*, p.180

35 Notes of conversation with the Duke of Wellington at Walmer, 25 October 1838, quoted in Stanhope, *Life of the Right Honourable William Pitt*, Vol. IV, pp.346–7

36 Ibid., p.348

37 Dacres Adams to Stanhope, 26 April 1861, Stanhope Mss U 1590 C405/15

38 Account of Oliver Ferrer, Twiss, *The Private and Public Life of Lord Chancellor Eldon*, Vol. I, p.499

39 Malmesbury, *Diaries and Correspondence of James Harris, First Earl of Malmesbury*, Vol. IV, p.347

40 Ibid., p.348

41 Corbett, *The Campaign of Trafalgar*, p.398

42 Notebook of Lord Fitzharris, 1805, Malmesbury, *Diaries and Correspondence of James Harris, First Earl of Malmesbury*, Vol. IV, p.349n

43 Stanhope, *Life of the Right Honourable William Pitt*, Vol. IV, p.347

44 Rosebery, *Letters Relating to the Love Episode of William Pitt*, p.37

45 Pitt to Harrowby, 29 November 1805, quoted in Rose, *William Pitt and the Great War*, p.542

46 Marshall, *The Rise of Canning*, p.296

47 Chevening Mss, quoted in Rose, *William Pitt and the Great War*, p.548

48 Marshall, *The Rise of Canning*, p.296

49 Stanhope, *Life of the Right Honourable William Pitt*, Vol. IV, p.362

TWENTY-EIGHT : 'How I Leave My Country'

1 Rosebery, *Letters Relating to the Love Episode of William Pitt*, p.46

2 Lady Bessborough to G. Leverson Gower, 23 January 1806, Granville (ed.), *Lord Granville Leveson Gower, First Earl Granville: Private Correspondence. 1781–1821*, Vol. II, pp.162–3

3 Stanhope, *Life of the Right Honourable William Pitt*, Vol. IV, p.363

4 Ashbourne, *Pitt: Some Chapters of His Life and Times*, p.360

5 Harrowby to Paget, 27 December 1805, quoted in Ehrman, *The Younger Pitt*, Vol. III, p.817

6 Canning to Pitt, 31 December 1805, Stanhope, *Life of the Right Honourable William Pitt*, Vol. IV, p.365

7 Raikes, *A Portion of the Journal Kept by Thomas Raikes*, Vol. IV, p.287

8 Rosebery, *Letters Relating to the Love Episode of William Pitt*, p.39

9 Stanhope, *Life of the Right Honourable William Pitt*, Vol. IV, p.366

10 Pitt to Castlereagh, 6 January 1806, quoted in ibid., p.367

11 Ibid., pp.367–8

12 Rosebery, *Letters Relating to the Love Episode of William Pitt*, p.41

13 Ibid.

14 Pitt to Wellesley, 12 January 1806, quoted in Stanhope, *Life of the Right Honourable William Pitt*, Vol. IV, p.374

15 Malmesbury, *Diaries and Correspondence of James Harris, First Earl of Malmesbury*, Vol. IV, p.352

16 Stanhope, *Life of the Right Honourable William Pitt*, Vol. IV, pp.44–5

17 Meryon (ed.), *Memoirs of the Lady Hester Stanhope . . .*, p.79

18 Tomline, draft account for his *Life of Pitt*, BL Add Mss 45107

19 Rosebery, *Letters Relating to the Love Episode of William Pitt*, pp.45–6

20 Stanhope (ed.), *Miscellanies*, pp.30–1

21 Tomline, draft account for his *Life of Pitt*, BL Add Mss 45107

22 Hinde, *George Canning*, p.140

23 Marshall, *The Rise of Canning*, p.296

24 Malmesbury, *Diaries and Correspondence of James Harris, First Earl of Malmesbury*, Vol. IV, p.353

25 Rosebery, *Letters Relating to the Love Episode of William Pitt*, p.46

26 Stanhope, *Life of the Right Honourable William Pitt*, Vol. IV, p.375

27 Rosebery, *Letters Relating to the Love Episode of William Pitt*, pp.46–7

28 Harcourt, *The Diaries and Correspondence of the Right Hon. George Rose*, Vol. II, p.223
29 Canning to Sturges Bourne, 8 January 1806, Canning Mss, William L. Clements Library, Michigan
30 Stanhope, *Life of the Right Honourable William Pitt*, Vol. IV, p.379
31 Rosebery, *Letters Relating to the Love Episode of William Pitt*, p.47
32 J. Stanhope, 'Notes of Mr. Pitt's Last Illness', quoted in Stanhope, *Life of the Right Honourable William Pitt*, Vol. IV, p.379
33 Ibid., p.380
34 Harcourt, *The Diaries and Correspondence of the Right Hon. George Rose*, Vol. II, p.230
35 Tomline, draft account for his *Life of Pitt*, BL Add Mss 45107
36 Harcourt, *The Diaries and Correspondence of the Right Hon. George Rose*, Vol. II, p.231
37 Marshall, *The Rise of Canning*, p.297
38 BL Add Mss 58909, fol. 101
39 Malmesbury, *Diaries and Correspondence of James Harris, First Earl of Malmesbury*, Vol. IV, p.354
40 Rosebery, *Letters Relating to the Love Episode of William Pitt*, p.48
41 Reilly, *Pitt the Younger*, p.345; see also Ehrman, *The Younger Pitt*, Vol. III, p.825
42 J. Stanhope, 'Notes of Mr. Pitt's Last Illness', quoted in Stanhope, *Life of the Right Honourable William Pitt*, Vol. IV, p.381
43 Ibid.
44 Ibid., p.382
45 Ibid.
46 Farington, *The Farington Diary*, Vol. III, p.166
47 Marshall, *The Rise of Canning*, p.298
48 Harcourt, *The Diaries and Correspondence of the Right Hon. George Rose*, Vol. II, p.258
49 Letter from Lord Wellesley, 22 November 1836, Stanhope, *Life of the Right Honourable William Pitt*, Vol. IV, p.396
50 *The Sun*, 24 January, 1806
51 *The Sun*, 23 January 1806
52 *The Times*, 24 January 1806
53 Lady Bessborough to Lord Bessborough, 23 January 1806, Granville (ed.), *Lord Granville Leveson Gower, First Earl Granville: Private Correspondence. 1781–1821*, Vol. II, p.162
54 Stanhope, *Life of the Right Honourable William Pitt*, Vol. IV, p.375
55 Sidmouth to Bragge-Bathurst, 22 January 1805, Sidmouth Mss, quoted in Ziegler, *Addington*, p.248
56 Stanhope, *Life of the Right Honourable William Pitt*, Vol. IV, p.391
57 *Morning Herald*, 28 January 1806
58 Meryon (ed.), *Memoirs of the Lady Hester Stanhope . . .*, p.69
59 Lt. Col. Taylor to the Bishop of Lincoln, 22 January 1806, Aspinall, *The Later Correspondence of George III*, Vol. IV, p.381
60 Rosebery, *Letters Relating to the Love Episode of William Pitt*, p.302

BIBLIOGRAPHY

MANUSCRIPTS

Bodleian Library, Oxford

Bland-Burgess Mss
Clarendon Mss
North Mss
Wilberforce Mss

British Library, London

Add Mss 75961–75962 Althorp Papers
Add Mss 34412–34471 Auckland Papers
Add Mss 69038–69411 Dropmore Papers
Add Mss 47566 Fox Papers
Add Mss 35349–36278 Hardwicke Papers
Add Mss 51318–52254 Holland House Papers
Add Mss 38734–38770 Huskisson Papers
Add Mss 33126–33130 Pelham Correspondence
Add Mss 45107–45108 Pretyman Papers
Add Mss 27918 Memoranda of the Duke of Leeds
Add Mss 28060–28067 Correspondence of the Duke of Leeds
Add Mss 37308–37313 Wellesley Papers
Add Mss 37842–37935 Windham Papers

Cambridge University Library, Cambridge

Pitt Mss

Devon Record Office, Exeter

Sidmouth Mss

Kent Archive Office, Maidstone

Chevening Mss
Stanhope Mss

West Yorkshire Archives, Leeds

Canning Mss

Public Record Office, Kew

Chatham Papers 30/8/101–363
Dacres Adams Papers 30/58/7
Pitt Papers 30/70

Suffolk Record Office, Ipswich

Pretyman Mss

William L. Clements Library, Michigan, USA

Melville Mss
Pitt Mss

PUBLISHED SOURCES

Historical Manuscripts Commission Reports

Report on the Manuscripts of J.B. Fortescue, Esq., Preserved at Dropmore, Historical Manuscripts Commission, XIII Report, Volume I, London, 1892–1927

Report on the Manuscripts of the Earl of Carlisle, Preserved at Castle Howard, Historical Manuscripts Commission, XV Report, 1897

Report on the Manuscripts of Earl Bathurst, Preserved at Cirencester Park, Historical Manuscripts Commission, London, 1923

The Manuscripts of His Grace the Duke of Rutland, G.C.B., Preserved at Belvoir Castle, Historical Manuscripts Commission, Volume III, XII Report, London, 1888–1905

BOOKS

Anson, W. R., *Autobiography and Political Correspondence of Augustus Henry, Third Duke of Grafton*, John Murray, London, 1898

Ashborne, Lord, *Pitt: Some Chapters of His Life and Times*, Longman, 1898

Aspinall, A., *The Later Correspondence of George III*, Volumes I–V, Cambridge University Press, Cambridge, 1962

Auckland, W., *The Journal and Correspondence of William Eden Auckland, Lord Auckland*, Volumes I–III, London, 1860–1862

Ayling, S., *The Elder Pitt*, Collins, London, 1976

Bagot, J., *George Canning and His Friends*, Volume I, John Murray, London, 1909

Barnes, D. G., *George III and William Pitt*, Octagon, New York, 1973

Bickley, F. L., *The Diaries of Sylvester Douglas, Lord Glenbervie*, Volume I, Constable, London, 1928

Black, J., *Pitt the Elder*, Cambridge University Press, Cambridge, 1992

Black, J., *British Foreign Policy in an Age of Revolutions*, Cambridge University Press, Cambridge, 1994

Bladon, F. M. (ed.), The *Diaries of Colonel the Hon. Robert Fulke Greville*, John Lane, London, 1930

Blanning, T., *The French Revolutionary Wars 1787–1802*, Arnold, London, 1996

Brooke, J., *The Chatham Administration*, Macmillan, London, 1956

Brougham, H., *Historical Sketches of Statesmen who Flourished in the Time of George III*, Volumes I–III, Richard Griffin & Company, 1858

Browning, O. (ed.), *Memoranda of Francis, Fifth Duke of Leeds*, Camden Society, London, 1884

Bruce, H. A., *Life of General Sir William Napier*, Volume I, Murray, London, 1864

Bryant, A., *Years of Victory 1802–1812*, Collins, London, 1944

Duke of Buckingham (ed.), *Memoirs of the Court and Cabinet of George III*, Volumes I–IV, Hurst & Blackett, London, 1853–1855

Burges, J. B., *Selections from the Letters and Correspondence of Sir James Bland Burges*, John Murray, London, 1885

Burke, E. (ed. J. C. D. Clark), *Reflections on the Revolution in France*, Stanford, California, 2001

Butler, C., *Reminiscences of Charles Butler*, Volume I, John Murray, London, 1822

Cannon, J. *The Fox–North Coalition*, Cambridge University Press, Cambridge, 1969

Christie, I. R., *The End of North's Ministry 1780–1782*, Macmillan, London, 1958

Christie, I. R., *Wilkes, Wyvill and Reform: The Parliamentary Movement in British Politics 1760–85*, Macmillan, London, 1962

Clarkson, T., *The History of the Rise, Progress, and Accomplishment of the Abolition of the African Slave-Trade by the British Parliament*, Volume I, Longman, London, 1808

Cleveland, Duchess of, *Life and Letters of Lady Hester Stanhope*, John Murray, London, 1914

Cobban, A., *Ambassadors and Secret Agents. The Diplomacy of the First Earl of Malmesbury at the Hague*, Jonathan Cape, London, 1954

Cobbett, W. (ed.), *Parliamentary History*, Volumes XXIII–XXXV, 1782–1801

Cobbett, W. and Hansard, T. C. (eds), *Parliamentary Debates*, Volumes I–XX, 1804–1812

Colchester, Lord, *The Diary and Correspondence of Charles Abbot, Lord Colchester*, John Murray, London, 1861

Coleman, T., *Nelson*, Bloomsbury, London, 2001

Copeland, T., *The Correspondence of Edmund Burke*, Volume VI, Cambridge University Press, Cambridge, 1967

Corbett, J., *The Campaign of Trafalgar*, Longman, London, 1910

Corbett, J. (ed.), *Private Papers of George, Second Earl Spencer*, Volume II, Navy Records Society, 1913

Cornewall Lewis, G., *Essays on the Administrations of Great Britain from 1783 to 1830*, London, 1864

Curzon, Lord, *The Personal History of Walmer Castle and its Lords Warden*, Macmillan, London,1927

Debrett, J., *History of the Westminster Election*, London, 1784

Debrett, J. (ed.), *The Parliamentary Register*, 1781–1803

Derry, J. W., *The Regency Crisis and the Whigs 1788–9*, Cambridge University Press, Cambridge, 1963

Dixon, P., *Canning*, Weidenfeld & Nicolson, London, 1976

Duffy, M., *Profiles in Power: The Younger Pitt*, Longman, Harlow, 2000

Ehrman, J., *The Younger Pitt*, Volumes I–III, Constable, London, 1969

Elofson, W. M., *The Rockingham Connection and the Second Founding of the Whig Party*, McGill-Queen's University Press, Montreal, 1996

Farington, J., *The Farington Diary*, Volume III, Hutchinson, London, 1923–1928

Farington, J., *The Diary of Joseph Farington*, Volume V, New Haven, 1978–1984

Feiling, K., *Warren Hastings*, Macmillan, London, 1954

Festing, G., *John Hookham Frere and His Friends*, J. Nisbet, London, 1899

Fitzmaurice, Lord E., *The Life of William Earl of Shelburne, 1st Marquis Lansdowne*, Volume I, Macmillan, London, 1875–1876

Fortescue, J., *British Statesmen of the Great War*, Clarendon Press, Oxford, 1911

Fortescue, J., *The Correspondence of King George III from 1760 to December 1783*, Volumes I–VI, Macmillan, 1928

Fremont-Barnes, G., *The French Revolutionary Wars*, Osprey, London, 2001

Furet, F., *The French Revolution 1770–1814*, Blackwell, Oxford, 1988

Furneaux, R., *William Wilberforce*, Hamish Hamilton, London, 1974

Gibbon, E., *Miscellaneous Works of Edward Gibbon*, Volume I, London, 1796

Gillespie Smyth, *Memoirs and Correspondence of Sir Robert Murray Keith*, Volume II, London, 1849

Granville, Castalia, Countess (ed.), *Lord Granville Leveson Gower, First Earl Granville: Private Correspondence. 1781–1821*, Volumes I–III, 1916

Hall, C. D., *British Strategy in the Napoleonic War 1803–15*, Manchester University Press, Manchester, 1992

Hamilton, Sir R. V. (ed.), *Letters and Papers of Admiral of the Fleet Sir Thos. Byam Martin, G.C.B.*, Volume III, 1901

Harcourt, Rev L. V., *The Diaries and Correspondence of the Right Hon. George Rose*, Volumes I–II, Richard Bentley, London, 1860

Haslip, J., *Lady Hester Stanhope*, Heron, Geneva, 1970

Hathaway, W. S., *The Speeches of the Right Honourable William Pitt in the House of Commons*, Volumes I–IV, Longman, London, 1806

Hayley, W., *Memoirs of the Life and Writings of William Hayley*, Volume I, London, 1823

Headlam, C. (ed.), *The Letters of Lady Harriot Eliot, 1766–1786*, Constable, Edinburgh, 1914

Hewitt, J. (ed.), *Eyewitnesses to Nelson's Battles*, Reading, 1974

Hibbert, C., *George III: A Personal History*, Viking, London, 1998

Hibbert, C., *Redcoats and Rebels: The War for America 1770–1781*, Penguin, London, 2001

Hinde, W., *George Canning*, Collins, London, 1973

Hoffman, R. J. S., *The Marquis: A Study of Lord Rockingham 1730–1782*, Fordham University Press, 1973

Holland, Lord, *Memoirs of the Whig Party*, Volume I, London, 1852–1854

Holland Rose, J., *William Pitt and the Great War*, G. Bell & Sons, London, 1911

Holland Rose, J., *William Pitt and National Revival*, G. Bell & Sons, London, 1911

Holland Rose, J., *Pitt and Napoleon*, G. Bell & Sons, London, 1912

Holland Rose, J., *A Short Life of William Pitt*, G. Bell & Sons, London, 1925

Horner, L., *Memoirs of Francis Horner*, Volume I, 1848

Ilchester, Earl of (ed.), *Letters to Henry Fox, Lord Holland*, Roxburghe Club, London, 1915

Jawett, P., *Pitt the Younger*, Purnell Book Series, 1974

Jenyns, S., *Thoughts on a Parliamentary Reform*, J. Dodsley, London, 1784

Johnston, E. M. (ed.), *Great Britain and Ireland 1760–1800*, Oliver & Boyd, London, 1963

Jupp, P., *Lord Grenville*, Clarendon Press, Oxford, 1985

Lecky, W. E. H., *History of England in the Eighteenth Century*, Volumes I–VIII, Longmans & Green, London, 1890

Lever, Sir T., *The House of Pitt*, John Murray, London, 1947

Lewis, W. S.. *Horace Walpole's Miscellaneous Correspondence*, Volume XI, Oxford University Press, Oxford, 1980

Lloyd Jones, D. M., *Darkness and Light, Ephesians 4.17–5.17*, Baker Book House, 1982

Lyall, Sir A., *Warren Hastings*, Macmillan, London, 1894

MacAlpine, I. and Hunter, R., *George III and the Mad Business*, Allen Lane, London, 1969

Macaulay, Lord, *Warren Hastings*, Phillips & Hunt, New York, 1886

Macaulay, Lord, essay contained in *Encyclopaedia Britannica*, eleventh edition, Encyclopaedia Britannica Company, New York, 1911

MacDermot, B. (ed.), *The Diary of Denys Scully*, Irish Academic Press, 1992

Malmesbury, Earl of, *Diaries and Correspondence of James Harris, First Earl of Malmesbury*, Volumes I–IV, Richard Bentley, London, 1845

Marshall, D., *The Rise of Canning*, Longman, London, 1938

Matheson, C., *The Life of Henry Dundas, First Viscount Melville*, Constable, London, 1933

Maxwell, H., *The Creevey Papers*, John Murray, London, 1923

Minto, Countess of, *Life and Letters of Sir Gilbert Elliot*, Volumes I–III, Longman, London, 1874

Mitchell, L. G., *Charles James Fox and the Disintegration of the Whig Party 1782–1794*, Oxford University Press, London, 1971

Mitchell, L. G., *Charles James Fox*, Oxford University Press, Oxford, 1992

Moore, T., *Sheridan*, Volume II, Longman, London, 1825

Mori, J., *William Pitt and the French Revolution 1785–1795*, Keele University Press, Edinburgh, 1997

Moritz, C. P., *Journey of a German in England in 1782*, Holt, Rinehart & Winston, New York

Namier, L., *England in the Age of the American Revolution*, Macmillan, London, 1930

Namier, L., *The Structure of Politics at the Accession of George III*, second edition, Macmillan, London, 1957

Pares, R., *King George III and the Politicians*, London, 1953

Pellew, G., *The Life and Correspondence of the Right Hon. Henry Addington*, Volumes I–III, John Murray, London, 1847

Phillips, K., *The Cousins' Wars*, Basic Books, New York, 1999

Phipps, E., *Memoirs of the Political and Literary Life of Robert Plumer Ward*, Volume I, London, 1850

Pollock, J., *Wilberforce: God's Statesman*, Constable, London, 1977 (reissued 2001)

Porritt, E., *The Unreformed House of Commons*, Volumes I–II, Cambridge University Press, Cambridge, 1903

Rae, W. F., *Wilkes, Sheridan, Fox: The Opposition Under George III*, Isbister, London, 1874

Raikes, T., *A Portion of the Journal Kept by Thomas Raikes*, Volume IV, Longman, London, 1856–1857

Reilly, R., *Pitt The Younger 1759–1806*, Cassell, London, 1978

Robertson, Sir C. G., *Chatham and the British Empire*, Hodder & Stoughton, London, 1956

Rogers, S., *Recollections by Samuel Rogers*, London, 1859

Rolo, P., *George Canning*, Macmillan, London, 1965

Romilly, S. (ed.), *Memoirs of the Life of Sir Samuel Romilly*, Volume I, John Murray, London, 1840

Romilly, S., *Letters to Ivy From the First Earl of Dudley*, Longman, London, 1905

Rosebery, Lord, *Pitt and Wilberforce*, published privately, Edinburgh, 1897

Rosebery, Lord, *Letters Relating to the Love Episode of William Pitt*, published privately, 1900

Rosebery, Lord, *Bishop Tomline's Estimate of Pitt*, John Murray, London, 1903

Rosebery, Lord, *Chatham: His Early Life and Connections*, Arthur L. Humphreys, London, 1910

Rosebery, Lord, *Pitt*, Macmillan & Co., London, 1918

Ross, C., *Correspondence of Charles, First Marquis Cornwallis*, Volumes I–III, John Murray, London, 1859

Rothenburg, G., *The Napoleonic Wars*, Cassell, London, 1976

Russell, Lord J. (ed.), *Memorials of Charles J. Fox*, Volumes I–IV, Richard Bentley, London, 1853–1857

Russell, Lord J., *Life of Charles J. Fox*, Volumes I–III, Richard Bentley, London, 1859

Rutland, Duke of, *Correspondence between the Right Hon. William Pitt and Charles Duke of Rutland*, London, 1842

Savage, G. and Finer, A. (eds), *The Selected Letters of Josiah Wedgwood*, London, 1965

Sichel, W., *Sheridan*, Volume II, Constable, London, 1909

Southey, R., *Letters from England*, April 1802, number 12, Cresset, London, 1951

Stanhope, Earl, *Secret Correspondence Connected with Mr Pitt's Return to Office in 1804*, Spottiswoodes & Shaw, London, 1852

Stanhope, Earl, *Address Delivered by Earl Stanhope at the Ceremony of His Installation as the Lord Rector of Marischal College and University, Aberdeen, 25 March 1858*, Aberdeen, 1858

Stanhope, Earl, *Miscellanies*, second edition, London, 1863

Stanhope, Earl, *Life of the Right Honourable William Pitt*, third edition, Volumes I–IV, John Murray, London, 1867

Stanhope, Lady H., *Memoirs of the Lady Hester Stanhope, as Related by Herself in Conversations with her Physician*, London, 1845

Stapleton, A. G., *George Canning and His Times*, London, 1859

Steuart, A. F. (ed.), *The Last Journals of Horace Walpole*, Volume II, John Lane, London, 1910

Taylor, W. S. and Pringle, J. H. (eds), *Correspondence of William Pitt, Earl of Chatham*, Volumes I–IV, John Murray, London, 1838–1840

Temperley, H., *Foundations of British Foreign Policy, from Pitt – 1792 – to Salisbury – 1902*, Cambridge University Press, Cambridge, 1938

Thackeray, Rev F., *A History of the Right Hon. William Pitt, Earl of Chatham*, Volume I, London, 1827

Thale, M. (ed.), *Selections from the Papers of the London Corresponding Society*, Cambridge University Press, Cambridge, 1983

Thorne, R. G. (ed.), *The House of Commons 1790–1820*, Volume IV, History of Parliament Trust, London, 1986

Tomline, G., *Memoirs of the Life of the Right Honourable William Pitt*, Volumes I–II, John Murray, London, 1821

Trevelyan, G. M., *Lord Grey of the Reform Bill*, Longman, London, 1920

Turner, M., *Pitt the Younger: A Life*, Hambledon & London, 2003

Twiss, H., *The Private and Public Life of Lord Chancellor Eldon*, Volume I, John Murray, London, 1844

Valentine, A., *Lord North*, University of Oklahoma Press, 1967

Waldegrave, Lord, *Memoirs from 1754–1758*, John Murray, London, 1821

Walpole, H., *Journal of the Reign of King George III, From the Year 1771 to 1783*, Volume II, Richard Bentley, London, 1859

Walpole, H., *The Letters of Horace Walpole*, Volume VIII, Bentley & Son, London, 1891

Walpole, H., *Memoirs of the Reign of King George III*, Volume III, Yale University Press, London and New Haven, 2000

Watson, J. S., *The Reign of George III*, Oxford University Press, Oxford, 1960

Whibley, C., *William Pitt*, William Blackwood & Sons, Edinburgh and London, 1906

Wilberforce, R. I. and S. W., *The Life of William Wilberforce*, Volumes I–V, John Murray, London, 1838

Williams, B., *The Life of William Pitt, Earl of Chatham*, Volume II, Longmans, Green & Co., 1913

Willis, R., *Bulletin of the Institute of Historical Research*, XLIV, no. 110, 1971

Windham, W., *The Windham Papers*, Volume I, Herbert Jenkins, London, 1913

Woodfall and Kinder, *The Correspondence of the Right Hon. John Beresford*, Volume I, London, 1854

Wraxall, N., *The Historical and the Posthumous Memoirs of Sir Nathaniel William Wraxall 1772–1784*, Volumes II–V, Bickers & Son, London, 1884

Wright, J. (ed.), *The Speeches of the Right Honourable Charles James Fox in the House of Commons*, Volumes I–VI, Longman, London, 1815

Wright, K., *Speeches in the House of Commons*, Volume IV, Longman, 1815

Wrigley, E. A. and Schofield, R. S., *The Population History of England 1541–1871*, E. Arnold, London, 1981

Wyvill, C., *Political Papers*, Volumes III–IV, York, 1794–1802

Yorke, P. C., *The Life and Correspondence of Philip Yorke, Earl of Hardwicke*, Volume II, Cambridge University Press, Cambridge, 1913

Ziegler, P., *Addington*, Collins, London, 1965

NEWSPAPERS

The Courier
The Gazetteer
Morning Chronicle
Morning Herald
Morning Post
The Sun
The Times
Whitehall Evening Post

INDEX